Global Problems, Global Solutions

In remembrance of my mother and father, Mary and Joseph Chirico, who taught me that we all are brothers and sisters, and with love to my children and grandchildren, Erin, Casey, Nathan, Natalie, A. J., Angel, and E. J.

Sara Miller McCune founded SAGE Publishing in 1965 to support the dissemination of usable knowledge and educate a global community. SAGE publishes more than 1000 journals and over 800 new books each year, spanning a wide range of subject areas. Our growing selection of library products includes archives, data, case studies and video. SAGE remains majority owned by our founder and after her lifetime will become owned by a charitable trust that secures the company's continued independence.

Los Angeles | London | New Delhi | Singapore | Washington DC | Melbourne

Global Problems, Global Solutions

Prospects for a Better World

JoAnn Chirico, Emeritus
The Pennsylvania State University, University College

Los Angeles | London | New Delhi
Singapore | Washington DC | Melbourne

FOR INFORMATION:

SAGE Publications, Inc.
2455 Teller Road
Thousand Oaks, California 91320
E-mail: order@sagepub.com

SAGE Publications Ltd.
1 Oliver's Yard
55 City Road
London, EC1Y 1SP
United Kingdom

SAGE Publications India Pvt. Ltd.
B 1/I 1 Mohan Cooperative Industrial Area
Mathura Road, New Delhi 110 044
India

SAGE Publications Asia-Pacific Pte. Ltd.
3 Church Street
#10-04 Samsung Hub
Singapore 049483

Acquisitions Editor: Jeff Lasser
Content Development Editor: Liza Neustaetter
Editorial Assistant: Tiara Beatty
Production Editor: Bennie Clark Allen,
                Jane Haenel
Copy Editor: D. J. Peck
Typesetter: Hurix Digitals
Proofreader: Scott Oney
Indexer: Molly Hall
Cover Designer: Gail Buschman
Marketing Manager: Kara Kindstrom

Printed in the United States of America

Library of Congress Cataloging-in-Publication Data

Names: Chirico, JoAnn, author.

Title: Global problems, global solutions / JoAnn Chirico, Pennsylvania State University, Beaver.

Description: Thousand Oaks, California : SAGE, [2019] | Includes bibliographical references and index.

Identifiers: LCCN 2018021123 | ISBN 9781506347783 (pbk. : alk. paper)

Subjects: LCSH: Social problems. | Globalization—Social aspects.

Classification: LCC HN18.3 .C45 2019 | DDC 306—dc23 LC record available at https://lccn.loc.gov/2018021123

This book is printed on acid-free paper.

18 19 20 21 22 10 9 8 7 6 5 4 3 2 1

Brief Contents

PART I: NOURISHING HUMAN CAPITAL

PART II: RESTORING CIVILITY TO SOCIAL LIFE

3 | Starving in the Shadow of Plenty 85

4 | Optimizing Human Capital: Good Health 111

5 | Expanding Horizons Through Lifelong Learning   144

PART II: RESTORING CIVILITY TO SOCIAL LIFE

6 | From Difference to Discrimination: Fault Lines of Race, Ethnicity, and Religion 166

10 | The Challenge of Political Violence — 303

PART III: SUSTAINING NATURAL AND MANUFACTURED ENVIRONMENTS

11 | Global Flows of Refugees

12 | Environmental and Economic Migration 368

13 | Destruction and Depletion of the Natural Environment 392

14 | Climate Change and Global Warming

15 | Urbanization: The Lure of the Cities   460

16 | A World Gone Awry? The State of Governance 495

Introduction

Neither the life of an individual nor the history of a society can be understood without understanding them both.

—C. Wright Mills, *The Sociological Imagination*

C. Wright Mills wrote *The Sociological Imagination* in 1959. Far from being outdated, it is arguably more relevant today than when it was written. Not only are the fates and fortunes of individuals, people like you and me, intertwined with the particular histories of our communities and our societies, but they are intertwined with the history of the world.

This book introduces you to the complexities of the major problems that confront us today—such as violent conflict, poverty, climate change, and human trafficking. Although individual people bear the burden of these problems, the problems originate in our collective histories. You are probably somewhat familiar with most of the issues in the book because they are a palpable part of our lives and they confront us daily in news accounts, political controversies, other courses you have taken, or even television programs that pull their stories "from the headlines." You probably know that social problems breed fear and distrust. They degrade our health and deplete our wealth. The social, psychological, and economic toll they take, and the cost to the quality of our lives, is difficult to quantify, but it is enormous.

If you watch the evening news or get a daily news feed, it's obvious that different societies and the people within them face somewhat different obstacles and have different opportunities. Some societies and some individuals fall victim to the ill effects of nearly all of the global problems, while others escape many of them. That is a good beginning for our analysis—social location matters. But the ways in which local, national, and global forces shape these different opportunities and vulnerabilities is not always obvious if you are relying solely on news accounts. In modern societies that are highly individualistic, it is all too easy and common to blame people for their plight. But what if a large percentage of people are poor, out of work, underpaid, starving, or victims of any number of problems? Can it all be due to their own failings as individuals? Could they all be lazy, ignorant, careless, or naturally violent? Or could their personal troubles stem from

social forces? That is where our sociological imagination provides insight.

We also need to consider that global problems present themselves differently in different parts of the world and to different groups of people within societies. Is poverty in the United States or the European Union shaped by the same forces as poverty in Africa or Southeast Asia? The answer is yes and also no. Poverty is shaped by the same global economic system wherever in the world it is found. But the ways in which the global economy flows through various locales, raising some people up and pushing others down, differ. We need our sociological imaginations to guide us through the study of global problems.

Social forces, like the physical forces of magnetism and gravity, are invisible to us. We do not see gravity, we see the apple drop. We know the forces of the physical universe through their observable effects—how they shape our world and the opportunities and vulnerabilities of countries and people within it. Similarly, we don't see social integration, a social force, or its absence directly. We see a world or community in which people can achieve their goals or a world or community in disarray with poverty, crime, war, pollution, and other problems. These problems—and their opposites such as wealth, security, and a healthy environment—are the observable effects of social forces.

Mills (1959) asked, "What are the major issues for publics and the key troubles of private individuals in our time? To formulate issues and troubles, we must ask what values are cherished yet threatened, and what values are cherished and supported, by the characterizing trends of our period." Choosing those that are most important from among the myriad problems that confront us is a daunting task.

Several good sources of national and global opinions can help us to identify them. The Pew Research Center is an excellent resource for finding out what is on people's minds, what people think is important, and ways in which people feel threatened. The center conducts dozens of global and national surveys annually to get up-to-the-minute readings of public opinion on the issues of the day.

Pew's 2014 survey in 44 countries asked people which of five threats they felt was the most dangerous. Although people in every region saw these issues as problems, the survey revealed geographic clusters reflecting internal and regional priorities. In most of the European countries and the United States, income inequality was seen most often as the greatest threat. For the United Kingdom and much of the Middle East, it was religious and ethnic hatred. Most of the African countries included chose AIDS and other diseases. In some South American and Asian countries, it was pollution and the environment. Nuclear weapons were top for most of the Eastern European countries. Figure I.1 shows the greatest perceived dangers by country. Social location matters.

The World Economic Forum (WEF) surveys experts drawn from businesses, academia, non-governmental organizations, and international organizations and governments to identify what experts think are the most serious risks facing the world over the next 10 years. The WEF draws its sample from advanced and developing economies and all regions of the world; however, nearly three quarters of the experts are male. The 2014 survey identified discrete risks related to economic, environmental, geopolitical, societal, and technological dangers—31 in all. The top 10 are primarily economic and environmental: severe inequality, unemployment and under-employment, environmental issues such as water crises, extreme weather and climate change, food insecurity, economic crises, political instability, social instability, and governance (WEF 2014).

The problems the world faces are complex and interrelated. Some have the same historical roots. When one worsens, such as climate change, so do the others, from food security to violent conflict and migration.

FIGURE I.1   Regional Perceptions of the Greatest Dangers in the World

While many people the world over share the same fears, their perceptions of the most dangerous problems vary by region.

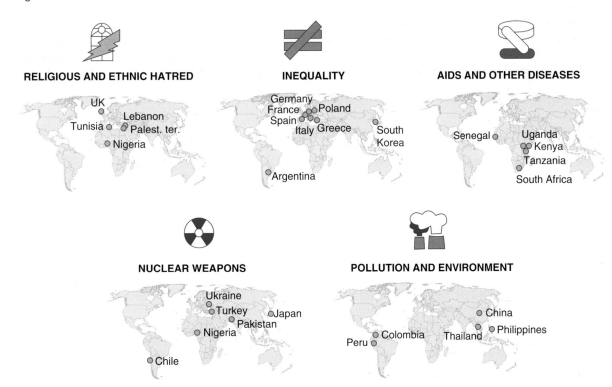

Source: "Greatest Dangers in the World." Pew Research Center, Washington, D.C. (October 16, 2014) http://www.pewglobal.org/2014/10/16/greatest-dangers-in-the-world/.

However, when one improves, so do the others. Action to improve one problem cascades out to the others. This is cause for hope.

This book is about hope. It is about people's "life chances"[1] and how we can improve them. Life chances are opportunities—the societal resources—people have to fulfill their potential. People with good life chances have access to the resources they need such as nutritious food, good health, and education. These people are less vulnerable to social problems. Having few resources restricts people's life chances. People's life chances depend on their social location. Social location refers to where people stand in the world. It can mean their geographic location such as a country or city given that some of us are lucky enough to be born in a wealthy area with more resources. Others are not so lucky, and their chances are fewer. Social location also refers to economic and social factors. Economic status, race, and gender are important social locations because they affect our life chances. Prejudice, based on one of these factors, severely limits people's access to important resources—including living wages, educations suited to their talents and ambitions, clean water and air, and basic sanitation—thereby limiting their chances at life and their opportunity to achieve their potential. Billions of people live with very meager life chances stemming from their social location based on one or more of these factors. When these factors lose their social meaning, they will not be social locations.

Inequality of life chances exists among societies and within every society regardless of the society's level of development or income. Whether economic, racial, ethnic, gender, religious, or a function of sexual orientation, inequalities are important for several reasons. First, they violate human rights. They are illegal wherever governments have ratified international treaties against discrimination or have national constitutions and other legal provisions guaranteeing equal treatment and equal access to society's fundamental resources. Inequality of opportunity degrades and diminishes the well-being of those who are discriminated against, taking years from their lives and stripping quality from their years. It costs all of us regardless of our personal life chances. Neither the world nor a society can afford to waste the talent, ingenuity, and/or ambition of any of its people any more than a corporation could expect to prosper if only a portion of its workforce were allowed to contribute. Inequality hurts everyone. Inequalities of one type or another—economic, political, or social—lie at the core of nearly every global problem, from those that seem to be the most personal such as suicide to the seemingly most impersonal such as climate change.

Chapter 1 is an introduction to sociological perspectives and analysis to get your sociological imagination going. Three broad themes organize the rest of the book. Sustaining and nourishing human capital is the theme of Chapters 2 to 5. They address the impacts of the economic, food, health, and educational systems on people's chances to live a productive and satisfying life and contribute to the common good.

Chapters 6 to 10 focus on our second theme—our civility and incivility toward one another. Chapters 6 and 7 address the impact of discrimination and persecution along the fault lines of identity—race, religion, gender, and ethnicity—the socially constructed categories that we use to identify "us" and "them." Chapters 8 to 10 address victimization through violent conflict and international crime.

The third theme is our environments. Chapters 11 and 12 address the changing landscapes related to people on the move, the flows of global migration. Chapters 13 and 14 investigate the effects of pollution and climate change in our natural environment. While climate change receives considerable attention, pollution is often overlooked—even though it continues to cause early death and loss of quality life years for millions of people. Chapter 15 considers our built environment—our cities. Half of the global population now lives in cities, and soon it will be two thirds. Finding strategies for cities to sustain a life of quality for so many people when so many cities are already overburdened is a problem for every country.

Global and national political environments—governance—is the topic of Chapter 16. The fates of countries and people within them are intertwined due to globalization. The problems the world faces spill over political boundaries. It isn't sufficient to study national problems or even national security without considering global problems and issues of global security. Multiple layers of governance and a multitude of actors affect how people live their lives, their potential for life chances, and the ultimate quality of their lives.

Throughout the book, you will find many stories of how social forces affect vulnerable individuals. You will also get a macro perspective by examining societal- and global-level data. The sociological imagination helps you to weave the narratives together, a necessary step in developing good policy and workable solutions. While we confront many severe global problems, the world is also full of promise for a better life for finding the common good.

NOTE

1. The term "life chances" was introduced into the social sciences by Max Weber. The concept emphasizes that people's successes and failures in life are influenced by many factors out of their control. Our social location— our economic class, race, and religion and the region where we were born, among other factors—bears significantly on the opportunities with which life presents us.

Acknowledgments

From the Penn State Beaver campus, I thank Linda Garlitz, who offered staff support, and the late Donna Kuga, who provided financial support. A number of people generously shared their work or patiently helped me to locate photographs and figures to enhance the stories this book tells. Antonio Rosa, a gifted photographer, generously shared his photographs—both haunting and beautiful—of children at work for this book and a prior book, *Globalization*. Lisa McKeon of the National Snow and Ice Data Center helped in sorting through glacier photographs. Steven Steinbrecher generously shared photographs of food storage huts that he had taken during his travels. Pat Fowlkes, Clemens Breisinger, and Oliver Ecker of the International Food Policy Research Institute shared their work and searched for high-resolution copies of maps and charts.

I appreciate all the efforts of the team at SAGE. Jeff Lasser's faith and patience in the project brought it to fruition. Tiara Beatty's diligence and attention to detail kept me organized. The excellence and skill of the production team, D. J. Peck and Jane Haenel, ensured minimal mistakes on my part and brought the book to life. I am extremely grateful for their over-the-top efforts on the project.

Finally, thank-you to the following reviewers:

Cari Beecham-Bautista, College of DuPage

Daniel Brook, San Jose State University

Virginia Brow, Purdue University

Sneha Dutta, Ohlone College

Paul Gray, Boston College

George Guay, Bridgewater State University

Robert Hollenbaugh, Irvine Valley College

Thomas Koenig, Northeastern University

Michael O'Connor, Upper Iowa University

Ann Powers, Acadia University

Neil Quisenberry, McKendree University

Christabel Rogalin, Purdue University

Beth Schneider, Winston-Salem State University

Richard Tardanico, Florida International University

Angel Valdivia, California State University

Michael Vasquez, Northern Arizona University

About the Author

JoAnn Chirico, emeritus, received her Ph.D. in sociology from the University of Pittsburgh. While originally a doctoral candidate in education, she found that sociology provided the theoretical tools to analyze the problems she investigated—the coincidence of the global rise of both progressive and fundamentalist movements in education, religion, and other dimensions of social life. Intrigued by Emile Durkheim's pronouncement that individual differentiation would proceed to such an extent that all we ultimately would have in common was our humanity, she began her study of globalization—the integration of humanity into a social order.

Most of her career was at the Beaver campus of Pennsylvania State University, where she emphasized the importance of research and evidence, the global perspective, and civic engagement in her classes. She has presented workshops on internationalizing the curriculum and engaging students in service learning at conferences over the years.

Her previous publications for SAGE include *Sociological Research Exercises for the Global Age,* a lab manual of mini research exercises for introductory sociology courses, and *Globalization: Prospects and Problems.*

1

Private Troubles and Social Problems

DEVELOPING A SOCIOLOGICAL IMAGINATION

FINDING SOLUTIONS: TARUN BHARAT SANGH (YOUNG INDIA ORGANIZATION) BUILDING FROM THE GRASSROOTS

Because the problems that we face are interrelated, so are the solutions. Affecting change in one problem can trigger a cascade of improvements in all areas of life if done correctly. This is what the villagers in the Rajasthan area of India discovered. Facing overwhelming problems, such as poverty, water scarcity, hunger, forest degradation, pollution from mining, and little education and health care, the villagers of Rajasthan partnered with Tarun Bharat Sangh (TBS). Energized and empowered, they overcame the odds. It started with water management but accomplished much more.

Rajasthan is harsh territory in northwest India—arid and semi-arid lands, mountains and desert. Like the rest of India, it is extremely vulnerable to climate change. Its temperatures range from 0°C (32°F) to 49°C (120°F). Nearly all of the water that arrives in the monsoon runs off the land or evaporates. The people are poor. Although Rajasthan is about 10 percent of India's land area, it has only 1 percent of India's water. Its forests are dying. As in many water-scarce communities, women and girls sacrifice education and employment opportunities to spend hours every day fetching water.

That was then, about 30 years ago. Today, although the climate is no friendlier, people's lives are much better. The key to the success in Rajasthan is the local community's involvement in and control of every phase of development. Spearheading a grassroots effort rather than coming in and taking over, TBS energized the

LEARNING OBJECTIVES

After completing this chapter, students should be able to do the following:

1.1 Distinguish between personal and social problems, societal and global problems

1.2 Understand how the political, economic, and cultural features of a society comprise its social location and influence both individual and societal vulnerability to global problems

1.3 Document global goals for improving people's life chances and progress made toward those goals

1.4 Apply theoretical frameworks to the analysis of global problems

1.5 Outline the major features of the global economy, global governance, and global culture

local communities to restore traditional water and resource management. In 1987, TBS helped villagers to construct a small *johad,* a traditional water management technique that directs rainwater underground to prevent evaporation and runoff. Seeing the success of this small demonstration, a johad craze overtook the region. The water table began to rise after decades of depletion. Rivulets ran year-round. Enriched, forests and scrub in the area came alive and prevented even more runoff.

Empowered by the recognition of their traditional knowledge and skills, the villagers have taken charge of water management and much more. The wells and aquifers are replenished. This has revitalized agriculture for both crops and livestock. Agricultural production for subsistence improved, and villages generate income from milk products made possible by the increase in biomass for livestock fodder. One of the major foci of TBS is the empowerment of women and girls. Women and girls no longer spend up to 18 hours a day hauling water, fodder, and fuel wood because of their scarcity. Relieved of much of this hardship, girls are more often in school and women assumed important roles in their communities in resource management, health, and education. They have revived traditional knowledge of herbs and healing and provide health care for the community. Primary schools are established throughout the area. TBS provides extensive training for the community teachers and infrastructure. Alternative educational centers for women provide training and platforms for self-help and discussions on topics such as girl education, child marriage, child labor, and rights and responsibilities.

The keys to success in Rajasthan are community inclusion and building on cultural traditions and values. Rather than taking over and excluding local people from development efforts, TBS worked at the grassroots level, promoting and nurturing village councils. It recognized the dignity of and value in traditional knowledge and practices. TBS supplies some funding and support, but villagers direct all aspects of the processes. They make the decisions through village councils and do all of the labor. At the village level, the council, Gram Sabha, is composed of representatives from all households. The council meets twice monthly, and all households must attend the meetings. There is no formal leader or hierarchy, and decisions are consensual.

At the regional level, The Avari Sansad (River Avari Parliament) meets twice a year, with representatives from 72 of the river basin villages. It is participatory, egalitarian, and decentralized, following Ghandian ethos. Parliament determines the best practices for water management and enforces the rules. Violations are handled in the community where they occurred through dialog and deliberation. Parliament decides which crops are recommended and those that are forbidden, which industries are allowed and where, whether or not boreholes may be drilled in the catchment area, grazing rights and limits, and other considerations that bear on protecting the natural resources and thus the health of the communities. Every decision is made with concern for long-term sustainability.

Empowered, the villagers learned to fight to protect their interests. Recognizing the importance of fish to the ecosystem, the communities fought off the government's efforts to allow a contractor to exploit the fish that had returned to the river. The people resisted, even though most are vegetarian, and won. They saw that mining was degrading their forests, disturbing the delicate balance in their mountains, threatening the animals therein, and affecting their natural water system. Despite violence against them by pro-mining elements, the people fought the mining operations. They succeeded in having 470 mines closed by an order of the Supreme Court of India.

TBS succeeded over the course of 30 years to restore the Avari River and its tributaries. Little of the monsoon rain is wasted. There are now more than 10,000 rain harvesting structures in the region. The entire region is revitalized, and people have life chances that seemed impossible just a short time ago. TBS has won national and global awards for its work. It is a model non-governmental organization.

Source: Adapted from Tarun Bharat Sangh (n.d.). See the website for more information: http://tarunbharatsangh.in.

IT WAS THE BEST OF TIMES, IT WAS THE WORST OF TIMES

It was the best of times, it was the worst of times, it was the age of wisdom, it was the age of foolishness, it was the epoch of belief, it was the epoch of incredulity, it was the season of Light, it was the season of Darkness, it was the spring of hope, it was the winter of despair, we had everything before us, we had nothing before us, we were all going direct to heaven, we were all going direct the other way—in short, the period was so far like the present period, that some of its noisiest authorities insisted on its being received, for good or for evil, in the superlative degree of comparison only.

—Charles Dickens (1859), *A Tale of Two Cities*

In 1859, Dickens thusly described the Paris and London of 1775, full of contradiction as the Enlightenment demands for the freedom and dignity of humankind challenged the heavy weight of tradition and monarchy. In its contradictions, the mid-1800s was equally stark. Each was a period overflowing with possibility and potential to provide a good life for everyone. Yet, each was a period in which much, if not most, of humankind was buffeted by forces beyond people's individual control—forces of which Dickens himself had been a victim, forces that pushed many into the abyss of despair. Each of these periods inspired great literature, philosophy, social theory, and scientific thought as reformers sought to combat forces that overpowered people, stripping them of their dignity and opportunity for a good life. This was the consistent theme across Dickens's work: how the personal and often tragic problems of individuals stem from the social and political forces over which they have no control.

The 21st century is a similar era; it could be the best of times. Like the 1850s, there is sufficient productive capacity in the world to give everyone a good life, a life of comfort. There is sufficient knowledge of how to do it sustainably in ways that will preserve our environment and resources. This is the promise of our era.

Yet, our world is full of contradictions. Vicious wars and violent conflicts still plague much of the world, killing hundreds of thousands and sending millions of people into life-threatening journeys to find refuge. Poverty and hunger still stalk many countries. People suffer violence, including violent death, because of their gender, race, ethnicity, religion, or sexual orientation. People reject environmental science. Many do not want to acknowledge fact, putting their trust in the fictions spewed daily but presented as reality. Xenophobia and prejudices are growing in many countries. Within societies, inequality is increasing. Where there could be plenty, we find despair.

There is still promise. We have made progress. Violent conflict has lessened since the mid-1990s. Extreme poverty was halved from 1990 to 2015. Fewer children die from preventable illnesses or waterborne ailments. Many more people have access to education and health care.

We can do better. In today's world, no people should be victims of tragic social problems any more than they should have been in Dickens's time.

PRIVATE TROUBLES, PUBLIC ISSUES

It is hard to imagine a place so devoid of opportunity, where people have so little to lose that they would walk thousands of miles to escape it. That is the story, though, of the "Lost Boys" of Sudan. Their story is a modern legend. It is incredible. It illustrates how personal and private troubles may be caused by social forces.

Victims of Circumstance: The Lost Boys

Sudan in the 1980s was a toxic mix of warfare, food insecurity, destruction, and death. Sudan was always an uneasy place; its borders, drawn by the British in 1947, merged an Arabic Muslim north with a Christian and animist south. During Sudan's transition to independence, it was clear that the peoples of the south would have little power, being ruled by the government in Khartoum. Even before its official independence at the close of 1955, southern troops rebelled. Civil wars and violent conflict followed. Arms poured into the country. In 1982, full-fledged civil war broke out again. Civilians were slaughtered. As is the case today in Sudan and South Sudan, both sides committed atrocities.

To escape the violence and warfare, 20,000 boys, many as young as 5 or 6 years, left their villages in southern Sudan (South Sudan was not independent until 2011). In large groups, they walked over a thousand miles to Ethiopia, but war there forced them to walk again, again through war zones, this time to refugee camps in Kakuma, Kenya. Dehydration, exhaustion, drowning in rivers, war, and wild animals had claimed thousands, nearly half of them, along the way. When they finally reached camp, they were given food and medication. Some learned English and other languages. Some were eventually reunited with their families, but most were not. In the early 2000s, about 3,600 were settled in the United States and thousands more were settled in other countries. By then they were adults, but they did not know snow, let alone electric light switches, butter, flush toilets, or even calendars. They excelled in their new homes, many graduating from colleges, many starting businesses. Some have returned to their hometowns to help the new generation of lost boys as the wars in Sudan and South Sudan continue (International Rescue Committee 2014).

There is no mistaking that these boys are victims. In their cases, it is easy to see the role of social factors. In other cases, with other problems, the social factors may be more difficult to discern. But if you look, you will find them.

To begin studying global social problems, we first need to distinguish personal or private problems from public or social problems. How do you recognize social problems?

Here is an analogy that I use in my classes:

Imagine that you are working as an admissions clerk in the emergency room (ER) of a hospital. Among your duties is recording information concerning what brings people to the ER: what is wrong with them and how they got sick or were injured. It is obvious that each person coming into the ER has a problem.

You notice over a period of time that many people have been injured in car accidents. Furthermore, many of these accidents occurred at a particular intersection of highways, let's say the intersections of U.S. Routes 119 and 22. The ER physicians are able to fix most of these people. They mend their broken bones and repair their injured organs.

Are they really solving the problems? Yes, but also no. Yes, they have solved many of the individual problems of the people admitted to the ER. But there is a larger problem, a social problem. What needs to be done?

Students are pretty quick to see that someone needs to repair the intersection. Maybe bushes have overgrown and are obstructing the view of oncoming traffic. Perhaps the merge lane is too short. Maybe there are potholes. It should be obvious that something is wrong with the structure of the intersection. People will always have problems. However, when a large number of people suffer from the same problem, it is likely to be a social or public problem.

The root cause is in the structure of the social group—whether a community, a society, or the world—just as the root cause of the accidents was in the structure of the highway.

Another important point: Not everyone who goes through the intersection has an accident. Consider what makes some people more vulnerable than others. In the case of the accident, there are a variety of possibilities. People who don't travel through that intersection are not vulnerable. Maybe people with old cars that cannot accelerate as quickly or reliably are more likely to have an accident. Perhaps people who are older cannot twist their necks far enough to see around the overgrown bushes. You can probably think of more factors that would make a person more likely than others to be vulnerable at that intersection. This doesn't mean that the accidents are personal problems. The vulnerable people would not have been vulnerable had the intersection not been faulty.

That is how we understand global social problems. Many individuals suffer the consequences, but the source of the problem is in the global order. The problems people share are larger than their own vulnerabilities, mishaps, or mistakes. Contradictions and dysfunctions in global systems can wreak havoc in individual lives.

Modern global problems affect young and old, rich and poor. No one escapes vulnerability to problems such as environmental pollution and terrorism. However, the people who bear the most severe victimizations are not randomly distributed. People are not equally vulnerable to global social problems. Some people and categories of people have liabilities not of their own making that

PHOTOS 1.1 AND 1.2 PERSONAL VERSUS SOCIAL PROBLEMS: If only a small number of people in a community are homeless, it may well be due to their individual personal problems. However, the presence of homeless encampments is symptomatic that homelessness is a social problem. What factors might make one society or another more vulnerable to homelessness? What might make one person more vulnerable than another person?

Credits: "Looking for Something?" by Adam James. Public domain (Photo 1.1); Cory Doctorow/CC BY-SA 2.0 (Photo 1.2).

aggravate their individual vulnerability. Their liabilities depend on their social location. The location could be geographical such as the country or neighborhood in which they live. It could be their age, gender, race, ethnicity, social class, or one of many other factors. However, being poor—a poor country or a poor person in a wealthy country—and being marginalized because of race, religion, ethnicity, or gender are among the most significant factors determining vulnerability. A sociological imagination helps one to see the social dimensions of problems in the global system, the contributing factors, and thus the potential solutions.

As with the faulty intersection, describing the scope of global problems and determining the people who are most often its victims comprise the first step in confronting them. Explaining the vulnerability of people in the operation of global systems is the second step. This helps us to identify the sources of the problems and point the way to viable solutions. Throughout this process, it is essential to remember that the individuals most vulnerable are akin to the "canary in the coal mine." They suffer the consequences first and usually the most severely, and the rest of us will probably suffer from them later or perhaps more subtly.

> What are some of the social problems that people face in your country? Can you identify some of the factors that make some people more vulnerable than others?

An Example: Suicide

Suicide is one of the problems that we think of as most idiosyncratic, that is, most subject to individual rather than social factors. It is true that most people who commit suicide have some type of personal problem; perhaps they are often depressed or unhappy. Many may have experienced a personal misfortune. But most people who are unhappy, are depressed, or have problems, even severe ones, do not commit suicide. Emile Durkheim studied suicide in 1897 to demonstrate that variation in suicide rates is a social phenomenon; rates of suicide vary with social structural variations. Rapid social change leaves people feeling anomic, without clear guidelines for life. Too few and/or weak bonds among people in society drains life of meaning, and too great an importance placed on the group in relation to the individual can make individuals'

lives seem inconsequential—as if it doesn't matter whether they live or die. All three of these social factors—rapid social change, lack of bonds, and diminution of the individual—cause spikes in suicide rates (Tables 1.1–1.3). Each of these social structural conditions is a mechanism whereby life loses meaning.

Durkheim noted that economic recessions increased suicidal tendencies. The financial crisis that began at the end of 2008 is a modern case in point. One study (Figure 1.1) found that at least 10,000 suicides occurred in North America and Europe as a result of the recession (Reeves, McKee, and Stuckler 2014). Whereas suicide in Europe had been decreasing in the years leading up to the recession, suicide reversed course and began an upward climb when the recession hit. It rose 6.5 percent by 2009 and remained elevated through 2011. In the United States, suicide had already been trending upward, but with the recession the rise accelerated 4.8 percent over the prerecession rate. Suicide in Canada increased 4.5 percent. In contrast, industrialized countries that escaped the recession did not experience an increase in suicide. That is not the whole story or even the most important part.

The increase in suicides was not inevitable. If the social structure, like the intersection on the highway, can be repaired or was not faulty to begin with, the suicide spikes could have been prevented (Figures 1.2 and 1.3). In a related study of 20 European Union countries, researchers found that greater investments in labor market programs and high levels of social capital (social trust) were significant in reducing suicides related to job loss. These social structural factors were effective, whereas suicides "were not significantly mitigated by higher rates of antidepressant prescription, unemployment cash benefits or the total per capita investment in social protections" (Reeves et al. 2015).[1] The authors noted that the suicides were not necessarily among people who became unemployed. Suicides may also occur due to increased economic anxiety. Rapid social change that leaves people with uncertainty, particularly in the context of a weak social fabric, makes people vulnerable. Strong fabrics protect them.

VULNERABILITY TO GLOBAL PROBLEMS

Global Vulnerability

Many challenges confront the modern world. We face a world of uncertainty. Whether in disease control, finance, the environment, or violent conflict, we increasingly face risks that defy rationality because we cannot calculate

A CLOSER LOOK
THE SOCIAL ELEMENTS OF SUICIDE

TABLE 1.1   Suicide and Social Change

Vienna: Economic Crisis (number of suicides)		Italy: Economic Prosperity (suicides per million)	
1872	141	1864–1870	29
1873	153	1874	37
1874	216	1877	40.6

Source: Adapted from Durkheim, Emile. (1951). *Suicide: A study in sociology.* 201, 204. Routledge Classics.

FIGURE 1.1   European Union Age-Standardized Suicide Rate, 2001–2011

Durkheim discovered the influence of social ties and economic shocks on the suicide rate more than a century ago. His theories hold today, as evidenced by the differing effects of the economic shocks of 2007 on suicides in Europe and the United States.

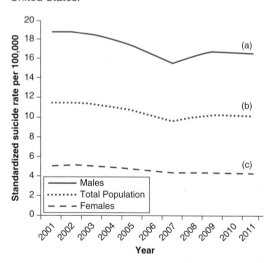

Source: Figure 1 from Reeves, McKee, and Stuckler (2014). Reproduced with permission.

TABLE 1.2   Influence of Family on Suicide

Family Status	Men	Women
Married with children	336	79
Married w/out children	644	221
Widowed with children	937	186
Widowed without children	1,258	322
Unmarried (age 45 men; age 42 women)	975	150
Unmarried (age 60)	1,504	196

Source: Adapted from Durkheim, Emile. (1951). *Suicide: A study in sociology.* 144-145, 155. Routledge Classics.

Note: Children have a protective factor for men and women, but marriage does so only for men.

TABLE 1.3   Influence of Religions and Community on Suicide

Territory	Protestant	Catholic	Jewish
Austria	79.5	51.3	20.7
Prussia	159.9	49.6	46.4
Prussia	187	69	96
Prussia	240	100	180
Baden	139	117	87
Baden	171	136.7	124
Aden	242	170	210
Bavaria	135.4	49.1	105.9
Bavaria	224	94	193
Wurttemberg	113.5	77.9	65.6
Wurttemberg	190	120	60
Wurttemberg	170	119	142

Source: Adapted from Durkheim, Emile. (2012). *Le Suicide Etude de Sociologie.* The Project Gutenberg.

Note: Where countries or territories appear more than once, the data are for different time periods.

A CLOSER LOOK
THE MITIGATING EFFECTS OF SOCIAL EXPENDITURES ON SUICIDE

Social spending on labor market programs prevented the spike in suicides experienced in countries that did not mitigate the effects of unemployment.

FIGURE 1.2   High Spending (>USD $135 per person, per annum) on Active Labor Market Programs

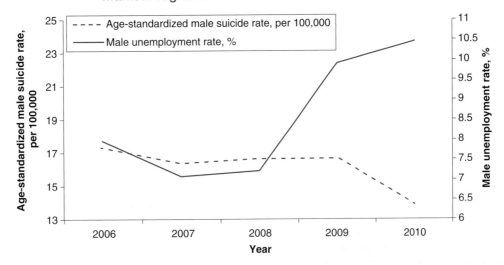

Source: Reeves et al. (2015). Reproduced with permission.

FIGURE 1.3   Low Spending (<USD $135 per person, per annum) on Active Labor Market Programs

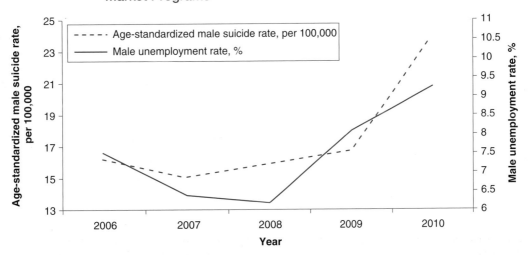

Source: Reeves et al. (2015). Reproduced with permission.

their consequences; they are unknown (Beck 1992). Consider the range of unanswerable questions posed by actions of our own human making. Here are but a few:

- How long will our water resources last if we continue to draw down freshwater resources? Can we replenish them in time?

- What do we do with the nuclear waste we are accumulating? Is there a way in which to dispose of it safely?

- Can we prevent terrorism?

- What do we do if antibiotics stop working against deadly infections?

- Is it safe to combine animal and human DNA to grow human organs in animals?

- Do genetically modified (GM) foods pose health risks or not?

- How high will the world's population grow? Can we slow growth? Should we?

Ironically, most of these are of our own making. They are manufactured risks (Giddens 2003).

- The ferocity and frequency of extreme weather events both are increasing, yet we continue to manufacture greenhouse gases.

- We have bountiful renewable and clean energy sources but are choking on the pollution from the combustion of fossil fuels.

- Natural disasters and ecosystem deterioration drive millions more people from their homes than does violent conflict.

- Violent conflict and persecution still threaten the world long after most of the world has recognized the importance and dignity of all humankind yet has failed to treat many with dignity.

- Tens of thousands of people starve to death every day. This is not because we cannot produce enough food. As a world, we throw away enough food to feed everyone who is hungry. (Waste and Resources Action Programme [WRAP] 2015)

These challenges and risks are synergistic, intensifying the effects of each other. Global agriculture produces more than enough food to feed the world. The economic value of food waste is estimated to be more than U.S. $400 billion per year and increasing (WRAP 2015). Growing the food that is wasted and decay of food waste emit greenhouse gases that add billions of dollars more to economic loss. Greenhouse gases cause global warming, which in turn contributes to hunger and violent conflict as once arable lands no longer support agriculture. Each of these contributes to waves of migration, which can destabilize surrounding countries and feed waves of resentment, discrimination, and persecution.

Because the threats to human security are interrelated, we live in a chronic state of "systemic risk." Systemic risk is the risk of "breakdowns in an entire system, as opposed to breakdowns in individual parts and components" (World Economic Forum [WEF] 2014). Systemic risks are characterized by the following:

- Modest tipping points combining indirectly to produce large failures

- Risk sharing or contagion as one loss triggers a chain of others

- "Hysteresis," or systems being unable to recover equilibrium after a shock. (WEF 2014)

While the synergy of interrelated risks and threat of systemic risk may appear daunting, it can also be cause for optimism. Synergy works both ways. Improvements in one challenge area can affect improvement in others. Mitigating climate change, for example, can lessen drought, affecting food security and decreasing violent conflict.

Individual Vulnerability

As you know, not everyone is equally vulnerable to global risks. Much depends on one's life chances. Very generally, your life chances are the opportunities or resources that you have to achieve your needs. Life chances depend heavily on a person's social location. The country in which you live is one social location. A child born in a Western European country has a much better chance to survive infancy and childhood than one born in a sub-Saharan country, Southeast Asia, or regions in the United States. The chances to obtain adequate food, clothing, and shelter, achieve your potential in physical, intellectual, and emotional development, get a good education, or have a job also vary by social class, gender, race, religion, and ethnicity. These are also social locations. Social location increases or decreases people's vulnerabilities to the risks of the world. This is one way in which, as Mills (1959) said, it is impossible to understand the history of the individual without understanding the history of the society or, for our purposes, the globe.

Locating Countries in the Global System

There are many labels commonly used to describe a country's position in the global system and the relationships among them. The assumption is that countries within any one category have a relatively common set of characteristics. They may be economic, political, or cultural depending on the specific labels and the context in which they are used. These labels are so often used that it is important to understand what they mean and some of the finer distinctions among them.

Developed and Developing

One delineation that social scientists use is "developed" as opposed to "developing." The classification is simplistic, but it is conventional shorthand to group countries that are similar in the characteristics important in determining people's life chances. One of these characteristics is wealth. Developed societies are generally wealthier and poorer societies are generally still developing.

The World Bank classifies countries into income categories according to their gross national income (GNI) per capita.[2] For the fiscal year 2018, the World Bank classifications[3] report uses the following classifications and thresholds:

Low-income economies	$1,005 or less
Lower middle-income economies	$1,006–$3,955
Upper middle-income economies	$3,956–$12,235
High-income economies	$12,236 or more

Source: GNI per capita, Atlas method by World Bank is licensed under CC-BY 4.0 (https://creativecommons.org/licenses/by/4.0/).

The World Bank reports on hundreds of development indicators relating to a country's economy, government, education, health care, and more. The income or wealth (total assets minus debt) of a country is related to life chances but is not sufficient to capture the complexity of life chances. Some countries do better at providing life chances than countries that have higher incomes.

To provide a measure better suited to gauging the actual life chances of people within a country, The United Nations Development Programme (UNDP) calculates the Human Development Index (HDI) to classify countries according to their level of development, defining development as enlarging human choices. The UNDP conceptualized enlarging human choices as a function of two primary dimensions: factors that directly enhance human capabilities and factors that create conditions for human development. Each of these has several components.

Factors that directly enhance human capabilities are a long and healthy life, knowledge, and a decent standard of living. Factors that create conditions for human development are participation in political and community life, environmental stability, human security and rights, and promoting equality and social justice (UNDP 2015). Each of these expands the "human capital" of a society and makes it possible for individuals to achieve their potential.

The HDI is a measure of a society intended to capture the opportunities that people in the society have. It incorporates GNI per capita, life expectancy as an indicator of health, and mean years of schooling and expected years of schooling as measures of knowledge. Countries are given a score from 0 to 1. The closer to 1, the higher the level of human development of a country, the more opportunities and choices people have, and the better their life chances are. Countries are classified as very high, high, medium, and low development. The HDI is not a perfect or complete measure but is a useful tool.

The Human Development Report provides a much more detailed rendering of many indicators that affect the basic four measures of the HDI and a person's life chances. It also provides alternative HDI measures adjusted to reflect how inequality and gender affect the HDI. The Inequality-adjusted Human Development Index (IHDI) considers the impact of three measures of inequality on each country's overall human development score. There is no society in which all people have absolutely equal life chances; however, some come close. In societies with very high levels of inequality, some people are much more privileged than others; some are so deprived as to have little to no choices in life. The Gender Inequality Index modifies the HDI by contrasting women's and men's scores on several important measures: health, labor market participation, and participation in government. As with the inequality-adjusted score, there is no society in which women are equal to men; in some societies, women have little or no control over their own lives.

East and West, North and South, and More

There are many other terms used to distinguish among systems of societies. For the most part, the definitions are not analytically precise. They refer to very general characteristics such as East or the Orient and West or the Occident. In this case, the reference is primarily to civilizational or, broadly speaking, cultural characteristics. These may appear stereotypical. Aspects of the civilizational differences deemed important are an orientation to group welfare taking priority as opposed to individual welfare, respect for and the place of elders in the society, formality and informality of social relations, dimensions of time, reverence for the natural world, and religious differences. Sometimes this delineation is used to refer to up and coming powers (the Asian "Tigers" and China) as opposed to older and declining powers (Europe and the United States) and often just "West" or "the West" to signify Western Europe, North America, Australia, and New Zealand. In these cases, it is referring more or less to the traditionally wealthier societies. Another distinction may refer to the type of government. The societies in the West are assumed to be more democratic than those in the "East," formerly associated with communism.

"North" and "South" are descriptors that refer to northern and southern regions of the globe. However, the implicit meanings of the terms are that the North is richer and dominant and the South is poorer and exploited. "First World," "Second World," and "Third World" are terms that have fallen out of favor, although they appear in older, particularly Cold War, literature about international relations. They infer political and economic characteristics. First World refers to capitalist industrial societies, on the one hand, and the North Atlantic Treaty Organization (NATO) alliance countries, on the other. Second World refers to the Warsaw Pact countries and the USSR—the less developed Eastern bloc. Third World countries refer mostly to nonaligned nations. In some contexts, the Third World and First World are used synonymously with South and North, respectively.

The Organisation for Economic Cooperation and Development (OECD), formed by a United Nations Convention in 1960, is an intergovernmental organization of the richest countries of the world. The purpose of the organization is to foster cooperation to promote one another's and global economic growth while maintaining financial stability. Originating with 20 members, it had 34 as of 2016. Several of the more recent members are emerging economies such as Mexico, Chile, Estonia, and Slovenia. In 2016, Latvia was invited to join and discussions were under way with a number of other countries in Eastern Europe and Latin America.

Throughout this book as well as in social science literature generally, any of these terms may be used. Each has assumptions that the societies being referenced

share important features in the context of the discussion. With respect to global problems, the labels are relevant as shorthand for referring to a cluster of countries with inference to the types and severity of problems they experience and the basic characteristics of their governments and economies.

USING A SOCIAL SCIENCE LENS

The social world is complex. Each social science views it from a somewhat different perspective, illuminating it in a different light. Each social science employs a variety of strategies and perspectives. Each contributes something to our understanding. That is to say that within the social sciences, there are multiple lenses through which we view social life. Each lens brings a different aspect of social life into focus. While some people think of them as competing, it is more useful to see them as complementary. Each of the perspectives is a tool that helps us to exercise a part of our sociological imaginations.

Shaping the Modern World

Taking our cue from Mills (1959), if we want to understand the global problems that plague individuals today, it is necessary to understand some of the history that has shaped the global systems, the societies within it, and people's lives within them.

The Great Divergence

There is not a clear beginning to what we think of as the modern era. A useful starting point is what Samuel Huntington called "the great divergence"—the period when some societies surged ahead of others in development. Although some social scientists date the beginning of the divergence in the 1600s, when the European countries gained dominance in trade and began outpacing societies of the East in wealth and power, others posit it nearly 200 years later, at the time of the Industrial Revolution. In the 15th century, European societies accumulated wealth through trade while India and China, which had enjoyed the highest standard of living in the world until then, did not. Still, until the mid-19th century, there was relative equality among societies (but great inequality within societies). Societies were agricultural, and there was little opportunity for people outside of the landed nobility and trading companies to accumulate wealth (Blinder 2006).

In the mid-19th century, with the Industrial Revolution and the colonization of Africa and Asia, the fortunes of Europe and North America advanced rapidly, separating them from the rest of the world, which remained poor. During the periods of trade expansion, followed by the Industrial Revolution and colonization, Europe created a vast overseas empire that lasted 500 years from the 15th century to the latter part of the 20th century (Figure 1.4) (Landes 1999).

Social scientists vary in the importance they place on one factor or another in the rise of European and later North American wealth and power over the rest of the world. It is unlikely that one factor or set of factors can account for the divergence The West benefitted from good

fortune with respect to geography, climate, topography, and resources that facilitated development. Reforms in social structure and culture such as modern democratic institutions, including balance of powers among government branches, laws to protect property and mechanisms for their enforcement, free education, electricity, and access to markets and financial institutions, as well as the embrace of science and pragmatic use of inventions, contributed to their growth. Many of these factors were not as favorable or lacking in other societies.

We may now be on the brink of a great convergence testing new models of development rather than following the models of the West. Following World War II, the Asian Tigers—Taiwan, Singapore, South Korea, and

FIGURE 1.4   Europe's Surge Ahead

Beginning in the 15th century, European development began to advance ahead of Asia. In the mid-19th century, however, with the Industrial Revolution and colonialism, it surged far ahead. Few countries have yet to catch up.

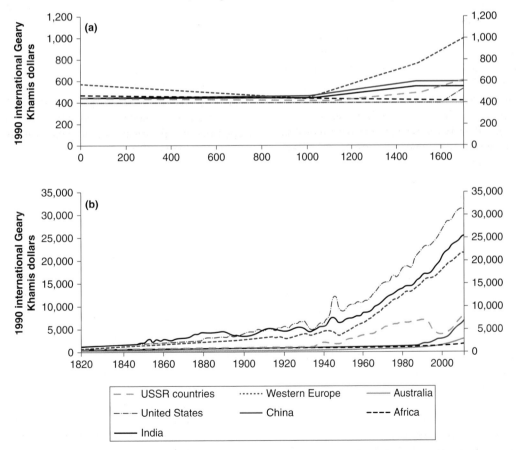

Source: The Australian Government the Treasury. *Economic Roundup Issue 3*, The Treasury available at https://treasury.gov.au/publication/economic-roundup-issue-3-2012-2/x under Creative Commons Attribution 3.0 Australia (CC BY 3.0 Australia). Full terms at https://creativecommons.org/licenses/by/3.0/au/.

Hong Kong—emerged with a roar and quickly caught up to developed societies. Succeeding them in the 1990s, the Asian "Cubs"—Indonesia, Malaysia, Thailand, and the Philippines—arose with growth rates that doubled their incomes. Although some may now be faltering, the "BRICS"— shorthand for Brazil, Russia, India, China, and

South Africa—exercise significant power on the global stage representing the rise of the global South and challenging the political and economic hegemony of Western powers. Even some of the poorest countries have made progress. In the 21st century, growth in developing societies has outpaced that in developed societies. Ethiopia,

GLASS HALF EMPTY OR HALF FULL?

The Achievements: The UN Millennium Development Goals

Although we often talk about global problems in the abstract, it is individuals who suffer the very real consequences of global problems. The United Nations Millennial Development Goals (MDGs) gave visibility to global efforts spearheaded by the United Nations (UN) to improve the lives of the poorest and most deprived people in the world. The goals were established in 2000, and the target date for attaining them was 2015. Comparing the severity of the problems is one indicator of the extent of global problems and a measure of the progress we have made in conquering them.

The primary focus of the goals was poverty reduction, although they cast a wide net encompassing many related factors. The 2015 Millennium Development Report (UN 2015) details significant progress toward reducing poverty and improving education, health, sanitation, living conditions, water and sewage, and gender equity.

The Eight Goals and Progress Achieved

1. To eradicate extreme poverty and hunger
   Extreme poverty rate in developing countries:

1990	47%
2015	14%

2. To achieve universal primary education
   Global out-of-school children of primary school age

2000	100 million
2015	57 million

3. To promote gender equality and empower women
   Primary school enrollment ratio in southern Asia

1990	74 girls to 103 boys
2015	100:100

4. To reduce child mortality
   Global number of deaths of children under 5 years old

1990	12.7 million
2015	6 million

Global measles vaccine coverage

2000	73%
2013	84%

5. To improve maternal health
   Global maternal mortality ratio (deaths per 100,000 live births)

1990	380
2013	210

6. To combat HIV/AIDS, malaria, and other diseases
   Global anti-retroviral therapy treatment

2003	0.8 million
2014	13.6 million

7. To ensure environmental sustainability
   Increased access to piped drinking water

1990	2.3 billion
2015	4.2 billion

8. To develop a global partnership for development
   Official development assistance

2000	$81 billion
2015	$135 billion

Source: From Millennium Development Goals: 2015 Progress Chart, by Statistics Division, Department of Economic and Social Affairs, United Nations, © 2015 United Nations. Reprinted with the permission of the United Nations.

for example, experienced double-digit growth. Tanzania doubled its gross domestic product (GDP). Rwanda's GDP growth averaged 8 percent a year.

Global health is much improved over 20 years ago. But improvement is not consistent year after year. As with most indicators, there tend to be ups and downs within overall upward trends.

Violent conflict certainly remains a serious problem, but the level of violent conflict is much lower than at its peak in 1991. War between two countries has all but disappeared from the global map. War among groups within countries has dominated conflict since the mid-1950s (Figure 1.5). Much of this was fueled by intra-societal struggles for dominance after independence and the Cold War. Since about 2010, there has been a bump up in violence. The overall trend, however, is toward greater peace.

The supply of freedom declined from 2005 to 2017, but the overall trend is improvement (Figure 1.6). People have more freedoms than before and during the Cold War period. More countries rate as free and more people live in freedom than at almost any other time, except 2005, in human history.

Despite the successes, serious global problems persist. Progress is uneven; some regions surpassed goals, while others had little progress. As goals approach completion, the remaining cases are the hardest to solve. For example, developing regions reduced their rate of extreme poverty by 69 percent; sub-Saharan Africa reduced its rate by only 28 percent (UN 2015). Globally, child mortality declined 53 percent; however, Oceania achieved only a 31 percent reduction (UN 2015). Aside from regional differences, achievement varies by gender, by the wealth of countries, and across urban and rural areas within countries.

The Challenges Ahead: The United Nations Sustainable Development Goals

As the MDGs approached their final years, the UN adopted the Sustainable Development Goals (SDGs),[4] which took effect in 2015. The target for their completion is 2030. With 17 major goals and a range of targets within each goal, the SDGs are more ambitious than the MDGs. In tackling a broader set of issues, they

FIGURE 1.5   Global Trends in Armed Conflict, 1946–2015

Few interstate wars have been fought since World War II. Most have been intrastate wars (within states).

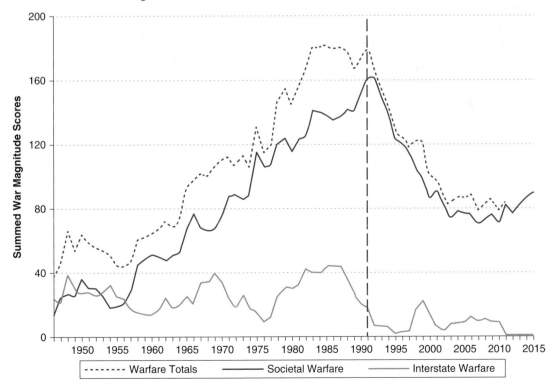

Source: Center for Systemic Peace (2015). Reproduced with permission.

FIGURE 1.6   Percentage of Countries by Level of Freedom, 1985–2015

The percentage of countries rated as free has declined since 2005 but remains well above 1985 levels.

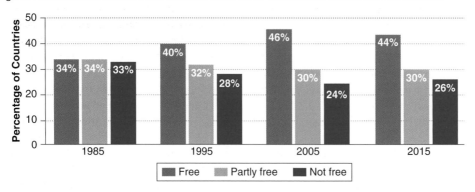

Source: Freedom House (2016). Reproduced with permission.

FIGURE 1.7   Sustainable Development Goals, 2015–2030

Recognizing that all societies need to improve equity and sustainability, the SDGs apply to developed and developing societies.

Source: The 17 Goals by The Global Goals for Sustainable Development (https://www.globalgoals.org/) licensed under CC BY 3.0 (https://creativecommons.org/licenses/by/3.0/).

acknowledge the interdependence of problems and the globe as a single system.

The SDGs apply to all countries, not just the least developed countries. Each goal stresses that every nation needs to improve. The first goal is to end poverty *everywhere;* thus, the goal of ending poverty includes indicators for both rich and poor countries. Each goal stresses "sustainability," acknowledging that development in the past has wreaked havoc on the environment. Life chances of much of the global population must improve, but if it is not done with concern for environmental health, we will not be able to maintain the gains and everyone will be worse off than before (Figure 1.7).

The SDGs pay more attention to the contributions of indigenous communities and traditional knowledge while emphasizing the importance of integrating science into policymaking and assessment. Too often, countries do not have the infrastructure or acumen to implement science-based policy. In such cases, developing countries will rely on foreign technologies and investment. On the other hand, developed societies are just beginning to acknowledge the importance of indigenous knowledge.

The goals are ambitious, but many countries, international intergovernmental organizations, and civil society groups acknowledge their urgency. They are goals that no country can achieve on its own, that require the involvement of civil society and corporations as well as countries and intergovernmental groups, and that require global coordinated action.

PERSPECTIVES FOR STUDYING PROBLEMS

The social world is complex. There are many lenses, many social sciences, through which to view social life. Each social science—sociology, political science, economics, psychology, or anthropology—employs a variety of strategies and perspectives that together make a more complete picture. Within sociology are several perspectives from which sociologists view the social world. Although many sociologists contributed to one or more of these perspectives, their basic premises and frameworks originated from the works of the classical sociologists, primarily Karl Marx, Emile Durkheim, and Max Weber.

Conflict Theory and the Forces of Production

Based in the work of Karl Marx, conflict theorists center their analyses on competition for and differences in power. Marx's focus was economic history—historical materialism—or how power in a society derives from a person's relationship to productive processes. But productive forces change and new ones inevitably emerge. Power shifts from one group to a newly formed group as social structure changes.

From feudal to capitalist societies, power gradually shifted from the aristocracy who controlled land to the bourgeoisie who controlled industrial activity. Transitions occur, Marx argued, because each era contains the seeds of its demise. The aristocrats of feudalism were

impossible without the peasants on whom they relied. But as the aristocracy adopted new methods of production, enclosed land, and grew cash crops, serfs and peasants were forced into the cities—ultimately becoming the workers of industrial capitalist enterprises. The bourgeoisie were impossible without the proletariat, the workers who performed the labor of production. Ultimately, as industrialization progressed along the never-ending quest to satisfy newer needs, Marx believed that professionals such as doctors, lawyers, merchants, and artisans would become absorbed into the working class until there were only two classes, the bourgeoisie and the workers. Workers would become increasingly exploited and alienated.

Because Marx saw survival as the most elemental societal function, those who controlled the forces of production controlled all other parts of the social system as well. Conflict theory focuses on how the bourgeoisie come to control the institutions of society and use them to their advantage. Thus, education prepares people for the jobs needed by the economy and helps to perpetuate inequality within class structure. Laws and policies are written to benefit the elite classes. Marx called religion the opiate of the oppressed. Religion keeps us duped—if not happy, at least not in terrible pain. For example, if you believe that the poor will be rewarded for all eternity and the rich and corrupt will be damned, or that the rich deserve their wealth because they have worked hard for it, you are not likely to rebel against the status quo.

Secular culture supports the power structure as well. Horatio Alger's 19th-century stories featured rags to riches plots of how poor boys of sterling character worked hard and rose to wealth. Called "the Horatio Alger myth," it remains a prominent theme in the United States. The belief that anyone who is willing to work hard can make it in the United States feeds antagonism toward welfare and other anti-poverty programs. Rugged individualism is a variation; people who have amassed a fortune, such as a Bill Gates and Warren Buffet, made their money on their own. These cultural ideals ignore the goods a society provides without which people could not have created their fortunes: the governmental structure of laws that protect their businesses, the roads, railways, ports, and airports their goods travel on and through, the public educational systems that educated their workers, their workers who work overtime and on holidays, the tax breaks, and the government-funded research that brought them to the point where they could make their enterprises a reality.

Who Benefits?

The irony of capitalism is that industrialization released so much productive power that everyone could have a good life. But instead, many all over the world remain in poverty and misery. Marx foresaw that capitalism would create a global economy. Multinational corporations, with the cooperation of elite classes in the poorer nations, developed an international bourgeoisie, a transnational capitalist class that extracts value from both workers and their countries and transforms them into their profit. Little accrues to the workers who create value. Not only the economies but also the political systems of many countries, rich and poor, continue to be controlled by, or at least serve the interests of, capital.

The conflict theory key to understanding the forces behind the essential problems of the world is "who benefits?" Whether it is understanding the relationships among societies or the individuals within societies, those at the bottom of the socioeconomic hierarchy suffer the most. Low achievement within educational institutions, the lowest wage jobs, lack of access to medical treatment, vulnerability to crime and violence—asking who benefits reveals the underlying power structure. Someone usually benefits from another's misfortune.

Contemporary conflict and critical theorists (a type of conflict theory) expand their analysis of conflict to include conflicts in values—such as those fueling the culture wars within and among civilizations—and other sources of domination based on gender, sexual identity and sexual orientation, race, ethnicity, religion, and other fault lines within societies. Conflict theorists operate within the tradition of critical theorists in that they seek not just to explain but also to transform the social order for the emancipation of humankind.

Structural Functionalism: Problems of Order Within and Among Systems

Structural functionalists view societies as living organisms. Organisms are composed of systems and structures, each of which has a set of functions. Human bodies, for example, have a skeletal system, a muscular system, a nervous system, and so on. Each system has a particular function that relates it to the other systems, and together they function to keep the organism alive. Viewing society as an organism focuses attention on structurally different systems such as the economic system, the political system, and the educational system, each of which has a different function but is related to and depends on the others. Together, they keep the society functioning.

The Importance of Solidarity

This perspective grew out of the work of the classical sociologist Emile Durkheim. The central intellectual problem of the fledgling science of sociology as Durkheim saw it was the problem of order. How was order possible in societies that stressed liberty and individual freedom? The answer for Durkheim was that people needed to feel connected to the social community; after all, people were social and did not exist except in a social group. With individualism and individual liberty, what would keep people from merely acting on their own selfish interest?[5] There needed to be some sort of moral code to connect them to the larger social order, to be the basis of solidarity. Collective values and beliefs were extremely important. Without them, society would be nothing but the war of all against all.

In *The Division of Labor in Society,* Durkheim (1893/1964) illustrated how the increasing division of labor in modern society—the differentiation of institutional systems—changed the nature of people's relationships and feelings of solidarity. In traditional societies, there was little diversity; people lived similar lifestyles in agricultural villages and towns. They had a shared set of collective values and beliefs that served as the basis of their solidarity. These values and beliefs prescribed very specific codes and guidelines for living. Consider, for example, the prescriptive nature of Amish life or Sharia law in which everything from clothing to recreation is prescribed. Durkheim called this mechanical solidarity.

However, in modern societies, the division of labor necessitates people developing different occupations and thus different lifestyles and outlooks. As millions of people migrated to the cities to work, live, and recreate together, an entirely different basis for social order emerged. Durkheim called this "organic" solidarity—organic as in held together by differences and thus interdependencies—rather than similarity.

A prescriptive basis of solidarity was impossible. A much more generalized set of values and normative regulations was necessary. In Western societies, people rally around the general values of freedom, equality, and privacy. Periodically however, what they mean in practice is vigorously debated.

Social order is more difficult in the context of organic solidarity than in that of mechanical solidarity. People were freed by the political revolutions and division of labor to be individuals but also made more vulnerable to anomie due to the relative lack of prescriptive guidelines and to egoism due to the lack of strong attachments found in traditional society.[6] This affects the frequency and severity of social problems. In both the global order and many societies, there is insufficient solidarity, either in terms of feeling that one belongs and thus bears some responsibility for common well being or in terms of insufficient consensus on governance and how problems should be resolved.

When the system operates well, everyone in the society, or the globe, acquires all of the resources necessary for them to fulfill their life chances. In traditional societies, economies may have failed to provide what people needed to survive because of insufficient knowledge or technology. People lived shorter lives. In today's world, there is enough knowledge and productive power to provide adequately for everyone in the world. Yet tens of thousands of people die from hunger daily, and violent conflict, international crime, shortfalls in health and education, and myriad other problems threaten people's life chances globally.

Function and Dysfunction

Structural functionalism prompts us to find the problems of order, the dysfunctions, within and among societal and global systems that give rise to these problems. For example, if people are starving, the economy is failing them—not providing them with the needs of survival. Is it because their wages are too low for them to buy healthy food? Do they have access to healthy food? Has environmental degradation or violent conflict resulted in food shortages in their country? Have local farmers been put out of business by agribusiness? Is it all of the above?

The contributions that a system makes to stability are its functions. Dysfunctions lead to instability. Functions and dysfunction may be manifest (intended and recognized) or latent (unexpected or unknown to many). Public housing projects, for example, were intended to be stable and secure housing for the poor; often and in many parts of the world, they replaced viable neighborhoods and became hotbeds of crime. The "green revolution" was intended to solve world hunger, but in many countries it destroyed farmland and put small farmers out of business. Each of these programs, however well intended, had serious unanticipated dysfunctions.

Function and dysfunction are not value judgments. Many things could lead to stability that many people would deem wrong or immoral. In addition, what is functional for the individual or segment of a social order might not be functional for the whole. For example, choosing to have or not have children is not judged as good or bad for most people. In developing societies, however, it may be functional for an individual family to have many children. Children may contribute to the economic health of the family. Where child mortality is high, families may have more children, recognizing that some may die young.

Children may care for parents in their old age and so on. However, for societies that are growing too quickly, more children are dysfunctional. Similarly, in developed societies, many families are having one child or no children. This is functional for the family; however, it is dysfunctional for the society experiencing zero or negative population growth.

Symbolic Interactionism: "If People Believe Something Is Real, It Is Real in Its Consequences"

Conflict and structural functionalist perspectives focus on social systems. Max Weber maintained that to understand social action, it was necessary to understand not only the context in which it occurred (as the perspective of the conflict theorist and structural functionalist) but also the meaning of action to the acting individual. According to Weber (1922/1978), social scientists had a much more difficult task than natural scientists. Social scientists needed to do all of the empirical work that natural scientists needed to do—collect data, find reliable patterns, and track down correlates and causes—and then some; they also needed to interpret what they found.

The objects of the natural world do not act on the basis of meanings. Two hydrogen atoms are not motivated to unite with oxygen to form water. They do not think about it. It does not need to be interpreted or empathized with to be understood. Not so in the social world. People act on the basis of the meanings that they attach to things, ideas, people, relationships, and so on. Weber stressed the importance of understanding people's actions. The social scientist needed to develop all of the quantitative skills of the natural scientist and also needed to develop *verstehen,* the ability to empathize and interpret what an action or belief means to the person acting.

One of Weber's (1905/1976) most influential books, *The Protestant Ethic and the Spirit of Capitalism,* demonstrated the importance of verstehen in understanding why capitalism developed in England and Germany, not in Catholic countries and not in the East. As discussed earlier in this chapter, the divergence in development did not depend on England or Germany's superior technology; for most of history, the technology of the East was superior. Nor was it an accident of fate. According to Weber, the culture of Protestantism, in particular Calvinism, propelled Protestant England into industrialization and the creation of wealth more quickly than either the Catholic countries of Europe or the Islamic and Buddhist countries of the East. The beliefs and values of Calvinism provided the motivations that shaped people's actions, including how they would use technology and wealth, giving rise to capitalism:

- If people believed that they were predestined to heaven or hell, as Calvinists did, wouldn't they want to know—to look for clues? And if they had a duty to God to work, as Calvinists had, wouldn't success in business be a sign that they were favored by God and destined for salvation? That should be enough to keep people working hard. (Our admiration of the wealthy and disdain for the poor is a remnant of this.)

- Having hard working workers means that a business is likely to turn a profit. (After all, workers do not need luxury, which is not in keeping with Calvinism.)

- What can business owners do with their profit? If Calvinism forbids luxuriating in food, wine, perfumes, and silks as French and Italian Catholics were wont to do, they must put their profit back into the work of God, back into the business. (Investment and reinvestment remains a pillar of the capitalist enterprise.)

- Because work was humans' duty, the natural world could not serve God in its natural state; like people, it could serve God only if it were transformed. Thus, a stone did not serve God by being a stone but rather needed to be transformed, by work, into a hammer, a road, a cathedral, or something else to service God. A tree was just a tree and of no service to God until it was transformed into a road, a tool, a chair, or a church.

The duty to transform natural resources through work became the motivation or justification to clear-cut forests, to appropriate the natural resources of Africa and Asia, and to view the environment only as a tool in the pursuit of progress.

Weber also stressed that economic class was not the only source of power in social interactions. Prestige and political office could also carry power because people ascribe meaning to certain statuses. In contemporary society, there is a lot of talk about "branding." People associate characteristics relevant to quality, trustworthiness, and so on to brands. The qualities or characteristics might well be deserved or might not. Nevertheless, the "brand" is only as valuable as the meaning that people attach to it.

Not fully recognizing the importance of verstehen has hampered aid efforts in the developing world and development in poorer areas of rich societies. For example, some feminist movements did not recognize the importance of family roles in traditional societies. It was not until they understood this that they could work meaningfully with the women they were trying to "help." Many people do not understand the importance of wearing a "burka" to some Muslim women who appreciate the freedom from people's eyes, particularly men's eyes. People have criticized the poor for having a "present time" orientation. It was not until ethnographers went into poor communities that they understood that the poor have a very clear understanding of the uncertainty of their futures. If the only thing certain is the present, then making the most of the present is a viable strategy. Understanding why farmers in developing countries might not want to use genetically modified seed when it is "free," why a woman in a poor country might not want birth control, why there are strenuous objections to developing sacred lands of indigenous peoples, in short, understanding any human action, requires that we use verstehen.

Like Marx and Durkheim, Weber did not believe that contemporary social structures necessarily (or even often) worked for the benefit of all of humankind. Using verstehen, he realized that as more and more of life became bureaucratized, people would feel increasingly trapped. His detailed analysis of bureaucracy led him to call it an "iron cage" in which people were imprisoning themselves. Marx, Durkheim, and Weber each probed the social order using multiple lenses to understand and solve the challenges, problems, misery, and social problems emergent at the time of the Industrial Revolution. Using these lenses in concert with one another helps us to understand the complexity of contemporary global problems.

UNDERSTANDING THE GLOBAL ORDER

About 2,000 years ago, the Stoics recognized that the political, racial, ethnic, class, and all of the labels that people use to divide people into "us and them" are artificial. The divisions are socially constructed and not part of the natural world. More than 100 years ago, Durkheim (1893/1964) predicted that societies were becoming so differentiated and people so diverse that at some point all we would have in common with others was our common humanity. In 1948, the Universal Declaration of Human Rights proclaimed that every person had rights as members of humanity and that political, ethnic, racial, and gender distinctions had no bearing on these rights.

Increasingly, people recognize this in their own lives. According to the World Values Survey, 72.1 percent of people in 60 countries agree or strongly agree that they see themselves as a world citizen. Exactly what each person means by this is not certain. At a minimum, if we see ourselves as a citizen of a place, such as a country, we must recognize that we are a member and, as such, we have rights and responsibilities. Most people, then, must think that they are part of the world as a whole and as such have both rights and responsibilities.

Global social problems arise out of the globe as a social system. By seeing themselves as citizens of the world, individuals recognize that they are enmeshed in global systems in the same ways that they are in societal systems. A number of specific theories based in the conflict, structural functionalist, and symbolic interactionist perspectives can help us to understand the globe as a system, inform the study of global problems, and discover the means to grant people's rights and fulfill our responsibilities as world citizens.

Theories of the Global Economy

The global economy is what most people associate with globalization and "the world system." Constant improvements in the speed and cost of transportation and communication have globalized every aspect of the economy. There are not many places or people that are not tied one way or another to the global economy.

Goods and services are produced from resources and components that come from all parts of the world and are distributed to all parts of the world. Production and consumption of goods occurs within a global framework. We are used to the idea that the products that are part of our daily lives may travel around the world before they reach us.

Every step of the production and distribution process adds value to the original raw material, increasing the price and providing jobs. The materials for one product, such as a mobile phone or computer or even the shirt on your back, may come from several countries. Perhaps the cotton in your shirt was grown in the United States or India. That is one cost, and the number of jobs depends on how it was grown and harvested. The cotton may be spun into thread in Indonesia, knit or woven into cloth somewhere else, dyed and sewed into a T-shirt in Colombia or Bangladesh according to the specifications of a designer in the United States, and then shipped around the world to retail and wholesale outlets. You might pick the shirt off the shelf at your local store or order it online from a merchant across the globe. Each step adds to the cost—value added—and provides jobs (Rivoli 2009).

Many of the raw materials needed for products come from the poorest societies. The precious metals needed for electronics come from some of the poorest countries in resource-rich Africa. Some are mined by children; unprotected by basic labor laws, they are regularly exposed to toxins that limit their life chances and work for pennies a day. Although their work is very valuable, little value is added to the cost of the product despite their life-threatening labor. The raw materials are manufactured into components and assembled into products in somewhat richer countries, perhaps China or Mexico. Most are delivered to the richer countries where they ultimately end up in the waste stream and are shipped back to poor countries for reuse or disposal, where the toxic materials have a second chance to pollute.

Few jobs are immune from being moved across country or across the world. Nearly everyone is in the global labor market looking for a job that will pay enough to live comfortably. Both manufacturing and service jobs are mobile. There is a global market for nearly any good or service that does not require hands-on labor such as plumbing or auto repair. The high-level service job market is not exempt; electronic communication facilitates the delivery of services from one side of the world to the other. Every service from reading x-rays, to accounting and engineering, to surgery (through robotics) that does not require hands-on labor can be done off-site or out of the country. Ironically, primary industry jobs are not mobile but can be replaced by technology as happened in agriculture and mining.

The world of investment and finance is borderless. Economic activity can be directed from anywhere in the world. The command centers of global corporations and the banks through which you do business need not be near to where stocks are bought and sold, checks are deposited or withdrawn, mortgages are applied for, or insurance is purchased. A recent advertisement for a global bank boasted that "in a changing world, you can unlock many markets with a single key." The bank has more than 180,000 employees in 70 countries claiming "local knowledge" and "worldwide expertise" (BNP Paribas 2017).

The globalization of capitalism refers to the evolution of capitalism from the early trading companies to a system of ownership, production, and control that incorporates nearly every country into global enterprises and markets. The globalization of capitalism also refers to the transition as formerly socialist-oriented societies transformed their state-controlled economies to free markets, privatizing industries and liberalizing trade. Many societies now have a mixed economy, differing in their balance of free market and state ownership and state planning or control. For example, China, calls itself "market socialism" or "socialism with a Chinese twist." In 1978, China abandoned its solidly socialist system, private enterprises were allowed, and many people became quite wealthy and helped others to advance into the middle class. The Chinese state still owns many of its largest businesses—from agriculture, to banks, to oil, to manufacturing—and much of the economic planning is done by the state. In much of Europe, mixed economies combine private enterprise and substantially free markets with strong social welfare programs. Denmark, Canada, Norway, Sweden, Finland, and Ireland are among the most free economies in the world. However, because each has an extensive social welfare system supported by taxation, they are called social democracies. The United States is mixed, with the largest share of enterprises privately owned, a smaller welfare program, and less regulation. Only North Korea and Cuba remain as socialist economies.

The benefits of the global economy are not shared equally among societies or the people within them. Where a country is located on the value-added chain—the level to which it has developed—determines how wealthy it can become. Each step along the supply chain adds value. Primary industry, the extraction of resources, is lowest on the value chain. Secondary industry, manufacturing, adds value to raw materials, provides better jobs, and increases the wealth of a society. A society that provides high-level services and tertiary industry, such as design, engineering, and financial services, adds "the most" value and can grow very wealthy. Where a country is located and where specific people are located within the country determine many of their life chances.

Inspired by Marxist analysis, world systems analysis and global systems analysis focus on economic relations and the expansion of capitalism at the global level as the source of inequality among countries and people.

World Systems Perspective

Rather than focusing on the division of labor within societies, world systems analysis[7] focuses on international power and the division of labor among societies. Its fundamental tenet is that a society's position in the global economy is more important to individual life chances than people's position in their society. Inspired by Marxist analysis, it focuses on the expansion of capitalism across countries and with it the economic domination of a few countries over many.

The power relations among countries are undeniably a potent force in shaping the internal dynamics of countries' economies. Conflict, competition, and exploitation characterize international relations as some countries maneuver themselves into dominant positions analogous to a global bourgeoisie, controlling the global economy, and other countries fall into subordinate positions, a global proletariat, supplying raw materials and low-level manufacturing and service.

According to the world systems perspective, global capitalism evolved in stages for hundreds of years. In the 16th century, Europeans began their global exploration and conquest. As they controlled and colonized more territory, they took raw materials from one country, used them to manufacture or buy goods in other countries, and sold them in a global market, including the society from which the raw materials came.

Thus, Europe began to establish increasingly complex commodity chains that eventually stretched across the globe. By about 1900, global capitalism was well established. The most developed societies controlled the markets and trade. They are the core of the economic system. Portugal, the Netherlands, Britain, and (since World War II) the United States have each had a turn in dominating the core and global economy as a whole. Other societies, the periphery and the semi-periphery, are less developed and more controlled.

The Periphery. The global commodity chain begins at the periphery. The periphery contains the poorest and politically and economically weakest societies. They are the least well integrated into the global system. A large portion of the labor force of these economies is employed in primary industries, such as agriculture, mining, forestry, and fishery, in which much of the work is insecure and pays very little. They supply raw materials to countries of the core and semi-periphery. Their secondary, or manufacturing, sector is typically composed of labor-intensive low-level technology products such as clothing and textiles. Similarly, their service sector tends to be a much smaller portion of their economy than in more wealthy societies, more concentrated in lower level services, often tourism, and contributes much less value to their gross national product than in higher-income countries.

Because these countries have less physical capital in terms of machinery, factories, and robotics needed for advanced productive capacities, every economic sector is much more labor intensive than in more developed societies. For, example, in the United States, cotton is a technologically managed crop. One large farm produced 13,000 bales of cotton in 2013 with only 13 employees and 26 machines. One machine, a cotton picker, costs about $600,000. This is not in the budget of a farmer in Pakistan, another major cotton-growing country, where nearly all of the picking is done by hand.

Who benefits from the peripheral societies' lowly position? Peripheral societies tend to have little negotiating power in the global political arena and have difficulty in generating fair trade deals, arrangements with multinational corporations, or terms with international financial institutions. Powerful governments and multinational corporations can manipulate prices and wages, at times in collusion with elites in the peripheral societies. For centuries, their resources and labor have been exploited by more wealthy nations. For example, as a condition of joining the World Trade Organization (WTO), developing countries needed to accept patented seeds and the partner fertilizers and pesticides that were created in tandem with them. Multinational manufacturers enter the countries for cheap labor, tax breaks, and weak environmental laws. All of these extract value from the country and force it to absorb part of the cost of production. Are these arrangements functional or dysfunctional, and for whom?

The peripheral societies have the lowest human development scores and greatest concentration of the poor. Finding solutions may be difficult, but it is not impossible. With greater economic diversification and political and technological development, they can rise from the periphery. Determining and establishing the conditions under which participating in global value chains enhances rather than stifles development is essential to providing a quality life in these societies.

The Semi-Periphery. Semi-peripheral societies are a step up on the commodity chain from the periphery. This is a very diverse level. Some societies at this level moved up from the periphery, and others fell from the core. As the middle level, they have a mix of core and periphery characteristics. Primary industries play a smaller role in their economies than in the peripheral societies. They are industrializing, but most industrialized at a later date than the core countries, so their industrial sectors tend not to be cutting edge or the highest value added but rather mid-range. They may manufacture automobiles and electronics but tend not to compete in the core countries. During economic downturns, their economies may benefit at the expense of the core by providing cheaper exports to other semi-peripheral countries and to peripheral countries.

Their institutional forms, government, education, health care, political parties, and so on are relatively more developed than the periphery but less developed than the core. Most of these societies gained independence during the 19th century and were able to take advantage of the migration of manufacturing from the North and West to the South. Brazil and many of the South American countries are in this group. Many Eastern and poorer European countries and rising Asian countries, such as China and India, are in the semi-periphery. Semi-peripheral societies may grow powerful and strong enough to challenge or move into the core, as did the United States.

The Core. These are the richest and most powerful countries. Controlling the highest levels of technology secures their place in the highest value-added sectors of the economy. In the age of imperialism it was shipping, in the industrial era it was high-level manufacturing, and in the service economy of today it is the design and marketing of high-tech products, information services, and finance. In the core society manufacturing sectors, one would find cutting-edge industries such as bioengineering, new materials science, and robotics. Like the United States, these societies may have very profitable and large agricultural sectors, but despite their size these comprise a small portion of their GDP. They have the economic and political clout to negotiate favorably with other countries and steer international organizations on such things as trade and finance. Aid and loans from the World Bank and International Monetary Fund have been directed toward the interests of core societies, particularly during the Cold War. Capital extracted from lower levels accumulates in the core societies. North American and Western European societies, along with Japan and Australia, comprise the bulk of the core. This domination began with industrialization and was enforced through colonialism, the Cold War, and neocolonialism.

World systems perspective is a very useful descriptive for the status of societies around the world and the relationships among them. They cannot explain all of underdevelopment. How, for instance, did the Asian Tigers escape the periphery? What about the new Asian Cubs? How was their escape from the periphery in spite of colonial histories accomplished?

Global Systems Theory

Like the world systems perspective, global systems theory (GST) (Sklair 1999) focuses on the spread of global capitalism. But rather than put states at the center of analysis, it focuses on economic classes. Following Marx, GST identifies classes primarily through their relationship to the means of production. Controlling the means of production in the contemporary world involves more than ownership. The transnational capitalist class (TCC) is the dominant force in the global economy. Nationality of members of the TCC is immaterial in this theory. Their control of the economy comes through the activity of transnational corporations in business, their influence in politics, and ownership of the media.

The TCC exerts control of global economic, political, and cultural systems. Unlike the origins of capitalism wherein the most important political, economic, and cultural processes occurred within countries, GST argues that they now occur without regard to national borders, not within or even among countries. The transnational capitalist class is composed of four "fractions": the leaders of the largest transnational corporations (the corporate fraction), the biggest media and merchant outlets (the consumerist fraction), politicians and bureaucrats (the state fraction), and the technocrats (the technical fraction). Together, they control the spread of the processes of production, from the extraction of raw materials to the delivery to consumers all over the world. Together, these fractions serve to advance the interests of capitalism, from the policy and law that regulate capitalist enterprises to the spread of consumerist culture through the mass media. Global cities are the "command centers" of capitalism, the hubs where corporate, media, and financial headquarters locate.

Just as the transnational capitalist class is spread across the world, so are the transnational labor movements, transnational social movements, civil society organizations, and transnational lower and middle classes. People's interests coincide with their transnational class more than with fellow nationals of another class. Whereas the transnational capitalist class is well organized and powerful, labor across the world is weak. There is no transnational union to represent labor and no effective transnational laws or treaties to protect workers. Even within developed societies, labor has lost much of the influence and capacity to argue for workers' rights that it once had.

Both world systems and global systems theorists predict that we are nearing the end of the capitalist era as we know it. World systems theorists maintain that a challenge to the existing core could come from semi-peripheral societies that are growing, such as China, Russia, and Brazil, or from a coalition of regional societies.

Or the threat to capitalism could come from within the nature of capitalism itself. Capitalism is less appealing if a high level of profits cannot be maintained. Environmental laws will force companies to clean up or not degrade environments. Labor will demand better working conditions and wages. Indigenous groups are claiming more rights to their resources—such as the Native American protests over the Dakota pipeline. All of these would cut into profits by making producers pay more of the cost of production. At the same time, the state, generally supportive of capitalism, is losing legitimacy. The continuing demise of the middle and working classes and concentration of wealth are making it harder for states to maintain order. Together, these forces may bring an end to global capitalism.

As the information society matures, will new productive forces displace capitalism? The information economy relies on a more creative workforce than an industrial economy. With outsourcing and contracting, will everyone become an independent contractor?

Global systems theorists predict that as human rights ideology advances, it will diffuse from political and cultural spheres to the economic sphere. Because capitalism is exploitative, human rights pose a serious threat. Environmental sustainability is another. Already, corporations recognize the threat that climate change poses to economic systems.

What comes after capitalism—perhaps a more authoritative regime with greater concentration of economic and political power or something better for all of humankind—remains to be seen.

Global Culture

There are two ways in which to look at global culture. One is to consider cultural diversity—how cultures of the world vary—to appreciate each for what it offers to enrich people's experience of the world and understand the world from another person's point of view. Cultural diversity enriches our experiences within the world and within societies. People have moved foods, clothing, music, and their values and lifestyles through trade, migration, and travel for millennia. Cities are hubs for these interactions. Nearly every city in the world offers a taste of the diversity of global cultures. Ironically, as cities become more diverse, they become more alike in their diversity.

If you aren't near a city, you can experience the world through modern communication. You can visit the Seven Wonders of the World online, watch news and entertainment from other countries, order products (even food), find recipes, and experience nearly any aspect of any culture. We all can become cosmopolitan and appreciate the beauty and value within other cultures.

Along with people and products, ways of thinking about the world, ideas, and values travel. Some are embedded within the products. Hip hop is a global phenomenon. Although the lyrics may vary, the style and "attitude" of male, and increasingly female, adolescent angst is embodied in the clothes, facial expressions, dance, and rhythms of the voice and music.[8] The near-global popularity of blue jeans signifies more than comfort. The independence and rebellion of youth, identification with the West, being modern, and the desire for equality (even though this may be a perverse charade in the case of expensive designer jeans, particularly those manufactured with rips, marks of wear, paint splatters, and already dirty) are woven into every pair, ironically now often made in the developing world (Crothers 2012).

Ideas spread globally through education, nongovernmental organizations, and intergovernmental organizations as well as through ordinary people in their travels. These diffuse different ways of looking at the world. We all look at the world from different perspectives depending on the context. At home deciding how to celebrate a holiday, we look to tradition. When we're studying for an exam, we use experience and consider what worked or didn't work the last time. When a child is born, many people look to religion even if they do not regularly practice. If we are deciding the best way in which to cure a disease or run a business, we turn to rationalization.

Rationalization is one of the most important components of global culture. It grew out of Enlightenment thought and has diffused globally. Rationalization is a way of thinking grounded in reason rather than in tradition, common sense, or religion. Through science, rationality helps us to create reliable and valid knowledge about the world and find the best ways in which to do things.

In addition to being a way of gaining knowledge, rationalization is a way of organizing the world. It emphasizes calculability—that everything can in some way be measured and arranged for the purpose of efficiency and predictability. It is a tool for organizing social life. Global trends in institutional arrangements, whether governmental, educational, hospital, military, manufacturing, or business enterprises, use rational, primarily bureaucratic, models. But as Weber lamented, bureaucracy might have appeared rational and functional but was highly dysfunctional. Bureaucracies were, in Weber's terms, "iron cages" that were alienating.

"Human rights" is another of the most important elements of global culture. The UN adopted the Universal Declaration of Human Rights in 1948. Representatives of all regions of the world formed the drafting committee. Although the declaration does not have the force of law, two treaties that followed, the International Covenant on Civil and Political Rights and the International Covenant of Economic, Social, and Cultural Rights of Indigenous People, do have the force of law. All three of these documents influenced every national constitution written or revised after it. Some rights, such as freedom of expression, of speech, and of belief, appear in nearly all (more than 90 percent) national constitutions. Although there may be disagreement about exactly how each right applies in a particular circumstance, this is no different from the diversity within any national culture. Regional conventions and covenants such as the Helsinki Accords adopted in 1975, the Arab Charter on Human Rights adopted in 1994, and the African Charter on Human and Peoples' Rights adopted in 1998 also recognize the universality of human rights. The UN Conventions, regional charters, and national constitutions that enshrine human rights have the force of law. They lay a normative groundwork for citizens in their relations to societies and the world's responsibility to people regardless of the country in which they reside.

Appadurai's Global "Scapes": A Theory of Global Culture

How culture diffuses around the world is the subject of Arjun Appadurai's five global "scapes." Appadurai (1996) used scapes to capture the nature of global cultural flows. A landscape is not static. It is constantly changing as water, wind, people, and animals flow or tread through it. Each of these creates paths in the landscape. Valleys are dug out by water, and dunes might be built by wind. People and animals create pathways and build habitats, dams, and roads that change the landscape. The landscape changes the flows as well. A river needs to bend around rocks or hills. The pathways of people and animals adjust to the terrain. Last, a landscape looks different from different vantage points and to the different people viewing it.

So too with global culture. The increased volume and ease of communication, which can be instantaneous from one side of the world to the other, and transportation, which can move masses of people from one side of the world to the other in a matter of hours, produced massive flows of information globally. Because people are on both the sending and receiving ends, the flows of information are shaped by and subsequently shape people's images of the world. As with the symbolic interactionists, the flows create a socially constructed reality shared globally but unique to every individual.

Appadurai identified five distinct but related flows that circulate culture globally:

- Ethnoscapes capture the flow of people for migration, for recreational travel, on business, to give assistance as part of a nongovernmental or governmental organization, and for any other reason. As people move about, their alliances, relationships, and communities morph and shift. They carry ideas and images with them, transmit them to others, and receive ideas and images from others. The communication among them is not perfect any more than any communication is; thus, we learn and in part invent the images and ideas of others that we both send and receive.

- Mediascapes are produced by mass and social media. They influence how people view other people in their own country as well as in other countries—how they understand the situation of others.

- Ideoscapes are the images of ideologies. They move within political domains and reach out to people through political parties, governmental and educational agencies, protest groups, and civil society organizations.

- Technoscapes are the flows of technology, high and low tech, mechanical and informational. This flow is important to determining the occupational structures of high- and low-wage jobs within countries, the movements of money (e.g., cell phones have become important in conducting business in developing countries), and the tools available to people for communication, education, and so on.

- Financescapes are the flow of currency and stock markets and of investment into and out of countries. These affect everything from the value of currency to the cost of goods. The financial crisis of 2008 demonstrated the interconnected nature of financial systems. Contagion spread globally in days, to some places within hours, shutting down banks and businesses.

Each of us develops our impressions, attitudes, and beliefs about the world and the people in it based on these flows with far-reaching consequences. Consider the situation of refugees. How you think of refugees may be influenced by knowing or working directly with refugees or perhaps pictures in the newspaper and accounts of their situations. Maybe you discuss the issues with your family, with friends, or in a class. Different accounts present us with different images and interpretations. Whether you decide that refugees are a threat or deserving of refuge, or whether you see them as a drain on the economy or a benefit, depends on how you assimilate these flows and convey them to others and is shaped by your own predispositions and prior knowledge and beliefs.

Global Governance: Who Gets What, When, and How

Complex social systems need a set of processes for regulation and coordination, enforcement, settling disputes, and deciding how resources will be distributed or used. These are the functions that we usually ascribe to governments. There is no global government. Instead, there is a relatively uncoordinated and often unaccountable multifaceted system of governance. Layers of governance are composed of individuals, states, intergovernmental organizations, non-governmental organizations, corporations, and civil society groups, each of which has a role, often unofficial, in determining "who gets what, when, and how," the defining function of politics according to Lasswell's (1960) famously titled book.

International Governmental Organizations. International organizations have several mechanisms to shape global norms. Their charters or constitutions lay out a set of principles—such as for human rights, fair trade, and/or environmental sustainability, among others—that members promise to uphold. To join most international organizations, countries must meet membership criteria. Membership criteria are a way of getting compliance to international or regional norms. Some, such as the European Union, might require a certain type of economic system, in this case a free market. Others require relationship commitments such as NATO's commitment to mutual defense—an attack on one member is an attack on all members. Members could be suspended or expelled for not maintaining the conditions of membership.

International organizations have authority to make and enforce policy and law within the boundaries determined by their member countries. Organizations that provide loans might require recipient countries to make structural adjustments to their economies in order to acquire a loan. The UN, the International Atomic Energy Agency, and the WTO, among others, legislate through treaties and conventions and have the authority to enforce them through some form of sanctions ranging from being "called out" in a report to diplomatic meetings, ending diplomatic relations, being excluded from international events, and economic sanctions. Military sanctions are generally reserved for humanitarian interventions.

These organizations shape global systems. Whether these organizations operate for the common good or in the interests of the most powerful members is a source of contention.

Civil Society Organizations. Civil society organizations (CSOs) are non-familial, non-state, and non-economic organizations that people voluntarily join to pursue their common interests. Their common interest could be anything from a Parent–Teacher Association at a local school to the International Red Cross. For the purpose of discussing global problems, the CSOs of most interest are those working domestically or internationally to effect solutions to people's problems.

CSOs have a decided impact on governance through their work. The decisions they make distribute resources and have direct impact on people's lives. They sit on expert panels and boards and influence governmental and corporate decision making and activities. The UN Integrated Civil Society Organizations System has entries for more than 24,000 organizations. The entries provide information on the region in which they work, the type of organization, and the issues on which they work. They address a range of issues such as economic and social development, peace, sustainability, conflict resolution, democracy development, and gender issues. Most engage in all aspects of advocacy for their issue from educating the public and policymakers, lobbying for policy changes, to delivering services "on the ground" where they are needed.

Non-governmental organization is a similar term that applies primarily to aid agencies. It is a type of civil society organization. Politicians or business owners may very well be members of CSOs, but not in their capacity as representatives of a government or their business.

Multinational Corporations. Any corporation that has facilities or offices, or even a mailing address, in more than one country is a multinational. These corporations can be very powerful and exert tremendous influence not only in the countries where they operate but also globally. Just in deciding that they will open a new facility, they influence policy within nations. Countries may compete for investment, sacrificing environmental quality, tax revenue, or their own development for investment money.

Corporate executives sit on global decision-making bodies as experts, influencing global regulations and policies. They lobby within nations and global bodies, currying favor and promising rewards for the countries or bodies that act in accord with their demands. Because their responsibility is to make profit for their shareholders, they act in their interests rather than in the common interest. Increasingly, however, some corporations are recognizing that social responsibility may actually make a positive impact on their bottom line.

Global Governance and Global Problems

Each of these actors in global governance—intergovernmental organizations, international civil society groups, and multinational corporations, along with states—operates independently as well as in concert. Even when each believes that it is operating for the greater good, their goals may be in conflict. Environmental organizations work for cleaner production of goods and energy. Workers' groups may fear that this will result in job loss.

Within international governmental organizations, countries often have their own interests in mind rather than the overall good. In most of these organizations, countries with greater economic power have a greater voice in deciding courses of action. Multinational corporations are accountable to stockholders and use their ethic to make profit as a rationale for moving to low-wage countries, avoiding taxes and strict environmental laws. International governmental organizations are accountable only to their funders. Even with good intentions, they may end up distorting local needs in pursuit of more global goals or neglecting needy groups in favor of ones with more popular causes.

There is no overarching body that can enforce cooperation among these groups or the pursuit of common goals. Global governance thus becomes a global competition for power and influence, with each group pursuing its own ends and accountable to its own stakeholders.

The Global Community: Global Civil Society

Our neighborhoods, our cities, our country, the world—these are the physical communities that we inhabit. Our clubs and organizations, our friendship groups, the places where we volunteer—these are the social communities that we inhabit. We build these communities through interaction.

A strong social community makes a country strong. When we belong to clubs and organizations or have friends and networks of acquaintances, we build ties to one another and throughout our communities. Some ties may become very strong such as with our closest friends or an organization with which we volunteer and to which we feel deeply committed. Other ties are weaker, perhaps only a face or name recognition, but both types are important. These strong and weak ties are the basis of civil society. The more robust and plentiful the ties, the more social capital (Putnam 2000) is in a neighborhood, a city, a society, or the world.

Capital is a thing of value that can be put to use to obtain a goal. For example, "human capital" is the total of resources inherent in the population of a community—the level of education and the overall health and the well-being of the people. The "higher" the human capital, the better equipped a community is to achieve its goals. "Economic capital" is the financial resources. A person's "social capital" is the value of the person's ties to others. People with a lot of social capital have many others on whom they can rely. They have people who they can call on for help, support, a favor, or advice. Some of these may be close friends, while others may be members of the same organization or people who know people they know. Social capital is a resource.

The global civil society is all of the formal and informal connections that people make throughout the world through travel, migration, education, and volunteer work. As travel and communication among people of different countries increase—think of how many students travel abroad every year—the global social fabric becomes more tightly woven with extensive networks of bonds connecting diverse people all over the world. The long-debated "six degrees of separation" thesis—that everyone in the United States is connected to everyone else by, on average, a chain of six people—seems to now hold at the global level.[9]

The connections people make the world over increase the social capital of the world. Especially important is "bridging capital." Bridging capital is capital that is built among people who are different from one another. Bridging capital "bridges" the fault lines among people—nationality, ethnicity, race, and social class—whether in a town, a country, or the world. Without bridging capital, it would be difficult for people to understand their common interests and goals. It would be difficult for people to understand one another's perspectives. Bonding capital is the capital built up among people who are alike in characteristics such as age, race, and social class. Both bonding capital and bridging capital are important; both build trust. As a community, large or small, a good measure of social capital means that people can work together to achieve common goals for the common good. It has collective efficacy.

A significant body of research on social capital has accumulated since the 1990s that confirms its importance. The OECD established a social capital project to look at the variety of ways in which social capital has been used in the social scientific literature. It found four distinct uses among the variety of definitions in the literature. Two apply to individuals: personal relationships and social network support. Two apply to collectives: civic engagement/trust and cooperative norms (Scrivens and Smith 2013). In studying global problems, social capital of the collective is most important, whether at the level of the community, society, or the world.

World Society Theory

World society theory (Meyer et al. 1997) is the counterpoint to global systems theory. Whereas global systems theory centers analysis on the global economy as the driver of global relations, world society theory argues that the global economy, global culture, and globalization generally grow out of the relationships among people—the global civil society—that exist outside of the formal operations of the economy or states.

The ideas that give shape to economies as they develop, to governmental bureaucracies, and to educational institutions emerge from the networks of people sharing ideas. As people adopt particular ideas and models, they spread and many will become part of global culture.

Ideas about human nature, the nature of knowledge, rationalization, and science, the nature of individualism, state sovereignty, human rights, the rule of law, the importance of environmentalism, and many more spread through civil society through the activity of intellectuals, people traveling for pleasure, the advice of experts, educational exchanges, and civil society groups—in general, through people interacting with others.

The ideas become a set of templates available to actors—whether individuals, organizations, governments, or corporations—the world over from which they can borrow. They serve as blueprints for the "good state," a "sound educational system," economic and political "freedoms," the good "global citizen," and so on. As the templates become more clearly defined, they crystalize and inform those in decision-making positions.

In other words, global culture develops through interactions in global society. Global culture, rather than the economy, shapes global life and subsequently the internal dynamics of societies as they adopt and conform to global models. The models available in the global culture inform the structures of economic and political systems, of education and governments, of non-governmental and intergovernmental organizations.

This is not to say that there are not competing global models. Clearly, there are. World Wars I and II, the Cold War, and the culture clashes within and among societies were and are clashes among competing global models.

SUMMARY

The study of global problems is complex. When studying social problems within a society, recognizing the social factors that give rise to problems and the factors that make particular individuals more vulnerable to them can be difficult. Studying global problems adds another level of analysis—identifying the global forces that give rise to global problems and the factors that make particular societies and the individuals within them more vulnerable to them.

Teasing out these forces and determining the impact of each requires understanding how the global systems that operate on societies evolved and how their momentum is likely to shape the future. If the forecast for the future appears good, knowing how it is developing can help to ensure it. If the forecast is not good, understanding how it developed can help to change the forecast.

Global culture has developed in such a way that the mandate for a good society is one that fulfills the potential life chances of all its members. A good world has the same mandate. The Universal Declaration of Human Rights has become the centerpiece of global culture. Human rights are everyone's rights as a member of global society. Upholding everyone's human rights is everyone's responsibility as a member of global society.

Throughout the course of this book, a select sample of global problems is analyzed. Each analysis begins with an examination of the data and identification of patterns in the data. Considering alternative explanations—guided by theories that suggest forces to examine—for societies' and individuals' vulnerabilities is the second phase. Finally, some of the people working in the field through civil society organizations, governmental organizations, or intergovernmental organizations to help solve these problems are spotlighted.

Not all global problems selected, or even every aspect of the global problems selected, can be covered completely. However, by studying some, working through the analysis, considering the questions, and doing related analyses, you will develop skills to examine and evaluate problems on your own—problems that plague the world now and ones that are likely to arise.

DISCUSSION QUESTIONS

1. What is the difference between a personal problem and a social problem? What indicators would you look for to determine whether an issue is a personal or social problem?

2. What are the problems that confront your community? Can you identify social factors at work? Are there any individual-level variables that make particular people more vulnerable than others?

3. Consider one of the problems confronting your community. Compare the approaches to the problem that would be taken by a conflict theorist, a structural functionalist, and a symbolic interactionist.

4. Do wealthy nations have a responsibility to help poorer nations raise their standard of living? Why or why not? If they do, how far does the responsibility extend? How would you balance the needs of "home" with the needs of people in poorer or violence-ridden countries?

5. Rank the sustainable development goals from highest to lowest in order of the priority you think they should have. What criteria did you use in deciding? In a small group, divide a budget among the goals, using 100 percent to represent all of the money in your budget.

ON YOUR OWN

1. Investigate the relationship between colonization and human development and/or societal wealth. Randomly select 10 countries from each of the Human Development Index categories from least to highest development countries. Using the Central Intelligence Agency *World Factbook,* find out whether or not a country was colonized and its date of independence. (Do not count countries that separated from another country as a former colony.) Does there appear to be a relationship between colonization and development?

2. There are many country and global maps of social factors such as poverty/wealth rates, unemployment, educational attainment, teen pregnancy, and homicide by state. Choose a selection of these or other maps. Describe the patterns related to severity that you observe. Compare and contrast the maps, noting which have similar patterns. Summarize your observations.

3. Compare the maps of country scores on the Cato Institute index of economic freedom with scores on the Freedom House index of political freedom. If you have access to Excel, SPSS, or another statistical program, find the correlation between these scores. Is there a significant relationship?

NOTES

1. Note that the associations in these studies are at the aggregate or country level, not the individual level. Causal statements at the individual level cannot be inferred.

2. There are fine distinctions among these three measures of income. Gross domestic product is the value of goods and services produced in a country. Gross national product (GNP) is the income produced by the nationals of the country, whether at home or abroad. Gross national income is similar to GNP with adjustments for taxes and receipts not otherwise accounted for in GNP.

3. Using the World Bank Atlas method, "The Atlas conversion factor for any year is the average of a country's exchange rate for that year and its exchange rates for the two preceding years, adjusted for the difference between the rate of inflation in the country and international inflation; the objective of the adjustment is to reduce any changes to the exchange rate caused by inflation" (World Bank n.d.).

4. See United Nations General Assembly Resolution 70/1, *Transforming Our World: The 2030 Agenda for Sustainable Development,* for the pledge made by states in adopting the SDG and a detailed list of the indicators within each goal. It can be found at http://www.un.org/ga/search/view_doc.asp?symbol=A/RES/70/1&Lang=E

5. Durkheim was very critical of Herbert Spencer and other utilitarians who thought that competition for and the signing of contracts that bound people based on their own self-interest was the source of social order. Spencer coined the term "the survival of the fittest" to

express the idea that contracts went to the winners of the competitions and that they would flourish while others would (and should) perish.

6. The solution to the dilemma, for Durkheim, was new intermediate structures similar to the voluntary groups that make up civil society and that Alexis de Tocqueville credited with strengthening democracy in the United States.

7. World systems perspective (also called world systems theory) was originated by Wallerstein (1974).

8. Keeler's (2009) study of rap in Burma found that the form was consistent with rap in the U.S. but the content avoided sex and violence and focused on love won and lost.

9. Most of us have experienced meeting a stranger, only to find that we have a common friend. We exclaim, "It's a small world." Milgram's (1967) chain letter may be the most famous test of the small world thesis, in which letters sent from people in Kansas and Nebraska reached targets in Boston moving only through people knowing each other on a first-name basis. The average number of links in the chain was only six. More recently, Watts (1999) used mathematical models to find that the small world phenomenon is very likely real and results in the rapid dissemination of information (and disease).

2

Socioeconomic
Fault Lines

INEQUALITY, POVERTY, AND DEVELOPMENT

WHAT IS GOLD WORTH?

Michelle, a 15-year-old Filipino girl, works at an underwater gold mine. She started when she was 8 years old. She, along with many of her friends, spends much of her day standing waist deep in a mercury-contaminated river panning for gold ore. When they find ore, they mix mercury into it in open wooden pans with their bare hands and then burn it, with nothing to protect them from the toxic fumes. Michelle and her friends report that they suffer from tremors and muscle spasms. They thought that the cold water caused their problems. No one told them that mercury was toxic.

Mercury is a toxin that attacks the nervous system. Mercury exposure can cause brain damage, tremors, partial blindness, deafness, memory loss, and spasms, among many other problems. Household use and many other uses are banned in the United States and other developed countries.

Some children at the mine are submerged for hours a day in the polluted water, digging gold ore out of the mucky river floor. Even though underwater mining is identified as being among the worst forms of child labor,[1]

LEARNING OBJECTIVES

After completing this chapter, students should be able to do the following:

2.1 Document the trends in inequality of income and wealth among and within the globe, regions, and nations as well as among individuals

2.2 Evaluate the consequences of inequality and poverty for people's life chances

2.3 Understand how globalization, historical, environmental, cultural, and geographic factors contribute to uneven development and inequality among countries

2.4 Distinguish developing countries from developed countries and know the basis on which they are classified

2.5 Understand the relationship between labor force participation in economic sectors and human development

2.6 Propose actions that international governmental organizations, the private sector, non-governmental organizations, and states can take to improve people's life chances

14 percent of children who live in the mining areas of the Philippines—about 18,000—work in the mines, underwater and underground. Many are 9 or 10 years old, some even younger. In addition to tremors and spasms, they complain of back, shoulder, hand, and other pain from carrying heavy loads of ore and from being submerged in cold water. Some children die from suffocation when their air compressors fail. None of them knew of hidden, long-term consequences they may be suffering.

The Philippines is the 20th largest producer of gold in the world. Small-scale mines are scattered through 30 provinces of the Philippines. Although children under 18 years are not permitted to labor in hazardous conditions, laws are rarely enforced in the small mines that produced 70 to 80 percent of the nation's 18 tons of gold in 2014. Tens of thousands of children work in equally hazardous conditions in the small-scale gold mines in Africa, Asia, and Latin America. Many toil with rarely a day off, and many never go to school, let alone enjoy the lifestyle of teens in the developed world.

Ruth, who was 9 years old when she started laboring in the mines, is now 15. She says, "There were times I would think about slashing my wrists because I couldn't take the hardship."

Is the gold worth the cost of these children's health, education, and future? What chance at life do Michelle and Ruth have?

Source: As reported by Kippenberg (2015), Human Rights Watch.

"The personal is political" was an anthem of the feminist movement of the 1970s. As a slogan, it insisted that the personal problems that women faced—from poverty, to inequality in the workplace, to lack of representation in the power centers of governments and the economy—were a function of systematic discrimination, not personal failing. The slogan applies not just to women. It also applies to the poor and to racial, ethnic, religious, and other minorities all over the world.

Despite the Millennium Development Goals' success in halving the number of people living in extreme poverty from 1990 to 2015 and continuing economic growth, more than 800 million people still lived in extreme poverty in 2015 (United Nations [UN] 2015b) (Figure 2.1). Poverty and inequality are widespread throughout the world and within societies but are not spread randomly. They are built into the global economy and enshrined in both national and global policies. Who benefits most from a country's economy and who receives the least is a function of both the society's position in the world and individuals' positions within the society. Their personal experiences of inequality are political.

This chapter examines the functions and dysfunctions of the global economy—who benefits and who does not. Poverty and economic inequality plague both global and domestic economies. Both affect an individual's life chances. This chapter explores the links among societal and global development, economic inequalities, and life chances.

HOW WELL DOES THE GLOBAL ECONOMY FUNCTION?

How bad can life be that families keep their children out of school and put them to work in dangerous conditions? How can the global community, which has so much wealth and plenty, allow this to happen? How and why has the global economy failed so many people?

We can evaluate an institution by how well it fulfills its primary functions. An economy should procure, produce, and distribute adequate means of survival for the people dependent on it. For the global economy, that is all of humankind. The means of survival include food, water, shelter, energy, and freedom from preventable

A CLOSER LOOK
PEOPLE LIVING ON LESS THAN U.S. $1.25 A DAY

The number of people living in extreme poverty has declined by more than half since 1990, but close to a billion people still qualify as extremely poor.

FIGURE 2.1   Extreme Poverty Between 1990 and 2015 (in millions)

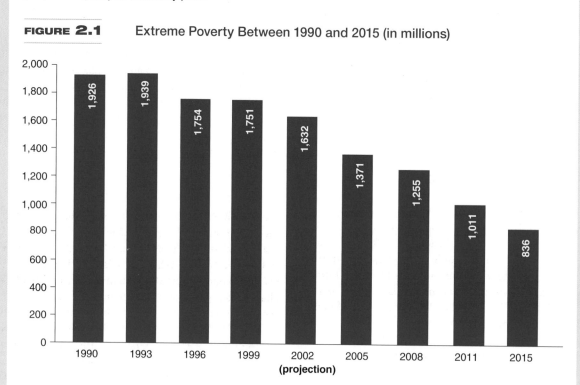

Source: From *The Millennium Development Goals Report 2015*, by the Inter-Agency and Expert Group on MDG Indicators led by the Department of Economic and Social Affairs of the United Nations Secretariat, © 2015 United Nations. Reprinted with the permission of the United Nations.

illness. The economy should not sully the necessities of life such as air, water, land, and other living things because health and long-term sustainability depend on them. The means through which the global economy provides for life chances are the subject of continual debate. What cannot be denied is that billions of people are living on the edge of survival and too many are not surviving. The global economy is failing many people in the world. Here is a sampling:

- 45 percent of childhood mortality is caused by hunger (World Health Organization [WHO] 2016).

- More than 800,000 children under 5 years die from diarrheal disease related to polluted water every year (Centers for Disease Control and Prevention [CDC] 2016).

- About 1 billion people lack adequate shelter; 100 million are homeless (United Nations

Educational, Scientific, and Cultural Organisation [UNESCO] 1998–2001a).

- 3 billion people do not have access to enough energy to meet their needs (UNESCO 1998–2001b).

- Approximately 7 million people died prematurely in 2012 as a result of air pollution exposure (WHO 2014).

- More than 900,000 children under 5 years die from pneumococcal diseases, preventable with a vaccine (WHO 2015).

- Nearly 4 million women, who would not have died if they lived in higher income countries, go missing each year (World Bank 2012).

It is not surprising that the opportunities to achieve our potential are not randomly distributed. For the most part, the statistics above are characteristic of developing countries. Living in a poor country makes a person more likely to be a victim of food scarcity, to live in a slum, to live without electricity, to be poisoned by air pollution, to lack basic health care, and to die early. People in developing countries are more likely to be victims of violent conflict, human trafficking, environmental destruction, and nearly every global social problem. That is the cost of global inequality among countries.

The relative position of individuals within societies also affects life chances. It goes without saying that those at the bottom of the economic pyramid, at both the societal and global levels, suffer more than those at the top. The poor in some rich societies have life expectancies, health, and education outcomes similar to those in many developing societies. In addition, it is important to note that in societies that have limited people's life chances through inequality, everyone suffers, not only those at the bottom. For those reasons, it is necessary to examine both global and domestic economies and inequalities.

UNDERSTANDING INEQUALITY

Measuring inequality is not as straightforward as it might seem. Both income inequality, usually measured as an annual flow of money accruing to an individual, a household, society, or the world, and wealth inequality, the total financial assets of these actors, are important. How much income comes from labor—a wage—and how much is earned through ownership of financial assets (stocks, bonds, real estate, etc.) is also important in understanding the capacity of an actor to accumulate wealth.

There are also several ways to measure inequality. The Gini ratio looks at the deviation of the actual distribution of income or wealth in comparison with perfect equality, with perfect equality being 0 and one person owning everything being 1. The Parma method looks at the relationship between the bottom 40 percent and the top 1 percent. Other methods look at some portion of the top (1, 10, or 20 percent) in relation to some portion of the bottom, or the earnings of people at the 90th percentile in comparison with people at the 10th percentile (the 90/10 inequality ratio).

Income Inequality Among Regions

The World Bank is a major source of data on income, inequality, and life chances. The World Bank reports that the value of the world production in 2014 was close to U.S. $78 trillion. While there is sufficient income to give everyone sufficient life chances, inequality of life chances is high. Growth has been uneven; while a few regions[2] are converging with higher income countries, many are relatively stagnant or have declined (Table 2.1 and Figure 2.2). Sub-Saharan Africa has only 6 percent of the gross national income (GNI) per capita of North America, and South Asia has less than 10 percent. GNI per capita of low-income countries is only about 1/60th that of high-income countries. There is also significant inequality among countries within regions.

Comparing the ratio of the incomes of developing regions to that of developed regions over time shows that inequality is decreasing; the line representing the developing world rises, indicating that the income gap between developing and developed nations has been decreasing since about 1990. However, as the lines for each region show, the increase is due to growth in East Asia, particularly the rapid growth of China and India at the end of the 20th century. The lines representing Latin America, Africa, and Oceania remain virtually unchanged, indicating that inequality between each

A CLOSER LOOK
INEQUALITY AND THE INCOME GAP BY INCOME LEVEL AND REGION

TABLE 2.1   GNI per Capita by Level of Development and Region

The GNI per capita of the lowest quintile is less than 2 percent of the Euro area income. The GNI per capita of sub-Saharan Africa is only 6.2 percent of that of North America.

Income Category	Low	Middle (lower and upper middle)	Lower Middle	Upper Middle	High	Euro Area	
GNI per capita	$629	$4,666	$2,012	$7,901	$38,274	$39,162	
Regions	East Asia and Pacific	Latin America and Caribbean	Middle East and North Africa	South Asia	Sub-Saharan Africa	North America	Europe and Central Asia[a]
GNI per capita (U.S. $, 2014 purchasing power parity)	$14,903	$15,226	$17,754	$5,298	$3,396	$54,748	$28,827

a. Europe and Central Asia includes the former Warsaw Pact countries in Eastern Europe, Russia, and the other former Soviet countries that comprised the USSR.

Source: Adapted from World Bank (2016b:52), World Development Indicators.

FIGURE 2.2   Ratio of Incomes in Developing Regions to Incomes in Developed Countries, 1990–2014

While world and Asian gross domestic product per capita rose from 1990 to 2014, other developing regions were stagnant.

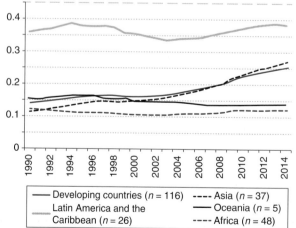

Source: From *Income convergence or persistent inequalities among countries? Development Issues No. 5* by Development Strategy and Policy Analysis Unit in the Development Policy and Analysis Division of UN/DESA, © 2015 United Nations. Reprinted with the permission of the United Nations.

of these countries and the developed world is virtually unchanged despite some fluctuation (UN 2015a).

Wealth Inequality Among Regions

Whereas income is an amount received over a period of time, wealth is the net assets, both financial and nonfinancial, minus debt. Because it takes money to make money, wealth inequalities are greater than income inequalities. Every region except Europe and North America has a lesser share of the world's wealth than their share of population (Table 2.2). The Asia–Pacific region is close to even. The more wealth in a region or country, the more it can invest in its people. The country and region into which people are born significantly affects their life chances.

A CLOSER LOOK
GLOBAL WEALTH

By comparing the percentage of the global population in each region with the percentage of its share of various forms of wealth and debt, it is evident that global wealth is very unequally distributed. How might this affect life chances?

TABLE 2.2   Distribution of Global Wealth Among Regions

Region	Percentage Share of Adults	Percentage Share of Wealth	Wealth per Adult	Financial Wealth per Adult	Nonfinancial Wealth per Adult	Debt per Adult	Median Wealth per Adult[a]
Africa	12.0	1.0	4,536	2,441	2,605	511	639
Asia–Pacific	23.8	18.4	40,505	25,270	22,297	7,691	2,711
China	21.2	9.1	22,513	12,752	11,704	1,943	7,357
Europe[b]	12.2	30.0	128,506	69,211	81,510	22,216	16,142
India	16.6	1.4	4,352	651	4,047	346	868
Latin America	8.5	3.0	18,508	7,682	14,093	3,267	4,034
North America[c]	5.7	37.1	342,302	271,267	129,303	58,269	59,737
World	100	100	52,432	33,659	27,442	8,668	3,210

a. Notice that this is median wealth per adult, not a mean. The mean income and wealth figures such as GNP and GNI per capita allow for comparisons in income and wealth among countries. However, they do not indicate the "average" person's income because people with extreme wealth skew the mean upward. The median is a much better indicator of how well the average person is doing. Because of inequality, the mean income in the United States is tens of thousands of dollars more than the median.

b. In this table, "Europe" includes Eastern European countries, not only the richer Western European countries.

c. According to the Credit Suisse 2015 *Wealth Databook,* the United States has 32 percent of global wealth and about 4.4 percent of global population.

(Continued)

(Continued)

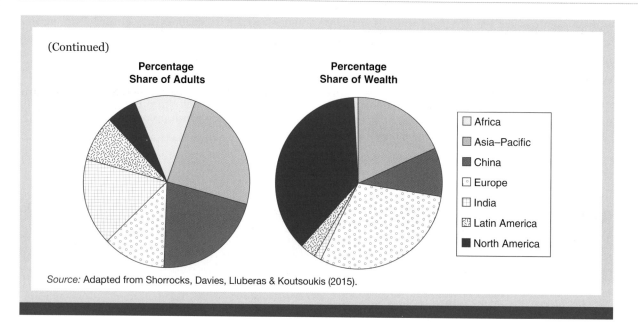

Percentage Share of Adults

Percentage Share of Wealth

☐ Africa
■ Asia–Pacific
■ China
☐ Europe
☐ India
▨ Latin America
■ North America

Source: Adapted from Shorrocks, Davies, Lluberas & Koutsoukis (2015).

FIGURE 2.3 Global Inequality of Income: The Lorenz Curve

Measuring global inequality of income using the Lorenz curve and Gini coefficient shows a decrease in inequality from 1992 to 2005 to 2015.

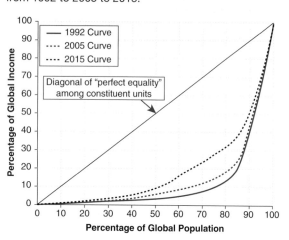

— 1992 Curve
---- 2005 Curve
···· 2015 Curve

Diagonal of "perfect equality" among constituent units

Source: Center for Systemic Peace (2017).

Note: Inequality is measured by the area inside the diagonal and the curves.

The disparity between the proportion of the world's population in each region and the proportion of global wealth highlights that there are sufficient global resources to alleviate the world's problems of hunger, malnutrition, water, and shelter. It is the distribution of resources,

particularly but not only income and wealth, that is the primary factor preventing people from having equal life chances.

Inequality Among Individuals

Global Inequality of Income

Estimating the distribution of income among individuals both globally and within societies provides another perspective on inequality.

The Lorenz curve visualizes the percentage of a given variable—in this case global income—that accrues to every percentage point of a population—in this case all of the people in the world (Figure 2.3). If there were perfect equality, every percentage point of the population would receive 1 percent of the global income, producing a straight line when graphed. The curve on the graph is the actual distribution. The innermost curve represents the actual share of income received by percentage of the population in 2015. The curve hugs the graph below 10 percent of global income until it reaches 50 percent of the population—indicating that half of the global population has hardly any of the global income—and shows that 80 percent of the population receives only 30 percent. The curve then rises rapidly, indicating the disproportionately large share of income accruing to the richest people in the world. The share of income of the richest 10 percent (640 million) of people based on the populations and GNI per capita of the richest countries barely changed during those years, claiming 42 percent of global income in 2010. The poorest quintiles barely changed either at only 1 percent (Conference Board of Canada 2011).

The Gini coefficient[3] is a measure of the deviation of the actual distribution from the line of perfect equality. The larger the Gini coefficient, the greater the inequality. The chart in Figure 2.4 shows a slight decrease in global inequality of income from 1992 to 2005 and a much more significant decrease in 2015. The decrease reflects the reduction of poverty in China and, to a lesser extent, in India, Brazil, and South Africa.

Median income doubled from U.S. $1,090 to $2,010 from 2003 to 2013, decreasing the 90/10 ratio from 37.6 to 30.2. The Gini coefficient decreased from 68.7 to 64.9. If growth rate projections hold, the Gini would decrease to 61.3 by 2035. The majority of decrease in inequality

A CLOSER LOOK
GLOBAL INCOME DISTRIBUTIONS AND PROJECTIONS

Global median income rose, or is expected to rise, from $1,090 to $2,010 from 2003 to 2030. The projection for 2035 is $4,000. As income rises above $7,500, there is little change.

FIGURE 2.4   Global Income Distributions and Projections

Incomes are adjusted for price changes over time and for price differences between countries (purchasing power parity (PPP) adjustment).

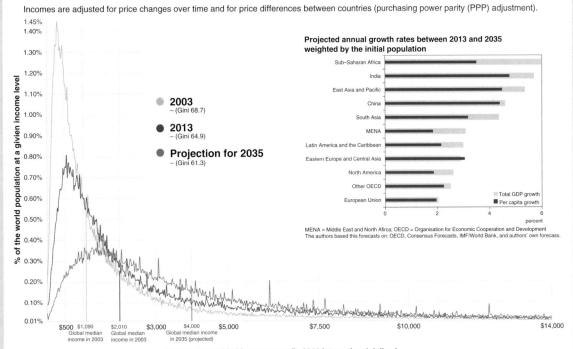

Source: "Our World in Data" by Max Roser. 2016. (https://ourworldindata.org/wp-content/uploads/2013/11/4-World-Income-Distribution-2003-to-2035-growth-rates.png). Licensed under CC BY-SA 3.0 AU (https://creativecommons.org/licenses/by-sa/3.0/au/deed.en).

would arise from increasing incomes at the bottom of the pyramid (Roser 2016).

The primary drivers of the decline in global inequality are China and India. From 1985 to 2000, China drove the decline almost single-handedly. After 2000, India has had a large effect on declining global inequality. As in most other countries, however, inequality within each of these countries increased (Milanovic 2011).

Inequality of Income Within Countries

Income inequality within countries persists and has grown in many countries over the past decades. From the mid to late 1970s, the primary beneficiaries of growth have been the richest people in the richest countries and an emerging middle class in developing nations such as China. Others, not so much.

The Gini coefficient calculated for a country measures inequality among individuals within the country. If the country Gini index is weighted by population, indicating inequality among individuals, it shows a steady decrease in inequality. Once again, if China is removed, it shows that the historical trend for most of the world has been increasing inequality among individuals (Conference Board of Canada 2011). Even before the recession of 2007–2008 hit countries all over the world, inequality within countries had been growing for decades. In 2011, the average income of the richest 10 percent of people within Organisation for Economic Cooperation and Development (OECD) countries was nine times the income of the poorest 10 percent (OECD 2011). Throughout history, as countries developed from the simplest to more complex economies, inequality increased. It peaked in the feudal agricultural societies in which nobility, a small portion of the population, had extreme wealth and peasants, the vast majority of people, had little. When societies industrialized, a middle class emerged, making societies more equal. However, as societies moved into the service and information economies, inequality began to increase again. This pattern of increasing inequality, then decreasing, and then increasing again is the "Kuznets curve" (Figure 2.5). It is not inevitable.

In many societies, inequality is increasing to extreme levels. The Bureau for Development Policy of the UN Development Programme (UNDP) found that between 1990 and 2010, inequality increased by 9 percent in

FIGURE 2.5   Inequality and Development: The Kuznets Curve

The Kuznets curve illustrates the relationship between inequality and economic stages of development. Diagram is for illustration only.

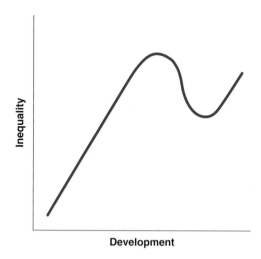

high-income countries and by 11 percent in developing countries (UNDP 2013). Countries with the highest inequality are clustered in Central and South America and southern Africa. Countries moving up the economic ladder, such as China, have greater proportions of income and wealth in the high and very high brackets (Canadian Conference Board 2011). Lower inequality is clustered in Europe; however, inequality is increasing as wages stagnate. Inequality varies significantly by country, but overall the top 10 percent of workers now take home more than twice their share and about the same portion of income (25 percent) as the bottom 50 percent.

With respect to wage inequality, inequality within enterprises now explains more of the inequality than inequality between enterprises. Most workers, including 80 percent in Europe, make less than the average wage of the enterprise where they work, indicating that salaries at the top pull the average wage far above what the median worker makes. Globally, those at the top of the income hierarchies continued to experience the most growth and take home large shares of total country income. The 1 percent of companies with the highest wages in Europe paid their top 1 percent of workers take-home wages of about €844 an hour in comparison with an average of €7.1 for

A CLOSER LOOK
THE BIFURCATED SERVICE INDUSTRY

PHOTO 2.1 The annual World Economic Forum meetings host a dinner for high-powered technology executives. Both they and the wait staff are parts of the "service economy"; however, their incomes and wealth place them worlds apart economically.

Robert Scoble/CC BY 2.0.

their bottom 1 percent in 2016 (International Labour Organization [ILO] 2016).

Growth itself does not correct inequality. Productivity drives growth, but productivity and worker compensation do not necessarily grow together (Figures 2.6–2.10 and Table 2.3). For example, China's rapid growth was accompanied by rapid increases in inequality. Inequality declined slightly as growth in China slowed, but more important was the increasing urbanization of the workforce that improved wages of the unskilled and migrant workers and increased the income stream into the rural areas as migrant workers sent money home (Shi 2016).

Neither did India's rapid growth increase equality. Much of the growth was in services that offer little in employment such as finance. The wage share of income dropped from 40 percent in 1990 to 34 percent by 2009; unearned income made the difference. Furthermore, a large part of the Indian population still toils in low-productivity agriculture. During early periods of growth, public spending to improve the situation of the poor was the primary stimulus. Recent financial policy—deregulation and tax and credit policy to stimulate spending among the wealthy—exacerbated inequality (Ghosh 2016).

Within the rich societies, the main reason for the increases in inequality is the explosive growth in income at the top of the pyramid (the "super-manager") and stagnation at lower levels. Corporate executive salaries are controlled by corporations' boards of directors

A CLOSER LOOK
INEQUALITY WITHIN COUNTRIES

FIGURE 2.6   Deepening Income Inequality, 1980–2014

A sampling of OECD countries illustrates the extent of deepening income inequality as greater shares of income accrued to the richest 1 percent in each of these countries.

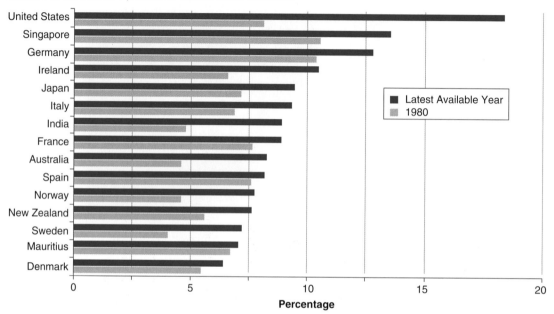

Source: Yates (2016). Reproduced with permission.

FIGURE 2.7   Country Income Inequality Within Regions

Each graph point represents a country; the lines are the regions. Income inequality within countries in all regions is rising. With the exception of two OECD countries, countries in developing regions had higher levels of inequality than OECD countries.

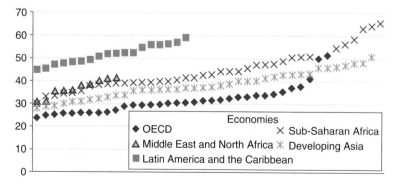

Source: Zhuang, Kanbur, and Maligalig (2014). Reproduced with permission.

TABLE 2.3   Inequality by Income Group

Inequality clusters in the low-income and lower middle-income countries. The richest countries, particularly with strong social welfare programs and policies, are more equal.

Income Categories	Income Classification Criteria: Gross National Income per Capita in 2009 (US$)*	Number of Countries	Country Examples	Total Population	Average Income in 2010 (constant PPP 2005 international $)	Secondary School Enrollment Rate, 2010**	Life Expectancy at Birth (years, 2009)	Infant Mortality Rate (per 1,000 live births, 2009)
High-income countries (rich countries)	Higher than $12,276	70	Canada, Poland, U.S.	1.1 billion	$33,232	100%	79.8	5.8
Upper-middle-income countries	$3,976 to $12,275	54	Brazil, China, Russia	2.5 billion	$8,731	90%	71.5	17.5
Lower-middle-income countries	$1,006 to $3,975	56	Guatemala, India, Nigeria	2.5 billion	$3,287	64%	64.8	51.7
Low-income countries	$1,005 or less	35	Bangladesh, Cambodia, Kenya	817 million	$1,099	39%	57.5	76.5

* The World Bank calculates gross national income using the Atlas conversion factor, which reduces the impact of exchange rate fluctuations when comparing national incomes across different countries.

** Ratio of enrollment in secondary school (regardless of age) to the population of the age-group that corresponds to that level of education.

Source: Conference Board of Canada (2011). Reproduced with permission.

(Continued)

(Continued)

FIGURE 2.8   Income Inequality in Europe

In Europe in 2010, the top 10 percent of earners collected 25 percent of the income.

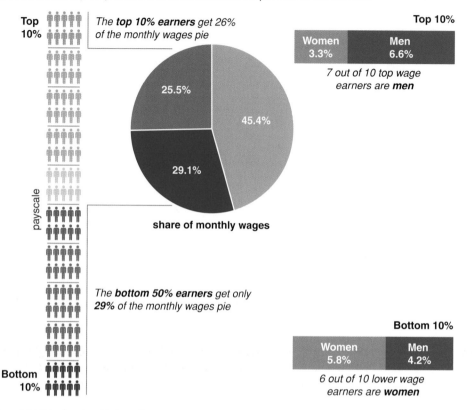

Source: Copyright © International Labour Organization 2016.

FIGURE 2.9   Income Inequality in China, 1981–2014

Rapidly increasing inequality in China accompanied its rapid growth.

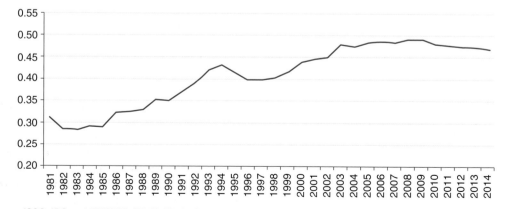

Source: ISSC, IDS and UNESCO (2016), World Social Science Report 2016, Challenging Inequalities: Pathways to a Just World, UNESCO Publishing, Paris. Licensed under CC BY-SA 3.0 IGO.

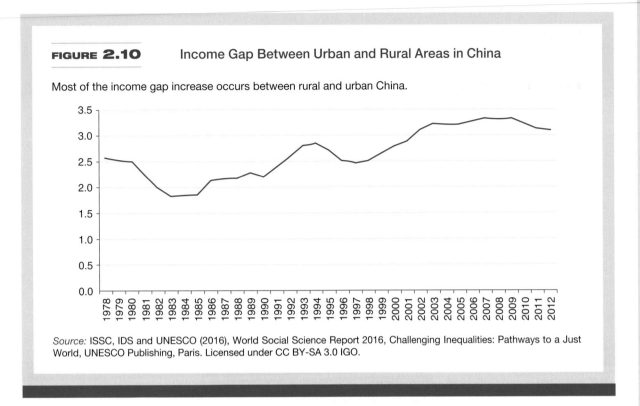

FIGURE 2.10   Income Gap Between Urban and Rural Areas in China

Most of the income gap increase occurs between rural and urban China.

Source: ISSC, IDS and UNESCO (2016), World Social Science Report 2016, Challenging Inequalities: Pathways to a Just World, UNESCO Publishing, Paris. Licensed under CC BY-SA 3.0 IGO.

composed of super-managers from other corporations or nonprofit organizations. At the same time, many transfer programs to assist lower-level workers have been cut.

Government policies affect equality. The inequities are decidedly more extreme in the Anglo-Saxon countries (the United States, Great Britain, Canada, and Australia) than in Continental Europe (France, Germany, and Sweden) and Japan. From 1960 to 1970, European countries were quite close in the share of income of the top percentile, ranging from about 6 to 9 percent, with the exception of Germany topping the list at 12 percent. The share going to the top decreased slightly from 1970 to 1980 but then rose dramatically in the Anglo-Saxon countries and rose less in other countries. The top 10 percent rose as well, but less in Continental Europe and barely at all in Southern and Northern Europe (Picketty 2014).

Wealth Inequality Among Individuals: The Global Wealth Pyramid

The world, as a whole, is wealthy. Global household wealth totaled about U.S. $256 trillion in 2016.[4] The global wealth pyramid depicts how wealth is distributed

among individuals, providing insight into how much of the world's wealth is held by people at the bottom or top of the wealth pyramid regardless of their country's wealth (Figures 2.11 and 2.12).

At the base of the 2016 pyramid are 3.5 billion adults, 73.2 percent of the adult population of the world, each of whose net worth is less than U.S. $10,000. Combining all of their assets, they own only 2.4 percent of global household wealth. Most of them live in developing societies, but about 20 percent of the base (about 700 million people) are in developed societies. Many may be there due to temporary setbacks such as prolonged unemployment; some may be elderly (Shorrocks et al. 2016).

Comparing the 2016 pyramid with the 2010 pyramid, increasing inequality is evident. In 2010, more wealth (4.2 percent) was held by a smaller portion of the global population (68.4 percent) living at the bottom of the pyramid than in 2016. The middle portion of the pyramid also lost in its share of wealth. In 2010, each 1 percent in the middle averaged 0.7 percent of the global wealth, while in 2016 that was reduced to 0.6 percent.

In 2016, only 18.5 percent of adults (about 900 million) possessed U.S. $10,000 to $100,000 in wealth.

A CLOSER LOOK
THE GLOBAL WEALTH PYRAMID, 2010 AND 2016

Comparing wealth pyramids of 2010 and 2016 illustrates deepening wealth inequality among individuals globally.

FIGURE 2.11   Global Wealth Pyramid, 2010

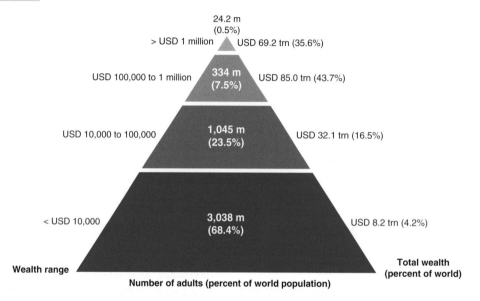

Source: Keating et al. (2010). Reproduced with permission.

FIGURE 2.12   Global Wealth Pyramid, 2016

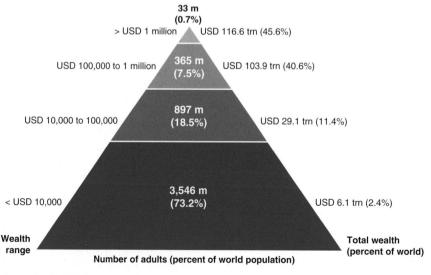

Source: Shorrocks et al. (2016). Reproduced with permission.

Country representation within tiers varies widely. For example, India and China have similar-sized populations, but 33 percent of the people in this tier are from China, whereas only 3.1 percent are from India. India's share has changed little in the past decade, whereas the portion that is Chinese has doubled since 2000 (Shorrocks et al. 2016).

There is greater concentration of wealth in the top two tiers of the pyramid. The top 8.2 percent of the global population had 86.2 percent of the global wealth in 2016, with most of that (45.6 percent) being in the possession of the top 0.7 percent. The average share of each 1 percent of the top 8.2 percent was 10.44 percent in 2016. In 2010, each 1 percent of the top 8 percent of the population possessed, on average, 9.9 percent of global wealth. Although this class is transnational and every region is represented, North America dominates the ranks of ultra-high net worth individuals, accounting for 49 percent of this class.

It is worth looking at some finer distinctions within the 2016 pyramid. The 50th percentile, the point at which half of all adults are above and half are below, is U.S. $3,210. Credit Suisse estimates that the bottom 50 percent of the global population has only 1 percent of the global wealth (Stierli et al. 2015). Many students in the developed world may meet the criterion to be included in the top half.

The global middle class, with assets of U.S. $50,000 to $500,000, expanded from 2000 to 2015. The expansion was dominated by China, but every region experienced some increase in adults reaching the middle-class threshold. It peaked before the financial crisis of 2007–2008 and had not recovered fully by 2015. In some regions, the middle class was still declining as of 2015. For example, in Egypt the middle class shrunk by half, and in Argentina it shrunk by two thirds. Growth in wealth flowed to the upper classes. For the world as a whole, wealth shifted 2:1 in favor of the upper classes. In North America, the shift was greater at 4:1 (Stierli et al. 2015).

Wealth Inequality Within Countries

As within the globe, wealth inequality within countries increased from the 1970s onward. In capitalist systems, inequality is thought to be necessary for growth by creating incentives for people to work hard, study hard, or take entrepreneurial risk. When inequality inhibits the opportunities for success, it operates like any form of discrimination and is dysfunctional not only for individuals denied their full life chances but also for the society. Society is denied the contributions of many people (Milanovic 2011). For example, the economic pie in the United States has been growing, but not everyone has benefitted equally.

Because it requires a surplus of income to create wealth and wealth creates more wealth, it is not surprising that wealth inequality is increasing in societies and that wealth is significantly more concentrated than income. The share of the country's income-generating wealth held by the top 20 percent increased, while the share of the bottom 80 percent decreased. Those in the top 20 percent also increased their share of the overall net worth of the country. Without access to income-generating financial wealth, middle- and low-wage workers will not decrease the gap. As illustrated in Figures 2.13 to 2.16, the level of wealth inequality within countries today is one cause of diminishing life chances for many people.

IMPACTS OF GLOBAL POVERTY AND INEQUALITY

This discussion of income and wealth focuses attention on the prosperity of the world as a whole and the inequalities in income and wealth among regions, countries, and individuals.[5] Inequalities of income and wealth would not be important if they did not affect the quality of people's lives and affect their life chances and well-being. But they do. The society into which a person is born and its level of wealth and inequality have a profound impact on the person's life.

Income sustains us day to day. Two people may have the same income but different levels of wealth. The one with more wealth has more opportunity. Wealth allows for investment, to use money to make money, or to move to a safer neighborhood or one with better schools or better recreational opportunities. A person with some wealth could invest in training for a new job or let his or her children develop their talents through music or art lessons. Even a little wealth can help a person recover more easily from unforeseen events. For example, when a car or hot water heater breaks down, a person with some wealth can have it repaired without going into debt.

For societies, it is the same. Wealth allows for investment in human capital such as education, health, nutrition, and welfare programs. It allows for investment in physical capital such as more productive machinery and infrastructure (e.g., roads). It allows a country to rebound more easily after unforeseen events such as

A CLOSER LOOK
WEALTH INEQUALITIES

FIGURE 2.13   Inequalities of Wealth in Select OECD Countries

Many European OECD countries have high levels of wealth inequality. Although the share of the top 10 percent is not as large in Norway as in several other countries, Norway's bottom 40 percent has negative wealth—more debt than assets. Norway has a generous social welfare program.

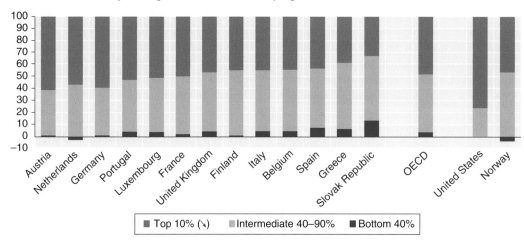

Source: Organisation for Economic Cooperation and Development (2017). Reproduced with permission.

FIGURE 2.14   Wealth Inequalities Within Countries

Gini measures of inequality show countries of high inequality clustered in Latin America and southern Africa.

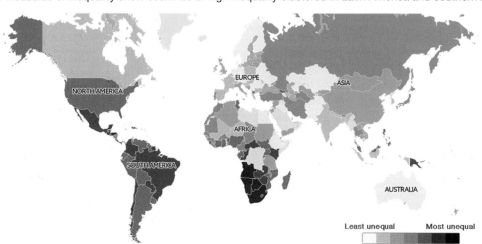

Source: World Economic Forum (2016). Reproduced with permission.

FIGURE 2.15   Distribution of Net Worth in the United States, 1983–2013

The distribution of net worth in the United States has become increasingly unequal.

	Total Net Worth		
	Top 1 percent	Next 19 percent	Bottom 80 percent
1983	33.8%	47.5%	18.7%
1989	37.4%	46.2%	16.5%
1992	37.2%	46.6%	16.2%
1995	38.5%	45.4%	16.1%
1998	38.1%	45.3%	16.6%
2001	33.4%	51.0%	15.6%
2004	34.3%	50.3%	15.3%
2007	34.6%	50.5%	15.0%
2010	35.1%	53.5%	11.4%
2013	36.7%	52.2%	11.1%

	Financial (Non-home) Wealth		
	Top 1 percent	Next 19 percent	Bottom 80 percent
1983	42.9%	48.4%	8.7%
1989	46.9%	46.5%	6.6%
1992	45.6%	46.7%	7.7%
1995	47.2%	45.9%	7.0%
1998	47.3%	43.6%	9.1%
2001	39.7%	51.5?/o	8.7%
2004	42.2%	50.3%	7.5%
2007	42.7%	50.3%	7.0%
2010	41.3%	53.5%	5.2%
2013	42.8%	51.9%	5.3%

Total assets are defined as the sum of (1) the gross value of owner-occupied housing; (2) other real estate owned by the household; (3) cash and demand deposits; (4) time and savings deposits, certificates of deposit, and money market accounts; (5) government bonds, corporate bonds, foreign bonds, and other financial securities; (6) the cash surrender value of life insurance plans; (7) the cash surrender value of pension plans, including IRAs, Keogh, and 401 (k) plans; (8) corporate stock and mutual funds; (9) net equity in unincorporated businesses; and (10) equity in trust funds. Total liabilities are the sum of (1) mortgage debt; (2) consumer debt, including auto loans; and (3) other debt. From Wolff (2017).

Source: Domhoff (2018). Based on data from Wolff (2017). Reproduced with permission.

(Continued)

(Continued)

FIGURE 2.16   Net Worth and Financial Wealth Distribution
in the United States, 2013

There is little opportunity in the United States for most people to acquire much wealth because financial
investment assets are owned by a small percentage of the population.

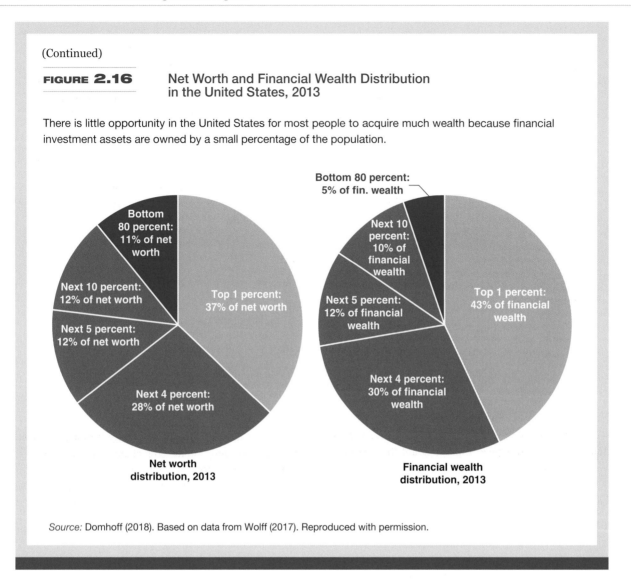

**Net worth
distribution, 2013**

**Financial wealth
distribution, 2013**

Source: Domhoff (2018). Based on data from Wolff (2017). Reproduced with permission.

natural disasters, extreme weather events, and economic
shocks.

Increasing divergence in income and wealth results in
increasing divergence in life chances:

- Despite the successes of the poverty reduction
  and related development efforts, many countries
  have failed to grow, much less thrive.

- Within regions, countries have different rates
  of success and have reached different levels of
  development.

- China, with about one third of the global
  population, has accounted for much of the global
  reduction in poverty, whereas other countries
  have had little to no reduction.

- Inequality, despite fluctuations, has increased
  since the 1970s.

How these trends developed, how they affect people's
life chances, and how they can be combatted are discussed
in the remainder of the chapter.

The UNDP measures and tracks many indicators on which the quality of life and life chances depend. The foundation of life chances are good health, appropriate education, nutritious food, adequate shelter, and sufficient wealth and income (a decent standard of living). The conditions that support the foundation are security, equality, a healthy environment, and a vibrant social and political community. Together, these form the Human Development Index (HDI) (Figure 2.17).

Life expectancy at birth, expected years of schooling, mean years of schooling, and GNI per capita are the four indicators that form the basic HDI. These are among the most standardized and readily available statistics as well as reasonable indicators of general well-being. The HDI scores approximate how well a country fares in providing life chances. It is also a point of comparison among countries and a means of assessing countries' improvement.

HDI varies widely by region (Tables 2.4 and 2.5). As would be expected, the two regions with the lowest income measures also have the lowest HDI. But given how far below the global average the South Asia region is in income, you might expect a much lower HDI. Similarly, the sub-Saharan Africa HDI is far below other scores, but its income is not as far below that of South Asia as one might expect. Income is not the sole determinant of HDI.

The relationship between income and human development is more complex than a straightforward correlation.

Including income in the HDI exaggerates the relationship between them. Note these anomalies:

- In the case of the Arab states, given an income measure significantly higher than the global average, one might expect a much higher HDI, one at least above the global average. However, it is lower. Their score would be much lower if income were not a component.

- Table 2.5 classifies countries by levels of development. A more direct relationship between income and HDI score is evident here. Note, however, that the world HDI is lower than those for high-income countries, but the gross domestic product (GDP) per capita is somewhat higher.

What do you suspect accounts for these anomalies? Is this because of the level of inequality across countries of the world? How might the level of inequality within regions and within countries influence the HDI?

Policy matters. There are many countries whose populations enjoy better life chances than people in countries with more income and wealth. Equatorial Guinea, for example, has roughly four times the GDP per capita of Vietnam (U.S. $21,056 in comparison with

FIGURE 2.17 Dimensions of the Human Development Index

The Human Development Index focuses on indicators related to health, education, and income—factors believed to be essential to achieving life chances.

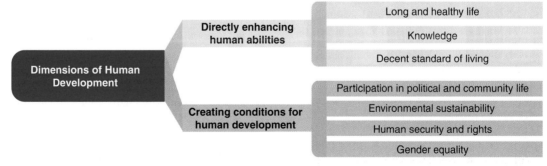

Source: United Nations Development Programme *Human Development Reports.* "What is Human Development?" by HDRO Outreach (http://hdr.undp.org/en/content/what-human-development), licensed under CC BY IGO 3.0 (https://creativecommons.org/licenses/by/3.0/igo/).

A CLOSER LOOK
HUMAN DEVELOPMENT MEASURES

GDP per capita and human development scores are related, but country income is not the only determinant. Good policy can increase a country's human development above that of richer countries. Bad policy can worsen it.

TABLE 2.4   Human Development Index Scores by Region

Region	Arab States	East Asia and Pacific	Europe and Central Asia	Latin America and Caribbean	South Asia	Sub-Saharan Africa	World
Number of countries and territories	20	24	17	33	9	46	188
HDI	0.686	0.710	0.748	0.748	0.607	0.518	.711
GDP per capita[a] (U.S. $, 2011 PPP)	$16,697	$10,799	$12,929	$13,877	$5,324	$3,339	$13,964

Source: Adapted from *Human Development Report 2015: Work for Human Development* by United Nations Development Programme (http://hdr.undp.org/sites/default/files/2015_human_development_report.pdf), licensed under CC BY IGO 3.0 (https://creativecommons.org/licenses/by/3.0/igo/).

TABLE 2.5   Human Development Scores by Development Group

Development Group	Very High	High	Medium	Low	Average Least Developed	Average OECD	World
HDI	0.896	0.744	0.630	0.505	0.502	0.880	.711
GDP per capita[a] (U.S. $, 2011 PPP)	$41,395	$13,549	$6,106	$2904	$2,122	$36,923	$13,964

a. Gross domestic product (GDP) per capita is stated in purchasing power parity (PPP) for better comparison across countries and regions.

Source: Adapted from *Human Development Report 2015: Work for Human Development* by United Nations Development Programme (http://hdr.undp.org/sites/default/files/2015_human_development_report.pdf), licensed under CC BY IGO 3.0 (https://creativecommons.org/licenses/by/3.0/igo/).

Note: Scores on the HDI range from 0 to 1. The higher the number, the better the human development.

U.S. $5,092) and an HDI of .587, yet Vietnam's HDI is higher at .666. South Africa has more than twice the GDP of Vietnam, yet they have the same HDI score of .666. The United Arab Emirates ranks about 10th in GDP per capita but drops to 41st in HDI. Cuba ranks in the high human development category, but its GDP per capita is only U.S. $7,301, comparable to the medium-scoring countries.

The HDI and economic status of a country are more significant in a person's life chances than a person's own talent and ambition. Living in a low-HDI country, a person does not have the same opportunity for an education or good health as a person in a higher HDI country. In a poor country, regardless of how hard they work and how smart they are, people do not have access to the same job opportunities or financial and physical infrastructure to "get ahead" as people in a richer country. Securing better life chances drives migration to higher HDI and higher income countries.

Societies with low HDI, particularly those with low income, experience the most social problems, including environmental destruction, violent conflict, and discrimination. However, not everyone in those societies suffers equally, nor does everyone in wealthy societies benefit equally from the opportunities wealthy societies afford.

The effects of income inequality within countries, even wealthy ones, are destructive. Income inequality stifles intergenerational upward mobility, leading to feelings of hopelessness and disaffection from the society. It stifles economic growth of the society as a whole, breeds social resentment, and can generate political instability. Oxfam International (2014), an international non-governmental organization, succinctly stated the dangers of extreme inequality:

> Extreme economic inequality is damaging and worrying for many reasons: it is morally questionable; it can have negative impacts on economic growth and poverty reduction; and it can multiply social problems. It compounds other inequalities, such as those between women and men. In many countries, extreme economic inequality is worrying because of the pernicious impact that wealth concentrations can have on equal political representation. When wealth captures government policymaking, the rules bend to favor the rich, often to the detriment of everyone else. The consequences include the erosion of democratic governance, the pulling apart of social cohesion, and the vanishing of equal opportunities for all.

Using three key indicators, the HDI computes an inequality *adjusted* index. The adjusted index accounts for the loss to a country or region in human development because of inequality. The more inequality in the region, the greater the difference between scores (Table 2.6 and Figure 2.18). Where there is inequality, portions of the population are not given the opportunity to develop their potential and the society does not develop human capital.

How the income and wealth of a country is used along with the distribution of income and wealth influences life chances and well-being. Countries that direct a greater portion toward public goods such as education, health, and building good governance and infrastructure will have better outcomes in terms of people's life chances than societies that invest less. When more income and wealth is directed to private consumption, it benefits only those individuals. When invested in public goods, the entire population benefits.

Even among rich societies, societies that are more unequal and spend less on public goods experience more social problems and quality of life issues than more equal societies. They may suffer more problems than some societies that are less wealthy but more equal. They tend to have lower overall educational attainment, poorer health, and more violent crime than they would have if they were more equal. In more equal societies and societies that use more wealth for the common good, the poor may have life chances equal to those in somewhat wealthier societies.

In societies that limit people's life chances through inequality, everyone suffers, not only those at the bottom. Research by Richard Wilkinson and Kate Pickett illustrates each of these points convincingly. The authors started with the simple question of why, "at the pinnacle of human material and technical achievement, we find ourselves anxiety-ridden, prone to depression, worried about how others see us, unsure of our friendships, driven to consume and with little or no community life" (Wilkinson and Pickett 2009). What they found might surprise some people.

A CLOSER LOOK
THE IMPACT OF INEQUALITY ON HUMAN DEVELOPMENT

TABLE 2.6   Regional Inequality and Human Development Index

HDI scores drop significantly in every region when controlled for inequality, indicating that the level of inequality diminishes people's life chances.

Region	Arab States	East Asia and Pacific	Europe and Central Asia	Latin America and Caribbean	South Asia	Sub-Saharan Africa
HDI	0.686	0.710	0.748	0.748	0.607	0.518
Inequality-adjusted HDI	0.512	0.572	0.651	0.570	0.433	0.345

Source: Adapted from *Human Development Report 2015: Work for Human Development* by United Nations Development Programme (http://hdr.undp.org/sites/default/files/2015_human_development_report.pdf), licensed under CC BY IGO 3.0 (https://creativecommons.org/licenses/by/3.0/igo/).

FIGURE 2.18   More Human Development Is Associated With Less Inequality

As evident in these graphs, the higher the level of human development, the less inequality there tends to be. Countries scoring below the lines are less unequal than would be expected; those scoring above the lines are more unequal.

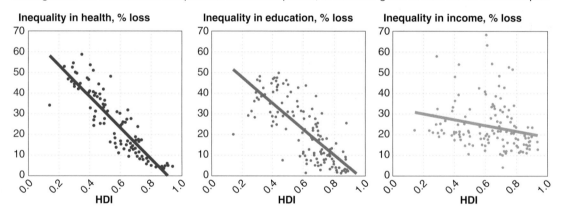

Source: United Nations Development Programme *Human Development Reports.* "Reducing inequality can significantly improve human development" by Selim Jahan (http://hdr.undp.org/en/content/reducing-inequality-can-significantly-improve-human-development), licensed under CC BY IGO 3.0 (https://creativecommons.org/licenses/by/3.0/igo/).

The severity of social problems and income are related when considering all societies—poorer societies have more problems. But among wealthy countries, there is no relationship between income and severity of problems. The wealthier are no better off, nor are the poorer suffering more. They are equal in their problems. However, there is a significant relationship between inequality and social problems. Among rich societies, the more unequal societies experience more severe social problems. Using data compiled by international organizations and national governments, they found that this relationship holds for all the problems

Wilkinson and Pickett (2009) tested, from measures of child welfare to violent crime.[6]

Among rich societies, more equal societies are healthier. More equal societies have less mental illness, longer life expectancy, lower infant mortality and obesity, and fewer teenage births and homicides. They have fewer people in prison, more social mobility, and higher levels of trust. In every measure in the United Nations International Children's Emergency Fund (UNICEF) index of child well-being, children in more unequal societies fare less well regardless of income level. States within the United States reflect the same relationships; states that are more unequal have worse outcomes than states of similar wealth (Wilkinson and Pickett 2009).

The most disadvantaged are most vulnerable and suffer the most, but inequality reaps destruction through all income levels of a society. When comparing the health of people in the same income levels across societies, people in more equal societies fare better than people of the same income in more unequal societies. This relationship holds true even for the poorest and wealthiest members of a society (Wilkinson and Pickett 2009).

Inequality, according to Wilkinson and Pickett (2009), is structural violence. It breeds family stress and breakdown. It entrenches an "us against them" mentality and discourages spending on the common goods such as education. It encourages us to compare among ourselves. These "psychosocial" factors—the fear of judgment, status competition, and status insecurity—create chronic stress. The authors cited a review of 208 studies showing that threats to social status, confidence in one's own competence, or belonging to a group perceived as inferior affects performance. In an experiment in which boys were asked to complete mazes, children from lower castes performed slightly better than those from upper castes. When asked to announce their names, as well as their fathers' and grandfathers' names, villages, and castes before completing the mazes, the performance of the lower caste boys dropped significantly.

Reducing the inequalities among us can improve the quality of life for all of us.

QUALITY OF LIFE ALONG LEVELS OF DEVELOPMENT

Statistics on poverty, inequality, and human development do not mean much without some basic understanding of people's lives at different levels of socioeconomic status.

The Bottom of the Pyramid

Franklin Roosevelt used the term "the bottom of the pyramid" to describe "the forgotten, the unorganized, but the indispensable units of economic power" (Roosevelt 1932). He was referring to the bankrupt farmers and workers who were at the bottom of the pyramid in the United States. He stressed their importance in rebuilding the U.S. economy from the bottom up. Many politicians and financial and industrial leaders of the period proposed "top-down" plans to revitalize the nation. They wanted to give money to big banks, railroads, and corporations. Roosevelt wanted to give at least as much help to the "little fellow" and to the little banks and loan companies that would help those at the bottom build themselves up again. There is still a bottom of the pyramid in the United States inextricably connected to the global bottom of the pyramid. People in the global "bottom" live in every country. Like the bottom of the pyramid of which Roosevelt spoke, it remains an indispensable unit of economic power both nationally and globally. Although myths about the poor being lazy abound, the poor are the hardest workers in the world and the foundation of the global economy.

Who are the people at the bottom of the pyramid? What are their lives like?

Slavery: It Still Exists

No one shall be held in slavery or servitude: slavery and the slave trade shall be prohibited in all their forms.

—UN Declaration of Human Rights, Article 4

At the base of the pyramid are slaves. Slavery is illegal in every country in the world but still exists. Sustainable Development Goals Target 8.7 calls for "immediate and effective measures to eradicate forced labour, end modern slavery and human trafficking, secure the prohibition and elimination of the worst forms of child labour, including recruitment and use of child soldiers, and by 2025 end child labour in all its forms."

There were 45.8 million slaves spread over 167 countries in 2016. Most of the slaves are in India, China, Pakistan, Bangladesh, and Uzbekistan (Walk Free Foundation 2016). However, slaves are found in every

CONSIDER THIS
WHEN A SOCIETY ACCEPTS SLAVERY

"Chains are for the slave who has just become a slave . . . but the multi-generation slave, the slave descending from many generations, he is a slave even in his own head. And he is totally submissive. He is ready to sacrifice himself, even, for his master."

—Boubacar Messaoud, son of slaves

Can slavery be so ingrained in a national culture that neither the enslavers nor the enslaved recognize that anything is wrong? Where slavery in inherited, generation after generation, it seems the natural order. It has the quality of destiny. Abdel Nasser Ould Ethmane, now an abolitionist in his homeland Mauritania, was allowed to choose his own birthday gift when he was 7 years old. Rather than a toy or candy, he chose Yebawa Ould Keihel, a dark-skinned boy who amused him. Yebawa tended the family's flocks in the hot sun, stood in the cold rain to support a tent to keep the family dry. Neither Abdel nor Yebawa questioned this. When Abdel went away to school, he encountered books on the French Revolution, human rights, and the abolition of slavery in other countries. At first, he thought the books were filled with lies. By age 16, he was convinced slavery was a grave injustice. He recognized that slaves deserved all the rights he enjoyed. He freed his slaves, but they did not know what freedom was, nor did they want to be free.

Mauritania did not abolish slavery until 1981 and did not make slave owning a crime until 2007. Still, there are hundreds of thousands in slavery. It is one of the poorest countries in the world, with 44 percent of its population living on less than $2 a day. Slaves have little hope for a life of plenty in or out of slavery. Many "masters" prevent them from leaving. Despite physical and sexual abuse, some do not understand that their enslavement is not their duty or destiny. Educating slaves to understand freedom and convincing them to want to be free are the first hurdles that SOS Slaves, founded by Abdel and Boubacar, and other abolitionist groups must overcome.

—as reported by John D. Sutter (2012), *CNN News*

---

country. Slavery goes by a variety of different names, including forced labor, involuntary servitude, bonded labor, debt bondage, child sex trafficking, child soldiers, human trafficking, and traditional slavery. Regardless of terminology, people held in compelled service are slaves.[7]

Slavery isn't just in Mauritania. It hides all over the world, in the supply chains of our clothing and electronic devices, in the kitchens and nurseries of the wealthy, in agriculture and mines, in virtually every industry.

Working Hard for Less than U.S. $3 a Day

Slightly above slaves in the socioeconomic hierarchy are people who earn less than $1 a day. They lack the basic necessities—food, clean water, and shelter. They may be among the "modern slaves" or live in a barter economy. They may be displaced from their homes by war, natural disasters, or civil strife. There are roughly 1 billion people living at this level.

A step above, those who earn $1 to $3 a day, are usually poorly educated and unskilled. They work as day laborers, migrant farmhands, helpers and assistants in petty trades, or temporary workers. They may have been displaced from their homes by conflict, natural disasters, persecution, famine, or other hardships. Their paychecks are unsteady. They might be able to afford only one meal a day, usually of substandard nutritional value. They are likely to lack improved sanitation, health care, and education. They may live in slums or shantytowns. There are about 1.6 billion people living at this level—a subsistence level (Rangan, Chu, and Petkoski 2011).

Work at these levels is insecure. When we talk about $1 or $1.25 or $3 a day, a worker is not earning that every day. For example, during harvest season, workers may earn more than their yearly average. On many days in the "off season," they might not earn anything at all.

Most of the very poor cobble together an income from several jobs doing different things—whatever work they can get. They lack the opportunity for a full-time job even at that low wage.

For example, the rural poor may have a small plot of land to farm but not enough to make a living or feed their families. In addition, they may work as day laborers or migrate for temporary work. Rickshaw drivers, for example, usually work only four days a week because of the hardship of the job. However, bad weather, police harassment, scarcity of riders, whether or not a rickshaw is available, and bad luck may mean that even a four-day week is not possible. They too work several jobs. In Guntur, India, a typical scenario for very poor women is to start off their day selling rice and bean breakfast pancakes. After that, they collect trash, make and sell pickles, maybe gather and sell fuelwood, fruits, and vegetables, and possibly work as laborers. A study of working poor by Massachusetts Institute of Technology economists found that the median family in villages in West Bengal, India, had three working members with seven different occupations among them (Radelet 2015).

Although there are non-cash assistance programs in wealthy countries such as the United States, there are still people working at an average of U.S. $2 a day or less. They share similar hardships. In their decades-long studies of poverty in the United States, Kathryn Edin and H. Luke Shaefer studied the plight of very low-income, particularly $2-a-day, workers. They found that the number of households living on $2 a day had roughly doubled from 1995, the latest era of welfare reform. In 2011, there were roughly 1.5 million households, about 4 percent of all households, living on $2 a day per person or less. They spanned family types, with one third being two-parent families. They spanned the races, with nearly one half being white, although the rate of growth among Hispanics and African Americans was higher than that among whites (Edin and Shaefer 2015).

Their work is irregular and unpredictable. A large pool of low-wage workers, many of whom were pushed into the workforce by lifetime limits on cash assistance, makes it easy for employers to demand that workers be available on call "24/7." There is no vacation time, sick leave, or health insurance. Even with food stamps and housing allowances, children go without regular meals and health care and sleep in substandard, overcrowded apartments. In at least one family living in the Mississippi Delta, the children reported that they often wished they were dead rather than be so pained with hunger (Edin and Shaefer 2015).

Just above them on the pyramid are the $3-to-$5-a-day workers.[8] This may not sound like a big difference, but even this little bit more means a more secure life. People at this level may have a few years of secondary education. They may work in such jobs as construction or petty trades, as drivers, or as staff in public or commercial establishments. They may own bicycles, televisions, and cell phones. There are approximately 1.4 billion people living at this level (Rangan et al. 2011). Their health is generally better at this level, so fewer days of work are missed. Their work not only pays more but also is more regular and secure.

The most success in the global struggle against poverty has been at these lowest levels, lifting people from extreme poverty to low income. An increase from less than U.S. $1.25 to just $2 a day makes a significant difference in people's lives. From $3 to $5 a day makes an even greater difference. These may mean a difference in food security or the chance to send children to school. It may mean being able to purchase tools to begin a small business. But even $5 a day is less than $2,000 a year and still poverty wages on the global pyramid. Many people in these lowest categories are among the modern slaves such as the migrant construction workers in the United Arab Emirates whose passports are taken away from them when they arrive. They work for about U.S. $167 a month (Walk Free Foundation 2016).

ORIGINS OF CONTEMPORARY INEQUALITY AMONG NATIONS

Prior to the Industrial Revolution, all societies were poor, and aside from a small elite class or caste, there was not a great deal of difference in how people lived from society to society or within societies. Nearly everyone lived an agricultural small town lifestyle. Nearly everyone was poor. A rough estimate is that in 1820, 94 percent of the global population lived on under $2 a day (in contemporary dollars) and 84 percent on under $1 (Radelet 2015).

Development and Economic Transitions

Traditionally, when social scientists refer to a society as developing, they refer to the process of economic transition, which leads to growth. In general terms, there are three sectors of economic activity: primary (agricultural), secondary (manufacturing), and tertiary (service) industries. The primary sector is that portion of the economy or labor force that involves securing raw materials and resources directly from the land. This can be thought of as the first step in a commodity or production chain. Agriculture, mining, fishing, and lumberjacking all secure raw materials from the earth. The secondary sector is manufacturing. This sector turns the primary resource into a product or goods. Manufacturing "adds value" to the resource. There are levels of manufacturing. Some are basic such as filleting and freezing fish and spinning cotton to thread. Examples of much higher levels of manufacturing are the chemical industry and new materials manufacturing. Higher levels of manufacturing add considerably more value than lower levels. Tertiary industry is the service industry. It is bifurcated with a low-level sector of low-skilled occupations that require little education and a highly educated, highly skilled workforce. The lower skilled sector performs many of the tasks associated with domestic work—from janitors, to launderers, to fast-food preparation, to child and home health care. The higher level service sector is in finance, marketing, upper management, and high-tech positions. Professionals—from technicians, to doctors, to teachers, to lawyers—are in this category.

Advances in technology propel societies along the developmental path. Technology releases people from lower level work, replacing them with increasingly efficient machines and robotics. In agriculture, for example, a few large expensive pieces of machinery can replace scores of workers. With further advances in technology, fewer workers are needed in manufacturing. Factories that employed thousands can get by with hundreds. The labor force moves into service. The occupational structure shifts from primary to manufacturing and then to service industries. The transitions are not easy, and workers are displaced.[9] As societies transition at different rates, they diverge from one another in the value they produce and subsequently their income and wealth.

The Industrial Revolution was the first opportunity for societies to significantly increase their income and accumulate wealth relative to other societies. Before the Industrial Revolution, the richest societies were only about three times richer than the poorest. In 1820, nearly everyone lived in absolute poverty. The first divergence among countries occurred with the Industrial Revolution (Figure 2.19). At this time, most of the world, some 75 percent, was still living under colonial rule and did not have the opportunity to develop independently. A small group of 17[10] countries industrialized and grew relatively rapidly and at similar rates during this early period of industrialization.

As manufacturing moved from the most advanced societies, it provided a second opportunity for development. Manufacturing began moving to less developed nations in the late 19th century. Latin America was free from colonization, but Africa and much of Asia were not. The 1950s were a take-off period for many societies from South America to East Asia. Among developing societies, a surge of growth from 1960 to 1990 produced a second divergence. Of the 108 developing societies, 11 experienced explosive growth, averaging more than 4.2 percent a year.

Other societies, about 40, grew at less than 1 percent, 28 grew at less than 0.5 percent, and 16 experienced negative growth. Some, such as Argentina, started out among the wealthier societies but went from wealth to poverty. Others, such as India, were already poor and grew so slowly that they grew increasingly poor in relation to global per capita incomes. The gap in per capita income between the richest and poorest grew 10-fold from 1870 to 1990, from about $1,286 to $12,662 (Pritchett 1997). In sub-Saharan Africa, the GDP per capita fell from one third of the richest nations in 1820 to one twentieth by the 2000s (Sindzingre 2005).

Because of differing rates of development, some societies remain heavily invested in agriculture and other primary industries in terms of both the proportion of their GDP that comes from the agricultural sector and the proportion of their labor force engaged in primary industry and agricultural work (Table 2.7). Manufacturing jobs typically pay more than primary industry jobs[12] and initiate the development of a middle class. As societies develop newer technologies, fewer workers are needed in lower level manufacturing. Ideally, they move to higher level manufacturing and services.

The proportion of GDP derived from each economic sector also indicates the level of development. A greater proportion of GDP is generated by "industry" and "services" in more developed countries (Table 2.8). Worker per worker, workers in higher level industries (except the low-level services) produce more value as measured by their contribution to GDP.

There is a general argument that people are poor because they must not work or work hard or because they do not have entrepreneurial talent or desires. Each of these arguments is false. As is evident in examining the "bottom of the pyramid," people in countries with low levels of development work hard—much harder, one might

A CLOSER LOOK
WAVES OF DIVERGENCE IN THE GLOBAL ECONOMY

In 1820, all societies were very poor. There were few wealthy individuals. By the 1970s, there were two distinct categories of nations. The largest category containing the bulk of the world's population did not develop and was not much wealthier in 1970 than in 1820. As development spread to more parts of the world, incomes in those regions increased. But most of the world is still relatively poor.

FIGURE 2.19   Waves of Divergence

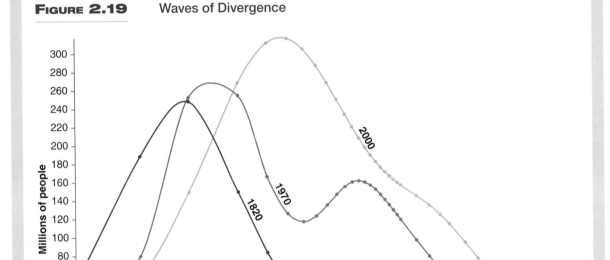

Source: Our World in Data by Max Roser (https://www.maxroser.com/roser/graphs/WorldIncomeDistribution1820to2000/World-IncomeDistribution1820to2000.html) licensed under CC BY-SA 4.0 (https://creativecommons.org/licenses/by-sa/4.0/).[11]

argue, than people in wealthy societies. But they work for less money. Their work, whether in agriculture, low-level manufacturing, forestry, or mining, is necessary for global growth but does not bear a living wage on the global market (Table 2.9). This makes it difficult, if not impossible, for individuals or the countries in which they live to provide adequately for a life of survival, let alone comfort. At the same time, global trade allows many goods made by these workers or made from materials collected by these workers, from T-shirts to toilet paper, to be purchased by consumers in wealthy countries for prices below their cost just 40 years ago.

Wages are the primary source of income in developed and developing societies alike. The opportunities that people have to earn an income are dependent on the jobs that are available where they live. What people are paid for their work varies by the distribution of jobs in the occupational structure of the society.

A CLOSER LOOK
THE RELATIONSHIP BETWEEN THE LABOR FORCE AND GDP

This sample of countries illustrates the level of employment in each industrial sector. As a general rule, the labor force transitions from agriculture into manufacturing and then into the services as workers reach advanced levels of development.

TABLE 2.7   Labor Force and Economic Sector

HDI Rank (Country)	Percentage of Labor Force in Economic Sector		
	Agriculture	Manufacturing	Services
Very High (United Kingdom)	1.3	15.2	83.5
High (Bulgaria)	7	30.1	62.9
Medium (Vietnam)	48	21	31
Low (Zimbabwe)	66	10	24

Source: Adapted from 4.2 World Development Indicators: Structure of output by World Bank (http://wdi.worldbank.org/table/4.2) licensed under CC BY 4.0 (https://creativecommons.org/licenses/by/4.0/).

TABLE 2.8   Percentage of GDP per Economic Sector in 2015

Higher-level manufacturing is distinguished from all industry in this chart, although it is included in the industry total. Manufacturing represents higher level industry.

Income level (GNI/capita)	Agriculture Percentage	Industry Percentage	Manufacturing[a] Percentage	Services Percentage
Low ($1,045 or less)	31	21	8	48
Lower middle ($1,046 to $4,125)	16	30	16	52
Upper middle ($4,126 to $12,735)	7	34	21	59
High ($12,736 or more)	1	25	15	74

a. These sectors are classification categories 15 to 37. They are included within "industry" percentages. They include the higher level manufacturing sectors such as chemicals, pharmaceuticals, electrical equipment, and machinery as well as some lower level sectors.

Source: Adapted from 4.2 World Development Indicators: Structure of output by World Bank (http://wdi.worldbank.org/table/4.2) licensed under CC BY 4.0 (https://creativecommons.org/licenses/by/4.0/).

TABLE 2.9   Percentage of Working Poor per Region

Many people think that the poor do not work. There are many people who work every day and are at or below poverty levels.

Percentage of Workers Living in Poverty (less than U.S. $1.25 a day)		Percentage of Workers in Developing Regions Working at Each Income Level (U.S. $)	
Developing world	11	Extremely poor (less than $1.25)	11
Oceania	18	Moderately poor (between $1.25 and $2)	16
Southern Asia	17	Near poor (between $2 and $4)	25

Percentage of Workers Living in Poverty (less than U.S. $1.25 a day)		Percentage of Workers in Developing Regions Working at Each Income Level (U.S. $)	
Southeast Asia	7	Total poor and near poor	52
Eastern Asia	3		
Latin America and the Caribbean	2		
Caucasus and Central Asia	1		
North Africa	1		
Western Asia	1		

Source: Adapted from *The Millennium Development Goals Report 2015* by the Department of Economic and Social Affairs, © 2015 United Nations. Reprinted with the permission of the United Nations.

FACTORS INFLUENCING VARYING LEVELS OF DEVELOPMENT

Why some societies broke from the historical record of slow growth, developed quickly, and became wealthy while others remained poor is a central question of the social sciences, including not just economics but also political science, geography, anthropology, and sociology.

Economic Growth

With the exception of the "Asian Tigers"—Hong Kong, South Korea, Taiwan, and Singapore—that successfully developed from 1960 to the 1990s, the developing world lagged behind the developed world for most of the post-World War II period. It was not until 2000 to 2009 that growth accelerated among other developing countries. When it did, it accelerated dramatically—7.6 percent, 4.5 percent faster than the developed world (Figures 2.20 and 2.21). If those rates had held steady, per capita incomes in the developing world stood ready to converge with those in the developed world in just 30 years. They seemed to be doing everything right—from improvements in education, to clamping down on corruption, to opening up markets to global trade and building infrastructure.

Growth was not evenly spread. East Asia, Eastern Europe, and the BRICS (Brazil, Russia, India, China, and South Africa) led in growth, with China accounting for the greatest share. Nevertheless, even the least developed societies, some 48 countries (34 in Africa, 13 in the Asia–Pacific region, and Haiti in the Caribbean), experienced rapid growth rates in that decade, peaking at 9.53 percent in 2007

(Figures 2.22 and 2.23). Since then, the growth rate has slowed to 3.553 percent in the least developed countries and dipped into negative numbers in Brazil and Russia for 2015.

A plethora of factors, both internal and external to societies, accelerate or inhibit economic growth. Competing theories—from geography, to institutions, to culture—all need to be considered because each is convincing in the evidence it brings to the debate and each may have an important role, whether in shaping historical development or explaining contemporary development and underdevelopment.

Extractive Institutions and Inequality

Institutions matter to development. Good institutions can influence every sphere of life, providing life chances and ensuring the rule of law. Acemoglu, Johnson, and Robinson (2001, 2002) and Acemoglu and Wolitzky (2011) looked to institutions for at least part of the explanation of modern inequality.

Former colonies and dependencies vary in their rates of growth post-independence. Paap, Franses, and van Dijk (2005) clustered countries according to their rates of growth. They found that on every colonized continent, there are a variety of growth rates (Table 2.10).

Different colonies presented Europeans with different opportunities for wealth. Consequently, Europeans developed two distinct institutional systems in their colonies. Europeans were highly susceptible to diseases found in Africa and Asia. In addition, those areas were densely populated when colonizers arrived. These factors limited the colonizers' opportunities to settle there, but population density offered an economic advantage—the

A CLOSER LOOK
GDP IN THE LEAST DEVELOPED COUNTRIES AND BRICS

While growth in developing countries and the BRICS did not keep pace with the rest of the world following World War II, GNI per capita rose rapidly beginning in 2000.

FIGURE 2.20   GDP per Capita in the Least Developed Countries

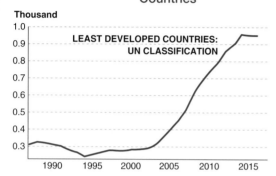

Source: Created from GNI per capita, Atlas method (current US$) by World Bank (https://data.worldbank.org/indicator/NY.GNP.PCAP.CD?locations=XL) licensed under CC-BY 4.0 (https://creativecommons.org/licenses/by/4.0/).

FIGURE 2.21   GDP per Capita in the BRICS

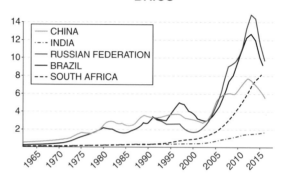

Source: Created from GNI per capita, Atlas method (current US$) by World Bank (https://data.worldbank.org/indicator/NY.GNP.PCAP.CD?locations=BR-CN-IN-RU-ZA) licensed under CC-BY 4.0 (https://creativecommons.org/licenses/by/4.0/).

Developing nations experienced rapid rates of growth beginning around 2000. The BRICS grew as they suffered few years of negative growth.

FIGURE 2.22   GDP per Capita Growth in the BRICS

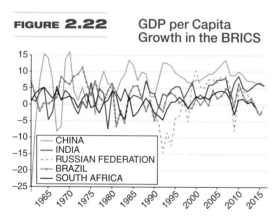

Source: Created from GDP per capita growth (annual %) by World Bank (https://data.worldbank.org/indicator/NY.GDP.PCAP.KD.ZG?locations=BR-CN-IN-RU-ZA) licensed under CC-BY 4.0 (https://creativecommons.org/licenses/by/4.0/).

FIGURE 2.23   GDP per Capita Growth in the Least Developed Countries

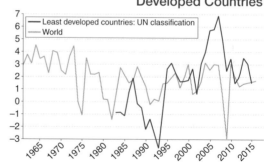

Source: Created from GDP per capita growth (annual %) by World Bank (https://data.worldbank.org/indicator/NY.GDP.PCAP.KD.ZG?locations=XL-1W) licensed under CC-BY 4.0 (https://creativecommons.org/licenses/by/4.0/).

opportunity for forced labor, whether on plantations or in mines. Where slavery had been practiced by indigenous groups, extractive political systems were already in place and people paid duty to powerful chieftains—much as in feudal Europe. In such cases, Europeans merely took control. Authoritarian and absolutist political systems developed that benefitted the few at the expense of the majority (Acemoglu et al. 2001).

A CLOSER LOOK
FORMER COLONIES BY GROWTH AND REGION

Former colonies within regions achieved various levels of success. However, none within Africa or the Middle East advanced to high levels of human development.

TABLE 2.10

	Low	Medium	High
Africa	26	8	0
America	7	6	1
Asia	2	5	6
Middle East	1	7	0

Source: Adapted from Paap, Franses, and van Dijk (2005).

Note: Low growth—Africa: Benin, Burkina, Burundi, Cameroon, Chad, Comoros, Côte D'Ivoire, Equatorial Guinea, Ethiopia, Gambia, Ghana, Guinea, Guinea Bissau, Kenya, Madagascar, Mali, Mozambique, Niger, Nigeria, Rwanda, Senegal, South Africa, Tanzania, Togo, Uganda, and Zambia; America: Argentina, Bolivia, Ecuador, Jamaica, Peru, Uruguay, and Venezuela; Asia: Bangladesh and Philippines; Middle East: Jordan. *Medium growth*—Africa: Congo, Cape Verde, Gabon, Lesotho, Malawi, Mauritius, Seychelles, and Zimbabwe; America: Brazil, Chile, Colombia, Dominican Republic, Paraguay, and Trinidad and Tobago; Asia: India, Indonesia, Nepal, Pakistan, and Sri Lanka; Middle East: Algeria, Egypt, Iran, Israel, Morocco, Syria, and Turkey. *High growth*—America: Barbados; Asia: China, Hong Kong, Japan, Korea, Malaysia, and Thailand.

"Extractive institutions" neither supported long-term development nor disappeared with the end of colonization. Lange (2004) discovered a long-term legacy of "indirect rule" in which the British colonial powers worked through intermediaries, such as chieftains, to exert control and administer the colonies. Chiefs were given power over all aspects of government. They existed as clients of the British, their patrons. Chiefs extracted wealth from the population for themselves and the British. The colonies were in effect clusters of kingdoms linked only weakly through a common colonizer. Looking at data for 33 British colonies, Lange found a robust negative association between indirect rule and "political stability, bureaucratic efficiency, lack of state regulatory burden, rule of law, lack of government corruption, and democratization" (p. 906). Indirect rule, he found, resulted in ineffective government and despotic decentralization, not bureaucratic rules.

In contrast to extractive institutions, North America developed inclusive, direct rule institutions. North America was lightly populated with a hospitable environment. Europeans settled there instituting direct rule characterized by formal rules, a centralized administrative structure, and a formal chain of command (Lange 2004). Acemoglu et al. (2002) identified a cluster of social, political, and economic institutions—the institutions of private property—necessary to ensure that a broad cross section of a society has the opportunity to develop. The political institutions were inclusive, for example, the town hall meetings of New England. The colonizers who lived there, whether of lower or higher social status, wanted their rights ensured.

The type of institutions a society developed made the biggest difference with respect to industrialization. Where rights were widely shared, there was incentive to take advantage of new technologies. The institutions that encouraged investment and protected private property facilitated development in the Americas, Australia, and New Zealand. Where rights were secure for only a small elite, neither the elite nor non-privileged classes were likely to take advantage of the new opportunities. The elite could take advantage of the new technologies only if they themselves had the entrepreneurial skills and ideas necessary for technological development. People other than the elite would not be motivated because their property would not be protected and their successes could be snatched away arbitrarily. In any case, elite classes would be likely to block efforts of others because they themselves would not benefit and their position could be challenged by new wealth. Successful industrialization requires a large number of people willing to make risks on investments. The United States, Australia, Canada, Japan, and Hong Kong were industrialized through the activity of their large middle classes (Acemoglu et al. 2002). Direct rule made it possible, whereas indirect rule subject to clientelism and the arbitrary decisions of intermediaries thwarted development.

To investigate the long-term legacy of colonialism, Nunn (2007) tested two variables: rates extraction and the resources devoted to securing property rights. The extractive institutions—land appropriation, tax systems, and forced labor—had a long-term impact on development. Highly extractive industries, the slave trade to start, reduced previously productive societies to low production. With high extraction, there is not motivation on the part of the populace to produce, and many people are motivated to engage in low-productive activities (securing the output of the producers through robbery, extortion, kidnapping, conflict, etc.), which discourages development. This low-production combination is stable and related to the decreasing development that many societies experienced post-independence.

In the case of African colonies, many were in a high-production equilibrium before contact with Europeans. Where there was high foreign extraction and unproductive activity, first through the slave trade and then through colonial rule, low-production equilibrium developed. In the case of Mozambique, as the slave trade increased, rice and wheat production fell. (It is now in the lowest 5 percent in human development.) A colonial administrator on the Gold Coast lamented that "the natives nowadays no longer occupy themselves with the search for gold, but rather make war on each other to furnish slaves" (Nunn 2007). Where colonizers chose lower levels of extraction and invested more in protecting property from "unproductive actors," people invested in productive activities and the colony was more likely to maintain development after independence. Where colonists settled, long-term development strategies held—in keeping with Acemoglu's theories concerning disease and development.

Extractive as opposed to inclusive institutions apply in the differences among the northern regions of North America and the southern regions of North America and South America. Land inequality and political inequality dominated the large plantation systems of the southern regions. They developed extractive systems based on slave labor and labor of indentured servants. Only an elite had property rights. In the north of the Americas, above the "Mason–Dixon line," the land was not suitable for large plantations but rather small landholdings. To this day, South America and the "Deep South" states of the United States are less developed and remain poorer than the north.

Easterly and Levine (2016) tested the effect of settler and non-settler colonization by measuring the relationship between the number of Europeans living in the colonies and their economic development in the late 20th and 21st centuries. They found robust evidence that current country income increases as the proportion of Europeans living in the colonies increases. In examining the population data, a "natural break" between what would be thought of as settler colonies and non-settler colonies fell at 12.5 percent. Testing only the colonies whose share of European settlers fell below 12.5 percent, a marginal increase in the percentage of European residents resulted in a greater increase in income than for the settler colonies. Furthermore, the positive effect on income of the proportion of Europeans living in the country during colonization remains when controlled for the proportion of Europeans living in the country today (Figure 2.24).

Easterly and Levine's (2016) evidence complements Acemoglu et al.'s (2002) reversal of fortune thesis that regions that were the most productive pre-1500 became the least productive after colonization and those that were the least productive pre-1500 became the most productive. Fewer colonizers settled in more densely populated colonies (an indicator of productive success); those colonies provided more opportunity for extraction because there was more for Europeans to tax away from the colonies and more labor force to exploit in plantations and mines. This inhibited development. Where there was lower population density, Europeans settled and brought human capital, more egalitarian political institutions, and other factors such as technology and knowledge of global markets that fueled long-term economic development. Even with small settlements, but above 4.8 percent, there is some benefit that offset the negative effects of the extractive institutions.

Colonialism lasted into the 1960s and 1970s, even later in some countries. While scientists in advanced economies sent people to the moon, majorities in many post-colonial societies remained uneducated. In 1960, only 10 percent of adults in the low-income countries were literate (World Bank 1978). The five best universities in Africa, according to the *African Economist* (2015), all are in South Africa, a Dutch settler colony. The next four are in Egypt. There is only one in the top ten not from these countries. It is in Tanzania. Even today, Africa has few scientists and engineers, about one for every 10,000 people in comparison with 20 to 50

A CLOSER LOOK

RELATIONSHIP BETWEEN PROPORTION OF EUROPEAN POPULATION DURING COLONIALISM IN RELATION TO INCOME

The greater the proportion of Europeans residing in the colonies, the greater their level of development today.

FIGURE 2.24   European Share at Colonization and Median Current Income

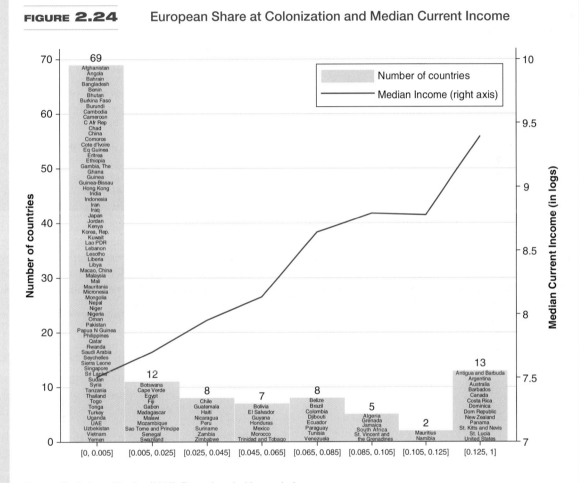

Source: Easterly and Levine (2016). Reproduced with permission.

per 10,000 in industrial nations. Although the African Union hoped for a scientific revolution in Africa to fuel development, improve agricultural productivity, fight disease, and preserve the environment, most countries have not followed through on commitments to advance science education (Mutume 2007).

Diversity and Conflict

While many rich countries, particularly the United States and Canada, welcome diversity as a source of creativity, energy, and entrepreneurship, diversity inhibits many developing societies. After shattering African states and kingdoms during the slave trade, colonial rule established political borders that fractured ethnic communities and combined them with others; some of them had developed animosities related to the slave trade. Colonizers imposed Christianity and Islam on indigenous religions, creating religious fault lines in addition to the ethnic ones. Ideological struggles during the Cold War pitted people against their fellow nationals. Despots of one ethnic or religious group led the persecution of the others. Many societies never developed a sense of national identity capable of encompassing all groups.

Diversity in these societies weakened rather than strengthened development. Intra-societal violence across ideological lines during the Cold War and religious and ethnic lines thereafter have ravaged populations and societies. While the human cost has been high, the economic effects are also high; the working-age population of many societies has been decimated, infrastructure destroyed, and the environment ravaged. Orphaned children and those living in refugee camps lose years of intellectual development, and physical growth is often stunted. Emotional and psychological trauma is extensive. A conservative estimate of the costs of a civil war to a country and its neighbors is about U.S. $64 billion. Over the past few decades, there have been two new civil wars a year on average. That brings the cost to about $100 billion a year, every year, for decades—double the foreign aid budget (Collier 2007).

In societies where diverse groups compete for power, developing institutions and spending money for the common good is not a priority. Only some of the population will thrive. A society cannot do well if only a portion of human capital is developed.

Corruption

Corruption is endemic to inequality and underdevelopment. The poorest societies also tend to be the most corrupt. Transparency International's (TI) 2016 Corruption Perceptions Index (TI 2017) found that corruption is even more strongly related to inequality than to income. The costs of corruption are high; the World Bank found that by controlling corruption, a country can realize a fourfold increase in income per capita, it can realize a 75 percent reduction in child mortality, and businesses can increase growth by about 3 percent a year.

The OECD (2014) publication "CleanGovBiz" cited corruption as one of the main obstacles to development for all economies. It listed four main ways in which corruption inhibits development:

1. Corruption increases the cost of doing business.

    o   The World Economic Forum estimates that corruption increases the costs of doing business by 10 percent on average.

2. Corruption leads to waste and the inefficient use of public resources.

    o   Gupta, Davoodi, and Tiongson (2001) found that child and infant mortality and student dropout rates are significantly higher in countries with high levels of corruption.

    o   African GDP loses 25 percent, U.S. $148 billion, to corruption every year.

3. Corruption excludes poor people from public services and perpetuates poverty.

    o   Because they cannot afford bribes, many of the poor are denied services.

    o   Corruption reduces government offerings to the poor.

4. Corruption corrodes public trust, undermines the rule of law, and ultimately delegitimizes the state.

    o   Bribery of public officials, bypassing regulations to protect the public, and corruption in political parties and elections undermine the foundations of democracy. This could lead to withdrawal of the public from political life or to protests and uprisings such as those that led to the Arab Spring in 2011.

Corruption, the unequal distribution of power, and economic inequality reinforce one another while the majority of people suffer (TI 2017). Bribery is a common form of corruption. People may need to pay bribes to get their children into school, to get a driver's license, or to get their trash collected. The World Bank (2004) estimated the global cost of bribery in the developing world, conservatively, to be U.S. $1 trillion a year.[13]

The World Economic Forum calls corruption the "hidden tax on global growth." This was a key topic at its 2017 annual meeting. Corruption undermines the development of countries in subtle ways. Olken and Pande's (2012) study of corruption drew from examples across a wide range of activities and a multitude of ways in which corruption costs societies. Efficiency costs are severe. For example, in Aceh, Indonesia, the authors found that truck drivers regularly paid bribes to avoid being forced off the road at weigh stations. Nearly all the trucks weighed in their research were overweight. Two in five were more than 50 percent overweight. This leads to rapid deterioration of the roadways. This is a hidden cost. In other cases, public expenditures might never reach their targets. In Uganda, one grant for special education sent by the central government had shrunk by 87 percent by the time it reached the local school.

Corruption by low-level officials and bureaucrats bears a high economic cost and a high cost in human capital, as when children lose out in education or nutritional and health care deficits lead to physical and mental stunting or infant and child mortality. Corruption at high levels, kleptocracy, steals from every institution and every person in the society and undermines the legitimacy of the government. With corruption, people go hungry while the corrupt live in luxury. Corrupt leaders of many former colonies enriched themselves at the expense of their people. Foreign aid channeled through corrupt leaders ended up in overseas bank accounts or was used to build lavish palaces with exotic animals. The World Bank found that about U.S. $20 to $40 billion of development assistance is stolen by high-level corruption.

Wealthy countries that shelter money for politicians or business owners are complicit in the corruption and benefit from it. *Financial Flows and Tax Havens* (Centre for Applied Research 2015) reports on recorded and unrecorded "net resource transfers" from poor to wealthier nations. Developing countries have been acting, in effect, as creditors to wealthier nations, with the balance of money flowing out from the poor to the rich nations. This is, of course, the opposite of what development efforts aim to accomplish. The report calls tax havens and illicit financial flows one of the greatest drivers, if not the greatest driver, of inequality in developing countries. The financial flow and tax haven study found that developing countries lost nearly U.S. $3 trillion in recorded transfers out of the countries and $13.4 trillion[14] in capital flight. These transfers are, in effect, loans to wealthy financial institutions in developed countries.

Political leaders guilty of grand corruption span the globe. Zine al-Abidine Ben Ali, the former president of Tunisia and the first leader to fall in an Arab Spring uprising, stole U.S. $2.6 billion from his country (TI 2017). Viktor Yanukovych, former president of Ukraine, lived in a lavish estate with an exotic zoo, a golf course, a spa with a salt grotto, and a full-sized Spanish galleon. Decorative items in his estate totaled in the millions of dollars. During the Cold War, corruption was endemic among heads of state of developing countries. Mobutu Sese Seko of Zaire (now the Democratic Republic of the Congo [DRC]), Suharto of Indonesia, Ferdinand Marcos of the Philippines, and many more of that era and beyond took trillions of dollars from their countries—much of it development aid—and contributed to the impoverishment and failure to develop or thrive of their people. In some of these societies, such as the DRC, development was more robust in colonial times than in independence.

Kleptocracy is not limited to the developing world. No nation is without corruption. In the United States, Illinois Governor Rod Blagojevich went to prison for trying to profit from his authority to appoint someone to fill the U.S. Senate seat vacated by Barak Obama when Obama became president. Ray Nagin, the mayor of New Orleans, profited from funds intended to help the recovery following Hurricane Katrina. Edwin Edwards, a long-serving governor of Louisiana, collected millions on the awarding of casino licenses.

The Resource Curse

Ironically, many countries that are rich in a resource such as oil or precious metals are poor. While being resource rich should be a boon to growth, it can also inhibit growth. One way in which this happens is through the "Dutch disease." When the Netherlands discovered large gas reserves in the 1960s, gas exports surged, bringing in foreign currency and driving up the value of Dutch currency. The increased value of the Dutch currency made Dutch exports more expensive and less competitive. Other industries suffered and unemployment increased.

Resources are also a curse if investors rush to invest in the resource, neglecting other development. The economy does not diversify. Many of the extraction industries do not employ many people once the wells are dug and the pipelines laid. While construction might employ thousands, operating the facilities often employs fewer than a hundred.

Dependence on one or two commodities is risky for a country. Prices are volatile, and supply and demand are not predictable. Consider oil prices. In less than 10 years, prices were slashed more than 50 percent. First, in the 2007–2008 recession, production virtually stopped due to decreasing demand for oil. China's growth is slowing, also decreasing demand. New natural gas wells in the United States increased the fossil fuel supply and decreased demand for oil. Prices dropped to below U.S. $50 a barrel, whereas they had been above $100 before the recession. Oil-dependent countries suffered.

How a country uses the profits from valuable commodities influences whether it will help or hinder development. China's growth fueled demand for Africa's natural resources. This could have revived Africa's manufacturing. Instead, Africa's industrial output decreased from 3 percent of global output in 1970 to half of that in 2016 despite the economic boom. Most African countries used the windfall to fund nonproductive programs. Some economists fear that this is going to be a repeat of commodity-driven boom and bust—a resource curse (Tafirenyika 2016).

Where governments control resources, authoritarian governments may use them to their own advantage to consolidate power. When Russia benefitted from the pre-recession increase in demand for oil, Vladimir Putin's authoritarian tactics did not seem to bother many Russians. After a short run with democracy in which the economy did not do well, they were happy with the stronger economy. The revenue stream from resources can pay for benefits as long as the commodity price holds. Populations can be kept satisfied with state-offered benefits. At the same time, politicians can enrich themselves with little public oversight of state-run enterprises. Corruption can thrive.

Resources are not necessarily a curse. Whether or not they are depends on human agency. Britain and the United States used vast coal reserves to industrialize. Ethiopia and Tanzania, while resource rich, experienced high economic growth without depending on their resource wealth. Whether it is a curse or a blessing depends on the governance structure and how the benefits from the resource are used. If they fuel diversification and industrial or service development, other industries can be built. Saudi Arabia, faced with falling oil prices and a public more restive due to the resulting decrease in benefits, recognized that the country could not depend on oil and is now trying to diversify its economy.

Climate Change

Climate change and pollution bear a cost to societies. The World Bank (2010) projected the costs for developing countries to range from about U.S. $75 to $90 billion annually for the years 2010 to 2050,[15] based on two different scenarios. The costs include such things as adapting agriculture, preventing and treating increases in vector-borne diseases, and harm to trade and fisheries, among many other impacts. This estimate does not include the cost of forced migration and illnesses such as heat stress, pollution, and increased allergen levels. Climate change also contributes significantly to violent conflict, particularly due to drought and food insecurity. Conflicts may be localized among groups competing for resources, as in Kenya and Uganda, or may evolve into civil wars. Terrorist groups also take advantage of drought conditions to control water supplies (as Al-Shabab has done in Somalia) or to lure recruits. These latter costs cannot be reliably estimated. However, they are, and will undoubtedly continue to be, in the billions.

In Africa, the costs of premature death due to pollution are high. In 2013, there were more than 250,000 premature deaths from ambient air pollution and more than 450,000 from indoor air pollution. The economic cost of these deaths was U.S. $447 billion. The United States also experiences thousands of premature deaths every year due to air pollution. No continent can afford to lose this much human or economic capital (Roy 2016).

The Global Economy

Participating in the global economy, the global division of labor, is essential for lifting countries out of poverty. Openness to the global economy, as measured by the percentage of GDP accounted for by imports and exports, is positively related to human development. Münch (2016) found that urbanization fosters specialization and facilitates integration into the global division of labor. Government expenditures on public goods, such as education, the rule of law, and health care, and the percentage of the population that is economically active enhance human development.

How a country participates is important. Developing countries have higher portions of GDP and labor in agriculture. The export of cash crops and raw materials, low value chain exports with easily manipulated prices, remains the mainstay of the least developed societies. They also tend to have high fertility rates. Both inhibit human development (Münch 2016).

For now, manufacturing remains critical for development in most countries. Without developing their manufacturing industries with reasonable wages, countries are less able to advance economically. Integrating into the supply chain of an international firm can help developing nations to advance, but they do not always benefit from a transfer of technology. This was something that the Asian Tigers insisted on, thereby facilitating their own growth.

While a developing country increases its total exports by entering a supply chain, it does not necessarily advance its own manufacturing sector.

VARYING PATHWAYS TO DEVELOPMENT

Societies exist across the continuum of development. As discussed above, most of the developed countries, those of Western Europe and North America, diverged at the time of the Industrial Revolution. Other societies never "took off" and are still growing slowly. There are at least two other patterns worth considering. Not all of the most advanced countries took the "Western" route, yet they advanced and took places among the wealthiest societies. Other countries showed rapid development and yet stalled. This section examines these alternate routes of development. Each provides a framework for thinking about global inequality and poverty in specific contexts.

Divergence in Asia: The Fast Growth of Japan and the East Asian Tigers

Landes (1999) contrasted the post-World War II success of Japan and the late 20th-century rise of the East Asian Tigers with the stagnation and decline of other societies. According to Landes's analysis, Japan's success grew from deep roots in every aspect of its society. Its success, and that of Hong Kong and Singapore, diffused through some other Asian societies as production and know-how spread through the region.

A fundamental feature of Japanese culture is the strong sense of family that extends up through to the nation. This translates to a sense of higher purpose, including in economic activity, serving the nation first, family second, other groups third, and the self somewhat further down the line. This dutifulness supports a strong work ethic that would make the Calvinists jealous. Education played an important role as well. Education has been important historically in Japan, being among the first countries to require universal primary education. Education includes willingness to learn from other countries. When manufacturing moved to Japan, companies did little to protect the intellectual capital in their products, believing they had nothing to fear from these "defeated" people. Japanese engineers quickly "reverse engineered" foreign technology, disassembling and learning from it. When traveling to factories abroad, they "humbly" asked questions, photographed, tape recorded, watched, and learned (Landes 1999).

Japanese engineers also invented, focusing on the highest technology products. They studied the markets and created products to meet demands. They developed more efficient production techniques. Their ethic of collective responsibility fostered a team approach and willingness of workers to submit to their superiors. Economic policy stressed protecting fledgling industries. When forced into open trade agreements, they instituted non-tariff barriers such as refusing some products due to the "different conditions" in Japan. Their economic policy was not to get the "lowest prices" and "discount distribution" but rather to build market share, capacity, and industrial and military strength (Landes 1999).

While the international financial institutions advocated import substitution—replacing imported products with ones manufactured domestically—the Japanese complied but developed export markets as well. When privatization was advocated, Asian governments established industries needed for development if the market did not. This is how Korea created one of the most efficient steel industries in the world, spurring its automotive and other industries, and how Taiwan created its Formosa Plastics industry (Stiglitz 2006).

Rather than choosing between an economy completely open to market forces and strict central planning, the Asian societies that grew quickly in the 1980s and 1990s took another path. They managed their economies but spread the benefits of development widely. Although specific policies varied, the main strategies included the following (Stiglitz 2006):

- Encouraging saving by creating savings institutions to ensure capital flow from stable domestic sources. Singapore took this a step further by requiring mandatory savings through wage attachments

- Opening their markets slowly while protecting fledgling industries

- Planning growth in export industries carefully, specifying which industries would be developed and how imports would be restricted

- Selecting foreign investment cautiously and requiring foreign companies to transfer technology and train workers

- Opening financial markets slowly and methodically

Development in these societies was successful but not trouble free. Too great an influx of foreign capital along with relaxing regulations led to short-term speculation and the financial crisis of 1997 (Stiglitz 2006).

Slow Growth or Income Traps?

The explosion of growth in the 2000s lifted many countries and people out of poverty and into low-income status. From 2001 to 2011, the poverty class shrank by 669 million people, about one third. Growth rates averaging about 6 percent a year in a few developing societies pushed people over the poverty threshold into low income. Every 1 percent growth per capita in a society reduced poverty by about 1.7 percent on average. Poverty dropped even more in more equal societies (*The Economist* 2013).

Does this mean that all societies will at some point converge? There has been mobility, but most mobility among people has been from poor to low income. Because growth did not move as many people from low income to middle income as from poor to low income, the low-income class grew by 694 million people (Figure 2.25).

From 1950 to 1980, there was significant mobility in terms of the numbers of societies that moved up income categories. From the postwar period into the 1980s, industry "unbundled" and manufacturing spread into poorer economies, lifting incomes in Latin America, parts of Eastern Europe, and Asia. Japan and Korea rebuilt with the help of the West after World War II and the war in Korea. The industrialized world turned toward more services and higher-level manufacturing (Baldwin 2006). Advancing through income categories took longer in the decades from 1980 to 2013 than from the 1950s to 1980. Although 31 countries moved from low-income status (1990 purchasing power parity less than $2,000) to lower middle-income status ($2,000 but less than $7,250) during the 1950s, 1960s, and 1970s, only 2 moved up during the three decades from 1980 to 2013 (Felipe, Kumar, and Galope 2017). Some societies have remained in low-income status for generations, as have 35 from 1950 to the present (Felipe et al. 2017).

Movement among societies from lower-middle to upper-middle class ($7,250 but less than $11,750) and from middle to upper income (above $11,750) is also

A CLOSER LOOK
GLOBAL ECONOMIC MOBILITY, 2001–2011

Poverty decreased from 2001 to 2011. Most people remained poor, and most mobility was from poor to low income. Fewer people moved from lower income to middle-, upper middle-, and high-income classes.

FIGURE 2.25   Percentages of Global Population by Income

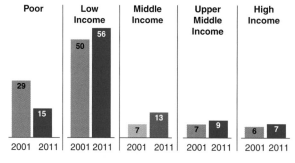

Source: "A Global Middle Class Is More Promise than Reality." Pew Research Center, Washington, D.C. July 8, 2015. http://www.pewglobal.org/2015/07/08/a-global-middle-class-is-more-promise-than-reality/.

progressing more slowly since 1980 than it did from 1950 to 1980. After 1950, the median number of years it took countries to advance to the upper middle-income category was 28. However, three countries in this group took from 50 to 54 years. Others advanced much more rapidly.[16] In addition, the number of high-income countries increased from 3 to 21 from 1950 (beginning in earnest in 1960) through the 1980s but increased by only 12 from 1980 to 2013 (Felipe et al. 2017).

Given their current growth rates and the year that they entered their income category, there are 10 countries undergoing slower than average transitions out of lower middle-income status and 4 undergoing slower than average transitions from upper middle-income to high-income status (Felipe et al. 2017). Countries now ranked as high-income status (U.S. $12,000 or above) enjoyed, at some point in their development, a high share of manufacturing employment—18 to 20 percent is the threshold for countries that are rich. The earlier that countries achieved their peak in manufacturing employment, the greater their GDP per capita was likely to be at that time (Felipe, Mehta, and Rhee 2018).

Are those countries that did not advance trapped in low- and middle-income status? There is no clear definition of a "middle-income trap." Using the term "trap" is misleading because countries can and do move up income levels, albeit at varying rates. Some move more rapidly and some more slowly, depending on a complex of circumstances that contribute to growth.

The 35 countries that have been in the lower-income tier since 1950 have high percentages of their workforces in agriculture. No country whose share of the labor force in manufacturing was below 16 percent ever achieved a per capita income of U.S. $6,000 or above. It may well be that increasing a country's manufacturing workforce is more difficult than it was in the past (Felipe et al. 2018). Certainly, mechanization must be a factor. So too are movements toward more service economies. Another problem is that in poor countries manufacturing activity tends to be in the lowest levels of the value chain. When the work is similar, it pays poorly in comparison with similar activity in other countries; for example, contrast textile workers in Bangladesh (among the poorest) with those in Colombia (middle income). Poor-quality employment and insecure employment in developing and emerging economies also sustain poverty. Maintaining their growth rates and securing adequate jobs will be essential for these countries to advance to higher income levels.

Is China Stuck?

In 1978, China moved from a centrally planned economy to a market-based economy, spurring the fastest expansion of any society in history, averaging about 10 percent a year. Manufacturing wages in China tripled from 2005 to 2016, rising above wages in countries such as Mexico and Brazil, helping to push all wages upward as workers could leave poorer paying jobs for better wages (Worstall 2017). The millions of Chinese that growth lifted out of poverty is a major factor in improving global poverty statistics. This was not accomplished without problems. Rising inequality, environmental issues, rapid urbanization, large debt, and an aging population each poses a serious challenge to growth (World Bank 2016a).

In 2015, China had its slowest growth in 25 years. With a shrinking labor force, labor activism, and rising wages, industry costs are pushing upward and China is losing some of its competitive edge. Economic hardships in other countries have weakened demand for its exports. Without more efficient use of resources and improvements in productivity and innovation, China may remain in the middle, unable to compete effectively with lower cost countries or high-developed ones (Johnson 2015). China became a lower middle-income country in 1992 and by 2009 had achieved upper middle-income status. It will not be until 2024 that it would be considered as slower than the median in moving into upper income (Felipe et al. 2017).

Are We All Getting Stuck? Wages and Workers

The International Monetary Fund's (IMF) World Economic Outlook Update (IMF 2017) projected that the global economy would grow somewhat faster in 2017 (3.4 percent) and 2018 (3.6 percent) than in 2016 (3.1 percent).

How does growth translate for workers? The ILO (2016) reported that global wage growth dropped from 2.5 percent in 2012 to 1.7 percent in 2015, its lowest level in four years. Excluding China, wage growth in 2015 was only 0.9 percent. Since the 2007–2008 recession, most of the global wage growth had been driven by emerging and developing economies. Among the developing countries in the G20—the largest developing economies—growth fell from 6.6 to 2.5 percent from 2012 to 2015. Wage growth increased somewhat in the United States and Germany but declined in Asia and the Pacific. In Latin America and the Caribbean and Eastern Europe, real wages declined (ILO 2016).

Unemployment in most developed societies has recovered from the recession, but wages have not. Many workers are working fewer hours, and many are working part-time when they would prefer full-time work (Figure 2.26).

Sluggish wage growth is a risk factor for overall growth. With less income, people spend less, and consumer spending is an important driver of growth. This could in turn shrink wage growth.

Wage Growth in the United States

In the United States, wages and productivity grew together from 1947 until they diverged in the 1970s. Wages peaked in 1973 at U.S. $22.41 (2014 dollars) and have not reached that level again—despite ever increasing productivity, increasing growth, and increasing job creation (DeSilver 2014).

A CLOSER LOOK
EMPLOYMENT STILL LAGS IN 2016

Fewer hours and more part-time employment impeded wage growth.

FIGURE 2.26   (a) Hours per Worker; (b) Involuntary Part-Time Employment, Share of Total Employment

a. Hours per Worker

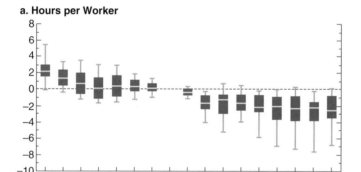

b. Involuntary Part-Time Employment, Share of Total Employment

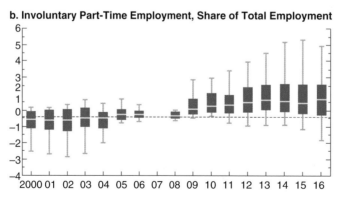

Source: International Monetary Fund. 2017. *Seeking Sustainable Growth: Short-Term Recovery, Long-Term Challenges.* Washington, DC, October.

Note: (a) Log level difference relative to 2007; (b) Percentage-point difference relative to 2007.

Labor's share of output diminished over time from the 1970s onward. Productivity growth outpaced wage growth, and the two diverged even further over time. Growing at an average of just below 0.2 percent from 1973 to 2017, wages overall rose 10 percent when adjusted for inflation. Not everyone's wages rose, however. People's wages in the bottom half of the wage earners have not grown. For the bottom quintile (20 percent of workers), wages decreased from 1979 to 2016. For those in the top quintile, they increased 27.41 percent from 1979 to 2016—significantly more than the 10 percent average (Figures 2.27 and 2.28) (Shambaugh et al. 2017).

The consequences of shrinking and stagnant wages are severe and limit people's life chances.

Minimum wage stagnation plays an important role in depressing growth. States and cities that increased their minimum wage experienced growth, not decreases, in low-wage worker income. Although not yet caught up to historic highs, minimum wage increases showed up in an overall wage increase in the bottom 10 percent since 2010. The increase was not as high as for the top two quintiles, but in states that increased the minimum wage the increase was 5.2 percent of real wage growth. In states that did not, it was 2.5 percent (Shambaugh et al. 2017).

Restricting worker power and choice also results in lower wages. This began in earnest in the 1980s. More than 28 percent of workers belonged to unions in 1956 compared with about 10 percent in 2016. Non-compete

A CLOSER LOOK
LABOR'S INCOME RELATIVE TO PRODUCTIVITY AND SHARE OF INCOME

FIGURE 2.27   Real Labor Productivity and Hourly Compensation, 1947–2017

Labor's compensation grew in tandem with productivity until the mid-1970s. Since then, compensation has declined relative to growth in productivity.

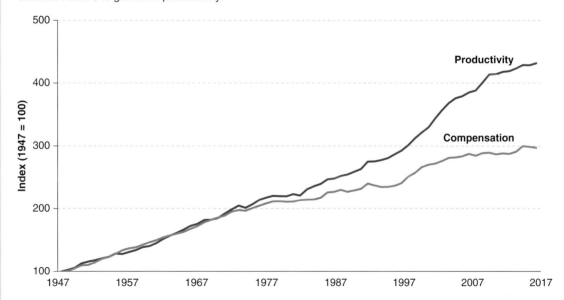

Source: Shambaugh et al. (2017). Reproduced with permission.

(Continued)

(Continued)

FIGURE 2.28   Labor Share of Income, 1973–2017

Labor's share of earnings in 2017 was a fraction of the share that accrued to labor in 1975.

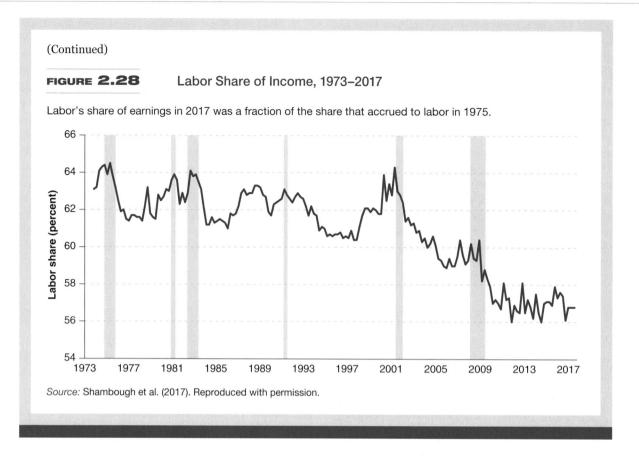

Source: Shambough et al. (2017). Reproduced with permission.

contracts (even for lower level workers) and collusion among firms also hurt worker wages. Worker mobility, which contributes to about 1 percent of wage growth per quarter as workers move to find higher incomes, declined nearly 50 percent from 1990 to 2016. Recessions, licensing requirements, non-compete contracts, and land use restrictions related to housing all contributed to decreasing mobility (Shambough et al. 2017).

Government policies can make a difference in wage growth. Minimum wage reform, collective bargaining legislation, and programs to increase labor productivity through education and training, research and development funding, tax incentives, infrastructure investment, and universal occupational licensing are actions governments can take. Income tax legislation—such as earned income credit—can distribute the gains of productivity more equitably. Corporations must consider reforming methods of determining executive compensation and providing fair wages commensurate with labor productivity. Ending non-compete practices for skilled and unskilled workers and other

practices that limit mobility can help workers to help themselves.

In addition to wages, stock options provide wage workers with opportunities to grow wealth. Stocks grant workers a share in corporate or company ownership and profit that grows (or decreases) in value as the corporation does.

FIGHTING POVERTY AND INEQUALITY

What is the secret to providing equal life chances around the globe? There has been significant progress, but many countries and many people within wealthy countries still lag behind despite decades of efforts. There is not a "one size fits all" answer to any global problem. Developing and developed countries have unique histories and needs.

Providing people with equal life chances to achieve their potential is increasingly recognized as a human right. Equal life chances do not guarantee or mean equal results. They mean an equal chance to succeed. Providing for equal life chances requires addressing the needs of the poor in general as well as target groups such as women, children, and ethnic and racial minorities. It involves a combination of programs and policies to guarantee human and civil rights, eliminate extreme income inequality and extreme poverty, provide social welfare remedies to supplement labor market weakness, and address non-economic forms of inequality.

Programs and policies to spur development and combat inequality and poverty at the same time must build an infrastructure for inclusive and sustainable growth. In many respects, these activities are governance activities because they determine the direction the society takes and the opportunities afforded to people in the society. Efforts of national governments, international governmental and non-governmental organizations, and the private sector must be coordinated to tackle these problems.

National Governments

Although the global economy has eclipsed the nation-state or country, national governments still have an important role to play in reducing inequality and poverty. International aid and governmental organization should assist in these domestic improvements, but national governments need to take the lead.

Direct Economic Growth

Economic growth is not the best measure of the health of the global economy or a domestic economy. It is not an indicator of general well-being of people. It is important, but economic growth does not guarantee an increase in the life chances of people. The past few decades have demonstrated that economic growth alone does not reduce inequality; in many cases, it exacerbates it. "Inclusive growth" that is shared across all segments of society will not happen without deliberate effort.

Since the early 2000s, many economies that grew quickly experienced "jobless growth," signified by an employment to population percentage that stagnated at about 60 percent (UNDP 2013). Economic growth needs to target incomes at the bottom of the pyramid. This means more jobs and jobs that offer a living wage, security, and safe working conditions.

The UNDP (2013) called on governments to facilitate the growth of small and medium-sized enterprises. These tend to be labor intensive and have proven to create more jobs faster than larger enterprises. Steps that governments have successfully implemented include the following:

- Working through central banks with public funds to guarantee loans, as has been done in China, Malaysia, Indonesia, and India.

- Offering education and information on new technologies, products, and markets.

- Offering incentives to larger enterprises to contract with smaller enterprises and procure materials and other inputs from them.

- Requiring a certain number or percentage of government contracts to go to small and medium-sized enterprises.

Governments also provide employment through public works projects such as infrastructure. These jobs have been shown to have a lower net cost per job created. These government-created jobs often create a "de facto" minimum wage and force other wages up to that minimum without minimum wage enforcement costs.

Tackle Inequality Directly Through Social Protection Programs

How growth diffuses through the globe and society matters. Where poverty and inequality efforts are not alleviated through work and wages, redistribution programs can substitute. Wilkinson and Pickett (2009) demonstrated that the strategy for achieving greater equality in a society does not affect the benefits to the society.

One strategy is social transfer. Finland, one of the most equal and wealthy societies, is also the most generous country. Its non-contributory social transfers—those to which neither the employee nor employer contribute—account for 43 percent of the income of households below the poverty line. Contributory transfers account for another 37 percent.

Social welfare programs cover few of the poorest people in the poorest nations. In sub-Saharan Africa and South Asia, which have the highest incidence of extreme poverty, only about 22 percent of the population has access to any type of social protection. Rural households tend to receive smaller amounts of income per capita than their urban counterparts (Figure 2.29) (Food and Agriculture Organization of the United Nations [FAO] 2015).

A CLOSER LOOK
SOCIAL WELFARE PROGRAMS

Most of the poor in low- and middle-income regions do not receive social welfare assistance.

FIGURE 2.29   Shares of Population Covered by Different Types of Social Protection Programs, by Region

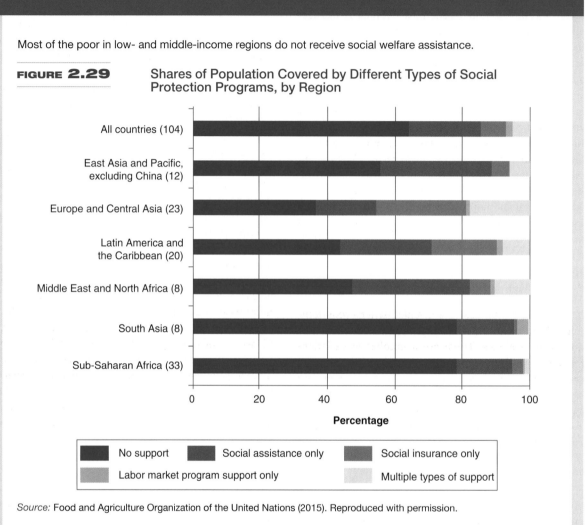

Source: Food and Agriculture Organization of the United Nations (2015). Reproduced with permission.

Closing the poverty gap through social protection programs for countries in Latin America and the Caribbean, the Middle East and North Africa, and East Asia would cost only about 0.1 percent of their GDP. It would take 1.6 percent in South Asia but 5.3 percent in sub-Saharan Africa, with some countries needing 10 percent. Even bringing the poorest up to U.S. $1 a day would cost 0.1 to 2 percent of GDP for most of the poorest countries but from 2.3 to 4.5 percent in others (FAO 2015). These programs are a good investment to ease populations displaced by structural transformations.

Ensure Dignity in Work

The international conventions requiring equal rights for all people have the force of international law, and their standing was reinforced by inclusion in national constitutions and subsequently other domestic laws. Elkins, Ginsburg, and Simmons (2013) confirmed that international treaties influence national constitutions and other domestic laws. Each has an independent effect on protection of rights, and international conventions act through domestic laws. Multiple levels of regulatory authority increase the likelihood that domestic mobilization in combination with international pressures increase actual respect for rights. Duplication of laws increases the probability that they will be enforced.

Ensuring that all segments of society have equal access to the tools of success is important for social justice and also for development. If a society develops only part of its human capital and prevents women and ethnic, religious, and indigenous minorities from achieving their potential, the society can never achieve its potential. Civil society groups, international governmental organizations, and other governments all have a role to play in ensuring that every government provides every member with the tools available to succeed.

Guarantee an Annual Income

This is an idea that has been circulating for a long time. It has been popular (and unpopular) in both liberal and conservative circles. There are a number of variations on the basic idea. One set of proposals would grant an annual cash amount to every adult. Another would limit it to those earning under a specified amount. For those plans that propose grants only for the poor, the amount is usually equivalent to a poverty income. Those proposals to offer grants to everyone are generally lower.

Switzerland held a referendum on a guaranteed basic income in June 2016. It was overwhelmingly defeated at the polls, with 77 percent against it to 23 percent in favor. It would have given about U.S. $2,555 to each adult and about one quarter of that for each child. The Finns experimented with such a program from 2017 to 2019 as a solution to a high (10 percent) unemployment rate. The Finnish plan gave a group of 2,000 randomly selected unemployed persons about U.S. $876 a month unconditionally and tax free. The trade-off is that it was to replace all of the social welfare programs. At the end of 2018, the Finns added a requirement that recipients work 18 hours within the first three months or enter a training program. The idea has not died. Sam Altman, a venture capitalist, is running his own experiment in the United States in Oakland, California (Donnelley 2018).

Provide Living Wage and Decent Work Positions

Work is the best poverty reduction program. Providing a minimum wage, or a living wage, can be part of an overall poverty reduction strategy. In developing societies, less than half of workers are covered by minimum wage policies (Grindling 2016). In many societies that have minimum wage laws, the minimum does not meet the standard to bring the worker or household to the poverty threshold.[17]

Minimum wage policies do not always affect the poorest workers. Increasing minimum wages will not help workers in the informal economy. In many countries, it does not cover workers in certain industries, certain sized companies, or other considerations. How many are employed in these sectors and the poverty rates among the self-employed have an impact on the effect of minimum wage increases. The effect of minimum wage increases on unemployment, whether there are losses and how significant they are, is also an important consideration.

While there is fear that increasing minimum wages might slow growth or employment, a number of studies show that modest increases in minimum wages need not do either. For example, in just 7 years in Brazil, the minimum wage was increased 80 percent (hardly modest). This was accompanied by a decrease in inequality, about 16 percent of it accounted for by the rise in minimum wage. In the case of Thailand, an increase in the minimum wage is expected to boost both employment growth and GDP growth (UNDP 2013).

In Brazil, while the minimum wage increase may have decreased poverty overall, the gap between the poorest and average workers increased. In Colombia, there were similar results, with minimum wage increases having little impact on the poorest. The conclusion of reforms in Nicaragua, Colombia, and Brazil is that when the minimum wage increase affects the heads of households, as opposed to secondary workers, poverty falls even if some secondary workers lose work (Grindling 2016).

Whether or not minimum wage increases have an impact on poverty and unemployment depends on country-level variables such as the nature of the labor market. To avoid increasing unemployment, some countries supplement employers to reduce their costs (OECD 2015).

Recognize Unpaid Labor

Work is a source of dignity for all of humankind. Recognizing the value of unpaid work could be a critical step in reducing poverty, particularly among women, who do the largest share of unpaid labor and comprise, along with children, the greatest proportion of the poor. Most of this unpaid labor is in household production.

Household production has a slight correlation to income; high-income households have a slightly higher level. As fewer hours have been spent on household tasks over time, household production has decreased; nevertheless, incorporating household production into income would have increased personal income by 30 percent in 2010 (Bridgman et al. 2012). Some form of payment to households, perhaps based on the number of members, would elevate the income of poorer households by a greater percentage than that of wealthier households, decreasing the inequality gap.

Education, Education, Education

Competing in a global economy requires skill and knowledge. Lifelong learning and skill training need to be available to all people. Whether this is a function only of government or of the private sector and government might be different in every country but is essential for all.

While the quantity of education need not increase in developed countries, the quality of public education and opportunities for adults in many countries needs to be improved. Even in developed countries, educational outcomes are strongly linked to parental background. Training and adult education opportunities are more available to higher skilled workers than to medium-skilled workers, who have more opportunity than lower skilled workers, even in the more equal Scandinavian countries (Förster, Nozal, and Théveno 2017). Countries that subsidize private schools through tax and other means can transfer that money to public schools, many of which are underfunded such as those in the United States (Milanovic 2011).

Intergovernmental and Non-governmental Aid Organizations

Target Foreign Aid

Foreign aid programs of governments and intergovernmental organizations and agencies expanded following World War II. Western nations formed the Bretton Woods institutions, the IMF, and the World Bank for reconstruction, for loans, and to stabilize exchange rates. Although the initial targets of stabilization and reconstruction were in Europe, the goals of the institutions evolved to concentrate both their efforts on developing economies.

Foreign aid has a mixed record of success. It might seem counterintuitive that aid could hinder a country's

PHOTO 2.2 Locally grown food programs fight hunger and combat poverty. This pepper farmer has been able to provide more for his children, put a new roof on his home, and earn a profit to reinvest in farming.

Sara A. Fajardo, Catholic Relief Services.

development rather than accelerate it. Aid to developing countries comes from a variety of sources. Not much comes without conditionality, in other words, with no strings attached. During the Cold War, aid from international institutions and governments was targeted to the strategic advantage of global powers. Aid came with few guidelines relative to development outcomes and more to UN votes. Much of the aid went directly into the pockets of dictators and their "cronies" who were appointed to oversee projects and whose lack of expertise doomed the projects to inefficiency or failure.

In 1995, the UN World Summit for Social Development adopted a foreign aid goal for rich nations equal to 0.7 percent of a their GNI. Only a few nations have met this goal.[18] The United States spent about U.S. $35 billion for foreign economic aid in 2014. This is about 0.2 percent of GNI.

In addition to the "bilateral" aid agencies of individual countries such as USAID (U.S. Agency for International Development), there are multilateral agencies such as the IMF and World Bank, many regional development banks such as the Asian Development Bank, and a number of UN aid programs and funds such as UNICEF. According to a Brookings Institute report (Easterly and Pfutze 2007), U.S. $103.6 billion in official aid was given to developing countries in 2006, for a total of about $2.3 trillion over 50 years. In their study of years of reports and evaluations of aid agencies, the authors offered an analysis of what went wrong with foreign aid and best practices for aid.

The major shortcomings that emerged from the analysis were the following.

Transparency. Recipient government reporting needs to be transparent to ensure that money is reaching the intended beneficiaries and is not channeled through corrupt officials or to less poor countries. Administrative and other cost reports of the agencies must also be transparent. Easterly and Pfutze (2007) found five agencies that do not report any data on their employment or budget. Multilateral agencies tended to do better than bilateral agencies, with the development banks doing the best. A few programs, primarily UN ones, had weak reporting mechanisms.

Fragmentation. Unlike the specialized bureaucracies and private corporations that specialize, aid agencies tend to split their assistance among too many projects and too many sectors. Specialization would streamline processes and create efficiencies. There is little coordination, which would also improve efficiencies. Coordination would reduce overhead costs and concentrate focus. Regardless of size, donors split among many projects, and this leads to almost insignificant worldwide flows such as the $5,000 to worldwide non-governmental organizations by Ireland in 2004. (This was not the total amount of foreign aid from Ireland.) Following the "trendy" projects is one mechanism that contributes to this (Easterly and Pfutze 2007).

Selectivity. It goes without saying that aid to countries that are not poor or to corrupt dictators does not stimulate inclusive growth. Countries that are not free (about one third) or partly free receive about 80 percent of aid. Easterly and Pfutze (2007) found that aid donors do not respond to changes in the level of corruption and aid goes to corrupt countries. On average, 68 percent of aid was going to corrupt countries. Aid to the least developed countries has increased over time, but at the expense of low-income countries rather than the middle-income countries. The share of aid going to least developed countries is 42 percent, and 22 percent goes to other low-income countries, leaving 36 percent to middle-income countries.

Aid agencies may be planning reforms in delivering aid to countries that are not free or have corrupt dictators. They may also be operating on the principle that beneficiaries in these countries need the aid the most. When aid is directed at middle-income countries, it may be perceived as nearing a tipping point where aid may make a significant difference in improving the quality of life. However, as Easterly and Pfutze (2007) noted, when aid is directed at "allies" who do not need it or are not spending it to benefit their poor, it is a misuse of aid.

Aid that requires recipients to buy goods and technical assistance from the donor country is a less effective form of aid. Aid that requires recipients to purchase food or goods from the donor country amounts to a subsidy to industries in the donor country. This frequently happened with food aid; the surplus product of the donor is "dumped" into the developing nation, often undermining local agricultural efforts. Many food programs now provide aid to support local producers. This spurs development and enhances inclusive growth. Technical assistance can pose a similar problem when given to promote the donor's interests. If it does not reap long-term benefits for the recipients, it is not aid (Easterly and Pfutze 2007).

Accountability and transparency, with respect to the benefits of aid, is the third response. Working closely with the beneficiaries, using aid to empower them is one of the most important criteria to affect long-term results. Accountability to the beneficiaries is different from that to donors. It entails constant feedback and participation of the beneficiaries in the development efforts. This is recognized by most aid agencies. However, adopting formal accountability measures has not kept pace with the intent. The Humanitarian Accountability Partnership (HAP) promotes standards for accountability, quality management, and transparency. About 100 aid agencies joined from its creation in 2003 to 2013 (Van Rooyen 2013).

Grant More Debt Relief

Debt has crippled many nations. For some countries, much of the debt incurred was seized through kleptocracy or crony capitalism. Like having a credit card where a person pays only the interest on the debt or only a minimal amount on the principal, the original debt grows far beyond the original loan. Servicing the debt consumes resources that could be better spent on human capital or physical capital improvements. This is a transfer of wealth from poorer to richer nations (or to the international institutions). Renegotiating the terms of the debt or some level of debt forgiveness is overdue.

In 1996, the IMF and World Bank launched a debt relief program for 39 Heavily Indebted Poor Countries (HIPCs). It is supplemented by the Multi-lateral Debt Relief Initiative (MDRI) funded by other lenders. The program does not include all of the heavily indebted countries. Nigeria, for example, is not on the list because it is not "poor" enough. Somalia is ineligible

CONSIDER THIS
PROVIDING ACCESS TO TECHNOLOGY—AS SIMPLE AS A MOBILE PHONE

In most of the developed world, we take mobile phones for granted. In the developing world, a mobile phone can make a world of difference. According to USAID (2015):

- An increase of 10 percent in mobile penetration can raise the GDP of a developing country as much as 1.2 percent.

- In Tanzania, mobile phones are used to deliver educational content to remote areas.

- Mobile phones are used by the Mobile Alliance for Maternal Action to deliver health information to pregnant and new mothers.

- When used to pay employees, mobile phones can cut out graft and corruption, as demonstrated in Afghanistan.

- Mobile phones provide access to markets, delivering important and timely information to farmers and buyers.

- Mobile phones can be used for financial services to people not served by the regular banking industry.

- By providing polling and voting information, mobile phones strengthened democracy in Haiti and Tunisia.

---

because it is too far in arrears. As of September 2015, 36 countries had met the criteria for debt reduction. A potential U.S. $76 billion in relief over time is provided for the HIPCs, and $41.6 billion by the MDRI is promised for relief for these countries. To qualify, countries needed to make and sustain progress toward achieving the Millennium Development Goals. The debt relief allows them to put more money into poverty reduction efforts (International Development Association [IDA] and IMF 2016). Expanding relief to the countries approved for relief and the criteria for which countries can qualify would make more money available for development.

The Private Sector

The private sector recognizes the importance of the "bottom of the pyramid" for corporate growth and profit in the new millennium. Although poor, that segment of the wealth pyramid has the most potential for market growth. Results of an online search of "bottom of the pyramid" brings up myriad business articles and books such as "The Fortune at the Bottom of the Pyramid." They contain money-making strategies for producing for and selling to the billions of the world's poor living on less than U.S. $2 a day—the last remaining untapped market. Whether or not the poor can be served in partnership with global capital—meeting genuine needs at reasonable cost—is an important question.

Secure Financial Services: Microfinance

Whether in developing or developed countries, the poor do not have access to the same financial services and opportunities as middle and upper classes. Without banks, checking accounts, or credit—the basics of finance—moving beyond the lowest levels of economic activity is difficult.

Not everyone needs thousands of dollars to start a successful business. One or two hundred dollars may be all that a person needs to get a business off the ground. Without collateral or a credit history, getting even a few hundred dollars can be impossible. Grameen Bank, for which its founder Muhammad Yunus received a Nobel Prize, provides loans, savings plans, checking accounts, and financial education to people who cannot qualify for conventional loans and in areas that are poorly served by conventional financial institutions.

Since its founding in 1976, Grameen Bank has loaned more than U.S. $19 billion to millions of people, primarily women, to start "cottage" industries, entrepreneurial activities that can lift a family out of poverty. The microloans range from about $100 to no more than about $1,500. While most people consider the poor as too huge a default risk to loan to them, Grameen Bank has a repayment rate close to 99 percent. The total month-to-month default rates[19] at conventional banks range from about 2 to 7.5 percent (Federal Financial Institutions Examination Council 2016).

Grameen Bank began with donor funds but halted donations in 1995 and is self-reliant. Its operations and loans are paid for by the interest received on the repayment of loans. It is not a commercial bank but has shown a profit in all but three years of its operation.

The Grameen "family" expanded to include related services: The trust's mission is to replicate the Grameen microfinance institutional model. By 2007, it was operating in 37 countries, including some developed countries. The fund expands its operations to small and medium-sized enterprises in Bangladesh. Grameen Telecom and Grameenphone make cellular service and mobile phones more available to the poor and in villages in Bangladesh. These are critical tools for conducting business. The Grameen Foundation, based in Washington, D.C., works with partner microfinance institutions around the world.

Checking and savings accounts and financial literacy are important components of the Grameen Bank. Loan recipients attend financial literacy classes. A checking account and deposits into a savings account are compulsory. The Grameen Banks become community enterprises, and member-borrowers assume ownership.

Most important, the banks are effective. Microloans buy everything from sewing machines, to livestock, to chickens, to refrigerators, to trucks—whatever people need to turn their business plans into reality. People receiving the loans create jobs for themselves and usually for their families, with a spillover into the larger community. For example, a study of 40 women clients of a microbank in South Asia found that the women employed their husbands. This took their husbands out of the local job market, making jobs available to others. This caused wages to increase. As a result, 40 microloans created 80 new jobs and resulted in 120 people being employed (UN Population Fund 2006).

There are more than 7,000 microfinance institutions around the world today. In the United States, there were six Grameen branches in New York and five in other cities. Grameen America had 18,000 members in 2013. Of more than U.S. $100 million loaned, most went to finance small businesses—tailoring clothes or selling flowers, baked goods, or clothing accessories—or to expand existing businesses. Grameen America is run on the Bangladesh borrower-member model, providing savings accounts, financial literacy education, and business consultation. Loans are less than U.S. $50,000, require weekly repayments, and post a 15 percent annual interest rate. Data collected by the Aspen Institute show that Grameen America creates jobs and increases income (Dewan 2013).

Patient Capitalism

Can capitalism accomplish what philanthropy tries to accomplish? Capitalism traditionally means getting the biggest return on investment in the shortest time possible. This can lead to disastrous results such as stock trades that create money for stock brokers and maybe the investor but create no value. This ethic has also led to "hot money" flowing quickly into developing countries and out again, speculating on currency exchange rates and leaving chaos in its wake.

Patient capitalism is an investment strategy developed by Jacqueline Novogratz. In 2001, she founded the Acumen Fund on the conviction that investing in worthwhile projects was better than fast cash that produced no value. She looks for investments that will make a profit and contribute social value to their communities. Rather than the short-term horizon of traditional investing, the Acumen Fund has a long-term horizon. Profit might take some time to realize, hence the need for patience.

In contrast to simple charity, the Acumen Fund finds long-term solutions to empower the poor. The fund provides long-term loans or takes an equity interest in early-stage companies. Where traditional investors avoid projects for the poor or anticipate a long-term rather than short-term profit, Acumen looks for them. Acumen focuses on specific areas that correspond to the critical goods and services needed by the poor—agriculture, housing, health care, education, energy, and clean drinking water. When a project has demonstrated success, it is scaled up and applied in more areas. Acumen does not fund unsustainable projects, a problem of traditional aid and philanthropy.

Unlike the microloans of Grameen Bank and other microfinance institutions, the Acumen Fund investments range from about U.S. $300,000 to $2.5 million. Acumen does not expect a high return, but it does expect a return, financial as well as social, in about 7 to 10 years. Acumen does take donations and will partner with governments, corporations, or agencies as long as doing so will benefit its clients.

In 2004, Acumen invested U.S. $600,000 in a startup called "WaterHealth International" to provide clean water to rural Indians. In the first year, WaterHealth opened two new systems, but neither met its deadline and both went over budget. With help from experts at Acumen, WaterHealth redesigned and found more efficient methods and built 10 new systems a year later. This caught the attention of other investors, and WaterHealth raised U.S. $11 million from private investors. It now operates more than 500 safe water systems and more than 5 million people have safe water because of its systems. WaterHealth is partnering with Coca-Cola, the American soft drink company, and Diageo, a British alcoholic beverage company, with a venture called "Safe Water for Africa."

Hundreds of Acumen Fund investments affect millions of lives, including teacher training for low-cost primary and secondary schools in India, data analytics so that the poor can access financial services through cell phone technology, small holder organic farmers who now bring organic produce into cities, and dairy farmers who now access markets through a dairy company.

Corporate Social Responsibility

Corporations responded to criticisms related to their exploitation of people and the environment by developing a variety of strategies to keep them mindful of social and environmental sustainability in their activities. The "Global Compact" facilitated by the UN is the largest corporate responsibility initiative, with more than 5,000 corporate members and more than 2,000 members from civil society, labor, philanthropy, and academia.

In signing the compact, businesses agree to 10 principles: to uphold human rights; recognize the right to collective bargaining; eliminate forced labor, child labor, and discrimination in labor; be cautious concerning environmental challenges; promote environmental responsibility and environmentally friendly technologies; and work against corruption, including bribery and extortion.

Member corporations submit annual progress reports detailing their efforts on behalf of the 10 principles, and groups such as civil society organizations report on their engagement activity—how they helped to advance the initiatives. Companies are rated as advanced, meaning that they are implementing "advanced" criteria and best practices; active, meaning that they meet minimum requirements; or learners, meaning that they do not meet one or more minimum requirements. As of early 2017, there were more than 2000 advanced companies, 25,839 active companies, and 4,053 learners rated by a panel of peer companies, multiple stakeholders, and an independent auditor.

World Economic Forum on Africa: Big Business and the Bottom of the Pyramid

In 2008, Bill Gates delivered a strong message to the World Economic Forum: "There are two great forces—self-interest and caring for others;" serving the poor is not always profitable, he argued, but it was in the self-interest of corporations to do good work. It enhances their companies' reputations, curries them goodwill with the public, and attracts better employees. The world is not getting better fast enough and is not getting better for everyone, he admonished. They, the corporate leaders, should do something about it (Figure 2.30).

That year, there was one overriding concern at the World Economic Forum—the recession of 2007–2008. With a global economic crisis, the people at the bottom of the pyramid looked attractive to corporate giants as the most rapidly growing market (recall the rapid rise of many from extreme poverty to low income) in the world. People who had what they needed would not be buying for a while because consumer demand was depressed. But the poor needed everything. It was clearly in the interest of big business that year to "do good," not just for the public relations and positive press that it would bring, as Gates suggested, but also for profit.

Thinking differently about opportunities among the poorest means thinking differently about them. First, the poor are to be treated with respect. The poor want high-quality goods, not stripped-down versions of goods served to others. Researchers report people commenting that "we have to look good. Otherwise, people will not take us seriously. . . . The teachers will write my children off as poor and not worthy of a good education" (World Economic Forum 2009). Thinking in terms of providing access, such as renting rather than buying goods, monetizing assets such as a good reputation to get a loan, and educating about products rather than acting as authorities, can help to leverage the capital of the poorest (World Economic Forum 2009).

Closing the Gap Through Fair Trade

Goal 17 of the Sustainable Development Goals is to "promote a universal, rules-based, open, non-discriminatory and equitable multilateral trading system under the World Trade Organization." Global trade has lifted many

CONSIDER THIS
A CORPORATION FOUNDED TO DO GOOD WORK

FIGURE 2.30   Newman's Own Logo

Source: Courtesy of Newman's Own Foundation.

"Newman's Own" wasn't started as a corporation in the usual sense. In 1982, it began when movie star Paul Newman began giving his homemade secret salad dressing to friends. It was a hit. He started a mass market food company. The intent was to make good food available at ordinary prices. The intent was also to make a profit and employ lots of people. The company, decades later, has grown to produce more than 200 products. It created jobs for thousands of people. All of the profits, more than U.S. $450 million, have gone to charities. While not everyone has the resources to start a company with the intent of giving away the profit, it does make one wonder how much profit, as opposed to wages, is really necessary to motivate people to do a good job.

people out of poverty. It has closed the gaps among some countries, decreasing world inequality. Trade can bring societies into the global economy, allowing for growth. Different countries or regions within countries have different capacities to take advantage of trade to boost growth. A World Bank study (Farole 2013) of 28 countries found that regional inequalities within countries were growing in 18 of the countries, incomes were converging in only 3 countries, and inequality was holding steady in 7 countries.

Free trade is not always fair trade. Fair trade is essential for developing societies to thrive. The fair trade movement is global with grassroots organizations, federations of organizations, and suppliers, producers, importers, and exporters the world over. The World Fair Trade Organization is a global network of such actors. Its membership includes regional fair trade organizations, more than a million small-scale producers, and 3,000 grassroots organizations. It is the main monitoring and certifying organization. There are thousands of fair trade stores throughout the developed world selling their products. They connect with every step along the supply chain.

The principles of fair trade are inclusive in ensuring that all potential effects of trade are addressed. They include creating better opportunities for disadvantaged producers, fair price, capacity building, gender equity, environmental protection, better working conditions, and transparency and accountability (Ruben, Fort, and Zúñiga-Arias 2009). Although most studies have shown only a modest or insignificant impact on disadvantaged people's incomes, other benefits, such as better access to credit, increases in the value of agricultural assets, and higher levels of animal stock, were found (Ruben and Fort 2012). In addition to those benefits, Ruben et al. (2009) found that fair trade improved farmers' organizations. Farmers' attitudes toward risk and investment improved, and farmers adopted a longer time horizon. Overall conditions for wage labor in the locality improved because the fair trade context provided a regional "floor" for working conditions and wages and other employers needed to come up to the standard. In the case of fair trade bananas, the fair trade production led to an overall increase in the price of bananas.

Although the effect on income at this point appears to be negligible, other improvements are worthwhile. With respect to "premiums" making only slight or negligible improvements in incomes, they may be put to use in increasing micro-credit programs, community loans, school fees, health insurance, technical assistance, and other ways that can have greater impact.

SUMMARY

Inequality, both among and within nations, limits people's capacity to fulfill their life chances. The consequences of inequality harm the entire society. They undermine trust and confidence in government, and a society cannot thrive without allowing all of its members to achieve their physical, intellectual, recreational, and occupational potential. At the level of the individual, inequality erodes the health of even those at the upper end of the economic hierarchy.

The roots of inequality go back hundreds of years but can be significantly mitigated by reforms in the institutional structures that shape daily life. International governmental and non-governmental agencies and organizations, national governments, and philanthropies all have the potential and responsibility to create the changes to establish a just world. Increasing inequality is undermining the stability of societies and the world. More equal societies benefit everyone.

Fighting poverty and inequality also depends on advances in the other problems discussed in this book. Climate change and water shortages, environmental destruction, conflict and discrimination, and lack of adequate food and health care are among the myriad issues that contribute to inequality and poverty and are made worse by poverty and inequality.

DISCUSSION

1. How would you describe inequality in the world to a person who has not studied this? What are the most important facts and concepts for him or her to understand? Try to answer this question in less than 200 words.

2. Complete a case study of the life chances of children in a poor country. Describe their daily life. What are their prospects for the future? How might this vary for children of different social classes in the society?

3. What is the foreign aid budget of the United States or your home country? To which countries does most of the money go? Can you determine for what purposes? For data on the United States, you can refer to the website ForeignAssistance.gov.

4. Which proposals do you think would have the most impact on increasing people's life chances and decreasing poverty?

5. What level of inequality is acceptable within and among countries? What criteria do you use to decide this?

ON YOUR OWN

1. Find the Gini ratio for a random selection of countries—10 from each category from very high, high, medium, and low levels of development. Plot them on a scatterplot or a cross-tabulation table. Do you see a relationship between level of development and inequality? If you can use Excel or another statistical package such as SPSS or STATA, run a statistical analysis using the entire dataset to test your observation and the significance of the relationship you observe.

2. Examine the lives of children globally. How do infant and child mortality rates vary across countries? Educational levels? Health problems from preventable illnesses? You can use the "Human Development Index" or "State of the World's Children" report for your research.

3. What provisions does the UN Declaration of Human Rights make concerning work? What constitutional provisions for work-related matters are specified in constitutions? The Constitute Project also allows for thematic investigations. It locates constitutions and the specific articles related to specific provisions.

    https://www.constituteproject.org/
    Click on "Explore Constitutions."

Type "work" into the search box, and provisions related to work will appear.

Find constitutional provisions related to each of the items.

Which do you find particularly important?

The Comparative Constitutions Project enables thematic explorations of national constitutions.

http://comparativeconstitutionsproject.org/

Under "Data and Analysis," find "Data Visualizations."

Here you can find the number and percentage of constitutions that mention work.

Move the slider to the most recent date and scroll through the items to select those related to work.

Interactive site: maps and tables, http://www.conferenceboard.ca/hcp/hot-topics/worldinequality.aspx

NOTES

1. The Worst Forms of Child Labor Convention.

2. There is also income inequality among countries within regions. Regional inequality is shown here to give a general idea of the extent of inequality.

3. The Palma ratio is another measure of inequality. It is the ratio of the top 10 percent's share of income or wealth divided by the share of the bottom 40 percent. The smaller the ratio, the more equal the society. The inequality-adjusted HDI reports both Gini coefficients and Palma ratios. See http://hdr.undp.org/en/composite/IHDI.

4. The wealth pyramid shows a general increase in inequality from 2015 to 2016. In 2015, there were 71 percent of adults globally at the base and 21 percent in the middle (China had 36 percent in the middle band and India had 3.4 percent). The share of income of the bottom two tiers decreased from 15.5 to 13.8 percent of income. There are slightly more people in the top two tiers, up from 8.1 to 8.2 percent. They hold a greater percentage of the wealth, from 84.6 to 86.2 percent (Stierli et al. 2015:24).

5. Income trends are important in understanding the fluctuations between economic progress and decline that are more readily apparent in income figures before in wealth. But wealth is the more important figure in terms of overall inequality and development.

6. Wilkinson and Pickett (2009) used income data from the UN. They measured inequality by the ratio of income of the richest 20 percent of the population to the poorest 20 percent. They also compared data for states within the United States and found the same relationships between inequality within states and social problems.

7. Although no one knows the precise number of slaves, and it is difficult to even estimate, The UN Office on Drugs and Crime (2014:9–11) reported that among detected trafficking victims, 53 percent are sex slaves, mostly women, but the number of children is increasing. As many as 33 percent of trafficking victims are likely children, two girls for every boy.

8. Target 1B of the Millennium Development Goals was to "achieve full and productive employment for all, including women and young people." Despite growth in the number of jobs, the percentage of people unemployed in the developing world has not changed significantly. Similarly, there has been a significant drop in the percentage of people in vulnerable employment—from more than 56 percent in 1992 to about 52 percent in 2000, the beginning of the Millennium Development Goals, to about 45 percent. The number in vulnerable employment increased in number from about 1.26 billion to 1.45 billion in 2015.

9. Societies with robust social programs to ease workers through these transitions make them with less difficulty. Where social safety net programs are weak, hardships abound.

10. Pritchett (1997) built on the groundwork laid by Maddison (1995), among others, in estimating early incomes, growth, and income gaps. Some economic historians, Pritchett noted, argue that the gap in incomes of the now developed and developing countries was smaller in the 1800s (Hanson 1988, 1991) or that there was not a gap (Bairoch 1993).

11. The website "Our World in Data" has an interactive chart on which different timelines may be displayed: https://www.maxroser.com/roser/graphs/WorldIncomeDistribution1820to2000/WorldIncomeDistribution1820to2000.html

12. In developed societies, some primary industry jobs, such as miners and workers in oil fields, make relatively high salaries. For example, in Australia a 25-year-old gold miner and high school dropout earned $200,000 drilling for gold (Miller 2011). This is unusual, but salaries in the upper middle-class ranges are not. In developing societies, as in the story that starts this chapter, it is quite different.

13. This does not include bribery in the developed world involving bribes between firms and public officials and politicians.

14. If China is excluded from the calculations, the transfers are U.S. $1.1 trillion and $10.6 trillion.

15. This is based on 2005 pricing.

16. Taking the East and Southeast Asian economies out of the equation for this group raises the median to 52 years.

17. Relative poverty wage is defined by the OECD as 50 percent of the median wage.

18. Those nations were Norway (1.05 percent), Luxembourg (0.93 percent), Sweden (1.4 percent), Denmark (0.8 percent), the Netherlands (0.8 percent), and the United Arab Emirates (1.4 percent) in 2015. The source of the OECD data is https://data.oecd.org (accessed June 21, 2016).

19. These data include real estate, consumer, and agricultural loans and leases written by commercial banks.

$\underline{3}$

Starving in the Shadow of Plenty

HUNGRY IN THE WORLD'S BREADBASKET

Loretta Schwartz-Nobel exposed the problem of hunger in the United States in heart-wrenching detail. The problems she brought to light were not only sad but also ironic—ironic because until well into the 2000s the United States was the "breadbasket of the world." The United States dominated global agriculture, exporting wheat, corn, and rice the world over. This sad irony characterizes many countries today. Millions of people are starving in countries that export agricultural products. Many, if not most, of the starving people work as agricultural laborers. Food insecurity haunts many in a world of plenty. Food insecurity is one of our manufactured risks.

No one would deny that food is a basic necessity of life. Without sufficient amounts of nutritious food, it is impossible to have a full chance at life. Inadequate supply is not the source of the problem. The world produces enough food for everyone on the planet to realize their potential for good health. There is enough food thrown away to feed all the world's hungry (Hoffman 2013).

Why, then, are millions of people chronically hungry? Why are so many undernourished? How could it be that in developing countries, where agricultural products can account for 20 to 60 percent of gross domestic product and as much 65 percent of the labor force, people are starving? How could it be that in the United States and Europe, the richest societies of the world, millions of people are food insecure?

LEARNING OBJECTIVES

After completing this chapter, students should be able to do the following:

3.1 Understand the importance of investing in sustainable food security and safety

3.2 Determine ways in which the current global food system neglects or diminishes the life chances of many people

3.3 Weigh the advantages and disadvantages of factory farming and traditional farming

3.4 Recognize how features of modern life have created or exacerbated food health and food security problems

3.5 Compare and contrast potential solutions to hunger and malnutrition problems for short- and long-term impacts

3.6 Evaluate the contribution of factory farming to overall global health

THE GLOBAL FOOD SYSTEM

The image of the farmstead and farming as an idyllic life producing "wholesome goodness" is a far cry from life on most farms today. Sometime between the hunting, gathering, and horticultural societies of prehistoric and ancient times to the agricultural systems of today, we lost our capacity to feed ourselves and care for the environment that sustains us. Hunger, undernourishment, and food insecurity are the most obvious problems of the global food system.

Industrialization transformed how we grow and what we eat. Even most dairy and meat products are no longer produced on traditional farms and ranches. We have the equivalent of dairy and meat factories where the cows are no more than extensions of machines that milk them, cows are just meat in a slaughterhouse assembly line, and chickens are simply egg-producing units. Agriculture moved, in large measure, from the family farm to the factory farm.

Farming is big business—agribusiness. As farms became larger and more mechanized, both the variety and quality of the world's food supply declined. Many of the poor depend on a few staples for their diet. While they may have sufficient calories, they are not getting proteins, vitamins, and/or minerals needed for good health. There is less access to nutritious food in many of the world's cities and rural areas than was had by the hunters, gatherers, and horticulturalists. Food deserts, where there is no access to fresh and nutritious food, exist in many of the world's richest cities. Food additives and many agricultural practices call food safety into question. Small farmers who often offer locally grown indigenous crops have been priced out of local and global markets.

Our capacity for producing richly nutritious foods suffers from neglect of environmental quality. The degradation of air and land, the depletion of surface and underground water related to agricultural practices, and the use of chemical fertilizers and pesticides threaten our very existence. Many agricultural workers suffer from hazardous conditions, receive substandard wages, and are starving. These are problems that we know. Each is a "manufactured risk" that we created. Unknown risks, such as the long-term impacts of genetically modified organisms, need to be understood. What we make, we can transform. Big business does not need to be bad business, and small farms can still play a vital role in rejuvenating the global food system.

Factory Farming

Many of the problems of the global food regime begin with the advent of large-scale "factory" farming. For most of human history, people fed themselves by hunting, gathering, and subsistence farming. For the most part, this was efficient and environmentally friendly. To ensure against hunger, societies developed elaborate norms of reciprocity and production. Some of these relied on forms of community ownership of the fruits of labor; some involved inter-group reciprocity or even raids on neighboring groups. Food shortages were primarily a function of local conditions of the natural environment—the season, the rainfall, the nature of the land, and people's skill in obtaining what they needed.

Although this may seem risky and inefficient, it worked fairly well. As societies became larger, more production per acre was necessary. Agrarian techniques and domesticating animals expanded the available food supply and its stability. Most of these food systems were sustainable, even "slash and burn" (where native vegetation was cut and the field burned so that crops could be planted). If the environment became temporarily exhausted, as it nearly certainly would, people moved. When the environment recovered, people could return and land could be resettled by the same group or a new group. Even the large agricultural systems, such as those that the Incas developed on the inhospitable slopes of the Andes, were sustainable. They fed thousands with plenty to spare. Indigenous crops were bred for hardiness and nutrition. The irrigation and anti-erosion techniques the Incas developed renewed and enriched the land and water as well as their people. This lasted until the Spanish occupation when the Incas were forced into the gold mines and forced to grow foods for the Spanish (Kendall 2005).

Scientific management techniques applied to agriculture have been a very mixed blessing. On the one hand, yields have increased dramatically. On the other hand, loss of biodiversity, environmental degradation, and treatment of living plants and animals as though they are nonliving factory inputs has serious consequences for stability, safety, and nutritional quality of the food system. The modern business model of agricultural production, the very large-scale factory farm, has broken the food system and many of the once abundant resources that supported it. Trade agreements favor large corporate agriculture and cash crops for export rather than the needs of local farmers, who could meet the nutritional needs of local people and support higher wage employment in rural areas. Varying conditions—from trade policies, to how food aid is distributed, to infrastructure for transportation of goods to markets and access to finance—determine who can benefit from the food system and who will go hungry.

Food for Profit: Agribusiness

What foods cost and where and how they are grown are not random or accidental. Choices of governments, nongovernmental organizations, corporations, and individuals dictate what is grown where and how it is distributed. For example, as in other sectors of the economy, protectionist policies such as tariffs on food can make imported food more expensive, shutting imported foods out of a market. Subsidizing an agricultural industry can make those foods cheaper on the global market and undercut domestic production. Who has influence to ensure that these policies work for their own advantage is often determined by power. The processes of agricultural production—from the giant machines that can work only in monocrop fields, to the chemicals needed to maintain the fields, to the irrigation systems, to "terminator" and patented seeds that cannot be saved from year to year, to the distribution systems—are largely managed through a small number of huge food and beverage companies[1] that have enormous influence in, if not control of, the global food system. National and global policies, jockeying for advantage in trade talks, the nature of food aid, and agricultural techniques all play roles in food security. The stakes are high. They are literally life and death for millions of people (Winders 2009).

Supply chains in the global food market are long and complex. The person who grows the food and the person who eats it not only never meet, they do not even know where in the world the other person is. Agribusiness is not new. In colonial times, local farmers were forced to abandon indigenous crops to farm the crops and agricultural products wanted in Europe. In the Americas, one of the first cash crops was tobacco. It fetched such a high price in Europe that many southern colonists abandoned food crops to use slave labor to farm tobacco on large plantations. They relied on trade with Europe and Native Americans for food. This plan backfired when about 70 percent of the Jamestown colonists starved to death in the winter of 1609–1610. This should have been a lesson. In many countries today, people—including agricultural workers—starve while crops are exported. Many rely on one or two staple crops that supply calories but not nutrition while they work in fields growing fruits and vegetables and commodities such as timber and rubber for export.

The Global Policy Forum (Paul and Wahlberg 2008) outlined a number of ways in which the global food system creates conditions for food insecurity. Agriculture for domestic production has declined in many developing countries while specialty crop production, such as coffee, cocoa, and sugar—hardly life sustaining—has increased. These countries must rely on imports of staples. This is encouraged by global trade policies. Despite arguing the importance of free trade, many rich countries, the European Union, and the United States subsidize their agriculture. Most of it goes to large industrial farms. This allows them to underprice domestic producers in developing nations. They can also enforce trade rules that allow tariffs on imports from these same countries. Domestic production in these countries declined, leaving people reliant on food imports and subject to insecurity related to the supply, demand, and prices on the global market.

Even most of the small farms, estimated to number about 404 million farms of under two hectares, that support a third of the global population must buy the bulk of their food. When prices are high, they face tough choices between food and education, health care, and other necessities (Hoffman, 2013).

While there are many small labor-intensive farms, more of the world's food is produced by large corporate "agribusinesses." These businesses are very profitable, but labor is very poorly paid. Large companies such as Cargill, Nestlé, Monsanto, Unilever, Kellogg, General Mills, and Archer Daniels Midland control the global market in grain, fertilizers, pesticides, and seeds in processing, distributing, and selling. According to Oxfam (Hoffman 2013), 500 companies control 70 percent of the global food supply. They have undue influence over international markets and policies. Just 4 of these companies (Monsanto, DuPont/Pioneer, Syngenta, and Bayer Crop Science) have 60 percent of the market share for agrochemicals, 35 percent for seeds, and 40 percent for biotechnology (United Nations Conference on Trade and Development [UNCTAD] 2010). Their supply chains have been known to employ child labor, pay substandard wages, and contribute directly to environmental destruction.

The high prices associated with chemical pesticides and fertilizers and the reliance on terminator and patented seed have put many small farmers out of business in developed and developing countries. After independence, many countries sold land, privatizing what was once part of the commons. Small farmers and the poor lost access to land on which they could have grown subsistence crops. Large land deals have continued, with foreign investors buying up large territories. Most of these investors will export what they grow, and much will go to fuel, not food (Oxfam International 2013). This reduces biodiversity and contributes significantly to environmental destruction. Rich countries with food surpluses distribute their surpluses as food aid. This undermines local producers by stealing their market. Exploitation of labor in agriculture is declining but still common, and slavery still exists in agriculture. There are reforms throughout the food supply chain. The Food and Agricultural Organization of the United Nations (FAO) has pledged to buy local food instead of bringing in imports as aid. Many, but not all, large companies have promised to look into the safety and labor conditions of their supply chains.

FOOD SECURITY

Food security is more than just absence of hunger. Food security depends on sufficient safe and nutritious food to ensure normal growth, normal development, and good health. For example, in Egypt the dietary supply of calories is 45 percent higher than adequate; however, stunting harms the life chances of 31 percent of children (FAO 2013).

The FAO (2015a) uses four categories to measure food insecurity:

Availability has to do with the adequacy of caloric supply generally and the caloric supply from animal protein, cereals, roots, and tubers.

Access measures societal features related to transportation, prices, and measures of adequacy.

Stability considers the stability and dependability of the food supply and factors such as arable land and violent conflict that affect stability.

Utilization assesses some symptoms of insecurity such as anemia, wasting, stunted growth in pregnant women and children, and vitamin A deficiency in the general population. Water and sanitation are also assessed in this category as they relate to food safety.

The key to improving the global food system is sustainability. Producing enough nutritious food to maximize everyone's life chances in ways that repair and preserve the health of the environment is a central challenge of our lifetime.

Availability: Hunger and Undernourishment

Calories are a measure of the energy that foods provide for us. The energy supply globally from food is more than plentiful given that it exceeds adequate levels by 45 percent. Nourishment is more than just calories, however. For proper growth and development, people need their calories divided among fats, proteins, and certain carbohydrates. People need micronutrients as well—vitamins and minerals. When people talk about hunger, they need to consider a combination of calories and nutrition. As is the case in Egypt mentioned above, stunting affects 20 to 45 percent of children in Benin, Malawi, the Niger, Kazakhstan, and Nicaragua, all of which have above-adequate supplies of calories (FAO 2013).

The two primary targets for hunger come from the Millennium Development Goals (MDGs) and the World Food Summit. The more modest MDG of halving the proportion of undernourished people came very close to its target; undernourishment in developing regions declined from 23.3 to 12.9 percent. A closer look shows that progress was very uneven across regions. Eastern and South-Eastern Asia surpassed their half-mark targets. People and/or children in Oceania, Southern and Western Asia, and sub-Saharan Africa did not fare as well. With respect to the number of people, although 200 million fewer people globally are undernourished, 795 million still are (United Nations [UN] 2015). Thus, the World Food Summit goal of halving the number of undernourished people by 2015 was far from being met in many countries. Even in developed regions, 15 million people were undernourished in 2014.

It is not surprising that poverty and hunger are related. Poverty leads to poor nutrition and poor health. Poor nutrition and poor health cause people to miss school and/or work. This, in turn, lowers their productivity and aggravates poverty. It is a chicken-or-egg question as to which comes first because they exacerbate one another. In Africa, the prevalence of undernourishment is 19.8 percent, but this percentage rises up to as high as 47 percent in Zambia (FAO 2015a).

Extreme poverty, we have seen, is concentrated in rural areas. This persists across regions despite regions' different rates of poverty (FAO 2015b). Ironically, the rural poor are more likely to be engaged in agricultural work than other rural households. Food accounts for an extremely large proportion of the household budget of the extremely poor—about 65 to 80 percent (FAO 2015b). In low- and middle-income countries, 45 percent of the total labor force is employed in agriculture, yet it produces only about 10 percent of the gross domestic product of these societies. This illustrates the low economic value placed on agricultural labor and products. In some of the poorest countries, the majority of agricultural workers are women, who have few opportunities in terms of finance, agricultural services, and markets. They have little opportunity to improve their productivity per acre and, subsequently, little opportunity to improve their income (FAO 2015b). This low valuing of agricultural labor is a major contributor to poverty.

Where there is growth in the agricultural sector, it stimulates more broad-based economic growth and can reduce poverty and hunger. This was the case in China. There, as urbanization grew from 1990 to 2012, the productivity of agricultural workers grew from U.S. $416 to $1,024 (FAO 2015b). Fewer people are needed in those cases as agricultural workers. They must find employment opportunities elsewhere.

Fruits, Vegetables, and Micronutrients

Fruits and vegetables are rich in vitamins, minerals, and other components of a healthy diet such as fiber and antioxidants. The World Health Organization (WHO 2014) estimated that insufficient consumption of fruits and vegetables accounted for 6.7 million[2] deaths in 2010. It is repeatedly on the WHO's list of the top 10 health risk factors. Consumption of fruits and vegetables varies widely across regions of the world and, surprisingly, by gender. In 2002, the global fruit and vegetable supply per capita was 173 kg. In the developed world it averaged about 200 kg, and in Asia availability was up to 180 kg; in Africa it was

A CLOSER LOOK
MEAT CONSUMPTION

As meat consumption increases globally, farming grain for animal consumption rather than human consumption rises.

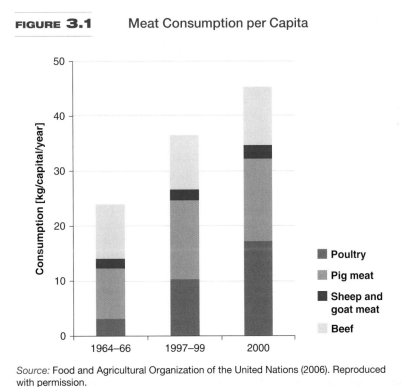

FIGURE 3.1   Meat Consumption per Capita

Source: Food and Agricultural Organization of the United Nations (2006). Reproduced with permission.

only 106 kg. In parts of Eastern Europe, Latin America, and South Asia, fruit and vegetable consumption was as low as 54 to 75 kg for young women (Weinberger and Lumpkin 2005). In 2004, figures for Africa showed consumption at a fraction of the recommended 146 kg per year (FAO/WHO 2011). In the United States alone, the direct medical cost of inadequate fruit and vegetable consumption from 2007 to 2009 was estimated to be more than U.S. $30 billion. The overall economic cost was estimated at more than $56 billion (Rosenfeld 2010).

In 2003, global fruit and vegetable production became a global priority. There has been significant progress. From 2000 to 2010, it grew at an average of 3 percent a year. In 2011, nearly 640 million tons of fruit and more than 1 billion tons of vegetables were produced globally (FAO 2013).

Ironically, food policy can decrease the availability of food. Food waste caused by the actual destruction of crops to maintain higher food prices is one such scheme. In 2001, one million tons of fruit and vegetables was destroyed at the same time diets in most countries were low in fruits and vegetables necessary for good health and development (Nicholson 2014). Use of food crops for fuel or livestock feed obviously reduces the food available for people. It also increases the price of food by depressing the potential supply. In 1997, David Pimentel figured that the grain fed at that time to cattle in the United States could feed 800 million people. In 2003, he figured that the livestock in the United States consumed seven times as much grain as people in the country did. That much agricultural product could feed an additional 840 million people on a plant-based diet (Pimentel and Pimentel 2003). As the appetite for meat of people all over the world continues to grow, the potential loss of food for people globally is enormous (Figure 3.1).

Biofuels production is also an inefficient displacement of potential food production. Producing biofuels is energy intensive. While biofuels appear eco-friendly at the gasoline pump, most (if not all) of this advantage is lost in growing it and getting it to the pump. This has been known for some time. Groom, Gray, and Townsend (2008) warned that alternatives to grains for biofuels, such as algae, should be used. Not only were current uses of grains environmentally unfriendly, but they also threatened food diversity and food supply. Corn, the authors concluded, was the worst possible of available alternatives for fuel.

Access

Part of the puzzle of starvation in the midst of plenty is access to food. Ironically, food sometimes goes rotting in

storage while people go hungry. India, for example, has the largest number of the world's hungry. Yet in 2012, it was the world's largest rice exporter and one of the largest wheat exporters. India had millions of tonnes of grain available. It had 62.8 million tonnes of grains (27.1 million tonnes of wheat and 35.7 million tonnes of rice) on hand—"good enough to meet the country's food requirement for another year"—and more was expected. Short of storage, after India filled its storage silos, much of the produce was lying in open fields, wasting (Rediff News 2013). Yet the hungry in India still starved.

Access to food depends on a combination of macro-social and economic factors and micro-level factors. Approximately 70 percent of developing countries are net importers of food. Food prices severely limit access to food for the poor. The 2007–2008 food price shocks sent many people in the United States, where food costs about 16 percent of a poor family's budget, rushing to the food banks. In countries such as Nigeria, where a poor family spends 73 percent of its budget on food, it was disastrous. Rising energy costs, increased demand for grain-fed beef, global warming, and the use of corn-based biofuels pushed prices up (Allen and Wilson 2008; *New York Times* 2008). Corn, sorghum, rice, and cassava, staple foods of many countries, increased in price as much as 61 percent from 2006 to 2008 (World Bank 2010). The economic crisis of the same time ensured that people could not afford the regular prices, let alone the inflated prices. The food index, the ratio of food prices to general purchasing power, is highest in the least developed countries that can least afford it. Food prices are trending high in developing countries (FAO 2013:78). The year 2014 brought some relief. Decreasing oil prices brought food prices to their lowest levels since 2010. This was a tremendous boon to the poor in food-importing countries (Fan 2015). While this may be good news in that it makes food more affordable for the poor, it of mixed benefit if it decreases the incomes of agricultural workers. Falling prices for potatoes, cereal crops, olive oil, vegetables, pork, beef, chicken, and eggs depressed worker pay throughout much of Europe (*Algarve Daily News* 2014).

While rising prices add more value to foods and boost the incomes of the agricultural sector, reversals of trade policies are necessary. Rather than developing countries lowering tariffs to make foods cheaper, higher tariffs could protect the domestic producers from unfair competition. Subsidies offered by rich countries to their own agribusiness undercut domestic production in developing countries. This forces many out of business. As with building the manufacturing sector in developing countries, protection of weak industries, rather than wealthy

CONSIDER THIS
INDIA'S TARGETED FOOD DISTRIBUTION

India has a larger number of the world's hungry than any other country. To create a more secure food system, India passed the National Food Security Act of 2013 that subsidizes grain for eligible families at greatly reduced costs. It is the largest food-based safety net in the world (Kaur 2014). Up to 75 percent of the rural population and 50 percent of urbanites—two thirds of India's population (some 800 million people)—will receive grain subsidies. Each person may receive 5 kg (11 pounds) of food grains a month. In its trial run in Odisha state, the program was a huge success. The Ministry of Consumer Affairs reported that 25 states had implemented the act and were distributing food subsidies, a huge benefit for the hungry (Department of Food and Public Distribution 2014, 2015).

The Targeted Public Distribution System (TPDS) cuts down on fraud and waste. State governments determine the criteria within their state that define poverty and food insecurity and, thus, eligibility for the program. Biometrics is used to identify the eligible participants. Each family has a designated Fair Price Store (FPS) where they must redeem their subsidy. Fully computerized, the TPDS has made tracking the food supply, distributing it, ensuring that there is not duplication of benefits among recipients, and financing it more efficient and transparent.

As expected in a program this large and complex, there are still issues that need to be resolved for the program to be of maximum benefit. First is the amount of grain and that only grain is distributed in most states.

The Indian Council for Medical Research recommends 14 kg of grain a month for adults and 7 kg a month for children (Arabi and Ramya 2013). The subsidy for 5 kg a month is far below that level. A diet of grain needs to be supplemented with other nutrients necessary for healthy development. Nearly half of India's children are underweight, 45 percent have stunted growth, 75 percent are anemic, and 57 percent are deficient in vitamin A (World Bank 2013).

FPSs are very common in urban areas and less concentrated in rural areas. The lack of competition has provided the opportunity for some FPS owners to take advantage of the system. When the FPSs have higher-priced buyers, they can divert food. In reserve, they have a captive market of needy families. Allowing people to redeem their subsidy at any FPS and allowing the subsidies to be used in other markets would reduce this fraud. This would also ease the burden for migrants who might not always be in the area of their designated store.

Another problem is that many of the food insecure are not eligible for the subsidy under their state laws. Owning a four-wheeled vehicle, having a family member in government service, and similar rules can disqualify many of the needy.

Would India need such an extensive food program if less agricultural product were exported and a wider range of food were grown domestically? It is an issue worth investigating.

---

ones, makes for more fair trade. Trade and other policies are discussed later in the chapter.

Weak infrastructure also inhibits food access. Transportation to and locations of markets are critical factors. Within the United States, pockets of people live without access to nutritious foods and fresh fruits and vegetables. In Detroit, 500,000 people live in such a "food desert." They are more likely than not to die prematurely of a diet-related cause. Research conducted in Chicago showed that people living in areas where good food was scarce were two times more likely to die of diabetes than people in more food-balanced areas. In many of these areas, people's main source of food is the local gas station shelves. Better access to a supermarket is related to decreased obesity, and better access to a convenience store is linked to increased obesity (Hesterman 2011). More than half (57 percent) of people living in low-income areas of the United States have very limited physical access to supermarkets or grocery stores (Hesterman 2011).

In developing countries, access or lack of access can be determined by something often taken for granted in richer countries—paved roads. In 2011, developing nations had, on average, only 46 percent of their roadways paved (FAO 2015b).

The price of food and roads, the wealth of the country, the depth of its food deficit, and the amount of a family budget that must be spent on food each affects people's accessibility to food and their life chances.

CONSIDER THIS
PLASTIC ROADS

In developed countries, we take our roads for granted unless we hit a pothole. We take for granted that we can get to wherever we want from wherever we want via our system of roads. In many developing countries, that is not the case. Many roads are simply local roads, perhaps not much more than paths. They do not get a person very far and might not hook up to any national or regional roads. Many are unpaved. Many wash out in rainy seasons.

Roads are important for the most basic necessities—access to food, to doctors and hospitals, to schools, and to markets for selling wares. Roads are expensive to build and maintain. It can consume from 2 to 5 percent of a developing country's gross domestic product (GDP) just to fix roads and repair vehicles from damage done on bad roadways.

Plastic roads might be the solution. Made from recycled plastic, modular pieces that fit together like a toy train track, these prove to be more durable than asphalt and more suitable for poor soil and extremes of temperature. India generates as much as 15,000 tons of plastic waste *daily,* and that is likely to increase. The Supreme Court of India has called this a "plastic time bomb." As of July 2014, about 3,000 miles of plastic roads had been laid in India. Multilayered plastics, which cannot be recycled, are perfectly well-suited for shredding and using along with other plastics in the roads. It is also much quicker and cheaper than other paving methods, the perfect example of *jugaad,* frugal innovation or turning garbage into gold. So while they seem unrelated, good roads are essential to healthy diets for getting locally grown foods and the people who need them to markets. Adapted from Kapur (2014).

Stability

The world's food supply is under constant threat. Many sources of instability are manufactured risks. One set of threats is environmental. Climate change, the depletion of water sources, and the degradation and disappearance of arable land wreak havoc on the still unpredictable patterns of our annual food supply. Another set of threats comes from human interactions. Violent conflict, migration, and discrimination all cause food instability and are caused by it. Yet another threat comes from the agricultural system itself.

Food Production Techniques

As food production moved from hunting and gathering to herding animals and horticulture, the stability of the food supply evolved along with the ability to feed larger populations and control food production. Native Americans were better stewards of America's breadbasket than the agriculturalists who settled it later. Native Americans practiced risk management techniques that evolved with their experiences in each particular climate. Their gardens were dispersed over their territories, leaving much of the plains undisturbed. They intercropped a wide variety of beans, maize (corn), and squash, including 13 varieties of corn. Their crops had a synergy; what one took from the soil, the other replaced. Crops were vulnerable to different risks.

While one was subject to drought or a certain pest, the others could resist, ensuring that the food supply was never subject to total devastation (Hudson 2011).

Large plantation systems and large plowed fields of the agricultural era ignored the balancing among crops. Industrial agricultural techniques that followed further exacerbated the instability of the food supply. The impact of agriculture on the environment is one of the most significant sources of instability and insecurity in the food supply.

Water systems are threatened by pollution and depletion. Industrial agriculture uses 2 to 3 times more fertilizers and 1.5 times more pesticides per kilogram of food than it did in the 1970s (UNCTAD 2010). Overuse of chemicals that are washed into rivers, water wasteful irrigation techniques, and climate change-instigated drought have lowered water tables and polluted water supplies all over the world, threatening the food supply long into the future. The Ogallala in the Great Plains of the United States is one of the world's largest aquifers. While aquifers normally recharge—restore to their usual level—as water recycles through the earth and atmosphere, the Ogallala water table has dropped 25 feet. Kansas farmers have switched from food production to cotton. To feed its growing population, China has added very water-intensive winter wheat to its crop rotations. China's groundwater usage has doubled every year since 1970

CONSIDER THIS
SUFFOCATED BY MANURE FUMES

In Montour County, Pennsylvania, in the eastern United States, a farmer was "agitating" the manure in his 124 × 12-foot storage tank. He walked around to the back of the tank, where he found his two sons, aged 2 and 4 years, unconscious. They had been riding their bikes on a road that ran along the side of the tank. While the older boy regained consciousness shortly after being moved to fresh air, the younger boy was unconscious for nearly 20 minutes (Penn State Live 2012).

Where there are large livestock factory farms, manure is produced as fertilizer in quantities too large to be used efficiently. Thus, it is often applied in quantities too large to be absorbed into the land, or it is stored in manure lagoons and tanks. Noxious gas emissions, such as ammonia and hydrogen sulfide, pose short- and long-term health risks to humans—from headaches, breathing problems, and skin rashes to neurological damage.

Runoff and manure "spills" contaminate streams, drinking wells, and groundwater with phosphorus, nitrogen, and bacteria, often killing fish. Bacteria can also be reabsorbed by the animals, and disease can spread quickly from one to another, threatening the health of the animals and safety of the meat.

Its aquifers may run dry in 30 years unless the country's water habits change (Yardley 2007).

Modern agriculture has been the definition of wasteful and destructive. Given the industrial machinery used on farms, the manufacture and application of fertilizers and pesticides, irrigation, and other modern farming techniques, it takes about 10 energy calories to produce 1 calorie of food (UNCTAD 2010).

Much of the world's land is used for agriculture, and much of that is threatened. Since 1960, about one third of the world's arable land has been lost through soil erosion and degradation. About 10 million hectares of land is lost each year. Increases in agricultural productivity yield more crops per acre but at the expense of healthy soil. When the land becomes too degraded for farming, it is abandoned in favor of more productive land. One estimate states that the amount of land abandoned in the last 50 years is equal to that farmed today (World Wide Fund for Nature n.d.).

Even our food tastes contribute to environmental degradation and, thus, decrease the stability of our food supply. In 2006, livestock grazing occupied about 26 percent of ice-free land on the earth, and another 33 percent was dedicated to feedstock production. Together, this comprised 70 percent of agricultural land (FAO 2006). As the world's appetite for meat increases even more, more land is needed for both grain and grazing. Each has the potential to diminish the land available for farming food or degrade arable land so that it is no longer optimally suitable for agriculture. Either the land's yield is diminished, or the soil must be supplemented with more chemicals. Increased livestock production will increase the emissions of methane, a greenhouse gas. Cattle, pigs, sheep, and other domesticated animals already produce 26 percent of the methane emissions in the United States as part of their digestive process. Their manure produces another 10 percent as it decays (Environmental Protection Agency 2017).

Industrial agricultural techniques are degrading the very resources, water, land, and air on which they depend.

Climate Change

Weather events can also increase instability of the food supply. While weather has always been an important factor in the food supply, the vagaries of weather associated with climate change have exacerbated this. Climate change has the potential to irreversibly damage every natural resource on which our food supply depends—arable land, fresh water, and clean air. By 2030, as many as 10 to 20 percent more people are expected to experience food insecurity due to climate change (World Food Programme [WFP] 2014). The global El Niño of 2015–2016 precipitated drought in many countries, from Latin America to Africa. In Guatemala, Honduras, and El Salvador, 2.3 million people were food insecure due to drought. In Haiti alone, 1.5 million were at risk. In Ethiopia, it was 10.1 million. In Papua New Guinea, 1.24 million people were put at risk by El Niño. Because 85 percent of their food is produced domestically, any disruption puts them at risk. El Niño is a natural weather event, but its intensity is heightened by climate change. It heightened drought across South Africa in mid-2016. Much of the risk due to drought is manufactured and thus avoidable risk. (WFP 2015).

CONSIDER THIS

ADVANCE WARNINGS—THE POTATO FAMINE AND DUST BOWL

In the 19th century, the great potato famine reduced the Irish population through starvation and emigration. Disaster befell the peasants, forced to farm potatoes on their scant plots to provide enough calories to feed their families, when their monocropped potatoes succumbed to the blight. The dust bowl of the 1930s, long before talk of climate change or the widespread use of chemicals in farming, was another warning that Western farming techniques might be on the wrong track. Misuse of land, clear cutting of the prairies, overplowing the fields, and monocropping stripped the soil of essential nutrients. When the drought came, the fields blew away—dust in the wind.

The threats of climate change to come are among the unknowns. Precise patterns of weather change in regions are not predictable at this point. Drought is not the only risk for food insecurity; flooding poses threats as well. Increasing temperatures may result in more rainfall overall, but it will not be evenly dispersed. Intense events that do the most damage are the least predictable. Rising sea levels threaten coastal and river delta agriculture and indirectly affect inland farming as freshwater supplies are salinized. Flooding destroys crops in the field and in storage as well as agricultural land and equipment (WFP 2014). Increases and decreases in temperature also take a toll. Evidence supports that global maize and wheat yields have shrunk 3.8 to 5.5 percent, respectively, compared with what they would have been without temperature volatility (WFP 2014).

The most climate change-threatened countries are in the developing regions of the world, which can least afford the damage. By 2080, there may be a 15 to 30 percent decline in agricultural output in sub-Saharan Africa and South Asia. The most threatened of the countries in these regions may experience a decline in product as high as 50 percent (UNCTAD 2010).

Energy Consumption

Modern agriculture is very expensive and energy intensive. This is not sustainable. In the United States, the food system produces approximately 1.4 Quads of food energy annually but consumes 10.3 Quads to produce the 1.4, more than a 7:1 ratio of energy input to output. Relying heavily on fossil fuels in every step makes food prices heavily dependent on energy prices. As the Center for Sustainable Systems (2017) study shows (Figure 3.2), most of the energy used is in the household. A little more than 20 percent is in production, and 40 percent of this is in making chemical fertilizers and pesticides. From 2014 to 2016, declining energy prices gave consumers a welcome break from rising food prices; however, lower energy prices are not guaranteed, and current energy consumption produces greenhouse gases.

Grain for biofuels is energy intensive. Because of industrial farming methods used in the United States to produce corn for biofuels, the amount of energy used in raising the corn is greater than the amount delivered in fuel energy. A total of 100 million tons of grain was expected to be converted into biofuels in 2008. That is enough productive capacity for food for 400 million people that will never reach the food supply. Some biofuels, such as the sugarcane used in Brazil and the palm oil of Indonesia, are more efficient, but all of them displace potential for food with fuel. Each is a driver of the food crisis and is unsustainable in the long run (Paul and Wahlberg 2008).

Violent Conflict

While food insecurity increases the likelihood of political instability and violent conflict, instability and conflict are also sources of food insecurity. Fragile and conflict-ridden countries often lack the infrastructure necessary for food security. Where present, it is often destroyed by conflict— "lack of passable roads, markets with few buying or selling offers and a lack of entrepreneurs, leading to less competitive markets and higher transportation costs" (Brinkman and Hendrix 2011). Violent conflict erodes a society's ability to produce food by destroying infrastructure, including land and water resources. In the breakup of Yugoslavia and the genocide in Bosnia–Herzegovina, people in once-thriving Sarajevo were reduced to gathering weeds for food. Food aid workers report that armed groups often steal food aid. They estimate that from 20 to 80 percent of food aid shipments to Somalia were stolen or confiscated by armed factions and then sold for money for arms (Nunn and Qian 2014).

High food prices ignited conflict in Syria, and food prices sextupled from the beginning of the war in March

FIGURE 3.2   Energy Flow in the U.S. Food System

The fossil fuel energy input in the food chain is unsustainable.

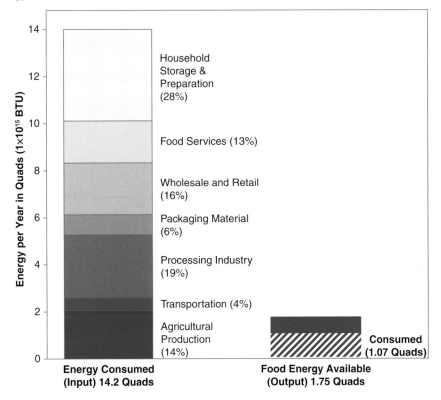

Source: Center for Sustainable Systems, University of Michigan. 2017. "U.S. Food System Factsheet." Pub. No. CSS01-06.

2011 to December 2012. This was due to decreased production, bombed factories, and increased shipment costs. Food denial was a war strategy used by the Sudanese government in the civil war for South independence. The government blocked aid from reaching the conflict zones. A World Food Programme (WFP) warehouse was blocked and food could not reach its destination. Regardless of their journeys, refugees fleeing conflict face the most severe food insecurities (Hendrix and Brinkman 2013). In 2015, 2.4 million people faced emergency conditions due to the protracted conflict (WFP 2015).

ISIS (Islamic State of Iraq and Syria) uses food as a weapon of war in both Syria and Iraq. By seizing land with wheat crops, wheat in silos and stockpiles, and poultry and livestock, ISIS gains money and support. It sells food cheaply. Because ISIS stole it, anything is a profit. While this gains the group some support among some Sunnis, it has deprived Christian and Yazidi groups of food and many farmers of their livelihood. As much as 40 percent

of Iraq's wheat production was under ISIS control in 2014 (Fick 2014).

The effect of violent conflict on food insecurity is evident in rates of child stunting, a measure of utilization. From 1990 to 2013, developing countries that had not experienced violent conflict made remarkable strides in diminishing or eliminating child stunting. Countries with civil conflict for the duration of the period made hardly any progress in combatting stunting. Countries that experienced conflict at only the beginning of this period made significant progress, while those that experienced conflict at only the end did not make much progress. None of these countries approached the rate of progress of countries that had no conflict (Figure 3.3).

Yemen, one of the poorest and most food-insecure countries in the world, made little progress from the 1990–1992 period to 2012–2014. Undernourishment decreased only 3 percent and food diversity decreased, increasing inadequate diet score by 41 percent. From

FIGURE 3.3   Violent Conflict Diminishes Progress in Reducing Child Stunting

The effects of violent conflict are far-reaching. Poor nutrition resulting in child stunting has a lifelong impact, diminishing life chances.

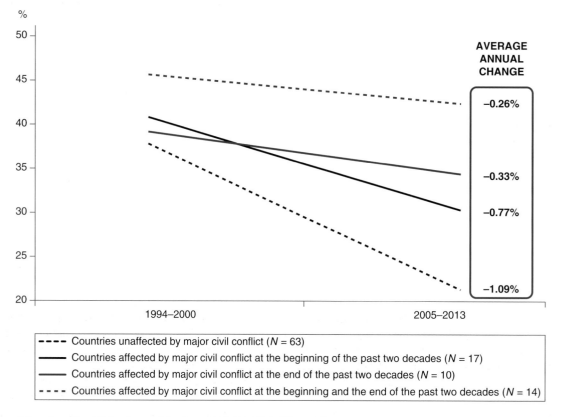

Countries unaffected by major civil conflict (*N* = 63)
Countries affected by major civil conflict at the beginning of the past two decades (*N* = 17)
Countries affected by major civil conflict at the end of the past two decades (*N* = 10)
Countries affected by major civil conflict at the beginning and the end of the past two decades (*N* = 14)

Source: International Food Policy Research Institute. *2014–2015 Global Food Policy Report* by Breisinger, C.; Ecker, O. & Tan, J. F. T. (https://www.ifpri.org/sites/default/files/gfpr/2015/feature_3086.html) licensed under CC BY 4.0 (https://creativecommons.org/licenses/by/4.0/).

2009 to 2011, 4.5 million people were severely food insecure and another 6 million were moderately food insecure. A combination of conflict, economic downturn, poverty, rising food prices, and low productivity makes Yemen particularly vulnerable to food instability. Although two thirds of the people depend on agriculture, the country's output is very low and it relies on food imports. Most of Yemen's revenue comes from oil. When oil production is down due to conflict or oil price decline, this creates even more instability (FAO, International Fund for Agricultural Development, and WFP 2014).

Other Threats to Stability

Anything that disrupts climate has the potential to disrupt agricultural stability. Climate events are shocks to the food system, affecting growing, producing, distributing, and pricing of food. Anything that affects employment also destabilizes food security. The most obvious reason is that without employment people cannot afford the quantity and quality of food needed. Sudden shocks to employment put people at risk. Epidemics and pandemics such as Ebola, hazardous work conditions, taking people out of the workforce, reducing wages for food, and reducing people in the food system hamper production and distribution. In developing countries, small producers are still the primary producers. Low investment in agricultural education and rural education and policy that impedes rather than enhances small growers and producers make the food systems less productive, decreasing productivity and stability.

Utilization

Utilization as it pertains to food security has a number of dimensions. As a general concept, utilization means that the ways in which food is grown (or otherwise produced such as with livestock, fisheries, poultry, and dairy), handled, distributed, and consumed are done safely and with the desired outcome in health and nutrition. It covers every step in the food system from farm to mouth to health outcomes.

Food Safety

Food safety is important to ensure maximum nutrition from food products and the absence of any contaminants and toxins—viruses, parasites, chemicals, and bacteria. The WHO released its first comprehensive publication on the global burden from foodborne diseases in 2015. This was the culmination of seven years of study. The WHO identified 31 global hazards that caused 32 specific diseases. These 31 hazards resulted in 600 million illnesses and 420,000 deaths. As with other social problems, the burden of these illnesses was not dispersed evenly across global regions. It was not dispersed evenly among demographic groups. The highest burden geographically was in Africa. Children under 5 years bore 40 percent of the foodborne disease burden (WHO 2015a).

The burden of disease is measured in disability-adjusted life years (DALYs). Foodborne diseases account for 33 million healthy life years lost every year (WHO 2015b). The highest rates were found in Africa, followed by the Southeast Asia region (WHO 2015b). Every region has a unique profile as to which contaminants and diseases it is most susceptible. *Salmonella enterica* accounted for the heaviest foodborne burden overall, 6.43 million DALYs. If all transmission sources of *Salmonella* are included, the burden is considerably higher at 8.76 million DALYs (WHO 2015b).

Foodborne illness is not limited to developing countries. In 2013 in the United States, there were 818 outbreaks of foodborne illness. In total, 13,360 illnesses, 1,062 hospitalizations, and 16 deaths resulted. Norovirus and *Salmonella* were the main contaminants. The incidence of *Salmonella* outbreaks increased 38 percent from 2012 to 2013 (Centers for Disease Control and Prevention 2013).

Food contamination can occur at any step in the food system from farm to dinner table. Consider these examples. They all can be fatal:

- Dioxins and polychlorinated biphenyls (PCBs) are produced in industrial processes. They enter the food stream through animals. They cause reproductive and developmental problems, interfere with hormones, and can cause cancer.

- Bacterial infections are among the most common. They may come from eggs, beef, pork, chicken, seeded vegetables, and unpasteurized milk, among many other sources. *Salmonella* most commonly causes fever, headache, nausea, and diarrhea, among other symptoms. These infections can be fatal.

- Norovirus and hepatitis A virus are usually caused by unsafe food handling, raw and undercooked seafood, and contaminated produce (WHO 2015a).

- Pathogens enter the vegetable supply from animal sources through contaminated irrigation waters and improperly treated organic fertilizers as well as through cross-contamination by food harvesters or equipment.

In livestock and other meat production, animals are treated no differently than a nonliving component in a factory assembly line. But they are living. Because this treatment is cruel, it activates stress hormones as it would in a human. This weakens an animal's immune system, making them subject to infections, parasites, and viruses that they can pass through the food supply. Although many factory livestock enterprises use antibiotics liberally, antibiotic-resistant bacteria are evolving that are dangerous to humans and animals alike.

Salmonella enters the food supply along multiple pathways. Hen housing systems that cage thousands of hens in unhygienic, extremely close quarters dramatically increase the risk of contamination over cage-free housing. Other cruel practices for the sake of "efficiency," such as withdrawing food and/or water to force an entire flock to molt simultaneously, also increase stress levels in chickens and increase the likelihood of *Salmonella*-infected eggs.

"Slaughterhouse waste," feed made from animals that are dying (including those that die from the forced starvation molting), is often contaminated with *Salmonella* and is fed to farm animals. A Food and Drug Administration study found that 50 percent of feed that contained slaughterhouse waste was contaminated (Ross 2010).

In emerging economies, changing food tastes are increasing demand for more of the riskiest foods—meats and vegetables. Their food systems are growing rapidly, and infrastructure and regulation are still weak. In some respects, this is a perfect storm for food safety. In Southeast Asia, avian influenza highlighted low levels of biosecurity on farms and lack of sanitation throughout the food system. There is a high risk of bacterial, viral, and

CONSIDER THIS
FACTORY FARMING AND FOOD SAFETY

Factory farming threatens the safety of our food supply. Pesticides and fertilizers and contaminants in irrigation water are retained in crops and jeopardize the food supply.

Cattle, pigs, poultry, and other animals kept in close quarters, hooked to machines, and trapped in cages experience stress. This is not only inhumane but also unhealthy for them (causing stress and decreasing their immune responses) and unhealthy for people, as discussed above.

Avian flu and swine flu are easily passed among animals in close quarters. In 2014, an avian flu epidemic hit the U.S. poultry industry, resulting in 48 million chickens and turkeys being "culled" (killed). A 2017 outbreak resulted in 73,500 chickens (to date) being culled. Although the flu cannot be passed to humans if the meat is properly cooked, it can be passed to humans through contact with the infected bird, its blood, or other contaminated environments. Avian flu (H5N8) cost duck farmers in France close to U.S. $3 million in 2016 and more than $3 million in 2017 as the flu swept through flocks.

Industrial agriculture has long been recognized as a breeding ground for bacteria. *Escherichia coli,* methicillin-resistant *Staphylococcus aureus* (MRSA), *Salmonella, Campylobacter,* and bovine spongiform encephalopathy (mad cow disease), among others, are potentially deadly when passed to humans. Thus, large doses of antibiotics are used to prevent the diseases in industrial agriculture and enhance growth, posing a health risk to humans as bacteria develop more antibiotic-resistant strains.

Artificial diets supplemented with hormones pass hormones to humans indirectly through water supplies and directly through consumption of animal products. The effects of the hormones and range of potential risks are still unknown but may affect growth rates and cancers.

---

chemical contamination in the food supply. Emerging markets have some of the highest incidents of foodborne disease (Grace and McDermott 2015).

In the poorest countries, there is probably a large incidence of unreported foodborne illnesses. However, people in these countries are somewhat protected by their lack of access to meats, fish, and leafy vegetables, which carry higher risks of contamination. Short supply chains and traditional methods such as fermentation and lengthy cooking also offer protection. Fungal toxins that grow in food staples pose greater risks. In Africa, because of their heavier reliance on staples, they bear the highest burden of those contaminants and the related illnesses (Grace and McDermott 2015).

Biodiversity and Undernourishment

As science replaced traditional agricultural methods of plant and animal breeding, biodiversity decreased. We are losing biodiversity at every level, "genes within species, species within ecosystems, and ecosystems within regions," so much so that it has been called a "biological meltdown" (Shand 1997). Biodiversity is important for the health of the earth and its people. And, as Shand (1997) argued, it is a political, economic, and social problem. The greatest factor in loss of crop and genetic diversity in livestock is high-input industrial agriculture and the displacement of more diverse, traditional agricultural systems.

With respect to food, biodiversity is critical for the vast array of micronutrients necessary for complete human growth and development.[3] The United States was once home to 7,000 species of apples. Fully 85 percent of them, some 6,000, are extinct (Shand 1997). Options for long-term sustainability and agricultural self-reliance are lost with loss of biodiversity. Shand (1997) pointed out that seeds are adapted to specific environments. When a community loses its community-bred seed, it loses its capacity to control its own food system. With the seed was a traditional body of knowledge about best growing conditions and potential risks and how to deal with them. With seed from outside, locals become dependent on outside resources and inputs. They can never be self-reliant.

Biodiversity is also important in livestock. Thousands of genetically diverse breeds developed in tandem with thousands of diverse cultures, carefully selected to meet environmental conditions and human needs. Each is adapted to certain environments, resistant to particular parasites or other threats; altogether, the variety provides a much more stable and safe food source.

The loss of biodiversity is evident in the cases of malnourishment due to micronutrient deficiency. The WHO calls micronutrients "magic wands." They are necessary for production of enzymes, hormones, and other substances needed for development. They are called "micro" because only small amounts are needed. But the small amounts are critical. Think of the multi-vitamin that you may take every day. It is a daily supply of select micronutrients. The best source of micronutrients is our food. Because many in the developed world have nutrient-poor diets, we take supplements.

Malnutrition is the "hidden hunger." It can be masked by getting adequate calories or even being overweight. The consequences are not hidden. Symptoms and consequences of malnutrition are best examined in children. They are the most vulnerable, and their health and development will determine the health and productivity of their society far into the future. In 2015, the UN International Children's Emergency Fund, WHO, and World Bank Group jointly issued a report on child malnutrition. It was the most comprehensive examination of malnutrition to that point. Here are their key findings:

- From 1990 to 2014, stunting prevalence declined from 39.6 to 23.8 percent. The incidence of child stunting was reduced by 96 million children, from 255 to 159 million.

- From 1990 to 2014, overweight prevalence went up from 4.8 percent to 6.1 percent, an increase of 10 million children from 31 to 41 million.

- In 2014, 7.5 percent of children were wasted, that is, 50 million or 1 of every 13 children, and 16 million of those children were severely wasted.

The consequences of micronutrient deficiencies are well established. Here are a few:

Iron Deficiency

- Every year, 115,000 women die during pregnancy due to iron deficiency anemia, and there are 600,000 stillbirths and deaths of babies within the first week of life.

- 18 million babies are born with a mental impairment due to maternal iodine and iron deficiency during pregnancy.

Folate Deficiency

- 150,000 babies are born with neural tube defects resulting from an inadequate intake of folate by their mothers before and during the early stages of pregnancy.

Vitamin A Deficiency

- Vitamin A deficiency causes no fewer than 350,000 children to become blind every single year (making it the biggest single cause of childhood blindness).

Micronutrients are critical for healthy brain development, from the time before conception until children are two or three years old. If children do not receive adequate nutrients in utero or beginning before 6 months of age, there are lifelong consequences for cognitive impairment and poor health throughout their lives. Breast-feeding for the first six months followed by a nutrient-rich diet thereafter is the best chance for overall health, school achievement, and a productive adulthood (Sight and Life 2012).

The chart in Table 3.1 summarizes some of the most important micronutrients and consequences of malnutrition associated with them.

HOW CAN WE FIX OUR BROKEN FOOD SYSTEM?

A 2014 report by the UN Special Rapporteur on the right to food had one answer to this question—agroecology. As the term implies, agroecology applies an ecological perspective and ecological science to food production. Conventional industrial agriculture, as we have seen throughout this chapter, has already reached the point of unsustainability by depleting and degrading the very natural resources on which it depends—land, air, and water. At the same time, the conventional food system has not fulfilled its obligation to feed everyone in the world sufficiently nutritious food to reach their potential in life chances. It has put small farmers out of business and left agricultural workers hungry.

For the food system to work for all, it must be sustainable and nutritious:

- It must promote stewardship of the resources on which the food supply depends and mitigate the threats associated with climate change.

TABLE 3.1   Micronutrient Deficiencies and Prevalence

Billions of people globally are at risk of devastating—even deadly—disorders due to micronutrient deficiency. The chart shows the major deficiencies, the risks, and estimates of the number of people at risk.

Micronutrient	Deficiency Prevalence	Major Deficiency Disorders
Iodine	2 billion at risk	Goiter, hypothyroidism, iodine deficiency disorders, increased risk of stillbirth, birth defects, infant mortality, cognitive impairment
Iron	2 billion	Iron deficiency, anemia, reduced learning and work capacity, increased maternal and infant mortality, low birth weight
Zinc	Estimated high in developing countries	Poor pregnancy outcome, impaired growth (stunting), genetic disorders, decreased resistance to infectious diseases
Vitamin A	254 million preschool children	Night blindness, xerophthalmia, increased risk of mortality in children and pregnant women
Folate (Vitamin B6)	Insufficient data	Neural tube and other birth defects, megaloblastic anemia, heart disease, stroke, impaired cognitive function, depression
Cobolamine (Vitamin B12)	Insufficient data	Megaloblastic anemia (associated with *Helicobacter pylori*-induced gastric atrophy
Thiamine (Vitamin B1)	Estimated as common in developing countries and in famines, displaced persons	Beriberi (cardiac and neurologic), Wernicke and Korsakov syndromes (alcoholic confusion and paralysis)
Riboflavin (Vitamin B2)	Estimated as common in developing countries	Nonspecific—fatigue, eye changes, dermatitis, brain dysfunction, impaired iron absorption
Niacin (Vitamin B3)	Estimated as common in developing countries and in famines, displaced persons	Pellagra (dermatitis, diarrhea, dementia, death)
Vitamin B6	Estimated as common in developing countries and in famines, displaced persons	Dermatitis, neurological disorders, convulsions, anemia, elevated plasma homocysteine
Vitamin C	Estimated as common in famines, displaced persons	Scurvy (fatigue, hemorrhages, low resistance to infection, anemia)
Vitamin D	Widespread in all age-groups, low exposure to ultraviolet rays of sun	Rickets, osteomalacia, osteoporosis, colorectal cancer
Calcium	Estimated to be widespread	Decreased bone mineralization, rickets, osteoporosis
Selenium	Common in Asia, Scandinavia, Siberia	Cardiomyopathy, increased cancer and cardiovascular risk
Fluoride	Widespread	Increased dental decay, affects bone health

Source: Tulchinsky (2010). Reproduced with permission.

A CLOSER LOOK
FOOD-RELATED POLICY

Regulations and policies from a variety of other sectors impact food systems.

FIGURE 3.4   Potential Policy Influences on Food Systems

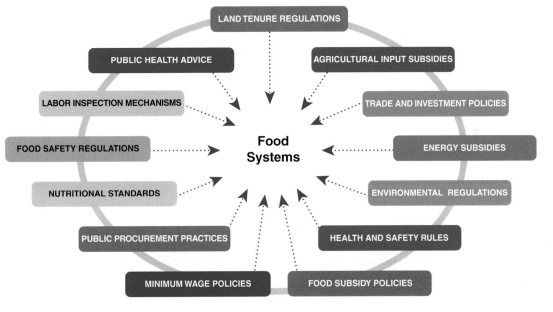

Source: International Panel of Experts on Sustainable Food Systems (2015). Reproduced with permission.

- It must restore biodiversity to the food supply in all corners of the world to eliminate malnutrition.

- It must support small-scale farmers and their organizations because they are best positioned to accomplish both stewardship and biodiversity.

As shown in the diagram in Figure 3.4, food systems are shaped by a broad array of policies. Some are enacted at global levels through trade agreements, and others are enacted locally.

Rebuilding Local Food Systems

Agribusiness occupies an increasing share of GDP in developing countries, yet 85 percent of farms worldwide are still small farms. In Africa and Asia, small farm holders farm 80 percent of the farmland. These farmers face significant problems that undermine their capacity to achieve their potential. Lack of access to natural resources, financial services, training and information, stable markets, and up-to-date knowledge and information are only a few of the obstacles they face. Improving the lot of small farm holders and agricultural workers, who are the most likely of workers to live on less than $1.25 a day, can improve food security, food diversity, and rural employment.

Promote Sustainable Agriculture and Agroecology

Sustainable agriculture is important to ensure an adequate food supply now and far into the future. Sustainable agriculture can have a significant effect in mitigating climate change because agriculture is a main contributor. Sustainable agriculture can preserve, rather than degrade, the resources needed for agriculture, land, water, and air. It is very compatible with smaller-scale farming and, thus, can improve the livelihoods and life chances of some of the world's poorest households. It provides a healthier, more nutritious food supply by relying on diverse crops and can build more diversity into the food supply.

Agroecology approaches agriculture as a self-sustaining ecological system. It engages symbiotic relationships among diverse component parts of the system from livestock to fish, forestry, insects, and organisms in the soil. This reduces or eliminates external inputs such as chemical fertilizers and pesticides or commercially developed seed. Soil and water are maintained, pests are controlled, and weeds are eliminated through carefully designed systems. These methods have been very successful in restoring degraded land and water. Agroecology has been shown to improve the biodiversity of agriculture as well as the nutritional diets and incomes of the poor. It does not require the use of purchased fertilizers or pesticides, and it preserves and restores land and water.

Examples from the 2010 Human Rights Council report on the right to food include the following:

- 350,000 hectares of land have been rehabilitated in Tanzania using agroforestry. In Malawi, nitrogen "fixing" trees sustain the corn harvest. This program, with help from Ireland, benefitted 1.3 million of the world's poorest people.

- An indigenous acacia species, widespread throughout Africa, takes nitrogen from the air and stores it in its leaves. The leaves are then incorporated into the soil. Their growing season is such that they do not compete with the corn for light or water. In Zambia, the trees are planted in the fields, making a "fertilizer factory." This increased yield nearly 3-fold while making the farms free of the expense of commercial chemicals and improving the soil.

- Stone walls built alongside fields in West Africa capture water during the rainy season, improving soil moisture and replenishing the water table. Livestock graze on the grasses that grow along the walls and fertilize the fields. Biomass production increased 10- to 15-fold.

- In Kenya, farmers inter-planted insect-repelling crops with corn. Insects repelled were attracted to Napier grass plots that trapped them. This was called a "push–pull" strategy. The *Desmodium* used to repel or push the insects away from the corn is used as fodder for livestock. Corn and milk production doubled, and the soil was improved.

- Fish and ducks in rice paddies in Japan, India, the Philippines, and China ate weeds, weed seeds, and pests and fertilized the paddies. They also served as a source of protein for the families. (De Schutter 2010)

Promote Small-Scale Farming

The vast majority of all farms are small, less than 1 hectare, but they occupy only 8 percent of farmland. Each farming community faces somewhat different obstacles. Mobilizing the community and helping them to articulate their unique needs is an important first step. Following this, local and national governments need to enact policies to overcome the obstacles. Some promising steps outlined in the 2014 Human Rights Council report include the following:

Increasing the productivity of smaller scale farmers for local and more distant markets has at least these four benefits:

- Increasing the diversity of food supply for local consumption

- Increasing the income of small producers and agricultural workers

- Combatting resource loss and climate change through sustainable agriculture

- Creating diverse employment opportunities across the food supply network

Policies that would build local small farm capacity:

- Increase subsidies and cash assistance as needed for agricultural inputs such as fertilizers (locally produced through livestock) and traditionally bred seeds.

- Ensure that low-cost financing is available to male and female small farmers.

- Eliminate formal and informal barriers to women in agriculture.

- Invest in education and training for processing and distributing local produce.

CONSIDER THIS
CLIMATE SMART PROFILES

Climate smart agriculture promoted by the World Bank strives to achieve sustainable food security and broader development goals by increasing agricultural productivity and resilience. Each participating country develops a custom smart profile. As of January 2016, there were 14 smart profiles, including 3 different ones to take into account the varying climates of Mexico.

Rwanda

In Rwanda, agriculture accounts for 33 percent of the country's GDP and employs about 41 percent of its population. Rwanda's agricultural exports, primarily tea, coffee, cattle, beans, and maize, are worth about U.S. $163 million. Nearly three fourths of its farms are very small, less than 1 hectare or about 2.47 acres. Rwanda is one of the most densely populated countries in the world. This has forced much of its agriculture onto very steep slopes, leading to soil erosion and a decrease in agricultural yields.

Unreliable rainfall and prolonged drought complicate the picture even more.

As part of Rwanda's climate smart plan, new irrigation methods (including water harvesting in small ponds), irrigation powered hydroelectrically and by hand pumps, compost training, and tree nurseries (among other innovations) increased productivity. Along with new agricultural practices, the programs offered crop handling, marketing, and business planning training. New enterprises focused on composting were developed. This particular program in Rwanda involved joint efforts of the Rwandan government, U.S. Agency for International Development (USAID), Canadian International Development Agency, International Development Agency, and Global Agriculture and Food Security Program and helped more than 100,000 people. It created jobs for 22,000 farmers, reduced crop loss with new drying and storage facilities, and increased soil fertility 3- to 10-fold for crops such as soybeans, maize, beans, and Irish potatoes.

Source: World Bank/International Center for Tropical Agriculture (2015).

- Invest in infrastructure to support local supply chains and horizontal integration of food processing and distributing networks bringing produce into urban areas. This creates higher-value employment opportunities.

- Purchase local produce for school meal and other food aid programs.

- Encourage small farmer organizations. These serve a variety of functions such as increased buying power, exchange of ideas and best practices, co-ops, and credit unions.

- Provide land for community gardens in urban areas.

- Protect the fishing rights of small-scale fisheries and protect them from development projects that threaten their livelihood.

Policies to protect small-scale farmers:

- Protect small farmers' access to land through such things as security of tenure, tenancy laws, development plans that do not disrupt land rights, and regulation of land markets.

- Develop national and local markets and food chains from growing to processing to distributing and consuming.

- Regulate agribusiness to ensure fair trade agreements, ensure that food aid does not undermine local producers, and protect the right to food.

- Protect local ecosystems through enforceable regulation on agribusiness. (De Schutter 2014)

As power has become more concentrated in agribusiness, farmers and their organizations need to be brought back into decision and policy making. This needs to be coupled with a shift in emphasis from quantity to nutritional quality, diversity, and environmental concerns.

The International Panel of Experts on Food Systems (2015) acknowledges that the interrelations of components of the modern food system, such as export policies, trade policies, and influence of the powerful industrial players, make this very challenging.

Protect Seed Rights

For centuries, farmers have used the best seed from one year's crop to plant the next year. This traditional breeding method evolves seeds, called landraces, well-suited to local farming conditions. It produces genetic diversity and stable yields because farmers would usually plant several varieties. Contemporary laws and trade agreements threaten traditional seed breeding.

One of the most important things that a government can do for small farmers is to protect their rights to develop, use, and sell their own seed.

Laws enabling and protecting seed patents originated in the United States and Europe, but now 72 countries belong to the Union for the Protection of New Plant Varieties (UPOV). UPOV prevents anyone who does not belong to the organization from producing seeds for commercial purposes. A farmer who uses such a developed seed must purchase it annually because of a patent or because terminator seeds are not capable of reproduction. Ironically, the engineered seeds usually begin with seeds traditionally bred and encompass the wisdom and work of generations of rural communities. Making a few alterations gives industrial agriculture the right to patent and control them, charging farmers for the use of knowledge that they once held collectively (Montenegro 2015).

Climate-resistant seeds are an example of patented seeds that are presented as a way to achieve climate justice for the most vulnerable countries. The seeds are engineered to resist various climate stresses such as drought, higher temperatures, and too much rain. Producers present them as ensuring good yields in countries whose food supplies are most affected by climate change. In advertisements, the seeds are promoted as "needed against hunger" or developed for "our hungry world" (quoted in Saab 2015:225). Climate justice movements see this differently. They see it as another way of making poor countries dependent on large corporations. Because they are patented, the seeds benefit the corporations, not the hungry poor. Six corporations[4] held the patents on 77 percent of climate-resistant seeds (Saab 2015).

Farmers' intellectual property rights over the varieties of plants that they have improved need to be protected in the same way as corporate rights are. This has not been the case. Although they are recognized in theory, as in the International Treaty on Plant Genetic Resources for Food and Agriculture (ITPGR) of 2004, they are not generally enforceable.

Because of the peculiarities of some trade agreements, farmers circulating their own evolved seeds, landrace, may be accused of undercutting trade agreements by giving unfair advantage to local producers.

Protect Agricultural Labor

Not all agricultural laborers are small-scale farmers. Many work on farms and for agribusiness. They often work in the most hazardous occupations for substandard wages.

- Ensure that workers are paid a living wage.

- Reduce the number of laborers who are working outside of the formal economy.

- Monitor compliance with labor legislation.

- Ratify all International Labour Organization treaties relevant to agriculture.

- Protect child laborers and workers from hazardous or abusive working conditions.

- Protect women from abuse in agricultural settings.

Assurances for the protection of workers can come only from a transparent supply chain.

Reform Abuse of Animals

Will raising animals with attention to the quality of their lives improve ours as well? Factory farm cows, poultry, and pigs are raised in conditions that even some farmers who produce them admit are not just inhumane but also unhealthy for humans. Compassion in World Farming is a non-governmental organization whose primary goal, in a nutshell, is to end the practice of factory farming of animals globally. This is to preserve animal health and, consequentially, human health. The "Business Benchmark on Farm Animal Welfare" is its annual report.

Restore and Fortify Women's Roles in Agriculture

As agriculture became more commodified, many traditional contributions of women were devalued. Women lost access to land. Large-scale farming left little land for foraging for indigenous medicines and foods. Traditionally, women used agricultural

CONSIDER THIS
BUILDING LOCAL CHAMPIONS

International aid organizations have learned that top-down and cookie-cutter answers to the world's problems seldom work. The Africa Lead[a] and Feed the Future programs build local capacity to advance the transformation of agriculture in Africa. The key component is identifying champions, local male and female leaders who can discover, develop, and promote the evidenced-based changes in policy and structures to end hunger and poverty in Africa.

The program is heavy in workshops and meetings for local and regional stakeholders and public and private organizations, ensuring participatory decision making. Providing advice and assistance in developing local capacity to manage sustainable agriculture is the key to maintaining the best practices discovered. As of March 2015, Africa Lead had supported 915 local and regional organizations and trained 615 champions.

a. Africa Lead is a USAID-led consortium in partnership with Development Alternatives Inc., Training Resources Group, Management Systems International (MSI), and Winrock International.

byproducts to replenish and keep soil healthy. There was little waste and sustainable practices. Agricultural reform must guarantee women's access to land rights, credit, technology, education, and roles in agricultural organizations. Women are still a large portion of small farmers. Denying them the resources needed to farm sustainably will perpetuate rural poverty and hunger.

FOOD SAFETY NETS

Rebuilding the food system starts with better agriculture and continues with more efficient food distribution.

Improving Agricultural Infrastructure

In both developed and developing nations, significant food loss results from improper handling, storage, processing, and distribution. One estimate is that one third of all food produced, some 1.3 billion tons, is lost every year. This wastes not only the food itself but also all the resources consumed in its production. If the world is to reach the Sustainable Development Goal of zero hunger, food loss must be eliminated.

Food reserves are critical for maintaining food supply and price stability. Reserves need to be available to protect the most vulnerable from food shocks due to natural disaster, conflict, or price spikes. Reserves are wasted without proper storage to protect them from contamination and rotting (Figure 3.5).

How much reserve a country can and should maintain depends on its storage capacity, the capacity for distribution, and the types of food aid policies it employs. India's Food Security Act of 2013, for example, promised to extend subsidized food distribution and uses public reserves in its school-based feeding programs. This requires significant storage as well as handling, processing, and transportation infrastructure. Countries that rely more on cash transfers than on food distribution need only maintain reserves for food shocks, requiring significantly less infrastructure. Nigeria has no policy for food distribution. It maintains reserves for emergencies only. This presents another set of problems. How can the food be stored for emergencies but not wasted if emergencies do not materialize regularly? Old food stocks must be rotated out and released before their quality is compromised and replaced with new stock.

In Zambia, the problem is different yet. Zambia produces an abundance of white maize; it must store grain from the surplus and then export it to other countries. In 2014, the Zambian government estimated that it lost 30 percent of its grain to inadequate storage (Shukla and Gupta 2014).

Keeping food safe and of high nutritional quality is a complicated process. Public–private partnerships seem to be the recommended route for solving problems of storage. Silos must have appropriate machinery for receiving grain and discharging it, aeration, monitoring temperature, and other processes to maintain safety and quality in storage and handling. Getting food to market requires handling and storage on trucks, trains, and ships

A CLOSER LOOK
GLOBAL FOOD LOSS

FIGURE 3.5   Global Food Loss States Along the Production/Supply Chain

Food is lost at every step along the supply chain. In the developed countries, the major portion of loss is in the consumption phase; in developing countries, it is in storage.

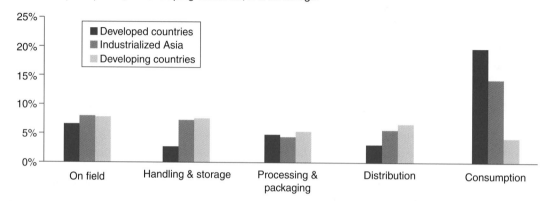

Source: World Bank Group. 2014. *Grain Storage Public-Private Partnerships.* Handshake. Washington, DC: World Bank. © World Bank. https://openknowledge.worldbank.org/handle/10986/28464 License: CC BY 3.0 IGO.

Traditional food storage huts leave food vulnerable to weather, insects, and rodents. New storage facilities can eliminate this source of food waste.

PHOTO 3.1A Burkina Faso food storage.

World Food Programme/Agbessi Amewoa.

PHOTO 3.1B Taken on the Island of the Los Uros people, Lake Titicaca, Peru, January 13, 2013. This is a photograph of a typical Los Uros village food storage hut.

Steven A. Steinbrecher.

PHOTO 3.1C Taken at the Maori village at Te Puia, Rotorua, New Zealand, January 5, 2018. This is a typical communal Maori Marae (communal village).

Steven A. Steinbrecher.

and at ports. Food may travel through several transportation hubs before reaching the final destination. Food safety and infectious disease inspections are required at every port. From ports to processing to packaging and distribution, each step is an important component of the food supply chain.

School Feeding Programs

The major safety nets employed worldwide are school feeding programs, food for work, and cash transfers. School feeding is a critical food aid program. Children, because their bodies and brains are still developing, are particularly vulnerable to undernourishment. In response, many countries have domestic school feeding programs. The national school lunch program of the United States feeds free or low-cost lunches to more than 31 million children every school day. The WFP is the primary provider of school meals globally. In 2014, it fed 18.2 million children in 75,500 schools in 65 countries and assisted governments in another 9 countries with their own school meal programs. Inclusive of all school feeding programs, about 368 million children are fed every day. The largest programs are in India (114 million), Brazil (47 million), the United States (45 million), and China (26 million). At least 43 countries have more than 1 million children enrolled (WFP 2013).

School feeding programs linked with other programs have a synergistic effect. By buying food locally whenever possible, the WFP helps to sustain small farmers and delivers better nutrition.

School meals also motivate families to keep children in school. Brazil took this one step further with *Bolsa Familia* program in 2003. While children receive meals in school, families receive cash for keeping their children in school. Studies have shown that most of this money is used to buy food and other necessities for the children. This is part of Brazil's *Fome Zero* (Zero Hunger) program.

Guaranteeing Food Aid

There are many food aid programs—foreign, domestic, and run by international agencies such as the UN's WFP. Most work on a combination of direct food aid, cash transfers, vouchers, and building sustainable local food systems.

New food aid programs work to build local capacity. The intent is not just to give food. Many food aid programs of the past simply bought food from their own domestic producers to provide to other countries. This resulted in undermining farmers in the recipient societies and reduced surplus or subsidized farmers and agribusiness in richer countries.

The best new programs combine nutrition interventions with programs to develop sustainable agriculture, increase yields of climate-appropriate and resilient crops, build on the best indigenous knowledge and modern technology, and help to expand fair trade opportunities.

CONSIDER THIS
THE MCGOVERN–DOLE SCHOOL MEALS FUND

Operated by the WFP, this school feeding program uses locally grown food to improve nutrition and education for children and economic development for farmers. Parents are more likely to send their children to school and keep them there if there is a food program. This is particularly effective for retaining girls in school. For the local farmers, the schools are a new market. The WFP also helps the farmers to improve the quality and yield of their crops. "Home-grown school feeding programs" are now operating in many countries. They have proven to be so successful that many local governments have assumed the responsibility for operating them.

The European Commission, for example, provided funding to 54 countries in 2014. Its program, the new Food Assistance Convention (FAC), provides cash assistance when there are adequate food supplies in the local markets, thereby boosting the local economy. It provides food in crises where it is not available locally. Livelihood programs support development of local agricultural capacity and integrated nutrition, health, and employment programs.

- In Kenya, the integrated approach funded health care projects, veterinary services, and animal fodder to protect the livelihoods of pastoralists, vouchers for the most at-risk people, and other necessities to overcome drought.

- In Darfur, people were given milling vouchers so that they would not need to sell part of their grain to have the rest milled.

- In the Democratic Republic of the Congo, cash assistance was given so that displaced families could buy from local markets and manage their spending to suit their individual needs. (European Commission 2015)

The WFP pledged to provide food aid by purchasing food from local sources wherever possible. In 2010, it purchased 80 percent from local purveyors. This supports sustainable agriculture, reduces transportation costs and related pollution, and matches food aid to cultural tastes and local needs. The WFP Purchase for Progress program helps small farmers to reach global markets and achieve fair prices by developing skills in every step of the business process. It pays particular attention to female farmers. This helps countries to achieve food self-sufficiency and contributes to a healthier global food supply (WFP 2017).

What Can Consumers Do?

Consumers can affect the food supply. The right action can increase the global supply of healthier foods and reduce waste, energy consumption, and environmental degradation:

- Eat less meat. Rich countries consume much more meat protein than needed. A vegetarian diet consumes half the energy of a meat-based diet. Less meat and more vegetables improve nutrition and reduce the ill effects of meat production.

- Plan meals efficiently. Shop for the freshest foods, locally and organically produced, as is possible. This reduces food waste at home and reduces the energy consumption required for refrigeration and transportation.

- Diversify your diet.

- Grow some of your own food at home and in community gardens. Use natural fertilizers and pesticides.

- Join campaigns to educate yourself about the food system and show support for efforts to ensure that governments, food companies, and others along the food supply chain enact and uphold fair and environmentally sound policies.

SUMMARY

The global food system is broken. Many modern methods of food production consume too much energy, harm the environment, and diminish the quality of our food. Much food is wasted while people starve. We know how to do better. Sustainable and resilient food systems are necessary. Educating people about food issues and acting on the knowledge is necessary to help fulfill people's life chances and the life chances of our environment.

DISCUSSION

1. What are the benefits and drawbacks of factory farming? In your assessment, does it have more benefits or drawbacks?

2. Compare factory farming with traditional farming. What advantages do traditional farming methods have over factory farming? Do traditional methods have a place in modern societies?

3. How can chemical pesticides and fertilizers backfire and cause more harm than benefit?

4. What are the short- and long-term priorities to ensure that everyone has sufficient and sufficiently nutritious food?

ON YOUR OWN

1. Investigate whether or not there are food deserts in your region. If there are, how severe are they? What are the income levels and racial and ethnic composition of areas identified as food deserts? You can use zoning maps for your city or town to identify areas and locate food stores or farmer markets within.

2. Look up data for three (or more) of your favorite foods on the website "Behind the Brands" (https://www.behindthebrands.org/brands). How does Oxfam rate their contributions to global well-being? Are there areas in which they excel? What are the areas in which they need the most improvement?

3. Compare the rates of child labor in developed and developing countries, using UNICEF data (https://data.unicef.org/topic/child-protection/child-labour). Examine the major international instruments regulating child labor internationally. What are the major provisions? (http://www.ilo.org/global/standards/subjects-covered-by-international-labour-standards/child-labour/lang--en/index.htm).

NOTES

1. The largest of these companies are Monsanto, Archer Daniels Midland, Associated British Foods (ABF), Coca-Cola, Danone, General Mills, Kellogg, Mars, Mondelez International (previously Kraft Foods), Nestlé, PepsiCo, and Unilever (Hoffman 2013).

2. The estimates for deaths attributed vary depending on the precise non-communicable diseases included in the measure. For a discussion and further resources for the 6.7 million estimate, refer to http://www.who.int/elena/titles/bbc/fruit_vegetables_ncds/en/

3. Biodiversity is also important for health care in seeking treatments and preventive medications. This is discussed in a later chapter. Shand (1997) made the point that humans may be losing more knowledge than we are creating through the destruction of biodiversity and the ignorance of traditional sources of knowledge. Companies trying to patent and control some of these traditional medicines and knowledge are a threat to human health.

4. These corporations are Bayer, Syngenta, BASF, Dow, DuPont (Pioneer), and Monsanto.

4

Optimizing Human Capital

GOOD HEALTH

COMMUNITY-CENTERED CARING FOR BETTER HEALTH

Violet Shivutse is a farmer in Kenya. Her community is her focus, but she is influencing women's lives globally. Women have traditionally played vital roles in African agriculture. Despite their labor in the fields, the women in Shivutse's community made few farming decisions and were not able to take out loans or take advantage of the agricultural extension programs. Lacking medical attention, many of her community's women farmers were dying in childbirth. The nearby hospital blamed the traditional birth attendants.

Shivutse worked with the local hospital to incorporate the traditional attendants into the outreach program, combining resources and upgrading care. She organized the attendants and agreed to be the group's secretary because many were illiterate. This was the beginning of the Shibuye Community Health Workers. They have since expanded services to include other health issues such as measles outbreaks, diarrhea, and education in sanitation, nutrition, and family planning.

But Shivutse was not done. In the mid-1990s, the HIV/AIDS pandemic hit Kenya, creating a national health emergency. Kenya's caregivers assumed responsibilities for the treatment and long-term care of AIDS patients in addition to their regular workloads. They also ensured that if a woman fell sick, her fields were tended and her land rights were defended. Still, the caregivers were not included in higher-level policy discussions that affected them and the quality of care they could provide. In 2003, Shivutse realized why. A donor told her that because the caregivers nationwide were a fragmented group, it was hard to bring them to the larger decision-making table to affect policy.

Shivutse returned home to create a branch of the Home-Based Care Alliance. Today, the Kenyan branch has 3,200 members. She has scaled up her work and now helps other communities to forge working relationships

LEARNING OBJECTIVES

After completing this chapter, students should be able to do the following:

4.1 Understand the importance of investing in people's health as a matter of human rights and the common global good

4.2 Determine ways in which current health care systems neglect or diminish the life chances of many people globally

4.3 Recognize the factors of contemporary life that increase risk of communicable diseases and non-communicable diseases

4.4 Assess potential strategies for improving global health and diminishing the long-term global risks

4.5 Explain forms of child labor and its cost to children, their society, and the world

with health care facilities. She often represents caregivers at global meetings. But it is her rootedness in her community from which her success grows. She says that she was not "handpicked to sit on a committee" but rather to serve a community.

Shivutse's story highlights the problems of health care globally. Access to even the most basic care is limited. Urban lifestyles encourage unhealthy habits. Non-communicable diseases left untreated become chronic conditions. Infectious diseases once thought conquered, such as measles, are resurging, and new infectious diseases, such as AIDS, are emerging. Antimicrobial-resistant bacteria, viruses, and fungi pose deadly threats. Sometimes the solutions are simple—community health care centers and trained attendants. Other times the solutions, such as finding new antimicrobials for new diseases, are more perplexing.

—as reported by Clar Nichonghaile in *Progress of the World's Women 2015–2016*

THE GLOBAL BURDEN OF DISEASE

We are each born with a different potential for a healthy life. But in the chance to fulfill that potential, we are all to be equal. That is a human right, articulated in Article 21 of the United Nations (UN) Declaration of Human Rights. Global efforts through the Millennium Development Goals reaped significant progress. Child deaths declined 53 percent from 1990 (12.7 million) to 2015. Still, nearly 6 million children died before their fifth birthday in 2015—nearly half from communicable diseases (UN 2015:5). UN Sustainable Development Goal (SDG) 3 pledges to "ensure healthy lives and promote well-being for all ages." In all, there are 50 health-related indicators monitored in the SDGs, spread across several goals. In 2016, the second year of the SDGs, country SDG health index[1] scores (0–100) ranged from 11 (Afghanistan, Central African Republic, and Somalia) to 87 (Singapore) (SDG Collaborators 2017).

As you probably expect, the chance to live to age 5 years is not evenly spread through the world; the burden of disease is not shared equally. Social location plays an important role in this ultimate life chance. Children born into poverty are two times more likely to die than the richest children, and children in rural areas are more than one and a half times more likely to die than children in urban areas (UN International Children's Emergency Fund [UNICEF] 2016). In general, people in lower socioeconomic status and poorer regions of the world are less healthy. However, health outcomes are not totally dependent on wealth or location. Improved water supplies and sanitation systems, dissemination of health care education, nutrition, the efforts of civil society, international governmental organizations and states, and maternal education all have a synergistic effect in improving health. In contrast, political and social unrest, war, climate change, natural disasters, and large-scale migrations adversely affect physical and mental health directly and reduce access to health care (Roth et al. 2017).

Nearly every aspect of our lives influences and is influenced by our health—the city or country where we live, the work we do, the food we eat, the education we acquire. While we are improving health care on some fronts, such as by an improved water source, we are manufacturing risks on others, such as by increasing pollution or processed foods. Nearly every global health problem results in some measure from the unintended consequences of our own actions.

HOW OUR LIFESTYLES HARM US: NON-COMMUNICABLE DISEASE

The UN officially recognized non-communicable diseases as a major concern for global health in 2011. The SDGs call for a one-third reduction (Roth et al. 2017). Of particular concern in the UN report are cardiovascular disease, diabetes, cancer, and respiratory diseases. Not only do they contribute substantially to the burden of disease, but they also have common risk factors that can be tackled simultaneously (Alleyne et al. 2013).

Non-communicable diseases are the leading cause of death, killing 40 million people yearly, accounting for 70 percent of all deaths globally. Without intervention, this will increase by 15 percent from 2010 to 2020 (Alwan et al. 2011) and by more than 50 percent in low- and middle-income countries by 2030 (Alleyne et al. 2013). Certainly, not all cases of non-communicable disease can be prevented or cured, but four behavioral factors exacerbate and/or give rise to them: tobacco use, alcohol use, physical inactivity, and unhealthy diets. These raise our blood pressure, our body weight, and our blood cholesterol and glucose levels. The risk factors vary by country income groups:

- Alcohol consumption, physical inactivity among women, total fat consumption, and total cholesterol had the highest prevalence in high-income countries.

- Upper middle-income countries have the highest rates of obesity and overweight among adults.

- Tobacco use has the highest prevalence in the lower middle-income countries of Europe and the Western Pacific Region.

There are some mitigating trends that should slow the rise. Western Europe, North America, and parts of Latin America are making dietary and other behavioral changes. Less smoking, reduced salt and fat intake, less harmful alcohol use, and more physical activity can reduce some rise in these diseases (Alwan et al. 2011).

The World's Biggest Killer: Cardiovascular Disease

Cardiovascular diseases (CVD: heart diseases and stroke) account for one third of deaths worldwide (Roth et al. 2017). The rate of CVD generally increases with improvements in the sociodemographic status (sociodemographic index [SDI]) of a country moving from the lowest quartile to the middle with a slight shift in the burden of mortality from women to men. It decreases only gradually from the middle 50th percentile to the 75th percentile of development (Figure 4.1). High-SDI countries have less than one fifth the rate of the lowest countries (Roth et al. 2017). The high-SDI countries accounted for most of the global decrease in CVD. Global progress has stalled; the rate of improvement from 2010 to 2015 was negligible in comparison with the rate over the prior 25 years.

After the cardiovascular diseases, cancers, respiratory diseases, and diabetes claim the highest burden of mortality. Within SDI levels, country results are very mixed. Variation in modifiable risk factors (such as behaviors), access to care, rising rates of obesity, the diffusion of interventions, air pollution, and changes in average temperature affect the burden of each disease in each country.

Lack of progress and the expected rise of disease in many developing countries are related to urbanization. Changing patterns of lifestyle that accompany urbanization—even rural people are adopting urbanized lifestyles—are related to rising non-communicable diseases. Diets high in saturated fats, refined foods, and sugars and low in fiber and decreasing physical activity increase the risk of chronic diseases. The World Health Organization (WHO) advocates for health promotion strategies that empower people to act both individually and collectively. It emphasizes the importance of monitoring to find patterns of disease, prevention programs to change lifestyles, and managing care through multiple sectors—education, health care delivery, civil society and local community groups, and governments (Habib and Saha 2010). If the major lifestyle risk factors could be eliminated, 40 to 75 percent of these diseases could be prevented.

Obesity: Disease of Development

Obesity is a global health challenge. As recently as the 1980s, only the United States was suspected of having an obesity problem. Now it is global, with particular concern for Asia, Latin America, the Middle East, and Africa as the health effects are felt at lower levels than the standard body mass index overweight thresholds (Popkin, Adair, and Ng 2012). There are different criteria for obesity; WHO, Centers for Disease Control and Prevention (CDC), and International Obesity Task Force use somewhat different indicators, making comparison across studies difficult, but there is consensus that obesity among children and adults is dangerously high and rising. The prevalence of obesity doubled in 73 countries and increased continuously in most others from 1980 to 2015. A meta-analysis of thousands of data sources established that in 2015 more than 1 million children and 6 million adults were obese (GBD 2015 Obesity Collaborators 2017). Euromonitor estimated 2017 obesity rates of 42.7 percent for the population age 15 years and over in North America and 19 percent for that in Western Europe. Overweight and obesity in China surged from 7.2 percent for adults age 20 years and over to 30.4 percent in 2015, and it increased from 3.5 to 16.3 percent for children age 19 years and under. In developing countries, more people are overweight than underweight—both may be undernourished.

The health risks associated with obesity are life threatening. Poor diet is the major cause of death and morbidity globally (MacGregor 2015). Obesity heightens risk for diabetes, heart disease, kidney disease, some cancers, and muscular–skeletal disorders. Obesity contributed to 4 million deaths, most due to cardiovascular disease, and 120 million disability-adjusted life years in 2015 alone (WHO 2017b). Genetics and certain medications make

A CLOSER LOOK
BURDEN OF DISEASE AND SDI

The burden of diseases differs by gender and level of human development in terms of both overall susceptibility and degree of vulnerability to particular diseases.

FIGURE 4.1   Cardiovascular Disease and Gender

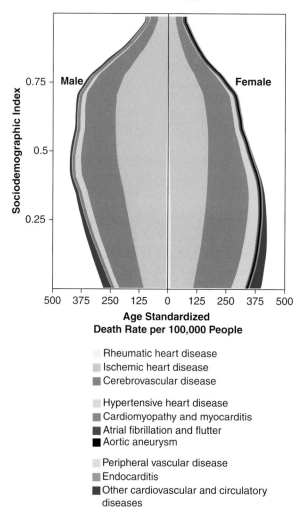

Rheumatic heart disease
Ischemic heart disease
Cerebrovascular disease

Hypertensive heart disease
Cardiomyopathy and myocarditis
Atrial fibrillation and flutter
Aortic aneurysm

Peripheral vascular disease
Endocarditis
Other cardiovascular and circulatory diseases

some people more vulnerable to obesity. However, it is lifestyle changes, in diet and declining physical activity related to development and urbanization, that account for the rapidly rising rates. Major culprits in the obesity pandemic are fast-food restaurants and packaged and ultra-processed foods—high in sugar, salt, cholesterol, trans fats, and calories and low in nutrition (Figure 4.2). In the United States, which leads the world in obesity, two thirds of calorie intake comes from such ultra-processed, ready-to-eat, ready-to-heat foods (Baker and Friel 2016).

Fast-food restaurants have meaning beyond just a quick meal. They are among the markers of middle-class life. In developing countries, eating at a fast-food restaurant may be a sign that individuals are upwardly mobile, modern, and cosmopolitan. It is a sign that they have some extra time and money to spare (Herkenrath et al. 2005). They are eating "foreign" foods from the developed world. With an expanded menu of Western foods, adapted somewhat to Chinese tastes, Pizza Hut offers the Chinese middle class a very Western experience. There, patrons often eat with knives and forks rather than chopsticks, and Pizza Hut provides them with a fine dining experience with spotless facilities and excellent table service (Chan and Zakkour 2014).[2]

In the United States as well, it is the middle class that most often finds itself at a fast-food chain. Even though 76 percent of Americans say fast food is not too good for you, or not at all good for you, 50 to 51 percent of those with incomes above U.S. $30,000, including those with incomes above $75,000, find themselves at fast-food restaurants weekly, in contrast to only 42 percent of those with incomes below $29,000 who go to fast-food restaurants weekly (Dugan 2013).

Fast-food retailers are multiplying quickly. Five of the major U.S. fast-food chains together have about 138,855 outlets—21.6 for every million people globally. Subway leads with nearly 43,000 to McDonald's 35,000. In the five years from 2010 to 2015, KFC increased its presence in China by 59 percent with 3.4 outlets for every million Chinese. Together with the other four of the big five—KFC, Subway, McDonald's, Starbucks, and Pizza Hut—there are 7.1 per every million people (Economist 2015).

A CLOSER LOOK
FAST-FOOD CONSUMPTION AND BODY MASS INDEX

Increases in fast-food consumption per capita and body mass increases are positively related.

FIGURE 4.2   Fast-Food Consumption per Country

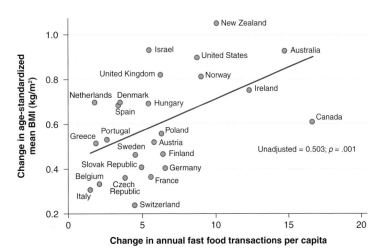

Source: DeVogli, Kouvonen, and Gimeno (2013). Reproduced with permission.

A CLOSER LOOK
CONSUMPTION OF ULTRA-PROCESSED FOODS

Consumption of ultra-processed foods is becoming dominant in the global food system. As countries develop, people eat more ultra-processed foods.

FIGURE 4.3   Development and Caloric Intake

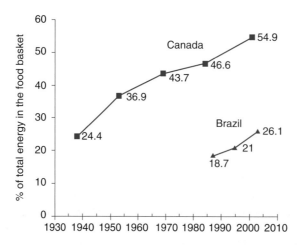

Source: Monteiro et al. (2013). Reproduced with permission.

FIGURE 4.4   Processed Food Consumption

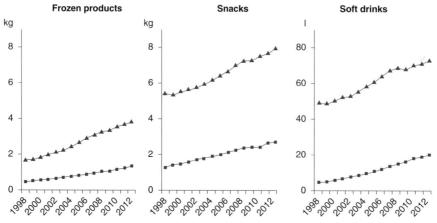

Source: Monteiro et al. (2013). Reproduced with permission.

Ultra-processed packaged food has much the same aura as fast food. It is relatively cheap, tasty (due to added salt, sugar, and fat), high calorie, very low in nutrition, and readily available as snacks as well as packaged meals. Ultra-processed foods already dominate the food supply of high-income countries (Figures 4.3 and 4.4). Traditional diets of developing countries are also giving way to ultra-processed foods (Monteiro et al. 2013). In 2002, the packaged and processed food industry sales stood at more than $3 trillion, while fresh foods were less than $1 trillion. While at this time 60 percent of these packaged and processed sales were in high-income countries, those sales were decreasing while sales in developing countries were increasing (Gehlhar and Regmi 2005).

Although changing patterns of agriculture are in part responsible—indigenous food crops are giving way to cash crops such as sugar in many developing countries—a large portion of responsibility is borne by the globalization of the food industry. Transnational food and beverage corporations, through their market concentration and power, have the capacity to shape the contours of local food systems, including availability, price, nutritional quality, desirability, and consumption (Baker and Friel 2016). They expand their market shares by moving into middle- and lower middle-income countries.

By providing easy access to tasty, ready-to-consume, and relatively cheap foods, transnational industries have found ways in which to make money even from people near the bottom of the pyramid. Nestlé has a long history of purveying questionable food strategies in developing nations. In the 1970s, Nestlé and other infant formula companies promoted baby formula in developing countries. With full knowledge that in some countries households lacked the indoor washing facilities to sterilize baby bottles—or even wash hands—and that many mothers could not read the instructions in any case, they continued to promote formula. Using salesgirls dressed as nurses and giving free bottles with purchases of formula made the costly formula seem like the best alternative. Babies suffered malnutrition and infection—even death—as a result (Muller 1974).

Now, Nestlé reports that 42 percent of its sales of snack foods are in developing markets. In Brazil, it uses a highly refined strategy to sell to the poor. Using local women who are familiar with the neighborhood (and who know when Bolsa Familia checks come in), they make personal calls selling door to door. Nestlé allows purchases on credit, allowing a month's time to make payment. Many women believe that the snack foods are nutritious, packed with vitamins, and their children eat them because they like the taste. The snack foods contribute to not only obesity but also malnutrition. This is tragic for the individual and the society—because it diminishes human intellectual and physical capital—and the economic productivity of the society as a whole.

DISCRIMINATION IN HEALTH CARE

Indigenous peoples suffer discrimination in every institutional sphere—health, education, political representation, and the economy. Infant mortality is a sensitive measure of overall health. It reflects maternal health and nutrition as well as access to health care. As reflected in WHO data, within countries' infant mortality rates of indigenous people are considerably higher than for the countries in general (Figure 4.5). Other revealing health measures include these facts:

- Suicide rates among Inuit youths in Canada are among the highest in the world.

- The diabetes rate among Aboriginal and Torres Strait Islanders in some Australian regions is 26 percent, six times higher than the general population.

- More than 60 percent of childbirths among ethnic minorities in Vietnam take place without prenatal care—twice the rate of Kinh, the ethnic majority.

- Poor sanitation and lack of safe water are many times higher for the ethnic Twa than for the general population. (WHO 2007)

As China has developed, there have been improvements in education, health, and many aspects of life chances. Health indicators in nine provinces show that the improvements have not been consistent between Han and minority ethnic groups. Since 1989, the health and nutrition gap between Han and minority group preschoolers has increased drastically. The gaps experienced by school-aged children and adults also have increased significantly (Ouyang and Pinstrup-Andersen 2012). Higher infant and maternal mortality rates and lower life expectancy are also documented among minorities in Yunnan Province, and minorities are more vulnerable to HIV/AIDS (Myers, Gao, and Cruz 2013).

A CLOSER LOOK
HEALTH DISCRIMINATION MEASURED BY INFANT MORTALITY RATES

In each of these countries, the infant mortality rate is significantly higher than that of the population in general. The differences in Australia, Canada, and New Zealand might look slight, but they are higher by 20 percent or more for indigenous groups.

FIGURE 4.5   Infant Mortality by Indigenous Groups

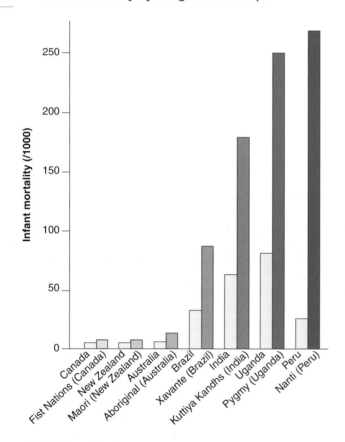

Source: Stephens et al. (2006). Reproduced with permission.

ANOMIE IN THE 21st CENTURY: MENTAL HEALTH CONCERNS

There is a global mental health crisis. Depression is the single largest contributor to global disability, account-ing for 7.5 percent of years lived with disability. Anxiety disorders are the sixth largest, accounting for 3.4 percent (WHO 2017c). Suicide is in the top 20 causes of death at 1.5 percent worldwide in 2015. In the Eastern Mediter-ranean region, 12-month prevalence of mental illness ranges from 11 to 40 percent, with the highest rates being in the higher-income countries of that grouping (Charara et al. 2017).

Mental disorders are diagnosable diseases. Some mental illnesses have biological roots that are independent of social environment or that may make a person more vulnerable to the social environmental stressors. A mental illness may be directly related to social and economic stressors—whether unemployment, poverty, traumatic events, marginalization, harassment, or bullying—particularly in the case of children or teens. Mental illness in combination with alienation and anomie—lack of a supportive social structure and culture—can contribute to suicide.

The Canaries in the Coal Mine: Deaths of Despair

The United States has never had the best health care ratings. Western Europe and Japan, among others, have consistently better life expectancies and infant and child mortality rates. This has been largely a function of inequality in the U.S. health care system and society generally. However, as in other countries, these measures of health had been improving—until recently.

In the United States, the mortality rates for non-Hispanic white men and women without a college education rose in all five-year age-groups from ages 25 through 64. Whereas in 1999, mortality for white non-Hispanics with only a high school degree was 30 percent lower than for blacks, in 2015 it was 30 percent higher. The gap between non-Hispanic whites and blacks, with high school or less than high school, closed significantly due to a decrease in black mortality rates and an increase in white mortality rates (Case and Deaton 2017).

Drug overdoses, alcohol-related deaths, and suicide rates, increasing with each birth cohort after 1945, account for the rise in mortality. These are "deaths of despair." Deaths of despair began their rise during the 1990s, but their increase was offset by decreases in other causes of mortality. As the decline in mortality from other causes slowed, continuing increases in deaths of despair increased the overall mortality rates, offsetting decreases for children and the elderly and from cancer and heart disease. Life expectancy at birth declined from 2013 to 2014, and overall life expectancy declined from 2014 to 2015. In other wealthy countries, mortality continued to decline (Case and Deaton 2017).

White non-Hispanics in the United States with a high school education or less are the "canaries in the coal mine." Not easily explained by objective trends in income and unemployment, subjective feelings of hope or hopelessness appear to be the best explanation. Working-class whites experienced a long and steady deterioration in their job opportunities beginning in the early 1970s.

Along with other changes in society—fewer and failing marriages, fewer prospects for their children, declines in membership in religious and voluntary organizations—people have fewer secure social supports and structure. If people succeed—and success in all of these areas is more likely with education—it is fine. But if it doesn't work out, lack of direction and lack of supportive structure and ties play out as in Durkheim's (1897/1966) famous study *Suicide*. When meaning is drained from life, deaths of despair increase (Case and Deaton 2017).

The United States is not alone in deaths of despair, although such deaths are not yet called that in other countries. Alcohol use as a cause of death and disability rose from eighth place in 1990 to fifth place in 2010 (WHO 2014). Globally, there were 3.3 million deaths, 5.9 percent, attributed to alcohol in 2012. The highest levels of morbidity and mortality are in the European region, with the large portion being in Eastern European countries (WHO 2014).

Suicide is also increasing globally—up 60 percent overall in four decades (WHO 2015b). The European region had the highest rate of suicide in 2015, again dominated by Eastern Europe. The highest rates globally are among men in the low- and middle-income countries, accounting for 78 percent of suicide. High-income countries as a whole have the next highest rate at 442 per 100,000 (WHO 2017c).

Suicide and mental illnesses are related—depression and alcoholism in particular. Most people with mental illness do not commit or attempt suicide, and not all suicides or suicide attempts are related to mental illness. Depression or another mental illness may be a proximate cause of suicide; the cause of the mental illness—whether biological or social, in combination with the lack of social or cultural supports—would be the root cause. As with other social problems, treating individuals, in this case for depression, is not enough of an answer. Finding the root causes of the high rates in the social systems and correcting those is.

As inequality in societies increases and people recognize, at least tacitly, that their lives are not improving, deaths of despair may claim more lives if progress for minorities stalls. Whites in the United States of lower education and socioeconomic status are a warning—a harbinger of trends that may move vertically across countries where inequality is increasing.

Teens and Adolescent Vulnerability

Suicide and accidental death from self-harm was the third leading cause of death globally for adolescents aged 10 to 19 years. In Europe, suicide is the second leading cause of death among adolescents and young adults aged 15 to 35 years; in Sweden and Korea, it is the leading cause (Choi and Kim 2015; Werbart Törnblom, Werbart, and Rydelius 2015). In England, suicide nearly doubled among university students from 2007 to 2017 (Marsh 2017). As with adult suicides, the rates are particularly stark for Eastern European adolescents aged 15 to 19 years, whose rate is 19 or 20 suicides per 100,000 in comparison with Organisation for Economic Cooperation and Development (OECD) countries' average rate of about 7 percent.

Gender Intergenerational and Gender Conflicts

Almost universally, males are more likely to commit suicide than females, and females are more likely to *attempt* suicide. Males are likely to use more violent, and thus more lethal, means or to be under the influence of alcohol, resulting in their greater completed suicide rate. Among adolescents, the male to female suicide completion ratio is 2.6:1. However, in countries such as China and India, female rates are higher than male rates, particularly in rural areas; the rate is 1.6:1 in China (McLoughlin, Gould, and Malone 2015), and it is 2.6:1 in parts of India (Radhakrishnan and Andrade 2012). In these societies, as egalitarian norms are growing, so are feelings of suppression and helplessness among females related to their low status within societies that are still very patriarchal. The rapidity of change in such societies leaves some females are caught between the older traditional paternalistic values and modern egalitarian values. The abundance of pesticides in these countries and their ease of use in suicide also contribute to the female suicide success rate (McLoughlin et al. 2015).

Indigenous Populations

A variety of studies in diverse countries—New Zealand, Canada, the United States, Ireland, and Australia—report that indigenous youths are much more likely (up to 30 times) to die from suicide than their peers. Causation is both historic and personal. Historical "transgenerational trauma," loss of land and culture, diminished family functioning, exclusion from the mainstream, unequal education, cultural clashes with parents, and economic hardship all play a role. Such life circumstances bring on greater prevalence of substance abuse, mental illness, and suicide (McLoughlin et al. 2015).

Bullying

Developmental psychology has long reported that peer relations, being accepted and part of the peer group, are important to identity development of the adolescent and carry tremendous meaning. In studies from very diverse countries, bullying, both cyber and in person, exacerbates depression and leads to increased suicidal ideation and suicide (McLoughlin et al. 2015). In some cases, bullying and other victimizations produced shame for failing to live up to one's own or another's expectations or for blaming one's self for abuse. Whatever the dilemma, the individual youths felt alone. Although they may have asked for help, they did not get the help they needed (Werbart Törnblom et al. 2015).

Low self-esteem and depressed moods can lead to health-damaging and life-threatening behaviors such as substance use, problem drinking, and eating disorders. Low self-esteem, associated with a stressful environment, increased in importance as a correlate of adolescent suicide from 1984 to 2007 as bullying became an increasingly salient social issue (Kokkevi et al. 2011).

The iGeneration

Has the smartphone created a mental health crisis among teens? Twenge (2017) called this generation, born between 1995 and 2007, the "iGen"—not only because these individuals grew up with social media, in particular the iPhone or smartphone, but also because it is shaping their lives.

In the United States, the amount of time teens spent in face-to-face social activities decreased rapidly, coinciding with the increasing use of cell phones and increasing unhappiness. While there may be many sources of unhappiness—uncertain economic futures and the high cost of college—use of social media and decreasing social activities appear to have independent effects.

One of the mechanisms is increasing loneliness. Teens "hang out" with friends less, date less, drive less, even have sex less than their counterparts as recently as the 1990s. Teens are spending more time alone in their rooms and on social media. When they do go out with friends, they remain active on social media. They announce their activities, however mundane, over multiple forms of social media, posting pictures of themselves with one another. This makes those not included in the event—however short it may be and regardless if there were 2 or 20 people—feel left out. Not receiving affirmation of one's online posts also brings angst to teenagers (Twenge 2017). Social media also provide an outlet for bullying and make bullying easier and a potential round-the-clock, seven-days-a-week opportunity to bully others.

Teens are losing sleep. Three or more hours a day on electronic devices increases the likelihood of less than seven hours of sleep each night. This alone compromises their well-being. It is related to weight gain, high blood pressure, depressed immune system function, compromised reasoning, depression, and anxiety. Spending all this time online isn't even making teens happy or even making them think that they are happy. More time on screens is associated with more self-reported unhappiness. More face-to-face interaction is associated with more happiness (Twenge 2017).

Many of the correlates of adolescent suicide reflect underlying problems of anomie, of not fitting in, and of not seeing a way forward. While these are social issues, they give rise to mental illness. Mental health treatment is necessary, and in many areas—outside of Europe and the Americas—there were no mental health services for children and adolescents in place (McLoughlin et al. 2015).

Trauma-Induced Stressors

Extreme events in the life of an individual, such as homelessness, abuse, and personal violation, produce post-traumatic stress, depression, anxiety, and other forms of mental illness. Disasters, such as hurricanes, wars, floods, refugee flight, and terrorism, affect millions of people every year and generate a severe burden of disease, mental as well as physical.

Invisible Wounds of War (Tanielian and Jaycox 2008) is an extensive study documenting that among soldiers engaged in the post-9/11 wars, the mental wounds, brain injury, post-traumatic stress, and depression were as severe as, or more severe than, the physical injuries. For many, the effects of trauma last a lifetime. Violent conflict and war leave civilians with long-lasting psychological trauma. Life in refugee camps, repeated victimizations, loss of family, dislocation, and disruption of community all bear psychological costs.

A meta-analysis of 17 studies on the aftermath of extreme weather events in developing countries revealed mental disease in an average of 30 to 40 percent of the populations affected in the first year. After two years, morbidity declined, but in one example, among students living in the city most devastated by 1998 flooding in Nicaragua, prevalence ranged from 2.6 percent in the mildest area to 90 percent in more affected areas (Rataj, Kunzweiler, and Garthus-Niegel 2016).

As such events increase in number, severity, and populations affected, planning for them needs to include the long-term psychological consequences. Enhancing resilience is a way to "pre-plan" to mitigate psychological trauma after disaster events. The risk for trauma following disasters is closely associated with fear of the disasters. One example, in the case of earthquakes, is earthquake simulation treatment. Teaching only what to do during an earthquake simulation is not enough; addressing and overcoming the fear and distress as well can mitigate post-event trauma. Preparedness involves all the same organizations and agencies that would be involved post-disaster—from primary and secondary health providers, to employers, to media and all the governmental and non-governmental agencies involved in relief. The primary goal is for community outreach to disseminate knowledge—informing people of how people are affected by trauma and the best ways to deal with trauma stress—as widely as possible. Rather than people feeling powerless, programs to disseminate materials and information equip people to feel more in control and enhance resilience. Appropriate pre-disaster preparation for many can be accomplished through self-care (Başoğlu and Şalcioğlu 2011).

As with pre-disaster care, some people may receive enough benefit from self-care post-disaster. Again, wide dissemination of materials and information is essential. Post-disaster screening is necessary to identify those who need additional outreach. Because trauma from disaster may last for years, periodic screening needs to continue. Where extreme events are common, pre- and post-disaster periods may be one and the same.

Building pre-disaster resilience is important for both developing and developed countries. Although developed countries might not suffer the same extent of visible physical damage, the mental health consequences, especially as disasters are increasing in intensity, are significant. Successful models used pre- and post-disaster in developing and developed countries are likely to be different. The general principles are the same, however—recognize the long-term consequences of trauma, build resilience and capacity for self-care pre- and post-disaster, identify victims who need more intensive treatment, and provide long-term care and periodic reassessment.

Mental Health and Discrimination

As with other minorities, indigenous people are likely to have significantly poorer mental health as well. Australian Aboriginal adults suffer psychological distress at a rate 50 to 300 percent higher than that of non-indigenous adults. While adolescents did not demonstrate more psychological problems than their non-indigenous peers, they did experience significantly more behavioral problems (Jorm et al. 2012). A study of Māori in New Zealand (Harris et al. 2006) documented the association between racism and mental health. First, the authors found evidence of significant differences in racial discrimination expressed toward Māori and ethnic European (non-indigenous, non-minority) groups. Measures of discrimination were verbal and physical attacks, unfair treatment, and overall number of types of discrimination experienced. As reported in Table 4.1, Māori experienced significantly more discrimination than people of European descent.

In comparing health outcomes of Māori and Europeans, researchers controlled for age and gender and found significant differences in self-rated health, low physical functioning, mental health, and cardiovascular disease. When they controlled for age, sex, and number of types of discrimination, Māori were still in poorer health, but the gap was reduced. Similarly, a reduction in inequality was found when deprivation was controlled along with age and sex. When age, sex, deprivation, and number of types of discrimination all were controlled, the gap nearly closed. These results indicate that discrimination had a deleterious impact on physical and mental health.

A CLOSER LOOK
SELF-REPORTED EXPERIENCE OF RACIAL DISCRIMINATION BY ETHNIC GROUP

Racial and ethnic minorities often report discrimination in health care. Māori in New Zealand report significantly more abuse than individuals of European descent.

TABLE 4.1   Lifetime Prevalence of Self-Reported Experience of Racial Discrimination by Ethnic Group

Type of Attack	Māori (n = 4,108)		European (n = 6,269)	
	Number	%	Number	%
Physical	284	8.5	204	3.4
Verbal	889	24.5	691	10.3
Setting of unfair treatment				
Health related	214	4.5	100	1.5
Work related	234	5.6	136	2.1
Housing related	339	9.5	49	0.7
Number of types of discrimination				
1	796	21.1	718	11.5
2	303	8.3	176	2.5
3+	116	4.5	34	0.5

Source: Adapted from Harris et al. (2006).

CONSIDER THIS
CLIMATE CHANGE AND HEALTH

Climate change presents serious threats to human security. While one threat might not necessarily be more serious than another, the threat to human health is as severe as any threat and sometimes unexpected.

The damage to the Fukushima nuclear reactor from the earthquake and tsunami that hit Japan in 2011 had ripple effects the world over. One that did not garner much attention was the price of iodine. The weather events damaged Japan's iodine-producing wells and refineries and caused a global shortage of iodine. With Japan responsible for one third of the world's iodine, the price tripled. Cambodia, dependent on imported iodine (an essential nutrient), could not afford it. Cambodia's diet enrichment programs stopped using iodized salt. A 2014 sampling of iodine levels in children showed a 30 percent drop from 2011. Children's brain development in Cambodia is at risk unless iodine is restored to their diets (McNeil 2017).

Both El Niño and La Niña weather events are expected to increase in frequency and intensity with climate change. The effects of each vary depending on the specific location. El Niño has increased the probability of cholera, malaria, and dengue fever. La Niña has been associated with chikungunya, dengue, yellow fever, Zika, and influenza epidemics. Climate change is probably one of the key drivers in the increases in outbreaks of infectious vector-borne and airborne diseases (Flahault, Ruiz de Castaneda, and Bolon 2016). The risk of mosquito-borne diseases, including Zika, is increasing. Since 1980, the mosquito season in many of the 76 major cities in the United States increased by a month to a month and a half. In at least 20 major cities, there are now at least 200 days of mosquito season. One bright spot is that in a few of the hottest southern cities, the season is shorter due to the excessive heat (Climate Central 2016).

INFECTIOUS OUTBREAK, EPIDEMIC, PANDEMIC

Urbanization, violent conflict, travel, trade, climate change, limited health care—each heightens risk of infectious outbreak. Globalization and its effects facilitate the spread of infectious pathogens that would have remained localized and had less impact, as discussed above. Time and distance are no longer obstacles to infections. They spread quickly and over broad geographic ranges.

Many infectious diseases have multiple hosts—humans and animals. Many have multiple modes of transmission—direct contact and indirect contact through a live vector, air, water, soil, or food. Old diseases are resurging, and new ones are regularly discovered. From just 1970 to 2007, 1,420 new pathogens were discovered. Not all infect humans, but if they mutate quickly, as have others before them, they may eventually jump to human hosts or develop new means of transmission.

Measles, for example, remains a leading cause of death globally, killing 15 people every hour, 134,200 in 2015—primarily in the developing world. Although that is still far too many, as recently as 1980 it killed 2.6 million people a year.

Measles can be eradicated. In the early 1960s, nearly all children had measles before they were 15 years old. In the United States, 3 to 4 million people were infected with measles every year. In the year the measles vaccine became available, 1963, 400 to 500 people died, 4,800 were hospitalized, and 4,000 developed encephalitis. With a public health campaign to vaccinate infants and update vaccines with "boosters," measles was declared eliminated in the United States in 2000—an achievement of modern medicine (Centers for Disease Control and Prevention [CDC] 2017). Similar results were achieved in other developed nations.

Now, it is making a comeback. Fearing harm from the vaccine, harm that is disputed by experts, some people stopped vaccinating their children. Unvaccinated people can carry measles with them, and just one person can infect hundreds—primarily others not vaccinated. Every year since 2008, the United States experienced an outbreak of measles. In 2014, 667 people in 27 states came down with measles. In the first four months of 2017, 61 people caught it (CDC 2017). The United Kingdom also experienced a sharp rise from 2001, reporting 2,016 cases in 2012 and 1,287 in 2013. Throughout the European Union, 10,271 cases were reported in 2013. The extent of the annual figures shows how measles can move through

CONSIDER THIS
TOURISM, TRAVEL, AND BATS!

Rabies is the bat-borne disease that most of us are familiar with, but bats—for all the good that they do—carry a much higher risk of disease. Histoplasmosis, like rabies, is found all over the world. Other diseases have been more location specific, but globalization may bring them closer to home for many people.

Marburg hemorrhagic fever is bat borne and Ebola, its cousin, is suspected to be. Nipah (which causes encephalitis), Hendra virus, and coronaviruses (related to severe acute respiratory syndrome [SARS]) all are bat related. Closer relations between humans and "the wild,"

via tourism, and travel can spread any of them beyond their natural habitats.

The rainforests of Borneo are among the most beautiful places on the earth. Tourists from all over the world visit to see the exotic plant and animal life. Gomantong Cave is one of the major attractions. Deep in the forest, it is home to swiftlet birds, millions of bats that keep the forests pollinated, and cockroaches that feed on the bat guano that covers every surface. Hidden in the bat guano and the neighboring forests, researchers found 48 new viruses, including one in the guano related to SARS (Doucleff and Greenhalgh 2017).

---

a population where many are not vaccinated (Oxford Vaccination Group 2017).

Humans are the only host for the virus, so even though it is highly contagious—passed by contact and through the air—it can be virtually eliminated within a population that is adequately vaccinated against it. Mass immunizations in countries where there are high death rates, primarily in the developing world, can bring it under control for about U.S. $1 per child immunization. Approximately 85 percent of children received one dose of vaccination before their first birthday in 2016. Two vaccinations are necessary to ensure immunity. Eradication of measles requires elimination in every country.

Infections Spread From Animals to Humans: Zoonotic Disease

The Bubonic Plague devastated much of Asia and Europe in the 14th century. While its precise geographic origin is subject to debate, it traveled along Silk Road trade routes and via military operations, killing millions in its path through China, India, Central Asia, on to the Middle East, Iran, and Europe. Bubonic Plague is carried by rats and small mammals. Fleas are the usual vector into the human population. If it develops in humans into pneumonic plague, it can be transmitted person to person. Estimates of the death toll vary, but it claimed somewhere from 50 to 75 million victims. Similarly, movements of the troops as World War I was winding down facilitated the spread of the Spanish (swine) flu or H1N1. Once in a human population, it is highly contagious. The 1918 pandemic

killed an estimated 20 to 50 million people. Diseases that originate in animal infections are zoonoses.[3] While plague and swine flu do not kill as many people today, both of them and other deadly diseases that move from animals to humans continue in the 21st century.

The older zoonoses, such as cow pox, chicken pox, and swine flu, are still problematic, but more worrisome are new zoonoses. Increasing contact between humans and wilderness, increasing meat in people's diets, and the ability of pathogens to adapt quickly make the emergence of new zoonotic disease unpredictable. More infectious diseases are jumping cross species from one animal to another, including to humans. About 75 percent of new infectious diseases are zoonoses, in comparison with about 60 percent of previously known infectious diseases (CDC 2016b). Many—"mad cow" disease, HIV, Ebola, avian flu, and SARS—have captured headlines, spreading justly founded fears of epidemics or pandemics. Contemporary lifestyles practically ensure that they can spread around the world in a day. When infectious microbes move into a new environment, whether across the country or across the world, or to a human host from an animal, lack of immunities heightens the risk that outbreak will become a local epidemic or global epidemic (pandemic).

Most epidemic diseases began as zoonotic diseases. The deadliest contemporary virus is HIV, which started as a zoonosis. Different strains originated in chimpanzees, monkeys, and other primates, hosts to Simian immunodeficiency virus. Several strains moved to the human population, probably through hunting and the consumption of "bushmeat." It evolved quickly to human-only variants.

CONSIDER THIS
VECTOR-BORNE DISEASES

More than 1 billion illnesses and 1 million deaths every year, 17 percent of infectious disease, result from vector-borne diseases. Most vectors transmit disease by ingesting pathogens during a blood meal and then injecting them into the host of their next meal.

Ticks, fleas, some types of flies, and mosquitos are common vectors. The diseases they carry are spread-ing unpredictably to continents where they had been unknown. Some spread disease from animals to humans, and others spread from one human to another. Controlling the vectors that transmit disease is critical to stopping an outbreak from becoming an epidemic or pandemic. Being aware and being alert are the best ways in which to protect yourself and your community.

A CLOSER LOOK
SPREAD OF HIV AND AIDS

HIV/AIDS has been the worst epidemic of the 20th and 21st centuries to date. Although education has reduced its spread, there are still hundreds of thousands of documented cases each year. The estimated annual number of new HIV infections in 2016 was 39 percent lower than in 2000.

FIGURE 4.6   Number of People Newly Infected With HIV

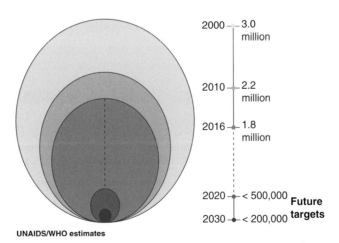

UNAIDS/WHO estimates

2000	3.0 million
2010	2.2 million
2016	1.8 million
2020	< 500,000 **Future**
2030	< 200,000 **targets**

Source: World Health Organization Global Health Observatory Data.

(Continued)

(Continued)

FIGURE 4.7   Migration of HIV Infections

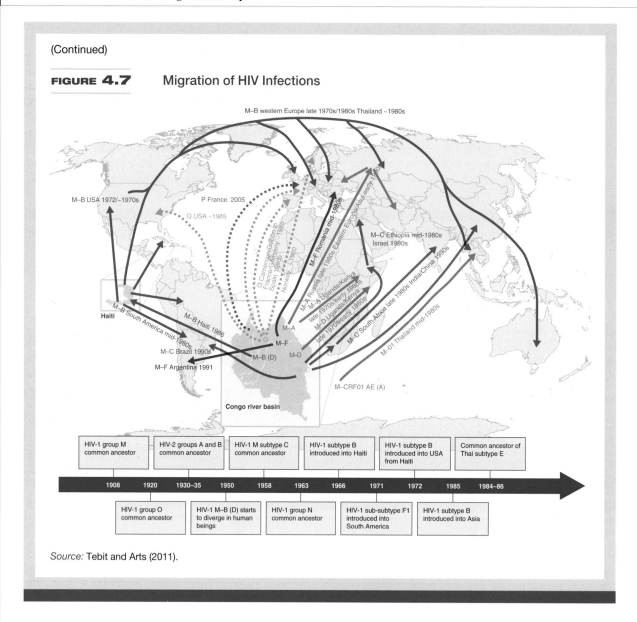

Source: Tebit and Arts (2011).

First noted in Cameroon, it traveled to Kinshasa, a global hub, in the 1920s and spread slowly at first, reaching Brazzaville in 1937—120 miles away. HIV strains moved with their human hosts along many paths—following migrants from small villages in the forests of the Congo river basin into cities, moving with refugees and through the sex trade out of conflict regions. As it branched out, it traveled more rapidly; by 2015, 70 million people were infected and 35 million had died. There are still new infections yearly, although prevention education has reduced their number (Figures 4.6 and 4.7).

The spread of pandemics to the developed world in the 21st century came as a surprise. Even experts believed that advanced health care systems and high standards of living would prevent the pathogens that wreaked havoc in Africa and Asia from spreading to wealthy nations.

West Nile virus arrived in metropolitan New York City in 1999 and within three years had spread to 44 states (Sejvar 2003). Two more pathogens never before seen in the United States appeared in 2003: SARS and monkey pox.

SARS likely spread from contact with infected animals—brought into human contact through the wild animal trade—and now through person-to-person contact, including coughs and sneezes. One man reportedly brought it from China to Hong Kong, from where it spread globally. Within a year, it infected more than 8,000 people and caused 774 deaths (Alam and Hammerschlag 2004). In 2009, H1N1 spread rapidly to all corners of the globe, killing from 123,000 to 203,000 in eight months from April 1 to December 31 (Simonsen et al. 2013).

Some zoonotic diseases remain relatively contained. Monkey pox is carried by Gambian rats but can infect other rodents and mammals (including monkeys). Handling these animals or consuming infected meat is the primary mode of transfer to humans. In the case of the United States, rats transported or caged along with prairie dogs infected them. Person-to-person transmission is possible with close contact with infected fluids; however, person-to-person transmission is not enough to sustain it in a population. It remains a rare disease (WHO 2016a).

Vector-Borne Diseases

The *Aedes aegypti* mosquito is responsible for spreading Zika and other viruses such as dengue and chikungunya. Perhaps due to immunity in Africa and Asia, the subtlety of its symptoms, or its symptomatic similarity to other viruses, only 14 cases of Zika in humans were detected from the first in 1952 until 2007. Many cases undoubtedly went unnoticed.

Zika took the world by surprise when it began to spread out of Africa and Asia. From 2007 to 2016, Zika spread to 62 countries and territories, becoming a global health state of emergency. The first significant outbreak was on Yap Island in the Pacific Islands in 2013, followed by four more outbreaks in 2013 and 2014. In French Polynesia, 10,000 cases were registered. It was then that the connection to birth defects was first suspected. The real danger is during pregnancy. It can be passed from a pregnant woman to her fetus and can cause birth defects, including microencephaly and brain and eye abnormalities. It can also trigger Guillain–Barré syndrome.

Outbreak reached the Americas, primarily South and Central America, in 2015, quickly turning Zika into a pandemic. Theoretically, Zika may be transmitted through saliva, but this is very improbable. Sexual transmission is also possible. An American working in Senegal in 2008 brought it home and infected his wife in the first documented sexually transmitted case. There have been other sexually transmitted cases, but the mosquito bite is the usual mode of transmission.

Climate change, urbanization, and poverty all accelerated the spread of Zika. Rising temperatures provide a much longer breeding season for mosquitos. As climate change increases temperatures, habitats conducive to mosquito breeding intensify. Researchers also noted that the areas in Brazil hard hit by El Niño were also hard hit by Zika. During droughts and anytime the water supply is insecure or remote, people store water. This is the mosquitos' breeding ground (Upton 2016).

SPECIAL SECTION

Children at Risk at Work

Children are both the source of hope for a better global future and the most vulnerable global citizens. While the global economy has grown, many children in both rich and poor societies have been left behind by global progress and progress in their countries. Many do not have a fair chance at life simply for being born in the wrong place and at the wrong time. This not only limits the fortunes of individual children deprived of the opportunity to thrive but also limits the health of societies and the world.

When you were 5 years old, you were probably enrolled in kindergarten or preschool. You may have a lot of good memories of playing with friends and family. This is our hope for all children. But for millions of children as young as 5 years, toiling in a field, baking bricks over an open oven, or shining shoes or trinkets is a daily reality. There is no time for school or friends.

CONSIDER THIS
WHAT ARE HER LIFE CHANCES?

We hear a lot about the dangers of working in a mine. Is this how you picture a miner? This young girl is one of millions of children who work in very dangerous conditions with short- and long-term health consequences.

PHOTO 4.1 Young miner.

Antonio Rosa. Reproduced with permission.

Children at the "bottom of the pyramid" bear special attention, not only because they are unwitting victims of forces far beyond their control, not only because they cannot protect themselves, and not only because it is inhumane. If we are ever to eliminate the worst forms of poverty and the social problems that go with it, we must improve the lives of children.

More than 264 million children aged 5 to 17 years are employed. About 168 million children, 11 percent of the child population as a whole, are classified as child laborers. The label "child labor" implies that the conditions of work do not meet permissible conditions in type of work, hours worked, or age of the child. About half of the child laborers, some 85 million, are engaged in hazardous work—work deemed physically, socially, or morally dangerous (International Labour Organization–International Programme on the Elimination of Child Labor [ILO–IPECL] 2013). Although the proportion of child laborers is highest in the poorest countries at 22.5 percent, lower middle-income countries have the greatest number of child laborers, more than 900,000 (ILO–IPECL 2013).

Many are startlingly young, with 44 percent of child laborers being only 5 to 11 years old. The older groups, 12 to 14 and 15 to 17 years, each comprise about 28 percent of child laborers (ILO–IPECL 2013). Boys in child labor outnumber girls—approximately 100 million boys to 68 million girls (ILO–IPECL 2013). These numbers give us an idea of the enormity of child labor, but even these estimates are probably low because many children are not counted yet work long hours in hazardous conditions (Table 4.2).

A CLOSER LOOK
CHILDREN AT WORK

Nearly 300 million children are employed. Many, nearly 168 million, are classified as child laborers, and more than 85 million are in hazardous work conditions, the most life-threatening and dangerous work for anyone.

TABLE 4.2   Children in Employment, Child Labor, and Hazardous Work, 5–17 Years Old, 2000–2012

	Children in Employment		Child Labor		Hazardous Work	
	('000)	%	('000)	%	('000)	%
2000	351,900	23.0	245,500	16.0	170,500	11.1
2004	322,729	20.6	222,294	14.2	128,381	8.2
2008	305,669	19.3	215,209	13.6	115,314	7.3
2012	264,427	16.7	167,956	10.6	85,344	5.4

Source: Marking progress against child labour – Global estimates and trends 2000–2012/International Labour Office, International Programme on the Elimination of Child Labour (IPEC) – Geneva: ILO, 2013.

The life of a child laborer or a child working in hazardous conditions is difficult for many of us to imagine. It includes work underground and underwater in mines, at dangerous heights, with dangerous machinery, and exposed to hazardous substances. Children, at the base of the supply chain of Apple and other electronics companies, dig tin ore out of mines with their bare hands, ever fearful of landslides but unaware of the toxins that threaten them.

The greatest number of child laborers, 98 million, work in agriculture. While farm work might conjure visions of an idyllic farm setting, that image is far from reality. Life in the agricultural sector is neither more humane nor less dangerous than other forms of child labor. A Human Rights Watch (HRW 2002) study based on interviews with children describes the inhumane conditions of child labor in agriculture despite being in violation of international treaties and covenants. The majority of children on farms work 9 to 13 hours a day, every day. They are regularly exposed to pesticides. Some children are sprayed right along with the crops as they work in the fields. Children, because they are still developing and have smaller body mass, are more vulnerable to pesticide toxicity than adults. Many of the pesticides are considered highly hazardous by the WHO. Children experience symptoms of toxin exposure—headaches, rash, diarrhea, and convulsions in the short run. Over time, they may experience cancer, brain damage, infertility, birth defects, coma, and death.

Agricultural laborers, particularly children, suffer high rates of injury. They have been crushed and maimed by machinery. They suffer back injury from heavy lifting and bending over in the fields. Many lack access to clean water for drinking and hand washing. Some are forced to drink the polluted water draining from the fields into canals (HRW 2002). Abuse of agricultural workers occurs not only in poor nations but also in the wealthiest nations.

The United States and other developed countries are not immune from the ills of child labor. U.S. law allows children as young as 12 years to work in agriculture with parental approval, and there is no minimum age for working on small farms. In 2014, tobacco farms in the United States and around the world were cited by HRW for hazardous child labor practices. Aside from working 50 to 60 hours a week in extreme heat, being exposed to dangerous machines, lifting heavy loads, and climbing to heights of several stories to the tops of barns, all common in child labor, children on tobacco farms suffer from nicotine poisoning. The 141 children, aged 7 to 17 years, whom HRW interviewed complained of "nausea, vomiting, loss of appetite, headaches, dizziness,

CONSIDER THIS
WALKING DOWN THE GRAIN

It sounds innocent enough, but farming is one of the most dangerous occupations in the United States, and "walking down the grain" is one of the most dangerous jobs. It involves entering a grain silo and loosening the grain that has adhered to the sides. It takes only a few seconds to become trapped and under half a minute to become completely submerged. A 6-foot man can become engulfed in the grain in 25 seconds. Despite deaths every year related to grain entrapment, including the well-publicized deaths of two teens, aged 14 and 19 years, who died together after being hired to walk down the grain,[a] 2014 had the highest number of grain entrapments and fatalities since 2010. Children are prominent among grain entrapment

victims. Boys from 10 to 15 years of age account for 20 percent of the victims in grain transport vehicles (Pack 2015).

In 2011, the Department of Labor proposed updating child labor laws relating to agriculture. Agricultural and other groups opposed it, and it was dropped. Proposals to ban employing children under 18 years of age from working in the industry made it to the U.S. House of Representatives and U.S. Senate committees in April 2015. As of January 2016, both were still in committee. In the meantime, the tobacco industry adopted a resolution in 2014 recommending against employing children under 16 years in the industry. It does not protect 16- and 17-year-olds.

PHOTO 4.2 This worker is equipped with a safety harness. Training is not always provided, equipment is not always available, and regulations are not always followed—as in the case of child workers. Given the vast size of grain silos, it is easy to see how a person could become trapped in the grain, unable to breathe.

John Poole/NPR.

[a]For coverage of child fatalities in the grain silos, see the special reports "Buried in Grain" (National Public Radio 2013).

skin rashes, difficulty breathing, and irritation to their eyes and mouths" (HRW 2014). The possibilities of long-term brain damage and cancer are very real. Because their families need the money, children work even while sick.

A study of child workers in the United States (Rauscher et al. 2008) found that most youths are employed in service and retail. Approximately 300,000 are employed illegally in non-agricultural work. Extrapolating from their findings, they estimated that as many as 888,000 may be laboring, engaged in violation of hazardous occupation orders.

A CLOSER LOOK
CHILDREN AT WORK

These children all are in Latin America, but the world over children work dangerous jobs in agriculture, mining, brick making, and other situations where they are exposed to numerous dangers and toxins.

All photos by Antonio Rosa.

Approximately 12 million children globally labor in manufacturing. Small hands, capable of doing fine needlework, and small bodies that can fit into small spaces make children desirable in a number of industries. Factory owners exploit children as they did in the textile and other industries of Western societies at the beginning of the Industrial Revolution. In Pakistan, children labor in the carpet industry, where their small hands create beautiful, delicate, complicated patterns. This beauty comes at great cost. Children may spend 15 or more hours a day over looms. They suffer respiratory disease, damaged eyesight, and spinal injuries. Most of the children in the carpet industry are in debt bondage, needing to work off payments made to their parents. In Bangladesh, they make garments. Many children were among the 1,137 workers who died in the 2013 Rana Plaza factory collapse in Bangladesh. In India, children as young as 7 years sew soccer balls for children in richer countries to play with (Lillie 2013). As terrible as all of these are, they are not the worst forms of child labor.

Millions of children are forced into the worst forms of child labor—children forced to engage in criminal activity, children exploited for prostitution and pornography, and children as soldiers in war. It is estimated that 5.5 million children are in forced labor. There is some overlap with those counted in hazardous work, but the numbers are difficult to estimate (ILO–IPECL 2013).

Eliminating the Worst Forms of Child Labor

Many people think that boycotting products made by child labor will end the practice. The UN Global Initiative to Fight Human Trafficking (UN.GIFT), however, maintains that this will only drive child labor further underground and increase the level of exploitation. They suggest supporting policies that promote fair trade practices. A holistic approach is necessary, combining the efforts of national governments, international governmental organizations, and non-governmental organizations.

The Hague Global Child Labor Conference (2010) detailed a blueprint for eliminating the worst forms of child labor by 2016. Programs and policies will need to vary across societies, depending on their specific weaknesses. Essentials for combatting child labor are similar to those needed to combat human trafficking:

- A strong framework for regulation and enforcement, specifying what constitutes hazardous work

- Strengthening labor laws pertaining to age of employment and hazardous work

- Strengthening punishments

- Devoting more personnel for training of labor inspectors and criminal investigators

- Better enforcement of labor and criminal law

- Better coordination of government efforts

- Better data collection and analysis.

All countries need to work to rehabilitate child victims.

Child labor fell by about a third from 2000 to 2012. While this shows promise, the pace of change was too slow to meet the goal of eliminating the worst forms of child labor by 2016 and all child labor by 2030. The 2015 Millennium Development Goals report called attention to the large disparities in life chances for children. It called for much more attention and intervention for children, particularly the most vulnerable: "girls, children belonging to minorities and nomadic communities, children engaged in child labour, and children living with disabilities, in conflict situations or in urban slums" (UN 2015).

Long-term improvement in quality of life chances in developing societies must begin with improving the lives of all children. Keeping children in school and out of work must be a priority. The lives of many children will be visited as we work through the chapters of this book devoted to specific problems that the world and the world's children face.

How do children fare where you live? Do you know how many children are working in your country? Do you know how many drop out of school before they complete secondary education? Are there indigenous, ethnic, or racial groups that are more likely to have limited life chances?

CONSIDER THIS
A $3 CERVICAL CANCER CURE

Not every medical need requires a highly trained physician or nurse practitioner. Even a disease as life threatening as cervical cancer can be prevented with a simple procedure administered by a nurse.

But it needs to be caught early. A swabbing with vinegar identifies precancerous lesions immediately by turning them white. Lesions can then be frozen and removed with a simple tool, a cryoprobe. This in-office procedure can save hundreds of thousands of lives and can be conducted by trained nurses.

MAKING HEALTH CARE WORK

The global health regime is shifting emphasis from a reactive posture emphasizing disease and disaster to a proactive posture promoting health and wellness. Finding solutions to some of our health care problems is a matter of behavioral change for some and political will for others.

Providing all people with their best chance at developing their potential for good health requires effort by and partnerships among governments, the private sector, and civil society.

Improving health outcomes requires a coordinated global strategy for tackling non-communicable as well as infectious diseases in all corners of the globe. Below is a sampling of the steps needed to ensure better health outcomes and some of the programs and ideas implemented to realize them.

Delivering Health Care in Remote Areas

In underdeveloped countries or neighborhoods in rich countries, from basic to more advanced, many people have little access to health care. The WHO (2013) anticipates a global shortage of 12.9 million health care practitioners by 2035—up from a shortage of 7.9 million in 2013. The increases in communicable diseases, aging of the health care force, attractions of better-paying jobs, and migration of health care workers to more desirable areas create global imbalances, leaving people at risk.

"Brain drain" is not just a phenomenon of developing nations. Whether in developed or developing countries, remote areas are underserved, while many wealthy urban areas have more physicians and specialists than necessary. In the United States, for example, one might not expect that there is a health care shortage. However, in May 2017, the federal government designated thousands of areas of the country with health care shortages—6,789 in primary care, 4,720 in mental health care, and 5,584 in dental care (Health Resources and Service Administration 2017).

Access to quality health care does not need to mean a physician for every service. Community engagement interventions are effective in improving health outcomes. "Frontline" community health workers include midwives, peer counselors, health educators, and nursing aides as well as registered nurses, physician assistants, and nurse practitioners. Whether in remote areas or urban slums, community health workers can deliver quality care and preventive medicine in the community where they live.

A series of randomized trials of community-based interventions for maternal and neonatal health produced dramatic results. The trials were held in Africa, Asia, and Europe. Health care workers in the trials included outreach workers, lay health workers, community midwives, community and village health workers, and trained birth attendants. Among other results, neonatal deaths were reduced by 24 percent and maternal illness by 25 percent. These promising results show the potential of training community people at a variety of skill levels to improve community health (Dye et al. 2013).

This level of community engagement is empowering, for individuals and the community. To improve health outcomes, community engagement must involve the community in all levels of decision making from planning, to delivering, to governance.

A CLOSER LOOK
COMMUNITY HEALTH

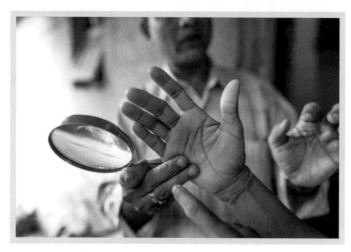

PHOTO 4.8 Community engagement programs to combat NTDs show great promise, reaching more than a billion people with vaccines and treatment.

Getty Images/Bloomberg.

PHOTO 4.9 Using community health workers enables aid organizations to reach many more people. Rebati in India vaccinates babies and children for polio and other life-threatening illnesses.

Pippa Ranger, Innovation Advisor, DFID/CC BY-SA 2.0.

Making Headway With Neglected Tropical Disease

Many parasitic and bacterial diseases that have been eliminated in most of the developed world continue to plague conflict areas and the poorest and most marginalized regions of the world. These are the "neglected tropical diseases" (NTDs). More than 1.5 billion people globally suffer from one or more of these diseases. The CDC lists 17 NTDs, 6 of which are fairly common.[4] Nearly every country in Africa, Central and South America, and South Asia has at least one NTD. These diseases cause physical and developmental disabilities, including blindness, stunting, anemia, and disfigurement. Many can be controlled through safe and efficient treatments (U.S. Agency for International Development [USAID] 2017).

In Bangladesh, the NTD program employs novel techniques to get the message and cure out. The "Little Doctor" program is one of them. Using children as peer educators, the entire primary school system is used to deliver basic public health initiatives. Hygiene, nutrition, sanitation, and the importance of deworming to combat soil-transmitted helminths (STHs) all are covered. The program accomplished an increase of mass treatment of 3 million schoolchildren for STHs in just three years.

The USAID (2017) NTD program works in countries across sub-Saharan Africa, Latin America, the Caribbean, and Asia. From 2007 to 2016, the program delivered 2 billion treatments to 935 million people. As a result, millions live free of one or more of the diseases. As with other health programs, working at the local level with community people in education, monitoring, and treatment proved to be essential in all of the programs' successes.

Transferring Knowledge to Action on the Ground

Managing the largely unpredictable health emergencies of the 21st century means getting knowledge to thousands, if not hundreds of thousands, of health care workers where they are, on the ground. In the early days of the Ebola outbreak, more than 800 health care workers died from the infection. In response, WHO's Health Emergencies Programme developed "OpenWHO," an online platform accessible to 250,000 users at a time. It enables community health care workers to respond quickly to infectious disease outbreaks. Information packs that contain everything about a disease are readily accessible any time of any day, preventing such a tragedy from happening again.

Infrastructure: A Necessity

Prevention is an important component of delivering health care. Access to good health requires clean water, sanitation, and electricity for refrigeration. Many remote areas and urban slums lack one or all of these. Urbanization shows no signs of slowing. Much of this growth will be in the developing world. Africa and Asia house 90 percent of the world's rural population, and they are urbanizing at the world's fastest pace. By 2050, Africa will be 56 percent urban and Asia will be 64 percent urban (UN 2014). Infrastructure in urban areas of the developing world is already overwhelmed. Without significant infrastructure improvements in electricity, water, and sanitation, the outlook for public health is bleak.

The Importance of Vaccines

Vaccines may have saved more lives and added more quality life years across the globe than antibiotics. There are vaccines available for about 25 diseases, many of which are potentially deadly. From 2000 to 2015, the measles vaccine alone saved 17.1 million lives, but progress toward new vaccines and increased vaccination stagnated from 2010 to 2015 (WHO 2015a). One in five children still do not receive necessary immunizations. Vaccination efforts must increase to include everyone and expand to include more emergent diseases.

A disease can be eliminated regionally by saturation level vaccination. Smallpox is the only disease eradicated. Eradication requires elimination everywhere. Measles is close to elimination in four of six WHO regions. Close to elimination, in the case of measles, means that more than 95 percent of a population has had a two-dose vaccination regimen. To be close to elimination, a disease does not occur indigenously and an importation does not spread significantly. A combined measles, mumps, and rubella vaccine regimen could potentially eradicate all three (Andre et al. 2008).

Vaccines have reduced the incidence of polio by 99 percent since 1988, yet it remains endemic in 3 countries—Afghanistan, Nigeria, and Pakistan—and 18 more countries are at risk. Eliminating polio and ensuring that it does not spread means reaching all children or a significant enough percentage of them to protect everyone from outbreak or epidemic (WHO 2017a). Similarly, diseases such as diphtheria, pertussis, and tetanus (DPT) are now rare in developed countries, due to routine vaccination regimens (often with a combined DPT vaccine), but are still threatening in developing countries.

Pertussis, for example, sickens 16 million people and kills nearly 200,000 children yearly (CDC 2016a).

In some cases, "herd protection" can be achieved with a 70 percent rate of vaccination. Hib (a type of influenza), cholera, and diarrheal diseases can be largely eliminated from a region in this way. "Source drying" is similar in that the reservoir population is targeted for vaccination to reduce the disease in the entire population. In controlling typhoid or hepatitis A, an occupational group such as food handlers may be targeted (Andre et al. 2008).

Development of new vaccines for emerging diseases is critical. So too is ensuring that everyone who needs them has access to them. Shortening the lag from the use of a new vaccine in the developed world and its introduction into developing countries is critical. In the case of pneumococcal conjugate, there was a lag of one year. This is a vast improvement over the decades it took earlier vaccines to be introduced to the developing world and even longer for them to penetrate sufficiently to eliminate diseases.

Making Superbugs: Antimicrobial Resistance

Antimicrobial[5] drugs are one of the greatest global health success stories. Antibiotic, antiviral, antifungal, and antiparastic drugs have saved countless lives and play a large part in the increase in life expectancy and healthy years of life. Increasing resistance compromises their life-saving properties. Already, this has cost lives. Globally, as many as 700,000 people die every year due to drug-resistant infections, primarily strains of malaria, HIV/AIDS, and tuberculosis. This is a global public health crisis and is likely to get much worse, killing perhaps as many as 10 million people a year if the problem of resistance is not solved (O'Neill 2016).

Ironically, the more we use antimicrobials, the less useful they become. Bacteria, fungi, viruses, and parasites adapt more quickly than our capacity to combat the diseases that they cause. Whether through genetic mutation—natural selection whereby those organisms that survive a treatment reproduce—or acquiring a gene from another microbe, microbes are adapting and preventing antimicrobials from working against them.

Bacterial resistance was evident as early as 1959, and there are virtually no antibiotics to which resistance has not been documented. While new antibiotics have been developed, progress has slowed.

Epidemiology studies show a direct relationship between antibiotic consumption and resistance. Overprescription, inappropriate prescription, and using an antimicrobial prophylactically to prevent illness in people who have been exposed or where resistance is suspected all contribute. A study of intensive care units found that 30 to 60 percent of antibiotics prescribed were inappropriate, unnecessary, or suboptimal. In the United States in 2010, the equivalent of one dose of antibiotic was prescribed for every person. In some U.S. states, there were more courses of antibiotic treatment prescribed than people in the state (Ventola 2015).

The overuse of antimicrobials in medicine is only a part of the problem. In the United States, more antibiotics are used to promote growth in animals bred for food than for medicine. When this was discontinued in Denmark, no appreciable effect on animal growth was noted. Better hygiene, vaccination, and nutrition are more effective methods of promoting growth. This same strategy can be applied to fish farming, where better conditions rather than overuse of antibiotics can produce the same results. Beekeeping, aquaculture, horticulture, ethanol production, food preservation, antifouling paints, and domestic products such as soaps and shampoos all contribute to antibiotic resistance. Antibiotics from all sources of use contaminate water supplies and coastal waters, exacerbating the problem. Antibiotic-resistant zoonoses are increasingly passing from animals to humans (Meek, Vyas, and Piddock 2015).

To retain the life-preserving capacity of antibiotics and other microbials, uses aside from medicine must be halted. There are alternative strategies for nearly every other use. Some classes, antimicrobials, must be preserved for human use only, and new ones must be developed that are not used in both animals and humans.

COORDINATED ACTION

Ensuring that everyone has a chance to fulfill their potential in health—as with all global problems—requires a global strategy that works horizontally connecting levels of care, communities with communities, and nations with nations as well as vertically linking communities to global networks. From research through implementation of strategies, whether responding to a crisis or providing primary care, necessary partners include government, civil society, the private sector, universities and research centers, and international governmental organizations.

An example of one such coordinated action is United to Combat NTDs. In 2012, civil society groups, philanthropies, government agencies, and private sector companies signed onto the London Declaration pledging to control or eliminate 10 of the 17 NTDs. They call these "diseases of inequity" because these diseases leave more than 1 billion people in the poorest areas of the world behind, hindered, if not prevented, from realizing their life chances. Trained village volunteers monitor and map the diseases and refer infected persons to the care centers. Mapping allows vaccination programs to be targeted to improve efficiency (Uniting to Combat NTDs 2015). Drug donations make the program affordable for endemic countries. In 2015, they received enough for 1.5 billion treatments (Uniting to Combat NTDs 2015). The Economist (2017) called the London Declaration partnership "the largest and most successful public health initiative in history."

There are a number of partnerships to develop new vaccines and ensure that all children are inoculated with existing ones. The WHO's (2013) Global Vaccine Action Plan 2011–2020 declared that decade "The Decade of the Vaccine." It is one of the largest partnerships, endorsed by 194 governments and involving 1,100 individuals in the planning process, including health professionals, researchers, drug manufacturers, global governmental agencies, civil society, the media, and philanthropies. The leadership of this alliance includes the WHO, Bill & Melinda Gates Foundation, GAVI Alliance, UNICEF, and U.S. National Institute of Allergies and Infectious Diseases (WHO 2013).

The Coalition for Epidemic Preparedness Innovations (CEPI) grew out of discussions at the 2015 G7 Summit and 2016 World Economic Forum Annual Meeting. The unpredictability of new outbreaks calls for innovative methods. When an outbreak such as Ebola in 2015 occurs, vaccines in the pipeline are typically not far enough advanced to use immediately. In that case, it cost potentially thousands of lives that could have been saved. The CEPI initiative develops vaccine pipelines, taking the candidate vaccines as far as possible before an outbreak occurs, making it possible to halt an outbreak in the early stages. This is a "just in case" and "just in time" strategy ready for final trial at the time of the outbreak, with small stockpiles ready to go. By partnering all the necessary stakeholders, research and development, regulatory approvals, drug manufacture, and other processes are streamlined for efficient and affordable implementation (CEPI 2017).

Funding Global Health

Health care is expensive. At U.S. $1 for a vaccine, distributing millions amounts to millions of dollars. The Global Vaccine Action Plan estimates that the cost to reach the goal of eliminating all vaccine-preventable diseases will be $50 to $60 billion over the "Decade of the Vaccine." Most of the cost will be to expand existing programs and add additional vaccines to them. Doing nothing, however, is more expensive. Ten vaccines, administered through the decade for a cost of $42 to $50 billion, will save 24 to 26 million lives (WHO 2013). Malaria alone costs the African continent U.S. $12 billion every year in economic productivity loss. The 2015 Ebola epidemic killed more than 11,000 people and resulted in an economic loss of $2.2 billion.

It goes without saying that how health care is funded determines who gets health care and the care they can get. It is an important aspect of governance because this has a significant and lasting effect on individual people's life chances and the well-being, economic productivity, and development prospects of countries. Transparency is critical in all aspects of health-related activity. Because health care programs and efforts are disjointed, it is difficult to determine where there is overfunding and where the gaps are. This knowledge is important in improving coordination of efforts.

There is no central repository to fund global health. It is virtually impossible to determine the exact amount spent on health care. Money flows from private and public sources to various civil society groups and governmental and intergovernmental agencies. The OECD reports "official development assistance" for health by donor category. Although it has the appearance of precision, McCoy, Chand, and Sridhar (2009) reported that official development assistance is often inflated because disbursements might not equal the commitments. A task force charged with calculating funding going to health gave up after two years because funding comes from many sources; there is no global data collection for foundations, civil society groups, and the corporate sector (McCoy et al. 2009).

The OECD (n.d.) compiles data on official development aid. Official development assistance for health has increased annually, reaching more than U.S. $7 billion in 2015. This does not include expenditures by private individuals, corporations, civil society organizations, and philanthropies. Private individuals give primarily through civil society organizations. Médecins Sans Frontières receives 87 percent of its income through private donations—mostly individuals. However, corporations, philanthropies, and public funders also channel some of their money through civil society organizations. Billions more go to health care through these channels (Figure 4.8).

Health research is another important consideration. Viergever and Hendriks's (2016) index of public

A CLOSER LOOK
HEALTH AID FLOWS BY DONOR AND CAUSE

Although precise figures are not available, this chart provides a glimpse of the donors to health care and the causes to which they donate.

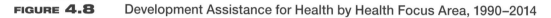

FIGURE 4.8   Development Assistance for Health by Health Focus Area, 1990–2014

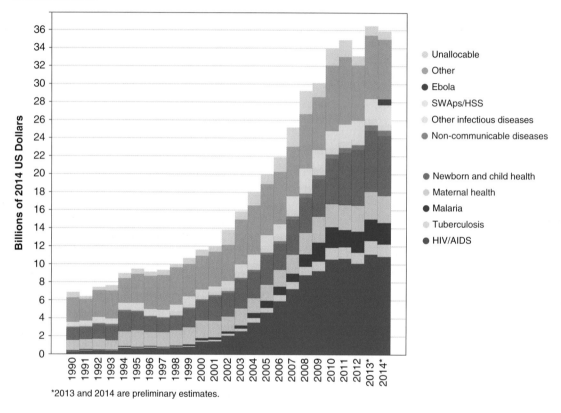

*2013 and 2014 are preliminary estimates.

Source: Institute for Health Metrics and Evaluation (2017). Reproduced with permission.

and philanthropic health care funders listed more than 200 funders.[6] The largest government funders were U.S. National Institutes of Health (U.S. $26.1 billion), European Commission ($3.7 billion), and U.K. Medical Research Council ($1.3 billion) (Viergever and Hendriks 2016). Some of the public funders, such as USAID, channel through official development assistance (ODA); thus, there is a degree of undetermined overlap with

the ODA figures. The largest health research related philanthropic funder was the Wellcome Trust at $909.1 million. Together, the 10 largest funders—public and private—gave $37.1 billion. This represented 40 percent of funding for health care research from high-income countries. Because corporations tend to conduct research in areas where higher profits are expected, areas that are not anticipated to be profitable are generally funded by public and philanthropic sources. They develop new knowledge in neglected diseases and increasingly develop new antibiotics.

Given the large sums of public money, more attention needs to be paid to how priorities for funding are determined. Too often, these decisions are made based on political and other special interests rather than the most need and promise.

Universal Health Care

Devising and implementing plans for universal access to health care must address both financing and delivery of services. There are vast discrepancies among countries, and between the rich and poor within countries, in access to services and ability to pay for universal health care. In 2005, country members of the WHO committed to reforming their health financing system so that everyone would have access to health services and not need to suffer financial hardship in paying for them. All UN member states promised to try to achieve universal coverage by 2030 as part of the SDGs.

There are roles for national governments, international governmental organizations and aid agencies, philanthropy, and the private sector to make universal health care a reality. Suggestions of the WHO (2010) include making domestic revenue collection more efficient. Many tax dollars are lost through tax avoidance, loopholes, and inefficiencies in collection. Indonesia realized benefits to all of government spending and health care in particular by revamping its tax system. Reprioritizing budgets to donate a larger percentage to health care and looking for innovative financing—such as taxes on airline travel—could also be used to finance health care.

Demand for payment at the time of service prevents many people from getting preventive care or the care that they need. Payment due at the time of service can be eliminated through prepay systems. One strategy is to establish a pool of funds—at least 15 to 20 percent of the total health care budget—to offset payment at the time of service to help people access health care without undue worry. The pool would be similar to an insurance plan whereby everyone is covered for a range of essential services. Everyone would need to pay into the fund through a payroll or insurance premium. The size of the pool, who would be covered, and the services covered would vary by country.

Ensuring access requires that services be available in all geographic regions and urban and rural areas. Making better use of community health workers, nurse practitioners, and physician assistants increases accessibility to high-quality care. Successful strategies for attracting health care professionals to underserved areas include visa waivers, educational scholarships or loan forgiveness, tax credits, rotating assignments, and government loans or grants for establishing private practices in underserved areas.

Promoting Mental Health Care

In urban areas of wealthy countries, it seems as though there is a psychiatrist or psychologist office on every corner. International human rights covenants require domestic mental health policies and laws, but only two thirds of WHO members have mental health-specific policies and only one half have mental health laws. In many cases, they are not in keeping with requirements of international laws. Treatment is unavailable in many countries and is inaccessible in many more due to cost. Discrimination against people with mental illness is widespread. Many countries with great need are significantly short on services. Only 1 percent of the global workforce works in mental health, and 45 percent of the world's population lives in a country with less than one psychiatrist for every 100,000 people. Mental health services need to be an integral component of health care.

Monitoring, Reporting, and Mapping Health

All aspects of health need to be continuously monitored at the local level and included in global information networks. Discovering an emerging disease or an outbreak of a known one is critical to combatting and containing it. Outbreaks, antimicrobial resistance, and even trends in non-communicable diseases (which should be treated as epidemics when they escalate in a population) need to be monitored and reported.

Mapping is also essential. When Doctors without Borders arrived in Guinea in 2014 to combat the Ebola crisis, they found themselves with little information on where the first outbreaks occurred, how Ebola was spreading geographically, and where it was most concentrated. The only digital map they had to start mapping the disease showed just two roads. They enlisted the help of Humanitarian OpenStreetMap Team, a digital mapping organization, to build them a map of the area. Within 12 hours, 200 volunteers from all over the world built maps of three cities online using satellite imagery (Hodson 2014).

Mapping and reporting are important health functions that can be completed by trained volunteers or lower-level health workers. Local health workers are the front line in monitoring and would be ideal for mapping training. Using information technology, they can be trained to be alert to disease threats, recognize them when they see them, and respond appropriately—even capturing them on video to communicate vertically and horizontally to other stakeholders. Going door to door, workers can map disease house by house, neighborhood by neighborhood, and intervene as needed. This empowers communities to take control of their health issues.

However, sometimes there is resistance to reporting. Publicity concerning outbreaks may prove to be costly to a community or nation—affecting trade, tourism, and global confidence in its food and other products. When public health suffers, officials may fear that their competence will be questioned. Descriptions of outbreaks are sometimes veiled in ambiguous terms to hide the outbreaks or prevent panic (Keusch et al. 2009).

To encourage reporting, it is critical to minimize reputational and economic damage to the country of the outbreak. The earlier an outbreak or trend is discovered, the less it will cost, so early reporting is advantageous to a country. Assistance for outbreak control is arguably the most important external motivation for countries to cooperate in reporting. In sub-Saharan Africa, the assistance of WHO in providing meningitis vaccines for countries affected provided an incentive for their cooperation. In another case, Indonesia did not cooperate in reporting an influenza outbreak. The influenza samples officials provided were tested there but designated to produce vaccines for developed countries, not Indonesia. The country did not cooperate with disease surveillance (Keusch et al. 2009).

While some export and travel restrictions are undoubtedly required in the case of an outbreak, caution to not overreact is also needed. With accurate monitoring, risk assessment, and reporting, overreacting is much less likely. To reduce the potential losses to a country, trade, travel, or other precautions can be zoned for specific regions or compartmentalized to specific products (Keusch et al. 2009). Careful handling of an outbreak, not just medically but also politically, is important for overall success.

Healthier Eating

While busy lifestyles may prohibit three home-cooked meals a day, increasing the nutritional value of snack and fast-food meals can offer a reasonable alternative. Street vendors of locally produced ready-to-eat traditional fare are a much healthier alternative to the ultra-processed snacks of the multinational food corporations. Household production of street food also provides an alternative livelihood for small-scale farmers. Micro-scale processing, a step above household processing, can provide employment for several people (Fellows and Hilmi 2011). The food carts growing more popular in developed countries are a few steps above the street cart and usually provide healthier food than the multinational fast-food restaurants and packaged ready-to-eat foods.

Monitoring the food industry also promotes better health. After more than a decade of struggle, the United Kingdom published voluntary salt reduction targets for processed foods. The British Food Standards Association, along with a civil society organization, monitored the progress of individual companies and the salt content the urine of a random selection of the British population. As salt content of food dropped, so did the salt in the sample—with no loss of sales. Most important, population blood pressure dropped and mortality from stroke and heart disease dropped. Unfortunately, after only four years the program was all but abandoned due to a change in government and lack of monitoring. Sign-on for future targets is poor. Big companies such as McDonald's, Unilever, and Kellogg are not signing on. With no enforcement or monitoring, they see no need (MacGregor 2015).

Lobbying by the food industry is thought to be responsible for the ultimate failure of the U.K. salt reduction program (MacGregor 2015). The global food industry is very powerful and has successfully defeated many attempts at greater regulation. Brazil's health surveillance agency, Anvisa, sought to curb obesity through regulation of the food industry in everything from additives to sponsoring sporting events. But armed with donations of U.S. $158 million to more than half of Brazil's legislators (threefold over 2010 donations), the food lobby—including executives from Nestlé and Unilever who sat on the Brazilian Association of Food Industries—defeated the proposed regulations (Jacobs and Richtel 2017).

Establishing Health as a Human Right

"[T]he enjoyment of the highest attainable standard of health is one of the fundamental rights of every human being. . . . [Health is] a state of complete physical, mental and social well-being and not merely the absence of disease or infirmity." —Constitution of the World Health Organization

Ethnic and racial minorities bear more than their fair share of disadvantage in health and health care. The barriers to good health are similar from country to country. While poverty is certainly an important determinant and needs to be addressed systematically, there are many features of health care delivery that affect health directly, resulting in worse outcomes for indigenous people and for ethnic and racial minorities. WHO (2007) identified access to health services and the timeliness of access, cultural sensitivity, quality of services, and discrimination in health care systems as factors that affect indigenous groups' and ethnic and racial minorities' chances to achieve their potential in good physical and mental health.

The recommendations of WHO (2007) for boosting those chances include the following:

- Increasing research into the impacts of discrimination and monitoring of disadvantaged groups' health

- Providing training, skill building, and awareness raising for health care professionals relevant to the human rights dimension of their work

- Targeting specific health inequities involving individuals and communities in collecting information and using it and involving them in every aspect of decision making about their health and planning for it

- Enacting comprehensive legislation outlawing discrimination and conforming to human rights practice, with significant civil and criminal penalties for violations

- Having sufficient financial resources to ensure prevention, promotion, and care programs

- Creating national programs, including affirmative action, to equalize health chances

- Putting a special emphasis on women and children, particularly abandoned and exploited children

- Stopping eco-racism and providing healthy environments free from industrial pollution and contamination with relocation as needed

In response to their own recommendations, WHO developed a series of seven modules for training and awareness. Fully 80 percent of new staff at WHO headquarters and 90 percent of global staff completed all seven of the modules by September 2016. The number of female staff in professional and higher categories increased to 45 percent in 2017. WHO created a handbook for monitoring and evaluating health care and outcomes and for enabling them to target low- and middle-income countries for evidence-based practices, programs, and policies. An innovative approach of eight steps put into play will steer analysis, help develop plans to address health inequalities and gender equity, and make health as a human right a reality. It is based on the SDGs' commitment to "leave no one behind" (WHO 2016b).

SUMMARY

Threats to health globally arise from a variety of sources, and they are surprisingly similar the world over, from increasing vulnerability to non-communicable disease—including mental health disease—to the potential for the rapid spread of communicable disease. Climate change, bad habits associated with economic growth, population density and overwhelmed infrastructure of urban areas, migration, population aging, overuse of antimicrobials, stagnant economies, and violent conflict all contribute to a world in which good health is becoming harder to maintain.

Meeting these challenges requires concerted and coordinated action from local to global governments, civil society groups, the private sector, and international governmental agencies.

DISCUSSION

1. Describe the features of globalization that contribute to the burden of non-communicable diseases around the world.

2. What preventive steps can we take, as individuals and collectively, to halt the emergence of microbial-resistant organisms?

3. How have urbanization and globalization contributed to the spread of infectious diseases, particularly new zoonoses?

4. People engage willingly in hazardous labor when there are no other choices. What steps can be taken to eliminate the worst forms of hazardous labor, particularly for children?

5. How has depression become a symptom of a disorder in modern life as opposed to a purely biologically caused mental illness?

6. What are the most important features of a comprehensive national or global health program?

7. Is health care a right or a privilege? Choose a country that has achieved universal health care, or is close to doing so, and outline the major features of its system. Assess the country's system, looking at the percentage of its gross domestic product spent on health care and its health statistics. Some information can be found on the WHO Universal Health Coverage Data Portal (http://apps.who.int/gho/cabinet/uhc.jsp).

ON YOUR OWN

1. In the Global Health Observatory data repository (http://apps.who.int/gho/data/node.home), you can find country-level data for health indicators such as heavy alcohol use. Compare and contrast the risks of a country rated high in human development and a country rated low in human development.

2. The Institute for Health Metrics and Evaluation keeps annual updates on the SDG health-related targets for 188 countries. The data visualization project enables users to construct global maps for the SDG index and each of the variables. Users can also find index and indicator scores by country as well as trends over time.

   Select six indicators, three related to communicable diseases and three related to non-communicable diseases. Investigate and assess progress in those indicators.

   Are regional patterns evident in the global map? Are there outliers for any region (ones that do significantly better or worse than a regional pattern)?

3. Choose the country where you live or go to school. How does its health compare globally? What are its strongest indicators, and which are the weakest?

4. Investigate disability-adjusted life years (DALYs) for mental illnesses using the Global Health Data Exchange (http://ghdx.healthdata.org/gbd-results-tool). Depressive orders are coded B.7.4, bipolar disorder is B.7.5, anxiety disorders are B.7.6, and eating disorders are B.7.7. Using the locations tab, determine which SDI has the most loss for each of the disorders listed. Or choose your country or region. What are the costs of the mental illnesses listed in your region or country?

5. The World Obesity Federation maintains a World Obesity Atlas. With the interactive world map, users can explore obesity statistics, drivers of obesity, health impacts, and policies undertaken to combat obesity.

   • Investigate a country of your choice and prepare a country report. Find the obesity rates (at this time, it is given for men, women, boys, and girls separately). What are the major drivers and impacts of obesity? Assess the policies the country has enacted.

NOTES

1. The SDG health index is based on 37 of the 50 health-related targets.

2. KFC dominates fast-food franchises in China, having 4,563 outlets. Others include McDonald's (1,957), Pizza Hut (1,264), Starbucks (1,367), and Subway (484).

3. Zoonotic diseases (zoonosis) are infectious diseases that originated in animals. When a pathogen acquires a strictly human variant or transmits readily from human to human, independently of an animal host, it is no longer directly zoonotic.

4. The six most common are guinea worm disease, lymphatic filariasis, onchocerciasis, schistosomiasis, soil-transmitted helminths, and trachoma.

5. Parasites and fungi that are unicellular are microbes. There are a number growing more resistant to drugs that are multicellular. Unless otherwise specified, *microbe* is used generally to refer to all of these pathogens.

6. Viergever and Hendriks's (2016) index was constructed as a byproduct of research for the top 10 public and private funders. Thus, it is not complete. In addition, the funding cannot simply be added to arrive at a total because there is an undetermined overlap in some funders such as the European Union and European Commission.

5

Expanding Horizons Through Lifelong Learning

CHILDREN WHO WOULD RATHER BE IN SCHOOL THAN ON HOLIDAY

It's two in the afternoon in a village in Bhang, Nepal. As the bell rings, signaling the end of lunch break, 11-year-old Lalita Bohara runs to her classroom, opens her notebook, and sits down on a bench along with her classmates while waiting for their teacher.

Amidst the excited chatter of the students, their English subject teacher is cheerfully greeted with "Good afternoon, Sir" as he enters the classroom. Lalita and the other third-grade students immediately start paying attention to him.

"I would have gone hungry had there been no meals on school days," says Lalita at dismissal time that day. "The meal helps me pay attention to the teachers while studying."

At home, Lalita, despite her young age, already helps her mother do a number of chores such as fetching water, cutting vegetables, and cleaning the house. On holidays, she also collects firewood—a six-hour journey on foot from her house. Unlike most kids, Lalita prefers to go to school and wishes there were no holidays.

"I don't like holidays since I have to work at home. I like coming to school because I get to eat *haluwa* for lunch and learn so many new things. I also enjoy playing with my friends," she says while her friends giggle.

Haluwa, a nutritious porridge-like meal consisting of a fortified wheat–soya blend with sugar and vegetable oil, is provided to young children during school hours every day. Because of the meal, children like Lalita are able to continue their studies and receive the nutrition they need, increasing their ability to learn and eventually [become] productive members of their communities when they grow up. (Lalita's story appears here as reported by Deepesh Das Shrestha, 2013)

Source: Das Shrestha (2013).

LEARNING OBJECTIVES

After completing this chapter, students should be able to do the following:

5.1 Understand the importance of investing in people—in their education appropriate to their ability and ambition

5.2 Determine ways in which current education systems neglect or diminish the life chances of many people globally

5.3 Evaluate the contribution of education to improving the lives of individuals, societies, and the world

5.4 Understand the inequalities in global education and the potential reforms that can ameliorate them

PHOTO 5.1 For many children the world over, school meals are a critical part of their diet.
Getty Images/Wendy Stone.

In our world, knowledge is power, and education empowers. It is an indispensable part of the development equation. It has intrinsic value—extending far beyond the economic—to empower people to determine their own destiny. That is why the opportunity to be educated is central to advancing human development.

—Helen Clark, United Nations Development Programme administrator, quoted in *Education 2030* (United Nations Educational, Scientific and Cultural Organisation 2015a)

Imagine primary school children dressed smartly in their red uniforms, backpacks in tow, pulling their desks into the street. They want the world to know that they want an education. "We want our school. We want to study in school," they chanted. Joined by their parents and teachers, they protest because their school was torn down without notice. This was not the first time a school was torn down. Corrupt officials in Kenya sell multiple deeds for the same land. They make extra cash, but children lose when a more lucrative developer buys a deed for the land on which their school stands (Gramer 2017). In Kenya, medium level in human development, people complete only 6.8 years of schooling on average, not enough to achieve their potential in life chances.

Zainab, another primary school child, sits in the middle of a group of 50 girls. Born in Pakistan as a refugee, her family could not afford to send her to school. On returning to Afghanistan, she is just starting school at 10 years old. Now, she loves school for the learning and the opportunity to be with friends. Her school in the Gamberi returnee settlement serves about 600 students with six teachers. More than 100 other children, aged 10 to 15 years, do not get to go to school, including Zainab's siblings. She worries that next year neither will she: "I don't want to stop here," she says. Across Afghanistan, returnees share the hope that their children can finally go to school (United Nations International Children's Emergency Fund [UNICEF] Afghanistan 2017). But in Afghanistan, a mere 3.6 years of schooling is the national average. What chance do these children have? What chance does the world have?

In comparison with some other countries, even Zainab's situation seems fortuitous. Some children are in classes of well over 100 students, some go in the open air where there are no classrooms, some share textbooks with 10 or more other students, and the global shortage of teachers is so great that many are taught by untrained and poorly educated teachers. Many children with disabilities, 93 million, and even more girls do not go to school at all. Children with poor nutrition may go to school, but their malnutrition will cause cognitive stunting as well as physical stunting (*Global Citizen* 2014).

Education is essential for the development of the individual and the society. The benefits of education to individuals, their families, communities, and societies are indisputable. The whole world benefits. For individuals, education improves their personal health and that of their families. A person with just a primary education is much less likely to contract HIV. Just six years of schooling improves rates of prenatal care, assisted childbirth, postnatal care, and immunization. For each year of schooling in a poor country, a person's income increases 10 percent.

Because women bear primary responsibility for agriculture in the developing world, female education leads to more productive farming and decreases in malnutrition. Education promotes the growth of civil society and the economic growth of the society. A study of 19 developing societies demonstrated that a country's long-term growth increases 3.7 percent for every year's increase in average years of schooling in the adult population (Roudi-Fahimi and Moghadam 2003).

ACHIEVING UNIVERSAL EDUCATION

Global norms dictate that one of the requirements of a modern and good society is that it provides education. Although today it is taken for granted, this was not always the case. In agricultural societies, people learned most of what they needed to know at home. Formal schooling was a private function rather than a public function. From the late 18th century to the 19th century, education became a public matter rather than a strictly private matter in then developing societies. Both in Prussia and in the United States, an influx of immigrants convinced the reformers of the period, and eventually most of the public, that universal education paid for by the public, not parents, was necessary to transform immigrants into citizens and a productive workforce.[1] Education, like other large formal organizational systems, followed the model of bureaucratic organization and scientific management principles that globalized in that period.

The dual function of education and the provision of universality achieved through public funding globalized, as did the bureaucratic model. Mass education spread along with the internationalization of the state system—irrespective of a society's income or industrialization. As late as 1820, more than 80 percent of people alive had no formal schooling (Roser and Nagdy 2016). By 1870, nearly every developed nation had achieved more than 10 percent enrollment of 5- to 14-year-olds in school. Until

World War II, enrollments grew at about 5 percent on average; by World War II, only 10 to 15 percent of societies had reached the 10 percent enrollment mark. As nations integrated further into the system of states, schooling expanded, with enrollments growing at about 12 percent a year (Meyer, Ramirez, and Soysal 1992). After the war, the implied normative standard of mass schooling as an indicator of a good state became explicit with the United Nations (UN) Declaration of Human Rights, Article 26, which declares education a human right.

In the 21st century, primary school enrollment is almost universal and secondary is close. The Millennium Development Goal (MDG) effort achieved nearly a 50 percent reduction in primary school-aged children who are out of school, reducing the number from 100 to 57 million. Primary school enrollment in developing countries rose to 91 percent. Literacy among youths aged 15 to 24 years rose to 91 percent globally (UN 2015) (Figures 5.1 and 5.2).

These are enormous achievements. But, there is still much to be done. MDG successes inspire a global effort to reach further. The children still left out of school are the hardest cases to enroll. Many are in conflict or refugee situations. Others are in extreme poverty or remote areas. The number of females out of school in both primary and secondary education is greater than the number of males out of school. This is primarily a function of sub-Saharan Africa. It is also striking that the number of children out of school decreased significantly from 2000 to 2007 and then remained relatively constant from 2007 to 2012 (and was 57 million in 2015). Of these primary school-aged children, probably 23 million will never enter school. The economic return on investment in education is significant—U.S. $5 gained for every $1 spent in education. If every child in low-income countries achieved basic reading skills, 171 million people would be lifted out of poverty, decreasing global poverty by 12 percent (Global Partnership for Education [GPE] 2017).

Simply being in school is not good enough, however. The Sustainable Development Goals (SDGs) call for improvements in the quality of education as well as 100 percent completion of both primary and secondary school and access to vocational or tertiary education for all.

MEASURING QUALITY EDUCATION

Defining a "quality" education is debated. Whether to measure "input" or "outcomes" is part of the debate. Certainly, measuring inputs is easier. How many students, qualifications of teachers, expenditures, resources,

A CLOSER LOOK
WHO'S OUT OF SCHOOL

Figures 5.1 and 5.2 show the numbers of children out of school in both primary and secondary education.

FIGURE 5.1   Out-of-School Children of Primary School Age by Region and Sex, 2000–2012

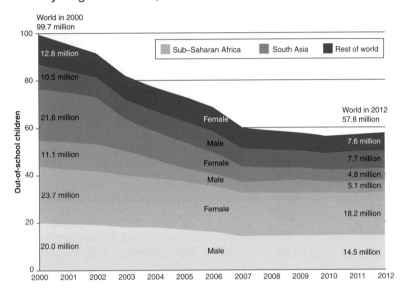

FIGURE 5.2   Out-of-School Adolescents of Lower Secondary School Age by Region and Sex, 2000–2012

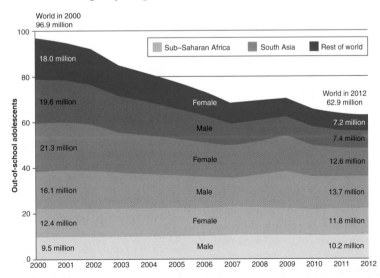

Source: UNESCO Institute for Statistics (UIS) and UNICEF (2015). *Fixing the Broken Promise of Education for All: Findings from the Global Initiative on Out-of-School Children.* Montreal: UIS. http://dx.doi.org/10.15220/978-92-9189-161-0-en.

PHOTO 5.2 These children, refugees from the Darfur region of Sudan, attend school in Djabal camp. Nineteen teachers hold classes for 690 students. There are six primary schools in the camp with 4,496 children. In this camp, 60 percent of the refugees are under 18 years old.

UNHCR/F. Noy/December 2011.

and courses offered all are reasonable ways in which to tally and evaluate the inputs, among others. Outcome is harder. Debates concerning the goals of education are important in deciding which outputs define quality. Completion rates, test scores, and skills gained all are reasonable measures for strictly academic output. What about values as output—whose values? Should preparing citizens and socializing them to national values be included in defining quality? Should education prepare us for life? If so, what does that mean? Should all students meet the same criteria, or should each person develop as a unique individual? And how do scores on tests relate? These debates are far from settled.

School Attendance and Completion

Despite significant improvement, primary school attendance fell short of meeting the MDG universal education target. Universal secondary education exists in only a few countries. The main barriers of cost, distance to school, and the need to earn an income are relevant in both primary and secondary school attendance but are even more pronounced in secondary education. In some of the worst areas, violent conflict makes education difficult if not impossible.

As reported above, about 91 percent of primary-aged students are in school, whereas about 83 percent of lower secondary-aged children are in school (primary or secondary). Attendance rates in West and Central Africa are the worst. Attendance in primary school was only about 74 percent, with about 60 percent of lower secondary children in school (UNICEF 2016).

Progress is uneven and inequalities persist, as is evident in Figures 5.3 and 5.4. Inequality in attendance by income, residence (urban or rural), and gender all are greater in secondary school than in primary school (Table 5.1). Gender equality has been attained in two thirds of countries, but in Africa, the Middle East, and South Asia many girls are still kept out of school, resulting in an overall gender gap in both primary and secondary education. Secondary school completion rates in the developing world lag far behind those in the developed world. This is a significant detriment to economic progress. Inequality in income and residence increase as the level of educational achievement increases. However, the gender gap in Latin America and in East Asia and the Pacific favors females.

The gender gap in education in the least developed societies is particularly troubling. Women's education has far-reaching effects on the physical, economic, and social health of a family and the larger society:

- A 1 percent increase in girls' secondary education reaps a 3 percent payoff in gross domestic product (GDP).

A CLOSER LOOK
PRIMARY AND SECONDARY SCHOOL ATTENDANCE RATES

Inequalities in attendance rates by income, rural and urban residence, and gender persist but are more pronounced for secondary school attendance than for primary school attendance.

FIGURE 5.3   **Adjusted Net Enrollment Rate Among Children of Primary School Age by Sex, 2000–2015**

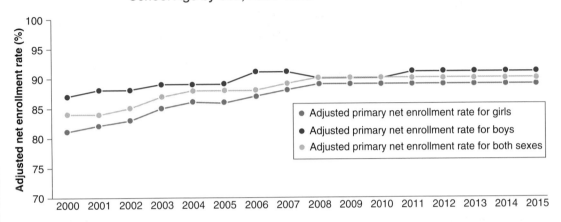

Source: United Nations International Children's Emergency Fund Global Databases (2017).

FIGURE 5.4   **Adjusted Net Enrollment Rate Among Children of Lower Secondary School Age by Sex, 2000–2015**

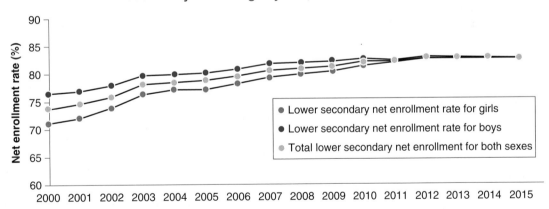

Source: United Nations International Children's Emergency Fund Global Databases (2017).

(Continued)

(Continued)

TABLE 5.1   Secondary Education Completion Rates: Developing Regions Data Averages, 2009–2015

The upper secondary completion rate is based on the population 3 to 5 years above secondary graduation age.

Countries and Areas	Total	Sex		Residence		Wealth Quintile				
		Male	Female	Urban	Rural	Poorest	Second	Middle	Fourth	Richest
Sub-Saharan Africa	24	28	21	40	12	4	7	15	24	46
Eastern and Southern Africa	19	20	18	28	7	2	4	7	12	33
West and Central Africa	29	34	24	45	16	5	10	21	34	55
Middle East and North Africa	47	48	48	55	40	28	33	43	53	74
South Asia[a]	30	34	27	44	24	6	15	24	36	59
East Asia and Pacific[a]	49	49	50	66	36	18	34	47	63	82
Latin America and Caribbean	58	54	63	–	–	–	–	–	–	–
Europe and Central Asia	68	71	66	72	59	47	61	68	76	88
Least developed countries	17	20	15	31	11	3	6	10	17	39

a. Excludes China and India.

Source: United Nations International Children's Emergency Fund Global Database (2017). Reproduced with permission.

- Every additional year of a woman's education beyond the average raises her eventual income 10 to 20 percent.

- Every additional year of girls' schooling
  - adds one-half to one-third additional year to their children's education.
  - avoids two maternal deaths per 1,000 girls.
  - lowers child mortality 5 to 10 percent.

- Females with secondary education are three times less likely to become HIV infected.

- An increase of four years of education reduces a woman's fertility by one child.

- Educated women are less likely to be a victim of domestic violence, more likely to participate in political and civil affairs, and four times more likely to oppose female genital cutting (Tembon 2008).

- Women's education provides them with more control over resources, which results in more spending on food and education for children (Revenga and Shetty 2012).

- Women's education leads to them having a greater voice in political decisions, which generally results in greater expenditures on public goods such as sanitation and water (Revenga and Shetty 2012).

Completion rates of secondary education in developed societies are considerably higher but not nearly universal. A high school degree in developed countries is the minimum credential needed for a job. The percentage of 25- to 34-year-olds who had completed high school or its equivalent in the Organisation for Economic Cooperation and Development (OECD) countries in 2015 ranged from 98 percent in Korea to 45 percent in Mexico. The OECD average was 84 percent (McFarland et al. 2017).

Inequality in access to tertiary education by income is still striking. Among OECD countries, the number of adults aged 25 to 34 years who had completed any type of tertiary education by 2015 ranged from 69 percent in Korea to 21 percent in Mexico. The OECD average was 42 percent (McFarland et al. 2107).

Inequities in Student Achievement

Getting to school and staying in is only the first step in building a quality educational system. Being in school does not ensure learning. Of the 250 million children who cannot read, write, or count well enough to meet minimum standards, half have been in school for four years or more.

Literacy is the first test of student achievement. Literacy in the developing world among youths aged 15 to 24 years is 91 percent, up from 83 percent in two decades. There are still 115 million illiterate youths in the world. Their life chances, not only in terms of earning an income but also in terms of health and participation in civil society, are also hindered. So too are the life chances of their children.

As is the case with enrollment, illiteracy is concentrated in specific regions—West and Central Africa and South Asia, where overall literacy is lower than 80 percent. In some countries, however, it is below 50 percent. In these regions, females suffer from illiteracy at a greater rate than males (UNICEF 2016). The gender parity is particularly important because the payoff to a family and

the society for female education, as discussed above, is significant.

The Program for International Student Assessment (PISA) tests reading, mathematics, science, and financial literacy. OECD and OECD partner countries participate. The gaps in scores across countries and within countries reveal sharp inequalities. In mathematics, for example, the scores of OECD countries, primarily very developed economies and some emerging economies, range from 408 (Mexico) to 532 (Japan), with a mean of 490 and a median of 494. The partner countries, mainly emerging economies, range from 328 (Dominican Republic) to 495 (Vietnam) (OECD 2015). The PISA scores reflect a "virtuous equity-efficiency" in that countries with higher PISA scores have lower inequality (Freeman, Machin, and Viarengo 2011).

The influence of family background on PISA scores also varies across countries. For OECD countries as a whole, family background accounts for 22 percent of variation in scores. However, in Japan it accounts for 14 percent and in Hungary it accounts for 38 percent. Students from single-parent families score 5 points lower on average than students from two-parent families. In the United States (where family-friendly policies are near nonexistent), the gap is particularly large at 23 points. Yet in some countries, there is virtually no difference in the scores of children from single-parent families (OECD 2010). The importance of noting these differences is to point out that many factors related to poor performance can be addressed through policy relating to children and their welfare. Family supports can affect achievement gaps for children from vulnerable family structures.

Inequality in Education and Life Chances: Select Examples

Ethnic and racial minorities still lag in educational achievement. The higher the level of educational attainment, the larger the gap. Inequality in educational achievement is not mysterious. Research has well documented that the 1954 *Brown v. Board of Education of Topeka* (Kansas) decision in the U.S. Supreme Court was correct in maintaining that separate schools are not equal schools. Educational attainment depends on a number of variables—affordability, the need to work along with going to school, the perceived benefits of higher education, and the achievement of learning outcomes. The National Assessment of Educational Progress (NAEP) is a series of tests that measure achievement in reading, mathematics, and science across the United

States in 4th, 8th, and 12th grades. It is disaggregated by race and ethnicity, dividing the school population into five groups: white, black, Hispanic, Asian/Pacific Islander, and American Indian/Alaskan Native (Native American). Whites outperform blacks, Hispanics, and Native Americans at all grade levels. Across all grade levels, Asians outscore the other groups in mathematics. Asians are also considerably more likely to take advanced mathematics courses than all other groups (Musu-Gillette et al. 2016).

In reading, the gaps among all groups are somewhat smaller than in mathematics. Asian and white scores were close for most years and grade levels. Both were higher than Hispanic, black, and Native American scores (Musu-Gillette et al. 2016). Both reading and math scores are related to absence rates. However, controlling for absence, Asians still maintain the highest scores, followed by whites. Hispanics outscore blacks and Native Americans, but the gap is not as large as that between whites or Asians and the other groups (Musu-Gillette et al. 2016). Native Americans in the United States had the lowest graduation group of any racial or ethnic group at 69.7 percent compared with 70.7 percent for blacks, 75.2 percent for Hispanics, and 86.6 percent for whites (Musu-Gillette et al. 2016).

Diminishing Returns in Income and Lifestyle

The gap between white and black households has narrowed very slightly since the civil rights movements of the 1960s. In 1967, median income for black households was 55 percent of that for white households. By 2014, it had increased to only 60 percent (Pew Research Center 2016).

Equal educational attainment does not translate to equal wages. Controlling for college, Asian men earn more than white men, followed by Hispanic and black men. Black men with a college education make only 78 percent of what white men make. Although the discrepancy is much smaller, white women earn more than women in the other groups and earn more than black and Hispanic men. Men within every racial or ethnic group earn more than women within their group (Pew Research Center 2016) (Figure 5.5). While much of the discrepancy is related to fields of study, occupational segregation, and career choices, discrimination is also at play. Choices of fields of study and careers themselves need to be investigated.

The "American Dream" to own a home is realized more often by whites than by blacks. White home ownership is 72 percent in comparison with 43 percent of

blacks (Pew Research Center 2016). Both blacks and whites recognize that there are institutional barriers to black success. Both recognize that failing schools and lack of jobs hold blacks back. However, whereas 75 percent of blacks recognize the role of low-quality schools, only 53 percent of whites do. Even fewer whites, 45 percent, recognize the lack of jobs as a factor, whereas 66 percent of blacks do. The two races are close in their perceptions of family instability and lack of role models. A slight majority of both blacks and whites perceive these as factors.

The largest discrepancies are in discrimination. Fully 70 percent of blacks perceive discrimination as holding them back, while only 30 percent of whites do. More of both blacks and whites think that individual discrimination is more of a problem than institutional discrimination, although it is 70 percent of whites and only 48 percent of blacks. Only 19 percent of whites, but 40 percent of blacks, see institutional discrimination as a bigger problem (Pew Research Center 2016). (These figures do not add to 100 percent because 11 percent of whites and 12 percent of blacks did not answer or indicated that they did not know.)

Education in South Africa

The effects of inequality are evident in the chart of comparisons among countries in Figure 5.6. Of the comparison countries, South Africa has by far the greatest percentage of students ranking at the bottom. In an OECD study of mainly rich countries, South Africa scored 75th out of 76. The gap between the highest and lowest scoring quintiles is more than that in nearly every other country tested.

Countries that are poorer but more equal than South Africa had better scores. In South Africa, 27 percent who had attended school for six years could not read. That figure is 4 percent in Tanzania and 19 percent in Zimbabwe. Only 37 percent of South Africa's children pass the matriculation exam, and only 4 percent earn a degree.

Until 1994, children attended segregated schools. Black schools received only about 20 percent of the funding that white schools received, and many black schools did not teach much math or science. Even now, with better funding for poorer schools, students are not learning. One reason is the teacher's union in the state schools. It is rampant with corruption and ill-prepared teachers. One study showed that 79 percent of teachers scored below the grade level in mathematics that they were teaching.

A CLOSER LOOK
EDUCATION, RACE, AND GENDER IMPACTS ON EARNINGS

Even among the college educated, Asian and white males earn more than other males and women.

FIGURE 5.5   Median Hourly Earnings Among Those Ages 25 and Older With a Bachelor's Degree or More

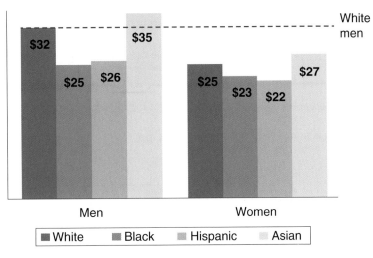

Source: "Racial, gender wage gaps persist in U.S. despite some progress." Pew Research Center, Washington, D.C. July 1, 2016. http://www.pewresearch.org/fact-tank/2016/07/01/racial-gender-wage-gaps-persist-in-u-s-despite-some-progress/.

With adequate teachers and curriculum, students can catch up fast. One low-cost private school in South Africa has a longer school day, 10 times the teacher training, and the same cost per pupil of the state schools. The students there are a year ahead of their peers in the state schools (Economist 2017).

The Special Cases of Indigenous Peoples

Indigenous peoples' chance to achieve their potential in intellectual development is far from being realized. The poor outcomes in school enrollment, retention, and achievement levels result from a variety of impediments—poverty, child labor, ethnicity, language barriers, gender norms, traditional practices such as early marriage, and lack of basic services. The International Work Group for Indigenous Affairs (IWGIA n.d.) outlines many of the difficulties.

As with some other ethnic and racial groups, the educational system relates to and is relevant to the mainstream culture and neglects to reflect or relate to indigenous cultures. For example, most educational systems ignore the history, values, norms, and traditions of the indigenous culture. Education is taught in the national language with little bilingual instruction. Traditional cultures, including their languages, are often devalued. School schedules do not adjust to the daily or seasonal structure of indigenous livelihoods such as those in pastoral and nomadic societies. Most non-indigenous teachers do not have the training they need in cultural understanding, and indigenous elders are not involved in goal setting for the schools.

A CLOSER LOOK
INEQUALITY AND EDUCATION

The poor performance of South African students in international comparisons highlights the inequalities in their educational system.

FIGURE 5.6   Selected TIMSS Math Scores, 2015 (percent of pupils)*

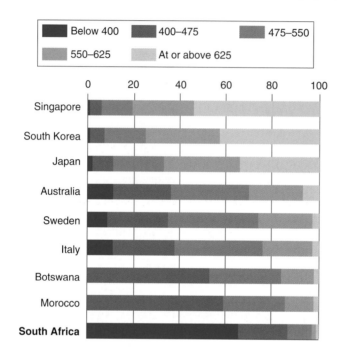

*500=Average

Source: The Economist (2017). Reproduced with permission.

There are many physical dimensions of schooling that may hinder enrollment and achievement. Location of schools, for example, may be a problem. Indigenous communities may be set apart or remote—not easily accessible. Mobile school facilities or culturally appropriate boarding schools (not necessarily a desirable alternative because they remove children from families) may be necessary. The costs of schools—even if tuition is free—in terms of materials, uniforms, meals, and transportation may be prohibitive. The physical infrastructure of schools, such as desks, chalkboards, ventilation, and lighting, is often inadequate. Last, security to and from schools needs to be ensured (IWGIA n.d.).

CONSIDER THIS
IMPACT OF EDUCATION ON INDIGENOUS PEOPLES IN AUSTRALIA

Australia maintains detailed statistics on the indigenous population. Noting the 20.5 percentage point gap in employment between indigenous and non-indigenous Australians, it poses the question of what the size of the gap would be if health, education, and geographic dispersion were the same for both groups. Figure 5.7 shows the gap in labor force participation as it stands. Figure 5.8 illustrates the gap in education, and Figure 5.9 portrays the gap in health. Figure 5.10 shows how the labor force participation gap would close with equalization in each of the life chances—health, education, remoteness, education and remoteness together, and the combined effect of all three—by more than two thirds, dropping from 19.9 to 6.3 (Australian Bureau of Statistics 2014).

A CLOSER LOOK
LIFE CHANCES OF INDIGENOUS AND NON-INDIGENOUS AUSTRALIANS

Indigenous peoples in Australia suffer discrimination in realizing each of these areas that affect their life chances.

FIGURE 5.7   Labor Force Participation by Indigenous Status

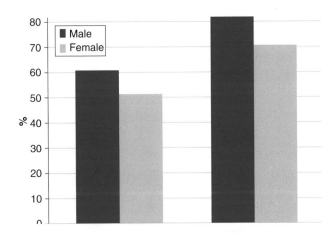

Source: "Exploring The Gap in Labour Market Outcomes for Aboriginal and Torres Strait Islander Peoples" by Australian Bureau of Statistics (http://www.abs.gov.au/ausstats/abs@.nsf/Lookup/4102.0main+features72014) licensed under (CC BY 4.0) (https://creativecommons.org/licenses/by/4.0/).

(Continued)

(Continued)

FIGURE 5.8   Level of Highest Educational Attainment by Indigenous Status

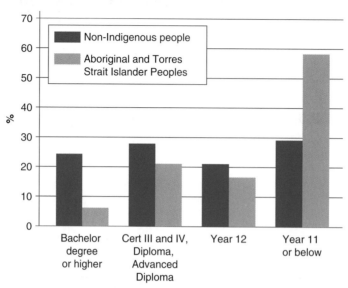

Source: "Exploring The Gap in Labour Market Outcomes for Aboriginal and Torres Strait Islander Peoples" by Australian Bureau of Statistics (http://www.abs.gov.au/ausstats/abs@.nsf/Lookup/4102.0main+features72014) licensed under (CC BY 4.0) (https://creativecommons.org/licenses/by/4.0/).

FIGURE 5.9   Health Status by Indigenous Status

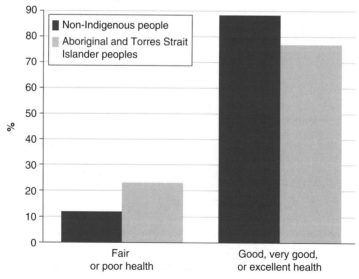

Source: "Exploring The Gap in Labour Market Outcomes for Aboriginal and Torres Strait Islander Peoples" by Australian Bureau of Statistics (http://www.abs.gov.au/ausstats/abs@.nsf/Lookup/4102.0main+features72014) licensed under (CC BY 4.0) (https://creativecommons.org/licenses/by/4.0/).

FIGURE 5.10   Labor Force Participation After Equalization of Life Chances

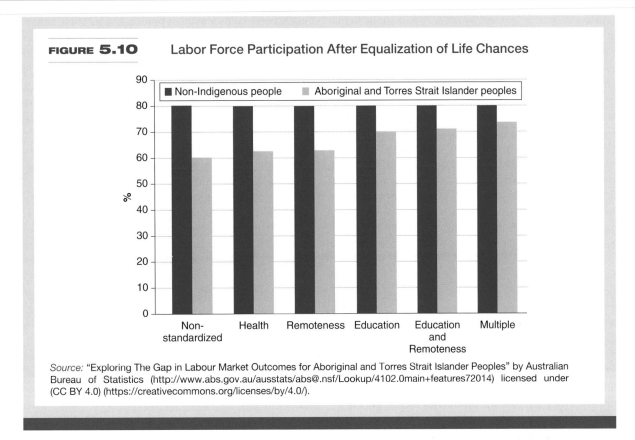

Source: "Exploring The Gap in Labour Market Outcomes for Aboriginal and Torres Strait Islander Peoples" by Australian Bureau of Statistics (http://www.abs.gov.au/ausstats/abs@.nsf/Lookup/4102.0main+features72014) licensed under (CC BY 4.0) (https://creativecommons.org/licenses/by/4.0/).

Teachers and Teacher Qualifications

There is a global shortage of teachers and of teachers explicitly qualified in their subject areas. In the United States in 2015, the pupil-to-teacher ratio, overall, in public schools was 16 to 1 and in private schools was about 12 to 1 (McFarland et al. 2017). In many developing societies, it is much higher—in the 30, 40, and 50 to 1 range. By 2030, it will require more than 1.5 million more teachers to attain universal primary education and more than 5 million more for lower secondary education If the current trend holds, not all of these teachers will be qualified. In one out of three countries, less than 75 percent of the teachers are trained to standards in their nation (Global Citizen 2014).

The developed world faces the issue of underqualified teachers as well. In the United States, the most recent Schools and Staffing Survey (2011–2012) showed that only 70 percent of public high school mathematics teachers had a major in mathematics, and only 46 percent of physical science teachers had a major in physical science (Hill, Sterns, and Owens 2015). England faces a similar dilemma. The Department for Education hoped to train 1,055 physics teachers for the 2015–2016 school year but got only 739. It also fell short on biology, chemistry, and mathematics teachers (Bawden 2016). In the United States, many districts are importing teachers from overseas. Teaching salaries are too low in some school districts to attract highly educated U.S. workers. The pay is attractive to the educated from developing countries. As it does for other occupations, the Philippines specifically trains teachers to be desirable for overseas employment. More than 250 teachers came from the Philippines on J-1 work visas. The money that they send home as remittances will help their families and country.

THE PIVOTAL PROBLEM OF FUNDING

Whether the problem is enrolling more students in school, retaining them for a longer time, or improving the quality of education offered them, more funding is needed. From 1999 to 2012, 38 countries increased funding by 1 percentage point of national income. Education for All and the MDGs set the target for national education funding at 15 to 20 percent by 2015. Progress toward the goal was uneven. Sub-Saharan African countries allocated the largest median share of their budgets at 18.4 percent; East Asian and Pacific countries allocated 17.5 percent. Ethiopia and Niger both exceeded the 20 percent mark. At the global median average of 13.7 percent reached in 2012, universal education cannot be attained (United Nations Educational, Scientific and Cultural Organisation [UNESCO] 2015b).

The final report on the 2000 to 2015 MDGs (UN 2015) recognizes that the world has made progress in achieving universal primary education. However, low-income countries achieved only about a 64 percent completion rate, and lower middle-income countries achieved about an 85 percent completion rate. The 2015 MDG report called attention to the large disparities in educational attainment and to the specific groups for whom more intervention is needed—girls, children belonging to minorities and nomadic communities, children engaged in child labor, and children living with disabilities, in conflict situations, or in urban slums.

Governments of low-income countries cannot meet funding goals on their own. Donor governments, philanthropies, development banks, and international organizations all are needed. The GPE estimated that from 2018 to 2020 donor governments need to invest U.S. $3.1 billion to meet the 20 percent budget allocation for education, and philanthropies and the private sector will need to increase their targeted contributions. This is to replenish the funding for education. After replenishment, $2 billion a year is needed to continue to scale up and maintain education. Health, prosperity, and peace will depend increasingly on education (GPE 2017).

REACHING MORE WITH EDUCATION

Success in enrolling more children in school requires a variety of strategies, depending on the local factors. Best practices, randomized trials, and pilot programs offer promise that universal quality education from childhood through adult life can be achieved.

Reducing or Eliminating the Costs Borne by Households

The cost of education is one factor preventing many children from going to school. Although the developed world is accustomed to free public education with minimal household contribution to supplies, in the developing world households are major funders of education. School fees may cover everything from uniforms, books, and other learning and teaching supplies to teacher and administrator fees. These fees can add up to hundreds of dollars. The proposals listed here are "stopgap" measures. As the SDG for education states in target 4.1, education must be free. All barriers to cost must be removed or education will never be equitable and will never provide children with the life chances to which they are entitled. Education fees and other costs continue to make education unaffordable for many.

Education is expensive. Ironically, some of the people with the least money spend the most on schooling. Ugandan households bear 57 percent of the cost of education. In Benin (U.S. $402 per child), Chad, Côte d'Ivoire ($637 per child), Guinea, and Niger, education expenses run from 20 to 25 percent of GDP per capita. It is more than 30 percent in Togo. In most rich nations, it does not exceed 5 percent. In some countries, even primary school can be expensive. In El Salvador, for example it averages $680 per child (UNESCO 2017). In 12 African countries, learning and teaching materials ate up 56 percent of household budgets (UNESCO 2015b).

A strategy as simple as providing uniforms rather than charging for them can increase school attendance and other related outcomes. In randomized trials in Kenya, uniform programs proved to be successful. While uniforms seem insignificant in the developed world, in Kenya the cost of a uniform was about 2 percent of per capita GDP. In 2003, per capita GDP was U.S. $850, so a uniform was about $17. To put this in perspective, in the United States in 2003, a uniform costing 2 percent of per capita GDP would have been about $900. The test programs had measurable results. Students stayed in school one-half grade longer, reduced their absences, reduced dropout rates, and among sixth-grade girls reduced childbearing (Kremer and Holla 2009).

Cash subsidies have proven to be one of the most effective strategies in many countries. In countries where children labor for cash, subsidies have the effect of reducing child labor and increasing child school attendance. Bolsa Familia is one of the most well-known programs. Begun in Brazil in 2003, the program gave subsidies to poor families in exchange for parents keeping their children in school and participating in preventive health care programs. The program successfully kept children in school—the chances of a 15-year-old girl being in school increased 21 percent by 2013. The World Bank credits the program with increasing school attendance and retention, reducing child labor, reducing child mortality, increasing prenatal medical visits, increasing immunization, and helping to slash poverty. The program has been efficient, costing about .6 percent of GDP while helping millions of families. Brazil, in conjunction with other aid agencies, exported the program around the world to more than 40 countries by 2013 (Wetzel 2013).

PROGRESA, a program instituted in Mexico, provides three years of monthly cash grants to poor mothers whose children maintained an 85 percent school attendance rate. Grants equaled about 25 percent of the average income for poor mothers. The program increased attendance in grades 1 through 8. Since primary education was near universal, the program adjusted to concentrate on the higher grades. This program expanded to 25 mostly middle-income countries. The PROGRESA program produced some desirable effects and other undesirable spillover effects. Within households receiving grants, household work increased for children not receiving the grants. But school attendance increased among students above the poverty threshold and among friends of children receiving the grants. The positive spillover resulted from peer effects (Kremer and Holla 2009).

Programs instituting merit scholarships covering all costs for the last two years of primary education effectively raised student scores not only among the sixth-grade girls competing for scholarships but also among those with little or no chance of winning them. The spillover effect may have been a peer effect, but teacher behavior changed as well. Teacher absence from school declined 4.8 percent.

Schools are increasingly used to provide basic health care. This is important for public health but also for school attendance. Hookworm, roundworm, whipworm, and schistosomiasis are particularly common among school-age children. They have serious health consequences such as anemia, protein malnutrition, and pain. These are expensive to diagnose but can be treated for pennies and without serious side effects. Twice-yearly treatments dispensed by teachers in areas of high worm diseases improved school attendance by 8 percentage points. These programs also had a spillover effect of increasing attendance among students in the same schools but not in the deworming program. Nutrition supplements also increased attendance (Kremer and Holla 2009).

Many of these strategies are low cost. Providing information concerning increased earnings potential for years of education increased attendance, a very low-cost strategy. Girls' attendance at the "one teacher" literacy education centers in India increased when a second female teacher was added. Where costs are higher, as in the cash subsidy programs and providing meals, the payoffs, as with other transfer programs, achieve future benefits beyond school attendance.

Children With Disabilities

The right to education of children with disabilities is protected by national laws. However, globally, children with disabilities are the most likely to be excluded from education. They are less likely to start and less likely to transition to secondary school. Lack of understanding of disabilities, lack of proper teacher training, and stigma keep them out of the classroom, severely limiting their life chances and denying them the opportunity to contribute to their community and society.

Quality inclusive education is one of the SDGs for education. Inclusive education is necessary to accomplish all of the other goals as well. The International Disability and Development Consortium (IDCC) designed action points to help educators target reforms to make education inclusive for students with disabilities—early childhood education, proper teacher training, equal access to scholarships, disability-compliant infrastructure, access to appropriate vocational and tertiary education, and gender- and disability-sensitive learning environments that are safe for all. In other words, children with disabilities need and are entitled to all of the educational benefits of any other child. Only then can a society even hope to accomplish the SDGs and promote full development of the society.

Caring for Children in Conflict Areas and Disaster Situations

One of the great tragedies of the contemporary world is the state of children in conflict areas. About 21 million, or 36 percent, of the world's out-of-school children are in conflict areas (UNESCO 2016). These children cannot be left behind, nor can those who are displaced by disaster or discrimination.

The Interagency Network for Education in Emergencies (INEE) sets minimum standards for children in these harsh situations. The standards, 19 in all, recognize the universal right to education but also the importance of education in emergency situations. Education asserts people's dignity, symbolizes hope for the future, and serves as a focal point for building community. Education is a critical component of the humanitarian response and is no longer seen as something that could be set aside until post-disaster.

Intergovernmental and non-governmental organizations have implemented the INEE standards around the world. In Iraq, for example, the standards were used to rehabilitate five schools in Fallujah after the fighting had forced people to flee their homes. Using the standards as guides, students, parents, teachers, and community members met in focus groups to prioritize their rehabilitation program. As a result, they focused first on getting water, sanitation, and classrooms ready. The Community Education Committee was formed and sent female members to identify reasons for low female participation. Safety emerged as the main reason, and this was addressed through arranging for students to walk in groups and a transparent recruitment program to ensure that male teachers were reliable and professional. Early planning activities and understanding the context of the local area are part of the foundational standards (INEE 2012).

The standards and their successful application in many areas demonstrate that quality education can be delivered in conflict and disaster situations. INEE provides guidelines and toolkits that show how.

Adult Education for Literacy and Jobs

Education for all must include adults as well—in both developing and developed countries. There were about 757 million adults (age 15 years and over) who could not read and write in 2013. This population is not confined to developing countries. Illiteracy is found in middle- and high-income countries as well. In Europe, 20 percent of adults have poor literacy skills. Illiteracy prevents people from fully participating in the benefits of society. They are more likely to suffer from unemployment, lower wages, and poor health. They are less likely to have a voice in the political life of their society (UNESCO 2016).

In developed societies, adult education is sometimes necessary for literacy, particularly for immigrants needing to learn the language of their new home. It is also needed for undereducated adults and a changing economy.

Extending Education to Pre-primary Education

The benefits of pre-primary education are undeniable. Both developed and developing societies benefit from it. It improves educational outcomes of children from disadvantaged backgrounds, and it frees women to pursue income-producing jobs. The global gross enrollment in early childhood education grew significantly from 1999 onward. It reached 54 percent in 2012 but was only 20 percent in sub-Saharan Africa. However, children from richer families and urban families attend pre-primary school considerably more than children from poor rural families. One year of pre-primary education would help close the gaps (UNESCO 2015a). One way in which governments have tried to provide greater access is through contracting with private partners to deliver pre-school education and paying the school fees for families (UNESCO 2015a).

In urban sub-Saharan Africa, demand for pre-primary education is strong. Parents expect learning, not just babysitting. In some areas, more than 80 to 90 percent of children are enrolled—almost exclusively in private schools. Roughly 70 to 84 percent of children from the poorest quintile are enrolled. However, not many of the teachers were trained for early childhood education, and the pedagogy is not always appropriate, with many preschoolers sitting at desks for teacher-led instruction (not necessarily in their home language) and sitting for exams. In contrast, in South Africa the government gives one year of pre-primary education—the reception or grade R. In Soweto, nearly all of the students—aged 5 and 6 years[2]—are in government schools. The instruction in the public and private centers is much more child centered, with play centers, group learning, and home language. Greater government involvement in sub-Saharan schools can increase the number of programs available, lower cost for parents, and provide better educational experiences (UNESCO 2015a).

Public education campaigns concerning the nature of pre-primary school and differences from primary schools have been successful in Thailand and Ghana. Cultural context must also be respected and used to shape the pre-primary school experience, building on local language materials and norms. These considerations boost enrollment as well as learning (UNESCO 2015a).

IMPROVING THE QUALITY OF EDUCATION

Schools for Life

What would happen if schools in developing countries did not adhere to Western models of education? Are there other possibilities? A more effective model of education may look quite different. Many students do not stay in school because they do not see it as relevant to their lives and, thus, not worthwhile in terms of the expense or relative to income they could be earning. The *Stanford Social Innovation Review* suggests a model similar to the ideas that John Dewey proposed in the industrializing United States in the 1920s. It is a model of education that prepares students to succeed at life—life in the society and world in which they live. The keys are relevant content, practical implementation, and student empowerment—a body of skills and attitudes that will serve students whether they move onto higher levels of education or directly into employment.

Teaching methods should engage students. "Schools for Life" is a model arguably more appropriate to the needs of developing countries. Rather than work toward achieving standardized learning outcomes, students learn how to have a positive impact on their communities—student-centered strategies that require them to work in teams tackling real problems, health modules, and entrepreneurship models are the centerpiece. They develop higher-level skills and concepts through active learning (Epstein and Yuthas 2012).

The Escuela Nueva model is such a "school for life." Clara Victoria Colbert founded Escuela Nueva in Colombia in the 1970s to improve the quality of rural schools. It was, in its own way, a part of the political revolution. As a sociologist, Colbert recognized that nothing could be accomplished without education. Using the model, teachers are equipped with learning guides in which concepts from all subject areas are applied as they would be in their lives to complete projects and solve problems. Students work at their own pace. Some of the simpler, but important, homework assignments are to check to see whether their siblings have had all of the immunizations and whether the water cisterns are bug free. Applying progressive, democratic education theories of Dewey, among others, the system helps students to develop academic skills in meaningful contexts. Teachers can teach themselves the system using the guides. The model has spread across Colombia, and 16 countries have replicated it. It is now a global model (Kamenetz, Drummond, and Yenigun 2016).

The schools of Finland have been a curiosity around the world. Their students are among the highest achieving in the PISA tests, although Finnish educators say that they don't pay much attention to the tests because they don't do much testing themselves. They do not pay their teachers the top salaries in the world, but their teachers are drawn from the top 10 percent of graduates, who then need to get a graduate degree in education. Teachers spend less time in the classroom than in the United States and spend more time planning. Every school has the same funding and same curriculum, so children get the same quality education no matter where they live. There is little difference between the top and bottom performers. More

than 93 percent of students graduate from an academic or vocational high school, and 66 percent go on to college. It helps that a generous social welfare program provides for preschool, paid maternity leave, and subsidized day care. Most important, however, as in Escuela Nueva, each child is provided with the time and attention that he or she needs to learn. The schools "prepare kids for life," in the words of one of the school principals (Hancock 2011).

Reforming the System

The OECD (2010, 2017) proposed policy recommendations for improving education that apply to developed and developing societies. Among them are the following.

Additional Support to Disadvantaged Schools and Students

Low-performing schools and low-performing students should be targeted early and helped through special curriculum, learning materials, and economic assistance. Students marginalized due to disability, ethnicity, socioeconomic, or other status should be included wherever possible in mainstream schools and classes. Tracking should be postponed, not started early.

The Finnish model provides extra money for schools with a disadvantaged population. In Espoo, a school received an extra 82,000 euros to meet the financial requirements of extra aides, special materials, and so forth. In "Hedgehog Road," the oldest low-income housing project in Finland, the school receives an extra 47,000 euros each year. This "positive discrimination" money ensures that "equality" is the most important word in Finnish education. Its special education teachers are paid somewhat above the average teacher scale because they have an extra year, a sixth year, of university study. Their job is demanding, and they have aides to help. Teachers work together collaborating on how to help each student. Each student is targeted based on his or her needs. The result of the extra money, time, and attention is that nearly 100 percent of the ninth graders in Hedgehog Road go on to upper secondary school. Those who do not will go to one of the vocational schools, attended by about 43 percent of Finnish students. They teach for life, not for tests (Hancock 2011).

Improve Teaching Quality and Teachers' Career Prospects and Incentives

Large classes, poor pay, and poorly equipped schools confront teachers in disadvantaged areas throughout the developing world and in areas of many developed nations. This makes it difficult to recruit enough teachers who are well enough trained and knowledgeable in their subjects to deliver high-quality education.

Millions more teachers are needed to achieve universal education. In developing countries, "contract" teachers are often used to help overcome the shortfalls. They could be untrained and not experts in the subject area. They are paid less than the regular civil service teachers and are often placed in the most remote or disadvantaged areas, compounding the disadvantage found there.

To lure the right people away from more lucrative jobs or better working conditions to enter classrooms, significant reforms must be made. For teachers to achieve the best possible results, systemic reforms also need to be addressed. The connection between teacher salary and student achievement is not linear. Students in Finland, for example, outperform those in many countries. Yet teachers in Finland are paid less than in most of those countries. What teachers there do have is respect. It is a highly valued and sought after occupation. This is not to suggest that teacher salaries should not provide them a salary befitting their education. But teachers who are valued and who are trusted with more autonomy over how to achieve educational goals in their schools and classrooms can achieve better results. This requires sufficiently decentralizing education so that more planning and development occurs at the school level where teachers know their students and how best to help them.

Strengthen Connections Between Education and Industry

While all students should receive a liberal education so that they acquire the skills for lifelong learning and familiarity with the great ideas of the civilizations, not everyone wants to or should go to college. Better secondary and post-secondary vocational programs attuned to student needs and the needs of the labor market are appropriate for traditionally aged students and adults in the developing and developed worlds. University education should also be linked closely with the needs of an ever-changing economy and world.

Establishing Education as a Human Right

The universal right to education is recognized in a number of international documents and treaties, beginning with the UN Declaration of Human Rights, which states in Article 26 that everyone has the right to a free education and, at least in elementary stages, that it be directed to the full development of personalities' and that parents have the right to choose the kind of education they prefer for their children. Education is related to income, health, and even participation in democracy. Without educational opportunity, achievement in other important life dimensions cannot be fulfilled to a person's potential.

These basic rights have been expounded on in a number of international instruments—in particular UNESCO's Convention against Discrimination in Education of 1960, the International Covenant on Economic, Social and Cultural Rights of 1966, and the UN Convention on the Rights of the Child of 1989. The right to a free education is guaranteed in 65 percent of constitutions and encoded into many national laws.

UNICEF argues for a rights-based approach to education. The principles that inform a rights-based model recognize the unique characteristics of indigenous peoples and minorities. Free and equal access cannot mean treating everyone the same. It must mean accounting for and remediating the differences among children and providing the education that is appropriate. These principles should inform education from primary through tertiary levels as well as through vocational education and job training for adults. The principles and how they apply to the education of groups of concern in this chapter are as follows:

- *Universality and inalienability:* The rights belong to everyone; they may not be given up or taken away by anyone. In this context, the principle means that every measure needs to be taken to ensure that all people have access to an education appropriate for them.

- *Indivisibility:* All rights are essential to the dignity of every person. The right to education cannot be subordinated to any other right, nor can any right be subordinated to it. In this case, a parent's right to choose other options for a child, whether that be the child's right to security or health care, cannot deny the child the right to an education. For example, children in need of security must also be educated in a manner appropriate for them. Whether in a refugee camp, foster home, or homeless shelter, children must also be educated.

- *Interdependence:* Some rights are interdependent. The right to education might be dependent on the right to information. Knowledge of one's rights is essential.

- *Equality and non-discrimination:* This principle does not mean treating everyone in the same way. It does mean that as services are delivered, the unique vulnerabilities of every child need to be considered. For example, bilingual education, education sensitive to cultural values and customs, living arrangements, and a plethora of other distinctions need to be addressed in providing an equal education. Any element not manifesting this principle—for instance, a culturally biased textbook that reinforces power imbalances—needs to be eliminated. Gender stereotypes and negative representations of indigenous or minority groups cannot be tolerated. Children with disabilities must be educated with the appropriate interventions such as Braille and sign language.

- *Empowerment:* The purpose of education is to develop the capacity of individuals and communities, thereby giving them power and control over their own lives. Children's views should be valued, showing respect for their families, cultures, and traditions. All forms of humiliating punishments are forbidden. Empowerment primarily is the capacity of people to claim and achieve their rights.

- *Accountability and rule of law:* Institutions must be held accountable for fulfilling human rights and if they violate those rights. Those who hold the duty to fulfill the rights need to be identified, and their capacity to fulfill their obligations must be assessed. They must be given the tools to develop their capacity wherever weaknesses exist. (UNICEF/UNESCO 2007)

Whereas the period from 2000 to 2015 explicitly addressed gender discrimination, those years saw gender gaps in education close significantly, with girls achieving at higher levels of attainment than boys. Discrimination against minorities in education needs to be targeted with the same intensity in order to reduce inequality.

Socioeconomic background remains the single most predictive factor of student achievement. Socioeconomic background of individuals within a school and segregation of schools according to socioeconomic background both affect educational equality in outcomes. Both segregating students by background within schools and segregation of schools by socioeconomic background increase inequalities in outcomes. Reducing the effect of family background characteristics through social welfare programs that reduce inequalities in living conditions increases students' opportunity to learn. Reducing inequalities among schools reduces educational inequalities in outcomes. Where social welfare programs are not politically supported, changes in policy and practice can reduce educational inequalities even when inequalities of background characteristics persist. Educational equality interventions, in turn, reduce overall inequalities in adult life chances, including occupational status, income, and health.

The opportunities for students to learn vary dramatically across and within school systems. Many factors related to the distribution of material and human capital affect inequality of learning outcomes. Class size, money spent per pupil, access to technology, and the range of the curriculum all may be important factors. Determining which factors and interventions can have the most impact is important. A World Bank study of more than 100 countries (Ferreira and Gignoux 2013) found that educational opportunity accounted for up to 35 percent of all disparities in educational achievement. This held not only for developing societies but also for developed societies. Among the findings of the study is that increasing the share of public educational expenditures spent in early primary grades increases the level of equality of opportunity and the equality in the chance to achieve. Because children come to school with different levels of preparation related to background factors such as parental education and income, targeting early years of schooling helps children to make up for some of that disadvantage. The researchers also found that increasing tracking—putting students into different educational programs as measured by vocational school enrollment in secondary education—decreased educational opportunity. The track placements tend to be significantly determined by early inequalities related to parental and other background factors. Thus, tracking exacerbates entry inequalities rather than mitigates them. Each of these factors related to opportunity affected inequality of achievement. Studies in the United States also confirm that efforts to use early education as a vehicle for ameliorating background disadvantages improves educational attainment.

A study of the dispersion of learning outcomes in school systems for more than 50 countries (Montt 2011) found that the distribution of teachers and of better teachers across the schools in a system, the absence of tracking, and the intensity of schooling all played significant roles in reducing negative educational outcomes. Although the factors may be related across school systems, and where one is found the others may be more likely, they have independent effects. For example, an equal distribution of opportunities does not produce equal results where intensity of schooling is not equal.

Opportunity to learn is essentially a measure of resources. The qualifications of the teachers, material resources, class size, and tracking of students into different educational programs all affect opportunity to learn. The Montt (2011) study found that ensuring equal distribution of qualified teachers reduced inequality in attainment. This variant is particularly important in increasing achievement of minority students. Montt also found that tracking students into different programs increased inequality, as Ferreira and Gignoux (2013) also found. Furthermore, the earlier the tracking occurred,

the greater the resulting inequalities. Class size was not an important variant with respect to inequality. This is in keeping with many prior studies.

Education from a rights-based perspective demands that policy and program work to give all children an education appropriate to their cultural, social, structural, and individual needs. It also demands that schooling be structured to overcome family and school background characteristics that lead to inequalities in educational outcomes. This is necessary not only to fulfill individual life chances but also to create a more robust society and increase potential for overall growth in both the economy and political participation. In societies such as the United States, where neighborhood segregation is increasing, school interventions for equality are critical.

SUMMARY

Education, matched to one's abilities and desires, is a human right. It is necessary to achieve one's potential in life chances. Too many children and adults are left behind because they have not received an education or have not received a quality or meaningful education. They are left

behind economically, socially, and in the health of themselves and their children. Global investment in education to ensure that everyone has this life chance is essential to developing a peaceful and prosperous world.

DISCUSSION

1. What would a comprehensive school system look like? What forms of education would be provided? Consider the spectrum of learners who need to be educated.

2. How should education be funded? What strategies work to achieve equality of education? What should be the role of private schools in educational systems?

3. How can educational systems make up for some of the disadvantages students face that limit their optimal potential success at school?

ON YOUR OWN

1. Investigate inequality for your home country, using the PISA data online. Under each academic category, scores are discriminated by a number of variables. For example, if you click on the arrow to the left of "Science Literacy," this menu appears:

- Average Scores
- Proficiency Levels
- Percentiles

- Gender
- Student Economic, Cultural, and Social Status (ECSS)
- School Poverty Indicator
- Race and Ethnicity

The last four variables measure the influence of inequalities on achievement. Assess the impact of inequalities on achievement scores. For each score, which form of inequality has the most effect? Which score is overall the most affected by inequality? Compare your home country with a country that is considered more equal than yours and one that is considered less equal. http://pisadataexplorer.oecd.org/ide/idepisa/dataset.aspx

2. The Human Development Index includes considerations of inequalities between males and females. The "Dashboard" presents this as ratios of the percentage ratio of females to males in a given variable. For example, Norway's ratio is 98 for pre-primary education and 111 for secondary education. This means that 2 percent fewer females go to preschool and 11 percent more females are enrolled in secondary school in comparison with males.

Life Course Gender Gap: http://hdr.undp.org/en/composite/Dashboard1

In which countries do you see the greatest gender gaps in education? In which countries are females attaining more than males? (Scores are color coded into three same-sized groups, with the darkest being the most equal. Whether a score is skewed to the favor of females or males is not considered, just the degree of inequality.)

3. Not all countries have constitutional provisions for education. Using the Constitute Project, find the countries that provide for education in their constitutions and the rights that they provide. The Constitute Project search page is found at this URL: https://www.constituteproject.org

Click on "Explore Constitutions."

Type "education" into the search box. How many constitutions mention education specifically? How many provide for "Free education?" "Compulsory education?" "Access to higher education?" "Equal education?"

You may also search under other terms related to education. What provisions are made by your country with specific regard to education? Some societies have "equal protection" articles or amendments that are used to provide for life chances such as health or education.

NOTES

1. Whether the motives of the reformers and others promoting public schools was to create docile and obedient citizens and workers or simply productive citizens and workers is debated. The Prussian system that was studied by American reformers may have had authoritarian motivations that many Americans may also have desired. It may also reflect dysfunctions of the growing bureaucratization of life.

2. Students younger than 5 years must go to private school.

6

From Difference to Discrimination
FAULT LINES OF RACE, ETHNICITY, AND RELIGION

WHEN YOU ARE NOT A PERSON IN YOUR OWN COUNTRY

[W]hat we know now in the 21st century is that the true wealth of a nation can be found in the human resources of a country and their ability to freely build, invent, excel, and express themselves. Countries that fully unleash this potential, that invest in the health, prosperity, security, and diversity of their societies, will thrive in the 21st century no matter the abundance that they have or don't have in traditional measures of wealth and strength.

—Antony Blinken (2016)

Arafa Begum lives in a concentration camp with her five daughters in her native country, Myanmar. Since 1982, Myanmar has refused to recognize Arafa and her children or any of the Rohingya, the ethnic group to which she belongs, as citizens. Now, because they are considered illegal immigrants, their country does not provide them with education, health care, jobs, or food.

Their persecution escalated in 2012 when genocide against the Rohingya began in earnest. As of fall 2017, 606,000 Rohingya have fled the country, fully two thirds of them just from late August through early September. Thousands have been killed or packed into concentration camps, and thousands have fled to other countries because their villages were destroyed and their houses were set on fire (Rushing 2017). Fearing that her family would not survive in Myanmar, Arafa was forced to face the risks of death at sea or slavery in brothels for herself and her daughters if they were going to escape. They fled by a ship equipped with little food or water and run by human traffickers. The ship, loaded with human cargo, needed to evade the Thai Navy to reach Malaysia.

LEARNING OBJECTIVES

After completing this chapter, students should be able to do the following:

6.1 Analyze how the social construction of meaning influences categories of race and ethnicity

6.2 Assess the impact that race, ethnicity, and religion have on life chances in different contexts

6.3 Examine how persecution and discrimination destabilize societies and global security

6.4 Analyze international conventions and national constitutions for recognition of religious rights and understand the dimensions of religious freedom

6.5 Distinguish social hostility toward and government regulation of religion and explain how they interact and reinforce one another

6.6 Discuss strategies to reduce persecution and discrimination within countries

After 50 days at sea, the ship was forced to turn back to Myanmar. Finding herself back in a concentration camp, Arafa will try to escape Myanmar again (Kristof 2016).

In a world plagued with ethnic and religious conflict and discrimination, Amnesty International calls the Rohingya the most persecuted ethnic group in the world today. Both a Yale Law School study (Lindblom et al. 2015) and a study by the International State Crime Initiative at Queen Mary University of London (Green, McManus, and de la Cour Venning 2015) found that in 2012 the government of Myanmar escalated decades-long persecution. The government engaged in genocide and failed to prevent genocide, attempting to destroy, in whole or in part, the Rohingya group.

In 2016, persecution intensified further. Rapes, torture, beheadings, shootings, and worse of men, women, children, and babies were reported by independent sources and the survivors of the fall 2017 attacks on more than 200 villages. Aung San Suu Kyi, who won the Nobel Peace Prize for her staunch opposition to Myanmar's military dictatorship and became Myanmar's de facto leader, has been criticized internationally for her years-long silence on the treatment of Rohingya and support of the military.

The Rohingya are one of many stateless groups throughout the world who are seen as foreigners in their own countries.

DEFINING DIFFERENCE: DIVERSITY AND MEANING

Although we are all human, we have socially constructed an array of categories through which to divide ourselves into "us" and "them." Sexual identity, hair and skin color and texture, eye shape, sexual orientation, the god or gods we do or do not worship, the ways in which we worship all have been invoked to generate solidarity, find targets for hate, and mobilize people to discriminate. Notwithstanding the advance of civilization and the universal recognition of human rights, we act on old hatreds and invent new ones.

There is no easy way to talk about either race or ethnicity, not only because people's prejudices emerge and test their tolerance. That happens. It is difficult to talk about race and ethnicity because they are slippery concepts. In China, *zu* refers to lineage without differentiating race from ethnicity. The terms do not have a biological or genetic meaning and cannot be defined with a comfortable degree of analytical specificity. Lineage, language, customs, norms, and values all have a role in establishing a racial and ethnic identity.

Race and ethnicity are socially constructed concepts and have differentiated differently in different parts of the world. Ethnicity is based on lineage and kinship. An ethnicity is a community of people who share a common culture, usually including a common language, history, and sets of values and beliefs. They identify "us" and others who are "them."

Before the advent of the nation-state, most regions of the world were occupied by many ethnic groups—hundreds of them. As nations formed uniting communities of varying ethnicity, ethnicities became subsumed under nations. Rather than existing as autonomous communities, ethnic groups became subjects of the state (although not always full citizens). As the many separatist movements and conditions of domination, discrimination, persecution, and genocide attest, this has not been unproblematic.

Race came later as a social construct, generally associated with the African slave trade. No one has had any success in identifying a genetic basis for differentiating races. Scientists long ago rejected racial naturalism, the view that there is a set of biological features shared only by members of a certain race. There are seven genes that combine in different ways to create the phenotype, the physical characteristics that we see. Ancestry mapping tools demonstrate that most of us draw our ancestry from many parts of the globe. We all are mongrels, and that fact is undoubtedly a source of strength for the human species.

Racial classifications are usually based on physical characteristics or how people look—the color of their skin, hair, and eyes; the shape of their face, especially eyes, nose, and mouth; their height; the texture of their hair; and varying combinations of all of the above. There is a presumed shared biological heritage that gives rise not only to visible physical features but also to personality characteristics such as intelligence, honesty, and a work ethic. In this regard, concepts of race and ethnicity are barely, if at all, distinguishable. In some cultures, race and ethnicity are interchangeable.

Race, while meaningless as anything but a social construct, is real in its consequences for people's life chances.

PHOTO 6.1 Manufacturing Race. Twins, one "black" and one "white," are not particularly uncommon. Can they really be of a different "race"? These twins celebrate their differences.

Worldwide Features/Barcroft Me via Getty Images.

Although defined differently country by country, and fluid[1] and changing within countries, race determines life chances. The labels are fault lines that run through society, bestowing prejudice and discrimination on one side and favor and privilege on the other. Even though there are not any real races, we need to understand how people think about them in order to understand how conceptions of race motivate action and affect the experiences people have (Appiah 2005).

Religion is another fault line in societies. Most people acquire a religious identity through birth, but in most societies people are free to change their religion or to decline to identify with one religion at all. Religious categories are also socially constructed, and to all believers their religion is the one that is true. Still, many religious persons practice "tolerance" and believe that allowing a diversity of religions to flourish enhances all religions. For others, belief is accompanied by righteousness—righteousness that empowers people, in their own eyes, to impose their beliefs on others or punish them for not believing or for believing otherwise.

All contemporary societies have some degree of racism, ethnic prejudice, and religious discrimination. Which boundary has the most meaning varies by the time and place. In some societies, religion is the fractious boundary, as in some of the Arab League countries divided by Islamic sect. In other societies, such as Rwanda and Burundi where the Hutu and Tutsi conflict cost millions of lives, that boundary is ethnicity. In the United States and South Africa, it is race. Regardless of how these classification schemes evolved, they are real in their consequences. People divide themselves into "us" and "them" and find ways to discredit and then discriminate against "them."

Where boundaries of race, ethnicity, and religion overlap, they might not be so divisive. Any two people may be divided by one boundary but united by another. Where boundaries are coterminous, separating people along all dimensions, they are more divisive. Regardless that nearly every government's constitution makes a general guarantee of equality, race, ethnicity, and religion become fault lines of inequities. Whether discrimination is encoded into law or not, people may be privileged in all three or have life chances denied, finding themselves on the outside—the wrong race, the wrong ethnicity, or the wrong religion.

BURNED BY THE SUN OR WHITE LIKE THE ICE: THE SOCIAL CREATION OF RACE

Skin color, perhaps because it is the most varied of our physical characteristics, can be used to separate people on the basis of the degree of lightness or darkness. Racialized conceptions of desirability are now globalized (Figure 6.1); lighter is better and darker is worse, so much so that skin lightening creams are a multi-billion-dollar global business.

How the color of a complexion, meaningless in and of itself, became "racialized" and laden with meaning powerful enough to reduce one person's life chances and enhance another's is a story of inequality.

The ancient world did not know color prejudice. Africans had a presence throughout Europe, particularly Greece and Italy, that was neither servile nor the object of prejudice and discrimination. Greek and Roman texts described noble people, the Ethiopians (Aithiopians) who lived under the torrid rays of the sun south of Egypt.

They bore the marks of the sun's heat—blackened skin ("scorched complexions") and "frizzly" or "wooly" hair. Ancient texts wrote of the piety and justice of Ethiopian rulers who outlawed the death penalty and required offenders to contribute to civic improvement and who instructed soldiers to take their enemy alive. Africans were loved by the gods for their justice—so just that they had no need for doors. In the writings of Homer, the Ethiopians were a favorite of the gods (Snowden 1971).

Snowden's (1971) account was drawn from interpretations of extensive writings, literature, and art of ancient Greece and Rome and early Christianity that portray a view of color in which difference was recognized and portrayed without any semblance of modern-day racism.

A CLOSER LOOK
RACISM AS A GLOBAL TRAGEDY

The World Values Survey of 81 countries shows that racism, as measured by how many people would not like a person of another race as a neighbor, is still a force in the world. Because admitting to racism might not be acceptable in some countries, the figures may actually be higher.

FIGURE 6.1

Source: Fisher (2013). Reproduced with permission. Based on data from the World Values Survey.

Cultural customs had no bearing on the value of the peoples or persons. Beauty came in all colors. Ethiopian men were often depicted as among the most handsome in the world, and the women were depicted as among the most beautiful. "Natural bent," not race, determines nobility, and excellence is found in "all men" whatever their race, wrote Menander, a Greek dramatist (Snowden 1971). This is not to say that ethnocentrism did not exist; rather, ethnocentrism was more an appreciation of one's own, not an aversion toward the other. Although the color black representing evil and white representing purity was common imagery, it did not apply to skin color, and virtue applied equally to both black and white persons.

The Emergence of *Homo Europaeus* and *Homo Afer*

Slavery is as old as war, when captured enemies were routinely enslaved. The association of race with slavery is much more modern. The concept of distinct races evolved in the Western world in a gradual process from about the 16th century, but it was never universally accepted. Confronted with the nature of indigenous Americans, the Spanish questioned how to treat them—as "dumb brutes" to be enslaved or "truly men capable of understanding the Catholic faith." Eventually, the argument that Native Americans had immigrated from Asia to America—that they were fully human—held sway but did not prevent enslavement of both the indigenous and Africans in the Americas.

In England and the Americas, social class was the main dividing line, not color. Africans and European indentured servants both were enslaved and often worked together. Each could earn freedom. In 17th-century America, as fewer Europeans immigrated as servants (presumably having heard of the harsh conditions) and the Native American population declined, African labor became crucial.

A means of enslaving Africans for life and replenishing the cadre of slaves was essential for the plantation economy. Slavery and colonialism demanded justifications for subjugating an entire continent of people. Africa became portrayed as a barbaric and uncivilized continent, and Africans were portrayed as better off in servitude than left to their own devices. The line between white and black servitude was drawn. Social class began to give way to color as a dividing line. Poor whites, elite whites, and small farmers began to identify as a group apart from black Africans. In the 1660s, Virginia built the legal framework to hold Africans in slavery for life. First,

this legal framework declared that people's status of freedom or bondage would be inherited from their mother, not their father. Second, it removed the stipulation that if slaves converted to Christianity, they would be freed. From this point onward, Africans, slavery, and inferiority became linked (Wood 1995).

As the slave trade continued, "scientific" views on race emerged. Linnaeus and other scientists of the era who classified plant and animal life, classified humans too. His categories evolved over time but each iteration specified physical, social, personality, and even clothing characteristics of each category. He delineated four sub-species of *Homo sapiens*: *europaeus, asiaticus, afer,* and *americanus*. Although these sub-species were not separated as different races, Linnaeus attributed different characteristics to them. In addition to their physical qualities, Linnaeus called *Homo europaeus* inventive, acute, and governed by laws; *Homo asiaticus* were melancholy, avaricious, haughty, and governed by opinion; *Homo americanus* were obstinate, merry, free, and governed by customs; he called *Homo afer* crafty, indolent, negligent, and governed by caprice (Smedley and Smedley 2011).

Justifying slavery during and after the American Revolution while proclaiming the natural rights of mankind proved to be difficult but possible. Thomas Jefferson advanced the ideology of the inferiority of Africans when he wrote in the "Note on the State of Virginia" that he suspected that blacks were mentally inferior to whites—a point disputed by Benjamin Banneker, an astronomer. Banneker sent Jefferson an Almanac, the first done by a black man. Banneker accused Jefferson of "the most criminal act" that he presumably detested in others (Gordon-Reed 2000).

The U.S. Constitution, which denied black men—free or enslaved—the right to vote, established a racial hierarchy and racist ideology in the United States. Racism was further institutionalized by a series of laws, policies, institutional practices, and individual acts of discrimination that continued to disadvantage African Americans and, subsequently, Asian, Southern European, and Mexican immigrants.

One of the last arguments buttressing theories of inequality among races was Darwin's theory of evolution. The theory of evolution argues that all animals developed from a common ancestor. To the abolitionists, this meant that all people—whether European, Asian, African, or American—had a common ancestry; however to the slave holders, it confirmed their belief that Africans were inferior.

A CLOSER LOOK
LEGAL FRAMEWORK AGAINST RACISM

There are four major international instruments concerning racism that have the force of international law:

- International Convention on the Elimination of All Forms of Racial Discrimination (1965)
- International Bill of Human Rights and associated covenants (1966)

- International Labour Organization Convention No. 111 concerning Discrimination in Respect of Employment and Occupation (1958)
- United Nations Educational, Scientific, and Cultural Organisation Convention against Discrimination in Education (1960).

Uniting Under the Yellow Emperor and Creating Ethnic Divides

Discrimination has a long history in China. In the 8th century, Uyghurs were forbidden to try to pass themselves as Chinese (Roberts 2012). In the Ming and early Qing dynasties, mid-17th century, Han Chinese referred to themselves as the "Yellow People" well before Europeans used the label "yellow." For the Han, it was a testament to lineage going back to Emperor Huang-ti, the "Yellow Emperor," and proof of their claim to purity and superiority.

More than 90 percent of Chinese are ethnic Han, but there are hundreds of small ethnic groups throughout China. Most of the ethnic minorities originate from rural areas along the borders with China's neighbors with whom they share a common culture such as the Manchu, Uyghurs, Kazaks, Mongols, and Tajiks. Each ethnic minority is small as a portion of China's population; the largest, the Zuang, is only 1.3 percent of the population. Together, they would be the 11th largest nation in the world and occupy more than half of China's land (Tuttle 2015).

Contemporary conceptions of racial and ethnic hierarchy crystallized in the late 19th century and were used to support the Han claim to superiority. Chinese intellectuals cited the flawed ideas of social Darwinism, applying natural selection to human races, to rejuvenate the race and to propose the superiority of the Chinese vis-à-vis their neighbors. Their hierarchy was yellow and white on top, red and black below. They recognized the ethnic groups of Asia of the "yellow" race but not as equal to the

Han. Prejudice was such that Zhang Binglin, a radical reformer of the period, accused the Qing dynasty of failing to protect the purity of the Han, leading to China's demise and defeat in the Opium Wars against Britain and France (Pfafman, Carpenter, and Tang 2015; Yamamoto 2005).

Throughout their history as a republic, attempts to equalize the ethnicities failed. Sun Yat-sen, the first ruler of the Republic of China, wanted to abolish all lines and cleavages of ethnicity. His goal was to establish one China, one nation with one cultural and political core. Mao Zedong's Communist government encouraged class unity but held up the Han as the vanguard of the revolution. The Han were to lead the other, less advanced minority groups toward eventual assimilation into the Chinese culture.

Under Mao, the hundreds of non-Han groups were recategorized into 56 ethnicities, presumably with the intent of making them easier to manage (Myers, Xiaoyan, and Ceconi Cruz 2013; Tuttle 2015). Mao brought the ethnic groups under China's control but did not incorporate them into the government. He arrested some minority group leaders and did not offer them leadership roles in the Communist Party. The government produced a series of films depicting the ethnic groups as primitive, savage, and backward—in need of being civilized and saved by Communist China. Despite the Communist ideology of equality, social Darwinist ideas of the hierarchy of races continued throughout the Communist era. Discrimination against ethnic groups remains significant (Yamamoto 2005).

CONSIDER THIS
CHINESE AND JAPANESE RELATIONS

China and Japan are geographically close neighbors, but according to a 2016 Pew Research Center poll, their relations could hardly be cooler. Only 11 percent of Japanese have a favorable opinion of China, and the Chinese return the favor with only 14 percent having a favorable view of Japan. Large majorities in each country see the other as arrogant and violent. Hardly anyone in either country sees the other as honest. Nor do many (less than 50 percent in each country) see the others as hard-working. In general, their views of one another are not getting any better. In most of the qualities rated, favorable opinions declined since 2006 (Stokes 2016).

Attitudes Toward Indigenous Peoples: Foreigners in Japan

Racism is "profound" in Japan, as described by a United Nations (UN) report in 2005, and has a long and deeply ingrained history. Much like when the English settlements in North America displaced indigenous peoples, when the Japanese migrated to the archipelago, they pushed the native peoples into marginal territories. From the 17th century to the mid-19th century, the Tokugawa feudal period, "Japanese" distinguished themselves from the Ainu, Ryukyuan, and "lesser" lineages. People labeled "eta," meaning outcast, and "hinin," meaning nonperson, were ostracized, were not able to intermarry with the majority, and passed their status down to their children. These categories of people were not physically distinguished from one another (Yamamoto 2005).

During the Meiji years from the mid-19th century to the early 20th century, Japan developed from a decentralized, backward feudal society to an industrial world power. As Japan developed, it strove to establish a single and superior Japanese identity based on the claim that the lineage of the Meiji emperor traced back to the original Yamoto clan and that the Japanese were related to the emperor. As in China and the West, the Japanese used social Darwinism to claim their superiority over indigenous groups and their neighbors.

From the Sino–Japanese War at the end of the 19th century to the end of World War II, Japan acquired (at least temporarily) islands that had been under Chinese, Russian, and German control. In 1871 it acquired the Ryukyu Kingdom, and in 1910 it acquired the Korean Empire. This last acquisition led to the Korean migration that swelled the Korean population in Japan from 3,989 in 1915 to 625,682 by 1935. The Japanese expanded the category "otherness" beyond the indigenous peoples to include Chinese, Vietnamese, Koreans, and Latin Americans of Japanese descent as well (Yamamoto 2005). A series of legislative acts following World War II stripped Korean ethnic groups of citizenship and treated them as foreigners even though they were generations born in Japan. In 1991, Koreans born in Japan acquired special "residency" (Park 2017).

Racism is now one of Japan's most severe social problems. The right-wing extremist group Zaitokukai (whose official name translates to citizens against the privilege of Koreans in Japan) is calling for Koreans to be killed. Its members try to dehumanize Koreans, calling them cockroaches and criminals and encouraging their extermination (Park 2017). The leader of this extremist group ran for governor of Tokyo in 2016. He did not win but garnered 110,000 votes with a platform built on abolishing public assistance for non-Japanese. Children are bullied at school, and discrimination in housing and hotel bookings is well documented. Japan inaugurated a hate crimes law in response, but because there are no penalties, the law has little effect (McCurry 2016).

Many establishments display "Japanese only" signs, and many practices limit Korean children's right to education. Filipinos, Thais, and Koreans have been attacked. Korean schools have been attacked. Some local governments deny or suspend funding for Korean schools. Hate speech and discrimination against Chinese and Koreans is common (Park 2017). Between 2012 and 2015, ultranationalists held more than 1,000 hate rallies.

A 2017 survey of foreign residents of Japan revealed widespread discrimination. More than 40 percent of respondents (4,252) claimed to have suffered discrimination in housing; 30 percent suffered derogatory remarks from strangers, bosses, colleagues, and subordinates; 25 percent were denied jobs; and 20 percent were paid less due to discrimination (Hurst 2017).

Fissures of Race, Religion, and Caste in India

Racism comes in many varieties in India. Being of a lower caste, of a darker complexion, an ethnic minority from the border areas, a Christian, or a Muslim all subject a person to discrimination in India. The most well-known is structured into the caste system—one of the most rigid and all-encompassing systems of inequality. Regional and ethnic prejudices, as well as racism against "foreigners" or aliens, are also abundant. "Scheduled castes" are untouchables, the most discriminated against caste, and "scheduled tribes" also suffer from severe discrimination. They receive some considerations similar to affirmative action. However, not all the ethnic groups subject to harsh treatment are covered by these laws.

Similar to China, a geographic divide exists between "mainstream India" and the Northeast, where the ethnic minorities originate. The populations living along the Northeast borders share ethnicity and culture with their neighbors—Bangladesh, Bhutan, Burma, China, and Nepal (Figure 6.2). They have a physical appearance similar to Chinese and other East Asians. The Mon-Khmer and Tibeto-Burman communities are "scheduled tribes." Other ethnic groups in the Northeast corridor, although not among the scheduled tribes, are also victims of discrimination and violence.

A CLOSER LOOK
THE SEVEN STATES OF INDIA'S NORTHEAST BORDER REGION

People in this region bear cultural and physical similarities with people of bordering countries—Myanmar, Bhutan, China, and Bangladesh.

FIGURE 6.2   Northeast Region of India

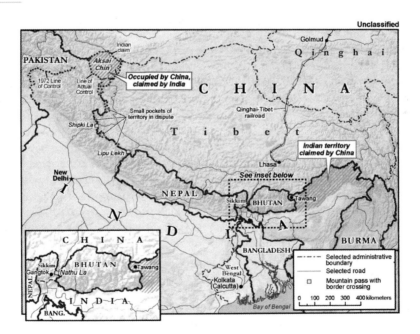

Source: United States Central Intelligence Agency. (2006) *China and India*. [Washington: Central Intelligence Agency] [Map] Retrieved from the Library of Congress, https://www.loc.gov/item/2006626895/.

This Northeast area is derogatorily referred to as the "Mongoloid fringe." Indians consider those who live there a different race and subject them to derogatory names such as "chinky." Although a diverse group with conflict and a number of rivalries among them, these marginalized people increasingly identify with one another because they all are subject to the same prejudice and discrimination, including violent attacks and homicide. Many Northeasterners migrated to Indian cities in the mainland to escape the violence and find economic opportunities. From 2005 to 2011, migrants from the Northeast, primarily of working- and lower middle-class backgrounds, increased 12-fold. Rather than escape the violence, targeted attacks and murders followed them. Northeasterners responded first with fear.

In 2012, however, was a tipping point. A young Northeasterner was murdered in an argument over a TV remote. A series of protests and vigils followed, and fear of future attacks sent a wave of migrants who had been living in the cities back home to the Northeast, depriving many businesses of a large part of their workforce—from ethnic restaurants to cleaning and security firms (McDuie-Ra 2015).

Color is also an important line of demarcation in India. Africans and people of African descent report widespread discrimination. An African American called India the most racist society in the world in an Indian newspaper. Most of the Indians who responded to the column agreed. The World Values Survey data concur; more than 40 percent of Indian respondents indicated that they would not like someone of a different race living next door (Fisher 2013).

Although the origin of castes is debated, color discrimination plays a role in all explanations. "Brahman was of white color, Kshatriya of red color, Vaishya was of yellow color, and the Shudra of black color . . . the untouchables are below Shudra" (Ambedkar 1979, quoted in Ayyar and Khandare 2012). Another interpretation is that the castes originated from two divisions: the dark-skinned are conquered indigenous peoples and the light-skinned are the descendants of Aryan conquerors and thus are superior. Yet another theory is that castes arose from work categories that also reflected the assignment of darker-skinned people to lower occupations (Ayyar and Khandare 2012).

The association of color and status remains strong even among the educated. The "Aryan belt" is known as the location of ideal beauty. Even within lower castes, those of lighter skin are preferred. In contrast, women of darker complexion are stigmatized (Ayyar and Khandare 2012). As in other parts of the world, skin lightening treatments are a billion-dollar business.

THE RIGHTS OF INDIGENOUS COMMUNITIES: THE "FIRST" PEOPLES

Children born into indigenous families often live in remote areas where governments do not invest in basic social services. Consequently, indigenous youth and children have limited or no access to health care, quality education, justice, and participation. They are at particular risk of not being registered at birth and of being denied identity documents."

—United Nations (2005), Permanent Forum on Indigenous Issues

Ironically, in many countries, it is the "first people" of a land who are the most marginalized. Although there is no hard-and-fast internationally accepted definition of "indigenous," it is generally recognized that indigenous peoples are the ones who were inhabiting a territory before colonial or imperial conquest—the Inuits, native of Alaska; the many Native American tribes throughout North and South America; the ethnicities that spread across Africa such as the Berber, Dinka, Maasai, and Nuer; the Aborigine of Australia; the Kachin and Uyghur of China; and the Ainu of Japan are among them. There are 3 to 4 million indigenous persons in the world, and about one third of them live in extreme poverty.

Colonial powers seized the lands that indigenous people occupied, often drawing political boundaries cutting through their territories, dividing language and cultural groups and joining them with others. Many indigenous people retain their original languages and maintain traditional customs and practices. They tend to live in harmony with land rather than try to control it. Many live on protected lands, home to 80 percent of the world's biodiversity. Where their lands are rich in resources, governments and private companies are wont to appropriate, sell, or pollute their land, leading to displacement. Displacement pushes indigenous people onto the least desirable lands, where it is hard to maintain their traditional lifestyles and hard to survive.

Despite the protections, indigenous people have been denied many of the rights and freedoms guaranteed them under international law. These rights include the following:

A CLOSER LOOK

THE LEGAL FRAMEWORK FOR THE PROTECTION OF INDIGENOUS PEOPLES OF THE WORLD

There are several main international instruments pertaining to indigenous populations that have the force of international law:

- International Labour Organization (ILO) Convention No. 169 concerning Indigenous and Tribal Peoples in Independent Countries (1989)
- Convention on the Elimination of All Forms of Racial Discrimination (1965)

- Convention on the Rights of the Child (1989), specifically Articles 17, 29, and 30
- A number of international conferences relevant to policies and programs implementing ILO Convention No. 169, including the following World Conferences: Rio de Janeiro (1992), Vienna (1993), Cairo (1994), Copenhagen (1995), Beijing (1995), Istanbul (1996), Rome (1996), Durban (2001), and Johannesburg (2002)

- Recognition by states of the physical and cultural existence of indigenous peoples

- The real and effective ownership of traditional lands and territories and of the resources (both material and spiritual) that they contain

- Their own understanding of their history

- Participate in and propose policies and projects for development, health, education, and other areas

- Effective mechanisms to protest against or oppose legislation, administrative measures, projects, policies, and programs that have a negative impact on the life, economy, or environment of their communities

- Real and effective recognition of indigenous legal systems and religions and the contributions that indigenous cultures have made to the progress of humanity, especially in relation to the environment, agriculture, philosophy, mathematics, and other fields (Telles 2007)

Indigenous Sovereignty

Although indigenous people are located within countries or nation-states, many are granted sovereignty by treaty.

That is to say that they have control over their own affairs. Sovereignty grew out of the Treaty of Westphalia in 1648 that established the sovereign nation-states of Europe. It is inarguable that indigenous peoples were self-governing on the arrival of colonial people and occupying powers. The UN Covenant on Economic, Social, and Cultural Rights clearly states that indigenous people have the right to freely determine their political status. This is one of the most controversial elements of the Covenant. On the one hand, it can be argued that if every other people or nation has the right of sovereignty, why should indigenous people be the only ones denied this? On the other hand, it can be argued that if indigenous people have the right to sovereignty, it will breed instability and undermine peace in established states.

In most cases, freedom to determine their political status or sovereignty, as applied by indigenous people, does not mean separatism and the establishment of a totally distinct nation-state, although there are many separatist movements—Scotland in the United Kingdom and the Catalonians in Spain, for example. Most groups pursue autonomy within the context of citizenship within a larger nation. Modes of self-determination other than secession are integration within an independent state or association with an independent state. If the independent state grossly violates its obligations to the indigenous nation, it loses legitimacy and the indigenous people retain the right to secession.

Under the UN Covenant on Economic, Social, and Cultural Rights, the right to self-determination contains four sets of freedoms that indigenous people may pursue: political status and social, cultural, and economic development for their own ends. Economic self-determination includes "the right to freely dispose of its own natural wealth and resources" (Article 2, paragraph 1). Given the importance of land and natural resources, this is a frequent point of contention between indigenous people and the dominant government. Economic self-determination also includes control over enterprises and taxation of enterprises within its territory, the types of enterprises such as casinos, and the distribution of funds from their operation (International Work Group for Indigenous Affairs [IWGIA] 2016).

Cultural dimensions of self-determination include the right to maintain cultural practices, language, religions, identity, and other aspects of heritage. Many of these cases end up in courts. In Canada, for example, the parents of a child suffering from cancer wished her to be treated with traditional tribal medicine. The hospital sued. Citing both the 1982 Canadian Constitution Act and the UN Declaration, the judge determined that it was in the best interests of the child to remain within the bounds of her parents' decision making. After several months, the sides came together and the child received treatments. Cases such as this benefit from a balancing of right and duty (IWGIA 2016). This balance overlaps with the people's rights to control their lands because they are intimately connected to the land through deeply held religious and spiritual beliefs. This right is recognized in the UN Declaration on the Rights of Indigenous Peoples.

Social dimensions include social development and social justice. These include education, health, and the means to thrive as well as access to justice—to legal and political process to secure rights and freedoms. In some cases, this process refers to tribal justice systems; in others, it may be enforced through the larger independent national government.

In the United States as in other countries, only those tribes officially recognized by the federal government are granted the rights of self-determination. U.S. states may recognize tribes, but that does not guarantee federal recognition. In any case, government courts, congresses, or parliaments of the larger independent countries have the final say on the degree of self-determination of indigenous peoples.

The Special Case of South Africa

South Africa is the only country in which the indigenous population, black Africans, is the most oppressed and the numerical majority. Whites, the dominant group, are only about 9 percent of the population. From colonization by the Dutch in the mid-17th century to subsequent takeover from the British and establishment as a republic in the 20th century, various systems of laws, culminating in apartheid in 1948, denied blacks the rights of citizenship. Similar discriminatory laws applied to Indians brought to work on plantations and Chinese brought to work in the mines, with both groups most frequently classified as "colored." The laws covered all aspects of life—disenfranchisement, segregated residences, education, employment, health care, business opportunities, association among races, land ownership, and even family life. Babies born to black or colored parents who looked white were taken from the parents.

In a cruel irony, in the 1970s, the government awarded Taiwanese, Koreans, and Japanese immigrating to South Africa status as "honorary whites." Other Chinese began receiving better treatment and in the 1980s were released from some of the discriminatory laws—such as not needing to use segregated facilities. In 2008, the Chinese in South Africa before 1994 were recategorized as "black" so that they could receive reparations (Canaves 2008).

Apartheid was not fully dismantled until 1996. Decades later, blacks, Indians, and Chinese have not closed the gaps in life chances with the white majority.

Land Rights Are Fundamental Rights

As peoples, we reaffirm our rights to self-determination and to own, control, and manage our ancestral lands and territories, waters, and other resources. Our lands and territories are at the core of our existence—we are the land and the land is us; we have a distinct spiritual and material relationship with our lands and territories, and they are inextricably linked to our survival and to the preservation and further development of our knowledge systems and cultures, conservation, and sustainable use of biodiversity and ecosystem management.

—The Kimberley Declaration (Indigenous Peoples Council on Biocolonialism 2002)

CONSIDER THIS
LIFE CHANCES OF THE INDIGENOUS IN MEXICO

Mexico is home to one of the largest populations of indigenous people, nearly 13 million comprising 13 percent of the population, nearly all (about 80 percent) of whom live in extreme poverty. They have the lowest rate of running water and electrification. They are in poor health, with little access to resources. Children have high rates of malnutrition. Because many speak their native language and have not had the opportunity to learn Spanish, they are excluded from public schools, employment, and the political process. Like minorities in many countries, they are treated unfairly and arbitrarily in criminal courts.

In 2016, Pope Francis apologized to the people of Chiapas for the crimes of the Catholic Church against the indigenous peoples of the Americas in the colonial era. He also condemned the continuing marginalization and discrimination they face.

The pope commended the indigenous people for maintaining their traditions and being custodians of the earth. This continues his work in seeking social justice and on the importance of preserving the environment.

Land is integral to the identity of indigenous peoples. Their land empowers them to live according to their traditional ways of life, preserving their culture. This is not a superficial concern. Ownership of land affects how people provide for themselves, how they practice religion, and how they structure family and other institutions. It enables communities to continue sustainable practices that preserve land for the generations that follow. For many, specific lands are sacred, imbued with spirits or consecrated by centuries or more of living and dying on the land. Unlike the lands on which churches, mosques, or synagogues are built, their land cannot be desacralized.

Indigenous people need to fight continuously to preserve their rights to their land. As recently as 2015, indigenous leaders defending their territory were "arrested (Russian Federation), harassed (Burma), threatened (the Philippines), and murdered (Nicaragua, Brazil, and the Philippines)" (IWGIA 2016).

The root of the socioeconomic poverty of many indigenous peoples is the denial of their land and resource rights. Legal and illegal encroachments on their lands occur regularly. Agribusiness and infrastructure development and extractive industries often force their displacement. In Ethiopia, the government allows foreign agribusiness to lease large tracts of land with no return of value to the indigenous peoples. The government resettles the people into villages with promises of amenities that are never provided. Half a world away, in Bolivia, the government granted agribusiness the right to expand the agricultural frontier from 3.7 to 20 million hectares, taking land from indigenous communities (IWGIA 2016).

Extractive industries result in displacement as well as exploitation and pollution of land. Norway, Botswana, Russia, Mexico, and the United States are but a few countries where extractive industries threaten the health of the land and the health of indigenous people. New leased copper mining in Norway threatens the reindeer population and fisheries of the Sami people. Hydraulic fracking and mineral prospecting are expanding in a world heritage site, game reserve, and transfrontier park in Botswana. Expansion of the oil frontier threatens ancestral and fragile areas in Ecuador. Oil and mining industries in Mexico, Russia, Bolivia, Peru, Indonesia, Malaysia, and other countries are favored over land rights and environmental protection (IWGIA 2016).

The stories of displacement of indigenous people nearly always end in hardship and death. Destruction and degradation of their land does as well. In the United States and Canada, the latest battle between the governments and Native Americans in their long-running battles is over pipelines. In 2015, along with environmental groups and other Nebraska landowners, seven tribes managed to block, at least temporarily, the Keystone XL Pipeline. The Keystone XL was slated to run near the Rosebud Sioux and Pine Ridge Indian Reservations, threatening culturally sensitive lands and water supplies. The Keystone XL is more threatening than the Montana pipelines that twice spilled more than 50,000 gallons of oil into the pristine Yellowstone River and poisoned the drinking water of thousands. Keystone XL is nearly twice as large, carries much more oil, and was to run across the Ogallala aquifer, one of the world's largest aquifers.

In 2016, Native Americans united again, camping out for months at Standing Rock, North Dakota. President Barack Obama halted the pipeline on environmental grounds. More than 20 oil pipeline projects—some completed and some in progress or stalled—throughout the United States threaten drinking water, religious sites, and treaty and land rights of tribes. The relative powerlessness of indigenous communities leaves them particularly vulnerable (Hersher 2017).

HUMAN RIGHTS, LIFE CHANCES, AND DISCRIMINATION

Discrimination against racial and ethnic minorities and indigenous peoples prevents them from achieving their potential in the pursuit of life, liberty, and happiness. The right to freely pursue good health, an education, employment at a fair wage, adequate housing, and a family though legal marriage all are essential components to achieving our potential. They are routinely denied people perceived as "minorities." Every case of discrimination against every group and every country cannot be reviewed here, but below is a sampling of cases drawn from a variety of countries and against a number of different groups. Education and health are reviewed in separate chapters.

Persecution and Discrimination in China

Although China's ethnic population is small in terms of the percentage of China's overall population, it is numerically the largest minority population in the world. China's laws and policies that forbid discrimination are ineffective, as is the case in many countries. Affirmative action laws for employment and university admissions

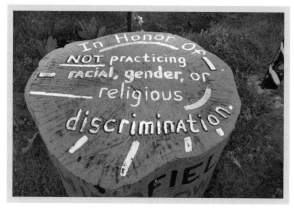

PHOTO 6.2 Discrimination comes in many forms as illustrated on this stump from a sculpture garden in Tennessee.

"No Discrimination" by Lindsey Turner/CC BY 2.0.

are ignored. Racial profiling of Tibetans results in law enforcement stopping them arbitrarily for questioning. Chinese hotels deny them accommodation. All Chinese over 16 years of age are required to carry identity cards with ethnicity marked, making discrimination easy, even when the physical characteristics of a person are ambiguous, as they usually are.

As would be expected, there are significant socioeconomic differences between minorities and Han. Han children are favored over minority children "in terms of parents' presence at home, parents' education, the economic development of provinces in which they reside, household's access to flush toilet, [and] household wealth." Interestingly, minority children were better off in access to electricity (Ouyang and Pinstrup-Andersen 2012).

Boundaries of ethnicity and religion overlap in China; in particular, the persecution of and discrimination against both the Muslim Uyghurs, a Turkish-speaking ethnic group in the Xinjiang autonomous region, and the Buddhist Tibetans are based on ethnic and religious grounds.

Religious control of the Uyghurs is extensive. Religion is to be subordinate to the goals of assimilation with mainland China, national unity, and economic reconstruction. The Uyghurs' discrimination and persecution is written into law and adopted as policy. Imams are vetted by the government. Schools are under strict regulation. University students are prohibited from fasting and are monitored in cafeterias to ensure that they eat on Muslim days of fast. The government arrested 10 middle school children in Guangzhou on alleged terrorism charges (Human Rights Watch [HRW] 2017).

The Chinese government regularly scrutinizes travel abroad for Uyghurs and Tibetans, among others. The Chinese issued a blanket recall of passports in Tibet in 2012 and in Xinjiang in 2015. The government is keeping the passports for safekeeping, a practice that effectively eliminates foreign travel for Uyghurs and Tibetans. Passport requirements established in 2016 for residents of Tibet and Xinjiang are onerous. Applicants must supply a voice recording, a DNA sample, fingerprints, and a three-dimensional image. Passports are subject to annual review. Although the policies have not been put into place in all of Xinjiang, it is now virtually impossible for Tibetans and Uyghurs to travel abroad, a restriction that also denies them the right to participate in religious pilgrimages (HRW 2015, 2016).

In Tibet, the Chinese government conducted massive military exercises using targets that appeared to simulate private homes and vehicles and civilian "enemies." The exercises were to send the message that popular dissent and protest would be met with armed force (Richardson 2016).

China does not have any protections on the basis of sexual orientation or gender identity. However, in 2016 Chinese courts agreed to hear cases of discrimination against LGBT (lesbian, gay, bisexual, and transgender) individuals. A case filed against the Bureau of Civil Affairs for refusing to issue a marriage license to a homosexual couple was defeated. Another against a mental health hospital that tried to cure a man of homosexuality was accepted. Despite this small crack in the government's posture against LGBT rights, China voted against initiating an expert post on LGBT affairs at the UN (HRW 2017).

Afro-Descendants in the Americas

A rich diversity of race and ethnicity comprise the Americas. Approximately 30 percent are of African descent. Yet they are among the poorest groups in the hemisphere, suffer discrimination in virtually every life domain, and subsequently have lower life chances. Resulting disadvantages begin at birth with high infant mortality and persist through death, with a lower life expectancy. The extent of discrimination and resultant disadvantage in the United States is well documented. For the rest of the region, data are less available. One difficulty is the problem of separating race and ethnicity from the variety of ways in which self-identity is expressed.

Despite this difficulty, several features of note and a common situation of structural disadvantage exists across the region, as shown by an extensive study by the Organization of American States (OAS) published in 2011. For example, geographic racialization and segregation, the concentration of Afro-descendants in specific spaces, persists across the region. In Peru select coastal districts, in the United States the southern states and "Rust Belt"

PHOTO 6.3 The Black Lives Matter movement arose to raise awareness of the shootings of unarmed blacks by police.

"I hope I don't get killed" by Johnny Silvercloud/CC BY-SA 2.0.

inner cities, and in other countries specific districts, regions, or "departments" are racially concentrated. In these areas, Afro-descendants typically hold subordinate positions in public policies.

Structural discrimination occurs in access to housing, loans, and quality health care. Across the Americas, people of African descent are concentrated in the poorest areas with the highest housing deficits and exposure to crime and violence. Transportation is inadequate. African Americans occupy the lowest rungs on the job hierarchy, often confined to the informal sector. Even within the same job categories, their wages are lower than those of others. Often job seekers do not even reveal their true addresses for fear it will automatically exclude them from consideration. Discrimination may be subtle, such as rejecting a candidate on the basis of not having a "good appearance," which is code for not white. In Canada, 52 percent of Afro-descendants age 15 years or over reported discrimination in work, employment applications, and promotions (OAS 2011).

During the era of the slave trade, Brazil imported more slaves than any other country, about 4 million. Consequently, more people of African descent (self-identified as black or mixed race), 51 percent of the population, live in Brazil than in any country other than Nigeria. Despite the strength of their numbers, many Afro-descendant groups lost title to their lands. The *quilombos* are communities in the interior of Brazil established by escaped slaves. They are home to hundreds of thousands or as many as a million Brazilians. But housing is fragile, drinking water and sanitation are scarce, and access to schools and health care is difficult. There are more than 151,000 students living in the communities. There are few teachers, and many are not properly trained. Many communities do not have a primary school (Gaspar 2011).

As with Native Americans in the United States, land rights in quilombos are insecure. Always threatened with eviction, the 1988 constitution of Brazil granted quilombo inhabitants—as a community—permanent right to the land that their ancestors settled. A 2003 expanded definition of quilombo swelled the number of potential titles from 29 to 2,400 (5,000 according to Branford 2017). Only a small portion, by either accounting, actually received titles. Once removed from the cities, some of the quilombos have been swallowed up by the favelas, and others are gentrifying (Planas 2014) and are now desirable locations. Still others are wanted for development by agribusiness (Branford 2017).

The 1991 Constitution of Colombia granted Afro-descendants the traditional lands of the "black communities." Legislation in Nicaragua in 2002 established a

"Communal Property Regime" for indigenous peoples and Afro-descendants. Ecuador also established a system for granting title deeds (OAS 2011). Reparations for African Americans in the United States have been discussed repeatedly, but the government has not made any reparation since 1865 when 40 acres of land confiscated from Confederate landowners and a mule were to be distributed. Repealed shortly after the legislation was passed, few former slaves, only about 2,000, actually benefitted from the promise.

Diminished Life Chances

The American Convention on Human Rights, Article 1, states the following:

> The States Parties to this Convention undertake to respect the rights and freedoms recognized herein and to ensure to all persons subject to their jurisdiction the free and full exercise of those rights and freedoms, without any discrimination for reasons of race, color, sex, language, religion, political or other opinion, national or social origin, economic status, birth, or any other social condition.

Similarly, the OAS Charter promises "the fundamental rights of the individual without distinction as to race, nationality, creed or sex," as does the Inter-America Democratic Charter. These proclamations have yet to be realized.

Discrimination persists in health care and education. Availability and accessibility, the quality of care, culturally insensitive or inappropriate approaches to treatment, and lack of treatments, medications, or policies relevant to diseases that affect primarily Afro-descendants all result in lack of care or of quality care (OAS 2011). Only a small portion of Afro-descendants reach and/or complete university education. Lower-level education is insufficient to prepare for college, illiteracy is high, and school achievement is lower. Methods and educational programs that may be inappropriate for the population and education costs are barriers (OAS 2011).

Afro-descendant women suffer a triple threat from gender, race, and poverty. Like women in general, they are poorer and have less access to housing, health, education, and good-paying jobs than men of the same race or ethnicity. As noted earlier, they are underrepresented in political and other decision-making bodies in comparison with both men and other women. They comprise only 1 percent of national legislatures throughout the region and only .03 percent in Latin America. In comparison with white women, their life expectancy is 8 years lower, their unemployment is higher, and they work for lower

wages and in less secure jobs. They have higher rates of both maternal and infant mortality. Racist attitudes of health care staff have been reported as well as an ultimate discrimination, forced sterilization (OAS 2011).

Concepts of race are passed from generation to generation through culture and in opportunities in social structure. While individual discriminations are actions by individuals that treat people unfairly, institutionalized discrimination is built into the social structures of everyday life and forms the basis of unequal life chances within a society even when prejudice seems to have diminished and laws are enacted to enforce equality.

The struggle for equal life chances in the United States did not end with the abolition of slavery. The Civil Rights Act of 1866 promised that every person of African descent brought to or born in the United States was a citizen. It gave every male citizen of the United States the same rights that every white male already had. The bill was passed by a two-thirds majority of both houses of Congress over the veto of President Andrew Johnson, who was later impeached.

The Civil Rights Act of 1875 guaranteed equal access to all public accommodations. It was short-lived, being declared unconstitutional by the U.S. Supreme Court in 1883. It was not until 1954 that another Supreme Court decision ruled that segregated schools were not equal. Even that didn't end discrimination. The Civil Rights Act of 1964 tried again, forbidding discrimination in public places and employment on the basis of religion, ethnicity, sex, or race. Since then, the Fair Housing Act and Voting Rights Act have reaffirmed rights and prohibited discrimination in housing and voting. These acts have been among the most powerful pieces of legislation in U.S. history. Still, they have not guaranteed equal rights or ended discrimination for racial, religious, and gender minorities. Voting rights in particular have been weakened given that 17 states with histories of voter discrimination passed restrictive laws after the requirement that they submit changes in their laws to the Department of Justice for review expired.

Despite the Civil Rights Act of 1964 and subsequent amendments, the only racial and ethnic minority to achieve parity with white Americans and surpass them in many measures is the Asian minority—although there is wide disparity among the Asian ethnicities, with some faring very poorly in quality of life dimensions.

Discrimination Begins at Birth and Continues Through the Lifespan

Poor life chances begin at birth. Minorities in the United States have significantly higher rates of mortality for

CONSIDER THIS
STATELESS FROM BIRTH

Most of us acquire citizenship through our parents. In some countries, a woman who is married to a non-citizen cannot pass citizenship on to her children in that they do not share in this right despite pledges of gender equality in their constitutions. There are 27 such countries: 12 countries in North Africa and the Middle East, 8 in sub-Saharan Africa, 5 in Asia–Pacific, and 2 in the Americas.

In some of these countries, there are restrictions on a man's rights as well—for example, if he is stateless or the child is born out of the country—but nowhere is there a blanket prohibition on men. Some countries have modest provisions to limit statelessness, but statelessness occurs in those countries as well.

The impacts of statelessness even on those born to citizen mothers are severe. Many rights granted to nationals in education, employment, health care, and social security are denied to the stateless. The psychological effects range from anger and resentment to depression. The stateless become quickly marginalized, and their lives are financially insecure (United Nations High Commissioner for Refugees 2014).

infants under 1 year old than non-Hispanic whites. For those of African American descent, the rate of infant mortality was double that of whites in 2013—11.11 per 1,000 babies born in comparison with 5.06. Nearly all of the disparities in mortality are preterm related (Centers for Disease Control and Prevention 2015).

Many preterm births reflect the health or age of the mother, which can be a function of lifelong institutional discrimination resulting from poor access to health care, poor education about health, poor nutrition, and/or teen pregnancy. Poor areas of wealthy countries have more in common with poor countries than with their fellow citizens. The African American infant mortality rate is higher than those of infants in Bulgaria, Serbia, Cuba, Lebanon, and the Ukraine (United Nations Development Programme 2015, Table 9).

Discrimination continues throughout the lifespan. In the United States, 71 percent of black adults report that they have personally experienced discrimination—11 percent regularly and 60 percent from time to time (Pew Research Center 2016a). Segregated neighborhoods result in segregated schools, diminishing life chances in education. Lower-quality education carries over to diminishing prospects for quality job opportunities. This diminishes the life chances of the next generation in health, education, and employment. African Americans are discriminated against in the criminal justice system. They are nearly 30 percent of all arrests while only 13 percent of the population. African Americans are incarcerated at five times the rate of whites, comprising 34 percent of those in correctional institutions. They are imprisoned on drug charges six times more often than whites, although

they use drugs at similar rates. Together with Hispanic Americans, they comprise 56 percent of the incarcerated population (and 32 percent of the population) (National Association for the Advancement of Colored People 2017). This has a snowball effect, resulting in diminished opportunities for housing, employment, and education as well as the opportunities of the next generation.

These are discussed in more detail in the chapters on education and health.

FALLING BETWEEN THE CRACKS: STATELESSNESS IN A WORLD OF STATES

Everyone needs to have been born somewhere and everyone needs to live somewhere. Everyone's ancestors originated somewhere. These are the usual tests for citizenship. Nevertheless, there are millions of people, perhaps as many as 12 million, who are not citizens of any country. They are stateless. With no guaranteed rights anywhere, they are among the most persecuted people in the world. In 1955, the chief justice of the U.S. Supreme Court said that statelessness was a form of punishment more primitive than torture.

National laws within each state determine who is or is not included. In Kenya, people may not leave their home without identity papers. It is a crime. If you are stateless, you do not have papers. As one such person said, if you are stateless, "How do you live? How do you look for a job or open a bank account?" You don't without risking arrest.

Being stateless means having no legal identity. Often denied access to education, health care, employment, property ownership, and/or political participation, the stateless have little opportunity to effect change in their status. Without identity documents or birth registration, their mobility is limited, closing off emigration or other routes to improving the quality of their lives.

Stateless persons are found throughout the world. In some instances, an entire ethnicity is stateless within the country where the people live. While some within an ethnic group may have citizenship in one country, their kin who are living in another country might not. Some individuals are stateless because their identity papers were lost in conflict or their births were never registered. One third of the stateless are children, and if they have children they will also be stateless—denied rights, denied opportunity, and destined to repeat the cycle—unless something changes.

Hundreds of thousands of Russian-speaking people living in Latvia and Estonia became stateless when the Soviet Union dissolved. Roma are scattered throughout Europe. Thousands of Roma became homeless when nationalism in Yugoslavia marginalized them, and thousands more became homeless when they fled the genocides in Bosnia. If they have papers at all, they are from a country that no longer exists. When Bangladesh gained independence, Bihari ethnics were not granted citizenship. A constitutional ruling in 2013 denied citizenship to thousands of Haitians living in the Dominican Republic.

In many countries, being born within their borders does not guarantee citizenship. In such countries, citizenship is determined by parentage. The Rohingya live in the Rakhine state of Myanmar. Although they have lived there for centuries, the Myanmar government does not recognize them as citizens. The government has subjected them to the worst forms of discrimination—killing, torture, rape, and arbitrary detention. Their homes and villages have been destroyed, and their land has been confiscated. They have been forced into labor. The government has even denied them the right to call themselves Rohingya.

The UN launched a 10-year program to end statelessness. International pressure and civil society advocacy groups have won change for thousands.

Another form of statelessness is that of a nation that has no country—no state—to enable the people to self-govern. They live under the rule of other peoples, and although they may be recognized as citizens in some of those countries, they long for self-rule or at least more autonomy. This is the situation of the Kurds, whose lands were divided among the states formed from the Ottoman Empire following World War I, and the Roma, whose

statelessness is primarily due to discrimination. Wherever they live, they live as oppressed minorities.

HAVING THE WRONG RELIGION COULD COST YOU YOUR LIFE

"Having the wrong religion could cost you your life," said Agustinus Wibowo, an Indonesian Buddhist in Kandahar who was repeatedly mistaken for a Hazara. This could have cost him his life. "Being a Muslim is not enough," he said. "They need to know whether you are a Sunni or Shiite."

—Karmi (2011)

Some religious groups have lived for hundreds of years in a country and been a large portion of the population but still are afforded minority status and treatment. They may have migrated along with an occupation or may have fled persecution elsewhere. The Hazara are one such group with a complicated past. They probably arrived in Afghanistan as Buddhist pilgrims from Asia. At least part of their genetic heritage suggests that they descended from Genghis Khan along with ethnic Tajiks, Turks, and others who traveled the Silk Road. Settled primarily in central Afghanistan's Bamiyan and Daikundi regions, they look different from other Afghanis and are a different Islamic sect than most of Afghanistan, Shia rather than Sunni. Although they are the third largest ethnic group in Afghanistan, persecution over centuries has forced thousands of Hazara to flee to Pakistan, Iraq, Iran, and Syria. But persecution followed them given that wherever they go they are either the wrong ethnicity or the wrong religion. Despite this, the Hazara occupy some of the more peaceful regions of Afghanistan and might be the best hope for Afghanistan (Zabriskie 2008).

Religious hostility in the forms of prejudice, discrimination, intimidation, and violence occurs on a daily basis. No country is immune. In some countries, it may occur subtly through institutional discrimination. Sometimes it is formal governmental regulation. In these cases, discrimination is written into laws and policies that grant privileged groups rights that others do not have or overtly deny rights and privileges to others. Social hostility, both violent and nonviolent, against religious minorities is widespread. Regardless of the form that it takes—institutional or individual, government regulation or social hostility—discrimination denies equal life chances to disempowered groups. It violates human rights.

After the horror of World War II, with human rights documents in place, there was hope that the world would be rid of religious and other forms of persecution. That is far from the case. While persecution of religious minorities has been a feature of many developing societies in the 20th century, in the 21st century religious prejudice, discrimination, and violence against religious groups emerged from the shadows into the mainstreams in developed Western societies.

Government favoritism and restriction, along with social hostility, lead to persecution, discrimination, and violent conflict. In contrast, religious freedom and lack of government favoritism is less disruptive (Finke and Martin 2014). Given the extent of religiously fueled terrorism, violent conflicts, and political dysfunction, illuminating the factors that enhance religious freedom and mitigate religious restriction and social hostilities is critical to restoring and preserving peace.

Religious Freedom as a Human Right

Religion, according to Emile Durkheim, reinforces solidarity among a community of believers. Believers' beliefs connect them to what they perceive as sacred, that which is to be revered. Religious practices and rituals are essential elements of demonstrating reverence and, for many religions, are essential for salvation. Practically, ritual also reinforces the solidarity of the group and the truthfulness of belief. As such, for true believers, religion serves as a central element of their individual and collective identity.

Religious freedom is well established as a human right, as stated in the UN Declaration of Human Rights as well as in regional declarations. Because of its importance in the lives of individuals and in international conventions, religious freedom is nearly universally recognized as a civil right in national constitutions. This is a hallmark achievement of cultural globalization. Despite this widespread recognition, complete religious freedom is still rare. Governments have uneasy relationships with religion, and as a result it often serves as a source of social unrest and conflict.

Freedom of religion or belief is complex. It empowers individuals in every sphere of religious and non-religious conviction and in the right to practice alone or in a community of believers. It includes developing a religious identity, being able to bear witness to that identity, communicating freely with others, organizing a community around religious life, transmitting religious belief to your children, building an infrastructure of support such as schools and charities, and the freedom to change your religion or express religious doubt (Bielefeldt 2016). As such, religion and religious organizations have a unique relationship with society.

Religion poses unique challenges and risks associated with the guarantee of religious freedoms, as discussed below.

Religion is institutionally organized. Institutions are part of the social structure of a society and, thus, must in some way be related to the state. The relationships may vary from strong alliances between a dominant religion and the state, to relations with little to moderate state interference in religion, to situations of antagonistic relationships with religions. In each case, religious organizations and persons come under some regulation and perhaps persecution if a religion is perceived to be a threat to the state or a more dominant religion. Thus, among these general types or relationships, there nearly always exists a variety of arrangements with varying levels of advantage or disadvantage for specific religions (Finke and Martin 2014).

Because religions institutionalize in order to sustain their religious community, religions compete with one another and with secular ideologies. Theories of religious economies assert that where there is religious pluralism without government interference, religion thrives. Religions will emerge to match the diversity of religious preference in an area. The more religions that are allowed, the more likely that people will find one that appeals to them. If it is in any way costly for a religion to participate in a community, it serves as a restriction. With restrictions—perhaps costs related to taxation, space, registration, hostility, and the like—some people's preferences go unaddressed. Even if it is only minority religions that are restricted, that restriction diminishes the entire supply of religion and stifles religious innovations (Finke 2013). In the contemporary United States and Canada, religious pluralism thrives in comparison with most monopoly churches. Low restriction generally leads to harmonious relations. In this regard, theories that separation of church and state, urbanization, and pluralism lead to the demise of religion are essentially wrong (Finke and Stark 1988).

Religious rights are also unique in the historical and cultural relationships that dominant religions share with the society. In combination with the capacity of religious devotion to mobilize group action, they can give a religious group social and political power. Many people think of themselves first in terms of their religious identity and second in terms of their nationality (Finke and Martin 2014). Religious organizations can mobilize believers for social and political movements to pressure for legislation in their favor and restrictions for other groups. Groups can call on cultural traditions to cast minority religious traditions or new religious movements as dangerous and engender strong social pressures to restrict or outlaw them. This pressure to curry favor and restrict others operates at local and national governmental levels, often with greater success at local levels.

In the United States, for example, many people appeal to the Judeo-Christian (or sometimes just Christian) tradition to influence local schools to teach creationism and abstinence sex education or to influence local city halls to display variations on Christian or quasi-Christian themes around holidays, grant local establishments the refusal to serve same-sex weddings, or challenge gender identity bathrooms. At the national level, the rise of the political right in the United States has used social action to pressure for a number of legislative proposals by pushing a religious agenda into the political realm, thereby preventing for decades the recognition of same-sex marriage, trying to outlaw a woman's right to abortion, and making provisions for birth control optional for religious employer-sponsored health insurance. Often the phrase "real American values" is substituted for a particular religious view. The "anti-cult" movement of the 1960s through 1990s was a near global movement that convinced many people that the cults were brainwashing their adherents and holding them captive, violating freedom of belief and assembly.

Because religions are embedded in institutions, they tend to compete for resources. A dominant religion has a good chance of winning the competition because an alliance of religion and state benefits both in the short run. The dominant religious organization gains privilege vis-à-vis the state and gains opportunity for financial and legislative support of its agenda. Political leaders gain the political and ideological support of the religious organization's adherents. They also gain effective control over the dominant religion. The societal price is increased religious restriction over competing religions or cultural groups (Finke 2013; Finke and Martin 2014).

Religious identities, because they generate such intense loyalty and demand that adherents organize and practice their beliefs, can threaten not only the dominant religion but also state and secular ideologies. Even where there is not a dominant religion or the state does not form an alliance with it, a state may try to eliminate religions generally such as during the Cultural Revolution in the former Soviet Union (Finke 2013). Falun Gong was originally welcomed by the Chinese government because it was based in Chinese traditions. The government awarded its founder, Li Hongzhi, the Award for Achievement in Science of the Mind and Metaphysics. Although Falun Gong made no direct accusations, the Chinese government perceived that its doctrines that physical illnesses resulted from social problems were dangerous. By the time it had attracted 70 million adherents, making it larger than the Communist Party, the government clearly saw it as a threat. Imprisonment, exile, or death followed for thousands of members (McDonald 2006).

Religious restrictions designed to enhance state control and public order are likely to produce conflict and violence. Religious restriction rarely functions as intended. Religious groups have the capacity to mobilize significant numbers of believers. If their agendas are in opposition to the state or just perceived to be in opposition, they pose a threat that states may try to neutralize by restriction or persecution. France's commitment to *laïcité,* meaning freedom of conscience, has become a state ideology of secularization and for many French a fundamentalist version at that. The extreme right in particular garnered influence at least in part to its demand for a strict adherence to laïcité, restricting any public expression of religion. The restrictions on such things as wearing religious symbols in public schools, although applied across the board to all religions, were not enacted until 2004. The ban on wearing burkas in public was enacted in 2010. These were a direct response to Islam. Some analysts suspect, with cause, that such restriction contributes to radicalizing youths (Zaretsky 2016). When social movements or political parties mobilize along religious lines, as is occurring in every region of the world, it is a powerful predictor of violence (Finke 2013; Finke and Martin 2014).

Contact across religious groups may increase or decrease conflict depending on its context. Where there are shared goals and interests, equal status, interdependence, and the support of authorities to facilitate interactions, relations will be good. This is a common tactic in combating prejudice and in peacemaking. Different interests and goals, inequality, lack of support, and competition will generate conflict. When there are favored religious groups and social restrictions, contact is likely to be minimal but confrontational when it occurs.

The results of government restriction and social hostility are clear. Harassment is a form of conflict that covers many forms of hostility, both violent and nonviolent, from physical assault and arrest to desecration of holy sites, discrimination in employment, and verbal assaults. In many countries, religious groups ae harassed by the government, social groups, and individuals. Religious groups experienced harassment in 159 different countries in 2014. This is down from the peak of 166 in 2012 but represents an overall increase from the 2007 baseline of 152 (Pew Research Center 2016b). In 2014, Christians were harassed in 108 countries, Muslims in 100 countries, and Jews in 81 countries. Other religious groups were also harassed. The largest increase was for Jews, whose peak in 2014 included social harassment in 30 more countries than in 2007, from 51 to 81 countries. Muslims and Christians experienced significantly more harassment by governments, in 80 countries for Muslims and 79 countries for Christians, and similar levels of social harassment in 85 countries for Christians and 81 countries for Muslims.

Measuring Religious Freedom and Religious Restriction

There is some level of government restriction and/or favoritism and social hostility in every country. The French ban on religious symbols in public schools was an obvious response to the increasing appearance of headscarves given that prior to the legislation Christian crosses, the Jewish yarmulke, and other symbols were tolerated. Many other countries are following suit. China and Russia cite the French example to justify their own, typically more burdensome, regulations.

Many regulations have an obvious intention of discriminating against "undesirable" religious organizations. A number of European societies do not recognize Scientology as a religion. Scientology, along with Jehovah's Witnesses, the International Society for Krishna Consciousness, the Unification Church, and the Worldwide Church of God, all are on the list of "cults" that are potentially dangerous. The burdens associated with entering the religious "marketplace" are rising. The percentage of governments that require registration of religions rose to about 90 percent by 2015; not all registration requirements are discriminatory, although many are. For example, the percentage of countries requiring state approval of their doctrines before being registered increased from 13 to 18 percent, and the percentage of countries that denied approval of religions increased from 22 to 27 percent (Finke, Mataic, and Fox 2015).

Many governmental, international governmental, and non-governmental organizations monitor infringements on religious freedom.[2] The U.S. Department of State (USDOS)[3] and Pew regularly issue detailed reports of government restrictions and social hostilities. The USDOS report, the "International Religious Freedom Report" (IRFR), ranks countries of concern for violations of religious freedom into categories according to the level of persecution, issues detailed reports annually, and reports any U.S. action and policy in response to violations. The U.S. Commission on International Religious Freedom (USCIRF), an independent commission, also issues a report to the USDOS. The commission issues detailed reports of abuse, suggests country classifications, and makes sanction and policy recommendations. The USDOS is not bound by its report, and political concerns are more likely to determine its responses rather than strictly the violations.

The Pew report codes information from 19 sources—governmental, international governmental, and non-governmental organizations, including the USCIRF and IRFR—and assigns countries two scores: social hostility and government restriction (Table 6.1). Because it is the most comprehensive data source and develops scores for nearly every country or territory (198 in 2016),[4] it is relied on most heavily here for scoring while details on specific cases of persecution and hostility are drawn from other sources.

The good news is that the 2016 Pew report showed religious persecution to be declining for the second year in a row. The number of countries with high or very high government restrictions decreased from 57 (29 percent—the 2012 peak) to 48 (24 percent) in 2014. Social hostilities rooted in religion also declined from the 2012 peak of 65 countries (33 percent) to 45 countries (23 percent). However, because many of the countries experiencing high rates of persecution are also highly populated, the number of people living under high and very high religious restriction declined only slightly, from 77 percent in 2012 to 74 percent in 2014. The bad news is that the rate of persecution remains high; both social hostility and government restriction are above the 2007 baseline adopted by the Pew Research Center (2016b), and religion-related terrorist activity, including attacks against religious organizations and people or on behalf of religious organizations or people, increased.

Government Restriction and Persecution

Many religious freedom issues are well known; others might be known only among those who suffer the consequences. Countries define and delineate the right to religious freedom differently. Atrocities by governments against religious minorities are not limited to situations of war, violent conflict, or authoritative regimes. China, Iran, Russia, and North Korea are governments whose violations of religious freedom are generally familiar, but many more governments, including the United States, France, and the United Kingdom, discriminate as well. Motivations for restrictions vary. Intolerance and authoritarianism are not the only ones. Governments may use religion to forge a homogeneous national identity. Widening power gaps, social fragmentation among groups, and economic and social disparities all are possible motivations that governments use to support or persecute particular religions. This can erode trust in public institutions.

Pew measures government restriction of religion using 20 indicators, including considerations as diverse as how religion is treated in national laws and whether a country favors one or more religions over others to harassment, intimidation, and physical violence against

A CLOSER LOOK
RELIGIOUS PERSECUTION IN DECLINE BY NUMBER AND PERCENTAGE OF COUNTRIES

From 2012 to 2014, the number and percentage of countries experiencing government restriction of religion and social hostility toward religion both decreased. However, religiously motivated terrorist activity increased.

TABLE 6.1   Religious Persecutions and Terrorist Activity

	Government Restriction		Social Hostility		Overall	Terrorist Activity[a]		
	Number	%	Number	%	% of Countries With Government Restriction and/or Social Hostility	Number	%	% Countries With Injury or Death
2012	57	29	65	33	43	82	41	60
2014	48	24	45	33	39	73	37	51

a. Data are from 2013 and 2014.

Source: Adapted from "Trends in Global Restrictions on Religion." Pew Research Center, Washington, D.C. June 23, 2016. http://assets.pewresearch.org/wp-content/uploads/sites/11/2016/06/Restrictions2016-Full-Report-FINAL.pdf.

members (Figure 6.3). This is in keeping with the view of the UN that religious freedom is multifaceted. Freedom pertains to belief, identity, and practice; to the creation of religious schools, charities, and organizations; and to the equal treatment of all religions.

Although government religious restriction decreased slightly overall from 2013 to 2014, the longer-term picture is more instructive. Many serious violations of religious freedom increased significantly during the seven-year period from the baseline year 2007 to 2014. Governments exercised more restrictions through the following:

- Interfering with more religions' worship and religious practices (from 16 to 25 percent of countries)

- Interfering with worship and religious practices as a general policy (from 18 to 29 percent of countries)

- Limiting public preaching by some or all religious groups (from 28 to 33 percent of countries)

- Prohibiting conversion from one religion to another (from 16 to 19 percent of countries)

- Limiting religious literature and broadcasting (from 34 to 46 percent of countries)

- Regulating wearing of religious clothing or symbols (from 11 to 24 percent of countries)

- Practicing widespread intimidation (from 18 to 42 percent of countries)

- Neglecting to interfere in cases of discrimination (from 20 to 23 percent of countries)

- Using a coercive organization to regulate religious affairs (from 13 to 23 percent of countries)

- Trying to eliminate an entire religious group from the country (from 1 to 8 percent of countries)

- Requiring religious groups to register while using a process that clearly discriminates (from 27 to 41 percent of countries)

- Using force against religious groups that resulted in destruction of property, imprisonment, displacement, physical injury and abuse, or death (from 31 to 41 percent of countries) (Pew Research Center 2016b)

A CLOSER LOOK
GOVERNMENT RESTRICTIONS ON RELIGION BY REGION

Regional scores of government restrictions are not surprising—the Middle East scores highest and the Americas score lowest—but regional scores obscure significant differences within regions. For example, within Europe, France and Greece both had a Government Restriction Index (GRI) of 4.4 and Bulgaria had a GRI of 5.5. They are more restrictive than Bahrain (3.0), Kuwait (3.0), Morocco (1.3), Qatar (0.6), and others in the Middle East–North Africa region.

FIGURE 6.3   Government Restrictions on Religion, by Region

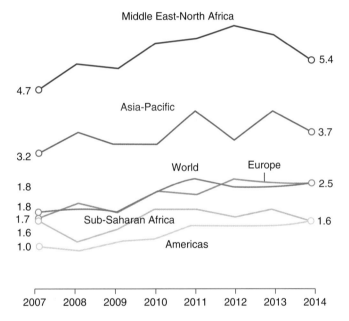

Median scores on the Government Restrictions Index

Source: "Trends in Global Restrictions on Religion." Pew Research Center, Washington, D.C. June 23, 2016. http://assets .pewresearch.org/wp-content/uploads/sites/11/2016/06/Restrictions2016-Full-Report-FINAL.pdf.

The USCIRF monitors Western Europe because of concern over increasing government restrictions and social hostilities, mutually reinforcing forces. Contrary to European Union (EU) law that exempts religious ritual slaughter of animals from stunning requirements, Denmark, Luxembourg, and Sweden ban all slaughter without stunning. Other Europeans, although not in the EU, also enforce prohibitions. Some towns in France ended a common practice of providing non-pork alternatives to Muslim and Jewish schoolchildren. In the Netherlands, a bill proposing prohibiting Muslim and Jewish children in educational, health care, and government buildings and on public transportation was pending at the end of 2015. These were just a few of the growing number of restrictions (USCIRF 2016). A number of European countries have restrictions on wearing clothing and symbols that are religious markers in various places. France and Belgium, for example, ban full-face Islamic veils anywhere in public. Switzerland has banned building any more minarets, the traditional topping of a mosque, anywhere. This was voted in by citizens in a popular referendum that has the force of law. The worst offenders in Europe, however,

CONSIDER THIS
THE DALAI LAMA AND CHINA

The current Dalai Lama, the 14th, continues to be the spiritual and moral compass of Tibetan Buddhism and is admired by religious and non-religious people alike. At one time, from the occupation of Tibet in 1950 to the Tibetan revolution in 1959 and until 2011 when the Dalai Lama handed political leadership of the Tibetan government in exile to a democratically elected prime minister (Kalon Tripa), the Dalai Lama was the political leader as well. At over 80 years old, he is one of the most inspirational, charismatic, and powerful global figures.

The Dalai Lama travels the world, giving public talks attended by thousands and carried over popular media, leading Buddhists and non-Buddhists alike in observing Tibetan religious traditions and pilgrimages, conducting empowerments, and meeting with world leaders. His global stature has garnered support for autonomy for Tibet and called attention to persecution of Buddhist monks, among others. As such, he is perceived by the Chinese government as a grave threat to the continued incorporation of Tibet into China.

---

are Russia, Belarus, and Bulgaria, all of which scored above 5 on the Pew Government Restriction Index (GRI) (Pew Research Center 2016b).

In the Middle East and North Africa, 12 of 20 countries scored above 5 on the GRI. In the countries with high government restriction, violations bear very severe sanctions. Imprisonment, physical punishment, and death sentences are imposed for activities classified as freedom of belief and expression in Western democracies. In Pakistan, 40 people are on death row for blasphemy. In Sudan, 27 Muslims were detained for maintaining that the Quran is the sole source of religious authority, which is in violation of the government's official view, which also recognizes the hadith. A Palestinian poet, Ashraf Fayadh, was sentenced to death in Saudi Arabia, reversing his sentence of four years in prison and 800 lashes. Courts subsequently overturned the death sentence for a sentence of eight years in prison and 800 lashes. His crime: disparaging remarks about Islam. Saudi Arabia carried out dozens of death sentences against Shia individuals who protested in 2011 and 2012 for greater religious rights. Several Shia clerics were sentenced to death (USCIRF 2016).

In the Asia–Pacific region—which includes Afghanistan, Azerbaijan, Burma, Indonesia, Iran, Kazakhstan, Kyrgyzstan, Laos, Malaysia, Maldives, Pakistan, Singapore, Tajikistan, Turkey, Turkmenistan, Uzbekistan, and Vietnam, all of which rated higher than 6 on the Pew GRI—China and Turkey stand out with the highest scores in the world, 8.6 and 8.1, respectively.

China had the highest level of government restriction as reported by the Pew Research Center (2016b). Any aspect of any religion that is deemed threatening to the interests of the government, Communist Party, or social stability is subject to punishment. China grants freedom of "belief" but not of practice. The government determines which religions are allowed to legally hold religious services: Buddhist, Catholic, Taoist, Muslim, and Protestant. Nevertheless, belonging to an approved religion does not guarantee freedom. Foreigners may practice their religion but are not allowed to try to convert others. People from both approved and non-approved religions have been arrested, imprisoned, tortured, and killed. Based on data from the 2005 and 2008 USCIRF reports on China, between 50,000 and 100,000 people were physically abused or displaced because of their religion (Association of Religion Data Archives n.d.).

The IRFR for 2015 (USDOS 2016) documents China's continuing abuse, imprisonment, torture, and killing of adherents of registered and unregistered religious organizations. Uyghurs, who are Muslim, were shot in their homes and in their houses of worship by assailants claiming that the people they targeted were terrorists and separatists. Tibetan monks, nuns, and laypersons are also targeted based on alleged separatist and independence activities. A protest in front of a police station resulted in 87 deaths and numerous other injuries. When 25 Uyghur women and girls refused to uncover their faces, covered by headscarves, they were jailed. More than 1,500 crosses were removed from Christian churches and destroyed. Many church buildings were bulldozed, reportedly for zoning violations. Falun Gong continues to report abductions, detentions, and deaths in police custody. Uyghurs and Tibetans report discrimination in employment, housing, and business opportunities. China has been a "country of particular concern" since the first reporting under the International Religious Freedom Act of 1998 (IRFA). U.S. sanctions include public expressions of concern about China's human rights violations and violations of religious freedom by the president and secretary of state as well as the restriction of exports related to crime control and detection (USDOS 2016, China).

Iran, a Shia government, uses religious restriction to discriminate against minority religions and converts to any sect other than Shia. Iran has executed "at least" 20 people, placed a number of Sunni preachers into custody awaiting possible death sentences, and imprisoned another 380 or so people—250 Sunnis, 82 Baha'is, 26 Christians, 16 Sufis, 10 Yarsanis, and 2 Zoroastrians—for membership in or activities of religious minorities (USDOS 2016).

Because access to North Korea is severely limited, the IRFA report (USCIRF 2016) relies on the UN Commission of Inquiry (COI) and non-governmental organizations outside of the country. According to these sources, North Korea continues to deny nearly all religious and other human rights. The government presented the state-controlled churches to COI observers as evidence of religious freedom. But religious practice outside of the state-controlled churches results in punishment. Any activity not explicitly allowed by the government—as simple as reading the Bible or praying—could lead to imprisonment as a political prisoner. Members of underground churches are arrested, beaten, tortured, and killed.

The inquiry on North Korea concluded that the government perceived Christianity as a grave threat because it challenges the cult of the personality (which in North Korea accounts for Kim Jung Un, his father Kim Jong Il, and his grandfather Kim Il Sung being viewed as gods) and provides a platform for social protest. A Canadian pastor was detained and sentenced to life in prison for "anti-DPRK [Democratic People's Republic of Korea] religious activities" that were not specified. Christians are confined to the lowest social class in North Korea's "songbun" hierarchy. This disadvantages them in education, health care, employment, and residence. Many rights, according to the COI, are so severely restricted and violations sanctioned that they constitute crimes against humanity (USDOS 2016, DPRK).

Social Hostility Toward the People, by the People

With religious based harassment occurring in 159 countries, professing the wrong religion in the wrong place can mean a death sentence, not only at the hands of a government but also at the hands of fellow citizens. Government restriction and social hostilities are mutually reinforcing. On the graph of the 25 most populous countries (Figure 6.4), a general positive relationship between the two is apparent. Government restrictions "give people permission" and provide justification for discrimination. Where there are legal codes with draconian punishments for blasphemy or desecrating the Quran, they are used to justify mob violence. Pakistan had the highest level of social hostility. There were 40 people on death row in 2016, primarily for being members of religious minorities, and 62 people have been killed by mobs since 1990 for this same "crime." In one case, a village mob accused a Christian couple of blasphemy and burned them alive in a kiln. In another case a Hindu man was accused of desecrating the Quran and a Hindu temple was set on fire in retaliation.

In the United States, government restriction is at a moderate level and social hostility is high. The rise in hate crime and hate speech associated with the campaign leading to the 2016 presidential election was striking. While hateful rhetoric inflamed crowds, responses of the crowds encouraged more hateful speech. Escalating social hostility provides the government with the social mandate to pass legislation or escalate discriminatory treatment under the law—or in spite of the law. Where people—particularly the powerless—are perceived to have attacked the dominant or official religion or are seen as a threat to people's way of life, even in a secular society, penalties may be severe. No continent or country is completely free of social hostilities against religious groups and individuals.

China leads the world in government restrictions, but the Chinese people score only 3.3 on social hostilities. While this is above the world average and above the average for every region except the Middle East–North Africa, it is below that for France, the United States, Italy, and the United Kingdom, all of which are considerably lower in government restrictions. Perhaps because the Chinese government is restrictive against all religions and does not favor a dominant religion, people for the most part do not feel threatened by any of them. Religion is not very important, or not at all important, to 80 percent of Chinese (Inglehart et al. 2014), which may be another reason for low social hostility (Figure 6.5).

Pew uses 13 indicators to develop the social hostility index. Crimes and violence counted below refer to those

A CLOSER LOOK
RESTRICTIONS ON RELIGION

Government and social hostility are mutually reinforcing. Countries low in one tend to be low in the other, and countries high in one tend to be high in the other.

FIGURE 6.4   Restrictions on Religion Among 25 Most Populous Countries

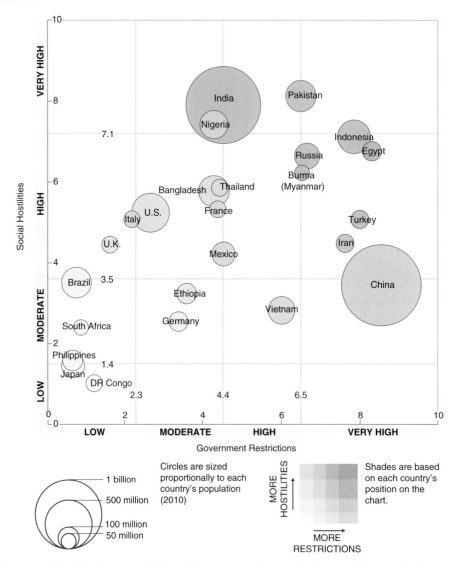

Source: "Trends in Global Restrictions on Religion." Pew Research Center, Washington, D.C. June 23, 2016. http://assets .pewresearch.org/wp-content/uploads/sites/11/2016/06/Restrictions2016-Full-Report-FINAL.pdf.

A CLOSER LOOK
SOCIAL HOSTILITY BY REGION, 2007–2014

Despite an overall decline from 2012 or 2013 to 2014, social hostility increased in every region of the world from the 2007 baseline. The social hostility chart closely resembles the government restriction chart, with the exception of Europe. Europe social hostilities were consistently above the global rate from 2007 onward.

FIGURE 6.5   Social Hostilities Involving Religion, by Region

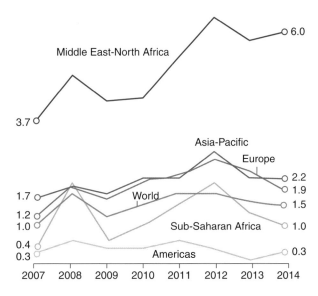

Median scores on the Social Hostilities Index

Source: "Trends in Global Restrictions on Religion." Pew Research Center, Washington, D.C. June 23, 2016. http://assets.pewresearch.org/wp-content/uploads/sites/11/2016/06/Restrictions2016-Full-Report-FINAL.pdf.

motivated by religious bias or hatred. Indicators that increased from 2007 to 2014 were the following:

- Crimes and malicious acts, including harassment and intimidation, property damage, detentions and abductions, assaults, and deaths (from 66 to 70 percent of countries)

- Countries experiencing multiple types of crime (from 50 to 62 percent of countries) (increased), countries experiencing only one type of crime (from 28 to 20 percent) (decreased), countries

not experiencing crimes (from 34 to 30 percent) (decreased), and countries experiencing six or more types of crime (2 percent) (held steady)

- Mob violence with no deaths (from 7 to 11 percent of countries) (increased) and mob violence with deaths (5 percent) (held steady)

- Sectarian violence between religious groups (from 8 to 10 percent of countries)

- Religion-related terrorist groups (from 30 to 41 percent of countries)

- Religion-related war or armed conflict (from 11 to 13 percent of countries)

- Physical violence as a result of tensions between religious groups in numerous cases (from 11 to 22 percent of countries)

- Groups that used force or coercion to dominate public life or prevent some groups from practicing in the country (from 43 to 45 percent of countries)

- Women harassed for violations of religious dress codes (from 7 to 23 percent of countries)

- Hostility over conversion from one religion to another—nonviolent (from 12 to 15 percent of countries) (Pew Research Center 2016b)

As with government restrictions, regional scores obscure variation within regions. In Europe, social hostility scores are relatively high in some countries. Russia's score (6.6) is not surprising given the tight controls placed on religion. However, France (5.4), Italy (5.1), Kosovo (5.1), Georgia (4.7), Ukraine (4.7), Sweden (4.6), the United Kingdom (4.1), and Greece (4.1 but down from 2007) are the highest in Europe, most representing increases from the baseline of 2007 due perhaps to the populism rising in response to migration. Although religion is not important in many of these countries, fear of terrorism ignited hostility toward Muslims.

Most social hostility scores in the Americas, 74 percent of them, were under 1. Many of the countries are small and homogeneous. In contrast, larger and more diverse societies experienced more social hostility. For example, Colombia (from 3.3 to 2.2) and Mexico (from 5.5 to 4.2) decreased, while Brazil (from 0.08 to 3.5) and the United States (from 1.9 to 5.2) increased in social hostilities. Canada, one of the most diverse countries, with 20 percent of its population foreign born, had little hostility.

The United States had the highest rate of social hostility toward religion in the Americas in 2014 and a significant increase over 2013. In the United States, many of the social hostilities toward religious groups, if reported, would be classified as hate crimes (Table 6.2). Pew attributes the increase in hate crimes to a portion of the increase in social hostilities, with the rise of crimes against Muslims being the most significant. Of the nearly 7,000 hate crimes in the United States in 2015, nearly 20 percent were crimes against religions. That anti-Jewish crimes accounted for more than half continued the historical trend (Federal Bureau of Investigation [FBI] 2017). Anti-Semitism, as with prejudices against other minorities, increases as the visibility of the Jewish communities and individuals within them increases. Larger Jewish populations, Orthodox rather than reform Jews, experience greater rates of hostility.

Terrorism and Religious Freedom

The ultimate aims of terrorist groups are overthrow of a state or establishment of a new one. Eliminating competing ideologies is a goal that serves the larger cause. Terrorist groups deliberately target communities of religious followers whose views challenge their own. Even though social hostility against religions had a modest decrease from 2013 to 2014, the number of countries that experienced religious-related terrorism rose to 82, with injury or death in 60 of them. The countries were spread the world over: 18 countries in the Middle East and North Africa, 18 in Europe, 17 in sub-Saharan Africa, 7 in the Americas, and 22 in the Asia–Pacific region, where the increase was the highest.

ISIS has terrorized the Yazidi to the point where ISIS's campaign of murder and rape can only be categorized as genocide. In addition to Yazidi, ISIS terrorizes Buddhists, Hindus, Sikhs, Jews, and anyone who does not submit to their brand of Islam, including other Sunnis who are not devout enough in ISIS's eyes. Al-Shabaab carries out most of its terror in Somalia and Kenya. In an attack on Garissa University in Kenya, the group killed more than 150 students, primarily Christians. In northern Kenya, Al-Shabaab exercises strict control, forcing groups to practice in secret. However, in Mandera, Somalia, Muslims stood up to Al-Shabaab, refusing to separate from Christians and saying, "You kill all of us or none of us" (European Parliament 2016).

Boko Haram, active primarily in Nigeria, also uses terrorist attacks against secular and religious targets, the most infamous being the 2014 capture of nearly 300 schoolgirls in Chibok who were forced to convert to Islam and were kept as wives and sex slaves. Many gave birth while in captivity. Some escaped while en route to camps. Others managed to escape their camps, and some were exchanged for prisoners. As of May 2017, 113 were still not accounted for.

The Lord's Resistance Army is a radical Christian terrorist group that originated in Uganda but has spread through the Central African Republic and Sudan. The

A CLOSER LOOK
HATE CRIMES IN THE UNITED STATES

Anti-Jewish hate crimes are consistently the most numerous in the United States, but anti-Muslim crimes doubled from 2012 to 2015.

TABLE 6.2   Hate Crimes in the United States, 2012–2016

	2012		2013		2014		2015		2016	
Total hate crimes	%	6,705	%	5,922	%	6,385	%	6,837	%	6.063
Religious	17.3	1,166	19.6	1,163	17.1	1,092	19.8	1,354	21	1,273
Anti-Jew[a]	59.7	696	59.2	689	58.2	635	51.3	695	54.2	684
Anti-Muslim[a]	12.8	149	14.2	165	16.3	178	22.2	301	24.8	307
Anti-multiple religions[a]	7.6	89	4.4	51	4.7	51	4.2	57	3.1	34
Anti Catholic[a]	6.8	79	6.4	74	6.1	67	4.4	59	4.1	62
Anti-Protestant[a]	2.9	34	3.6	42	2.6	28	3.5	47	1.3	15
Anti-atheist[a]	1.0	12	.6	7	1.2	13	.1	2	0.4	6
Anti-other[a]	9.2	107	11.6	135	11.0	120	13.6	193	12.1	165

a. Percentage is that of religious bias hate crimes committed against that religion.

Source: Adapted from Federal Bureau of Investigation (2013–2017).

group killed thousands and recruited children to be soldiers and sex slaves. In India, the National Liberation Front of Tripura, a Baptist group, wanted everyone in Tripura to convert to Christianity. One year in the early 2000s, the group slaughtered more than 400 people. In the United States, the Christian terrorist groups Christian Identity and Soldiers in the Army of God bombed abortion clinics, killing workers and doctors who performed abortions, forcing their religious views on those who disagreed. Attacks on Jewish and African American religious groups in the United States also qualify as religiously motivated terror.

"The Revolt" emerged in 2016 in the West Bank among young Jewish settlers. They carried out a series of attacks against Palestinians, including killing a toddler and his parents. They also attacked a church atop Mount Zion. The Jewish Defense League, no longer active in the United States, was responsible for crimes against Palestinians and Arabs, among others such as Nazis and Russians.

In 2016, Russia instituted "anti-terrorism" laws that prohibit extremist views and provide authorities with the legal tool to restrict religious practice. People may also be arrested for violating generally accepted norms of social behavior. Missionary activities were redefined to include activities of praying, preaching, and passing out literature—anything that takes place outside of an approved religious site.

CONFRONTING DISCRIMINATION AND PERSECUTION

As noted by the UN Special Rapporteur on religious freedom, violations of human rights do not fall within the internal affairs of countries. Governments have the primary responsibility for respecting human rights within their countries, but their responsibility is not exclusive. Human rights are a national and international concern. As with all global problems, international governmental organizations, global civil societies, the private sector, and national governments and civil societies all must play a role.

International Organizations

The UN Office of the High Commissioner on Human Rights has primary global responsibility for protecting human rights. It partners with national governments, civil society organizations, other UN agencies and offices, regional governmental associations, and the private sector, among others, to set standards for human rights, monitor human rights, and implement human rights policies and reforms. It maintains a presence on the ground through field offices the world over.

One of the major initiatives is the National Human Rights Institutes (NHRIs). These help governments to weed out human rights violations—such as torture and illegal arrest—and to develop necessary infrastructure to ensure human rights, from national laws to educational systems.

"Discrimination can both cause poverty and be a hurdle in alleviating poverty" (HRW 2013). HRW developed very specific strategies for discrimination and persecution for the UN to implement within the framework of its development goals. These suggest that the UN do the following:

- Target the social and economic needs of the most marginalized and discriminated against groups

- Develop a definition of discrimination consistent with international human rights laws

- Establish a framework to identify the most marginalized groups in every country and their social and economic needs, particularly the most urgent needs

- Evaluate the laws of each country and the institutional structure for discriminatory elements as well as the actions of private parties

- Address and ensure the rights of indigenous peoples, including their land and cultural rights and the free, prior, and informed consent necessary to ensure their rights

- Collect and analyze data that are disaggregated according to the discriminated against groups such as by gender, locale, religion, or ethnic background

- Address the social and cultural needs of the poorest two quintiles in each country and target closing the gap between the richest quintile and the poorest quintiles (HRW 2013)

Regional governmental associations must insist on respect for human rights within member countries and be ready to act on established sanctions when human rights are violated. Regional governmental bodies must also ensure that domestic laws of member countries prohibit discrimination and political systems ensure representation as detailed below.

The EU issues an annual report, "Human Rights and Democracy in the World." The African Commission on Human and People's Rights requires member countries to submit national reports on human rights concerns every two years. Within the African Commission, a number of "Special Rapporteurs" focus on specific types of violations. The Association of South East Asian Nations (ASEAN) also has an Intergovernmental Commission on Human Rights. The Inter-American Commission on Human Rights represents members of the OAS. The United States and many other countries issue reports to their parliaments or congresses. The USDOS issues annual reports on all countries that receive assistance and UN member states to Congress. This is mandated by the Foreign Assistance Act of 1961 and the Trade Act of 1974. Each of these international organizations issues recommendations and takes actions, from reprimands to diplomatic and economic sanctions and (in extreme cases) interventions, to encourage reforms upholding human rights.

National Constitutional and Legislative Reforms

Where governments have signed international treaties regarding human rights, they must be held to task by the international community to enshrine equal rights and protection to racial and ethnic minorities, religious minorities, and all gender identities and sexual orientations in their national constitutions. Purging domestic laws of discriminatory and prejudicial provisions should follow.

Where governments have committed to rights in international treaties, national constitutions, and domestic law, they are more likely to respect those rights. There is more leverage for international and domestic civil society groups to establish monitoring, reporting, and enlisting other governments and intergovernmental organizations to pressure the governments for honoring their commitments. Constitutional and legislative reforms should encompass equality in all aspects of life relative to life chances but should contain a special provision for full participation and representation in the political realm.

Gaining Political Representation

Politics is power. Global norms demand greater inclusion and representation of all groups within a society. The legitimacy of governance depends on how well the government can represent and meet the needs and interests of its entire constituency. Ethnic, racial, and religious minorities are underrepresented in the decision-making bodies of their countries. Some are completely disenfranchised in both democracies and authoritarian regimes. The potential for and actual disenfranchisement threatens all societies. Although different strategies are more effective for different types of minority status—religion, ethnicity and race, and gender, for example—gaining a voice requires structural changes in how parties put forward candidates, how electoral systems are structured, and how the broader political fabric of a country is constituted.

Political Representation

In the United States, minorities—including African Americans, Native Americans, Asians, and Hispanics—made up only 17 percent of representatives in the 114th Congress that was seated in 2015 (Figure 6.6). This percentage compares poorly with their combined total of 38 percent of the U.S. population. Only 35 percent of African Americans, 22 percent of Hispanics, 12 percent of Asians, and 8 percent of Native Americans are represented by someone of the same race or ethnicity (Krogstad 2015).

As long as whites continue to diverge so widely in their perceptions and minorities have such scant representation in politics, it is unlikely that there will be significant legal change to ensure equal rights.

Quotas are often used to ensure greater minority inclusion in elective offices. This can be done successfully but needs to proceed cautiously. Ethnic and religious group boundaries (unlike gender) tend to be coterminous with partisan cleavages and societal divides such as class. Quotas for religious and ethnic groups can increase divisions in societies because election can depend on appealing to a single constituency—and often the extremities because they are most likely to vote. This can "ghettoize" minority candidates and concerns. Working across class, religious, and ethnic boundaries to establish a broad inclusive base of support results in a healthier political process.

Despite these difficulties, quotas are used in a number of societies. They have mixed results (Reynolds 2006). The number and size of ethnic or religious groups, their geographic dispersal, the competitiveness of parties, and access to information all influence how effective quotas can be in achieving empowerment, as opposed to serving as "window dressing" or supporting the status quo and dominant party.

Bird (2014) differentiated three broad categories among the 28 countries with rules for establishing ethnic quotas while warning that no two systems are completely alike. The categories are systems that guarantee seats to ethnic groups, incorporate ethnic groups into pan-ethnic parties, and create special electoral districts for ethnic groups.

Electoral systems designed to guarantee minorities seats through a proportional or threshold system by working through ethnic parties[5] give a proportionate number of seats to each. This tends to result in the government co-opting a preferred ethnic party or parties at the expense of other more threatening ones. Because parties need to build coalitions to succeed in passing legislation, concessions may be made to the interests of an ethnic party. These are often minor and may serve only to advance a few (usually male) ethnic leaders, who may be motivated by self-interest to work through the ruling party. If this system is to work to empower minorities, it must be in the context of true competitiveness within the parties for the representative seats, strong ethnic media to provide information on candidates and issues, and citizens' access to the records of their representatives. This system also requires the support of strong democratic institutions (Bird 2014).

The second system, pan-ethnic parties, is the least likely to result in meaningful inclusion of ethnic groups in democracy building, according to Bird (2014). The main reason is that the ethnic representatives ultimately

A CLOSER LOOK
DIVERSITY IN THE U.S. CONGRESS

Although diversity is increasing, the U.S. Congress is still not representative of the U.S. population.

FIGURE 6.6   Number of U.S. House and Senate Members by Race and Ethnicity

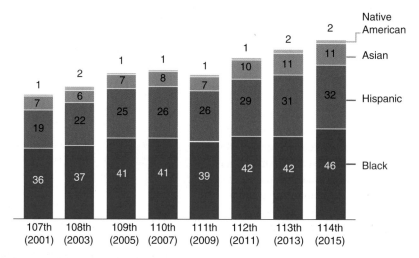

Source: "114th Congress is most diverse ever." Pew Research Center, Washington, D.C. (January 12, 2015) http://www.pewresearch.org/fact-tank/2015/01/12/114th-congress-is-most-diverse-ever/.

elected are beholden to the party for their positions. In practice, this strategy—as in Singapore, Jordan, and Lebanon, among other countries—has tended to maintain and buttress the ruling party rather than introduce real reform.

The third system, in which districts are designated as ethnic districts, tends to create cleavage by suggesting that representatives from other districts need not be responsive to minority concerns. If the district is not competitive or the representative is put forward by a central party, the representative might not be responsive to local concerns. Enabling special districts within a mixed member system, as in New Zealand, ensures minority representation and more inclusive dialog (Bird 2014).

There are more effective strategies for increasing minority representation. Putting more minority candidates on ballots or in positions where they may be beholden to dominant parties is not enough. One of the mistakes that parties make is running minority candidates

against one another in minority districts. This is a waste of an important resource, minority candidates, and does little to increase representation.

Important lessons grew out of the 2010 British parliamentary elections. With many incumbents retiring from their seats, the 2010 elections provided a unique opportunity to make meaningful progress in minority representation. Each of the main parties had sufficient incentive to elect minority candidates. The incentives ranged from recognizing the need to develop a more inclusive image to better representing all the members of society.

Four strategies proved to be effective. Each defied traditional thought concerning minority electability. For example, putting minority candidates on the ballot in "white" districts defies common logic. People simply expect that they would lose. But the Labour Party put minority candidates in "safe" white districts that Labour had little chance of losing. The districts elected the minority candidates. The minority candidate thus represents a broad swath of the public, not just minorities. Cultivating local minorities to run in districts that had never elected a minority before also succeeded. Local candidates proved to be more acceptable in ethnically diverse districts than were candidates culled from a centrally developed list. Spreading candidates over more seats rather than running them against one another, while it might not guarantee a minority win in any particular district, resulted in more minority candidates being elected. Posting an "A" list of candidates (now discontinued) with minorities in top spots also resulted in greater minority wins and also provides more representation (Sobolewska 2013).

Finances

The costs of financing a campaign for elective office can be prohibitive for potential minority (and women) candidates. Poverty, low wages, and family financial commitments compel many to disqualify themselves from running for office. Political finance reforms can help to mitigate the cost of elections. Public financing of political parties may be made dependent on requirements for the inclusion of minorities. Inclusion should be required at all levels—from training at local and national levels, to all party activities, to leadership roles, to candidacy.

Training and Mentorship

Many minorities and women within developing countries have been excluded not only from channels of power but also from a political education. Although it is important to get women and minorities into political offices immediately, long-term efforts should also cultivate a future cadre of women and minorities. One step is including building talent through scholarships for university education in politics and law. Internships in political offices can enhance training and provide mentorship opportunities. Training should begin at local levels to develop channels through which candidates can move from local to national levels.

Minority Sections

Minority sections within parties can provide support for candidates, including specialized training and designated fundraising. These sections may broaden and refine the discussion of minority issues, educate the party on the issues, and develop platforms to address them. These sections can also monitor the party. Minority sections can interact with and enlist civil society organizations and groups to provide the information they need, assist in ensuring that laws for their participation are enforced, and exert pressure on governments and international organizations to follow through on commitments for equal representation.

Combatting Violations of Religious Rights

The UN Special Rapporteur 2016 report called on the international community to act on all violations of religious freedoms from governments and non-state actors. They must protect refugees, recognizing that many are fleeing religious persecution. They must not refuse refugees whose religious beliefs are different from their own on the basis that it would erode their own religious identity or composition. This is "territorialization of religion and goes against the most fundamental religious freedom dictate" (Bielefeldt 2016).

Every year, the United States issues two reports on religious freedom authorized by the IRFA. The independent USCIRF annual report issues recommendations to the secretary of state, president, and Congress. Government responses to violations of religious freedom vary according to not only the gravity of the violation but also the strategic relationships among countries. The USDOS also issues a report to Congress. Government officials take the recommendations into account in their interactions with other countries or non-state actors.

The president and USDOS have the obligation to consult with humanitarian agencies and other interested parties before acting in order to assess potentially dangerous impacts of sanctions on those who are discriminated against. But being listed in the reports as a country that has violated religious freedoms is a public criticism and a sanction in and of itself. Beyond this, the sanctions authorized by the IRFA range from a private "demarche" or statement of reproach concerning the violations, to public statements, to barring entry of officials from the offending country into the United States, to a range of financial restrictions. These are usually accompanied by consultations concerning how the action should be addressed by the violating country or actor in question. For example, in 2014 John Kerry (U.S. secretary of state) issued a warning on a visit to Nigeria that the United States would deny entry to any person who incited or engaged in violence during the upcoming elections (USCIRF 2016).

The United States included sanctions for the violation of religious freedoms in the package of sanctions against Iran in 2010. Executive orders by the Obama administration instituted visa bans and asset freezes on 19 Iranian officials and 18 entities for violations of religious rights. Similar visa bans and frozen assets are in place for Russian officials and the Chechen president, Ramzan Kadyrov (USCIRF 2016).

Within the United States, the prosecution of hate crimes on the basis of religion is one way in which violations of religious freedom are combatted. It is a recognition by the government that non-state or social actors must respect religious freedom. The Civil Rights Division prosecutes the well-publicized violations such as attacks on places of worship—synagogues, mosques, and churches—and religiously motivated shootings. It also prosecutes less attention-getting crimes such as forcibly pulling a headscarf from a Muslim woman. Federal courts have struck down local zoning laws, and the Department of Justice has filed suits against states when codes were written to prevent building houses of worship and religious schools, whether Christian, Muslim, or Jewish (U.S. Department of Justice 2016).

The European Parliament also ranks upholding religious freedom among its global priorities. The Intergroup on Freedom of Religion or Belief and Religious Tolerance annual report in 2016 assessed religious restrictions and made recommendations for action to the EU Parliament. The 2015 report called attention to "failed states" that are extremely unstable (Afghanistan, Central African Republic, Libya, Somalia, Syria, and Yemen) and recommended that the EU help to prevent any group within these countries accused of violating human rights from generating income by selling raw materials or artifacts. The EU promises to be generous in humanitarian aid and to support basic security in failed states (European Parliament 2016).

The 2016 EU report also identified "focal countries" chosen not only for their violations of religious freedom but also for the pressure that the EU can exert on them based on their bilateral relations. The recommendations are similar to those of the USCIRF in the United States. For example, the report recommended that the EU institute a reward-based system whereby Burma receives enhanced partnerships and agreements for making and complying with human rights reforms. It suggested supporting nongovernmental organizations in China to strengthen their advocacy and reporting and maintaining asset freezes and travel bans in Iran (European Parliament 2016).

Civil Society and Governmental Organizations

Civil society organizations and governmental agencies that work on the ground bridge local actors, national governments, and international agencies. They can be effective change agents, especially when working in partnerships. The U.S. Agency for International Development (USAID), for example, works with religious groups and civil society groups, providing resources and advice and helping them to partner with one another. A 2016 "World Faith Africa" meeting in Nigeria brought USAID together with Religions for Peace, The Global Women of Faith Network, The Council of African Religious Leaders, and the GHR Foundation to develop strategies to counter religious extremism that incites violence.

The crisis of Boko Haram resulted in the deaths of more than 30,000 Nigerians, the displacement of 2.5 million people, and the abductions of 50,000 more. The World Faith Africa meeting stressed the need to combat religious extremists such as Boko Haram on the psychological, socioeconomic, political, and ideological fronts. Religious and community leaders from all faiths pledged to work together to mentor the vulnerable to help them reject violent ideologies. They recognize that they must build reconciliation within communities.

The International Association for Religious Freedom (IARF), founded in 1900, is the world's first international inter-religious organization that works for freedom of religion globally. There are 73 member organizations spread over 26 countries. It has consultative status at the UN. Most of its work is local—on the ground. For example, to reduce social hostility, the IARF offers workshops bringing together educators from different religious traditions to teach one another how to educate about their own religious tradition. In multi-religious societies such as India, the IARF offers workshops on building a common cultural heritage that embraces all religions. In Costa Rica, it held conferences on dispelling intolerance toward religious and cultural minorities.

Christian Solidarity Worldwide (CSW) is a civil society organization that promotes religious freedom of all religions. It is one of the groups that monitors and reports on religious discrimination to the United Kingdom, the United States, the UN, and the EU. More important, it provides human rights advocacy training locally in 20 countries. At a 2016 conference in South Asia, CSW brought 25 lawyers from Pakistan, Indonesia, Bangladesh, Sri Lanka, and India to share their political advocacy best practices in contesting discriminatory legislation and getting it changed. In 2016, CSW held a protest at the Chinese Embassy to demand the release of Li Heping, a civil rights attorney who was detained in a massive crackdown that targeted more than 250 human rights workers. He was released and given a suspended sentence in April 2017. Civil society groups, along with international governmental organizations and other governments, are critical in monitoring human rights abuses and pressuring violators to relent.

SUMMARY

Race, ethnicity, and religion are social constructs—ways that people have invented to divide "us" from "them." This is not necessarily harmful when and if mutual respect and bridging social capital are abundant. However, in the competition for resources, bigotry and ignorance, if allowed, can erode the social landscape, creating deep divides. The price of bigotry is high. Individuals, whole societies, and eventually the world suffer the consequences. The consequences for a society range from lower productivity and economic growth to the erosion of trust. Lower productivity and economic growth exacerbate poverty and inequality, and many people's life chances are harmed. Erosion of trust is very likely to bring violent conflict. The spillover effects have global consequences.

DISCUSSION

1. Try to develop definitions of race and ethnicity. If possible, try to do this in a small group and write definitions with which everyone agrees. Did you or your group succeed? Evaluate your efforts.

2. What are the essential guarantees that a society should provide in the name of religious freedom? How does this relate to the tension among religious groups in the world today? Consider some of the contemporary issues.

3. Weigh the land and other rights of indigenous people against the claims or desires of other segments of society, as in disputes over pipelines in the United States or religious symbols in France. What criteria would you use to resolve these competing claims and needs?

4. What strategies might be used to reduce social hostilities among groups within societies? Devise a plan to address such a matter in your community or society.

5. How do prejudice and discrimination destabilize societies? Provide examples from contemporary world or national news.

6. Hate crimes have been on the rise in many countries. Examine a national/international newspaper for one week. What acts of social hostility or hate crimes were reported? In which countries were they committed? Who were the victims, and who were the offenders?

ON YOUR OWN

1. Minority groups, however they are defined, suffer from poorer life chances than other groups. Find current health, education, employment, or income for a group identified as a minority in your country.

2. a. The Southern Poverty Law Center reports on acts of hate and hate groups. Investigate its "hate map." Which states have the highest number of hate groups? You can find this by selecting a state and selecting "all groups." The groups are listed along with the number of hate groups in the state.

   Which type of hate group has the largest number of groups nationwide? You can find this by selecting a type of group and selecting "all states." Which type of group is the most numerous?

   or

2. b. The Federal Bureau of Investigation collects hate crime statistics. They are not complete but give an idea of the types of hate crimes most frequently committed. The Hate Crime Statistics Report can be found at https://ucr.fbi.gov/hate-crime/2015

   What percentage of hate crimes fell into each bias category? What group was most often victimized in each of the categories?

3. The Pew Research Center rates countries on social hostility to religion and government restrictions on religion. The full report released in 2017 can be accessed at http://www.pewforum.org/2017/04/11/global-restrictions-on-religion-rise-modestly-in-2015-reversing-downward-trend.

    In the full report, how many of the 198 countries rated fall into the high or very high categories in government restriction and social hostility? Of the 45 countries in Europe, how many report social hostilities toward Muslims? Toward Jews? Toward Christians?

    Examine "Appendix B," the Social Hostilities Index, of the countries rated high or very high in social hostilities. Which are generally considered "free countries/consolidated democracies"?

    Explore the report for the types of social hostility experienced in the democratic countries. You can also follow hyperlinks in the report to the U.S. Department of State reports on religious freedom for specific countries.

4. The Comparative Constitutions Project provides data on the rights and freedoms enacted in national constitutions. Using its "Data Visualizations" function, you can determine how many and what percentage of constitutions grant each particular right and freedom.

    http://comparativeconstitutionsproject.org/ccp-visualizations/

    a. Choose the "Rights Motion" chart. Here users can investigate when each right first appeared and the percentage of constitutions in which it is currently included.

    b. Find rights relevant to religious freedoms and racial and ethnic equalities.

    c. In the Comparative Constitutions Project, users can search constitutions for mention of specific rights and freedoms. The texts of relevant articles are displayed.

    Investigate the constitution of a country (or countries) that ranks high in racial and ethnic discrimination or regulation of religion. Compare the text with a country that is low in discrimination or regulation. Analyze the texts for similarities and dissimilarities.

About the project: http://comparativeconstitutionsproject.org/about-constitute

Interactive database: https://www.constituteproject.org

5. The World Values Survey provides for online analysis of values. Investigate how people feel about having neighbors of a different race, religion, sexual orientation, or other common bias.

    Go to the World Values Survey Online Analysis: http://www.worldvaluessurvey.org/WVSOnline.jsp

    Select Wave 6. 2010–2014. Select the country or countries you would like to explore.

    Click the survey questions. Click "show tree." Scroll to the folder labeled "Would not like to have as neighbors." Choose one bias.

    The next screen gives you a breakdown of how people in the country answered. By choosing a variable under the menu "Cross by:", you can see how the answers varied by something such as education, religion, or any of the other questions.

    You can also explore the connection among values related to religion: importance of religion (V9), religious denomination (V144), and whether or not people would or would not like to have neighbors of a different religion (V41).

6. The Center for Systemic Peace maintains a global database of major political violence conflicts. Information on each is provided, including whether or not it is an ethnic war or ethnic violence. Choose one of the ongoing ethnic conflicts of magnitude over 1,000. Investigate the country. What is the root of the conflict? What ethnic groups are involved? Are there historical factors that come into play?

    http://www.systemicpeace.org/warlist/warlist.htm

    The CIA World Factbook is a good reference with which to start.

    https://www.cia.gov/library/publications/the-world-factbook

NOTES

1. In the United States, Italians and Jews, among others, were not considered white until they advanced up the socioeconomic ladder. They got whiter as they got richer. Chinese were considered black. As they got wealthier, they lost the label of black and became considered "non-white."

2. Religious freedom cannot be absolute in any case; nor can any freedom—that of speech, press, association, and so forth. Each is subject to some legal restrictions. The lines between state requirements, such as registration and restriction, can blur. Some would call any form of registration a restriction. But where registration grants tax-exempt status, it is an advantage. If not used to disadvantage some groups and advantage others, or to inhibit practices or beliefs that do not violate other rights in any way, a registration or other regulation might not necessarily be considered a restriction. For example, where states should or should not prohibit female genital mutilation is controversial. However, because it is practiced on children, it is generally not considered a restriction. However, denying Jews male circumcision, as is proposed in some countries, is considered a restriction.

3. The USDOS reports annually to the U.S. Congress on religious freedom in the world, in keeping with legislation passed in 1998 as part of the International Religious Freedom Act of 1998. The report classifies countries as "countries of particular concern" if violations of religious freedoms are deemed sufficient to warrant further action by the United States.

4. The 2016 report is based on 2014 data.

5. In a threshold system, a minority gets a seat if the minority party receives a certain percentage (threshold) of votes—for example 10 percent—that a "regular candidate" would need to obtain a seat.

7

You Can't Empower Us With Chickens
GENDER THROUGH THE LIFESPAN

WOMEN, GIRLS, AND THE SPOILS OF WAR

Yazidi men in Iraq fought to save their communities from ISIS (Islamic State of Iraq and Syria) brutality. Losing battles, parents watched as their children died from hunger and thirst or the horror of beheadings. Women and children watched as men were slaughtered. The United Nations (UN) declared the ISIS rampage against Yazidi in Iraq a genocide. Supporting this claim were the mass graves found on sites that had been Yazidi towns.

As spoils of the war, ISIS took thousands of women and girls who survived the genocide into sexual slavery. A rescue network run by Yazidi activists, Ameena Saeed Hasan and Khaleel Al-dakhi, struggles to save as many as it can but has reached only a small percentage of what it believes to be about 3,700 captives. Its work started with one phone call to a mother in a refugee camp in Kurdistan, Iraq. A kidnapped girl had managed to stay in contact with her mother by cell phone. The mother put Hasan and Al-dakhi on the phone with her daughter, who was beyond desperation and wanted to commit suicide. They agreed to help her and quickly put together a team to smuggle her out of Mosul, where she was held captive. Others heard of the rescue. Their one-time rescue grew into an underground operation.

Women and girls call every day, dozens a week, from cell phones that they manage to smuggle, begging to be rescued. The network rescues and rehabilitates victims. Hasan and Al-dakhi won the Trafficking in Persons Award of the U.S. Department of State. They also won the 2016 Human Rights First Award. They had rescued more than 170 women and girls by the fall of 2016.

Rape as a war tactic or one of the "spoils" of war is ancient. Rape is used systematically to spread terror, destroy communities, facilitate genocide, infect women with HIV, destroy the family structure, and provide sex for soldiers, among other objectives. Not until thousands of Muslim women had been raped in Bosnia–Herzegovina did the International Criminal Tribunal identify the systematic rape of women and girls in war as a crime against humanity.

LEARNING OBJECTIVES

After completing this chapter, students should be able to do the following:

7.1 Understand the concepts of sex and gender as social constructs

7.2 Identify ways in which discrimination throughout the lifespan limits women's and girls' life chances

7.3 Analyze cultural motifs that contribute to prejudices and discrimination against women and girls

I long to hear that you have declared an independency. And, by the way, in the new code of laws which I suppose it will be necessary for you to make, I desire you would remember the ladies and be more generous and favorable to them than your ancestors. Do not put such unlimited power into the hands of the husbands. Remember, all men would be tyrants if they could. If particular care and attention is not paid to the ladies, we are determined to foment a rebellion, and will not hold ourselves bound by any laws in which we have no voice or representation.

—Abigail Adams in a letter to John Adams, March 31, 1776 (Allen 2016, Library of Congress Blog)

Females were not always relegated to secondary status. In most hunting and gathering societies, women and men were equals. Not every society differentiated sex and gender into two simplistically divided categories. As societies developed beyond subsistence and achieved a surplus of goods, control of the surplus became a critical question. Gender inequality and the bifurcation of gender accompanying it are arguably among the oldest and most pervasive forms of inequality. Before race, ethnicity, or religion divided a society into "us" and "them," gender differentiated the dominant from the subservient.

Most nations have signed onto the Convention on the Elimination of All Forms of Discrimination against

A CLOSER LOOK
MAJOR INTERNATIONAL INSTRUMENTS RELEVANT TO GENDER

The following UN conventions have the force of law for countries that are party to them. The UN declarations are statements of global norms. While they do not have the force of law, they serve as models and set standards:

1. Convention on the Elimination of All Forms of Discrimination against Women (CEDAW) (1979) and Optional Protocol to the Convention (1999)

2. Protocol to Prevent, Suppress, and Punish Trafficking in Persons, Especially Women and Children, supplementing the United Nations Convention against Transnational Organized Crime (2003)

3. Convention on Consent to Marriage, Minimum Age for Marriage, and Registration of Marriages (1962)

4. Convention against Discrimination in Education (1960)

5. Discrimination (Employment and Occupation) Convention (1958)

6. Convention on the Nationality of Married Women (1957)

7. Convention on the Political Rights of Women (1952)

8. Equal Remuneration Convention (1951)

9. Convention for the Suppression of the Traffic in Persons and of the Exploitation of the Prostitution of Others (1949)

10. Declaration on the Elimination of Violence against Women (1994)

   - Declaration on the Protection of Women and Children in Emergencies and Armed Conflicts (1974)
   - Declaration on the Elimination of Discrimination against Women (1967)
   - UN Human Rights Council: Special Rapporteur on violence against women, its causes and consequences.

Source: Women's Watch (n.d.).

Women and the Beijing Declaration and Platform for Action. Many regional and national constitutions and other laws claim women's equality in all matters. Inequality persists, however, in all countries due to weak laws or weak enforcement.

GENDER INEQUALITY AND HUMAN DEVELOPMENT

Despite international conventions and national constitutions, there is no country yet that provides women with opportunity to reach their full potential. Sustainable Development Goal (SDG) 5 calls for gender equality and empowerment of all women and girls. However, due to women's pivotal role in family and community, their empowerment is essential in achieving many other goals, especially in hunger, health, and education. From sex selection before birth to unequal access to health care, education, and paid employment, to domestic violence, kidnapping, forced marriage, and rape, to punitive practices that demand death for the slightest infractions, women remain captives of ideologies and cultural attitudes with deep roots in patriarchal societies. These same attitudes, rooted in the doctrine and dogma of sex and gender, deny homosexual and transgender individuals their natural rights and subject them to cruel and unusual, formal and informal, punishment all over the world.

Given that females are discriminated against even before they are born, it is not unexpected that gender inequality affects human development. The situation of women and girls varies widely around the world. In developed societies, equal wages, fair opportunities to achieve according to ambition and talent, representation in the

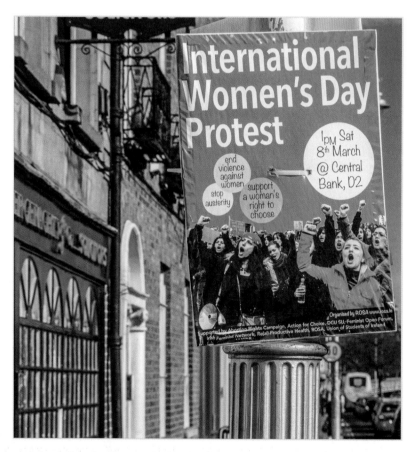

PHOTO 7.1 The United Nations began celebrating International Women's Day in 1975 to recognize both women's achievements and struggles.

International Women's Day Protest by William Murphy/CC BY-SA 2.0.

political arenas and corporate life, and sexual violence and harassment are among the paramount concerns. Even in Norway, long considered one of the most equal societies, women face barriers, particularly women in minority and indigenous communities. In developing societies, the needs are much greater, with violence even more normative, often openly and legally.

The Human Development Report issues a Gender Inequality Index (GII) in addition to the Human Development Index (HDI). The GII incorporates five indicators into three measures to derive a female reproductive health index, female empowerment index, and female labor market index. Together, these form the female gender index. The male empowerment index and male labor market index form the male gender index. The higher the GII, the more inequality between males and females. A gender inequality-adjusted HDI is calculated for each country. There is not one country that does not have a lower inequality-adjusted HDI than unadjusted one, indicating that there is not one country in which gender inequality does not inhibit development and the quality of life, particularly (but not exclusively) for women. Women of minority groups suffer from intersectionality, the combined effect of membership in two or more marginalized groups (Figure 7.1).

In North and South America, Eastern and Western Europe, Australia, and much if not most of Africa and Asia, people proclaim that women's rights are important. A 2015 Pew survey of 38 nations showed that majorities said equal rights for women were important or very important in every country except Burkina Faso. The median of response of "very important" was 68 percent. In countries where support for women's rights is near universal, in the 90 percent and above range, men and

A CLOSER LOOK
THE COMPONENTS OF THE GENDER INEQUALITY INDEX

FIGURE 7.1   Gender Inequality Index (GII)

The Gender Inequality Index is based on measures of health, empowerment, and employment. Countries are scored on each indicator, and an overall score is calculated. These are reported in Table 5 of the Human Development Reports.

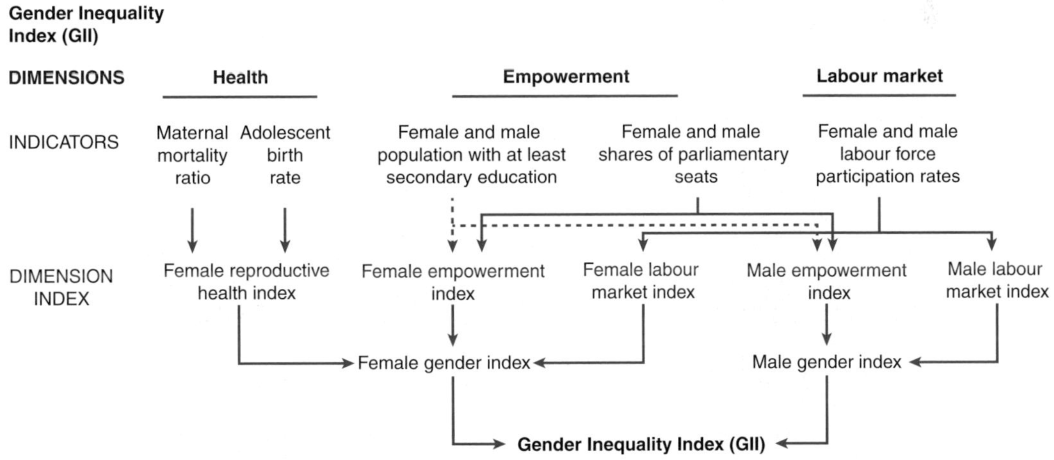

Source: Human Development Report 2016 Technical Notes by United Nations Development Programme (http://hdr.undp.org/sites/default/files/hdr2016_technical_notes.pdf), licensed under CC 3.0 IGO (https://creativecommons.org/licenses/by/3.0/igo/legalcode).

A CLOSER LOOK
IMPORTANCE OF GENDER EQUALITY

Majorities in all but one world region believe that gender equality is important.

FIGURE 7.2   Survey Results on the Importance of Gender Equality

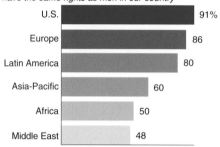

Regional median saying it is very important that women have the same rights as men in our country

U.S.	91%
Europe	86
Latin America	80
Asia-Pacific	60
Africa	50
Middle East	48

Source: "Many around the world say women's equality is very important." Pew Research Center, Washington, D.C. (January 19, 2017) http://www.pewresearch.org/fact-tank/2017/01/19/many-around-the-world-say-womens-equality-is-very-important/.

FIGURE 7.3   Survey Results on the Rights of Women

% saying it is very important that women have the same rights as men in our country

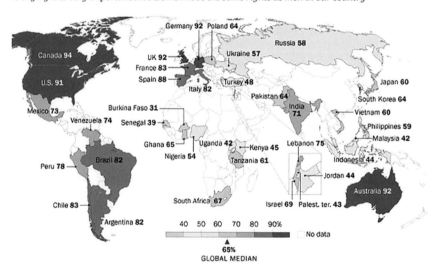

Source: "Many around the world say women's equality is very important." Pew Research Center, Washington, D.C. (January 19, 2017) http://www.pewresearch.org/fact-tank/2017/01/19/many-around-the-world-say-womens-equality-is-very-important/.

women are not significantly different in their support, with the exception of the United Kingdom (Figures 7.2 and 7.3) (Fetterolf 2017).

Still, women do not have life chances equal to those of men. A significant gap, 5 percent or more, between men's and women's response of "very important" was seen in 24 of the 38 countries. In 12 countries, the gap was in the double digits. Where there is significant difference between women's and men's valuing of equality, men are likely to have significantly more political power as well, making it very difficult to pass equalizing legislation or enact equalizing policies.

Women struggled for, fought for, and finally won—in theory at least—equal rights in the developed countries bit by bit in a centuries-long struggle. Although it varies by country and the rights in question, women's rights in the developing world are at about the level developed societies were 50 to 100 years ago. And women in the developed

regions of the world still lag behind men in measures of empowerment—earnings, wealth, and political voice.

The World Economic Forum (WEF 2017) Global Gender Gap calculated the global gender performance index at 68 percent. That is to say that there is a gap of 32 percent. Overall, men are 32 percent ahead of women in the four indexes measured: economic participation and opportunity (gap of 42 percent), educational attainment (gap of 5 percent), health and survival (gap of 4 percent), and political empowerment (gap of 77 percent) (Tables 7.1 and 7.2) (WEF 2017).

The prognosis is not promising. At the current pace of change, taking into consideration that some scores have eroded from earlier peaks, the global gap[1] for the 106 countries included in the first report, in 2006, will close in about 100 years, longer than the 83-year estimate from the previous year. The most promising index is education. The progress of women in education has been steady,

A CLOSER LOOK
GLOBAL GENDER GAP 10 BEST AND 10 WORST COUNTRIES

Gender ratios range from Iceland's 88 percent to Yemen's 52 percent, leaving gaps from about 12 percent in Iceland to 48 percent in Yemen. The overall global ratio is 68 percent.

TABLE 7.1   The 10 Best Countries

1.	Iceland	.878
2.	Norway	.830
3.	Finland	.823
4.	Rwanda	.822
5.	Sweden	.816
6.	Nicaragua	.814
7.	Slovenia	.805
8.	Ireland	.794
9.	New Zealand	.791
10.	Philippines	.790

Source: Adapted from World Economic Forum (2017).

TABLE 7.2   The 10 Worst (from Worst)

1.	Yemen	.516
2.	Pakistan	.546
3.	Syria	.568
4.	Chad	.575
5.	Iran	.583
6.	Mali	.583
7.	Saudi Arabia	.584
8.	Lebanon	.596
9.	Morocco	.598
10.	Côte d'Ivoire	.604

Source: Adapted from World Economic Forum (2017).

and the gap could be closed in 13 years. In the case of politics, although the gap is currently the largest, it is closing the most rapidly. At this pace, the gap could close in 99 years—a rather long time to wait. The economic gender gap will not close for another 217 years (WEF 2017). This rate of progress is not acceptable. The well-being not only of women and girls but also of all humankind is at risk.

GENDER INEQUITIES THROUGHOUT THE LIFESPAN

It Begins Before Birth

Many people might prefer to have at least one son rather than none. In the United States, a 2011 Gallup poll discovered that 49 percent of men polled said that if they were to have only one child, they would prefer it be a boy. Women were nearly evenly divided among a boy preference and a girl preference, but more had no preference, 36 percent of the female vote (Newport 2011). Where patriarchy is strong, son preference may be more than just a wish. It is likely to become a practice. Preference for sons originates with a variety of economic, cultural, and social motives—the need for sons to perform religious rituals, the belief that sons are better equipped and more likely to provide security for parents in their old age, the likelihood that girls leave home while boys remain within the parental homestead and contribute to the economic well-being of the home, and the desire to carry on the family lineage through male heirs. With or without one-child policies or the legality or illegality of abortion, cultural norms for son preference affect family size and composition. The underlying bias favoring males continues to affect females throughout their lives.

People practice son preference in one of three ways; by having children until they reach their desired number of sons, by selective abortion, and by infanticide. Each of these has a different impact on the society in question and the well-being of girls. Differential stopping tends not to disrupt the sex ratio of a society, whereas selective abortion does. Selective abortion and infanticide show up in "missing" females. The practice of son preference at birth (as opposed to differential treatment alone) may be hidden where there is not a dearth of females and an excess of males.

In Turkey, for example, there is a decided son preference. Families are more likely to stop having children after a male birth or after the desired number of males are born. While there is not an unbalanced sex ratio in the society, there is within families. The sex ratio at last birth is highly skewed to males—indicating families stopping with the

birth of a male and the likelihood of males growing up in smaller families. In access to resources, smaller family size advantages males and larger size disadvantages females.

Turkish families with a female firstborn are 6.7 percent larger on average than those with a male firstborn. The child mortality rate is slightly higher for males, as in most countries. In Turkey, even though education, urbanization, and higher age at marriage reduce fertility, additional births in response to the absence of a son persist. Differential stopping is also evident in Egypt, Central Asia, and the United States, but it has not affected the overall sex ratio in those societies (Altindag 2016).

In Turkey and India, female health suffers from son preference. Sons with an older female sibling are favored in health investment. Among third and later-born children, the female advantage in child mortality disappears for females with an older female sibling. The gender gap in mortality shifts to advantage males. Altindag (2016) proposed that without a son preference, boys and girls would have similar numbers of siblings. This would create a more equal resource allocation. Differences in resource allocation—with the quality of allocation decreasing as the number of siblings sharing resources increases—is documented in the case of education in Korea, another society with a son preference (Altindag 2016), and Pakistan (Zaidi and Morgan 2016).

Polling of more than 50,000 Indian women in 2006 revealed that nearly 60 percent of them wanted at least two sons, with 33 percent wanting one son. While an overwhelming majority of women, 87 percent, wanted at least one daughter, not many wanted more than one daughter. However, discrimination against daughters occurs—by 5 years of age, 6 percent more girls than boys are stunted and 1 percent more girls are unvaccinated. The discrimination is based on the gender of girls' older siblings in a similar fashion as in Turkey. If a family already has sons and no daughters, the family is more likely to nurture a daughter. Girls with two or more sisters are the most discriminated against, whereas boys with two or more sisters are not. Unlike Turkey, India does have an unbalanced sex ratio at the societal level as well as at the family level. Selective abortion, in addition to differential stopping, is practiced (Pande and Malhotra 2006).

In Pakistan, son preference is strong, but families also wish to have at least one daughter. The happiest families are those with two sons and one daughter. Contraception use is low in Pakistan and abortion is illegal. Still, contraception—differential stopping—is the preferred method of practicing son preference. Contraception use is lowest among those with only daughters and is higher among those with sons. Pakistan has a relatively high rate

CONSIDER THIS
SON PREFERENCE AND MATERNAL HEALTH

India has one of the highest rates of maternal and adult female mortality in the world. Strong son preference encourages women to practice fertility methods that are injurious to their health:

- Frequent pregnancies, intervals shorter than 24 months between pregnancies, and unsafe abortions increase the possibility of maternal mortality.

- Women whose firstborn is a girl have significantly higher rates of anemia up to 30 years of age caused by close spacing of children or past pregnancies.

- Among uneducated women, those whose firstborn is a girl are 3.6 percent more likely to experience severe violence than those whose firstborn is a boy.

Source: Adapted from Milazzo (2014).

of abortion, but there is not clear evidence of sex selective abortion. There is not an unbalanced sex ratio at birth. With increasing contraceptive use and norms encouraging smaller family sizes, it is an open question whether or not sex selective abortions will rise. As in Turkey, India, and other societies, son preference dilutes the resources a family has to allocate to its children, reinforces patriarchy, and disadvantages girls (Zaidi and Morgan 2016).

Where smaller families and sons both are desired, modern technology has made selective abortion a potential son preference practice. Statistically, if families desire one son, 99 percent will achieve that if they are willing to have six children. If the desired goal is one son with a maximum of two children, 25 percent are likely to need to practice sex selective abortion (Pörtner 2015).

Sex selective abortion is reflected in a country's sex ratio, as is evident in the cases of Azerbaijan, Armenia, Georgia, Montenegro, Albania, Vietnam, India, Pakistan (109.9), and China. As recently as 2013, each of these countries had a sex ratio of 110 or more boys for every 100 girls. Without interference, the norm is about 105 given that more males are born than females. Other societies, such as South Korea and Nepal, have unbalanced ratios but not as extreme as those countries (Gilles and Feldman-Jacobs 2013). Many families will spare a firstborn girl because she can help with chores and raising younger siblings. But sex selective abortions increase with the number of pregnancies resulting in a female. The sex selection ratio skyrockets to as high as 200 boys to 100 girls for thirdborn children in some provinces of China. The effect on the demography of the society is an unbalanced sex ratio, with an excess of males. These societies are "missing" millions of women.

In India, the main users of sex selective abortion are women with eight or more years of education. These women also have the lowest rates of fertility. As fertility declines, sex selection is occurring earlier in the sequence of births, although there is no evidence of it on the first birth. There is some evidence that boy preference is declining somewhat as smaller families are increasingly desired, but it has not slowed the sex selection practice, at least not in India. Legal restrictions have not discouraged the practice. In fact, sex selective abortions have increased 5 percent for highly educated urban and rural women since they were made illegal nationwide in 1994. With education, women are both more likely to want smaller families and have access to sex-determining technology—primarily ultrasound. For every 100 women in their childbearing years, there are about 9.4 abortions for urban women and 10.5 abortions for rural women among those highly educated. The sex ratio among these women favors boys, 53.7 percent urban and 53.4 percent rural (Pörtner 2015). Women who are poorer are more likely to practice more closely spaced pregnancies in seeking to give birth to a son. In India, sex ratios and mortality statistics suggest that sex selection is not practiced by lower-caste Hindus or Muslims despite them being poorer. Muslims have lower child and infant mortality (particularly among girls), have higher female-to-male sex ratios, use contraception less, and tend to have a preference for greater numbers of girls as well as boys (Borooah et al. 2009).

Most of the attention in the popular press has followed the case of China, where a one-child policy in the 1970s resulted in widespread son preference practices that together created a complex set of problems. As problems became apparent, the government adapted some policies for various parts of the country. It enacted policies such as allowing a second child if the first was a girl in some provinces, permitting parents who were only children to have more than one child, and in 2015 it instituted a two-child policy for everyone. While many societies have a sex ratio that favors boys, China's is the largest. World Health Organization data from 2000 measured China's ratio at 119 boys born for every 100 girls. Despite adjustments, restricting fertility in combination with son preference norms created a gender crisis and a dramatic increase in China's dependency ratio—the number of working adults to the number of youths and elders.

Declining fertility in China was well under way before the one-child policy, having dropped from six births per woman in 1960 to fewer than three by 1980. With fertility overall in China at 1.6, a reversal or at least neutralization of son preference norms is evident in some areas, particularly those below fertility replacement. More couples are choosing not to have children, and more couples do not differentially value sons and daughters. The fertility rates in Hong Kong, Beijing, and Shanghai all are below 1. The sex ratio is about the world norm. In contrast, a 2014 study found that having a son as a second child was 7.4 percent more likely among women with a high school education than among women with no formal schooling. While in some areas of China, developed urban areas, the sex ratio may be normalizing, overall it remains high, driven particularly by rural areas, measuring 118 boys for every 100 girls in 2013 (Gilles and Feldman-Jacobs 2013). In the long run, China's sex ratio may even out, but the problems it caused reach into the future, affecting social movements, legislation, urbanization, media, education, and the labor market (Pande and Malhotra 2006).

Son Preference and Infant and Childhood Mortality

Where small families are desired and sex typing technology cannot be afforded, the grisly impacts of son preference on childhood are too often infanticide and abandonment. Female infanticide is not new. In India, it dates at least as far back as 1789, where reports indicate that in some areas it was so widespread that one province had only five families that had not killed their newborn daughters. In 2000, infanticide increased 19.5 percent over 1999 (foeticide increased 49.2 percent). Dowry and poverty are the primary reasons reported for female infanticide. Safety for the girl and son preference for carrying on lineage were secondary but very important rationales (Tandon and Sharma 2006). An old saying in

India expresses the sentiment that bringing up a daughter is like watering a neighbor's plant. It is an investment on which there is no return. In China, girls are sometimes called "spilt water," a waste because they neither carry on the family name nor provide for their parents' old age.

In India, in 2011, 90 percent of the 11 million abandoned children were girls. Many die. Of those who do not, most will never find a home. In the years 2010 to 2015, only about 4,000 to 6,000 children were adopted annually through the Central Adoption Resource Authority (2016) established to facilitate in country and inter-country adoptions of orphaned, abandoned, and surrendered children. The thousands of babies adopted every year from China are a small fraction of those who need homes. It would be a mistake to believe that all parents who abandon their children do not love them. Many are placed where they are sure to be found and are protected from harm as much as possible.

Differential stopping results in less access to resources such as health, education, and food and disadvantages girls with respect to having more work at home. The presumed effects of sex selective abortion on the lives of girls and women are mixed. It may be that access to sex selection means that girls who are born are wanted or else they would have been aborted. With sex selection, there is often more space between the birth of the first child, if a girl, and the births of subsequent children, improving her life chances—even if she is no more wanted than before. Because the women practicing sex selection are better educated, their children have better survival chances independent of spacing or selection. Abandonment, unless the girls are adopted, severely limits girls' life chances.

Where traditional norms continue to dominate, more sex selection is likely even as fertility decreases. By contrast, in Korea, which traditionally reflected a high rate of sex selection, the sex ratio of boys to girls is declining—although not yet to normal levels. Industrialization, urbanization, economic development, media campaigns, and—perhaps most important—laws and policies to promote gender equity and female employment will increase the status of women and increase the desirability, or at least diminish the undesirability, of girls.

The cultural view that female babies are undesirable, and at worst disposable, reinforces views that discrimination and violence against girls and women are acceptable even if officially illegal. An excess of single men also tends to increase crime. In societies such as India and China with deep cultural bias against women, and where females have long been seen as disposable, it is not surprising that crimes against women—particularly rape and murder—are high. Sometimes women are victimized simply because they are female or sometimes because of a perceived failure in some duty prescribed for their role—such as bearing their husband sons or not coming with sufficient dowry. Whether India can manage the social impact of an extra 28 million men of marriageable age that it is expected to have by 2020 is doubtful. Its police and judicial systems are not adequate to handle current crimes against women, let alone the swell expected to come (Hundal 2013).

Among the consequences of sex selection is an active marriage market for brides. With a changing sex ratio, some women may benefit from a surplus of men in the marriage market. For others, it provides another opportunity for them to be exploited and victimized. Kidnapping has been on a continual rise in India, increasing 67.9 percent from 2004 to 2014, reaching 77,237 in 2014. The majority of kidnapping victims, 74.6 percent, were female. Marriage was the primary reason, followed by illicit intercourse—forced sex and rape. Many victims are kidnapped from Muslim areas such as West Bengal and Assam, where sex selection is not practiced, and taken to Haryana and similar areas, where the woman shortage is most severe (National Crime Records Bureau 2014). Hundreds of women and girls are kidnapped in Vietnam to be sold in China. In some cases, women are hired to pose as brides and then run away when the price is paid. Human traffickers may lure girls and young women from poor areas where they are more plentiful. Traffickers may then sell them to poorer or less educated men in provinces such as Haryana, one of the regions with the highest male-to-female ratios.

In an ironic twist, a married daughter, particularly a beautiful and educated one, may in fact prove to be more desirable than an unmarried son (Pörtner 2015). Wealthy men pay thousands of dollars to agencies, "love hunters," who scout upscale shopping malls for the perfect bride. Looking for perfect skin, an elegant face, and virginity, one love hunter was promised U.S. $30,000 if she found the perfect bride. Just three miles away, parents stood advertising their sons with homemade signs. One woman stopped and asked a parent, "Does he own an apartment?" Upon hearing the answer "no," she moved on (Larmer 2013).

Child Marriage

On the day of her marriage at 11 years of age, Noora was enjoying all of the attention. The celebration was three days long. Each day, women dressed her in a different beautiful dress and put jewelry on her. She was given gifts. There was wonderful food—spiced lamb and rice—and music and dancing. But then, the celebration ended and she was taken away from her home by a man more than three times her age. He undressed in front of her, wanting sex. She ran away. After 10 days of crying and avoiding sex, she was warned that she was disgracing the man—now her husband—and her family. The first time she had sex with him, her body, only 11 years old, went into shock. Although she was taken to the hospital, she was returned to the man. Noora's treatment was not considered abuse; he was her husband. Despite beatings, she survived and bore three children by the time that she was 15. As with many girls forced into marriage, her dreams of education and a job seemed unattainable (Ramdani 2013). Although Noora was married in the late 1970s, marriage of girls under 15 in Yemen, Afghanistan, Tanzania, Sudan, Bangladesh, Malawi, Nepal, Mozambique, Cameroon, and other poor regions is still common.

Child brides, bought and sold, are among the most disadvantaged and discriminated against women in the world. Every country has a minimum age at which girls may be married. In most countries, it is 18 years, although younger marriages may be allowed with parental permission. Consent of the parents does not protect girls from child marriage because it is the parents who most often arrange it. The girls may be unaware of the arrangement until their parents tell them. One young girl reported that a man showed up at her house, and her father told her that he was her husband because he had paid the price (Children's Dignity Forum [CDF] 2009).

In the developing world, even though it is near universally officially condemned, one in three girls is married before 18 years of age, one in nine before age 15 (United Nations Population Fund [UNPF] 2012). Marriage marks the end of many of these girls' hopes, their dreams, and sometimes even their lives. Child marriage is a violation of a child's—male or female—human rights. Most of these young girls not only are physically and emotionally too immature for marriage but also know nothing of sex. One young bride reported that she expected her husband to be like an older brother and protect her. Although pressured to have children, these girls might not know anything about raising them. The only positive is that if supported by older women, most enjoy being mothers. Financial security and resources, food, clothing, and medication for their children are their biggest concerns in being a mother (CDF 2009).

Girls' families do not sell the girls only for the money or pay a dowry just to be rid of them. They often do it for

CONSIDER THIS
SUSTAINABLE DEVELOPMENT GOAL 5.3

One of the SDG targets is to end child marriage by 2030. Although outlawed almost everywhere, child brides are still too common:

- 15 million girls are married every year.

- 28 girls are married every minute.

- 1 girl is married every 2 seconds.

The consequences are severe for the girl, any children she may have, and the society as a whole:

- Child marriage impedes girls' education. Most often, the girls drop out of school because attending is either impractical or illegal. Every year of primary school adds 15 percent to a girl's future income.

- Child brides experience physical and sexual violence at high rates.

- Pregnancy and childbirth are among the leading causes of death in girls aged 15 to 19 years in low- and middle-income countries. The rates of stillborn babies and infant mortality increase by 50 percent for young women.

- Child brides are at high risk of contracting AIDS.

- Child brides have little or no power in controlling their sexual relations. They are vulnerable to sexually transmitted diseases, including HIV.

- Child marriage violates a child's human rights to safety, health, education, and choice of marriage partner.

- Child marriage traps girls in poverty.

Source: Girls Not Brides (n.d.).

love—to protect the girls and secure their future. Many deliberately circumcise their girls at a young age so that they may be married younger, immediately after circumcision. Younger brides are more desirable because they are more likely to be virgins. Once a girl has had sexual relations, she is not good "bride material" by the custom in many countries. Another factor influencing child marriage is the importance of maintaining a strong authoritarian family structure. A bride typically moves into the groom's family, where she could potentially disrupt family harmony if the conjugal bond is stronger than the parent–son bond. For this reason, many brides do not meet their grooms until the wedding day, as is the case in 80 to 90 percent of child marriages in North India. Along with the youth of the bride, this practice eases the transition into a family structure where a bride is most likely to fall under the authority of her husband's parents, specifically her mother-in-law (Vanneman, Desai, and Vikram 2012).

Child marriage occurs primarily in poor and rural communities. Poverty and child marriage go hand in hand. One study found that 16 percent of girls in the richest 20 percent of developing societies were married, whereas 54 percent in the poorest 20 percent were married (Wallach 2016). Stress on a poor family may be relieved by not needing to support a daughter, and the daughter may benefit by having someone else to support her. In Madagascar, where climate change has wrought drought and starvation, people are crushing chalky stones and cooking ash to make soup. There, Sojona, one of whose daughters is 10 years old, would marry her off if he could. Then, her husband would have the responsibility of feeding her. He is torn between knowing that marrying her so young is wrong but finds it a better choice than letting her starve. "I don't feel like a man anymore," he says. "I feel guilty because my job was to care for my children and now they have only red cactus fruit" (Kristof 2017). For this reason, some researchers fear that raising the age of marriage for girls will increase the cost of raising daughters and may have the unintended consequence of increasing female infanticide or sex selection (Suarez 2017).

A daughter may be a family's most valuable commodity in a society where a bride price is paid. Younger girls generally fetch a higher price. A family might be motivated by giving the girl a better life with a richer and older man than the family can provide for her. Conflict situations place girls at high risk. Marriage is often protection for a young girl. Rape is a tactic of violent conflict, and a girl is less marriageable should she be victimized. It may be a race to marry off a daughter before she can be violated as an act of war. Furthermore, marriage affords the girl protection by the husband's family. Girls' futures are similarly uncertain in refugee camps.

In conflict situations, in refugee camps, and in economically distressed areas, child marriage increases. In Syrian refugee camps, the rate of child marriage increased significantly—"alarmingly"—above Syria's usual rate. Among the refugee girls, 24 percent of those 15 to 17 years old are married. As one mother reported, her cousin, out of the "goodness of his heart," offered to marry her daughter, who is 15, and support her entire family (UNPF 2017).

Child marriage is not always voluntary on the part of the family of the girl. Weak law enforcement and bad law facilitate the exploitation and abuse of girls. In 2016 in Tunisia, a judge approved the marriage of a 13-year-old girl to a 20-year-old man who had raped her. The Tunisian Ministry of Women's Affairs tried unsuccessfully to annul the marriage. Under Tunisian law, a rapist can be acquitted if he marries the girl. It is up to the Parliament now to change the law that allows abusers and rapists to escape prosecution if they marry their victims (Stowe 2016).

In Nigeria, a similar situation ensued. Years before Boko Haram began its reign of terror on young girls, girls had been subject to kidnapping. There, Habiba, a 14-year-old girl, was abducted on her way home from school. She was forced to marry one of her abductors. The Emir, ruler of the province, approved the marriage after being paid a dowry by her abductor. Her father, desperate to get her back, went first to the police, who condemned the act but did not release Habiba to her father and sent the girl back to the Emir's palace instead. Her father went to the palace, was intimidated by the Emir, and was forced to sign an apology to the Emir. Even with the help of human rights groups, he has been unable to secure Habiba's release. This is not an isolated case. From 2011 to 2016, more than 40 Christian girls were abducted. Their captors claimed that they left voluntarily and have converted to Islam. Applying sharia law that allows for marriage of underage girls, the Emirs claim that the marriages are legitimate even though the girls are minors under the Nigerian constitution. Only a few girls have been released, and only a few of their abductors have been prosecuted. Abduction and subsequent forced marriage is a national crisis (World Watch Monitor 2016).

Although child marriage occurs throughout the world, it is much less common in Western Europe and North America than in Africa and Asia—under 6 percent, in fact. Nevertheless, the impact on girls is the same. Child marriage in the United States is associated with physical and psychological harm. With respect to physical harm, child marriage is associated with sexually transmitted diseases, including HIV, and with cervical cancer, unwanted pregnancy, maternal mortality, and infant malnutrition. Low educational attainment may be among the causal mechanisms for some of these poor health outcomes. Isolated from their family of birth and friends and pulled out of school, child brides are physically and psychologically vulnerable. Girls who marry are more likely to experience abuse than older women, to believe that a spouse is justified in violence against them, and to suffer mental health problems (Le Strat, Dubertret, and Le Foll 2011).

Child marriage is so entrenched in some areas that it may be a struggle to eradicate. In sub-Saharan Africa, about 40 percent of girls under 18 years of age are married. The African Union launched "The AU Campaign to End Child Marriage" in 2014. As of June 2016, 14 African nations had signed on. Urbanization and economic development help because they make more opportunities available for women, increasing girls' worth in the eyes of a very traditional society. Attacking the underlying norms using media to raise awareness and conduct gender equality campaigns can have an impact where economic development and urbanization alone cannot. Social welfare programs for the elderly must also play a role, relieving children of the sole support of their parents.

Advantages and Disadvantages at School

"Are you going to school?" the man on a motorcycle asked Shamsia Husseini one morning in late 2006 when she was in fact on her way to school. He pulled the burka from her face and sprayed her with acid, scarring her face and blurring her vision. Her mother, who cannot read or write, and her father encouraged her not to quit but rather to keep going, no matter what, even if she were killed. She did return to school, as did others in her school who had been attacked with acid. The people who burned them, her parents told her, want them to be "stupid things" (Filkins 2009).

Malala Yousafzai was 17 years old and campaigning for girls' education when she was shot in the head in Pakistan. She survived and won the Nobel Peace Prize in 2014 for conducting a global campaign for girls' education in the face of constant threat. These attacks were in Pakistan and Afghanistan, the focus of publicity on school-girl attacks. But attacks on girls' education occur regularly and are widespread. From 2009 to 2014, there were attacks on schools in 70 countries. Attacks directly on girls and their teachers include acid attacks, rapes, and murder, among other forms of violence (UN Office of the High Commissioner on Human Rights [UNOHCHR] 2015).

Attacks on girls' education stem from different reasons in different circumstances. Education is a transformative force and is resisted by people who resist social change. Groups like ISIS, the Taliban, and Boko Haram view globalization and modernization as threatening.[2] Education, particularly of girls or education based on secular values, is a threat. Armed conflict limits all education but particularly that of girls because many are forced to stay home or turn to child marriage for protection from sexual and other violence that accompanies conflict. In some cases, attacks on girls' education are extensions of the general violence and oppression of girls. Despite the attacks, Shamsia and Malala returned to school. So do most girls when they have the chance.

Education is a right guaranteed in nearly every international human rights treaty and national constitution. Refugees, asylum seekers, and stateless persons all maintain their right to education. Not every girl has a chance at education equal to her ambition or ability. However, when girls get a chance at education, they outperform boys on many measures. This is becoming a global phenomenon. According to the WEF Global Gender Gap, women are close to closing the gap with men in education. In 2017, the overall educational attainment index was 95 percent, leaving a gap of only 5 percent.

Literacy rates provide a brief look back in time. Literacy is a basic need. Literacy contributes to a better job, better health, and more active community engagement and political participation. It improves one's own life and the lives of one's family members. In many countries, particularly where development and literacy are low, women are disadvantaged in comparison with men. Males have higher literacy rates than females in all the developing regions except Latin America and the Caribbean. Adult literacy rates reflect access to and quality of primary education in a country. The more disadvantaged education is in a country, the more disadvantaged women are in comparison with men. In the least developed nations, nearly two thirds of adult women are illiterate. Where there are large literacy gaps among adults, it reflects past generations of disadvantage for girls (Table 7.3).

A CLOSER LOOK
LITERACY PERCENTAGE BY REGION AND GENDER, 2005–2013

TABLE 7.3   Literacy by Region and Gender

In several regions, females are close to parity with males in literacy. Their progress is slowest in sub-Saharan Africa.

Region	Female	Male
Arab states	86.9	93.1
East Asia and Pacific	98.7	98.8
Europe and Central Asia	99.3	99.7
Latin America and Caribbean	98	97.6
South Asia	74.3	86.3
Sub-Saharan Africa	62.7	74.7
Least developed	65.9	75.5

Source: Adapted from World Bank (2012, Statistical Annex Table 10).

Contemporary progress in school enrollment is one of the success stories of the Millennium Development Goals, particularly for girls. Primary school enrollment in developing countries stands at 91 percent, up from 83 in 2000. The number of children out of school has been halved, from 100 million in 2000 to 57 million in 2015. Looking at the totality of countries, gender parity has been achieved. In many parts of the world, the educational attainment of young women has surpassed that of young men. Young women are scoring higher on many measures of achievement, going to college at higher rates, and graduating at higher rates. However, disparities exist across regions. As in the cases of Shamsia and Malala, the world still witnesses the horror of girls maimed or even killed for going to school and having their schools burned down.

In Western Asia, girls lag slightly behind boys in primary and secondary school, but because a greater rate of girls than boys who graduate go on to higher levels, they are at parity in tertiary education. The situation is similar in the Caucasus and Central Asia, but girls are slightly ahead in tertiary schooling. In Southeastern and Eastern Asia, girls are at parity with boys in primary and secondary school but are ahead of them in tertiary education. In contrast, girls are behind boys at all levels in sub-Saharan Africa.

In Latin America and the Caribbean, Europe, and North America, the gender gap has reversed. Young women now achieve higher levels of both secondary and tertiary education than young men, a reversal of just a decade or so ago. Men drop out of secondary education more than women in 26 of 28 countries in the European Union (EU). Women outnumber men in higher education in 19 of 22 countries in Western Europe and North America and in 23 of 25 countries in Central and Eastern Europe (United Nations Educational, Scientific, and Cultural Organization 2015). This imbalance has generated a call for attention to boys and their underachievement. Overall, girls tend to outperform boys in reading, boys outperform girls in mathematics, and the two are about equivalent in sciences. However, among the highest 10 percent of scorers, boys score 11 points higher than girls. Boys outperform girls in thinking like a scientist. In only one country, Qatar, do girls outperform boys in formulating situations mathematically, a skill that requires thinking like a scientist. Girls' lesser self-confidence and less willingness to make mistakes or learn by trial and error seem to lie at the root of these differences. These characteristics are critical to the scientific process. Similarly, girls have less self-confidence and more anxiety in mathematics performance (Organisation for Economic Cooperation and Development [OECD] 2015).

Boys' underperformance in reading appears to stem from the amount of time that they spend reading, what they read, and the pleasure that they get from reading. Reading anything is better than not reading at all, and even reading comic books and magazines improves reading scores. Reading for enjoyment declined among both girls and boys from 2000 to 2009 but declined even more for boys, widening the gender gap. Whereas girls are likely to be frequent readers of fiction and more likely than boys to read magazines, two thirds of boys read newspapers for enjoyment and are more likely than girls to read comic books. If boys enjoyed reading as much as girls do, their scores on international tests would be 23 points higher than they currently are (OECD 2015).

Boys also spend less time doing homework than girls, and spending more time on homework is related to higher achievement. This has interesting impacts relative to the gender gap. Where boys and girls spend equal time on homework, the mathematics gap between girls and boys widens, boys outperform girls in science, and the reading gap narrows (OECD 2015). This is strong evidence that the factors relevant to self-confidence and anxiety are major factors in the lower achievement of girls, and time spent on homework is depressing boys' scores. These gender differentiations carry over into college, where men and women study different fields.

Boys' attitudes toward school and learning are less favorable than those of girls. They are more likely to skip school and arrive late. They are more disruptive in class, more likely to talk out of turn, and less likely to listen to directions and follow instructions. These differences in behavior grow wider as students mature. Boys increasingly disengage and withdraw in class (OECD 2015). This may explain the increasing gap between boys and girls in tertiary education.

The most surprising data come from the Middle East and North Africa (MENA). Most of these are Arab countries along with Israel. Although the women there are among the most oppressed, they are also among the best educated in their countries. Some MENA countries are among the most rapidly advancing in human development, particularly in health and education indicators (World Bank 2013). Girls outperform boys in the oil-rich Arab nations as well as in Jordan and Palestine. Contrary to a near global trend, they outperform boys in science and mathematics in Saudi Arabia. They outperform boys in math in Bahrain, Dubai, Oman, and Qatar. In Jordan, girls outperform boys in nearly every subject and they have done so for decades. Twice as many women as men go on to college, where they outperform men in computer science, mathematics, and engineering, among many other subjects. As in most other parts of the world, more women in Arab nations as a whole go on to tertiary education than men (Ripley 2017). These nations and their girls, however, do poorly in comparison with the wealthy OECD nations. Jordan, for example, scores near the bottom of the 69 countries participating in the Programme for International Student Assessment international tests administered to OECD and select other nations (Education GPS 2015).

Women at Work

Where girls are disadvantaged in education, the disadvantage follows them through to the workplace and political realm. But the reverse, women's equality and advantage in education, does not follow them into the world of work and politics. Equal education does not translate to equal opportunity or equal pay. This is especially true of women in the MENA countries, where despite advances in education they have the lowest female labor force participation in the world, far below that of men in their countries.

The WEF indicators of economic participation and opportunity are labor force participation, wage equality, female legislators, officials, and managers,[3] and professional and technical workers. The overall global wage gap is 77 percent. If there were a direct impact of education on work life, the gap would be only 5 percent.

Despite women's increasing levels of education, the global gender gap in labor force participation decreased only 2 percent. Despite women entering the workforce in larger numbers with increasing levels of education, earning gaps persist (Figure 7.4). There is no single reason for the gaps; instead, many factors coalesce, resulting in lower participation and lower earnings. Different factors weigh differently depending on the circumstance.

What is common across regions and circumstances is that gender inequality in labor force participation and earnings contributes heavily to women's overall disadvantage in realizing their life chances. It is directly related to the feminization of poverty—the significantly higher percentage of women in poverty than men. As with all worker wages, women's wages have not kept up with increases in productivity. Eliminating both the wage gap and the productivity gap would increase women's wages more than 70 percent (Figure 7.4).

Cultural attitudes and stereotypes, although diminished in many countries, still disadvantage women. Where there is near universal acknowledgment that women should be able to work, the valuing of men's work over women's work lingers. In the World Values Survey of 59 countries, 39 percent of people agreed that "When jobs are scarce, men should have more of a right to jobs than women." When asked whether men make better business executives than women, 42.9 percent of respondents agreed or agreed strongly (Inglehart et al. 2014).

In the United States, 30 percent of people think that women are better at being honest and ethical and at providing fair pay and benefits, while less than 5 percent think that men are better at either of these. More than 30 percent think that men are more willing to take risks, but overall people do not see a big difference between men and women. Majorities of both men and women believe that the quality of life for women would improve if there were more women in leadership roles (Pew Research Center 2015). Nevertheless, the economic gender gap in the United States is 24.8 percent.

Years of school is significantly related to income. But women, as well as minorities, do not get the same return on their investment in education (Figure 7.5). Women and minorities with equal educations earn less than men at every educational level. Furthermore, the earnings gap increases with increasing levels of education (UN Women 2015).

Occupational segregation is part of the equation. Women are over-represented in clerical work and support roles and under-represented in managerial and skilled work. Many work below the status that their educational bracket would warrant. Within low-skill occupations, women are concentrated in lower-paying domestic and cleaning work, while men are in manufacturing and mining, higher-paying jobs. Women outnumber men in fields that pay less—such as education, life and social sciences, and the humanities—whereas men are more likely to study computer sciences, engineering, mathematics, higher-paying medical specialties, and the physical and chemical sciences. Many female-dominated fields such as early child education and home health care, in which women care for society's most valuable resource, children, and the most vulnerable, the elderly and ill, do not pay as much as male-dominated fields of lesser social value.

Outdated gender roles and outdated knowledge of occupations contribute to occupational segregation. But sexual harassment in traditionally male fields leads women to avoid or leave their jobs, both skilled and unskilled. An EU survey found that 75 percent of women in managerial positions, and 61 percent in the service sector, experienced sexual harassment. Among the traditionally male trades in the United States, one third of women reported that they always or frequently experienced harassment (UN Women 2015).

A CLOSER LOOK
CLOSING THE GENDER AND PRODUCTIVITY GAPS

FIGURE 7.4   Median Hourly Wages for Men and Women

Eliminating the gender inequality gaps would raise women's wages significantly.

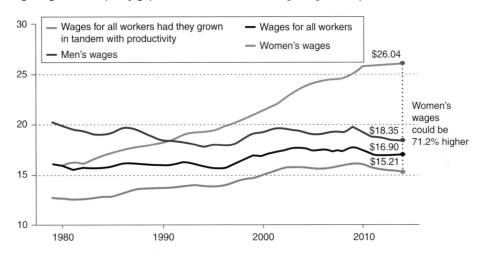

Source: Davis and Gould (2015). Reproduced with permission.

FIGURE 7.5   Median Weekly Earnings by Education, Gender, and Race, United States (2014 annual averages)

Women earn less than men at every educational level. As the educational level rises, the gap increases.

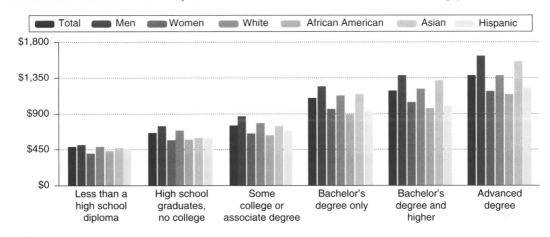

Source: Bureau of Labor Statistics (2015). Reproduced with permission.

Within occupational categories, the earnings gap persists. In the United States, the Bureau of Labor Statistics (BLS) collects data on the proportions of men and women in occupational categories and the average weekly wages in each category by gender. Overall, the median weekly earnings for men is $949 and for women is $770, about 81 percent of men's wages. The size of the gap varies by occupation. For example, for personal financial advisers, women earn 59 percent of men's wages. For engineering technicians, it is 80 percent (BLS 2017, Table 39). In minimum wage and union jobs, men and women have more parity, but in neither case is it equal. Union jobs are controlled by contracts featuring pay grades and years on the job. A study of 26 European countries found a "glass ceiling" in 11 countries. At the high end of occupations, women experienced a large gap with men's pay. Some countries had a "sticky floor," a large gap at the low end. Three countries had both sticky floors and glass ceilings (UN Women 2015).

Cultural stereotypes about men's and women's work and their aptitudes account for part of occupational segregation. Availability of child care, policies relative to family care, flex time, work from home options, and men's contributions to care work influence the occupations that women choose. Needing to juggle child care or care work with a career can turn women away from time-intensive and demanding occupations. Ironically, women's concentration in low paying domestic work allows some women to pursue these careers.

The "mommy penalty" and "daddy bonus" also contribute to the gap. Whereas men get a bonus with marriage and parenthood, women get a penalty. Apparently, the thinking is that with parenthood, men will need more money and women will be taking time off from work. In the United Kingdom and United States, about 40 to 50 percent of the pay gap is thought to be due to parenthood (UN Women 2015). Women's time away from the workplace on maternity leave hinders advancement in their career paths. Policies that enable women to start from where they would have been without maternity leave, even if it requires additional training when returning, are necessary to remedy this. Societies must keep in mind that bearing children, bringing new members into a society, is an important function for social health and is not solely of benefit to women or their families. Women should not be penalized because only they can bear children.

Everyone has a "second shift," work over and above their paying jobs, that is necessary to run a household. Women assume much more responsibility than men for this unpaid work. It inhibits their earnings potential.

In some households, the second shift includes unpaid work producing goods and services for family consumption that would otherwise be bought. Some second-shift activities produce products for sale in the market with no direct pay to the women. The second shift includes cooking, cleaning, collecting firewood or water, caring for the elderly and children, and many more tasks without which economies would suffer. In some regions, the necessary task of collecting water, nearly always assigned to women or girls, can take hours a day.

Across nearly all societies, women's second shift is longer than men's second shift. When paid and unpaid work is totaled, women devote more hours to house and care work than men and fewer hours to paid work. Women, on average, spend 8 hours and 39 minutes a day working. More than half of that time, 4 hours and 47 minutes, is unpaid. In contrast, men spend 7 hours and 47 minutes working, only 1 hour and 30 minutes of which is not paid (WEF 2017). Women spend fewer hours in leisure than men. This affects their health, as well as earnings, and decreases women's productivity regardless of the nature of their employment. Women have fewer hours to work for pay, although they spend more hours in value-generating activity.

In the MENA countries that have made strides in educating women, jobs for women are scarce. Most women who are employed find work in the public sphere, particularly in education and health services. Public sector expansion, however, is unlikely to be able to meet women's demands for more employment opportunity, especially in the poorer countries. The private sector is also limited, and women are more constrained in the private sector. Private employers perceive women as too costly and not as productive as men. In the private sector, women fear for their safety. They often lack the skills demanded for the private sector. All of these factors need to be addressed.

You Can't Empower Us With Chickens: Economic Empowerment for Women

The focus of too many empowerment efforts for women have been on short-term metrics such as how many women increased their household income with chicken farming or how many girls enrolled in school—even if they rarely attended. Establishing equality in economic power requires a much more significant effort, conquering cultural attitudes and structural constraints. You can't empower women with chickens (Zakaria 2017).

Women's empowerment is critical not just for women's life chances but also for the entire society. Women make up a large portion of the agricultural labor force. It is the major source of employment for women in South Asia and sub-Saharan Africa. In the developing world overall, they are about 40 percent of the agricultural workforce. In some countries (such as Bangladesh) and regions (such as Eastern Africa), they comprise more than 50 percent of the agricultural workers (Raney et al. 2011). The gender gap in lack of resources in agriculture not only limits women's life chances but also holds back entire societies. Global agricultural output would increase by 2.5 to 4 percent and reduce hunger and poverty by closing the gender gap.

Women suffer in comparison with men in wage work and opportunities for entrepreneurship as well. When more women work, for themselves or for others, it reaps faster economic growth for the entire society (Klasen and Lamanna 2009). The greater the share of income controlled by women, the more children benefit, improving the future of the society (World Bank 2012). To promote women's economic development, interventions must address needs of women as wage earners, as entrepreneurs, and in agriculture.

Strengthening Wage and Equal Opportunity Laws

Wage and equal opportunity laws are the most frequent remedies to advance the economic power of wage workers. The minimum wage is an important consideration in looking at gender inequalities. First, minimum wage workers are among the poorest. Second, low-wage work is dominated by women; two thirds of minimum wage jobs in the United States are held by women. Third, even among minimum wage jobs, there are inequities. Fourth, many domestic and piecework employees, predominantly women, are not even covered by minimum wage laws. Reforms of minimum wage policies and laws can help to raise incomes among all of the lowest paid workers.

The International Labour Organization (ILO) passed "Minimum Wage Fixing Machinery" Conventions in 1928, 1951 (applying to agriculture), and 1970[4]—including more categories of workers with each convention. These encouraged governments to pass minimum wage laws to protect disadvantaged groups of workers from unduly low wages. The conventions and related documents highlight that the minimum wage should be dynamic and adjusted periodically to the country's economic growth and that minimum wage standards should be sufficient to "satisfy reasonable human needs" and raise the standard of living for all workers. The Equal Remuneration Convention in 1951 specifically addressed the principles of equal pay for men and women and equal wages for work of equal value (ILO 2014).

With respect to national laws, New Zealand passed the world's first national minimum wage law in 1894, ahead of the ILO. Several other countries—Australia, France, Norway, and the United Kingdom—soon followed. The first federal minimum wage law passed in the United States in 1938[5] was intended to stabilize the economy in response to the "Great Depression" of 1929 to 1939. Nearly all countries—90 percent of the ILO's membership—now have minimum wage laws. Measured against the standards delineated by the ILO to protect workers from low pay, combat poverty, satisfy human needs, and equalize or reduce inequality, the laws fail.

Countries define the "wage" included in the minimum using different standards. Workers in some countries, for example, may receive benefits "in kind" such as food, housing, and/or uniforms that may be included in the calculation of their minimum wage, whereas in other countries it is not. Some include overtime, whereas others do not. Workers whose "tips" are included as wages are among those most visibly affected by how wages are defined. These, most often in the United States, are wait staff and are predominantly women. Many, if not all, countries include tips in the wages, and the minimum guaranteed by the employer may be much lower than the minimum wage for other job categories. In Canada, for example, the minimum wage for tipped personnel is 15 percent lower than the general standard. In France, if the tips workers receive do not bring them up to the general minimum wage, the employer must make up the difference. In the United Kingdom, employers must pay tipped employees the national minimum wage regardless of tips (ILO 2014). In the United States, employers of tipped staff may pay significantly less, U.S. $2.13[6] an hour in 2017 in comparison with the national $7.25. Employers must make up the difference. While for workers in expensive and busy industries tips may pay more than the minimum, for most workers it results in the minimum wage. About 15 percent of tipped workers in the United States earn below the federal poverty level.

Some countries establish regular reviews of the minimum wage or call for automatic increases. The ILO Convention of 1970 stipulates that not only worker needs but also family needs be considered in setting the minimum wage. Many countries peg the minimum wage to the mean wage. Azerbaijan keeps the minimum wage at 60 percent of the mean wage. In Bosnia–Herzegovina, it cannot be below 55 percent. In Belarus, it must not fall below one third (ILO 2014).[7] The average hourly earnings of private sector employees in the United States ranged from U.S. $39.57 to $15.50 in November 2017, with an overall average of $26.55. The $7.25 minimum wage is just about 28 percent of the mean.

Not all countries increase their minimum wages with economic growth or inflation. In the United States, there is not an automatic increase or reconsideration of the minimum wage. It rose every three to five years from 1938 to mid-1968, when it peaked at U.S. $1.60 or more than $11.00 in 2017 dollars. In 1968, the minimum wage was about the poverty level for a family of three. It is now well below the poverty level for a family of two.

Pay gaps between men and women persist in minimum wage jobs in systems that allow different minimums by occupation or industrial sector. Globally, where the minimum wage for jobs is assumed to be differentiated on the basis of skills, responsibility, and working conditions, it turns out that gender plays a significant role. In Mauritius, job categories are defined as male or female and the female jobs pay less. Within the tea, salt, and sugar industries, women's jobs pay 20 percent less. In many countries, the jobs are not specifically labeled male or female, but many job categories thought of as "female" are underpaid. They are not evaluated on the basis of objective criteria (ILO 2014). In Australia, the country with the highest overall minimum wage, women paid in the minimum wage sectors earn, on average, 10 percent less per hour than men. Because the wages are set, the difference is not a result of employer discrimination, higher male productivity, or men's better negotiating skills. Health care workers, for example, earn less than road transportation workers. Hospitality workers—overwhelmingly female—work in hot and loud environments with often physically demanding tasks. Equal pay for equivalent value or conditions does not hold (Broadway and Wilkins 2017). In countries where minimum wages are set by representatives of worker organizations and employees, women—including representatives from women's organizations—must receive equal representation (ILO 2014).

Ensuring that all low-wage work is covered by minimum wage laws, that minimum wages are pegged to increases in mean wages and set at a level to meet the needs of a family of three, that the proportion of employee representatives in negotiations is equal to the proportion of women in an industry, and that equal pay for equivalent work is achieved will help to advance the economic empowerment of women, and workers generally.

Equal pay for equal jobs does not mean identical jobs but rather jobs that are equivalent in value, working conditions, skills, and so forth. This is particularly important because occupational segregation, a problem in and of itself, separates men and women into different job categories. Many of the service jobs of great value—from teachers, to child care workers, to nurses, to social service workers—are dominated by women and are paid lower salaries than jobs of comparable skill and less social value. As stated above, ILO conventions specifically require equal pay for work of equal value, as do many national and regional laws.

Many European countries adopted national action plans for reducing the gender pay gap that require businesses (of a certain size that varies by country) to report regular analyses of their pay structures. These countries adopted definitions of indirect discrimination similar to the EU Employment Equality Directive that covers equal pay for work of equal value. Firms that do not comply can be sanctioned (European Commission n.d.). Companies in the United States are subject to prosecution under the Equal Pay Act.

Access to Resources, Finance, and Training

In many countries, women do not have equal access to the resources needed to make money. Relieving time constraints, the ability to get sufficient financial resources, meaningful education and training, and rights of land tenure or ownership all potentially increase women's incomes. So too does overcoming cultural norms requiring that women have male guardians in public, prohibiting socialization between males and females, and limiting women's participation in legal matters. Successful interventions must also attend to the needs of poor versus non-poor women, young versus old women, rural versus urban women, and other differentiating characteristics.

All women need access to capital, but the impact differs depending on the size of the woman's enterprise. Small subsistence enterprises do not benefit to the same degree as larger ones or those run by men. Women-owned small enterprises generally face more constraints that limit their growth. Women, particularly poorer women, are more likely than men to be pressured to divert a money grant or loan to family needs rather than growing their business. This "kin tax" is particularly powerful when cash loans are visible to family and close relatives are present. In these cases, more privacy regarding the transfers, such as that accorded by the use of mobile phones or in-kind transfer of capital through inventory

PHOTO 7.2 In southern Afghanistan where contact between men and women is limited, these Afghan police and U.S. military officers play critical roles in helping ensure women's safety.

U.S. Army photo by Pvt. Andreka Johnson, 1st Stryker Brigade Combat Team, 25th Infantry Division Public Affairs/CC BY 2.0.

purchasing programs, helps women to keep money to grow their businesses in their businesses. Savings accounts also improve women's economic performance. A study in Western Kenya found that access to savings accounts yielded a 45 percent increase in business investments above that of women without accounts. The savings accounts had a similar effect with respect to privacy and a greater psychological effect related to ownership. This had a lasting effect (Buvinić and Furst-Nichols 2016). Delivering financial services through mobile phone technology is an adjustment that is also important to women with little mobility (Buvinić and Furst-Nichols 2016).

The time and money requirements of skills and business training programs frequently limit their success with women. Many have high attrition rates due to the constraints that women, particularly poor women, face in contrast to the fewer constraints faced by men. Such programs need to be designed with women in mind. Scheduling class times and location with attention to women's availability can decrease attrition and increase efficiency and effectiveness (Buvinić and Furst-Nichols 2016). Subsidies while women are in training programs increase the likelihood of them finishing the longer-term programs that are more effective than the shorter programs.

Equitable land rights are critical for strengthening women's role in agriculture. Land is more than just an economic asset to produce income or wealth. It is "security, status, and recognition" (Rao 2011). In many developing countries, land is controlled by men and kinship groups headed by men. It is common for a woman to lose rights to land that she has worked with her husband after his death. In Zambia, for example, one third of women lost their land when their husbands died. One compromise has been separating ownership from right to use. In Ghana, for example, land is titled to a husband, but he cannot sell it without consent of, or providing benefit to, others affected. Community ownership of rights where water, grazing, and sanitation are shared can be established to give everyone equal rights. Women, considered minors in Swaziland, cannot own land. However, some women were able to persuade a female chief to intervene with other chiefs to grant them their land after their husbands had died. Joint ownership and right of inheritance need to be institutionalized (Kimani 2012).

Women face similar constraints in Asia. Their agricultural contribution is equal to or exceeds men's contribution, but most are landless. Land rights systems vary across Asia. In communist states, governments own and households acquire rights. In some' land passes only through males, and in some it passes bilaterally or through females.

While there has been some success in acquiring assets for women on a case-by-case basis, this is inefficient and time costly—time that is lost to other income-producing activity. Implementing existing laws is a first step. Governments must be pressured by domestic and international civil society groups, other governments, and private interests to end discriminatory practices and policies, correct any discriminatory laws, and ensure that women have equal access to all resources—land, credit, tools, memberships in organizations, marketing, and so on—necessary for successful production. The UN must strengthen monitoring commitments that countries have made under international treaties, research and unmask institutional constraints on women securing rights, and maintain a database of land holdings indicating ownership by men, women, and jointly. Where foreign business interests have acquired land (often to secure food for export), as is happening in much of Africa and Asia, the impact on current land owners and tenants, including women, must be considered. Last, as with activities in other economic realms, women need sufficient representation on all decision-making bodies that affect their livelihoods (Rao 2011).

Infrastructure investment designed with women's constraints in mind promotes development in all three areas of concern: farming, wage work, and entrepreneurship. Coupling women's economic empowerment by incorporating gender policies into infrastructure improvements ensures that women are not left behind. Providing access to energy, technology, and transportation opens windows of opportunity for women, particularly those with heavy household responsibilities. In Bangladesh, women provided with business skills and technology made significant contributions to rural electrification. Mobile phones granted women in a number of countries opportunities to produce income and greater independence. Mobile phone technology, in addition to strategies discussed above, can alert women to market conditions and training opportunities and allow them to buy and sell goods. A road connecting women to markets cuts down on travel time in Bangladesh. In combination with reserved spaces in the markets and separate toilet facilities, women became major traders in the local areas (Nandera 2016). These and similar considerations in infrastructure development can empower women as they improve the overall economic situation.

Access to capital investments is another hurdle. Government or intergovernmental programs should require a percentage of grants or loans to be reserved for women's enterprises—whether in agriculture or other businesses. Bank account ownership lags among women, particularly in the poorest countries and in rural areas. Globally (including developing countries), about 58 percent of women had accounts in 2014 in comparison with 65 percent of men. However, in developing economies, the ratio was 50 to 59 percent, a wider gap (Demirguc-Kunt et al. 2014). Because internet use is very limited in some countries, mobile phone technology can provide account access and enable cashless transactions. Account ownership encourages saving by providing a safe place, provides privacy as discussed above, allows for more financial resilience, and facilitates trade—both buying and selling.

Training in every link of value chains from procuring resources, to financing, to production, to transportation and marketing must be made accessible to women—whether in agriculture, manufacturing, or services. Making women key players in every step of a value chain empowers everyone.

Family-friendly work policies are necessary if women are to achieve equality in economics whether they are running a business, working for wage labor, or working in agriculture. Women should not be punished by the "mommy penalty" because only women can bear children. Quality child care at reasonable or no cost provided as an extension of educational systems, significant paid family leave that can be shared by spouses, quality medical care and insurance, and reservation of job seniority without penalty for time off for family leave all are necessary to achieve equality at work. The EU gender equality laws consist of a series of European Commission Articles and Directives. Together, they protect women from direct and indirect forms of discrimination, the crux being that if a practice or policy affects one gender more than the other (such as the fact that women, due to family circumstances, must more often work part-time or anything related to pregnancy), it is illegal (Burri and Prechal 2008).

Many countries still have laws that blatantly discriminate against women in economic (among other) matters. Inheritance and property laws, as well as laws related to employment, constrain women's opportunities, keeping them dependent and reinforcing stereotypes. Equality Now (2015) lists a sampling of laws from both poor and wealthy nations. For example, in Saudi Arabia, where there are both sons and daughters, the sons inherit twice as much as the daughters. In Chile, husbands are granted control over their wives' property as well as their own. In the United Kingdom, there are restrictions on women in the military serving in close combat or on the front lines based on gender, not on qualifications. As argued by Rao (2011), country laws and practices need to be scrutinized and any hint of direct or indirect discrimination needs to be eliminated if women and the society in general are to achieve their potentials in life chances.

Women in Politics

Increasing women's numbers in political office is important for individual women to have opportunities equal to men's and for advancing issues important to women. The arguments for stimulating women's political participation range from basic fairness to the ways in which women's participation advances the common good of a society. Cross-national surveys document that both men and women perceive democratic institutions as more legitimate when women are elected in significant numbers. When women participate in parliaments, those parliaments are thought to function more effectively. Women tend to influence more collaboration. Female representation is associated with increasing women's engagement in political processes such as calling or writing their representatives, engendering greater accountability. They address more women's and family issues such as education, violence, and health (Inter-Parliamentary Union [IPU] 2018). In the U.S. Congress, women are more likely than men to introduce "women's issue" bills. The bills, however, are much less likely to be enacted into law than bills in general (1 vs. 4 percent) or "women's issue" bills sponsored by men (1 vs. 2 percent). That pattern has persisted from 1970 to the present (Volden, Wiseman, and Wittmer 2016). In Latin America, women's representation is growing, but their participation is often marginalized, being assigned to less powerful committees (Schwindt-Bayer 2010). Greater participation of women in legislative bodies means both more votes for legislation and policy that support issues perceived as "women's issues,"[8] and that women could not as easily be forced into marginal roles. More female legislators generally translates into more women's issue policy becoming law or regulation and women having more influence in policy and law generally (Schwindt-Bayer and Mishler 2005).

The good news is that from 1995 to 2005, the number of women in parliaments around the world doubled. The bad news is that parliaments globally were only 23 percent female by June 2015. There is significant variation by country. Rwanda's lower house of parliament was 63.8 percent female in 2015—the highest ever in the world. Bolivia was the only other country in which more than 50 percent female representation was achieved. There is significant regional variation globally, but there was not one region overall in which female representatives reached 50 percent (Table 7.4).

Both the progress in women's empowerment and the impediments are the result of country-specific factors and globalization. On the one hand, globalization has rendered gender equity more prominent as an indicator of a country's progress. Political participation is one important measure. Regional and international declarations reinforce the importance of female participation. The CEDAW stipulates that countries must take measures to end discrimination against women in political and public life. Many national constitutions prohibit discrimination in politics. As patriarchal values diminish, fewer cultural expectations impede women. However, cultural norms in many countries still favor male dominance in politics (among other aspects of life). Country reports to the UN vary, but in Burkina Faso, Bolivia, Italy, Indonesia, the Philippines, and Zimbabwe cultural attitudes and stereotypical views of women and gender roles remain obstacles. Furthermore, the 2010–2014 round of the World Values Survey of 60 countries indicates that 49 percent of the total sample agreed or strongly agreed that "On the whole, men make better political leaders than women."

Factors other than cultural ones, from financial to personal, are also stumbling blocks. Where women cannot obtain financial independence, it is unlikely that they can afford the time or expense of political campaigns or gain political party support (UN 2013). The male power structures in place favor male candidates. Party leaders tend to support men. The channels needed to move up the political ladder from local offices into higher office are male dominated. Structural changes are needed to engender more political party support for women and minority candidates. Until women participate equally in the parties, their candidacy is limited.

The Pew Research Center found that opinion in the United States as to why there were not more women in top political jobs include both cultural and structural issues. Respondents identified higher standards for women (38 percent), the populace not being ready to elect women leaders (37 percent), women not having sufficient connections and party support (27 percent), family responsibilities not leaving enough time (17 percent), and women not being tough enough (8 percent) as important factors

A CLOSER LOOK
WOMEN IN GOVERNMENT

TABLE 7.4   Women in Parliament or Congress (as of December 1, 2017)

Women still lag behind men in political representation in all regions.

	Single House or Lower House	Upper House or Senate	Both Houses Combined
Nordic countries	41.4%	–	–
Americas	28.6%	28.1%	28.5%
Europe–OSCE member countries, including Nordic countries	27.3%	26.2%	27.1%
Europe–OSCE member countries, excluding Nordic countries	25.9%	26.2%	26.0%
Sub-Saharan Africa	23.7%	23.2%	23.6%
Asia	19.7%	16.0%	19.4%
Arab states	18.3%	12.6%	17.5%
Pacific	15.5%	37.1%	17.9%

Source: Inter-Parliamentary Union (2018). Reproduced with permission.

Note: OSCE, Organization for Security and Cooperation in Europe.

impeding women's progress. When the same respondents were asked about qualities of men and women that make them suitable for political jobs, they indicated that there was little difference between genders. About one third indicated that women are better at compromising and being ethical. The majority reported no difference between men and women in being more willing to work to improve the U.S. quality of life in general and standing up for their beliefs. The majority, 70 percent, also believe that more women in leadership roles would make life better for all women (Pew Research Center 2015).

Structural changes in electoral systems can overcome cultural impediments. Responses to the statement "Women should have the same chance of being elected to political office as men" in Afrobarometer Round 5 (2011–2013) and Round 6 (2014–2015) showed no correlation to actual representation. Countries with weak support for the statement did not have any worse representation than countries with strong support. Countries in which significantly more women than men agreed with the statement were no different in female representation than countries in which there was a smaller gender gap or different than Malawi, where more men agreed than women. Religiosity did not appear to be an impediment either. Predominantly Muslim countries in Africa and Asia have only slightly lower rates of representation. As discussed in the next section, quotas can overcome the influence of culture and religion to achieve better representation of women in politics (Tripp 2016).

Less discussed is the possibility that women may be more "election averse" than men. In an experimental comparison of men's and women's likelihood to volunteer, as opposed to enter, an election, men and women make comparable choices when deciding whether or not to volunteer for a task, but women are less likely to choose to enter a competitive election for the opportunity to perform similar tasks (Kanthak and Woon 2015). This hesitancy can be overcome as well.

Overcoming Obstacles to Political Participation

The 2017 UN Women Commission on the Status of Women Report reiterates Abigail Adams's wish of 1776. Representation in politics is one of the most important strategies to improve the situation of women, whether in developed or developing societies. Ensuring that women have full voting rights is only the first step. Getting women elected to office and ensuring that their voice is equal to men's voice are the critical next steps.

Training women to run for elective office is essential to promoting their participation. Mentoring programs run by political parties, academic institutions, and civil society organizations increase the pool of women willing to run for political offices. Workshops should cover the range of topics important for running for political office such as public speaking, fundraising, using technology, gaining endorsements, exercising leadership, networking, and managing diversity issues. Some programs reach into colleges and schools to engage girls and young women in running for offices in their schools and universities. Programs focus on running for everything from local school boards and town councils to state and national representatives. These programs build a pool of talented women who will be ready to run for political office when the time comes.

In countries where political parties receive public funding, rewarding the parties with enhanced funding for increasing their share of women elected to office is an effective strategy. Georgia, Bosnia–Herzegovina, Mali, Niger, Colombia, and Bolivia have tested this strategy. Some countries require that political parties use a portion of their funds for programs to develop women's political capacity.

The 1995 Beijing Conference on Women adopted a target of 30 percent as the minimum standard for women's representation—considered a significant enough proportion to give women a voice. One of the more successful strategies for getting more women into office relatively quickly is quotas. Most quota systems do not guarantee women winning, but if structured properly they generally do boost the chances. Algeria increased its proportion of women in the lower house of parliament from 8.0 to 31.6 percent after introducing a new quota law in 2012. The law required that 20 to 50 percent of candidates put forward by parties be women. Parties were rewarded with state funding based on how many female candidates they elected. Tunisia had similar success, increasing its share of women in parliament to 31.3 percent by requiring that parties put forward equal numbers of men and women. Men's and women's names must be alternated down the party list. The 50 percent goal was not achieved; nevertheless, progress was significant (IPU 2018).

Legal candidate quotas such as those used in Algeria and Tunisia require political parties to put forward a certain or equal number of female candidates. Sometimes, as in the case of Tunisia, there are requirements for positioning candidates on the ballot. Voluntary candidate quotas by parties is another (less effective) quota strategy. Reserved seats for women is a third strategy. It guarantees women a specific portion of seats. This is particularly effective if, after winning a reserved seat and developing a record and name recognition, women move from the reserved seat competition and run for non-reserved seats, leaving the reserved seats to bring more women into office.

Many African countries established 50–50 campaigns in the early 2000s. Of the 20 countries with the highest proportion of women in parliament, 15 had some form of quota system (IPU 2018). Even among Arab nations, long considered among the most repressive for women, quota systems achieved representation for women surpassing many of the wealthy developed democracies. Quotas can overcome many of the obstacles faced by women, from lack of party support to lack of confidence and risk aversion.

When quotas are established, the proportions of women running for office usually increase significantly. In a study of quotas in Jordan's municipal elections, the number of women running increased from 40 before the quotas to 355 after quotas were established. Women reported that it was the quotas that encouraged them to run (Nanes 2015). As of 2014, more than 100 countries had quota systems in place to ensure women's representation in political institutions. Many studies have confirmed that international pressures on poor countries to qualify for aid and conform to international norms of being a modern society are effective in encouraging these countries to adopt some form of a quota system. In turn, quota systems encourage women who would not have otherwise considered running for public office (Nanes 2015).

While quotas and electoral systems can increase women's chances of being elected, there need to be more extensive efforts to reach all groups of women. Gender quotas have so far benefited a greater portion of majority women than minority women. Too often, when minority representation increases, it is dominant group women and ethnic men who acquire seats. Strategies to ensure that minority ethnic women are included and represented are critical. True political voice for minorities and women means that they have direct representation and are not marginalized by majority women or minority men. It is too easy to fall between the fault lines of identity politics. Young women are also underrepresented in comparison with both older women and young men.

The structure of the electoral system can promote women's representation. In 2013, 32[9] of the 35 countries that had 30 percent or more women in their legislatures had either proportional representation or mixed electoral systems (UN 2013). The basic feature of a proportional system is that each district elects a number of seats that are divided among competing parties or groups according to the proportion of votes that the party gets. There is not a single winner for a district. If, for example, there are 10 seats in a district and a party gets 30 percent of the votes, 3 seats go to that party. The three chosen candidates would be the top vote getters of that party. In a mixed system, some seats within the district are won by proportion and others are won by majoritarian vote. Both of these methods are more likely than "winner takes all" to increase women winning seats. In addition, half of the countries also had quota systems in place requiring parties to put forward a certain percentage of female candidates.

How ballots are constructed also affects whether women win elections. Many parties require alternating male and female names. However, if a man is at the top of the list and the party wins only one seat, it goes to a male. In some cases, parties must alternate not only within a ballot but also the gender at the top of each ballot.

Women's movements are successful in increasing women's participation. In Africa, women's representation in legislatures tripled from 1990 to 2015. Proportionately, there are more women in cabinet positions than in any other part of the world, 22 percent in comparison with 18 percent. The most significant factors in this achievement were women's movements and coalitions. In Senegal, Algeria, and Mauritania—countries where conventional wisdom suggests that women's representation would lag—women hold 43, 32, and 25 percent of legislative seats, respectively (Tripp 2016).

Violence Against Women

In much of the world, gender-based violence remains behind closed doors, unseen, the victims silent. The cases we do hear about are the most egregious. Some societies have only recently acknowledged domestic violence as criminal. Recognizing that what goes on behind closed doors within a family is of public concern and not just a family matter, China passed its first national law against domestic violence in 2016. Other countries have not yet recognized it. In Pakistan, 1,100 girls and women and 88 men were killed in 2015 for violating their family's honor. There are many ways in which a woman or girl can dishonor her family—from refusing a marriage partner, to marrying someone of whom the family has not approved, to committing adultery, to becoming too "Westernized," to being the victim of a rape. These are human rights issues, and these acts should not bear any punishment, least of all capital punishment. Typically, there is no or little punishment for honor killings. In October 2016, Pakistan passed new laws that mandate life imprisonment for honor killings and rescinded laws that allowed murderers to go free if the family of the victim forgave them. Whether these laws will end honor killings in Pakistan is doubtful. Many occur beyond the reach of the central government. Honor killings continue in Afghanistan, India, South Asia, North Africa, and the Middle East as well as in Western nations where migrants have brought the practice with them.

UN Women (2016) reported that 35 percent of women globally have experienced physical or sexual violence, or both, and that in some countries the rate is as high as 70 percent. Violence is widespread in private and public venues and includes physical, sexual, psychological, and emotional components. It includes the practices of forced marriage, child marriage, sex trafficking, honor crimes, forced pregnancy, intimate partner and stranger violence, and violence in conflict situations.

Although complete information is difficult to collect, the UN Women's Global Campaign to Stop Violence against Women reveals these facts on the extent of violence:

- In the 28 EU states, 43 percent of women have experienced some form of psychological intimate partner violence.

- Half of all female homicide victims globally and 6 percent of male homicide victims were killed by intimate partners or family members in 2012.

- A 2012 study in New Delhi, India, found that 92 percent of women reported having experienced some form of sexual violence in public spaces in their lifetime and 88 percent of women reported having experienced some form of verbal sexual harassment in their lifetime.

- Slightly more than 10 percent of women have experienced forced intercourse or another forced sexual act. The most common offenders are current or former intimate partners.

- Human trafficking is primarily a crime against females. Women and girls account for 70 percent of trafficking victims. Girls are two thirds of the children trafficked.

- About 10 percent of women in the EU report have been harassed online after 15 years of age, including receiving unwanted and offensive sexually explicit emails, SMS (text) messages, and advances on social networking sites.

- School-related violence victimizes 246 million girls and boys every year. Girls are at greater risk than boys of sexual violence, including harassment and exploitation. School-related gender-based violence is a major obstacle to universal schooling and the right to education for girls.

- Girls and women in indigenous communities suffer some of the worst atrocities.

#MeToo

Long before Twitter, Tarana Burke sat and listened to a 13-year-old describe the sexual abuse she endured. Ten years later, in 2006, Burke started the nonprofit Just Be Inc. to help victims of sexual assault and harassment. She also gave her movement a name, the words she could not speak 10 years earlier to the young victim she consoled, "Me, too." A black activist in Harlem, New York City, Burke wanted to spread awareness about the severity of sexual violence against minority women.

Ten years later, a front-page news article in the United States detailed allegations of sexual harassment and sexual abuse perpetrated by Harvey Weinstein, a famed Hollywood producer (Kantor and Twohey 2017). More stories of alleged abuse, rapes, and payoffs by Weinstein appeared as more women came forward. A week after the article appeared, actress Alyssa Milano "tweeted," "If you have been sexually harassed or assaulted write 'me too' as a reply to this tweet." Overnight, tens of thousands of women, and some men, responded, and the hashtag "#MeToo" spread internationally. In less than a month, it was retweeted in various languages and forms 2.3 million times from 85 different countries—#YoTambien (Spain), #BalanceTonPorc (France, "snitch out your pig"), #QuellaVoltaChe (Italy, "that time when"), and various Arabic translations. Across the world, dozens of powerful men—politicians, movie and television stars, broadcast and print newsmen—were forced to resign their positions, were dropped from television and film programs and projects, and lost endorsements (Powell 2017).

PHOTO 7.3 #Metoo spread globally. This march was on March 8, 2018, in Paris.

#Metoo photo by Jeanne Menjoulet under Attribution 2.0 Generic (CC BY 2.0).

Well-publicized trials, charges, and allegations against famous and powerful people, resulting in resignations and dismissals, had been increasing for a few years before #MeToo. The pictures of 35 women who accused beloved comedian and television star Bill Cosby of sexual assault and rape appeared on the cover of *New York* magazine in 2015. Roger Ailes, creator and head of Fox News, lost his position in 2016 as a flood of allegations of sexual assault and harassment came out. Fox News star Bill O'Reilly lost his job as word of multi-million-dollar settlements for sexual harassment and assault cases came out in early 2017. But, building on the gathering momentum, #MeToo became a turning point. Victims of sexual assault and harassment, both male and female, determined that it was time for a reckoning with the commonality of widespread sexual harassment and assault. Although it was long talked about, not much had been accomplished in bringing the scope of the violence to light or holding perpetrators accountable. #MeToo drew attention not only to assaults but also to the everyday indignities that women suffer from sexual innuendos and offers to unwanted touching that never make the official statistics or headlines but normalize the objectification and degradation of women.

Campaigning civil society groups captured the public attention and attention of power brokers and managed to increase political participation by women. Maybe the renewed attention on sexual violence and harassment will have an equal effect. Hopefully, by keeping harassment in the headlines and intensifying the call to men to speak out and to refuse to participate where women are treated unfairly or degraded, #MeToo will have lasting effects even after the hashtag fades.

Changing Laws and Changing Culture

The same cultural—or global—values and norms that give rise to female foeticide and infanticide, and to underrepresentation in work and politics, give rise to harassment and violence; women are to be subordinate to men, women and girls are objects, women and girls are of little value, in some way women are responsible for their abuse, power and money bestow privilege, and boys will be boys and men will be men—so expect no less. That it took a white woman or women for the abuses to capture worldwide headlines speaks to the vicious reality of racism. While each of these attitudes may vary by degree or pervasiveness country by country, they are present in every country and minorities in every country bear the highest costs.

Changing cultures and the behaviors that follow from them is difficult but possible. Cultures evolve as social conditions change, and their evolution can be hastened. While laws prohibiting sexual violence and harassment are well established in international and domestic laws, justice suffers from weak laws and weak enforcement of good laws (Equality Now 2016).

Equality Now's (2016) survey of laws in 82 countries (as they stood from 2014 to late 2015) reveals startling weaknesses. Weak laws not only violate justice in particular cases but also reduce the perception of the severity of violence against women generally. Among them:

- In at least 10 of the countries studied, it was still legal for a man to rape his wife.

- In 9 countries a man could escape punishment by marrying his victim, and in 12 countries he could escape punishment by making a financial settlement with the victim or her family.

- In some countries, paid sex with a minor is significantly lower than other forms of rape of a minor.

- A total of 68 countries do not have laws against sexual harassment.

Pressure from other countries can be effective in promoting positive change. If civil society groups within countries with strong laws pressure their governments to use carrots and sticks to pursue abuses of women in other countries as human rights violations, laws might be strengthened and enforced.

Among the 122 countries that do have laws, many violations are never reported. A U.S. Equal Employment Opportunity Commission (EEOC) study (Feldblum and Lipnic 2016) reported that gender harassment is the most common form of harassment, affecting about 25 to 75 percent[10] of women. In the United States, 90 percent of people who say they were harassed at work (including any form) never report it. One factor is that although they might experience the behavior as hostile, they do not define it as harassment. Another is fear of losing their job or retaliation from others who might see them as troublemakers. The most common responses to harassment generally are to avoid the harasser, downplay its severity, ignore it, or just endure it. Least common (6–13 percent) is filing a formal complaint (Feldblum and Lipnic 2016).

Enforcing liability laws against companies in harassment cases might alert corporations to take harassment seriously, not cover it up, and ensure that perpetrators are prosecuted and victims are compensated without any form of retribution. Harassment claims are costly to corporations. Cases in the private sector in the United States in 2015 resulted in U.S. $125 million for employees when cases were filed and resolved pre-litigation with the EEOC, and an additional $39 million was secured for employees through litigation. Corporations lost about $356 million in court and settlement charges of harassment litigation in 2012. The costs extend beyond these direct monetary costs to lost productivity of the victims, including psychological distress, anxiety, post-traumatic stress, and depression. Physical ailments include headache, gastric and sleep disorders, and exhaustion (Feldblum and Lipnic 2016). The public image of the company also suffers, particularly in class action suits—which have more than one victim—and in cases with well-known perpetrators.

As with the #MeToo movement, public shaming and prosecution or firing of individual perpetrators, particularly those in positions of power, may put other perpetrators and potential perpetrators, as well as their workplaces, on notice.

Variations of Sexualities and Defining "Normal"

Narrow definitions of sexual orientation and gender normalcy leave many people outside of the boundaries. In some countries, just being who you are, if it is not perceived to be within the boundaries, can be a crime; in other countries, falling outside of the boundaries of sexual normalcy might be called a sin or an illness.

The UN and international law make it clear that countries have an obligation to protect all persons from violence, torture, and cruel, inhumane, or degrading treatment, specifically mentioning LGBT (lesbian, gay, bisexual, and transgender/transsexual) and intersex persons in many of its documents. This entails the obligation to protect rights such as free speech and assembly and to protect from discrimination and social hostility, including hate crimes, and prosecute such illegal behaviors. It also includes protection from practices such as "so called 'conversion' therapy, forced genital and anal examinations, forced and otherwise involuntary sterilization and medically unnecessary surgery and treatment performed on intersex children" (UNOHCHR 2015).

Homosexuality is criminalized in 73 countries concentrated in Africa, the Middle East, and South Asia. The penalties are severe, ranging from fines and a month's imprisonment to death, a possibility in 13 countries. In 5 of these countries, just being homosexual can result in a death sentence. As with other forms of discrimination, government restriction and social hostilities exacerbate one another. Government restrictions give people permission to discriminate and persecute. Social hostility reinforces government's reckoning that discriminatory laws are acceptable.

In Africa, 34 of 54 countries criminalize same-sex relations among men, and 24 countries criminalize them among women. Two important court cases from those countries resulted in steps forward. In 2014–2015 in Kenya and Botswana, courts upheld the principle that although homosexual acts were illegal, being a homosexual was not. As such, homosexuals were not to be denied their rights as persons under the law. They were to be afforded rights to equality and dignity. Both of these cases arose in the context of the right to form organizations and the "freedom of association." In Zambia in 2015, the High Court upheld a lower court ruling that advocating for the rights of people (in this case homosexuals and sex workers) was different from soliciting for sex—upholding the defendant's freedom of speech. These rulings open the door for combatting other forms of discrimination in, for example, employment, housing, and education (Meerkotter and Reid 2015). Whether the new interpretations will effect change remains to be seen.

Freedom of association is under attack in other parts of Africa. For example, in Nigeria the "registration of gay clubs, societies, and organizations, their sustenance, processions, and meetings is prohibited" and carries a punishment of up to 10 years in prison, according to a 2014 law. A challenge to the case in 2016 was struck down by a federal court (Carroll 2016). Social attitudes in Nigeria may be slowly changing. Polling in Nigeria shows that from 2015 to 2017, 9 percent more people supported equal rights for LGBT people, up from 30 to 39 percent. A reverse trend was noted regarding criminalization of same-sex behavior, up from 86 to 90 percent of people favoring criminalization (Nwaubani 2017).

Only 65 countries have laws barring discrimination based on sexual orientation in at least part of their territories (United Nations Development Programme [UNDP] 2016). But even in those societies, the laws do not halt the attacks on people with alternative gender identities and sexual orientations. In the United States in 2015, the EEOC ruled that discrimination on the basis of sexual orientation was indistinguishable from discrimination on the basis of sex and, thus, is prohibited under the law by Title VII of the Civil Rights Act of 1964. This gave people

A CLOSER LOOK
HATE CRIMES

TABLE 7.5   Hate Crimes in the United States: Single Bias Offenses With a Gender Bias

Anti-gay male hate crimes dominate hate crimes committed with a gender bias.

	2012		2013		2014		2015		2016	
Total hate crimes	%	6,705	%	5,922	%	6,385	%	6,837	%	7,227
Total related to gender bias[a]	19.6	1,318	24.7	1,465	20.8	1,327	20	1,366	19.2	1,384
Total sexual orientation[b]	NA	1,318	95.7	1,402	88.8	1,178	89.2	1,219	88	1,218
Anti-gay (male)[c]	54.6	720	60.6	849	58.0	683	62.2	758	62.8	765
Anti-lesbian[c]	12.3	162	13.2	185	14.3	168	13.8	168	11.6	141
Anti-LGBT[c]	28	369	22.6	317	23.6	278	19.3	235	21.5	262
Anti-heterosexual[c]	2.0	25	1.7	24	1.5	18	1.9	23	1.9	23
Anti-bisexual[c]	3.1	41	1.9	27	2.6	31	2.9	35	2.2	27
Total gender bias[b]		N/A	2.	30	3	40	2.1	29	2.6	36
Anti-male[c]			16.7	5	30	12	27.6	8	28	10
Anti-female[c]			83.3	25	70	28	72.4	21	72	26
Total gender ID[b]		N/A	2.3	33	8.2	109	8.6	118	9.4	130
Anti-transgender[c]			75.8	25	63.3	69	63.6	75	85.4	111
Anti-gender nonconfoming[c]			24.2	8	36.7	40	36.4	43	14.6	19

a. Percentages of total hate crime.

b. Percentages of total related to gender bias.

c. Percentages of "b" category directly above.

Source: Adapted from Federal Bureau of Investigation Hate Crime Statistics for 2012 to 2016 (FBI 2013, 2014, 2015, 2016, 2017).

Note: In 2012, gender bias and gender identity were not disaggregated. Some may be included in the total sexual orientation hate crimes.

protection in states that did not have workplace protection based on sexual orientation, and the reasoning could be applied in other areas such as Title VIII and housing. However, in 2017 the US Justice Department filed a brief in a court case regarding a skydiving instructor who was fired because he was a homosexual. The brief argued that the law applies only to treating men and women differently. Because the EEOC enforces discrimination laws, the Justice Department argued that it is up to the legislature and courts to determine what they mean if the EEOC decisions are challenged. This leaves protections based on sexual orientation undecided in the United States (Zillman 2017).

Hate crimes related to sexual orientation and gender identity account for about one fifth of recorded hate crimes in the United States. Because LGBTI (LGBT and intersex) people comprise only about 2.1 percent[11] of the U.S. population, crimes against them occur at a rate of more than eight times the rate expected based on their share of the population and their share of hate crimes. Furthermore, they are much more likely to suffer a violent crime than other targeted groups (Table 7.5) (Potok 2011).

In just the first eight months of 2017, there were 36 hate homicides of LGBTI and HIV-positive people, one a week. Of these, 75 percent were people of color. More than half were black (Waters and Yacka-Bible 2017).

Discrimination on the basis of sexual orientation and identity occurs on a daily basis throughout Europe as well despite its illegality. A survey of more than 93,000 people conducted in 2012 by the European Union Agency for Fundamental Rights (FRA) found that a third of respondents felt discriminated against in the past 12 months in at least one of the areas of housing, health care, education, social services, and access to goods and services, and one in five believed that they were discriminated against in a job or in looking for a job. Transgender people reported more bias than LGB people, especially in employment and health care. Younger people (18–24 years) reported less tolerance than older groups and were the most likely to report violence and discrimination harassment (FRA 2014).

A quarter of respondents were physically (nearly all were physical threats or attacks) or sexually attacked or threatened in the five years preceding the survey, 10 percent in the past year. Nearly 60 percent believed that the attack was wholly or partially because of their sexual orientation or sexuality. Transgender respondents were most likely to report violence or violent threats in the past

five years (34 percent) and in the past year (15 percent). Transgender individuals also had the highest incidents of violence per 1,000 respondents, 512, with the next highest being 273 among bisexual men (FRA 2014).

About a third of respondents were harassed in the year prior to the survey, and three quarters of those believed that it was because they were LGBT, that is, 19 percent of all respondents. Lesbian women (23 percent) and transgendered men (22 percent) were most likely to have experienced harassment. Overall, the average for the EU was 1,012 harassment incidents per 1,000 respondents, ranging from 1,794 in Bulgaria to 683 in Spain. Ridicule and name calling were the most frequently reported forms of harassment (FRA 2014). Most of these cases were never reported to the police or any other organization. If reported (only 9 percent of the most serious incidents), more than half, 5 percent, were reported to an LGBT organization. The social atmosphere is such that 80 percent reported that offensive language and jokes are common. Respondents in Belgium, the Czech Republic, Denmark, Finland, Luxembourg, the Netherlands, Spain, and Sweden reported a more favorable social atmosphere than respondents in other EU countries (FRA 2014).

Social hostilities are being aggravated and encouraged by media campaigns in many countries. In Algeria, television programs are calling homosexuality a social problem that must be "cured" from society. They conflate homosexuality with pedophilia, rape, and killing children. Some celebrities have appeared on these programs to promote state-run centers to cure homosexuality through psychology or torture (Carroll 2016). An LGBTI activist in Algeria maintained that the government is behind the television campaigns that appear on government-affiliated stations. Many governments do not want to officially crack down because if they do they may be condemned by international organizations. Instead, they turn the population against homosexuals. A religious leader reported on television that the war against homosexuals should be a priority over the war against ISIS. Activist groups have suspended activities because of the media attacks. Where homosexuality is illegal, homosexuals cannot report attacks against them to the police because they themselves would be arrested (Arab Foundation for Freedom and Equality 2015). Tactics of dehumanizing and demonizing a minority group are the same as those used in genocides. In this case of the television programs, homosexuals are being called "devil worshipers" in addition to being accused of rape and pedophilia. The programs accuse the West of planting the homosexuality.

verbal attacks against homosexuals by
...ficials erupted in 2015. Indonesia had no
...ptions against homosexuality, and in this case
...t hostility followed social hostilities. Attacks
...I events by fundamentalist Muslim groups had
...poradic for about a decade. In 2015, fundamental-
...uslim religious leaders issued a fatwa condemning
...mosexuality as a vile act and calling for the death pen-
...lty. In 2016, government cabinet ministers spoke out
against LGBTI rights. The education minister called for
banning the LGBTI community from universities so as
not to undermine morals and values. The defense minister claimed that LGBTI people were more of a threat than
nuclear weapons. The mayor of Bandung called for banning any discussion of LGBTI matters on social media.

Anti-LGBTI politicians and religious leaders in the
United States are much more hostile than the general
public. Although they try to associate homosexuality with
pedophilia, they generally take a non-criminalization
approach. Recognizing in the late 1990s that hateful rhetoric would not get them very far with the vast majority of
the U.S. public, leaders within the far and religious right
recommended this softer but no less hostile approach.
Presenting LGBTI persons as ill and capable of being
cured became the focus of extensive ad campaigns in the
early 2000s.

Being Transgender or Intersex

It is widely recognized that people cannot be divided
neatly into existing social categories of race, ethnicity,
sex, and gender. Categorization may ultimately prove to
be futile. People have only recently begun to pay attention
to the discrimination faced by people who do not fit neatly
into the sex and related gender binaries of male or female,
man or woman, girl or boy. The binary is as much a social
construction as the fault lines created by conceptions of
race. While transgender and trans are the most common
umbrella labels with which people identify, a rich array
of identity terms captures the diversity of identity. "Two-
spirit," "gender fluid," "gender non-conforming," "non-
binary," and a number of others may be used in addition
to, or in place of, transgender or trans (James et al. 2016).
Transgender persons are those whose physical appearance does not match the identity that they feel they are or
that their chromosomes label them. They may or may not
have undergone surgery or treatment to align their identity and physicality. There are many aspects of human
biology linked to sex—reproductive organs, secondary
sex characteristics, chromosomes, elements of brain

structure, and hormones. They align in many combinations. To be intersex is to have some physical variation
from what was traditionally considered male or female.
Many persons who are intersex have been subjected to
unnecessary surgeries before the age of consent. Many
physicians now consider this a violation of a person's
human rights.

The U.S. Transgender Survey (James et al. 2016)
documents many forms of discrimination against people
of non-conforming identity. They result in meager life
chances, poor statistics in mental and physical health,
and limited opportunities to enjoy the benefits of a developed society such as home ownership.

Twice as many transgender people lived at the poverty level (29 percent) than the U.S. population in general. Unemployment was also high, at 15 percent, three
times the national average (James et al. 2016). This is
despite higher than average educational attainment.
Fully 65 percent of transgender persons had some college
or an associate's degree, and 17 percent had a bachelor's
degree or higher. This is in contrast to 46 percent and 10
percent of the general population, respectively (James
et al. 2016).

Many transgender persons experienced at least one
form of rejection (44 percent), although most overall had
supportive families (60 percent). Having a supportive
family was the most important determinant of quality of
life for transgender persons. They are more likely to be
employed and are less likely to have done sex work, been
homeless, suffered from psychological distress, or committed suicide (James et al. 2016).

The various forms of identification that people carry
play important roles in their lives. Typically, they have
a gender marker as well as the person's name, which is
usually also indicative of a gender. Establishing conformity among these documents and a person's true identity raises complex and expensive legal issues. Changing
a name and changing an identity marker are separate
processes, but currently both are important to full access
to the rights and privileges of society. Only about a third
of respondents tried to change their names. Transgender
men and women were most likely, more than half, to try.
Most (88 percent) who applied for name changes were
granted them, and most reported that they were treated
with respect in the process. Some who wanted a name
change ultimately quit the process due to time or money
(James et al. 2016).

Changing gender on identification documents was
more difficult. Most had never tried to change any of their
IDs. Denials on birth certificates were the most common

denial at a rate of 15 percent, while changing a driver's license was denied only 2 percent of the time. Those who identified as non-binary typically did not try to change because neither male nor female fit their identity. Many others never tried to change their gender because they believed that they could not unless they had undergone medical treatment to change genders or could not afford it.

Identification documents are problematic because they need to be presented to obtain goods or services and to receive privileges such as voting and driving.

When presenting identification that is incongruous [with] physical appearance, people have been harassed, de[nied] services, assaulted and faced other negative treatme[nt]. This was particularly the experience of those of M[id]dle Eastern, American Indian, or multi-racial heritag[e] (James et al. 2016).

The world is just beginning to recognize transgender and intersex individuals; nevertheless, their problems bear the mark of familiarity—discrimination, violence, and persecution.

SUMMARY

The roots of gender-related discrimination lie in the vestiges of patriarchy that vested power, and thus value, in males over females. From conception throughout the lifespan, women's and girl's life chances are constrained by cultural values and social norms. Even though many countries still have laws that discriminate, unequal life chances may arise from just "doing business as usual." Discrimination and persecution of homosexual, transgender, and intersex persons are rooted in the same patriarchal values. Challenges to the male role challenge male empowerment and are met with resistance. Globally, women and girls, as well as LBGTI individuals, share similar problems of violence and discrimination just for being who they are. Equal rights for all is not a suggestion but rather a mandate under international and domestic laws. Making them a reality is one of the critical challenges of the 21st century.

DISCUSSION

1. Investigate countries that score well on the Global Gender Gap. Some among the top 10 might be surprising. What features of the developing countries such as Rwanda, Slovenia, the Philippines, and Nicaragua account for their performance in the top 10? Contrast their reports with those of some wealthier countries, such as the United States (No. 49) and the Netherlands (No. 32) that do not score as well.

    http://www3.weforum.org/docs/WEF_GGGR_2017.pdf

2. Are labels such as "male" and "female" necessary, or should they be abandoned or revised? Compare the functions and dysfunctions of the labels. If you think that the labels should be revised, what should they be?

3. Design a plan for securing more representation of women in political positions and business positions of power. Should there be policies adopted for increasing the representation of LGBTI individuals in positions of power as well?

ON YOUR OWN

1. Create a brochure that would educate potential victims and perpetrators concerning sexual harassment at work or school. The EEOC information is a good resource:

    https://www.eeoc.gov/eeoc/publications/promising-practices.cfm

2. Find the countries with the highest rates of child marriage. What factors do you hypothesize correlate with these rates? Compare and contrast at least five countries with high child marriage rates with five countries with low child marriage rates on five different variables. You can use the UNDP Human Development

...k World Development Indicators, ... Warlist, and other online sources for ...a on child marriage see Girls Not Brides

...orld Values Survey asks a number of questions ...erning attitudes toward women's roles at work, ...politics, and in the family. It also asks a question concerning tolerance toward homosexuality. Researchers can study a country's attitudes over time or compare countries. When you select questions under

"Show Tree," there are relevant questions under "Would not like to have as neighbors," "Work," "Family," and "Justifiable."

4. Investigate occupational segregation in the United States. Compare and contrast majority "male" and "female" occupations and their salaries. Are there occupations with equal value but unequal wages? What are some occupations that are of equal value and equal wages?

NOTES

1. The health gap is on a general downward trend. The WEF (2017) did not calculate a closing date.

2. Some people in deeply conservative countries react to the threat of change that accompanies all education. Some conservative groups in modern societies also resist some forms of education and stress religious and traditional views over aspects of science and history education.

3. Legislators are included in the political category.

4. A number of other international instruments address fair remuneration for workers, including human rights instruments—the European Social Charter, the African Charter on Human and Peoples' Rights (followed by principles and guidelines for implementing them), and the South Asian Association for Regional Cooperation Social Charter—and some trade agreements such as the North American Free Trade Agreement (NAFTA).

5. Minimum wage laws presumably enacted to protect all workers appeared in some states in the United States in the early 20th century. Their purpose was quite different from that of today's laws. Their objective was to drive women and ethnic and racial minorities out of the labor market. If employers were forced to pay the same price for women and minorities as for native-born white males, they would be less likely to hire them, effectively eliminating them from the competition for jobs.

6. This minimum has not increased in 25 years.

7. For a more detailed look at more countries and minimum wage increases, see ILO (2014).

8. Women are not a homogeneous group. They and their interests cut across class, religious, age, racial, and other divides. However, a general recognition that women tend to be more supportive of health, education, and violence-related issues tends to hold across the divides. These concerns are also apparent in the research on how women use their incomes as well as their votes.

9. The countries were a reasonable sample of countries that varied in levels of development, geography, and culture; in total, 12 were developed, 9 were sub-Saharan, 8 were Latin American and Caribbean, and 3 were from Eastern Europe and Central Asia.

10. Depending on how the sample was drawn and how sexual harassment was defined (or not defined), the number of women admitting to sexual harassment varies.

11. This study was conducted at the Southern Poverty Law Center using data from the 1995 to 2008 Hate Crime Statistics, including only crimes against persons, not property.

8

When Life Becomes a Commodity

HUMAN AND WILDLIFE TRAFFICKING

COMING BACK FROM SLAVERY

From 3 am to 8 pm, James Kofi Annan, not yet 6 years old, worked in a fishing village with other children. Like the other children with whom he worked, he was sold for labor. He moved from village to village working in fishing villages, usually with one meal a day, no medical care, and little sleep. When he was 13, he managed to escape and returned home to the relief of this mother and the ire of his father, who had received ongoing payments. Despite ridicule for his poverty, he enrolled in school, learned to read, and excelled—eventually being one of only a few to attend college. He then worked for five years at Barclay's Bank of Ghana. After five years, he resigned to devote his efforts full-time to "Challenging Heights," an organization he established to rescue, shelter, and educate child slaves, especially about their rights. The organization works in prevention and advocacy and educates parents about the dangers of trafficking and the opportunities that school and health care open up for their children. Annan has won a number of awards, including the Frederick Douglass Freedom Award in 2008. He uses award money to further his work.

Source: End Slavery Now (2015).

LEARNING OBJECTIVES

After completing this chapter, students should be able to do the following:

8.1 Analyze the features of modern life that contribute to the opportunity and motivation for international crime

8.2 Understand the types and prevalence of human trafficking

8.3 Analyze global and societal factors that contribute to offending and vulnerability to victimization

8.4 Evaluate the effectiveness of the current anti-trafficking regime and suggest improvements

8.5 Assess programs to rehabilitate the variety of victims of human trafficking

8.6 Evaluate the strengths and weaknesses of the legal framework for combatting trafficking in wildlife

EFFECTS ON CRIME

e dangerous and dark effects of global-
globalization of crime. More open borders
n technological advances in communication,
ation, and manufacturing create opportunities
crimes and for conducting old crimes in new, more
nt, less risky ways. Just as the market for legal goods
services is global, so is the market for illegal goods and
ervices. There are at least 52 activities that fall into the
category of transnational crime. They range from trafficking in arts and antiquities to trafficking in human organs.

Improvements in transportation and communication did not cause globalization, but they increased its
pace exponentially. The volume of transportation of both
people and goods through sea and airports is such that
identifying every illegal shipment is impossible. In 2007,
2.2 billion people traveled globally on 29 million flights
among 3,750 airports. In 1996, 332 million tons of goods
traveled across the seas; by 2007, it was 828 million tons
(United Nations Office on Drugs and Crime [UNODC]
2014). How can this many people or this much cargo be
inspected effectively?

The anonymity, speed, and new modes of communication serve transnational crime well. Mobile telephones,
"burner" disposable phones, and the capacity to route
communications through several countries in seconds
before reaching the final destination make it hard to pin-
point the geographic locations or identities of the people
communicating. Encryption makes it difficult to decode
and read illicit messages. In 2009, there were close to
240 million websites (and there will probably be many
more by the time this gets to print). Policing this many for
crimes as diverse as child pornography, money laundering, and human trafficking is a near impossible task.

Anything that can be gotten legally can be obtained
illegally, and many forbidden goods and services from
drugs to slaves are available through international crime.
With high-quality printers and copiers and digital video
and audio recorders, making counterfeit goods from
purses to watches and pirating movies and music is easier
and the goods are harder to distinguish from the genuine
ones. From counterfeiting to the sex trade, new technologies make old crimes easier and make many new "cybercrimes" possible.

The costs of transnational crime were enormous,
about U.S. $870 billion, comparable to 1.5 percent of
global gross domestic product (GDP) or 7 percent of the
world's exports of merchandise in 2012—a figure that
has surely risen significantly since then (Interpol 2014;

UNODC 2012). Drug trafficking, the most lucrative of the
crimes, reaped profits of about $320 billion in 2012, coun-
terfeiting made about $250 billion (hundreds of billions
more if domestic counterfeit sales and digital pirating are
included), human trafficking about $32 billion, smug-
gling migrants about $7 billion, and trafficking in timber
about $3.5 billion. Elephant ivory, rhino horn, and tiger
parts from Africa and Asia produced $75 million annually
in criminal turnover (UNODC 2012). However high the
economic costs, it is the political, social, and human costs
that are most severe. Millions of lives are lost or ruined.
The corruption that transnational organized crime (TOC)
breeds destabilizes governments. The costs of TOC are
burdensome for all societies, but like all social problems
they fall most heavily on developing countries. Even in
healthy societies, transnational crime threatens states,
democracy, and development.

INDIVIDUAL AND ENVIRONMENTAL VULNERABILITY TO TRANSNATIONAL ORGANIZED CRIME

Anticipating where organized crime might arise and who
might fall prey is important to preventing and combatting
TOC. Uncovering patterns of individual and environmental vulnerabilities that "push" people toward organized
crime or make them victims of it helps to understand
how trends in TOC develop. Markets in drugs, arms, and
people expand and contract as societal conditions change.
Factors such as unemployment, a labor market closed to
women, gender discrimination, lack of opportunity, poverty, persecution, collapse of social infrastructure, conflict,
and war "push" people toward crime. The lure of better
conditions or illicit opportunities, along with demand for
goods or services, may "pull" them toward traffickers or
other victimizations (Europol Public Information 2011).

Environmental Factors

Determining the environments in which TOC will thrive
and those that will be resistant is not as easy a proposition
as it might seem. Political, social, economic, and cultural
factors all play a role. Their synergy in different configu-
rations alters the relative importance of each from case to
case. These factors are those that also relate to disorder
generally, from domestic crime to violent conflict. Some,
such as a strong ethnic identity, are relevant only in the
context of others in determining the nature of the crime
or disorder that emerges.

Political Factors

Rule of law is one of the most important factors related to the infiltration of organized crime in a country. Where these factors are present, countries are less vulnerable:

- Government and its officials, private entities, and individuals are accountable under the law.

- Laws are clear, publicized, stable, just, and applied evenly.

- The processes by which laws are enacted and enforced are accessible, fair, and efficient.

- Justice is timely delivered by competent, ethical, and independent representatives who have the resources they need and reflect the makeup of the communities they serve. (World Justice Project 2016)

Rule of law depends on the quality of its institutions and the people who occupy them. People must perceive the institutions as legitimate. Laws need to be fair and applied equally. This requires independent and accountable branches of government. The justice system, for example, must not hold any person above the law and must serve the country, not special interests. Lawless spaces create an environment ripe for crime. With no one to enforce or uphold it, there is no law.

Crime thrives where there are weak institutions and weak rule of law. In West Africa and East Africa, governments of failing states are overrun by criminal networks. As with the traditional crime networks, organized crime uses its own people and methods to fill in for legitimate institutions. In February 2016, Operation Adwenpa in West Africa positioned 100 local and Interpol officers at border points in Benin, Côte d'Ivoire, Ghana, Nigeria, and Togo. In just 10 days, the officers arrested a Ghanaian wanted by Brazil for drug trafficking, a French national wanted by Benin, and another Ghanaian who was smuggling two children into Togo; six children being trafficked for labor were rescued; and 900 kg of narcotics, seven stolen vehicles from Canada, France, Germany, and Italy, and gold, jewelry, ivory, and counterfeit passports were seized (Interpol 2016a).

In countries and regions with little state capacity for regulation and enforcement, "might makes right." These countries become incubators for crime. The weakness and void within failed and failing states provide a haven for criminal activity. In some areas, the only governing force is transnational crime. In Guinea–Bissau, for example,

South American drug cartels have taken over, making it a hub on their trafficking routes. Drugs provide a better income for the people and the country as a whole than its cashew exports. The government and drug traffickers are indistinguishable, and the valuable drug trade is protected by the military. It has been called Africa's first "narco-state" (Mungai 2015).

Where states are in transition, even from autocracy to democracy, they are at their most fragile. Laws and institutions are in flux. It takes time to build a stable government. State structures weaken before new strong ones are established. Conditions of anomie in developing nations and countries in transition after the breakup of the Soviet Union and Warsaw Pact rendered them vulnerable to TOC. These countries sit along drug transit routes from both Asia and Latin America. Traffic in drugs, arms, and people passes through these routes.

Strong authoritarian states also provide opportunities for organized crime. Authoritarian states are not accountable to anyone. The legislature and judiciary may serve the executive branch, not the people. Corruption is almost always present. Unlike the situations of weak states, organized crime operates within the limits established by the state authorities. It is at the service of, rather than in opposition to, the government. Collusion between the state and criminals in these conditions is under control of the state, not the criminals, and state officials as well as their friends and families grow wealthy (Williams and Godson 2002).

Violent Conflict

Violent conflict and hostility destroys the economy, infrastructure, and social relations within a society. It depletes resources. War-torn societies in the Middle East and the former Yugoslavia illustrate this dramatically. Black markets and negative social relations develop to fill the void. Its effects last long after a conflict has ceased. Supplies needed for conflict fuel black market trafficking not only for arms but also for many goods, including people trafficked for conscription into armed groups or for sex slaves to serve them. One of the greatest challenges to postwar recovery is the expansion of organized crime. Skilled militants with an oversupply of arms take advantage of the economic and political vacuums. The insecurity from violent conflict diffuses outward to neighbors; it increases tensions among states and among social groups within states. When the conflict has ceased, armed groups remain (Marshall and Cole 2014).

Civil war gave rise to piracy along the shores of East Africa. Somalia has not had a functional government since

1991. Fishermen in Somalia have become pirates because legitimate employment opportunities are few and far between and there is no functioning government to patrol the waters. Somali piracy peaked in 2011, but pirates are still active there as well as in West Africa and Southeast Asia. In recognition of the weaknesses of many governments and the lawlessness of the seas, some governments have gone so far as to encourage merchant companies to hire private security forces and arm their ships, effectively handing over government's traditional monopoly on the use of force (Urbina 2015).

Economic Factors

Where the economy is weak, organized crime often pays better and offers more security than conventional jobs, even jobs in the police and military. In these situations, many officers are corruptible, from the local police to military generals.

When an economy is transitioning from a command market to a free market, particularly in the context of a political transition, organized crime is likely to become deeply entrenched in the economy. As mentioned above, authoritarian states and organized crime share interests. When the regime falls or transitions, the power often shifts to the criminals. They can seize control over many businesses, particularly in export sectors. They can demand "protection" from small and large businesses, banks, and other financial institutions (Williams and Godson 2002).

Rebel and terrorist groups turn to organized crime to finance their activities. From FARC (Revolutionary Armed Forces of Colombia) in Colombia to more recent conflicts in the Middle East, there are close links between terrorism and TOC. FARC, the Taliban, al Qaeda, and Hezbollah all participate in the drug trade in various capacities to fund their activity.

Cultural and Social Factors

Cultural norms might disguise or contribute to trafficking. When laws passed by the central government conflict with traditional norms, the traditional norms often dictate practice. The rule of law often does not extend far beyond urban areas if enforced even there. Traditional forms of justice often prevail. Sexual mores that condone and promote violence against women play a role in justifying or morally "neutralizing" trafficking in women and girls for both sex and labor. Norms relevant to child labor may suggest that a child is a resource to be put to work, however dangerous the job.

There is a very thin line between seeing a woman as of less value than a man or a child as a resource and selling that woman or child to a trafficker. Child sex tourism and child domestic servitude and labor are no longer acceptable in international law or in any domestic law regardless of custom or traditional norms. Ironically, diplomatic personnel have been among the most visible abusers of these customs. The Organization for Security and Cooperation in Europe (OSCE) has produced a handbook as well as guidelines for preventing diplomats from using trafficked labor and settling disputes when they arise (OSCE 2014).

"Favors" for friends and family in the context of business or government is considered corruption in most modern societies and contrary to rule of law outside of a family-owned business. But it is normative in traditional societies. Family and friends are expected to benefit from one another's positions. This extends into some societies as quid pro quo or clientelism through which political and economic favors are exchanged. These expectations reinforce social relations between organized crime and a populace, between organized crime and politicians, and it solidifies loyalties and relations within the organized crime group itself. The Italian Mafia and Chinese Triads were based on these principles. Nigerian politics is still based on "prebendalism" in which those in political office are expected to use the office for their benefit and that of their faction. Along with authoritarian rule, this cultural norm helps to explain the rise of Nigerian organized crime (Williams and Godson 2002).

Markets also explain the strength of organized crime. In some cases, as happened with alcohol and prohibition, legalizing alcohol broke the grip of organized crime.

Some markets, of course, cannot be legalized. But even among those where legalization is possible, it does not necessarily push out organized crime. For example, the legalization of prostitution in Amsterdam did not force the sex traffickers out of the business.

Individual-Level Factors

In assessing individual vulnerability, three main categories of risk are worth considering:

- *Personal vulnerability:* any characteristics of the individual such as youth or old age, physical disability, gender, mental disability, cultural difference, and family situation

- *Situational vulnerability:* legal status in a country or marginalization due to cultural, religious, social, and linguistic isolation

CONSIDER THIS
THE PROTECTION OF COMMUNITY

A San Diego State University researcher discovered that approximately 38,000 Spanish-speaking workers in San Diego County, California, are victims of abuse and human trafficking. Most were in the construction sector, followed by food processing and janitorial work. Agriculture was the lowest. Most abuse occurred at the workplace rather than during capture or transportation. Workers were confined to the workplace, forbidden from contact with relatives, and subjected to physical and sexual violence as well as having their identity papers confiscated. The low level of trafficking among these farm workers was surprising. The research revealed that the close-knit network of agricultural workers might have reduced the potential for trafficking and abuse (Zhang 2012).

- *Circumstantial vulnerability:* unemployment and economic destitution (Daniel-Wrabetz and Penedo 2015)

Age

Children are particularly vulnerable. As economic liabilities in conditions of poverty, they may be lured or sold into the labor or sex market. At the other end of the age spectrum, older adults are also vulnerable. People at the upper end of working age are still able to work but may be left out of the job market, particularly where jobs are hard to come by. Desperate for work, they are more easily lured into high-risk opportunities. Desperate for money, and perhaps ignorant of modern technologies and finance, they become victims of a variety of emerging crimes. The handicapped and mentally disabled, excluded from many opportunities, may be lured by offers of love or jobs.

Children are the most powerless victims. Sold by her parents in Egypt, Shyima Hall was later smuggled into California by her captors. She worked 20 hours a day while suffering physical and verbal abuse. Her captors kept anything from her that might teach her English. Four years into her captivity, a neighbor filed an anonymous report of her captivity. At the time of her rescue, she could speak only three English words (U.S. Department of State [USDOS] 2014).

Shyima is one of many who were sold by their parents. In Svay Pak, a neighborhood in Phnom Penh, Cambodia, half of the population lives on less than $2 a day. It is the global epicenter of child sex trafficking. Desperation drives many parents and relatives to sell one or more of their children. Neoung sold the virginity of her 12-year-old daughter, Kieu. Kieu was held in a brothel for three days and raped by three to six men a day. Upon her return, her mother sold her a second time and then a third time. It was then that Kieu knew that she needed to flee. When interviewed by CNN, Kieu's mother said she was heartbroken to sell her daughter but had no choice because of debt. Ann, facing $6,000 of debt, also sold her daughter. The money lenders promised her "big money" for her daughter's virginity. She had seen others do it, so she did it too. In the neighborhood, some of these mothers are mocked for giving away their daughters. Others think it is fine. Deep in poverty and debt, a daughter's virginity is often a family's most valuable asset. In Cambodia, United Nations International Children's Emergency Fund reports that a third of the 40,000 to 100,000 people in the sex trade are children. In countries where corruption is high, prosecutions happen but are difficult to bring forward because many police are involved in the trafficking. In a society like Cambodia devastated by violent conflict and genocide, poverty and corruption combine in a lethal mix.

Agape International Missions now works in Svay Pak, providing loans, rescuing girls, housing them, and giving them factory jobs. Shyima's story illustrates all three levels of vulnerability, common in Cambodia. However, there is no country immune from child trafficking as a source country, a destination country, or both. In China, the one-child policy is blamed. In India, it "makes sense" to sell girls off at a young age. They are financial liabilities; a girl will ultimately leave home, after her parents pay for her marriage, and move in with her husband's family. Selling girls, perhaps as child brides, saves this expense.

Although it is impossible to count the victims of child trafficking, estimated to be at about 1.2 million, and determine how many are sold by parents, the number is

CONSIDER THIS
CHILDREN, THE MOST VULNERABLE SEX WORKERS

Sex trafficking is the fastest growing organized crime. National and global sports events are among the "hottest" venues for sex trafficking. Among the sex workers are children. The Federal Bureau of Investigation (FBI) estimates that 200,000 children in the United States are at risk for being trafficked for sex every year. Many, if not most, are sold online. In 2008, the FBI found 2,800 advertisements for children online.

Thorn, an NGO, combats online child trafficking with "intelligent technology." Its program, "Spotlight," identifies victims online and illicit online networks. In 2016, the organization collaborated with the FBI, the Alameda County district attorney, and police in Oakland, California, to identify victims at Super Bowl 50 (Artega 2016).

---

surely in the tens or hundreds of thousands. Children are trafficked for sex, for cheap and unpaid labor—domestic labor and hazardous work—and for soldiering.

Marginalization

Marginalized people and marginalized communities are also among the most vulnerable. These groups face discrimination, persecution, violence, and abuse. The Roma are a people without a homeland. They face discrimination and prejudice throughout Europe, although they are citizens of the European Union (EU) and the countries in which they live. Not only poor, they also face extreme marginalization and little access to social services such as education, health care, employment, and credit. They end up taking loans in the informal sectors of money lending at exorbitant interest rates, putting them into debt and making them vulnerable to traffickers. They lack the protection of law enforcement and distrust it, exacerbating their vulnerability. Many have been prosecuted for crimes—from prostitution, to burglary, to illegal entry—that they were forced to commit while victims. Threat of turning victims over to law enforcement after they have been forced to commit crimes is one method of coercion. This dilemma confronts minority ethnic groups worldwide, particularly in countries with weak governments or governments that violate the rights of minorities within their population. There are hundreds of such marginalized groups globally.

Marginalization of lesbian, gay, bisexual, and transgender (LGBT) people makes them particularly vulnerable. Many countries criminalize people on the basis of sexual orientation. This elevates the threat of violence and precludes them from educational and employment opportunities. Many are rejected by family and their communities. This is a twofold dilemma. The discrimination and lack of opportunity leads them to seek opportunity outside of traditional channels and prohibits them from turning to law enforcement for help. Non-governmental organizations (NGOs) in Argentina found that transgender women were promised jobs but had their passports stolen by traffickers and were forced into prostitution. South African LGBT children were coerced into prostitution by threats to expose them to their families (USDOS 2014).

THE LEGAL FRAMEWORK TO COMBAT TRANSNATIONAL ORGANIZED CRIME

International conventions and treaties have the force of law, binding the countries that ratified them to uphold them and promote international cooperation in achieving the objectives. Because TOC differs from traditional "organized crime" in several ways, considering the differences is important in constructing legal frameworks that combat TOC in all of its dimensions.

Traditionally, organized crime groups develop territorially in areas marginal to or neglected by the state. They offer services such as credit, jobs, and security where conventional opportunities do not exist. These activities devolve into loan sharking, "protection," and positions in the criminal hierarchy. Traditional syndicates supply a range of goods or services, diversifying rather than specializing. They secure loyalty within their territories by intimidation but also by providing services that the government does not or cannot provide. Criminal control can force peace in a violent and conflict-ridden region, a *Pax Mafiosa,* the Mafia's peace. Even Joaquín Guzmán Loera ("El Chapo"), head of the Sinaloa Cartel, is a folk hero in his home state, where homicide is two and a half times the national average. People celebrate him for helping out local people, for providing them with jobs in the trade, for his intelligence demonstrated in having amassed a fortune, for winning against the government for many years, and for keeping their state relatively calm. When he escaped from jail, he returned to his state and many people were glad because it would keep worse drug gangs out of the area (Neuman and Ahmed 2015).

Now, TOC is increasingly composed of loosely structured networks rather than the hierarchically structured groups of traditional organized crime "syndicates" (UNODC 2014). A study of 40 crime groups from 16 countries distinguished five types of crime organization: the crime network, the traditional rigid hierarchy, regional hierarchies, clustered hierarchies, and core group organizations. The traditional rigid hierarchy characterized only one third of the groups and was mostly associated with groups having a strong social or ethnic identity. Regional and clustered hierarchies are composed of groups that may be distributed across countries or regions. Component group networks grant more autonomy than in the rigid hierarchies, and the core group structures are small, tightly knit flat structures surrounded by a loose network (van Dijk and Spapens 2014).

These smaller, decentralized, more fluid and agile criminal structures are better adapted to changing conditions. For example, after the Cali and Medellin cartels of Colombia disbanded, hundreds of smaller, more fluid, more sophisticated groups took over cocaine trafficking. They proved to be nimbler in face of stronger law enforcement and court adjudication (van Dijk and Spapens 2014). Mexico, which acquired a more significant role in trafficking after the demise of the Colombian cartels, underwent similar transformations. The structure of the Sinaloa cartel, perhaps the most famous of the drug cartels, rose to power after the fall of the Guadalajara cartel in the 1980s. It adapted its structure in the last 20 years, operating as a federation of affiliated cells. It allies with other cartels in adopting a less hierarchical, more decentralized structure overall. Each subgroup has significant autonomy in its own operations (Harris 2014). Each subgroup has its own hierarchy.

Smaller, more fluid, and more agile groups also adapt quickly to the opportunities of globalization. More open borders facilitate movement of people and goods. Internet and mobile phones facilitate communication. Global financial systems make it easier to move money. Racketeering is less profitable for traditional groups that are weakened by arrests and social changes, the ethnic diversity of urban areas, easier credit, the decline of powerful unions, and transparency in government contracts. More regulation and prosecution at the national level has pushed crime to the global level, where many gaps in regulation and security open new opportunities. The new networks are low profile and fill the market gaps left by the decline of the larger, very visible traditional groups. The scenario of organized crime today is "less a matter of a group of individuals who are involved in a range of illicit activities, and more a matter of a group of illicit activities in which some individuals and groups are presently involved" (UNODC 2010). If the groups and individuals are caught, the activities continue as the market and incentives remain.

The capacity of small groups to engage in a broad network of supply and transit links in a variety of markets is illustrated by the story of two FBI cases. One Albanian group was caught smuggling in 100 kg of heroin. The group's U.S. ties were in the cities of Chicago and Detroit and in the state of Texas. The group had international ties in Albania and Macedonia. The heroin traveled from Afghanistan and probably through Turkey on its way to Albania. This small group was allegedly also dealing in illegal pharmaceuticals, gambling, ecstasy, and stolen goods. This was a very loosely organized group with no clear leader. Another group was headed by a Vietnamese woman who lived in Canada and for six years managed to traffic millions of ecstasy pills into the United States. She was the leader and pivotal link in a small Asian drug trafficking network (Bjelopera and Finklea 2012).

The 2000 UN Convention against Transnational Organized Crime is the major treaty governing international efforts to combat TOC. Because of the complexity of TOC structures, the convention is carefully crafted using rather broad definitions to expand the responsibilities of governments as needed to prosecute newly emergent crimes and fluid forms of organizations that commit them.

An act is considered *transnational* if it occurs in more than one state, if part of the preparation or control takes place in another state, if the organized criminal group has activities in more than one state, and if it has substantial effects in a state other than where it was committed (UNODC 2000, Article 3).

Crimes to be prosecuted under the act include money laundering, corruption, obstruction of justice, participation in a criminal group (as defined above), and "serious crime" (UNODC 2000, Articles 5, 6, 8, and 23).

The *serious crime* stipulation casts a wide net. It is defined by the length of the potential sentence in the country where the act is committed. Any crime for which the sentence could be a maximum of four or more years of incarceration is covered (UNODC 2000, Article 2).

Under the convention, an *organized criminal group* is one with the following characteristics:

- A group of three or more persons that was not randomly formed

- Existing for a period of time

- Acting in concert with the aim of committing at least one crime punishable by at least four years of incarceration

- Acting to obtain, directly or indirectly, a financial or other material benefit (UNODC 2000, Article 2)

The convention considers participation in an organized criminal group very broadly as well. It includes participation directly in the crime, of course, and also agreeing to take part in a crime of the criminal group or doing anything that could contribute to the crime being fulfilled, including giving advice (UNODC 2000, Article 5).

These broad definitions give the act the scope and flexibility to adapt to unforeseeable developments in the nature of the organization and the nature of crime.

Every country that ratifies the convention agrees to incorporate the terms of the convention into their domestic laws. This would include criminalizing the acts mentioned in the convention, institutionalizing methods for prevention, and securing the rights of victims, rather than prosecuting them as criminals, which is critical to divert them from criminal enterprises.

Revising domestic law in line with the convention ensures two mechanisms with which to hold states accountable: the international convention and their own laws. States can be called to task for violating either mechanism. In general, such carryover from international law to domestic law, rather than simply being redundant, increases enforcement (Simmons and Hopkins 2005).

All serious crimes with an international component as described above are included in the convention.[1] For specifically targeted crimes, three protocols supplement the convention: one for trafficking in persons, especially women and children, a second for smuggling migrants, and a third for manufacturing.

HUMAN TRAFFICKING: WHEN PEOPLE BECOME A COMMODITY

Data on human trafficking are based on cases that have been detected. There is no generally agreed on or methodologically sound estimate of the number of victims. Thus, the data reported on victims detected should not be assumed to represent the gender and age breakdown of all victims. Crimes involving female victims, by far the largest group of detected victims, may be more frequently detected than crimes involving male victims.

The State of Trafficking in Persons: Prevention and Prosecution

There is no accurate count of victims of human trafficking. The USDOS estimates that there are approximately 20 million victims currently. Each year, countries report[2] the number of traffickers they convict and the victims they identify. While many have been saved, millions are still captive (Tables 8.1, 8.2, and 8.3).

Forms of Human Trafficking

The main forms of human trafficking are sexual exploitation (53 percent), forced labor (40 percent), and organ removal (0.3 percent).

Sex Trafficking

In two separate incidents in London, Border Force officers stopped young girls traveling alone. The ages on their passports indicated that they were adults. They were in transit from Lagos, Nigeria, to Paris, being trafficked as prostitutes. They were placed in protective custody, but their captor eventually caught up with them. He tried to move them to Spain, but border patrols refused one girl entry. This gave Interpol an opportunity to capture their captor, who is now serving 14 years in prison in London (Interpol 2014).

Many children and others trafficked in the sex trade never get out alive. Sex trafficking haunts every continent and, more than likely, every country. It is the most common form of human trafficking. It is impossible to know how many victims there are globally or within any one country. In the United States alone, there are thousands, both U.S. citizens and foreign nationals. One estimate is that there are about 4.5 million people globally trapped in forced sexual exploitation (Polaris Project 2015). They may be working alongside victims of forced labor in the

A CLOSER LOOK
VICTIMS OF HUMAN TRAFFICKING

TABLE 8.1   Regional Trafficking by Servitude Category

Based on the victims rescued, regional patterns of human trafficking vary in the proportions of victims in various categories of servitude.

Region	Sexual Exploitation	Forced Labor	Other[a]
Africa and Middle East	53%	37%	10%
Americas	48%	47%	4%
East Asia, South Asia, and Pacific	26%	64%	10%
Europe and Central Asia	66%	26%	8%

a. Other includes organ removal, armed combat, petty crime, forced begging, benefit fraud, baby selling, pornography, forced marriage, illegal adoption, and rituals.

Source: Adapted from Federal Bureau of Investigation Hate Crime Statistics for 2012 to 2016 (FBI 2013, 2014, 2015, 2016, 2017).

TABLE 8.2   Detected Victims of Human Trafficking by Age and Gender, 2011

Sadly, the numbers of children victimized seems to be rising, based on counts of detected victims. From 2004 to 2011, the percentage of victims who are girls increased from 10 to 21 percent and the percentage of victims who are boys increased from 3 to 12 percent, although the ratio of children to adults varies by region.

Women	Girls	Men	Boys
49%	21%	18%	12%

Source: Adapted from Federal Bureau of Investigation Hate Crime Statistics for 2012 to 2016 (FBI 2013, 2014, 2015, 2016, 2017).

TABLE 8.3   Children and Adult Victims of Trafficking per Region

Region	Children	Adults
Africa and Middle East	62%	38%
Americas	31%	69%
East Asia, South Asia, and Pacific	36%	64%
Europe and Central Asia	18%	82%

Source: Adapted from Federal Bureau of Investigation Hate Crime Statistics for 2012 to 2016 (FBI 2013, 2014, 2015, 2016, 2017).

CONSIDER THIS

SELLING CHILDREN ONLINE—AVAILABLE TO BE RAPED

Every day, thousands of children, some boys but mostly girls, are advertised for sale. Some are runaways and gullible, some are simply naive and gullible, and some are kidnapped. However they got there, they are captive and available to be raped—20 or 30 times a day, depending on the number of buyers. One of the most notorious of these sites operates openly—globally. "Backpage" hosts 80 percent of the online sex ads in the United States. Anyone can post an ad, reply to an ad, and buy anything from antiques to children.

Operators of the site know that children are being sold. With profit nine times the average for online service sites, it is worth hundreds of millions of dollars. Children's lives are ruined before they have a chance at life. The U.S. government has tried for years, and is still trying, to shut the service down. How could the most powerful country in the world fail repeatedly to protect its most vulnerable?

agricultural camps, mines, or other remote and isolated industries, where government presence is minimal. Bolivian and Peruvian women and girls supply forced sex work in the mining areas of Peru. In the mines of Surinam, Guyana, Madagascar, and China, and in the U.S. state of North Dakota, women and children are exploited in the sex trade. This is a short list of the countries involved.

As in other forms of trafficking, the promise of a legitimate job is often used as bait. Kidnapping, buying and selling children, and selling young girls as "brides" all are techniques to coerce victims into the sex industry. Like other forms of trafficking, the internet opened up more opportunities. In addition to "mail-order brides," escort services, dating services, and thinly veiled online advertisements for prostitution make marketing sex cheap and easy.

Some victims are captive within their homeland, and others are captive in places where they do not speak the language, making escape even more difficult.

Fully 79 percent of female and 8 percent of male trafficking victims who have been detected are trafficked for sexual exploitation. In some cases, women have been tricked into sexual labor through the mail-order bride industry. Many women enter these marriages willingly to escape poverty. Some, after entering the marriages, are sold by their "husbands," who turn them over to sweatshops or brothels. As with child labor, some children are sold as brides to pay off family debts. "Opium marriages" involving girls to settle debts are common in Afghanistan. This was the fate of Khalida. When she was 9 or 10 years old, her father's opium crop was wiped out in the government's war against the drug trade. Unable to pay the

drug trafficker the U.S. $2,000 he had borrowed, he sold Khalida to the 45-year-old trafficker. Such marriages may involve girls as young as 5. In these cases, the girl is a domestic servant until she is old enough to consummate the marriage. Suicide among these children is also not uncommon (Aronowitz 2013).

Nicholas Kristof, a *New York Times* columnist, spent decades investigating human trafficking. The stories he collected are outrageous and common. Poonam was taken from her home in Nepal. The recruiter told her that she could earn a lot of money and make her father proud. She was 12 years old. He took her to a brothel in Mumbai, India, where he sold her for $1,700. Given "falsies" and a skimpy dress, she was ready for customers. Determined to make a big profit, the brothel owner sold her 20 to 25 times a day—every day. There were no holidays, no days off, and no pay. One day when she was hurt and bleeding, Poonam refused. She was beaten and burned with cigarettes. She was rescued when the police raided the brothel. Although she told the police that she was older, she feared a beating that the brothel owner told her she would get from the police. The police realized that she was a child and took her to Maiti Nepal, an anti-trafficking organization (Kristof 2015).

Although it is not a money-making prospect, terrorist groups, including Boko Haram and ISIS (Islamic State of Iraq and Syria), have kidnapped thousands of women and girls; Boko Haram alone kidnapped more than 2,000 just in 2014 and 2015. Most are used as domestic or sex slaves, sometimes through forced marriage. When 200 women and girls were rescued by Nigerian forces, the victims reported that they were forced to change their names, raped, and forced into marriage and other forms of slavery. In a manner similar to how traditional organized crime groups rationalized their crimes, ISIS developed elaborate rules concerning when raping "sex slaves" was allowed and when it was not (Dearden 2015).

Sex Tourism

Globalization provides opportunities for tourism and sex tourism (as well as for medical tourism and receiving trafficked human organs). Sex tourism is such big business that it supplies as much as 2 to 14 percent of the GDPs of Thailand, Malaysia, the Philippines, and India (Aronowitz 2013).

Child pornography and child sex tourism are the darkest sides of this dark business. The Centers for Disease Control and Prevention (CDC) estimates that there are about 2 million children sexually exploited globally. It warns that under U.S. law, any residents of the United States who engage in sexual or pornographic activity with children anywhere in the world can be prosecuted when they return to the United States (CDC 2013). Any child engaged in sex work is considered trafficked. In 2012,

U.S. federal agents uncovered 123 children exploited sexually for the purposes of pornography, 5 of whom were only 3 years old. The investigation spanned 46 U.S. states and six countries (ICE Newsroom 2013).

Child sex tourism is found all over the world. Sex tourism along both sides of the U.S.–Mexican border is big business. In some cases, it is affiliated with the drug cartels. Flows of traffic in child sex tourism follow patterns. U.S. residents and Canadians generally travel to the Mexican border and Latin America, with Costa Rica and Mexico being the favored spots, followed by Brazil and the Dominican Republic. Europeans travel primarily to Africa, where there are reportedly 10,000 to 15,000 girls being trafficked off the coast of Kenya. Australians go to Southeast Asia, primarily Indonesia, the Philippines, and Thailand. Asians tend to travel within their own regions (Table 8.4) (Aronowitz 2013).

Ironically, the legalization of prostitution does not seem to diminish sexual exploitation. In the Netherlands, where prostitution is legal, human trafficking has always infiltrated prostitution. Human traffickers take advantage of licensing differences in local laws. Licensing prostitutes should provide law enforcement with a chance to

A CLOSER LOOK
CHILD SEX TOURISM

TABLE 8.4 Major Known and Emerging Destinations of Child Sex Tourism

Although child sex tourism is more prevalent in developing countries, it exists all over the world. Major sporting events, such as the Super Bowl in the United States and FIFA (Fédération Internationale de Football Association) championship games, attract tourists for the sports and the sex trade that accompanies them.

Region	Countries
Africa	Cameroon, the Gambia, Kenya, Senegal, South Africa
Southeast Asia	Indonesia, Cambodia, Laos, the Philippines, Thailand, Vietnam
Central and South America	Brazil, Colombia, Costa Rica, Dominican Republic, Guatemala, Honduras, Mexico
Northern Russia, Eastern and Southeastern Europe	Romania, Moldova

Source: Adapted from *Transnational Crime and the Developing World* by Channing May (https://illicittrade.com/reports/downloads/Transnational_Crime-final.pdf) licensed under CC BY 4.0 (https://creativecommons.org/licenses/by/4.0/).

CONSIDER THIS
CHILD SLAVES IN NEW YORK

Beginning at 9 and 11 years of age, the young Korean brother and sister slept in a basement with no mattress. They worked daily keeping house, being masseuse to the homeowner, and later in a grocery store, although they needed to turn over their salaries. They were beaten daily and kicked routinely. They did go to school. One day after six years of captivity, the boy, then 14, decided to tell his teacher of the nightmare they had been living. Later that day, their captor was arrested at her home in Flushing, New York. (Colangelo and Schapiro 2016)

recognize victims. Utrecht, a municipality that requires licenses for "window prostitutes," interviews each one for about an hour before she is licensed. Whether or not this is helping is debated. Many West European prostitutes may have disappeared into the illegal sector to avoid registration. Non-location-bound prostitution and prostitutes working in "houses" of prostitution are less visible, and it is harder to enforce regulation (Dutch National Rapporteur on Trafficking in Human Beings and Sexual Violence against Children 2013).

The U.S. 2015 Trafficking in Persons Report recognizes the Netherlands as a Tier 1 country for its laws and efforts to combat trafficking and help victims. It registered 1,561 victims in 2014, up from 2013. Approximately 80 percent of trafficking victims in the Netherlands are victims of sexual exploitation.

Human Trafficking in the Global Supply Chains

The image of victims of trafficking are often pictures in isolated areas, perhaps with a cruel overseer keeping them captive. Contrary to this image, many victims, an estimated 19 million, are working in the corporate supply

A CLOSER LOOK
VICTIMS IN FORCED LABOR BY REGION

TABLE 8.5   Detected Victims in Forced Labor

Overall more males are trafficked for forced labor than females, nearly twice as many. However, this varies by region.

Region	% Boys and Men	% Girls and Women
Africa and Middle East	45	55
Americas	68	32
East Asia, South Asia, and Pacific	23	77
Europe and Central Asia	69	31

Source: Adapted from *Transnational Crime and the Developing World* by Channing May (https://illicittrade.com/reports/downloads/Transnational_Crime-final.pdf) licensed under CC BY 4.0 (https://creativecommons.org/licenses/by/4.0/).

chains of the world's most visible industries and largest corporations. This is very big business given that forced labor generates U.S. $150 billion annually (Table 8.5) (International Labour Organization [ILO] 2016).

Trafficking exists throughout the global supply chains in agriculture and the food industry, in nearly every consumer or business-to-business product, and even in the services, particularly the hospitality industry. Global supply chains make trafficking in persons easy to conceal. A multinational corporation procuring raw materials from several countries, manufacturing in several others, assembling in still more, and shipping to others may have little knowledge of the workers hired by subcontractors and by subcontractors of the subcontractors. Giant hotel chains may have little knowledge of who is hiring the personnel cleaning their rooms, making the beds, or making the sheets they put on the beds. Possibly, the corporations do not care to know. Human trafficking exists in every link in the chain.

Victims of trafficking work in every industry—from sophisticated industries such as electronics to the incredibly dangerous brick ovens, from our necessities such as food, clothing, and construction to recreation soccer balls. Even chocolate candy is tainted by human trafficking. Trafficked children, some sold by their relatives, work the cocoa farms of West Africa swinging machetes and wielding chainsaws while exposed to toxic chemicals for 12 or more hours a day.

Marginalized groups, migrants, the disabled, and minorities are most at risk. Industries that are seasonal or have peak periods of demand may turn to traffickers to meet periodic needs for an influx of labor such as to bring in a harvest, roll out a new product, or construct a highway within a limited time. In East and South Asia, the garment industry turns to forced labor to meet periods of high consumer demand (USDOS 2015).

Major global corporations are not exempt. Toyota subcontractors trafficked laborers from China, Vietnam, Indonesia, the Philippines, Brazil, and Thailand. Workers had been stripped of their passports and threatened with deportation if they tried to leave. Like most companies when their supply chain is exposed, Toyota promised a full investigation and restitution (National Labor Committee 2008). But people's lives were already ruined. Human rights activists, NGOs, and international governmental organizations brought trafficking in the supply chain to public attention and are making corporations accountable. Corporations are promising to investigate and hold all phases of their supply chain accountable. Ignorance is no longer considered an excuse.

Fishing and Seafaring

Slavery and human trafficking in the seafood industry has become notorious. An award-winning (Easton 2015) Associated Press (AP) investigation (McDowell, Mason, and Mendoza 2015) found Burmese victims of human trafficking in fishing and shrimping in Thailand and Indonesia. Their fish flow into the supply chains of Fancy Feast, Meow Mix, and Iams pet foods. Fish caught and shrimp caught and peeled by trafficking victims were found in stores throughout the world, including Kroger, Safeway, Albertsons, Walmart, and Sysco, the world's largest food distributor. They are also sold to restaurant suppliers and throughout Europe and Asia. According to the AP investigation, some suppliers, such as Santa Monica Seafood and other independent suppliers, go to great lengths to try to ensure that their supply chains are trafficking free. They admit that despite the effort expended and cost incurred, they still cannot guarantee their supply chains.

Workers interviewed by the AP investigative team and workers who spotted them cried out for help and begged to be taken away. They reported that the captains force them to drink unclean water and work them for 20 to 22 hours a day. They are routinely whipped or beaten. "I think our lives are in the hands of the Lord of Death," one said. Men are maimed by the beatings, and deaths resulting from their conditions and abuse are common. When a man dies, the body is tossed overboard to be devoured by sharks. "If Americans and Europeans are eating this fish, they should remember us," said Hlaing Min, 30, a runaway slave from the Indonesian island of Benjina. "There must be a mountain of bones under the sea. . . . The bones of the people could be an island, it's that many" (McDowell, Mason, and Mendoza 2015).[3]

Nestlé commissioned an independent investigation of its own industry. The company found that the fish in its Purina brand pet foods were caught by trafficked labor from Myanmar and Cambodia. One of the laborers interviewed reported that after 10 years of backbreaking work, he had nothing to show for it. Nestlé found underage workers and workers working long days without rest and given minimal food and water. With their own papers confiscated, the fake identities provided by traffickers or companies hid the illegality of the workers.

Trafficking in the seafood industry is not limited to Asia. The nature of the work, often out of sight on seafaring vessels, renders it less visible than in the cases of sex workers who are filling a market and have direct interaction with clients. Not all trafficked workers are unskilled labor. Ukrainian men trafficked to Russia, Turkey, and South Korea, for example, tended to have relatively high levels of professional identity. They were skilled professionals, having studied at technical colleges. However, like other victims of trafficking, age made them vulnerable. They tended to be older or younger and inexperienced, both categories that are less desirable on the legitimate job market (Surtees 2015).

Garment Industry

Ironically, Patagonia, one of the founding members of the Fair Labor Association and whose website is an education on environmentalism and social responsibility, has had a difficult time in cleansing its supply chain. Patagonia found a problem with its first-tier manufacturers—those who make their clothes from cloth. Its 2007 investigation resulted in Patagonia eliminating 33 of its contracted manufacturers, reducing to 75 from 108. In a subsequent investigation, Patagonia disclosed that it had discovered that most of the subcontracting Taiwanese factories that spin its raw materials into yarns, and that knit yarns into cloth, were guilty of trafficking and exploitation. The factories were using labor "brokers" who charged workers exorbitant fees, U.S. $7,000, for their jobs. The brokers also charged an additional monthly fee for the workers to keep their jobs. The traffickers deposited the workers' paychecks into accounts from which brokers deducted their fees. Patagonia found that the further down the supply chain the exploitation occurs, the harder it is to identify (White 2015).

Patagonia is far from the only clothier subject to human trafficking. Like other consumer products, the clothing industry is decentralized. Material components come from many suppliers and are manufactured in phases that move materials globally from one subcontractor to another. Investigations uncovered victims in the supply chains of clothing sold in Walmart, Sears, and JC Penney, among others. Some companies have made restitution to the victims (National Labor Committee 2003).

Electronics

Apple designs and sells electronic consumer products. It does not mine the metals, manufacture the components, or assemble them into finished products. Foxconn builds about 40 percent of the world's electronics, including many of Apple's. It employs hundreds of thousands of workers, widely dispersed globally such as in China, Brazil, and the Czech Republic. It supplies Apple along with Dell, Hewlett Packard, and many others in the industry. Foxconn doesn't make the components from which it builds the products. Apple, for example, gets the parts that Foxconn assembles from companies such as Flextronics—both of which contract with the biggest names in electronics. Based in Singapore, Flextronics has factories across four continents in 30 countries.

Flextronics, Foxconn, and similar factories recruit labor through thousands of "brokers." Brokers scour the poorest regions of the developing world; in the case of Flextronics and Foxconn, this would include Indonesia, Cambodia, Myanmar, Vietnam, and Nepal. Brokers sell the jobs. Desperate for work, people or their families pay as much as a year's wages, sometimes more.

Workers may be kept captive. Some factory managers confiscate and lock workers' documents in safes, preventing workers from leaving. They may be trapped for years while trying to pay back the debt and interest. In 2008, Apple tried to stop the abusive practices and limit broker fees to one month's pay. A "daisy chain" of brokers and recruiters from the factory all the way back to workers' home villages makes that near impossible because each broker charges a fee. In 2012, Apple found that workers were overcharged U.S. $6.4 million (Simpson 2013).

The story of one man, Bibek Dhong, illustrates how this works. When Apple announced the iPhone 5, the short time horizon for production and delivery set off a hiring frenzy to staff the Flextronics International factory in Malaysia, where the cameras for the phone would be manufactured. Although Apple said that workers should not pay a fee for the jobs, brokers subcontracted to subbrokers, who apparently always charge. A native of Nepal, Dhong was recruited in the drive for labor. His first contact was a local broker who promised him a good overseas job. Dhong paid him U.S. $250 and was sent up the chain to a broker who was registered with the government. Dhong surrendered his passport to this broker, who wanted $350. When Dhong finally reported to the airport for passage to the job, he was ordered to pay another $400. Borrowing at every step, Dhong was $1,000 in debt before he started working. The broker warned that if Dhong mentioned the fees, he would be punished, fined, and sent back to Nepal.

Within a month and a half, the factory lost the contract due to camera defects. Dhong and thousands of others were without work but were kept in the factory hostel for two more months, without adequate food for most of that time. With expired visas, their passports were returned with a one-day travel stamp to get them back to Nepal. Owing money, many needed to sell their land. Dhong, working in a shoe factory for $3 a day, owes

U.S. $300 a year in interest on the loans for a job that lasted only briefly (Simpson 2013). Flextronics and Apple promised to repay workers for fees charged.

Flextronics is one of Apple's main suppliers. Apple is far from its only client. Flextronics claims to be in the supply chain of nearly every customer in the electronics chain. This includes consumer electronics but also Lockheed Martin (aircraft), Ford Motor (automobiles), and more than 1,000 customers in nearly every line of business (Simpson 2013).

Shipping

In one of the largest human trafficking cases in the United States, Signal International shipyard brought 500 Indians to Mississippi, each expecting a good job and a green card. Each worker paid between U.S. $10,000 and $20,000 to the recruiter in India. Instead of jobs and green cards, Signal gave the Indians very restrictive work permits and inhumane working conditions. They lived under armed guard, as many as 24 in a space the size of a double wide trailer. Signal called these "profit centers" and deducted $1,050 a month from their pay, making $730,000 on the housing. Signal fined them $250 to $500 for having alcohol or guests. They were regularly searched and were threatened with deportation if they complained or questioned the legality of the situation. The Southern Poverty Law Center organized lawsuits for the men. Along with the American Civil Liberties Union, Asian American Legal Defense and Education Fund, and dozens of prestigious law firms, it worked pro bono for seven years on the cases. In February 2015, a jury awarded $14 million to five victims. In July 2015, another suit was settled for $20 million. Other cases continue. But Signal lost $34 million and declared bankruptcy (Desai 2015; Yachot 2015).

Trafficking in Organs

People the world over live longer, and medical procedures such as organ transplants are now commonplace. While this is progress, there is a sinister side. The number of people needing an organ transplant far exceeds the available supply. In most countries, the average wait time for an organ transplant is counted in years. In the United States alone, 22 people die every day while waiting.

As in every other form of transnational crime, where there is unmet demand, there is an opening for crime—in this case, for trafficking in human organs. People on both sides of the exchange are desperate—the people who desperately need organs to save their lives and the people who need money to save their lives and/or those of their families. It makes for big business. One of the top 10 illegal moneymaking activities, it makes about U.S. $1.2 billion (De Compostela 2015). The World Health Organization estimated in 2012 that about 10,000 black market operations occur yearly. Many of these organs, primarily kidneys and livers, are trafficked. Economic and political crises plunge people into the hands of human traffickers. Nearly every country is a source of desperate people willing to sell an organ in hopes of getting out of debt or maybe getting out of the country.

The Palermo Protocol specifically prohibits removal of organs as exploitation. Laws of the Council of Europe, the United States, and many other countries also prohibit

CONSIDER THIS
ORGAN WATCH

Global commerce in organs seems to have begun in the 1970s and 1980s in South Asia. A 1990s report on 131 transplants revealed that wealthy patients from the United Arab Emirates and Oman traveled to India, where local brokers scoured the slums of Bombay recruiting people so desperately poor that they would sell their "extra" kidney for $2,600 to $3,300. Researchers Nancy Scheper-Hughes and Lawrence Cohen began to investigate the medical ethics of such "transplant tourism." What they uncovered, however, was "the entrée of international organized crime into the secret world of illicit transplant surgeries" that spanned continents. Calling the global trade in organs "the new cannibalism," they founded Organ Watch in 1999. Their interviews with organ sellers uncovered stories of deception, physical threats, false imprisonment, confiscation of documents, and beatings—the techniques common to human traffickers the world over.

Organ Watch fights traffickers in courts and has tracked down traffickers in person, confronting them on behalf of victims—both sellers and recipients. (Scheper-Hughes 2015)

A CLOSER LOOK
ORGAN TRAFFICKING

TABLE 8.6   Prominent Countries Involved in Organ Trafficking Networks

The people who sell their organs are located primarily in poorer or developing countries, while the buyers are located in wealthy countries.

"Selling" Countries	Facilitating or Operating Countries	"Buying" Countries
Argentina, Bangladesh, Brazil, China, Colombia, Egypt, India, Iran, Iraq (until the Iraq War), Israel, Moldova, Romania, Pakistan, Palestine, Peru, the Philippines, Russia, United States, Turkey	China, India, Iran, Iraq (until the Iraq War), the Philippines, Romania, Russia, South Africa, United States, Turkey	Australia, Canada, France, Gulf States, Iran, Israel, Italy, Hong Kong, United Kingdom, United States, Taiwan

Source: Adapted from Scheper-Hughes (2015).

the selling of human organs. Despite this, courts sometimes see this as a victimless crime and prosecution is very difficult. In one such case in New Jersey, U.S. federal prosecutors had a hard time believing that prestigious U.S. hospitals could be involved in trafficking or that the victims had been coerced. Despite a decade of trafficking, the defendant was sentenced to only two and a half years in a low-security prison because, as the judge said, "everyone got something out of the deal" (Scheper-Hughes 2015).

Trafficking in organs is a complex process and involves an extensive network from the person who identifies the victim, to medical personnel who perform the surgeries on the victim donor and on the recipient, to persons who transport the organ, to organ banks, and to any other "middlemen" who may be involved. The network for any one transplant may involve actors from four or five countries. As with other forms of trafficking, the patterns may shift depending on law enforcement activity or new actors entering the "business."

The complexity and complicity involved is evident in the trafficking patterns in the Middle East. Wealthy recipients from Israel, Kuwait, Oman, and Saudi Arabia originally traveled primarily to India. Traffic then moved toward Turkey, Iran, and Iraq, and then to Russia, Romania, Moldova, and Georgia. One common pattern connected participants from four countries. Israeli kidney buyers flew to Turkey, where Turkish and Israeli doctors transplanted the organs of sellers from rural Romania or Moldova. Brazil and South Africa joined the traffic in the last 20 years (Table 8.6) (Aronowitz 2013).

COMBATTING HUMAN TRAFFICKING

Human trafficking is, unfortunately, big business. According to the FBI, it is not only the third largest criminal enterprise in the world but also the fastest growing. Combatting trafficking depends on preventive and enforcement efforts from the local community up to the global level. This is a monumental task and requires the coordinated efforts of NGOs, local and national governments, and international governmental agencies. Each of these entities is charged with "due diligence" under international law to uphold rights.

Efforts to stem human trafficking stretch back over a century. In 1902, in an effort to prevent the trafficking of women and girls in prostitution, 13 European countries adopted the International Agreement for the Suppression of the White Slave Trade. In 1921, the League of Nations passed a Convention for the Suppression of Traffic in Women and Children. The UN adopted the Convention for the Suppression of the Traffic in Persons and of the Exploitation of the Prostitution of Others in 1950. It did not consider other purposes for trafficking and, like the other human rights treaties of the time, had weak monitoring and enforcement mechanisms. It was not until the end of the Cold War, with the opening of borders and the rapid increase in goods and people flowing across borders, that developed countries felt threatened. This was the impetus for a vigorous transnational regime for human trafficking generally. Human trafficking became perceived as a criminal problem as opposed to only a human rights problem (Lloyd and Simmons 2014).

The Palermo Protocols

Regional and national laws and agreements concerning human rights multiplied quickly throughout the 1990s. Many of these specifically referred to human trafficking among other provisions, and some related indirectly to human trafficking as in the protection and rights of migrant workers, children, or domestic workers (Lloyd and Simmons 2014). As a supplement to the 2000 Convention against Transnational Organized Crime, the UN Protocol to Prevent, Suppress, and Punish Trafficking in Persons, Especially Women and Children (the Palermo Protocol) entered into force on December 25, 2003. With an agreed-on definition for trafficking in persons, it provides a framework for convergence in national law and coordination of international investigation and prosecution. The protocol binds ratifying countries to "prevent and combat trafficking in persons," "protect and assist victims," and "promote cooperation among States Parties" (Article 2) (Office of the United Nations High Commissioner for Human Rights 2000).

The protocol is important for recognizing the variety of forms trafficking may take, many of which had been neglected in national laws. For example, Article 3 makes clear that the threat or use of force is not the only means of trafficking. Fraud, deception, abuse of power, and payment or benefit given to persons having control over the person all are prosecutable as trafficking. In other words, any form of direct or indirect coercion is trafficking. Even when a person voluntarily engages the trafficker, if deceit or fraud was involved (as in the many false promises of good and legal jobs), it is trafficking. Transporting a person from one location to another is not necessary for a person to be trafficked; it is the coercion and exploitation that constitute trafficking. Each of these provisions allows prosecutions that previously would not have been covered by many national laws.

CONSIDER THIS
CARING FOR VICTIMS

Guidelines for a good anti-trafficking law based on the Palermo Protocol include mechanisms designed to make prosecution easier and ensure the care of victims. They include the following:

- A broad definition of coercion that includes all forms—financial, physical, reputational, anything that would compel people to continue their activity to avoid harm

- A well-articulated definition of trafficking to include all forms, not just recruitment and transportation

- Provision for complete care of the victim—medical, physical, legal, emotional, and psychological

- Immigration relief for victims regardless of their legal status

- Legal services to address compensation for the crimes committed against them (USDOS 2010)

Like other countries, the United States offers victims of human trafficking "continued presence" immigration status and protection while their cases are investigated and prosecuted. They are offered counseling, medical care, job skill training, housing, and other assistance. Their immigration status may be made permanent depending on their circumstances. They are not considered criminals regardless of the acts they were forced to perform. The "Continued Presence" brochure can be found on the Immigration and Customs Enforcement website (https://www.ice.gov/doclib/human-trafficking/pdf/continued-presence.pdf).

PHOTO 8.1 This girl is but one of many child casualties of the drug trade in Afghanistan. She was sold by her parents to settle a debt with drug traffickers.
Reuters/Parwiz.

Exploitation, according to Article 3, includes sexual exploitation, forced labor, anything resembling slavery, and removal of organs. Any form of involvement with the trafficking of children—from recruiting, to harboring, to transferring, to receiving—is prosecuted as trafficking. A child is anyone under 18 years old. These definitions make possible many more strategies of trafficking and more of the people involved than had been possible under most national laws. Like the convention on TOC, these same criteria are to be encoded into national laws.

In combination with provisions for prevention and victims' rights, the protocol constitutes a vigorous global regime. "Traffickers," claimed Jana, a survivor of sex trafficking, "are extremely well connected. We need to be too" (USDOS 2015). That is what the convention and protocol hope to accomplish.

Governmental and Intergovernmental Agencies

Since the Palermo Protocol, a number of governments established mechanisms to monitor human trafficking globally. Besides the UN Convention Against Organized Crime, a Committee of the Parties was established to monitor provisions of the convention. In addition, The UN Special Rapporteur on Human Trafficking is empowered to take action on violations against trafficked persons, visit countries to assess their prevention and prosecution efforts, make recommendations, and submit annual reports. Although the original mandate was for three years, it has been extended repeatedly. In July 2017, The Human Rights Council extended the mandate for an additional three years. In the United States, The Victims of Trafficking and Violence Protection Act passed into law in 2000 mandates that the USDOS issue a "Trafficking in Persons" report annually. It assesses countries' activities to combat human trafficking. Those countries not compliant with the international rules stipulated in the Palermo Protocol may be sanctioned by the United States. Countries are rated from Tier 1, those that meet or surpass the minimal level of compliance, to Tier 3, the lowest level of compliance. The Council of Europe adopted a European Convention against trafficking. The Group of Experts on Action against Trafficking in Human Beings (GRETA) and the Committee of the Parties monitor the European Convention across parties to the convention. Many agencies within these governmental and intergovernmental organizations play a role in monitoring. In addition, many local and global civil society organizations are very active in monitoring human trafficking.

Monitoring, publicizing the results, and sanctioning have been shown to be effective in coercing countries to root out and prosecute human trafficking more vigorously. It also significantly improves the lives and future life chances of victims.

Enacting comprehensive laws, conducting investigations to root out trafficking, ensuring enforcement, and providing comprehensive victim services all are necessary actions required of governments under international law.

Incorporating the international protocols into domestic law, from local to national, is important to reinforce enforcement and norms. As of 2018, many countries had yet to ratify or assent to the Palermo Protocol against human trafficking. These countries were primarily developing countries in Southeast Asia, Oceania, and Africa. Recent parties include Japan in 2017 and South Korea in 2016 (United Nations Treaty Collection 2018).

Even among those countries that have ratified the Palermo Protocol, many are ranked in Tier 2 or 3 of the USDOS Trafficking in Persons Report. Tier 2 countries are not meeting minimum standards of international law but are making significant efforts to come into compliance. Among Tier 2 countries, there is a watch list of countries whose number of victims is increasing or who have not provided efforts to combat severe forms of trafficking. Tier 3 countries are not making efforts to comply. Tier 2 countries are primarily middle- to low-income developing countries. These countries need support from other international governmental and non-governmental agencies to meet their goals. Tier 3 countries are among the most authoritarian governments or are failed states. Those countries that are failed states will need international assistance and enforcement. For those that are authoritarian, international pressure and sanctions may be needed to bring them into compliance. Many of these countries are themselves under sanction for human rights violations.

The state of California has been called the epicenter of TOC in the United States, including human trafficking along with drugs and arms trafficking and related activities (Harris 2014). California is also one of the largest agricultural states and home to many vulnerable migrants. As such, it has developed model laws, among them the "Transparency in Supply Chain Act" of 2012. It requires all corporations with gross receipts of more than U.S. $100 million and sales in California of more than $500,000 to report on their efforts to trace their supply chains and eradicate any human trafficking found. This has affected nearly every major corporation, not just foods. Many of these reports are public and online such as those from Patagonia and Nike.

In 2016, the U.S. Congress passed a law modeled somewhat after California's; it gives the government the right to confiscate any goods that are suspected of being made with child or forced labor. It requires Customs and Border Protection to file an annual report on enforcement.

Many states as well as the federal government have set up special units and task forces. Trafficking in Persons is one of the special units of the FBI dedicated to all forms of human trafficking that issues regular reports. While the special units bring forward and obtain convictions on many cases, they are only a fraction of the estimated 600,000 to 900,000 victims thought to be in or passing through the United States every year.

Government training so that personnel who work at borders and in customs and immigration can recognize victims is essential. Border enforcement is one of the most effective ways of tracing trafficking routes and saving victims of trafficking as well as illicitly trafficked goods. Not only government employees but also personnel working for private companies, whether in transit hubs or on planes and trains and along highways, need to be trained. In the Netherlands, a railway inspector spotted an older man with two young Hungarian women. The women had bags of sexy lingerie. Suspicious, the inspector notified police that the group had boarded the train at Sittard, headed for Utrecht. There, the man was arrested. In another case, a flight attendant recognized a young girl in need on an Alaska Airlines flight to San Francisco. She noticed that the girl was ill at ease and left a note for her in the restroom. The girl replied with a note crying for help. Rest stops along highways are another "hot spot" for human traffickers. Airline Ambassadors and Truckers against Trafficking deliver training to private companies so that their employees become lookouts for trafficking victims. The greater the awareness, the more victims can be saved.

Combatting Trafficking in the Supply Chain

Cleansing the global supply chain of trafficked victims is essential. While many corporations are making the effort, not all are and it has proven difficult to combat trafficking. Partnership for Freedom, a non-governmental agency, announced a competition for the best technological solutions for combatting trafficking in the private sector.

Mobile phones and online sources are becoming important tools in developing countries for everything from small-scale finance where banks are not available to communicating market conditions. Each of the five finalists in the competition has proposed a way to extend these technologies to people at risk or in close proximity to them. Solutions include using mobile phones to get regular data directly from workers to track data on labor conditions globally. Another proposal would monitor, collect, analyze, and map social media and public internet sources for indicators of labor exploitation. Others would communicate directly with ships at sea in the fishing industry to gauge conditions or to pay migrant workers and get feedback from them, thereby increasing transparency and accountability in recruitment (Partnership for Freedom 2016).

The ILO launched the "Fair Recruitment Initiative" in 2015 as part of a larger "Decent Work" initiative. If businesses can prevent deceptive recruitment, they can prevent victims from entering the supply chain. Four steps form the basis of the initiative:

- Study the migration pattern. One important specific suggestion is to find alternatives to private recruiters such as worker cooperatives, accredited employers, and public employment agencies.

- Improve laws and policies. An important suggestion here is to work with legislators and train inspectors with respect to regulating recruiters and employment agencies.

- Promote best fair business practices, particularly in cross-border recruitment, by providing online access to tools and strategies.

- Empower and protect workers—work with trade unions and civil society organizations and use social dialog mechanisms to address and obtain early warnings of unfair recruitment practice. (ILO 2015)

The "Fair Recruitment" pilot program was set to operate from 2015 to 2018, with the ILO, trade unions, media professionals, governments, and civil society organizations working together and coordinating their efforts.

Everyone Can Play a Role

Although many victims are out of sight while locked in basements or brothels, others circulate in public view and even serve the public in hotels, restaurants, and brothels. Awareness of human trafficking and recognizing the signs are critical. Neighbors may get an occasional glimpse of a domestic laborer. Victims of sexual exploitation work along highways at truck stops. Recognizing the signs of victimization may save lives. There are many resources that educate about warning signs and indicators related to human trafficking.

PHOTO 8.2 In 2014, religious leaders from around the world met at the Vatican to sign the Declaration of Religious Leaders Against Modern Slavery.

Reuters/L'Osservatore Romano.

Recognizing Victims

Across the United States, hundreds of thousands of people are victims of human trafficking. Some are smuggled from other countries. Some enter legally, recruited for what they thought were legitimate jobs, only to have their papers stolen and be forced into servitude. Some are U.S. citizens. This is the case throughout Europe, Asia, South America, and Africa.

How would you recognize a victim? The U.S. Department of Homeland Security, which offers trainings for first responders, law enforcement, and federal workers, lists these indicators:

- Does the victim possess identification and travel documents? If not, who has control of these documents?

- Did the victim travel to a destination country for a specific job or purpose, and is the victim engaged in different employment than was expected?

- Is the victim forced to perform sexual acts as part of employment?

- Is the victim a juvenile engaged in commercial sex?

- Does the victim owe money to an employer or does the employer hold wages?

- Did the employer instruct the victim on what to say to law enforcement or immigration officials?

- Can the victim freely leave employment or the situation?

- Are there guards at the work/harboring site or video cameras to monitor and ensure that no one escapes?

- Does the victim have freedom of movement? Can the victim freely contact family and friends? Can the victim socialize or attend religious services? (U.S. Immigration and Customs Enforcement 2013)

Polaris Project (2018), a non-profit, lists potential red flags that anyone might notice in his or her community having to do with work and living conditions, mental health, autonomy, and general sensibility or disorientation:

- Are the people free to come and go, and are they fearful, anxious, or depressed?

- Do the people lack health care or appear to be malnourished?

- Do the people have inconsistencies in their stories?

- Do the people know where they are and how they got there?

- Are the people not able to speak for themselves?

- Do the people have few possessions, and are they in control of their own money, bank accounts, or other finances?

- Do the people's living conditions seem to have high-security measures such as high fences and barbed wire?

Educating Communities

Educational campaigns that reach into the communities most vulnerable to human trafficking are one of the most effective tools. U.S. Agency for International Development (USAID) uses a multifaceted approach on the ground, working with community leaders, NGOs, and the private sector to strengthen local capacity to prevent and combat trafficking. USAID teaches local leaders about the techniques of traffickers, the costs of victimization, and victim services. Information tailored to the community is communicated by locals through schools, community activities, pamphlets, and neighborhood watches. It also works to strengthen local governments and civil society. USAID's (2006) activities include the following:

- Strengthening government surveillance and monitoring

- Monitoring private contracts to ensure adequate labor standards

- Enacting legislative reforms, including training prosecutors and judges

- Raising public awareness of traffickers' techniques and safe migration practices

- Mobilizing community resources for awareness campaigns

- Developing local capacity for helping victims and joining with NGOs to develop reintegration and rehabilitation programs that include shelter, health care, and psychological services

- Providing literacy, life skills, self-esteem, and vocational programs for victims

CONSIDER THIS
WHAT CAN NGOs DO? LA STRADA INTERNATIONAL

La Strada International (LSI) focuses its advocacy work on female victims of trafficking in Europe. Established in the Netherlands in 1995, its member organizations are based in Eastern European countries where poverty, violent conflict, and weak social safety nets increase women's vulnerability. Given the scope and depth of the conditions that give rise to human trafficking and the financial and legal constraints placed on NGOs within many countries, LSI asks, "What can anti-trafficking NGOs offer?"

It turns out that, in conjunction with one another, they can—and do—accomplish a lot.

Advocacy and Lobbying

One of the key roles of any civil society organization is advocacy. LSI was organized in 1995, before the emergence of the intergovernmental organizations and major treaties relevant to human trafficking. LSI, along with other human rights groups, was influential in every step of developing the European human trafficking regime. It lobbied governments for ratification of the Council of Europe Convention and was instrumental in the EU directive and the European hotline and in evaluating the GRETA missions. Gaining status as a participant in international governmental organizations gives civil society groups a direct channel to governments that have the power to prosecute and sanction. LSI sits at the table at a number of such organizations. Chief among them is the Organization for Security and Cooperation in Europe (OSCE), Alliance Expert Coordination Team made up of representatives of the UN, EU, and OSCE as well as other major NGOs. Working with other NGOs also helps to build civil society capacity in local and national communities.

Prevention

Prevention takes many forms, including direct outreach to potential targets of traffickers and education within the most vulnerable countries and within destination countries. Raising awareness among targeted groups is essential. Educational campaigns stressing the deceptive techniques used to lure people and educating victims about their rights are critical. LSI runs a 24-hour hotline with trained consultants who register victims and help them to find needed support. They provide safety tips and information as to where victims can get emergency help if needed.

Monitoring has a preventive effect given that countries experience pressure to conform to international norms. Prevention efforts also require education in the source and destination countries. How to recognize victims of trafficking or the traffickers themselves and how to report such information are important. Disseminating information concerning the extent and types of forced labor can expand eyes and ears on the ground and save lives.

Social Support Services

This is LSI's core mission. This service depends on each individual victim's needs and the resources that can be garnered. Emergency and long-term care are provided. Basic necessities of food, clothing, and safe shelter, replacing identity documents and acquiring travel documents, psychological and emotional support and counseling, health care, legal aid and support, education, and job training or help in finding a job are among the services that nearly all victims need. They may also need transportation back home and help in resettling when they arrive. In 2013, Google, along with LSI, Polaris Project, and Liberty Asia, established an international information sharing collaboration between hotlines and nonprofits. This facilitates case management and victim protection across borders. Victims are starting over with nothing. Unless these services are provided, victims may never escape.

Compensation

Victims of trafficking have the right to compensation for material and immaterial damages. They rarely receive any. The COMP.ACT project coalition worked to identify and overcome obstacles that prevented victims from receiving compensation. It formed national coalitions to present recommendations to governments on achieving justice for victims. Many partners worked directly with lawyers to support victims in pursuing compensation claims. In the years from 2009 to 2012, they secured compensation for more than 50 victims. The highest award granted was €54,000.

As a result of their activity, intergovernmental organizations included compensation in their agendas. The EU Directive on combatting and preventing trafficking in human beings and the EU Strategy toward Eradication of Trafficking in Human Beings both cover compensation.

Source: Hoff (2011), La Strada International (n.d.).

MTV EXIT (End Exploitation and Trafficking) Foundation incorporated as a nonprofit in Europe in 2003. MTV and USAID joined forces in 2004 to produce MTV EXIT. Because youths are the most vulnerable to trafficking, the program maintains that youths are also the most powerful to end it. The program is a high-quality production of educational campaigns and youth trainings using social media, live events, and activities with rock musicians, movie and television stars, documentaries, dramas, animated videos, and videos of live events. MTV EXIT claims to have been the largest behavioral change campaign in the world. By 2014, it held 40 concerts in 18 different countries, hosted 1.8 million people through its live events, reached 83 million viewers of its programs, and sponsored 570 community outreach events. Detailed instructions are posted online to help local communities train youths aged 18 to 25 years using MTV videos and materials. Australia Aid and the Association of Southeast Asian Nations were also involved (MTV EXIT Foundation 2014; USAID n.d.). The 10-year MTV EXIT project ended in 2014, although concerts continue and videos are still available online.

TRAFFICKING IN WILDLIFE: FLORA AND FAUNA

Nearly every lucrative trade is a temptation for organized crime; trafficking in wildlife is one of the increasingly lucrative specialties. While globalization makes transportation of products and communication among criminal networks of buyers and sellers easier, it also circulates information on the purported medical and magical properties of wildlife, expanding their allure. Although poverty is a motivation for trafficking in wildlife on the supply side, increasing wealth is motivation on the market side. Consumer demand is the most important driver of wildlife trafficking. Increasing wealth enables people to pay high prices for a rare species that they believe can cure a disease or bring good fortune or simply so that they can have something rare and exotic as a symbol of their wealth. Rhino horn, more expensive pound for pound than heroin or cocaine, is consumed in Vietnam not just for its supposed curative powers but also to flaunt wealth (May 2017).

Thousands of animals are trafficked daily. The World Wildlife Seizure Database (World Wise) lists more than 7,000 species seized for illegal trafficking. No one species accounted for more than 6 percent of seizures (UNODC 2016). Parrots, freshwater turtles, and even great apes are among those animals that become pets to satisfy someone's need to have an exotic animal. Sea life provides caviar. Rhinos and elephants are prized for their ivory. Some, like the totoaba fish, are thought to have medicinal value. As with other crimes, harm extends beyond the immediate victims. The totoaba are found only in the Gulf of California. Once plentiful, they were overfished due to demand for their swim bladder, used in traditional Chinese medicines and soups. One totoaba sale to a trafficker can net a Mexican fisherman one month's salary. Illegal trade in totoaba also threatens other marine life that gets caught in the nets. Among them is the vaquita, a small dolphin that is the most endangered marine animal in the world. Only about 100 are thought to still exist (Bale 2016).

Illegal animal trafficking is second only to habitat destruction in its danger to animal species. The threat to animals whose populations are being decimated is important in its own right. There are other costs as well. Wildlife trafficking undermines conservation efforts. It undermines the economic viability of communities that depend on wildlife biodiversity and ecotourism. By bypassing public health controls, it has the potential to introduce zoonotic infectious diseases into human populations, domestic animals, and other wildlife. Invasive species, such as the vine mealy bug, damage crops. Like other organized and transnational crime, wildlife trafficking undermines the rule of law and fuels corruption. It threatens global security.

Worldwide illegal animal trafficking is the third largest illicit trade in goods, after guns and drugs. The perception that it is a low-risk, high-return crime attracts organized crime groups, making trafficking in wildlife increasingly lethal to both animals and humans. The value of the trade is impossible to measure. About a decade ago, the USDOS estimated a cost of U.S. $10 billion (Bergman 2009). A number of recent estimates placed it at about $20 billion in 2012 (Havocscope 2016).

Fairly reliable global estimates on trafficking and poaching are available for the largest animals—elephants, rhinos, and tigers. African elephants are poached at an unsustainable rate. Poachers killed more than 100,000 in just three years from 2010 to 2012 (Udell 2015). Their population declined 20 percent in the last decade, dwindling to 400,000 (USDOS 2015). More than 1,000 rhinos on average were poached each year from 2012 to 2015 just in South Africa alone (USDOS 2015; Udell 2015). Of the five rhino species in the world, three are endangered. Only 5,000 black rhinos are left in the wild. Their slaughter began with rumors that their horns, ground into dust, could cure cancer. However, the alleged magic keratin is the same as is found in fingernails (Mathewson 2016).

CONSIDER THIS
PANGOLINS IN DEMAND

Little heard of in the West as of yet, pangolins are in high demand elsewhere. Described as artichokes with legs, their scales, which are used in Chinese medicine and sell for up to $6,000 a pound, have long been valued. Now, their meat is considered a delicacy. In the last 10 years, more than a million pangolins have been trafficked. They are the most trafficked animal in the world. With a diminishing supply in Asia, traffickers are turning to Africa. All eight species are being considered for the endangered species list.

Sources: Mathewson (2016); Northam (2015).

PHOTO 8.3 Considered a delicacy, all eight species of this little-known mammal are endangered. The adult pangolin resembles an armadillo.

2630ben/iStockphoto.

For many people, it is hard to imagine the grandeur of a tiger being used as decoration. But for others, it is a sign of status, putting tigers on the brink of extinction. Already three of eight subspecies are extinct, and the remaining five are endangered. The last sign of a tiger in Cambodia was in 2010. Vietnam's tiger population may be 10 or fewer (Global Tiger Initiative Secretariat 2013).

Habitat loss related to development is one cause for tigers' decline, but the main threat is poaching. Their bones are used in traditional Asian medicines, and their pelts (the most frequently seized item) and other body parts, such as teeth and claws, are made into decorative items. From 2000 to 2012, there were 645 seizures of tiger parts, representing about 1,425 tigers, across 12 countries. India has the largest tiger population and was the country with the most seizures. China and Vietnam, with small wild tiger populations, are zones of large consumption. As with other illegal goods, the seizures are only a fraction of those traded (Stoner and Pervushina 2013). In 2010, tiger range countries met to devise an enhanced surveying and protection plan involving governments, NGOs, local communities, and philanthropists. The good news is that the tide may be turning for tigers; for the first time in 100 years, the tiger population may be growing. The World Wide Fund for Nature (2016) reported recently that from 2010 to 2016 the tiger population had increased from 3,200 to 3,890.

The Special Case of Latin America

While many of the big animals come from Asia and Africa, Latin America is the source of 25 percent of wildlife seizures. As one of the most biodiverse regions of the world, Latin America is particularly vulnerable to wildlife trafficking. Ecuador, for example, has 1,600 known species of birds in comparison with the 900 of the continental United States (Bergman 2009). One bird, a wild scarlet macaw, could fetch U.S. $150, more than people could make hauling other cargo up and down the rivers in Ecuador in a year (Bergman 2009). Brazil is reportedly home to 15 to 20 percent of the world's biodiversity and the source of 5 to 15 percent of the illegal trade in wildlife. In Colombia, wild animal trafficking is a $17 million industry—the fourth largest illegal industry after guns, drugs, and human trafficking. Animal trafficking from Colombia follows the same routes to Europe and the United States as do the drugs. In just one year, 2012, 46,000 illegally trafficked animals were rescued in Colombia, far fewer than were trafficked (Wight 2013).

Birds, reptiles, turtles for their eggs and meat, caimans for their skins, marine life such as shark fins and the totoaba bladders, sea cucumbers, and conch as well as monkeys, frogs, scorpions, spiders, and even jaguars are trafficked. Although many are traded domestically, there is a thriving international trade as well. Birds are the main commodity on Latin America's illegal market, making up 80 percent of Brazil's illegal market. Of those, 60 percent serve the domestic market and 40 percent serve the international market. In Mexico, it is 90 percent of 65,000 to 78,500 parrots. That still leaves 6,500 to 7,850 parrots for the international market. A wild finch from Guyana would sell for $5 locally. In the United States, it would bring $500 to $10,000, depending on the appeal of its song. About 73 million sharks are killed to supply the global shark fin market. Shark fin soup, a sign of status and wealth, can sell for $100 a bowl in China (Neme 2015). It is not hard to see how wildlife trafficking became a multi-billion-dollar business for TOC (Tables 8.7 and 8.8).

The United States is a destination country for much of the illegal trade in wildlife, especially that coming from Latin America. From 2004 to 2013, U.S. consumers imported 7,111 illegal animals, 47,914 illegal wildlife products, and 81,526 illegal pounds of wildlife. Demand was highest for meat, eggs, and shoes (Goyenechea and Indenbaum 2015).

A CLOSER LOOK
THE GLOBAL WILDLIFE MARKET

TABLE 8.7 Poacher Versus Consumer Prices (U.S.$)

From poacher to consumer, the price of wildlife increases exponentially.

	Commodity	What the Poacher Receives	What the Consumer Pays	Rate of Markup (%)
Live	Macaw	$2 to $20	$800 to $10,000	29,900% to 49,900%
	Chimpanzee	$50	$20,000	39,900%
	Falcon	$500	$50,000 to $100,000	9,900% to 19,900%
Product	Pangolin meat (per kilogram)	$22.50	$250 to $350	1,011% to 1,456%
	Bear gall bladder (whole)	$100 to $150	$5,000 to $10,000	4,900% to 6,567%
	Tiger pelt	$1,500	$16,000	967%

Source: Transnational Crime and the Developing World by Channing May (https://illicittrade.com/reports/downloads/Transnational_Crime-final.pdf) licensed under CC BY 4.0 (https://creativecommons.org/licenses/by/4.0/).

(Continued)

(Continued)

TABLE 8.8   Estimated Value of Select Illegal Trade in Wildlife

Based on these and other estimates of the United Nations Office on Drugs and Crime, illegal trade in wildlife is thought to be the third largest revenue stream of transnational organized crime.

Animal or Animal Part	Value of Trade
Ivory	$100 million value of annual trade
	$15 per kilogram in Africa
	Up to $850 per kilogram in Asia
	Carved ivory is not priced by weight
Rhino horn	$8 million value of annual trade (price in source country may be only 1 percent of final retail price)
Powdered rhino horn	Up to $20,000–30,000 per kilogram
Tiger parts	$5 million value of annual trade
Tiger skin	Up to $20,000 in China for one skin
Tiger bones	Up to $1,200 per kilogram
Indonesian timber	$4 billion value of annual trade

Source: Adapted from "Environmental Crime: trafficking in wildlife and timber" by UNODC, ©United Nations.

Cost to the Ecosystem

Trafficking in wildlife robs a country of some of its most valuable resources. Whereas the sale of protected wildlife is illegal, in many countries indigenous communities depend on these animals and plants for food and medicines. Poaching deprives them of important resources and a potential revenue stream in ecotourism. While exotic animals bring extremely high prices in their final destination, the community of their origin receives very little.

When animals are poached and their natural numbers are reduced, not only is species diversity in terms of one animal threatened, but also entire ecosystems become unbalanced, harming many more. Tigers, for example, are at the top of their food chain. If tigers become extinct, the biodiversity and balance of the entire ecosystem would become unbalanced. The populations of deer, wild boar, and other tiger prey would increase rapidly. This would deplete the vegetation on which they, smaller animals, and insects depend because regrowth would not keep up with consumption. Not only could the forest be lost, but

also forest animals and insects would probably migrate to nearby areas—most likely agricultural—thereby threatening another human food supply.

Contemporary poachers have little regard for the ecosystems in which they operate. Other species than those targeted are often killed in the process of capturing the prize.

Like other forms of transnational crime, wildlife trafficking contributes to corruption and violence, bringing greater harm to the ecosystem. Traps and nets do not discriminate; they capture prey as well as other animals. In capturing some birds, whole trees are felled.

The Legal Framework for Combatting Trafficking in Wildlife

The Convention on International Trade in Endangered Species of Wild Fauna and Flora (CITES) is the main international instrument for combatting traffic in endangered species. It subjects international trade to controls with respect to species threatened with extinction, species whose trade must be controlled to prevent their use in ways that threaten their survival, and species under protection in at least one partner country that has asked for cooperation from others in controlling trade in those species. CITES was first drafted in 1963 but did not go into force until 1975. By 2016, there were 181 parties to CITES and 35,000 species under some degree of protection.

Despite international treaties, convergence in domestic laws is weak. For a treaty such as CITES to be effective, the convention must be enforced at the national level. Using Indonesia as just one example, tigers are listed at a sub-species level in domestic law and only two are named. Before any prosecution may occur, the sub-species needs to be proven. With only two listed, forensic tests may be inconclusive and charges must be dropped (Stoner and Pervushina 2013). Because trade in certain species is legal in some countries and illegal in others, enforcement of the law is complicated. Furthermore, in many countries there are technicalities that make certain kinds of trade legal but others illegal, even with respect to the same species. For example, in many Latin American countries, selling sharks is allowed, but shark finning (removing the fins) is not allowed. Some traffickers have gotten around the law by leaving the fins attached to the spine, "shark spining." In Ecuador, "incidental" catching of sharks is legal, but intentionally catching them is not (Neme 2015).

In 2012, the UN recognized trafficking in wildlife as a new form of TOC, made it an issue of highest concern, and called for a greater response. In illicit trade in tigers, roughly 10 percent of the suspects, but probably significantly more, are part of organized crime groups. In Russia

and Nepal, major organized crime elements have been identified in the trade (Stoner and Pervushina 2013).

Interpol established the Environmental Compliance and Enforcement Committee[4] in 2012 with 190 member countries. Interpol partners with national and international organizations on "projects" and "operations" that cover many of the endangered species of fauna and flora. Environmental "projects" include Predator on "big cats" and other species, Project Wisdom for elephants, Leaf for timber, Scale for fishing, and Eden for waste, particularly electronic (Interpol 2016c). Its operations cover nearly every continent. Interpol operations are precisely targeted and facilitate information sharing and cooperation in enforcement as needed in the case of any transnational crimes (Interpol 2016b). In another action, Interpol joined with four other intergovernmental organizations[5] to form the International Consortium on Combatting Wildlife Crime. It supports national and regional law enforcement. Created during the International Tiger Forum in 2010, it models similar initiatives that emphasize cooperation across agency and national borders—local, regional, and global efforts.

Transnational criminal groups do not necessarily specialize. Making money in one crime can finance illegal activities in another area. In 2011, Europol linked the Rathkeale Rovers (aka Irish Travelers), an Irish organized crime group, to 67 rhino horn thefts networked across 15 European countries. Using traditional organized crime tactics of intimidation, aggravated burglary, and violence, the group preyed on antique dealers, museums, zoos, private collections, and virtually any sources. The group sold through auction houses throughout Europe. Its activities

CONSIDER THIS
CRUSH AND BURN

In 2015, the United States, China, Ethiopia, Mozambique, Thailand, Republic of the Congo, and the United Arab Emirates crushed or burned all, or a significant portion of, their stockpiles of seized ivory. This global demonstration raised awareness of wildlife trafficking and showed that trafficking will not be tolerated (Welch 2015).

In May 2016, Kenya had its biggest ivory burn ever. President Uhuru Kenyatta lit the match and set fire to U.S. $105 million worth of ivory. He demonstrated Kenya's zero tolerance for poaching and the terrorists that transnational

crimes such as poaching, human trafficking, and drugs and arms trafficking attract (Gettleman 2016).

In 2017, two tons of ivory jewelry, statues, and trinkets representing tusks of about 100 elephants was crushed in New York's Central Park. Many of the pieces were extremely valuable, including a pair of ivory tower sets worth U.S. $850,000. Since 1989, more than 270 metric tons of ivory, representing tusks of about 20,000 elephants, was burned or crushed by 22 nations (Associated Press 2017).

were not limited to ivory or Europe. The group also trafficked in drugs, counterfeit products, money laundering, fraud, and organized robbery. Beyond Europe, the Rathkeale Rovers committed crimes in North and South America, China, South Africa, and Australia (Udell 2015).

The secrecy of financial enterprises enables illegal transnational criminal activities. Shell companies, jurisdictions that protect the privacy of financial matters over the public good, allow transnational crime to flourish—without the easy flow of money across borders, often protected by national laws, transnational crime would be harder to conduct and easier to prosecute. This is discussed in Chapter 9.

SUMMARY

Transnational crime is one of the most serious threats to human security in the 21st century. The scale of these crimes in loss of life and money is staggering. Human trafficking and trafficking in organs are among the fastest growing crimes. Desperation drives people to risk slavery for themselves or their children, lured by promises of jobs that never materialize. Literally worked to death, they are deprived of any chance at life. Their countries of origin lose as well, robbed of many of their working-aged populations, robbed of their young, and leaving many children orphaned and many husbands and wives widowed. Others, also driven by desperation, pay smugglers for passage to refuge or pay off a debtor with a part of their body. Others, equally desperate, buy the organ. Both risk life-threatening complications. Ultimately, ending these crimes and wildlife trafficking requires ending the desperation—the poverty—that drives people to victimization, thereby ending the supply.

Eliminating the market would also put an end to transnational crime. If people were unwilling to buy another human, human trafficking would not exist. Probably only scientific advances will end the desperation of people selling their organs. Many of these people probably do not think of themselves as criminals. Public education to help people recognize victims of trafficking and public exposure (as well as just punishment) of those who have kept victims captive both are important in diminishing the market.

Convergence of international law concerning human and wildlife trafficking is essential. Particularly important is convergence in the financial industry so that money cannot be so easily laundered or hidden. If the profit can be taken out of trafficking, there will be little motive.

DISCUSSION

1. What features of modern life and globalization contribute to increases in human trafficking. In wildlife trafficking?

2. What is the role of poverty in international crimes? Consider human and wildlife trafficking especially.

3. How does convergence in laws across countries help to combat trafficking?

4. Why should the global community be concerned about trafficking in wildlife?

5. How does transnational crime contribute to corruption?

ON YOUR OWN

1. The Polaris Project collects data on human trafficking. It also educates the public about how to recognize victims of human trafficking. Based on the information on its website, what are indicators that you could watch for to recognize a potential victim? You can also reference the UNODC.

https://polarisproject.org/human-trafficking

https://www.unodc.org/pdf/HT_indicators_E_LOWRES.pdf

2. Analyze the USAID and/or other countries' programs to combat human trafficking. Does the program take a holistic approach?

3. Investigate up-to-date statistics on wildlife trafficking. Has any progress been reported? Have there been changes in laws or in enforcement techniques? The World Wildlife Reports are a place to begin investigation. The 2016 report can be found at this URL:

https://www.unodc.org/documents/data-and-analysis/wildlife/World_Wildlife_Crime_Report_2016_final.pdf

4. Analyze news reports of the connection between human trafficking and terrorism.

NOTES

1. As a point of clarification, the "International Classification of Crime" is used for statistical purposes to allow for better coordination across countries and includes serious and "non-serious" crimes, many of which are not covered by the convention.

2. Reporting is a requirement of the Palermo Protocols to which 173 countries are party.

3. The 2015 Associated Press investigation led to the freeing of 2,000 slave laborers. The four journalists—

Robin McDowell, Margie Mason, Martha Mendoza, and Esther Htusan—won the Bartlett and Steele Award for Investigative Business Journalism (Easton 2015).

4. This replaced the Environmental Crime Committee.

5. The five organizations are CITES Secretariat, Interpol, UNODC, the World Bank, and the World Customs Organization.

9

Transnational Property Crimes

A RISKY BUSINESS: SELLING ILLEGAL ARMS TO THE U.S. GOVERNMENT

Efraim Diveroli was only 19 years old when he enlisted his friend, David Packouz, 23, to partner with him in his company, AEY. It was 2005. Packouz was a massage therapist in Miami. Diveroli, who had worked for his uncle's arms business, struck out on his own in 2004. Diveroli's strategy was simple. Rather than go for a high volume of customers as most dealers would, he would pursue only one—the U.S. government. Daily, he scoured the federal government's postings for bids for arms contracts. By 2005, he had close to U.S. $2 million in the bank. Impressed, Packouz joined him.

In 2006, the U.S. government was equipping the Afghan military with arms and ammunition to battle al Qaeda and the Taliban and was outsourcing the job. Diveroli and Packouz, working from their apartments equipped with cellphones and an internet connection (and getting high most of the time), scoured the world for low-cost suppliers and strategies for getting the arms to Afghanistan. Despite a record including risky corner cutting and some failed government contracts, AEY procured a U.S. $298 million contract in January 2007 by outbidding major league competitors. The company became the major supplier of munitions to Afghani police and military.

Finding contacts throughout Eastern Europe, including those on the federal list of illegal arms dealers, AEY connected suppliers with transport and with the military in Afghanistan. Diveroli and Packouz dealt with military and government officials daily in and outside of the United States. They found cut-rate deals on old and obsolete stockpiles of the former Communist bloc. As long as the equipment worked, they said, it didn't matter how old it was. Using a shell company registered in Cyprus as an intermediary, AEY could purchase cheaper, even if far less than optimal, weaponry from Albania. A legal trick used often in illegal sales, this disguised the origin and endpoint of the sales. Another trick Diveroli tried was to rebox the ammunition to disguise its manufacture

LEARNING OBJECTIVES

After completing this chapter, students will be able to do the following:

9.1 Evaluate the strengths and weaknesses of the legal framework for combatting transnational organized crime

9.2 Understand the individual and societal level vulnerabilities to victimization

9.3 Understand the role of legitimate businesses and consumers in supporting transnational organized crime

9.4 Assess the global and national security risks posed by transnational organized crime

9.5 Propose measures to combat transnational crime, including a global legal framework

in China in 1966. He convinced a friend, Alex Podrizki, that because it was procured in Albania, it did not violate U.S. law against munitions procurement from China.

When the boxes were split open at their destination in Afghanistan, the ammunition spilled out onto the floor. It was obviously old, and the origin of every casing was marked. An Afghani colonel exclaimed, "This is what they give us for fighting. . . . It makes us worried because too much of it is junk" (Chivers 2008). A U.S. military lieutenant colonel reported that none of the ammunition had misfired but that some was in such poor condition that it was discarded (Chivers, Schmitt, and Wood 2008).

A congressional investigative committee issued a 28-page report of its findings detailing AEY's known violations and government failures in the procurement process (Congressional Committee on Oversight and Government Reform 2008). Both Diveroli and Packouz were convicted on several federal charges of fraud. Diveroli began a four-year sentence in 2011. Packouz was sentenced to seven months of house arrest, and Podrizki was sentenced to four months of house arrest. Both received probation following their house arrest (Elfrink 2016).

Source: As reported by Lawson (2011), Chivers (2008), and Chivers, Schmitt, and Wood (2008).

In many respects, the world is a lawless land. When Emile Durkheim wrote at the turn of the 20th century, he warned of anomie. The world was undergoing very rapid social changes. Industry was replacing agriculture as the primary source of jobs. Agricultural workers and artisans were leaving farms and their craft shops behind in rural areas and villages to move to cities and work in factories.

It was the most massive movement of people and rapid change in lifestyle that the world had known. Social, cultural, and economic dislocation characterized the times as the close-knit communities of familiar people, routines, and lifestyles gave way to the poverty, drudgery, filth, anonymity, and powerlessness of city life and factory jobs. The city, Durkheim saw, was a place of turmoil. Crime and suicide were high.

The world is in the throes of another massive dislocation wrought by globalization and another seismic economic transition. In developing societies, urbanization is proceeding even more rapidly than it did during the Industrial Revolution. Developed societies experience social and cultural dislocation as the service/information economy replaces manufacturing. The internet, as well as the "darknet" that lurks encrypted within it, provides new opportunities veiled in secrecy and anonymity for global trafficking of most any commodity from guns to people.

Crime is high in developing societies, much of it driven by the markets for illegal goods in the developed world. The global supply and demand chain of illegal goods and services fuels and creates violent conflicts and encourages corruption in government. Emerging transnational crimes—cybercrime, identity-related crime, trafficking in cultural property, environmental crimes, organ trafficking, fraudulent medicine, and piracy—diversify the global criminal economy beyond the traditional weapons and drugs.

Many more transnational crimes exist than can be discussed in this chapter. As regulations are enacted or tightened, organized crime groups find new revenue sources by skirting them. Environmental crimes such as toxic dumping and trade in some of the exotic or endangered species grew out of such new environmental regulations. Sales of stolen art and cultural artifacts generate revenue of about U.S. $1.2 to $1.6 billion a year (May 2017). Resources such as timber, oil, and precious metals and jewels, practically any good or service that can be provided legally, is also provided illegally by transnational groups.

Although the chapter is organized by types of crimes, transnational criminal groups do not specialize. Any one group might be involved in drug trafficking, human trafficking, counterfeiting, or any other combination of crimes. The darknet provides illicit transactions with a veil of secrecy provided by encryption. Illicit drug sales over the darknet increased by about 50 percent a year over the last few years. Ecstasy, cannabis, LSD, and new psychoactive substances such as "bath salts" and K2 were the drugs most often purchased online (United Nations Office on Drugs and Crime [UNODC] 2017a).

The processes of globalization that empower criminal network growth proceed much more quickly than the capacity of law enforcement to prevent them. It is not an exaggeration to claim that transnational organized crime is a security risk to every country in the world. The crux of much of the problem is regular people. In many of the cybercrimes, we are unwilling victims. But in many others, the consumer market—the demand for illegal and cheaper goods and services—is the engine that drives transnational organized crime.

THE WAR ON DRUG TRAFFICKING

More is known about drug trafficking than about human trafficking. Nevertheless, it is hard to fathom the global volume of illegal drug trafficking, the many networks of people, and the violence and harm involved. Drugs and drug trafficking kill people, provide financial support for organized criminal and terrorist groups, erode the fabric of society, and threaten governments.

Attitudes and perspectives on the use of drugs shift as policies succeed or fail and mores evolve. From regulation to criminalization, from tolerance to punishment, from seeing drug use as a personal choice to a moral failure to a sickness, effective strategies to reduce harm are hard to develop.

From the 16th century to the 19th century, opium was commercialized by European powers as they enlarged their commercial and colonial presence in Asia—first the Portuguese, then the Dutch, and finally (and most expansively) the English. Throughout the 19th century, they encouraged cultivation and opium became one of the most significant commodities in the international market, so significant that it reversed the British trade balance with China. The British demand for exquisite Chinese silks, china, and teas resulted in a trade deficit. Although they were well aware of the harm opium caused, the British solved the deficit by selling opium transited through India to the Chinese. Realizing the human cost as well as depletion of their stock of silver, the Chinese attempted many times in the 18th and 19th centuries to end opium sales. In the mid-19th century, the question was settled by war. Although the British public and many powerful politicians opposed opium sales (It was illegal in Britain) and did not want to wage war to protect the opium trade, British merchants and some free trade advocates did not want to lose such a lucrative market. The British parliament ultimately voted for war. China lost the opium wars (and lost Hong Kong). By the turn of the 20th century, one quarter of the Chinese male population was dependent on opium (UNODC n.d. b).

By the turn of the 20th century, narcotics production was at record heights in Asia. The British were not the only colonial powers using their colonies in the opium trade. Spain and the Netherlands both had significant economic interests in narcotics trade. For more than 50 years, along with the British, they cultivated and sold opium throughout Southeast Asia. The Dutch and British pharmaceutical companies expanded coca production from South America into Asia as well. Peru's development strategy was based on export of coca paste (Buxton 2010).

In a twist of fate, Chinese immigrants migrating to California in the 1800s brought opium introduced by Europe with them. In New York in the early 20th century, Chinatown was the center of the East Coast black market in opium.

Evolution of the International Narcotics Regime

The United States had kept out of the narcotics trade and debates. Increasing rates of addiction in the United States, including to morphine and other derivatives of opium, prompted President Theodore Roosevelt to initiate the International Opium (Shanghai) Commission—the first attempt at the international regulation of drugs.[1] It convened in Shanghai, China, in 1909 to develop common policy and coordinate international efforts to stem drug use and trade. Thirteen countries attended the meetings: the United States, Austria–Hungary, China, France, Germany, the United Kingdom, Italy, Japan, the Netherlands, Iran (then Persia), Portugal, Russia, and Thailand (then Siam). Whereas the Americans and Chinese were hoping for universal prohibition, the commission issued a less vehemently opposed statement. It affirmed all the countries' intent to regulate or prohibit the use of opium for other than medical reasons, to gradually suppress opium smoking, and to prohibit exporting opium to countries where it was illegal (UNODC 1959). Unfortunately, in the United States the debate had been fueled by racism and moralizing directed against the Chinese and African Americans. The attitude shifted from tolerance to punishment and criminalization.

Three years later, as follow-up to the Shanghai Commission, the Hague Opium Convention was signed. Europe, China, and the United States had varying views. The European powers profited handsomely from lucrative markets for drugs in their overseas colonies and in the pharmaceutical market in Europe and the Americas. Furthermore, the "war on alcohol" between gangs and organized crime and law enforcement in the United States did little to inspire confidence in the benefits of criminalization of drugs, which China and the United States favored.

Europe resisted. Both China and the United States walked out of the preparatory talks. However, the United States continued its crusade against drugs[2] at the League of Nations, succeeding in passing the 1936 convention that criminalized certain drug offenses internationally. It was a hollow victory; only 13 nations signed the convention (Jelsma 2011).

From the first Hague Conference, through the interwar period, and after World War II, the League of Nations and subsequently the United Nations (UN) adopted a number of drug conventions, each adding to the international regime and scheduling drugs according to the harm perceived by the World Health Organization (WHO) commission. In 1961, the UN consolidated the conventions.

Three major international drug control treaties form the focus of the global regime to combat drug trafficking:

- The Single Convention on Narcotic Drugs of 1961 (as amended in 1972)

- The Convention on Psychotropic Substances of 1971

- The United Nations Convention against Illicit Traffic in Narcotic Drugs and Psychotropic Substances of 1988

Together, these treaties codify measures to combat trafficking and facilitate, albeit imperfectly, international cooperation, particularly in prosecuting cultivation and related money laundering. The conventions established two international organizations charged with oversight functions:

- The Commission on Narcotic Drugs is the central policy-making body. It recommends new strategies and policies for combatting trafficking and recommends new drugs for addition to the conventions. It consists of representatives from 53 member states elected to four-year terms.

- The International Narcotics Control Board is an independent board of 13 members elected to five-year terms on the basis of their personal expertise. They serve as individuals, not member country representatives. Among their major duties, they monitor implementation of the conventions and make recommendations to states.

The conventions and organizations emphasize criminalization of the supply chain. The U.S. "war on drugs," declared in 1971 under President Richard Nixon and expanded under President Ronald Reagan, instituted a hardline approach—expanding drug control forces and instituting mandatory sentences for drug offenses. It dramatically increased the incarceration rate, disproportionately for minorities (UNODC n.d. b)—a legacy that persists.

Despite the punitive government approach, the overall mood in the United States and the world was more forgiving. More money was devoted to treatment than to law enforcement. Many countries, individual U.S. states, and the U.S. federal government considered legalizing marijuana. In the mid-1980s and 1990s, the mood in the United States swung back to law enforcement. The war on drugs was back on full-scale in the country, with militarization of drug law enforcement units and mass incarceration for drug-related offenses. This continued through most of the first decade of the 21st century.

Not until the 2010s would the mood begin to shift again. With the opioid death[3] epidemic, most alarming in the United States but significant in middle-income and other developed countries as well, the tide may be turning to tolerance and treatment within countries, while the war on trafficking still rages internationally.

THE HUMAN COST OF ILLEGAL DRUGS

Death by Drugs

As with other forms of trafficking, if there weren't a market, there would not be a crime. Misuse of prescription opioids (primarily hydrocodone, oxycodone, and tramadol) and heroin and fentanyl use are at crisis levels in North America and are on the increase globally. The market for drugs is so large, and the risks so high, as to warrant a detailed examination. Although the rate of drug use has been fairly stable, ranging from a low of 4.6 percent in 2008 to a high of 5.3 percent in 2015, the volume of the global market for illegal drugs grew by 47 million people, from 208 million in 2006 to 255 million in 2015. The number of problem users increased 3.5 million since 2006 and is at nearly 30 million,[4] or 11 percent of users in 2015 (UNODC 2017a).

Drug-related deaths are rising globally. Reporting criteria by country vary because some report only overdoses and others report deaths attributed to drug use disorders. The UNODC claims that the estimate for 2015 of 190,900 deaths probably underestimates the actual number, perhaps by as much as half. North Americans accounted for more than 25 percent of these deaths in 2015 (UNODC 2017a). Both the United States and Canada have experienced alarming increases in overdose deaths since the turn of the 21st century, with heroin and the synthetic opioid fentanyl causing the majority of overdoses in both countries. The market share of fentanyl continues to surge and is reportedly twice as likely to result in overdose as heroin and eight times as likely as injecting other opioids (UNODC 2017d). Carfentanil, a synthetic opioid that is 10,000 times stronger than morphine and 100 times stronger than fentanyl, made it into the consumer market in 2016. Overdose deaths in the United States soared above 64,000 in 2016, up from 52,404 in 2015. The number for 2017 was expected to be higher yet (Figure 9.1).

The United Kingdom accounts for a large portion of overdose deaths, up 10 percent from 2014 to 2015. England, Wales, and Scotland all reported increases of 10 to 15 percent from 2014 to 2015. The aging addict population and purity of heroin are the most likely causes of the increase.

As with other social problems, the rates of overdose deaths in the United States and Canada vary widely across regions. In 2016, only two Canadian provinces[5] had rates of more than 150 per million, while several had rates of less than 50 per million. The British Columbia overdose death rate was 285 per million in 2016 (Health Canada 2017; UNODC 2017a). In the United States, 10 states had between 210 and 415 overdose deaths per million in 2015. West Virginia had 415 per million, but some states had as low as 69 per million (Centers for Disease Control and Prevention 2016).

Australia is witnessing a similar crisis. Overdoses among 30- to 59-year-olds doubled from the early 2000s to 2015; most were fentanyl driven, although overdoses from amphetamines doubled as well. In Australia, Queensland and West Australia had the highest rates (Pennington Institute 2017). A number of studies have demonstrated the relationship between overdose and economic decline. In the United States, on average, a 1 percent increase in unemployment is related to a 7 percent increase in overdose emergency room visits and a 3.6 percent increase in overdose deaths per 100,000. The relationships reflect adverse relationships among whites in particular (Hollingsworth, Ruhm, and Simon 2017). In the United States, Canada, and Australia, the cities, provinces, and states of the highest overdose rates are those most associated with economic decline, joblessness, and a cumulative effect of diminishing life chances (Figure 9.2) (Case and Deaton 2017).[6]

While the greatest percentages of people in drug treatment in North America, Europe, and Asia are seeking treatment for opioids, in Latin America and the Caribbean it is cocaine and in Africa it is tranquilizers and cannabis. Cocaine overdoses are also on the rise globally, primarily due to lacing cocaine with fentanyl. Overdoses from the cocaine–fentanyl combination doubled from 1999 to 2015 (UNODC 2017a).

Information on opiate and opioid use in Asia and Africa is limited. Opioid use is increasing, however, in some African countries. Tramadol is the most abused in Africa, but heroin use is increasing as well. Running counter to the overall global trend, heroin use is continuing to increase in North America and Africa, while decreasing in other regions. The sharpest increase was in Africa (Figure 9.3), probably related to the increasing traffic on the "southern route" out of Afghanistan. In Asia, heroin use declined but is still above the 2000 levels. Trafficking patterns seem to also be related to increases of

FIGURE 9.1   Overdose Deaths in the United States: 1999 to 2015

Overdose deaths from synthetics other than methadone, primarily fentanyl, skyrocketed, accounting for twice the deaths from heroin in 2015. Overdose deaths rose to more than 64,000 in 2016.

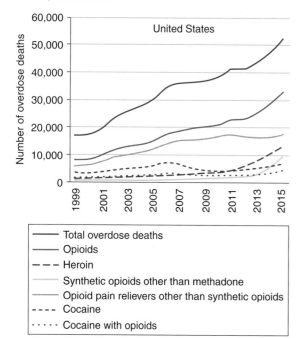

Source: United Nations Office on Drugs and Crime, *World Drug Report 2017* (ISBN: 978-92-1-148291-1, eISBN. 978-92-1-000020-0, United Nations publication, Sales No. E.17.XI.6).

A CLOSER LOOK
DRUG-RELATED MORTALITY

FIGURE 9.2   Drug-Related Mortality by Region

Drug-related mortality is far above average in North America and Oceania.

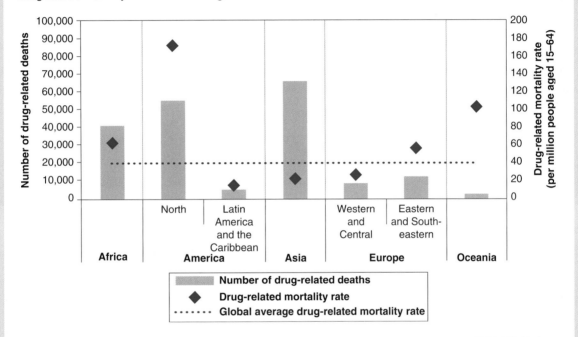

Legend:
- Number of drug-related deaths
- ◆ Drug-related mortality rate
- ······· Global average drug-related mortality rate

Source: United Nations Office on Drugs and Crime, *World Drug Report 2017* (ISBN: 978-92-1-148291-1, eISBN: 978-92-1-060623-3, United Nations publication, Sales No. E.17.XI.6).

heroin use in some of Afghanistan's neighbors, including Iran, Pakistan, Tajikistan, and the United Arab Emirates (UNODC 2017b). Overdose statistics are not available.

Overdose is not the only route to early death by drugs. Drugs exacerbate or cause disease and chronic conditions that lead to early death. It is difficult to estimate the precise toll of infectious diseases on drug users because people's associations with drugs are often unknown. The estimates here represent a median within a range.

People who inject drugs (PWID) are most at risk for contracting infectious diseases that cost years of life. HIV, hepatitis, and tuberculosis are the primary killers. Globally, 11.8 million people (ranging from 8.6 to 17.4 million)

injected drugs in 2015. China, Pakistan, Russia, and the United States together account for more than half. Among PWID, more than half have contracted hepatitis C—more than 6 million people. Hepatitis C is even more debilitating on a global scale than HIV; in 2013 alone, it cost about 225,000 lives and more than 7 million disability-adjusted life years. HIV is less common among PWID than hepatitis; prevalence is rising, however, and reached 19.9 percent in 2014, up from 13.2 percent in 2009. HIV attributable to PWID cost more than 50,000 deaths in 2013 and close to 3 million disability-adjusted life years. People who use drugs, whether they inject or not, are particularly susceptible to contracting tuberculosis, usually

A CLOSER LOOK
HEROIN USE

FIGURE 9.3   Heroin Use Perception Index, by Region

Africa experienced a sharp and fairly steady rise in heroin use from 2000 to 2015.

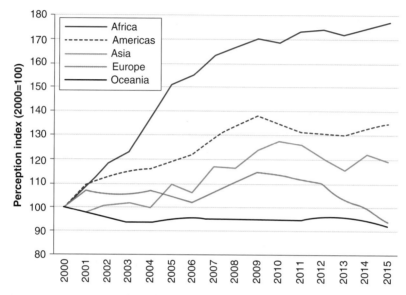

Source: United Nations Office on Drugs and Crime, *World Drug Report 2017* (ISBN: 978-92-1-148291-1, eISBN: 978-92-1-060623-3, United Nations publication, Sales No. E.17.XI.6).

related to living conditions such as homelessness, poverty, and incarceration. Among PWID, the prevalence is even higher, about 8 percent in comparison with 0.2 percent of the general population (UNODC 2017a).

There are effective treatments for HIV, hepatitis, and tuberculosis. New treatments for hepatitis C cure 90 to 95 percent of chronic cases within months. Australia, France, Georgia, and Morocco offer universal treatment for hepatitis. Australia made PWID and prison populations a priority to slow the spread. Ending tuberculosis is a Sustainable Development Goal, and the WHO is launching a global strategy. Stalling the global effort is that those who use drugs are unlikely to be treated. Due to either ignorance of infection or availability of treatment, lack of access or resources, or stigma, the most vulnerable are least likely to be treated.

DEATH AND VIOLENCE ALONG TRAFFICKING ROUTES

Drug trafficking creates war zones. Whether rival transnational criminal organizations battling one another for control of a country or rival gangs battling for control of a neighborhood, the routes of drug trafficking are deadly. When involved with rebel or terrorist groups and activities, the toll of violence in drug trafficking—as with all transnational crime—is compounded. While a few people may become very wealthy and powerful, most people are left poorer and more desperate.

Drug trafficking is more easily cultivated along routes already in disarray. Misfortunes of history and geography coalesce, resulting in the drug cultivating regions and trafficking patterns. Civil war and violence destabilized many of the regions along the drug route corridors before they became major highways for illicit trade. For decades, civil conflicts and transnational crime were intimate partners.

Cocaine and the Americas

Needing high altitudes and high humidity, coca plant cultivation is extremely difficult outside of Colombia, Peru, and Bolivia, the major three countries where it is grown. Among nearly every other South and Central American country, decades of war between authoritarian governments and rebel factions created conditions of disorder that facilitated, but did not cause, coca cultivation and related drug trafficking. For more than half a century, four-pronged war raged in Colombia; Revolutionary Armed Forces of Colombia (FARC) and ELN (National Liberation Army) rebels, the government's military, the powerful drug cartels, and paramilitaries working for landowners and oil and gas companies battled in shifting alliances, giving the country one of the highest murder rates in the world.

FARC grew out of the peasant movements of the 1920s. Plantation owners dominated the lands for coffee cultivation. Peasants had no land rights and worked under harsh conditions. The peasant movement evolved into FARC, formed in 1964, which grew to be a formidable armed rebel organization by the 1990s. The jungles became war zones, the government fighting peasant rebels, with many peasant farmers caught in the crossfire. In the meantime, peasants pushed off farmlands settled in the jungles, where the most profitable crop was coca. Marijuana traffickers began bringing small amounts of cocaine in suitcases to the United States. Others saw an opportunity for big business.

In the early 1970s, Pablo Escobar was a petty thief in Medellin, Colombia, with much grander visions. Seeing the potential of cocaine, he and his gang joined forces with the marijuana smugglers. As they expanded the business, they became more sophisticated and more violent, not only killing in battle but also killing hundreds of government officials, judges, prosecutors, journalists, and those caught in the crossfire.

Escobar's Medellin cartel dominated the American and European markets. It splintered into specialized groups after he was killed by police. They were followed by the Cali cartel, which was in part responsible for Escobar's killing by police. After the downfall of these two large hierarchical organizations, the cocaine trade, like other transnational criminal organizations, fragmented into smaller, more agile groups. There are hundreds there in the Andes today.

The new groups' pattern of transnational crime involves a network of nodes 'independent but linked' so that if one group falls, the gap will be quickly filled by others. They are called the BACRIM (bandas criminals) by the Colombian authorities, who say that they are almost invisible.

One constant through these transitions has been FARC. Pressed for finances, its members became active taxing growers, processors, and transporters in the areas they controlled. In 2012, FARC began peace negotiations with the government in which FARC promised to cooperate with the government in eradicating coca and the cocaine business. But a peace deal brokered by FARC and the government won't necessarily bring peace. As FARC demobilizes, it leaves a power vacuum in rebel-controlled territories. The government says that the drug trafficking gangs, many including former paramilitaries, rebels, and youths who worked for them, are the greatest threats. They even offer signing bonuses and high salaries to former FARC members who will join them. The gangs control their territories with extreme violence and extortion. Tumaco and Buenaventura, the major ports for cocaine export, are hotly disputed territories once held by FARC. Local officials and citizens are worried about homicides and struggles to control drug exporting among rival gangs. Other areas are also left vulnerable (Yagoub 2016a, 2016b, 2017). After years of decline, coca cultivation increased 30 percent from 2013 to 2015, with most of the increase being in Colombia (UNODC 2017a). It is perhaps related to groups moving into areas once controlled by FARC where production had diminished.

Peru and Bolivia faced similar wars. Peru is currently the world's largest cocaine producer. Shining Path, although greatly diminished since its height, still controls many drug trafficking regions and works with traffickers. Murders in Callao, a drug (and other illicit good) export port, rose every year from 2011 to 2015 and are about double the national average. In contrast, in Lima, the capital and largest city, they did not rise. The rise is related to rivalries between trafficking gangs (Yagoub 2016b).

Foothold in Central America

Violence follows cocaine up the trafficking route through Central America (Figure 9.4). Panama, Honduras, Guatemala, Nicaragua, El Salvador, and Mexico all experienced civil wars against dictators of the right and left before and

A CLOSER LOOK
TRAFFICKING ROUTES

FIGURE 9.4   Land, Air, and Sea Trafficking Routes From Colombia

Drug routes through Central America destabilize countries in their paths.

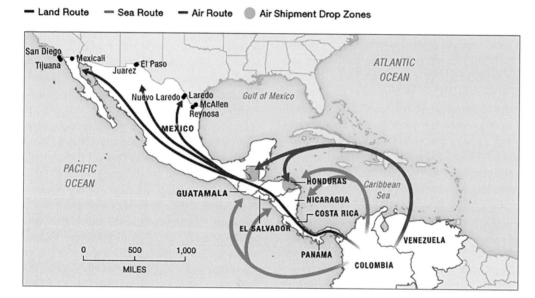

Source: NPR, STRATFOR Credit: Stephanie d'Otreppe/NPR.

throughout the Cold War facilitating the infiltration and establishment of organized crime.

Trafficking cocaine from South America moved into Mexico in the 1970s, when most of the traffic was driven out of the Caribbean. When the Colombian cartels splintered into smaller organizations, the most influential cocaine (and heroin) cartels were in Mexico and violence followed north, into the major trafficking zones of Mexico. There, five cartels control drug traffic; the Sinaloa cartel, a federation of crime groups, is reputedly the most powerful in the world (McDermott 2013).

Escobar was aided by Manuel Noriega, president and dictator of Panama, in laundering drug money and running drugs through Panama to the United States. Although the U.S. government knew this, it relied on Noriega, a right-wing dictator responsible for thousands of deaths, as a buffer against communism. It was not until 1988 that the U.S. government turned on Noriega. By this time, trafficking through Central America was well established. Panama remains a major transport state moving drugs up from Colombia further into Central America.

The Northern Triangle of Central America—the trio of Guatemala, Honduras, and El Salvador—is now the most violent region in the world. Two levels of organization operate there. The larger handle, *transportista,* transport through the country for the cartels. They corrupt the law enforcement system from police to judges. Whom they cannot corrupt, they kill. The smaller neighborhood gangs sell in their territories. Violent rivalries at both levels have sent thousands of refugees fleeing the violence, the forced conscription of their sons, and the raping of their daughters north into Mexico and some on to the United States.

Since former President Felipe Calderón of Mexico intensified the campaign against the drug cartels, the war on drugs cost some 100,000 lives. Included in the tally are students, journalists, police, politicians, and government officials. Some got in the cartels' way; others were just bystanders.

Fighting these groups and gangs is complicated. Ironically, in some respects, the successes of the U.S. government and Calderón's attempts in Mexico to destroy the cartels intensified the violence. In the late 1980s, the United States broke up Caribbean networks that trafficked cocaine from Colombia cartels into the United States. Mexico then became much more important in the supply chain. With their power came money and the capacity to bribe enough Mexican officials to ensure their supply routes. In 2000, a transition in the ruling party brought a wave of violence directed by the cartels at the government in an attempt to maintain control. In 2006, Calderón declared war on the cartels. With help from the U.S. military, 25 of the top 37 drug kingpins were killed. Instead of bringing more peace, the cartels splintered into upward of 60 smaller drug trafficking gangs. Battles over territories and leadership and against government ensued. The gangs killed 100 mayors and former mayors as well as dozens of municipal leaders. Gangs kidnapped and extorted to supplement their incomes (Lee and Renwick 2017).

Opiates From Afghanistan

Since the 19th-century Opium Wars in which tens of thousands of Chinese were killed, the opiate industry has been the deadliest and most destabilizing of the drug trades, although all leave very bloody trails. More people die from opium drug overdosing, from participating in the trade, from enforcing the law, and from innocently standing by than from any other drug. The primary routes of trafficking from source to destination established in the 17th, 18th, and 19th centuries persist. Commercial crops of poppy (along with cannabis and coca) still contribute to people's livelihoods throughout Asia as they have for centuries.

One of the three relatively established routes for heroin traffic from Afghanistan is the Balkan route, which traverses Iran and Turkey and then on to Southeastern Europe to Western and Central Europe. Stronger border controls between Afghanistan and Iran and between Iran and Turkey have pushed some of that traffic along a southern route. The southern route goes through Iran or Pakistan and on to Asia and Europe via Kenya and Tanzania in East Africa. Increasing traffic along the southern route detour is responsible for increasing opiate use in Africa. The northern route passes through Central Asia to Russia. Opiates from Afghanistan reach North America via West Africa. Fully 90 percent of heroin reaching Canada originates in Afghanistan, mostly (although not exclusively) through the southern route—50 percent via India, Iran, and Pakistan. Each of these routes passes through countries at war with themselves over ethnic and religious conflict.

Drug Trafficking and Support for Terrorism

There is a complicated relationship between drug trafficking and terrorism. Many terrorist groups acquire a good share of their financing through the drug trade. Afghanistan is the primary source of illicit opium. Nearly all cultivation, some 85 percent, occurs in territories related in some way to the Taliban, which relies on the opium trade for half of its annual income. Villages with poppy cultivation are much more likely to be under Taliban or ISIS (Islamic State in Iraq and Syria) control than to be under government control (61 to 33 percent); three fourths (75 percent) of those without poppy cultivation are under government control (UNODC 2017d).

Since 1979 and the decade-long Soviet invasion, followed by the relentless decade-long civil war through which the Taliban gained control of nearly all Afghanistan, Afghanistan has been characterized by fractiousness and insecurity. Although Afghanis had grown small amounts of opium poppy for centuries, large-scale production did not begin until the Soviet invasion. When the central government lost control of the provinces, warlords controlling the territories used opium cultivation to raise money for arms to fight the Soviets and, when the Soviets retreated, to fight one another. The Taliban allowed the opium trade to flourish, benefitting financially from support of the trade. In 2000, successful in securing most of the country, the Taliban outlawed opium production and it quickly dropped more than 90 percent within one year. Cultivation rose again, to its highest point in 2016, with the Taliban in control of the majority.

In Myanmar, there is a weak but still significant relationship between the number of people killed in terrorist attacks and the area under opium cultivation. Cultivation and deaths due to terrorist attacks peaked in 1996, and cultivation declined steadily through 2006 before they began to rise again. The terrorist attacks declined rapidly from the 1996 peak and stayed relatively low, even reaching zero in 2006. They rose again very rapidly from 2013 to 2015, accompanying a tripling in the acreage under cultivation (UNODC 2017c). As Myanmar is losing its place in opium production, crystal meth production is increasing (Figures 9.5, 9.6, 9.7, and 9.8).

A CLOSER LOOK
DRUG CULTIVATION AND TERRORIST ACTIVITIES

Terrorist operations in drug cultivation regions come to rely on drugs as a source of revenue.

FIGURE 9.5 Persons Killed in Terrorist Attacks and Area Under Opium Poppy Cultivation: Afghanistan, 2000–2016

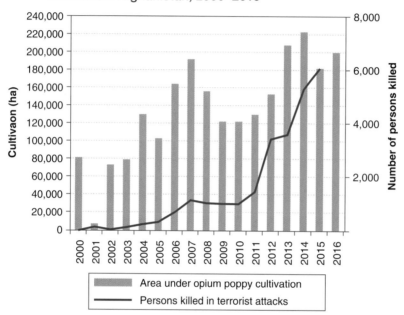

Source: United Nations Office on Drugs and Crime, *World Drug Report 2017* (ISBN: 978-92-1-148291-1, eISBN: 978-92-1-060623-3, United Nations publication, Sales No. E.17.XI.6).

FIGURE 9.6 Registered Victims of Non-state Armed Violence and Area Under Coca Cultivation: Colombia, 2000–2016

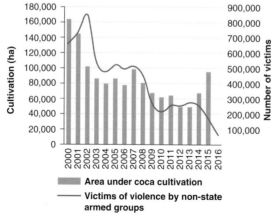

Source: United Nations Office on Drugs and Crime, *World Drug Report 2017* (ISBN: 978-92-1-148291-1, eISBN: 978-92-1-060623-3, United Nations publication, Sales No. E.17.XI.6).

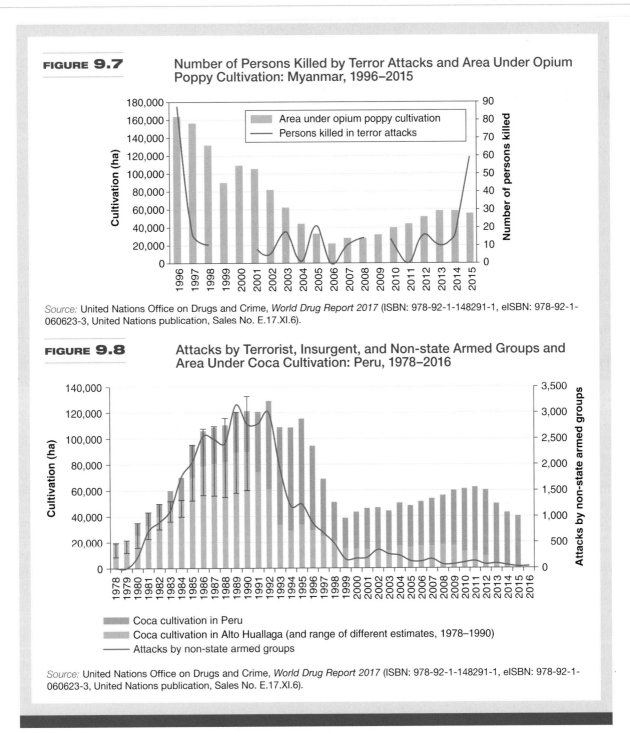

FIGURE 9.7 Number of Persons Killed by Terror Attacks and Area Under Opium Poppy Cultivation: Myanmar, 1996–2015

Source: United Nations Office on Drugs and Crime, *World Drug Report 2017* (ISBN: 978-92-1-148291-1, eISBN: 978-92-1-060623-3, United Nations publication, Sales No. E.17.XI.6).

FIGURE 9.8 Attacks by Terrorist, Insurgent, and Non-state Armed Groups and Area Under Coca Cultivation: Peru, 1978–2016

Coca cultivation in Peru
Coca cultivation in Alto Huallaga (and range of different estimates, 1978–1990)
Attacks by non-state armed groups

Source: United Nations Office on Drugs and Crime, *World Drug Report 2017* (ISBN: 978-92-1-148291-1, eISBN: 978-92-1-060623-3, United Nations publication, Sales No. E.17.XI.6).

The terrorism connection is also significant in South America. Coca bush cultivation decreased steadily from 2007 to 2013, down from 180,000 hectares to less than 121,000 hectares. Most of the decrease has been in Colombia. Peru and Bolivia historically have accounted for a smaller share of production, their production has held steady at about 20,000 hectares for Peru and 50,000 hectares for Bolivia.

The source pattern for cocaine shifted with successes of law enforcement. Terrorist activity shifted as well. As fields and laboratories were eradicated in one country, they moved to another country. Terrorist activity in

Colombia and Peru aligns with these shifts. From World War II to about the 1970s, Peru and Bolivia were the primary growers and Colombia processed. From 1978 through the early 1990s, both cultivation and terrorist activity, primarily Shining Path in the Alto Huallaga region, were high, and both decreased through the mid- and late 1990s.

As the air traffic from Peru to Colombia was disrupted, Colombians began growing. By 1997, Colombian cultivation surpassed that of Peru. Both terrorist activity and cultivation in Colombia were high in the early 2000s. Large-scale eradication efforts of the United States and Colombia cut production in Colombia. Cultivation declined by 70 percent from 2000 to 2013. Terrorist killings by FARC fell 60 percent. Peru and Bolivia picked up some of that decline. Peruvians developed refining techniques and began growing again; however, cultivation did not increase in the Alto Huallaga region, the area that had been associated with Shining Path (UNODC 2010, 2015a, 2017c).

Destabilization and Drugs

Corruption is one of the major destabilizing effects of drug trafficking.

West Africa became a hub for drug traffic as use of traditional routes was curtailed by U.S. and UN law enforcement (African Economic Development Institute n.d.). Now drugs come by sea and air. A coastal country with scores of islands off its coast, Guinea–Bissau, became the perfect haven for drug traffickers in transit from South America to Europe. Plagued by poverty and a government destabilized by coups, civil wars, and assassinations, Guinea–Bissau has been a nearly lawless land for decades. When the drug market entered, many of the police, military, and government officials joined it. The drug trade is much more lucrative than cashews, its main legitimate export, or government service.

In Guinea–Bissau, the military protected the drug shipments, even helping traffickers to unload planes. They have had standoffs with the police. When police do manage to make an arrest, they must turn the traffickers and seizures over to other government officials. The drugs and traffickers often disappear, released by corrupt officials. As has happened in Mexico and other trafficking hot spots, those trying to expose or end the corruption are threatened or assassinated. A new president, Jose Mario Vaz (Jomav), was elected in 2014, promising reform.

With a UN peacekeeping force in place and money from African and Western donors, it may succeed. The government began by dismissing the former head of the army, General Antonio Indjai, listed by the United States as a drug kingpin. Next, the government planned to cleanse the army, 500 at a time, starting with coup leaders and others on the European Union's (EU) sanctions list (Farge and Pereira 2015). As of 2018, reforms in police, military, justice, and other government offices have not been sufficient to bring stability.

ECONOMIC COSTS OF DRUGS AND ALTERNATIVE DEVELOPMENT

Drug trafficking is the second largest—after counterfeiting—source of transnational crime revenue,[7] bringing in about 25 percent of its total income. In the EU, the drug market in 2010 was equivalent to 0.23 percent of gross domestic product (GDP). In the United States, it was more than three times that amount, 0.7 percent. In Afghanistan, the value of opiate exports ranged between 7 and 16 percent over the period from 2011 to 2016 (UNODC 2017d).

It could be argued that drug money is functional in that it contributes to a country's GDP and boosts investment and employment, especially in countries that are poor and drugs are a larger part of the economy. Following this reasoning, putting an end to the violence and harm of the illegal drug trade relies on accomplishing one (or both) of two things: eliminating the market or eliminating the supply. Eliminating the market is an educational, health, and public policy proposition that will be discussed later in the chapter. Eliminating the supply depends on breaking the hold that drug dealers have on growers—hundreds of thousands of farmers, most of whose livelihoods depend on the trade. Providing farmers with an alternative crop is a promising strategy for combatting the supply of illegal drugs.

Many non-governmental organizations, governmental agencies in the United States, Germany, Thailand, and the EU, and intergovernmental agencies fund and/or operate alternative development programs. UNODC has programs in Afghanistan, Bolivia, Colombia, Lao PDR, Myanmar, Thailand, and Peru. UNODC evaluates the programs not only by declines in drug crop cultivation but also by the improvements in quality of life for the farmers and environmental sustainability.

CONSIDER THIS
THE COCA RUSH

To make a living, farmers need to grow and sell crops. When Colombia opened its markets to international trade, many of its own staple crops became unprofitable, with the prices being undercut by imports from other countries. Between 1945 and 1984, the contribution of agriculture to the national economy dropped from 40 to 22.5 percent (Cook 2011). It is not hard to understand how in the 1970s coca—hardy, capable of thriving in poor soil, grown without complicated irrigation or expensive fertilizers, and easily made into a non-perishable paste—became an attractive crop for poor Colombian peasants.

Poppies, Not Potatoes

When the onion and potato harvest of the Guambiare Indians in the mountains outside of Popayán, Colombia, failed, the first to reach out to help them was a North American. He gave them seeds, fertilizer, four months' worth of groceries, and a promise to buy their harvest. While this started with a few Guambiare, it was not long before 70 percent had given up food crops to grow the wild poppies the North American brought (Schemo 1998).

When there are no alternatives, drugs are a reliable cash crop. Farmers are often victims of transnational drug traffickers. Helping farmers to make a living with legal and profitable cash crops, and offering protection as needed, is essential in combatting drug trafficking.

In Lao PDR, Oudomxay Province, home to 1,082 Hmong, the primary commodity was poppy. Through the Thai Royal Project Foundation, the Highland Research Institute, and UNODC, farmers received technical assistance, materials, greenhouses, and improved water supply and storage systems to cultivate fruit and vegetable varieties. Sy Chan, a leader among the farmers and the cooperative that they formed, reports that demand for their produce is so high that they cannot produce enough. Her family's living conditions and food security improved dramatically. As of 2013, Oudomxay Province was free of poppy (UNODC 2016a). Similar success stories from UNODC, U.S. Agency for International Development, and others abound. However, not every attempt is a success.

For alternative development to work, a basic infrastructure needs to be in place. This is not always the case in drug cultivation regions. Ideal conditions for alternative development are as follows:

- Effective control of the area by central government and an absence of counter-pressure from insurgent groups

- The provision of an enabling sustainable economic environment at the national and international levels that facilitates the presence of market forces that make illicit cultivation less attractive

- Consistently applied disincentives through law enforcement and eradication (UNODC, n.d. a)

Given these constraints, alternative development is best approached not just, or even primarily, as a drug cultivation control program. Better, it is approached as a sustainable rural development and poverty reduction program. This focuses attention on the root causes of the supply side of the drug economy; "poverty, violence, weak political and judicial systems, absence of public institutions and control mechanisms, well-established trafficking networks for drugs, and the lack of infrastructure and alternative development, and access to legal markets are the main factors pushing farmers to grow drug crops" (Gesellschaft für Internationale Zusammenarbeit 2013), the same factors that give rise to other global problems.

TRAFFICKING IN FIREARMS AND WEAPONRY

The 2001 Protocol against the Illicit Manufacturing of and Trafficking in Firearms, Their Parts and Components and Ammunition (Firearms Protocol) is the most significant piece of the international firearms regime. Illicit trafficking is defined in Article 3(e):

> the import, export, acquisition, sale, delivery, movement or transfer of firearms, their parts and components, and ammunition from or across the territory of one State Party to that of another State Party if any one of the States Parties concerned does not authorize it in accordance with the terms of this Protocol or if the firearms are not marked in accordance with Article 8 of this Protocol.

As with other international laws, it is most effective when supported by domestic law and there is convergence in national laws across countries. In the case of firearms, there is considerable latitude in domestic regulations. In some countries, illicit trafficking includes transfers domestically. Laws concerning registrations also vary. Some narrow definitions of trafficking treat firearms as contraband and do not establish it as a criminal offense. Another complication is that there may be both legal and illicit dimensions of any one trafficking incident.

The Nature of the Market: Crime and Conflict

The actual value of the illegal arms trade is difficult to determine. The UN Comtrade estimated value of the legal trade was about U.S. $17.3 billion and that of the illegal trade was about $1.7 to $3 billion in 2014, making it about 10 to 20 percent of the legal trade. Arms trafficking is the largest source of revenue for transnational organized crime.

Wherever there is crime or conflict, there is a market for illicit arms. Street criminals are usually in the market for concealable weapons and generally obtain guns diverted from the legal market. Where countries have strict gun controls, guns are usually trafficked from regional neighbors with a less regulated market; nearby guns are more easily acquired and cheaper. The farther arms travel and the more intermediaries that transport them, the higher the price grows.

In Mexico, there are no legal gun shops; only the military is permitted to make legal sales. The maximum weapon a private owner may have is limited at .38 caliber. Despite these tough laws, there are roughly 15.5 million firearms in civilian hands, 10 million of which are not registered.

The United States, Mexico's neighbor, has the most heavily armed citizenry in the world. Guns bought legally in the United States are relatively cheap and are easy to purchase legally via straw buyers[8] or at gun shows where permits are not required. With millions of people crossing back and forth across the borders, smugglers can take guns in small quantities in passenger vehicles, evading suspicion of organized crime trafficking. One smuggler can take as many as 500 weapons a year across the border. To illustrate how lucrative this business is, 12 percent of the 55,000 registered gun dealers in the United States—6,700 of them—are along the U.S.–Mexican border. More than two thirds of the guns seized in Mexico between 2004 and 2008 came from Texas, California, and Arizona. The largest clientele for these firearms? The drug cartels, which use them to maintain their operations and enforce their rules. The drug trade resulted in more than 10,000 gun deaths in Mexico nearly every year from 1990 to 2008 (UNOCD 2010).

More than half of the arms seized by Mexican federal law enforcement from organized crime groups were long arms, primarily assault rifles. While some may have originated in the United States, military arms are more likely the source of these weapons, particularly for the cartels. The Los Zetas drug cartel recruited Mexican military to form its military branch. The military brought weapons with them. The civil wars that plagued Nicaragua, El Salvador, and Guatemala left stockpiles of weapons in reach of corrupt military that were easily stolen. Arms are also trafficked along with cocaine from Colombia and Venezuela or ephedrine from China (UNODC 2010).

There are stockpiles of weapons from fallen regimes all over the world. Muammar Gaddafi of Libya amassed a huge armory of conventional and biological weapons and explosives during his four-decade rule. Even while under sanction and embargo from 1992 to 2003, he managed to buy weapons from Belarus—a country whose dictator was known for his disdain of international treaties and fondness of other dictators. Gaddafi maintained strict control over his stockpiles but diverted weapons to groups or governments that supported him and his anti-American predilections regardless of their barbarism. After Gaddafi was beaten to death at the hands of rebel forces, his small arms arsenal of 250,000 to 700,000 firearms started to flow through West Africa, and the more sophisticated weapons were likely transported to the Middle East. UNODC (2013b) estimated that about 2.5 percent of the arsenal had been trafficked. The supply of guns to armed groups can prolong the conflicts in this unstable region.

Weapons from Gaddafi's arsenal still circulate. Hundreds, and possibly thousands, of shoulder-held missile launchers are not accounted for. A London investigator tracking small arms encountered a group of fighters who had bought weapons, including shoulder-held anti-aircraft missiles, from nomadic smugglers on their way to illicit weapons bazaars in Chad, loaded up with weapons from the Gaddafi cache. Many of Gaddafi's weapons are believed to be in the hands of ISIS and other jihadists (Broder 2016).

The arms trade fuels violent conflict. Because arms are durable goods, their trafficking follows conflict around the world. The market for arms is high in a country when conflict is high and fades with peace. The arms move on to the next conflict. The Group for Research and Information on Peace and Security (GRIP) points directly to Western countries for their complicity in the arms trafficking that devastates so many developing countries. They sell arms liberally to regimes that violate human rights and to groups rebelling against regimes that they would like to see toppled (GRIP 2016). These arms, legacy weapons from past and recent conflicts, live on and move on to future conflicts through transnational crime groups. Weapons from old conflicts are a major source of weapons trafficked through West Africa along with weapons sold by or rented from corrupt officials and transferred to militant groups from sympathetic governments.

The dissolution of the Soviet Union left stockpiles of arms and ammunition throughout Eastern Europe. Destroying them or securing them is a monumental task. The Ukraine housed 30 percent of the Soviet military industrial complex, including 7 million small arms and large weapons systems—the third largest stockpile in the world after China and Russia. Much of the stockpile has ended up in the Democratic Republic of the Congo, South Sudan, Chad, Darfur (in Sudan), Equatorial Guinea, and Kenya. From 1992 to 1997, more than U.S. $32 million of Ukrainian weapons were stolen and sold abroad. While this was before export rules were strengthened, the government officially authorized 20 percent of the sales. Arms are trafficked from the stockpiles of other Eastern European countries as well (UNODC 2010). Even when arms are deactivated, they can be recommissioned and live on to fight in more conflicts. Many countries have very lax laws concerning sales of deactivated arms. The machine guns used in the magazine *Charlie Hebdo* attacks in Paris in 2015 are thought to have come from Slovakia. They were sold legally as deactivated.

Among the many questions arising from the November 2015 attacks in Paris that killed 129 people is where the assault rifles came from. France has very strict gun control laws, yet Kalashnikov-style rifles were evident in both attacks. They are thought to have come from Eastern Europe after the fall of the Iron Curtain (Axe 2015). It is not hard to understand how in such situations arms fall into the hands of criminals; in authoritarian countries, the most organized groups outside of the government (although sometimes complicit with the government) are criminal groups. The chaos surrounding conflict provides an opportunity for organized criminal groups to operate more openly, sometimes taking on leadership roles in the conflicts, often serving both sides, and often growing from domestic to transnational stature.

The former Yugoslavia had the fourth largest military in Europe. As the wars broke out in the 1990s, weapon stockpiles came under control of the Serbian government and many were diverted to criminal groups that became militant groups active in the conflicts. Bosnia and Croatia, being under embargo during the war, needed to smuggle in arms. During the two years from 1993 to 1995, U.S. $308 million worth of arms were smuggled into Croatia and $207 million worth of arms were smuggled into Bosnia, reaching $800 million by the end of the war. In 1997, when the Albanian government fell, 643,220 small arms were looted. Only 15 percent were recovered (Carapic 2014). During the Balkan wars, loosely organized criminal groups and networks became active fighting in the war efforts and in smuggling the arms to fuel them as well as petrol, cigarettes, and other commodities. In Kosovo, long a hub of the international drug trade, the Jasheri drug smuggling clan grew into the Kosovo Liberation Army. Russia's recent redesign of the AK-47 will put massive stockpiles of the older models on the market throughout Eastern Europe and into other regions (Axe 2015).

After the wars in Eastern Europe, criminal groups—still the most organized and well financed—opened legal businesses, focusing on white-collar crime. Many continue to participate in criminal networks throughout the region, trafficking in narcotics as well as weaponry. Their presence is so pervasive that a 2010 Gallup poll revealed that 37 percent of people in the Balkans say that organized crime affects their lives on a daily basis (Carapic 2014).

Many of these guns and grenades they trafficked reached Western Europe via the "ant trade." Individual operators, the ants, can move weapons from their source in Eastern Europe one at a time relatively easily across the open European borders. A long enough trail of "ants," making the journey back and forth often enough, can move a lot of arms.

CONSIDER THIS
THE IRAN–CONTRA AFFAIR

One of the most infamous incidents in arms trade was the Iran–Contra affair. In 1985, the U.S. government had an arms embargo against Iran in place. However, Iran, then at war with Iraq, made a back-channel request to buy arms from the United States. Using Israel as an intermediary, senior officials in the Reagan administration made a deal—arms for the release of seven hostages being held in Lebanon by Iranian-supported terrorists. Officials sold missiles through Israel to Iran. With the money from the sale, they supported the "Contras," counter-revolutionaries fighting the Cuban-supported Sandinista government in Nicaragua. This intricate arrangement was orchestrated to bypass other legislation passed by the U.S. Congress that forbade assisting the Contras. Fourteen people in the Reagan administration, as well as a number of private parties, faced criminal charges for their role in the affair. President George H. W. Bush pardoned most of them pre- or post-trial. One case was dismissed. Most of the private parties received probation and fines. One was sentenced to prison for tax fraud.

Trafficking Patterns

Armed groups get their weapons in four main ways: seizure, donations, purchases, and local production. Seizures may occur on the battlefield, by looting stockpiles, and by small-scale thefts. Armed groups may seize munitions from government stockpiles, particularly after a governmental failure as in Libya, from rival groups, and even from peace operations. Arms may be donated through transfers by governments or other groups with common interests. Individuals, perhaps politicians or citizens, may contribute arms or support for them. Groups with sufficient financing, such as those that are state supported, buy arms directly. Corrupt officials may sell government weapons. Craft or local production shops can convert weapons from one type to another and recommission deactivated weapons. Although rare, factories may be seized. Most weapons are originally legally purchased and then diverted illegally and circulated for decades (Berman and Racovita 2015).

Government tracing and seizure reports submitted to the UN are one method of determining trafficking patterns. The numbers of arms seized by any country can vary widely year to year for any number of reasons from policy changes to having a particularly large seizure in a given year. The UN report does not reflect the amount of illicit trade. Reasons for the seizures also vary. In some countries, the majority of seizures can be for trafficking offenses, other criminal offenses, or administrative violations.

While it does not reveal the volume of illegal arms trade, tracking is important for establishing trafficking routes. Comparing where a weapon was seized with its country of manufacture provides evidence as to whether or not it was trafficked across borders. Tracing reports establish a tentative link of weapons between those countries and indicate which countries require cooperative operations with one another. Tracing helps to identify weaknesses in national laws or enforcement that need to be rectified to tighten controls and reduce trafficking via that route.

Most seizure and tracing reports suggest that regional traffic is the most prevalent. Trafficking from one region to another, although less common, it is still a significant problem. Firearms from the United States reached Europe, Latin America, and the Caribbean. In Brazil, shipping containers transporting furniture of U.S. citizens moving to Brazil from Miami also contained firearms. Traffickers hid Kalashnikov-type rifles and ammunition from China, Romania, and Hungary in mattresses. Firearms from Europe have reached Africa and the Americas. From Asia, they have reached Central America (UNODC 2015b). As the volume of global trade increases, so will arms trafficking across regions. The increasing ease of transportation as well as the greater burden on inspectors makes this very likely.

West Africa is a hub for arms trafficking as well as drugs, people, and oil. Because West Africa does not produce its own arms, the arms in circulation were imported from outside of the region. In Mali, armed groups use weapons trafficked through circuitous routes from many countries. Most come from the former Soviet Union, China, and Eastern Bloc countries (Bulgaria, former Yugoslavia, Poland, Romania, former Czechoslovakia, and former East Germany). But other source countries include Algeria, Egypt, and North Korea.

As mentioned above, weapons are durable goods and have a long life. After the Libyan stockpiles were diverted in 2011–2012, arms sold legally to Qatar by Pakistan that had been transferred to Libya decades later ended up in Mali—along with arms sold by Belgium to Libya (Anders 2015 and personal communication).

Most of the flow of arms coming into West Africa is from legal stocks illicitly obtained. They fall into five categories:

- Legacy weapons from past conflicts

- Weapons from recent conflicts in neighboring regions

- Weapons sold or rented from corrupt security officials

- Weapons transferred by sympathetic governments

- A small number of weapons imported from outside Africa (UNODC 2013b)

Depending on their supply and their needs at any given time, countries may be a source, a transit hub, and/or a destination. Reports from the Yugoslav Republic of Macedonia illustrate that it is such a country. In 2012, Macedonia found that legal companies falsified documents claiming that some of their weapons were stolen. They then sold the weapons illicitly, making them a source. Firearms and explosives entered Macedonia from neighboring countries, primarily Albania, Kosovo, and Serbia. They were to be resold in other parts of the Balkans (including two-way traffic in and out of Albania), Greece, and Scandinavia. In this, Macedonia was a transit hub. One of the shipments bound for Crete was seized at the Bulgarian border in transit. Macedonia is also a destination, particularly for firearms that are converted there to fire explosive ammunition and resold to other countries (UNODC 2015b).

An increasingly significant vehicle of all transnational crime, the darknet facilitates and is a major force in firearms trafficking as well. A Rand study (Persi Paoli et al., 2017) provides an overview of trafficking in the darknet. Purchases are hard to trace and may occur through cryptomarkets that host many vendors or individual vendor markets that single vendors operate on their own. Some vendors are on the cryptomarket and have their own site. Another strategy to avoid detection is to ship weapons in

parts over several shipments or hidden in other items. Vendors have shipped arms in old television sets, printers, and musical instrument cases—to avoid detection. At least one vendor offered to ship firearms along with drugs for a discounted shipping cost. Shipping firearms in parts also bypasses some regulations relating to intact firearms that do not apply to component parts (Persi Paoli et al. 2017).

Pistols were the most often traded arms on the darkweb, followed by rifles and submachine guns. With the exception of the submachine guns, which were mostly replicas, nearly all of the weapons were "live" or operable as is. Curiously, whether the weapons were new or used was often not listed. Most purchasers bought ammunition with firearm purchases. "How to" manuals on making bombs and explosives at home or manufacturing a firearm from a 3-D printer are also commonly sold (Persi Paoli et al. 2017).

Experts report that because of the limitations of infrastructure in conflict zones where many people lack internet access and shipping services may be limited, the darkweb is not likely to be the trafficking choice of groups in armed conflict but may serve well "lone wolf" terrorists or small gangs (Persi Paoli et al. 2017). Minors, people with criminal or mental health records, and others not able to buy guns through legitimate means may also be attracted to the darknet sales (Persi Paoli et al. 2017).

Combatting the Arms Trade

The Protocol against the Illicit Manufacturing of and Trafficking in Firearms, Their Parts and Components and Ammunition to the UN Convention against Transnational Organized Crime is the major transnational instrument on combatting arms trafficking. To enforce the protocol, the UN "Program of Action to Prevent, Combat, and Eradicate the Illicit Trade in SALW (small arms and light weapons) in All Its Aspects" was adopted by all UN member states in 2001. Biennial reviews reinforce states' commitment to the program. Because arms circulate for generations, most of the attention in the protocol and program focuses on controlling stockpiles of weapons. Among the items to which parties agreed at the Fifth Biennial Meeting in 2014 were the following:

- To manage their stockpiles, identify specific requirements for stockpile management, particularly after conflict situations, and coordinate this with disarmament

CONSIDER THIS
FACEBOOK AND FIREARMS

Social media facilitate many transactions, with arms sales being among them. The Small Arms Survey (Jenzen-Jones and McCollum 2017) found that social media hosts an active arms bazaar in Libya. During the Gaddafi regime, arms sales were strictly controlled. With the fall of the regime, stockpiles were raided, opening the gate for a large illicit arms trade. Social media, with its veil of anonymity, became a popular vehicle. Researchers included eight social media sites in the study. Most of the sellers focused on Tripoli and surrounding areas. Most of the participants appeared to have ties to armed groups. Most of the weapons were from the Cold War era.

Facebook, with more than a billion visitors monthly, became one of the largest marketplaces for firearms, both legal and illegal, in the world. In response, Facebook banned private sales of firearms on its site and on Instagram in 2016. It will rely on users to police the site, reporting violations of the policy (Goel and Isaac 2016). Many of the firearms sales through Facebook, including handguns, grenades, guided missiles, and heavy machine guns, seemed to target terrorists and militant groups (Chivers 2016).

- To cooperate, assist, and share expertise and technology on stockpile management, destruction and disposal in environmentally friendly ways and assist countries as needed

- To promote the role of women in combatting illicit trade and include them in policy making, planning, and implementing programs of management and physical security

- To implement measures for effectively identifying and tracing weaponry and keeping and sharing the information (United Nations General Assembly 2014)

A second instrument, "International Instrument to Enable States to Identify and Trace, in a Timely and Reliable Manner, Illicit Small Arms and Light Weapons," is an important tool in international cooperation to illuminate trafficking patterns. It is imperfect, and many states do not have the capacity or records to trace arms back to their manufacturers. Coordinating reporting and improving participating in tracking is important for more reliable results.

As in other areas of transnational crime, varying national laws relevant to the sale of arms and the size of the arms manufacturing and export industry in many powerful nations impede the development of a strong international regime of control.

INTELLECTUAL PROPERTY CRIME: TRAFFICKING IN COUNTERFEIT AND PIRATED GOODS

All consumers buying counterfeit goods enjoy the great bargain that they're getting on a purse, jewelry, clothing, drugs, or even auto parts at a fraction of the cost of the authentic brand. They might consider how lucky they are to get a new release movie before it is up for sale through a traditional outlet or is available for streaming. What they might not consider is that they are the ultimate target of a global criminal network of manufacturers, distributors, and retailers.

Counterfeiting and piracy[9] are certainly not new crimes, but as with other forms of organized crime, globalization provides opportunity for growth:

- Outsourcing manufacturing to factories in countries with little regulatory oversight provides ample opportunity for unauthorized manufacturing. Many counterfeit products, made by the same people making the authentic products, cannot be distinguished from the legitimate ones.

- The increasing volume of trade provides more opportunity to move counterfeit products as well as legitimate products. It is impossible for every shipping container to be inspected.

- Global media, from television and movies to social media, create demand for "brand name" products.

- With a good internet connection and printer, copying the design and packaging of a branded consumer good is easy.

- Pirated movies and video games are easily copied and packaged to resemble the original ones. They are sometimes for sale in the underground market before they are in legitimate distribution in stores or theaters.

- Trade through online auction and social media sites provides a global marketplace for counterfeit goods.

Everything that can be made legally can be made illegally as well. From cigarettes to watches, to meats, to alcohol, anything can be, and nearly everything is, counterfeited or copied somewhere in the world. Intellectual property crime is relatively low cost and high profit. The costs of research, design, original production (as in movies, video games, music, and other pirated commodities), trademark, and marketing all are borne by the authentic owner of the brand or copyright. Even the reproductions can be accomplished on the cheap because there is little concern for quality control and reproductions are, unfortunately, often associated with human trafficking.

An accurate reading of the volume of counterfeit goods is impossible. Judging from the numbers of seizures, it takes a very significant toll on the global economy (Table 9.1). Based on seizure reports from 38 countries,

A CLOSER LOOK
LOUHU COMMERCIAL CITY

PHOTO 9.1 China has become the center of the world for counterfeit goods. Louhu Commercial City within Shenzhen, a major export city, is a shopper's paradise for illegal and counterfeit goods. An indoor mall of thousands of stalls sells counterfeit watches, purses, shoes, scarves, clothes, electronics, and toys for a fraction of their usual prices.

JoAnn Chirico.

physical counterfeiting in China accounts for about 12.5 percent of its exports and 1.5 percent of GDP. China and Hong Kong together produce about U.S. $396 billion each year.

Economic Cost of Counterfeiting

The economic loss to the company whose product has been copied, to the country where the goods are manufactured, and to the country where the goods are ultimately sold is significant and passed on to legal purchaser, so we all pay:

- Counterfeit products evade taxation at several steps in the supply chain. When counterfeit goods are smuggled in, import taxes are also avoided.

- Because the goods are not sold through legitimate retailers, sales taxes are avoided.

- Because counterfeit goods are produced below the radar of law enforcement, many are produced in sweatshops where people are denied fair income, exacerbating poverty.

- Companies lose market share to the counterfeit products.

- Illicit manufacturing does not abide by environmental laws, externalizing that cost of production onto the country.

Trade in counterfeit products is an annual loss of $500 to $700 billion to legitimate companies and a related loss of 2.5 million jobs. This translates to a $125 billion loss to developed countries in taxes and increased welfare spending (Denis 2014). Where counterfeit products are manufactured, there is no oversight to ensure worker safety. Often these goods are produced in sweatshops. The losses due to cigarette smuggling alone are enormous. About 25 percent of cigarettes smoked in the United Kingdom are counterfeit or smuggled. This costs the government about U.S. $2 billion every year in lost taxes (Interpol 2014:31). Cigarette smuggling in Spain became so extensive that sales in shops selling cigarettes fell 40 percent in 2012 (Interpol 2014).

Despite the luxury consumer goods, the tens of thousands of watches and purses, cigarettes are counterfeiters' most popular products. They are light and very portable. Governments impose taxes on cigarettes that inflate the purchase price far above the cost of manufacture. Three

strategies are employed in this crime. They all are low risk and high profit. Organized crime is deeply involved at all levels. Terrorist groups, notably the Northern Ireland IRA (Irish Republican Army), raise money through illicit cigarette trade as well. The Congolese rebel group CNDP (National Congress for the Defense of the People) allegedly received funds donated by a Rwandan cigarette smuggler. One strategy is to source legally produced, authentically branded cigarettes in one country and illegally smuggle and sell cigarettes in another country. Cigarettes are also manufactured illegally and packaged in counterfeit packaging as a brand product. Another strategy is to legally manufacture or buy cheap cigarettes in a country that allows it and to bring them, "illicit whites," illegally into other countries (Interpol 2014).

The total for global physical counterfeiting is about U.S. $461 billion (Global Intellectual Property Center [GIPC] 2016). Only a fraction is seized. The retail value of goods seized in the United States, had they been genuine, would have been U.S. $1.383 billion—41 percent in the form of watches and jewelry (Table 9.2) (U.S. Customs and Border Protection [CBP] 2017).

Dangers of Counterfeit Goods

Counterfeiters do not worry about protecting their "brand." As a result, counterfeit goods are usually of inferior quality. While this may be frustrating to consumers whose shoes or purse fall apart after minimal use, it is not particularly harmful. In many counterfeit goods, however, low quality can be life threatening. The global dispersion of technology for higher-level manufacturing expanded the range of goods that can be easily made illicitly. More than one fourth of the goods detained at the European border in 2013 were daily use products proven to be dangerous to consumer health and safety. These products can include harmful chemicals and substandard component parts. Among the dangerous products were shampoos that caused chemical burns, cosmetics that contained toxins, and batteries and laptop and phone chargers that caused explosions and fires (Europol and Office for Harmonization in the Internal Market 2015). Pharmaceuticals that have worthless or harmful chemicals are especially dangerous.

The list of hazardous products would number in the hundreds of thousands. Here are a few examples of the many dangerous fakes circulating:

- The U.S. Department of Defense found 9,356 counterfeit products in its procurement system. These products, from electrical components to bolts, rivets, and screws, pose risks to soldiers on and off the battlefield.

- Counterfeit condoms from China offered little protection against pregnancy and sexually transmitted diseases. They burst, leaked, and did not contain spermicide. The condoms were found in discount stores in New York, Virginia, and Texas (GIPC n.d.; Interpol 2014).

- Counterfeit Tamiflu became the number one seller of fake pharmaceuticals during the H1N1 flu virus threat (GIPC n.d.).

- Counterfeit perfumes contained antifreeze, harmful bacteria, and urine (GIPC n.d.).

- Personal mobile devices are vulnerable to explosion and harming users (GIPC n.d.).

- Rat meat sold as lamb and horse was in meat supplies in Shanghai and Europe (Interpol 2014).

- 156,000 hazardous toys were seized at a port in Baltimore, Maryland, in one day in February 2015 (U.S. CBP 2015).

- Antifreeze, rubbing alcohol, and methanol caused tens of thousands of deaths in the early 2000s and as many as 12,000 in 2010 (Interpol 2014).

- Infant milk laced with melamine victimized 300,000 infants and caused the deaths of six babies in China (Interpol 2014).

A CLOSER LOOK
GOODS SEIZED AT THE EU AND U.S. BORDERS

TABLE 9.1   Countries of Provenance of Goods Seized

China and Hong Kong lead the world in the percentage of counterfeit articles circulated and the value of counterfeit articles.

Country of Provenance % Provenance by Articles (2016)				Country of Provenance % Provenance by Value (2016)			
European Union		United States		Europe		United States	
China	80.65	China	52	China	72.21	China	45
Hong Kong	7.79	Hong Kong	36	Hong Kong	16.17	Hong Kong	43
Vietnam	1.71	Singapore	2	Turkey	2.52	India	1
Pakistan	1.71	Germany	1	UAE	1.59	Singapore	<1
Cambodia	1.5	Turkey	1	Unknown	.84	Cambodia	<1
Turkey	1.09	Others	8	Pakistan	.77	Pakistan	<1
India	1.08			India	.63	Bangladesh[a]	<1
Others	4.47	Total number	31,560	Others	6.4	Others	8

a. Colombia, Korea, and Mexico also accounted for less than 1 percent of provenance by value.

Sources: Adapted from U.S. Customs and Border Protection (2017) and European Union (2017).

(Continued)

(Continued)

TABLE 9.2   Counterfeit Goods Seized at EU and U.S. Borders, 2016

Smaller items are more easily transported and, like jewelry and watches, have high profit margins. Even these counterfeit "Super Bowl rings" can be bought for the right price.

Major European Union Seizures by Manufacturer Suggested Retail Price		US Seizures by Manufacturer Suggested Retail Price	
Commodity Categories	Percentage	Percentage	Commodity Categories
Watches and jewelry	17.6	47	Watches and jewelry
Toys	14.3	17	Handbags and wallets
Bags, wallets, and purses	10.4	9	Consumer electronics/parts
Perfumes and cosmetics	8.2	8	Wearing apparel/accessories
Sports shoes	6.9	5	Pharmaceuticals/personal care
Clothing (ready to wear)	6.7	4	Transportation parts
Cigarettes	5.5	4	Footwear
Sunglasses	5.0	1	Computers/parts
Games	3.4	1	Labels/tags
Mobile phone accessories	3.1	< 1	Optical media
Mobile phones	2.7	3	All others
Total value	€672,899,102	U.S. $1,382,903,001	Total value

Sources: Adapted from European Union (2017) and U.S. Customs and Border Patrol (2017). Reproduced with permission.

PHOTO 9.2 Counterfeit Super Bowl rings seized by U.S. Customs and Border Protection.

U.S. Customs and Border Protection/Photo by Glenn Fawcett.

Counterfeit pharmaceuticals are among the most dangerous counterfeit goods. According to the GIPC, 96 percent of all online pharmacies are operating illegally. That does not mean that all of the drugs they sell are counterfeit, but there is a high level of risk. In the United States alone, sales of counterfeit pharmaceuticals rose $11 million from 2010 to 2011, an increase of nearly 200 percent. In Europe, one in five people buy prescription medications without a prescription, leaving them particularly vulnerable to fakes on which they spend about €10.5 billion. Topping the list are weight loss drugs and flu and erectile dysfunction medications (GIPC n.d.).

Interpol Operation Heera coordinated more than 1,150 law enforcement officials from seven countries in West Africa. From mid-May to mid-June 2017, pharmacies, factories, warehouses, vehicles, and shops were raided and authorities seized more than 420 tons of illegal pharmaceutical and medical products. They were valued at more than U.S. $28 million, and 150 people were arrested or put under investigation (Interpol 2017). This disrupted a major transnational criminal effort and probably saved many lives by getting dangerous products off the market.

Not only is transnational organized crime deeply involved in the counterfeiting and smuggling business, but also many groups channel money to conflict groups. Counterfeiting is a fast and relatively easy way to make a lot of profit. The 900 percent profit margin is hard to match in any industry. Interpol and the Federal Bureau of Investigation report that millions of dollars from counterfeiting is diverted to al Qaeda, Hezbollah, and other terrorist groups (GIPC 2016).

New Trends in Moving Counterfeit Products

Counterfeit goods are transported or smuggled the world over using the same carriers as legitimate goods. In sheer volume, the postal service far exceeds any other means, and this method of transport increased rapidly from 2010 to 2016. This coincides with the increases in online retail activity. When calculating means of transportation by the number of articles or value, the picture changes. The greatest number of articles and greatest value are carried by sea (Figures 9.9, 9.10, and 9.11).

The traditional retail outlets for counterfeit and pirated products are ordinary shops, outdoor markets, private residences, street vendors, bars and pubs, and (of course) the open trunks of cars. Most of the time, we recognize these as counterfeit outlets when we see them.

A CLOSER LOOK
COUNTERFEIT GOODS SEIZED BY EU CUSTOMS, 2016

The most seizures were articles transported by post. More articles and more value seized were transported by sea.

FIGURE 9.9   Cases by Means of Transport

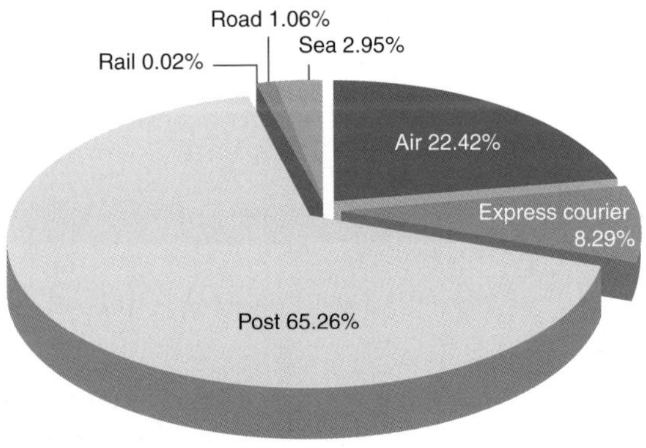

Road 1.06%
Sea 2.95%
Rail 0.02%
Air 22.42%
Express courier 8.29%
Post 65.26%

Source: European Union (2017). Reproduced with permission.

(*Continued*)

(Continued)

FIGURE 9.10   Articles by Means of Transport

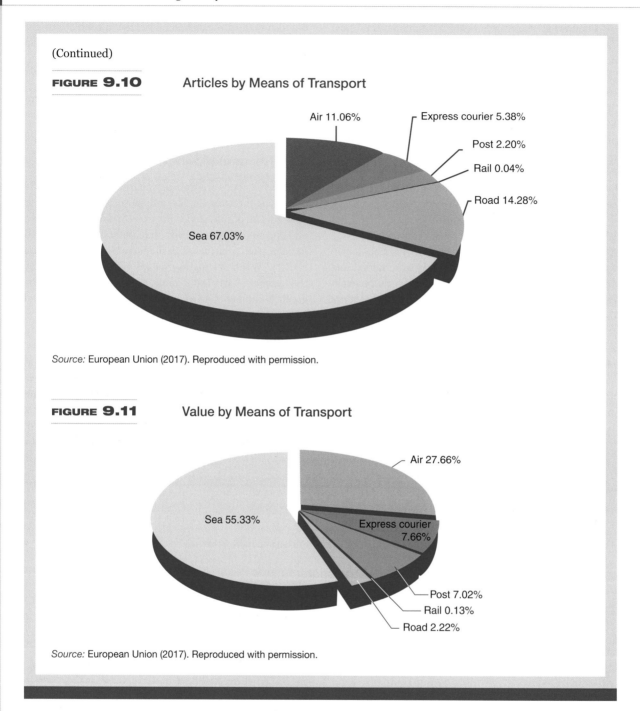

Source: European Union (2017). Reproduced with permission.

FIGURE 9.11   Value by Means of Transport

Source: European Union (2017). Reproduced with permission.

Widespread access to the internet is changing the retail marketplaces of illicit goods as rapidly as it has changed the marketplace of legitimate business and authentic products.

First, online auction and sales platforms, such as Amazon, eBay, and retail websites, expanded markets. While these are still problems, social media sites seem to be attracting much of the counterfeit and pirating

CONSIDER THIS
BRINGING DOWN A BUSINESS

Alibaba was the world's largest online e-commerce company. With headquarters in China, it commands 80 percent of the Chinese online market. With $170 billion in sales in 2012, it outsold Amazon and eBay combined. Early in 2015, the Chinese government released a white paper accusing Alibaba of not effectively policing its online merchants. Counterfeit goods were common on the site.

The government accused the company of not regulating what merchants could sell, inadequate product information, and a flawed system of ranking merchants. Alibaba's stock share price tumbled 20 percent with the warning. It was a temporary setback for Alibaba but a very stark warning of the dangers of selling counterfeit goods online (Team Wall Street Survivor 2015).

---

business away from them. Social media sites are even less costly and less visible than other online sites established specifically for trade. Social media sites may have already become the main vehicle used by counterfeiters. In the United Kingdom, investigators found more than 30,000 images of counterfeit goods on Facebook in just one day. In only a few weeks, an interagency task force in the United Kingdom took down 4,300 Facebook sites and 30 profiles. It seized £3 million of goods and diverted 11 million views to a page with an official police warning (Commercial Crime Services 2015).

In Hong Kong, the customs technology crime investigative unit developed an artificial intelligence program, SocNet, to troll through social media sites and recognize suspect postings. The program communicates with the site posing as potential buyers. In the first six months of 2014, 79 percent of online counterfeit sales verified were on auction sites. In the same period in 2015, 65 percent were on social media sites. As counterfeiting gravitates to social media, more young people are involved, at least in Hong Kong, where 40 percent of the arrests were secondary school and university students. Many of them reported that they believed selling the goods was legal as long as they disclosed that they were counterfeit (Schindler 2015).

As self-storage units become more common, they are also more commonly used in the supply chain of counterfeit goods in transit. Working with self-storage businesses is a new avenue for combatting this crime. In the United Kingdom, the "Tick Box" initiative is a partnership between self-storage facilities and local Trading Standards offices. It is a simple list of procedures that the facilities commit to following that clarifies the information they refer to the Trading Standards office. They display posters throughout the facility clarifying their practices to users (Intellectual Property Crime Group 2015). Regardless of

what is counterfeited, it is an intellectual property crime and may be prosecuted under national and international trade laws.

EMERGING CRIMES

New threats to international security emerge from the same sources as legitimate activities—new technologies, changing tastes opening up new markets, and shifting boundaries between legitimate and illicit activities as new harms, such as to the environment and endangered species, are discovered.

The Impact of Cyberspace: Traditional Crimes in New Ways and New Crimes

Cybercrimes are a top national security threat to the United States and any nation whose government, citizens, or industries have an online presence. Infrastructure control systems, such as electricity grids and gas lines, and valuable information, such as medical, financial, and banking records, all are vulnerable.

The internet, providing instantaneous audio and visual communication, revolutionized many aspects of life. Crime is far from the least among them. Drug trafficking, human trafficking, pornography, counterfeiting, and piracy all are made easier and cheaper with access to instantaneous global communications. Traditional organized crime caught on quickly, acquiring cyberskills and moving into cyberspace (McAfee 2005). Online security, legislation, and law enforcement lag behind the ever-changing landscape of the internet and the technologies that drive it. Cloaked in anonymity of both the creator and receiver levels, child pornography thrives online. Many countries, 93 of 187 by one recent study, do not even have legislation to address child pornography. Of those that did at the time of the survey, 24 did not have provisions for crimes carried out online (UNODC 2010). The online marketplace *Backpage* sells women and children along with automobiles, real estate, and jobs. After repeated investigations, grand jury inquiries, and federal lawsuits, *Backpage* shut down its adult section. Sex trafficking of children simply moved to the dating section.

Medicare fraud is a crime as old as Medicare, and the use of cyberspace makes it much more profitable. In 2010, in the largest Medicare fraud case by a single criminal organization, 73 individuals were indicted for fraudulent charges totaling more than $163 million. The Armenian American-organized crime enterprise Mirzoyan–Terdjanian established 118 fake clinics in 25 states and stole the identities of doctors and thousands of patients. But there were no brick-and-mortar "fake clinics," no one posing as doctors, and no patients, real or otherwise, signing up for treatments. The clinics, services, and people all existed only in "cyberspace." The leadership was based in Los Angeles and New York. Others were scattered throughout Armenia and the United States. One of those indicted, Armen Kazarian, was known as a *vor v kazone*. This is Russian and translates roughly as "thief-in-law." A *vor* is a criminal of great influence who uses his influence to settle disputes, using violence or threat of violence as needed. This was Kazarian's role. It was the first prosecution of a *vor* (Department of Justice 2010).

Cybercrime is a catch-all category for any crime that occurs in the borderless realm of cyberspace anywhere, that is, on the internet. New forms of financial crimes, identity theft, and crimes against individuals, corporations, and governments flourish online. For many of these, there is no need for a physical presence at the "scene" of the crime and there might not even be a tangible product that can be seized. The potential profits and losses from cybercrimes outstrip those that require the physical movement of goods or people.

Cybercrime, an invention of the late 20th century, expands opportunities for million-dollar (or more) financial crimes that were once available only to those in white-collar occupations. Although transnational organized crime has a significant presence, a person need not be involved in an organized crime group to make millions from transnational cybercrimes.

Reliable accounting of cybercrime losses is hard to come by. As with conventional crimes, police records report only crimes that come to the attention of the police. In a survey of 24 countries, only 21 percent of people claimed to have reported their victimizations to the police (UNODC 2013a). In gauging the extent of cybercrime, police data must be used in conjunction with other sources. International victimization surveys are the most comprehensive. The victimization rate for the common cybercrimes of credit card fraud, identity theft, responding to a phishing attempt, and unauthorized email access was between 1 and 17 percent, depending on the country. This is a higher rate of victimization than that for conventional crimes of burglary, robbery, and car theft, which in these same countries was under 5 percent. Countries with lower levels of development had higher rates of individual victimization than countries with higher levels of development. In Europe, rates of victimization in private sector enterprises for crimes such as data breaches, confidential business documents, stock records, and other intellectual property ranged from 2 to 16 percent (UNODC 2013a).

The Internet Crime Complaint Center (IC3), a division of the FBI, tracks crimes that are reported to it by businesses and individuals across the globe. Since its inception in 2000, the IC3 had received 4,063,933 complaints through 2017. Over the years 2013 to 2017, 1,420,555 complaints were received for a total loss of U.S. $5.52 billion. Criminals use the anonymity of the internet to prey on people's sympathy, generosity, and vulnerabilities, often discovering these through social marketing techniques. Among the complaints the IC3 receives are frauds such as charitable contributions fraud, identity theft, phishing, reshipping, auction fraud, repayment fraud, counterfeit goods, check fraud, payment fraud, investment fraud, pharmaceutical fraud, non-shipment of goods, and work-at-home scams. It also investigates money laundering and intellectual property theft (IC3 2018).

As the internet grows, so do criminal opportunities. The surfaces both from which to strike and from which to be victimized have expanded rapidly and are continuing to expand. McAfee, the international security firm, estimated that from 2015 to 2019–2020 there would be double the global network traffic, close to five times the data traveling through the networks, 25 percent more users, and about 10 billion more connected devices (McAfee 2015a). In the same way that it became harder to discriminate legal activities from illegal activities as the volume of people and goods moving by train, plane, or ship increased exponentially, it is harder to distinguish legal cyber activity from illegal cyber activity as internet traffic increases. Network anonymity, bitcoin, and other virtual currencies exacerbate the difficulties.

CONSIDER THIS
SPIES HUNTING SPIES HUNTING SPIES

Israeli intelligence officers followed Russian government hackers as they wormed their way through computers around the world in search of U.S. intelligence programs. The Russians had found a back door into Kaspersky security software, turning it effectively into spyware. The Israelis also entered systems through Kaspersky, finding the Russians there. Kaspersky ultimately noticed the activity in its systems and found a newer and much more powerful version of the Israeli- and American-developed Duqu (related to Stuxnet) malware. The United States was not involved in this, but among Russia's activities in this operation, the Russians stole classified U.S. National Security Agency (NSA) documents from an outside contractor who had them on his home computer.

Kaspersky admitted that it did download secret NSA hacking files, but only after they were flagged as malware due to the contractor's computer being infected, and the company immediately deleted them. Kaspersky was investigating a hacking group, Equation (allegedly NSA), when the hacking tools were obtained by the Shadow Brokers who subsequently released many (hackers with ties to Russia) (Perlroth and Shane 2017).

Kaspersky is a Russian corporation and is one of the largest computer security corporations globally. U.S. government agencies that used Kaspersky antivirus software were ordered to remove it.

In another case, Firas Dardar is wanted for committing hacks against the U.S. government, media, and private organizations. His alias when working under the Syrian Electronic Army (SEA) was "The Shadow." He is also wanted for a variety of extortion schemes against American and other international companies.

In January 2016, seven Iranian nationals were indicted in a denial of service conspiracy targeting the U.S. financial sector and companies. The defendants were employees of Iranian computer security companies that do work for the Iranian government (Federal Bureau of Investigation [FBI] 2016).

When a government sponsors attacks on another government's agencies or its vital institutions, is it crime or war?

As the internet has grown more sophisticated, so has the cybercriminal. The once lone hacker, the cyberdelinquent, has grown up and joined a criminal gang. The evolution of cyberattacker profiles progressed from recreational hackers to cybercriminals, "hactivists" and "hacktors," organized crime, and state-sponsored espionage and cyberwar (McAfee 2015a). Organized groups, some for economic gain, such as Pawn Storm and Guardians of Peace, and some for political gain, such as CyberBerkut and the Syrian Electronic Army, replaced the lone wolf hacker.

Criminals devise ever more ingenious attacks, and the security industry that needs to anticipate and thwart them plays a cat-and-mouse game. As in other transnational crimes, cybercriminals cooperate across countries. Criminals share techniques in a variety of ways. When one group exploits a vulnerability or develops a new attack, it is decoded and copied by others. Criminal hackers sell their malware, bugs, and viruses, creating an entire new big business with a cost to the global economy of about U.S. $400 billion, perhaps much more. Thus, cybercrime is now a full-fledged criminal industry with the network structure found in other forms of organized crime—"suppliers, marketers, service providers, financing, trading, and a proliferation of business models" (McAfee 2015b).

Phishing and Spear Phishing

"Phishing," sending out hundreds or even thousands of emails in the hope that someone will take the bait, is one of the oldest internet crimes. It is still popular and has grown more sophisticated. The Nigerian letter scam, the 419 scam, is one of the oldest. It had roots in real events. When dictators in Africa fell, many people needed to move out of the country. Letters appeared in people's emails stating that the sender had millions to send out of the country and would share with the recipients. All the recipients needed to do was send an advance fee to help the sender move the money. In some cases, the "phisher" asked for a bank account number. Of the potentially thousands of people who received the emails, only a few needed to respond for the phisher to make a lot of money.

The letter scam spawned many variations. Phishers pose as government officials requiring that recipients pay a fine "or else." Some claimed that the recipient was the sole surviving relative of royalty or a millionaire and had inherited a fortune. This scam gained the moniker "419" from the number of the Nigerian penal code section prohibiting it.

"Spear phishing" is a newer and more sophisticated form of phishing. The emails are not generated randomly by hackers. Spear phishing is targeted toward specific organizations or individuals within them. It contains some item of interest to catch the attention of the target or appears to come from a trusted source. These more sophisticated phishing scams are usually used to gain a foothold into a network or obtain information rather than money. Asking you to click on a hyperlink in the email opens your computer to attack.

Criminal organizations and state-sponsored actors use spear phishing techniques to install malware on users' computers. Gaining access to one user's computer allows them to infiltrate the network, moving at will through it. In a spear phishing campaign of just 10 emails, there is a 90 percent chance that one person will open it and click on the hyperlink. Verizon reports that 23 percent of users open phishing emails and 11 percent click on the attachments. Fewer people than in the past are giving up passwords when asked or clicking on phishing sites. But because the first click on one of these messages typically comes in less than a minute after it is sent, there is not much time to prevent damage done by those users who follow through on the scam (Verizon 2015).

Ransomware

One of the newest cybercrimes, discovered first in Russia in 2005, "ransomware" holds your computer hostage without it leaving your physical possession. Ransomware infects computers through malicious emails, other malware, or a visit to a malicious website. New forms are constantly in development. The infection prevents the legitimate owner or users of the computer from accessing or using one or more of its functions or apps. Instead of the usual display, users get the message to pay a ransom or never see their files again. Some programs impersonate law enforcement agencies telling the user that they have committed an illegal act and owe a fine; others just demand the ransom. Most schemes demand payment in prepay cards, bitcoin, or another non-traceable currency. Vulnerability is high. Targets include media sites such as *The New York Times* and British Broadcasting Corporation (BBC), academic and financial institutions, businesses, and government agencies. Although many security firms advise against paying the ransom, others advise paying. Victims have little choice. This was the case at Hollywood Presbyterian Hospital when its computer systems were ransomed for $17,000 in bitcoin in February 2016.

Ransomware is costly, but the overall costs in lost productivity outweigh the actual costs of the ransom. Ransomware attacks are growing at about 350 percent annually, costing about U.S. $325 million in 2015 and rising to an estimated $5 billion in 2017. Dozens hit the health care industry in 2016 and 2017, inflicting potentially life-threatening damage (Morgan 2017a). The largest ransomware attack to date, the WannaCry outbreak in May 2017, hit approximately 700,000 computers the world over. Hospitals in France and the United Kingdom turned away patients. Manufacturing at Renault and Honda shut down. The ransom paid out was slight, about U.S. $55,000 in bitcoin (Kaspersky 2017). Even if everyone affected paid the ransom, it would net only about $60 million, but the overall cost estimate was $1 billion in damages—lost records, lost productivity, training to avoid attacks, and other indirect costs—in four days. Whether money or destruction motivated the attack is uncertain (Morgan 2017b). ExPetr and BadRabbit were the second and third major attacks in 2017, both confined to Russia, Ukraine, and Western Europe (only Germany in the case of BadRabbit). These attacks primarily targeted networked businesses and organizations. Businesses lost significant amounts of data. Even among those who paid the ransom, many lost some or all of their data (Kaspersky 2017).

Microsoft Office, Adobe PDF, and graphics files were the first and most often targeted, but other file extensions will undoubtedly be vulnerable as ransomware becomes more sophisticated. In 2016, cybercriminals attacked a Mac operating system for the first time. Over one weekend in March 2016, 6,500 Mac users downloaded the infected software (Victor 2016). Ransomware expanded beyond computers and now can lock mobile phones. The number of mobile attacks increased fivefold from 2014 to 2015, from 18,478 to 94,344. Of all mobile attacks, the percentage of ransomware attacks went from 1.1 to 3.8 percent (Unuchek and Chebyshev 2016).

Zero Day Bugs and Attacks

Virtually all new programs have bugs. When a new program is released, it is a race to see who will find the bugs

CONSIDER THIS
BEWARE OF MALWARE

Malware is the generic term for any intrusive and disruptive software. It may be a worm, a bug, a virus, or even a "Trojan horse." It may ask you for ransom, take remote control of your device, steal information, disrupt operations, and perform any number of other unwanted actions from the merely mischievous to the criminal. It slips into an internet-connected surface through a "back door" in a program, a website, an email attachment, or other contaminated file. By one count, five malware events occur every second (Verizon 2015).

McAfee Labs reported more than 40,000 new malware events in the first quarter of 2016 for a total of 550,000,000 that quarter (McAfee 2016).

first—criminals, hackers, or governments that might want to exploit it or the company and its users who want to close it. These vulnerabilities, "zero day" bugs, are big business.

The cost of zero day attacks, exploiting the vulnerability of bugs, has escalated. About 20 years ago, reporting a bug to the company might get you a T-shirt or some credit toward purchases. Now, zero day attacks are common and costly. Whoever finds the bugs before the program is attacked has a cadre of eager buyers. Governments and criminals purchase bugs to use them whenever the need arises. The going price for a zero day bug can be anywhere from $5,000 to $250,000, depending on its sophistication and how many variants of a system it can expose (Hesseldahl 2015). Companies, including Google, Facebook, Dropbox, Microsoft, Yahoo!, PayPal, and Tesla, pay hackers thousands of dollars in bounties to find the bugs before a zero day attack. This problem is so pervasive that Microsoft and Google formed "Project Zero," employing hackers to scan the internet looking for holes (Perlroth 2015).

Identity-Related Cybercrimes

The U.S. Federal Trade Commission received more than 490,000 reports of identity theft cases in 2015. Most victims do not report on the site; thus, this number is the "tip of the iceberg." The Bureau of Justice Statistics estimates that about 17.6 million people age 16 years and over were victims in 2014. The total loss to the economy is more than $50 billion. Most victims, 79 percent, experienced one type of victimization; the other 21 percent experienced more than one type. Most of the victimizations, 85 percent, involved the fraudulent use of an existing bank, credit card, or other existing account such as a telephone account. New accounts were opened in a small number of cases. Only about one third of victims knew how their identity was stolen. Many, 48 percent, discovered the fraud only after a bank or other institution contacted them (Harrell 2015). In just the first three months of 2015, identity theft cases in the United Kingdom totaled 32,058, up 31 percent from the same time in 2014. Fully 80 percent of these were committed online.

Stolen identity refund fraud is popular around tax time in the United States. With a stolen Social Security number, a thief can use online tax preparation software or a corrupt tax preparation company to file a completely fraudulent claim. Social Security numbers are easier to obtain than we would like to think. Numbers can be bought online, stolen from medical and employment records, or coaxed out of unwitting victims through impersonating a government official. The individuals might not realize that their numbers were stolen until they file their own tax returns and learn that someone using their names has already claimed a refund. The account to which the refund was directed might well have been emptied before the scheme was discovered.

Not all identity theft is for financial gain. Israeli Mossad agents used the Australian passport of an Israeli citizen living in Australia, and passports of other Israeli citizens to enter the United Arab Emirates to carry out an assassination against a ranking member of Hamas. Now those citizens fear retaliation from the Palestinian terrorist group (Information Security and Artificial Intelligence 2013).

Attacks on the Internet of Things

More devices connected to the internet mean more targets for attack. Watches, appliances, automobiles, and

CONSIDER THIS

APPLE VERSUS THE FBI AND SONY VERSUS NORTH KOREA

What do you do if the FBI wants you to hack into your own system? To look for connections between the San Bernardino shooters and potential terrorist networks or cells, the FBI wanted Apple to find a zero day bug in its iPhone 6. The problem with that is that if Apple finds the vulnerability, it compromises the security of users. It also puts Apple in a compromising position if other countries use that as a precedent to make similar requests.

Apple refused, so the FBI took the company to court. The FBI withdrew its suit against Apple when it received a credible offer from someone who could find it for them. This let Apple off the hook with the FBI and let the FBI off the hook for setting a precedent. But what comes next? Does the FBI have an obligation to give Apple the bug so that it can prevent zero day attacks, or does the FBI keep it so that it can exploit it if needed again?

In 2014, Sony experienced one of the most widely publicized zero day attacks. Reportedly, "Guardians of Peace" entered Sony's network in September through spear phishing attacks that inserted malicious code into emails. The vulnerability in the computer systems gave the attackers free access to other parts of Sony's network in an attempt to destroy the corporate network (Hesseldahl 2015). They attacked in November. They revealed studio secrets such as about unreleased movies, embarrassing emails, and employee data, including salaries. The attack was allegedly launched by North Korea in retaliation for Sony's release of the movie *The Interview,* which contained a satire of North Korea's dictator, Kim Jong-un (Schneier 2014).

many devices that we use daily are increasingly internet connected, and many lack the depth of security necessary for protection. The "internet of things" is expected to grow exponentially. Verizon predicts growth from 1.2 billion devices in 2014 to more than 5 billion by 2020. Whether or not a device needs to be secured depends on the function of the device. Other considerations are cost of security for the device, digital space available in the device, and space required for security (Verizon 2015). In 2016, McAfee Labs found that 5,000 mobile apps installation packages, from 21 different apps, had colluding codes embedded. When they share information, they may be malicious (McAfee 2016).

The market for connected automobiles is expected to grow at a compound annual rate of 45 percent; that is 10 times faster than the regular car market, representing 75 percent of new cars, approximately 200 million shipped globally by 2020 (Greenough 2015; McAfee 2015a). New cars have at least 14 surfaces susceptible to attack. These include the engine, transmission, steering, and braking. All of these will require software that ensures secure connections between the hardware and external systems. Because no system is 100 percent secure, rapid and remote fixes to vulnerabilities are

necessary for safety. As of the end of 2015, there were 1.4 million vehicle recalls affecting four manufacturers. Only one manufacturer was able to issue a patch remotely. The rapid increase in connected hardware along with the lack of depth in its security poses a substantial risk that could easily result in loss of life (McAfee 2015a).

World War Cyber Style?

Governments readily seize the opportunities presented by viruses, bugs, worms, and other cyber methods to spy on or attack other governments, their corporations, and nationals. The United States, China, Russia, and Israel created cyber-focused units within their militaries (Geers et al. 2014). As in other cyber realms, the international norms of cyberspace in state relations lag behind states' capacity to spy, attack, or otherwise wreak havoc on other countries' systems. Verizon (2015) warned that if a state-sponsored intruder wants into your system, only another state-sponsored actor can help you defend against it. Attacks originating from state sponsors are different from ordinary attacks, and the differences could prove disastrous (Korolov 2014).

Cyberattacks come into play in conventional wars and disputes. Hacker wars involving everyone from amateur but patriotic hackers, to cyber militias, to organized criminal gangs have supplemented or substituted for nation-state conflict since the 1990s, replacing government assets with nongovernmental assets (Hollis 2011). North and South Korea, as well as India and Pakistan, use attacks against one another in their decades-old conflicts. Even during "peace" time, they can conduct cyberwar. Pakistan installed malware on India's popular music sites. The "Pakistani Cyber Army" shut down the website of India's Central Bureau of Investigation. In turn, India launched a large-scale cyber espionage attack on Pakistan targets, including military, financial services, food services, information technology (IT), mining, engineering, and legal, among many others (Geers et al. 2014).

The United States and Russia have the most sophisticated hacking cyber regimes. In the Ukraine conflict, a cyberattack linked to Russia shut down a power grid affecting 225,000 customers. Hackers installed malware that enabled them to remotely switch breakers, cutting the power. They then spammed the call center, preventing customers from reporting the outage (Volz 2016). Russia also used cyberattacks to deal with uprisings in Georgia and Estonia. In the Georgian case, Russian physical assaults on Georgia were synchronized with cyberattacks. Georgian hackers were able to retaliate against some of Russia's hackers (Hollis 2011).

Spotlight: China

China's cyberwarfare might not be as sophisticated as that of the United States or Russia, but it more than makes up for that in its "brute force" tactics. With more than four times the population of the United States, it can overwhelm cyber defenses with quantity if not quality (Geers et al. 2014). The Chinese government employs thousands of hackers and manages "cyber militias" made up of experts from academia and industry. The Chinese have hacked the National Aeronautics and Space Administration, the U.S. Department of State (USDOS), the U.S. Department of Defense, the U.S. Commerce Department, the U.S. Naval Academy, the World Bank, and the U.S. presidential campaigns of John McCain and Barak Obama, among many other U.S. departments, agencies, and corporations. In some cases, computers needed to be offline for weeks. In other cases, departments within agencies needed to throw away all of their computers (Rogin 2010).

In 2016, the U.S. Treasury Secretary criticized the Chinese for their state-sponsored cyberattacks. The Chinese are suspected of being behind the theft of millions of records of former and current U.S. government employees. In addition, China has hacked Google, Intel, Adobe, Morgan Stanley, the U.S. Chamber of Commerce, the Department of Homeland Security, Lockheed Martin, and the Army Corps of Engineers. These intrusions provide the Chinese with sensitive communications, research and development data, proprietary information, and in one case plans for the F-35 fighter jet, the most advanced in the United States.

"Comment Crew" is more traditionally organized than the fluid networks of modern transnational crime—a hierarchical bureaucracy with an elite set of creative and strategic thinkers atop a layer of specialists that design and produce malware in "industrial fashion," with hordes of "foot soldiers" below who are the brute force attackers carrying out extensive cyberattack campaigns. Fortunately, this structure may prove to be their downfall because mistakes made at the bottom in the execution of a program leave telltale signs recognizable by cyber defenders.

"Iron Tiger" is a newer and more sophisticated Chinese attack strategy. Actors gather information about specific individuals within the organization it targets. They study how an organization formulates its email addresses to determine which individuals to target and set about getting solid information on the targets. In their "spear phishing" emails, they use names that relate to subjects' interests such as "BBC" for the British Broadcasting Corporation. While the emails are typically short, file attachments and hidden images contained the malicious files. Using "Iron Tiger," Chinese actors infiltrated high-tech and defense contractors in the United States (Chang et al. 2014).

Chinese attacks on Europe included governments and businesses. In India, officials worry that Chinese disruption of their networks could give China permanent "denial of service" capability. In South Korea, they compromised computers of government officials and assaulted the portal containing information on 35 million Koreans. In Japan, they attacked government, military, and high-tech networks (Geers et al. 2014). Even old disputes can inspire modern attacks. Every September 18, China attacks Japan's websites. The cyberattacks are fueled by recent events but timed to commemorate the Sino–Japanese conflict of 1931 (Pawlak and Petkova 2015).

CONSIDER THIS

NEW CYBERWARFARE?

Russian meddling in the 2016 U.S. presidential election raised alarms around the world. Among the things that we know is that President Vladimir Putin gave Russian officials specific orders to engage in an ongoing cyberattack to damage or defeat Hillary Clinton and boost Donald Trump, according to a Central Intelligence Agency (CIA) report. Further investigations by U.S. intelligence revealed that the FBI found that Russian intelligence-affiliated hackers broke into Democratic National Committee (DNC) computers.

A private security firm, CrowdStrike, identified "Cozy Bear" and "Fancy Bear," both affiliated with Russian intelligence, as the DNC hackers. Information from the site was leaked throughout the summer and fall of 2016 by "Guccifer 2.0," identified by CrowdStrike as a Russian intelligence operation. Wikileaks also released thousands of DNC emails stolen during the hacks. Emails from Clinton and Nancy Pelosi were also released by Guccifer 2.0 during the summer and fall of 2016. Then candidate Donald Trump declared in a "tweet" that Russia leaked the documents because Putin likes him. The CIA, NSA, and FBI confirm that Putin ordered the Russian interference in U.S. elections to help Trump's campaign.

On another cyber front, Russians used social media—including Facebook, Twitter, and blogs—while posing as Americans to spread false information about Clinton and support Trump. Much of the information about Clinton was blatantly false and inflammatory. Twitter shut down 201 accounts of Russian operatives in September 2017. Russian operatives bought advertisements praising Trump and attacking Clinton on Facebook, YouTube, and Gmail. On Facebook alone, there were thousands of such ads.

Sources: Paletta and Barrett (2016); Entous, Timberg, and Dwoskin (2017).

Hactivist: The Hacker Activist Call to Cyberarms

"Hactivists" attack governments, corporations, organizations, and individuals for what they perceive as civil disobedience for political or social justice. The most famous of these groups, the Guy Fawkes masked "Anonymous," claimed responsibility for attacks against government targets as diverse as Iran, India, Israel, Malaysia, Syria, and the Spanish police. The group perpetrated attacks against groups such as the Klu Klux Klan, Muslim Brotherhood, and Church of Scientology and businesses such as Koch Industries, Sony, and Bank of America. Anonymous has a very loose network structure with no real leader. As such, many hackers may pose as Anonymous or Anonymous-linked hactivists. Their motivation and methods seem to be the only way to distinguish Anonymous from posers, cybervandals just out for wreckage, and ordinary profit-motivated cybercriminals.

In January 2015, after the Paris attacks on the magazine *Charlie Hebdo,* Anonymous posted a video declaring war on the terrorist group ISIS, its supporters, and other jihadist networks. The group's campaign against ISIS intensified after the November 2015 Paris attacks that killed 130. Although difficult to verify who was responsible, more than 1,500 Facebook, Twitter, and other websites vanished within weeks. "Operation ISIS," a network of hackers from all over the world, claimed responsibility (Saul 2015). Although the hactivists cannot keep ISIS offline, they push them further underground, into a theater with which Anonymous and associated hactivists are very familiar.

COMBATTING CYBERCRIME: THE LEGISLATIVE FRAMEWORK

As with other forms of transnational crimes, convergence in domestic laws and forging channels of international cooperation are essential. Fragmented legal systems with conflicting laws and broken communications between agencies provide free spaces for crime to operate. This is particularly true of crime in cyberspaces.

As of 2013, 82 countries had signed at least one cybercrime multilateral treaty. The main treaties are the Council of Europe Cybercrime Convention (Budapest Convention), the League of Arab States Convention, the Commonwealth of Independent States Agreement,

CONSIDER THIS

HACKERS SEND SHOCK WAVES THROUGH U.S. FINANCIAL INDUSTRY

Officials revealed that hackers had penetrated Experian, a credit rating agency, and the U.S. Securities and Exchange Commission (SEC) within weeks of one another. The Experian hack exposed and compromised 143 Americans' financial data. The SEC hack compromised financial records and corporate records that could be profitably used for insider trading or manipulating stock markets. The SEC hack was in 2016 but was not revealed until September 2017 when it was connected to illegal trading.

the African Union Convention, and the Shanghai Cooperation Organization Agreement. These do not yet form a comprehensive or coordinated international regime concerning the substance of criminal codes or seriousness of offenses that would rise to the level of crime as opposed to civil or administrative violations. As progress is made in these agreements, greater harmonization of national laws and cross-country coordination should result (UNODC 2013a).

The most extensive international agreement is the Budapest Convention on Cybercrime. It opened for signatures by both European Council members and non-members in November 2001. As of November 2016, it had been ratified by 50 countries and signed by 6 more, with 12 more invited to join. Its influence extends beyond member countries because regional organizations and national governments are looking to it as a beginning in best practices (Microsoft Secure Blog Staff 2016).

The treaty requires parties to it to enact and enforce domestic laws relative to cyber security. It covers four broad categories:

- Offenses against the integrity of computer data and systems

- Computer-related offenses such as fraud and forgery

- Content-related offenses such as child pornography

- Criminal copyright infringement

Although it is adaptable to criminal developments, the convention is limited because it does not cover the full range of cybercrimes. Obvious omissions are identity theft, spam, and sexual grooming of children (Clough 2014). It is not yet an adequate basis for international harmonization of laws. Societal variation in norms and rights regarding freedom of speech and privacy may prevent international consensus, while other crimes were not anticipated by the convention. Periodic reviews may correct some of these deficiencies, and regional agreements may achieve greater consensus (Clough 2014). The convention also includes provisions for cooperation and assistance in investigation, establishing jurisdiction, and extradition (Clough 2014).

As with other transnational crimes, countries vary significantly in their capacity to collect and analyze evidence. This is particularly problematic with electronic evidence. UNODC (2013a) reported that of six countries surveyed in Africa, none had sufficient resources. In Europe and America, 60 percent of the samples reported sufficient capacity. In Asia and Oceania, about 70 percent reported adequacy.

People should not rely on government investigation and enforcement as their first line of defense. Institutions, organizations, and individuals must keep security software up to date. Network protection and vigilance on the part of users is most important. Double factor authentication makes hacking into networks more difficult. Keeping up-to-date security software in such things as removing spam emails can eliminate many potential clicks onto malicious sites.

Verizon (2015) found that a surprising number of errors by system administrators led to a significant number of breaches. Deliveries to the wrong addresses, publishing proprietary information on public sites, insufficient capacity, and insecure disposal of records were the most common errors. Another area requiring greater vigilance on the part of organizations is the installation of patches for found vulnerabilities. Rather than installing corrective patches immediately after software companies released them, many were not installed until months or years later. Old vulnerabilities do not go out of date. Whereas most vulnerabilities are exploited within the first two weeks of release, vulnerabilities discovered in 1999 were still exploited in 2014 (McAfee 2015b; Verizon 2015).

Although organization and company IT must be vigilant, consistent caution by individual users is also necessary. McAfee (2015), the security company, collects data on real-world attack patterns. It found that every hour, there were 6.7 million attempts to lure its customers to risky sites and its customers' networks were exposed to 19.2 million infected files. These were just two of the criminal attempts. Although the security suggestions seem like common sense, as with the system administrator's mistakes, sometimes common sense does not win out. Protect your password, consider keeping important records on a computer that is not connected to the internet, be cautious when opening emails and examine addresses carefully, don't visit pop-up sites, buy only from trusted online sources, ensure that your network is secure, keep anti-virus software up to date, and so on. Suggestions for individuals are published regularly by the FBI's IC3.

Synergy Links Among Transnational Crimes, Criminals, and Terrorists

It is increasingly difficult to separate transnational criminal organizations and terrorist organizations, whether international or national. Particularly with regulations on contributions to terrorist groups tightening, they have looked increasingly to various forms of transnational crime to finance their activities. While it appeared that links among terrorist and organized crime groups would be temporary and situational, they are becoming increasingly interrelated. What may have started as "activity appropriation," or borrowing of one another's methods, has evolved to buying and selling services—such as passport forgery, transportation, protection, and of course financing—to and from one another (Interpol 2014).

After the al Qaeda terrorist attacks in the United States on September 11, 2001, the United Nations Security Council (2001) noted "with concern the close connection between international terrorism and transnational organized crime," including money laundering; human, drug, and arms trafficking; and movement of chemical, nuclear, biological, and other deadly materials. In 2011, UNODC Director Yury Fedotov warned, "Thanks to advances in technology, communication, finance and transport, loose networks of terrorists and organized criminal groups that operate internationally can easily form links with each other. By pooling their resources and expertise, they can significantly increase their capacity to do harm" (UNODC 2011).

Just as terrorist and criminal groups were cooperating, cooperation by countries on all the related fronts, from money laundering, to terrorism, to drug trafficking, to arms trafficking and corruption is necessary. This was reiterated in 2014 with Security Council Resolution 2195 (United Nations Security Council 2014).

Transnational organized crimes are major sources of financing for many terrorist organizations and dwarf the proceeds that can be made by other crimes. Even before the forces of globalization made legal and illicit transnational activities much easier, FARC, one of the oldest terrorist groups in the world, and Shining Path profited from the drug trade. They taxed traffickers and provided protection services. Despite the Islamic denunciation of drugs, the Taliban, al Qaeda, and Hezbollah have profited from the drug trade. In some cases, the terrorist groups become transnational criminal groups, taking over the trade.

Terrorist groups make money in many ways. ISIL (Islamic State of Iraq and the Levant) sells oil from wells in territories that it seized. Kidnappings, robbery, protection, and extortion are among the many crimes ISIL uses to finance its terror. ISIS and other terrorist organizations battle online as they try to recruit globally while hactivists and governments try to keep shutting down their sites and replacing ISIS messages with messages of their own. Terrorist and transnational criminals overlap in human trafficking as well. In Nigeria, Boko Haram kidnapped thousands of women and children. Their leader released a video saying he would sell them into slavery (Reuters 2014).[10] Children as young as 12 years are forced to be soldiers by armed and terrorist groups in Asia and Africa.

The lines among organized crime groups, insurgents, and terrorists are blurred and often invisible. This is common in the trafficking hubs, where organized crime and terrorist networks cross and overlap. In northern Mali, drug, arms, commodities, and people traffickers coalesce and use the same routes. Cocaine travels through from South America on its way to Europe. Arms travel through on their way to Northern Africa. The traffickers ally with armed groups to protect their economic interests. They have close ties to corrupt political actors and use construction projects to launder money. Mokhtar Belmokhtar, who founded the jihadist group Al-Mourabitoun, was

"Mr. Marlboro," so named because of his cigarette smuggling. Rebels, jihadists, and transnational criminals organize convoys, modernizing the traditional caravan trade, trafficking through Mali (Anders 2015).

COMBATTING TRANSNATIONAL CRIMES

The impact of transnational organized crime is growing along with other dimensions of globalization. Sustainable Development Goal target 16.4 calls for reducing illicit financial flows, recovering stolen assets, and combatting all forms of organized crime. The increasingly globalized finance, web of communications, ease of transportation of goods and people, and quantity of goods and people on the move all make transnational crime easier to commit and harder to combat. Structural adaptation of organized crime groups, from rigid hierarchical organizations to fluid horizontal networks, makes them harder to detect. A fluid and flexible coordinated network of law enforcement, intergovernmental agencies, and civil society groups is necessary to prevent and defeat transnational crime.

There are four strategies necessary to reduce transnational crime:

- Establish and coordinate global norms regarding the legal framework of crime, prevention, and enforcement measures

- Establish and enforce the rule of law, increasing national capacity to combat crime

- Remediate the contextual situations that give rise to crime

- Decrease demand for the goods and services that criminals supply

The Importance of Transnational Conventions

Combatting transnational crimes requires international cooperation in every aspect of the criminal justice procedure. Harmonizing domestic laws so that there is no "safe haven" from which transnational actors can launch or conduct crimes, in whole or in part, without surveillance or fear of prosecution is essential. Differing laws related to finance allow criminal organizations and tax evaders to easily launder money through Switzerland and other countries. With international pressure mounting, Switzerland began a series of reforms in 1997, but 20 years later the country was still a major port for illegal gains.

International cooperation in investigation requires mutual assistance and sharing evidence within transparent channels of communication and cooperation. This is important in the prevention of crimes before they occur as well as in the prosecution of crimes after damage is done.

Transnational crimes, by their definition, cross jurisdictional borders; thus, guidelines concerning where a transnational crime should be prosecuted need to be established in advance to ensure rapid prosecution. Regional treaties on extradition appeared as early as the turn of the 19th century with the inter-American Montevideo Convention. The Arab League treaty followed in the 1950s. The European Convention on Extradition, the Benelux Extradition Convention, and the Nordic treaty were signed in the 1960s. In the 1990s the UN adopted the Model Treaty on Extradition. Regional alliances also developed concerning "mutual assistance on criminal matters." Extradition agreements need to be established where there are none.

The level of harmonization and cooperation required can be addressed only through transnational regimes. This is easier said than done. Within-country rights of individuals, particularly with respect to privacy and speech, vary across countries and must be taken into account in transnational law. Protecting the sovereignty of countries with respect to enforcing laws and conducting investigations that reach into other countries' territories is also important. Most conventions require that countries respect the territorial boundaries of other countries; however, doing so can impede investigation and prosecution if countries are not fully cooperative.

As of yet, no convention on transnational crime achieves perfect convergence on definition of crimes, investigation, or jurisdiction. Even though transnational crime does not respect political boundaries between countries, the countries must. International treaties are most effective when encoded into domestic law. They are mutually reinforcing and result in better enforcement (Simmons and Hopkins 2005). Where there is not convergence and domestic legislation is inadequate, treaties are not effective.

Establishing the Rule of Law

Establishing the rule of law and the capacity to enforce it in poor countries requires international effort. Weak countries have enacted laws but do not have the institutional means to support them. This is important in enforcing laws against criminals and, even more important, in giving everyone in the society access to justice. Bringing marginalized groups into their full rights could substantially increase their economic potential and reduce the likelihood of co-option into transnational crime networks. Ensuring that farmers are well paid for growing and harvesting crops of value, such as local foods, has kept some farming communities from growing crops for illegal drugs.

Rooting out the corruption that results in collusion between crime and government and/or military is necessary for effective rule of law. The International Commission against Impunity in Guatemala incorporated the coordinated efforts of civil society organizations, churches, and the UN to use modern techniques to investigate and prosecute official corruption. It has been successful in bringing many corrupt officials, including an ex-president, to justice. Although far from perfect and not completely successful, this model could be improved and incorporated into other countries where governments, police, and military collude with criminals and benefit from crime (Call 2017).

Because money is at the root of crime, global norms and enforcement regarding money laundering and seizure of illicit gains need better articulation and implementation. Money laundering itself is a transnational crime. The World Bank, UN, International Monetary Fund, many regional alliances, and countries have anti-money laundering initiatives. International conventions on transnational crime also have anti-money laundering provisions. Money laundering could not continue without the involvement and cooperation of banks and businesses. Seizure of the proceeds from crime, vigorous enforcement of regulations, and significant sanctions against the countries, banks, and businesses that do not cooperate with international norms and laws are necessary to make it costlier to shelter criminal proceeds.

Developing nations cannot do all of this on their own. The "Panama papers" revealed significant weaknesses in Panama's fight against money laundering (almost exclusively from drug trafficking). Lack of communication among government agencies, inexperience of investigative staff, inconsistent enforcement, an overburdened judicial system, and corruption such as tipping off criminals (USDOS 2017)—these vulnerabilities are common in developing countries. The Council on Foreign Relations (Lagon 2012) suggests creating a "Global Trust" for the rule of law. As it stands, there is no international body that is focused on building a country's capacity for rule of law. The UN Human Rights Council has a very limited mandate, and the International Criminal Court comes into play only after crimes against humanity have been committed.

A Global Trust could mobilize and coordinate the efforts of governments, non-governmental organizations, multilateral institutions, and private entities. A regionally representative governing board drawn from developing and developed nations and representatives of the agencies and institutions involved should be universally perceived as legitimate. The main responsibility of the board would be issuing grants evaluated by committees of experts who report to the board. A strong team of inspectors would ensure that awardees appropriately administered the funds.

Reducing Supply

Alleviating the conditions that make people vulnerable to organized crime can reduce the supply of illegal goods and services. These are development and poverty alleviation issues. Civil society groups, as well as international agencies, have an important role to play. From the anti-corruption efforts of Transparency International, which help to reduce corruption, to alternative development, which provides farmers with crops more lucrative than drugs, civil society efforts can reduce the numbers of people vulnerable to coercion in supplying the goods and services required by organized crime.

Where supply cannot be diminished at its source, it may be intercepted. Border and customs control to combat human trafficking and smuggling of illegal goods need to be strengthened. Trafficking routes of international crime groups—whether for drugs, guns, or counterfeit goods—are often the same or meet at hubs. Law enforcement has had some success by concentrating in these areas.

Reducing Demand

Without demand for the illegal goods and services that transnational crime supplies, it stands to reason that there would not be transnational crime. Education, while not a panacea, is an effective tool in many cases. International agencies and organizations successfully reduced demand for endangered wildlife in many countries through educational programs. Counterfeit goods are often bought by people who might never think of themselves as thieves or consider other crimes.

Approaching drug abuse as a public health issue in addition to approaching trafficking as a law enforcement issue can decrease demand. Drug trafficking ravages every society in its path from the source society, through the transit societies, to the consumer societies, primarily in the developed world. Reducing demand depends on recovery of users and prevention of future users. Public funding and health insurance coverage for better and longer rehabilitation programs to treat those already addicted are needed. Access to quality mental health care can decrease drug use of those who are self-medicating.

When drug use is perceived as risky, drug use declines. Although many educational efforts to reduce drug use have failed, there are evidence-based best practices programs for prevention.

SUMMARY

Transnational criminal groups no longer specialize in one type of crime. Of the drug trafficking groups operating in Europe, for example, two thirds are involved in other crimes, whether human trafficking, weapons, or counterfeit goods trafficking. Terrorist groups are intimately involved in transnational crimes, either participating directly or benefitting by offering protection to criminal groups. Organized crime groups are destructive beyond the direct costs of the crime. They destabilize governments through corruption. They cause or exacerbate violent conflicts. They destroy generations of lives. This contributes to poverty and underdevelopment holding entire societies hostage.

DISCUSSION

1. What features of modern life and globalization contribute to increases in international crime?

2. What is the role of poverty in international crimes? Consider human and drug trafficking especially.

3. How does convergence in laws across countries help to combat international crimes?

4. Many people consider buying and selling counterfeit goods a "victimless crime" or not even a criminal act. Why is it a crime? Who are the victims and what is the harm?

This UNODC publication is a good reference: https://www.unodc.org/documents/data-and-analysis/tocta/8.Counterfeit_products.pdf

5. How should societies differentiate between cyberwar and cyberattacks? To help clarify your thoughts, consider this NATO (North Atlantic Treaty Organization) video. You do not need to agree. http://www.nato.int/docu/review/2013/Cyber/Cyberwar-does-it-exist/EN/index.htm

ON YOUR OWN

1. Investigate how other countries attempt to control the harm related to the use of narcotic and other strong drugs and marijuana. What strategies have been successful in harm reduction?

2. Study one of the major cybercrime reports. These reports vary in some of the crimes reported and the time span covered. Prepare a report on victimization based on one of the reports.

   - The FBI publishes an IC3 report annually. The 2016 annual report can be found at https://pdf.ic3.gov/2016_IC3Report.pdf

   - McAfee Threats Reports are issued quarterly. To find the most recent ones: The September 2017 report is located at https://www.mcafee.com/ca/resources/reports/rp-quarterly-threats-sept-2017.pdf

   - Verizon Data Breach Investigations Reports are published annually. The 2017 report can be located at http://www.verizonenterprise.com/verizon-insights-lab/dbir/2017

3. The World Economic Forum publishes an annual Global Competitiveness Report. The 2017 report includes 138 countries. Rankings of the

countries are found in Table One on page 44 of the 2017 report.

Choose 10 high-ranking countries and 10 low-ranking countries.

Organized crime is indicator 1.15. Find the values for organized crime of each of the countries. Although this is one factor of many, do you find a relationship between the overall ranking and the organized crime value? (The lower the value, the more problematic is organized crime.)

http://www3.weforum.org/docs/GCR2016-2017/05Full Report/TheGlobalCompetitivenessReport2016-2017_ FINAL.pdf

NOTES

1. When the United States acquired the Philippines from Spain, it was forced to consider a position on opium. The Spanish had established retail outlets for opium in the Philippines. The first inclination of the United States was to allow them to continue in order to finance education. Christian missionaries met this with hostility, and the first U.S. regulations of narcotics and later alcohol, criminalizing them, developed.

2. The United States repealed its prohibition against alcohol in 1933.

3. In the United States in 2016, there were more than 64,000 drug overdose deaths and countless overdoses.

4. The estimated range is from 15.3 to 43.1 million people aged 15 years and over.

5. The average for Canada was 88 per million.

6. Case and Deaton (2017) did not single out Canada, but their data reveal that the United States, Canada, and Australia show the highest rates of death and despair. National statistics show that these areas have high unemployment. For example, Queensland had the highest rate of unemployment in Australia in 2017.

7. This varies by country and region. In the EU, it is the third source of revenue after counterfeiting and tax fraud (UNODC 2017d).

8. Straw buyers or purchasers are people with clean records who purchase arms and ammunition. They can spread their purchases over many dealers to avoid the reporting of sales requirements. Semi-automatic assault rifles can also be purchased this way.

9. A counterfeit good is one that bears the trademark, or a mark that cannot be distinguished from a trademark, and infringes on the owner of the mark. A pirated good is an unauthorized reproduction of a copyrighted product.

10. The video can be seen on *The Guardian*'s website under the heading "Boko Haram leader: We will sell the girls on the market" (http://www.theguardian.com/world/video/2014/may/06/boko-haram-sell-girls-market-video).

10

The Challenge of Political Violence

REHABILITATING CHILD SOLDIERS

Melida left home when she was just 9 years old. Lured from her family by the promise of soup, she found herself conscripted by the Revolutionary Armed Forces of Colombia (FARC), one of the oldest rebel groups in the world, fighting one of the oldest ongoing violent conflicts in the world. At age 16, she escaped and found her way back to her village in Caldas. She was carrying a pistol and grenade. At first, no one recognized her. When she told them her name, villagers insisted that Melida had disappeared and was dead. Then, her grandfather spotted a birthmark on her cheek. Nevertheless, the reunion was short-lived. The next day, the military surrounded Melida's house. Her father[1] had turned her in for the promise of money, a promise the authorities did not keep.

Now 20 years old and living in a camp for former child soldiers, Melida sometimes wishes for her return to the rebels. Life as a civilian is hard—so hard that Leila, a cousin and a fellow conscript of the rebel forces, committed suicide. Rebels raised thousands of child soldiers, thousands of whom are now young adults like Melida and Leila, to fight, and their educations are confined to the ways of guerilla tactics and the lessons of Marxism. The FARC, as it is for other children conscripted by rebel or guerilla groups, was home, family, and school for Melida and Leila.

Vulnerable children face a similar fate throughout the world. Although the incidence of child soldiering has decreased in the last decade, it is still too common. Thousands of child soldiers are still fighting, some for rebel groups and some for governments.

If the final peace accord signed between the FARC and the Colombian government on August 24, 2016, holds, a zone of peace will extend through the Americas. Together with most of Europe, East and Southeast Asia, and Southern Africa, about 80 percent of the world's population lives in a zone of peace, free of active armed political conflict.

LEARNING OBJECTIVES

After completing this chapter, students will be able to do the following:

10.1 Identify factors that create vulnerabilities to violent conflict

10.2 Distinguish micro-level and macro-level factors that contribute to violent conflict

10.3 Identify conflict trends in developing and developed countries

10.4 Compare and contrast types of warfare and violent conflict

10.5 Assess efforts of the international community to avoid reoccurrence of violent conflicts

Despite this statistic, 2014 was the most lethal year since the end of the Cold War. Although violent conflict decreased when the Cold War ended, it began rising again in 2012. The total number of deaths, 37,000, was the largest increase, 80 percent, in the previous 15 years. Humanitarian crises affect more than 125 million people, displacing 60 million of them (Pettersson and Wallensteen 2015; Taranco 2016). Many are concentrated in the region from Pakistan to Nigeria (Pinker and Santos 2016)—a region vulnerable to many problems.

THE NATURE OF WAR, ARMED CONFLICT, AND POLITICAL INSTABILITY

Global systems of the 20th century were designed to address inter-state tensions and civil wars. War between nation-states and civil war have a given logic. . . . 21st century violence does not fit the 20th century mould. . . . Violence and conflict have not been banished. . . . But because of the success in reducing inter-state war, the remaining forms of violence do not fit neatly either into "war" or "peace," or into "political" or "criminal" violence.

—*World Bank (2011), quoted in Kaldor (2013)*

The Volume of Combat

How do we understand today's violent conflicts?[2] When we think of war, we generally think of political conflict among states—interstate war. Following World War II, wars between or among states became less common. Trade and treaty enveloped Europe in a "zone of peace" that eventually evolved into the European Union.[3] After the Cold War,[4] interstate war became a rarity. The last interstate war in South and Central American nations was the 1995 border dispute between Ecuador and Peru. With the peace agreement between FARC and Colombia, an intra-state conflict, the Americas would become another zone of peace (Pinker and Santos 2016).

FIGURE 10.1   Violent Conflict by Type

Interstate wars have diminished since World War II. Most wars and violent conflicts are intrastate.

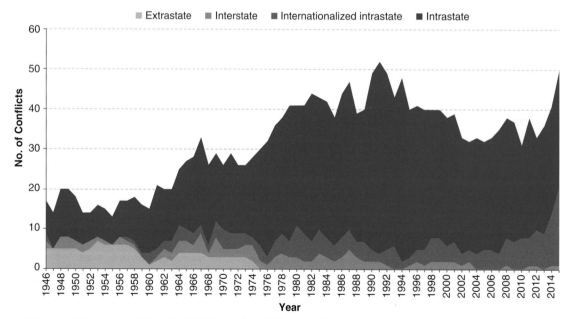

Source: Melander, Pettersson, and Themnér (2016). Reproduced with permission.

From the end of the Cold War to 2014, there were fewer than 20 onsets of interstate violence (Figure 10.1). Only 5 of these rose to the level of war: Georgia and Russia in 2008 over the territory of South Ossetia, the U.S.-led overthrow of Sadaam Hussein's regime in Iraq and the subsequent sectarian conflicts in 2003, Eritrea and Ethiopia in 1998, Armenia and Azerbaijan in 1990, and the Gulf War between Iraq and Kuwait in 1990. Including the 2001 bombing of the U.S. World Trade Center and Pentagon by al Qaeda as an interstate war, although al Qaeda is not a state, brings the total to 6.

The wars in Afghanistan and Iraq may well be the last traditional, 20th-century style wars—large-scale, multi-year ground invasions of one country by another (Slaughter 2011). Interstate violence accounts for more conflict than interstate war, but still for only a small fraction of total violent conflict. In 2014, of 40 active conflicts, there was only 1 interstate conflict, that being between Israel and Palestine.

Today's conflicts erupt along fault lines within societies rather than between or among them. From the late 1940s to 1989, the Cold War years, the level of intra-societal civil conflicts more than tripled, erupting along the ideological divide of capitalism and communism. Goals of civil wars tend to be one of two kinds: take-over of the government or secession from the state and establishing an independent state. Marxist and leftist insurgents fought revolutionary civil wars to overthrow capitalist-oriented governments, and capitalist-oriented insurgents fought to overthrow socialist- or communist-oriented governments. Military governments became relatively common during the Cold War era throughout Latin America, the Middle East, and Africa—presumably as a defense against such groups.

Following the Cold War, the number of violent conflicts declined steadily. The fault lines shifted. Religious and ethnic rivalries became the primary divides. Even more than during the Cold War era, today's civil and ethnic conflicts are "irregular wars." They have no declared battles and battlegrounds; an entire country may be the battleground. Civilians and combatants are often

FIGURE 10.2   Estimated Annual Deaths From Political Violence, 1946–2011

Many more noncombatants die in political violence than formal or informal combatants.

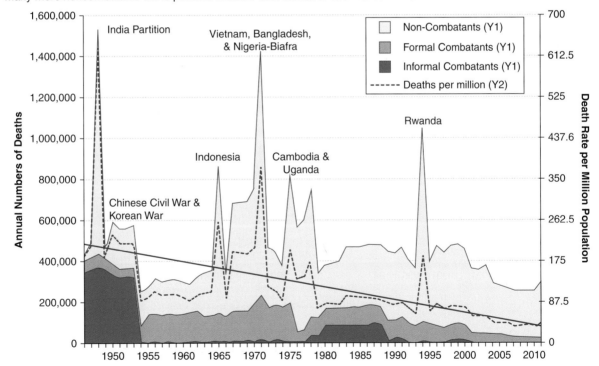

Source: Center for Systemic Peace (2014–2017). Reproduced with permission.

difficult to distinguish and may in fact change from one day to the next. An entire ethnic or religious group—not just combatants—may be demonized by its enemy and targeted. In the Rwandan genocide, every Hutu was called to take up arms and rid Rwanda of every Tutsi "cockroach." During the Sudanese wars, Omar al-Bashir, then president, called the South Sudanese "insects" and vowed to overthrow their "insect" government when South Sudan gained independence. Crimes such as rape and the massacre of civilians are tactics in these wars, not latent dysfunctions (White 2008). More civilians than official or unofficial combatants die in contemporary wars and political conflict (Figure 10.2).

With the exception of the political violence in Colombia, the longest running conflicts active in 2016 are ethnic and sectarian wars and violence. Conflicts in Myanmar, India, the Philippines, and Israel have lasted more than 50 years. Dominated or oppressed by others, groups fight

A CLOSER LOOK
FATALITIES IN ORGANIZED VIOLENCE

FIGURE 10.3   Fatalities in Organized Violence by Type of Conflict, 1989–2015

State-based violence has accounted for the greatest number of fatalities in most years. The genocides in Rwanda, Bosnia–Herzegovina, and Democratic Republic of the Congo are exceptions.

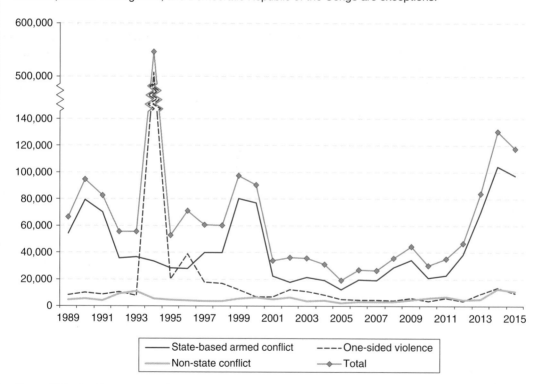

Source: Melander, Pettersson, and Themnér (2016). Reproduced with permission.

to establish their own state, gain more autonomy, and/ or overthrow the government. The Kosovars in Serbia, Georgians in Russia, East Timorese in Indonesia, and Christian South Sudanese in Sudan all succeeded in their wars of independence—at great cost. Kurds, whose "territory" spans parts of Turkey, Iraq, Iran, and Syria, are fighting for a homeland at the same time that they battle ISIS (Islamic State in Iraq and Syria) forces.

As has been the case throughout the civil wars in Arab Spring countries—Egypt, Libya, Syria, and Yemen—there may be two or more rebel groups within any one conflict. Different groups are likely to have different motives. In each of these countries, moderate and radical Islamic groups fought alongside secular democratic groups. While all groups fought to overthrow a dictator, the type of government that they envisioned would follow differed among them. As a result, violence often continues among ethnic and/or religious groups. In Ethiopia, for example, the Tigrean People's Liberation Front wanted to take over the state, whereas the Eritrean Liberation Front wanted to secede. With victory, each group obtained its goal (Collier and Hoeffler 1998). However, violent conflict continues to plague each country.

As noted above, 2014 was the most lethal year since the end of the Cold War, with an estimated battle-related death toll of more than 130,000. That year also had the highest number of conflicts since 1999, with 40 active conflicts having more than 25 fatalities and 11 conflicts rising to the level of war, having more than 1,000 fatalities in that year. While Syria accounts for a large proportion of the fatalities, it did not account for all of the increase in 2014. Of the 10 most deadly conflicts, 8 intensified in 2014 (Pettersson and Wallensteen 2015). The number of fatalities decreased to 118,000 in 2015, but active conflicts increased to 50 driven by ISIS expansion (Melander, Pettersson, and Themnér 2016).

Analyzing Irregular Warfare: The "New" War

As is evident in the prior discussion, since the end of World War II and the Cold War in particular, violent conflicts have been within states rather than between or among them (Figure 10.3). This leaves the question, "If states are not fighting one another with government armed forces, who is fighting?" Contemporary conflicts are classified into three types: state based, one sided, and non-state conflict. State-based conflict involves one government and its army fighting organized groups but not another state. One-sided conflict is one group—such as a terrorist group like ISIS, the Taliban, or Boko Haram—against

civilians. Non-state conflict involves two or more organized groups. Scholars use a variety of terms to describe these irregular forms of combat: hybrid wars, degenerate warfare, privatized wars, wars among the people, and postmodern wars, among others. The new nomenclature calls attention to various aspects of contemporary conflicts: degenerate, state decaying, hybrid (or mixing private and state forces), motives, technologies, and so on. Most of these descriptors single out one dimension of conflict. Kaldor (1999, 2013) prefers the label "new wars" to distinguish them, as analytical type, from the "old wars" of the 19th and 20th centuries. She specifically looks to the intensification of political, cultural, economic, and military connectedness—globalization—as the cause of this transformation of warfare.

Globalization has eroded the state's monopoly on the legitimate use of violence and has made it nearly impossible for one state to use force unilaterally against another state. On the one hand, the transnationalization of military forces—alliances such as NATO (North Atlantic Treaty Organization), the United Nations (UN) Security Council, and arms control agreements—all limit a state's capacity to act unilaterally against another state, as does the destructive capacity of modern military technology and the risk that its use poses. International norms also prohibit force. Within states, the failure of political and economic systems, particularly in autocratic and anocratic regimes, creates a vacuum for organized criminal groups, paramilitaries, and rebel factions, among others who use violence for their particular ends.

Differentiating New and Old Wars

Kaldor (2013) advanced a four-dimensional framework to differentiate new wars from old wars that emphasizes the social relations of war (Table 10.1). First, states are not the actors in most contemporary wars and violent conflicts. Rather than the state's military, various groups within societies—rebel groups, religious factions, militias, warlords, criminal organizations, and/or mercenaries, among others—fight one another and/or the state in shifting alliances. Many of the armed conflicts within sub-Saharan Africa and North Africa do not involve state forces at all.

New wars tend to be decentralized; many different groups with different objectives engage in the combat—often with rivalries among one another in addition to their common enemy. Within a failed or fragile state, the state has completely lost its monopoly on violence, clearing the way for violence along factional lines. Communication

A CLOSER LOOK
"OLD" AND "NEW" WARFARE

TABLE 10.1   Kaldor's Four Dimensional Framework

New warfare contrasts in many respects with older forms of warfare among the regularized forces of states.

Dimension	Old	New
Actors	Regular armed forces of states	Networks of state and non-state actors, internal and external
Goals	Geopolitical interests or ideology Winning power to carry out a program	Identity politics; religious, ethnic, or tribal interests or ideologies Winning power in the name of a group
Methods	Battle, capturing territory through military means	Population displacement, violence against civilians, forcible removal of people from territory
Forms of finance	State coffers, taxation, outside patrons	Predatory means: looting, pillaging, kidnapping, or smuggling people, oil, diamonds, or precious minerals; seizing or taxing humanitarian aid

Source: Adapted from Kaldor (2013).

technologies allow for instantaneous communication among groups to spread their messages, recruit combatants, and construct political networks. Conflicts often spill over borders, destabilizing nearby countries. Combatants cross state boundaries to join in conflicts alongside ethnic or religious compatriots, as do mercenaries for economic gain. Groups and individuals migrate from all over the world, globalizing the conflicts. Diaspora communities provide financial and moral support, often prolonging rather than shortening the conflicts.

Goals of the new conflicts tend to be identity based, in contrast to ideological or territorial motives on behalf of a state interest or reforming a state of older wars. Whereas identity politics is voting, organizing, or working for policy changes to benefit a particular group, new wars are "identity wars." Political or social change goals aim to restore the group to a past glory or fulfill the global promise of nationhood. Old hatreds and animosities are revived. As in the case of the Bosnian and Rwandan genocides, the goal was not only to attain power in the name of a religious or ethnic group but also to eliminate the group perceived as "other." This is one reason why combatants target civilians and the conflicts persist for longer periods and often erupt after a period of relative peace.

The corresponding method of war is not just to capture territory through military takeover but also to cleanse a territory by removing an undesired population through intimidation, fear, terror, and (too often) genocide. There are no rules. What was war crime is now war strategy. Kaldor (2013) sees this as a symptom, almost apocalyptic, of the cleavage between cosmopolitanism and particularism, the global and local forces that emerged with the globalizing norms of universalist and multicultural values.

Financing new wars requires new strategies. Because the fighting units in new forms of war are not states, financing cannot come from taxation. At its height, ISIS was an exception in that it collected about $1 billion in taxes and in selling electricity, water, and other commodities to the people in towns it controlled (Chodorow 2015). Money for most groups comes from a variety of external sources. Those who have the opportunity become entangled in international crime. They may offer protection or participate directly in human trafficking, drug and arms trade, or the illegal sale of oil, rare metals, or diamonds. Kidnapping, hijacking humanitarian assistance goods, and other forms of plunder are also common. Remittances from a diaspora community and support from other governments are important sources of revenue. These external revenue streams tend to prolong wars rather than shorten them.

Why are these differences important? Decision makers must meet the challenges of the new wars with new research and policy strategies. Recognizing that the conflicts are wars, the Kaldor framework differentiates war from other forms of illegitimate violence. This is an important distinction because criminal violence, as some are prone to view terrorism, requires a policing response, whereas wars require a military and political response. The new wars cannot be treated as old wars or as barbarism, savagery, or ancient rivalries. They are organized violence and thus war, but they are organized in a way that calls for changed policy to match their changed character (Kaldor 2013).

The new war model deepens our insight into security analysis. Traditional definitions of security emphasize the military defense of territory. The new war agenda focuses our attention on the political, economic, social, and environmental threats to human security—threats such as poverty, disease, hunger, crime, pollution, human rights abuses, and unorganized violence. Models of international politics based on state control over territory do not reflect contemporary reality. The new war model updates older models by emphasizing that state sovereignty is not just about territory but also about supplying human welfare and rights. All states are not equally legitimate and thus are not equally deserving of legal respect. States failing in this new definition of sovereignty based on responsibility should not enjoy "inviolable territory" or "sovereign prerogatives." The new war model stresses the broader normative model (Newman 2004; Williams 2014).

The non-traditional sources of threats open policy makers to more forms of preventions and interventions than military action and more forms of peace building than ceasefires and peace agreements. Focusing on non-state actors calls attention to the need for new international laws and for new ways of dealing with the criminal

methods employed in new wars. Focusing on the economy of new wars and how they are sustained might stop other states from prolonging these wars through various external financing. Reducing criminal activities may shorten, if not prevent, wars by combatting the financing through illegal trade in humans, arms, drugs, and other resources, as was done with "blood diamonds" (Williams 2014).

Actors of the New Wars: The "Non-State Actors in New Conflict Dataset"

Who are the actors in the new wars? With new wars, it is not enough to know about states, as with conventional wars. Factors such as whether combat will escalate or deescalate the potential length of the conflict and the type of outcome—whether rebel victory, government victory, or negotiated settlement—depend as much on the characteristics of rebel groups as on those of states. Rebel groups are very diverse in many respects. This diversity is largely neglected in the research on such conflicts (Cunningham, Gleditsch, and Salehyan 2013).

The "Non-State Actors in New Conflict Dataset" (NSA dataset) provides detailed information on rebel groups necessary to analyze conflict situations and how combatant characteristics might influence the outcome. For example, whether the group is affiliated with a political party and the relationship of that party to the state, influences how the government responds to the political wing and the capacity of the group to push through for policy changes. This is one factor coded into the data set.

The number of troops that a group commands in relation to the military strength of the state is an important factor in whether the group can challenge the government militarily and whether the group will be able to maintain the challenge. This factor is measured by a number of variables: how much popular support the group has relative to the state, how able it is to procure weapons, and how effective it is at fighting. Each of these measures is important in gauging how likely a group is to pose a serious threat to the state. Cunningham et al. (2013) cited the example of the Tutsi rebels, the Rwandan Patriotic Front (RPF). This rebel group was composed primarily of Tutsi refugees who had fought for years, ultimately successfully, to overthrow the Ugandan government. A rough calculation of the threat that they posed to the Rwandan government would score them low on their capability to mobilize forces, as ethnic Hutu are the majority in Rwanda. Their ability to procure arms was about the same as that of the Rwandan military, yielding a moderate score on that category. Finally, the RPF had years of experience in guerilla fighting and was more skilled than the Rwandan military, so the rebels would score high in effectiveness in fighting.

The control that the command structure exercises over troops is another characteristic. The score is based on whether the group has a command structure and the degree to which it exercises control over the troops. Groups that do not have clear leadership are simply labeled "insurgents" such as "Kashmiri" insurgents and "Sikh" insurgents. Groups that have leadership are scored on how much control the organization exerts. For example, the Eritrean People's Liberation Front (EPLF) was highly organized and coordinated. When rebel groups were successful in gaining independence from Ethiopia, the EPLF in effect became the government of Eritrea, while the other, less organized, groups did not (Cunningham et al. 2013). The Taliban, in its takeover of most of Afghanistan in the 1990s, acted as the government, and at one point some sympathetic governments recognized it as the government, of Afghanistan from 1996 until it was toppled by the United States in 2001.

Controlling territory, the degree of control, and external supports also influence the dynamics of conflict. Cunningham et al. (2013) pointed out that in the Congolese civil war, the Liberation of Congo established control to the degree that it had administrative control and collected taxes, whereas the Rally for Congolese Democracy had only nominal control over some territories. Because insurgencies usually involve multiple rebel groups, the relationships among the groups and their donors are important variables. Often these groups have different goals even though they are involved in the same conflict against the same states or other actors.

Having the support of a transnational constituency can sustain a group beyond its own capacity. Support may come in the way of recruits, money, arms, and/or finding sanctuary in another country. Whether this external support is from a diaspora community, others who are sympathetic on ideological or religious grounds, or another government may increase or decrease a group's chance of success. Such external support may also prolong a conflict, increasing fatalities and the long-term cost of the conflict (Cunningham et al. 2013). In the Syrian civil war, both Bashar al-Assad's regime and rebel groups received external support—Assad receiving it from Russia and Iran and the rebels receiving it from the West. ISIS was also fighting in the Iraq–Syria area. As of this writing, the conflict was in its seventh year, with more than a half million fatalities.

In assessing the overall context of rebel groups, the NSA dataset (Cunningham et al. 2013) reveals that 85 percent of combat groups are weaker than the state they battle. As an aggregate, the highest measure of their strength is their capacity to mobilize people. However, even in this measure only 7.5 percent have high capacity and 36.9 percent have moderate capacity. The majority of rebel groups score low in capacity, even though this is their strongest element. Close to half of rebel groups, as well as states, receive assistance from external actors, most often in the form of military aid. How each of these factors weighs in a conflict bears on potential avenues of success for the international community in quelling conflicts.

Case Study: Scoring ISIS as a Combatant

Examining ISIS[5] through the lens of this NSA dataset is informative. ISIS began as al Qaeda in Iraq, fighting the United States along with other Sunni groups. It transformed itself with the move into Syria, becoming ISIS and alienating al Qaeda with its claims to be the caliphate, the Sunni Islamic state. It shocked the world in its capacity to mobilize people globally to its cause of establishing a Sunni caliphate. It used social media very effectively, recruiting thousands not just to support or sympathize but even to join ISIS in combat. At its peak, about 2,000 recruits were flooding monthly into Syria, primarily across the border from Turkey. By December 2015, about 32,000 fighters from 89 countries had joined. However, as the fortunes of ISIS changed in 2015 and 2016, the flow trickled to 50 per month in 2016 (Witte, Raghavan, and McAuley 2016).

While most recruits were from the Middle East, ISIS has also attracted youths from Russia, the United States, Canada, Australia, New Zealand, Indonesia, and European countries. What lured them? While many analysts highlight economic factors related to poverty, unemployment, and inequality in source countries, isolation in ethnically homogeneous countries seemed to be the root cause (Benmelech and Klor 2016).

Allegedly, ISIS is the most funded terrorist group in history. It started by hiring fundraisers to seek out financing from wealthy sympathizers in the Persian Gulf, many from Qatar, where anti-terrorism laws are not as strict as in other countries. ISIS also used social media to solicit funds as well as recruits. As it gained in strength and took over territories, it secured financing through fines, taxes, extortion, pilfering, and oil, probably its most profitable form of finance. ISIS also engaged in human trafficking. UN Security Council Resolution 2170 requires governments to ensure that their nationals, banks, companies, and individuals are not financing terrorism and black market activities. Social media companies can also be sanctioned if money is flowing through their sites to support terrorism. As governments have been more vigilant on money laundering and funds going to terrorists, support from some external sources has diminished (Lister 2014).

Assessing the capacity of rebel groups involves comparing their strength with the capacity of their foes, whether a state or other group. In the case of ISIS, there are a number of foes. The civil war in Syria began in 2011 with rebellion by domestic secular groups, domestic Sunni and Shia religious groups, and Kurdish forces hoping to secure a homeland for themselves. Those groups gained the support of the United States, while Assad, president of Syria, gained the support of Russia, Iran, the Iranian-funded terrorist group Hezbollah, and, in word if not in deed, China. ISIS did not exist as an entity at the time. ISIS moved into this mix in 2014, taking advantage of the chaos in Syria and in neighboring Iraq and Libya, where it has also taken territory. While its success in gaining funding, recruiting fighters to the area, and securing territory was rapid, it has faced combined attacks by Syrian rebel groups, Shia Islamic groups, Kurds, and Turkey—by about 60 countries, including other Arab nations such as Egypt, Jordan, Bahrain, and United Arab Emirates as well as Western powers such as the United States, Canada, and Australia. Even other Sunni groups, including al Qaeda and affiliates, battled ISIS. Although helped by Russian attacks on other rebel groups fighting Assad, the alliances of forces fighting ISIS may have proved to be too potent a mix for it. In 2014, ISIS controlled 126 key areas across Syria and Iraq. These areas included cities where ISIS taxed and fined people, provided some services, and controlled oilfields through which it gained revenue. Despite apparent control and its capacity to secure weapons, ISIS lost 56 of its key sites, 25 percent of its territory, by mid-2016 (Almukhtar, Wallace, and Watkins 2016).

CORRELATES AND CAUSES OF VIOLENT CONFLICTS

Regardless of the goal, there is never one single factor that leads to violent conflict. A number of political, social, and economic variables that limit people's life chances make a country vulnerable—closed political processes that do not allow for discourse or opposition party participation, marginalization and exclusion of groups from the mainstream opportunities for development, unemployed youths, impoverishment, inadequate public services, human rights violations, and migratory flows (Organisation for Economic Co-operation and Development [OECD] 2001). Each of the factors discussed below may be relevant to a conflict situation. The weight that any one contributes will vary from situation to situation.

Governance and Political Instability

Violent conflict is a failure of governance. One way of classifying governments is to assess the degree of freedom they provide, as rated by the degree to which they grant their people civil liberties such as freedom of speech and assembly and political rights such as the rights to form political parties and vote. Autocracies are characterized by elite rule and few rights and liberties, with resulting low levels of freedom. At the other end of the spectrum are democracies, in which people have more rights and freedoms. The Polity Project of the Center for Systemic Peace (n.d.) rates countries on a scale from −10 for the most autocratic societies to +10 for the most democratic societies. Societies that fall in the middle are called anocracies because they have some democratic and some autocratic features. Many of these societies are in transition, becoming democracies or sliding from democracy into autocracy. The annual polity scales, calculated back to 1946, show transitions and trends for each country (Figure 10.4).

Political instability, including revolutionary or ethnic war, lethal violence by the state against a social or political group, and/or a regime change (transition toward either democracy or autocracy), occurs most often in anocracies (−5 to +5). Autocracies and unconsolidated democracies have substantial and similar levels of risk. The most stable government is a "fully institutionalized" (+10) democracy. A full democracy is likely to have strong institutions and have achieved higher levels of development and equality. Anocracies that are in transition to democracy have not formed strong enough economic or political institutions. Anocracies resulting from adverse regime change toward autocracy are likewise not strong enough to stabilize society through repression.

Goldstone et al. (2010) developed a model to predict the onset of political instability within a two-year time frame. They used data from 117 instability onset cases and 351 stable control cases, 3 of which were matched to each of the instability cases. Episodes of instability within a country that occurred in rapid succession were treated as one event. Unique to their study was a more complex delineation of regime type. Rather than use a

A CLOSER LOOK
POLITICAL INSTABILITY AND REGIME TYPE

FIGURE 10.4   Polity and the Onset of Political Instability, 1955–2006

Historically, anocracies have been the most unstable regime type.

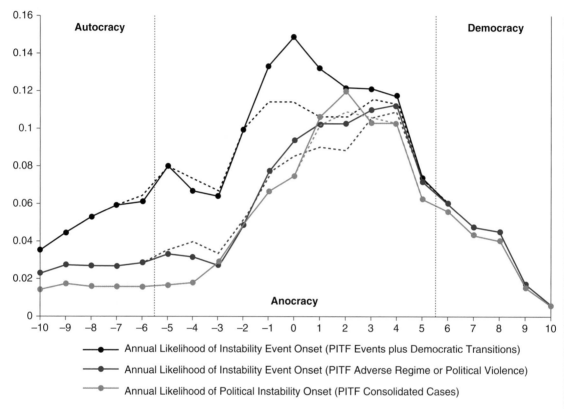

Source: Center for Systemic Peace (n.d.).

Note: The dotted lines represent countries scored -77 and -88, where governments have collapsed or lost control or where foreign authorities maintain local authority.

simple democracy/autocracy binary, which is too crude a distinction, or the three-category measure of autocracy/anocracy/democracy, in which anocracy is very ambiguous (it could result from either adverse or positive regime changes), they used a five-category model. The categories ranged from full democracy to full autocracy, with three intermediate categories: partial autocracy, partial democracy with factionalism, and partial democracy. These three categories all would be classified as anocracies in the three-category typology.

In this model, full autocracy and full democracy were no more or less likely than one another to experience instability. Partial democracies without factionalism and partial autocracies had significantly higher likelihoods of instability than the full regime types. However, partial autocracies had higher likelihoods of both civil war and adverse regime change. Partial democracies without factionalism were no more prone to civil war than full democracies and autocracies. They were significantly more likely to experience adverse regime change such as the overthrow of a government by a radical regime, the contested dissolution of federations such as in Yugoslavia, and the collapse of state authority such as in Somalia (Goldstone et al. 2010). Partial democracies with factionalism had by far the greatest likelihood of instability—more than 30 times greater than that of full autocracies.

Partial democracies with factionalism had a very high level of risk for the onset of civil wars in comparison with the others and an even higher level of risk for adverse regime change.

State Fragility

It is not surprising to find significant relationships between state fragility and violent conflict. A number of nongovernmental groups and "think tanks" measure state fragility. In general, state fragility refers to the stability of the government. A society without a stable or strong

---

A CLOSER LOOK
FRAGILITY AND CONFLICT

TABLE 10.2   Fragility Scores, 2014

The higher a state scores on fragility, the more likely it is to experience violent conflict.

Fragility Score 2014	Number of Countries	Conflict Status of Countries (war, conflict within last 5 years, and conflict within last 20 years)
Extreme (20–25)	8	8 war
High (16–19)	17	8 war 2 within last 5 years 7 within last 20 years
Serious (12–15)	26	4 war 1 within last 5 years 11 within last 20 years
Moderate (8–11)	33	3 war 16 within last 20 years
Low (4–7)	33	5 war 10 within last 20 years
Little or no (0–3)	50	

Source: Adapted from Marshall and Cole (2009).

government may erupt in violent conflict or become a haven for those engaged in violent conflict elsewhere. Although there is not a specific definition for state fragility, organizations that offer measures use similar criteria. The Brookings Institution's Index of State Weakness rates states on 20 points divided into four categories: economic, security, political, and social welfare (Rice and Patrick 2008). These same four dimensions are used in the OECD (2016) Fragility Framework along with environmental security. Typical indicators include gross domestic product (GDP), rule of law, transparent institutions, human development, control over territory, and violent conflict, among many others.

The Center for Systemic Peace (Marshall and Cole 2009) takes a slightly different approach by measuring state fragility using four functions of a state's capacity, although many of the same indicators may be included within the functions. The functions are as follows:

- Manage conflict, make and implement public policy, and deliver essential services

- Maintain system coherence, cohesion, and quality of life

- Respond effectively to challenges

- Sustain progressive development

The Center for Systemic Peace correlates fragility with major violent conflicts. Fragile states are on the brink of becoming "failed states," states that cannot perform their basic functions—governing, policing, educating, providing for production, and providing security (Table 10.2).

Economic Considerations

One of the most striking features of political violence since World War II is that conflicts occur in the poorest countries. These countries have vulnerable populations and weak infrastructures, with little capacity to manage conflict. The International Peace Research Institute found that in 1993, 65 of 126 developing countries experienced war or sub-war violence[6] (less than 1,000 people killed in the year). Violent conflict was concentrated among the poorest of these poor countries, with 31 in the poorest third of developing nations and 24 in the middle third (Figures 10.5 and 10.6) (Smith 1994).

Collier and Hoeffler (1998) used both income per capita and natural resources as proxies for the taxable base that a rebel group would hope to control with a successful rebellion. In considering civil wars from the 1960s to about 1994,[7] they found that high per capita income decreased both the likelihood and duration of war. With other variables held at the mean, the likelihood of war when income per capita was half of the mean of other countries was .65 but was only .15 if the country had income double the mean.

Infant mortality, a sensitive indicator of development, also showed a significant relationship to instability. In the Goldstone et al. (2010) study, countries with an infant mortality rate at the 75th percentile had seven times the rate of countries at the 25th percentile. As an indicator, infant mortality remained significant when controlled for both civil war and adverse regime change.

With respect to natural resources, the researchers found that the presence of natural resources increased the likelihood of civil war up to a point. The countries in the sample had a share of resources[8] that contributed on average 15 percent to their GDP, and the maximum for any country in the study was 67 percent. War became most likely—with a probability of .56—at a 27 percent share, in comparison with a probability of only .12 for a country without natural resources. The presence of natural resources is an attraction to rebels who wish to capture control. When a country had more than a 27 percent share, the likelihood of war decreased. The presence of natural resources, then, increased the likelihood of war unless there was a lot of them, in which case they decreased the likelihood of war because they enhance the financial stability of the government and its capacity to defend itself.

Ethnic Factionalism and Inter-Rebel Conflict

Countries with factionalism have twice the fragility of countries without factionalism (Marshall and Cole 2014). Of the 36 major violent conflicts active in 2015, 25 were ethnic wars and violent conflicts (Center for Systemic Peace 2017). It is tempting, then, to think that ethnic factionalism is a cause of war. The question is, under what conditions does ethnic factionalism produce violent conflict? Diversity alone is not sufficient. In the Goldstone et al. (2010) study, ethnic factionalism, defined as "sharply polarized and uncompromising competition" in combination with a "partial democracy," resulted in the highest probability of state instability, particularly with respect to civil war. Partial democracies without factionalism (unlike partial autocracies) are no more likely to experience civil war than full democracies or full autocracies. With factionalism, partial democracies are 30 times more likely to

A CLOSER LOOK
ECONOMIC DEVELOPMENT AND CONFLICT

Whereas the highest economic quintiles have enjoyed relative peace since World War II, warfare has concentrated in the bottom two quintiles. As recently as 2010, the poorest quintile of countries had warfare at six times the rate of the richest quintile.

FIGURE 10.5   Societal Capacity and Warfare, Lower Three Quintiles, 1946–2016

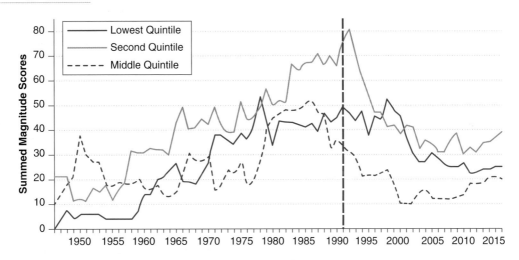

Source: Center for Systemic Peace (2017).

FIGURE 10.6   Societal Capacity and Warfare, Higher Three Quintiles, 1946–2016

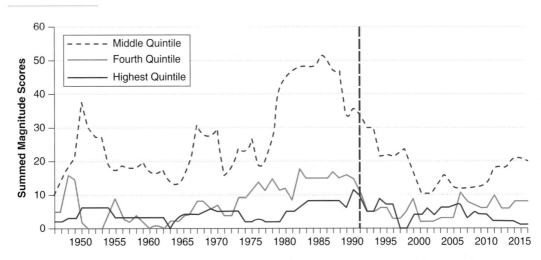

Source: Center for Systemic Peace (2017).

fall into ethnic and civil wars and adverse regime changes (Marshall and Cole 2014). State-led discrimination against minority religious groups triples the likelihood of civil war over states without state restriction of religion. Government restrictions legitimize and are closely associated with the emergence of social hostilities (Grim and Finke 2011).

Attaching emotive content to political concerns increases volatility. Individuals may transfer loyalties among groups according to whoever they perceive as having common interests and values. They congregate to express concerns and frustrations and to empathize with one another. The groups provide an opportunity to vent, to demonstrate the importance of an issue to the government, and to have a voice in the political realm. If emotions come to define political action, it can become more contentious, divisive, and even counterproductive. There may be a synergistic effect in which the issue gains more acceptance among not just active but also previously inactive members of the group. The latter become mobilized and the issues expand beyond the initial interests of the core group (Marshall and Cole 2014). Ad hoc groups may form, heightening the emotive content. This dynamic in the United States gave rise to the "white lives matter" movement among white supremacist group members in response to the "black lives matter" concern over police brutality against black men and boys.

Government actions are critical in managing rising conflicts. They may dissipate the emotive content through accommodation. This is most appropriate for single-issue demands. In cases of multiple-issue activism, accommodation may increase conflict if the concession is seen as a reward for the conflict itself. The state may also stimulate or escalate activism by denying or rejecting claims. Repression may quell dissent temporarily if the government uses it to allow time for a suitable accommodation. Repression alone, however, is likely to increase the transfer of emotive content and loyalty away from the state to the identity groups that provide an alternative source of authority. Civil society groups acting in this regard might not pose any immediate dangers. However, if militant groups link to civil society groups, the militant groups are likely to be emboldened by the political turmoil; they are increasingly likely to act out, legitimize force in conflict resolution, and open the doors to protracted social conflict. Protracted conflicts have a tendency to devolve further into extremist violence, as in the cases of 43 genocides since 1955 (Marshall and Cole 2014).

In the cases of the Arab Spring countries, these various outcomes are evident. Countries that capitulated, such as Egypt (which has since regressed into authoritarianism) and Tunisia, or those that made some concessions to protests, such as Morocco, did not erupt into extreme violence. Libya and Syria remained plagued by continuing violence. Many rebels have been co-opted, and extremist groups, some of whom were not in the area, have migrated to it, taking advantage of the turmoil.

Rebel Versus Rebel Violence

The manner in which civil and revolutionary conflicts are often reported conveys the impression that there is a single unified rebel force against a state; often, however, there are a number of groups, each pursuing its own goals. These goals may be compatible, for example, if all want to establish a democratic state, or they may be incompatible, for example, if some want secular democracy and some want theocracy. In contemporary conflicts, violence often results from fighting among various rebel groups, not just against the state. Such battling seems counterproductive because it squanders resources that the groups could otherwise use to combat the government. Considering, however, that the groups would ultimately face competition from one another over control of the government, it is not surprising.

Fjelde and Nilsson (2012) studied armed conflict among non-state actors from 1989 to 2007 to find out why fighting among rebel groups occurs in some conflicts against the state but not in others. While fighting among rebel groups may reflect local concerns, such as revenge for past harms or greed, more generalizable dynamics related to rivalry over material resources and political influence can also be discerned. They found that resources such as drugs, territorial control, the strength of rebel groups relative to others, and state weakness influence whether or not rebel groups will fight one another. In the case of resources, it is well known that many rebel groups finance their activities through the appropriation of a country's resources. But will they fight one another over this source of funding? The preliminary finding suggests that different resources have different effects. Neither oil and gas production nor gemstone production had a significant effect.[9] Drug production did. It was associated with increased combat among rebel groups. Fighting over the drug market among rebel groups is similar to fighting among criminal gangs to create "a monopoly of predation."

Territorial control, rebel group strength, and state strength are significantly related to the likelihood of combat among rebel groups. If a group controls a territory that acts as a type of haven from government, it can attend to rival groups. Combatting rival groups while also

CONSIDER THIS
CLIMATE CHANGE, FOOD, AND CONFLICT

Climate change is the number one security threat to the world. It is the single biggest cause of resource scarcity and human migration. Would Arab Spring have occurred without climate change? Would the level of violence in East and Central Africa have escalated without climate change? Climate change creates extreme weather events and long-term damage. Water supplies disappear, crops wither, and livestock dies. Climate volatility creates resource and food scarcity, which leads to conflict.

When livelihood becomes impossible in one area, people move to another area, establishing competition for resources there. For example, pastoralists in East Africa typically followed well-established routes with customary rules and regulations for resource sharing that evolved over long periods. When climate change disrupts their traditional patterns, it forces them into routes where they might not share a common heritage. Conflicts over resources, as happened in Kenya, Ethiopia, and Sudan, turn violent. Rather than trying to quell the intergroup conflicts, elites in Kenya, Ethiopia, Uganda, and Rwanda escalated violence, using it as cover to oppress their opponents and win the support of their constituency groups (Mobjörk and van Baalen 2016).

The exhaustion of people living under cruel dictatorships may have been enough to ignite the uprisings that swept through the region. Climate volatility hastened it. Global drought in many parts of the world drove food prices up globally, particularly in the Middle East, which is heavily dependent on imported food. The most severe drought ever recorded in the Syria–Turkey–Iraq neighborhood drove millions of people into cities from 2007 to 2010, exacerbating already explosive conditions throughout the region. In December 2010, Mohamed Bouazizi, a street food vendor in Tunisia, ignited himself in a desperate protest that set off the Arab Spring rebellions.

Lake Chad in Sahel Africa has evaporated to less than one tenth of its size, displacing millions of people. Millions more are in desperate need of humanitarian aid, a situation that Boko Haram has been able to work to its advantage.

As climate volatility worsens, food insecurity, rising sea levels, and escalating migration threaten to destabilize more world regions. This could escalate conflict not only within countries but also between them.

---

in combat with the government is much costlier (Fjelde and Nilsson 2012). With all other factors held constant, the likelihood of intergroup conflict doubles when one group controls a territory. This is complementary to findings that when a rebel group controls a territory, conflicts are protracted and drawn out longer than they otherwise would be. The most significant risk for inter-rebel conflict is for groups that are weaker than the other groups. This effect is stronger than for dominant groups or groups that are not inferior to the others. Both of these effects are strong and often independent of one another. When the authority of the state is diminished, the primary determinant of a group's position in a post-conflict society is dependent on its power with respect to other groups. Eliminating other groups is incentivized, making fighting among rebel groups likely (Fjelde and Nilsson 2012).

Several control variables within the Fjelde and Nilsson (2012) study were also significant. Support from external actors, particularly governments, increases the likelihood of inter-group conflict. This dynamic is evident in Syria, where the Turkish government supports groups that will fight the Kurds, with whom the government has

been in conflict. Where ethnic factionalism, as opposed to politics or ideology, is the basis for rebel groups, conflict among groups results from competition for the loyalty of their common ethnic constituency. This is similar to the conflict between al Qaeda and ISIS, both of which court the loyalties of Sunni terrorists and fighters.

Understanding the dynamics of conflict and combat among rebel groups is an important dimension of understanding contemporary civil wars. These conflicts may prolong war and are serious detriments to establishing peace afterward. Armed conflict among rebel groups merits the same attention as conflicts between groups and states. Not differentiating among rebel groups or treating rebel groups as a unified front is perilous in preventing and ending conflict and establishing peace.

Neighborhood Effects

"Bad neighborhoods"—those in which four or more neighboring countries experience violent conflict—also make a country vulnerable to violent conflict. Countries in bad neighborhoods have similar vulnerabilities and share many of the same causes of instability. Contagion is powerful in these circumstances. In the Goldstone et al. (2010) study, bad neighborhoods had a significant effect on the onset of civil war. Close to half (77) of the countries studied (160 in all) had four or more neighbors, and of those 11 of the problem onset cases, about one tenth, had four or more neighbors in conflict. While the requirement of four or more neighbors in conflict may be extreme or rare, that increases its significance in being found in such a high percentage of cases.

Bad neighborhoods may have several effects. Conflicting parties may flee to a neighboring country for refuge or to regroup. Where there are ethnic or otherwise sympathetic compatriots, conflict may spread. Success in one country may embolden a rebel group to spread into others. A state may follow these parties into the neighboring state or enlist the help of that government to quash the rebellion. Boko Haram, for example, spread from Nigeria into Niger, Chad, and Cameroon.

CONSEQUENCES AND COSTS OF VIOLENT CONFLICT

The costs and consequences of violent conflict extend far beyond the lives lost and the military expenditure, however vast those might be. There are profound social, political, and economic consequences. Public health, mental health, educational attainment, child physical and intellectual development, and investment capital are among many factors important to life chances that diminish in the aftermath of conflict. Furthermore, the consequences last for decades beyond the period of active warfare. This outcome, in turn, may increase the likelihood of further conflict. Violent conflicts and their consequences often spill over into neighboring countries, destabilizing entire regions.

The Stockholm International Peace Research Institute (SIPRI) gauged the effect of violent conflict on the Millennium Development Goals (MDGs). SIPRI found that countries that experienced conflict lag significantly behind in progress toward the MDGs. Using the examples of Burkina Faso and Burundi, SIPRI noted that these countries had similar levels of growth from the 1960s until Burundi's civil war in the 1990s. While Burkina Faso's growth took off in the 1990s, post-Cold War, Burundi's fell, losing three decades of growth. By 2010, Burundi had still not recovered (Gates et al. 2015).

To calculate a more precise measure of consequences, SIPRI compared the development of countries that experienced median-sized conflict of approximately 2,500 deaths over a five-year period with that of similarly situated countries that did not experience conflict. While progress in each indicator dropped sharply in the years of the conflict and immediately afterward, Table 10.3 illustrates long-term impacts.

The relationship between educational attainment and economic development is well established. An analysis of the decades-long civil conflict in Turkey confirms the link between conflict and education attainment. Using security force casualties as a measure of the intensity of violent conflict in the counties of Turkey, Kibris (2015) found that students in conflict counties suffer not only in fewer years of schooling but also in lower-quality schooling. The counties where conflict was the most severe scored significantly lower on university entrance exams. This outcome, in turn, is likely to inhibit Turkey's economic and political development. Kibris's study also found more significant gender differences in mathematics and science achievement in conflict counties in comparison with non-conflict counties. Males might not suffer as much disadvantage as females because they may participate in out-of-school activities such as their family businesses or other jobs that make up for some lost learning. This difference, however, can reinforce gender bias and discrimination. As cited in Kibris (2015), numerous other studies in Guatemala, Cambodia, and Rwanda confirm the long-term relationship of violent conflict to educational attainment, income and earnings, and the political development of the countries.

Beyond delayed progress on the MDGs, war creates humanitarian crises. Millions of refugees and internally displaced persons live in sub-standard conditions, often for generations. Refugees pouring into neighboring states can destabilize fragile countries that cannot afford to provide for them. Financial aid from the international community is rarely enough to offset costs. Even in Europe, the flood of refugees from the Middle East has created political conflicts in countries whose citizens fear that the migrants will bring terrorism with them and/or dilute their cultural purity or because they resent the cost of housing and caring for refugees.

Children in Conflict

The cost of conflict to children is the most horrific cost of violent conflict. The UN International Children's Emergency Fund (UNICEF 2016a) reported that 1 in every 200 children in the world is a refugee. That is 50 million children:

A CLOSER LOOK
VIOLENT CONFLICT AND DEVELOPMENT GOALS

TABLE 10.3   Long-Term Impacts of Violent Conflict on Millennium Development Goals

The effects of war can last generations beyond the end of the war.

Millennium Development Goal	Consequence of Median-Level Conflict After 25 to 30 Years
Undernourishment	Increase in proportion of population undernourished by 3.3 percent
Economic growth	Decrease in gross domestic product per capita by 15 percent
Life expectancy	Decrease by one year
Infant mortality	Increase of 10 percent
Educational attainment	Average loss of three to four years of schooling with minor conflict in neighborhood in comparison with a non-conflict neighborhood
Access to clean water	Access to clean drinking water cut off for 1.8 percent of population

Source: Adapted from from *The Millennium Development Goals Report 2015*, by the Inter-Agency and Expert Group on MDG Indicators led by the Department of Economic and Social Affairs of the United Nations Secretariat, © 2015 United Nations. Reprinted with the permission of the United Nations.

- Within the first six months of 2015, 350,000 children landed on Europe's shores. (Those were the lucky children who escaped to [relative] safety.)

- 250 million children are living in areas of prolonged violence.

- Conflict in South Sudan displaced 490,000 children in less than one year.

- UNICEF helped 2,813 child soldiers escape in the Democratic Republic of the Congo.

- Whereas children were a small percentage (9 percent) of civilian deaths in the first two years of the war in Syria, it rose to about 25 percent from 2013 onward. More than 17,000 children lost their lives in the Syrian conflict by the end of 2016 (Guha-Sapir et al. 2018).

In South Sudan, UNICEF reported that 3.75 million children are at risk. They suffer from severe malnutrition that leads to physical and mental stunting. More than half of the children in South Sudan are not in school, losing years of development. This is the highest percentage in the world. Children face severe psychological damage as well as physical harm. Wherever they are, when children are in the midst of conflict, their situation is the same.

In 1996, a report to the General Assembly of the UN spurred the UN to establish a special office on children and armed conflict. The UN Security Council adopted a resolution to address the protection of children affected by armed conflict. With the intent of enhancing child protection, the council listed six of the most egregious violations of children. Called the six grave violations, they are as follows:

- Killing and maiming of children

- Recruitment or use of children as soldiers

- Sexual violence against children

- Attacks against schools or hospitals

- Denial of humanitarian access for children

- Abduction of children (UN 2013)

Every year, the Office of the Special Representative of the Secretary-General for Children and Armed Conflict issues a report. The report lists groups that engage in these most serious violations. In most countries, the list includes multiple groups—among them terrorist and

CONSIDER THIS
THE CHIBOK SCHOOLGIRLS

One of the most infamous attacks on children was the Boko Haram kidnapping of 276 young girls from their boarding school in Chibok, Nigeria, on April 14, 2014.

Of these kidnapped girls, 57 escaped shortly after being abducted, while still in transit. A few others managed to escape and return home later. At the end of 2016, about 200 remained captive, scattered in clusters throughout Nigeria's northeast Sambisa Forest. Boko Haram has forced some girls to become suicide bombers, including one girl who turned herself in while a bomb was still strapped to her, and others were forced into sexual slavery and to bear children to Boko Haram fighters. Many of the girls were returned in 2017 as part of a prisoner swap with the terrorists. Now in their 20s, many of the Chibok students are living at and studying in the university. As of 2018, about 100 were still missing.

After taking over the town of Damasak, Nigeria, Boko Haram kidnapped more than 300 elementary school children and 100 women and held them in the school from November 2014 until the kidnappers fled with the children in March 2015 when they were chased from Damasak by a multinational force. The force also found mass graves containing hundreds of bodies. Townspeople have returned, but up to 500 children and women are missing.

From 2009 to 2014, Boko Haram killed thousands—6,644 in 2014 alone—often by beheading, and displaced millions, including close to 1 million children. Education is the figurative front line of Boko Haram's battleground. Between 2009 and 2015, the group killed more than 611 teachers, forced 19,000 to flee, destroyed 910 schools, and forced more than 1,500 schools to close. (Abubakar 2015; Human Rights Watch 2016; Nossiter 2015; Searcey 2018)

rebel groups, government militaries, UN peacekeepers, and other international forces. Detailed reports for many countries cite thousands of killings, abductions, and rapes. Children are deliberately targeted to heighten the terror of attacks.

In Syria, Afghanistan, Yemen, Somalia, and South Sudan, among other countries, thousands of children were recruited, used, killed, or maimed by rebel, terrorist, and insurgent groups or government forces. In Yemen, there was a 500 percent increase in children recruited in 2015 over 2014 and a 600 percent increase in children killed. In Somalia, there was a 50 percent increase in reported violations against children, and Afghanistan recorded the highest number of child casualties since recording began in 2009.

Increasingly, children are used not only as soldiers but also as suicide bombers. On August 21, 2016, a child no older than 12 or 14 years became a statistic in a long list of child suicide bombers. He attacked at a wedding in Turkey, killing more than 50 people, close to half of them children themselves. Used because they are less suspect, children, along with women, comprise an increasing share of recruits and captives used as suicide bombers. The Taliban has long used children and women, as has Boko Haram and now ISIS. In the Nigerian regional conflict, child suicide bombers increased from 4 to 44 from 2014 to 2015 (UNICEF 2016c). UNICEF helped to free 1,775 child soldiers there in 2015, but the growing violence led to a renewed surge in recruitment (UNICEF 2016b), including, as mentioned above, nearly 3,000 from the Democratic Republic of the Congo (UNICEF 2016a). The number of child soldiers in Afghanistan doubled from 2014 to 2015. Some of those recruited went to government forces. However, the Taliban recruited the majority of these children, using the religious schools in Afghanistan and Pakistan as recruiting grounds.

Reintegrating children-turned-soldiers who have escaped or who were rescued from FARC and other conflict groups is essential. Rehabilitation, very difficult at best, is critical to saving them and to building a lasting peace. If not reintegration, what hope is there for them—trafficking or joining a paramilitary group? (recounted in Casey 2016). The tendency in some countries is to treat these children as security risks rather than as victims—a tendency that does more harm than good. Reintegrating them is an international responsibility.

The annual report to the UN Security Council (UN 2013) detailed cases of the six grave violations reported from countries in conflict globally. Children are no longer "collateral damage" but rather are targeted in order to maximize casualties and increase terror. They not only are used as suicide bombers but also are turned into executioners. Millions are displaced from their homes, often becoming orphaned or separated from their parents or other caregivers. Nearly 100,000 unaccompanied children applied for asylum in 2015. Children in camps, especially those separated from their parents, are at very high risk of abduction, sexual violation, and other grave violations. Children are victims in these horrific ways and in subtler ways. Infectious disease spreads more rapidly in camps for refugees or internally displaced persons. Cholera, hepatitis, and malaria are hard to control in camps. Food, sanitation, education, and health care are scarce. Children lose years of physical and mental development. Helping all of the children victimized by violent conflict will take a monumental international effort. There can be no price tag put on this effort.

THE CONFLICT TRAP

The Central Africa Republic's (CAR) toxic mix of economic and political issues, religious and ethnic fractionalization, militant extremists, limited resources, landlocked geography, and neighbors experiencing war has contributed to its being in or nearly in conflict since its independence in 1960. Stability for more than a few years has proven to be elusive, including three coups from 1965 to 1995. A brief period of moving toward democracy at the end of the Cold War was followed by the eruption of factionalism and an abrupt decline to autocracy and classification as a failed state by 2014 (Marshall and Gurr 2016).

The CAR is not the only country in this situation. What keeps a nation in conflict—off again, on again—for so long? Of the billion people at the very "bottom of the pyramid," 73 percent experienced civil wars in the last decades. Unlike other civil wars, however ghastly, that were over relatively quickly and did not repeat, the wars at the bottom of the pyramid tend to repeat. Often a fragile peace is achieved, only to break down months or a year or two later.

Armed conflict leaves a country fragile, even more so for the poorest countries. As conflict exacerbates conditions of limited employment, low economic growth, and low levels of physical, mental, and social development— the very factors that increase vulnerability and motivate rebellion—this leads to a downward spiral, increasing the likelihood of further conflict, an outcome that Collier et al. (2003) called the "conflict trap."

Conflict, economic stagnation, and resource dependency all make a country more vulnerable to the conflict trap. In countries more vulnerable to civil war to begin with, periods of peace may be too brief to allow for recovery. Violence between previously conflicting parties in six countries—Azerbaijan, India, Mali, Myanmar, between India and Pakistan, and between Israel and Lebanon— resumed in 2014. While some of these conflicts had simmered in the years between periods of major conflict, in 2014 the number of fatalities in each rose to more than 25. Burundi, Cameroon, and Yemen joined the list when all experienced new outbreaks of violence in 2015.

PROTECTING PEACE AND PROBLEMS OF PEACEMAKING

Sustainable Development Goal 16 calls for just, peaceful, and inclusive societies. Governance, development, and conflict resolution strategies are inextricably intertwined in ending conflict and building a lasting peace. These require global effort. One form of crisis or another afflicts 125 million people. The internally displaced and refugee populations stand at more than 60 million. It is not an exaggeration to say that one or more of these conflicts affects every society, every corner of the globe, directly or indirectly. Death, misery, and economic loss haunt people having nothing to do with the conflict. Within the neighborhood of violence, incomes and mortality suffer, even in countries not experiencing violence internally. On the global stage, conflict plays a role in the spread of crime, drugs, disease, and terrorism (Collier et al. 2003).

PHOTO 10.1 Kurdish People's Protection Units (YPG) were among the most effective and reliable troops fighting ISIS in Syria and loyal allies of western governments.

Kurdish YPG Fighters by Kurdishstruggle/CC BY 2.0.

How to achieve lasting peace is one of the most important questions of the new millennium. It is in the interest of the global community to prevent conflict and preserve peace, not only because of spillover effects but also because international and global forces have often been at the root of the conflicts. Collier et al. (2003) stressed that although the context of each country is unique, countries at similar levels of development and those in post-conflict situations can benefit from similar strategies.

Preventing Violence: A New Deal for Engagement in Fragile States

Just as the UN and Bretton Woods Institutions grew out of a global partnership devoted to ensuring that there would never be a World War III, a new global partnership is needed to address the conflicts afflicting so many regions of the world today.

The New Deal for Engagement in Fragile States, called for by UN Secretary-General Ban Ki-moon at the World Humanitarian Summit, provides a blueprint for such a partnership. The partnership engages leadership of the G7+ (the most powerful and wealthy nations), civil society, and development partners in coordinating efforts to identify and address the causes and consequences of conflict and fragility. Rather than just targeting aid, the new partnership will manage aid.

The International Dialogue, a key aspect of the New Deal, is a forum allowing the 40 countries and organizations who are members to identify, propose, and

PHOTO 10.2 A celebration of the fifth anniversary of the United Nations Security Council Resolution 1350 on Women, Peace, and Security was held in Mogadishu, Somalia, on October 28, 2015. The resolution underscores the importance of women in conflict prevention and peace building.

UN Photo/Omar Abdisalan.

PHOTO 10.3 The Andi Leadership Institute brings young women from conflict areas together to lead peace-building efforts in their communities. This is the inaugural group of eight women in 2013.

Inclusive Security and Andi Leadership Institute/CC BY 2.0.

coordinate measures to achieve peacebuilding, state building, and Sustainable Development Goals while paying special attention to women and youths (Taranco 2016). The membership agreed to five peacebuilding and state building goals (PSGs), five FOCUS principles that are action plans, and five TRUST principles for better coordination and more effective management of resources.

International involvement, such as the New Deal and International Dialog, is essential in preventing violent conflict. There are two categories of countries at risk for violent conflict, even though it might not yet be overt: countries that have been developing successfully and poor countries. A priority for the international community is to prevent conflict from breaking out in these countries. For countries that have been developing successfully, the primary mechanism for maintaining peace is to cushion these countries from shocks that can destabilize them. The international community must provide financial cushions to mitigate financial shocks. Without financial cushions, changes in economic policy will do little to reduce the risk of conflict.

In these countries, political reforms are more important than economic reforms. However, political reform must be undertaken with caution because the conflict risk within regimes that are inconsistent is high. The key recommendation is to distribute power more equitably throughout society. Specific policy to prevent narrow interests from gaining undue power and to protect the power of minorities through electoral systems that guarantee representation without producing deeper cleavages may vary from country to country (Collier et al. 2003).

CONSIDER THIS
WORLD HUMANITARIAN SUMMIT INTERNATIONAL DIALOG

Peacebuilding and State Building Goals

Legitimate politics: Foster inclusive political settlements and conflict resolution.

Security: Establish and strengthen people's security.

Justice: Address injustices and increase people's access to justice.

Economic foundations: Generate employment and improve livelihoods.

Revenues and services: Manage revenue and build capacity for accountable and fair service delivery.

FOCUS Principles

F: Conduct periodic *fragility assessments* to identify causes and aspects of fragility and resources of resiliency.

O: Develop *one national vision and plan*.

C: Honor the unique *compact* developed for each country based on input from all stakeholders and reviewed annually.

U: *Use* the PSGs to monitor progress for each country.

S: *Support* inclusive political dialog and build leadership capacity in civil society and institutions, specifically by fostering women and youth participation.

TRUST principles

T: Ensure *transparent* use of aid through monitoring, tracking, record keeping, and budgeting by states.

R: Identify *risk mitigation* strategies and approaches to risk management; use joint mechanisms to reduce and manage risk.

U: *Use* and strengthen country systems; identify oversight and accountability measures and strengthen public financial management systems; increase percentage of aid delivered through national systems as a country improves its management targets.

S: *Strengthen* capacities of civil and state institutions.

T: Increase the *timeliness* and predictability of aid by projecting three- to five-year estimates and by collecting and providing reliable data to ensure regular and accurate reports on volatility.

Source: International Dialogue (2016).

PHOTO 10.4 Forced by the Lord's Resistance Army to become a soldier at age 13, David says that "without this training, I possibly would be dead. I would have been pushed into stealing for food."

Department for International Development/Pete Lewis.

For countries that are poor but at peace, economic policies are a priority. Although not at war at any given time, risks of war for these countries have been increasing. Some of their strategies are clearly working, while others may be wasteful or counterproductive. While increasing military spending may seem wise, it has not had a deterrent effect on rebellion. Similarly, regional arms races do not have a deterrent effect on international conflict. Rather than increases, regionally brokered reductions in regional military spending are more effective in preventing conflict (Collier et al. 2003).

Countries can take a variety of steps. Cutting off channels of financing for rebellions is a priority. One priority is preventing rebel groups from appropriating natural resources and extorting resource companies. Efforts to protect resources and prevent companies from paying ransoms have been successful in reducing, but not eliminating, this

CONSIDER THIS
RESOURCES AND CONFLICT

The international community has taken significant steps to ensure that resources are not used to finance potential and actual conflict situations. The Kimberley Process (discussed below) for certification of diamonds went into effect in 2003. This process has reduced, but not eliminated, the capacity of rebel groups to sell black market diamonds. Gold and precious minerals used in high-tech applications, oil, and even timber are resources for which there are significant illegal markets that terrorist groups have used to finance their activities. The U.S. Dodd–Frank Act of 2010 had implications for these sales. By requiring two-tiered audits in the electronics industry, it left many, but not all, mines that provide lithium and other rare metals used in high-tech devices demilitarized and conflict free. Investigating gold and other mines and bringing them into the formal economy can prevent or at least shorten conflict situations by shutting down one stream of revenue.

financing stream. Eliminating corruption in government and industry is necessary to maintain public trust. Having transparency in managing natural resource revenues that the government receives and monitoring how these revenues are spent and distributed are essential. The international community must help countries to either develop programs for meeting these goals or adapt successful templates from other countries (Collier et al. 2003).

Protection from negative shocks, such as price crashes and natural disasters, is also important in countries that are poor but at peace. Collier et al. (2003) suggested various forms of financial loan and grant arrangements managed by the World Bank and International Monetary Fund that would adjust loan repayments and aid to mitigate the effect of shocks. Trade policies can and should be negotiated to protect against price shocks.

PHOTO 10.5 The Trans-Sahara Counterterrorism Partnership builds peace and security through community engagement. This U.S. Army soldier is passing out soccer balls to local youth in Bamako, Mali.

U.S. Air Force photo by Tech. Sgt. Roy Santana.

Whereas economic growth does not have a significant impact on reducing conflict in countries that are developing well, it is important for poor countries. Increasing the growth rate of poor countries by 3 percent nearly halves the incidence of violent conflict. Many poor countries are dependent on a primary commodity. Diversifying the economies of poor countries has been one of the most successful strategies for growth. Where this is not possible, as in the case of countries with few options, good management of the primary resource is necessary. Botswana is a case in point. With few options, it has made its diamond industry work well for growth. Aid, sound economic policy reform, and access to markets all produce growth (Collier et al. 2003).

Nearly half of the countries in the "poor but peaceful" category are dominated by one ethnic group but have a number of minority groups. Ensuring group and individual rights and protecting them with institutional avenues of addressing grievances protects the peace. Here, Switzerland is a good example. While 75 percent of the population is German speaking, quotas in employment, decentralization that empowers communities, and multilingual education afford some protection to the Italian and French minorities. Where the minority (or minorities) is wealthier than the majority (as in South Africa), gradual redistribution is suggested. In Malaysia, gradual redistribution increased the majority Malay share of GDP by 15 percent. Because the economy was also growing, minority incomes grew as well (Collier et al. 2003).

Remittances have varying effects on the likelihood of violence and conflict. If used to finance rebel groups, remittances generally prolong violence. However, remittances also alleviate economic pressures in poor societies and avoid conflict. Remittances can release poorer voters from dependence on the dominant party or regime for social welfare or clientelism. "Economic autonomy" makes poor voters more willing to vote against or challenge local authorities with whom they do not agree and move the society in a more democratic direction. Remittances also provide financing for opposition parties. Thus, remittances can foster political change, particularly in a more democratic direction, lessening the likelihood of violent conflict. However, in regimes that do not allow elections or where opposition groups and parties are banned, remittances may increase the likelihood of violent conflict (Escribà-Folch, Meseguer, and Wright 2015). The ramifications of remittances are discussed further in the chapter on migration.

PROMOTING PEACE AND GETTING OUT OF THE CONFLICT TRAP

Some conflicts erupt repeatedly, persisting for decades. As discussed earlier in the chapter, the most significant predictor of a violent conflict breaking out is having had violent conflict in the past. If past conflict is the best predictor of future conflict, getting countries out of the conflict trap is essential.

In countries that have been at war for decades, conflict becomes a way of life. Conflict situations tend to become longer and longer. A two-pronged strategy for shortening conflicts and reducing post-conflict risk is necessary.

Shortening or Ending the Conflict

If there were a blueprint for shortening and ending conflict, there would not be the level of violence that we witnessed in the 1990s or that persists today. However, at least two points should be addressed: the importance of cutting off funding and the potential advantages and disadvantages of outside involvement.

Stopping the Flow of Finances

As with countries that are at peace but fragile, cutting off the financing to bring groups to the negotiating table is a priority. Fighting is lucrative for rebel leaders. Access to funding increases the capacity of rebel groups. Collier et al. (2003) reported that Jonas Savimbi, an Angolan rebel leader of UNITA (National Union for the Total Independence of Angola) in the 1990s, was one of the richest men in the world, valued at some U.S. $4 billion. There is not much motivation in such cases for rebel leaders to give up the fight. Cutting off their access to the commodity markets that made them wealthy is one action that can make war less appealing. In the case of Savimbi and Angola, cutting off access to the diamond market, and thereby stopping the sale of "blood diamonds," was a decisive step, along with Angola's increased military expenditures, in both UNITA's defeat and the defeat of RUF (Revolutionary United Front) in Sierra Leone.

The drug trade has proven to be more difficult to eradicate. However, when Britain raised the penalties on the illegal use of drugs and supplied addicts legally, the illegal market shrank. In the case of the Khmer Rouge, its lifeline was timber. Both the Cambodian and Thai governments largely allowed the illegal trade from Cambodia across the border to Thailand. Before international pressure and sanctions forced the governments to end the trade, the Khmer Rouge benefitted. Ending the timber trade accelerated the demise of the Khmer Rouge. Any policy that can discount the price of the illegal markets can reduce funding to rebel groups profiting from them.

Remittances are the largest source of foreign aid. Unfortunately, diaspora communities abroad send money home that is used to finance rebel and terrorist groups, prolonging wars. This was the case in Sri Lanka. The Liberation Tigers of Tamil Eelam (Tamil Tigers) received an estimated U.S. $450 million a year that they used to buy arms. The Kurdish Workers Party received about $50 million in 1992 alone. Government bans on providing money to specific organizations and improved policies for scrutinizing cash flows are the best ways in which to control these flows. For example, the British ban on the Tamil Tigers dried up a significant source of their income. This factored into forcing them to the peace table (Collier et al. 2003).

Outside Involvement

Determining whether to become engaged in a foreign conflict and, if so, how best to engage are always problematic. In their review of studies, Collier et al. (2003) found mixed results for outside intervention. They found that diplomatic intervention did not systematically shorten conflicts to any significant extent. Certainly, this finding is borne out in the recent case of the war in Syria, at least as of 2018. Two attempts at peace accords negotiated by Russia, the United States, various rebel groups, and the Assad regime did not hold, and fighting resumed within days or weeks of the accords. Perhaps this is because, like Syria, these were the most difficult conflicts. Perhaps the conflicts would have lasted longer without intervention. Military intervention on the side of the rebels has worked to shorten some conflicts.

Different results were reported by Pettersson and Wallensteen (2015). Rather than helping to settle conflicts, outside support often prolongs them. By providing troops, arms, or other resources, external military support allows the fighting to extend beyond the capacity of the conflicting parties. This leads to a longer conflict with more fatalities. Involving other parties can forestall successful negotiation if external supporters do not approve of the agreements or if they bring their own interests into the process. The strategy and role of outside intervention—economic, military, or diplomatic—must be approached with caution. Again the conflict in Syria is a case in point given that China, Russia, the United States, and Turkey support different parties and have different motivations for engaging in the conflict.

A Different Path to Peace

The history of peacemaking bears a legacy of violence. Michael Collins was a leader in both the struggle for Irish independence from Britain and the negotiations that achieved independence for the southern counties. Some members of the Irish Republican Army (IRA) that Collins represented were unhappy with the compromise that left Northern Ireland behind and vowed to fight on as the "real" IRA. On a trip to the north, former fellow rebels ambushed and killed Collins. Northern Ireland has yet to establish total peace. Long after the peace agreement of the 1920s, "the troubles" broke out in Northern Ireland. They lasted 30 years, from 1968 to 1998, claimed well over 3,000 lives, and injured tens of thousands more people. The "peace walls" still divide Protestant and Catholic sections within the cities of Northern Ireland.

Negotiations toward peace in the Israel–Palestinian conflict has had its martyrs. The Egypt–Israel Peace Treaty signed in 1978 has held despite continuing warfare in the region and the Arab Spring revolutions. It cost Nobel Peace Prize awardee Anwar Sadat, president of Egypt, his life when he was assassinated by religious zealots angry with, among other things, the peace accord. An extremist angry with the Oslo Peace Accords that Yitzhak Rabin, prime minister of Israel, signed with the Palestinians assassinated Rabin to halt or stall the peace accords.

In contemporary conflicts, it is not just a lone target who is the victim of post-conflict peace. Often entire rebel factions continue the war against the new or reformed government. Total peace necessitates compromise, with more than just those groups willing to lay down arms. It requires motivating all groups to lay down arms. Because not all rebel parties and their supporters are united in their goals, what one group may accept, others may reject, with intentions to fight on.

Reaching an inclusive peace, in which all parties are signatories to the agreement, is an ideal, but is a partial peace valuable? The question as to whether violence by outside actors, non-signatories, will erode the partial peace is important. In other words, is partial peace better than no peace? Can a partial peace hold in a context of continuing violence by others? These questions were addressed by Nilsson (2008) using data on government and rebel group behavior following peace agreements.

Reasoning that rebel groups and governments are strategic actors implies that they have estimated the costs of violence by outside actors before they sign an agreement. It is reasonable to expect that the peace among signatories will hold even if not all conflict groups are included in the agreement. Using the Uppsala Conflict Dataset that tracks the behavior of all groups engaged in a conflict and all peace agreements, Nilsson (2008) found that rebel groups that sign a peace agreement are likely to see peace prevail, while non-signatories are twice as likely to experience post-settlement armed conflict. This finding is subtly different from findings by others. The common understanding is that a partial agreement does not maintain peace. But by examining dyads, it is evident that peace is likely to hold between signatories. There is no significant difference in the likelihood of armed conflict among signatories and the government whether the agreement is all-inclusive or partial. This reflects the experience of partial peace in countries such as the Philippines and Burundi, where peace was achieved with some groups but not all groups.

Where total peace is not achievable, partial peace should not be overlooked. Examining the endurance of peace for signatories and non-signatories, Nilsson (2008) found that non-signatories experienced peace for about two years, while signatories experienced peace for eight years (p. 491). Where the conflict was particularly devastating and where the conflict was over government as opposed to territory, conflict was more likely to resume. Where there was power sharing, peace prevailed for a longer period. Lastly, UN peacekeepers were not very effective in maintaining peace.

These results, showing that partial peace reduces the overall prospect for peace in comparison with all-inclusive peace, are not surprising. But the finding that partial peace does not affect whether signatories maintain the peace is an important one. Partial peace is possible and reduces the scope of conflict and presumably the loss of life and degradation of the quality of life for many people, potentially millions.

Escaping the Conflict Trap

Support from the international community in the first decade of peace is critical if a country is to avoid falling into the conflict trap (Collier et al. 2003). It requires significant effort, but the benefits in reduced risk of conflict resurging are likely to outweigh the costs. The two priorities for the first 10 years are demobilization and timely aid.

Continued or increased military mobilization, as often happens, breeds distrust. Demobilization and reintegration of combatants is critical to ensure both the domestic and international communities that the peace commitment is genuine and secured. This requires involvement of the international community. A military presence is necessary during these years, but it must come from an outside source. Whether that source is the UN, a configuration of bilateral or multilateral forces, or a regional one will vary by the specific situation. What is critical is that the military presence is perceived as legitimate and that it is prepared and permitted to fight, if necessary, to preserve the peace. But it is also critical that the military does not overstay its "welcome."

Demobilizing in stages is important for reintegrating combatants and ex-military into society in productive citizen roles. Successful reintegration can be a long and complex procedure. Any quartering of combatants should be as short as possible. Support from communities and families is important for the most successful reintegration. Some combatants may have committed crimes against, or in other ways harmed, their home communities. Sources of the original conflict might not be settled. Many combatants need help with trauma or need other psychological or social healing. Communities need strengthening to increase their capacity to take in combatants.

Fears of increasing crime are common with demobilization. Targeted interventions, identifying those likely to turn to crime, and providing help in returning to economic activity can create conditions for successful demobilization. Transparency in the processes is important to retain legitimacy. Such transparency should reduce risk of conflict resurgence and help to spur growth by building back the labor force. In the Ugandan case in the 1990s, demobilization generally did not increase local crime rates. But soldiers without access to land were 100 times more likely to commit crimes than the average Ugandan.

The timeliness of aid is also critical. In the first decade post-conflict, economic growth tends to be higher than normal. During the first few years, growth in a post-conflict society proceeds at normal rates; even though aid is highest at this time, it does not affect the growth rate. Early investment in post-conflict societies needs to be directed at reforming and implementing social and structural policies. Social policies that promote inclusion are the priority, even more so than macroeconomic policies to promote growth. For example, post-conflict policies need to be different from those in societies at peace. In potential trade-offs between policies that promote peace and policies that promote growth, peace-oriented policies must prevail. Territories controlled by rebels, for example, might be those where it is most difficult to promote growth. Growth could increase faster in urban areas or areas where private investments are most active. Public investment in these areas might make the most sense for rapid growth, but people in more disadvantaged areas may see that investment as unfair. Such policies may present cause for grievance or even a return to rebellion. Governments may need to sacrifice quicker short-term growth to prevent further conflict. Managing growth transparently may reduce such conflict (Collier et al. 2003).

Aid has the most impact at the fourth and fifth years post-conflict. Growth during these later years accounts for the above-normal growth rates typical of the first decade. Appropriate policies, infrastructure, strategies, and other mechanisms to make the best use of aid are not in place in the first few years. Aid during those years is necessary, but rather than being diminished after those years, it should be ramped up for the fourth and fifth years. In these years, the amount of aid that a country can use productively doubles. With policy reform and demobilization accomplished, domestic and international actors can be encouraged to bring investment back into the country, assured that it will be well spent. Infrastructure, for example, is one such wise investment. Conflict inevitably damages, if not destroys, infrastructure, which is essential for growth, and growth is essential to escape the conflict trap. The return on investment in infrastructure is high. In post-conflict Uganda, the World Bank road repair returned 40 percent on investment. Road and other infrastructure improvements can affect inclusion, for example by connecting rural areas to urban markets.

The diaspora community can play an important role in post-conflict countries. Its members may be involved through remittances and financial aid but also more actively by sharing skills and opportunities. Conducting trade with domestic businesses, providing expertise in nation building and economic activities, volunteering as teachers, and sending books and other supplies to bolster the recovery of education are among the potential productive roles for the diaspora community.

If by the end of the first post-conflict decade, with the help of well-timed aid and a peacekeeping force, a country can institute sound and fair policy, achieve a 2 percent increase in annual growth, and diversify its economy by a mere 2 percent of GDP away from primary commodity dependence, the risk of conflict can be halved, from 44 to 22 percent. If the country can sustain development, the risk may drop to 12 percent over the next decade. After an additional five years of peace, the country has more likely than not escaped the conflict trap.

SUMMARY

Increasing democratization, economic development, international governmental organizations, and regional, bilateral, and multilateral treaties and trade all have contributed to decreasing violent conflict and war between countries. The fault lines that divide people in the 21st century more often erupt within societies.

Sovereignty, the right of nations to independence and self-rule, has inspired separatist movements of oppressed minorities to demand their own states. Other movements press for more autonomy but not necessarily their own states. Political instability, inequalities in the access to resources and benefits of societies, perceived threats to religious and ethnic identities, food insecurity, and persecution and discrimination in societies breed grievances. If people have no recourse to pursue justice, without the help of the international community, violent conflict may be their only option.

DISCUSSION QUESTIONS

1. Who should decide whether or not a people should be recognized as a sovereign state (their own country)? Should it be the people themselves, the UN and other countries, the International Court of Justice, or the country from which they are separating?

2. Should the role of UN peacekeepers be revised to allow them to participate more in ending violent conflicts within countries?

3. How did the history of colonialism and the Cold War help to set the stage for violent conflicts within societies?

4. What must be accomplished in order to prevent post-conflict societies from erupting into violence again?

5. Why are countries in transition fragile? Are there strategies that the international community can employ to help them stabilize?

6. How do facets of globalization and modern life contribute to violent conflict?

ON YOUR OWN

1. Using the Systemic Peace Warlist, Human Development Index (HDI), and Freedom House designations, explore the relationship among violent conflict, human development, and freedom.

   a. Select 20 countries most recently involved in violent conflict.

   b. Find their HDI score and their freedom score.

   c. Does there appear to be a relationship between human development and violent conflict?

   d. Does there appear to be a relationship between the freedom scores and violent conflict?

If you have access to a statistical program, you might do a more complex analysis.

2. The "Mapping Militant Organizations Project" presents a map for militant groups that details the evolution of the groups, their associations with other groups (ally or rival, merger or split), and the areas where they operate. It also provides detailed profiles of the groups.

http://web.stanford.edu/group/mappingmilitants/cgi-bin/maps

Choose a group in which you have an interest. When did it emerge? Did it split from or merge with other groups? How large is it? Does it operate in more than one country? What is its objective?

3. The Global Conflict Tracker (2016), developed by the Center for Preventive Action, presents information on active conflicts. It looks at the conflicts from the perspective of the interests of the United States and whether they are of critical interest, significant interest, or limited interest to the United States. Conflicts in any of these categories, and most likely all of them, have serious humanitarian consequences.

Compare the Global Conflict Tracker's analysis of a conflict in which the United States has a critical interest with one in which it has a limited interest. What criteria did the tracker use in determining the classification of each?

4. It is always problematic in deciding what to do in conflict situations. What criteria would you use to classify the effort we should put into conflicts of varying types?

Watch the video *The Humanitarian Crisis in the Eastern Congo* (https://www.cfr.org/sub-saharan-africa/democratic-republic-congo).

What should other countries and intergovernmental organizations do in this conflict and others like it?

NOTES

1. Her father had searched for her when she first disappeared, even confronting rebel groups.

2. Various listings of violent conflicts vary by the size of conflicts that are included. The Center for Systemic Peace War List lists only major conflicts that brought 500 deaths in a year. The Uppsala Conflict Data Program lists conflicts in which 25 deaths per dyad occurred. Some studies include political instability such as coups even though the death counts may be small. Most experts count wars as conflicts with 1,000 fatalities in a year. This chapter addresses listings and studies as they are relevant to the topics at hand, distinguishing war, major violent conflicts, and political instability in keeping with the original sources.

3. The future of the European Union is uncertain. Disagreements among states on austerity and stimulus packages, the crippling debt of some states, and the torrent of refugees from conflicts in Middle Eastern countries have strained the capacity of countries and relations among them. In 2016, the United Kingdom voted to leave the European Union.

4. During the Cold War years, a near global conflict between democratic and socialist states, the United States and the Union of Soviet Socialist Republics, avoided direct confrontation even as they supported insurgent factions warring within countries or the governments they battled. Cold War "proxy" wars raged throughout Central and South America, Asia, and Africa.

5. ISIS is also known as ISIL (Islamic State of Iraq and the Levant), IS (Islamic State), and Daesh.

6. Most experts consider war to be conflicts in which there are more than 1,000 fatalities within a year and sub-war violence to be less than 1,000 fatalities.

7. Collier and Hoeffler (1998) used the dataset compiled by Small and Singer (1982) and Singer and Small (1994). A civil war in the set is defined as a war in which one of the primary actors is the government in power, the stronger force experiences at least 5 percent of the fatalities of the weaker force, at least 1,000 battle fatalities occur per year, and there is significant military action. Eliminating countries from which there is insufficient data on all of the variables examined resulted in a database of 98 countries, 27 of which had civil wars during the period from the 1960s onward.

8. Collier and Hoeffler (1998) gauged a country's share of natural resources by the percentage of primary commodity exports to its GDP.

9. Fjelde and Nilsson (2012) reported that gemstone production was negatively correlated but insignificant. Oil and gas production was positively correlated and insignificant. Based on studies by others, they speculated that rebel groups may take time off from fighting for the extraction of gemstones. The measure of gemstone production used was during the years of rebellion.

11

Global Flows of Refugees

AWAY FROM THE WAR WITH A GLIMMER OF HOPE

At 62 years old, Aisho Warsame fled Mogadishu, Somalia. She had held out in the war-torn city until she thought she would either go crazy from the constant noise of the bombing and shelling or be killed. With her husband already murdered and her house bombed, she took her four children and six grandchildren first on foot and then by bus to Galkayo, a city about 435 miles north. Now, they reside in a camp with thousands of others. A makeshift shelter is their home, and they have close to nothing by way of possessions. The luxury that she enjoys is the knowledge that she will not end up as one of the bodies—all that can be seen, she said, on the streets of Mogadishu.

According to the United Nations (UN) security rating of refugee camps, Galkayo is a "Level 5 Security Phase." Level 6 is the most dangerous. No UN or U.S. Agency for International Development (USAID) tents are in sight; people make their shelters out of rags and twigs. Naomi Steer, the director of Australia for the UN High Commissioner for Refugees (UNHCR), watched one man making a bed from oil cans while a woman constructed another of rocks. Children's bellies swelled with malnutrition. In Galkayo, the complex story of migrants and the interlocking factors that forced their displacement are all too vivid, from the shriveled limbs and swollen bellies to gunshot wounds. Like Aisho, some fled the violent conflict; others fled famine, their crops and livestock having dried up from drought and hunger.

In the midst of this desperation, there is one spot of hope—a spotless facility, a hospital. Far from his home in Italy, "Dr. Gaima" and his staff, supported by Australia for UNHCR, provide medical care for the violent crime

LEARNING OBJECTIVES

After completing this chapter, students will be able to do the following:

11.1 Compare and contrast causes of voluntary and forced migration

11.2 Present an argument in favor of or against international responsibility for refugee protections in international law

11.3 Analyze the societal- and global-level causes of refugee migration in general and in specific cases

11.4 Evaluate the conditions in refugee camps in relation to obligations under international law

11.5 Explain the difficulties in resettlement and repatriation of migrants

11.6 Compare and contrast the potential advantages and disadvantages of repatriation, local integration, and resettlement of refugees

11.7 Propose strategies for preventing refugee crises and improving conditions for refugees

PHOTO 11.1 Ethiopia hosts about a quarter of a million refugees.

YONAS TADESSE/AFP/Getty Images.

cases, such as rape and gunshot wounds, and for the chronic problems that plague Somalis who have gone a lifetime without medical care (Steer 2011).

TYPES OF MIGRATION

"Migrant" encompasses a variety of people who differ widely in their circumstances. Economic, political, social, environmental, and physical insecurities push people from their usual residences. What the migrants have in common is that they left their homes, presumably, for a better life elsewhere—some elsewhere in their homeland, some in other countries. Some leave voluntarily; others have little or no choice.

Those forced to leave are "displaced persons." The label is ugly, suggesting that they have no place where they belong. But it accurately describes an increasing number of people. In 2016, 1 of every 100 people were forcibly displaced from their homes, more than any time since record keeping began in 1951. Migrants displaced by war and violence, whether conflict or crime, may be those with whom you are most familiar. Civilians, women and children in particular, are the majority of victims of violent conflict across the world. Pictures of the horrific conditions under which they flee violence and the deaths suffered along the way are seared into the global consciousness. The Mediterranean and Aegean seas are mass graveyards where thousands lie underwater,

drowned while seeking a safe haven. No guarantee of safe haven exists even for migrants who succeed in escaping to another country or a less violent area within their own country. As the flow of migrants escaping violent conflict or persecution increased, pressure on governments to deny them entry also increased.

In 2015, violent conflict, war, and persecution forced about 12.4 million people from their homes. Most, 8.6 million, remain in their homelands, although conditions there are generally less secure than flight to another country would be. Some 3.7 million flee abroad as refugees or asylum seekers, mostly to poor nations. Migrants fleeing persecution in fear of grave harm or death on the basis of race, ethnicity, sexual orientation, political ideology, or religion have protected status on the global stage. Most of the migrants in these categories flee their homes as a last resort before there is no hope left and it is too late to escape. They take little with them. But many leave much behind—professional jobs, comfortable homes, and families, their fates altered by conflict and persecution. Others, already stricken by extreme poverty, leave little behind.

Environmental degradation and extreme weather events displace an even greater number of migrants than persecution, violent conflict, and war. Natural disasters,

CONSIDER THIS
CATEGORIES OF MIGRANTS AS CLASSIFIED BY THE UNHCR

Who qualifies for the protection of international refugee law is not always clear-cut. Refugees and asylum seekers are categories defined by the United Nations' 1951 Refugee Convention and its 1967 Protocol. To be granted this status, people must have a well-founded fear of returning to their home country because of persecution on the basis of their religion, nationality, race, membership in a protected social group, or political opinion.

People fleeing violent conflict are afforded the protections offered by the UNHCR and are included in the UNHCR, World Bank, and other statistics on refugees. Governments in developed countries do not automatically grant refugee status to populations fleeing war or violent conflict, although most governments make provisions on humanitarian grounds to accept such refugees and grant some level of temporary protection or even permanent asylum.

The UNHCR offers "complementary" and "temporary" protection and status as individuals in "refugee-like" situations to others facing risk of harm.

Asylum seekers are those who applied for refugee status but whose status as a refugee is not yet determined.

Internally displaced persons (IDPs) have fled their usual residence due to armed conflict, natural disaster, violence (such as criminal violence of the drug trade), or human rights violations but who remain in the country. Only IDPs from conflict situations are included in the UNHCR statistics.

Returnees are refugees who returned to their country of origin but are not fully integrated. Returned IDPs are similar in having returned to their usual residence but are still under the UNHCR's protection and are provided with assistance.

Stateless persons are not recognized as citizens of any country. They fall under the UNHCR statelessness mandate of protection. The UNHCR is also committed to preventing and ending statelessness. Stateless persons are usually classified as "people in refugee-like situations" (UNHCR 2016a).

Migrant is a general term used to describe people who have left their usual residence, whether voluntarily or involuntarily and whether they have crossed an international border or not. When the terms migrant and IDP both appear in a publication, migrant often refers specifically to international migration.

---

such as hurricanes and typhoons, floods, earthquakes, tsunamis, fires, and landslides, are more frequent and more intense due to climate change and will continue to increase in both frequency and intensity. Environmental events along with environmental destruction caused by pollution and ill-planned land use forced 3 to 10 times more people from their homes than conflicts or wars in 2015, approximately 19.2 million (Norwegian Refugee Council 2016).

Economic migrants vary in life circumstances. Some are pushed by poverty and unemployment. Others, a privileged few, pursue better occupational and lifestyle opportunities. Economic migrants are the largest category of internal and international migrants.

Nothing tests the goodwill of a country or its people in the same way as migration. When a country needs a larger labor force, migrants are recruited and welcomed. However, if the complexion of the country begins to change color or spoken accents sound too foreign, fear may set in and countries react by changing laws or policies to block further immigration of particular groups. This happened when "too many" people of Southern European

and Eastern European descent flowed into the United States. The Immigration and Naturalization Act of 1924 effectively stopped migration from these regions until the mid-1960s.

Migrants fleeing war, as with the Jews of World War II and the Syrians of 2015, may be refused help if they are feared as collaborators or sympathizers with the enemy. While countries recognize their failure to protect Jews, hostility toward refugees from the Middle East repeats history. Fleeing a natural disaster may force people into neighboring countries or territories that are not significantly better off than their own. Forced from their homeland and often not welcome in their new land, the crisis of displaced people is one of the major crises of the modern world.

The flow of global displacement from 1996 to 2011 occurred in waves; the number of displaced persons increased or decreased by only a few million from year to year. The overall volume of displaced persons increased by only about 5 million people in the 15 years from 1996 to 2011. That changed with a significant upward trend that

A CLOSER LOOK
GLOBAL DISPLACEMENT

FIGURE 11.1   Trend of Global Displacement and Proportion Displaced, 1997–2016

In 2000, there were 173 million international migrants. By 2015, the stock of international migrants had grown to 244 million. This is the largest number of international migrants on record. This swell in the numbers of migrants alarmed many people in both sending and receiving countries. Although the number of migrants of all types increased rapidly along with the global forces that push them from their homelands, the percentage of people living outside of their homeland increased by only 1 percent from 2000 to 2015, rising to 3.3 percent from 2.3 percent (UN 2016).

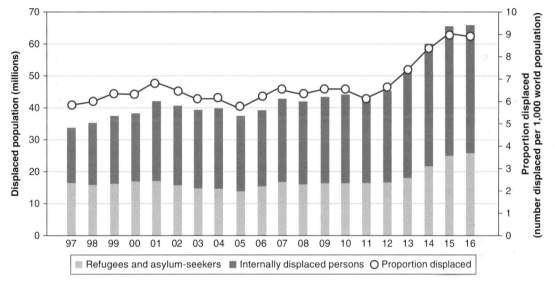

Source: United Nations High Commissioner for Refugees (2017). Reproduced with permission.

began in 2012. From 2012 to 2015, the number of people displaced increased by more than 40 million. The flow of displaced persons swelled from 10 people displaced every minute in 2010 to a peak of 30 per minute in 2014. It decreased slightly, to 24 per minute, in 2015 (Figure 11.1) (UNHCR 2016a).

These global flows of people present the international community with a unique and complicated set of issues:

- Large waves of migrants may, at least temporarily, increase insecurity and destabilize their host country, particularly if the country is poor.

- Refugees from conflict-torn countries may inadvertently or deliberately carry the conflict with them across borders, increasing ethnic tensions in neighboring countries with similar ethnic mixes.

- Insurgents may cross borders and carry out attacks from neighboring countries, sometimes with and sometimes without the support of nationals within the host country.

- Networks of migrant communities may be enlisted or coerced to facilitate trafficking people and goods for ethnically based organized crime.

CONSIDER THIS
THE LEGAL FRAMEWORK ON FORCED MIGRATION AND DISPLACEMENT

There are five main international instruments that protect the rights of refugees:

- The 1951 Convention Relating to the Status of Refugees

- The 1967 Protocol Relating to the Status of Refugees

- The 1990 International Convention on the Protection of the Rights of All Migrants and Members of Their Families

- The 2000 Protocol to Prevent, Suppress, and Punish Trafficking in Persons, Especially Women and Children

- The 2000 Protocol against the Smuggling of Migrants by Land, Sea, and Air

Together with the instruments on the rights of migrant workers adopted by the International Labour Organization, these form the basis of the international normative and legal framework on international migration.

- When waves of migrants reach a level that people in the host country perceive as threatening to their physical, economic, cultural, or social well-being, they often react with discrimination, hate speech, hate crimes, and persecution.

- Migrants often live in extreme physical and economic deprivation, with their conditions worsening the longer they are confined. Generations may be deprived of education, adequate health care, and nutrition. They also suffer psychological trauma. The present and future welfare of the migrant community, and perhaps that of their home and host countries, are jeopardized.

Global trends have complicated the status of displaced people and the strategies to solve their problems. The distinctions between types of displacement—refugee status and "ordinary" migrant status, voluntary and involuntary migration—are blurred as global forces interact in complex ways, creating conditions intolerable and inhospitable to human well-being.

GLOBAL FLOWS OF REFUGEES

Refugees have a specific status in the international community, receive protection, and are granted rights under international laws. Refugees are persons who cannot live safely in their homelands. No country has an obligation to accept migrants, but all the signatories to the United Nations "1951 Convention on Relating to the Status of Refugees," its protocol, and subsequent conventions have an obligation to accept and provide for the well-being of refugees.

The global total of people living displaced by conflict or persecution, internally or in another country, topped 65.3 million people in 2015. That is more than nine people per thousand in the global population, more than double the number of just two decades ago and a total higher than at any time since World War II. Most of this global total, 41.8 million, represents internally displaced persons (IDPs). They are still within their country of origin. More than 21 million fled to other countries (Figure 11.2). About half are children, many unaccompanied by adults. Asylum seekers, traditionally defined as those who have applied for refugee status in the country they have reached, numbered 3.2 million in 2015.

Despite the special status and protections due asylum seekers, refugees, and people living in refugee-like status, they face perilous conditions beginning with their flight from danger, in seeking refuge, while in refugee camps and asylum detention, and even after resettlement or repatriation.

Who Are the World's Refugees?

The status of a refugee is ordinarily defined in terms of membership in a group that is suffering persecution. The 1951 Convention Relating to the Status of Refugees, Article 1, Paragraph 2 stipulates the following:

A CLOSER LOOK
GLOBAL REFUGEE POPULATION

FIGURE 11.2   Refugees, Including Refugee-Like Situations (in millions of people)

The global population of refugees has topped 21 million people.

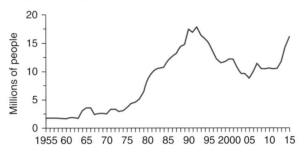

Source: International Monetary Fund. 2016. *World Economic Outlook: Subdued Demand: Symptoms and Remedies.* Washington, October.

A person who, owing to a well-founded fear of being persecuted for reasons of race, religion, nationality, membership of a particular social group or political opinion, is outside the country of his nationality and is unable or, owing to such fear, is unwilling to avail himself of the protection of that country; or who, not having a nationality and being outside the country of his former habitual residence as a result of such events, is unable or, owing to such fear, is unwilling to return to it.

In War and Violent Conflict

The surge in forced displacement since 2012 ignited debates over who does and does not qualify as a refugee. Under the 1951 Convention, persons fleeing violent conflict are not *normally* considered refugees. However, guidelines on the implementation of the convention and the 1967 Protocol stress that situations of armed conflict and long-term consequences can amount to violations of human rights. As the Assistant High Commissioner for Protection argued in 2016, "most conflicts today target groups of civilians *because of their real or perceived ethnic, religious, social or political affiliation*" (emphasis added) (UNHCR 2016c).

Treatment of people fleeing war and other violent conflicts as refugees has been inconsistent across countries. The Organization for African Unity and signatories of the Cartagena Declaration in Latin America recognize those fleeing violent conflicts as refugees. Many countries, unwilling to accept refugees from the multiple crises in the Middle East and North Africa, reject the premise that fleeing violent conflict qualifies a person as a refugee, and they require each individual to demonstrate that he or she specifically, as an individual, is targeted and thus in danger.

The UNHCR urges countries to recognize that the devastation wrought by armed conflict—both immediate such as the deliberate killing of civilians and long term such as hunger—rises to the definition of human rights abuses. This makes those fleeing protracted conflicts refugees, and this consideration should be applied globally to ensure protection to those who need it—both inside and outside their countries of origin—without relying on individual verification. This does not prohibit governments from denying refuge on an individual basis.

Refugee Status Due to Ethnicity

Many ethnic groups rejected and persecuted in their homelands have little choice but to flee the country or be relegated to a camp in their home country. The Lhotshampas are ethnic Nepalese. Their homeland, however, is Bhutan and has been for more than 300 years. As happens with many migrants, Bhutan originally recruited Lhotshampas as laborers. Although anywhere from 25 to 30 percent of the population is ethnic Nepalese, the Lhotshampas became increasing unwelcome in the 20th century. Wanting to preserve "ethnic purity," Bhutan expelled more than 100,000 in the 1990s. Recognized internationally as refugees, most fled to Nepal, living in UNHCR refugee camps for the next 15 to 20 years. Most who fled to the refugee camps have now resettled, divided among several developed countries. The Lhotshampas who remain in Bhutan face severe discrimination. The Bhutanese government excludes as many as possible from citizenship, which denies them business, education, and employment opportunities, hoping to force them into exile (Mørch 2016).

Persecution of ethnic groups in Burma forced tens of thousands to flee to surrounding countries. People born there or brought there as children know no other country, and elders who have been there for decades have forgotten what their homeland, which rejected them, was like. More than 140,000 refugees from Burma, ethnic Karen and Karenni, Rakhine, Mon, and Pa-o, are scattered through nine refugee camps in Thailand, Bangladesh, India, and Malaysia. More than 1 million Rohingya live in Burma and have for generations. Burma denies them citizenship; thus, they are stateless, without any rights anywhere except as refugees. Amnesty International calls them the most persecuted ethnic group in the world. Most are concentrated in camps, and tens of thousands have fled.

The Hmong were the last refugee group from the Vietnam era to receive relief from their persecution in Laos. While many have been resettled, others still live in camps in Thailand.

A CLOSER LOOK
MAE LA OON REFUGEE CAMP

PHOTO 11.2 In Thailand, the Mae La Oon camp is under constant threat of closing. These refugees from Burma have nowhere else to go. Returning to Burma risks their lives.

Burma Link.

In Africa, Kunama refugees fled from their homes in Eritrea to camps in Ethiopia, a country unable to resettle them even with UNHCR assistance. Burundians had been living in refugee camps in Tanzania.

These are just a few examples of the many persecuted groups forced to flee their homelands, with refugee status being their best chance of survival.

Refugee Status Due to Sexual Orientation and Identity

People who experience persecution based on sexual orientation (lesbian, gay, bisexual, transgender, and queer people) represent an increasing percentage of asylum admissions globally. They fall within the membership category "particular social group." While much of the world increasingly recognizes the rights of homosexual, transgender, and non-binary individuals, many countries still consider any but the cisgendered male and female identity and heterosexual sexual orientation to be criminal. In 2016, homosexuality could bring a death sentence in 12 countries. Persecution based on sexual orientation is widespread in many countries. Ironically, most of the cases coming to the United States originate from elsewhere in the Americas, where homosexuality is legal. The Americas account for 9 of the top 25 source countries to the United States (Millman 2014).

Finding asylum does not always bring freedom from persecution. Immigrant communities from countries where homosexuality is criminal or subject to social discrimination may bring hostile attitudes with them. Although not in fear of arrest, sexual minorities may still fear banishment from the community or family.

Refugee Status Due to Violence and Violent Conflict

Patterns in the flow of refugees change as new conflicts emerge. The international flow represented by the total number of refugees in any given year reflects new conflicts and situations of persecution as well as protracted conflicts. The "top 10" list provides a quick glance at major flows. Countries with smaller populations may also experience prolonged or intense conflict and persecution, but due to their smaller populations, they contribute less to the global flow. In Table 11.1, Afghanistan appears at or near the top of the list in all three of the sample years, as it has since 1980. Other countries of protracted conflict and/or histories of minority group persecution, such as Sudan, Somalia, Eritrea, and the Democratic Republic of the Congo (DRC), are also evident from their repeated appearance on the lists.

New or escalating conflicts and persecution can be determined by the appearance of countries on the list. The devastating impacts of the genocide in Bosnia, the wars following the bombing of the World Trade Center and Pentagon in 2001, and the Arab Spring are evident in the numbers of refugees fleeing those countries.

The Most Vulnerable Refugees

Women and children make up a large share of the world's refugees, including those from Syria. Children under 18 years are 51 percent of the global population of refugees. This is an increase from 41 percent in 2014. People aged 18 to 59 constitute 46 percent, and only 3 percent are over 60. Females comprise 47 percent of refugees, and they range from 48 to 50 percent of every age category, from children to the elderly (UNHCR 2016a, Table 14).

Women make up a somewhat higher percentage of refugees residing in Syria (52 percent) and Afghanistan (51 percent). Curaçao and Togo have the highest percentage of females at 56 percent (of only 48 refugees). Mauritania (55 percent), Serbia and Kosovo (53 percent), and Niger (55 percent) have relatively high percentages. Where the refugee population is predominantly male, they tend to be very small refugee populations—some in the single digits, many only in the hundreds, and most below 10,000 (UNHCR 2016a, Table 14).

Geographic Flows of Refugees

The pattern of flow to refugee-receiving countries mirrors the outward flow of refugees because most people remain within their region, usually in neighboring countries, often to where they can walk (Table 11.2).

Hosting refugees is an international responsibility, one assumed by every country party to the UN conventions relating to refugees. Nevertheless, refugees concentrate in a few regions, primarily in developing countries. Overall, more than 25 percent of refugees, 4.4 million, were hosted in sub-Saharan Africa and more than 25 percent, 4.39 million, were hosted in Europe—primarily Eastern Europe. Sub-Saharan Africa, Ethiopia, Kenya, Uganda, the DRC, and Chad were among the top 10 countries hosting refugees at the end of 2015. Although the UNHCR operates refugee camps, the major burden is borne by those who can least afford it.

Seeking Refuge From Middle East War

Worsening conditions in Syria and surrounding areas sent millions of refugees fleeing for their lives. Although

A CLOSER LOOK
COUNTRIES OF ORIGIN FOR REFUGEES

TABLE 11.1   Top 10 Countries of Origin for Refugees and Persons in Refugee-like Situations, 2000, 2010, and 2015

The initiation, escalation, and end of violent conflict can be discerned in the flow of refugees.

Major Source Countries, 2000	Total	Major Source Countries, 2010	Total	Major Source Countries, 2015	Total
Afghanistan	3,587,366	Afghanistan	3,054,709	Syria	4,872,585
Burundi	568,084	Iraq	1,683,579	Afghanistan	2,666,452
Iraq	526,179	Somalia	770,154	Somalia	1,120,000
Bosnia–Herzegovina	504,981	DRC	476,693	South Sudan[a]	778,700
Sudan	494,363	Myanmar	415,670	Sudan	628,800
Somalia	475,655	Colombia	395,577	DRC	541,400
Angola	433,760	Sudan	387,288	Central African Republic	471,100
Sierra Leone	402,807	Vietnam	338,698[b]	Myanmar	451,800
Eritrea	376,851	Eritrea	222,460	Eritrea	411,300
DRC	371,713	China	184,602	Colombia	340,200

a. South Sudan became independent in 2011. Its figures would be included in Sudan's figures in prior years. War continues in both Sudan and South Sudan.

b. 300,000 Vietnamese refugees are well integrated and in the protection of the government of China.

Sources: Adapted from United Nations High Commissioner for Refugees (2002; 2011, Annex Table 2; 2016a, Annex Table 2); World Bank (2018, World Development Indicators, Interactive Database, 2000 data).

many in the United States fear being overwhelmed by people fleeing Syria, few have been accepted into the country (Figure 11.3). The majority of the refugees from Iraq, Afghanistan, and Syria remain in nearby countries, particularly Lebanon, Jordan, and Egypt, East Africa and the Horn of Africa, and elsewhere in the Middle East. Millions of refugees risked their lives to gain entry into Europe. Europe experienced a more than 300 percent increase in the number of refugees. In 2014, approximately 280,000 migrants arrived in Europe; in 2015, 1.3 million refugees arrived. Thousands died en route in this "European migrant crisis." Millions slept outdoors in Turkey, waiting for the chance to work their way to countries farther inland (Connor and Krogstad 2016). Many could not. More than half, 2.5 million, of the refugees in Europe at the end of 2015 remained in Turkey, one of the poorest European countries. European Union (EU) entry points in Italy and Greece also housed large numbers of displaced persons; in 2015, 118,047 refugees and 60,156 asylum cases were pending in Italy and 56,578 refugees and asylum cases were pending in Greece (UNHCR 2016a, Table 1).

A CLOSER LOOK
TOTAL REFUGEES AND PEOPLE IN REFUGEE-LIKE SITUATIONS

TABLE 11.2 Total Refugees and People in Refugee-Like Situations, 2000, 2010, and 2015

For the first decades of the 20th century, most refugees stayed within the region of their origin. This changed with the influx of refugees to Europe from the wars of Arab Spring.

UNHCR Region of Asylum or Residence[a]	Total Refugees and People in Refugee-like Situations		
	End of 2000[b]	End of 2010	End of 2015
Central Africa and Great Lakes	N/A	976,300	1,189,241
East and Horn of Africa	N/A	893,159	2,739,375
Southern Africa	N/A	146,162	189,842
Western Africa	N/A	168,334	294,953
Total Africa	3,627,130	2,408,676[c]	4,413,411
Americas	637,064	803990	746,788[d]
Asia and Pacific	5,383,418	4,014,115	3,830,255
Europe	2,309,885	1,606,639	4,391,419
Middle East and North Africa	N/A	1,940987	2,739,554
Total	12,062,075[b]	10,396,500	16,121,427

a. This does not include asylum seekers.

b. 2000 statistics were reported differently. The total includes Oceania as a separate category with 68,578 refugees. N/A, not available.

c. This total is for Africa as defined as UN major region and includes North Africa.

d. Of these, 337,698 are in Latin America/Caribbean and 273, 202 are in the United States.

Sources: Adapted from UN High Commissioner for Refugees (2011, Annex Table 1; 2016a, Annex Table 1).

Many European countries rejected the obligation to host refugees or accepted few relative to the countries' wealth and population density. Slovakia and Hungary sued the EU over regulations that established a quota system for countries' acceptance of migrants. Bulgaria, Hungary, and Slovenia built walls to stop refugees from crossing into their countries. Exceptions were Germany and Sweden. Germany accepted a total of 316,115 refugees and people in refugee-like situations and had 420,625 persons with asylum cases pending at the end of 2015. Sweden, considerably smaller than Germany, had 169,520 refugees and 157,046 persons with asylum cases pending (UNHCR 2016a, Table 1).

Governments made some accommodations. The EU revised asylum regulations to allow asylum seekers to move through the EU without needing to apply to the first

A CLOSER LOOK
ADMISSIONS TO THE UNITED STATES FROM SYRIA

FIGURE **11.3**   Syrian Refugees to the United States

With the flood of refugees pouring out of Syria, many believe that their countries are being overwhelmed, including many in the United States. The number of refugees from Syria who make it to the United States, however, is negligible. From 2011 to 2015, only about 2,000 refugees from Syria came to the United States.

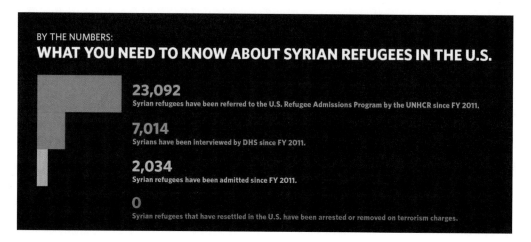

BY THE NUMBERS:
WHAT YOU NEED TO KNOW ABOUT SYRIAN REFUGEES IN THE U.S.

23,092
Syrian refugees have been referred to the U.S. Refugee Admissions Program by the UNHCR since FY 2011.

7,014
Syrians have been interviewed by DHS since FY 2011.

2,034
Syrian refugees have been admitted since FY 2011.

0
Syrian refugees that have resettled in the U.S. have been arrested or removed on terrorism charges.

Source: White House Archives (2015).

EU country they reached. They were also able to apply for asylum outside the borders of the country to which they applied. At the end of 2015, other European countries hosting refugees and asylum seekers (refugees/asylum cases) were France (273,136/63,057), the United Kingdom (123,067/45,870), Italy (118,047/60,156), the Netherlands (88,536/28,051), Switzerland (73,336/32,701), Austria (72,216/80,057), Norway (50,389/25,316), and Finland (12,703/24,366). Although they accepted refugees from Syria, Afghanistan, Somalia, Sudan, and others among the major outflow countries, none of these wealthier European countries were among the top 10 hosting countries. Not all of those requesting asylum would be granted status as refugees. The number of refugees hosted by a country in relation to its population and its gross domestic product (GDP) per capita is important in understanding how the obligation to protect refugees, whether required by law or humanitarian ethics, is shared among countries (Figures 11.4 and 11.5).

Seeking Refuge From Drug Violence in Central America

While much of the attention has been on refugees escaping Asia and Africa, they are not the only regions with refugee crises. Rather than war, it is gang violence in Central America that is responsible for the fivefold increase in the outflow of refugees from the region—from 20,900 people in 2012 to 109,800 in 2015 (Table 11.3). Coming almost exclusively from El Salvador, Guatemala, and

A CLOSER LOOK
WHERE DO REFUGEES GO?

Many countries, among the poorest, host refugees beyond their capacity given their wealth and population density.

FIGURE 11.4   Refugees per Million Dollars GDP at the End of 2016

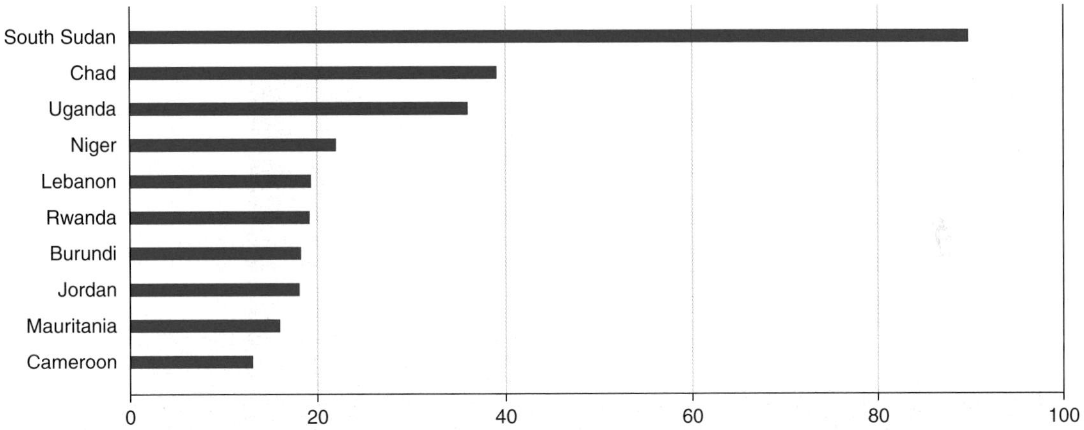

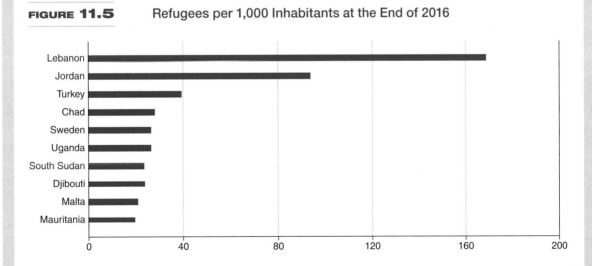

Source: United Nations High Commissioner for Refugees (2017). Reproduced with permission.

FIGURE 11.5   Refugees per 1,000 Inhabitants at the End of 2016

Source: United Nations High Commissioner for Refugees (2017). Reproduced with permission.

A CLOSER LOOK
FLEEING VIOLENCE IN MEXICO AND CENTRAL AMERICA

TABLE 11.3   Migration From Central America and Mexico

People trapped in areas controlled by drug gangs need to choose among known dangers of forced labor for the gangs, being killed by the gangs, and the perils of flight. They hope to find safety in the United States and other Central American countries.

	Fiscal Year 2013	Fiscal Year 2014	Fiscal Year 2015	Fiscal Year 2016
Unaccompanied children	38,759	68,541	39,970	59,692
Family units	14,855	68,445	39,838	77,674
Individuals	360,783	342,385	251,525	271,504
Totals	414,397	479,371	331,333	408,870

Source: U.S. Customs and Border Protection (2016).

Honduras—the "Northern Triangle"—about half seek asylum in the United States, while others seek asylum in Mexico, Belize, and Costa Rica (Semple 2016).

Although many refugees travel in groups and families, unaccompanied children are prominent among the flow. Unaccompanied children apprehended at the U.S. border surged in 2014. Historically, most unaccompanied children apprehended have been from Mexico. This pattern held through to 2011, when the violence in the Northern Triangle of Central America drove thousands of children out of the region. The number of unaccompanied children peaked in 2014 at 68,550—three quarters from the Northern Triangle. Family unit apprehensions followed a similar pattern but peaked in 2016. The gang and organized crime violence from which families and children flee and the violence and dangers they confront on their journeys are a humanitarian crisis of the utmost severity. Providing a safe path to refuge is a challenge to all of the countries involved.

Some refugees from Central America are on the run for years. Most report that they never wanted to leave their country. They had no choice. They comply with the gangs, die, or leave. They leave behind businesses, prospects of school, and their churches. One family fled from their home in El Salvador when a gang tried to recruit their son as a drug mule and their daughter as a "child bride." Each parent left behind a successful business, and the children left behind the prospects of college. They fled first to northern El Salvador and reestablished their business. The gang found them and they fled again, this time to Mexico, where they await a decision on their asylum application. Similar stories abound. Gangs force boys to serve as drug mules and "lookouts." Gangs take girls to make them brides. They kill anyone who gets in their way or refuses. Many, even those applying for asylum in Mexico, hope to reach the United States. One Honduran migrant who the gangs tried to recruit said the migrants are not going north to seek the "American dream. . . . You go for your life" (Semple 2016).

In response to the crisis, a coordinated international effort was initiated. Mexico increased its acceptance rate from 45 percent of the cases it heard in 2015 to 62 percent in the first six months of 2016 (Semple 2016). The U.S. Customs and Border Protection takes referrals of vulnerable migrants to facilitate legal entry. The UNHCR spearheads an international effort to increase the number of safe lodgings. Agreements forged among international partners in Central and North America focus on creating "safe zones" within the countries of origin and in those to which refugees flee (UNHCR 2016b).

CONSIDER THIS
DISCOURAGING REFUGEES

As sentiment against refugees rises in wealthy countries, they are publicizing the dangers and difficulties inherent in migrating to safer areas. A "Danger Awareness" campaign launched by the U.S. Customs and Border Patrol stressing the perils of immigration—the arduous and deadly journey, the likelihood of detention while awaiting a hearing, and the consequences of illegal immigration—did little to affect whether or not people decided to migrate. Particularly unlikely to be discouraged by the likelihood of danger were those who were already the victims of one or more crimes. They are, understandably, the most likely to migrate. Well aware of the risks and dangers of migration, the dangers at home weighed more heavily in their decisions (Hiskey et al. 2016).

Europe, also under pressure from citizens to reduce migration, launched campaigns in Afghanistan emphasizing the dangers of being smuggled and the difficulty of settling in Europe if refugees make it there. As with the U.S. efforts, they are largely symbolic, having little effect. What they accomplish, however, is to "shift the risks of the journey to the [refugees] themselves rather than the restrictive border regimes" (Oeppen 2016).

LIFE AS A REFUGEE

Women, children, and the elderly are at risk for exploitation, violence, and abuse in many societies while merely going about their daily activities. Where there are stressors such as persecution and discrimination by their governments and violence and conflict that disrupts or corrupts law enforcement, destroys infrastructure, and halts most legitimate economic activities, people's vulnerabilities are heightened and they are easier targets for exploitation by predators. Escaping such situations often means enlisting smugglers who take refugees on perilous journeys crammed into cargo containers, trucks, or vans with little air, food, water, or sanitation. Many die en route. Photographs and videos of people, including children, drowned or being pulled from the Aegean and Mediterranean seas attempting voyages in leaky and overfilled vessels are real-life nightmares watched in real time around the world. Travel by land is no easier.

By Sea or by Land: Danger

Médecins Sans Frontières (MSF) works in refugee camps all over the world. During the summers of 2015 and 2016, MSF went over and above its usual work to rescue migrants at sea. While the stories of violence in the countries they fled, however horrific, were expected, the extreme violence—including beatings, sexual violence, and murder—on their migration journey was alarming even to the seasoned humanitarians of MSF. Hundreds of stories depicted similar exploitation to that experienced by Agnes, a migrant from Eritrea: "I was beaten with bare hands, with sticks, with guns. If you move, they beat you. If you talk, they beat you. We spent two months like that, being beaten every day (Cornish 2016). Aside from the danger of the travel itself, smugglers may collude with human traffickers and sell their human cargo into forced labor and sexual slavery.

On August 27, 2015, Austrian police opened an abandoned refrigerated truck and instead of foods found 71 people, all of whom were dead. They were smuggled into the country, nearly half from Iraqi Kurdistan. Five people, whose passage was arranged by a young Iraqi named "Sevo" who calls himself a guide, traveled by car, by bus, and by foot from Iraq through Turkey, Bulgaria, Serbia, and Hungary to reach the van to take the 71 people into Austria. Some had fought against ISIS (Islamic State in Iraq and Syria), but without pay, for months and decided to risk fleeing (Coles and Nasralla 2015).

Violence in Iraq and elsewhere has meant big business for human smugglers. More than a million Kurds fled Iraq during the reign of Saddam Hussein. In 2003, when the regime was toppled, many returned. Now, they flee again; the most valuable cargo leaving Iraq is human.

On the Way, the Calais "Jungle": Mini City or Refugee Camp?

With a "Main" Street with ethnic restaurants, an art gallery, a theater, a nightclub, the "Jungle Books" library, a playground, mosques, churches, convenience stores, a charging station for phones and computers, language lessons, and even an information center for those who hope to be just passing through, and with more than 9,000 residents, Calais, France, has all the markings of a small city or at least a village.

The wooden shacks, however, were built by charity groups, and the information center dispenses advice from human rights attorneys about how to get asylum in the United Kingdom. The artwork is varied, but much of it depicts scenes of England, reflecting the desired destination. Recreation during the day features dominoes and football/soccer. At night, the mood changes. Groups of people-smuggling gangs try to stop cars and trucks to stow away on them. British Islamic militants infiltrate, posing as aid workers (White 2015).

The Calais camp arose informally with makeshift shelters and squatting in abandoned buildings—as a jumping-off point to the United Kingdom. With a tunnel and a big and very heavily trafficked port between France and the United Kingdom, Calais is a magnet for people trying to reach the United Kingdom. Restrictive laws make entering the United Kingdom difficult, so illegal entry followed by a claim for asylum is many refugees' best hope.

The "camp" is actually about nine encampments around the town of Calais. With thousands desperate to reach the United Kingdom, Calais developed all of the worst characteristics a refugee camp could have—trafficking, sexual exploitation, and squalor. The camp became a symbol of the failure of two wealthy nations to deal with the refugee crisis.

In the fall of 2016, the French decided to clear the camp for the second time. Many were bused to reception centers, where people had been protesting against their arrival (Lima and Nossiter 2016). Thousands fled to Paris, which *The New York Times* (Nossiter 2016) called "the new Calais."

More than a thousand unaccompanied children, about 10 to 17 years old, were in Calais. Some of these children were admitted into England if they had relatives there. Others were promised resettlement in France. After enduring the dangers of their journeys, their fates are unknown but hardly secure.

A Tale of Two Camps

It might not in actuality be the best refugee camp in the world, but it deserves its reputation as at least one of the best. Kilis, a camp Turkey built set along the Syrian border, provides refugees with tiny houses resembling shipping containers, 10 feet wide and 23 feet long. Each has three rooms, including a small kitchen area and bathroom. Although still far from ideal, electricity, a satellite dish for television, and windows make it homier. Many amenities of a community lessen the trauma of living in a camp. Residents drop off their laundry at one of several camp laundries, where it is washed free of charge. Street lights line the brick-paved, regularly swept streets. Sanitation and clean water reduce the likelihood of disease. An activities building provides looms and weaving lessons, among other events. A small clinic with free care provides transportation to a local hospital as needed. Three grocery stores operated by three private companies are available for refugees. Refugees are given debit cards and a monthly allowance. And, perhaps most important, there are schools.

The grocery stores and debit cards have proven to be both efficient and cost-effective. Run by local merchants, they support the local economy. USAID and the World Food Programme are copying the system in other camps where feasible. Residents interviewed by journalists report that there is not the violent crime, black market, and/or crimes against women that are common in other camps.

In Kilis and other camps like it, life is relatively comfortable, but it is not ideal. "There is not purpose in a life like this," as one refugee reported. Even camps such as these cannot be permanent solutions.

The Syrian refugees in Kilis are relative newcomers to refugee status, there for only three or four years as of 2016. Even though it seems that the Turkish government thought their stay would be shorter, it is a fraction of the time some refugees have been in camps. In Kenya, Dadaab (a collective name for several camps that were built outside of Dadaab, a Kenyan village) is more than 20 years old. Built to hold 90,000, it held more than 420,000 by the end of 2015. It is not the oldest camp in the world, but it is the largest and deserving of its reputation for being among the worst.

Asad Hussein was born in Dadaab in 1996, just five years after the camp opened for Somalis fleeing the civil war. It now hosts refugees from other countries as well as Kenyans escaping drought-caused famines. Like Asad, many have lived all of their lives in Dadaab. Kenya threatened to close the camp, asserting that terrorist attacks in Kenya by al-Shabaab are planned in Dadaab and that Dadaab is a recruiting ground. A Kenyan judge blocked the move, calling it illegal and discriminatory.

Kenya has threatened closure before. The government promised Asad and his family resettlement in 2004 when it threatened the refugees with camp closure. His family underwent the medical exams and investigations required for resettlement. Perhaps, he thinks, his family's papers were sold to another family. Each time closure is threatened, some refugees return to Somalia; why stay, they ask, if Kenya does not want them? Although officially leaving under this threat is voluntary, Human Rights Watch (HRW 2016) claims that it is not. The refugees have no real choice. They lose a U.S. $400 stipend if they do not leave and wind up being deported. They do not have accurate information about the conditions in Somalia. Kenyans in the camp are expected to reintegrate in Kenya, but Somalis are not promised resettlement. Asad calls himself, and the generation of children like him, stateless; neither Kenya, where he was born and grew up, nor Somalia accepts him. He is, he says, a child of the UNHCR (Hussein 2016).

Asad's parents finally left the camp in 2017 after 22 years there. They joined his sister who had made it to the United States in 2005 along with her husband and child. In October 2017, Asad went to Somalia, a country he had never seen. He, along with others, paid a driver U.S. $60 each to take them. In preparation to pass through al-Shabaab territory, he cut his hair, hid his cellphone and notebook, and wore loose pants. They traveled on al-Shabaab-controlled roads, stopping as the rules required at each black flag, signifying an al-Shabaab checkpoint. At first, they paid a fee and were issued a receipt. Traveling through al-Shabaab-controlled towns, he listened to an al-Shabaab-controlled radio station and obeyed all of the al-Shabaab-determined rules. (You can follow Asad on Twitter: twitter.com/asadhussein.)

The Risks Faced by Refugees in Camps

If the dangers of travel are survived, refugee camps pose additional sets of risks. Conditions like those found in Kilis are rare. Viral and bacterial infections spread rapidly through camps, aided by the malnutrition, overcrowding, unsanitary conditions, open sewage, and trash found in most camps. Even shortages of simple everyday items such as soap for hand washing heighten the risk of disease significantly. Cholera, typhoid, influenza-like illnesses, diarrheal disease, and severe acute respiratory infections threaten all refugees. Vector-borne diseases spread by mosquitoes, ticks, and rodents find optimal conditions for their survival in the camps. Skin and blood infections spread from contact with waste and infected wounds. Eye infections result from infected dust and fumes, and intestinal infections result from flies and insects that feed on the plentiful waste and garbage.

Danger of violent and sexual crime, kidnapping, and seduction by human traffickers within camp are well documented. Women are vulnerable as they go about their daily activities, venturing outside of camp grounds to collect firewood or other construction materials and going to the latrines, which may be located far from their shelters.

Camps may also be vulnerable to night raids. Unaccompanied children are in danger in camps, particularly in danger of recruitment as child soldiers by armed groups. Armed groups provide food and family that the camps do not offer (Achvarina and Reich 2006). In addition to the physical dangers and disease, mental health of refugees deteriorates. People suffer from depression, post-traumatic stress, and suicidal ideation. They live in fear for themselves and their children (Getanda, Papadopoulos, and Evans 2015).

Refugees find the most security in countries with which they share important characteristics—ethnicity, culture, language, religion, and/or other bonds. These are more important than the wealth of a host country or its democratic leanings. For this reason, Iraqi refugees found better treatment in Syria than in most other countries meeting their needs in food and water, free education, and health care (al-Miqdad n.d.). These countries, like the refugees that find their way there, are likely to be poor. Although the UNHCR and other aid and humanitarian organizations from many countries assist poorer countries that host refugees, life for the majority of refugees is far from comfortable. The goal of the UNHCR and international aid organizations for refugees is to return them to security and a life of dignity. The international community, led by the UNHCR, pursues three long-term strategies as durable solutions to refugees' problems: return to their homeland, local integration into the society of their new residence, and resettlement into another host country. Unfortunately, for many refugees, these goals are elusive, and many remain in refugee status for decades. They remain in camps or makeshift settlements in limbo, not having full asylum, not ready or willing for repatriation, and not chosen for resettlement in a third country.

Dadaab, described above, is not the only camp where generations of refugees have been born, grown up, and died. Refugee populations of 25,000 or more who have held refugee status for five or more years are said to be "protracted refugee situations."[1] At the end of 2015, there were 6.7 million refugees living in protracted status. They represented 32 different "situations" or nationalities spread among 27 host countries.

Afghans are the largest refugee group living in protracted status under the UNHCR mandate. For nearly four decades, since 1979 and the Soviet invasion, Afghan refugees have lived in Iran and Pakistan. At the end of 2015, nearly 1 million Afghan refugees were in Iran and 1.6 million were in Pakistan, with the camps growing as flows of new refugees continue arriving and babies are born into refugee status. Another 10 nationalities have been in refugee status for more than 30 years, 12 have been refugees for 20 to 29 years, and 9 situations have lasted 10 to 19 years.

The first wave of Palestinian refugees, counted separately from other refugees, have lived in protracted status since 1948. A second wave joined them in 1967. By the end of 2015, there were 5.2 million Palestinians living in protracted status, some of whom fled wars and some of whom were born into refugee status.[2]

Considering the Palestinians and refugees in protracted status, millions of people are growing up and growing old in conditions of physical, economic, social, and mental insecurity, many without adequate food and clean water and with little or no education, no employment or training, vulnerable to violent crime and human traffickers. As described above, even those in the most secure camps are not living a "real" life. This is a global tragedy and a global security threat.

MSF claims that Western governments shirk their moral, if not legal, duty to migrants, which exacerbates the dangers and risks that they face. Because of this, MSF Canada rejected further funding from EU countries. Wealthier governments, MSF argues, use aid and political incentives to avoid resettling refugees in their own countries and shift the burden to poorer countries, exemplified in the EU's "outsourcing" migrant responsibility to Turkey. Instituting restrictive policies such as limiting access to health care, putting obstacles in the way of migrants seeking asylum, and holding migrants in detention for unduly long times are attempts to dissuade migrants from staying in host countries. Migrants who make it to wealthy nations undocumented are forced to stay underground because of policies designed to deter refugees. Fearful of seeking basic services and medical care, their physical and mental health conditions deteriorate further (Cornish 2016).

THE "SOLUTIONS"

Most refugees want to go home and will go voluntarily when it is safe. In 2015, 201,400 refugees were repatriated—returned to their country of origin. This rate of return was the third lowest of the last 20 years. Of the 12.9 million returnees of the 20 years from 1996 through 2016, most returned before 2010; only 10 percent returned from 2011 through 2016—the lowest rate of any five-year period. The decrease in the flow of repatriation was probably due to the increasing violence in North Africa and the Middle East.

Returning refugees home is a complex process. Under UNHCR regulations, repatriation must be voluntary. The refugees must agree to return based on full knowledge and accurate information of the current situation in their home country. The UNHCR, the host country, and the home country share the obligation to provide the information by means that are both accessible and understandable to the refugees. The home country must cooperate fully to ensure the refugees' safety. International agencies, including the UNHCR, are obliged to participate in the repatriation process and assist reintegration into the home country. These conditions are rarely met.

In 2015, the largest groups of returnees were Afghan (61,400), Sudanese (39,500), Somali (32,300), and people from the Central African Republic (21,600). Other countries with somewhat smaller but still significant numbers of returnees were Ivory Coast (12,059), Mali (4,088), and the DRC (8,438). Because all of these countries were still experiencing violent conflict, it cannot be assumed that these refugees returned to safety and a life of dignity, both conditions of repatriation promised by the UNHCR and the international community.

Repatriation to Afghanistan is a case in point. Attempts to settle the Afghan refugee crisis through a concentrated focus on repatriation have had unintended consequences. Rather than working for the best interests of the refugees and the country, which is war torn and poor, large-scale repatriation strained Afghanistan's resources and exacerbated existing problems. Security deteriorated, shelter is scarce, health care and education are inadequate, and land ownership and tenure are problematic because returnees' land has been occupied and papers documenting ownership have been lost. Returnees have trouble gaining employment. Many return home only to become internally displaced.

On the other hand, many refugees who remain in the host country, as in the case of many Afghan refugees in Pakistan, try to "fade in" and stay. They compete, in the case of Afghan refugees, with Pakistanis for jobs and other resources, creating prejudice against them. Countries in conflict or post-conflict situations—or experiencing other destabilizing events—must be carefully assessed to determine their absorptive capacity (Schmeidl 2009). It appears unlikely that this is being adequately done.

Repatriation of Somalis living in Dadaab camps in Kenya is equally controversial. HRW (2016) researchers interviewed Somali refugees and asylum seekers living in Dadaab, government representatives, and UNHCR representatives. They investigated the process of repatriation as it was being implemented. They found that people felt coerced and pressured to "volunteer" to return. Authorities did not provide them with information on alternatives or information on conditions in their home country. The Kenyan government, Somalia, and the UNHCR signed an agreement to repatriate refugees in 2013. The UNHCR

CONSIDER THIS
A WORLD-FAMOUS REFUGEE

In 1985, a young girl's picture appeared on the front of *National Geographic*. Sharbat Gula, then 12 years old, became a symbol of the plight of Afghan refugees and the generosity of Pakistan in hosting them.

After more than 30 years as a refugee in Pakistan, Gula was arrested by Pakistani officials, who deported her back to Afghanistan. Her crime was falsifying identity papers. Thus, in 2016, she acquired new symbolic significance. Although personally presented with a key to an apartment by Afghanistan President Ashraf Ghani, she now symbolizes the plight of Afghan refugees in Pakistan, arbitrarily rounded up and arrested for forced deportation (Nordland 2016b).

Gula and her children, who have known life only in Pakistan, will be forced back to Afghanistan along with many others who have never lived there or have not lived there for decades. Subject to routine harassment, the mistreatment of the refugees by Pakistan has often been in retaliation for actions by the Afghanistan government. Despite this, most refugees wish to stay in Pakistan. Forcing them back is a breach of the principle of "non-refoulement" that mandates voluntary returns.

Source: Amnesty International 2016; Wararich 2014.

reportedly knew that conditions in Somalia were not conducive to return. In Somalia, it was aware that continuing attacks against civilians, kidnappings of women and children, sexual violence, and massive displacement were common. As in Afghanistan, many returnees end up internally displaced. Thousands of others who left eventually returned to camps in Dadaab. Conditions were far from secure. One woman returned because she feared that her son would be kidnapped by al-Shabaab. Another refugee returned because he found others living on his property and he could not reclaim it. Many who returned to Dadaab were not accepted back into the camp. They lost their placement and food rations and were left with nothing, homeless in Kenya.

In 2016, the Kenyan government again announced that the camp would definitely close; this time in November 2016. However, conflict in Somalia, crimes against civilians, and activity of the terrorist group al-Shabaab were ongoing. Refugees were told that they would receive U.S. $200 on leaving the camp and $200 on arrival in Somalia. They were given little information. Many feared that if they did not leave voluntarily before the closing they would be deported and would not be given any of the stipend. Most of those interviewed felt that they had no choice. Such conditions do not meet the requirements of the UNHCR.

In Pakistan, Kenya, and similar situations, HRW recommends that refugees be assured that return to their country of origin is voluntary. If refugees repatriate but are unable to establish themselves in their homeland, they should assume their status and the rights that go with it if they return to the country of asylum. The UNHCR should not facilitate or assist repatriation unless the movement is entirely voluntary and refugees have been given accurate information. There needs to be on-site assessment of the situation in the country of origin before refugees return and honest reporting of the situation to potential returnees. Refugees need assurance that they will be able to stay in the country of asylum if they choose. There needs to be greater effort to resettle refugees in other countries where safety can be assured.

Reintegrating into a homeland presents a number of difficulties. When the Taliban lost dominance in Afghanistan, millions of refugees returned home—5 million from 2002 to 2008. This was the largest UNHCR-assisted repatriation program in 30 years and was more complex and challenging than foreseen. The rate of return outpaced the rate of reintegration. Afghanistan was poor and struggling after decades of war. The return was destabilizing for the returnees and the country. Many could not return to their place of origin. Most returnees lacked documents to prove ownership or tenure on their land since it was occupied by others. Choices ranged from moving onto yet someone else's land, to living with extended family, to increasing stress on those communities or in urban areas without access to basic services. Land that returnees were promised often did not materialize or was far from the urban centers where at least the possibility of employment existed. Thousands lived for months in makeshift settlements in the desert with tents of plastic and water brought in by tanker (Al Jazeera 2008; Schmeidl 2009).

Repatriation is a monumental task. An International Labour Organization (2013) report documents the extensive assistance that organizations and agencies involved in the Afghanistan reintegration effort provide in helping to rebuild every aspect of daily life. Infrastructure within the country or particular communities needs to be rebuilt—from roads, to financial services, to civil society. People need assistance in reestablishing themselves on the land or in jobs. Job training, education for financial literacy, inputs for agriculture—from seed, to irrigation, to veterinary services for livestock—and many more services need to be coordinated. Afghanistan, even with assistance, was not equipped for this level of effort. It is likely that the repatriation effort worsened the conditions and diminished chances for a final peace in Afghanistan.

In 2016, Pakistan launched another ambitious campaign to force Afghans out, threatening expiration of their refugee status, increasing arbitrary arrests, shutting down refugee schools, and using other intimidation tactics. The UNHCR bowed to Pakistan's pressure and increased the stipend for documented refugees who leave voluntarily to U.S. $400 per person. Along with an announcement that stipends would end in December 2016, this effectively coerced more refugees to leave but did not provide enough money to establish a life of dignity and is irrelevant in reducing the physical dangers they faced in Afghanistan. Close to a million documented and undocumented refugees returned in 2016 alone, and the campaign continued through 2017. This was the largest forced deportation, to that date, in history and was a severe violation of refoulement prohibitions.

The situation in the home country is critical to repatriation. In the first wave of massive repatriation, Afghanistan struggled with providing for those who still remained behind. With conflict escalating in Afghanistan in 2016, instability was rife even without the addition of the refugees. Most of these returnees, like those before them and others the world over, are likely to find themselves displaced in their homeland.

The situational context of the migrants needs to be part of the equation as well. The length of their asylum, why they were in the particular country of their asylum, and whether or not they desire to go home are important. For some, particularly those born and matured in the country of asylum, home may be the host country. Repatriation is often not a viable solution if safety and security are the goals. Durable solutions need to be found for refugees wherever they are. Repatriation should not be assumed to be the best or priority solution. All solutions need to be considered in context.

Integration Into Host Country

Local integration into the country where a refugee finds asylum is potentially a durable solution and the second most common after repatriation. Refugees may be able to obtain housing and jobs and contribute to the welfare of the society. Local integration is not clearly defined, but Article 34 of the 1951 Convention states that the end goal of local integration is naturalization. Because not all countries keep records differentiating naturalized citizens who were refugees from those who were not, the total number of refugees fully integrated is not reliable. At a minimum, 32,000 refugees were naturalized in 28 different countries in 2015 (UNHCR 2016a).

The EU instituted regional protection programs (RPPs) as a pilot program in 2004, implemented by the UNHCR, in the Great Lakes region of Africa to improve refugee protections and find durable solutions. A second began in 2009 in the Western Newly Independent States (Ukraine, Belarus, and Moldova). The UNHCR prioritized local integration and voluntary repatriation. Initial evaluations determined that resettlement was the primary solution in the regions (although not necessarily all through the RPPs). Three more were established in 2011 and 2012. According to critics, the EU plan was motivated both by protecting refugees and protecting its own borders. No new funds were allotted, and the direct support of migrants did not occur until the last phase (Bruns and Zichner 2016).

While historically not always the preferred solution, the tide may be changing with respect to local integration. In Africa, some governments recognize that the best way in which to deal with the flow of refugees is integration into the local economy. Tanzania granted citizenship to 200,000 refugees and gave them access to land and political rights. Uganda, host to a large population of refugees, gives them small plots of land and the right to start their own businesses. This integrates them into the local community and contributes to the local economy (Diop 2016).

Angolan refugees who fled to Zambia in waves, first in 1966 and again in the 2000s, demonstrate that local integration can be a very successful strategy. They have integrated both socially and economically. Although they find difficulty in making enough money to feed their families and pay school fees, this is true of native Zambians as well. Settled in defined areas where they have land to farm or the ability to start businesses, they achieved economic self-reliance and no longer depend on aid, a primary indicator of economic integration. Social integration is extensive. Zambians welcomed the Angolans, with whom they share cultural ties. They inter-marry, attend school and church, and enjoy recreational activities with native Zambians in neighboring communities. The refugees interviewed felt safe and protected in Zambia.

Similar ethnic and cultural backgrounds facilitated the integration of the Angolans, but a number of government actions also paved the way. Angolans were given access to land, to schools, and to health clinics. They were also able to move outside of settlement areas for work opportunities. In Zambia, Angolan refugees were located in established settlement areas and were also able to self-settle. This information is based on reports from refugees in the government settlements, so the welfare of those who self-settled may be different (Development by Training Services [DTS] 2014). Another sign of success is that permanent residence has been offered to 10,000 refugees, and in 10 years they will be eligible for citizenship. A detailed settlement program is in place for the Angolans who receive permanent residency.

Not all of the details are decided in the case of Angolans in Zambia. Angolans raise concerns that in their integration they would lose the homes and businesses in the refugee settlements without compensation, whether or not infrastructure will be ready for them when they move, whether there will be sufficient credit available for them to start new businesses, and whether those who farm will have access to markets to sell their produce, among other concerns. Because only those refugees who arrived before 1986 are eligible for local integration so far, those who do not qualify and do not wish to repatriate are concerned that they will lose assistance in such things as housing and medical care (DTS 2014).

In some respects, Africa can serve as a model for the world. While governments in Europe and the EU are pulling out of agreements they forged concerning refugee resettlement, governments in Africa are collaborating on how to best serve refugees and internally displaced persons. The five nations of the Great Lakes—Burundi, Tanzania, Rwanda, the DRC, and Uganda—met in June 2016 to cooperatively propose regional solutions to problems of forced displacement. A total of 25 African governments signed the "Kampala Convention," the African Union Convention for the Protection and Assistance of Internally Displaced Persons in Africa, legally binding them to protect the well-being of IDPs (Diop 2016).

A New Approach? Integrating Humanitarian and Development Needs

With its refugee camps overflowing, Tanzania agreed to be a pilot country for the Comprehensive Refugee Response Framework (CRRF). Part of the New York Declaration for Refugees and Migrants adopted by the UN in September 2016, CRRF approaches the situation of refugees holistically, combining humanitarian and development concerns. It engages governmental authorities, international and regional organizations, civil society, and the private sector.

The Comprehensive Regional Protection and Solutions Framework is an annex to the New York Declaration, applicable to situations of large-scale migrations of refugees. Members commit to best-practice strategies in four key areas:

- Reception and admission measures
- Support for immediate and ongoing needs
- Support for host countries and communities
- Enhanced opportunities for durable solutions (Americas Bureau, UNHCR 2017)

Resettlement of Refugees and Asylum Seekers

Resettlement requires finding a new country where refugees may live permanently. This is the least common of the durable long-term solutions. Most refugees resettled are referred by the UNHCR, although it cannot ensure anyone's acceptance into a country. This is a decision subject to each country's discretion. Year to year, the UNHCR recommends about 8 percent of refugees for resettling. The percentage has been consistent, with the number rising and falling as the number of refugees increases and decreases.

To be considered, resettlement must be the most appropriate solution and must fall into one of seven resettlement categories: legal and/or physical protection needs, lack of foreseeable alternative durable solutions, survivors of violence and/or torture, women and girls at risk, medical needs, family reunification, or children and adolescents at risk. The first four listed account for nearly all of the referrals (UNHCR 2015).

In the decade from 2005 to 2014, the number of refugees submitted for resettlement by the UNHCR doubled. Most of the refugees resettled in 2015 originated in countries plagued with extreme violence or persecution—Syria, the DRC, Iraq, Somalia, and Myanmar, accounting for 80 percent of all resettled refugees (Figures 11.6 and 11.7).

Resettling refugees employs a number of different strategies. Private sponsorship programs, medical and student visas, family reunification, labor mobility, and academic scholarships all provide opportunities for resettlement in a third country. Formal and informal groups of people, as well as religious organizations and official resettlement agencies, help refugees to make new lives. In each of 2014 and 2015, wealthy countries accepted just over 100,000 refugees for resettlement (UNHCR 2016a). There were 37 resettlement countries[3] as of 2016. Of the resettlements in 2015, the United States accepted more than half and Canada accepted more than one fifth (UNHCR 2016a).

Refugees resettled in new countries may also face discrimination. Even before the Syrian crisis spread largely unfounded fears that terrorists were flooding into Europe and the United States among the refugees, discrimination against refugees and asylum seekers was widespread in the general public. Pakistan scapegoated Afghani refugees for the rise of fundamentalism in Pakistan by accusing them of harboring extremists in the camps. On Human Rights Day in 2009, the High Commissioner on Human Rights called attention to the widespread discrimination against refugees, from detention for long periods to discrimination by landlords, employers, and state authorities. Refugees are "stereotyped and vilified by some political parties, media organizations, and members of the public" (Pillay 2009).

Refugees in Protracted Situations

The UNHCR prioritizes refugees in protracted situations. Usually this requires coordination of several countries. The United States is actively involved in six of

---

A CLOSER LOOK
REFUGEE RESETTLEMENT NEEDS

Global resettlement needs are dominated by refugees from four countries. More than a million refugees were in need of resettlement in 2016. The UNHCR Resettlement Data page has an interactive chart of country trends over time with details on countries of origin, asylum, and resettlement and UNHCR submissions (http://www.unhcr.org/en-us/resettlement-data.htm).

FIGURE 11.6   Refugee Countries of Origin

Most of the refugees submitted for resettlement from 2005 to 2014 came from just 13 countries, more than one quarter from Myanmar.

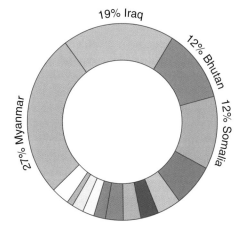

7% Congo (DRC), 4% Afghanistan,
3% Eritrea, 3% Syrian Arab Rep.,
3% Islamic Rep. of Iran, 2% Sudan, 2% Burundi,
2% Ethiopia, 1% Colombia, 5% Other

Source: United Nations High Commissioner for Refugees (2015).

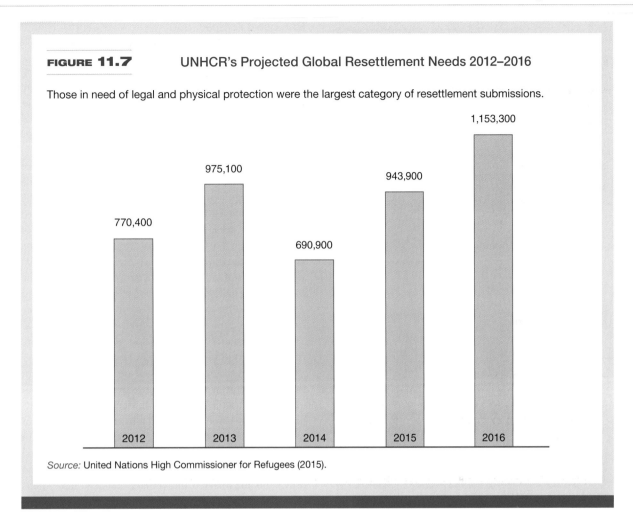

FIGURE 11.7   UNHCR's Projected Global Resettlement Needs 2012–2016

Those in need of legal and physical protection were the largest category of resettlement submissions.

Year	Value
2012	770,400
2013	975,100
2014	690,900
2015	943,900
2016	1,153,300

Source: United Nations High Commissioner for Refugees (2015).

the protracted refugee situations: Afghans in Pakistan, Lhotshampas (ethnic Nepalese expelled from Bhutan) in Nepal, Burmese in Thailand, Croats and Bosnians in Serbia, Liberians in West Africa, and Somalis in Kenya.

In each of these situations, coalitions pursue multiple strategies simultaneously, including resettlement, repatriation, integration in the host country, and improvements in the quality of life in camps. Coalition efforts have had considerable success. The protracted situation of the Lhotshampas in Nepal spurred countries, including Australia, Canada, Denmark, the Netherlands, New Zealand, Norway, the United Kingdom, and the United States, to coordinate resettlement efforts in 2006. Beginning in 2008, after two years of planning, their resettlement began. By 2016, most had resettled in the coalition nations: Australia (5,554), Canada (6,500), Denmark

PHOTO 11.3 The Bhutanese refugee community often gathers in one another's homes for religious and cultural programs. This community is in Charlotte, North Carolina.

Photo of Bhutanese refugees by Kevin Beaty/CC BY 2.0.

PHOTO 11.4 Water is brought into camp in Kivu, Democratic Republic of Congo.

Photo of bringing water into camp in Kivu DRC by Julien Harneis/CC BY-SA 2.0.

PHOTO 11.5 These Syrian children made it safely to the largest refugee camp in Jordan, where they receive assistance from international agencies.

EU/ECHO/MERAN ANABTAWI.

(874), New Zealand (1,002), the Netherlands (327), Norway (566), the United Kingdom (358), and the United States (84,819) (Das Shrestha 2015). This was one of the largest refugee resettlement efforts ever undertaken until the war in Syria.

Guaranteeing basic services for those refugees remaining in Nepal, about 18,000, is under way. Plans for improvement and consolidation of the camps (there are seven camps of Lhotshampas in Nepal), initiated by the UNHCR and approved by Nepal, are promising. Due to extensive international efforts, the Nepalese camps, as reported by independent monitors, provide considerably more assistance to the refugees than do many others. There are schools, medical care, and adequate food and water.

Refugees, Asylees, and Resettlement in the United States

The United States has a long history of accepting refugees. Hundreds of thousands of Europeans who could not return to their homes following World War II settled in the United States. Since 1975, the United States has admitted approximately 3 million refugees (Figure 11.8).

The flow of refugees mirrors the state of the world. In 1975, the Indochina Migration and Assistance Act made way for a large wave following the war in Vietnam. The wars in Afghanistan from the 1980s onward produced another, now decades-long flow. In the 1990s, streams of refugees fleeing the former Soviet Union and Eastern Bloc arrived, and the flow from Africa increased with genocidal wars and terrorism. The Patriot Act, passed in response to the attacks on the World Trade Center and Pentagon in 2001, reduced the flow of refugees dramatically. The flow swelled again, however, with the rush of Somalis in 2004. The Near East and South Asia dominated the last wave, from about 2008 to 2016 (Igielnik and Krogstad 2017).

In the United States, refugees are processed through the Department of State. Every year, the president submits a report to judiciary committees of Congress outlining proposed refugee admissions, the nationalities of refugees proposed for admission along with the reason for admission, their current location, and processing plans. The proposal sets ceilings for each category and provisions for referred individuals. Referred individuals are those individuals in danger of harm due to personal characteristics, such as sexual orientation, or perhaps their political activities, such as dissidents.

The time a person is referred to the United States as a refugee to the time of the person's arrival is 18 to 24 months. Historically, the United States has admitted more than half of global resettlement refugees. The 2015 ceiling set for refugee admissions to the United States was 70,000. The actual number admitted was 69,933—one third from the Near East and South Asia, the majority from Iraq; one third from Africa, primarily Somalia and the DRC; one quarter from East Asia, nearly all of whom were from Burma; 3 percent from Europe, more than half of whom were from Ukraine; 3 percent from Latin America and the Caribbean, nearly all of whom were from Cuba and Colombia; and about 10,000 Syrian refugees referred from the UNHCR.

In 2016,[4] the United States accepted 84,995 refugees for resettlement. They came from 79 different countries, but 70 percent came from just five countries: the DRC, Syria, Burma, Iraq, and Somalia. Acceptances in those

A CLOSER LOOK

FLUX AND FLOW OF REFUGEES IN THE UNITED STATES

FIGURE 11.8   Number of Refugees Admitted to the United States, by Region of Origin of Principal Applicant and Fiscal Year

The flow of refugees to the United States mirrors conditions of conflict and persecution.

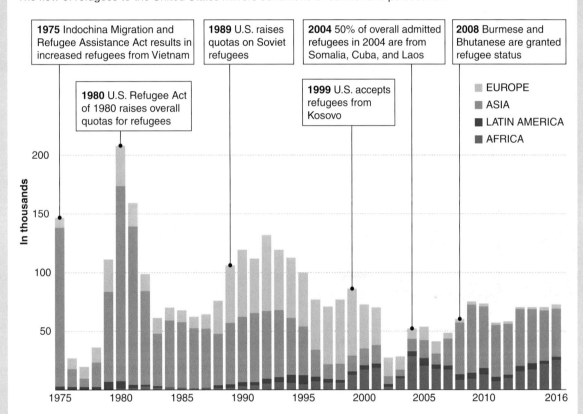

1975 Indochina Migration and Refugee Assistance Act results in increased refugees from Vietnam

1980 U.S. Refugee Act of 1980 raises overall quotas for refugees

1989 U.S. raises quotas on Soviet refugees

1999 U.S. accepts refugees from Kosovo

2004 50% of overall admitted refugees in 2004 are from Somalia, Cuba, and Laos

2008 Burmese and Bhutanese are granted refugee status

■ EUROPE
■ ASIA
■ LATIN AMERICA
■ AFRICA

Source: "The shifting origins of refugees to the U.S. over time." Pew Research Center, Washington, D.C. (September 15, 2016) http://www.pewresearch.org/ft_16-09-14_refugeeskeyfacts_originsovertime/. Data from Refugee Processing Center.

years pale in comparison with the volume of admissions from 1990 to 1994 following the dissolution of the Soviet Union and Eastern Bloc, when 100,000 to 120,000 were admitted annually (U.S. Department of State 2017).

In contrast to the refugees who are processed through the Department of State, asylum seekers are processed through immigration. There are two main routes to asylum. Seekers may be granted asylum through a U.S. Citizens and Immigration Service officer. This is referred to as an "affirmative" application. If applicants for asylum are denied, they are referred for removal proceedings. That is their second chance to be granted asylum. They are then brought up for removal hearings; they submit a "defensive asylum" application. The process is more extensive than many people recognize, and many people are misled concerning the origin of asylees. If people are

CONSIDER THIS
GENEROSITY OF STRANGERS

A former school teacher, poker buddies, lawyers, artists, book club friends, hockey moms, and other simply "ordinary" people with big hearts banded together in small groups across Canada to sponsor and resettle refugees. While the government had committed to accepting 25,000 refugees, it has raised the total to accommodate the demand of Canadians to help out in this humanitarian crisis.

Their job doesn't end with the refugees' arrival. The volunteer groups house the refugees, help them to find doctors and enroll in school, and in general do whatever is needed to help them adjust to life in Canada.

The Canadian helpers are joined by communities, religious organizations, families, and just groups of friends who "adopt" refugees. Throughout the world, similar groups open their neighborhoods and even their own homes. In Pawtucket, Rhode Island, a single church adopted about a dozen refugee families.

---

in the United States and undocumented, they are also brought to trial for removal. They also may apply "defensively" for asylum in removal proceedings before an immigration judge. In either case, to be granted asylum, people must show that they meet the criteria for a refugee. Spouses and children of asylees may apply for asylum on grounds of family unification.

In 2016, 20,455 people received asylum in the United States; most, 11,729, were granted affirmative asylum through the Office of Immigration and Citizenship. The remaining 8,726 were granted asylum defensively through the U.S. Executive Office of Immigration Review (Office of Immigration Statistics 2018). There is not a limit on the number of people who can be admitted as asylum seekers. The trend from 2011 to 2015 has been a decrease in the rate of asylum grants.

There are different countries of origin for refugees and asylum seekers (Tables 11.4 and 11.5). China accounted for the greatest number of acceptances from 2010 to 2015—3,610 cases, or 44 percent, of the total in 2015. Following China were Guatemala, Honduras, India, El Salvador, Ethiopia, Nepal, Mexico, Russia, and Somalia.

In response to the flood of refugees and asylum seekers that began in 2012, many countries reformed their asylum procedures to allow for "in-country" processing whereby refugees could apply for asylum in their country of origin. The United States allowed refugees from Iraq, Cuba, Eurasia, and the Baltic states, as well as children from El Salvador, Guatemala, and Honduras, to apply for in-country processing beginning in 2015. It reflects recognition of the global humanitarian crisis.

Some asylum seekers have the good fortune to live in communities while they await decisions on their cases. They are allowed to obtain work permits. However, the uncertainty of their status inhibits their finding jobs and stable housing. Those living in communities are more likely than those living in detention centers to have legal representation at their hearings, enhancing their chance of acceptance.

Life for most begins in a detention facility, of which there are about 180 in the United States. Detention centers resemble prisons. Whether the applicants are criminals or people who have suffered extreme forms of persecution, all detainees receive the same treatment. Although there are family detention centers, families are often separated. They may be in a detention center for months, some for years. Although refugees have rights under international law, there are no universal standards regarding medical and mental health care, religious services, access to telephones, legal services, or even libraries while in detention seeking refugee status. Much as in the refugee camps, life in detention centers leads to mental and physical health problems, including infections, post-traumatic stress, and depression.

Refugee Adjustment in the United States

Once granted asylum, a person can qualify for eventual naturalization. About 3.2 million people in the United States in 2016 were refugees, about 8 percent of the immigrant population. A 2016 study of Hmong, Bosnian, Somali, and Burmese refugees (Kallick and Mathema 2016) shows that they have integrated well economically, socially, and culturally. Because these groups come from three different continents, have diverse cultures and religions, arrived with varying levels of education, and arrived at different times, they represent a good cross section of the U.S. refugee experience.

Using data from the American Community Survey, Kallick and Mathema (2016) found that although there is variation among the groups with respect to some measures of integration, the overall trend of successful integration is common to all four refugee groups. While recent refugees lag somewhat behind their native-born counterparts, by the time they have reached 10 years of residence in the United States, they match native-born citizens in most measures and surpass them in some.

Language and education are important measures of integration. Within 10 years, more than two thirds of refugees in all four groups spoke English well or very well. Among those refugees who came as children, three refugee groups complete high school at rates comparable to their U.S.-born peers (Somalis' high school graduation rates are in the range of 80–86 percent, somewhat lower rates).

Refugee men integrate into the labor force rather quickly, usually beginning in low-level jobs. As the length of residence in the United States increases, so do their salaries to rates comparable to those of native-born men.

A CLOSER LOOK
ORIGIN OF REFUGEES AND ASYLEES IN THE UNITED STATES

There are about 2.5 million refugees currently living in the United States. The countries of origin of refugees and asylees are different.

TABLE 11.4   Top 10 Refugee Groups in the United States

Country	Number	% of Total Refugees
1. Vietnamese	526,874	21
2. Russian	460,772	19
3. Iraqi	152,352	6
4. Bosnian–Herzegovinian	145,278	6
5. Laotian[a]	141,727	6
6. Burmese	137,081	6
7. Somali	121,985	5
8. Iranian	96,120	4
9. Cuban	93,222	4
10. Cambodian	88,526	4
All other refugee groups	513,917	21
Total	**2,477,854**	**100**

a. These are Hmong refugees.

Source: Adapted from Kallick and Mathema (2016).

(Continued)

(Continued)

TABLE 11.5   Individuals Granted Asylum by Country of Nationality, 2014 to 2016

Country	2016		2015		2014	
	Number	Percent	Number	Percent	Number	Percent
Total	11,729	100.0	17,787	100.0	14,624	100.0
El Salvador	1,404	12.0	1,860	10.5	183	1.3
China, People's Republic	1,381	11.8	2,573	14.5	3,912	26.8
Guatemala	1,317	11.2	1,700	9.6	311	2.1
Honduras	885	7.5	1,099	6.2	89	0.6
Egypt	690	5.9	1,513	8.5	2,580	17.6
Syria	660	5.6	865	4.9	849	5.8
Iraq	611	5.2	697	3.9	533	3.6
Mexico	455	3.9	662	3.7	469	3.2
Iran	381	3.2	639	3.6	572	3.9
Venezuela	328	2.8	466	2.6	318	2.2
All other countries, including unknown	3,617	30.8	5,713	32.1	4,808	32.9

Source: Office of Immigration Statistics (2018). Department of Homeland Security.

Note: Ranked by 2015 country of nationality.

Women integrate into the labor force more slowly, but after 10 years their labor force participation is comparable to that of native-born women. The Burmese refugees who arrive with the highest levels of education fare the best, with median wages of $54,000 for men and $50,000 for women after 10 years. Where certification requirements inhibit qualified immigrants from getting jobs in fields for which they are qualified, programs for retraining and/or help through the certification process are essential. Denying refugees the opportunity to use their skills is a waste of brain power that no society can afford. Preventing "brain waste" lifts the limits on individual earnings and boosts local economic growth.

Refugees help to build local economies. They not only have high rates of employment but also start businesses and provide employment for others. For example,

in Utica, New York, Bosnian and Burmese refugees play important roles in the economy. They brought entrepreneurial activity and filled much of the labor force need for a local medical equipment manufacturer. They bought and renovated deteriorating housing and thus revitalized neighborhoods (Kallick and Mathema 2016). Similar stories abound throughout the United States. The plentiful success stories make anti-immigration and anti-refugee sentiment hard to understand.

Resettlement in Europe

Nearly 700,000 asylum seekers fled to Western Europe in 1992 after the fall of the Iron Curtain. That record was nearly doubled when in 2015 1.3 million people risked their lives to seek refuge in Europe (Figure 11.9). Among them were more than 100,000 unaccompanied minors, about 7 percent of the first-time asylum seekers. While refugees were still migrating from Kosovo and other Eastern European countries, half of those arriving in 2015 were from Syria, Iraq, and Afghanistan.

Along with the UNHCR, the EU and its member countries manage resettlement and relocation of refugees. Resettlement brings a refugee from outside of the EU into the EU. Relocation moves a refugee from one EU member country to another. Humanitarian admissions are also accepted, but they are temporary placement, not a durable solution. Beginning in 1990, asylum seekers would need to apply for asylum in the first EU country that they entered, the original "Dublin regulation." Because the surge of refugees arrived primarily on the shores of Greece

and Italy, Germany agreed to drop this requirement and accept asylum applications of anyone who arrives there regardless of where the person first entered the EU. Later this requirement was dropped by the EU as a whole. The regulations established in the Common European Asylum System manage the flow of migrants, coordinating migration among member and other European countries. The EU has tried but failed to develop uniform standards for asylum seekers across member countries. Acceptance remains a country-by-country decision, and some countries resist taking refugees.

To ease the burden on refugees, some EU members, including Austria, Italy, the Netherlands, Denmark, and Spain, implemented in-country processing and other protected entry procedures, eliminating some of the ordinary

A CLOSER LOOK
NUMBER OF ASYLUM SEEKERS IN EUROPE SURGES

FIGURE 11.9   Number of Asylum Applications Received by EU-28 Countries, Norway, and Switzerland, 1985 to 2015

Flows of asylum seekers to the EU surged at the end of the Cold War and the war in Kosovo. Those flows seem mild in comparison with the flood of people fleeing the turmoil in the Middle East and North Africa, Syria in particular.

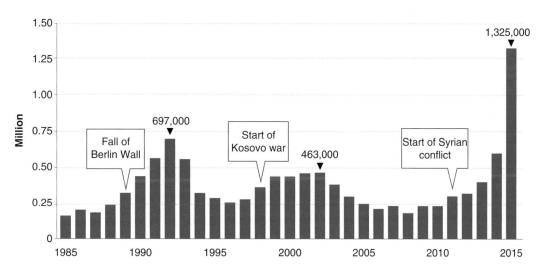

Source: "Number of asylum seekers in Europe surges to record 1.3 million in 2015." Pew Research Center, Washington, D.C. (August 2, 2016) http://assets.pewresearch.org/wp-content/uploads/sites/2/2016/08/14100940/Pew-Research-Center-Europe-Asylum-Report-FINAL-August-2-2016.pdf. Pew Research Center analysis of Eurostat data.

visa requirements. Others, including Austria, France, Germany, Italy, and the United Kingdom, accepted more people through UNHCR humanitarian evacuation programs. These programs offer temporary protections where massive evacuations are necessary such as what happened in Kosovo and Macedonia. Countries around the world have responded similarly. Brazil, for example, has allowed protected entry for Syrians and others affected by that war. Rather than show sufficient finances, a job, or a return ticket, refugees just need to show that they belong to a nationality at risk from the war.

Other strategies for dealing with the flood of refugees from the chaos and carnage in the Middle East have slowed rather than accelerated the process of resettlement. The EU and Turkey agreed to allow the EU to return irregular migrants to Turkey. In return, the EU promised more aid for the refugees in Turkey, more liberal passage of Turkish nationals into the EU, and expedited resettlement of refugees (Organisation for Economic Cooperation and Development 2016). Allegedly, this serves two purposes: to placate EU citizens alarmed by the flow of refugees from Syria and to eliminate the business of smugglers leading refugees on the dangerous journey across the Aegean Sea from Turkey into Greece. Human rights advocates widely criticized the deal. On the one hand, the return of refugees legitimately in danger violates international law and the EU's own principles. If the agreement is enforced with compliance to the legal framework, it is likely that very few will actually be returned to Turkey. The hope seemed to be that the threat of return will dissuade refugees from making the crossing over the Aegean Sea from Turkey to Greece. It also raises the possibility that countries may believe that they can buy their way out of their obligation to refugees (Collett 2016).

Of the millions that arrived in Europe, EU countries approved fewer than 300,000 asylees in 2015 (Table 11.6). Of those, Germany accepted nearly half. Most of the refugees admitted were from Syria, Eritrea, Iraq, Afghanistan, and Iran (BBC News 2016). Relocation has proceeded slowly. The EU approved plans to relocate 160,000 of the refugees staying in temporary shelters in Greece and Italy in 2016. One year later, fewer than 6,000 people achieved relocation. Denmark and the United Kingdom opted out of the program. Austria, Hungary, and Poland, while not officially opting out, did not accept any refugees for relocation (HRW 2016).

In contrast, 2016 experienced a significant decrease in the flow of refugees into the EU and a significant increase in the outflow of migrants returning to their countries of origin. The International Office of Migration reported that 69,000 refugees returned to their home countries in 2015. If the trend of the first six months of 2016 would continue to the end of the year, approximately 100,000 would return. Most of them were leaving from Germany,

A CLOSER LOOK
EUROPEAN UNION ASYLUM APPROVALS

TABLE 11.6   European Union Asylum Approvals, 2015

European asylum approvals fell below targets in 2015.

Germany	140,910
Sweden	32,215
Italy	29,615
France	20,630
The Netherlands	16,450
United Kingdom	13,905

Source: Adapted from Human Rights Watch (2016).

CONSIDER THIS
WAR, REFUGEES, AND RESETTLEMENT

The civil war in Syria increased the global flow of refugees to a torrent. With more than 4.8 million new refugees in the course of just a few years from just one country, Syria, the world experienced its greatest tragedy of refugees since World War II. Syrian refugees have strained the resources of surrounding countries—Turkey, Jordan, Lebanon, Egypt, and Iraq. The Syrian flood joins the flow of refugees from Afghanistan, Iraq, and Somalia, among others who enter Europe through Greece and Italy.

The 1951 Geneva Convention and 1967 Protocol regarding refugees establish global norms that define a signatory country's obligations toward refugees. Countries must submit annual reports to the UN specifying the status of refugees that they are hosting and any domestic legislation regarding refugees. Consequently, refugees are defined and processed similarly in most countries, following the UNHCR definitions and protocols. They are granted international protections outlining their rights and the benefits they are to receive. They are guaranteed freedom of religious practice, the right to food, and the right to secure shelter. Countries may expand on these rights but may not restrict them. If they do, they may be sanctioned under international law.

Using the United States as an example, refugees of the first priority are those referred by the UNHCR, second priority are those of special humanitarian concern, and third priority are family reunification cases. All refugees submit to a screening process and medical exam before they are able to travel to a new country, even when referred through one of these mechanisms. Once they are approved, they are assigned a sponsor to help them through their resettlement.

Asylum cases fall into a different category. Although the requirements are the same as for refugees, the process is different. For the most part, asylum seekers are those who have already reached the country in which they wish to remain and are seeking protection. They may have come to the country of their own accord such as those fleeing the violence in Central America or escaping persecution in Africa on the basis of their sexual orientation. The EU has a common system for member countries, the Asylum Procedures Directive for processing asylum seekers and a Qualifications Directive that sets minimum standards for protections such as work, health care, education, social welfare, resettlement assistance, and travel documents.

---

the largest recipient of asylum applications, 442,000 in 2015. Germany expects to refuse as many as half of the Afghan applications; some 150,000 Afghans arrived in Germany in 2015. Germany is conducting an active campaign to encourage voluntary departures, including financial incentives.

One young migrant from Afghanistan, Arian, explained that after 10 months in Germany, he realized that he had made a mistake. His journey had taken him over the Aegean Sea, where he almost drowned when the dinghy capsized. He walked through Greece to Hungary and on to Germany, sometimes lost and in the rain. Once in Germany, he was put into a migrant reception center, a camp. He was not interviewed or processed for asylum. Although the social workers were kind, the townspeople seemed hostile.

The Syrian refugees, in contrast, were given passports and language lessons. Social workers told them that Syrians were invited, while Afghans were not. Afghans protested that there was war in Afghanistan and they did not want to return. Arian was moved to another camp but still was not processed. He slowly realized that he would not be allowed to stay. He was sent home on a charter flight with 125 other Afghans. His family had spent most of their savings and needed to sell a car and some land to pay smugglers U.S. $7,500 for his trip to Germany (Reeves 2016). Arian's story is common. Most of the world sees the refugees from Afghanistan as economic migrants rather than refugees fleeing war.

A Note on Asian Countries

Despite their own pressing needs, poorer Asian countries—the Philippines, Indonesia, Malaysia, and Thailand—have more than their share of refugees. In contrast, the more developed Asian nations have done little to mitigate the refugee crisis. Refugees—as with other migrants—are often seen as a threat to the state and to

A CLOSER LOOK
STATUS OF ASYLUM CASES

TABLE 11.7   Status of Asylum Cases, Global

There are millions of migrants waiting for their cases for asylum to be heard and recognized as refugees in need of protection. The backlog of cases pending at the beginning of 2015 was close to 2.5 million; by the end of the year, it had risen to more than 3.2 million despite more than 1 million cases closed that year.

Pending, Start of 2015	Received UNHCR Assistance	Applied During 2015	Outcome of Decisions During 2015						Pending, End of 2015
			Positive				Otherwise Closed	Total	
			Convention Status	Complementary Protection Status	Rejected				
Total									Total
2,417,627	588,153	3,094,276	443,307	236,027	504,405		1,037,267	2,221,006	3,219,941

Source: United Nations High Commissioner for Refugees (2016a, Annex Table 9). Reproduced with permission.

racial homogeneity. Japan did not launch a resettlement program until 2010 and accepts on average fewer than 20 refugees a year—all originally migrants from Burma after stays as refugees in other countries. Facing international pressure, Japan accepted 30 Syrian students who qualified for their universities along with their immediate families in 2016 (Williamson 2017).

South Korea accepts refugees from North Korea, who usually arrive from a third country. It accepted its first non-Korean refugee, an Ethiopian, in 2001. It has accepted a small number, 22, of refugees from Myanmar who had been living in Thailand. As of late 2016, South Korea had taken in only 600 non-Korean refugees from 18,800 applicants. While there are a few hundred refugees from Syria in Korea, they are not recognized as refugees by Korea; thus, Korea avoids granting them the rights of refugees under international law. Admitted under humanitarian aid, they renew their applications annually, cannot bring their families to join them, and cannot receive health and other benefits. Acceptance as a refugee in Korea depends on past persecution, not escaping war or future persecution. Despite promises by South Korea to expand its role in the refugee crisis, it seems that the importance of racial homogeneity to the nation wins over international aid (Sang-Hun 2016).

In China, the situation is more severe. By the end of August 2015, there were only 9 refugees and 12 asylum seekers from Syria in China. Nearly 800 persons of concern from parts of Africa and Iraq were in China temporarily while they awaited transfer to a permanent location. In *People's Daily,* Chinese officials argued that the United States and its allies in the West created the refugee crisis through the arrogance of their democratization program in the Middle East, and therefore China bears no responsibility. They also claimed that taking refugees violates their policy of non-interference in other countries. By accepting refugees, they implicitly take one side in the conflict. That said, China has a long-standing antipathy to accepting non-Chinese migrants. They have little bureaucratic structure for processing permanent residency. Although they accepted 300,000 refugees from Cambodia and Vietnam during that war, the refugees were primarily of Chinese ancestry. And although China has 56 officially recognized ethnic groups, it does not consider itself a diverse nation. As one country, all the ethnic groups share a common Chinese history and narrative (Pan 2016).

Meanwhile, one of the worst refugee crises played out in the Bay of Bengal and the Andaman Sea. In 2015, thousands of Rohingya fled Myanmar headed for Malaysia. Not expecting anything out of the ordinary, along with Bangladeshi refugees, they crowded onto ships run by smugglers over a well-traveled route. When Thai authorities announced a crackdown on human smuggling, smugglers abandoned ship, leaving 5,000 to 8,000 stranded, adrift at sea. At first, no country would take them. For weeks, they remained onboard. Thailand, Malaysia, and Indonesia provided them with fuel, water, and supplies but sent them back to sea. At least 70 people died at sea from starvation, dehydration, or abuse. Malaysia and Indonesia eventually relented under the intense international pressure, agreeing to accept 7,000 refugees between them. Thailand promised to stop turning away boats. As of December 2015, 1,000 were still unaccounted for (Vongkiatkajorn, 2015). Since then, hundreds of thousands more Rohingya have fled Myanmar and thousands remain, their persecution so intense as to be genocide.

Deportation

Not all asylum seekers are granted refugee status or other protective measures and are allowed to remain in the country in which they seek asylum. In both 2008 and 2009, about 600,000 asylum seekers were deported from Europe. In 2014, 487,000 migrants were deported; in 2015, it was 551,000.

In October of 2016, the EU and Afghanistan, the country from which the second highest number of asylum seekers in the EU come, signed an agreement that the EU may send back to Afghanistan any Afghans who are not granted asylum in the EU. This holds whether or not they leave voluntarily and even applies to unaccompanied children. Afghanistan, with only 10.4 percent of its GDP derived from domestic revenue, is extremely dependent on foreign aid. It has ample motivation to accept the deal in spite of ongoing conflict (Rasmussen 2016).

By acting on the agreement with aggressive deportations, including of women and children, the EU joins Norway, which has been the most aggressive in involuntary deportations. Norway has rejected 90 percent of all Afghan claims, in contrast to 40 to 50 percent rejection in most other European countries (Nordland 2016a).

In the United States, deportations focus on removal of people who are threats to national security. From 2008 to 2011, most removals occurred from among those already within the United States. From 2012 to 2015, most occurred at the borders—70 percent in 2015. Based on these statistics, U.S. Immigration and Customs

CONSIDER THIS
TWO FACES OF NORWAY

Massoud Mosavi was planning to spend Friday, August 12, 2016, celebrating his seventh birthday jumping on trampolines with friends at his party. Instead, Norwegian police entered his home at 2:30 am, handcuffed his parents, and arrested his older brother and him along with his parents. That day, they were put on a flight back to Afghanistan, accompanied by 11 Norwegian police. Their crime—nothing. There was no crime—except perhaps committed by the Norwegian government.

Norwegians pride themselves on a fierce commitment to equality and human rights. But on this test of humanitarianism, they failed. Despite their wealth, they take few refugees and much of their population seems to resent those who they do take. Norway is among the most aggressive in sending Afghans back to Afghanistan, even if they are officially recognized as refugees. No other European country has had as many forcible repatriations/deportations as Norway. Norwegians claim that Afghanistan is "safe enough" because there are pockets where the war hasn't worsened—although most of the country is more insecure than at any time since 2001.

In the meantime, Massoud, who speaks only Norwegian and English, not Dari, and his family are trying to make a home. His sister, about to graduate from high school, was allowed to stay in Norway on humanitarian grounds. Having been separated from her family in Turkey, she was the first to arrive in Norway. She is allowed to stay because she is considered to have established a strong connection to Norway through her years of schooling. Even though her family had been flown to Norway as part of family reunification, even though her brothers have also received nearly all of their schooling in Norway, and even though they are ill-equipped for Afghanistan, they are forced back. There they will join millions of other internally displaced Afghans, vulnerable to suicide bombings, improvised bombs, and all the dangers of a country at war.

Source: Nordland (2016a).

Enforcement (ICE n.d.) reports that illegal border crossings, with the exception of one year, were at their lowest levels in 40 years (Figure 11.10).

More than half, 59 percent, of the total removals, and 91 percent of those apprehended within the United States, had a previous criminal conviction. This was in tandem with the United States' increasing emphasis on removing convicted felons and others considered public safety threats over non-criminals.

Nevertheless, 96,045 people removed had no criminal conviction. They may have an immigration violation such as overstay of their visa, working without a work visa, trying to enter illegally, or other immigration violations. In addition to removal, "returns" are people who are deemed inadmissible or deportable but who leave the United States without an order of removal.

INTERNALLY DISPLACED PERSONS

Due to the increases in protracted conflicts, extreme weather events, natural disasters, and climate changes, forced migrations are expected to increase. As with the situation of refugees, the number of IDPs surged after 2011, peaking in 2014. Most people who are forcibly displaced are not refugees but rather remain within the boundaries of their homeland. More than 30 million people were internally displaced by conflict and disasters[5] in 2017 alone; more than half of those were from just three countries: Syria, the DRC, and Iraq (Internal Displacement Monitoring Center [IDMC] 2018). The largest number of IDPs displaced by conflict and violence is in Syria, which for the first time displaced Colombia. Both countries have more than 6 million IDPs. Of the 10 countries[6] with the greatest numbers of IDPs, all had more than 1 million IDPs and all except Colombia and Turkey are in Africa or the Middle East (IDMC 2016).

The 1951 UN Convention does not address IDPs. Most do not fall under the protection of the UNHCR, and there is no other international agency with responsibility for them. Because they reside in the country where dangers confront them, their situations are often more precarious than those of refugees who reach a relatively greater degree of safety in another country. Not only might their situation be socially untenable due to persecution, but also physical conditions—whether war, disaster, or government restrictions—may prevent humanitarian aid from reaching them.

A CLOSER LOOK
U.S. ICE REMOVALS

FIGURE 11.10   FY 2008–2015 ICE Removals

The number of ICE deportations has decreased, and the portion with criminal records has increased.

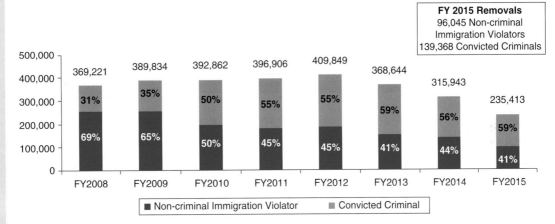

FY 2015 Removals
96,045 Non-criminal Immigration Violators
139,368 Convicted Criminals

Source: U.S. Immigration and Customs Enforcement (n.d.). Reproduced with permission.

Issued a mandate by the UNHCR in 1992, international legal experts crafted a set of "Guiding Principles" from a compilation of existing international laws. The principles, presented to the UN in 1998, recognize the ethical and legal obligations of the international community and governments to IDPs.

The principles affirm the rights of IDPs as members of humanity and as citizens or residents of the country in which they reside, their homeland. Regional alliances that encourage their member states to adopt domestic laws based on the principles give the principles greater force. The Organization of American States, the Great Lakes Protocol on the Protection and Assistance of IDPs in Africa, and the Council of Europe mandated that their signatories incorporate the principles into their national laws. The principles specify protections from arbitrary displacement, protection during displacement, and guarantees for safe return, resettlement, or integration. In short, accepting the principles obligates a country to prevent displacement insofar as is possible, mitigate crises that may arise, and end displacement as quickly as possible in such a way that is safe and provides the IDPs with

a secure life—a durable solution, as is to be the case with refugees. This required the concerted effort of governments, aid agencies and organizations, and international agencies.

Where governments accepted the principles, and developed domestic laws and policies to implement them, they have had positive effects. Aid agencies also use them as operational guidelines, serving as benchmarks for protection standards and practices. Four ways in which they have benefitted IDPs are through raising awareness of IDP needs, mobilizing support from the international community, directing field staff toward solutions, and assisting governments (Ferris 2008).

The IDMC makes the important point that we need to think of displacement in a more holistic fashion that affords all forcibly displaced people protection, whether refugees or internally displaced (IDMC 2016). The same factors that produce refugees produce IDPs—violent conflicts, natural disasters, climate change, persecution, and violations of human rights.

While some IDPs live in camps, others are dispersed. As in situations with refugees, the strain on their host communities may lead to resentment and conflict. Yemen, the poorest country in the Middle East, had the largest number of newly displaced IDPs in 2015. Overshadowed by the war in Syria, Yemen has received little attention. Renewed violence by Houthi rebels, supported by Saudi Arabia, forcibly displaced 2.2 million people, one tenth of its population. Hospitals and schools have been bombed indiscriminately, and children are starving. All of the governorates, aside from one, were affected by the violence.

In addition to Yemen's suffering from political violence, two typhoons struck that same area, forcing another 56,000 from their homes. Every region of Yemen had people living displaced in 2015. They live in overcrowded rented places, schools, other public buildings, tents, and makeshift shelters. Many families are separated, leaving many children unaccompanied. Fully 82 percent of the population is in need of humanitarian assistance, including the most basic food and water. Although this displacement is new, there are no durable solutions in sight, so the plight of these people is likely to become protracted and deteriorate further (IDMC 2016). As of 2018, the situation in Yemen had only worsened.

In the meantime, blockades of Yemen's ports put up to search for weapons on their way to the Houthi rebels slow the delivery of humanitarian aid to displaced persons. The searches, conducted by the UN Verification and Inspection Mechanism, composed of a coalition from the United States, United Kingdom, EU, the Netherlands, and New Zealand, cleared nearly 200 commercial ships. However, despite presumably the best intentions, thousands of metric tons of food were delayed or never offloaded. Disputes with the rebels over customs fees also hamper the delivery of aid. This is not in keeping with the Guiding Principles. As of the end of 2016, the United States has been the major grantor of humanitarian aid to Yemen.[7] Still, the aid request made by the UN is 57 percent below target in pledges (Sharp 2016).

Conflict, drug trafficking, the war on drugs, and threats by rebel groups forced millions of Colombians out of their homes. It is called Colombia's "invisible crisis." Drug traffickers and rebel groups, in Colombia as elsewhere, have become barely distinguishable and often overlap. Most of the people displaced in Colombia are from remote rural areas where armed groups compete for territory and force recruitment into their ranks. Physical violence, sexual violence, and psychological violence all take a toll. In addition to the war on drug traffickers and with the rebels, war on the drug crops by way of aerial spraying of herbicides also forces people from their land.

Colombia has one of the longest periods of protracted displacement. Although Colombia has made much progress in economic development, has developed better relations with its neighbors, and participates in continued talks for a final peace agreement with rebels (voters rejected a 2016 agreement between the government and rebel groups), its troubles are far from over. The number of IDPs continues to grow, reaching 6,939,067 at the end of 2015, the highest number of IDPs in the world at that time.

A 2015 report for the Council on Hemispheric Affairs (Højen 2015) details the plight of the IDPs in Colombia. Indigenous persons and Afro-Colombians are the majority of those internally displaced. They are, as would be expected, among the poorest, those living in poverty and extreme poverty with an average monthly income of U.S. $63 per family. IDPs are pushed from their land by both the rebels and traffickers. As of 2012, they lost approximately 6.8 million hectares (nearly 17 million acres). Most of the displaced, 80 percent, move into the cities for the anonymity it affords. However, they cannot afford city life where a free education does not include the cost of uniforms and books. In the event that an IDP family could afford the uniforms and books, like other migrants, they may lack the identification papers necessary to receive education, health care, and other government benefits. Urban jobs are hard to come by for illiterate farmers. Their situation is as dire as many in refugee camps.

Even before the UN adopted the Guiding Principles, Colombia passed national legislation on behalf of IDPs. Legislation and policy elevated the position of the IDPs, calling for such things as payment of restitution and damages, but there has been little implementation. In at least one case, the government acted violently against IDPs who had illegally constructed makeshift shelters in Bogotá by tearing down the shelters, their only homes (Højen 2015).

Second only to Colombia, millions of people are displaced within Syria, 6,563,642 at the end of 2015. Tens of thousands of people are trapped in between rebels and the border with Turkey. As with refugees, IDPs must often move and move again. In 2016, half of the residents of a camp for IDPs in Syria, 8,500 people, needed to flee yet again, terrified for their lives.

The most displacements occurred in 2016, however, in the DRC, where nearly a million (997,000) people were displaced, primarily by conflict. In 2016, nearly 15,000 people were displaced nearly every day in Africa (IDMC 2017).

"Invisible" Displacement Crises

People forced from their homes by criminal or generalized violence, slow onset disasters, and development[8] are often "unseen" or "underreported" in the ranks of the IDPs. Their situations, however, are similar. Although the line between involuntary and voluntary migration is harder to draw in these cases than in the situations of typhoons, earthquakes, and wars, the plight is the same. People are forced to leave their homes or face the probability of physical harm or even death.

For the purpose of identifying those forced from their homes by criminal violence, a research project launched in 2013 in Honduras cited these factors: "forced recruitment, extortion, murder, threats, injury, sexual violence, insecurity in the community [conflict, shootings], kidnapping, forced disappearance, torture, discrimination, arbitrary detention and dispossession of land and dwellings" (IDMC 2016). If people moved for any of these reasons, they should be considered displaced. In Honduras, an estimated 174,000 people fit this definition of IDPs, including children born in displacement. Another measure relating displacement due to criminal violence in Honduras is the correlation between rates of displacement and the homicide rate (IDMC 2016). This confirmed similar correlations found in a 2012 study in Mexico (IDMC 2016).

Although the data are vague, an estimated 1.7 million people fled criminal violence in Mexico from 2006 to 2011. In 2012 in El Salvador, about 130,000 people, or 2.1 percent of the population, moved because of threat of criminal violence. A reasonable estimate of IDPs as a result of criminal violence in El Salvador, Mexico, Guatemala, and Honduras is at least 1 million.

SUMMARY

Commitment to human rights necessitates that countries cooperate on protecting and finding durable solutions for refugees and others in need of humanitarian assistance. In addition, every country has a selfish interest in securing safety and a life of dignity for refugees. The issues that drive refugees from their home and the problems that they face while in refugee status and beyond affect the entire world. The years of inadequate food, health care, and education along with psychological trauma and physical injury are tragic not only for individuals suffering but also for the peace and prosperity of the world.

While most refugees wish to return home, it is not always the most durable solution. Refugees in protracted situations might not have ever been in their "homeland." Others have nothing left there. Too often, repatriation is forced and refugees end up displaced in their country or the one they just left. Resettlement or integration into the host country may be the best course to secure the safety and life of dignity that refugees are promised.

Preventing the situations that give rise to refugee flight and internal displacement— persecution, discrimination, war and violent conflict, and violations of human rights—must be a priority. Failing that, providing safe passage, for refugees' security and well-being, and a durable solution is a responsibility.

DISCUSSION

1. Defend or refute the argument articulating the need for an international agreement for the protection of refugees as stated in the 1951 Convention and Protocol Relating to the Status of Refugees and the 1967 Protocol.

2. What protections do you think should be guaranteed to refugees fleeing violent conflict and war? If possible, discuss this with a group and negotiate an international agreement on protections.

3. What are the potential benefits and drawbacks of repatriation, resettlement, and local integration for both countries and refugees?

4. Choose one of the protracted refugee situations. What international efforts are under way to find durable solutions? Evaluate the solutions in terms of the safety and well-being of the refugees in question.

ON YOUR OWN

1. There are a number of sites through which to research the U.S. responses to refugees.

   a. Based on the Center for American Progress reports, assess the success of refugee integration into the United States. Provide the evidence to support your assessment.

   The citation for the report:

   Kallick, David Dyssegaard and Silva Mathema. 2016. *Refugee Integration in the United States.* Washington, DC: Center for American Progress. https://cdn.americanprogress.org/wp-content/uploads/2016/06/15112912/refugeeintegration.pdf

   b. There are nine agencies that contract with the U.S. government to resettle refugees. This map shows where each agency settled refugees. According to the Pew Research Center, more than half of the refugees were settled in just 10 states. https://www.google.com/maps/d/viewer?mid=1EnG5uN8ba5x2c8VGYDdUyUEBZFg&hl=en_US&ll=40.37776040145107%2C-108.71451697500004&z=3

   Go to the website of one of the agencies. Investigate its settlement program. How does the agency see its mission? How does it accomplish its goals? How does the agency form partnerships to carry out its work?

   c. The United States runs the largest refugee resettlement program in the world. Read this Fact Sheet about refugee resettlement. http://www.migrationpolicy.org/research/ten-facts-about-us-refugee-resettlement?gclid=CNXEkbac1dQCFYmKswodYpEPlA

   What do you think are the most important things that people should know?

   Do these facts support the opinion that the United States could accept more refugees or that the United States should not accept more refugees?

2. Compare maps of refugees and IDPs with maps of GNP per capita. What relationships are apparent? Summarize the forces that coalesce in the patterns.

   Maps of refugees and IDPs can be found in the UNHCR's *Global Trends: Forced Displacement in 2016.* http://www.unhcr.org/5943e8a34.pdf

   To compare more precise data, Annex Table 1 lists by region.

3. The scale of the flow of refugees into Europe is hard to imagine. This interactive map makes it somewhat easier to picture.

   http://www.takepart.com/article/2015/10/28/map-that-shows-how-huge-europes-refugee-crisis-really-is

   The bar at the top of the map moves across time from 2002 to 2015. If you hold the cursor on the timeline, you will see migration to the whole of Europe from the Middle East, Asia, and Africa. If you hold the cursor on a country, you will see the flow from that country for the point on the timeline.

   The chart below shows the monthly migration from and to each country.

   Examine the flow at the beginning of the timeline, a point in the middle, and the end of the timeline. How do the flows from sending countries and receiving countries change?

   What world events may be related to the change?

NOTES

1. Protracted status refers to the group living in refugee status. Not every individual in that group may be in protracted status for the duration. Some individuals may repatriate or resettle. Some die while in refugee status, others are born, and there are new flows. In the situations where refugee status has endured for decades, many will spend the duration or significant portions of their lives in refugee status.

2. The right to return of Palestinians is one of the major obstacles to peace between Israel and Arab countries.

3. As of 2016, the resettlement countries were Argentina, Australia, Austria, Belarus, Belgium, Brazil, Bulgaria, Canada, Chile, Croatia, Czech Republic, Denmark, Estonia, Finland, France, Germany, Hungary, Iceland, Ireland, Italy, Japan, Republic of Korea, Latvia, Liechtenstein, Lithuania, Luxembourg,

the Netherlands, New Zealand, Norway, Portugal, Romania, Spain, Sweden, Switzerland, United Kingdom, United States, and Uruguay.

4. The fiscal year (FY) runs from October 1 to September 30. The refugees admitted in FY 2016 would actually be those admitted from October 1, 2015 to September 30, 2016. Numbers from different sources may vary whether based on a fiscal year or a calendar year.

5. About 11.8 million (39 percent) due to conflict and about 18.8 million (61 percent) due to disasters (IDMC 2018).

6. Syria (6.8 million), Colombia (6.5 million), Iraq (2.6 million), the DRC/Sudan (2.0 million), Nigeria (1.7 million), Yemen (2.0 million), South Sudan (1.9 million), Ukraine (1.8 million), Afghanistan (1.3 million), and Turkey (1.1 million).

7. In December 2016, the United States also stopped selling weapons to Saudi Arabia. Saudi Arabia has been a major aggressor in Yemen, trying to restore the former government. With one hand the United States was supplying aid, and with the other it was facilitating Yemen's destruction.

8. Migration due to environmental change and development are considered in other chapters.

12

Environmental and Economic Migration

WHERE DO THEY GO NOW?

"The lake was our mother and our father." Adrián Quispe is, or at least was, a fisherman. Along with his four brothers and hundreds of other Uru-Murato people in Llapallapani, Bolivia, he depended on the lake for sustenance for himself and his family. The Uru-Murato lived from the bounty of Lake Poopó for millennia. The original inhabitants of the area, they survived incursions of the Incas and the Spanish, but the hopes of their surviving climate change are dim. Once Bolivia's second largest lake, Lake Poopó is just a dry salty expanse. Cyclical El Nino droughts made worse by water diversion gradually shrank the lake. But in December 2015, the lake simply disappeared. With too little water in the lake, the seasonal winds kicked up too much silt for the fish to breathe. Tens of thousands of stranded fish rotted, filling the air with their stench for weeks. With the fish dead, the flamingos, ducks, and other birds died or left. Hundreds of families left as well. Their livelihoods and homes are no longer viable.

There is even more at stake. The Uru-Murato were so connected to the lake that many took Mauricio as their family name after the fish that they called mauri. Their lifestyle revolved around the lake and fishing—ritual prayers to St. Peter (a fisherman), rituals to mark the beginning of the fishing season, weeks on the lake following schools of fish with many women working alongside their husbands. While scientists knew for decades that the lake would eventually die, its life expectancy was centuries more—not years more. With the lake gone, most of the families have gone, leaving their adobe homes behind. They work in mills, mines, and farms. Many are hundreds of miles away. They can no longer teach their children to fish. Their lifestyle and the culture that depended on it will probably die as well. "Without this lake, where do we go?" Quispe asks.

—Adapted from reporting by Casey (2016)

LEARNING OBJECTIVES

After completing this chapter, students will be able to do the following:

12.1 Differentiate voluntary and forced migration

12.2 Recognize the societal- and global-level causes of migration

12.3 Assess the costs and benefits of migration to sending and receiving countries

12.4 Explain the difficulties in resettlement and repatriation of migrants

WHAT IS A MIGRANT?

Migration is one of the most significant globalization processes of the 21st century. If all of the world's migrants would occupy a single country, it would be the fifth largest country in the world with 244 million people, 3.3 percent of the global population. The United States hosts a larger number of immigrants than any other country, but it is only 14 percent of the U.S. population. In contrast, 28 percent of Australia's population is foreign born, as is 22 percent of Canada's population. In the Persian Gulf, Kuwait, United Arab Emirates, and Qatar all are nearly 75 percent foreign (Connor 2016). Most migrants in the Gulf states are foreign workers. In 2013, the percentage of foreign-born population in Organisation for Economic Cooperation and Development (OECD) countries ranged from 43.7 percent in Luxembourg to less than 1 percent in Greece, Turkey, Mexico, and Poland (OECD 2018).

"Migrant" encompasses a broad array of people whose only common characteristic is that they are on the move. Due to the immediacy and desperation of their flight and the dangers they face daily, refugees capture the most headlines; however, migration due to environmental disasters and environmental degradation and migrations of people looking to make a better living, receive an education, and/or reunite with family account for the largest number of international migrants and displacements within countries. Although migrants generally are not protected by international law, like all people they are protected by international human rights laws.

Forced migration or displacement, voluntary migration, and similar terms do not have legal standing or universally accepted definitions. Forced migration usually refers to displacements from war, violence, environmental disaster, urbanization, and many other circumstances that leave people with only two realistic choices: move or have a life of hardship, perhaps even death. People often report multiple reasons for moving. If, for example, farmers' land is no longer arable due to drought and they cannot make a living or feed their families from the land, they could be said to be forced by environmental change.

The Special Rapporteur of the Commission on Human Rights suggested the following definition of migrants, but it does not have official standing. These persons should be considered as migrants:

- Persons who are outside the territory of the state of which they are nationals or citizens, are not subject to its legal protection, and are in the territory of another state

- Persons who do not enjoy the general legal recognition of rights that is inherent in the granting by the host state of the status of refugee, naturalized person, or similar status

- Persons who do not enjoy general legal protection of their fundamental rights by virtue of diplomatic agreements, visas, or other agreements (United Nations Educational, Scientific and Cultural Organisation 2017)

This definition differentiates migrants from refugees and people who are displaced or move internally. Although refugees are sometimes referred to as migrants, refugees are a specifically defined category afforded international protections. People who do not cross international borders fall outside the limits of this definition, but some of the most powerful forces compelling people to leave their homes—natural disasters and urbanization—displace people internally and account for the greatest number of migrants.

While not considered refugees, many migrants—both internal and international—face equally dire circumstances. They may travel journeys on treacherous routes, arriving illegally and facing struggles to find homes and jobs and to integrate. Others, such as highly skilled professionals, may seek a better life, arriving along regular legal routes and finding opportunity to start a business that grows into a multinational corporation.

There is one convention and two protocols specific to migrants. As of November 28, 2017, only 51 states were party to the 1990 International Convention on the Protection of the Rights of All Migrant Workers and Members of Their Families (United Nations Office of the High Commissioner on Human Rights 2017). The International Labour Organization also protects rights of migrant workers. Together, these instruments offer protections to a small fraction of the total migrant population. The 2000 Protocol to Prevent, Suppress, and Punish Trafficking in Persons, Especially Women and Children and the 2000 Protocol against the Smuggling of Migrants by Land, Sea, and Air are part of the Palermo Protocols annexed to the Transnational Convention on Organized Crime. These have near universal ratification.

One of the powerful storylines of the 2004 movie *Crash* was portrayed Maria, a Hispanic woman who left her home, husband, and children behind, and to be cared for by others, so that she could care for and nurture a wealthy California family. The story portrayed the dilemma of thousands of women who must leave their families to be able to provide financially for them. Their

A CLOSER LOOK
MIGRATION PATTERNS

FIGURE 12.1   Percent of Migrants by Major Area of Destination

Most international migrants move within their region of origin. Latin America and the Caribbean and North America are the exceptions.

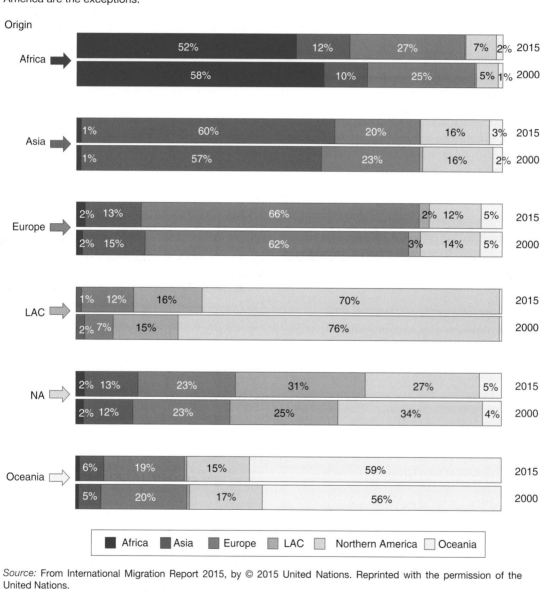

Source: From International Migration Report 2015, by © 2015 United Nations. Reprinted with the permission of the United Nations.

Note: LAC = Latin America and the Caribbean; NA = Northern America.

CONSIDER THIS
THE LARGEST MIGRATION IN HISTORY

Some moves were voluntary and some forced. Some were forced by central planning and some by ecological degradation. In 2016, Guangzhou (formerly Canton) and Shenzhen, two of China's four largest cities, had populations of more than 13 million and close to 11 million, respectively. In 1970, Guangzhou's population was only about 1.5 million; Shenzhen's was only 22,000 and in 1950 was only 3,000. The extremely rapid growth of these cities is part of the story of "the largest migration" in the history of the world.

When China opened to private enterprise and to the world, 160 million people moved from poor rural areas to urban areas. As recently as the late 1970s, China was only 20 percent urban. From 1990 to 1995, 10 million moved; from 1995 to 2000, 32 million moved; and from 2000 to 2005, 38 million moved. Mass migration was responsible for 20 percent of China's economic growth from 2001 to 2010. The gross domestic products (GDPs)

of coastal provinces are comparable to those of Austria and Switzerland. Tens of thousands of villages have been swallowed up, torn down, or abandoned in the wake of China's development (Economist 2012).

Then the trend began to reverse. Manufacturing is moving inland. Wages in rural areas are rising, and the time away from family, pollution, and transportation to and from the coastal cities make staying inland very attractive. Although people continue to migrate to the largest cities, the government is moving to develop its middle and smaller cities, promoting growth there. But a middle Chinese city is a large one nearly anywhere else in the world.

One billion people will live in cities in China by 2025 if current trends continue. There will be 221 cities of more than 1 million, 23 will have more than 5 million, and 8 will be megacities with more than 10 million people (Woetzel et al. 2009).

---

stories are at the intersection of the globalization of "care work" and the importance of remittances to people living in developing countries.

PATTERNS OF MIGRATION

As with refugees, the trends in global population flow depend on global forces and shift with changing global circumstances. Patterns of migration differ according to the type of migrant (Figure 12.1). As would be expected, there is virtually no flow of migration from advanced to less developed or emerging economies. People in advanced economies are less vulnerable than those in lesser developed countries, and lesser developed and emerging economies generally offer fewer opportunities.

There are some common misconceptions about migrants. For example, most migrants originate from middle-income countries (157 million, nearly 65 percent, in 2015), and this is the most rapidly increasing migrant category. Most international migrants stay within their region of origin—60 percent of Asians, 66 percent of Europeans, 52 percent of Africans, and 59 percent from Oceania remain within their region. The exceptions are migrants from Latin American and the Caribbean, most of whom move to North America, and North Americans,

more than 50 percent of whom move to Latin America (31 percent) or Europe (23 percent) (United Nations [UN] 2016a).

As would be expected, migrant flows from emerging economies to other emerging economies are low and have remained relatively constant, contributing about 2 percent to the population composition of emerging economies. Most economic migrants move from poorer and emerging economies to richer nations.[1] Wealthy countries host more than two thirds, 71 percent, of the global total of international migrants and an even larger percentage, 81 percent, of 21st-century migrants (UN 2016a).

DISPLACED BY CLIMATE CHANGE AND ENVIRONMENTAL DISASTER

Climate change is arguably the greatest 21st-century threat to human security and every country's national security, stemming from the potential for massive displacements of people—caused by food shortage, extreme weather, and exacerbated "natural" disasters. The environmental events due to climate change are already the largest single source of forced migration. Yet people recognized as victims of climate change and disasters are denied status as refugees.

It is difficult to overestimate the cost of disasters in people's lives. Disasters may come on quickly with little or no warning, as in the case of a volcanic eruption, an earthquake, a tsunami, or a flash flood, or they may emerge slowly, years in the making, such as famine due to environmental degradation (Figure 12.2). From 2008 to 2014, environmental disasters displaced, on average, 26.4 million people annually, 1 person per second. The yearly totals range from 42.4 million in 2010 to 15 million in 2011. Weather hazards accounted for 86 percent of the displacements, 22.5 million people, about 82,000 per day. Geophysical events such as volcanoes and earthquakes displaced the remaining 14 percent. Because many small events, particularly those that displace fewer than 100 people, do not get reported, the official figures are smaller than the actual total displacement (Norwegian Refugee Council 2015). The year 2015 brought 19.2 million new displacements due to natural disasters throughout 113 countries (Internal Displacement Monitoring Center 2016), more than any other source of migration.

A CLOSER LOOK
DISPLACEMENT FROM DISASTERS

FIGURE 12.2   Protracted Displacement Following Disasters Worldwide in 2014/2015

Environmental events displace people the world over. In these situations, people were still displaced years after, some decades after, the actual events.

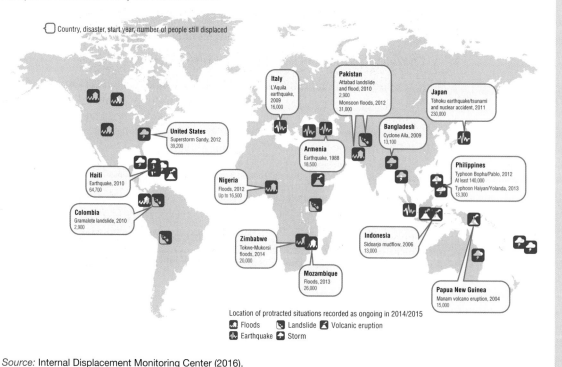

Source: Internal Displacement Monitoring Center (2016).

Many more people are vulnerable to disasters than have been in the past. Population growth is one factor. Population growth in the urban areas is another. People are attracted to urban areas by economic opportunities; commercial buildings and residences may be hastily built or built in areas near rivers or along coasts that are susceptible to floods. As the factors coalesce, they multiply people's vulnerability. Population growth, urbanization, and extreme weather events are the recipe for a "perfect storm."

As with other global problems, developing societies suffer the most severely and have the least capacity to rebound from these events. From 2008 to 2014, 95 percent of the people displaced were from middle- and low-income developing countries, primarily South and East Asia. People in the very lowest and highest income countries experience less than their share of displacement. In the lowest income countries, urbanization is much lower than in middle-income countries; people are less exposed. In middle-income countries, they are more vulnerable than in high-income countries, even when they are equally exposed. For example, the Philippines and Japan are equally exposed to tsunamis, yet the Philippines experiences a much higher level of displacement. High-income countries have better emergency response and early warning systems. In high-income countries, however, those with low incomes suffer more and longer displacements, as was the case with Hurricane Sandy in the United States and the 2011 flooding in Canada (NRC 2015).

Asia experienced the highest rate of displacement from 2008 to 2014, with more than 5,000 people per

CONSIDER THIS
THE SPECIAL CASE OF HAITI

PHOTO 12.1 Although its landscapes are beautiful, Haiti—unlucky in its geography—is vulnerable to earthquakes, hurricanes, and floods. Disasters pile on one another, not allowing Haitians to catch their breath, let alone recover from one disaster before the next one strikes. With a small population of less than 11 million, Haiti accounted for about one sixth of disaster-related deaths from 1996 to 2015, more than any other country in terms of absolute numbers or relative to its population (United Nations Office for Disaster Risk Reduction and Centre for Research on the Epidemiology of Disasters 2016). After Hurricane Matthew struck in 2017, Haiti needed clean water to prevent the spread of disease along with food, shelters, material for rebuilding, and agricultural supplies. The good news was that cholera was able to be controlled.

U.S. Navy photo by Mass Communication Specialist 3rd Class William S. Parker

million displaced on average. Latin America and the Caribbean was second, North America was third, Europe was fourth, and the Middle East and North Africa had the lowest rate of displacement. This is in keeping with their rankings in global economic and human development.

Although displacement from environmental change and unforeseen extreme weather events is the largest category of forced displacement, there are no international protection instruments to ensure humanitarian aid for the victims, whether they move internally, as most do, or across borders. Because displacement due to disaster and climate change will worsen, the mandate of the UN Commission on Human Rights (UNCHR) is expanding to include the protection of victims of natural disasters. Five climate change scenarios that are likely to provoke massive and chronic human displacement far into the future are the following:

- Extreme weather events related to water such as floods, hurricanes/typhoons, and mudslides

- Population areas that have become too dangerous for human habitation

- Environmental degradation and slow onset disasters such as salinization of fresh water or land, desertification, and recurring flooding

- Submersion of small island states

- Violent conflict triggered by climate change-caused scarcity of essential resources such as land, water, and food (UN, n.d.)

The scenario for the future is one of chronic humanitarian disasters. The question that confronts the global community is one of global justice. Developed countries created the early conditions and momentum of climate change. With millions of lives at stake from extreme weather, geological events, and deteriorating environmental conditions that make it impossible to meet their basic needs—and the conditions of violence that often result—can environmental migrants be refused the right of refuge?

DEMOGRAPHIC, ECONOMIC, AND SOCIAL IMPACTS OF MIGRATION

What is the most important question in considering migration? Whether or not migrants do well when they arrive at a destination country? Whether or not the receiving country, most often wealthy, is advantaged or disadvantaged by migration? Collier (2013) suggested that the most important question is whether or not there is a net overall good, especially in consideration of the impact on the billions of people in the home countries of migrants, most of which are characterized by poverty and devoid of many of the political and social liberties that can lead to prosperity.

Both sending and receiving countries can benefit from migration in their demography, economic growth, and social life. For receiving countries, as discussed below, migration is a source of demographic growth. Emigration from countries with high unemployment of working-age youths may relieve social stress. Although this diminishes the labor force, remittances may generate an income stream that lifts families out of poverty. The Philippines trains people, from domestic workers to highly skilled health care practitioners, specifically to increase their emigration value and the opportunities for greater remittances. Wealthier countries also benefit economically whether the migrant is low or high skill. Despite people's fears, most of the research on migration concurs that the overall effect of migration on both the sending and receiving countries is generally positive when migration is well managed at both the sending and receiving ends.

Demographic Impacts of Migration

One benefit of immigration to wealthier receiving countries is the demographic impact. Because many rich nations have at or below replacement fertility levels, migration has helped to balance global population growth, redistributing population from overpopulated to underpopulated countries. For those wealthy countries, net increases in migration could compensate for zero or negative population growth.

The current trend of migration to Europe is not enough to completely compensate for the decline in fertility; however, Europe's population loss would be even greater without migration. Without net positive migration, the population of Europe would have declined between 2000 and 2015 (UN 2016a:21). Three quarters of the population increase in the European Union (EU) and European Free Trade Association (EFTA) resulted from the increase in the foreign-born population. North America would also experience population decline with zero net migration. On the side of sending countries, net negative population migration in Latin America and the Caribbean slowed population growth there, accelerating their aging (Figure 12.3) (UN 2016a).

CONSIDER THIS
MIGRATION, FERTILITY, AND POPULATION AGING

A dependency ratio is the ratio of the number of people of working age in relation to those too young or too old to work. Positive net immigration and higher fertility rates among immigrant populations than native populations help to lower the dependency ratio in the United States. If fertility rates among immigrants continue to decrease, maintaining the dependency ratio depends on increasing immigration of working-age migrants.

Population aging in developed countries occurred gradually, over about 100 years depending on the country, as lifespan increases with better sanitation, medicines, and health care. In Latin American and Caribbean countries, the population aged rapidly in a generation (20 years). Their fertility has declined to only slightly above replacement. Their dependency ratio is thus growing rapidly. This presents a challenge for these countries to support a sufficient workforce and welfare programs to care for an aging population.

A CLOSER LOOK
IMMIGRANT CONTRIBUTIONS TO THE WORKFORCE

FIGURE 12.3   Immigrant Percentage of Working Age Population (aged 25–64 years old)

In many advanced economies, immigrants make up a significant portion of the workforce. Without these immigrants, labor shortages would be likely.

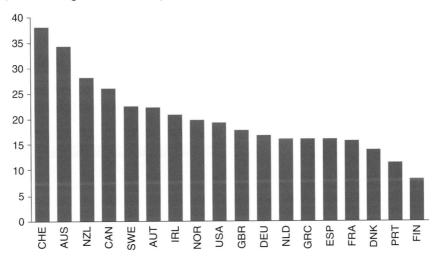

Source: Jaumotte, Koloskova, and Saxena (2016). International Monetary Fund. Reproduced with permission.

Note: CHE = Switzerland; AUS = Australia; NZL = New Zealand; CAN = Canada; SWE = Sweden; AUT = Austria; IRL = Ireland; NOR = Norway; USA = United States; GBR = United Kingdom; DEU = Germany; NLD = The Netherlands; GRC = Greece; ESP = Spain; FRA = France; DNK = Denmark; PRT = Portugal; and FIN = Finland.

The demographic characteristics of the migrant population, not just the numbers of people, are critical to the benefits of migration. Most international migrants, 72 percent, are of working age. This is a much higher percentage than the average of the total global labor force (UN 2016a). For developed countries experiencing zero or negative population growth, international migrants boost an important segment of their population—their working-age population. From 1990 to 2010, migrants contributed about half of the growth in the working-age population in high-income countries where it was measured (see Figure 12.3) (Jaumotte et al. 2016). This reduces the dependency ratio of a country—the number of people capable of working in relation to those who are too young or too old to work. Furthermore, most migrants have higher fertility rates than the native-born population of receiving countries. This has a longer-term impact on a country's age structure, helping to maintain a sufficient labor force—at least until their birth rates decrease to those of the native-born populations.

In the United States, immigration is critical to growth in much of the country, particularly areas losing domestic migrants—that is, about half of the country's 100 largest metropolitan areas. International and domestic migrants tend to congregate in different cities. Domestic migrants tended toward the Sun Belt. Port cities where ethnic niches had been established tended to attract international migrants, but there has been greater variability over the course of the 21st century, spreading the benefits of immigration more broadly. A total of 47 metropolitan areas had domestic migration losses that were at least partially offset by international migration gains. In 19 of them, international migration exceeded domestic losses (Frey 2017).

There can be costs to this shift in population to the sending country. Its labor force can be diminished and become less productive. But where youth unemployment is high, emigration can alleviate social and political pressures.

Economic Impacts of Migration on Host Countries

Aside from being well-known corporations and seemingly so American as to be "household" words, Tesla, Zumba, Panda Express, Kraft, Chobani, and Kohl's, along with the tech companies Yahoo!, Google, Amazon, and eBay, were founded by immigrants. Immigrants or their children founded or co-founded more than half of the U.S. 2017 Fortune 500 companies—57 percent of the top 35 (Center for American Entrepreneurship 2017). The immigrant-founded Fortune 500 firms employed 18.9 million people and generated billions in gross national product (GNP).

Immigrants are overrepresented among small business owners. Given that moving to a new country is fraught with risk, it is not surprising that immigrants are twice as likely to start businesses as the native-born population. Immigrants own more than half of the U.S. grocery stores and nearly half of the nail salons. The businesses owned by the 2.9 million immigrant entrepreneurs comprised 20.6 percent of entrepreneurs and generated U.S. $65.5 billion in 2014. Not only do these small businesses support themselves, but in 2007 they employed nearly 6 million workers (Center for American Entrepreneurship 2017).

CONSIDER THIS
MIGRATION CHAINS

Migration tends to encourage more migration—an effect of reducing the investment cost of migration, particularly from poor countries far from wealthier ones. Knowing someone or knowing of someone from one's town or village who can help in getting established and acclimated encourages others to follow. Networks emerge in the home country. Niches emerge in the host country.

Residential neighborhoods such as "Chinatown," "Little Italy," "Old Deutschtown," and "Polish Hill" and occupational niches such as ethnic restaurants, food stores, nail parlors, entertainment, construction, and finance multiply human, social, and economic capital in a community and facilitate immigrants' economic, social, and cultural integration.

From 2004 to 2014, migration contributed 47 percent of the growth in the U.S. workforce and 70 percent of the growth in Europe's workforce (OECD 2014). Although many people resist the evidence, immigration of both high- and low-skilled migrants can boost a host country's economy. In high-income countries, a 1 percent increase in working-age migrants increases a host country's economy 2 percent in the long run. Labor productivity and the increase in the ratio of working-age population to total population are the primary factors producing the gain. Because this test was applied to high-income countries, it is a more demanding measure than if calculated for both high- and low-income countries. Without their immigrant population, GDP per capita would be 5 percent lower on average, according to an International Monetary Fund study of 18 wealthy countries (Jaumotte et al. 2016).

Although the specifics vary by country, how well migrants integrate into a country's economy is a key factor. Within high-income countries, the effect may be larger or smaller depending on variables such as the migrant mix, the labor market, and the complementarity of migrant and native skills (Jaumotte et al. 2016). Where migrants' skills are similar to those of native-born workers, migrants compete with natives, their integration is slower, and they may affect wages in the short run until the market adjusts. Where, however, migrant skills are complementary, they integrate more quickly and increase overall productivity in both the short and long runs. Complementarity also increases the diversity of the labor force. Low-skilled migrant women entering the labor market of a wealthier country can be quickly employed in domestic work and child care, enabling higher-skilled native-born women to enter the labor force or transition from part-time to full-time or even overtime work.

Complementarity is most likely to exist in aging societies with rising educational levels. These societies are more likely to have gaps in employment sectors, especially low-skilled non-tradable jobs. These are readily filled by immigrants. With immigrants filling lower-skilled jobs, natives are more likely to improve their own education and move into other more complex or more skilled labor categories. Female labor market participation also increases; immigrants increase the supply of child care and household services. Complementarity results in filling positions where native labor is in short supply, advancing technological progress when there are highly skilled migrants, and increasing demand (Blagrave, Saxena, and Vesperoni 2016).

Despite these positive outcomes, recent migrants have lower employment rates than longer-term migrants, who have lower employment rates than natives (OECD 2016). A number of factors contribute to this: language, credentials not recognized by the host country, skills not applicable to the labor market in the host country, inaccessibility of public sector jobs, unfamiliarity of local customs and norms, and lack of contacts for networking (OECD 2016).

Migrants are usually the first fired in a downturn. They work for less pay, longer hours, and under some of the worst conditions in their host societies (UN 2016a). Many countries restrict access to health care for migrants. Mexican immigrants in the United States, despite their long history there, have limited access to health care, even those who work. In 2003, 52 percent of Mexican immigrants did not have health care coverage, nor did about 36.7 percent of other immigrant groups from Latin America and the Caribbean (Wise and Covarrubias 2007).

Social Impacts on Host Countries

One of the most often overlooked social impacts of immigration is that, at least in the United States, areas with large immigrant communities have lower crime rates than areas with a lower percentage of immigrants. A quick review of the data based on several studies (Ewing, Martínez, and Rumbaut 2015) establishes that immigrants commit fewer crimes than the native-born population. This is true of both property and violent crimes and has been true for decades. Misconceptions about criminality of immigrants leads to overly punitive policies and harsher punishments for immigrants than native-borns would receive for the same or more severe crimes. Immigrants have been deported and detained for traffic offenses (Ewing et al. 2015):

- From 1990 to 2013, the immigrant proportion of the population grew from 7.9 to 13.1 percent. Illegal immigrants more than tripled from 3.5 to 11.2 million. Federal Bureau of Investigation (FBI) data report that the violent crime rate fell 48 percent and the property crime rate fell 41 percent in this period.

- Crime is generally high among adolescent and young adult populations. Native-born males, aged 18 to 39 years, are incarcerated at a rate of 3.3 percent, while immigrant males of the same age are incarcerated at only a 1.9 percent rate.

- Among less educated males aged 18 to 39 years, native-borns had an incarceration rate of 10.7 percent in comparison with 2.8 percent among Mexicans and 1.7 percent among foreign-born Salvadorans and Guatemalans of the same age and education. (FBI 2017)

Criminologists have known this for more than a hundred years, documented in academic studies and government commissions. "If you want to find a safe city, first determine the size of its immigrant population," according to Jack Levin, who minced no words when he reported his findings and those of other criminologists. Immigrants come for a better life; they don't want to risk that. If they are undocumented, the stakes are even higher for them. Immigrants are "success oriented," having given up a lot (quoted in Balko 2009). Of the 32 cities with populations over 500,000, El Paso (Texas), San Diego (California), and San Antonio (Texas) are among the safest cities in the country.

One of the keys traditionally has been how a group is welcomed and integrated into society. Canada and the United States have been more welcoming than when the Irish and Italians and other earlier ethnic groups arrived. Arab Americans have integrated well, with high average incomes and little crime. In France and Germany, where they have been marginalized, there are waves of crime and rioting (Balko 2009).

El Paso, with one of the most heavily immigrant populations, ranks consistently as the first or second safest city in its size category. El Paso (population 687,193 in 2016) had 17 homicides in 2016. In comparison, Pittsburgh (population 302,443 in 2016) had 57 homicides. El Paso is considered one of the best places in the United States to live, in part because of its low crime rate. Also in contrast, the homicide rate for all cities of 500,000 to 999,999 population in 2016 was 12.9 per 100,000. For cities smaller than El Paso, the rate was 12.3 per 100,000, or 84.5 homicides for a city of 687,193. Other cities with high immigrant populations also fare well.[2]

Since 2011, the education profile of immigrants to the United States aged 25 years and over has changed. Prior to 2011 college graduates and immigrants with less than a high school education were roughly equal, 28 and 30 percent, respectively. Among immigrants arriving from 2011 to 2015, 48 percent were college graduates (or better), considerably better than the 31 percent of college graduates among all U.S. residents, and only 19 percent had less than a high school education. The increase in educational attainment may be a function of an increasing percentage of Asian immigrants (Frey 2017).

Economic Impacts in Home Country

Remittances are the most direct benefit of migration to the sending country. Diaspora populations generate significant resources for their countries of birth, often providing a significant percentage of the GNP. On the global level, remittances that migrants send home are a larger source of income than either foreign aid or foreign investment. In 2014 migrants from developing countries sent home U.S. $436 billion, and in 2015 they sent home $440 billion. This was well over official development assistance and foreign investment, excluding that of China (UN 2016a).

However, if remittances are simply a "safety valve," they may hinder progress rather than help long-term economic development efforts. In Mexico, for example, remittances have been a major source of external income. About 8 percent of families receive remittances. For 47 percent of these families, it is their primary source of income. Most remittances go into meeting basic needs, health, and education. About 10 percent go into savings and small-scale investment such as housing, land, livestock, and small businesses. Remittances act as a buffer against poverty, but depending on how they are used, they do not necessarily contribute to long-term development (Wise 2007).

Remittances certainly are not a panacea or replacement for development. Remittances do not necessarily alter underlying political, social, and economic infrastructures. They can be used as a tool to aid in development. To maximize the effect of remittances as a resource for promoting development, Carling (2008) suggested adopting a broader definition of remittances than is commonly considered, enabling receiving and sending countries to construct effective policies for the totality of money generated by migration movements. In addition to money that individual migrants send back home, measures of remittances should include worker compensation earned abroad such as by cross-border commuters, temporary and seasonal workers, and embassy workers as well as money moved from country to country as workers move.

Other forms of transfers than from individuals should also be counted among remittances. Special policies for money from collectives such as religious organizations, governments in terms of social security transfers, and businesses such as with company pensions can motivate their use in the home country for development. Similarly, receivers of remittances may include migrants who send money home for their own use, charities, and taxes or levies in addition to the intra-family transfers usually included in discussions of remittances (Carling 2008). Without policy and planning for the full range of remittance revenues, countries may miss out on important development opportunities.

Because migrants may be perceived as privileged in their home country, it is important to avoid policies that could create tension or resentment between migrants and non-migrants by giving migrant money special treatment. Policies that target migrant money indirectly, providing incentive to invest in the home country, can have long-term developments. For example, by issuing bonds that provide interest, remittance money can be used for development and earn money for the migrant or recipient. India and Israel have issued these bonds and funded infrastructure projects with them. Nigeria is preparing such bonds. With just 10 percent of global diaspora savings put into bonds, U.S. $50 billion could be spent on infrastructure (World Finance 2015). Policies offering tax and other financial considerations for increasing the volume of remittances, directing them toward development purposes, stimulating direct investment, directing remittances used for consumption, and providing financial literacy for recipients all can result in better use of remittance revenues (Carling 2008).

In addition to remittances, channels of communication and travel between migrant populations and countries of origin can transfer knowledge, both technical and "know-how," back to the home country. Maintaining links to multiple locations and travel among them, circular mobility patterns, can be transformative in leading to poverty reduction (International Organization for Migration 2015). On the other hand, migration out of the country (emigration) can cripple long-term growth. Losing people means losing human capital. Whether professional, white collar, blue collar, or general labor, migrants tend to be among the most skilled in their work category. Losing the top echelon of each labor category weakens the skill composition of a country's labor force, depresses productivity, and decreases a country's taxable income base. "Brain drain" and "skill drain" are distinct disadvantages to the nations that migrants leave. They take the knowledge and skills that their country or their privilege provided them away from their homelands, some of which may be in desperate need of those very skills.

The emigration of talent from countries where it is desperately needed is one of the greatest challenges of globalization. Between 1990 and 2003, an average of 20,000 highly educated Africans left their homelands every year (Mutume 2003). In 2010, 1 in 9 Africans with a college education lived in an OECD nation. For Latin America it was 1 in 13, and for Asia it was 1 in 30. Fully 90 percent o people with tertiary degrees from Uganda live outside of Uganda. Small island nations have the highest rates of talent emigration. In Barbados, Trinidad and Tobago, and Haiti, more educated people lived outside of their homelands than within them. A number of other countries had emigration rates of the highly educated in the range of 30 to 40 percent. High-population non-OECD countries, such as India, China, and Russia, have rates below 3.5 percent (OECD–United Nations Department of Economic and Social Affairs 2013).

More than 20 percent of nationals holding degrees emigrated from many of the world's poorest countries (OECD 2016). The health care industry is among those that suffer most acutely. Better wages, working conditions, support, and career opportunities motivate highly trained practitioners to emigrate to wealthier countries. The United States, United Kingdom, Australia, and Canada employ 72 percent of the nurses and 69 percent of the doctors who emigrate to OECD countries. As in other industries, they fill in gaps such as in rural areas that native health care workers find less desirable. While some of these practitioners might not desire to work in rural areas of developing countries, in OECD countries they accept these opportunities and have chances for moving to more desirable areas as they advance their careers (Cometto et al. 2013). While the density of health care practitioners is increasing in those countries, it decreases in those that need health care the most. Sub-Saharan Africa is home to about 25 percent of the world's infectious disease cases but only about 2 percent of the global supply of health care practitioners. Only 50 of 600 practitioners trained in Zambia remained there. Manchester, England, has more practitioners from Malawi than Malawi does (United Nations Population Fund 2006).

Social Impacts on Home Countries

Migration may also affect the political climate of a country. Whether it encourages improvements in governance or worsens governance is not easily determined. On the one hand, if minority and dissident populations leave, it lessens the voice of people. More educated populations demand more democracy, so if the most educated people leave, it lessens pressure for democracy. In this way, emigration can act as a safety valve for bad regimes. In the case of Zimbabwe, millions fled to South Africa. From South Africa, they were neither able to influence the political situation in Zimbabwe nor able to convince the South African government to change its posture toward the regime of Robert Mugabe in Zimbabwe.[3] Had they remained, and remained vocal in their opposition, they may have been able to effect some change. However, if the diaspora community can exert pressure from outside, or release the poor from dependence on the government in countries where they can vote a government in or out, it may be able to effect improvements in governance. In Cape Verde, diaspora populations relayed democratic ideals back to their country of origin. In Cape Verde, households with a migrant were more likely than those without a migrant to lobby for political change (Collier 2013).

International students are an important stream in the flow of migration. Three million international students were enrolled in OECD countries in 2013—800,000 in the United States and 1.4 million across the EU, primarily in the United Kingdom (420,000) and Australia (250,000). Overall, the social sciences, business, and law attract the most students. In the United States, Germany, and Scandinavian countries, the sciences and engineering prevail. The higher the level of tertiary education through bachelor's, master's, and doctoral degrees, the greater the concentration of international students. Among doctoral graduates from OECD countries, 23 percent were international students. The higher the level of the degree, the greater the concentration in the sciences and engineering. Among international doctoral graduates, 55 percent earned degrees in science or engineering (OECD 2016).

International students are highly prized by the countries to which they migrate. They enrich the diversity of the learning environment for domestic students, they often stay and become valued workers or entrepreneurs, and they fill the ranks of tertiary institutions. Many countries expedite their entry while taking some caution not to burden local coffers. A number of countries created programs to enable graduates to remain in their countries on special visas for post-graduate work or job searching. When the U.S. government announced its initial ban of migrants from seven majority Muslim countries in 2017, the loudest outcries were from universities and businesses.

A number of studies demonstrated that some of the loss in human capital with respect to education is recaptured through remittances received, increasing educational attainment in the households that receive them. While the empirical evidence among studies is inconsistent, it is also possible that the possibility of future migration to a host country with a greater payoff for education may inspire investment in education, increasing the overall supply in the country of origin as would remittances used for education (Dustman and Glitz 2011). Circular migration, whereby people spend time working or being educated abroad and return to put their enhanced knowledge to work at home, mitigates brain drain.

POPULIST BACKLASH TO IMMIGRATION

According to Collier (2013), countries vary in how well they assimilate immigrant groups. He found that sustained rapid migration is most likely to have adverse effects. Social and political risks arise most often when migrants do not integrate well or compete with native workers. He maintained that children growing up in the United States inevitably assimilate U.S. values, whereas in Europe they do not. There, he argued, children more often adopt a self-identity different from the national identity of the country in which they are living. Whereas U.S. identity includes, at least traditionally, "welcoming strangers" and is values based, European identity is based on "nationality." Furthermore, major immigrant groups to the United States are Hispanic, more linguistically and culturally similar to the diversity of U.S. citizens than European immigrants are to the less diverse cultures of European nations. This, according to Collier, has the potential to undermine trust and social capital while increasing antipathy, particularly in cases of rapid mass immigration. In California, one of the richest U.S. states, public services eroded in response to rapid immigration of diverse groups. This undermined empathy for lower-income folks who were no longer seen as "like us" but rather as less fortunate (Collier 2013).

The most dangerous impacts of migration have been political backlash, anti-immigrant rhetoric and sentiment, and hate crimes. Both Europe and the United States experienced intense political backlash in response to the flood of millions of refugees from the Middle East. Even though relatively few of these refugees were ultimately accepted into the United States or most Western European countries, populist movements gained strength on anti-immigration sentiment affecting the presidential contest in the United States, the vote to exit the EU in the United Kingdom, and the strengthening of populist parties in France (National Front Party), the Netherlands (Dutch Freedom Party), and Austria (Freedom Party).

Anti-immigration populism in the Scandinavian countries is also on the rise. Sweden, Finland, and Norway were among the most popular destinations for refugees and asylum seekers. Once among the most generous—Sweden took in more refugees per capita than any EU member state and offered them permanent residency in 2013—in 2015 the Scandinavian countries began making policies more restrictive. Sweden withdrew its permanent residency policy in favor of a temporary residency. Finland reduced its stipend for refugees. Norway, as mentioned earlier, is aggressive in deportations. In each of these countries, populist parties—the "Finns," the Sweden Democrats, and Norway's Progress Party—increased their share of support in polling and voting (Benton and Nielsen 2013). Mughan and Paxton (2006) found that anti-immigration sentiment and populist appeal in the 1998 Australian election rose from perceived material and assimilationist threats—the fear that the immigrants would not become like Australians. In 2013, the elections were won on an anti-immigration plank.

Populist slogans are the same throughout these countries. They perceive immigration to be a threat to their way of life, in addition to their economic well-being, either through loss of jobs or through demands on social welfare systems. Throughout Europe, the United States, and Australia, hate crimes and demonstrations against Muslims or immigration in general rose. In the United States, hate crimes against Muslims in 2016 spiked 67 percent, reaching their highest level since 2001. In the wake of the 2015 ISIS (Islamic State in Iraq and Syria) attacks in Paris, hate crimes against Muslims—primarily against girls and women in the immediate aftermath—in the United Kingdom rose. From July 2014 to July 2015, there was a 70 percent spike in hate crimes (Johnson 2015).

These developments are in keeping with Collier's (2013) proposition that racially and ethnically distinct immigrants arriving in large numbers at a rapid pace are likely to be perceived as cultural and material threats. In the case of Europe, the immigrant population of Muslims began as guest workers, primarily Turks, in the 1950s and 1960s. It swelled with family unification and high birth rates. Muslims from former French and British colonies also immigrated. From 1990 to 2010, the Muslim population swelled from about 4 million to 11.3 million (Benton and Neilsen 2013). The visibility of the immigrant population coupled with the rapid increase had already given rise to anti-immigration rhetoric before the terrorist attacks in Europe. The attacks and the flow of young Europeans to join extremist groups in the Middle East exacerbated it.

Immigration policy is a contentious issue. The immigrant population of the United States is the largest in the world. Immigrants also comprise their largest proportion of the population since World War II. The scale of immigration in the United States generated fears and debate on the impact of immigration on the economy. In 1965, the United States was opened to immigration after three decades during which immigration dropped to nearly zero. Since then, the foreign-born population increased from 9.6 million to 45 million by 2015, 14 percent of the U.S. population. Together with their offspring, this added 72 million people (immigrants and their offspring) to the U.S. population. Half of the foreign borns are from Latin America, and one quarter are from Asia. In 1965, non-Hispanic whites accounted for 84 percent of the population; in 2015, they accounted for 62 percent (Pew Research Center 2015). The complexion and accent of the country has been changing—and rapidly. While anti-immigration groups traditionally have seen Latin Americans and Asians as the major economic and cultural threat, Muslims are perceived as a security threat, resulting in calls for religious tests for entering the United States during the presidential campaign and after the election in 2016.

Immigration is also perceived as threatening in parts of Asia. Many East Asian nations take pride in racial purity. One can see how, if immigration from outside of racially and ethnically similar countries is stepped up in East Asian countries, social integration may prove to be difficult. Although a number of officials in these countries recognize the need for immigration to increase the workforce, public resistance is strong. As a case in point, 44 percent of South Koreans, 33 percent of Japanese, and 20 percent of Taiwanese view immigrants as undesirable neighbors (Inglehart et al. 2014).

CONSIDER THIS
MAKE AMERICA GREAT AGAIN?

The 2016 presidential election in the United States witnessed extreme vitriol not evident in presidential politics for decades. Racist rhetoric calling Mexicans rapists and drug dealers, calling Muslims terrorists, and promising a ban on Muslim immigration on the part of candidate Donald Trump were matched in venom by his supporters turning the slogan "Make America Great Again" on its head by proclaiming "Make America White Again."

A Promising Note

Despite populist rhetoric and demands to halt the flows of migrants in response to the flows of refugees that became more pronounced following the Arab Spring wars and terrorist attacks, an Amnesty International (AI 2016a)[4] poll of 27,000 people in 27 countries showed that not all people are turning their backs on refugees. This poll demonstrated that most people would welcome migrants into their country. Many people globally would be willing to host refugees in their own home, about 10 percent on average, and 30 percent would welcome refugees into their neighborhood. Nearly half would welcome refugees into their town, city, or village. More than 8 in 10 would welcome them into their country. Two thirds of people, 66 percent, believe that their governments should do more to help refugees.

China was the most welcoming. Nearly half, 46 percent, of Chinese would welcome refugees into their own home. Ironically, Germany and the United Kingdom were the second and third most welcoming. The Merkel government in Germany has been under fire and populist movements have gained strength in response to the government's offers to host refugees. In the United Kingdom, the "Brexit" vote to leave the EU was in part a reaction to the idea that floods of refugees would pour through their borders from other EU countries. The United Kingdom was second behind China on the percentage of people, 29 percent, who would allow refugees to live in their home. People in both countries, Germany (96 percent) and the United Kingdom (87 percent), were very high in willingness to allow refugees into their country.

At the bottom of the welcome index were Russia, Indonesia, and Thailand. Russia, however, was the only country polled in which less than a majority did not approve of accepting refugees fleeing war or persecution into their country. Indonesia was tied with the United States at 72 percent, while Thailand was only 1 percent behind at 71 percent.

MITIGATING THE CHALLENGES OF MIGRATION

Theoretically, free labor migration and free trade operate on the same principle—free movement, whether of people or goods, facilitates the optimal allocation of goods or people across countries. Some economists argue that barriers to and quotas on migration are inefficient. Elimination of immigration controls could possibly double the world's real income or, according to the more conservative economists, increase it 5 to 12 percent (Bradford 2013). If the theory held up in practice, eliminating the barriers would eliminate many of the challenges of migration. However, the barriers are not likely to fall soon.

The challenges faced globally by the flows of migrants in danger, whether internally displaced or international refugees, whether from conflict, persecution, natural disasters, or violent conflict, are not likely to quell soon. Mitigating and improving the impact and situations of migrants as well as sending and receiving countries has potential for ensuring that migration not only is well managed but also maximizes benefits for all parties.

Improving the Situation of Migrants

Managing migration for positive outcomes requires attention to every step of the migration process, from initial exodus from the country of origin through the physical and bureaucratic journey to a new permanent home to integration in a country of resettlement or return to the homeland and protection from illegal detention and deportation afterward. As discussed, half of the world's refugees live in only 10 countries and only 30 countries offer resettlement places, falling far short of the need. Even the basic necessities required for support and protection are in short supply.

People on the Move

AI initiated an "I Welcome" campaign and toolkit for activists and anyone who wishes to see the refugee migration crisis well managed. It asks people to take an "I welcome refugees" pledge, noting that in their recent survey an overwhelming majority of people globally did welcome refugees into their country. In addition to taking the pledge, AI calls on governments to work together to ensure legal "pathways" to safety for refugees. The pathways can be opened quickly in emergency situations such as the Syrian crisis. Pathways such as family reunification, academic scholarships and study visas, and medical visas open opportunities for refugees to travel to host countries in organized, legal, and safe ways.

According to AI (2016b), wealthy governments do too little to protect and resettle refugees. Nearly all of the burden is borne by poor and middle-income countries. As an example, the organization cited the United Kingdom, which has hosted only 5,000 refugees since 2011 (although England has many Eastern European migrants). In contrast, Jordan, with a GDP of slightly over 1 percent of the United Kingdom's and a much smaller population, has more than 665,000 refugees. In Australia, there are a mere 57,594 refugees and asylum seekers, compared with Ethiopia's 739,156. AI suggests that states collectively establish objective criteria—such as a country's wealth or population size, among other criteria—defining each state's responsibility based on its capacity to host refugees.

A global transfer mechanism to move refugees from countries that have reached a threshold number of refugees, no more than 10 percent of its determined capacity, could manage and direct flow. Because there is no transfer system in place now, a country's population of refugees is determined only by how many refugees make it across the country's border. Because countries of first arrival are likely to be the only ones who reach their threshold, a third factor is that states must be obliged to increase funding. Refugees need sufficient food, clothing, shelter, sanitation, medical care, and education. Few states bulging with refugees are able to provide even the most basic needs for all refugees. The EU was criticized for trying to buy its way out of accepting refugees with its deal to increase subsidies to Turkey for allowing refugees to be sent back to Turkey or retaining refugees there. However, AI warns that financial assistance is not a substitute for refusing resettlement of refugees, refusing transfers, and/or turning down asylum seekers at the border.

Streamlining refugee status determination for large groups fleeing, AI maintains, is necessary for their protection. When thousands, hundreds of thousands, or millions flee en masse as in the Syrian crisis, status determination on an individual basis is inefficient and leaves most refugees unprotected. Accepting particular groups on a presumptive basis is warranted. The organization argues that this can increase rather than decrease security because it would then allow processing in an orderly manner, thereby making assessing security risks easier.

These recommendations may work to alleviate the condition of refugees and forced migrants from the exit of their country of origin to the time of resettlement.

Arrival at Immigration

Once a migrant has arrived in a country for refugee resettlement or as an economic migrant, the process of integration is the next challenge. All aspects of integration into society are intertwined and affect one another. Success in integrating migrants is very uneven, determined in most part by their skill set, educational level, language proficiency, mental and physical health, and age. The total foreign-born population in OECD countries was 120 million in 2014—46 percent in the EU and EFTA (with 80 percent of the population growth in the area from 2000 to 2014) and 35 percent in the United States, amounting to about 13 percent of their total populations on average. Some countries have foreign-born populations as high as 44 percent (Luxembourg) and 29 percent (Switzerland, Australia, and New Zealand) (OECD 2016). Integrating immigrants must be a priority to secure the well-being of the immigrants and their new countries.

The "Vision Europe Summit" (Papademetriou and Benton 2016) advocated a holistic approach to integrating migrants into the EU. Labor market integration is one key because it may facilitate integration along social and political dimensions. In the EU in general, differences in labor market integration are not large for the totality of migrants in comparison with the native born, but differences are larger for specific categories. For example, in 2015, 61 percent of foreign-born people were employed,

CONSIDER THIS
OF MUTUAL BENEFIT: TRADE AND MIGRATION

An impact of immigration often overlooked is the effect on trade. A 2014 World Bank study of African emigration and trade found that migration increased bilateral exports particularly with respect to trade between African countries. The more physically and ethnically different the African countries from one another, the stronger the effect on trade.

The positive impact is explained primarily by migration mitigating the dampening effect of weak institutions on trade. Strong institutional infrastructure enhances trade by reducing risks. Where institutions are weak, regulations may be weak, mechanisms for enforcement may be weak, and information concerning products may be nonexistent.

Informal networks across the countries strengthen market information sharing about products, familiarize one another concerning cultural differences, and (more important) establish networks of trust.

Countries are beginning to put diaspora communities to work in trade councils, trade missions, and business networks in Africa, in Europe and the United States. In this way, migrants play an important role in opening markets for exports from their home countries. (Ehrhart et al. 2014)

---

in comparison with 66 percent of native-born people; the percentage of people economically active was 70 percent for foreign-born people and 77 percent for EU nationals. Men, however, fare much better than women, labor migrants fare much better than family migrants (many of whom may be women or face cultural norms discouraging working) or refugees. Refugees in particular, because they are not selected for entry into the country based on skill, are less likely to fit neatly into the local economy. They also have less control over their destinations and their careers. After spending years in refugee status, they may find that their skills are outdated or that they have lost skills they had no opportunity to use. They may face labor market restrictions or might need to spend time in orientation programs that delay their entry into the job market. Educational levels of migrants, as a whole, tend to be lower than those of native-born people. While educational level can be an assist in the labor market, this works better for migrants who received their advanced degrees in the destination country.

Whether the country one comes from or enters into bears more influence on a person's successful integration is debated. In the United States, it appears that country of origin is better correlated with how a refugee fares than settling in the United States. Country of origin influences an individual's educational and skill level and cultural characteristics. In Europe, it is harder to determine which matters more across European countries. Where immigrants are visibly different, they fare less well. It is clear that discrimination plays a role. Visible minorities, Muslims and those from sub-Saharan Africa, suffer more from unemployment than any other group except the Roma, a national minority. In Italy, South and Southeast Asians outperform natives. In the United States, Asians have the highest income of any racial or ethnic group.

Second-generation integration is a better overall measure of integration. It would be expected that people born and raised in a country would be fully integrated. However, there are sharp differences between the EU and the United States and Canada. In the United States and Canada, there is little difference in the reading levels of children with native-born parents and immigrants. In the EU, however, children with two immigrant parents lag significantly behind in reading at 15 years of age. School dropout rates, however, are similar. In the United Kingdom, second-generation immigrants are less likely to drop out, although the dropout rates for the second generation are higher in Austria, Denmark, Finland, and France. Reading level is only one measure of integration. Aside from some Asian populations, children of ethnic and racial minorities do not fare as well in school as white majority children regardless of the origin of their parents.

Policy to Integrate Migrants

Most OECD countries are instituting policies to allow for more efficient integration of migrants into the labor force. This applies to both economic migrants and refugees, many of whom have advanced skills or professional backgrounds. Programs include language courses, programs to recognize or upgrade professional and labor certifications that migrants acquired in their countries of origin, and supplemental trainings to fill gaps between homeland and new country work requirements. These help migrants to integrate more quickly and prevent "brain waste." Labor force participation can facilitate political and sociocultural immigration. Many countries maintain work requirements for permanent residency and naturalization into citizenship for immigrants or to bring family members into the country. Work requirements generally do not apply to refugees or asylees.

Immigration reforms in some countries make entry easier for less skilled workers. Japan, for instance, created employment agencies through which domestic workers may be hired. Canada also initiated special policies for caregivers. Construction and shipbuilding workers who previously were trained and worked in Japan are allowed to return and work up until the 2020 Olympics. Germany is loosening requirements for labor from the West Balkan countries. Caps for temporary workers in New Zealand were raised.

In contrast, responses to the flood of refugees from war-torn countries of the Middle East are mixed. The Migration Policy Institute (2016) found that European countries tried to limit and control immigration by moving to secure their borders and building fences; some even temporarily suspended passport free mobility among countries in the Schengen area.⁵ The U.K. vote to withdraw from the EU was seen largely as a move to protect its borders as well as gain more control generally over decisions affecting the United Kingdom (Migration Policy Institute 2016). In March 2016, the EU issued a warning to economic migrants moving among the flood of refugees that they should not risk their lives or money. They would not be admitted into Europe.

Terrorist attacks by European citizens who became radicalized, the flow of youths to support Islamic fighters in the Middle East, and fears of terrorism raised concerns about assimilation in Europe. On the one hand, those who recognize the failures on the parts of government and civil society to assimilate Muslim migrants call for programs to alleviate tensions between Muslim communities and mainstream society. On the other hand, support for policies antagonistic toward Muslim migrants and Muslims in general has grown throughout Europe, the United States, and Australia, as discussed in the prior section.

Africa, South America, and Southeast Asia, where international immigration has historically been low in comparison with most OECD countries, moved to freer mobility. As an example of the more liberalizing changes in South America, Chile made major changes to its migration regime in 2016. The country eased its application procedure for its Antofagasta region. This region attracts many workers. Chile created a new visa for people marrying or forming a common union that allows them residency and work privileges. It granted health services for vulnerable immigrants and agreed that children under 14 years of age would not be subject to migration penalties (OECD 2016:248). These changes follow policy changes that granted temporary work visas in 2015 for those with signed employment contracts. They may work for an entire year before reapplying and may switch employers during that time. In 2014, Chile extended health care for migrants whose applications were pending approval (OECD 2015).

Also in the works are plans for continent-wide citizenship. In Africa and South America, continent-wide citizenship and removal of visa requirements were discussed as real possibilities. In South America, a letter of commitment was signed in 2016. It is an expansion of the Mercosur Residence agreement that allows for two years of work and residence in a member country with a pathway to permanent residence. It also provides for work rights, family unification, and access to education for children. The 54 African Union member states launched an African passport that allows entry without visas into all member countries. While it does not involve residency or work arrangements, it is a step toward greater mobility by improving opportunities for cross-border tourism and commercial activity (Migration Policy Institute 2016).

With the East Asian emphasis on racial purity, policy efforts have stressed increasing return of the diaspora community and/or its members' offspring. China and Japan both have launched programs to try to win back their nationals who left and their children who were born and educated abroad. South Korea has long given dual citizenship and special treatment under immigration law for people of Korean ancestry. In Southeast Asia, the Association of Southeast Asian Nations Economic Community inaugurated a program to allow for more free mobility of labor by recognizing academic and professional credentials of other member nations. High-skill, high-education fields have not witnessed much mobility due to visa stumbling blocks, but the tourism industry is moving ahead quickly (Migration Policy Institute 2016).

In 2016, Germany adopted new policies for all immigrants to accelerate integration. Although not all immigrants will stay in Germany, it reasons that it is better in the long run to risk investing in immigrants who might leave rather than not investing in those who will stay. All immigrants are treated as though they will become permanent residents. The priority test, which forbids an immigrant from being hired for a position if there was a qualified national available, was dropped. The Vocational Education and Training program was opened to more asylum seekers. The program allows for three years of vocational training and two years of work after that. It also provides language and introduction programs to all asylum seekers. Not only is this approach less risky than failing to integrate those who stay; those who do return to their home countries are better able to contribute to growth and productivity in their country of origin. This seems to be a strategy that would be wise for all countries to follow.

Policies to Prevent Brain Drain

Brain drain in poorer countries is brain gain in wealthier ones. While wealthy countries can work to improve the lives of immigrants in their countries by facilitating integration and full use of their skills, this may impede the well-being in developing countries. Health care is among the primary areas in which brain drain can have an enduring impact on the well-being of a country of origin. Cometto et al. (2013) posed policy reforms for both sending and receiving countries.

Higher salaries and the improved lifestyle that wealthy countries offer are a draw that sending countries cannot match. However, higher salaries are not the only vehicle for lifestyle improvements. Neither can poorer countries match the specialized training and research opportunities of wealthier countries. Nonetheless, poorer countries can improve working and living conditions. Housing allowances, rotations from harder to serve and more isolated regions to more centrally located ones, time off and sabbaticals, and even child care for practitioners' children on-site all can improve work life without huge financial drains. Diversifying the skill mix and associated credentials of health care practitioners can make them less apt to migrate. A variety of credentialed health care practitioners on-site can alleviate the workload of the more advanced practitioners, improving work life. Because most credentialing is recognized only in the country of origin, it also makes migration more difficult.

Although this runs counter to concerns for integrating migrants into destination countries, it may prevent some from leaving. Policies that make it attractive for migrants to return home after study or short-term practice abroad not only are a brain gain but also provide for knowledge transfer from developed to developing countries.

Wealthy countries need to consider what is best all-around for development. They need to consider helping to alleviate brain drain problems in developing countries. By developing their own labor force to fill the labor gaps that draw highly skilled and educated migrants, fewer skilled professionals and laborers will be tempted to leave their countries—particularly when coupled with improved conditions in home countries. Directing government spending in education to fields where there are shortages may attract students from college majors whose graduates face high unemployment rates. Scholarship money can be directed toward graduates that will work in underserved areas or occupations. Cost-effective ways to educate health professionals and other needed professionals make study in these fields more attractive. Training for a varied skill mix, such as nurse practitioners, physician assistants, emergency technicians, medical assistants in health care, and technicians and engineers in technical and scientific areas, can fill gaps rather than concentrating the labor force in some areas while others are neglected. Finally, Cometto et al. (2013) suggested that wealthy countries refuse to hire professionals from countries with shortages.

Sustainable Development Goals

Migrants remain among the most disadvantaged people in the world. While presumably under international protection, they may go generations without adequate health care, education, clean water, sanitation, adequate nutrition, and other necessities even as the quality of life in these matters improves for the world as a whole. Measures to achieve the Sustainable Development Goals (SDGs) will also affect the flow of migrants. Improving the quality of life in developing countries mitigates the push factors that forcibly displace people. Climate change, food security, violent conflict, poverty, inequality, and persecution all increase flows of migration, and achieving SDG targets should improve the lives of migrants wherever they reside. Although not included for consideration in the Millennium Development Goals, explicit concerns for migrants are included in the SDGs:

- Goal 4 on quality education and lifelong learning calls for "increasing the number of scholarships for students in developing countries, particularly the least developed, to study in developed countries." This may be a legal managed entry for migrants, particularly refugees.

- Goal 5 targets gender inequality and empowering women and girls, calling particular attention to human trafficking.

- Goal 8 promotes economic growth and decent work for all, including protecting the labor rights of migrants, particularly female migrants. Domestic workers, a common occupation for female migrants, often find themselves outside of the protection of labor laws.

- Goal 10, aimed at reducing inequalities, mentions international responsibility for planned and well-managed migration and reducing the cost of migrant remittances.

- Goal 16 aspires to peaceful and inclusive societies. Given the insecurities many migrants face in their journeys and destinations, this goal cannot be accomplished without managing migration.

Many of the SDGs, while not specifically mentioning migrants, will improve their lives. For example, migrants displaced by climate change and environmental degradation outnumber every other type of forced displacement. The SDGs' calls for international action protecting the environment can potentially slow this form of forced migration. In refugee camps, migrants often lack basic necessities. Migrants, even when resettled or integrated, often lack the same access to health care, particularly reproductive care, as native-born people. Improved access to education is an SDG that must be applied in refugee camps, in detention centers, and for migrants' integration when resettling, repatriated, or integrating into the community of their first refuge. All of the SDGs need to be applied to migrants, whether forced or voluntary, economic migrants or refugees, for them to be considered successful.

Good Governance for Refugees and All Migrants

The dangers of migration and the threats felt in receiving countries tend to grab the headlines. Successful migration programs and the contributions of migration get less popular attention. Often overlooked is that migration can reap benefits for both the host country and the country of origin. Given the potential demographic, economic, and social benefits to receiving and sending countries, it is in every country's interest to plan for migration. Maximizing the benefits and minimizing the dangers and threats of migration requires managing migration well. The private sector, public sector, and civil society all should be involved in these efforts.

The "Migration Governance Index" (Economist Intelligence Unit [EIU] 2016) is one of many frameworks to assist in developing governance tools. It helps countries to assess the scope of their policies in five dimensions of migration governance: institutional capacity, migrant rights, safe and orderly migration, labor migration management, and regional and international cooperation. It aids in discovering gaps in policies and insights that could lead to improved programs and better managed migration. The model addresses sending and receiving countries to maximize benefits for both.

Institutional Capacity

Institutional capacity refers to ability of the structures and processes of an entity such as a government, corporation, civil society, or any organization or group to accomplish its goals. Whether a sending or receiving country, managing migration successfully depends on an infrastructure of policies and laws, with agencies and organizations to implement them, in a coordinated and seamless fashion and migration strategies that work in conjunction with national and local societal socioeconomic development efforts to maximize the potential benefits of migration.

Sending countries need to cultivate their diaspora community in development efforts. These reach far beyond remittances to encourage circular migration and the return of emigrants, both of which advance technology, talent and knowledge, and migrant investments in their homelands. Receiving countries' policies should promote filling workforce needs where there are labor shortages and shortages of critical skills. Countries that do well in developing institutional capacity clearly articulate their migration policies in easily understood language and ensure that they are readily available in user-friendly formats to potential migrants. Conditions of leaving and return and benefits of investing in the country and processes for doing so are critical types of information for potential emigrants. The types of visas available and regulations relevant to them, policies such as how to obtain permanence and citizenship, and the status of family are types of critical knowledge for immigrants (EIU 2016). Transparency enables migrants to make sound decisions and progress through migration processes with less difficulty.

Migrant Rights

Migrant rights facilitate adjustment and integration into a receiving country. Integration is impossible without basic services such as appropriate education, health care, employment, and security. Some countries bar migrants from basic services, and others grant them but migrants fail to take full advantage through lack of knowledge, lack of interest, fear, or other non-legal factors. Countries tend to offer greater protections for rights to work and long-term paths to citizenship and less for social services and other costlier items. Some countries, such as Italy and Canada, offer some basic services to both undocumented and legal migrants, but in most countries these rights are ambiguous. Granting rights may strain finances of receiving countries and cause resentment if they are, or are perceived to be, burdensome (EIU 2016). Sweden offered a broad range of social services for regular migrants, but in 2017 it reduced services, cutting back on paid parental leave and monthly cash benefits (Economist 2017). For most migrants, the end goal is citizenship. With respect to citizenship, the general trend has been for countries to streamline processes at the same time that they tighten requirements. Sweden led the OECD countries in percentage of foreign-born residents naturalized, 6 percent, in 2014. The average for OECD countries was only 2.5 percent (OECD 2016).

Safe and Orderly Migration

Government policies can exacerbate the difficulties of migration. It is easy to understand how the flood of migrants from Iraq, Afghanistan, and Syria challenges the policy and infrastructure designed for significantly smaller flows of migrants. Civil society groups, philanthropies, governments, and non-governmental organizations all try to provide protections that include everything from rescue at sea, to transitional care, to permanent settlement. At the same time, many government policies make the journey more treacherous. Actions such as disbanding the camp at Calais, refusing

entry to the Rohingya, and building barriers at the borders play into the hands of human traffickers and predatory smugglers.

When borders of one country are open but borders of the next one are closed, migrants may get trapped in "transit hubs" on the way to their ultimate destinations. Migrants fleeing from Africa to Europe traveled from Libya to Italy, then to Morocco, and then to Spain. Others fled from Syria to Turkey, to Greece, and then farther inward. Thousands of migrants were trapped when first Austria closed borders with the Balkans and then Macedonia, Croatia, and Serbia closed its borders with Greece. Many migrants were headed for Germany, but passage was blocked and very few were admitted through; the rest remained trapped.

The worst cases emerged in Libya. The EU tried to stop the flood of migrants from Libya by sending the boats headed for Italy back to Libya or paying for the boats to never embark. Witnesses from Doctors without Borders reported thousands of people concentrated in detention camps packed on top of one another without ventilation. Rape, kidnapping, extortion, and physical abuse by security officers were common in official detention centers. After being raped, women were forced to call home and ask for money to be sent. Men were forced to run until they collapsed from exhaustion. There were no basic services (Liu 2017).

Not only must governments offer safe and orderly passage as well as settlement, but also greater coordination among governments is necessary to ensure migrant safety (EIU 2016).

Labor Migration Management

Sending and receiving countries must coordinate labor migration (EIU 2016). The gains in a younger population for developed societies need to be weighed against the loss of human capital of sending countries. Granting visas tailored to attracting immigrants with specific skills needed in receiving countries, considering the employability of students immigrating for study, and validating the skill sets that immigrants acquired outside of the host country will help to ensure that migrants can integrate into the host society and contribute to economic goals.

Effective labor management must ensure worker safety and protections through enforcement of the International Labour Organization conventions or similar codes. These promote at least minimum standards for working conditions, family reunification, and collective bargaining, among other provisions. Going beyond the minimum to prohibit discriminatory pay, provide occupational rehabilitation instead of deportation in the case of worker illness or injury, and other measures that foster humane treatment stabilizes the labor force and the society.

Sending countries need to assess the impact of emigration. Very often, emigration of talented people—at all skill levels—leaves shortages in the labor markets. Assessing these movements and trying to counter them with policies that stem the flow of needed knowledge and skill is critical. Certain policies—tuition reimbursement, extra compensation for serving in hard-to-populate regions or skill sets, rotations among regions, and similar incentives—can be effective in keeping talent at home.

Regional and International Cooperation

Sending and receiving countries need to coordinate efforts through regional consultative processes, bilateral arrangements, and international conventions. Some of these are binding, some are voluntary initiatives, and some are diplomatic arrangements. They cover a host of issues from migrant flows to regulations regarding human trafficking, to visa requirements, to labor and temporary work arrangements, to technical assistance, to funding (EIU 2016). In many situations, effective governance requires extensive decentralization delegating administrative responsibility for services, investment decisions including flows of foreign investment and remittances, raising revenues, and other fiscal matters to the cities or other local governments along with central support and cooperation (International Organization for Migration 2015).

The New York Declaration for Refugees and Migrants adopted in 2016 is a set of commitments to uphold the rights of refugees and migrants. Like the UN Declaration of Human Rights, it does not have the force of international law. But it should serve as a guide as countries develop domestic policy and form international treaties and partnerships based on the following principles:

- Protect the human rights of all refugees and migrants regardless of status (this includes the rights of women and girls and promoting their full, equal, and meaningful participation in finding solutions)

- Ensure that all refugee and migrant children are receiving education within a few months of arrival

- Prevent and respond to sexual and gender-based violence

- Support those countries rescuing, receiving, and hosting large numbers of refugees and migrants

- Work toward ending the practice of detaining children for the purposes of determining their migration status

- Strongly condemn xenophobia against refugees and migrants and support a global campaign to counter it

- Strengthen the positive contributions made by migrants to economic and social development in their host countries

- Improve the delivery of humanitarian and development assistance to those countries most affected, including through innovative multilateral financial solutions, with the goal of closing all funding gaps

- Implement a comprehensive refugee response based on a new framework that sets out the responsibility of member states, civil society partners, and the UN system whenever there is a large movement of refugees or a protracted refugee situation

- Find new homes for all refugees identified by the UN High Commissioner for Refugees as needing resettlement and expand the opportunities for refugees to relocate to other countries through, for example, labor mobility or education schemes

- Strengthen the global governance of migration by bringing the International Organization for Migration into the UN system (UN 2016b)

Although the needs and circumstances among sending countries and among receiving countries vary significantly, work on a common set of principles and guidelines based on the New York Declaration, the Global Compact on Migration, started in April 2017. In 2018, the General Assembly was scheduled, at the time of this writing, to hold an international conference on the compact and adopt it in 2018. In November 2017, the United States backed out of the Global Compact, stating inconsistencies with U.S. policy and infringement on national sovereignty.

SUMMARY

Migration, whether forced or voluntary, poses challenges and opportunities for individual and global well-being. Natural disasters and climate change force more migrants from their homes than any other circumstance. Forced migration results from some form of trauma, food shortages, dire poverty, violent crime, and/or escape from threat of kidnapping or physical harm, among other atrocities. Yet none of these categories of migrants officially comprises refugees. In the migration journey, many migrants face death, disease in camps, violence, and victimization. Preventing the disasters that force people from their homes is, of course, the best answer. But safe passage for migrants from the beginning to the end of the journey must become a global priority.

Economic migrants face another set of difficulties. Migrants, both forced and voluntary, may face discrimination and prejudice in their destination countries. Because wages have been stagnating in many countries, resentment is often directed at immigrant groups for taking jobs and depleting social service resources.

In general, regardless of the skill level, migrants are among the most skillful at their level in their home countries. This can produce "brain drain" and loss of productivity in the sending country. Developed countries attract high-achieving students from less developed countries and often create special programs for them to stay. While remittances that they send home are important sources of revenue for developing countries, the loss of knowledge and talent is harmful. Policies and practices whereby the sending country can benefit from its most talented at every skill level need to be negotiated.

Integrating migrants into the fabric of receiving countries is important to the life chances of migrants and realizing the benefits of migration for the countries. For countries that are overpopulated, strategic emigration may enhance their development by balancing the demographic pyramid as long as they are empowered to receive the benefit of productive diaspora communities.

DISCUSSION

1. What do you believe should be your country's responsibility for assisting international migrants? What criteria did you use to determine your answer? Do you think that different countries should have different responsibilities? Why or why not?

2. Discuss the pros and cons of extending the mandate of the UNCHR to include the protection of victims of natural disasters and climate change.

3. Should people fleeing violent crime, such as in Central America, have the same rights to refuge as people fleeing persecution?

4. Develop a scoring matrix to determine which countries benefit the most from migration, receiving or sending countries. Test your matrix on a pair of countries.

5. Design a holistic strategy for local communities to integrate migrant populations that benefits migrants and the community. The strategy may involve philanthropies, the private sector, other government levels, and civil society organizations.

ON YOUR OWN

1. The Migrant Integration Policy Index uses eight indicators to rate countries on how well they integrate migrants. How does the index define each of the indicators? Choose one high-ranking country and one low-ranking country based on their overall scores.

   http://www.mipex.eu/play

   Compare and contrast the high- and low-ranking countries by examining each country's individual country report.

   http://www.mipex.eu

   What issues is each country facing? What are the countries' strengths and weaknesses?

2. In 2015, 67 percent of international migrants lived in just 20 countries. The countries are listed in the *International Migration Report 2015* (p. 7).

   http://www.un.org/en/development/ desa/population/migration/publications/ migrationreport/docs/MigrationReport2015_ Highlights.pdf

   Working from these data, investigate the age and gender demographics of the receiving countries.

   What is their age structure? Is continued migration likely to be harmful or beneficial given the age structure of their migrant population?

3. The OECD Interactive Database enables users to create charts and graphs relevant to migration topics. "Permanent Immigration Flows" provides data for total immigration, work, family unification, free movement, family accompanying workers, humanitarian, and others. It also provides data for a variety of variables relating to foreign- and native-born populations such as employment and participation in the labor force.

   Compare the employment and unemployment rates for foreign- and native-born populations for the OECD countries listed. For which countries is foreign-born unemployment lower than native-born unemployment? Investigate the labor force participation rates for these countries. Which population participates at a greater rate? Investigate the policies of one such country to see why this may be.

   https://data.oecd.org/migration/permanent-immigrant-inflows.htm#indicator-chart

NOTES

1. Refugees have a different migration pattern from the overall population of migrants. Most refugees, 86 percent, migrate to and from developing countries and the very least developed countries took in 25 percent of the global total of refugees (UN 2016a:9). Although the flow of refugees dominated much of the discourse concerning migrants to OECD countries, they remain a small portion of the total flow.

2. These statistics are based on the FBI's (2017) *Crime in the United States 2016* reporting.

3. Mugabe was forced out of office by a military coup in November 2016. As of this writing, the degree to which reforms may follow is unknown.

4. Detailed data of the poll can be found at https://www .amnesty.org/en/latest/news/2016/05/refugees-welcome-index-shows-government-refugee-policies-out-of-touch.

5. The Schengen Agreement guarantees free mobility among 26 European states. It covers most of the EU states and the four EFTA states.

13

Destruction and Depletion of the Natural Environment

INVISIBLE THREATS

In Pesarean, Indonesia, metal smelting is a traditional craft. Rather than the knives, swords, and temple gongs of the traditional crafters, electrical, automobile, and motorcycle parts dominate the smelting craft today. In 1978, no longer able to make a living making tin buckets, Pak Pat, a smelter, turned to disassembling automobile batteries. He drained the acid onto the ground, with the vapors disappearing into the air. He made lead ingots from the metal. He worked outside of his home, and although he prospered economically, the human cost was high.

Pak Pat was not the only one in his village disassembling metal batteries and other electronic devices. By smelting the metals in their yards or homes, they released toxic vapors. The waste they produced, slag, is composed of charcoal ash, leftover metal, and other byproducts. Not wanting to keep it near their homes, they created a dump for the slag in the middle of the village.

In 2010, the Indonesian government created an industrial zone for smelting about a half mile (1 km) outside of the village, but the slag heap remains. People walk through it every day. Children play there, eating their snacks while they play. All the while, they are inhaling and ingesting lead. Adult blood levels measured in 2015 were nearly double those measured in 2010. Children's levels weren't taken, but children living near smelting demonstrate stunting and cognitive and physical developmental problems.

The cost to Pak Pat's family was high. Of his 10 children, 3 died as infants, 3 are brain damaged, and 1 has never spoken. Another child does not have brain damage but has severe respiratory problems and requires regular hospital visits. The son of Pak Pat's nephew Tasiri was born with half his body paralyzed. He developed respiratory problems while a toddler. Tasiri moved away, and his son's lungs recovered.

In May 2016, Pure Earth submitted a remediation plan for the slag heap to the Indonesian government. It was approved. If you follow Pure Earth on social media, you can keep track of its progress. (Bernhardt 2016)

LEARNING OBJECTIVES

After completing this chapter, students will be able to do the following:

13.1 Identify and assess the sources of pollutants of land, air, water, and forest systems

13.2 Explain the potential dangers and long-term consequences of pollution to humans and the natural environment

13.3 Describe the magnitude of the consequences of the destruction and depletion of natural resources

13.4 Compare and contrast the impacts of developed and developing societies on the environment

13.5 Develop a plan—local, societal, or global—to combat environmental pollution

CONSIDER THIS
ARE WE POISONING OUR CHILDREN?

Phillip Landrigan, primarily responsible for regulations to get the lead out of gasoline and paint, says it is critical to see whether there is a connection between autism, asthma, attention-deficit/hyperactivity disorder, Type 2 diabetes, childhood obesity, and other disorders and chemical toxins, many of which are in widespread use. All of these are on the rise. Rates of childhood leukemia and brain cancer, he notes, are up 40 percent since the 1970s. The Columbia Center for Children's Environmental Health that he directs has already established the connection between bisphenol A (a widely used plastic) and irreversible brain damage to a developing brain (Lombroso 2015).

A nerve gas developed by Nazi Germany, chlorpyrifos, is in Dow Chemical Company's agricultural and outdoor pesticides. (It is banned for indoor residential use.) Because it is a nerve gas, it does as would be expected. It damages our brains. It also causes tremors in children and is linked to cancer and Parkinson's disease in adults. In 2012, it was found in the umbilical cord blood of 87 percent of newborns tested in a clinical study. It was on the EPA's list of chemicals to be banned for outdoor and agricultural use in the spring of 2018. The ban was blocked by the administration. While there is no direct evidence of tit for tat, could the ban be related to a U.S. $1 million donation by Dow Chemical to the 2017 inauguration (Kristof 2017)?

We inhabit many environments in our lifetimes. Everything we do affects them, making them healthier, more supporting of life, or unhealthy. They provide us with the necessities of life. With respect to the natural environment, we call these *ecoservices* and they are plentiful. It has taken centuries for us to understand the natural environment enough to recognize the harmful effects of our actions. Over time, there has been a degree of predictability in nature's cycles that allows us to anticipate nature's patterns and plan for agriculture, for conservation, and for life. That level of predictability may be coming to an end. Nature's patterns are no longer reliable. Ice caps and glaciers are melting, changing ocean and wind currents. Disruptions in nature's cycles have already multiplied many-fold the number of extreme weather events in ways that we do not fully understand. Zoonotic diseases such as Ebola, HIV, avian flu, and Zika virus are on the rise. What other changes lie ahead are, at least as yet, unpredictable. Our knowledge of our environment built over centuries, which helped to improve lives all over the world, may become obsolete (Gail 2016).

It seems as though we often forget that we entrust our lives to our environments, the source of all that sustains us. We begin in utero, the environment of a mother's womb. What does it mean that decades after the U.S. Environmental Protection Agency (EPA) banned DDT (dichlorodiphenyltrichloroethane), a pesticide toxic to humans, it is found in the bloodstream of fetuses? A 2005 study by the Environmental Working Group found DDT, other pesticides, and on average more than 200 chemicals in the bloodstream of very young fetuses, fetuses too young to have developed a blood–brain barrier to provide them protection against contaminants. Among the chemicals they found, 180 are known to cause cancer in humans or animals, 208 cause birth defects or abnormal development in animals, and 217 are toxic to the human brain and bloodstream (Environmental Working Group 2005).

Ongoing research, beginning in 1998, at the Columbia Center for Children's Environmental Health (2015, 2016a, 2016b) tracks the toxicity of the air in New York City. The center recruited 725 pregnant women to wear backpacks containing equipment to measure toxins they inhaled as they went about their daily routines. Within two days, the toxins showed up. Each woman's pack identified at least one pesticide along with other toxic pollutants, including carcinogens, endocrine disruptors, and others with consequences for neurological, mental, and physical development. The same toxins were identified in the cord blood of their babies when they were born. Mothers had passed the pollutants on to their children while they were in utero. While all possible developmental, neurological, and other effects could not be known initially, 15 percent of the children in the study had at least one identifiable developmental problem. As the children grew, more effects developed. Early developmental

CONSIDER THIS

SILENT SPRING

Rachel Carson changed the way in which we see chemicals in our daily lives and environment. Deeply appreciative of nature, she worked for the U.S. Fish and Wildlife Service after receiving her master's degree in zoology. As early as the 1950s, when colleagues reported fish and birds dying, she questioned what had happened to their habitat—their environment—that could cause such disaster. She published her answers in *Silent Spring* in 1962.

DDT, produced by the powerful company Monsanto, was responsible for the deaths of wildlife and contaminating the food supply. Met with hostility by the chemical industry, the quality of her research was above reproach and she was vindicated by the President's Advisory Committee. DDT was regulated and eventually banned. She awakened public awareness. The alarms she sounded—cancer, the potential deaths of species, toxicity in the food chain—got the public's attention. She changed the way in which the world sees nature and people's place in it (Carson 1962).

delays, attention-deficit/hyperactivity disorder, behavioral problems, learning and cognitive developmental difficulties, emotional problems, smaller head circumference, and lower IQs were among the consequences associated with the toxins.

Among children, the world's most precious resource, "chemical exposure has been estimated to play a significant role in 100 percent of the cases of lead poisoning, 10 to 35 percent of asthma cases, 2 to 10 percent of certain cancers, and 5 to 20 percent of neurological problems (Wilson, Chia, and Ehlers 2007).

We depend on our environments to provide us with the resources we need to sustain life. What chance at life do people have if their environment in the womb is poisoning them? What chance do people have if their environment is degraded with air, land, and water pollution? What chance do they have if the biodiversity of their environment is dwindling and entire species are threatened with extinction? What chance do they have if clean fresh water sources are depleted?

SCOPE OF ENVIRONMENTAL PROBLEMS

Air, land, and water are contaminated. Lakes and forests are disappearing. Glaciers are melting. Extreme weather events have multiplied exponentially. Oceans are acidifying, killing coral reefs. Only about 10 percent will survive. Many animal and plant species have become extinct before their time. From 1998 to 2014, a span of just 17 years, the earth experienced its 10 warmest years on record. In some cities, residents wear face masks, hoping to protect their lungs from small particulates in the air. The "four Ds"—degradation of air, water, and land, depletion of natural resources, deforestation, and waste disposal—are at the root of these troubles. Each threatens the health of the environment and subsequently human development.

CHEMICAL CONTAMINANTS

We live in the age of chemicals. Under most kitchen sinks, in garages, in our bathrooms, and in basements, an array of chemicals is on hand for cleaning, gardening, painting, dealing with pests, laundering clothes, polishing furniture, and a host of other household tasks. Personal care products such as lotions, shampoos, deodorants, and medications that seem harmless may contain chemical compounds dangerous in the environment. Thousands of chemicals used in our houses, industry, and agriculture were created synthetically following World War II; most were put in use without testing for safety. The chemicals discussed in this section, among many other chemicals, have serious health consequences. Many are carcinogenic. Some affect our respiratory system and lead to pneumonia and death. Many attack other organs such as the heart, kidneys, and liver. The endocrine disruptors affect our neural pathways or glands and subsequently the hormones that control physical and mental development. We are regularly exposed to these chemicals through the air we breathe, the food and water we ingest, and absorption through our skin.

PHOTO 13.1 This satellite photograph captures the haze over Bangladesh on January 21, 2007, just south of the Himalayas. Sediment collecting at the mouth of the Ganges is exacerbated by industrial land use.

NASA Visible Earth.

Persistent Toxic Substances

Persistent toxic substances are naturally and synthetically created substances that persist for a long time in the environment, often traveling across continents from their origin. They are harmful to the environment and all living things within it. Many exist in various phases—for instance, evaporating from water or land into the air, where they travel on airborne particles and come back to the land and water bodies in rain, snow, and mist. They are emitted from products, many of which we use in our homes. Many bioaccumulate, building up in bone, an organ, or fatty tissue. Many biomagnify, increasing in concentration as they move up the food chain from lower, such as single-cell organisms, to higher, such as animals and people.

Chemical contaminants present one of the most serious threats to humankind. The 2015 annual report of Pure Earth and Green Cross of Switzerland (PE and GCS 2016) focused attention on the world's worst pollutants. The "winners" for 2015 were lead, radionuclides, mercury, hexavalent chromium, pesticides, and cadmium. Human exposure to any one of them, some in their elemental form and others in mixtures or compounds, can cause debilitating and life-threatening diseases.

Together, those six contaminants affected the health of 95 million people in the 2,300 sites included in the study and cost them 14.75 million disability-adjusted life years (DALYs). Five of the contaminants have been in the top six since 2010. In 2015, cadmium replaced arsenic. The 49 countries and 2,300 sites included in the study are only a fraction of the sites contaminated by persistent toxic substances that should be priorities for remediation. For example, in Ghana alone, 1,944 sites are in need of remediation. The EPA identified more than 300,000 sites in need of remediation.

Persistent bioaccumulative toxic chemicals have serious health consequences. Many are suspected carcinogens; others cause developmental and neurological problems. They may affect blood composition, function, and blood cell production. They can cause arrhythmia and heart failure. Some affect the liver; others affect the immune system and/or respiratory system. They cause emotional and behavioral problems and even a loss of IQ points.

Given the potential human disorders brought on or intensified by these (and other) pollutants, it is not at all surprising that pollution causes millions of early deaths and millions more people suffer with physical and mental health problems.

Not everyone is equally vulnerable. The risks posed by specific toxins vary according to the following:

- Individual characteristics such as age (in utero is generally most susceptible), sex, metabolic rate, genetic makeup, and prior exposures

- How the chemical is used, released, or disposed

- The type of exposure (inhalation, ingestion, or contact)

- The length of exposure

- How quickly the chemical breaks down into less toxic substances

Heavy Metals and Radionuclides

Heavy metals and radionuclides persist in the environment circulating among air, water, soil, animals, and plant life. They do not break down into less toxic substances. As elements not synthetically created, they occur naturally. Human activities from mining, to electricity generation, to the processing and use of agricultural, household, and industrial chemicals release them into the environment, where exposure is harmful to human, plant, and animal life. Their danger is exacerbated because of biomagnification; they become more toxic as they rise through the food chain.

Most rock phosphates contain heavy metals and radioactive elements. Using rock phosphates as fertilizers introduces them into the ecosystem, as does mining, processing, application, and disposal. They may travel through the air, enter the soil and water, and be ingested by microorganisms, thereby contaminating the food chain. In the soil, they enter plants and are ingested by animals and humans. In water, they contaminate up the food chain to fish and shellfish. They accumulate in the body with high potential for severe health consequences (Lema et al. 2014).

Because they can be transported over long distances, they are a global problem regardless of where they are released. A Global Environment Facility (GEF) report of chemical concerns to human and environmental health ranked heavy metals as the number one concern in four of the five regions of developing and transitioning economies (Bouwman 2012). Only those listed by PE and GCS as the most serious threats in their 2016 report are discussed below.

Mercury

Mercury is a neurotoxin. Even small amounts cause serious health problems affecting "kidney, heart and respiratory problems, tremors, skin rashes, vision or hearing problems, headaches, weakness, memory problems, and emotional changes" (GEF 2013). Children mining for gold in Latin America and Africa suffer mercury exposure daily in the air they breathe and the water in which they stand. Mercury is also used in industrial processes such as zinc smelting, in products such as lighting and dental work, and in hospitals. Although banned for use in some home products, mercury remains problematic in developed societies, as you will see later in the chapter. One of the top six toxins identified by the GEF,[1] mercury is among the top ten of the World Health Organization (WHO). It affects brain and neurological development, memory, language, fine motor, visual, and spatial skills, attention, and fine motor development (WHO 2016b).

The Minamata Convention on Mercury was signed in 2013. It has 128 signatory countries and 25 ratifications, as of 2016, that pledge to reduce the use of mercury in products and industrial processes; control air, land, and water releases; and address storage and disposal. It also bans new mercury mines and phases out existing ones.

The example of mercury highlights the work that needs to be done to rid the environment of dangerous pollutants. Mercury is an element that cannot be created or destroyed. It is ubiquitous—found all over the world, discharged into air, land, and water. Only 10 percent of mercury emissions into the air are natural, 30 percent are humanly made, and 60 percent are reemissions, primarily from human sources in the first place (United Nations Environment Programme [UNEP] 2013). It is used in industrial processes and is a byproduct of non-ferrous metal production. Many products contain mercury, primarily measuring devices, batteries, dental products such as tooth fillings, lighting and lamps, and switches and relays. It is released in coal combustion and cement making. Phasing these out is the most effective way in which to reduce mercury in waste.

Mercury contamination remediation is necessary. It requires substitutes for mercury in products and processes and safe storage of mercury already in the environment. It also requires rehabilitation, as much as possible, of the people sickened or developmentally delayed by exposure. The small artisanal gold mines where so many people, including children, suffer the consequences of mercury exposure provide the economic support for entire families. As many as 13 million people work in poorly or unregulated artisanal mines in 55 countries throughout Latin America, Africa, and Asia. Many are women and children. The dangers faced vary by the minerals mined and the methods used. But the health consequences are severe (Hinton, Veiga, and Beinhoff 2003). Remediation is expensive, but it would be more expensive not to remediate. No price can be put on our health and lives.

Because of the dangers posed by mercury in mining, the GEF has made mercury a priority. Its program of action includes education concerning the dangers of mercury, sponsoring locally built, more efficient gold processing techniques that will reduce mercury use emissions and exposure by about 50 percent. GEF-5 funds remediation projects in the mines of the Philippines, Ecuador, Peru, Burkina Faso, Senegal, and Mali. It commits about U.S. $2.5 million of GEF funds along with about $6 million in co-financing. Projects to reduce air emissions and waste management of mercury dovetail with efforts to reduce persistent organic pollutants (POPs) such as non-incineration waste treatment, reducing waste, and replacing mercury- or POP-containing products. These efforts are funded with more than $250 million for the cycle. Work supporting countries in meeting their obligations under the convention will continue through at least the cycles leading into 2020 (GEF 2013).

Chromium

Another naturally occurring mineral, chromium, is found in foods, including broccoli, garlic, and grape juice. Although the supporting evidence is unclear, dietary guidelines in the United States (National Institute of

Health 2016) state a minimum daily requirement for chromium, but the European Food Safety Authority (2014) found no beneficial effect of chromium and does not recommend an intake guideline. Chromium occurs naturally in the environment, and chromium compounds are released into the environment through natural emissions, mining, and industrial uses. Exposure through inhaling chromium dust, skin contact, and ingestion is toxic. Many common industrial processes, including leather tanning, metal processing, auto body repair, the ceramic and glass industry, cement production, electroplating, corrosion control, photography, dyes and pigments, coal and oil combustion, copy machine toner, and wood preservatives, release chromium into air, land, and water (Agency for Toxic Substances and Disease Registry 2013).

Depending on the medium of exposure, the effects of chromium vary. Inhalation causes respiratory problems, including cancer. Workers are most at risk for inhaling chromium. Occupational exposure occurs through inhaling chromate dust and fumes and through contact with eyes and skin. The toxicity of inhaled chromium is not debated. Higher rates of lung cancer in chromium workers have been documented as far back as the 1930s. Nasal perforation leaves workers more susceptible to other respiratory ailments as well. The Occupational Safety and Health Administration in the United States requires protective measures for workers in danger of exposure to chromium. In low- and middle-income countries, workers have little protection from contamination in low-tech, low-cost industrial processes, such as tanning leather, that are widespread there.

European Union (EU) legislation restricts hexavalent chrome solutions found to be carcinogenic and mutagenic. They are not to be used in EU production or in products imported into the EU. This includes items as diverse as leather products (shoes, gloves, purses, and other products that come into direct contact with skin) (World Footwear 2014) and chrome plating on automobiles (Classic Cars for Sale 2014). The ban on leather products and other lower-level manufacturing products may easily hurt the economies of developing countries or lower-level workers in middle-level economies.

Exposure to the general public is primarily through ingesting contaminated water. While the relationship between ingestion via water and cancer is debated, a study in Greece (Linos et al. 2011) added to the mounting evidence of a significant relationship. Although the study was relatively small, it found elevated cancer levels related to water contaminated by hexavalent chromium, its most toxic form.

Without comprehensive wastewater control and treatment, chrome processing and tannery operations pose health risks. There are more than 300 toxic chromium sites globally, and together they pose a risk to 16 million people and account for 3 million DALYs (PE and GCS 2016). Entire communities can suffer the consequences of hexavalent chromium exposure where tanneries are concentrated and waste is not adequately handled. For example, Hazaribagh in Bangladesh is home to 200 tanneries. They produce 7.7 million liters of liquid waste and 88 tons of solid waste daily. The waste is discharged directly into surface and groundwater sources, contaminating them with chromium along with companion cadmium, arsenic, and lead. People wash clothes, swim, and bathe in the water and also use the water for irrigation. Polluting water and land, it enters food through fish and crops. In some areas, the waste is used in feed, resulting in contaminated poultry and eggs. One quarter (25 percent) of a sample of chicken livers from the region contained hexavalent chromium.

Remediating the ground water, converting hexavalent chromium to trivalent chromium that is less toxic, and treating contaminated soils is possible, although expensive. Salt-tolerant bacteria, bone charcoal, worms, molasses (on which bacteria feed) added to soil, or electron donor enrichment cultures added to water are potential methods to lessen or detoxify the environment (PE and GCS 2016). Although expensive, the long-term consequences of not remediating are more severe.

Lead

Lead has been banned from gasoline and paint in the United States and many developed countries, but it remains the fifth most important metal in the U.S. economy and 85 percent of lead used in the United States is produced domestically. Although the amount of lead in piping is controlled, there are still major U.S. cities that have solid lead piping. In some non-lead pipes, there is lead solder at the joints (Plumbing Manufacturers International 2016). Old housing stock may have lead-based paint. Paint chips containing lead have a sweet taste that is appealing to children.

In developing societies, lead use is widespread. Lead is still used in some places in "paints, dyes, ceramic glazes, pesticides, ammunition, pipes, weights, cable covers, car batteries and sheets used for protection against radiation" (PE and GCS 2016). Lead enters the environment through mining, metal smelting, iron and steel production, and pigment production. It enters the air and settles into the soil and water. It enters the food supply, accumulating in plants and animals. Approximately 26 million people are at risk for lead exposure.

Lead rises to toxic concentrations in people through ingestion or inhalation. It can be absorbed through the skin, but not usually at toxic levels. Children, because of their developmental level and body mass, are particularly susceptible. The list of maladies that result from lead toxicity is extensive, including neurological damage and loss of IQ points, more impulsivity, loss of memory and dementia, infertility, joint pain and chronic headaches, anemia, decreased concentration, nerve disorders, infertility, increased blood pressure, and chronic headaches. It can also cause seizures and death at very high exposure levels (PE and GCS 2016).

Several studies have documented a relationship between lead exposure and delinquency and violent crime. In a study of delinquency in Pittsburgh, Pennsylvania, researchers found greater bone lead concentration in boys who exhibited more aggressive and delinquent behaviors. Because lead affects brain development, children with toxic levels of lead are more likely to exhibit developmental problems than are others (Feigenbaum and Muller 2016).

Radionuclides: Radon, Radium, and Uranium

Radiation exists naturally in air, food, and water. Exposure of millions of people to dangerous levels coincided with the beginning of the nuclear industry in the 1950s. There is no level of exposure to radioactivity that is considered safe. Even low-level background exposure increases the risk of infant mortality, cancer, and low birth weights. Low-level exposure such as to those people who work in the nuclear industry, about 10 million people, can cause chromosome and genetic mutations (PE and GCS 2016). Prenatal exposure may cause brain damage.

The toxic effects vary with the type of nuclide, whether exposure is acute or chronic, and the strength of the nuclide. The radionuclides uranium, radon, and radium vary in their half-life and type of radiation emitted on decay. Large-volume sources are from uranium mining, weapons production, and nuclear reactors. Mining may release radioactivity into the air, or radioactivity may leak into water sources. People may be poisoned by inhaling, ingesting, or contact. Improper storage and waste disposal of radioactive materials puts the environment and people at risk.

Radiation poisoning causes hair loss, fatigue, weakness, fever, diarrhea, disorientation, dizziness, low blood pressure, and death. Psychological costs include post-traumatic stress disorder, diminished well-being, depression, anxiety, and suicidal ideation. Because their developmental processes are ongoing, children are more susceptible than adults. The psychological consequences of exposure or threat of exposure in children are hyperactivity and emotional, conduct, and peer problems (PE and GCS 2016).

People working in or living near the nuclear industry, in mining, in energy or weapons production, or in scientific and medical applications are at greatest risk. Nuclear waste from mining uranium, particularly dust from open pit mining, may contaminate soil and water and spread through the environment. Food and water sources can become contaminated. Approximately 800,000 to 1 million people are at direct risk from the 91 uranium mining and processing sites identified through the Toxic Sites Identification Program. The full burden of disease from the range of radionuclides is difficult to estimate due to the many avenues of exposure. Studies of the nuclear accident at Chernobyl, Ukraine, report that more than 10 million people still suffer physical and psychological health effects. A study of the 2011 accident at Fukushima, Japan, reports that 385,000 people suffer psychological trauma from the event. We do not know the full range of effects on the people working in the nuclear industry who are exposed to radiation on a daily basis (PE and GCS 2016).

Cadmium

Cadmium and cadmium compounds are known carcinogens. As far back as the 1500s, cadmium was released into the rivers and riverbeds of Fuchu, Toyama, Japan, through gold, silver, copper, zinc, and lead mining. Women living there had long suffered from itai-itai (ouch ouch), a renal and bone disease. In the 1950s, scientists finally linked the contaminated rivers to the irrigated rice fields that contaminated foods grown there. Despite this knowledge, release of cadmium into water continues. In 2012, a mining company spilled a large quantity into the Guangxi River, which caused massive fish death and contamination of the water supply. More than 150 sites around the world continue to pose a health risk to 5 million people at a loss of 250,000 DALYs (PE and GCS 2016).

Cadmium is an impurity found in most phosphorus and zinc ores. The global overuse of phosphate

CONSIDER THIS
THE TRAGEDY IN FLINT, MICHIGAN

Lead received significant attention in the United States in 2015 when it was found in the drinking water in the former heavy industrial town of Flint, Michigan. Flint, once a center of the automotive industry, declined rapidly after the auto industry left town. It has a poverty rate of 40 percent. In April 2014, hoping to save $200 million over 25 years, authorities switched the Flint water supply from Detroit to the Flint River. This was a temporary move until a pipeline could be built connecting Flint to the Karegnondi Water Authority. However, the switch occurred without testing for the corrosive effects that the new water supply might have on the distribution grid. Within a month, residents were complaining of the smell and color of the water. In August, *Escherichia coli* (*E. coli*) and other coliform bacteria were found in the water. Authorities advised residents to boil the water, and they increased the chlorine levels in the water supply. This prompted General Motors to switch its own water supply in October 2014, fearing the corrosive effects of chlorine on its machinery.

In January 2015, the Centers for Disease Control and Protection found Flint to be in violation of the Safe Drinking Water Act. The chlorine interacted with organic matter in the water and produced too high a level of trihalomethanes, some of which are carcinogenic in humans. In February, high levels of lead were found in homes.

It wasn't until January 2016 that a state of emergency was declared in Flint. The human cost of this avoidable poisoning will not be known for years to come. (Kennedy 2016)

---

fertilizers where soils are low in phosphate results in a concentration of cadmium. Industrial wastes, mine waste rocks, smelting waste, and tire ash are often added to fertilizers to enrich the zinc levels, raising levels of cadmium as well. Chemical phosphate fertilizers caused metal contamination of agricultural soils in Australia, New Zealand, and Norway. Cadmium bioaccumulates; concentration in soils from fertilizers or in water from runoff contaminates food—fish, shellfish, and rice in particular. In Southeast Asia, where there are few fertilizer regulations, rice grown in cadmium-contaminated soil may cause kidney disease. Feed additives of zinc phosphate may also have concentrations of cadmium, as was found in Belgium (Bouwman 2012).

The major sources of cadmium in the atmosphere are non-ferrous metal production, zinc refining, nickel–cadmium battery production, some pigments, iron and steel production, fossil fuel combustion, incineration of municipal waste, and manufacturing phosphate fertilizers.

In industrial settings (metal plating, battery, pigment, and plastic production), exposure is primarily through inhalation. Nickle–cadmium batteries, banned in Europe in 2009, are still fairly common globally. When contained in a battery cadmium is not toxic, but when ingested it is more toxic than lead.

Persistent Organic Pollutants

Another category of PTS contains organic compounds, meaning that they have carbon, the element at the basis of life on the earth. Persistent organic pollutants[2] is an umbrella term for a variety of chemicals with serious health consequences for plants, animals, and humans. Although they are not elemental forms and most are humanly made, they resist degradation. They are very difficult to eradicate from the environment, persisting for decades. Carried by air and water, they circulate globally from continent to continent.

Most POPs are fat soluble and thus accumulate within the fatty tissues. As they move up the food chain, their concentration increases, making them persistent bioaccumulative toxins (PBTs). Their health consequences are better understood in animals than in humans, but they include cancers and developmental, reproductive, and neurological delay and damage.

Once released or disposed into air, water, and land (Figure 13.1), POPs can be transported across continents and oceans. They persist in the environment, being found decades after their use was banned. They accumulate in the food chain, with particularly high levels in fatty tissues of fish and marine animals. They affect vegetation, animals, and humans. Exposure of humans is primarily through ingestion in the food chain. Because they persist in land, air, and water, nearly every food type is a potential source.

FIGURE 13.1   POPs Circulate Through the Environment

Persistent organic pollutants enter the food chain through air, land, and water before being ingested by humans potentially thousands of miles from their source.

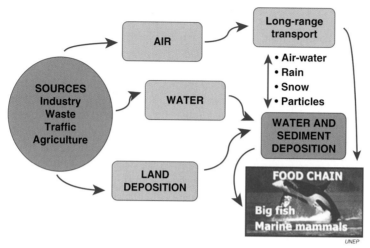

Source: World Health Organization (2008).

Polychlorinated biphenyls (PCBs) are the most widely used POPs and most widely found in the environment. There are 209 PCBs in all. Vegetables, fruits, and cereals absorb them through land pollution. Milk, other dairy products, and meats are susceptible as cows and other animals feed on contaminated corn, hay, and grasses. Fish, shellfish, and other aquatic life absorb them through water. They can also migrate from packing materials into foods.

Pesticides are another widely used category of POPs, putting agricultural workers at great risk. Despite an international "code of conduct" for the use of pesticides, its implementation is weak. Cheaply produced pesticides are used widely in low- and middle-income countries. Of the 10 most commonly used pesticides, 7 are among the most dangerous. In addition to exposure of workers, storage and containment methods are weak, resulting in leakages and releases. Workers in Asia report nausea, convulsions, headaches, and dizziness. WHO estimates that 3 million agricultural workers suffer from acute pesticide poisoning in addition to the 20,000 deaths and 735,000 chronic illnesses reported annually.

Volatile Organic Compounds

Like other organic compounds, volatile organic compounds (VOCs) contain carbon. Characterized by their low boiling point, they are volatile in that they readily change into vapors or gases at normal room and outdoor temperatures. Found in many household products as well as industrial processes, VOCs pose significant health risks as indoor and outdoor air pollutants.

Sources are plentiful, as anyone who has caught a whiff of gasoline or "that new car smell" can attest. Although so ubiquitous in modern life that we take them for granted, VOCs are dangerous, as demonstrated by the deaths due to "huffing" or inhaling these products. In many households in developed nations, these products are so frequently used that indoor air quality is more hazardous from the VOCs than is the outdoor air. The risk with respect to indoor VOCs is relative to the specific chemical, ventilation, and individual characteristics such as the amount of time spent indoors (not just in homes but also in all indoor facilities, including schools, office buildings, and stores), age, and health. The health effects of chronic exposure include kidney and liver damage, central nervous system damage, and cancer. Short-term exposure can worsen asthma and cause dizziness, headaches, nausea, and eye, nose, and throat irritation.

Methylene chloride and benzene are among the most toxic VOCs. Methylene chloride is found in solvents such as paint strippers and aerosol sprays. The body converts it to carbon monoxide, where it can create symptoms of carbon monoxide exposure. Benzene is in auto emissions, tobacco smoke, paint supplies, and fuels. It is a human carcinogen (EPA 2016c).

Indoor air is very toxic where wood is burned, as in the wood stoves common in developing countries. Wood smoke contains VOCs, particulates, polycyclic aromatic hydrocarbons (PAHs),[3] and carbon monoxide. In low- and middle-income countries, alternative fuels such as coal, biomass (including dung and crop residue), paraffin, liquefied petroleum, and gas double the risk of childhood pneumonia. In South Africa, 40 percent of the population still uses alternative fuels, 90 percent in rural areas (Vanker et al. 2015). WHO estimates that 2,000,000 children under 5 years of age die every year from acute respiratory illnesses, most related to the use of alternative fuels for cooking and heating.

Many of the indoor air pollutants are not regulated in the United States, Europe, and developing countries. Those used in construction and paints are the most frequently regulated. There are labeling standards being developed for household and related products, but terms and criteria are not standardized and are hard to interpret. Manufacturers in some countries are to limit the use of VOCs to the "lowest concentration" based on the concentration in the final product.[4]

In the outdoors, cars and other gasoline-burning engines, power plants burning fossil fuels, chemical and petroleum industries, and industrial solvents emit the VOCs contributing to outdoor air pollution. In the air, VOCs react with nitrous oxides to form smog, ground-level (tropospheric) ozone. In the United States, outdoor VOC emissions created by human activities (excluding wildfires) decreased markedly, 47 percent, from 1990 to 2011. The largest decrease was from on-road vehicles. In Europe, VOC emissions decreased 63 percent from 1990 to 2010. Improvements in solvent management and solvent efficiency are the most significant sources of the reductions. Despite these reductions, more needs to be done both to protect our physical and mental health directly and to slow global climate change.

AIR, LAND, AND WATER DEGRADATION AND DEPLETION

Persistent, toxic, and bioaccumulative substances degrade fresh, sea, and underground water supplies, the soil and everything that grows in it, and the air necessary for healthy plant and animal life. In 2012, polluted air, water, and soil accounted for 8.4 million deaths in low- and middle-income countries. Air pollution alone accounts for 200,000 early deaths in the United States every year (Caiazzo et al. 2013).

Degradation depletes resources. Fresh ground and surface water is not infinitely renewable. It is diminishing. The supply of healthy air is diminishing. The earth's water and air often destroy life rather than support life. Land is becoming uninhabitable, becoming unsuitable for agriculture, and disappearing into the seas. Forests are being destroyed by urbanization, logging, and pollution.

For the world to move ahead, sustainable development means protecting air, land, and water.

Toxic Releases to Air, Water, and Land

The EPA identified six principal air pollutants: carbon monoxide, lead, nitrogen dioxide, ozone, particulate matter, and sulfur dioxide. There are 182 more toxic air pollutants. Many are emitted as particulates or VOCs capable of migrating long distances to be deposited in water and soil.

Many industries use toxic chemicals and release toxic chemicals as waste. In developing societies, toxic mercury flows freely in mining processes. Children and adults working in the mines suffer from mercury poisoning. In developed nations, industries are better able to contain contamination but not completely. Every day, poisons are released into the air and water and are injected into various types of underground wells or landfills where, if not properly contained, they migrate to the surface.

Both the United States and EU report toxic release data annually. In the United States, EPA collects release data on more than 650 chemicals from thousands of facilities. Published in the Toxic Release Inventory (TRI), the EPA tracks both source reduction (using less material) and releases.

U.S. Toxic Release Inventory

The TRI[5] tracks how thousands of industries (21,783 in 2014) manage toxicants that they use or produce as byproducts. Among the 650 chemicals tracked are more than 180 carcinogens, all of which pose health threats to humans and the environment. Many people are not aware of the volume of toxicants released directly into air, water, and land. The TRI tracks the volume of pollutants recycled or released into land, air, and water. Sixteen specific chemicals and PBT chemicals, lead and lead compounds, mercury and mercury compounds, dioxin and dioxin-like

CONSIDER THIS

POLYVINYL CHLORIDE — THE DEADLIEST PLASTIC?

Polyvinyl chloride (PVC) plastic products are common. Their production uses more chlorine gas than any other industrial process. Huge amounts of chlorine-rich hazardous waste are produced along with bioaccumulative toxins, lead, other heavy metals, and phthalates (which provide some of the flexibility and are also a health hazard). There are at least 12 POPs produced at some point in the PVC lifecycle.

These toxins are released in production and are emitted from PVC products. Although outlawed by regulation for toys, PVCs are a common building material. Children are at risk from vinyl floorings, wall coverings, and other materials in schools and homes. PVCs are related to autism, cancer, immune suppression, reproductive impairment, and endocrine disruption in children and adults. (Thornton 2002)

compounds, hexabromocyclododecane, and polycyclic aromatic compounds (PACs) are of special concern, and reporting requirements are more stringent for them than for others. The TRI does not cover toxins released by motorized vehicles, consumer product and chemical residues in food, or industries not required to report.

"Release" means discharged into the air or water or disposed of through some means into the land. Land disposals vary in their security and may leak from their storage. Overall, the quantity of toxic releases has decreased over time, although it varies by the particular chemical and the source of pollution. The *TRI National Analysis 2014* (EPA 2016b), which was updated in 2016, covers the period from 2003 to 2014 (Figure 13.2). Releases declined 13 percent, primarily through decreases in releases into the air, which declined 55 percent. The share of total releases into the air declined from 36 to 19 percent. Land releases increased, particularly underground injection.

Lead, Mercury, and Dioxin Releases in the United States

Releases of lead fluctuated during the decade, ending with an overall increase of 72 percent from about 400 million pounds to just under 750 million pounds. Most of the releases of lead and lead compounds, 91 percent in 2014, originated in metal mining. Excluding mining, releases decreased 30 percent from just over 80 million pounds to about 60 million pounds. Electric utilities and metal mines drove most of the decrease (EPA 2016b).

Emissions decreased 45 percent, from close to 140,000 pounds to about 75,000 pounds. Electric utilities decreased their emissions 51 percent primarily by using fuels other than coal for combustion. Electric utilities, including coal and coal-fired plants, accounted for 57 percent of mercury emissions in 2014.

TABLE 13.1   Toxin Release Decreases in Europe

Releases of several toxicants decreased in Europe. Progress was uneven, and some countries increased their releases.

From 1990 to 2013	Percentage Decrease	Countries With Increases
Hexachlorobenzene	96.45	Latvia, Estonia
Polychlorinated biphenyls	76.7	Portugal, Spain
Polycyclic aromatic hydrocarbons	62	Denmark, Iceland, Malta, Liechtenstein
Dioxins and furans	84.54	Malta, Latvia

Source: Adapted from data by European Environment Agency (2016).

A CLOSER LOOK
RELEASES OF TRI-REGULATED CHEMICALS

FIGURE 13.2   Disposal or Other Chemical Releases, 2003–2014

Releases in regulated chemicals decreased over time due primarily to decreased releases into the air. Land releases increased.

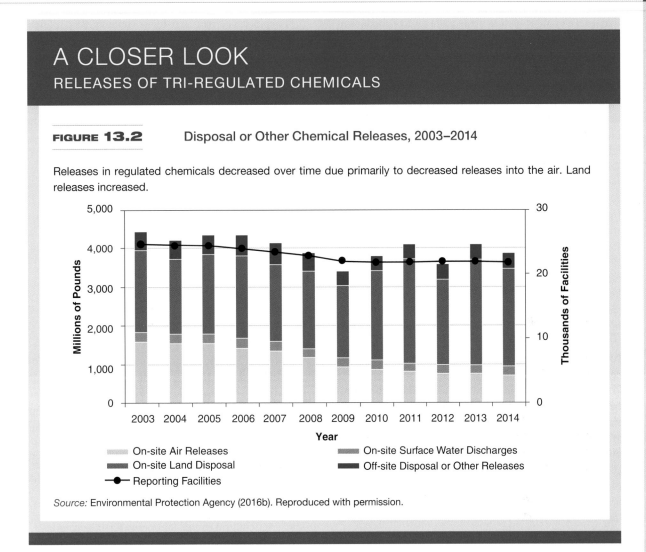

Source: Environmental Protection Agency (2016b). Reproduced with permission.

Total releases of dioxins decreased by 14 percent overall from 2003 to 2014. However, they increased from 2010 to 2014, when congener (dioxin-like) information was first collected, with grams TEQ (toxic equivalent) increasing at a faster rate than dioxins overall grams.

Releases in Europe

A total of 33 countries belong to the European Environment Agency. The primary sources of their POP emissions are commercial, institutional, and household combustion (mostly for heating), industrial metal production, and road transport. From 1990 to 2013, emissions of POPs decreased significantly.

Toxic release reports do not capture all pollutants or toxic substances. Only required chemicals and only industries required to report are included. Nevertheless, they provide a good idea of what hazardous substances are entering the environment, how they enter, and trends in managing them.

DEVELOPING NATIONS AND TOXIC DUMPING

The costs of environmental pollution in the developing world are enormous. Pollution accounts for 20 percent of the burden of disease in developing countries and costs approximately 8.5 million lives every year. Some of these are the "traditional" hazards relevant to poverty and underdevelopment such as inadequate sewage and lack of clean water. Others, the chemical or "modern" hazards, come from industrialization without the safeguards of more modern cleaner technologies.

In developing nations, the population, particularly in the rapidly urbanizing areas, suffers from both modern and traditional hazards simultaneously. Water is contaminated with human and animal feces and industrial chemicals. Air is polluted by burning dirty fuels and industrial byproducts. Land is spoiled by traditional household garbage and medical waste. Electronic waste, a modern hazard, is an increasing risk.

At 20 to 50 million tons and growing, electronic waste from computers, mobile phones, televisions, cameras, wiring, and so on is the fastest growing waste stream in the world and a major environmental challenge. Many of the materials being thrown away when we toss out our electronic devices are not only valuable, such as gold, palladium, and other precious metals, but also highly toxic, such as mercury, lead, and endocrine disruptors (e.g., brominated flame retardants) (Ajero et al. 2012).

Richer nations often ship toxic wastes to developing societies for disposal or recycling to take advantage of cheaper labor and weaker environmental laws. Ferrous and non-ferrous metals, plastics, glass, and wood all may be recycled for other uses. Valuable metals such as gold, silver, copper, steel, and aluminum can also be salvaged. While capturing the valuable waste can be a profitable business for these countries, it exacerbates the severity of their pollution problems and has hefty long-term costs. The methods of disposal and recovery, from open fires to strong acids, release POPs, lead, mercury, cadmium, PVCs, dioxins, hexavalent chromium, and other toxic contaminants into the environment. Their presence is well documented in the food chain. Because the recycling and recovery is usually accomplished with little worker protection, it is a direct threat to human health (Scientific and Technical Advisory Panel of the GEF [STAP] 2012). Reducing open burning will reduce some contamination, however international efforts are necessary to address importing toxic waste, open burning, and sewage issues to make the most impact on pollution in the developing world (STAP 2012).

Water Security

Safe and clean drinking water is a human right. Clean water is essential for life, and thousands of people die every day because they lack this basic resource. In 2010, the UN General Assembly officially recognized this and passed Resolution 64/292, "The Human Right to Water and Sanitation":

"Deeply concerned that approximately 884 million people lack access to safe drinking water and that more than 2.6 billion do not have access to basic sanitation, and alarmed that approximately 1.5 million children under 5 years of age die . . . [the UN General Assembly]

1. *Recognizes* the right to safe and clean drinking water and sanitation as a human right that is essential for the full enjoyment of life and all human rights.

2. *Calls upon* states and international organizations to provide financial resources, capacity-building and technology transfer, through international assistance and cooperation, in particular to developing countries, in order to scale up efforts to provide safe, clean, accessible and affordable drinking water and sanitation for all. (UN General Assembly 2010)

Water security is critical to public health and economic development in both the developed and developing worlds. WHO (2012b) estimates that economic losses attributable to inadequate water supply and sanitation alone amount to U.S. $260 billion a year. No country can take water security for granted.

In addressing the global water challenge, Joseph Alcamo, the UNEP chief scientist in 2011, provided this "short list" of threats:

- Agricultural runoff containing fertilizers and POPs

- Unidentified and unmonitored residues from medicines and other new chemical products

- Global climate change that will elevate water temperature and alter the dilution capacity of freshwater systems

- Air pollution deposition into aquatic systems from local and distant sources (nitrogen and sulfur compounds and sometimes heavy metals, organic compounds, and other toxic pollutants)

- Expansion of coverage of the public water supply without making adequate provision for facilities to treat its returning wastewater (Alcamo 2011)

CONSIDER THIS
A CAUTIONARY TALE

Poor water management created one of the worst environmental and public health crises of the 20th century. In the 1950s, the Aral Sea was the fourth largest saline lake in the world. It supported more than 40,000 jobs and several prosperous towns, supplying one sixth of the USSR's (Union of Soviet Socialist Republics) fish. The government detoured its two largest tributaries to grow cotton and other crops in the surrounding desert, disturbing the balance of evaporation and inflow that had sustained the sea. Without its replenishing inflow, it evaporated. The more it evaporated, the faster it shrank, due to its decreasing depth and lower salt concentration on the water's surface. Within 20 years, it was destroyed.

Salt concentration in the sea rose from 10 parts per thousand (ppt) in 1960, a year in which the sea yielded 43,430 tons of fish, to 92 ppt in 2004. By 1980, there were no fish caught. The damage spread.

As the groundwater declined, salinization of the soil increased. Fertilizers were added to compensate. This further degraded the land, and runoff further polluted the sea.

Vegetation began to die. As the vegetation died, the effect of winds intensified, blowing dust, salt, and pollutants from the fertilizer. Ten major dust storms now occur annually. Dust from the Aral Sea region was found as far as 500 km away. As many as 43 million metric tons of salt blew from the seabed from 1960 to 1984. About 6 million hectares of agricultural land was destroyed.

The destruction of the sea also contributed to climate change and increasing temperatures. The sea surface no longer disrupts frigid north winds. It does not contain enough moisture to feed snow into the surrounding mountains and more distant regions. The dust and salt are coating glaciers, decreasing the overall volume of ice. Wildlife is vanishing. Water is scarce.

The worst impact has been on public health. Anemia, respiratory disease, kidney troubles, tuberculosis, infections and parasites, typhus, and hepatitis increased dramatically. The child mortality rate is the highest in the region, and maternal mortality is 120 per 10,000 births.

Recovery efforts have made some progress. It is doubted that a full recovery is possible.

Source: Howard (2014).

 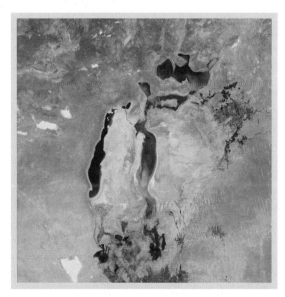

PHOTOS 13.2A AND 13.2B Degradation of the Aral Sea, 2000 to 2017. As these NASA (National Aeronautics and Space Administration) satellite images show, the Aral Sea is a small fraction of its former size and the surrounding area is a bed of salt.

NASA Earth Observatory.

Agricultural production, mining, industrial discharge, deforestation, precipitation from air pollution, over-irrigation, and power generation all contribute to the degradation and depletion of water, but agriculture and industry are the major culprits. Industry dumps 300 to 400 million tons of toxic chemicals, sludge, and waste into water each year. In the United States, agricultural runoff of manure and fertilizer is the greatest source of water pollution. Agricultural runoff from the Mississippi Basin is creating a dead zone in the Gulf of Mexico averaging 5,309 square miles each year.

To complicate the problem, water does not respect national boundaries. There are 286 transboundary river basins in the world. A total of 151 countries include territory within at least one transboundary basin, and 39 countries have 90 percent of their territory within one or more transboundary river basins (UNEP–DHI and UNEP 2016). There are 200 transboundary aquifers. This means that water security is an important international issue and a potential trouble spot in international relations. Use upstream may very well result in pollution and depletion downstream in another country. Underground aquifers are often shared among countries. Overuse in one country depletes the freshwater supply in other countries. Air or land pollution in one country can travel across borders and contaminate the water supply in other countries. This global problem requires international and global solutions. Water quantity, quality, and availability are critical issues moving forward in the 21st century.

POLLUTION IN THE DEVELOPING WORLD

While the developed world experiences water pollutants due to toxic discharge from industry and runoff from agriculture, the developing world experiences these toxins as well as those coming from untreated sewage.

Although the Millennium Development Goal target for improved drinking water was met ahead of schedule, and the situation in developing countries improved, hundreds of millions still lack this fundamental human necessity. Degradation of the water supply due to inadequate sewage is a major problem in the developing world.

In 2016 in India, only 209 of the 3,119 towns and cities had even partial sewage and treatment facilities. Many bodies of water, even the mythical Ganges River, are open sewers. More than 1.3 billion liters of household waste and garbage flow into the Ganges yearly (Dakkak 2016).

This scenario is repeated in thousands of cities, towns, and villages all over the world:

- 663 million people still use unimproved drinking water sources—surface water, springs, and unprotected wells. About half of these people live in sub-Saharan Africa, and one fifth live in South Asia (United Nations [UN] 2015).

- 801,000 children under 5 years of age die from diarrhea every year, that is 2,200 daily (down from 5,000 daily), mostly in the developing world and mostly due to lack of clean water (Centers for Disease Control and Prevention [CDC] 2015).

- Where people lack adequate sewage and sanitation, open defecation is widely practiced and approximately 1.7 million people die unnecessarily every year, many as a result of diarrhea (CDC 2015).

- Unsafe drinking water and poor sanitation result in millions of people being infected with tropical diseases, including Guinea worm disease, Buruli ulcer, trachoma (the world's leading cause of blindness), and schistosomiasis, every year (CDC 2015).

- Lack of adequate sanitation contributes to approximately 1 billion people becoming infected with soil transmitted helminths.

- In 2011, 589,854 cases of cholera, including 7,816 deaths, were reported to WHO by 58 countries (WHO 2012a).

- Malaria kills more than 1.2 million people annually, mostly African children under the age of 5 years, due to poorly designed irrigation, water, and sewage systems (WHO 2016a).

- Antimicrobial-resistant bacteria and their genetic material are increasingly present in wastewater, complicating treating infectious disease (WHO 2015).

In addition to household and human waste, industrial discharges and agricultural runoff pollute water where laws regulating industry and agriculture are weak. About

CONSIDER THIS
WATER AND GOLD

Global demand for gold strains the freshwater supply in the developing world. A large-scale surface mine can use from 16 to 26 million gallons of water a day. Mining boom towns are springing up the world over, bringing severe water pollution with them. In Peru, rivers that once brought drinking water to Guyana's indigenous population are too polluted for drinking. Mercury and cyanide used in processing ore also pollute fresh ground water, surface water, and soil. About 400 billion pounds of waste is dumped into water annually. "One wedding band is equal to 20 tons of mine waste." (Kozacek 2012)

260 million liters of industrial waste, 6 million tons of agricultural runoff of pesticides and fertilizers, and thousands of animal carcasses flow into the Ganges every year (Dakkak 2016).

In Rio de Janeiro, Brazil, where the Summer Olympics were held in 2016, the water of the famous Copa Cabana beach is so polluted that experts in public health called it an "extreme environment" where infection of the athletes was very likely. Swallowing just three teaspoons of the water is 99 percent likely to result in infection. Testing of the waters in July and December showed the presence of viruses from human sewage at 30,000 to 1.7 million times higher than what would be highly alarming in the United States or Europe (Associated Press 2016).

In many developing regions, there is barely any treatment of wastewater; as much as 90 percent is dumped or flows directly into rivers and streams (Figure 13.3). As countries in the developing world improve their standard of living, meeting the increasing needs for energy and food will exacerbate water stress from pollution and depletion (Corcoran et al. 2010).

WATER POLLUTION IN THE DEVELOPED WORLD

Although releases of chemicals from industry into water sources have been curtailed, serious contamination problems still exist in wealthy countries. Agricultural fertilizers and pesticides also pollute fresh water and coastal areas. Oil spills and the chemical agents used to clean them (which have not tested for safety) have done inestimable harm. Newly emergent concerns such as those related to pharmaceutical and medicinal wastes, the longevity of hormones from human excretion in water supplies, and nanoparticles arise regularly.

In the United States, the majority of the thousands of chemicals used in industry, agriculture, and personal care are not tested for safety. Of the 3,000 high-use chemicals,[6] only 43 percent had been tested as of 1998. There is no reason to expect that this has changed significantly because the study has not been updated and regulations have been weakened. Along with other known toxins, they end up in water resources (World Wildlife Fund n.d.). Wastewater is treated and then discharged directly into surface and ground water. Pollutants that are not regulated may well end up in drinking water. A new EPA initiative studied the water supplies of 30 water plants, specifically choosing plants that handle many types of wastewater—human, industrial, business, and agricultural. It found more than 250 chemicals and microbiological pollutants that are not yet regulated (EPA 2017).

Nanoparticles are just beginning to capture the attention of environmental researchers. Nanoparticles are one billionth of a meter in size. They have broad applications in pharmaceuticals, personal care products, food packaging, and cosmetics. The number of consumer products using them is increasing at about one per day. Nevertheless, little is known about how they will interact in the environment or the effects on biological systems (Kulacki and Cardinale 2012).

Production of nanoparticles is expected to increase to about 58,000 tons by 2020. Assuming that production processes will be regulated, most releases into the environment will probably be through human activities and consumer use of nano-enabled products. The human activities involve combustion of fossil fuels and mining, already known as significant sources of pollution. These release carbon- and metal-based nanoparticles into the air or water, where they are implicated in many pulmonary diseases. The synthetic nanoparticles are newer and less well known. Anti-microbial and ultraviolet (sun)-blocking

A CLOSER LOOK
WASTEWATER TREATMENT

FIGURE 13.3   Ratio of Treated to Untreated Wastewater by Region

The ratio of treated to untreated wastewater reaching water bodies for 10 regions is shown. An estimated 90 percent of all wastewater in developing countries is discharged untreated directly into rivers, lakes, or oceans.

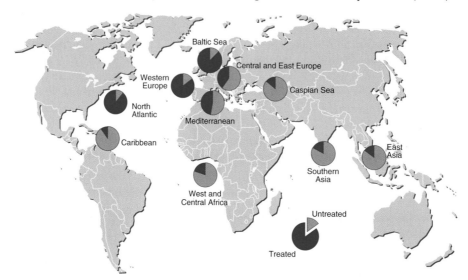

Source: GRID–Arendal (2010), Hugo Ahlenius. http://www.grida.no/resources/7599.

clothing, pharmaceuticals, next-generation batteries, and many other products will use nanoparticles. These may be washed out of clothing, end up in landfills, or be disposed of in many other ways where they pose hazards (Lohse 2014).

ENVIRONMENTAL ASSESSMENT IN THE UNITED STATES

The EPA assesses land, air, and water regularly. With respect to water bodies, measures of health include the following:

- Biological quality: Considered the most comprehensive indicator of water body health;

measures how well the water body supports a diversity of macroinvertebrates such as crustaceans, worms and mollusks, and fish life

- Human health indicators: Mercury in fish and bacteria

Stressors measured include the following:

- Chemical stressors: Eutrophication (nutrient pollution by phosphorus and nitrogen), salinity, and acidification

- Habitat stressors: Disturbance by human activity, deterioration of vegetation along the river corridors, and excess fine sedimentation

Last, the change in stream conditions from 2004 is also measured.

The 2008–2009 National Assessment of Rivers and Streams (EPA 2016a) results for the lower 48 states[7] are shown in Table 13.2. The threat that each stressor poses to the environment is figured by assessing three factors:

- The extent of the risk or the percentage of rivers and streams rated poor

- Its relative risk or the severity of its impact on water condition or how much more likely a water body is to be rated poor when the stressor is high in comparison with low

A CLOSER LOOK
RIVER AND STREAM QUALITY

TABLE 13.2   The 2008–2009 National Assessment of Rivers and Streams Results for the Lower 48 States

Rivers and Streams: Indicators	Percentage Good	Percentage Fair	Percentage Poor
Biological quality: Macroinvertebrate	28 percent	25 percent	46 percent
Biological quality: Fish	36 percent	19 percent	32 percent
Human Health Indicators			
Mercury in fish[a]	38,519 did not exceed criteria		13,144 exceeded criteria
Enterococci bacteria	70 percent did not exceed human health threshold		23 percent exceeded human health threshold
Stressors[b]			
Phosphorus	35 percent	19 percent	46 percent
Nitrogen	38 percent	20 percent	41 percent
Habitat stressors			
Excessive sedimentation	55 percent	29 percent	15 percent
Vegetative cover	56 percent	20 percent	24 percent
Disturbance	34 percent	46 percent	20 percent
Change in stream conditions			

a. Fish were sampled in only 51,663 miles of rivers and streams. Percentages cannot be extrapolated to the entirety of rivers and streams or the target population of the 1,193,775 miles of assessment.

b. Salinity and acidity are not reported here. Acidification was rated "poor" less than 1 percent for every region. Salinity was rated 3 to 4 percent "poor" for every region. A significant number of rivers and streams in the United States pose significant risk to plant, animal, and human life.

Source: Adapted from Environmental Protection Agency (2016a).

- The attributable risk or how important that stressor is in determining the quality of the water (EPA 2016a)

Those stressors with the most attributable risk would be those that should take priority in planning and action.

For all regions, the greatest risk to macroinvertebrates is eutrophication from phosphorus and nitrogen. With respect to fish, except for the western United States, where riparian vegetation cover and excessive sedimentation

had the highest attributable risk, phosphorus and nitrogen again posed the greatest threat. In considering human health, the presence of the enterococci bacteria indicates that disease-causing agents, such as viruses, bacteria, and protozoa, may also be present. Swimming in contaminated waters may result in gastrointestinal distress as well as eye, ear, respiratory, and skin diseases. Eating fish and shellfish from contaminated waters causes illness. Closing beaches due to contamination brings economic costs (EPA 2016a).

A CLOSER LOOK
NITROGEN POLLUTION AND THE WATER CYCLE

FIGURE 13.4   Overview of the Aquatic Nitrogen Cycle and Sources of Pollution With Nitrogen

Intensive agriculture, energy production, industrialization, and urbanization contribute to the pollution of European water systems. Less than half of all water bodies have a "good" status.

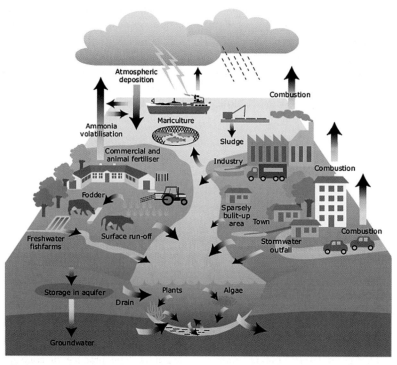

Source: European Environment Agency (n.d.).

CONSIDER THIS
ALGAE BLOOM AND DEAD ZONES

Nitrogen and phosphorus from agricultural runoff and other sources fertilize algae in freshwater and saltwater bodies in the same way that we use them to fertilize crops and flower beds. As the algae grow, they block light and deplete oxygen; other plants and sea life die.

Algae growth can create a dead zone where other plants and fish cannot live. In the Gulf of Mexico, a dead zone develops every spring fed by runoff from farms along the Mississippi River Basin. At 5,000 square miles, it is the second largest in the world. It becomes a "biological desert" with economic consequences of about $82 million.

There are about 200 dead zones in the United States and about 400 known worldwide. Because not all have been counted, there may be as many as 1,000 (National Resources Defense Council 2014).

In Chesapeake Bay, runoff from chicken farms creates a dead zone in which fish, crabs, oysters, and other animals suffocate and wash onto shore.

As if this weren't bad enough, some species of algae, phytoplankters, produce biotoxins.

In water, microorganisms transform mercury into the toxic organic mercury, methylmercury. It bioaccumulates and biomagnifies, appearing in higher concentrations in fish that eat fish than in fish that eat microorganisms. In humans, methylmercury causes damage to the nervous and immune systems; fetuses in utero are particularly vulnerable. Toxic levels were found in fish in 13,144 of the 51,633 miles of rivers sampled (EPA 2016a).

In data collected from 2006 to 2014 on a wider variety of stressors, the EPA's assessment of water body pollution in the United States found that pathogens contributed the most frequently to causes of impairment,[8] followed by nutrients, metals other than mercury (i.e., lead, arsenic, aluminum, zinc, cadmium, barium), oxygen enrichment, PCBs, sediment, mercury, caustic (acidic) conditions, unknown (impaired biota), temperature, turbidity, salinity (chlorides, sulfates), and pesticides (EPA 2016a).

Ground water is also contaminated. The contaminants that we put into air and land can seep through into ground water. Ground water supplies the drinking water of 114 million people[9] in the United States, nearly one third of the population, yet there was little regulatory oversight until 2006. Disinfection is required only when deemed necessary and must reduce the virus concentrations by 99.99 percent. Where there is not disinfection, contaminated tap water accounted for 6 to 22 percent of acute gastrointestinal illnesses and as much as 63 percent among children under 5 years of age (Borchardt et al. 2012).

Europe experiences similar problems (Figure 13.4). Industry, agriculture, energy production, urban development, and land use all threaten the water supply through chemical pollution and overuse. Eurostat and the Organisation for Economic Cooperation and Development both administer questionnaires to EU countries and prospective members. Because participation is voluntary and national regulations differ, the data are not consistent across countries. An independent study of 4,001 sites throughout 91 river basins of Europe (Malaj et al. 2014) confirmed that chemical pollution in Europe is a widespread continental problem. The study examined chronic and acute risks of 223 chemicals[10] for three major organism groups: fish, invertebrates, and algae. The study also documented eight land-use types that drove the chemical risks.

At least one of the organisms studied posed a chronic risk in 42 percent of the sites. The actual risk would be much greater if a wider variety of organisms and chemicals were studied. Pesticides are the highest risk chemical, implicated in 81 to 96 percent of sites with chronic and acute risk. Despite regulation, pesticides continue to threaten species other than the target pest. Herbicides were most responsible for risk threshold exceedances for algae, and insecticides were most responsible for those for fish and invertebrates. Organotin compounds are primarily leeched from the hulls of ships, and flame retardants are primarily leeched from consumer products (brominated diphenyl ethers). Agricultural and urban (household and industrial) land uses are the major contributors. The practice of concentrating agriculture to preserve other lands for conservation does not appear to be a viable solution to agricultural runoff, and even small streams with runoff can contaminate entire catchment areas. Buffer strips of vegetation between farm land and water to absorb runoff are a better solution. Better treatment technologies for urban waste are necessary.

DEPLETION OF WATER RESOURCES

Freshwater systems are not sustainable given the pressures put on them. Not only has humankind degraded water through pollution, but also water resources, once considered renewable, are depleted as well. The amount of fresh water on the earth that is accessible is very small—only 2.5 percent. Increasing populations and increasing development reduce the amount of water available per person every day. Mismanagement of water resources, common all over the world, exacerbates the scarcity of water and related stresses. Water is not a renewable resource.

Development, raising the standard of living for billions of people worldwide, increases the demand for energy, material goods, and better food, all of which require more water. Climate change, already a significant contributor to water scarcity, will continue to accelerate it. Rising temperatures will increase evaporation and precipitation. Surface water will have a higher temperature,

and flows are expected to decrease. The rise in sea level will contaminate much of the fresh water with salt water as oceans move inland. Droughts, floods, and heat waves will be more severe. Drought can diminish the capacity for hydropower, causing reversion to fossil fuels (International Energy Agency [IEA] 2012). Economic growth in developing regions could decline by as much as 6 percent of gross domestic product (GDP) due to climate-caused water stress, according to the World Bank. By 2050, freshwater supplies in cities may decrease by as much as two thirds in comparison with 2015 levels (World Bank 2016).

Most of the earth's fresh water, about 70 percent, is locked into glaciers and ice caps (Figure 13.5). Surface water contained in rivers, streams, and lakes is another source of fresh water. Much of the surface water in lakes at high altitudes is not accessible to many of the world's populations. Other lakes, in arid regions, are susceptible to evaporation and may become too salty to support life. The Dead Sea, the Caspian Sea, the Aral Sea, and the Great Salt Lake are examples.

Ground water accounts for about 30 percent of total fresh water and is the largest source of accessible fresh water. Aquifers, which are something like underground reservoirs made of porous rock and sand, are a

---

FIGURE 13.5   Freshwater Availability

The earth's freshwater supply is not evenly distributed around the world. Many areas of water scarcity are also conflict zones.

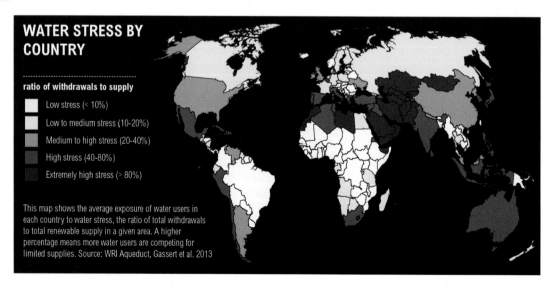

major source of drinking water for about one fourth of the world's population and a major source of water for irrigation. The problem is that we may be overusing and degrading the aquifers, the primary water source for more than 2 billion of the earth's people.

NASA (National Aeronautics and Space Administration) satellite images of aquifers, taken from 2003 to 2013, show that 21 of the world's largest 37 aquifers were past their sustainability tipping points; more water was being taken out than could be replenished during the decade of the study. This is a long-term problem that is likely to get worse as the demand for water increases. Aquifers took thousands of years to fill. While water can be removed easily, aquifers replenish slowly through rainfall and snowmelt. These hidden reservoirs are increasingly stressed because drilling for water increases with drought and the need for irrigation. Although NASA was able to document the extent of depletion, how much water is in each aquifer is harder to determine (Richey et al. 2015). However, there are symptoms that indicate when an aquifer is running low.

The costs of groundwater depletion are high; surface water flow diminishes or dries up, wells run dry, land can subside as its support is gone, salt water may fill the voids left by freshwater (contaminating soil and water), and contaminants from fertilizers and pesticides used on irrigated lands may concentrate and contaminate remaining water. People lose their source of drinking water, irrigation, and industry.

In the North China Plain, China's premier agricultural area, water tables are dropping at a rate of 1 meter annually. From 2003 to 2013, researchers calculated net water use for six crops grown in experimental beds (Yang et al. 2015), measuring the moisture content of soil to calculate net use and recharge of the ground water for different crop rotations. They found that the most prevalent pattern of crop growth and rotation (winter wheat and summer maize) was the worst possible combination of crops studied for water conservation. The dilemma is that this combination provides the most income for farmers there.

Ecological damage is already evident. There has been land subsidence caused by the water drawdown and increasing salinity along some coastal areas. Natural streams and surface waters have disappeared. With poor treatment, wastewater often goes right back into the supply. Unless agricultural patterns change, the aquifers may run dry in 30 years (Yardley 2007).

Earlier estimates of global aquifer depletion underestimated the rate at which they are being used. NASA found that the most stressed aquifers are the Arabian Aquifer on which 60 million people depend, the Indus Basin in India and Pakistan, and the Muzuk-Djado Basin in Libya and Niger. Many of these aquifers are located in regions where social, economic, and political tensions are already high. The study raises red flags in these areas, hopefully making them priorities for intervention to protect lives and livelihoods (NASA 2015).

Freshwater withdrawals in the United States doubled from 1950 to 1980 and decreased somewhat from 2005 to 2010. Groundwater withdrawals did not decline and remain more than double, at 76 billion gallons a day in 2010 as compared with 34 billion, the 1950 rate of withdrawal. Nearly 80 percent of water withdrawals are from surface waters. The total water usage in 2010 was 355 billion gallons a day, with irrigation and energy production accounting for the largest withdrawals at 115 and 161 billion gallons a day, respectively. This is important because a large proportion of water withdrawn is lost, a consequence of consumptive use. More than half of the water withdrawn for agriculture and one fifth of the water withdrawn for energy and other uses is never returned (Center for Sustainable Systems 2016).

In the Great Plains of the United States, the Ogallala aquifer supplies irrigation to one third of the nation's corn and drinking water for seven states. But it is diminishing rapidly; the water table dropped 25 feet. In Ulysses, Kansas, the Ogallala no longer feeds its rivers and streams. Farmers are switching to the less water-intensive cotton and bringing in bottled water. While most of the Ogallala remains uncontaminated, shallow areas and those farthest downstream show signs of contamination, with chemicals seeped into the aquifer along with the irrigation water (Gurdak 2010b). Rain rarely reaches the aquifer, evaporating before it soaks down (Gurdak 2010a).

Water and Energy Codependency

Energy and water are interdependent. Water is needed to generate energy, and energy is needed to pump, distribute, and treat water. As development progresses, water supplies will be increasingly stressed from use and pollution in the process of producing more energy.

Every form of energy requires water somewhere in the production process. For coal and oil, water is required in extracting these from the earth. It cools thermal power plants. It irrigates biomass crops. Whether or not there is enough water, given known sources, to sustain a population of 9 billion, the expected global population in 2050, is a serious question.

Climate change threatens water supplies even in countries and regions that historically enjoyed reliable water resources. Hurricanes Katrina and Rita caused extensive damage to the U.S. energy infrastructure, shutting down natural gas and oil delivery infrastructures. The impact was felt by energy markets as far away as New York and New England. Too much water, as in rising sea levels and hurricanes, and too little water, as in wildfires and heat waves, are significant threats to energy systems.

Water requirements for energy production, whether nuclear, oil, gas, coal, or biomass combustion, hydropower, or even some solar systems, are already difficult to meet given water shortages and temperature requirements.[11] Water shortages will constrain energy production at many existing facilities and may constrain new plant development (Dell et al. 2014). Nuclear power and carbon capture and storage systems, strategies that some advocate for reducing greenhouse gases, both are highly water intensive. Even with modifications, such as reducing energy demand through conservation, fewer coal-powered plants, retiring inefficient plants, more advanced cooling systems, and increased reliance on biomass, an 85 percent increase in water use is still likely (IEA 2012).

THE GLOBAL WATER REGIME

Altogether, the international water regime has about 3,600 international agreements (United Nations Department of Economic and Social Affairs [UNDESA] 2014). The first treaty of any kind may have been the treaty of 2500 B.C. between the Sumerian city-states of Lagash and Umma over use of the Tigris River. Water security is so critical to any nation that stability is prized even if it means signing a treaty with a country with which you are at war. In the last 50 years, while 150 treaties have been signed, only 37 acute disputes over water broke out. From 1957 and throughout the Vietnam War, the Mekong River Commission—a pocket of security among warring Laos, Cambodia, Vietnam, and Thailand—functioned. The India and Pakistan Indus River Commission survived two wars between those countries. The Nile River Basin serves 10 countries and is shared by 160 million people. They cooperate on the use of the basin to spur economic development and fight poverty in all 10 countries (UNDESA 2014). The UN 1997 Convention on Non-navigational Uses of International Watercourses established principles for agreements between countries. The two principles are not to cause "significant" harm to neighbors and to establish "shared and reasonable use."

The groundwater regime is much less developed than surface waters. Most agreements are between countries and apply to specific waters, as opposed to offering global regulation, and very few are devoted specifically to ground waters. It was not until 2009 that the UN moved to develop provisions to the 1992 Convention on the Protection and Use of Transboundary Watercourses and International Lakes. The provisions are guidelines rather than regulations. They call on countries to take measures to avoid harming, through contamination or depletion of groundwater supplies, and to cooperate on water management (United Nations Economic Commission for Europe [UNECE] 2014). The 1992 convention also has protocols providing for protection of human health in managing transboundary water supplies (UNECE 2000).

A GLOBAL VIEW: AIR POLLUTION

One of the most important environmental success stories is "getting the lead out" of gasoline globally. Car companies incorporated lead (tetraethyl lead) as their gasoline additive for two main reasons: lower cost and alcohol prohibition in the United States. By 1924, people were already calling it "looney gas" because it killed production workers in the first production factories. In 1925, scientists warned that its public health effects were serious and would not show up for years to come. By 1970, there were as many as 250,000 lead poisoning cases a year in the United States. Through the 1970s, Europe and then the United States started to replace lead in gasoline, perhaps primarily because it was not compatible with the catalytic converters being installed in cars to combat air pollution rather than the health effects. Nevertheless, by 2013, nearly every country had phased lead out of gasoline.

Air pollution success stories are few and far between. Outdoor air pollution accounts for 3.3 million premature deaths every year (Lelieveld et al. 2015). The heaviest burden of mortality is in the developing world, primarily in Asia, particularly China and India. The Lelieveld et al. (2015) study is one of the most comprehensive and explicit studies in linking fine particulate matter (PM2.5) and ozone (O_3) and their emission source categories to the burden of premature death. Air pollution is linked to chronic obstructive pulmonary disease, acute lower respiratory illness, cerebrovascular disease, ischemic heart disease, and lung cancer. The categories of source emissions, ranked from first to last globally, include residential and commercial energy, agriculture, power generation, industry, natural sources (sulfur and nitrogen

CONSIDER THIS
A TOOL FOR TERROR

The strategy of ISIS (Islamic State of Iraq and Syria) to amass power and money through the control of oil fields and refineries is well publicized. ISIS's strategic use of water is less well known. In Syria and Iraq, the control of water may be more critical than the control of oil.

In 2014, ISIS captured Mosul Dam, a critical source of energy in Iraq. With the help of U.S. air support, Kurdish fighters were able to recapture it. They tried to capture Haditha Dam but failed. In Fallujah, ISIS successfully controlled the dam, using it to cut off water and cause flooding in districts with Christians, Kurds, and Shiites. Even after ISIS left some villages, it still controlled the water by turning off and on electricity needed to draw water from wells (Ramaswami 2014; Shapiro 2014).

from volcanic activity, lightning, forest fires, decay, particulate matter from airborne desert dust), and land traffic. Source emission rankings vary by countries' level of development and particular circumstances such as regulations and the importance of each economic sector.

Not all particulates are equally toxic. The Lelieveld et al. (2015) study treats the carbonaceous particles and sulfates, nitrates, and crustal particles such as ash and dust from the earth's crust as of equal toxicity. The researchers ran a secondary study treating the carbonaceous particles as more toxic and found that their risk factor increased. Vulnerability as measured by premature mortality is high in developed and developing countries. The 10 countries where people are most vulnerable are China, India, Pakistan, Bangladesh, Nigeria, Russia, the United States, Indonesia, Ukraine, and Vietnam. Germany and Japan fall within the top 15.

The major sources of particles and pollutants in the air vary by region and level of development. Some sources are natural, while others are humanly caused. Desertification and drought might be considered "natural" sources of particles and pollutants in the air. Both, however, are exacerbated by climate change and constitute, in part, a manufactured risk. If these impacts of climate change increase, they increase the risk from "natural" sources even as we decrease those from energy generation.

Developed countries reduced their levels of many, but not all, air pollutants. In just a few days in January 2016, several streets in London had already surpassed their annual limit for nitrogen dioxide emissions. Due to this and other pollutants, 29,000 people in Britain die prematurely every year (Vidal and Helm 2016). Agriculture, however, is the primary source of air pollution in Europe.

In the United States, lead and lead-related hazardous toxicants remain a primary source of air pollution. In 2003, close to 1,250 million tons of lead and lead compounds were released into the air. This dropped to about 400, or by 65 percent, in 2014. Metal and metal mining account for most of the release in the United States (EPA 2016b).

As countries develop, so does pollution. Few countries have regulations in place, and measurements are hard to come by. WHO measures outdoor pollution in Africa by satellite data, inventories of pollution sources, air current modeling, and occasional ground monitors.

The global morbidity and mortality rates due to air pollution are high:

- *Indoor smoke,* primarily from the use of solid fuels in domestic cooking and heating, kills an estimated 1.6 million people annually due to respiratory diseases.

- *Urban air pollution* generated by vehicles, industries, and energy production kills approximately 800,000 people annually.

- *Lead exposure* kills more than 230,000 people per year and causes cognitive effects in one third of all children globally. More than 97 percent of those affected live in the developing world.

- *Unintentional poisonings* kill 355,000 people globally each year. In developing countries, where two thirds of these deaths occur, such poisonings are strongly associated with excessive exposure to, and inappropriate use of, toxic chemicals and pesticides present in occupational and/or domestic environments. (WHO 2016a)

LAND DEGRADATION

Land resources and the ecoservices that they provide are dwindling. In just the last half century, half of the world's wetlands have been lost, 80 percent of grasslands are suffering from soil degradation, and 20 percent of drylands are close to becoming deserts. Every minute of every day, 28 hectares of forest is lost (World Bank n.d.).

Land is degraded through many mechanisms. Chemical contamination from air pollution enters soil through acid rain and as particulates. Salinity from rising sea levels makes vegetation impossible. Direct release of toxins into the land from mining, manufacturing, and energy production into landfills or other storage is another mechanism. Unsustainable agricultural practices rob the soil of vital nutrients, leaving soils infertile. Overgrazing strips land of vegetation and packs soil, preventing rebound. At worst, these end up in tragedies such as the Dust Bowl of the 1930s that killed hundreds with the "brown plague" and forced millions out of their homes or flooding and mudslides, which have killed millions more.

Land use and the pressures on land change as people's needs change. Population pressures and improving the life chances and standard of living for people the world over will continue to pressure ecosystems, including land resources and land ecosystem services.

Industrialization and Toxic Sites

Industrialization benefitted many people through improvements in the standards of living. The costs have been high; air pollution was perhaps the first noticed. Pollution of land came as a later realization. All over the world, but particularly in the most developed countries—European countries, the United States, and Russia—millions of old industrial sites contaminated with cyanide, lead, and other heavy metals pose hazards to animals, plants, and people. Some have been remediated; many more, approximately 100,000, are in need of immediate remediation.

The Toxic Site Identification Program (TSIP) identifies and studies toxic sites in the developing world. The TSIP has identified more than 3,000 sites that affect 54 million people. A total of 84 sites have been remediated, improving the health conditions of 4.2 million people. Another 12 were in progress of being remediated as of 2015.

Solid waste management presents a potential dilemma or a potential opportunity for rapidly urbanizing countries. Within the next 20 years, half of Africans will live in cities. As urbanization increases, so will the amount of waste generated. With an infrastructure already strained, solid waste generation is expected to double in low-income cities in Africa. Similar problems are expected in Asia as well. While this is an acute health risk, it is also a sustainable development opportunity. Waste recycling is already a source of income for many of the poorest in developing countries. Six African universities are investigating how best to establish environmentally sound waste management while providing secure well-paying jobs for the "waste recyclers." This requires technology transfer from the developed countries, private sector investment, and strengthening institutional capacity (UNEP 2016).

The greatest volume of waste in the United States is released into the land, 65 percent in 2014; the largest share of these disposals, about 70 percent, is from metal mining. The overall volume of land disposals increased from 2003 to 2014; however, if metal mining is excluded, the overall volume decreased. Metal mining is among the most toxic of industrial activities. In the United States, the EPA identified tens of thousands of sites in the country needing remediation, with more than 1,300 being high priority (Pure Earth 2015).

THE FORESTS

The earth's forests have inspired poetry, art, philosophy, religion, and science for thousands of years. They are home to innumerable species of plants and animals, many of which we have yet to discover. We call them the "lungs" of the planet because they "breathe in" carbon dioxide (CO_2) and, along with water and energy from sunlight, convert it to energy-storing rich sugars, starches, and oxygen, which they "exhale."

The forests, like other green plants, are essential for our survival. Their ecosystem services include much more than the alchemy that they perform on our CO_2 emissions. Forests are one of the greatest reservoirs of species biodiversity, housing 90 percent of terrestrial biodiversity. They purify both water and air, holding 650 billion tons of carbon, more than is in the atmosphere (GRID–Arendal 2014). More than 1.5 billion people in the Dominican Republic, Peru, the Democratic Republic of the Congo, and elsewhere depend on the forests for everything that they need—fuel, medicines, and subsistence income. Forests are the focus of their material and non-material cultures. The forests even protect us from extreme weather. Tropical storms killed thousands in 2004 in Haiti in mudslides and flooding. In the Dominican Republic and Puerto Rico, the storms were not as devastating. In southeastern Haiti, the source of the flooding, mountain forests, had been stripped nearly bare and afforded no protection. By comparison, the forests in Puerto Rico and the Dominican Republic had been restored as the countries moved from agriculture to industry. The forests reduced soil erosion and flooding, saving lives (Aide and Grau 2004).

Forests are particularly important to women and children. Forests are a rich source of protein (bush meat) and other nutrients children need for proper growth and development. Forest products are used for sustenance and are traded in informal markets. Women's collection and trade activities in this regard provide them with a more equal footing in the household. This household-level activity fights poverty and should be encouraged through legislation to protect the rights of the small-scale forest users. Economically, the forests are worth billions of dollars in timber, pharmaceuticals, and paper (GRID–Arendal 2009; World Bank n.d.).

The quality of life for everyone diminishes with the degradation and destruction of forests. The many different definitions of forest degradation make it difficult to measure how much or to compare rates globally. Different nations, environmental groups, and intergovernmental organizations use different indicators such as the composition and quantity of biomass, timber volume, fragmentation, and/or crown coverage; others focus on function such as carbon sequestration, soil protection, and/or biodiversity conservation. Harmonization of definitions would support better international conservation efforts and enhance assessment (Ghazoul et al. 2015; GRID–Arendal 2009; van Lierop et al. 2015). The two main sources of data on deforestation, the Food and Agriculture Organization (FAO) and the University of Maryland, agree that, however measured, tropical forests are disappearing at an alarming rate (GRID–Arendal 2014). However, all of the various indicators are important and point to deterioration and diminishing forest ecosystem services.

There is unanimity concerning the interrelated causes of forest degradation. Human activity has taken a direct toll through urban expansion, unsustainable logging, clear cutting for agriculture, and use of wood for fuel. Air pollution, forest fires, diseases, and pests also take a heavy toll. Despite successful reforestation programs in Europe, China, and the United States, forest loss continues in poor countries (Sloan and Sayer 2015). About 20,000 hectares of forest is lost every day; that is 835 hectares every hour (GRID–Arendal 2009). From 1990 to 2015, total forest areas decreased from 4.28 to 3.99 billion hectares (FAO 2015). Planted forests are meeting some of the demand for forest products, but pests, pathogens, and climate changes—in particular extreme events such as droughts, floods, fires, and cyclones—will affect planted forest health, requiring continued work on forest management and pollution and climate control (Payn et al. 2015).

Air pollution enters the forests as dry deposits or as washed out of the air by rain. It causes damage to animal life and vegetation, from minor damage to destruction of entire forests. Some of the harmful effects have been known from the beginnings of the Industrial Revolution. Trees absorb pollution through leaves and roots, inhibiting their capacity to produce or absorb nutrients. Sulfur dioxide (SO_2), mono nitrogen oxides (NO_x), O_3, aluminum, and other pollutants all harm trees. SO_2 and NO_x combine with atmospheric moisture to form acid rain. With damaged leaves, trees have less capacity to conduct photosynthesis and create nutrients and are weakened, making them more vulnerable to disease and pests. Acids reaching the soil soak in and displace nutrients such as calcium and magnesium, which are washed away from the rooting zone. In soil, they release aluminum toxic to animals, plants, and trees while also depriving the trees of nutrition (National Oceanic and Atmospheric Administration 2008; Tomlinson 1983). Where exposure is prolonged, such as in high mountain regions often surrounded by fog, trees are particularly susceptible. They grow more slowly or may stop growing and die.

While regulations limit SO_2 emissions in most of Europe and North America, in China, India, and other developing countries SO_2 emissions still cause widespread damage. As natural gas and oil production increases, gas flares and "sour gas" are growing problems. Gas flares burn off waste gases in various forms of oil production, petroleum processing, and natural gas drilling. Gas flares emit CO_2 and, if not flared efficiently, waste gases (SO_2, NO_x, and carbon monoxide [CO]), particulates, VOCs, hydrogen sulfides (H_2Ss), and other contaminants are released. In Nigeria, the acidification of air, water, and soil in combination with the hot climate degrades the forests and other vegetation and even reduces the nutritional values of crops (Ajugwo 2013).

More than half of the world's forests are tropical and sub-tropical forests located in Latin America, Central Africa, and Southeast Asia and Oceania. About one third are circumpolar taiga, the boreal coniferous forests of north-ern-most lands, and just over 10 percent are temperate in North America, Europe, and parts of Asia (GRID-Arendal and United Nations Environment Programme 2009). Because the decline of temperate forests has been reversed, this chapter concentrates on tropical forests.

The Tropical Forests

The drivers of degradation and deforestation vary among regions and forest types. The Amazon is the world's largest tropical forest, 60 percent of the world's forest. Its richness is unsurpassed. It is habitat for more species than any other place on earth; 30,000 plant species, 4,200 butterfly species, 2,500 fish species and likely many more species still to be discovered. Approximately 385 different ethnic groups, speaking more than 300 languages, make their homes there. Devastation in the Amazon has been on an equally large scale, having lost 216,000 km^2—almost equivalent in size to the United Kingdom—from 2000 to 2010.

The Amazon rainforest spans several countries—Brazil, Peru, Surinam, Guyana, Bolivia, Ecuador, Colombia, and Venezuela. Brazil and Peru contain the most. The rate of deforestation in Brazil decreased significantly from 2006 to 2010 in comparison with 2001 to 2005 and earlier. The primary drivers have been ranching and industrial-scale soy farming. In Peru, little deforestation occurred, but degradation due to legal and illegal logging is widespread. There are also oil and gas concessions and wildcat gold digging, suggesting that the deforestation will continue at its current rate or increase. Conflict over forest resources has plagued Bolivia and Colombia, which suffer a higher than average deforestation rate for the area. Ecuador, Surinam, and Guyana have not experienced much defor-estation. Hopefully, expansions of gold mining there will not change that (GRID–Arendal 2014).

Central Africa hosts the second largest rainforest. Its riches rival those of the Amazon. It is home to 75 million people, nearly all of whom depend on it for food, medicine, and their livelihoods. Rich in fish and bush meat, the Congo supplies protein for 30 million people. Researchers regu-larly discover new species, but 10,000 plants, 1,000 birds, and 400 mammal species are already on record. About 500 plant species and 85 animal species are harvested, along with other forest products, providing for people's liveli-hoods whether they are consumed directly or traded. The Congo holds 20 percent of the world's tropical forests and stores about 25 percent of the carbon stored in forests.

Data for deforestation in Central Africa is not reliable. Measurements are difficult, and the sources vary signifi-cantly. There is agreement on the need for better moni-toring and that deforestation is likely to increase. In West Africa and Madagascar, the forests are already severely degraded. In the Congo Basin, there has been much less deforestation and degradation; large areas of the forest are still intact. The severity of the region's violence may have been the forest's safeguard, keeping large industrial enterprises away. As prices of forest commodities, from precious minerals to food and fuel increase, the area may come under greater threat. Demand for palm oil and cash crops may lead the way to unsustainable forest develop-ment and deforestation (GRID–Arendal 2014).

The rainforests of Southeast Asia and Oceania are the world's most devastated, deforested by logging, rubber, and palm oil. Like the indigenous people of the Congo and Amazon, the forests provide them with all of life's needs. With traditional knowledge of plants and animals and cultivation, those living on one of the reserves con-tinue to maintain traditional culture and preserve the for-est. While the forest in the protected reserve is thick and diverse, plantations can be seen on neighboring hills.

Drivers of Deforestation and Degradation

Drivers of deforestation and degradation[12] vary from type of forest and the region. When roads are built in an area for mining or logging, they open new areas and "invite" agriculture. When decimated of trees by logging, an area may be converted to agricultural use. As demand for agricultural and forest products increases, better forest management is critical to ensuring that the riches of the forests and their valuable ecoservices are preserved.

Agriculture

Agriculture is the proximate cause of 80 percent of deforestation globally. Large-scale commercial farm-ing is the main driver in Latin America and about one third of deforestation in Asia and Africa (Kissinger et al. 2012). Industrial-level soybean production in Brazil accounted for 25 percent of Brazil's deforestation from 2000 to 2005. In Brazil, Argentina, Bolivia, and Para-guay, millions of hectares of forest are left seasonally dry for soy production, most of which goes to China for animal feed (Aide and Grau 2004). As soy production expands, often on land used for cattle pasture, it pushes cattle farther into the forests, causing new devastation (GRID–Arendal 2014).

In Southeast Asia, palm oil is the key driver of deforestation. It is the cheapest oil in the world and is very versatile—used in foods, cosmetics, animal feed, and biofuels. It is not surprising that palm oil accounts for one third of the world's oil consumption or that production increased 43 percent globally in just 20 years. Already devastated by palm oil plantations, Indonesia plans to double palm oil production (GRID–Arendal 2014).

With the exception of a few countries, commercial enterprises are responsible for more degradation in Latin America and Southeast Asia than subsistence. Commercial enterprises are heavily invested in cattle ranching, fuel wood collection, charcoal production, and livestock grazing in these regions. Timber logging, commercial forest extraction, accounts for 70 percent of degradation (Kissinger et al. 2012).

Subsistence agriculture is also a problem; it accounts for 30 to 35 percent of deforestation in Central Africa and subtropical Asia (Kissinger et al. 2012). Although subsistence slash-and-burn agriculture was practiced for thousands of years without harm to the environment, population pressures make it unsustainable and it is destroying forests. Other forms of subsistence degradation include fuel wood collection, charcoal production, and livestock grazing. Including these factors, subsistence factors account for 50 percent or more of the degradation across Central Africa.

About 40 percent of harvested wood goes to making paper and paperboard. Latin America and Southeast Asia have been hardest hit, responsible for 70 to 80 percent of degradation, but logging concessions are increasing in Central Africa. While timber plantations on degraded land outside of forests would relieve pressure on the forests, often they are placed within the forests on logged or degraded lands. This increases, rather than relieves, the pressure on forests.

Population growth, economic growth, and the development of export economies are indirect drivers of deforestation and degradation. These are likely to increase demand for forest products and forest land use until 2050 and perhaps beyond—increasing demand for food, including oils, meat, and feed for livestock. Demand for metals has been increasing, giving rise not only to industrial mining, especially in Africa, but also to small-scale and illegal mining (Kissinger et al. 2012). Global shortages of land may make forests even more attractive to

commercial enterprises. In Ghana, 61.6 percent of land considered suitable for agriculture is already acquired by foreign direct investment; in Ethiopia, it is 42.9 percent (Kissinger et al. 2012).

Violent conflict, poor governance, and poor infrastructure preserved much of the Congo Basin forests from commercial enterprises. Reconciling current and anticipated pressures for growth and development with forest preservation and the needs of indigenous people while curtailing commercial exploitation is essential to the health of the region and globe and requires international assistance. This provides people in the basin with opportunity to pursue green economic growth, coupling economic policy with sustainable practice (Megevand 2013).

THE GLOBAL CHEMICAL REGIME

United Nations Conventions

Chemicals and waste are regulated globally by a series of conventions.[13] The most significant of these are the Basel, Rotterdam, Stockholm, and Minamata Conventions, their accompanying protocols, and the Strategic Approach to International Chemicals Management.

The Basel Convention is arguably the most significant agreement with respect to disposal of chemicals. Adopted in 1989, conveners fashioned it as a response to the discovery that richer countries exported toxic waste to Africa, Eastern Europe, and other developing countries, taking advantage of cheaper disposal. Its provisions set out safeguards and standards for the safe disposition of hazardous materials. It also established guidelines for "trade in waste" agreements among countries. The treaty prohibits export of waste to Antarctica and countries not party to the convention. It allows agreements between and among countries for the import and export of waste providing that the agreements are, at minimum, as environmentally safe as Basel requirements. It also provides for training and technology transfers among nations to improve waste management and decrease waste byproducts (UNEP 2011).

The Rotterdam Convention, adopted in 1998 and entered into force in 2004, provides stipulations for trade in banned or severely restricted pesticides and industrial chemicals. The chemicals to which it applies are listed in Annex III of the convention and are updated regularly. The convention tries to ensure that there is transparency

CONSIDER THIS
LIVING IN THE RAINFOREST—ITOMBWE PROTECTED AREA, CONGO

Indigenous peoples living in the forest and the local communities rely on the forest. As one villager in Bionga, Democratic Republic of the Congo, explained, they have everything they need there. "The air in the forest is different from in the village, it's better for the body. There is a closeness, a special psychological dimension about being in the forest. We feel at ease here, and whoever is used to it will always have the urge to come back to the forest" (GRID–Arendal 2014).

Their knowledge protected the forests for centuries. In the Congo, their wisdom is guiding many of the conservation efforts. "Pombo" is the period of gestation for forest animals. Hunting and trapping are forbidden. From February to April, dumping chemicals into the rivers is forbidden as fish are moving from rivers to the streams to spawn. Sacred forest and river sites are preserves where no human activity is allowed. Local forest communities are insisting that these rules be respected as conservation laws are established. These commonsense rules, determined and enforced by the local chief or "Mwami," are a model for other Congolese communities. Integrating local communities—often indigenous peoples displaced by conflict or edict—is a right of people who have lived on and conserved the land not just in the Congo but everywhere (GRID–Arendal 2014).

On the other side of the world in a village in the Morowali forest in Indonesia, a formally educated woman who had tried town life found towns noisy and polluted. She echoed the sentiment of the Bionga villager, "Here inside the Morowali forest I've got what I need and life is better" (GRID–Arendal 2014).

in trade agreements concerning these pollutants. Its two primary provisions are "prior informed consent" (PIC) and information exchange. PIC is the mechanism through which a country notifies that it will or will not receive shipments of a particular chemical listed by the convention and ensures that exporters comply with the decisions and conditions of trade. The information exchange serves to provide up-to-date information concerning potentially hazardous chemicals, chemicals that governments have banned domestically, and chemicals causing problems in developing countries or countries in transition. All parties to the treaty receive this information regularly. If an exporting country has banned a chemical domestically, it must inform importing countries of the ban and the reasons for the ban before it ships any quantity of the chemical. This enables countries to make sound decisions. It prevents richer nations from dumping chemicals it does not itself use such as happened with the export of DDT to poor nations.

The Stockholm Convention remains the most important international agreement specific to the production, use, and control of POP chemicals in the environment. Adopted in 2001, it now has 152 signatory countries. Most (but not all) signatories, including the United States, Israel, and Italy, have ratified it. When enacted in 2001, it listed 12 primary POPs for elimination or at least reduction of their production, use, and release. Most developed countries, including the United States, no longer produce the original 12 POPs. Developing nations have more recently taken strong action to eliminate them. As science advances, more POPs have come under the terms of the convention. Another 9 chemicals were added in 2009.[14] These are pesticides, industrial chemicals, and byproducts.

Sound management of chemicals and waste is essential for sustainability. Not all countries have the resources to address the integrated approach needed on their own. The "special program" instituted by the UN provides for financial assistance to nations to incorporate sustainability with respect to chemicals and waste into their national development plans. Developing nations must strengthen their institutional capacity to develop, monitor, and enforce the treaties. A special program of the UN provides financial assistance to developing countries, coordinates aid to avoid duplication, and identifies which programs to assist.

Regional Agreements

There are many regional agreements affecting use and disposal of chemicals into the environment. Some of the regional treaties, such as the 1979 Geneva Convention on Long Range Transboundary Air Pollution in Europe, are components of regimes within UN agencies. Each of the regional economic commissions[15] has environmental agreements relevant to member states.

Europe began limiting pesticides regionally in the 1980s. In 1992, the EU began reviewing pesticides in use and toughened its regulations, requiring risk assessments and approvals of pesticides across the EU rather than country-by-country regulation. The new regulations alone resulted in many chemicals being discontinued by their manufacturers. Some were discontinued because they were obsolete, but others were discontinued because it was known by the manufacturers that they would not pass scrutiny. Approval for use does not mean that a chemical is safe. There are maximum residue standards that must be adhered to, especially in the cases of food products.

National Regulations

We like to think that all of the chemicals we use in our homes and gardens, all that are in our personal care products, and all that are released into our environment by industries and agriculture are tested and regulated for safety to humans and the environment.

In the United States, the Toxic Substances Control Act (TSCA) was not legislated until 1976 as the damaging effects of many chemicals were just becoming known, 25 years after the liberal use of pesticides and other toxins began. Under the act, pesticides and pharmaceuticals must be tested, but most industrial chemicals and chemicals in our personal care products do not need to be cleared for safety. They must be tested only if the EPA can show that there is a potential risk. However, if the EPA does not act within 90 days of notification of the product, it cannot require testing. The EPA met this timeline only five times since the act became law: for PCBs, dioxin, hexavalent chromium, asbestos, and CFCs. In some of these cases, the ban is only for certain uses. As a result, nearly all of the 85,000 industrial chemicals in use have never been tested (Urbina 2013).

Several states—California, Maine, Maryland, Minnesota, New York, Oregon, Vermont, and Washington—acted on their own to ban chemicals they deemed hazardous. In 2016, the U.S. Congress passed legislation strengthening the TSCA to allow the EPA to require testing and impose user fees on industry to expand the testing program. States will still be able to impose their own rules by way of a federal waiver. The bill[16] passed with bipartisan support and support from the chemical industry. Environmental groups were split in their support because the bill provides a window of 3.5 years for the federal review before a state may impose its own restrictions. During this time, states are not able to pass regulations protecting their citizens as they see fit (Eilperin and Fears 2016).

Canada's Environmental Protection Agency (CEPA) adopted legislation in 1999 that required an inventory of all chemicals used in Canada. CEPA completed an inventory of 23,000 chemicals in 2006 and developed a management plan for 200 (Chemical Hazards and Alternatives Toolbox [ChemHat] n.d.).

The European Chemical Agency, an agency of the EU, registers and regulates chemicals used or imported into the EU. REACH (Registration, Evaluation, and Authorization of Chemicals) legislation that took effect in 2007 requires manufacturers and users of chemicals to register their chemicals and list potential adverse health effects of each one. Chemicals of special concern will be subject to further authorization (Breithaupt 2006). China developed policies similar to REACH (ChemHat n.d.).

Most other developing societies are further behind. A GEF report on chemicals in developing countries and "countries with economies in transition" found chemical management issues in these countries to be complicated by poverty, lack of regulation or enforcement, accidents, illegal manufacturing, transport, and uses of chemicals (Bouwman 2012).

Better harmonization of the regulation of chemicals and adhering to the highest standards benefits all societies. On the one hand, better regulation means a healthier environment. On the other hand, better regulation opens up markets to societies that otherwise would be closed to them.

In 2015, the United Nations Development Programme (UNDP) worked to help 65 nations develop regulations and national implementation plans in accordance with the Stockholm Convention. For example, in Turkey, UNDP helped to develop national regulation and policy as well as programs to eliminate current POP stockpiles and wastes, high-concentration PCBs, and PCB-containing equipment stockpiles, build sound management practices for future PCB stockpiles, reduce unintended POP release, and other sustainable, environmentally sound practices. UNDP modeled these on best practices and trained personnel in best environmental practices and techniques (Ministry of Environment and Urbanization, Republic of Turkey 2015).

CONSIDER THIS
SOURCE REDUCTION

Ozone in the stratosphere, as opposed to ground-level ozone, protects us from some of the harmful effects of ultraviolet radiation. Chlorofluorocarbons (CFCs) are one of the primary substances responsible for depletion of the ozone layer. They have a variety of uses as varied as aerosols and refrigeration. CFCs are on the list of substances to be eliminated under the Montreal Protocol. Using a source reduction strategy, hydrochlorofluorocarbons (HCFCs) replaced CFCs in most uses. This was one of the most successful environmental campaigns, saving the ozone layer. Unfortunately, HCFCs have a very high global warming potential. Most developed nations have already banned them. They are now listed under the Montreal Protocol and are to be discontinued in 2030.

ESCAPING THE TOXIC: LIVING GREEN

It is often overlooked that what is good for the people's health and the health of the environment may also be good for business, industry, and economic growth. We all are probably familiar with the mantra "Reduce, Reuse, Recycle" for conservation and pollution control in our daily lives. That applies to agriculture, services, and industry as well.

Green chemicals, green construction, and green energy seem to be just such smart strategies. Green chemistry is the catch-all terminology for capturing sustainable development strategies that reduce the level of toxins and toxicants in the environment, conserve resources, and reduce emissions of greenhouse gases. Below are a few waste release and reduction examples.

Industrial Source Reduction

Source reduction can combat chemical pollution and climate change using a few basic strategies:

- Substituting non-toxic and non-polluting alternatives for hazardous substances

- Using less of a hazardous substance in a product or process

- Substituting lighter-weight materials to reduce transportation pollution

- Substituting reusable products for disposable ones

- Replacing products, such as our high-tech devices, less often

- Using recycled and recyclable materials

As people the world over are becoming more environmentally aware, demand for greener and less toxic products and processes is increasing. This demand ranges from consumers in rich European countries looking for less toxic personal care products to farmers in developing countries looking for less toxic fertilizers and pest control strategies. Greener regulatory standards will close markets to products that do not conform. After three years of attempts, The TSCA received an update from the U.S. Congress in 2016. Although many health and safety groups argue that it is not as strong as it needs to be, it affords some additional protections for the public. One key provision is that any group who will be disproportionally exposed (such as workers) or vulnerable (such as children) to a pollutant needs to be protected, not just the "average" person.

A University of Massachusetts and Blue Green Alliance study (Heintz and Pollin 2011) proposed that green chemistry could be leveraged to create thousands of good jobs and promote better health for people and the environment. Employment in the industry (excluding pharmaceuticals) fell 38 percent from 1992 to 2010 even as productivity increased. That represents a loss of 300,000 jobs. To increase employment, demand for products will need to increase and the average number of jobs for a given amount of production will need to increase. If only 20 percent of petrochemical-based plastics were replaced with bio-based plastics, 104,000 new jobs would be created even if output remained the same.

Products redesigned to reduce or eliminate polluting and toxic substances must perform as well as those they replace. Household chemicals, building materials plastics and synthetic fibers, industrial cleaners, personal care products, and pesticides are among those where demand for greener products is high and potential is great.

A CLOSER LOOK
SOURCE REDUCTION

Significant reduction in toxic waste can be achieved through source reduction strategies. For various reasons, not all companies have invested in them.

FIGURE 13.6   Source Reduction Activities and Estimated Decrease in Waste, 2014

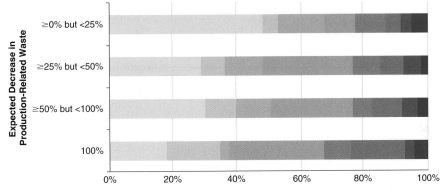

Source: Environmental Protection Agency (2016b).

FIGURE 13.7   Reported Barriers to Source Reduction, 2014

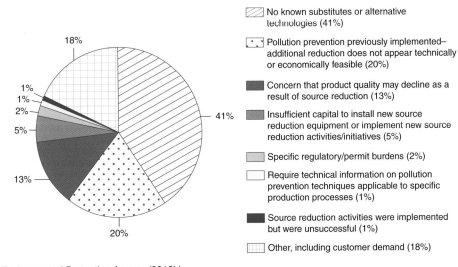

Source: Environmental Protection Agency (2016b).

Through a number of legislative initiatives, California prioritized the green chemistry industry. By creating a clearinghouse of information for consumers and strengthening the regulatory function of its state's EPA, it motivated companies to fill the demand for less hazardous products. One company that developed a stainless-steel water bottle to replace plastic increased employment sixfold. Two computer giants eliminated brominated flame retardants, which helps them to compete in global markets. A pharmaceutical company reduced the solvent in one of its medications and cut costs as well as hazardous waste (Heintz and Pollin 2011). These products not only are "green" but also improved employment and company market share.

Source Reduction

Source reduction is not new but is not used to its fullest extent. Between 1991 and 2012, companies reporting to the TRI initiated 370,000 source reduction programs. These programs were researched and evaluated by Abt Associates[17] and the EPA (Ranson et al. 2015). In the year when they were implemented, source reduction programs, as a whole, averaged a 9 to 16 percent reduction in releases of the targeted chemicals.[18] The effect lasted for five years. The researchers classified the strategies into eight categories, finding considerable variation in effectiveness among them. Inventory control had no effect, and good operating practices had only a small effect. Significant reduction in releases came from raw material modifications (20 percent), cleaning and degreasing (15 percent), and product modifications (13 percent). In evaluating the overall effect of the programs, the research concluded that without these strategies, releases would have totaled 51.6 to 61.3 billion pounds rather than the actual 46.9 billion pounds (Ranson et al. 2015).

In 2014, 13 percent of TRI-reporting facilities initiated new source reduction programs and 87 percent did not. Not having an alternative material or technology was the most frequent reason cited. A nickel–cadmium battery manufacturer, for example, reported not being able to find a substitute for the nickel (Ranson et al. 2015). In 2013, the European Parliament instituted a ban on mercury in button batteries to begin in the autumn of 2015 and a nickel–cadmium battery ban to begin in December 2016. Once current supplies were exhausted, they would be allowed only in emergency systems and lighting. They believe this will spawn innovation as well as reduce toxic pollutants in the environment (Chatain 2013).

The Problems of Plastics

Plastics date back to the 1800s, but modern plastics did not appear on the scene until after World War II and were still quite a novelty until the late 1970s when low-density polyethylene made mass production possible and cheap. Over the past 50 years, production of plastics has continued to rise unabated despite the pollution problems they present. Over the past 20 years, the world's production of plastics increased on average 5 percent every year. After food and paper, plastics are the major component of urban waste—plastic packaging, plastic bottles, plastic bags, and a multitude of other goods. Rapid urbanization and development is driving consumption of plastics faster in developing countries than in developed ones. In Dhaka, Bangladesh, 140 tons of plastic waste are thrown away every day. Developing countries are least equipped to deal with this volume of waste. Although some is picked out through the informal sector, newer lighter wastes are seldom worth the trouble. Left in landfills, they not only take up valuable space but also create anaerobic pockets and aid in the formation of methane, a potent greenhouse gas (International Environmental Technology Centre [IETC] n.d.).

In 2013, 299 million tons of plastic were produced globally. UNEP estimates that 22 to 43 percent goes to landfills. About 10 to 20 tons go into the ocean each year, where a total of about 268,940 tons are currently floating. This bears an enormous cost. Plastic entraps marine life. Like miniature cargo ships, it transports microbes, algae, fish, and other marine life to regions where they upset the local ecosystems. It pollutes beaches. Altogether, it accounts for a U.S. $13 billion loss to marine systems every year. Only 26 percent of post-consumer plastic in Europe is recycled, and only 9 percent is recycled in the United States. Plastic collected for recycling is often shipped off to developing countries that have less regulation. China receives the majority of the waste. Although it began to implement controls in 2010, much is still processed in family enterprises or incinerated for energy by industries that afford no environmental protections (Gourmelon 2015).

In Europe and the United States, packaging is the major source of consumer plastics. Reducing our reliance, such as by forgoing plastic bags and using non-disposables at the grocery store and finding better anti-theft measures than enlarging the packaging, is a good start. Turning the waste into a resource is another; that is the basic strategy of the "circular economy." Plastics are made from petroleum, so it makes sense to turn plastics back into fuel. To make recycling plastics economically viable, they must be converted to a resource in high demand. To address this, the IETC, a division of UNEP, instituted two pilot projects in Thailand and one in the Philippines where plastics would be converted into fuels using environmentally safe strategies (IETC n.d.).

In India, the government mandates that road developers mix plastics into asphalt. Plastic has the added advantages of making the roads water resistant and better adapted to weather changes. It can reduce the cost of roads for developers, and plastic recycling can be a revenue stream for municipalities that sell plastic to road developers (Arora 2015). A Dutch company is planning to build roads entirely of plastic recycled from oceans and incineration plants. The all-plastic road can survive temperatures as high as 80° and as low as −40° Celsius. Its lifespan is estimated at 50 years while unaffected by corrosion, thereby requiring less upkeep. Plastic roads will also help to eliminate pollution from asphalt, which adds 1.6 million tons, or 2 percent, of transport emissions of CO_2 into the atmosphere every year (Saini 2015).

No Waste: Creating a Circular Economy

The current economy can be summarized briefly as "We take, we make, we use, we throw away." The "circular economy" is a circular supply chain promoting sustainable use of materials. One person's waste is another person's resource. A circular economy can reduce the use of source materials and waste. Europe "loses" 600 million tons of waste every year that could be made into 600 million tons of resources (European Commission n.d.).

The ideas are simple. Many of the products that people use have relatively short lives before they end up being disposed of in a landfill or incinerated. The goals of the circular economy are the following:

- No waste
- Make products that last longer, with parts disassembled and repaired

- Provide recycling streams for materials, including toxic substances
- Capture materials from waste and find a use or recycle them to make new products
- The more a material can be reused or recycled, the better, prolonging the life of resources if not actual products

In some circular economy strategies, consumers become "users." They do not own but rather rent or share durable products. After being used, products are returned for recycling or reuse of the product, its parts, or its material composition (World Economic Forum [WEF] 2014). This requires a change in mindset that seems to be developing, as is evident in car leasing and short-term car and bike rentals. Airbnb is a variation on the sharing theme. Bought products would also need to have provisions for return built in.

> *Have you bought jeans at H&M? If you have, they may have been part of the circular economy. H&M, a Swedish company, buys end-of-use jeans. They ship them to Pakistan, where the material is disassembled, spun into new fiber, and made into new jeans. (WEF 2014).*

Moving to a circular economy would require changes on the part of manufacturers as well. Making products that are easy to disassemble, to recover materials and parts, is a different approach to manufacturing. Many countries are already formalizing the concept. In the EU, plans for targets and regulations are being negotiated. The European Commission-suggested targets for circular economy implementation are to recycle 65 percent of municipal waste and 75 percent of packaging waste by 2030 (European Commission n.d.). A survey of 10,618 companies across the EU found that 70 percent are implementing circular economy strategies. The larger the company, the more likely it is to have a program—72 percent of small businesses in comparison with 89 percent of large businesses. About 50 percent of businesses are trying to reduce, reuse, or sell their waste. Fewer businesses, about 34 percent, are using less or recycled

CONSIDER THIS
PLANT CHICAGO

Question: How do an aquaponics fish vegetable farm, a brewery, a craft food business, an anaerobic digester, a power plant, and a bunch of flies all get along?

Answer: Just swell in a collaborative circular economy in which one person's waste is another person's resource.

Spent grains from the brewery feed the fish, whose waste fertilizes the produce. These are used to make nutritious foods. Food waste feeds an anaerobic digester, which powers a heat and electricity generator. Food scraps also feed black flies, whose larvae are fed to the fish.

Bonus: A mushroom farm grows inside an old repurposed refrigerator.

Plant Chicago (n.d.) is a nonprofit organization (http://plantchicago.org).

---

materials, 19 percent are trying to reduce water consumption or to reuse wastewater, and 16 percent are trying renewables (Senet 2016).

The circular economy reduces the amount of new resources used, thereby providing a buffer from resource scarcity, price volatility, and political instability. A circular economy increases competitiveness by reducing material costs. It can create new jobs. The European Commission (n.d.) projects up to about 170,000 new jobs in the EU and a boost to GDP of 3 percent. Perhaps the most important benefits are the reduction in greenhouse gases by more than 500 million tons from 2015 to 2035, a reduction in pollutants, and reducing landfill emissions.

Economic savings of a circular economy are also significant. Each ton of clothing collected and sorted could generate U.S. $1,975 in revenue or a gross profit of $1,295 from reuse. Clothing can cascade down to being worn again, being made into upholstery stuffing, being made into insulation, or being recycled into yarn to make new fabrics. Circuitry in manufacturing from office machinery to automobiles could save up to $630 billion in one year in the EU alone (WEF 2014). There are billions of dollars at stake.

It may be that developing countries not far along the industrialization path will have an easier time in building a circular economy. The mindset of scarcity is one to which they are accustomed. Infrastructure can be designed from the beginning with a "waste out" target rather than be redesigned and outfitted. They can learn from the mistakes of the developed world. Conservation, "no till" agriculture, rice grown with less water (and more profit), and the dike–pond system used in China synergize land and water ecorelations to create food and bioenergy for the entire system and are "no waste" examples that are already in place. "Pay as you go" business models are increasing their presence in Africa, Asia, and South Africa, providing access to services, even electrification, without needing to own (Raksit 2015).

As urbanization continues, housing will be in high demand. Bamboo as a sustainable building material is already zero waste. Its distinct advantages as a building material in the developing world are that it is much faster growing than wood and uses less fossil fuel to grow, has no emissions compared with cement making, does not contribute to deforestation, and aids in combatting global warming because it is a super storehouse for carbon. Bamboo is well ventilated to provide zero energy cooling. It withstands earthquakes and can be built elevated to withstand flooding. Overcoming its stigma as a poor person's house is the major obstacle.

The WEF reports that social forces are aligning that make this the right time for the circular economy:

- Consumers are starting to favor services over ownership. Zip cars allow you to have a car when needed without the expenses of owning.

- Increasing urbanization should result in many cost reductions such as of asset sharing services, collecting and treating end-of-use materials, and more frequent waste collection, preventing leakage.

- Urbanization has potential for developing integrated systems that share resources and use one another's discarded materials or byproducts. An example is Plant Chicago (see box).

Finding alternatives to hazardous substances, reducing the resources that we use, and implementing strategies to turn waste into resources seems like a sensible way to live that allows the world's richest to improve the quality of life for everyone through sustainable development.

Managing and Reclaiming Wastewater

The water crisis is one of the most dire and dangerous threats that humans face. Inadequate treatment of wastewater not only exacerbates the problem but squanders a valuable resource. In South Africa, Cape Town faced a crisis that was unresolved as this was being written—running out of water. Predicting a "Day Zero" when water would run out, the city of 4 million faces turning off its running water taps, forcing residents to travel to distribution centers for fresh water. The potential for social unrest is high.

Leaky pipes and partisan squabbling worsened the crisis, but a once-in-a-century drought, too severe for the dams to handle, was at the root. Close by in the desert, Windhoek, Namibia—also ravaged by drought—has no water crisis. For 50 years (since 1968), Windhoek has recycled wastewater, removing the sewage and converting most of it into drinking-quality water. The technique used in Namibia is one among many uses that can convert wastewater into fresh water—at prices much lower than desalination. Not only did the water treatment avert water shortage crises, but the treatment reduced morbidity and mortality from waterborne disease.

In Orange County, California, where some communities are running out of water, one of the largest (and oldest) plants that converts sewage into drinking water feeds the treated water back into the groundwater supply, ultimately reaching about 70 percent of the Orange County population. As in Singapore, which also recycles wastewater, the reclaimed water exceeds health standards.

Water that is too "gray" is used for irrigation. Windhoek now recycles 80 percent of its wastewater. It does it as nature does—using bacteria. Even untreated, wastewater handled properly provides agricultural services. Used in irrigation, wastewater filters through the soil, improving soil fertility rather than introducing contamination downstream. Many farmers prefer wastewater because it saves fertilizer costs, being rich in nitrogen, phosphorus, and potassium (Corcoran et al. 2010).

Recycling water is more energy efficient. Pumping ground water as supplies diminish requires more energy. Transporting water over distances to regions where supplies have run out also requires energy. Recycling on-site eliminates or reduces both of these energy costs. Because water used for different purposes has different purity standards, recycling water to meet these lower standards—such as for irrigation where contaminants may be assets—energy is saved by reserving the highest cost treatments for drinking water.

SUMMARY

It is vital that the public recognize the dangers of chemical pollutants used on a daily basis in households and industrial processes. The use of chemicals and chemical compounds became widespread in the developed world before their toxicity was fully recognized. Although the dangers are now well known, many of these toxins and toxicants remain unregulated and in widespread use, particularly in the developing world.

Because these toxins and toxicants have long-term effects and remain dangerous for long periods, it is imperative that their use be banned where possible. Substitutes must be found. Where banning is impossible, they must be regulated for the protection of workers and the environment. Pollutants degrade our land, air, and water, threatening human health.

Whereas lack of infrastructure results in water contamination in the developing world, outdated or decaying infrastructure results in contamination in the developed world. Old pipes of lead or containing lead solder are a major public health hazard in the United States. Clay pipes, leaky because of age or invasion by tree roots, result in spillage of sewage into the ground and eventually groundwater resources. Rebuilding the infrastructure is a multi-billion-dollar project in many communities.

DISCUSSION

1. How do you weigh the choices among environmental protection, regulation of toxic chemicals, and economic growth?

2. Consider the responsibility that richer nations have to poorer nations based on the following facts:

   a. Developed nations used hazardous chemicals that persist in the environment with abandon before the harmful effects were well known or regulated.

   b. Many of the processes that contaminate the environment and harm the health of people in the developing world are for products used in the developed world.

   c. Developed countries were able to raise their standard of living without concern for the effects of the fossil fuels that enabled them to industrialize and advance.

3. What changes can you make at home, at school, and in your community to practice "green" living? What effect would each change have on your life and on the planet?

ON YOUR OWN

1. The World Health Organization interactive map allows you to investigate countries' levels of air pollution. Which regions have the highest levels? The lowest? Choose a country that scores high and one that scores low. What factors contribute to the country's high or low score?

   Notice that you can filter by region and look at the scores for individual countries. http://gamapserver .who.int/gho/interactive_charts/phe/oap_exposure/ atlas.html

2. Investigate toxins in your area. How would you describe the environmental health of the area? What factors contribute to the good or poor health of the area.

   Link to Interactive Maps, the 2014 TRI Report, Quick Facts, and more. You can search by zip code, city, or state.

   https://www.epa.gov/trinationalanalysis/where-you- live-2015-tri-national-analysis

   TRI Explorer: Interactive Site from which reports on releases by industry, state, or type can be generated.

   https://iaspub.epa.gov/triexplorer/tri_text.background

3. What is in your drinking water? You can investigate at this site:

   Drinking water reports for U.S. major metro areas: http://www.uc.edu/gissa/projects/ drinkingwater/

   Drinking water contaminants and sources and health consequence: http://www.uc.edu/gissa/projects/ drinkingwater/contaminant_list.html

4. Coral reefs not only are beautiful but also perform ecosystem services valuing more than U.S. $29 billion a year. Explore the reefs on the GRID–Arendal website: "Endangered Reefs, Threatened People."

   https://grid-arendal.maps.arcgis.com/apps/Cascade/ index.html?appid=2f440e93fefa4cce8e660c259bd23b50

   a. Where are the reefs found?

   b. How many people do they protect, and what protections do they offer?

   c. Which regions are the most thermal stressed due to climate change?

   d. Which regions are the most stressed due to acidification?

   e. What steps can be taken to save those reefs that can be saved?

NOTES

1. The Global Environmental Facility is a partnership of 182 nations and 10 intergovernmental agencies, many non-governmental organizations, and private sector corporations. It is the largest public funder of projects to improve the environment. Its grants are concentrated in issues related to biodiversity, climate change, land degradation, international waters, the ozone layer, and POPs. The Intergovernmental Negotiating Committee of the Minamata Convention selected GEF to fund its implementation (GEF 2013).

2. The original 12 POPs are the pesticides aldrin, chlordane, DDT, dieldrin, endrin, heptachlor, hexachlorobenzene, mirex, and toxaphene; the industrial chemicals hexachlorobenzene and PCBs; and the byproducts hexachlorobenzene, polychlorinated dibenzo-*p*-dioxins and polychlorinated dibenzofurans, and PCBs. POPs added in 2009 are the pesticides chlordecone, alpha hexachlorocyclohexane, beta hexachlorocyclohexane, lindane, and pentachlorobenzene; the industrial chemicals hexabromobiphenyl, hexabromodiphenyl ether and heptabromodiphenyl ether, pentachlorobenzene, perfluorooctane sulfonic acid, its salts, and perfluorooctane sulfonyl fluoride, tetrabromodiphenyl ether, and pentabromodiphenyl ether; and the byproducts alpha hexachlorocyclohexane, beta hexachlorocyclohexane, and pentachlorobenzene.

3. PAHs are also among the POPs. There are more than 100 different forms, many of which are believed to be carcinogenic as well as having other health risks.

4. For information on European regulation, see the European Solvents VOC Coordination Group (http://www.esig.org/about-us). For information on VOCs in the United States, see the EPA's *Technical Overview of Volatile Organic Compounds* (https://www.epa.gov/indoor-air-quality-iaq/technical-overview-volatile-organic-compounds).

5. Another reporting system, the Discharge Monitoring Report, focuses on discharges into water.

6. High-use chemicals are those used at volumes of more than 1 million pounds per year.

7. There may be considerable variation by region for any of the stressors and indicators. For more detailed reports by region, see the original report.

8. This is as measured by "causes of impairment." The list would be similar, but ordered slightly differently, if measured by total maximum daily load (TMDL). Charts detailing national cumulative TMDLs by pollutant causes of impairment, as well as a state-by-state accounting of impaired waters, may be found at https://iaspub.epa.gov/waters10/attains_nation_cy.control?p_report_type=T#status_of_data. There is also an interactive site where users can create detailed reports of impaired waters at https://iaspub.epa.gov/apex/waters/f?p=ASKWATERS:DOC_SEARCH.

9. The Groundwater Foundation puts the figure at 51 percent of the U.S. population (99 percent in rural areas) depending on ground water for drinking water.

10. The chemicals analyzed can be classified into insecticides, fungicides, organotin compounds, herbicides, PAHs, brominated flame retardants, and other compounds (PCBs, halogenated alkanes, and phenols, with each of these "others" acutely affecting five or fewer sites).

11. Thermal pollution degrades water by increasing (or decreasing) its ambient temperature from releases of warm water (such as from combustion or industrial processes) or cool water (such as from hydroplants). This causes thermal shock and changes the biological composition of the ecosystem.

12. Definitions of deforestation and degradation vary. The definitions used by Kissinger, Herold, and De Sy (2012) are as follows: "6. Deforestation here is defined as the conversion from forest into other land use categories, with the assumption that forest vegetation is not expected to regrow naturally in that area. 7. Forest degradation is defined as reduction of the canopy and loss of carbon in forests remaining forests, where the human disturbances are not associated with a change in land use and where, if not hindered, the forest is expected to regrow or be replanted."

13. Unless otherwise noted, the information in this section is found at the Secretariat of the Basel, Rotterdam, and Stockholm Conventions website (http://synergies.pops.int).

14. See Note 2.

15. The Transboundary Air Pollution Agreement for Europe is a component of the environmental policy of the UN Economic Commission for Europe. The UN Economic Commissions for Africa, for Asia and the Pacific, for Latin America and the Caribbean, and for Western Asia all have an environmental policy component.

16. The bill is called the Frank R. Lautenberg Chemical Safety Act for the 21st Century. It was named after the late U.S. senator who fought for years for correctives to strengthen the TSCA.

17. Abt Associates is a global research firm committed to "research and program implementation in the fields of health, social and environmental policy, climate change, and international development," according to the Abt website (http://www.abtassociates.com/About-Us/At-a-Glance.aspx#sthash.HQbR5F0E.dpuf).

18. The research employed several statistical models to determine the effects. Two models were tested for the programs as a whole. One model found a 9 percent reduction, and one model found a 16 percent reduction. For the reduction levels of the specific strategies, two models were used. Both models had statistically similar results, as reported here.

14

Climate Change and Global Warming

UNDER WATER IN THE UNITED STATES

Violet, her husband, and two children live in a small trailer behind the ruins of their former house, destroyed by Hurricane Gustav in 2008. The trailer is moldy from regular flooding. They cook on a hotplate because their stove was ruined by flooding. Suffering from lupus, Violet worries that she won't be able to reach a doctor when needed if the bridge that connects the island she lives on to mainland Louisiana is flooded. Dreams of college for her children dim further every time they miss school because the bridge is flooded, which is often.

Isle de Jean Charles, where Violet and approximately 60 others live, is ravaged by climate change. In addition to flooding, the pecan and banana trees once plentiful on the island are all but gone—victims of salt water soaked into the soil. More than 90 percent of the island's land has disappeared—washed away through the channels cut across the island by loggers and oil companies, washed away by hurricanes. Flood control measures block the free-flowing rivers that brought fresh water and sediment to replenish the island. There are few animals to hunt or trap; the land is not arable. The island is not habitable.

What little is left of their island is likely to be under water as ice caps melt and the sea level rises. The islanders are identified as among the most vulnerable in the United States to climate change. Their island cannot be saved. Even if it were rebuilt, rising seas and extreme climate events continue to threaten and destroy it. They are slated to be the first U.S. climate change refugees. The community, lives, and culture of the islanders are in danger. Isle de Jean Charles is tribal land. The islanders' families have lived there for hundreds of years. Although the government's plan is to move the entire community to a new location, hoping to preserve the culture, some islanders do not want to leave. Others, like Violet, see nothing except misery ahead on the island. "I just want to get out of here," she proclaims. (Davenport and Robertson 2016)

LEARNING OBJECTIVES

After completing this chapter, students will be able to do the following:

14.1 Identify the variety of signs or symptoms of climate change

14.2 Analyze the sources of climate change related to human activity

14.3 Assess the threats to global stability posed by elements of climate change considering rising sea levels, extreme weather events, food insecurity, and violent conflict

14.4 Evaluate the potential of various methods proposed for improving the earth's health and limiting climate change

14.5 Compare and contrast the measures that should be taken at global, societal, and local levels to combat climate change

THE THREAT OF CLIMATE CHANGE

As with Violet and the residents of Isle de Jean Charles, some forced displacements occur gradually. They don't often make the headlines. Forced by rising sea levels that make homes uninhabitable and fields infertile with salinity, Violet and her family are likely to be joined by hundreds of thousands more refugees forced out by rising seas. Pacific Island nations are among the most vulnerable. Kiribati, an atoll with about 100,000 residents, lies only 6 feet above sea level. The Maldives, Tuvalu, the Marshall Islands, Micronesia, the Caribbean, and Mauritius, among others, all are endangered by the rising sea levels.

National security experts from all over the world, including James Mattis, U.S. President Donald Trump's secretary of defense, cite climate change as one of the greatest threats, if not the greatest threat, to national and global security. Knowledge that climate change creates conditions of instability is not new. In 2007, an authoritative report compiled by military and intelligence officials warned that climate change debates focused on economics and neglected, for the most part, foreign policy and national security issues (Busby 2007).

Climate change and its effects are threat multipliers in regions already facing security challenges. The potential and likely direct and indirect consequences of climate change are severe for both developed and developing nations. Extreme weather events increasing in frequency and intensity can overwhelm the capacity of authorities to respond, causing widespread death, public health crises, and a breakdown of law and order. Less direct but even more deadly are the long-term effects of climate change. Increasing temperatures, drought, desertification, and food shortages devastate regions and spawn social unrest. The Paris Agreement plans deign to prevent a global 2° C[1] rise in temperature by 2100. In sub-Saharan Africa, temperatures already reached the 2° C rise and could reach a 4° or 5° C rise by 2100 (Pereira 2017; Serdeczny et al. 2016). Precipitation in the region decreased. Desertification is expanding. Every year, 12 million hectares of land turn to dust—land that could have grown 20 million tons of grain (British Broadcasting Corporation 2017).

Africa has been the region most vulnerable to climate change. Vulnerability is not confined to the driest areas, but 80 percent of armed conflicts in 2007 occurred in dry ecosystems (United Nations Convention to Combat Desertification n.d.). Desertification brings food shortages. Food shortages bring conflict and rioting. It was food shortage that ignited the rioting in Tunisia and gave rise to Arab Spring across North Africa. Syria had faced its driest years in five years and most devastating crop failures perhaps in its history, leading to its long-lasting civil war.

Shoreline erosion, coastal flooding, and agricultural destruction threaten hundreds of thousands of people in Asia. In Bangladesh, efforts continue to reclaim land to house the roughly 200,000 people whose lands are washed away by erosion. Anywhere from 20 to 25 percent of Bangladesh's land will be under water if sea levels rise 1 meter—an event expected by the end of the century and displacing approximately 18 million people. Migration of Bangladeshis into India has already created tension and incited violence. On another front, rivers originating in Kashmir supply the majority of water needed for Pakistan's agricultural irrigation. As the region becomes drier, India's dam building on these rivers deprives Pakistan of this much-needed water. Similarly, river basins that originate in China on which India depends are threatened (Lone 2015). Kashmir is a flashpoint between India and Pakistan, inciting three wars since World War II between these two nuclear armed states.

Discovering Climate Change

Studying climate change is not new. In 1859, John Tyndall wondered what caused the glaciers across Europe to melt. In his lab, he discovered that while most of the sun's heat radiated back from the earth and passed easily through the atmosphere, several gases could trap heat waves. He found that water vapor was a powerful block. In combination with carbon dioxide (CO_2), its heat-trapping potential was exacerbated.

In 1896, Svante Arrhenius discovered that concentrations of CO_2 regulate water vapor and that cutting the CO_2 in the atmosphere by half would lower the temperature in Europe by 4 to 5° C (7–9° F).

Arrhenius's friend, Arvid Högbom, calculated that factories and industrial sources were adding CO_2 to the atmosphere and would cause the earth's temperature to rise. They did not see it as much of a problem at the time because at the rate CO_2 was being generated in 1896, they calculated that it would take 3,000 years for the temperature to rise significantly. By 1908, however, Arrhenius suggested that the warming might occur in 300 years. Now, of course, we know that we are generating much more CO_2 and other greenhouse gases than these early climate scientists could have anticipated. Consequently, the earth's temperature rose and continues to rise much more quickly than they predicted (Weart, 2016).

Popular Opinion and Climate Change

People in the developing world are the most likely to experience the most harm from climate change. It is not surprising that a Pew Research Center (2015) Global Attitudes and Trends poll showed that people in Latin America and Africa are the most concerned about climate change as a serious problem and how it can hurt them personally. In Europe, where a majority (54 percent) agree that climate change is a serious problem and 60 percent believe that it is already harming people, only 27 percent are "very concerned" that it will harm them personally. Americans and Chinese, who create the most greenhouse gases, are the least concerned.

What people are most concerned about is drought and water shortages. When asked to choose their biggest concern from among these four choices—all of which kill people—they choose in this order of concern:

- Drought/water shortage (44 percent)

- Severe weather such as intense storms and floods (25 percent)

- Long periods of unusually hot weather (14 percent)

- Rising sea levels (6 percent)

With the exception of rising sea levels scoring above unusually hot weather in the United States and Europe, this pattern of priority was the same across all regions (Pew Research Center 2015).

Experts the world over agree that the effects of climate change are far-reaching. They include agriculture, health and disease, energy supply and demand, increased intensity and frequency of wildfires and extreme weather events, coastal and marine ecosystems, water quality and supply, transportation, and a factor often overlooked— the national security of every nation.

Climate Change Cycles and Feedback Loops

The earth's climate is changing. Across the earth, the regional patterns of temperature, precipitation, and seasons that scientists have relied on for centuries to predict weather are changing, each in different ways. Some seasons are shortening, some lengthening. Some regions of the world are getting more rain and snowfall, some less. The overall temperature of the atmosphere and seas is changing. These changes are occurring significantly more rapidly than would be the case if the changes were occurring from natural cycles. With these changes in climate come day-to-day changes in weather patterns making them less predictable and making extreme weather events more frequent and more intense.

The singular most important cause is the accumulation of CO_2 and other gases in the earth's atmosphere (Figure 14.1). Combustion of carbon-based fuels spews CO_2 into the atmosphere. Along with nitrous oxide from both combustion and fertilizers, methane from decomposing human, animal, and other organic wastes, and fluorinated gases from industrial processes, these gases form a barrier around the earth that, like a greenhouse, traps heat and causes the earth's temperature to rise. The gases and rising temperature create condensation increasing atmospheric water vapor, the most abundant greenhouse gas. Clouds and precipitation enhance the greenhouse effect. Deforestation complicates this further, weakening the earth's ability to absorb CO_2, increasing its concentration in the atmosphere.

The increase in the earth's atmospheric, oceanic, and land temperatures causes the climate changes that the earth experiences. Overall, the earth's average temperature increased 1° F in the 20th century. It does not sound significant, but it already has created a cavalcade of climate events. Small changes in temperature have oversized effects. Already we have experienced the following:

- Sea level rise from melting of glaciers, snow, and ice

- Less reflection of radiation back out of the atmosphere because of loss of ice and snow

- Increase in ocean temperatures, which also causes sea level rise

- Acidification of oceans

- Increased vulnerability of coral reefs

- Decreasing plant and animal biodiversity in many ecosystems

- Changing ocean current and wind patterns

- Increase in extreme weather events

- Imbalance in hydrological cycles—drought in some areas, flooding in other areas

- Desertification

- Shifting animal habitats and patterns of animal migration

- Decreasing biodiversity and potential extinction of many plant and animal species

THE SYMPTOMS OF A CHANGING CLIMATE

Climate change discussions often focus on one or two aspects of it; rising temperatures and rising sea levels. These are critical but not the only aspects of climate change, nor are they the ones that most of us experience directly.

Climate change is reflected in long-term patterns in seasons, temperatures, precipitation, and ocean and wind currents. Hadley's cell, El Niño, and La Niña are climate patterns. Trends of climate over long periods tend to be relatively stable. Understanding them enables us to predict the weather and ecosystem characteristics. Weather is the day-to-day, or even minute-to-minute, fluctuations in temperature, precipitation, and so on.

As climate changes, it affects weather patterns. It is weather that we notice day to day. Weather is becoming less predictable. This is one cost of climate change. The costs of climate change, the externalities, are not paid by the industries doing the polluting or supplying the oil and coal companies that furnish combustible fuels; they are borne by everyone in damage to our health, our natural environment, and our built environment.

A CLOSER LOOK
EVIDENCE OF CLIMATE CHANGE

Data on atmospheric CO_2, ocean temperature, earth temperature, and precipitation all point to a rapidly changing climate.

FIGURE 14.1　　CO_2 Levels Through History

This graph compares samples of atmospheric CO_2 from ice cores with more recent samples. It provides evidence of the increase in CO_2 since the Industrial Revolution.

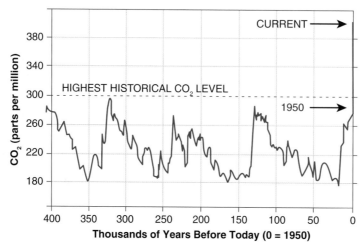

Source: National Aeronautics and Space Administration (2017a).

FIGURE 14.2   Temperature Increases From 1880

Climate scientists from four research centers have little disagreement on the degree of the earth's temperature changes.

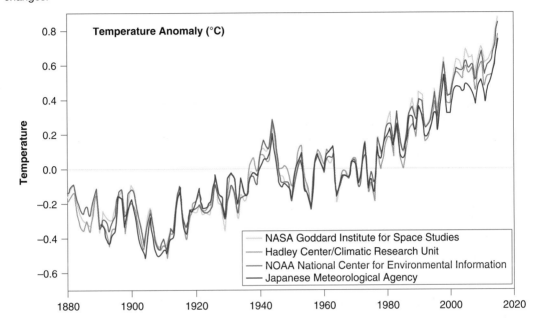

Source: National Aeronautics and Space Administration (2017b).

Boulder Glacier in Glacier National Park has nearly disappeared, as shown by these comparison photos.

PHOTO 14.1A   Boulder Glacier, Montana, 1932

TJ Hileman, GNP Archives.

PHOTO 14.1B   Boulder Glacier, Montana, 2005

G. Pederson, USGS.

Surface Temperature

Thousands of measures of the earth's land, water, and air temperatures are taken every day by hundreds of independent monitors. Many governments and scientific organizations have tracked temperatures over the last hundred or more years. These consistently show an increase in average air, water, and land temperatures to the point that as of 2017 16 of the 17 hottest years on record have occurred since 2001 (National Aeronautics and Space Administration [NASA] 2017c).

Every year since 1970 has been above the global 1951 to 1980 average (NASA 2017c). At 99° C, this is a full 1° higher. Contrast this with average variation of less than 1° over the last thousand years and 4° to 7° over the last million years (World Meteorological Organization [WMO] 2013). Each of the last three decades has been progressively warmer than any preceding decade since 1890, and 1983 to 2012 has likely been the warmest 30-year period in 1400 years (Intergovernmental Panel on Climate Change [IPCC] 2014). The first 16 years of the 21st century were among the hottest 17 years on record, which dates back to 1880 (1998 is the third hottest year) (National Oceanic and Atmospheric Administration [NOAA] 2016b). The warmest year on record dating back to 1850 was 2016 (Figure 14.2) (Met Office Hadley Centre and Climatic Research Unit 2016).

It is not the case that every day will be warmer than the average for that day or that the earth will be uniformly warmer. Some regions such as the Arctic, which so far has been warming most rapidly, warm more quickly than others. Some days, months, or years may have cooler than average temperatures. That does not mean that overall the earth is not warming, but it is reason to use "climate change" to capture the full range of effects and global warming more specifically, even though it is the crux of climate change.

When a weather event such as a drought or flood occurs in one part of the world, it is not in isolation. There is a global pattern of variability. With global warming, increased evaporation becomes balanced by increased precipitation. The hydrological cycle is intensified; wet areas become wetter and dry areas become drier. At the same time, subtropical dry zones expand poleward. This will cause regions such as the U.S. Southwest to dry.

Scientific evidence supports the argument that the increase in the earth's temperature is due to human activities. Worldwide greenhouse gas emissions increased by 35 percent from 1990 to 2010 (Environmental Protection Agency [EPA] 2016). CO_2, methane, and nitrous oxide can be measured in the earth's atmosphere, and their concentrations have increased markedly. Scientists have also known since the mid-19th century that these gases trap heat. In fact, many of the instruments flown by NASA use this basic knowledge to navigate.

Oceans: Sea Level, Salinity, and Acidity

The effects of pollution and climate change on the oceans are profound. While most of the greenhouse gases accumulate in the atmosphere, causing the greenhouse effect, most of the excess energy produced, as much as 90 percent, is stored in the oceans, increasing the ocean temperature. Since 1969, the top 700 meters of the ocean warmed 0.302° F, significantly more than the average for the earth's surface (NASA 2017c). In regions where evaporation dominates precipitation, ocean surface salinity increased. In regions where precipitation dominates, surface salinity decreased. This is indirect evidence of changes in the water cycle associated with greenhouse gases (IPCC 2014).

The oceans are also affected by glacier melting. Glaciers and the ice sheets associated with them are land ice and hold the largest stores of fresh water. They are melting, and as they melt the fresh water eventually winds its way to the salty seas, raising the temperature and affecting salinity. To get an idea of how fast glaciers are melting, consider Glacier National Park in the United States (Photos 14.1A and 14.1B). In 1910, Glacier National Park had 150 glaciers. Now there are 30 and the melting continues. Glaciers in the Garhwal Himalaya are melting so quickly that they may be gone by 2035, and 80 percent of the "snows of Kilimanjaro" have disappeared. In Indonesia, Peru, Switzerland, and Greenland—all over the world—glaciers, ice sheets, and snow caps are shrinking fast (Glick n.d.). The effect is synergistic; as snow and ice melt, the thinner layer left melts more quickly, increasing the rate of melting.

The Antarctic ice sheet is the largest repository of fresh water in the world. Since 2002, it has been losing ice at a rate of 134 gigatons per year. The Greenland ice sheet is melting even faster, at a rate of 287 gigatons per year (NASA 2017d). Snow and ice act like mirrors. As the ice sheets melt, the earth also loses reflective capacity (albedo) and global warming is intensified. Snow and ice reflect back nearly all of the sunlight, 85 percent, that strikes it. The open water left by ice melt reflects back only 7 percent.

These are the two mechanisms causing the rising sea levels: expansion and melting ice and snow locked into glaciers, snowcaps, and other land formations. Like other consequences of the greenhouse effect, sea level doesn't rise uniformly across the world. In some places it is not rising at all, and in others it is decreasing. Overall, the sea level rose about 8 inches from the beginning of the 20th century. It could rise by 3 feet or more by the end of this century (Figure 14.3) (NASA 2017e).

The increase in temperature and changing salinity affect the habitat of marine life. Another threat to the oceans posed by greenhouse gases is the direct effect of CO_2 in the oceans. Not all of the greenhouse gases emitted remain in the atmosphere. About 25 percent of the CO_2

we create is absorbed by the oceans, increasing its acidity. The increase in temperature, the increase in acidity, and changes in salinity all disturb the delicate balance of the oceans, endangering plant and animal life, including the coral reefs (IPCC 2014).

Permafrost Thaw

In the coldest parts of the world, only the upper layer of the earth, the active layer, thaws in spring and summer. Below the active layer is an "ice-rich layer" and below this is permafrost. As its name implies, permafrost remains frozen all year round.[2] Through various mechanisms, such as disturbance of soil or vegetation, surface water and groundwater interaction, and loss of snow cover, rather than direct response to air temperature, climate change is causing permafrost thaw in many

A CLOSER LOOK
SEA LEVEL CHANGE

FIGURE 14.3   Sea Level Changes, 1870–2000

Sea level has risen about 8 inches from the beginning of the 20th century. Even if global warming slows, the rise will continue. This NASA chart is online in interactive form, giving precise reading of the increase in sea level year by year.

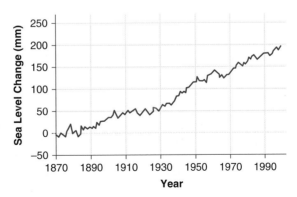

Source: National Aeronautics and Space Administration (2017f).

regions (Hong, Perkins, and Trainor 2014). Twice as much carbon gas is locked into permafrost of the Arctic and boreal forests as is in the atmosphere. Some of these gases have been locked there for thousands of years from the decay of organic matter.

Permafrost thaw feeds back into climate change and is one of the most significant contributions of land ecosystems to the atmospheric warming. Over time, the release of greenhouse gases into the atmosphere from permafrost thaw outweighs the uptake of carbon from any increase in vegetation that arises from the warming (Schuur et al. 2009). The Artic permafrost alone stores 1.5 trillion tons of carbon gases, including methane. Methane, which is being released at a rate of 50 billion tons a year and heats the atmosphere 25 times more efficiently than CO_2,[3] accelerates global warming. The East Siberia Arctic Shelf also contains significant stored methane. Subsea permafrost thawing and decrease in ice are expected to significantly increase methane emissions there as well (Shakhova et al. 2017).

Permafrost thaw poses hazards in addition to greenhouse gas release. Different types of permafrost are affected to a greater or lesser extent by thawing, but all types decrease in stability. This poses risks to ecosystems and human infrastructure. Permafrost is a critical component of a soil ecosystem. Permafrost thaw poses significant hazards:

- Dependent on drainage, the thaw is likely to create subsidence and overly saturated soils. This can cause trees to die. In an area of good drainage, it will improve the drainage and create drier conditions.

- Because permafrost affects vegetation, thaw can result in boreal forest being replaced with steppe-like habitats when drier conditions result or with wetlands where more highly water-saturated conditions result. Over the long term, thaw will produce better drainage and dry conditions stressing vegetation, shrinking ponds within the area and affecting aquatic life.

- Microbial activity will increase, releasing CO_2 and methane.

PHOTO 14.2   This apartment building was destroyed due to settling caused by permafrost thaw.
Professor Vladimir Romanovsky, University of Alaska Fairbanks

- Infrastructure damage to roads, buildings, airports, and facilities due to thaw and permafrost settlement poses significant expense. Many structures may need to be abandoned if funding is not available for continued repairs. (National Snow and Ice Data Center 2013)

Sea Ice and Animal Life

Arctic Sea ice is measured by the extent of its coverage and its depth. The period 2005 to 2010 recorded the lowest summer's end (September) ice coverage ever, dipping to a low in 2007 of 4.26 million km^2 (1.65 square miles), 39 percent below the long-term average. This record low was broken in 2012 with summer ice extent diminishing to 3.42 million km^2, 18 percent lower than 2007 (WMO 2013). As with land ice, when sea ice melts, albedo is diminished and more energy is absorbed, increasing the temperature. Perovich and Polashenski (2012) found that once sea ice had melted, the seasonal ice that followed in its wake on the next freezing did not rebound to the reflecting capacity of the multi-year ice. A study by Lund University (2015) found that sea ice loss not only affects the oceans but also affects ecosystems farther away and on land. The increase in temperature from Arctic sea ice melt stimulates microorganisms in the Arctic tundra ecosystem to release more methane.

Maximum and minimum sea ice levels and when each level occurs are important measures of the sea ice. The maximum extent is reached toward the end of winter, in March, and the minimum extent is reached toward the end of summer, in September. For the sea ice year beginning in October of 2014, the maximum was reached 15 days earlier than average on February 25. This means that warming started earlier in the year. Its maximum extent was the lowest value on record, dating back to 1979. The minimum in September was the fourth lowest on record. There was also twice as much "first-year" ice as there was 30 years ago. The loss of sea ice and increased temperatures are forcing warm water fish communities in both the Atlantic and Pacific oceans farther north. The Atlantic Ocean meets the Arctic Sea at the Barents Sea. Larger predator fish, such as cod, beaked redfish, and long rough dab from the southwestern Barents Sea are entering the north parts in large numbers.

As the climate is changing, the water temperature is now more favorable to these predator fish than the Arctic fish species native to that area. The Arctic fish tend to be smaller and have a more specialized diet, and they are not likely to withstand a move farther north (Fossheim et al. 2015).

Walruses in the Arctic

Walruses use sea ice throughout the seasons for mating in winter, birthing in spring, and haul out (congregating) platforms throughout the year. Because they can also use land, they are not as threatened as other species. Two types of walrus exist in the Arctic, and their habits and habitats are somewhat different. The Pacific walrus population probably declined significantly from 1980 to 2000. On the one hand, its population had reached the carrying capacity of the environment. On the other hand, the carrying capacity was diminished by the loss of sea ice. The loss of sea ice reduced Pacific walruses' access to prey, affecting the health of female walruses, resulting in less healthy calves. In addition, using land-based haul out platforms increases mortality of young walruses due to trampling events. Besides the loss of sea ice, threats to walruses in the Arctic include declines in the clam population, acidification of the sea, oil and gas extraction, and disease and contaminant risks from fish species new to the Arctic (Kovacs et al., 2015). Both Atlantic and Pacific species of walrus were decimated in the past by hunting. Hunting the Pacific walrus is not prohibited by the United States, Canada, or Russia, in part because of its importance to Arctic natives, although there are controls in place. The Atlantic walrus is listed as a species of "special concern" by the Committee on the Status of Endangered Wildlife in Canada (Committee on the Status of Endangered Wildlife in Canada 2011). The Pacific walrus was to be considered for the U.S. Endangered Species Act protection in 2017.[4] It is fully protected in Norway, and while the ice melt is dramatic there, the ban on hunting and reserve areas where they are not subject to human interference have allowed the population to resurge. Greenland also has put protections in place (Kovacs et al. 2015).

Polar Bears at Risk

Polar bears are at greater risk from climate change than are walruses. Polar bears are ice dependent. Arctic sea ice is necessary to their survival. Along with the "ringed seal," their prey, they are the "canary in the mine shaft" indicators of the state of climate change in the Arctic. Polar bears need 60 percent more calories than realized,

CONSIDER THIS
BLACK CARBON IN THE ARCTIC

Black carbon, soot, is one of the keys to understanding climate change in the Arctic. Because the Arctic has no direct sources of pollution, the likely culprit is gas flares from oil extraction. They spew black carbon, gas nitrogen dioxide and particles, and/or aerosols. Until recently, gas flares were overlooked as a source of climate change. With the recent boom in oil exploration activity in Canada and the United States, significantly more greenhouse-generating soot and gases are reaching the Arctic, where even small disruptions are amplified (Li et al. 2016). The Arctic is particularly vulnerable to the effects of global warming. As snow and ice diminish, their reflective power is weakened, as discussed. More radiation will be absorbed, accelerating warming. Vegetation is increasingly moving north due to warming, which will also decrease reflection and increase absorption. These feedback effects result in the Arctic temperatures rising at twice the rate of the global average. Since 1978, Arctic sea ice is disappearing at an average rate of 3 percent per decade; portions are disappearing at a rate of 7 percent per decade. These are much greater losses than occur with normal fluctuations.

It has consequences. The hunting season of indigenous Arctic peoples is shorter. Their "drying" season is unseasonably wetter, making it difficult to dry food for storage to feed themselves in the fall and winter months. Reindeer and caribou will work harder to find food due to heavier snows and rain, depleting their populations. Shorter ice seasons and less ice mean that baby seals and walruses might not have enough time to wean and may die. Caribou and polar bears might not have enough ice path for migration (Union of Concerned Scientists n.d. b).

---

about 12,325 every day. They hunt from ice floes. As the ice melts, polar bears starve (Leahy 2018). Polar bears are uniquely adapted to the Arctic environment with wide paws that act something like snowshoes and strong legs and webbing between their toes that aid in swimming. Like Arctic ice, their transparent fur reflects light, but they have a black skin and thick layer of fat that insulates them, trapping heat (National Wildlife Federation n.d.). They are dependent on sea ice for breeding as well as feeding. In 2008, when they were considered for and placed on the endangered species list, scientists argued that melting sea ice could bring about their extinction in parts of Alaska and Canada. In 2003 and 2004, when the number of ice-free summer days rose to 135, their population dropped by 25 percent. In that period, researchers also observed emaciated bears, starving bears, drowning bears, and bear cannibalism—things they had never seen before. It was clear that climate change challenged their survival (Madin 2008).

A Complication: Polar Bears and the Endangered Species Act

The "poster child" of climate change, campaigns on behalf of the plight of the polar bear, such as the World Wildlife Fund (WWF) and Coca-Cola joint endeavor,[5] captured much of the public's imagination and helped people to understand the threat of climate change. Although polar bears are listed as a threatened species, it is not clear that the Endangered Species Act (ESA) can protect them. At issue is whether or not the ESA has the authority to combat global warming. Although by ESA regulations polar bears are clearly in danger, the decision to list them contained this caveat: "Listing will not stop climate change or prevent sea ice from melting" (Kearney 2014). In other words, the listing of polar bears as endangered is not cause to act on their behalf in fighting climate change, for instance, by requiring further regulations on greenhouse gas emissions.

The EPA should, on the face of it, be able to protect polar bears on the basis of the critical habitat designation (CHD) because Arctic ice is necessary for the survival of the species. CHD would provide special management of the habitat. In the 2013 case *Alaska Oil and Gas Association v. Salazar,* the court vacated the CHD designation (Kearney 2014). The ESA is currently powerless to protect any animal or plant species due to destruction of its environment from climate change. This would apply to Pacific walruses and others if they are added to the list.

A CLOSER LOOK
WALRUS HAUL OUT

PHOTO 14.3 In 2017, loss of sea ice caused the earliest walrus haul out ever. Diminishing sea ice leaves walruses with fewer and smaller ice floes, forcing more onto land. Because they are easily startled, human activity can cause stress and stampede, in which many may die.

U.S. Geological Survey, Public Domain.

A New Threat to Polar Bears

Now, the polar bear species faces a new threat. Polar bears and grizzly bears are the most closely related bear species, with their evolution having diverged only about a million years ago. Their habitats overlapped for some time in the western Canadian Arctic, where grizzlies had been showing up for about 50 years. The bears have mated in captivity, but the first instance in the wild was observed in 2006. At that time, it was too soon to tell whether this would become a regular occurrence resulting from climate change (Roach 2006). However, a decade later in 2016, many more hybrid bears have been found and it seems as though there have been decades of sporadic interbreeding. Islands off Southeast Alaska have bears that have polar bear DNA but look more like grizzlies. Scientists

PHOTO 14.4 As Arctic ice diminishes in area, it also diminishes in depth. This polar bear broke through the Arctic ice in 2009.

Canadian Coast Guard, Public Domain.

with long histories in studying Arctic bears fear that grizzly bears have more to gain than polar bears. Eventually, they fear, the polar bear population could dilute to where it does not exist at all (Popescu 2016).

EXTREME WEATHER AND DISPLACED PEOPLE

Developing countries will suffer the most from the weather-related disasters and increased water stress caused by global warming. . . . Even 2° C warming above pre-industrial temperatures— the minimum the world will experience—would result in 4–5 percent of African and South Asian GDP [gross domestic product] being lost, and developing countries are expected to bear 75–80 percent of impact costs.

—Zou Ji, quoted in World Economic Forum (2015)

Most people experience climate change through their day-to-day experiences with weather. The most noticeable of the weather changes is the greater frequency and intensity of extreme weather events—more and stronger hurricanes, winter storms, landslides, forest fires, heat waves, drought, and flooding. While the link between extreme weather and climate change took years to verify, climate scientists are now able to untangle the natural variability in climate and weather from the effects of global warming.

From 1995 to 2015, there were 6,457 weather-related disasters. Breaking this down by decade, there was a 14 percent increase for 2005–2014 over 1995–2004 and an increase of 200 percent over the level recorded for 1985–1994 (Table 14.1) (Center for Research on the Epidemiology of Disasters [CRED] 2015).

These events claimed 606,000 lives—that is, 30,000 lives on average per year—and affected more than 4 billion people. Low-income countries suffer the most, but high-income countries were not without death and

A CLOSER LOOK
EXTREME WEATHER EVENTS

TABLE 14.1   Extreme Weather Events, 1995 to August 2015

Extreme weather events of every type increased in frequency from 1995 to 2015, killing hundreds of thousands of people and affecting billions. Event types by percentage of total events and number of people affected are shown.

Event	Flood	Storm	Earthquake	Extreme Temperature	Landslide	Wildfire	Drought	Volcanic Activity
Percentage of occurrences by type	43%	28%	8%	6%	5%	5%	4%	2%
Number of people affected	2.3 billion	660 million	[a]	94 million		8 million[b]	1.1 billion	[a]
Number of deaths	157,000	242,000		164,000		20,000[b]	22,000	[a]

a. Data not given.
b. Landslides and wildfires combined.

Source: Adapted from Center for Research on the Epidemology of Disaster (2015).

injury. Because of greater infrastructure in higher-income countries, the economic loss was much greater than it was in low-income countries; however, it was a much smaller percentage of gross domestic product (GDP) (Figures 14.4 and 14.5).[6]

The economic cost of extreme weather events is also high. HSBC, one of the world's largest financial services firms, estimates the cost of extreme weather to G20 countries from 2005 to 2014 at U.S. $309 billion. Of the 2014 cost of $44 billion, $11 billion came from droughts and

$31 billion came from flooding. Indirect costs such as disruption of the supply chain, as happened when rain forced hard drive factories in Thailand to shut down, add significantly to the total (Holodny 2016).

The Summer of 2017

The summer of 2017 brought one natural disaster after another across the world. In Asia and Africa, the death toll was alarming. A heavy monsoon season brought

A CLOSER LOOK
THE COSTS OF WEATHER-RELATED EVENTS

Life lost due to weather events is greater in poorer countries than in higher-income ones. Economic damage is greater in higher-income countries, but in proportion to GDP it is greater in lower-income countries.

FIGURE 14.4   Total Numbers of Deaths Compared to Average Number of Deaths per Weather-Related Disaster by Income Group, 1995–2015

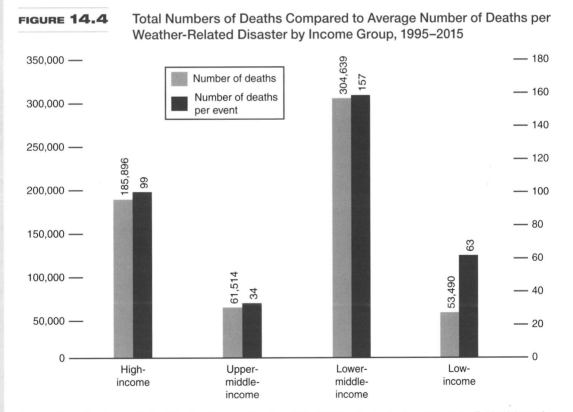

Source: From The Human Cost of Weather Related Disasters 1995–2015, by Centre for Research on the Epidemiology of Disasters CRED and The United Nations Office for Disaster Risk Reduction, © 2015 United Nations. Reprinted with the permission of the United Nations.

(Continued)

(Continued)

FIGURE 14.5   Economic Losses in Absolute Values as a Percentage of GDP From Weather-Related Disasters, 1995–2015

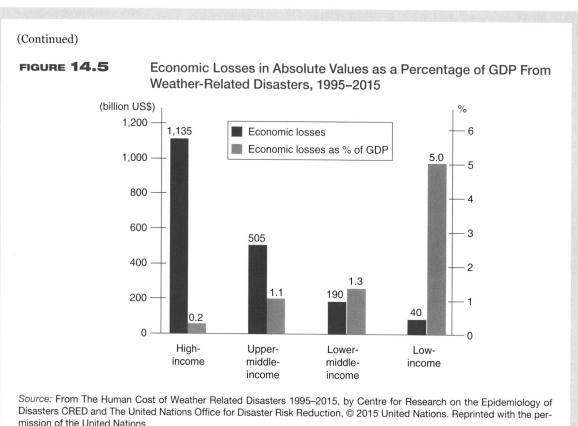

Source: From The Human Cost of Weather Related Disasters 1995–2015, by Centre for Research on the Epidemiology of Disasters CRED and The United Nations Office for Disaster Risk Reduction, © 2015 United Nations. Reprinted with the permission of the United Nations.

flooding that killed more than 1,200 people in India, Nepal, Pakistan, and Bangladesh and forced millions from their homes. In Mumbai, India, which had some of its heaviest rainfall in 15 years, a building collapsed, killing as many as two dozen people and injuring dozens more. More than 3,000 villages in India and one third of those in Bangladesh were submerged (Dhillon 2017).

Tropical storms, intense rains, and mudslides killed more than 1,200 people across Africa in August 2017. In Freetown, Sierra Leone, a mudslide destroyed hundreds of homes and killed more than 1,000 people. A mudslide also claimed more than 200 lives in a village in the Democratic Republic of the Congo. Thousands of people were evacuated in Niamey, Niger, due to flooding that killed at least 40 people. Intense rains displaced more than 100,000 people in Benue state, Nigeria (Kazeem 2017).

In one of the most active and devastating hurricane seasons on record, Hurricanes Harvey, Irma, Jose, and Maria devastated Texas, Mexico, and the Caribbean, all within a month of one another. It is rare for a hurricane to "sit still," yet Harvey hovered for five days, bringing 53 inches of rain along with devastation and death in parts of Houston. Irma's path of destruction swept through the Caribbean and Florida. In the two-island nation of Antigua and Barbuda, Barbuda is now deserted, left uninhabitable by Irma. About 40,000 people were evacuated from St. Martin. Six islands of the Bahamas were evacuated. The death and destruction tolls would take months to figure. Maria left millions of people, more than three quarters of the population, without power and more than a third without drinking water at home in Puerto Rico. Nearly a thousand people had died and hundreds were missing a month later. It would be months, and in many places years, before living conditions could be restored. Some places never may be.

In September, a massive magnitude 8.1 earthquake killed 100 people in Southwest Mexico. This was followed the next day by Hurricane Katia on the east coast, and less than two weeks later another massive earthquake, of magnitude 7.1, killed more than 200 people in Puebla near Mexico City and displaced thousands.

Strong winds, months of the highest ever recorded temperatures, heavy rainfall the previous winter, and years of prior drought combined to fuel wildfires that spread through eight California counties, more than 170,000 acres of California wine country (Figures 14.6 and 14.7). Fires are more frequent and larger throughout the western United States.

Hurricanes are a feature of the western Atlantic. They may form by Africa or Europe, but they cross the ocean to do their damage. Hurricane Ophelia behaved differently and in October struck in Ireland. It made the extreme event list for how strong it was for where it was. If the winds of 119 miles per hour on Fastnet Rock Island are verified, it would be the strongest ever to hit Ireland (Di

Liberto 2017). Hundreds of thousands of people were left without power. Most was restored within 10 days (Power 2017).

Even if we stopped emitting greenhouse gases immediately, it would not stop global warming and climate change. CO_2 stays in the atmosphere for hundreds of years. The feedback loops will continue. Extreme weather events will also continue into the foreseeable future.

HEALTH AND NUTRITION EFFECTS

Death and injury due to extreme weather events are the most dramatic cost to human life. But there are other significant health effects. The most well-documented effects on health are those due to the impact of climate on the

A CLOSER LOOK
SECOND WETTEST WINTER AND HOTTEST SUMMER ON RECORD IN CALIFORNIA

The second wettest winter on record combined with the hottest summer on record to feed the conditions that created the wildfires in October 2017. Deadly mudslides followed in January 2018 as the burned earth could not absorb the next winter's rains.

FIGURE **14.6**   Winter Precipitation in California, 1896–2017

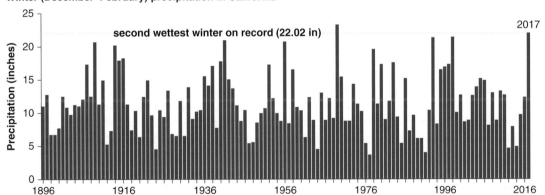

Source: Lindsey (2017).

(Continued)

(Continued)

FIGURE 14.7   Summer (June–August) Average Temperature in California, 1896–2016

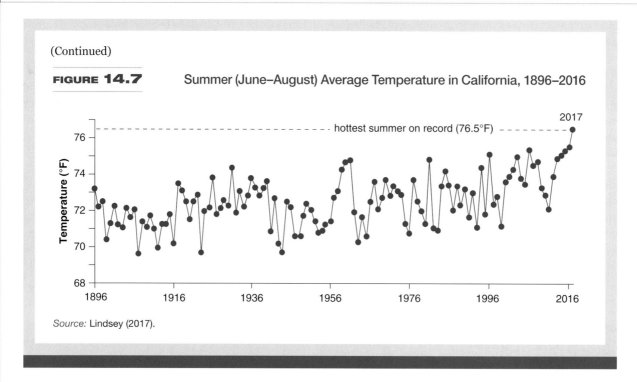

Source: Lindsey (2017).

environment such as degradation of agriculture due to drought, flooding, hurricanes, and tornados, and vector-borne[7] and parasitic diseases such as malaria, dengue, yellow fever, West Nile virus, plague, Lyme disease, and others carried by mosquitoes, ticks, and fleas. These types of disease account for 17 percent of deaths globally, and they are becoming more threatening.

As the climate warms and becomes wetter, vector-borne diseases may be more threatening for several reasons. As the climate warms, the habitat in which mosquitoes, fleas, and ticks can live expands. Their incubation time shrinks, which increases the period during which they can infect a host. Warmer temperatures increase their biting behavior. Increased rainfall increases stagnant pools and puddles, giving the parasites more breeding grounds. Drought pushes people out of rural areas into urban ones, increasing their likelihood of becoming infected. This means that more people spread over more regions are at greater risk of being bitten and infected over a longer period (World Health Organization–Western Pacific Region 2012).

For people with allergies and asthma, climate change will increase respiratory difficulties. Plant biology and plant growth are influenced by temperature, precipitation, and CO_2. This has been ignored in much of the literature on climate change impacts. The possible effects deserve serious study. Increased CO_2 contributes to plant growth and subsequently increasing growth and pollen production in trees, plants, and ragweed, intensifying respiratory allergies. As pollen production is increased several times with an increase in CO_2 and as pollen is seemingly becoming more allergenic, more people may become vulnerable (Ziska and Beggs 2012; Ziska, Epstein, and Schlesinger 2009).

Food supplies have received more attention. They are put into jeopardy with drought in some regions or too early of a snow thaw in others, whereby the water is present but earlier than it is needed and absent when it is needed. There is more to consider than that. Rising temperatures during the reproductive stages of plant growth can adversely affect fertility and fruit and grain production. Nutritional values of food are also affected. More CO_2 from pre-industrial times to the present has reduced the protein content and increased the carbohydrate content of spring and summer wheat. Rice paddy protein is decreased in the presence of higher temperatures and more CO_2. In some cases, increased CO_2 has increased nutritional value. Strawberry antioxidant capacity and mung bean omega-3 fatty acid increased with increased CO_2.

Increased CO_2, temperature, and precipitation all affect the efficacy of chemical weed and pest controls (Ziska et al. 2009). There are two potential scenarios. It could be that more crops are destroyed by pests, pathogens, and weeds that currently consume 42 percent of crops, or more chemicals could be applied. One of these decreases the food supply; the other increases harmful chemicals into the environment and degrades soil (Ziska et al. 2009).

Many questions remain to be answered. Which plant-based medicines will increase or decrease in potency? Will contact dermatitis (e.g., poison ivy and oak) increase in severity of cases, and will more people become allergic as the irritant urushiol increases in toxicity in reaction to increasing CO_2? Will poisons in plants increase in toxicity, becoming more lethal (Ziska et al. 2009)?

The earth's natural carbon cycle has been altered. Even if all greenhouse gas emissions are eliminated, those still in the atmosphere and the changes they caused will keep the earth warming "by about 6° C over the next century" (NASA n.d.). Where ice and snow have disappeared, water and land will absorb radiation that formerly ice and snow reflected back. This will increase water evaporation, and water vapor—the most potent greenhouse gas—will increase the greenhouse effect. These feedback loops will

A CLOSER LOOK
GREENHOUSE GAS EMISSIONS AND ECONOMIC SECTOR

FIGURE 14.8   Total Annual Anthropogenic GHG Emissions by Gases, 1970–2010

The rate of greenhouse gas emissions increased from 1.3 percent a year for 1970–2000 to 2.2 percent a year for 2000–2010. The largest increase (59 percent) was from CO_2 fossil fuels and industrial processes.

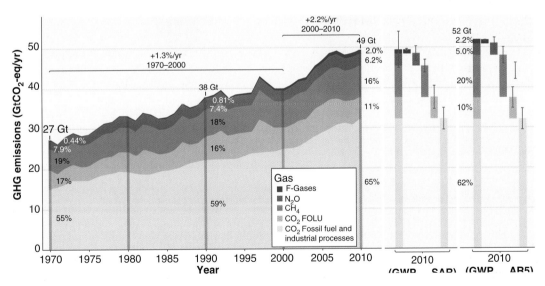

Source: Figure 1.6 from IPCC, 2014: *Climate Change 2014: Synthesis Report. Contribution of Working Groups I, II and III to the Fifth Assessment Report of the Intergovernmental Panel on Climate Change* [Core Writing Team, Pachauri, R.K. and Meyer, L. (eds.)]. IPCC, Geneva, Switzerland.

(Continued)

(Continued)

FIGURE 14.9   Greenhouse Gas Emissions by Economic Sectors

Electricity and heat production is the greatest source of greenhouse gas emissions.

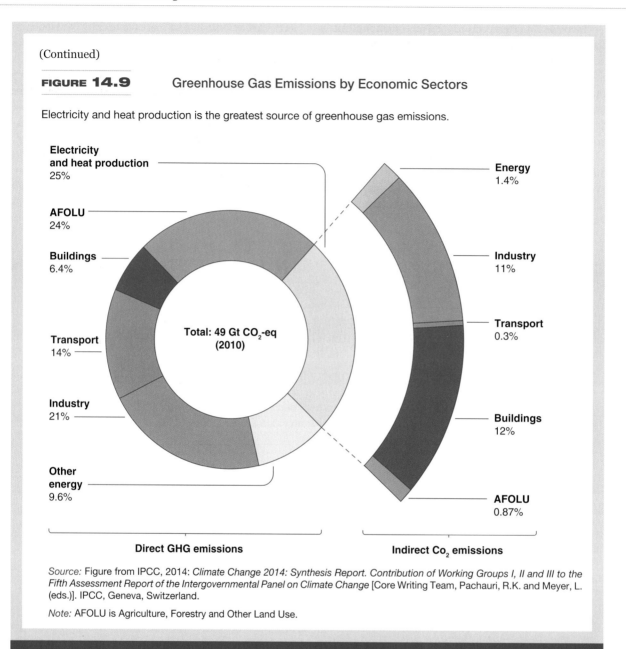

Electricity and heat production 25%

AFOLU 24%

Buildings 6.4%

Transport 14%

Industry 21%

Other energy 9.6%

Total: 49 Gt CO_2-eq (2010)

Energy 1.4%

Industry 11%

Transport 0.3%

Buildings 12%

AFOLU 0.87%

Direct GHG emissions   Indirect CO_2 emissions

Source: Figure from IPCC, 2014: *Climate Change 2014: Synthesis Report. Contribution of Working Groups I, II and III to the Fifth Assessment Report of the Intergovernmental Panel on Climate Change* [Core Writing Team, Pachauri, R.K. and Meyer, L. (eds.)]. IPCC, Geneva, Switzerland.

Note: AFOLU is Agriculture, Forestry and Other Land Use.

continue without greenhouse gas emissions. How long it will take for temperature to stabilize cannot be determined. What is not in doubt is that thermal inertia will keep it rising (Royce and Lam 2013). This makes action to mitigate climate change all the more urgent.

Greenhouse Gases

Energy fuels the modern economy. The economic break through of the Industrial Revolution was that it unharnessed massive energy stores found in fossil fuels that could do more work than humans and animals could do and could do it faster. This made electrification of homes and factories possible. It made mass production possible. The energy of fossil fuels and the machines that made use of them could produce enough food, clothing, and shelter for everyone in the world to live comfortably. The cost would not be realized until later. Before the Industrial Revolution, there was not significant inequality among nations. Most people in most nations were poor (Figures 14.8 and 14.9). With industrialization, some nations became wealthy and in doing so changed the climate.

As Europe and the United States took advantage of these productive capacities and became wealthy, greenhouse gases were accumulating. Although pollution by smoke and smog was abundantly evident in industrial towns of the 1800s, the long-term health and environmental effects of pollution and greenhouse gases[8] (CO_2, methane, nitrous oxide, ozone, chlorofluorocarbons, and water vapor) were not evident until much later.

Energy, whether for our homes, industries, agriculture, or transportation, is the main source of greenhouse gas emissions and the key to climate change.

The energy sector is the single biggest contributor to global greenhouse gas emissions, accounting for 35 percent of anthropogenic emissions and 49 percent of energy emissions in 2010 (Bruckner et al. 2014). It takes energy to power economic growth and development. As societies move from agrarian to industrial economies and GDP per capita grows, energy use will grow along with it. Population growth increases energy use as well, but energy use per capita varies by income, lifestyle, available resources, and available technology. Richer nations still consume more energy per capita and release more greenhouse gases despite cleaner technologies (Blanco et al. 2014).

Per capita greenhouse gas emissions are higher in Organisation for Economic Cooperation and Development

A CLOSER LOOK
GREENHOUSE GAS EMISSIONS BY WORLD REGION AND PER CAPITA BY WORLD REGION

Although Asia now emits the largest share of greenhouse gases, the OECD countries emit far more per person, reflecting their much greater energy consumption per person.

FIGURE 14.10   Aggregate GHG Emissions

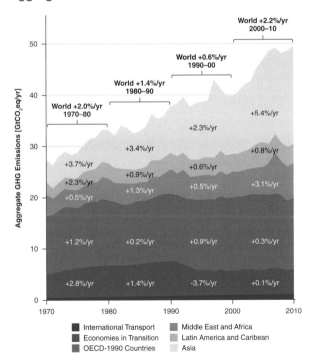

Source: Blanco et al. (2014). Reproduced with permission.

(Continued)

(Continued)

FIGURE 14.11   Per Capita GHG Emissions

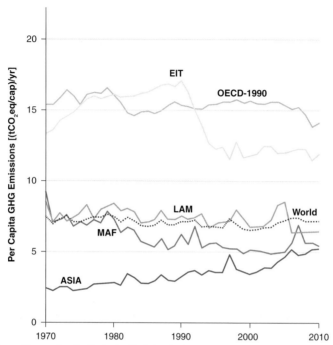

Source: Figure 5.2 from Blanco G., R. Gerlagh, S. Suh, J. Barrett, H.C. de Coninck, C.F. Diaz Morejon, R. Mathur, N. Nakicenovic, A. Ofosu Ahenkora, J. Pan, H. Pathak, J. Rice, R. Richels, S.J. Smith, D.I. Stern, F.L. Toth, and P. Zhou, 2014: Drivers, Trends and Mitigation. In: *Climate Change 2014: Mitigation of Climate Change. Contribution of Working Group III to the Fifth Assessment Report of the Intergovernmental Panel on Climate Change* [Edenhofer, O., R. Pichs-Madruga, Y. Sokona, E. Farahani, S. Kadner, K. Seyboth, A. Adler, I. Baum, S. Brunner, P. Eickemeier, B. Kriemann, J. Savolainen, S. Schlömer, C. von Stechow, T. Zwickel and J.C. Minx (eds.)]. Cambridge University Press, Cambridge, United Kingdom and New York, NY, USA.

Note: EID = Economies in Transition; LAM = Latin America and Caribean; MAF = Middle East and Africa.

(OECD) countries than in Asia, although Asia has more total greenhouse gas emissions. Key drivers vary by region. In OECD countries, the primary driver is GDP per capita. This is also the case since about 2000 in "economies in transition" (former Warsaw Pact centrally planned economies). Wealthier countries use more energy as the demand for electricity and goods grows and lifestyles of people change. In Asia, Latin America and the Caribbean, and the Middle East and Africa, it is fossil-based energy (territorial use). However, in Asia the second driver is GDP per capita, but in the other two regions the second driver is population (Blanco et al. 2014). In terms of per capita emissions, OECD countries increased energy use about 13 or 14 percent since 1990, whereas Latin America

and the Caribbean increased 60 percent, Africa and the Middle East 90 percent, and China 200 percent, reflecting their economic growth and development. However, these three regions are still using only half of the OECD rate per capita of the 1970s (Figures 14.10 and 14.11) (Blanco et al. 2014).While cleaner fuels and technology allowed countries in the developed world to decrease their emissions of CO_2 in recent decades, they still emit significantly more greenhouse gases per capita than the developing regions—10 metric tons per person per year as opposed to 3 metric tons in developing regions. As noted in the 2015 Millennium Development Goals report, the developing regions increased their emissions nearly threefold, from 6.7 to 19.8 billion metric tons per year, due to increasing

CONSIDER THIS
THE MECHANICS OF EXTREME WET AND DRY WEATHER EVENTS

The science behind temperature and extreme weather is well established. Hundreds more extreme weather events occur yearly than would occur without climate change. Others would have occurred in any case but with less intensity.

A few principles account for the basics of how various forms of extreme weather are produced. Greenhouse gases trap radiation in the atmosphere. This increases the temperature of the atmosphere. This heat is a source of energy. For every 1° C increase in temperature, moisture in the air increases 7 percent. The increase is not evenly spread around the globe. In some places it is higher, and in others it is lower. For example, Des Moines, Iowa, has had a 13 percent rise in moisture over 50 years.

The increase in moisture brings about an increase in precipitation, rain, and snow. There is a 2 or 3 percent increase for every 1° C increase in warming. The extra moisture plus the extra energy results in a 6 or 7 percent increase in extreme rainfall. Increased intensity of storms means more flash flooding.

When moist warm air meets cooler drier air, thunderstorms result. When there is a rotational source, such as the warm moist air from over the Gulf of Mexico meeting the strong jet stream from the west, tornadoes develop, as happened tragically in the string of tornadoes that hit in April 2011 (Smith et al. 2014).

Drought and Heat Waves

The Union of Concerned Scientists (n.d. a) differentiates three types of drought: *meteorological*, which is dryness relative to usual rainfall, *hydrological*, which relates to low water in water systems, and *agricultural*, which is when there is too little water to meet the demands of crops. The American Southwest is one of the most drought-sensitive areas of the world. Droughts cost the United States about U.S. $9 billion a year.

The consequences of extreme weather events extend beyond the immediate damage in lives lost and infrastructure destroyed. There are also long-term impacts on individuals and communities. While infrastructure may be rebuilt, communities are destroyed. Individuals move on, but the psychological costs and destruction of families continue.

---

demand for energy for development and the types of fuel sources (especially coal) they used. For example, although China is far behind the developed world in per capita emissions, it is now the largest emitter of greenhouse gases in the world. While China is now engaging modern technologies to continue its development, most developing countries lag. Because their energy production is still low in terms of their eventual energy needs and they lack sufficient capacity in modern technologies, their emissions will rise unless significant action is taken by the global community.

Another important aspect of these drivers is that the sharp increases in some countries' territorial use of energy and related emissions stem in part from manufacturing products and growing produce for export to OECD countries (among others). The decline in territorial emissions in OECD countries is more than offset by increases in other countries that are related to OECD consumption. It could be said that greenhouse gas emissions have been exported to developing nations.

In the least developed nations, agriculture accounts for nearly all greenhouse gas emissions, nearly 90 percent. As these populations urbanize, their energy use and emissions will increase. Help of more developed nations will be critical in mitigating related greenhouse gas issues. Other important drivers of greenhouse gas emissions are agriculture, forestry and other land use, transport, waste, and industry (Blanco et al. 2014).

THE ENVIRONMENTAL REGIME

The global environmental regime is a complex network of nongovernmental and governmental organizations at the local, national, regional, and global levels. It has grown slowly as people increasingly recognized the threat to environments posed by human activity. From its beginnings in the preservation of particular species threatened with extinction to concern for the global threat posed by climate change, it has grown to encompass treaties, regulations, and programs to analyze environmental problems, legislative provisions to combat them, and actions to remediate and solve them. Many other treaties such as those on trade and jobs also contain environmental concerns. International environmental associations, treaties, and intergovernmental organizations all now number over 150 (Meyer et al. 1997).

COP21, held in Paris in December 2015, was the 21st Conference of the Parties to the United Nations Framework Convention on Climate Change. The convention originated in negotiations at the Earth Summit in Rio de Janeiro, Brazil, in 1992 and entered into force in 1994. COP21, the Paris accord, is the latest conference and the newest set of accords. It will enter into effect after at least 55 countries that are party to the convention and whose total greenhouse gas emissions cumulatively represent 55 percent of the global total ratify it (Article 21). The convention reaffirms many of the provisions of past treaties and establishes responsibilities for monitoring their terms.

The substantive text of the treaty is in Article 2. The first point of Article 2 calls on countries to strengthen "the global response to the threat of climate change, in the context of sustainable development and efforts to eradicate poverty," including to do the following:

- Hold the increase in the global average temperature to well below 2° C above pre-industrial levels and pursue efforts to limit the temperature increase to 1.5° C above pre-industrial levels

- Increase the ability to adapt to the adverse impacts of climate change and foster climate resilience and low greenhouse gas emissions development in a manner that does not threaten food production

- Make finance flows consistent with a pathway toward low greenhouse gas emissions and climate-resilient development (United Nations [UN] 2015)

These provisions make it clear that poverty reduction and food security are important goals that must be achieved but within the context of sustainability. In other words, food security and poverty eradication must be achieved in such a way as to secure the long-term health of the world. Funding should be consistent with these aims. The second point in Article 2 makes it clear that different nations have different capacities to contribute to these goals. Thus, equity does not mean every country being treated in the same way or subject to the same expectations. Rather, within the overall goal, expectations for each country will vary in relation to its capacity.

Other articles of the agreement clarify that international cooperation, sharing of best practices and technology, and financing should be directed at building the capacity of countries to mitigate and adapt to climate change. Other expectations are for transparency in countries' actions and support of others. It also calls on "non-party" actors such as civil society groups, philanthropies, the private sector, cities, and other subnational authorities to support actions to reduce greenhouse gas emissions.

"GREENING" THE EARTH: SUSTAINABLE DEVELOPMENT

As this chapter emphasizes, even if we eliminated all greenhouse gas emissions, the globe would continue to warm and the climate would continue to change. That does not mean that there is nothing we can do. Mitigating climate change and adapting to it will increase the health of the planet and subsequently human health and well-being and that of animal and plant life as well.

Stalling Climate Change

Green chemistry and a circular economy, as discussed in Chapter 13, are important steps to reduce greenhouse gases, conserve resources, reduce hazardous substances, grow healthier food, and help restore our ecosystems. They are not enough to stop global warming and climate change. We need to significantly reduce or eliminate anthropogenic sources of greenhouse gases. How close to stalling global warming are we?

Carbon Reduction Through Carbon Pricing Strategies

Cap and trade (emissions trading system), carbon tax, clean coal, and carbon sequestering are strategies that aim to reduce carbon and other pollutants in the atmosphere by reducing the amount of source carbon or preventing carbon released in combustion from polluting the environment. The costs of greenhouse gases and other carbon pollution—the externalities—are staggering in all of the damage to health, the natural environment, and our built environment. Carbon pricing is a strategy to make the polluters pay for the damage they do.

Many environmental and industry groups support carbon pricing. Cap and trade is the most common form. Every country's programs are somewhat different, but all cover CO_2 and most major industrial sectors such as transportation, power generation, and manufacturing. The "cap" is an upper limit to the emissions allowed by a major pollution source. Each cap represents a portion of the reductions in greenhouse gases necessary for a country to meet targets. Polluters covered under the policies have a cap, or allowance, to release a certain amount of carbon. The caps are to be adjusted downward yearly.

The trade comes into play because a polluter may release more pollutants than its cap allows provided that it buys allowance from an entity that is emitting less than its cap. Allowances may be bought from any participating countries. This opens up an international market for emissions and puts a price on emissions, which should be motivation to reduce pollution. As of 2016, 35 countries, 17 provinces or states in the United States and Canada, and 7 cities (5 in China and 2 in Japan) were participating. When China began its national program in 2017, participants accounted for 49 percent of global GDP (International Carbon Action Partnership [ICAP] 2016).

The European Union initiated cap and trade for greenhouse gases[9] and all large industrial facilities in 2005, aiming at a 20 percent reduction by 2020. After the Paris meetings, an accelerated timetable was set for the 2020–2030 period aiming at a 43 percent reduction from 2005 levels to meet its new target—a reduction of 80 to 95 percent by 2050 (ICAP 2016). Through a combination of policies, the U.S. state of California reduced greenhouse gas emissions per GDP by 20 percent and per capita by nearly 15 percent from 2000 levels (ICAP 2016).

Cap and trade is one method of making industries pay for the privilege of polluting more than their allowance. A direct tax is another. Eighteen countries, cities, or states put a direct tax on carbon. The province of British Columbia reduced fuel usage 16 percent and per capita emissions 3.5 times faster than the rest of Canada. Industry leaders, academics, non-profits, and politicians credit the carbon tax for their success. Because every dollar that the tax generates goes to the public by way of reduced taxes, it has broad appeal. Plans to increase the tax in 2018 were under way.

One lesson to take away from the success of carbon pricing strategies is that industries can be weaned from carbon resources and that carbon pricing may motivate movement toward renewable resources.

Carbon Capture and Sequester

Nearly every plan to reduce climate change calls for reduced but continuing use of fossil fuels at least until 2050. What to do with CO_2 is a problem that cannot be ignored. Carbon capture requires separating carbon from other combustion emissions and trapping it before it escapes. This is an expensive process. After capturing carbon, it must be sequestered. This requires piping it as a gas or transforming it into a liquid so that it can be piped to a suitable location.

From southwest Colorado, drillers piped a huge bubble of CO_2 gas to west Texas to be used in oil recovery. There it is forced into the ground to force oil out of pockets to the surface. Hopefully it will stay there. Gas captures are now planned for power plants that will pipe the gas to oil fields. Storing CO_2 in gaseous or liquid form risks its leakage from storage. Necessary monitoring for leakage adds to the expense (Biello 2014).

Ideally, carbon sequester, if used, would lock the gas into a solid form. The CarbFix Project dissolves the gas with water, making soda water, and pumps it into basalt rock, where it forms calcite, turning it into stone. Experiments in Iceland, which is nearly all basalt, demonstrated that in less than two years 95 percent of the CO_2 turned to calcite. There are still problems to be overcome. The process would need to be scaled up enormously, and it consumes a lot of water. But salt water can be used, and basaltic rock is common along continental margins and the ocean floors (Fountain 2016). While this is not a fix for global warming, it may contribute to a solution for as long as we are burning fossil fuels. Carbon pricing can reduce the expense.

Renewables and Non-Carbon-Based Strategies

The technical capacity of renewables to meet energy demands far exceeds current use. A 2011 IPCC study of 160 scenarios modeled by more than 120 researchers reported that as much as 80 percent of global energy demand could be met by renewables by 2050, cutting greenhouse gas emissions by a third and keeping the global temperature rise below 2° C, the target set by COP21 in Paris.

Currently, close to 24 percent of global energy needs are met by renewables when nuclear energy is included as renewable. Renewables are not necessarily greenhouse gas neutral. The benefits depend on how the resource was acquired, how it is used, construction and operation of the facility, storage, and disposals of wastes. For example, low-grade uranium with a high energy input for mining and milling will have a larger carbon emission than a richer ore with less extensive mining and enrichment.

There are other variables to figure as well. However, nearly every renewable technology, other than charcoal and some other biomass methods, emits far fewer greenhouse gases per kilowatt hour than fossil fuel burning (Table 14.2).

The share of renewables of total energy is growing, albeit slowly. If we omit dams built decades ago from the data above, renewable energy's contribution is much smaller. If we omit all dams—China has been building many in recent years, not only in China but also in South America and Africa—it is smaller still. In developed

A CLOSER LOOK
RENEWABLE ENERGY

TABLE 14.2   Estimated Renewable Energy Share of Total Energy Consumption, 2015

Renewable energy is still a small portion of the global total energy used.

Type of Fuel	% Use in 2015	Type of Renewable	% Use in 2015	Type of Modern Renewable	% Used in 2015
Fossil	78.4				
Renewable	19.3	Traditional biomass	9.1		
		Modern renewables	10.2	Biomass/geothermal/solar heat	4.2
				Hydropower	3.6
				Wind/solar/biomass/ geothermal power	1.6
				Biofuels for transport	0.8
Nuclear	2.3				

Source: Adapted from REN 21 Secretariat (2017).

Note: Biomass and biofuels are renewable but vary in the amount of carbon and many other pollutants they generate. Some biofuels are considered carbon neutral because the CO_2 they produce is offset by growing them.

countries, there is little demand for growth in energy. Populations are not increasing (except in the United States), the energy infrastructure is in place, and there are large stocks of fossil fuels. In developing societies, the move toward industrialization and economic growth along with still increasing populations is driving a rapidly increasing demand.

The Energy Grid and Distributed Renewable Energy

In the developed world, energy grids may stretch across a continent. To get an idea of how large these grids are, consider what happened in a power failure, a blackout. In 1965, 30 million people across Canada and the U.S. Northeast had no power. In 2003, a power line in Ohio brushed against trees, shutting it down, and ultimately 50 million people in the U.S. Northeast and Canada were without power. In India in 2012, half of the country was left without power. Across Germany, Italy, France, and Spain, 10 to 15 million people lost electricity when a German power company switched off a line to allow a cruise ship to pass through the River Ems. China, Thailand, Brazil, and Paraguay all experienced major blackouts. In all of these, people were stranded in subways, in mines, on trains, and in elevators—often without water. People died.

Now the grids of developed countries are aging. Utility companies are talking about smart grids. But whether or not they are better or safe from a cyberattack is debatable. Increasingly, people are considering going "off the grid" or forming much smaller local grids. And in the developing world, where many people are still without electricity, distributed renewable energy is probably the smartest strategy.

Sub-Saharan Africa is one of the most energy-deprived regions in the world; two thirds of the people living there, more than 600 million, do not have access to electricity. Many of these people use dangerous and hazardous sources indoors such as kerosene lamps and inefficient wood-burning stoves. Although many of these people may someday be connected to grids, that prospect is far off for most or may never happen. "Power Africa" is a collaborative effort led by U.S. Agency for International Development partnering with African governments, global philanthropies, aid organizations of other developed countries, and more than 100 private sector partners. The commitment is to add 30,000 megawatts by supplying electricity to 60 million new homes and businesses that are currently without power. The project combines extensions of existing grids and off-the-grid projects. For this to be successful, policy, regulatory, financing, and technical expertise all need to fall into place. The projects need to be environmentally and financially sustainable. Bomi Safi, for example, is a one-woman company in Kenya. She mobilizes women to distribute solar-powered products such as cooking stoves. This type of simple but sophisticated off-the-grid answer can significantly raise the quality of life for millions (Makoye 2016; U.S. African Development Foundation 2016).

Electricity expands life chances; from refrigeration for food and medicines, to studying at night, to starting a small business with a sewing machine, every dimension of life chances is improved with power. Renewable solutions can be as simple as solar-powered lanterns to provide nighttime light or a biomass generator to run a sewing machine. Challenge Power Africa is a competition for entrepreneurs to bring off-the-grid solutions to underserved populations.

Award-winning off-the-grid small projects are wonderfully inventive. Here is a sampling. These were chosen as among the 10 weirdest energy innovations by Smart Villages:[10]

- GravityLight supplies 20 minutes of continuous light by lifting a bag of dirt with a pulley and letting it down slowly. There are no solar panels, no batteries, and no harmful fumes.

- SOCCKET II is a soccer ball (football) that, after 30 minutes of play, can power a lamp for 3 hours.

- Cloud Collective developed a device whereby tubes of algae could be connected to roads and bridges to feed off the transport CO_2 emissions. The crop could be harvested at some point to make a viable biofuel.

- Hydro Electric Barrel generates enough electricity to power refrigeration by spinning and bobbing in a stream or river.

- Sanitation for human waste and medical equipment is important to the developing world. An off-the-grid device using nanoparticles to concentrate sunlight to heat is so effective that it can turn icy water to steam for sanitizing in seconds. The Bill and Melinda Gates Foundation awarded this invention a grant for development. (Fitzgerald 2016)

The Solutions Project: 100 Percent Clean Is 100 Percent Possible

By 2050, 100 percent renewable energy could be a reality, according to a multi-institution research team centered at the Stanford University Atmosphere/Energy Program. The 100 Percent Project is an extremely detailed plan, a roadmap, of how each of 139 countries and each of the 50 U.S. states can reach the 100 percent renewable 2050 target and an 80 percent renewable 2030 target.[11] The plan does not figure in conservation measures that require "sacrifices" but rather is a "business as usual" plan. It does not rely on technologies that do not exist. It does not build any new dams or nuclear plants. All of the energy in the plan comes from water, sun, and wind.

Each roadmap calculates and includes the types of energy available in each country and strategies for using each. This includes the following:

- The future demand for every energy sector—electricity, transportation, heating/cooling, industry, and agriculture/fishing/forestry

- The number of wind, water, or sunlight energy generators and the footprint and spacing areas needed to meet demand for each case

- The rooftop areas and solar photovoltaic potentials existing on buildings, carports, garages, parking lots, and parking structures

- The adjusted costs of energy in 2050

The roadmap also includes, in great detail, the benefits that will be realized by the roadmaps:

- Reductions or elimination of millions of air pollution-related deaths and illnesses

- Reductions in trillions of dollars a year in pollution from mining for, drilling for, and transporting fuels

- Avoiding trillions of dollars a year in damage costs from acid rain and other pollution

- Reductions in trillions of dollars a year in ambient CO_2 and global warming costs

- 51.4 million jobs created globally, more than offsetting the expected loss of 27.1 million jobs in the old energy industry, for a net gain of 24.3 million long-term good jobs

- Price stability (oil prices fluctuate, sometimes wildly)

- The revenue that will be gained

- Energy efficiency (electricity has a higher work-to-energy ratio than combustion)

- Reduced international conflict over energy

- Elimination of "energy poverty"

- Reduced large-scale system disruption through power outages or terrorism

The roadmaps also supply a blueprint by way of a transition timeline and recommended policy measures to implement the roadmaps (Jacobson et al. 2016).

The Solutions Project does not include nuclear facilities, carbon capture, biofuels, or natural gas. It does not add any new hydropower plants but includes existing ones. The technologies that it uses and the contribution of each one to global energy are "19.8 percent onshore wind, ~12.7 percent offshore wind, ~40.8 percent utility-scale photovoltaic (PV), ~6.5 percent residential rooftop PV, ~7.0 percent commercial/government/parking rooftop PV, ~7.7 percent concentrated solar power (CSP), ~0.73 percent geothermal power, ~0.38 percent wave power, ~0.06 percent tidal power, and ~4.3 percent hydropower" (Jacobson et al. 2016).

For light ground transportation, battery electric vehicles and hydrogen fuel cells are planned. All processes relating to transportation by land, air, and sea can be electrified, many by 2030, such as small-scale marine, rails and buses, and heavy-duty truck transport. High-efficiency electric appliances, many of which are already in use, will replace the appliances and technologies that are now gas, oil, or coal driven, even for high-temperature industrial facilities (Jacobson et al. 2016).

SUMMARY

Climate change is the greatest global security threat. Extreme weather events, rising seas, and slow degradation of environments force more people from their homes than any other cause, including war. Climate-driven drought exacerbates food shortages and leads to social unrest. Unless stalled, climate change is likely to add millions more people to the refugee crisis. Although forces already set in motion, such as rising sea temperatures, cannot be immediately halted, climate change can be slowed and kept from becoming catastrophic.

The developed world grew rich through cheap and unlimited use of fossil fuels, filling the atmosphere with greenhouse gases and creating the conditions of climate change in the process. Population growth and improving the living standards in countries at low levels of development will increase demands for energy. These countries must be helped to invest in and rely on clean energies. Replacing fossil fuels with renewable energy and developing efficient mass transportation systems and low- or no-carbon vehicles are necessary steps. Preserving air, land, and water so that it may continue to support life is a necessity.

DISCUSSION

1. Compare and contrast strategies to combat climate change. Which hold the most promise? Consider those in the text and others that you may investigate.

2. The U.S. state of California has developed one of the most ambitious programs to combat climate change. Investigate its plans and report on its goals and strategies that you find promising or innovative. California's plan, the highlights, strategies for sectors, and legislation can be found at this site: http://climatechange.ca.gov. Specific plans for greenhouse gases are also at this site: http://www.arb.ca.gov/cc/cleanenergy/clean_fs2.htm.

3. Consider the Pew Global Report on attitudes toward climate change. How do you explain the differences in people's attitudes based on their political persuasion? Consider how they weigh economic issues and jobs against environmental health. http://www.pewglobal.org/2015/11/05/global-concern-about-climate-change-broad-support-for-limiting-emissions/climate-change-report-24.

4. The competing interests of generating or maintaining jobs and the cost of environmental protections are vigorously debated. Gather evidence on both sides of this debate and evaluate which side has the stronger argument.

5. Assess the impacts of climate change where you live. There are a number of sources for every continent. A few are suggested below.

In Africa: https://www.unicef.org/esaro/Climate_Change_in_Africa.pdf

In Asia: https://www.adb.org/news/infographics/climate-change-impacts-human-systems-asia-and-pacific

In Australia: http://www.environment.gov.au/climate-change/climate-science-data/climate-science/impacts

In Europe: https://www.eea.europa.eu/soer-2015/europe/climate-change-impacts-and-adaptation

In North America: http://www.ccsenet.org/journal/index.php/jsd/article/view/9793

In South America: http://www.worldbank.org/en/news/speech/2014/12/02/climate-change-impacts-in-latin-america-and-the-caribbean-confronting-the-new-climate-normal

In the United States: https://19january2017snapshot.epa.gov/climate-impacts/climate-impacts-northeast_.html

How have these impacts affected you or your community?

6. An important factor in solving every global problem is considering the responsibility of richer developed nations to poorer nations. Do richer nations owe poorer nations help in developing cleaner and healthier technologies? Why or why not? If they do, how much help should they provide?

ON YOUR OWN

1. *National Climate Assessment: Future Climate* has interactive maps of the United States that illustrate potential future climate and weather scenarios given both lower and higher emissions of greenhouse gases. It proposes scenarios for the following dimensions of climate: temperature change, soil moisture, precipitation, consecutive dry days, and sea level rise (http://nca2014.globalchange.gov/highlights/report-findings/future-climate).

2. What sacrifices are people willing to make for a sustainable environment? Investigate the survey questions concerning the environment asked in the World Values Survey. Choose a developing country and a developed country to compare and contrast. Compare answers within a country by age and educational level. http://www.worldvaluessurvey.org/WVSOnline.jsp

   Protecting environment vs. economic growth

   Past two years: Given money to ecological organization

   Past two years: Participated in demonstration for environment

3. Investigate the Solutions Project Roadmap for your country or U.S. state:

   http://thesolutionsproject.org/why-clean-energy

   How does its formulas for renewable energy potentials compare with those of the National Renewable Energy Laboratory?

   https://www.nrel.gov/docs/fy12osti/51946.pdf

   After reading both of these projections, how feasible is a 100 percent renewable plan? What are the advantages, and are there any disadvantages that the plans may be overlooking?

NOTES

1. The 2° C rise in temperature is in comparison with the 1951–1980 baseline.

2. Permafrost is land that remains at 0° C for at least two years.

3. For the greenhouse effect of greenhouse gases, see the EPA's *Overview of Greenhouse Gases* (https://www3.epa.gov/climatechange/ghgemissions/gases/ch4.html).

4. For a timetable of the 2013–2018 Endangered Species Act Listing Workplan, refer to https://www.fws.gov/endangered/what-we-do/listing-overview.html.

5. The WWF–Coca-Cola campaign raised $2 million in donations for polar bears. The polar bear has been the Coca-Cola mascot (WWF 2012).

6. Data on deaths, injuries, and economic losses are underreported for many low-income countries. For example, economic losses were reported for only 12.5 percent of disasters (CRED 2015).

7. Vector-borne diseases are those that are transmitted from one organism to another, usually by an arthropod such as a mosquito, tsetse fly, flea, or tick.

8. The EPA distinguished direct greenhouse gases, which are listed above. The indirect ones are "CO [carbon monoxide], NOx [nitrogen oxides], NMVOCs [non-methane volatile organic compounds], and SO_2 [sulfur dioxide]. These gases do not have a direct global warming effect, but indirectly affect terrestrial radiation absorption by influencing the formation and destruction of tropospheric and stratospheric ozone, or, in the case of SO_2, by affecting the absorptive characteristics of the atmosphere. Additionally, some of these gases may react with other chemical compounds in the atmosphere to form compounds that are greenhouse gases" (taken from the *EPA Inventory of U.S. Greenhouse Gas Emissions and Sinks: 1990–2013* published in April 2015: https://www.epa.gov/ghgemissions/inventory-us-greenhouse-gas-emissions-and-sinks-1990-2013.

9. Cap and trade was introduced in the United States in 1990 and used successfully in helping to reduce sulfur dioxide and nitrogen oxides in the environment, combatting acid rain.

10. Smart Villages held workshops in every region of the developing world—six workshops over a three-year period from 2014 to 2017—to bring energy innovations to policy makers, donors, and development agencies. Two final workshops were to be held in Brussels and Addis Ababa to bring all of the lessons learned to the UN and other global actors. There are many more inventions on the Smart Villages website (https://e4sv.org).

11. The Solutions Project roadmaps are a much more detailed and refined set of projections based on a series of earlier projections by the head authors, Mark Z. Jacobson and Mark A. Delucchi. "100 Percent Clean 100 Percent Renewable" is a motto of sorts for the project.

15

Urbanization

THE LURE OF THE CITIES

TALE OF TWO WOMEN

Nearly everything that can be manufactured, from the simplest toy to the most complex electronic device, is made in Dongguan, China. Girls by the millions pour into Dongguan, and cities like it, to escape the poverty of rural China. Lu Qing Min is one of them. She does quality control. We might see misery and exploitation in her job and the jobs of others like her—long hours, cramped living quarters of 10 to 15 in a room, 50 people sharing a bathroom, and low wages—but she sees opportunity. For her, her job is a chance to save some money, to have some extra money to spend, to send some money home to her husband and children, to move up perhaps to a secretarial position. She is young and sees this as a chance to do something with her life. What she makes doesn't matter. How little her job is in the grand scheme of things doesn't matter. She is not alienated. She is moving up in social class. Eventually, her husband and children will join her. Her girls will be city girls. They will be middle class (Chang 2008).

Norma Brion, at the time her story was published, had seen her children in person only twice in the last eight years. It was not because she was a neglectful mother or in jail. Quite the opposite—she was a devoted and hard-working mother, but taking care of her children meant emigrating from the Philippines and working taking care of someone else's children so that hers could have a better life. She was in Abu Dhabi, one of a half million Filipino women working in the United Arab Emirates. They are among 10 million Filipino women who are working overseas, usually as domestics, so that they can send money home to their families. And they do—$26.9 billion just from January to November 2016. For Norma and millions like her, the city is the place to be—sometimes in their own country, sometimes far away. In time, they will return to their families (Santos 2017).

LEARNING OBJECTIVES

After completing this chapter, students will be able to do the following:

15.1 Understand the multi-dimensions of sustainability—environmental and social

15.2 Understand the processes leading to greater urbanization

15.3 Analyze causes and consequences of problems of urbanization

15.4 Compare and contrast the concepts of megacities, global cities, and creative cities

15.5 Describe factors related to the fragility of cities

15.6 Describe the processes through which "slums" can be strengthened

15.7 Recognize the positive features of "slum" communities

15.8 Develop proposals to enhance the sustainability and resilience of cities

Neither Lu Qing nor Norma sees herself as a victim. While this is not reason to excuse the conditions under which most work or that force them to leave their families behind, it is important to recognize the dignity with which they work, how they live their lives, and their dreams for themselves and their children. The city is their hope.

WHAT MAKES A CITY?

All roads led to Rome, the center of commerce, politics, and culture of the empire. For centuries, continuous flows of migrants followed roads to Rome, seeking fortune or brought as conquests of war. All were made citizens and their presence gave rise to angst over the usual problems that accompany urbanization whether in the ancient world, the industrial era, or the 21st century. How should the congestion in people, traffic, housing, garbage, and sewage be made tolerable and safe? Were these new immigrants/citizens a drain on the Roman economy? Were the free handouts (grain in the case of Rome) destroying people's willingness to work (Beard 2015)?

Cities have long stood at the center of the intersecting roads of global life, forming and informing channels among civilizations. The "Silk Road"—from China to the Mediterranean—is one of the most famous channels. All along the road, migrants moved, forming hubs that became cities on the main routes, moving and mixing goods and cultures in the process. The cities stood, as they do today, at the nexus of ecological and social transitions—mountain to flatland, water to dry land, rural to urban, civilization to wilderness, rich to poor.

For most of history, the world's largest cities were in the Middle and Far East. Chinese cities dominated from about 1100 to 1850. But with industrialization, urbanization in Europe surged and Europe's cities, for a time at least, became the largest and most prosperous in the world.

Today's cities are in many ways similar in character to ancient cities. Teeming with diversity, they are the political, cultural, and commercial centers of the world. People come to the cities to make their fortunes or at least make a living. Flows of migrants to cities continue and show no sign of stopping anytime soon. Whether rich or poor, cities are connected through complex networks of people and materials that make them the pivotal actors in the contemporary world. There are more international organizations and networks of cities than of intergovernmental associations as cities band together to solve their own and the world's problems (Muggah 2017).

With the majority of the world's population living in cities and the majority of the world's economic growth produced there, cities will determine the world's future. Traditionally, urbanization has meant increasing prosperity and improved life chances. We have seen in earlier chapters that, for the most part, city residents live longer, healthier, and more prosperous lives than rural residents. Whether cities can sustain these strengths into the future is the 7 billion person question of the 21st century.

WHAT DOES IT MEAN TO BE URBAN?

Where the People Are

The increasing dominance of urban life affects every aspect of life, with potential for a more secure and sustainable future for everyone or increasing inequalities and social unrest. Whether due to climate change, conflict, economic opportunity, or just a desire to be where the "action" is, the flow of migration is to cities. There are about a billion people, one in seven, living outside of the area where they were born. Nearly one in five of these people live in global gateway cities. More than half of the world's population (54 percent) is now urban. Three million more people move to cities every week (International Organization for Migration [IOM] 2015). By 2050, nearly two thirds of us will be in urban areas. Some will have arrived by migration and some by natural increase—being born in the city. Housing, feeding, and employing the new urbanites strains the infrastructures of cities, many of which are already deteriorating under the burden of their current populations. There is no sign that the flow of people will relent. Most of the increase will be in the developing world, in regions that are the least prepared to cope with it.

Although we calculate statistics about urbanization, there is not a global definition of *city* or *urban*. Most countries define an urban area as having a population above anywhere from 1,000 to 5,000. There are exceptions; to be considered urban in Sweden, only 200 people need to agglomerate, whereas in Mali it requires 40,000 (McGranahan and Satterthwaite 2014).

The boundary dividing urban from rural is hard to find. Do the suburbs qualify as urban? What about the slums that surround cities in the developing world? Three

A CLOSER LOOK
TORONTO BY THE NUMBERS

FIGURE 15.1   Toronto

Toronto when defined by "city proper" is less than half the population of the "urban agglomeration" or "metropolitan area."

Source: From The World's Cities in 2016, by Department of Economic and Social Affairs, © 2016 United Nations. Reprinted with the permission of the United Nations.

geographic areas define concepts related to urbanization: the city proper, the urban agglomeration, and the metropolitan area. The political boundary delineates the city proper. Urban agglomeration is the contiguous area that is "built up" around a city. The metropolitan area may include several cities—large and small—as well as their suburbs.[1] It is defined by social, cultural, and economic connectivity.

Which is being discussed or compared makes quite a difference when discussing "city" size. Toronto, for example, has 2.6 million in the city proper, 5.1 million in the agglomeration, and 5.6 million in the metropolitan area (Figure 15.1) (United Nations, Department of Economic and Social Affairs [UN DESA] 2016). In some reports, various definitions are used. Urban agglomeration is used most frequently by the United Nations (UN) and others using its data unless otherwise specified.[2]

For all of the talk about the cities of millions, the majority of urban dwellers are not located in the largest cities. According to the UN classification categories, they are in the medium- and smaller-sized cities:

- There are about 28 megacities—cities with populations of more than 10 million. About 12 percent of urban dwellers, roughly 453 million, live in megacities.

- Large cities of 5 to 10 million house about 300 million people, or 8 percent of the global urban population.

- Most cities have fewer than 5 million inhabitants.

- Medium-sized cities have 1 to 5 million residents and account for 20 percent of urban dwellers, about 837 million. Medium-sized cities are expected to be the fastest growing, approaching 1.1 billion by 2030.

- Small to medium-sized cities of 500,000 to 1 million hold 10 percent of the urban population, about 420 million.

- The smallest cities of less than 500,000 house close to 50 percent of the urban population. This portion is shrinking but is still expected to house 45 percent of urbanites in 2030. (IOM 2015)

The Character of the Modern Cities

In 1800, only about 3 percent of people lived in urban areas. Cities in the 1800s developed rapidly. Drawn to the city for work, the young flocked to London during the 18th and 19th centuries. London's first reliable census in 1801 showed that it already hosted more than 1 million residents. In the next 50 years, however, the population exploded to more than 3 million. At least 38 percent of the residents were migrants to the city. Although most were from rural England, the "year of revolutions" and political upheavals in Europe drove internationals to London as well. Diversity became a hallmark of the city. Sizable immigrant communities from Ireland, France, Germany, Italy, and Spain formed throughout the city. In the latter part of the century, Chinese, Indian, and African communities grew, and Jews fleeing persecution in Russia and Prussia added thousands to the Jewish community that was already established. Economic opportunity also lured people to the city. By 1910, London had grown to more than 7 million (Emsley, Hitchcock, and Shoemaker 2015).

In many ways, classical sociology emerged as a response to the character of the modern city, as did much art and literature. Modern cities struck the social thinkers of the time as not only quantitatively different but qualitatively different from village life. Ferdinand Tönnies, Emile Durkheim, Georg Simmel, Max Weber, Karl Marx, and Adam Smith all saw both the promise and the peril of city life. The close and personal life of the village, what Tönnies (1887/2004) called *Gemeinschaft,* was replaced by the impersonality of formal rules and regulations guiding interaction—*Gesellschaft*. The common culture of lifestyle, values, and beliefs of mechanical solidarity broke down in the urban setting under the weight of the division of labor, diversity, and difference—organic solidarity[3] (Durkheim 1893/1964). The constant stimulation of the crowds, lights, sounds, and smells required an adjustment of consciousness, the emergence of the blasé personality—an indifference to much of one's surroundings—that became a hallmark of urbanity (Simmel 1903/1971). It seemed that coordinating masses of people, whether in factories, hospitals, or schools, required the impersonality and rigidity of the bureaucratic form of organization, trapping people in iron cages[4] of their own collective—not personal—making (Weber 1914/1978).

Although city life was quite grand in the upstairs of elegant townhouses and the entertainments of the wealthy, chaos often reigned in the industrial cities. Streets built in medieval times were crowded with traffic. Horses, hand-carried sedans, and pedestrians jostled for space. Fancy shops with luxury goods competed for attention with street vendors selling everything from fruit and fish to milk and pies and shouting out the virtues of their wares. Politicians making speeches, bare-knuckle fistfights, knife sharpeners, furniture menders, and craftsmen added to the urban excitement and spectacle. Despite the liveliness and adventure of the city, filth was everywhere; sewage with human waste ran through gutters in the streets; roads were dusty in summer and muddy in winter. Horse manure was left to rot in the sun. Dirt and pollution was so thick in the air that candles were lit during the day (White 2009).

Children worked at dangerous jobs that required nimble fingers and small bodies—cleaning chimneys and doing jobs in the cotton mills and factories. Despite the poverty, people continued to come from the countryside where machines had replaced farmhands. The commons disappeared as land was increasingly enclosed and privatized. A working class filled the factory floors as landowners transformed agriculture into a capitalist enterprise (Marx 1897/1992–1993).

Despite this mayhem, city life was in some respects liberating. People were freed from the prejudices of small town life (Simmel 1903/1971). With the increasing division of labor, people were freed—indeed forced—to cultivate their distinctiveness and difference (Durkheim 1893/1964). The diversity of people merging in the cities stimulated the creation of culture. Freed from the arbitrary inequalities bestowed by birth, people were freed to make their fortunes and, in the process, elevate the prosperity of all (Smith 1776/1982).

For better or worse, the metropolis was "one of those great historical structures in which conflicting life currents find themselves with equal legitimacy" (Simmel 1903/1971).

PHOTO 15.1 This illustration from *The English Spy,* published in 1825, depicts some of the glamour and bustle of High Street in London but little of the filth.

The English Spy, illustrated by Robert Cruikshank.

PHOTO 15.2 These young workers are waiting for the night shift whistle to blow at the Whitnel Cotton Mill in North Carolina on the U.S. East Coast. Some of them have been at this job for years.

Lewis Wickes Hines, 1908, Library of Congress.

CONTEMPORARY CITIES

Contemporary cities are diverse, not only from within but also among one another. Cities of the 21st century are probably larger, busier, noisier, and more congested than Simmel ever imagined. As recently as 1995, there were 22 large cities and 14 megacities the world over; by 2015, that had doubled to 44 large cities and 29 megacities (United Nations Human Settlements Programme [UN Habitat] 2016). Cities have spilled over their political boundaries. Most of the growth has been in the developing world.

Asia is once again, as before the Industrial Revolution, the most urbanized region of the world—48 percent urbanized and the residence of 53 percent of the world's urban dwellers. In the process of urbanization, Asia has become an economic powerhouse, moving many people from poverty into the middle class, although many are also left behind. China once again has a number of large cities but not the largest. Tokyo is usually ranked as the largest city in the world[5]—more than 38 million people as of 2017. Although Africa has urbanized at a faster rate, African urbanization has not brought the same level of overall prosperity (UN Habitat 2016).

Weaving the Global Social Fabric

The global social fabric is woven through city life. The interpersonal connections that knit back and forth, through and among cities, are plentiful and complex. They form the social infrastructure of the global systems. The economic connections resultant from the dispersion of manufacturing and finance and the political connections are the most visible forms. The human-to-human connections of migrants within a city to one another, and to the native born and back to their home country, are the connections of the global social community.

When women from the Philippines take domestic jobs—for which their government trains them—in Japan, the Gulf states, or, increasingly, in the United States and other Western countries, they bring their culture with them. Even though they are away from their families, the ease of communication makes it possible for them to continue directing activities of their own children at home. They transmit influences from the West. Children of the wealthy learn from their domestic workers as well as from their own parents. Family dinner tables of wealthy Westerners may be laden with ethnic dishes from exotic tropical locales. Migrant workers consume the services of the cities in which they live, many of which may be provided by other migrants. They

---

FIGURE 15.2   Foreign-Born Population in Major Cities

Major cities lure a large portion of the world's international migrants.

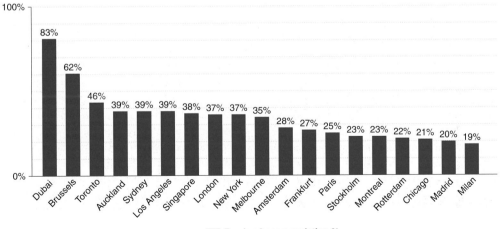

■ Foreign-born population %

Source: International Organization for Migration (2015).

may dine at ethnic restaurants owned by other migrants, who are also sending money to and communicating with those in their homeland. Migrants from different countries may attend the same religious services or shop at the same markets.

The size, power, and diversity of ties emanating from cities around the world may make them, as opposed to nations, the command centers of the contemporary world. As "islands of governance," cities may replace nations as the most significant political unit (Khanna 2010). Cities already are holding global summits. The "Mayors Summit" began in 2005. Now called the C40 Mayors Summit, it gathers political, private sector, philanthropic, and academic leaders to develop strategies for a sustainable urban future.

Around the world, cities are taking the lead in solving social problems. Cities drive innovation, are a positive force for sustainable development, and spur global change. In the United States, cities are leading the way in combatting climate change. When the Trump administration withdrew support from the Paris Accords in 2017, cities across the nation pledged to stay the course and make promised reductions. Similarly, many reinforced their position as "sanctuary cities" in response to the focus on deportations of undocumented immigrants who had not committed violent or other serious crimes. Given the population size and wealth of many cities, their actions may have more impact than some federal initiatives.

Cities sit at the crux of cultural globalization as well. Cultural globalization occurs through the entertainment that the elite class demands, but more important, it grows through the flows of people, rich and poor, through the cities. Both rich and poor are migrant classes. The rich follow the political and business networks, moving for opportunity and traveling the world for business and pleasure. The poor who serve them are also global travelers. Many migrate internationally for the opportunity to serve the wealthy. They may return home, bringing along knowledge and ideas as well as remittances. They may bring family and friends along after them, occupying occupational and cultural niches in the global cities. In their home countries, they also serve the wealthy from other nations who as cultural tourists seek an "authentic" cultural experience in developing countries.

Cities, whether global powerhouses, megacities, creative cities, fragile cities, or the informal cities of squatter communities, are the places where nearly all people make their homes. Understanding cities' makeup, structure,

problems, and potential provides the knowledge needed to make a better life for everyone.

The Global City: Global Powerhouses

Social scientists differentiate two types of the largest cities. Global cities are centers of international relations. These are the cities that gleam from glossy brochures advertising financial services, multinational corporations, expensive multi-million-dollar apartments, and world-class cultural activities.

With privatization, deregulation, the unbundling of processes at the task level, and the fast and relatively free flow of information, the global economy grew out of the nation-state framework. With the ease of communication and manufacturing spread all over the world, corporate heads found more value in being located centrally than with manufacturing facilities. Advanced services workers—finance consultants, marketers, stockbrokers, tax consultants, attorneys, business consultants, and the like—concentrate near corporate headquarters. Thus, the cities have emerged as command centers. Global cities and "city-regions" are important parts of the global architecture—hubs of the global systems connecting the global economy, politics, and cultural life around the world. Whereas industrial cities were agglomerations of manufacturing, global cities are agglomerations of the intellectual functions that control and service the global economy—creating a synergy among those in the knowledge and information networks. Just as particular industries concentrated in specific cities where they found comparative advantage—steel in Pittsburgh, automobiles in Detroit, and so on—global cities are sites of agglomeration—finance in New York, London, and Singapore; high-tech in the Silicon Valley; and so on (Sassen 1991, 2005).

The Global Cities Index analyzes cities along five dimensions: business activity, human capital, information exchange, cultural experience, and political engagement. Based on 27 indicators, the index provides a city's strength in each of these areas and an overall idea of how connected and influential it is.

Another measure, the Global Cities Outlook, looks at a city's potential through 13 indicators, measuring personal well-being, economics, innovation, and governance. The Global Elite are 16 cities that appear in the top 25 on both lists (Figure 15.3) (A. T. Kearney 2017). A city's profile on the Index and Outlook dimensions indicates whether the city is an economic powerhouse, based on the amount of business activity, trade, and finance, or whether it is an

A CLOSER LOOK
ELITE CITIES, 2017

FIGURE 15.3   The Global Elite Cities per the Index and the Outlook

The "elite cities" are those that have the most power and influence now and potential for the future. They rank in both the Global Cities Index, according to their performance, and the Global Cities Outlook, according to their potential.

Americas

New York, Index 1/Outlook 2
Chicago, Index 7/Outlook 15
Los Angeles, Index 8/Outlook 25
Washington, D.C., Index 10/Outlook 19
Toronto, Index 16/Outlook 20
Boston, Index 21/Outlook 5
San Francisco, Index 23/Outlook 1

EMEA

London, Index 2/Outlook 4
Paris, Index 3/Outlook 3
Berlin, Index 14/Outlook 18
Moscow, Index 18/Outlook 10
Amsterdam, Index 22/Outlook 16

Asia Pacific

Tokyo, Index 4/Outlook 23
Singapore, Index 6/Outlook 11
Melbourne, Index 15/Outlook 16
Sydney, Index 17/Outlook 13

■ Top 10 in both the Index and Outlook
■ Top 25 in both the Index and Outlook

Source: A. T. Kearney (2017). Reproduced with permission. https://www.atkearney.com/global-cities/full-report.

industry leader, based on university presence, patents per capita, and private investments. Developing these and other profiles can aid city, regional, and national governments in strategic decision making for growth and quality of life. It can also help businesses to make strategic decisions for growth (A. T. Kearney 2017).

Global Cities: The Nexus of Rich and Poor

The global cities, more than any other, are the nexus of the rich and poor—the most and least powerful global classes in intimate contact every day. While global cities are expensive to live in, many of the poor migrate to the global cities for jobs. The lifestyles of those who command and control demand that there is a class to care for them. Particularly in households with two parents working, the intimate needs of daily living—from cleaning to cooking, to doing laundry, to shopping to caring for children and the elderly—become the province of myriad low-paid service workers. Other low-paid

workers clean the offices, drive the taxis, work the hotels, and pick up, drop off, or do the dry cleaning. Many of these services demanded by the wealthy are labor intensive—hand-pressed rather than machine-pressed shirts, bespoke suits, multiple servers for each diner at expensive restaurants, and the like. Personal services to the elite class may comprise as much as 30 to 50 percent of the global economy, although no one gets rich providing them (Sassen 2009, 3).

Global cities are not necessarily among the largest cities in the world, although some may be. Megacities are big and most are continuing to grow. More will be added to the list by 2030. Although there is much poverty in the global cities, people continue to come to them.

The Megacity: The World's Largest

Six of the ten largest cities are in Asia. China is leading the way. Migration to China's cities increased by 500 million over just 30 years. By 2017, China had 15 megacities.

By 2030, 70 percent of China's population will be urban. But unlike in other developing countries where growth is most likely haphazard, Chinese cities grow by government planning.

Urbanization pulled millions of people out of poverty in China. As part of China's centrally planned economic development, the government channeled urbanization to villages, middle-level cities, and peripheral cities. From 1950 to 2010, the urban population of China grew from 13 to 45 percent. Unlike other developing countries, the growth was not concentrated in one or two of the largest cities. Those largest cities, Shanghai and Beijing, did grow, but not at the rapid rate of the others. Shenzhen, for example, was a fishing village of about 30,000 in the 1970s. From 1985 to 2015, its population swelled 6,040 percent. It is now a megacity of about 12 million and the fourth largest city in China. The crane—not the bird but rather the construction crane—is seen all over the city skyline. Rather than 52 percent of industrial output being concentrated in China's largest cities, it decreased to 22 percent, while middle-city output surged from 47 percent in 1978 to 75 percent by 2002. Growth in the second- and third-tier cities limited growth of China's largest cities (Airriess 2008).

Even though China has been urbanizing at a quick pace, each of its largest cities has only a small fraction of the country's total population, in contrast to many developing nations where 15 to 35 percent of the population may live in the largest city. China's urban expansion produced great wealth for a segment of the population and lifted many more out of poverty into lower-middle- and middle-class status.

Urban Vitality and the Creative City

Global finance, politics, culture, production, and people all flow through cities insofar as they can attract the human and economic capital necessary for development. In the competition for these resources, winners must be creative. Jane Jacobs's work in the 1960s chastised city planners of the era for "unbuilding" cities. City planners were suffocating the vitality of cities with oversimplified solutions to the demands of expanding cities. They did not understand the complexity of the city, how every "unique, intricate and interlocked detail" played into creating the vitality and character of the city (Jacobs 1961/1992).

Diversity, Jacobs argued, was the key to a city's vitality. The synergy of people with diverse cultures, ideas, talents, and skills; diverse sights, sounds, tastes, and smells; lights and music mixing on the sidewalks, in the parks, and in the stores—all this makes cities vital.

PHOTO 15.3 The rich run the global economy, but the poor keep the rich running by seeing to their most intimate needs—from cleaning their bathrooms, to doing their laundry, to caring for their children.

Brooklyn Street Scenes by Steven Pisano/ CC BY 2.0.

A CLOSER LOOK
URBANIZATION IN CHINA

PHOTO 15.4 China's urbanization has been part of an economic development plan. Special enterprise zones led to rapid growth of previously small cities or villages. Two generations ago, Shenzhen was a fishing village. Grand apartments and modern skyscrapers reflect new wealth.

JoAnn Chirico.

Decades after her warnings, and perhaps because of mistakes made, an entire industry has arisen to analyze and discover how the qualities of vitality that she recognized in a city interact to make cities successful.

The Rise of the Creative Class and the related Creativity Index, developed by Richard Florida, were inspired by Jacobs, among others. By focusing on the creative class, Florida (2002) wanted to extend the focus of economic development literature from firms and industries to people and places. The key economic resource, he maintained, is collective, shared, or intersubjective creativity. Creativity doesn't just occur by happenstance; it is nurtured in places. Industries cluster where there are clusters of talented people, and talented people cluster where there are "natural, cultural, and built amenities. Synergy involving everything from architecture to prestigious knowledge institutions—and most of all the presence of other talented people"—attracts talent (Florida 2014). Florida's thesis is that the vitality of a city—its economic potential—depends on its ability to attract "the creative class."

The Creativity Index is based on the "three T's": talent, technology, and tolerance. Survey research by Gallup and the Knight Foundation confirmed that people look for openness (toward immigrants, gays and lesbians, young singles, the poor, etc.), social offerings for entertainment, and physical beauty such as green spaces. Knight found these factors consistent over three years and across the country (Florida 2014).

Cities have paid attention to Florida's ideas and research, while sometimes misunderstanding the main lessons. The take-away for policy makers is that it is the little things that attract people—things that improve the quality of life rather than megaprojects such as stadiums, casinos, and convention centers. Community-driven local improvements such as parks and bike paths are more meaningful than casinos. Cities need to have friendly "people climates" rather than the "business climate" of low taxes, subsidies, and little regulation. They need to be inclusive and offer something for all types of people. They need quality of place. Quality of place is a combination of what is there, as in the natural and built environment, who is there, as in the diversity of people, and what is going on, as in the street life, cafes, culture, art, music, and outdoor activities (Florida 2014).

According to Charles Landry, who consults internationally on imagination and creativity in urban change, great cities meet seven criteria for their greatness: they are places where people feel at home and have a sense of stability; places that have both tradition and distinctiveness; places with a "can do" attitude; places where it is easy to connect through communication and networking; places where it is easy to interact and move around; places of inspiration where people can learn and self-improve; and places that are well put together through design (Landry n.d.).

The Creative Cities Index tries to capture how well a city is doing. Its difference from other indices is its holistic approach—drawn from the perspective of both an insider and an outsider—and its breadth over many domains (Landry n.d.)—that is, a city's creative ability and potential.

The World's Fragile Cities

Fragile cities struggle to provide the minimum in public goods—law and order and basic services such as clean water, electricity, and affordable food. They have difficulty in keeping their residents healthy and safe. Rather than improving, fragility is worsening over time. From 2000 to 2015, most of the world became more fragile, especially cities in lower- and middle-income countries but in high-income settings as well.

The Igarapé Institute metric of 11 indicators measures the fragility of cities. Unemployment, population growth, inequality, pollution, access to electricity, homicide, terrorism, and conflict events all contribute to fragility. According to data for 2015, of the 2,100 cities studied, 435 were rated above average in fragility and 11 percent (239) exhibited high or very high fragility. The majority (71 percent) were rated average and 13 percent were rated low. As can be seen in Figure 15.4, the number

A CLOSER LOOK
DOMAINS OF THE CREATIVE CITIES INDEX

The domains measured in the Creative Cities Index capture aspects of social, political, and economic life that facilitate people's aspirations for personal growth and fulfillment:

- Political and public framework
- Distinctiveness, diversity, vitality, and expression
- Openness, trust, accessibility, and participation
- Entrepreneurship, exploration, and innovation
- Strategic leadership, agility, and vision
- Talent development and the learning landscape
- Communication, connectivity, and networking
- The place and place making
- Livability and well-being
- Professionalism and effectiveness. (Landry n.d., Creative City Index)

of fragile cities has increased since measurement began. However, this has not been confined to developing countries (Muggah 2017).

The Complexity of Fragility

The combination of factors that affect fragility varies by region and city. In the Middle East and Central Asia, rapid population growth, terrorism, conflict, low access to electricity, and unemployment are the most significant factors. In Central and West Africa, they are conflict, unemployment, and lack of electricity. Weather events, inequality, homicide, and unemployment are significant in Central America and the Caribbean. Most cities in the United States are low fragility, but some, such as Baltimore and Albuquerque, are higher than would be expected, while some Mexican cities, such as Cuidad Juarez, are lower than would be expected (Muggah 2017).

Environmental factors such as the drought in Syria contributed to that country's fragility for years before the

A CLOSER LOOK
FRAGILE CITIES

FIGURE 15.4   Fragile City Scores, 2000–2015, by Subregion

Aside from a small decrease in South America, fragility rose steeply in all lower and middle developed regions from 2014 to 2015. All regions increased in fragility from 2000 to 2015, South America only slightly.

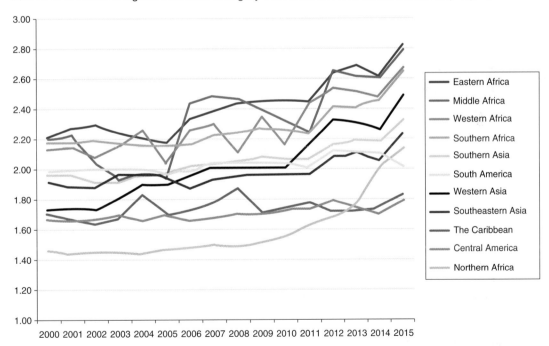

Source: Muggah (2017), Igarapé Institute.

revolution. It lasted 15 years and was the worst drought in 900 years. Between 2006 and 2011, 75 percent of Syria's farms failed and 85 percent of the livestock died. About 1.5 million people fled the rural areas into already crowded cities, increasing fragility and ultimately ending in war (Stokes 2016).

There are potentialities—threat multipliers—that worsen the conditions leading to fragility. Population density in urban areas make them more susceptible to epidemics that are worsening as contagions develop new strains resistant to antivirals and antibacterials and new zoonoses emerge. Natural disasters and the slow progression of climate change, if not halted, will force hungry millions from some of the poorest regions of the world into the cities, overburdening infrastructure.

The Challenge of Demographics to Fragile Cities

Developing and developed societies have different demographic profiles. The demographic profile of a society is significant in diagnosing the problems a society or city may encounter. Demography changes with urbanization. Urbanization generally offers women a better chance at equality, education, and employment and thus increases wealth. With opportunities, wealth, and better access to medical services decreasing infant mortality and increasing access to birth control, women postpone marriage and limit childbearing. Fertility declines. Declining fertility brings a "demographic dividend." The dependency ratio due to youths decreases, the proportion of workers and savers increases, and money that would have been spent on youths can go to improving infrastructure, capital investment, investments in higher education, and other development necessities.

Despite the fertility decline from rural to urban areas, many cities are missing out on the demographic dividend. Many of the world's cities experience rapid population growth. Some is through natural increase, due to the relatively young age structure in cities, and some is through migration into cities.

In many low- and middle-income cities, population growth is making cities more fragile. African and Asian countries with relatively high poverty are growing at "turbo" speed. High-speed growth is dangerous for a city. Karachi, Dhaka, Kinshasa, and Lagos, for example, are 40 times larger than they were in the 1950s. While infant mortality decreased with improvements in health,

fertility has not declined. In combination with migration, these cities have experienced a surge in youths, creating youth bulges in their demographic profiles. In some of these cities, 75 percent of the population is under 30 years old and the average age hovers near 16 years, in comparison with the old European cities where it is 45 years (Muggah 2015).

It is not just youthfulness that makes the cities fragile. The specific demographic of youths—underemployment, undereducated, and male—leads to violence and fragility. Violence among this demographic, "hot people," is transmitted like a contagion in patterned ways among this group. In contrast, where youths have a high rate of high school graduation and college enrollment, cities or neighborhoods have lower crime rates (Muggah 2015). Not everyone sees the African "youth bulge" in a negative light—as a fear to be tamped down. Critics of the UN, World Bank, African Development Bank, and other efforts to offer youths agricultural or low-level training and entrepreneur opportunities reject the image of youths as a security risk or an untapped labor pool to serve the status quo. They note that many youths are organizing—for instance, LUCHA (Struggle for Change) in Congo and *Y'en a Marre* (We've Had Enough) in Senegal—to protest for meaningful reforms in the economy, in education, and in land, thereby creating more fair societies (Kimari 2018).

Increasing access to the internet can also contribute to a rise in criminality in the fragile cities. Urban youth gangs use the internet to organize themselves, recruit, extort money, hire killers, and advertise their activities. This is particularly relevant to the narco gangs in Latin America but is also spreading among parts of Asia and Africa (Muggah 2015).

Another factor that could contribute to either city prosperity or fragility is the role of migration. Cities are at the forefront of the mass migration challenge. Cities must plan for migration and integrating migrants into the economic, social, and cultural fabric of the city. This can be affected by national policies that cities need to address.

Migration policies can have either positive or negative effects on cities. Labor policies that are too restrictive or unclear result in irregular migratory flows. Border policies may result in stranding migrants in "transit hubs" before they reach their destinations. Poorly managed migration leaves migrants to develop their own solutions to providing for their basic needs in housing, jobs, education, and health. This contributes to the growth of urban slums, unplanned areas, and hazard-prone areas (IOM 2015).

Uneven Economic Development

Cities drive economic development, generating more than their share of wealth for a society. Globally, 80 percent of the world's gross domestic product (GDP) comes from its cities. Whereas Paris has 16 percent of France's population, it generates 27 percent of its GDP. In developing societies, the ratio is higher. In Kinshasa, the 13 percent of its urban population generates 85 percent of GDP for the Democratic Republic of the Congo. The prosperity of a nation is, in large part, dependent on the performance of its cities (Figures 15.5 and 15.6).

Cities benefit from economies of scale. With a large and diverse population, businesses are better able to match their labor and supplier requirements, generating greater productivity. Through agglomeration, cities spur creativity and innovation. There is benefit to shared services. Sharing infrastructure among many users generates greater connectivity at a lower cost. Perhaps most important, the synergy created through the flow of ideas leads to more learning and innovation—enhancing human capital (UN Habitat 2016).

While the global picture of economic growth and urbanization is positive, it is not—as suggested earlier in the chapter—the case in all countries. When aggregated, urbanization in the least developed countries, particularly in sub-Saharan Africa, shows little or no effect on overall economic growth (UN DESA 2013). Urban life is increasingly precarious in most of these cities, although some

A CLOSER LOOK
CITIES BY POPULATION AND PERCENTAGE OF GDP GENERATED

Cities are the economic engines of the modern world. They generate more than their share of GDP.

FIGURE 15.5   Share of GDP and National Population in Selected Cities

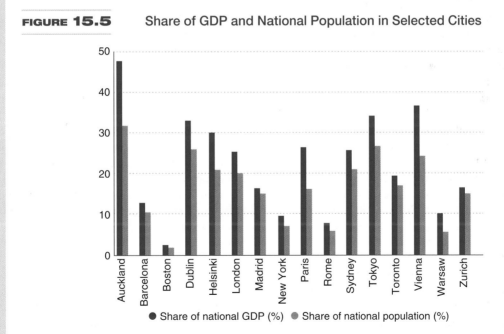

● Share of national GDP (%)   ● Share of national population (%)

Source: UN Habitat (2016). Reproduced with permission.

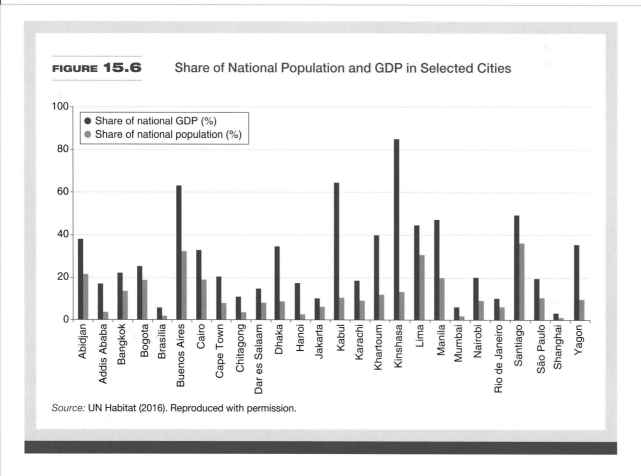

FIGURE **15.6**   Share of National Population and GDP in Selected Cities

Source: UN Habitat (2016). Reproduced with permission.

have made progress. Because most future urbanization will occur in the least developed countries, and most of it will be concentrated in what are now urban slums, the expectation that urbanization will bring greater prosperity cannot be taken for granted.

Increasing inequality in many cities along with racial, ethnic, and economic class segregation threatens social sustainability. Competition for resources and cleavages along fault lines of inequalities promote distrust and inhibit working for the common good. Social sustainability requires building and maintaining social capital that bridges identity groups and fosters cooperation rather than competition. Cities must foster equal life chances for all of their residents.

Historically, economic growth and urbanization have not been environmentally friendly.

Rising Inequalities

In general, urban residents have greater life chances than rural residents. However, there are inequities within urban areas that are hidden in the averages. Absolutely equal outcomes in health or education would not be expected because people have more or less vulnerable genetics as well as different talents and ambitions. When inequalities are patterned along dimensions of social location such as geographic region, gender, ethnicity, or class, they result from social forces, not individual variations. Inequalities are rising within cities in developed and developing countries. The larger the city, the greater the degree of inequality it is likely to have.

Cities are not sustainable where there is too great a degree of inequality. As cities have grown, investments in urban infrastructure have not kept pace. Africa experienced strong growth in the beginning of the 21st century. But most city dwellers live in slums, with many, if not most, lacking access to basic services such as clean water, sanitation, electricity, health care, and education. Without education or job prospects, inequality creates "demographic time bombs" (Cocco-Klein 2016).

In the United States, income inequality is greater than before the recession of 2007–2008. The large metropolitan areas and their large cities have greater inequality than the national inequality and greater inequality than in 2007. The more unequal incomes are, the more difficult it is to maintain a reasonably well-functioning city. As inequality increases, schools have difficulty in maintaining a mixed-income student body. Income-segregated schools do not harm the achievement of higher-income students, but integrated schools do boost the achievement of lower-income students.

Inequality narrows the tax base, and essential city services will likely suffer. Private sector goods may increase in price, making it harder for lower-income families to get by. Housing is less affordable for low-income families than in more equal cities. Even in cities such as Cleveland and St. Louis, where the housing prices themselves may be relatively inexpensive in comparison with other cities, the poor cannot afford housing due to low salaries. In cities where the poor make more money, such as in New York or Washington, D.C., housing is still not affordable because it is so much more expensive (Holmes and Berube 2016). Even middle-income families are finding housing to be unaffordable in many cities.

Inequality gives way to divided cities, spatially and socially. The economic and social development gains that urbanization should bring are not realized. Jobs in the formal sector are scarce in many countries. Latin America, for example, has the most unequal cities in the world. In Chile, 30 percent of people are employed in the informal sector; in Colombia, it is 60 percent. In the informal sector, there is a much greater chance of poverty, less job security, and much more inequality. Spatial and social divides created by inequality make mobility less likely and transmission of poverty from generation to generation more likely. Education, weak social safety nets, larger family size, and unemployment are also brought to bear. While Latin America experienced a reduction in poverty, the gains were not as pronounced as in other regions with greater equality (UN Habitat 2012).

A study of 42 countries in Africa, the Americas, and Asia shows how inequality in health outcomes results from social forces. For example, mortality under 5 years of age increases with each step down the economic ladder. Children from the poorest urban families are twice as likely to die under age 5 as are children from the richest ones. The magnitude of difference varies from 1.3 times as likely to 15.6 times as likely, depending on the country (World Health Organization [WHO] and UN Habitat 2010).

Poorer children in cities are also more likely to suffer from the chronic malnutrition that accounts for one third of all childhood deaths than their richer city neighbors. Child malnutrition is less common in urban areas than in rural areas, but inequities within the urban population are significant. Stunting is three times more common among the poorest children than among the richest children. The inequalities in child malnutrition result not only from family wealth but also from inequities in the mother's education and her partner's education. Wealth accounted for 30 to 76 percent of the discrepancy, mother's education accounted for 1 to 31 percent, and partner's education accounted for 8 to 18 percent. Both the region of the country and the child's biological characteristics had less impact (WHO and UN Habitat 2010). Many dimensions of health and health care differentiate poorer urban residents from wealthier ones. Access to skilled birth attendants, diabetes care, communicable diseases care, and piped water all favor the wealthy (WHO and UN Habitat 2010).

Cities within developed nations also reflect inequities in the basics of health. Japan is noted for excellent health care, but research has documented significant inequalities in incidence of tuberculosis by wards within all of the Japanese cities studied. Of the 13 cities studied, 9 had higher than national rates. The higher the rate, the wider the discrepancies between poorer and wealthier wards. These inequities are common in cities around the world. Neighborhoods in New York and the U.K. city of Preston also show inequities in access to essential health care. Data disaggregated for urban areas highlights which areas and populations are most in need of intervention if life chances are to be restored to everyone (WHO and UN Habitat 2010).

Inequities result in poorer families not keeping their children in school, lowering their skills and limiting their earnings. In Organisation for Economic Cooperation and Development (OECD) countries, an increase in inequality of about 6 Gini points decreases the likelihood of poor people graduating from college by 4 points. They cannot invest in opportunities. Inequality perpetuates and deepens economic and social divides.

Inequality is harmful to everyone, not just the poor. The long-term rise in inequality in OECD countries has lowered overall economic growth.

THE URBAN SLUMS: CITIES OF TOMORROW?

Rising income inequality and rapid urbanization give rise to the most profound problem facing every city—affordable housing. The flows of people from all economic levels into cities are not abating.

The sustainability or unsustainability of urban growth is most visible in a city's slums, its informal settlements. As

A CLOSER LOOK
URBAN SLUMS

FIGURE 15.7   Urban Slum Population, Percentage per Region

There were about 863 million people living in slums in 2013. That is up from 650 million in 1990 and 760 million in 2000.

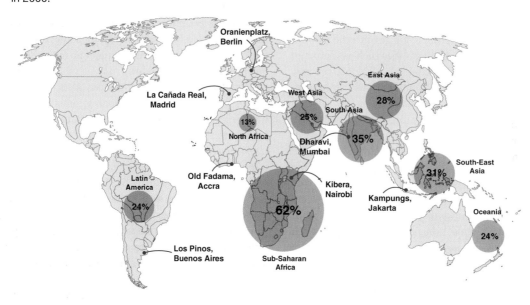

Source: International Organization for Migration (2015). Reproduced with permission.

more people move to cities hoping for a better life, housing is the first problem that they face. Based on current trends, there will be 1.6 billion people without secure and sufficient housing by 2025. While the percentage of people living in slums declined from 39 to 30 percent, the number of people in slums continues to grow (Participatory Slum Upgrading Programme [PSUP] 2016). Whether in developed or developing regions, the proportion of the global urban population living in slums is alarming (Figure 15.7), as high as 59 to 62 percent in sub-Saharan Africa, 25 to 31 percent in regions of Asia and the Pacific, and 21 to 24 percent in Latin America. Even in developed countries in Western Europe, more than 6 percent of urbanites live in precarious conditions, and even more do in Eastern and Southern Europe (IOM 2015; PSUP 2016).

In terms of households, 330 million urban households do not have adequate housing, and unless something is done it will increase to 440 million by 2025. Slum life can become a poverty trap. Contrary to a common belief that slums are temporary homes that people leave after a generation, many families remain for generations (IOM 2015; Marx, Stoker, and Suri 2013). Of the 10 million people who move to cities in sub-Saharan Africa every year, 7 million move into slums and only 2 million will ever move out unless current trends are reversed (PSUP 2016).

Slums vary widely in some characteristics. Some are crime ridden and some are relatively safe. Some are cities within themselves with shopping, doctors, barber and beauty shops, and artisans, and some lack most of even the most basic services. What they have in common are five criteria, only one of which must be present to define a slum: inadequate safe water, inadequate sanitation, poor structural quality of housing, overcrowding, and insecure rights protecting the right to reside on the land.

Preventing the cities of tomorrow from enlarging urban slums must be a global priority. Three policy efforts are proving to be promising in solving the challenge of unsustainable urban growth. First, the growth of substandard settlements must be curtailed, and those in place must be brought to acceptable standards. Second, rental markets must be stabilized, providing more security of tenancy for poor and low-income households. Third, underused properties in and near cities can be converted to affordable housing (King et al. 2017). What cannot be forgotten is that inside the slums are people—people who demonstrate resilience and strength in surviving and making a life against the odds.

ACHIEVING URBAN SUSTAINABILITY

Urban development offers extraordinary promise of better living, for both cities and rural areas, through synergies of urban life. Concentrating people spurs economic enterprise, cultural development, and innovation. It builds economies of scale in basic services.

The potential remains unfulfilled. Air, land, water, and noise pollution, crime, density, poverty, lack of basic infrastructure, sub-standard housing, and unemployment plague cities. Unless the trends in urban problems reverse, the quality of life will diminish even more. A sustainable city meets the needs of its residents in economic development, social development and inclusion, environmental management, and urban governance through strategies that maintain and continuously improve a high standard of living for everyone (UN DESA 2013).

Sustainable Development Goal 11 challenges cities to provide safe and affordable housing and sustainable transit, improve residents' health, reduce environmental impacts, and provide safe and accessible green spaces. Insofar as cities generate the major portion of prosperity for the country and the world, cities must meet the challenge.

Looking Inside Slums: Finding Resilience and Community

A slum might look different to an outsider looking in than to an insider looking out. From the outside, slums look ramshackle, spontaneously generated, unorganized, and chaotic. Inside, many are viable communities with their own economic, social, educational, recreational, and other opportunity structures. Dharavi, made famous by the movie *Slumdog Millionaire,* is deep within Mumbai, India. Rather than formed by migrants attracted to the city by the promise of a better life, Dharavi, like many "urban villages" found in the megacities of China, was originally a village, in this case a fishing village inhabited by the Koli. Mumbai grew up around it and encircled Dharavi. Joined by migrants to the city, it is now home to about 750,000 people—the best guesstimate—densely packed into an area smaller than Central Park in New York. Most remarkable is that within Dharavi, its low-tech "slum industries" generate between U.S. $600 million and $1 billion every year (Yardley 2011).

Dharavi is by no means ideal. It has open sewage, and most people's access to water is through outdoor taps that serve multiple families and operate only for a short portion of the day. The best communal toilets charge a fee. Nevertheless, using their ingenuity, people created schools and opened shops, and they ship many of their wares around the world (Yardley 2011). Anyone can shop in the online Dharavi market.

Dharavi is not the only urban slum to have created a community. Robert Neuwirth spent two years visiting four "squatter communities," a kinder term than slum. He calls them the cities of tomorrow because they will increasingly be home to more of the world's residents, perhaps as many as one third by 2050. In the squatter settlements, he found people building, literally and figuratively, their communities (Neuwirth 2005a, 2005b).

In Kenya, outside of Nairobi is Kibera, the largest squatter community in East Africa, bursting with entrepreneurial activity and energy. There are beauty parlors, bars, restaurants, a health clinic, a soda dealer, a grocery store, a church, and more—on just one of its many busy streets. The entire community is self-built (Neuwirth 2005b). People feel at home in Kibera, even though home improvement usually means a tarp over the roof of a mud hut to protect it from weather. "Kibera is very good," one woman told Neuwirth. "I don't feel as if there is any other place in Nairobi that I could feel so much at home. . . . If I have a problem, my neighbors will help. People here create a society." This sentiment was repeated throughout Neuwirth's interviews in Kibera and other informal settlements (Neuwirth 2005a).

While Kibera is bustling with economic activity, people have little control over their lives, homes, or land on which their homes are built. Most are tenants in their mud huts. Lack of tenure or ownership of the land that they live on is one of the most significant impediments to sustainable development. Even though the residents pay rents (most landlords are absentee but built the mud shacks), their tenancy is insecure. For decades

A CLOSER LOOK
KIBERA

Kibera, one of the largest squatter communities in the world, is teeming with entrepreneurial activity, from a butcher to streets with shops to children who make toys with the trash, that nearly overwhelms the community.

Photo of Kibera in Nairobi by Kaisu Raasakka/CC By 2.0.

Photo of a butcher sitting outside of his shop in Kibera by Thom Pierce/CC BY 2.0.

Photo of a market in Kibera by Kaisu Raasakka/CC BY 2.0.

Photo by Rob Barnes, Grid-Arendal, reproduced with permission.

Photo by Rob Barnes, Grid-Arendal, reproduced with permission.

while people lived there, the government classified the land as forest, although most of the trees had been cut for fuel and housing. The people were denied the right to vote for decades. In the eyes of the government, the people of Kibera, which means forest or jungle, were trees (Neuwirth 2005a).

The informal settlements are too large and are growing too quickly for governments to ignore. Never part of city planning, they need to be incorporated. Kibera upgrading started as part of a joint venture, Kenya Slum Upgrading Project (KENSUP), between the Kenyan government and UN Habitat. Like other governments, the Kenyan approach had been to evict and demolish. UN Habitat favors "in situ" upgrading—leaving communities intact after temporary disruptions. Residents are moved section by section into temporary decanting housing while new apartment buildings are built on the sites of their former homes.

In Southland, also outside of Nairobi, four men lived in a typical 10 × 10 hut of corrugated metal on a concrete slab. They had no running water. They bought tap water from a nearby tap owner. They shared a community latrine with 20 families, about 100 people. They had enough electricity, illegally tapped from a neighbor, for a single dim bulb. Such a home could be anywhere because nearly half of Nairobi lives in these conditions. Nevertheless, inside Southland, the men reported, was freedom. It was a simple life with no one controlling them. Southland has since been torn down to make way for development (Neuwirth 2005b).

Rocinha, the largest favela in Rio de Janeiro, is much more advanced than Southland or Kibera. Pieces of tile and signs, plaster on the brick, and color adorn the homes. Streets are paved. Most homes have electricity, much of it stolen by "grillos" who tap into the grid and wire the neighborhood, and running water, also diverted from the municipal supply through a maze of pipes (Neuwirth 2005b). Rocinha, once controlled by drug-dealing gangs, was cleared of crime in 2011 by the government in preparation for the 2014 World Cup and 2016 Summer Olympic Games. Now it's patrolled by local police. It is a "city within a city," listed as a destination in tour books of Rio de Janeiro. Guided tours roam through Rocinha on a daily basis. Rooms can be rented through Airbnb, and tours of its neighborhoods can be booked online.

In Brazil's favelas, the majority of slum residents earn middle-class salaries. Brazil's growth lifted many favela residents out of the poverty class. Many, if not most, remain in their neighborhoods, joined by other middle-class residents pushed out of the city by rising house prices. In their homes, most have refrigerators (99 percent), washing machines (69 percent), and microwaves (55 percent). Rocinha and the other favelas remain slums, however; neighborhood infrastructure such as transportation, education, sanitation, and access to health care are inefficient. It remains a slum despite decades of renewal efforts implemented with varying degrees of success (Gurgel 2014).

Turkey instituted two laws to protect squatters. One is that if you build your house overnight and do not get caught, you cannot be evicted. The other is that if 2,000 people are in the community, it becomes a legal entity with the powers to vote, collect taxes, and provide services as any other municipality. As a result, Sultanbeyli, which sits outside of Istanbul, achieved a higher level of development and resident investment than most other squatter settlements (Neuwirth 2005b).

In spite of slum conditions, the people within demonstrate creative energy and create viable communities. Despite the odds stacked against them, resourceful people in urban slums manage to make life work.

That is not to say that these slums are acceptable, but they must be recognized as neighborhoods and as part of the city. The flow of people into cities will not abate. One solution to housing is to build on the energy in the slums to upgrade existing slums and plan better for the continuing growth that will extend the world's cities.

Urban Rehabilitation and Community Preservation

There are at least two ways in which city planners can use the resilience, initiative, and willingness of people caught by circumstance without housing or in substandard housing. First, with the participation of the community, viable neighborhoods can be brought to meet adequate standards for health, safety, and security. Second, new affordable housing can be built on available land within or close to the city.

The usual course of governments in urban renewal, including of slums, is to tear down without much concern for the community that residents have established there. In Yerwada, a squatter settlement of seven neighborhoods on the outskirts of Pune, India, the government took a different approach. Wide streets that allow the sun to shine through have replaced dark and narrow alleys by building up rather than out. Small parks for children to play and yards for outdoor cooking are scattered throughout.

Brick-and-mortar houses have replaced the bamboo and asbestos huts. No one has been forced to move; the vibrant social structure of the community has been maintained even as the infrastructure has been transformed (Shiva 2015).

The success of the renovation is a lesson in best practices:

- Keep residents intimately involved every step of the way

- Retain as much of the social dynamic as possible by mapping the areas and using the map to plan open spaces and roadways as closely as possible to where residents had created them informally

- Retain permanent structures and keep residents in their same lots or as close as possible to their former home sites

- Create multistoried structures to preserve open space

- Use local labor

- Create life-sized models to solicit resident suggestions

Residents funded a portion, about 10 percent, of the overall cost (Shiva 2015).

Community participation resulting in community empowerment became the gold standard of urban revitalization in the 1990s. In urban revitalization, the goals of community participation range from the minimum, such as meeting housing needs, to increasing the political power of marginalized residents and improving their overall well-being and feeling of security in their tenure on their property. An upgrading project in Zwelisha, outside of Durban, South Africa, was deemed a success for fulfilling these functions, even though it was only the community development committee that was empowered. The community development committee did not consult with residents or gather feedback but rather acted on their behalf, coordinating them and mediating among them, the municipality, and the external experts. Residents' influence in the settlement through the committee remained intact after the project was finished, and thus the committee was able to enforce rules to which residents either agreed (no taverns) or disagreed (no shacks added to the property) (Patel, 2013).

Temporary Housing Solutions: Put Unused Land to Good Use—Squatter Cities and the Dignity Village Model

Homelessness is not confined to the developing world, and neither are squatter communities. Unaffordable and substandard housing is a global problem. In response, hundreds of squatter communities, tent cities, and tiny house villages have sprung up in developed countries. Paris, London, Seattle, Portland, Washington, D.C., San Francisco, Sydney, Tokyo, and many more cities house squatter communities that temporarily solve the problem of unaffordable housing for thousands. Like the favelas in Brazil and the slums that grow within and outside of urban centers of developing countries, tent cities and villages offer homes and communities for those who otherwise would be homeless. Some are officially recognized by their city governments and provided with land and some services, others are ignored, and some are shut down and bulldozed.

Seattle, Washington, lays claim to being "the home" of the tent city in the United States. In 1990, SHARE (now SHARE/WHEEL[6]) organized the first one. In 2002, the city adopted basic operating principles for its officially sanctioned tent cities and shelters. Residents in SHARE/WHEEL cities, like many others, are bound by strict codes of conduct—no alcohol, no drugs, no violence, and no disruptive behaviors. Organized security workers are on duty 24 hours a day, seven days a week, and a litter control patrols daily. There are port-a-potties, bus tickets for work and appointments, and evening meals brought in by volunteers. Under their agreement with the city, the tent cities move every three months to a new church lawn or other location that is permitted to host them. Some of their shelters are permanent. Other tent cities have varying degrees of structure and organization.

SHARE/WHEEL is not a social service agency; as in the informal squatter communities, people took charge and created their own housing solution. It is a self-managed self-help group that, as of 2017, had about 500 residents in 14 shelters and 2 tent cities in the Seattle area. The board of directors and committee members, all of whom are participants, are the decision-making bodies of the communities (SHARE/WHEEL 2017).

Dignity Village started in 2000 in Portland, Oregon, and grew to be an international movement. Like the Seattle tent cities, Dignity Village is self-help. It started when a group of homeless activists moved onto a vacant lot and built tiny homes. The original Dignity Village now

CONSIDER THIS

THE LESSONS LEARNED IN RIO DE JANEIRO'S FAVELA IMPROVEMENT PROJECTS

In many respects, Rio de Janeiro's struggles with urban revitalization is a story of two steps forward, one step back. Although impossible to get a definitive count, the 600 to 800 favelas that surround Rio are home to 25 percent of its population, about 1.5 million people. The earliest favelas date to latter decades of the 19th century as returning war veterans, freed slaves, and former plantation workers migrated to the city for work and could not find affordable housing. From their beginning, government and public opinion viewed the settlements as "unsightly" and a threat to the city.

The first attempts to revitalize them were around the turn of the 20th century. It appeared simple enough—evict the residents and reclaim the land. However, the favelas continued to grow. In 1937, favelas were prohibited. The city government tore down thousands of tenements and moved the people to "proletariat parks" where they were subject to strict curfews and other controls. The 1950s to 1970s brought more eradication, removal of residents, and resettlement in remote housing compounds. Nevertheless, the favelas continued to grow. There was no place else to accommodate the ever-increasing flows to the city (Perlman 2010).

Several phases of redevelopment and reform in Rio highlight urban development lessons from which all cities can learn.

Phase One: Let the People Take Charge

Busloads of favela residents began protesting at Rio's mayoral office and city council in the 1960s. Their demands were simple. As part of the city, they reasoned that they should receive city services; water, electricity, paved roads, streetlights, and security of tenancy in their homes. The favelas could no longer be ignored or razed. To conduct negotiations, city government required each favela to organize a residents association. The associations then organized into a federation of associations. This turned to the favelas' advantage, giving them some bargaining power and influence over candidates in elections (Perlman 2010).

Realizing that the favelas could not be eradicated, the city adopted a new strategy, *Operação Mutirão,* a partnership between the city and the favelas. Residents supplied the labor for an ambitious program of improvements and the government provided materials and engineering help. Another partnership, *Companhia de Desenvolvimento de Comunidades* (CODESCO, dedicated to improving

favelas), involved consultations among residents, architects, and economists for planning and securing long-term low-interest loans.

These programs were ahead of their time by focusing on community members and making their needs and goals the focus of the projects. Operação Mutirão lasted only a year and a half; CODESCO completed only three of its projects. Commercial interests of real estate developers quickly overcame the interests of justice, and from the late 1960s to 1975 more than 100,000 residents were evicted from communities across the city. That is the cost of insecure tenancy. Liberation theology activists helped some favela residents to fight for rights of tenure but they won few court contests (Osborn 2012a).

Many of the poor were resettled in *conjuntos,* government projects. If the quality of construction in the project was adequate or high, the poor could not afford to live there. If they couldn't afford it, the poor would sell the unit to someone wealthier and return to a favela. The conjuntos, such as *Selva de Pedra,* became middle-class housing. If the project was of poor quality, it deteriorated rapidly and most of the poor simply left and returned to favelas.

Eviction and resettlement did not work. Viable neighborhoods were destroyed. The stock of low-income housing was diminished rather than increased. Favelas continued to grow. Neither the needs nor the strengths of community were taken into consideration.

Phase Two: Favela–Bairro, a Mixed Record

The return of democracy to Brazil in the 1980s brought two important breakthroughs: city politicians recognized the voting power of the favela, and the 1988 constitution established some rights of tenure; after five years of occupation, land became the property of the resident (Jenkins 2014; Osborn 2012a). When the favela associations demanded waste collection, water and sewage, land title, urbanization, and street paving, left-leaning politicians favored adopting the policies. When a candidate from the favelas nearly won the mayoral election in 1993, it was clear that the favelas could not be ignored.[6]

Up to this point, the favelas still had not been recognized as part of the city. In 1994, the new mayor launched the most ambitious plan of neighborhood upgrading in the world, *Favela Bairro* (Favela to Neighborhood). Rather than evict and eradicate, the favelas and the city would be socially, physically, and economically integrated. All of Rio's medium-sized favelas were to be upgraded within 10 years. They would be supplied with the electricity, sewage, and other services they were denied or needed to steal. Widened and paved roads, staircases, ramps, and funiculars improved vehicular and pedestrian mobility in and out of the favelas. Plazas created meeting places and were placed within and around the edges of the favelas. They served both as civic meeting places and as transitional spaces connecting the favelas with middle-class areas, blurring the boundaries that had segregated them and eradicating stigma (McGuirk 2016).

With U.S. $180 million from the Inter-American Development Bank and $120 million from the city for each of Phases One and Two, Favela–Bairro not only provided a greatly improved streetscape but also established community buildings with social services such as children's centers, computer centers, and diverse trainings in such things as hygiene, community development, and land titling. In 2001, Favela–Bairro lost funding before the project was completed.

About 168 favelas benefited from Favela–Bairro improvements (Osborn 2012b). It improved the quality of life for hundreds of thousands of people with little displacement. Although residents approved of the program and its processes, in hindsight it was not as participatory and was more paternalistic than community inspired. It failed to affect the drug trade that controlled many favelas and did not trigger as much resident-initiated renovation of housing (McGuirk 2016). Favela–Bairro did not provide microcredit, which could explain why resident renovation of housing was so limited. In a similar vein, failure to foresee the need for literacy training accounts for the negligible success of the employment segment of the program. One of the important lessons of Favela–Bairro is the importance of meaningful community participation (World Bank 2001).

Phase Three: More Detriment than Benefit?

During the first decade of the 2000s, money trickled into the favelas. Then, in 2010, Rio's mayor announced the *Morar Carioca program* to great fanfare. Much more extravagant than Favela–Bairro, Morar Carioca was a significant component of Rio's 2012–2016 strategic plan to showcase Brazil in the 2016 Olympic Games. Designed to leave a lasting legacy, Morar Carioca was to benefit 232,000 households by 2020 (Siemens 2014). With a budget of Brazilian Real [R] $8 billion (about U.S. $4 billion in 2010) coming from the city, along with credit and loans from the federal government and the Inter-American Development Bank, Morar Carioca was to transform 815 favelas[7] (Brown 2016). In total, 40 architectural firms chosen from twice as many applicants implemented the program. Each team was staffed with at least one anthropologist and one social worker and assigned specific favelas to ensure that each favela was to be designed according to its particular needs (Osborn 2013). Because renovation of housing was a prime failure of Favela–Bairro, Morar Carioca prioritized housing (McGuirk 2016). Community involvement was a priority, and community members participated through surveys, brainstorming sessions, and presenting their ideas directly to city council (Brown 2016).

Broken promises soon followed. Facilities and amenities for the 2014 World Cup and 2016 Olympic Games competed with the favelas for development. In October 2010, Favela do Metrô residents protested plans for stadium parking that would displace 800 people (Waldron 2016). Within months after the 2012 elections, plans for some favelas were canceled without explanation.[8] In total, 344 families were evicted from Vila Autódromo to make room for roads to Olympic Park (Douglas 2015). After about 26 of a promised 117 apartments were built in Babilônia, the workers left and no one from the city offered the residents an explanation (Barbassa n.d.).

Residents of the favelas shuffled between favelas and transitional housing to accommodate renovations. In 2012, the residents of one favela were evicted to allow for upgrading, but one year later improvements had not been made. More than 400 families were priced out of another favela after it benefitted from upgrades and police services and rents soared by 300 percent (Brown 2016). While some people who were evicted were resettled close to their original housing, 8,600 families were resettled far outside of the city, making travel for work difficult if not impossible. Rather than improving transportation infrastructure for favelas, dozens of bus lines were eliminated, having a significant negative impact on jobs and mental health. Basic infrastructure in these areas was another concern. Lack of local schools or access to health care, critical problems of transit and distance from jobs, and more expensive utilities all erode the quality of life (Douglas 2015). As late as 2016, benefits of Morar Carioca to the favelas were negligible.

The city government's accounting presented a different picture. It reported that only Vila Autodromo was evicted in order to accommodate the World Cup and Olympic Games. Most evictions and relocations, 72.2 percent of the evictions, were due to faults in the location—subject to flooding, landslides, or other precarious situations (Rio Perfeitura 2015). During the first phase of Morar Carioca, the city government reported that 306,000 people in 69 communities benefitted

(Continued)

(*Continued*)

and that the second phase, from 2014 to 2016, would benefit another 328,800. The third phase, from 2017 to 2020, was scheduled to reach 436,000 people (Rio Perfeitura 2015). One reason for the large discrepancies between the media and residents' accounts may be that reportedly the program's name, Morar Carioca, was appropriated to use with any upgrade regardless of when it was originally planned, how it was funded, or whether the favela was in the program (Brown 2016). In some favelas, the most expensive projects were to benefit tourists; the elevator in Cantagalo, gondolas in Alemão and Providencia, solar-powered lights and a deck of recycled plastic in Babilônia all cost millions of dollars, but trash collection and letter delivery, two things that residents prioritized (at least in Babilônia), were not addressed (Barbassa n.d.).

Another issue raised by residents and media concerns safety. Complex de Maré is among a cluster of favelas that never received the police pacification units they were promised, although 40 other favelas did. Instead, it was among the victims of a military "occupation" and rash of police and military violence that killed more than 300 citizens in Rio in 2015 and more than 100 in the first five months of 2016. Most were from the favelas; most were young black men. Although this level of violence was significantly lower than the peak in 2007 preceding the Pan American Games, 2014 saw a 39 percent increase over 2013 and 2015 rose another 11.2 percent (Amnesty International 2016).

Was Social Cleansing the Intention?

The corruption scandal that wrecked Brazil's economy uncovered widespread massive corruption not only in Petróleo Brasileiro (Petrobras), its initial target, but in the construction and meat industries as well. Mismanagement and corruption diverted money intended to benefit millions in the favelas, and elsewhere, into the pockets of a few. Millions of dollars in bribes influenced the construction of World Cup and Olympic construction projects. Odebrecht and Andrade Gutierrez,[9] the largest construction companies in Brazil, paid politicians—including the mayor—for contracts. This was to the harm of the favelas, among others. For example, in 2013, the "People's Plan for Vila Autodromo" won the Deutsche Bank Urban Age Award design competition. The plan would have left the favela intact but vastly improved. Instead, the mayor went ahead with the demolition of the favela, a viable community that could have been made safe and secure. Real estate developers increased their profits substantially, even taking the bribes into account, on the Olympic contracts (Chade 2017). There was no attempt by the developer, Caravalho, to conceal that the Olympic

Village housing would be sold as luxury housing afterward. The Olympic Village and the related developments, such as swimming pools, tropical gardens, and a lake, would be for the privileged, those of good taste, the elite, he was reported to have said (Watts 2015).

Minha Casa, Minha Vida (My House, My Life) is the largest public housing program in Brazil's history. This federal program was initiated by President Lula de Silva in 2009 and expanded by his successor, Dilma Rousseff. Not specifically focused on favelas, it promised subsidized quality housing with official titles and mortgage payments based on income for all families earning up to U.S. $1,528 (R $5,000) (Rio Perfeitura 2015). Although criticized for corruption and inefficiency, critics acknowledge that the program has made a dent in the housing shortage. As of June 2016, the program had built 2.6 million low-cost homes across Brazil and 4.2 million were under contract at a cost of U.S. $67 billion. Still recovering from the worst depression in Brazil's history, the program faces cuts and most of the new housing might not be built (Arsenault 2016).

How much the failures to revitalize the favelas resulted from corruption over decades will probably not be quantified. However, several lessons learned are important for development efforts globally.

Throughout these and other phases of favela revitalization and efforts to meet the demands for low-income housing, despite successes and failures, the primary lessons remain the same:

- Many areas classified as slums or other informal settlements house viable communities that have already proven their resilience. Development efforts need to build on the strength of these neighborhoods rather than demolish them.

- Pushing the poor farther away from the city proper isolates them from the services that they most need— public transportation to jobs or jobs within walking/ biking distances, health care, and education. This exacerbates rather than solves problems.

- Gentrification of poorer communities and development of luxury housing and amenities cannot replace affordable housing if a city is to build resilience.

- Community participation and community preservation supported by partnerships across many sectors of government, civil society, philanthropy, education, and private enterprise are necessary for realistic and workable urban development.

- Keeping promises is also necessary.

houses about 60 residents in tiny houses. Designed to be an eco-friendly "green" community, it is constructed of recycled materials and has an organic farm, composting toilets, and 24-hour security. Only where there is medical necessity are the houses wired for electricity. A common area has television, and the entire neighborhood has access to Wi-Fi. The city provides waste removal and recycling (Lumpp 2013). Residents must contribute U.S. $35 a month and 10 hours of work weekly to maintain the community.

Residence in Dignity Village is restricted to two years except for community leaders. Potential residents are placed on waiting lists and given a 60-day guest residency when a house becomes available. During the guest residency, potential residents demonstrate conformity to rules of behavior—no violence, drugs, alcohol, theft, or any disruptive behavior—and participation in the community life. After 30 more days, they become a member if approved by a community vote (Dignity Village n.d.).

Dignity Village was built by its original residents, at least partially in protest of the status quo. Not-for-profits, churches, and some city governments adopted the idea and are building new affordable tiny house communities across the United States and the world. The objective of most, as for Dignity Village, is to provide transitional housing and help move people into permanent housing.

The villages vary according to their sponsors and needs of the area. Built by an interfaith group and construction company, Nashville's Infinity Village tiny houses are only 60 square feet but have electricity, a "Murphy" (wall) bed, heat and cooling, a mini-fridge, and a microwave. Nickelsville in Seattle began with a few tents, but with private donations it grew into an encampment of 14 tiny houses at a cost of about U.S. $2,200 each. As with many other encampments, there is electricity in each house, but water facilities are community shared.

An Austin charity, Mobile Loaves and Fishes, built the Community First! encampment of refurbished RVs and concrete platform tents. By adding 125 tiny homes, it will eventually house 250 residents. In addition to the homes, there will be a medical facility, an outdoor movie theater, gardens, places of worship, and other amenities. Rent will range from U.S. $200 to $350. Unlike the others, Community First! provides permanent residence.

Tent cities and little house villages are more akin to resident-run condominium associations than the traditional shelters run by governments or social service agencies. Most traditional shelters do not allow couples to stay together. They may exclude people who do not qualify for subsidies or have served any jail time. Shelters with strict in and out times do not accommodate nighttime work schedules. Most tent cities and little house villages are open to all homeless people who abide by the rules and participate in the community. As reported by the residents, they are small town neighborhoods where people support one another and feel safe. People have the dignity that comes with self-reliance and the autonomy to control their own lives.

People's Rights to Land and Voice

Policy can affect whether urban growth contributes to growth in slums. For the years 1990 to 2007, some countries experiencing explosive urban growth experienced nearly all of it (Nigeria and Pakistan) or most of it (Bangladesh and the Philippines) in the slums. Others such as Egypt, Mexico, India, and Indonesia saw declines in the proportion of slum residents even as urbanization increased. Others such as Brazil and China saw a much smaller increase in slums than overall urbanization (Marx et al. 2013).

It is highly unlikely that urbanization will stop. Policies trying to keep people in rural areas fail. Rather than allow urbanization to proceed haphazardly, cities can plan for sustainable urban growth. First, a city can designate land available to new residents. Even if the city or national government cannot afford to upgrade the land with utilities, people will settle there and, because their right to settle is provided by the government, are likely to feel secure in their tenure, invest in it, and over time see the community upgrade.

Formally recognizing land rights, at least in the new settlements, provides the security of tenancy that makes long-term investments in property more likely. While Neuwirth (2005b) agreed that security in tenancy makes the difference between a developed squatter community and an underdeveloped one, it must be appropriately secured. Too often, land rights are sold (sometimes involving corruption). This practice puts many low-income buyers in debt, and many need to sell their property to pay off the debt. This is not security.

One solution is the Turkish system discussed above—land pooling, through which adjoining smaller land parcels belonging to different owners are combined into one development and the land is then leased from the landlords. Government or a private entity must contract with the landlords for an orderly development. In land sharing agreements, residents in danger of eviction negotiate to continue to lease a part of the land on which they reside. The remainder can be leased to another. The drawback of this approach is an increase in density. It works best in lower-density settlements (Angel and Boonyabancha 1988).

Also included in the Turkish system are citizenship rights. These are critical. Unlike Kibera, where the people are "trees," people need voice in their communities. People in all communities, including squatter communities, have the right to engage their government. With that, of course, come responsibilities. This is an important step in upgrading—not just for housing, water, electricity, and so on but also for education, health, economic, and social opportunities.

Bringing squatter communities into the formal structure of government benefits the government as well. Not only will crime and environmental degradation decrease, but also revenue from the billions of dollars generated in these communities will broaden the tax base.

Making Cities Resilient

Being resilient means being able to adapt in the face of adversity or setback. Fragile cities are not resilient. They break down rather than bounce back. Preventing fragility is important but not enough to produce resiliency. Resilience, as applied to cities, "is the capacity of individuals, communities, institutions, businesses, and systems within a city to survive, adapt, and grow no matter what kinds of chronic stresses and acute shocks they experience" (100 Resilient Cities 2017).

To build resilience, cities must make a deliberate and concerted effort. The systems that make up a city are interdependent like the systems of a human body. During shocks or disasters, failure in one system cascades, causing failure throughout. For example, when Hurricane Sandy landed in New Jersey in 2010, roads were impassible. Trucks could not get out to restore electricity. Pumps had no electricity to pump gas. People were unable to get to work. Economic effects rippled through city sectors (Ehlen 2014). To survive and thrive in contemporary times, redundancy in backup plans needs to be in place to prevent one failure from prompting others. In a resilient city, rather than one system failure knocking out the others in a domino effect, multiple avenues in place for each system would prevent a catastrophic failure. City systems cannot just respond to crises as they arise but rather must plan for as many eventualities as they can foresee.

City governments cannot be the only important actors in building resilience. The 100 Resilient Cities project networks city governments, civil society groups, the private sector, and individual citizens globally to share strategies and assistance on becoming more resilient. The cities in the network vary from small to mega sized. Some are growing, while others are shrinking. Some are wealthy, while others are poor. Building resiliency is important for all of them.

Resilient cities share seven characteristics:

- *Reflective:* Using past experience to inform future decisions

- *Resourceful:* Recognizing alternative ways to use resources

- *Robust:* Well conceived, constructed, and managed systems

- *Redundant:* Including spare capacity purposely created to accommodate disruption

- *Flexible:* Willing and able to adopt alternative strategies in response to changing circumstances

- *Inclusive:* Prioritizing broad consultation to create a sense of shared ownership in decision making

- *Integrated:* Bringing together a range of distinct systems and institutions (100 Resilient Cities 2017)

Membership in the resilient city program requires a city to draft action steps that include specific plans and a commitment to use 10 percent of the city's budget for resiliency-related activities. Pittsburgh, Rotterdam, and Lagos are very different cities in their size, history, and level of development, in the problems they confront, and in their city governance, yet all are in the Resilient Cities network. Evidence presented at the 2017 Resilient Cities meeting demonstrated that cities are using their shocks and stresses profiles in project design, land use planning, and budget and capital planning (Armstrong 2017).

Pittsburgh: Are Immigrants the Answer?

Pittsburgh, Pennsylvania, with a city proper of about 300,000 in a metropolitan area of more than 2.3 million, was an industrial city, once the largest steel maker in the United States. It lost population, like many of the "Rust Belt" cities of the United States, as industry and steel making moved.

Pittsburgh was able to survive the loss of heavy industry due to the presence of two major and several

CONSIDER THIS
WHAT TO DO WITH WATER

As sea levels rise, water is a greater threat than ever. Two members of the Resilient Cities network responded very differently.

Rotterdam's Answer to Its Shocks and Stressors

Many of the world's largest cities hug bodies of water—the coastlines, rivers, and lakes. While convenient for transportation, struggles with the seas have been part of life for centuries for many cities. Rising seas now are a threat to their very existence. Resilience in the face of climate change is not a luxury. Bangladesh, New York, Shanghai, New Orleans, and Mumbai, among many other of the world's largest cities and island nations, face mass migrations unless they invest heavily in building resilience. No city better knows the threat and how to confront it than Rotterdam.

Much of the Netherlands is built atop land that was once under water. Much is below sea level, as is most of Rotterdam. Fighting back the water is an extremely expensive proposition. In fighting the water, Rotterdam would lose. In Rotterdam, resilience means accepting the encroachment of water rather than resisting and turning the threat into opportunity rather than a deficit.

The change in perspective concerning how to deal with the water began when flooding forced hundreds of thousands of people in the Netherlands from their homes in 1990. Building higher levees and living behind 10-foot walls was not a palatable option. A much more desirable option was learning to live with the water, to invite it in, control its path, and use it to create a more livable city—a "less divided, more attractive, healthier city" (Kimmelman 2017). Rotterdam still has levees and gates, one of which is a massive storm surge barrier completed in 1997. But those are only part of the solution. Rowing courses, water sports, and plaza fountains make good use of the water. Parking garages, gardens, basketball courts, harbors, canals, and parks all serve multiple needs as emergency reservoirs or retention ponds. At the individual level, people are encouraged to buy boats and use a free app that tells them where they are in relation to the sea. Children pass swimming tests fully clothed, and people dig out the concrete from their gardens so water can absorb. The economy is greener. This is all in an old industrial city that was once crime ridden and filthy (Kimmelman 2017).

Innovative investments throughout the city are making it not just safer but also more amenable and livable. It is a great example of urban resilience.

Lagos: A Win for the Wealthy, a Loss for the Rest

Central planning in Nigeria meant consistent losses for many of the people in its growing cities. None exemplifies this more than the chronic struggle with the waters that surround the islands of Lagos. To keep the sea at bay and mitigate flooding, the Nigerian government entered into contract with private funders and China Communications Construction Group to build Eko Atlantic City (EAC). It is a four-square-mile extension of Lagos protruding into the Atlantic Ocean protected by a 35-foot seawall. Not only protection from the water, the land extension will also increase land available for housing, another necessity to accommodate the rapid population growth (Berkowitz 2013).

The development is not built with the displaced migrants that continue to pour into Lagos in mind. It is a haven for the wealthy to reside in one of the many high-rise apartments under construction. Each of the five towers is named after a pearl—White Pearl Tower, Black Pearl Tower, and so forth—except for the Eko Energy Estate being built by an oil and gas logistics firm. It will house about 5,000 custom-designed apartments in 50 to 60 towers (Uwaegbulam, 2015). As of late May 2018, 3 towers were completed and 13 were under way (Ibukun, Mongalvy, and Sguazzin 2018).

Although it received international awards, EAC seems to have more adverse sustainability impacts than positive ones. Environmentally, the wall that protects EAC threatens, rather than protects, nearby islands. The water diverted by the wall must go somewhere. Surrounding islands are lower than EAC. Swaths of Lagos and its population are made extremely vulnerable by the wall (Onuoha 2017). In 2012, floods killed 16 people and displaced hundreds of citizens around Lagos. Environmental experts and residents maintain that waters that would have remained in the ocean in surges are forced by the EAC wall to flow into the neighborhoods (Adegboye 2017). Socially, it increases spatial divides and inequities in Lagos. It creates distrust of the government because it promotes government planning as a tool to benefit the wealthy. Like many of the other projects, development did not enhance the quality of life for any but elite Lagos residents (Lawanson 2016).

Rotterdam and Lagos are both 100 Resilient Cities members with water management a common chronic stressor.

smaller universities, a blossoming high-tech industry, and extensive health care facilities. The stated priority for Pittsburgh is equitable development so that everyone—low income, minorities, and immigrants—benefits from city growth. In practical terms, equitable development means construction of mixed income, diverse housing, improvements to make neighborhoods safer, and generating economic opportunities in low-income and diverse neighborhoods (City of Pittsburgh 2017).

While migrants are flowing into some cities, other cities and their regions have dedicated considerable time, energy, and money to attracting immigrants. An important component of building resilience in Pittsburgh is the Immigrants and Internationals Initiative that began in 2007. Realizing that immigration is essential to its future, the region's "Immigrant Community Blueprint"—a joint venture of city and county governments, educational institutions, philanthropies, civil society groups, economic development agencies, and interested residents—is an action plan across domains of life to make the region inclusive and attractive to immigrants, regardless of their current skill level or income.

Attracting immigrants is not enough. Sustainability requires keeping them. The Pittsburgh Blueprint includes steps to ensure that immigrants feel welcome. It includes action items for all realms of life, encompassing language access, health and well-being, education, economic development, civic engagement, and family success. Language access entails steps such as collecting language-related data, instituting language learning programs, and increasing the standards for interpretation services. Health and well-being requires providing regular and on-site interpreters or multilingual providers at social service and health care providers and training in cultural sensitivity for service providers, among other actions. Economic development includes entrepreneurship opportunities for new immigrants. In education, it means supporting early childhood education, ensuring that parents are included in their children's education, providing training programs for all skill levels, and ensuring post-secondary opportunities (Allegheny County 2017).

Lagos: Empowerment Through Organization

Lagos, Nigeria, one of the five fastest growing cities in the world, is already one of the largest, with more than 21 million residents. Roughly 70 percent of the population does not have access to the goods that a city has to offer—jobs, housing, transportation, education, electricity, and so forth (Hoelzel 2016). Lagos experiences shocks and chronic stresses such as coastal and tidal flooding, disease outbreak, rainfall flooding, and sea level rise (100 Resilient Cities 2017).

In 2015, *National Geographic* heralded Lagos as Africa's "first city" and celebrated its dynamic growth that pushed the entire country along. Closer examination revealed that city planning in Lagos explicitly prioritized making the city appealing to investors, tourists, travelers, and businesses with the intention of becoming not just a big city but also a "global city." China accepted Nigeria's call for foreign investment. Foreign investment benefits a city when it creates jobs for residents and the increased revenues are reinvested locally in infrastructure, education, and health for all. However, in Lagos, as happens in other cities and as discussed above, the projects overlooked residents, particularly the poor. Chinese engagement in Africa has been to employ Chinese on their projects and avoid responsibility for negative social, environmental, and/or economic impacts. Local employment was not increased, and profits from Chinese investments were not put back into the city to improve the conditions of the poor, although government agents may have reaped significant profit (Hoelzel 2016).

Why else didn't investment help the city? One reason lies in the structure of government. Planning for a city growing so rapidly that the census can only broadly estimate the population—somewhere between 13 to 20 million—is an enormous task. Complicating this task is the government structure. In Nigeria, there are no city mayors; thus, planning, along with governing, is a state and national function. Governing city planning from the state offices poses several difficulties. In planning for Lagos, efforts were disjointed, a unifying vision was lacking, and ministries often worked in isolation from one another and in contradictory ways (Ummuna 2016).

Similar lack of coordination existed in housing. Nine institutions in Lagos state have direct bearing on housing. A piecemeal approach to housing issues centralized at the state level neglected local governments and failed to develop plans or housing to meet the city's actual needs. The state did not solicit any community participation. There was no progress in some slums for more than 30 years (Lawanson 2016).

After Lagos joined 100 Resilient Cities, it joined with other cities to form the Nigerian Resilient Cities Network (NRCN) to embolden resilience thinking across the country. Membership is open to any city that commits to the principles of Resilient Cities. The NRCN helps member cities in developing resilient strategies and receives support from 100 Resilient Cities. Registered as a nongovernmental organization, NRCN acts on behalf of its member cities as a collective on state and national levels.

The Lagos state development plan for 2012–2025 did little to include local concerns. Planning procedures excluded broad segments of society from participation, and there were no mechanisms for accountability (Hoelzel 2016). By organizing local stakeholders, the NRCN might be able to force participation of local governments and residents, hold the state and national governments accountable, and achieve meaningful results. By organizing, Lagos is exhibiting the necessary qualities to build resiliency—reflective in recognizing how foreign investment left most of the city behind and resourceful, inclusive, and integrated by bringing cities together to consolidate their positions and power. Already it has had positive results. The NRCN Facebook page announced a U.S. $300 million project financed through credit from the World Bank for helping low- and middle-income families afford mortgages and to create jobs. Along with the announcement was this post: "Great news! Now to start a conversation about how best to spend the money. I will be making an argument for promoting self-build initiatives, NOT contractor or developer led approaches," proclaimed Simon Gusah of NRCN on the project's Facebook page (November 8, 2017). In mid-2017, the program was rated moderately satisfactory by the World Bank. The housing portion of the program is faring better than the jobs portion (Ayeyemi 2018).

Environmental Sustainability in the Cities

Cities can devastate the natural environment. Environmental threats are legion—concrete replacing greenery, diminishing biodiversity, traffic and industry billowing carbon dioxide (CO_2) and other toxins into the atmosphere, landfills of organic and inorganic waste occupying precious land and seeping into water supplies, and overuse of water and energy. Below are a few of the unsustainability statistics:

- Population in a global sample of 120 cities grew by 17 percent, but the footprint of these urban areas grew by 28 percent (UN Habitat 2016).

- Cities produce about 80 percent of the world's global warming potential (Riffat, Powell, and Aydin 2016).

- Compact cities produce less greenhouse gas emissions than sprawling cities due to transportation. Urban form is perhaps the most important feature in a city's global warming potential.

- Three quarters (75 percent) of waste is recyclable, but 70 percent is not recycled (Riffat et al. 2016).

- Buildings consume 40 percent of the world's energy use; more urbanization means more buildings (Mandyck 2016).

- A 50 to 60 percent increase in global food production is needed to feed the growing urban population.

Renewable energy, more efficient mass transit and vehicles that do not emit greenhouse gases, waste management and recycling, more compact city design by building up instead of horizontally, rainwater harvesting, urban gardening, and more resilient agriculture are familiar priorities on the environmental agenda. Food efficiencies, small city or neighborhood design, and building material issues strategies reduce the footprint of cities significantly.

Food Supply Chain Strategies

City expansion reduces farmland and extends the supply chain, increasing the distance of people from food. Food spoils in transit as much as 30 to 40 percent in the developing world. Longer supply chains emit more greenhouse gases and waste more food. Growing more food in the city or its immediate surroundings mitigates the greenhouse gas cost of transportation and unsustainability of food waste. Alternatively, "cold chain" technology, keeping food refrigerated in transit, keeps food fresh and eliminates pollutants and carbons related to growing 30 percent more food.

The savings of cold chains are enormous. Food waste related to inefficient supply chains generated about 1 gigaton of CO_2 equivalence in 2011—two thirds of the greenhouse gas emissions of total U.S. road transportation of 2012. Net savings in extending cold chains throughout the developing world is about 550 million tons of greenhouse gases, more than the total annual emissions of France (450 million tons) in 2012. Cold chain technology implemented in China would generate 40 percent of the savings (Bio Intelligence Service 2015).

The Garden City Strategy

New cities planning calls for carbon neutrality and sustainability. One model is a "return to the future." The Town and Country Planning Association (TCPA), a civil society organization working in the United Kingdom, encourages implementing the Garden City model first conceived in the late 19th century by Ebenezer Howard. The original Garden City model emphasized social, economic, and environmental cohesion. The principles are not too different from the best practices in urban development:

- Strong leadership and community engagement
- Community ownership of land and long-term stewardship of assets
- Affordable housing for ordinary people
- Strong and diverse local job markets
- Beautifully designed homes with gardens and opportunity for people to grow their own food
- Generous green spaces, biodiverse public parks, and tree-lined streets
- Walkable neighborhoods, including cultural, shopping, and recreational facilities
- One 21st-century update: low carbon transit and rapid transit networks linking cities for a full range of employment opportunities (Riffat et al. 2016)

The TCPA offers some key points for the new Garden Cities based on its study of developments built following World War II. Like other city planning efforts, the TCPA recommends that the local communities take the lead in choosing the site and that the effort be a private–public partnership to ensure the interests of the city residents. Legislation creating the cities should include provision for the long-term stewardship to maintain the quality of the cities. Because many previous urban renewal efforts were thought to be sterile, the Garden Cities should provide cultural, social, and recreational activities.

Zero Carbon Building

"Zero carbon building" (ZCB) programs encourage construction of new buildings or retrofitting older buildings to generate zero carbons on balance. All greenhouse gas emissions must be offset by generating clean and renewable energy on- or off site. In Canada, among other countries, certification is issued to buildings that demonstrate the net zero balance. For new buildings, the Canadian certification requires that 5 percent of the renewable energy generated is installed on-site and thermal energy heat loss is reduced. Regular reporting documents that the zero balance was achieved and is being maintained (Canada Green Building Council 2016).

Eco-efficient building materials, in addition to the more well-known photovoltaic cells and other renewable energies, are critical in Europe's "Smart Cities and Communities Initiative." Aiming for a 40 percent reduction in greenhouse gases in the urban environment, the zero-carbon home is of vital importance as people continue to expect greater levels of comfort, increasing energy use (Riffat et al. 2016).

Eco-friendly wood construction is on the rise. Developments constructed of wood are something like building forests of trees. It is ideal for ZCB, even contributing to carbon reduction while growing. Wood stores carbon over a long period of time; just 1 kg of wood stores 9 kg of CO_2. Wood produces no waste, and it harnesses solar energy. A 30-story wooden tower built in Vancouver, Canada, testifies to wood's versatility and strength (Riffat et al. 2016).

ZCB is not difficult with inventive use of plentiful materials. Recycled steel is another eco-friendly material. Six junkyard cars provide enough material for an average house. Insulating concrete forms (concrete with a layer of air and supports), plant-based insulation in place of fiberglass, stucco-coated straw bales, and lumber made from recycled plastic and wood are innovative and practical construction options (Anderson 2016).

Tackling Transportation

Urban transit contributes a significant portion of the urban footprint. Transportation knits the connections among diverse city systems and multiple stakeholders. Accessibility, bringing things closer to where they are needed, is a simple but single most important goal of transportation. As cities expand in population and area, transportation problems become thornier. Moving more people over greater distances with a minimum of air and noise pollution, land degradation, and time wasted commuting challenges city planning. Improvements in transportation improve economic productivity and personal happiness and well-being (Zielinksi 2012).

Because cities vary in the infrastructure in place—their structure, their terrain, and their capacity to build anew—no single solution for all cities exists. Denser cities cut traveling times and thus contribute less than urban sprawl. In planning for new cities or renovating old ones, compact designs must be considered. But it will not be a solution for every city.

But integration, as a guiding principle, works for all systems. Integrated transportation systems coordinate bus, subway, bike, car, and pedestrian traffic. With focus on connecting multiple modes, speed and safety of transportation increases. One strategy is creating more protected routes for bicycles and pedestrians. Connecting these routes to public transportation increases ridership and decreases traffic. Rather than building new infrastructure, promoting alternate transportation is more effective and sustainable for most cities.

Bike and car share programs exist in many cities to complement the traditional park and ride hubs; adding bike sharing and car sharing stations to the hubs increases their utility. Protected lanes for bikes promotes their use and prohibits cars from transforming them into an extra car lane or parking lane.

Streetcars, phased out of most developed countries in the mid-20th century, are making a comeback. Modern streetcars prove to be a more efficient, city-friendly public transportation alternative. Running on electricity rather than combustion motors, they are lighter and more environmentally friendly than buses. Most roads do not need to be fortified to handle streetcar traffic. Streetcars maneuver more easily through traffic.

More efficient bus service is one city's answer. Detroit, although it introduced streetcars, also revamped its buses. Installing interior and exterior cameras reduced crime on the buses by 62 percent. Reliability increased as safety improved. (Drivers had walked out in protest over the shooting death of a driver while on duty, and many buses never left the station on a given day for safety concerns.) More efficient routes, some with 24-hour service and others with limited service, and other improvements increased ridership.

Good Urban Governance

One of the most critical lessons gleaned from the experiences of cities and their revitalization attempts is the importance of good governance. Governance is not synonymous with government. Governance brings all of the stakeholders in a city together to design and implement plans for the common good. Socially, economically, and/or spatially divided cities are unsustainable. Urban redevelopment must be carefully planned to maintain viable communities; too often, in both developed and developing countries, neighborhoods are destroyed and city life is fractured.

Government and civil society organizations and agencies, small and large businesses, philanthropies, educational institutions, and citizens from across the economic and social spectra need to be brought to the same table. A coherent and integrated development approach is necessary to leverage resources wisely and ensure that all sectors evolve with regard to eliminating contradictory trajectories and goals and reducing the potential for shocks or chronic stresses to cause cascading failures. Building redundancy into systems may seem inefficient, but contingency backup is necessary in systems where there are uncertainties.

The scale and rapidity of migration to megacities and the lack of migration to some smaller cities threaten sustainability. Deliberate development of middle and smaller cities, rather than allowing sprawl to infinitely expand on the borders of the megacities, creates more sustainable urban development. Integrating migrants, making use of their talents, and recognizing that migrants are necessary for economic growth in cities (and countries) that have zero or negative population growth or building creativity build social cohesion.

China's migrations from rural to manufacturing and export centers is responsible for its growth. Yet the hukou system of registration denied millions of rural migrants essential benefits, such as education and health care, received by those registered as urbanites. Reforms of the hukou system under way ameliorate part of the problem but in practice still deny benefits to millions. Many of the international migrants working in Arab states are similarly denied. Most developed countries grant benefits to international migrants; however, social and economic integration for many needs improving.

Decentralized decision making and community engagement are necessary in every phase of city planning, from initial assessments of needs and strengths to final design and implementation. Every city's plan will be different based on local needs and strengths, including financial capabilities. Municipal leaders are critical to address the specifics of each city's specific needs, from the inequities in health and education and other basic services to global concerns such as climate change. Decentralization may be limited to the delegation of decision making and implementation on specific issues from a central authority to regional or local ones. This is often referred to as deconcentration. Devolution, a step beyond that provides financing to be managed at the local level, is critical to cities where infrastructures are overburdened if they are to carry out their plans.

Good governance can make the difference between cities that degrade and decay, becoming more and more fragile, and cities that are resilient. Haphazard development resulting in social and economic divides degrades the quality of life for all city inhabitants.

SUMMARY

Cities can be a positive force to drive prosperity. However, many cities are overburdened and their infrastructures cannot adequately provide for all of their residents. Migration and fertility stress some cities, while population loss and aging stress others. In the slums or squatter communities, residents are denied the most basic life chances—including, in many places, the right to be recognized as citizens. Problems from inequality to conflict abound.

Building resilience into cities requires a concerted effort by governmental and non-governmental stakeholders. The problems of cities extend beyond slums. From the wealthiest cities to the poorest ones, all cities face chronic stressors and shocks. All cities face increasing inequities in access to services that increase life chances, the resultant social divides, and environmental problems that challenge sustainability and resilience. Environmental and social sustainability are interrelated; one cannot exist without the other.

The corporations with gleaming headquarters in the global cities bear responsibilities not just in those cities but also in the megacities and smaller cities where their products—or those of their clients—are made. Civil society and philanthropies need to look beyond the cause of the day to coordinate services with all stakeholders and deliver services across all sectors. Planning must be coordinated horizontally and vertically with decentralization of authority and funding to the cities themselves.

Economic and social divides within cities separate neighborhoods not only by income but also by access to basic services from management of solid wastes to water quality, to education, to health care—all necessary for basic life chances and escaping poverty traps. Continuity of services is limited in many parts of cities, not just in the poorest areas. Social divides create distrust in government and lack of empathy and concern for those caught in poverty traps. The sustained economic growth expected from cities is unlikely to continue without healthier cities. No city is sustainable unless life chances are equitably granted to all city residents.

DISCUSSION

1. Study the strategy for resilience for one of the cities in the resilient city network. What are the city's major challenges, and what are the primary means through which the city will address them? Cities with strategies posted online are on this website: http://www.100resilientcities.org/strategies/#/-_

2. Develop a definition for urban sustainability and urban resilience. What characteristics does a sustainable city have? A resilient city? Why is local decision making important to improving city sustainability and resilience?

3. What are the benefits and drawbacks of immigration for cities? How can cities make a welcoming climate for immigrants? How can nations help to balance the flow of immigrants among cities that are overburdened and smaller and medium-sized cities?

4. Why are cities becoming more important actors in international and global relations? For ideas and information, visit the Mayors Summit website and reports: https://globalparliamentofmayors.org/annual-summit-2018

ON YOUR OWN

1. Investigate the most recent report of one of the creative cities highlighted on the United Nations Educational, Scientific, and Cultural Organization Creative Cities website: http://en.unesco.org/creative-cities/creative-cities-map

   What has the project accomplished?

2. Using the interactive maps on Igarapé Institute's website, select a city to investigate. What are this city's most vital issues? What trends are predicted for this city to 2030? What suggestions are there for strengthening this city?

   http://fragilecities.igarape.org.br

3. Investigate the Gini coefficients for U.S. cities. Are there patterns to the geographic locations of the most equal or unequal cities? How do they fare on quality of life measures?

   For information on U.S. cities: http://www
   .bizjournals.com/bizjournals/news/2014/01/31/
   gini-indexes-of-income-inequality-in.html

   For information on cities in developing nations: https://unhabitat.org/wp-content/
   uploads/2014/03/Table-3.1-Gini-Coefficient-for-Selected-Cities-and-Provinces.pdf

4. What is the closest city to where you live or go to college? Tour the city or a neighborhood within it to assess the quality of life. Consider these factors:

- Condition of the exteriors of homes, schools, and public facilities
- Occupancy and vacancy rates
- Employment
- Age structure
- Pollution
- Availability of food stores or markets

Are there noticeable inequalities in people's life chances?

The Community Toolbox is a service provided by the University of Kansas to help people build stronger communities and foster positive social change. Section (2) Understanding and Describing the Community offers a detailed guide for community analysis: http://ctb.ku.edu/en/table-of-contents/
assessment/assessing-community-needs-and-resources/describe-the-community/main

In the "Tools" tab, there is a "Community Description Worksheet" that can help you to organize. It has interview guides should you decide to include interviews in your analysis: http://ctb.ku.edu/en/table-of-contents/
assessment/assessing-community-needs-and-resources/describe-the-community/tools

NOTES

1. The Organisation for Economic Cooperation and Development (OECD) is beginning to use the concept of "functional urban area" defined by population density and economic function. The methodology is limited to OECD countries and thus is not useful in global analysis.

2. The UN DESA (2016) report *The World Cities in 2016* lists cities by population size and identifies the statistical concept used to determine the population. The report also lists the rate of growth and the proportion of the country that is urbanized.

3. Both Weber and Durkheim engaged Tönnies on his delineation of these terms. Both proposed correctives. For all the similarity in their concepts, Durkheim did not view the organic solidarity of the industrial society as "unnatural" or a lesser form of social life, as Tönnies did. Weber emphasized the different forms of thought from which each sprang—traditional versus rational.

4. Weber maintained that the bureaucratic form of life would persist until the last ton of fossilized fuel was burned. This seems to be coming to pass given that new forms of organization (the horizontal corporation,

learning corporation, etc.) are being tried and renewable forms of energy are increasingly replacing fossil fuels.

5. Determining the world's largest cities is a tricky business. The rankings change depending on whether it is just the city, as defined by its political boundaries, or the metropolitan area.

6. SHARE/WHEEL is a partnership of the Seattle Housing and Resource Effort and the Women's Housing, Equality, and Enhancement League (women only).

7. In 1993, Benedita da Silva, born in a Rio de Janeiro favela, nearly won the mayoral election.

8. The number of favelas varies by accounts. McGuirk (2016) put the number at 582 favelas housing more than a million people.

9. Plans for the Cordovil region in Rio de Janeiro's North Zone were canceled in January 2013 and not reinstated until May 2016. The region has largely depended on itself for upgrading and has five communities in the region slated for upgrades beginning in 2016 (Healy and Norris 2016).

10. Officials in both of these companies, along with dozens of politicians, have been convicted along with dozens of politicians on corruption charges related to the World Cup and Olympic Games construction projects, among other projects. Odebrecht alone paid out U.S. $800 million from 2001 to 2016. Odebrecht's dealings were not limited to Brazil. It has admitted to bribery in more than a dozen other countries, and others are suspected.

16

A World Gone Awry?

THE STATE OF GOVERNANCE

IS THE WORLD UNMANAGEABLE?

There are known knowns. These are things we know that we know. There are known unknowns. That is to say, there are things that we know we don't know. But there are also unknown unknowns. There are things we don't know we don't know.

—Donald Rumsfeld, U.S. Secretary of Defense, 1975–1977 and 2001–2006

We live in a chaotic world, a world of risk and uncertainty. Uncertainty is basic to the human condition because the future is essentially unknowable. Risk, as opposed to threats that have always existed, is a modern concept. Risk anticipates a future that can be planned based on facts, measurements, and rational processes. The foundation of actuarial science is the calculability of risk. It is how we cope with uncertainty (Beck 1992).

The dangers the world anticipates today are global catastrophes, manufactured risks, and uncertainties.

Manufactured risk and uncertainty are unique to contemporary times; they are characterized by delocalization (affecting the whole world), the incalculability of their consequences, and the non-compensability or irreversibility of the consequences. Climate change, terrorism, and financial crises are such manufactured risks, threats arising from people's decisions, not from nature (Beck 2009). As science (and rationality in general) has shaped much of the world, science has lost authority among some people. Ideology and cultural perceptions concerning the pros and cons of

LEARNING OBJECTIVES

After completing this chapter and related materials, students will be able to do the following:

16.1 Summarize and assess the goals, characteristics, and norms of good governance as stated by international bodies and states

16.2 Identify the multiple layers of state and global governance and explain how each contributes to or complicates good governance

16.3 Compare and contrast types of regimes, particularly liberal and illiberal democracies

16.4 Describe and prioritize the challenges facing state governments

16.5 Analyze the challenges of governance posed by populism, nationalism, and globalism

16.6 Relate the challenges of state governance to the challenges of global governance

16.7 Design or modify a plan of action for institutionalizing the essential components of good governance in a state and for global governance

various potential consequences of decisions form much of the public debates. It is tempting for people to simplify and pose one set of alternatives as safe and another set as risky (Beck 2009).

Risk is hard to manage in a world of manufactured uncertainty. The public debates in social media and polarized politics, and the allegations of "fake news" as well as the temptations to simplify problems and disregard science, reflect the difficulties of manufactured risks and uncertainties.

Where has governance gone wrong? Stabilizing countries and creating a more manageable world depend on good state and global governance. Democracy, human rights, the rule of law—these have formed the centerpiece of the emerging international order since the end of World War II, informing institutions both within and among states. International political bodies from the United Nations (UN) to the regulatory agencies, to the governmental and non-governmental aid agencies, to states themselves proclaim these principles but nevertheless failed in their common mission to build a world of peace and prosperity.

Not that there hasn't been progress. As previous chapters have discussed, there are millions fewer people living in the worst forms of poverty, war between states is nearly eliminated, violent conflict within states claims fewer lives than at its post-World War II peak, and millions of people are breathing cleaner air and drinking cleaner water. Carbon emissions have decreased. On average, people live longer and healthier lives than ever before. Globalization potentially affords everyone the opportunity to achieve their life chances.

But the progress is not distributed equally. Billions of people exist in very fragile circumstances. Food insecurity, oppression and persecution, and violence are everyday facts of life for many. Inequality is increasing in many areas, and political polarization is widespread. New diseases threaten as we narrow the buffer zone between civilization and the wilderness. We may have polluted and destroyed the natural environment beyond its capacity to support future generations of human life. Instead of fulfilling their life chances, these problems deny people years of life and lives of quality.

Are these failures of governance? While there was significant progress in the late 20th century toward global governance, it seems to have reversed since about 2008 or 2009. Trends in global integration, peace, and fair and free trade are reversing and integration is disintegrating (Talbott 2017).

People bear the cost of poor governance in the diminished quality of their lives and in lost years of life due to the problems discussed in prior chapters, but just as progress is not distributed evenly, neither is the cost distributed evenly. Depending on people's social location—geographic, social class, race, ethnicity, and gender—they bear more or less of the cost. Neither sources of people's problems nor the solutions to them are contained within political borders. The problems are generated, in whole or in part, by international relations and global forces. The solutions also must be.

GOALS OF GOVERNANCE

Goals of Global Governance

Although they are not clearly articulated or systematically defined, goals of global governance are emergent. The most significant modern attempts to establish institutions of global governance have been the League of Nations and the United Nations, each following on the heels of a world war in an attempt to provide for global collective security.

The Covenant of the League of Nations states the following:

In order to promote international co-operation and to achieve international peace and security

- by the acceptance of obligations not to resort to war,

- by the prescription of open, just and honorable relations between nations,

- by the firm establishment of the understandings of international law as the actual rule of conduct among Governments, and

- by the maintenance of justice and a scrupulous respect for all treaty obligations in the dealings of organized peoples with one another. (League of Nations 1924)

The covenant proposes general principles of appropriate behavior and responsibilities of states regarding such matters as provisions for citizens, a commitment to reduce armaments, a set of procedures for settling disputes among countries, and the promise that an act of war against one country would be an act of war against all countries.

The Preamble of the Charter of the United Nations broadens the scope of collective security to include equal human rights of all people and countries and a better standard of living for all people:

We The Peoples of the United Nations Determined

- to save succeeding generations from the scourge of war, which twice in our lifetime has brought untold sorrow to mankind, and

- to reaffirm faith in fundamental human rights, in the dignity and worth of the human person, in the equal rights of men and women and of nations large and small, and

- to establish conditions under which justice and respect for the obligations arising from treaties and other sources of international law can be maintained, and

- to promote social progress and better standards of life in larger freedom.

And for these ends

- to practice tolerance and live together in peace with one another as good neighbors, and

- to unite our strength to maintain international peace and security, and

- to ensure, by the acceptance of principles and the institution of methods, that armed force shall not be used, save in the common interest, and

- to employ international machinery for the promotion of the economic and social advancement of all peoples. (United Nations 1945)

In keeping with the expanded goals, the preamble offers a host of agencies and departments to achieve these goals.

Whether due to the work of the UN, other regional intergovernmental associations, or bi- and multi-lateral treaties, there has been relative peace among nations since World War II. Other global goals—security within many nations—is still elusive, as are global prosperity and freedom.

Goals of State Governance

The goals of state governance are not much different from those of global governance. National constitutions tend to be very similar, at least in part a function of globalization. The earliest written constitution still in use is the Constitution of the United States. Its preamble reads as follows:

We the People of the United States, in Order to form a more perfect Union, establish Justice, insure domestic Tranquility, provide for the common Defense, promote the general Welfare, and secure the Blessings of Liberty to ourselves and our Posterity, do ordain and establish this Constitution for the United States of America. (U.S. Constitutional Convention 1787)

Although the terms are somewhat vague, the government is to secure peace at home, defense from threats from abroad, general welfare, and the enjoyment of liberty. To do so, the constitution outlines the basic structure of a liberal democracy—the rule of law, the separation and independence of the branches of government, procedures for elections, the civil liberties that are the rights of citizens, and the preservation of these for the future indefinitely.

The preamble of a much later—1993—constitution is very similar in its focus on peace, equality, self-determination, well-being, and prosperity now and for the future:

We, the multinational people of the Russian Federation, united by a common destiny on our land, asserting human rights and liberties, civil peace and accord, preserving the historic unity of the state, proceeding from the commonly recognized principles of equality and self-determination of the peoples honoring the memory of our ancestors, who have passed on to us love of and respect for our homeland and faith in good and justice, reviving the sovereign statehood of Russia and asserting its immutable democratic foundations, striving to secure the well-being and prosperity of Russia and proceeding from a sense of responsibility for our homeland before the present and future generations, and being aware of ourselves as part of the world community, hereby approve the Constitution of the Russian Federation.[1]

Russia's constitution begins with promises of democracy and civil liberties and goes on to outline the independent branches of government, rule of law, procedures for elections, and promises to secure the well-being and prosperity of Russia now and for the future generations.

China's preamble is quite interesting in that it chronicles the struggle to establish and maintain the socialist People's Republic of China. Its goals, however, are very much the same as the others—to improve its institutions, including the legal system, develop prosperity and national defense, and make life better for the people. It emphasizes that China is a socialist democracy and also refers to adhering to the democratic dictatorship, presumably until a further stage of socialism is reached:

> *The Chinese people of all nationalities will continue to adhere to the people's democratic dictatorship and the socialist road, persevere in reform and opening to the outside world, steadily improve socialist institutions, develop the socialist market economy, develop socialist democracy, improve the socialist legal system and work hard and self-reliantly to modernize the country's industry, agriculture, national defense and science and technology step by step and promote the coordinated development of the material, political and spiritual civilizations, to turn China into a socialist country that is prosperous, powerful, democratic and culturally advanced.[2]*

China's 1982 constitution, its current constitution, was amended in 1988, 1993, 1999, and 2004, liberalizing its economy and securing private property rights, the rule of law, and safeguards for human rights (China Global Television Network 2018). Amendments enacted in 2018 reversed liberalizing trends, not in the economy but rather in politics. The 2018 amendments secured the position of the Communist Party of China, which apparently fears the possibility of opposition factions splintering and/or seeming irrelevant to a new generation. The amendments state that the leadership of the Party is the defining feature of Chinese-style socialism, making "Xi Jinping Thought" official policy, abolish term limits for the president, and give the party control over local agencies related to corruption and personnel (Babones 2018). The amendments were not well received among many within China's middle class, as reflected in social media posts, where sensitive terms were quickly censored (Jackson 2018).

As reflected in international documents and national constitutions (and reactions to them), people's expectations for their governments and the procedures to achieve them are similar worldwide. People also expect a range of political and civil rights that form the basis of liberal democracy.

> *What should be the goals of global and state governance? Who should decide them?*

LAYERS OF GOVERNANCE

Governance implies more than government. It involves many actors making decisions that affect people's lives. Multiple layers of governance play powerful roles in decision making at all levels, from local to global. They interact in a complex web of relationships, often unplanned and uncoordinated. Their internal dynamics, as well as how they relate to one another on the global stage, determine how well global governance functions.

The State System of Governance

Whether the states are just one set of actors among many or the central actors on the global stage, the character and quality of states are critical factors in determining whether people are advantaged or disadvantaged in achieving their life chances. Ineffective or corrupt state governance creates a range of internal problems, from poverty to violent conflict, that have spillover effects into the global arena, complicating the problems of global governance. Good global governance requires states to be effective internally and willing to cooperate on the global stage to solve global problems. State capacity, populism, and fear of terrorism erode states' willingness to do so.

> *Can the state system of governance serve as the basis of global governance? If each state is sovereign and free to act in its own interests, can global governance ever be effective for the common good?*

Challenges to State Capacity

For better or worse, challenges to state governments are eroding state sovereignty and the capacity of states to manage affairs within their borders and in international relations. The state system is no longer capable, if it ever was capable, of managing the globe effectively.

Government failures to effectively govern stem from three sources:

- The transnational nature of the problems that affect people's quality of life

- A material or organizational deficiency limiting state capacity

- Refusal to admit or address problems (Koenig-Archibugi 2002)

The transnational problems are obvious. From pollution to terrorism to international crime, no state can solve them effectively alone. They require more coordination and emphasis on the common good than some states are willing to make. State capacities with respect to material resources such as medicines, education, food, and infrastructure limits many states. They can prevent states from adhering to global norms. These can be alleviated with more international effort and cooperation.

Deficiencies in organizational resources are more difficult to solve. Some societies do not have strong institutions. Rule of law, transparency and lack of corruption, civil and political rights, and a functional government, including the parliament or congress and independent courts, all are necessary. Consider the organizational deficiency of the U.S. Congress. When a congressional leader declares that the mission of the party he represents is to ensure that the president is not re-elected,[3] it is clear that serving the people by governing is not the top priority. This severely constrains problem solving. Although not a guarantee, strong institutions can alleviate pressures that cause internal conflict.

If a government refuses to recognize problems, it cannot solve them and they are likely to get worse. For decades, President Thabo Mbeki of South Africa refused to admit that there was an AIDS epidemic in South Africa. Alan Greenspan, former chairman of the U.S. Federal Reserve, refused to acknowledge fraud in the financial industry or the housing bubble that ultimately sparked the global recession of 2008–2009. Within the U.S. government, there are climate change "deniers" and fossil fuel enthusiasts who fight regulations to reduce pollution and greenhouse gas emissions. In many of these cases, decision makers prioritized their own interests and ideology over facts and analyses.

Although states cannot meet the challenges of global problems on their own, they can and do mitigate or exacerbate them. Global problems will never be solved without solving problems within societies. Meeting the challenges of governance requires new models at the state and global levels.

The Challenge of Sovereignty

Sovereignty, the right of a nation, a people with a common identity, to self-rule and self-determination, was enshrined in the Treaty of Westphalia. It is the centerpiece from which other principles of statehood flow. Ironically, it is an ideal spread by globalization and, at the same time, it is challenged by globalization.

The rules established by Westphalia no longer hold. The principle of sovereignty needs rethinking and revision. Many aspects of law are now globalized through international treaties and membership in international organizations. Globalization demands that not only international affairs but also many intra-national affairs come under the scrutiny of the global community. From human rights to nuclear weapons, it is no longer the case that a government cannot be questioned about its handling of internal affairs.

Global norms and laws expand as connections among nations expand. Trade, which would seemingly involve straightforward negotiations of prices, expands into many areas because of its many ties to related issues such as the environment, working conditions, human rights, health protection, security, and other sectors (Cassese 2005). To be a member of the World Trade Organization (WTO), a country pledges to abide by laws in all of these areas.

Crimes against humanity are forbidden not only outside of but also within a country's borders. A country may be sanctioned by the global community for its pursuit of nuclear, biological, chemical, or other weapons of mass destruction. Membership in various regional or global international organizations binds states to such things as labor standards and commitments to reduce carbon emissions or institutionalize the rule of law that may impinge on a country's freedom to establish laws and regulations based on its perceived or short-term national interest.

Many state governments and people within societies resist and resent rules and regulations established by international bodies. One way in which states are responding to the challenge of regional and international agencies and organizations is to withdraw. When people in the United Kingdom voted to leave the European Union (EU) (the "Brexit" vote), the primary reason they claimed was that they did not want to live by rules concerning migration and open borders made in Brussels. They wanted their sovereignty back. In the United States, justification for backing out of the Paris Climate Accord, Trans-Pacific Partnership Agreement on Trade, Iran nuclear deal, and Global Compact on Migration was the pledge to "put America first." Whether such retreats will benefit or harm U.S. citizens and our relations with allies is debated and remains to be determined in the long run. They will, however, exacerbate global problems. Other countries resist global norms on a variety of issues that they perceive as restrictive—North Korea on nuclear weapons, Russia on Ukraine, and Myanmar on the Rohingya, among many others.

Countries resist global norms and external influences when local elites and their governmental allies perceive them to be not in their interest; we see this in environmental and energy concerns and human and labor rights, among other issues. Resistance may arise when norms are contradictory to or incompatible with national practices and values. Many cases of children's, women's, and human rights are resisted on these grounds—including the U.S. refusal to ratify the Convention on the Rights of the Child that requires universal health care for children. (Another reason why the United States did not ratify is that the convention forbids executing a person for crimes committed as a child, which the U.S. Supreme Court did not declare unconstitutional until 2005.)

Countries can continue to resist when they have nothing to lose. This makes powerful countries more immune to external pressures. North Korea, with near total control internally, does not need to bow to international pressures even as sanctions have brought misery to the nation. Iran was able to resist decades of negotiations on nuclear weapons. Significant sanctions were already in place by the West against Iran. Both Russia and China have economic and political relations with Iran. When both of these countries refused to block further UN sanctions, Iran stood alone. Both were instrumental in reaching agreement. Without their support and at times problem solving, the negotiations may not have succeeded. If the United States maintains withdrawal from the Iranian nuclear deal without reaching another, it could strengthen ties among Europe, Russia, and China and diminish the leadership role of the United States.

> *How does a country balance its claim to sovereignty against cooperation for the common good? Are there times when a state should forgo its short-term interest for the long-term interest of the common good?*

The Challenge of Nationalism

Ideally in a society, each community of people is granted voice and is politically equal to every other group—to the person. Indigenous ethnic groups and other ethnicities that are marginalized within countries but have a strong sense of identity are demanding more control over their own affairs. Three strategies are federalism, or gaining autonomy over a distinct territory within a state; separatism, or establishing a new and independent state; and revolution, or taking over a state.

Active separatist groups are on every continent (except Antarctica) and within many countries.[4] Sometimes, groups seek changes through the ballot box (as in separatist referenda in Canada, Scotland, and Spain, all of which lost). Other times, groups demand separation violently. Some separatist movements and civil wars, such as those in East Timor and South Sudan, have been successful but at the cost of tens of thousands of lives. In some cases, such as that between East Timor and its former occupier Indonesia, relations are supportive and cooperative. In the case of Sudan and South Sudan, relations remain hostile with intense violent conflict. The terrorist movement ISIS (Islamic State of Iraq and Syria) continues its brutal fight despite having lost all of the territory it had secured in Iraq and nearly all of its territory in Syria. The quest of ISIS is to establish a "caliphate," a state based on the strictest form of Islam. Although ISIS fighters have been losing on the battlefield and in recruiting, should they be successful in securing a territory, it is not likely that ISIS would be recognized as a state by any country, including the Arab states.

Nationalism has also played into the rise of populism. Fear of losing cultural identity and intolerance of diversity is on the increase in many developed countries. Economic nationalism, in promoting protectionism and disdain for free trade deals, ignores the reality of the impossibly interconnected supply chain—so international that the most made-in-America car in the United States as of 2017 was the Toyota Camry despite Toyota being based in Japan. It also ignores the importance of trade and economic ties for building alliances and exerting influence on other countries in realms important for risk management such as worker rights and environmental protections.

> *How would you define a "good state"? What expectations do you have of your government? How can governments better manage internal and external affairs?*

CONSIDER THIS
NATIONALISM AND DIVERSITY

Europeans, on average, are considerably less tolerant of diversity than Americans. Many Europeans believe that a strong national identity depends on upholding cultural traditions, national language, and being born in the country (Wike, Stokes, and Stewart 2016). A Pew Research Center survey found that anywhere from 22 to 63 percent of respondents in 10 European countries thought that diversity made their country a worse place to live. Fears of job loss and terrorism were their major concerns. Only 10 to 31 percent said that diversity made their country a better place. In the United States, only 7 percent thought that diversity made the country worse and 58 percent said that it made the country better—figures that dropped to 5 percent and rose to 64 percent, respectively, in 2017 (Doherty, Kiley, and Johnson 2017; Drake and Poushter 2016). Populist leaders of the right across Europe and in the United States have seized on these sentiments to bolster their support, in many cases securing political office even in countries where the majorities of people are more tolerant.

Civil Society Groups: The Importance of Association

The strength of the associations among people in a society strengthens its government. When Alexis de Tocqueville, the French political philosopher, visited the United States in 1831, he marveled at the vibrancy of American civic life. When "several inhabitants of the United States have taken up an opinion or feeling that they wish to promote in the world, they look for mutual assistance, and as soon as they have found one another out, they combine" (quoted in Kaldor 2003).

In *Making Democracy Work* and *Bowling Alone,* Robert Putnam called attention to the importance of civic engagement—active and involved participation in service groups, whether related to schools (such as Parent–Teacher Associations), places of worship, not-for profit social services, amateur sports, charities, labor unions, neighborhood groups, or others (Putnam 1993, 2000). These associations form the basis of civil society. Putnam feared that as participation in civic life waned, as it did in the 1960s, it endangered communities and the society as a whole, particularly democracy. According to Putnam, civil society groups form the foundation of democracy in that they are forums where people, often of diverse backgrounds, meet to pursue common interests. They practice democracy in these groups. While socializing, they build social capital that can bridge fault lines of class and identity within societies. As a bonus, people often discuss common problems and the issues of the day in these groups.

Voluntary association is an important part of belonging to a social community. This is how many civil society organizations, one of the most visible dimensions of a social community, arise, whether local, such as the early labor unions, or global, such as Bernard Kouchner calling together doctors concerned with the human devastation of war to found Médecins sans Frontières (also known as Doctors without Borders) or Peter Berenson, horrified at the treatment of prisoners, founding Amnesty International. Both Kouchner's and Berenson's organizations are now among the largest and arguably most successful non-governmental or civil society organizations in the world. Each began with one person who found other like-minded people from all over the world.

As part of its "Better Life" initiative, the Organisation for Economic Cooperation and Development (OECD) assesses people's well-being in OECD and some emerging economies. The assessment identifies civic engagement as one of the 11 core dimensions of a healthy life (OECD 2013). Global civil society organizations[5] are the most visible actors in global civil society. Their numbers have grown exponentially, aided by the formation of the UN in 1948, the civil rights and other global movements of 1968, the end of the Cold War in 1989, and the subsequent global call for human rights (Davies 2008). People might not participate directly in global civil society organizations (CSOs), but many people belong to local or national groups that do and thus connect them to the global level.

Global civil society shares most characteristics of domestic or national civil societies except that it is global. Global civil society has the following characteristics:

- Composed of non-governmental, non-economic, and non-familial local and global groups and organizations

- Conducted through interlinked social processes—sometimes tightly linked, sometimes loosely linked

- Civil—encouraging non-violence, mutual respect, and compromise

- Pluralistic, with strong conflict potential among or between groups

- Global—not confined to state boundaries or the interests of any particular nation (Keane 2003)

Global Civil Society and Democracy

Among their functions, civil society groups channel people's interests to the political levels, where the decisions that affect their lives are deliberated and decided. They serve as instruments of democracy in this regard.

Civil society groups are increasingly invited to participate at a global level, whether at the UN or other international intergovernmental organizations. There are, for example, 314 civil society organizations[6] from all over the world (some global, most national) recognized as "accredited" to the Conference of the Parties (COP 21) at the UN Conference on Climate Change in Paris in 2015.

Global civil society and CSOs can advance but not guarantee democracy. As in other realms of social life, not everyone's voice is necessarily heard or honored. Interests are not guaranteed recognition. Sometimes only the most powerful or influential local groups or causes advance to the level where decisions are actually made. Many deserving groups never attract the attention of the powerful global or domestic civil society organizations. Many groups, particularly those that are marginalized, do not have the necessary organizational structure, public relations skills, or financial resources to capture the attention of national or global audiences. Although deserving, their message might never be heard.

Although needing improvement, civil society organizations play an important role. The impact of civil society groups on governance can be powerful. In examining the history of social movements and change around the world, it is evident that civil society and engagement play a prominent role. Global social norms with respect to environmentalism and human rights developed within the networks of civil society and the activities of local and global CSOs. After organizing, they pressured governments to pay attention and forced other governments to adopt norms, encode them into domestic law, and create institutions within governments to enforce them (Meyer et al. 1997). Human rights groups working underground in Eastern Europe and collaborating with rights groups in Western democracies were instrumental in getting Western countries to pressure Eastern European countries to respect the human rights article of the 1975 Helsinki Accords (Thomas 2001). Groups such as the National Rifle Association have been effective in preventing firearms regulation and research in the United States, even though many national polls indicate that the majority of people want reasonable gun control legislation.

The benefits of civic engagement documented in the research literature covering many countries include gains in the following:

- Trust and cooperative norms

- Institutional performance

- Individual well-being

- Personal networks and skills (Scrivens and Smith 2013)

These four outcomes are mutually reinforcing. Where there is high civic engagement, it fosters less corrupt and more efficient institutions. Civic engagement allows citizens to be heard, makes them more sophisticated consumers of politics, gives them a more generalized community-oriented outlook, and encourages "consociational democracy" that bridges deep social divides (Scrivens and Smith 2013).

Civil society organizations are important actors in global governance. How can we ensure that civil society groups are brought into the domain of democratic governance? How can we ensure that all deserving groups have their interests represented at national and global levels?

Multinational Corporations: Do They Have Undue Influence?

Corporations are important to providing a higher quality of life by providing jobs, as well as important breakthroughs in medicine, technology, and communications, among many other areas of life. With respect to governance, it is important to recognize that multinational corporations wield enormous power. Directly, through the decisions they make, they influence the life chances of billions of people through the movement of jobs, working conditions and wages, their ability to shirk or pay taxes due, and their attention to environmental concerns. Managing the activity of corporations for the common good is difficult. The ethic of corporations remains primarily to maximize earnings for shareholders. Among most corporations, social responsibility is a secondary concern at best.[7]

Every January, the most powerful people in the world meet at the World Economic Forum in Davos, Switzerland. Although politicians and civil society groups are present, it began as a meeting of European business leaders and remains dominated by the largest global corporations. Their stated mission is "to improv[e] the state of the world . . . to shape global, regional and industry agendas." There, they plan the economic future of the world. Many of these multinational corporations are wealthier than some countries. For these countries especially, corporate investments are necessary for development. Until these countries reach a level of development where their workers can demand higher wages, they have even less power to shape corporate activity than do the developed countries. However, in all countries where there are low wages, lax or weakly enforced worker safety and environmental regulations, and/or tax concessions, corporations transfer part of the cost of doing business onto their host countries. While this does shape global agendas, it does not improve the state of the world.

Indirectly, multinationals wield tremendous power by lobbying, contributing to political campaigns, engaging in foreign investment, and serving as expert consultants on policy-making panels. Carl Icahn, a billionaire investor, became a special advisor on regulatory matters to candidate Donald Trump. Among his first investigations was regulations on the use of corn-based ethanol in gasoline. If the regulation were changed based on his suggestions, it would save CVR Energy U.S. $205.9 million. Icahn is a majority investor in CVR. In the roughly five months following Trump's election, the stock price of CVR soared, generating $455 million (Lipton 2017).

Lobbying itself is big business. Corporations spend about U.S. $2.6 billion annually on lobbying activities in Washington, D.C., alone. Some of the largest corporations have more than 100 lobbyists in Washington. For every $1 that public interest and labor groups spend on lobbying, corporations spend $34. The pharmaceutical industry is among the most powerful. Initially, the industry opposed a pharmaceutical benefit in Medicare to prevent bulk purchases by the government. Changing tactics, lobbyists worked to get the benefit approved on the condition that the government could not make bulk purchases. The industry reaped a $205 billion benefit via Medicare Part D over the next 10 years (Drutman 2015).

Public relations campaigns to influence public opinion and provide expert witnesses to policy-making bodies are powerful corporate tools to influence the decisions that governments and international governmental organizations make. In Britain, a high-speed train proposed on grounds that would benefit only a few commuters was going nowhere until the message was spun to pit the "wealthy Chilterns" and their worry about hunting rights against working-class jobs building the rail (Cave and Rowell 2015).

The tobacco and fossil fuel industries are giants in both lobbying and public relations. At least a year after the tobacco industry knew the cancerous effects of smoking, the major companies joined together to form the Tobacco Industry Research Council in 1954 for the sole purpose of misleading government and the public on the risks of smoking. One of their internal documents clarified how to deceive the public. "Doubt is our product. . . . Spread doubt over strong scientific evidence and the public won't know what to believe" (quoted in Saloojee and Dagli 2000). As early as 1992, Argentina discussed legislation prohibiting smoking in some public places and banning tobacco advertising. In response, the industry held a closed-door session with influential figures from sports and advertising, among others. Shortly thereafter, 129 articles—105 favorable to the industry's anti-ban position—appeared in newspapers and magazines, influencing public opinion enough that the president of Argentina could comfortably veto the legislation (Saloojee and Dagli 2000).

The fossil fuel industry employs the same tactics. In addition to lobbying, "clean coal," climate change denial, denial that human activity is responsible for climate change, and assertion that climate change is "just a theory" all are tactics to confuse the public about the safety of burning coal and other fossil fuels.

CONSIDER THIS
THE MILITARY INDUSTRIAL COMPLEX

The defense industry also wields enormous power. Dwight D. Eisenhower was a decorated World War II general before becoming president of the United States. From his unique vantage point, he saw the danger posed by the emerging military–industrial complex. The United States never had a permanent armaments industry until after World War II. In his farewell address as president in 1961, Eisenhower warned, "In the councils of government, we must guard against the acquisition of unwarranted influence, whether sought or unsought, by the military industrial complex. The potential for the disastrous rise of misplaced power exists and will persist" (Eisenhower 1961). Eisenhower worried that the growing industry would become an enemy of national interest, distorting the use of resources and generating unjustified expenditure.

Eisenhower's worry about the undue influence and wasted spending of the military–industrial complex became reality decades ago. The military industry is joined by many others whose undue influence has led public policy for their own gain rather than the national good.

More recently, it was revealed that Purdue Pharma executives knew at least as early as 1996 that its opioid MS Contin, and subsequently in 1998 OxyContin, was widely abused. They continued to ignore multiple warnings and market them as less addictive. Their concern reportedly was only for a potential credibility problem—decisions that resulted in hundreds of thousands of overdose deaths and the opioid epidemic. In 2007, three Purdue officials were found guilty of misdemeanors. Over the course of the next five years, enough pain pills were sent to West Virginia, an epicenter of the epidemic, to give every man, woman, and child 433 pills (Meier 2018).

Potential for Corruption: The Revolving Door and Conflict of Interests

"The revolving door" inserts the interests of business directly into government policy. Often people leverage their positions in the private sector to move into government or leverage their government experience and contacts to move into the private sector. On the one hand, the contacts that a government employee has may be valuable as business assets, whereas individuals moving from the private sector into government may bring with them a favorable disposition toward a former employer or the industry in general. This is very common practice and may very easily bring a pro-business bias into policy deliberations. Although having experts can be a benefit, there need to be guarantees against any conflicts of interest or quid pro quo from the relationships or biased policies.

Government officials may favor an industry or corporation in exchange for employment when they leave office. Although this favoritism might not be stated explicitly, it may be an expectation. Insider information from time in government service may be used after leaving government to give a new private employer an advantage. One of the most infamous cases involved Monsanto, an agricultural giant in the United States. A former Monsanto lawyer joined the Food and Drug Administration (FDA) in time to help draft regulations on agricultural biotechnology. The policy drafted not only applied in the United States but also became the model for regulations globally. Monsanto is the major global producer of genetically modified seeds. The lawyer left the FDA within a few years and returned to Monsanto as a vice president. Monsanto is involved in numerous lawsuits pertaining to its seed (Transparency International [TI] 2010). The regulations have protected the corporation many times.

In the EU in a given year, 50 percent of conflict of interest issues are unregulated, and the revolving door was the least regulated among them. During the Barack Obama administration, Dan Poneman came under criticism for taking a post as president and chief executive officer (CEO) of a nuclear enrichment company after leaving his position in the Department of Energy. The company allegedly received special treatment during his government tenure (Lazare 2015).

Dating as far back as the Franklin D. Roosevelt administration, financial industry executives have held powerful positions in the U.S. federal government. The financial firm Goldman Sachs is prominent among them.

In the Trump administration, five Goldman Sachs executives or former executives were appointed to prominent positions.[8] Goldman Sachs' stock prices rose 36 percent within a few months of Trump's assuming office. Relaxing regulations on financial firms and corporate taxes—policy changes proposed during the presidential campaign—should benefit Goldman Sachs among other financial firms (Kelly 2017). During Bill Clinton's administration, Gary Gensler (formerly of Goldman Sachs) helped to enact deregulation legislation that exempted some portions of derivatives trading from oversight. In a turnaround and change of heart after the crisis, he was a leader in enacting regulations during the Obama administration.

After their stints in government, executives move back into the industries they left. Robert Rubin went from Goldman Sachs to the Clinton administration, where he was instrumental in the repeal of the Glass–Steagall Act and its separation of commercial and investment banking, and then to Citigroup when he left government. Richard B. (Dick) Cheney went from government positions in the Richard Nixon and Gerald Ford administrations to secretary of defense under George H. W. Bush, then to Halliburton, and then to the U.S. vice presidency in 2001. Halliburton made millions of dollars in its role in the Iraq War, which Cheney had a role in instigating.

In the U.S. state of Georgia, the former governor, Sonny Perdue, appointed many business partners to government positions in which they oversaw state funding and then appointed former government officials to his new business when he left office. Perdue also met, while in office, with managers of the Georgia Ports Authority in order to lay "the groundwork so that when the governor leaves office they will be in a position to start up an operation" (O'Neil 2017). Perdue has owned several agricultural businesses, which called attention to many potential conflicts of interest in his new government post as head of the Department of Agriculture in the Trump administration.

The revolving door and other conflicts of interest rising from government officials' connections with business interests undermine citizens' confidence in their government. In the 2013 Corruption Perceptions Index, more than half of the respondents in 17 of 28 OECD countries said that their governments were entirely or largely run for the benefit of a few big interests looking out for themselves (TI 2013).

More regulation over conflict of interest problems is critical for accountability in the relations between corporations and government. Some countries enforce "cooling off periods" during which an individual cannot move from a government job to a corporate job. These should be applied to moving from a government position to a lobbying position as well. Few countries regulate this.

> *Multinational corporations have profound effects on people's lives—now and in the future. Is there any way that governments and international governmental organizations can manage the activities of corporations more effectively to work for the common good? Should corporations be required to ensure that their activities benefit people in general, people in their home countries, or their workers and not just their shareholders?*

International Political and Economic Institutions

Multilateral, regional, and global governmental organizations and agencies play important roles in governance. Their specific mandates are diverse, but in general they work on behalf of states to achieve regional or global goals. They influence state or sub-state activities through criteria for membership, negotiating and enforcing agreements and treaties, regulating state or organizational activities, and/or taking direct action implementing policies and programs. There are hundreds of these organizations and agencies.

Regional and International Intergovernmental Alliances and Organizations

Global organizations such as the UN; its agencies such as UN International Children's Emergency Fund (UNICEF) and UN Educational, Scientific, and Cultural Organization (UNESCO); bodies such as the UN Security Council; the World Bank, International Monetary Fund (IMF), and Asian Infrastructure Investment Bank; and the Universal Postal Union, among many more, have authority delegated by the member states to make decisions and act on behalf of members. The UN Security Council decides whether to deploy peacekeepers, defines their mission, and determines the size and scope of an operation. It can decide whether force or sanctions should be used in or against a country. It refers people to the International Criminal Court for prosecution for crimes against

PHOTO 16.1 The UN Security Council field missions work "on the ground" to investigate and help resolve conflicts. This mission in Colombia led by Uruguay and the United Kingdom met with FARC, government, and communities.

UK Mission to the UN/Lorey Campese.

humanity. UN members are obliged to abide by its decisions or face sanctions if they do not. The UN agencies work "on the ground" to implement UN policy and programs such as combatting child malnutrition through UNICEF, securing the safety of refugees through UN High Commissioner for Refugees (UNHCR), and protecting human rights through UN High Commissioner for Human Rights (UNHCHR).

The World Bank and IMF help to manage the global economy. The World Bank provides development assistance, grants, and loans from a pool of money provided by nations designated as "donor" nations. The grants and loans have "strings attached," policy prescriptions that the country must implement. In this way, the bank has influence over the internal affairs of many developing countries. The IMF works to encourage economic growth, stabilize the global economy, and stabilize and grow the economies of individual nations. By controlling how donor funds are dispersed and the conditions attached to their dispersal, the IMF also influences the affairs of many nations and has enormous impact on the global economy. For example, the IMF provided stimulus loans to developing countries to help them stabilize following the shocks of the 2008–2009 recession.

The Asian Infrastructure Investment Bank (AIIB), China's counter to the Western-controlled financial institutions, is new on the global scene, beginning operations in 2016. Its founding documents adhere to emerging principles of global governance relative to transparency, accountability, fairness, poverty reduction, and environmental sustainability. Although funding is limited to the Asia Pacific region, its funding membership is global. Voting power is based on money invested, but although China holds 28 percent of the shares, it cannot block the simple majority required for voting. The AIIB promises that its development projects will adhere each participating country's determined contributions to the environmental sustainability goals of the Paris Accords. It also promises transparency in its operations and adherence to international principles. Projects approved span energy, urbanization, water, and transportation sectors across the Asian region (AIIB 2014–2017).

The WTO provides a forum for countries to negotiate the rules for global trade. Member nations have "most favored nation" status requiring that they all be treated equally in trade among members. The WTO negotiates agreements to which all member nations are bound, settles disputes, and enacts safety regulations to prevent disease, invasive species, and other contaminants from spreading through trade. Its stated goal is to create fair markets to protect producers and consumers. The WTO mandates very basic worker protections, such as prohibiting child labor, but international labor standards are the province of another international organization, the International Labour Organization.

While not a global trade organization, China's trillion-dollar "One Belt, One Road" project promises to shape global trade through massive infrastructure investment across more than 60 countries establishing rail, road, and sea trading routes. For the price of its investment, China reaps trade, economic, and strategic alliances. Unlike the IMF and World Bank, China makes few policy demands on countries. At the Sixth Forum on China–Africa

A CLOSER LOOK
DEMOCRACY SCORES

FIGURE 16.1   Changes in Democracy Scores, 2007–2017

Several nations that joined the EU or are candidates for joining have suffered declines in democracy since 2007.

Source: Freedom House (2017).

Cooperation, while pledging investments from Chinese policy banks of U.S. $65 billion in Africa, President Xi reinforced China's commitment to Africa, their "win–win" cooperation, and mutual respect for "each other's choice of development path." He elaborated, reinforcing that "China strongly believes that Africa belongs to the African people and that African affairs should be decided by the African people" (Ministry of Foreign Affairs 2015).

Membership in international organizations mandates conformity to standards of membership in exchange for rights of belonging. Although credibility of some organizations suffers to the extent that they are not run democratically, they remain powerful. The UN Security Council, for example, has permanent and rotating members. Any of the 5 permanent members—China, France, Russia, the United Kingdom, and the United States—can veto a proposal even if all other 14 members vote in favor. In the IMF, countries get votes in accordance with the amount of money that they contribute. In the WTO, powerful corporations have undue influence over policies. Civil society and labor do not have the same level of influence. Poorer societies that may need the most help from these organizations are underrepresented.

These organizations must respond to demands for more accountability and fairness. With more transparency and communication with the communities they affect and the broader global public, they can raise their reputational accountability (Grant and Keohane 2005).

Regional associations—North Atlantic Treaty Organization (NATO), European Union (EU), Association of Southeast Asian Nations (ASEAN), Mercosur, North American Free Trade Agreement (NAFTA), and Commission on Security and Cooperation in Europe (CSCE)—vary in function. Some are economic, based on trade, such as NAFTA and Mercosur. Others are for security, such as NATO and the CSCE. There are qualifications for joining and, along with those, rights and responsibilities of membership.

Following the dissolution of the Warsaw Pact, many Eastern European countries applied to join the EU and many have succeeded. The Copenhagen criteria detail the political and economic conditions that every country must meet. Countries must demonstrate that they have a stable government that respects the rule of law along with the political institutions required to carry it out (an independent judiciary, political parties, free elections, etc.). They must have an excellent human rights record, including protecting minority rights. They must align their domestic laws with the EU laws. They must meet economic criteria such as a functioning market economy

and the ability to meet financial obligations of membership. Although several former pact countries ascended to the EU, several—Poland, Hungary, and Romania among them—suffered declines in democracy since 2007 (Figure 16.1).

> States are not treated equally in international governmental organizations. Would they be more effective if poorer countries were given more voice?

A NORMATIVE BASIS FOR GOOD GOVERNANCE

Defining good governance is difficult. One straightforward definition of good governance is a government's "ability to make and enforce rules and to deliver services." Although the focus is stated, this definition avoids the trap of equating good governance expectations and assumptions with a particular governmental form such as democracy. It focuses on how well agents carry out the wishes of a populace, not judgments about politics, policy, normative ends, or the goals that they set. Such a measure is applicable to both democratic and authoritarian regimes (Fukuyama 2013).

Considerations of good governance apply to both domestic and global governance. The ability to make and enforce rules is dependent on legitimacy. Legitimate governance conforms to widely accepted principles and values. Despite cultural diversity within and among societies, there are widely accepted norms for governance. Many are embedded in international treaties that establish rights and regulations and in national constitutions, as are procedures for enforcing them and the structures of governments and governance through which they are enforced. One principle underlying all of the norms is fairness. People trust systems that they believe are fair. They evaluate institutions on fairness, not just their own success within them (Keohane 2002).

The capacity of governance, both state and global, to deliver necessary services is challenged on many fronts. First, there are the problems; climate change, terrorism, international crime, new diseases, financial contagion and crises, fragile states, rogue states, and many more pose threats to states that they cannot meet and solve on their own. Attacking any of these problems requires consultation and coordination with other states. Potential solutions may require states to act for the common good, but such solutions—whether on nuclear programs, climate, trade, or a host of other issues—have proven to be difficult to negotiate among actors who perceive the terms of agreement as antithetical to their interests. Despite the severity of the risks the world faces, many people view programs and policies adopted through international governmental organizations as threats to national sovereignty.

The multitude of layers implicated in governance threatens domestic and global governance. Civil society groups of all ideological types, corporations deciding where to invest, and international regulatory agencies promoting adherence to international norms seldom act in concert and directed toward a common goal set. Depending on the level and effectiveness of their regulations, neither states nor intergovernmental organizations control many of the activities of these actors. Each layer of actors, each actor, has motivations and interests and the capacity to act on them. The special interests of these actors may conflict with one another or run counter to the goals of governance for the common good. This creates a potentially volatile global environment.

Good global governance can help everyone to navigate this turbulence. Good governance serves constituents, not special interests. While even good governance cannot promise a solution to every problem, it is the best start. There are a variety of datasets and indices[9] that measure aspects of state government and governance from the supply of democracy to the bureaucratic structure. Most are a combination of process and procedure such as rule of law; others are outcomes such as peace and prosperity. Many international organizations monitor these norms and rate countries accordingly. The World Bank's set of Worldwide Governance Indicators is a widely cited source. How a country scores on the indicators can determine whether it will be able to attract investment, financial or other forms of aid, and tourists' as well as establish a good reputation in general. There are six broad categories on which countries are scored. They are not democracy per se but rather features of democratic and other forms of governance. The criteria furnish a starting point for achieving good global and domestic governance. It should apply not just to governments or intergovernmental organizations but also to all actors involved in governance:

- Voice and accountability
- Political stability and absence of violence
- Government effectiveness
- Regulatory quality
- Rule of law
- Control of corruption

Voice and Accountability

Voice measures the degree to which people are able to express their priorities, needs, and wants to the government and the responsiveness of the government to the people—in short, the degree to which people can affect their government. Accountability measures the degree to which people can hold an entity to acting on their expressed voice or interests. This includes reliable and accessible records, public discussion of policy making and implementation, and (in the case of governments specifically) freedoms such as travel, assembly, speech, and press. To be accountable, any actors in governance must justify their activities to their constituents and those who are affected by their actions.

The demand for voice and accountability is increasing globally. Unfortunately, the record is mixed. Achieving voice at the global level, particularly if people's voices are channeled only through their national governments, is difficult but not impossible.

Holding powerful or wealthy states accountable is difficult. Regional associations can hold their memberships somewhat accountable to their peers. However, there is no guarantee. If powerful or wealthy states do not like the rules, they can leave rather than accept their responsibilities (Grant and Keohane 2005). The United Kingdom, deciding that it no longer wanted to be accountable to the EU, voted in 2016 to exit. People believed that they had more to gain by leaving than by staying and abiding by rules relating to open borders and immigration. The terms of the U.K. exit or "divorce" from the EU are to be negotiated politically or possibly be settled in the International Court of Justice or Permanent Arbitration Court, both located in The Hague, the Netherlands. In either case, the balance of power between the EU and the United Kingdom will factor in the settlement as one must decide which concessions to grant to the other for potential future returns.

Many states argue that internal accountability to their citizens outweighs their external accountability to the association. Thus, Greece argued strenuously that the austerity measures demanded by the EU were harmful to its citizenry and could not be accepted. Argentina has steadfastly refused to pay its debt to the IMF and other lenders

CONSIDER THIS
THE PROBLEM OF NORTH KOREA

Among the major problems of global governance are the nuclear ambitions of North Korea and the risk of a related nuclear war. Figuratively, between North Korea and the rest of the world stands China. North Korea is intent on developing nuclear weapons and the missile capability to deliver them, regionally threatening U.S. allies and trans-Pacifically threatening the United States itself. While Trump originally declared that if China would not help, the United States would do it alone, in a not-very-veiled threat to the country, Trump declared, "China will either decide to help us with North Korea, or they won't. . . . If they do, that will be very good for China, and if they don't, it won't be good for anyone" (Buckley 2017).

China, however, did not see the situation in quite the same way. While China is reportedly impatient with North Korea's nuclear ambitions, President Xi Jinping cautioned Trump to restrain himself. China is not a magician, and its influence, Xi said, is limited (Mullany and Choe 2017). China has called on the United States and South Korea to halt their joint "war games" and for North Korea to halt its nuclear development in order to ease tensions in the region.

After Russia flew bombers over the Korean Peninsula in early December 2017, China responded in kind, sending its own bombers out. With both countries eager to increase their influence in Asia and decrease that of the United States, China announced that it may cooperate with Russia. Both criticized the position of the United States "tweeted" by Trump that talking is not the answer (Tarabay 2017). On December 13, 2017, they did just that, conducting a joint six-day exercise of anti-ballistic missile computer simulations to counter cruise and ballistic missile attacks. Reportedly, the message for North Korea was that the two countries were preparing in the event of an outbreak of nuclear war. The message for the United States was that the Russia–China alliance would counter threats by the United States and its allies (Kwong 2017).

Internally, North Korea exerts total control over its economy, media, and citizens' movements. Few outsiders are allowed to visit. The people are among the poorest and most oppressed in the world. Within the Kim dynasty, Kim Jung-un, the current president, is the son of Kim Jung-il and grandson of the first leader Kim Il-sung. Many North Koreans seem to believe that the Kims protect them from external existential threats. Many worship them as gods. Thus, many people believe that the armaments programs are justified even though people are starving. The opposition is violently oppressed. Spies, the government claims, are everywhere, and suspects are imprisoned, perhaps along with their families.

North Korea is a particular problem for global governance. Neither negotiations nor economic sanctions have deterred North Korea in pursuit of its nuclear and military ambitions. How can problems like this be solved by the global community?

---

on the grounds that the money went to dictators and Argentina has no moral obligation to pay. Payment would also cause undue suffering for the people of Argentina. The Trump administration argued that the Paris Climate Accord and Global Compact on Migration were not in step with U.S. policy and withdrew. Legislation to restrict voting rights was enacted in many U.S. states and had a significant impact on the poor and minorities. In some cases, the legislation was rejected by the courts.

Citizens can sometimes hold more powerful states accountable. For example, citizens may demand that their state be more accountable for the obligations that go with power or take more responsibility for contributing to problems suffered by the poorer countries of the world, whether as a result of their colonialism, unfair trade, the activity of their multinationals, or climate change. Administrations supported by a more cosmopolitan base may be more responsive to these appeals, as was Obama in 2008, than other administrations (Jackman and Vavreck 2011). The unpopularity of changes to the Affordable Care Act (Obamacare) among citizens was instrumental in defeating legislation to amend it in 2017. In another case, the U.S. Congress did not bend to public opinion and legislated a highly unpopular tax reform package in 2017. Despite years of polling in the United States showing that the majority of U.S. citizens want more responsible gun control laws and more concern for the environment, citizen voices have not been heard. Holding states accountable will depend on more direct participatory citizen engagement.

The World Bank indicator for voice and accountability shows that from the first measure in 1996 to 2015, voice and accountability among states increased for lower-income countries but declined for high-income countries. Restrictions on information, voting rights, and freedom of assembly all erode voice and accountability.

Political Stability and Absence of Violence

Indicators in this category are peaceful transfer of power, internal and external conflicts, and other forms of social unrest. As might be expected, more wealthy nations are more stable than less wealthy ones. Political instability is not just a national problem; it spills over boundaries, destabilizing regions and exacerbating other global problems—it is a global problem.

State fragility is concentrated in sub-Saharan Africa, the Middle East and North Africa, and Southern Asia. These regions are plagued by violent conflict and weak or failing governments. Civil violence not only threatens people's physical security but also diverts resources from the development of public goods and private enterprises. It has long-term effects. Less noted but also important, violent crime has the same effect. In a controlled study, the World Bank (2006) determined that a 10 percent decrease in the homicide rate increased gross domestic product (GDP) by 0.7 to 2.9 percent over the next 5 years (cited in Haggard and Tiede 2010).

The Fund for Peace conducts annual ratings of fragility—178 countries in 2016. Its Fragile States Index includes 12 indicators that range from demographic pressures to conflict. Countries are scored from 1 to 10 on each one and are given a total score that is the sum of the 12 indicator scores. The average total score for the group of 178 countries for 2016 was 70.8—or an average across the 12 indicator scores of 5.9.

Putting the scores into context; the country with the lowest total score is Finland at 18.8 (average score of 1.57 over the 12 indicators). The highest is Somalia with a score of 114 (a 9.5 average over the 12 indicators). With the exception of Haiti, the most fragile quintile of countries (35 countries) all were in Africa or Asia. The top quintile is composed of primarily OECD countries. The weaknesses of the two groups are decidedly different. For the top quintile, group grievances, poverty and economic decline, and uneven development are the primary sources of fragility. The highest fragility scores reflect factionalized elites, followed by legitimate state or group grievances, uneven development, demographic pressures, external interventions, human rights and rule of law, poverty and economic decline, security apparatus, public services, human flight and brain drain, and refugees and internally displaced persons.[10]

> *How does understanding the variables related to state fragility help us to understand global problems? When the more stable and least stable countries have decidedly different problems, does it inhibit solving them?*

Control of Corruption

Corruption is the abuse of power for private gain. Costs extend beyond the immediate costs of the bribe, fraud, or other act. Corruption inhibits development, whether in poor or wealthy countries. It delegitimizes a government and can render it ineffective in achieving societal or global goals. It can bring down a government.

No country is free of corruption as measured by a variety of indexes.[11] According to TI, more than 6 billion people live in countries with serious corruption problems. Whether in government and public institutions or private enterprises, corruption erodes legitimacy of both the political and economic systems. Citizens pay the cost, whether in inflated prices of goods and services, lower-quality goods and services, or decreased quality of governance.

Both the left-leaning "occupy movements" that represent the "99 percent" and the far-right populist movements gaining currency globally mount their movements on the corrosive effect of corruption on the social fabric. Their claims are legitimate. While corruption is more widespread and visible in lower-income countries, corruption and inequality are closely related in both high- and low-income countries. It is not surprising that social exclusion and corruption are more closely related than GDP and corruption. Where there is strong social cohesion, there is likely to be less corruption. These variables interact in a vicious circle; corruption increases the unequal distribution of power, leading to social exclusion, which turns into an unequal distribution of opportunity and wealth (Figures 16.2 and 16.3) (Heinrich 2017).

PHOTO 16.2 "Occupy Protests" spread globally in 2011. While not having a direct impact on governance, concern about the elite "1%" became part of the popular discourse. This was day 36 in Zuccutti Park, New York City.

Day 36 Occupy Wall Street by David Shankbone/CC BY 2.0.

Relying simply on enforcement without addressing the underlying ethos is ineffective. Corrupt officials adapt as policy changes and reforms to curb corruption are enacted. They substitute alternative forms and methods of corruption (Olken and Pande 2012). It is not surprising, then, that the 2013 Corruption Barometer found that majorities in 88 countries thought that their governments were ineffective in fighting corruption. In only 11 countries did majorities think that they were effective (TI 2013). In gauging people's perceptions of corruption, political parties were thought to be the most corrupt, followed by the police and judiciary (TI 2013).

Bribery of Foreign Officials

Although some countries outlawed bribery in foreign business contracts in the 1990s, corruption remained "business as usual" in most of the world. Bribery was so commonly accepted that many multinationals routinely built cost of bribes into their contracts. Corporations can still deduct bribery costs from income taxes in many countries.

The OECD Convention on Bribery and Corruption went into force in 1999. As of 2017, there were 43 signatories—all 35 OECD countries and 8 others: Argentina, Brazil, Bulgaria, Colombia, Costa Rica, Lithuania, Russia, and South Africa. Although not every country is a member, the convention establishes global standards and norms. It suggests best practices for detecting and investigating corruption and policy measures, such as tax policy, that can combat bribery. For example, none of the parties to the convention explicitly permits tax deductibility of bribes, and 29 of them explicitly eliminated it as of 2016 (OECD 2017b).

Signatories submit annual reports detailing their anti-corruption efforts. Although the convention reports only bribes paid by companies or individuals to foreign officials, the corruption scores serve as a report card for the countries. Signatory countries benefit by being deemed safe for business. Together, these 43 countries account for 60 percent of global foreign direct investment, 50 percent of the world's exports, and 95 of the world's largest non-financial enterprises. Enforcing anti-corruption measures affects both sides of an international deal, spreading global norms. The OECD instituted anti-corruption networks or initiatives in every region of the world (OECD 2017b).

Despite the global norms, countries often continue to pursue what they perceive as being in the best interest of their corporations (Holmes 2009). Not all of the signatory parties have prosecuted corruption cases; of the 43 signatories, 23 have not concluded any cases. From 1999 to 2016, 443 individuals and 158 entities were sanctioned in criminal proceedings in the 20 member countries who

A CLOSER LOOK
CORRUPTION AND INEQUALITY

Corruption and inequality, as measured by social exclusion, are closely related in both high- and low-income countries.

FIGURE 16.2   Corruption and Social Exclusion in Non-OECD Countries

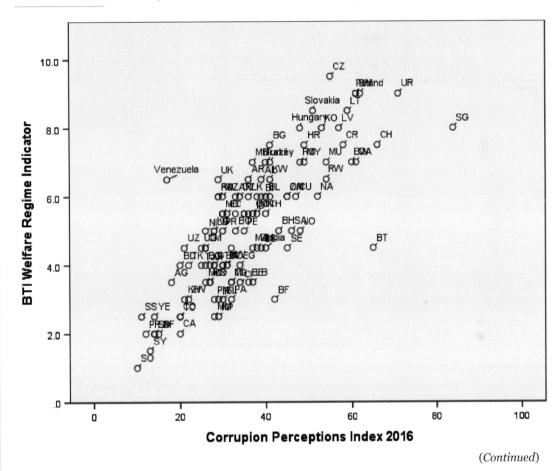

(Continued)

(Continued)

FIGURE 16.3   Corruption and Social Exclusion in OECD Countries

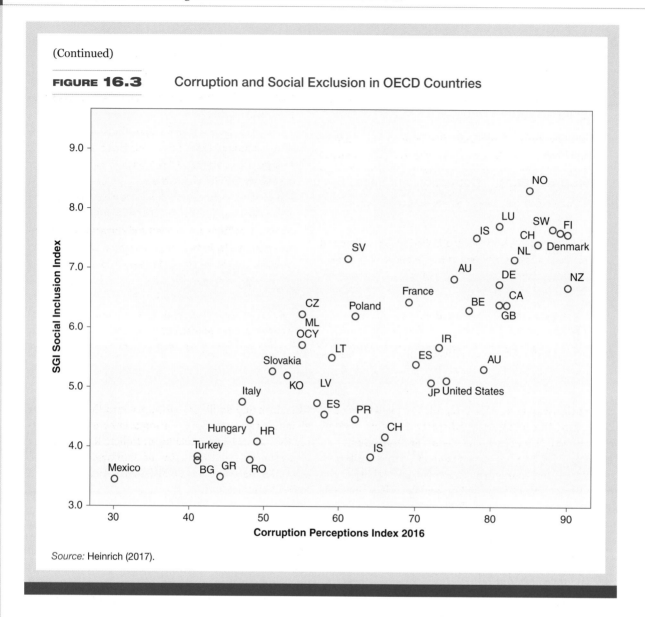

Source: Heinrich (2017).

concluded cases (OECD 2017b). As of 2016, 125 of the individuals received prison sentences (OECD 2017a).

The 2014 OECD Foreign Bribery Report revealed that most bribes are conducted at the highest levels of the corporations by management, including CEOs. On the receiving end, 53 percent of the bribes went to management—41 percent to managers and 12 percent to the CEOs. In at least 60 percent of the cases, large companies of more than 250 employees were involved. For example, the common perception is that rich country corporations are paying bribes to officials in the poorest

countries. However, from 1999 to 2013, two thirds of bribes were paid to officials in very high-income (21 percent), high-income (22 percent), and medium-income (24 percent) countries (OECD 2014). Over half, nearly 60 percent, were for the procurement of contracts. Second was for clearing customs, at only 12 percent. Preferential tax or other treatment, access to confidential information, and getting licensing or visas were the other categories in which the purpose of the bribe was known (OECD 2014).

Does bribery pay? For the corporations involved, it seems to pay. The amount of the bribes was not available

CONSIDER THIS
CORRUPTION AT HIGH LEVELS

High-ranking government officials accused or convicted of corruption include the following:

Richard Nixon: President of the United States resigned from office in 1974 so that impeachment proceedings on three articles adopted by the House Judiciary Committee—obstruction of justice, abuse of presidential powers, and hindrance of impeachment processes—would not go forward.

Bill Clinton: President of the United States impeached, for perjury and obstruction of justice concerning a sexual affair he had with an intern, but not convicted or removed from office.

Dilma Rousseff: President of Brazil removed from office in August 2016.

Park Geun-hye: President of South Korea removed from office in March 2017.

In the cases of Park and Rousseff, they were removed from office for lesser violations than activities of their predecessors that did not result in either charges or impeachment if charged. In the case of Rousseff, her main accusers were themselves under investigation or charged with bribery and siphoning public funds. After her removal, dozens of politicians were tried and convicted on corruption charges. Her immediate predecessor, Luiz Inácio Lula da Silva, was sentenced to 12 years in prison for money laundering and corruption.

It is likely that, as females, Rousseff and Park were held to a higher standard than men in countries where corruption has been widespread.

---

for all of the cases in the OECD report. The highest value bribe reported for the 224 cases where the data were available was U.S. $1.4 billion, and the smallest was $13.17. Altogether, U.S. $3.1 billion was paid out in these bribes. The value of the transaction to the parties making the bribes averaged about $837 million, and the bribes generally cost only about 5 percent of this value. Benefits other than monetary ones, such as entry into a market, a dominant position in the market, and establishing a monopoly, are not included in the dollar benefit of the bribes but add significantly to their value. Given the secrecy around bribes, these cases and amounts are only the tip of the iceberg (OECD 2014). Of 37 cases where the data were available, when caught and fined, 17 of the offenders were fined less than 50 percent of the profit, 5 were fined 50 to 100 percent, 7 were fined 100 to 200 percent, and only 8 were fined more than 200 percent (OECD 2014).

Because multinational corporations and governments are two of the most important layers of both state and global governance, bribery undermines trust in governments, businesses, and markets. It diverts money that should be used for the well-being of people into private pockets. Although people generally differentiate bribery from lobbying, others see no real difference. When asked by a reporter what the difference was between bribing public officials to turn their backs when bringing an illegal substance into the country or giving a large campaign donation to ensure that importing the substance is made legal, Robert Reich, while a professor at the University of California, Berkeley, answered that there was no difference—that a bribe is a bribe (Maiello 2009).

Rule of Law

Like other aspects of governance, the meaning of "rule of law" expands as globalization diffuses global norms and the emergence of new norms to manage the problems wrought by globalization. Originally, rule of law referred to political criteria. In the 1990s, it acquired an economic dimension after the Asian economic crisis of 1997–1998 revealed weaknesses that left sovereign economies and citizens vulnerable. Thus, rule of law now has three dimensions:

- Constraint on the state to ensure that public officials are kept within the boundaries of their offices and adhere to procedural and other laws

- Protection of individuals' security, rights, and access to just recourse if rights are violated

- Security of property and related rights

The rule of law affirms that everyone is subject to the law, regardless of power, money, or position. The separation of powers of the branches of government provides checks on power and balances powers so that no branch is either subordinate to or dominant over another branch. No people—or government officials no matter how high their office—can act arbitrarily and impose their will in deciding or administering justice. Rather, the laws must be established, enforced, and judged by procedures determined in a country's constitution. The law is thus both universal and objective. This contrasts with forms of traditional justice such as traditional monarchies, to whom laws did not apply and who could impose their will in arbitrary fashion, and tribal chieftains, who could settle disputes based on personal judgment. It also contrasts with authoritarian regimes, where rulers can impose their will on other branches of government.

Individuals are endowed with rights under the rule of law that protect them from the power of the state. The rights vary from country to country, depending on their constitutions. The rights of free speech, expression, and belief, freedom of the press, and the right to a fair trial, among others, are very common in upward of 90 percent of constitutions regardless of whether or not they are implemented. Individuals are also protected in that they cannot be prosecuted ex post facto—for something that was not a crime at the time of their act.

The economic dimension of the rule of law considers the importance of guarantees on the enforcement of contracts, the protection of ownership of property, checks on government reach, and corruption that threatens the balance of powers among branches of government. The rule of law is challenged in many countries where populist and authoritarian leaders manage to alter

A CLOSER LOOK
TRUST IN GOVERNMENT

FIGURE 16.4   Public Trust in Government, 1958–2015

Trust in government in the United States, while not at its lowest level, is far lower than in the 1950s and early 1960s.

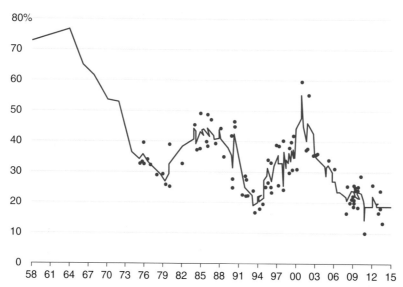

Source: "Beyond Distrust: How Americans View Their Government: Broad criticism, but positive performance ratings in many areas." Pew Research Center, Washington, D.C. (November 23, 2015) http://www.people-press.org/files/2015/11/11-23-2015-Governance-release.pdf.

constitutions or act unconstitutionally, with the assistance of an acquiescent court or legislature, to extend their power.

On the global level, rule of law applies to the activities of nations. The rule of law applies to countries' commitments to abide by international treaties, respect the sovereignty of other nations, and follow the regulations of organizations of which they are members. If they violate or do not meet their commitments, they are subject to sanctions by other nations. In this respect, international organizations legislate by enacting membership criteria and regulation, and they also serve as judge and jury by imposing sanctions. The formal judiciary of the UN—the International Court of Justice—settles disputes among nations that agree to submit to its decisions and other legal questions submitted by UN agencies or the General Assembly. The International Criminal Court, an independent court, hears cases of crimes against humanity.

Trust and Confidence in Governments

Confidence and trust in governments is weak in many countries globally. In the United States, public trust peaked in 1964. At that time, 77 percent of Americans thought that they could trust the national government to "do the right thing just about always or most of the time." In 2015, it was less than 30 percent. Trust eroded rapidly during the 1960s and 1970s—the time of the Vietnam War, the Watergate scandal, and the civil rights movement. Economic growth led to a recovery of confidence in the mid-1990s, and confidence soared after the terrorist attacks on the World Trade Center and Pentagon in 2001. That was short-lived as the economy worsened and trust declined rapidly until 2007. From 2007 to 2015, it remained around 22 to 25 percent (Figure 16.4) (Pew Research Center 2015).

Public perception of fairness corresponds very closely with trust in the government. People want to see that the government is run for the benefit of all people as opposed to a "few big interests" (Pew Research Center 2015; van der Meer 2017). Overall satisfaction with the state of the nation is also important. Periods of financial instability or crisis, as would be expected, are associated with dissatisfaction with the state of the nation and eroded trust. Economic growth increased both satisfaction and trust, but national satisfaction increased significantly more than trust in the federal government (Pew Research Center 2015).

The situation in other countries is not much better (Table 16.1). The 2010–2014 World Values Survey showed that, on average, 14 percent of people had a great

A CLOSER LOOK
WORLD VALUES SURVEY

TABLE 16.1   World Values Survey Question: How much confidence do you have in . . . ?

Around the world, with the exception of the military, confidence in government institutions and the UN is below 50 percent.

% Responding	UN	National Government	National Parliament	Civil Society	Multinational Corporations	Military
A great deal	10.06	14.19	9.93	16.55	11.14	29.46
Quite a lot	30.85	31.55	27.89	40.23	36.57	38.30
Total	40.91	45.74	37.82	56.78	47.71	67.76

Source: World Values Survey (n.d., Wave 6: 2010–2014) and Inglehart et al. (2014).

Note: The number of countries for each category varies slightly from 58 to 61.

deal of confidence in their national governments and only about 10 percent had a great deal of confidence in their national parliaments.[12] Ranking very high in confidence were China, Qatar, and Azerbaijan, all higher than 80 percent in total for "a great deal" and "quite a lot" of confidence in their national governments and from 60 to 80-plus percent for "a great deal" and "quite a lot" of confidence in their national parliaments.

Corruption is very closely related to trust. Corruption increases inequality, undermines efficiency, and demonstrates lack of accountability. This is related to procedural fairness. Fairness affects people's willingness to accept government decisions. Where citizens and decision makers interact, procedures are transparent and trust is built (assuming that the transparent procedures are fair). This is true of both democratic and non-democratic regimes (van der Meer 2017).

What drives your confidence or trust in the government?

MEETING THE CHALLENGES OF GOVERNANCE

There are no easy answers to meeting the challenges of governance. The effort requires stabilizing states and stabilizing the global order. Managing them can hopefully decrease risk and increase the desired outcomes—peace and prosperity.

Challenging Multiple Layers of Governance

Achieving a capacity for fairness in governance means holding all the actors in governance accountable. Accountability constrains power. Varying actors are accountable to different stakeholders. Because in one way or another decisions at every layer of governance affect people far beyond their immediate stakeholders, we all have a stake in their activity. A major deficit in the current systems of both state and global governance is a deficit of accountability. Making each level accountable to the common good, rather than to its special interest, is critical for fairness—and thus for good governance. Accountability is an attempt to ensure that governance responds to the voices of those governed.

In the multiple layers of governance, there are too many "veto players." Groups and individuals can block policy for the common good that is not aligned with their special interests. The more polarized their positions are, the less likely it is that innovative or negotiated policies will be adopted (Ames 2002).

At the global level, the problem of multiple layers of governance compounds problems of accountability. As discussed earlier, bodies such as the UN Security Council and IMF grant undue weight and power to a few countries. Forceful and coordinated global action is needed to solve global problems from terrorism to the refugee crisis, to environmental pollution, to hunger, to climate change, and so on. In some of these areas, different strategic interests complicate well-coordinated action. However, in others—such as climate change, hunger, and international crime—most countries have common interests.

Reforming Global Governance Institutions

The institutional framework for global governance grew out of World War II. Allies began drafting the United Nations Charter in 1941, before the war ended. The UN was the Allies' response to a need for international cooperation—in this case, the need for a forum for states to collaborate to secure their mutual interests in peace and in social and economic development. Also before the war ended, the Allied nations met at Bretton Woods in New Hampshire and established the IMF and the Bank for Reconstruction (precursor to the World Bank) to stabilize the global economy and secure funding to fight poverty. They recognized that global political stability depended on economic stability.

It is true that there have been few wars between or among countries since World War II, but wars within countries and other forms of civil strife are still too common. The world has changed since World War II, but the international institutions have changed very little aside from adding more countries and agencies. One criticism is that the very institutions of global governance do not conform to emerging values of governance. They are neither democratic nor transparent. The UN Security Council, for example, has five permanent members—the Allied nations of World War II: China, France, Russia, the United States, and the United Kingdom. Any one of those five can veto any resolution regardless of how the other members vote (the other members include 10 other countries elected for two-year terms). This provision affords those five nations undue power. The IMF is always headed by a European, and countries get votes according to the amount of money they contribute. The United States appoints the head of the World Bank, which is always headed by a U.S. citizen.

Historically, how the World Bank and IMF award money has depended not only on need but also on the political strategizing of wealthy nations. Thus, the accountability of international institutions is compromised by the undue influence of a few powerful states.

The IMF and World Bank both have issued reforms to move toward greater democracy in decision making. Previously, the quota system determined voting power based on economic size and openness. The 2010 reform shifted 6.2 percent of quota shares to developing and emerging economy countries. The reform was to go into effect in 2016. Executive directors of the IMF do most of the decision making. The larger and more powerful countries each have one executive director. Other countries may be part of a block, with one or more executive directors for the block.[13] Although most decisions are made by consensus, when voting occurs, the United States—even after reforms—still retains veto power. Its 16.46 percent quota can block any vote given that each vote requires 85 percent approval (Bretton Woods Project 2016).

The World Bank operates similarly; its rebalancing of shareholder power is expected to increase developing and emerging economies from 49.17 percent of shares to 52.76 percent. Civil society groups argue that this reform is not enough. Reforms that would give more representation to developing countries in voting and on the executive board and in leadership are necessary. They cite the reappointment of Christine Lagarde as managing director of the IMF for a second term without any challenger as an example of lack of democracy and transparency (Bretton Woods Project 2016).

The UN has improved on its record. Recognizing that states working through the UN cannot solve problems on their own, the UN Foundation develops partnerships with civil society organizations, corporations, individuals, and foundations all over the world (UN Foundation 2013). Agencies such as UNESCO, United Nations Development Programme (UNDP), World Food Programme, and UNICEF work directly on the ground. They have improved their operations by focusing more on developing a broad array of partnerships. Rather than developing programs and solutions for countries, they are developing them with people within countries.

Another criticism of the global institutions is that they do not work effectively as a seamless system. The problems that the world faces, as we have discussed in this text, are interrelated, with one problem affecting the others. The institutions are ill equipped to manage the global risks, from global warming to global epidemics, to global financial imbalances; they work on issue-specific mandates but need to work across sectors and work effectively in coordination with one another (Bradford and Linn 2007).

The "One UN" or "Deliver as One" program is an attempt to alleviate this fracturing of services. Countries implementing the strategy have one joint work plan for all of the UN agencies working in the country. The goal is to deliver services more effectively—including improving accountability and governance, increasing equity across regions, being more inclusive in policy and decision making, and implementing sustainable development. Within the One UN program, agencies coordinate activities and resources. Borrowing from economic theory, they implement programs jointly, with each agency acting where it has comparative advantage.

By fostering open dialog and greater coordination with civil society organizations that work on the ground, communicating with the broader global public—not just state officials—concerning their activities and effectiveness, and communicating with people in the countries affected by their decisions, international agencies can enhance their accountability and improve their reputations.

Earning a Seat at the Table: Holding Corporations and Civil Society Organizations Accountable

Although they are not part of formal government structures, corporations and civil society organizations play significant roles in governance at all levels, from the neighborhood within a city to the globe. They sit on expert panels, they interact with United Nations agencies, they lobby for legislation, and they act on their own behalf everywhere in the world. In the best of cases, they enhance legitimacy of policy making and improve people's lives. Yet no qualification other than their presumed expertise is required. They are accountable only to laws within the countries in which they operate (unless they can evade them) and to their stockholders or donors.

Being outside of the formal governance structure, corporate and civil society organizations are not held accountable to the common good, only to their special interests. However, because corporations and civil society organizations are political actors whose actions affect more than only their constituencies, they need to be held to standards of good local and global citizenship. Their good behavior cannot be assumed because of their mission statements or public relations efforts. Their activity must be transparent, and their good behavior must be demonstrable.

The only way in which to hold corporations and civil society organizations accountable is to bring them into the formal governance structure (Kuper 2007). To begin, their role in the governance structures must be defined. What exactly they are accountable and responsible for—in other words, their goals, the actions they will and do take, and the consequences of those actions, unintended as well as intended—must be clearly defined. If these roles and responsibilities are not clearly articulated, it is impossible to hold them accountable. In return, they get a seat at the decision-making tables in advisory roles. The level of their participation should depend on the benefits their actions have for the common good and any harm they may have caused.

Greater transparency and demonstrable good behavior are not undue burdens. All political actors should need to earn the privileges and advantages they accrue. Corporate and civil society organization reports can be used to grant or deny their participation in decision-making bodies. If these organizations do not adhere to standards of social responsibility, they can be denied opportunities to participate in or influence decision making. To sit in and provide advice to regulatory agencies, corporations should be required to pursue social justice goals included as part of their regular business functions (Kuper 2007). Good global citizenship includes considerations such as environmental stewardship, fair wages, safe working conditions, fair prices paid for resources, and fair practice with respect to taxes paid to national and local governments. Unless corporations meet the requirements for good citizenship, they should be denied a seat on any panel providing expert testimony or any political decision-making or advising body—from the G-8 or G-20, to the UN, to national and local committees, agencies, and boards.

Civil society organizations are thought of as holding governments and corporations accountable through their monitoring and reporting. But they must be held accountable too. For civil society organizations, accountability must extend beyond their donors and the legal requirements of countries in which they operate. They must also be accountable to the constituencies on whose behalf they work, the values and ethics of those constituencies, their staff, their mission, and fellow civil society organizations. The Istanbul Principles for CSO Development Effectiveness[14] and the International Framework on CSO (Civil Society Organization) Development Effectiveness provide guidelines endorsed by civil society organizations to regulate their own accountability (IBON International 2014).

The eight Istanbul Principles are the standards to which civil society organizations should be held accountable. They include considerations of the following:

- Human rights and social justice
- Gender equity
- People's empowerment and participation
- Environmental sustainability
- Transparency and accountability
- Equitable partnerships and solidarity
- Sharing knowledge
- Committing to positive sustainable change (Tomlinson 2012)

Civil society organizations that demonstrate a sufficient level of accountability would be recognized and given seats on advisory boards and, when appropriate, decision-making bodies. Accountability benefits corporations and civil society organizations, as it would any actor, by establishing legitimacy and trust and providing organizational knowledge.

Self-managing accountability mechanisms and guidelines with requirements for multi-stakeholder dialog and reporting emerged as the consensus at the 2011 Assembly of Civicus (World Alliance for Citizen Participation). The assembly's guidelines stress not only the responsibility of civil society organizations to continuously engage in consultation and reporting but also the responsibility of governments to provide a context in which they can work (Tomlinson 2012).

The contexts in which civil society organizations operate vary widely depending on the countries in which they operate. Their effectiveness is facilitated or hindered depending on how free or restricted they are. In some countries, civil society organization accountability efforts are deliberately hampered by corrupt governance or inadvertently by poor governance. Mandatory registration (Russia requires CSOs with international support to register as "foreign agents," undermining their legitimacy), confusing and expensive registration, contradictory regulations, arbitrary application of laws and regulations, and politically motivated legal proceedings, including arrest, inhibit effectiveness in many countries hostile to civil society organizations. These impediments are more common in authoritarian countries, but some have been reported in democratic societies (IBON International 2014).

Holding governments to their responsibility to civil society organizations is often difficult. Most governments support restrictive practices as protecting state sovereignty, promoting transparency and accountability, enhancing aid effectiveness, and national security matters (Rutzen 2015). In the 21st century, between 2004 and 2010, perhaps inspired by the revolutions in Georgia and Ukraine and the war on terror, 50 countries passed legislation or considered legislation restricting civil society organizations. Following the Arab Spring in 2011, 60 countries enacted or proposed more than 120 laws restricting freedom of speech or assembly. Many laws had to do with restricting international funding—from capping international funding, to routing it through the government, to bringing criminal charges such as treason against recipients (Rutzen 2015).

Pressuring such governments for change requires reaching outside of national boundaries to build transnational vertical and horizontal connections—horizontal to other civil society organizations and vertical to appeal to other governments and intergovernmental organizations. The appeals of civil society groups in Eastern Europe to civil society groups in Western democracies and Western governments contributed significantly to one of the most dramatic political events of the 20th century, ending communism in Eastern Europe and ushering in democratic reforms (Thomas 2001). In some cases, multinational corporations can be pressured to implement divestment strategies, as in the case of ending apartheid in South Africa.

Accountability, Stability, and States

Strengthening weak states must be a priority in ameliorating problems of global governance. Bad national policies and weak states affect a country's citizens but often have global effects as well. Countries with weak environmental and tax laws or that serve as tax or criminal havens and hubs of trafficking can wreak havoc all over the world. A housing bubble with weak financial regulation in one country can create a global recession. Conflicts spill over borders. The "butterfly wings" effect[15] has never been more pronounced.

Restoring democracy and building prosperity are the most proven ways to stabilize states. Anocracies have historically been the most unstable and fragile regime type. However, as Marshall and Cole (2014) noted, anocratic states have been relatively stable in the late 20th and early 21st centuries. There have been few reversions to autocracy or onsets of war. This recent relative stability of anocracies is due at least in part to proactive international engagement. The efforts of a variety of international actors in conflict mediation, election monitoring, accountability guarantees, and economic investment via foreign aid and direct investment all pay off in greater stability. More educated populaces with greater democratic expectations are a second factor. A third factor is a more professional military that is less likely to intervene politically or suppress the public opposition. Recognizing and managing the complexities of democratic transition and making extra and long-term support efforts will prolong the transition period to democracy but provide more stability in the meantime.

Historically, autocracies have appeared to be more stable than anocracies. Authoritarian stability, however, is an illusion; eventually it erupts (Klaas 2016). The Arab Spring erupted in and spread through autocratic states. Bamyeh (2011) identified contextual factors in Egypt that apply to the other revolutions and violent conflict generally: marginality and lack of inclusion, spontaneity (although some groups had called for protests, strikes, and civil disobedience, there was little advance coordination), a unifying civic character and political focus even though there was a diversity of groups, autocratic deafness, and refusal to recognize the severity of the people's resentments even as the protest deepened. Individually, most of these factors delegitimize the state; they are not fair.

The expectations of legitimacy and fairness have evolved over time and are still changing. Corruption of one form or another undermines legitimacy. Conflict and violence tend to be highest in states that are the most corrupt. States free from corruption can institutionalize transparency, the rule of law, inclusion, and respect for human rights without fear. In addition, states must recognize that globalization has winners and losers in every society, a theme from which populists garner support. Social welfare spending to cushion people through the effects of globalization is another factor of fairness essential to state stability.

Socializing States

States can be socialized into conformity with international norms. International norms and laws make a difference if they are made to matter. Enforcing global norms can increase human rights and the supply of democracy in a country. States respond to international pressures to conform. No one expected, for example, that Eastern European states would abide by the human rights norms written into the Helsinki Accords in 1975, not even the European Commission, which insisted that human rights be included. But once the accords were signed, dissidents energized by the opportunity formed a powerful network of civil society groups within Eastern Europe that reached out to international groups and to politicians in Western democracies to pressure their governments to pressure Eastern Europe nations to abide by the accords (Thomas 2001).

Finance is another area where international actors can motivate better state performance. When states commit to financial regulation, that commitment has a systematic impact on their behavior. They comply in order to preserve their reputation, which is important in financial competitions. The more states in compliance there are in a region, the more likely a state is to comply. Peer pressure is more important than pressure from either the IMF or domestic economic conditions (Simmons 2000).

The international community can also effect improvement in elections. Monitoring and sanctions by civil society groups, states, and regional organizations all are effective. The international community employs a variety of strategies, depending on the particular context, such as the state being monitored, its relation to other states, and the type of fraud. Shaming, by calling a government out in reports of civil society groups and official government reports such as those issued by the U.S. Department of State, rewards, and punishments all can improve election behavior (Donno 2013).

Regional organizations may also play an important role in socializing states. Although member countries, and some aspiring to membership such as Turkey, are faltering, membership in the EU motivated nations in transition out of the communist orbit to make democratic reforms. Regional intergovernmental organizations set requirements on countries in order for them to obtain membership and the privileges that go with it. The EU requires member states to have stable democratic institutions to ensure the rule of law, observance of human rights, and protection for minorities, among other stipulations relating to their economies and obligations to other members. Member countries that falter, such as Hungary, can be sanctioned, although they are more likely to be given chances to reform.

The Organization of American States, The African Union, and the Pacific Islands Forum all pledge to promote peace, stability, democracy, and good governance. Fiji, for example, was suspended from the Pacific Islands Forum from 2009 to 2014 for deterioration of human and democratic rights. Among the reasons for the founding of

Mercosur, the South American trading bloc, was to stabilize democracy on the continent. The bloc has had varying levels of success, with both Paraguay and Venezuela recently coming under criticism.

Diplomatic channels are another mechanism for socializing states. While there are certainly times when the hard power of the military must be used, soft power and diplomacy have historically produced better results. Richard Nixon's engagement with China; Jimmy Carter's success in bringing Egypt and Israel, after 31 years in a state of war, to a peace agreement that has lasted 39 years to date; the end of the Cold War; and the SALT (Strategic Arms Limitation Talks) and START (Strategic Arms Reduction Treaty) treaties that reduced nuclear stockpiles globally were achievements of diplomacy that have had lasting results. In contrast, wars such as those in Afghanistan and Iraq have multiplied the chaos in chaotic regions of the world. Violent conflicts in Africa and Asia multiply the misery.

None of these mechanisms can guarantee that states will be brought into compliance with global norms. History is replete with examples of states that have resisted in the face of diplomacy, sanctions, neighborhood effects, and even ratification of treaties for decades.

Enhancing Inclusion Through Deliberative Polling

Deliberative polling is a global experiment in civic engagement. The process is simple: choose a random sample of citizens affected by an issue, bring them together and provide them with educational materials, allow them to deliberate, and then poll them on their opinions or decision. This process facilitates citizens' voices by educating citizens about public policies and polling them on their opinions. In some cases, it has served as a strategy for citizen decision making. In China, the practices of deliberative polling and deliberative democracy improved decision making in local communities. Rather than making choices on the basis of the most personal appeal, citizens chose long-range projects that, while not glamorous, provided the best outcome for the common good (Fishkin et al. 2010). In South Korea, citizens gathered to educate themselves about and deliberate unification with North Korea. In Bulgaria, it was the conditions of the Roma with respect to housing, education, and crime that drew citizens into decision making. In Northern Ireland, Protestants and Catholics came together to discuss schools and arrive at mutually acceptable conclusions (Center for Deliberative Democracy n.d.).

Development efforts demonstrate the key role that civic engagement plays. Because governments cannot support broad-based development efforts alone, providing public services such as education, health care, and even rule of law depends on partnerships across civic associations and engaged citizens (Scrivens and Smith 2013). Governments and governmental agencies find that in both developed and developing nations, combatting crime—from "ordinary" street crime to international drug and human trafficking—works best with extensive community engagement. Deliberative polling is one way in which to accomplish educated citizen input. Through one mechanism or another, building social capital by engaging the populace (citizens and non-citizens alike) improves societal and global health.

The Individual Actor and Accountable Decision Making

Ultimately, it is individuals, alone or in groups, who make decisions. The problem for governance is how to structure decision making so that actors are accountable to the publics they serve and the broader common good while avoiding biases or errors in thinking. This is true whether the decision maker is in government, the private sector, a civil society organization, or an international governmental organization or agency. Lerner and Tetlock's (2003) research demonstrates that people's decision making is dependent on the institutional and social contexts. Accountability always influences decisions. The decision-making process can be engineered so that accountability motivates people to engage in deeper and more exploratory thought rather than just conforming to what they think people's views are or digging in and expending effort trying to cling to, bolster, or justify positions they have held but are incorrect—errors common in contemporary politics.

Typically, politicians try to appeal to the median voter (post-primary), according to Tetlock (cited in Beck 2017). However, when groups—in this case political parties and parts of the populace—retreat into their own "truth worlds," that retreat undermines the conditions of accountability. Under these conditions, people are not necessarily looking for facts and they are not generally well informed. People do not force the politician into deeper and more exploratory thought.

Checks and balances are one aspect of government that is supposed to force politicians into more complex thought. The judiciary places checks on both legislatures and heads of states, which also check on each other. To avoid "being checked," the idea is to anticipate the ways in which you could be wrong before others find them. You are more likely to avoid errors in this way. However, if you do make a mistake, the court can prevent illegal actions by the other two branches. With respect to legislatures and heads of state, it generally takes both or an overwhelming majority in the legislature to pass and enforce laws and policy. The world witnessed these checks on Trump when the courts blocked the U.S. president's executive orders banning people from six predominantly Muslim countries from entering the United States. Courts interpreted the action as a ban on a religious group due to commentary by people in the administration. The proposals would need to be rewritten until they could withstand court scrutiny, forcing deeper thought.

Holding Power to Account: The Role of the Media

The media are another important check on power. But when the public or large portions of it do not care to deal with facts or they are manipulated in such a way as to cling to their own truth worlds, accountability is weakened. Delegitimizing the media negates their capacity to provide a check. The media are prime targets of authoritarian leaders, often resorting to shutting them down or imprisoning journalists. In a less extreme case, when the media pointed out inaccuracies stated by the administration, Trump called them liars and "the enemy of the people" and "doubled down" on his false statements. People double down, according to Tetlock (cited in Beck 2017), when they have done something and cannot take it back or when they think a source of accountability is too intrusive.

In Latin America, public denunciations of the press were followed by revoking licenses, trying to break up companies, and imposing more regulation. Turkey and Hungary manipulated sales of media to more friendly ownership. In even more authoritarian countries, administrations increased efforts to control the media, shut down some telecommunications before elections and during protests, and extended restrictive laws. Globally, freedom of the press sunk to its lowest level in 13 years in 2016 (Abramowitz 2017).

New sources of information and reporting, such as through *Wikileaks,* offer new challenges to governments and the public. Online sources can publish much more, do so more quickly, and reach more people than traditional print or broadcast journalism. Although this "networked public sphere" provides a forum for non-traditional journalists such as bloggers, and their reach is global, they deserve the same constitutional protections as traditional journalistic outlets regardless of the country they operate from or write about. Legitimacy of the information they circulate is a legitimate concern that demands vigilance on the part of users.

An international regulatory regime outlawing the export of online surveillance technology to targeted countries would help to protect journalists (and dissidents) from surveillance. Spyware is big business for companies that create it and sell it to governments, or to intermediaries that then re-sell it, for the purpose of limiting freedom of information (Reporters Sans Frontières 2017).

Engineering the most well-thought-out decisions depends on the decision makers learning of their accountability prior to forming an opinion, their audiences' opinions being unknown, and the audiences being well informed, wanting accuracy, and demanding the reasons for the decisions made. These are difficult conditions to achieve in the contemporary political climate, where much of the populace, as well as politicians (at least in Europe and the United States), is not very comfortable with complexity, is firmly attached to pre-conceived "truths" it is unwilling to test, and social media outlets

are well positioned for spreading false reports (even those planted by foreign governments) and enflaming public opinion.

The complexity of the modern world is such, however, that even in the best of cases the experts can get it wrong. Predicting future events in such a complex world defies our usual definitions of making good judgments. People who derive their judgments from a wide range of reference points and who know a little bit about many things— "foxes," Tetlock (2005) called them—tend to do better in forecasting than those who know one thing really well— the "hedgehogs." Drawing from an eclectic mix, extrapolating from current trends, and improvising as events change works better than "single-minded determination."

There is no way to guarantee the accuracy of predictions. The nature of the risk that characterizes the modern world is that there are unknowns in every situation. However, risk can be reduced with good decision-making processes. Yet such processes cannot be obtained without all audiences demanding that decision makers, in every dimension of governance, pay attention to facts and evidence, commit to goals but not to points of view until the issue at hand is thoroughly explored, and be able to justify decisions based on reliable evidence.

SUMMARY

Both state and global governances are facing severe challenges. The problems that the world faces, such as climate change, increasing inequality, and international crime, defy easy solutions and require global cooperation. However, the multiple layers of governance are not coordinated toward common goals. Accountability and transparency are in short supply in many of the forums where decisions are made, whether intergovernmental organizations, governments, corporations, or civil society

organizations. Globalization spreads norms for good governance based on democratic principles, but the supply of democracy is in decline. Many states are fragile, and trust in state governments is eroding.

Building a system of global governance requires coordinated global effort of reform in every layer of governance. With the rise of nationalist populism and protectionism, the immediate picture for better global governance is bleak.

DISCUSSION

1. Do you think that the goals of global governance as stated in the United Nations Charter can be achieved?

2. What is more important to good governance—its characteristics or the outcomes?

3. How do the multiple layers of governance interact to the benefit, and also to the detriment, of good global governance?

4. How could global governance be institutionalized in such a way as to bring all the layers of governance into a formal system?

5. Can global governance be democratic? Explain why or why not.

ON YOUR OWN

1. The World Bank Worldwide Governance Indicators are available for online analysis. Users are able to create tables and charts for the any one of six governance indicators for a single country for a given year or time series. Users are also able to create global maps, tables, and charts for the world or groups of countries by region or income.

    Which dimension of governance is strongest in the world as a whole? Which is weakest? Why do you suppose these are so? Do strengths and weaknesses vary by region or income group?

    Explore issues related to governance using the online tools. Develop hypotheses concerning individual countries or groups of countries and dimensions of governance that are of interest to you. http://info.worldbank.org/governance/wgi/#reports

2. Using the Corruption Perceptions Index, which societies are rated as the most corrupt?

    Investigate the correlations between corruption and GDP per capita and corruption and level of violence.

    Investigate the World Bank records data on GDP per capita.

    The Center for Systemic Peace has violent conflict data. Go to its "Warlist."

    Corruption Perceptions Index: https://www.transparcncy.org/news/feature/corruption_perceptions_index_2017

    World Bank Data Market: https://datamarket.com/data/set/15c9/gdp-per-capita-current-us#!ds=15c9!hd1=6d.74.6u.6a&display=bar

    Center for Systemic Peace Warlist: http://www.systemicpeace.org/warlist/warlist.htm

3. The World Values Survey asks respondents questions concerning their confidence in various actors involved in governance and the type of political system that they prefer. Both of these are found under the heading "Politics and Society."

    You can start the online analysis at this URL. Choose the 2010–2014 Round of surveys: http://www.worldvaluessurvey.org/WVSContents.jsp

    In the 2010–2014 Round, Questions V127 to V130 ask about preferred political systems. Questions V131 to V142 ask about democracy. Questions V109 to V124 ask about confidence in a variety of governmental and other institutions. Depending on how in-depth you want to explore, you can compare a few countries or many of them.

    You can compare and contrast countries by their civilizational cluster. The map of cultural clusters is found at this URL: http://www.worldvaluessurvey.org/WVSContents.jsp

    To find the ratings for the entire set of countries surveyed in the round on a particular question, choose any country and then, under "Type of indicator to display," choose the "percentage of selected category." You will then see the percentage of respondents who chose that response for each country on the right-hand side of the page. These can be copied into an Excel file.

    You can compare the answers to one or more questions or control for several independent variables.

NOTES

1. The Constitution of the Russian Federation can be found at http://www.departments.bucknell.edu/russian/const/constit.html

2. The Constitution of the People's Republic of China can be found at http://www.npc.gov.cn/englishnpc/Constitution/2007-11/15/content_1372962.htm

3. Mitch McConnell, the Republican Senate minority leader at the time, proclaimed during an interview with the National Journal in 2010 that "the single most important thing we want to achieve is for President Obama to be a one-term president" (Kessler 2012).

4. A list of separatist, independence, and decentralization (autonomy) movements by country can be found on the Constitution Society website: http://www.constitution.org/cs_separ.htm

5. Notice that the definitions of civil society organizations used here stress "civil." They do not include groups that use violence to attain their means. Violence-using organizations are part of the global social fabric but are not civil. They have social capital, and social capital, like any capital, can be used for good or evil. Most discussion of CSOs does not include these groups.

6. The list of 314 civil society organizations accredited to COP 21 as of November 2015 can be found at http://www.unccd.int/Lists/SiteDocumentLibrary/CivilSociety/List-of-civil-society-organizations-having-confirmed-their-interest-in-remaining-accredited.pdf

7. See Chapter 2 for a discussion of the Global Compact, patient capitalism, microloans, and other movements to build social responsibility into corporate functioning.

8. The Clinton and Obama administrations each had two Goldman Sachs executives, and the George W. Bush administration had five.

9. The Freedom House, Polity Project, Varieties of Democracy, Bertelsmann Transformation Index, World Bank Worldwide Governance Indicators, and Quality of Governance Institute datasets are a few of these.

10. The 12 indicators are demographic pressures, refugees and internally displaced persons, group grievance, human flight and brain drain, uneven economic development, poverty and economic decline, state legitimacy, public services, human rights and rule of law, security apparatus, factionalized elites, and external intervention. For descriptions, see http://foreignpolicy.com/fragile-states-index-2016-brexit-syria-refugee-europe-anti-migrant-boko-haram

11. In addition to TI's Corruption Perceptions Index, the Bertelsmann Foundation Sustainable Governance Indicators, the Economist Intelligence Unit, the World Justice Project, the World Economic Forum, and the PRS Group's International Country Risk Guide are guides to corruption globally. The World Bank Country Policy and Institutional Assessment rates developing countries, and the African Development Bank rates African countries.

12. Combining a great deal of confidence and quite a lot of confidence increases the average of the global sample for national governments to 46 percent and national parliaments to 38 percent. The respective figures for the United States were 33 and 20 percent total, but only about 4 and 2 percent, respectively, expressed a great deal of confidence.

13. Sub-Saharan Africa, for example, has two executive directors for 46 countries.

14. The Istanbul Principles may be found at CSO Partnership for Development Effectiveness (2010).

15. The "butterfly wings" effect refers to an argument in chaos theory that small changes in one condition may cause dramatic changes in another—that the flutter of a butterfly's wings could cause a tornado.

References

Introduction

Mills, C. Wright. 1959. *The Sociological Imagination*. New York: Oxford University Press.

Pew Research Center. 2014. *Greatest Dangers in the World*. Washington, DC: Pew Research Center, Global Attitudes and Trends. Retrieved February 15, 2018 (http://www.pewglobal .org/2014/10/16/greatest-dangers-in-the-world).

World Economic Forum. *Global Risks, 2014*. Geneva: World Economic Forum. Retrieved February 15, 2018 (http://www3 .weforum.org/docs/WEF_GlobalRisks_Report_2014.pdf).

Chapter 1

Appadurai, Arjun. 1996. *Modernity at Large: Cultural Dimensions of Globalization*. Minneapolis: University of Minnesota Press.

Beck, Ulrich. 1992. *Risk Society*. London: Sage.

Blinder, Alan S. 2006. "Offshoring: The Next Industrial Revolution?" *Foreign Affairs* 85(2): 113–128.

BNP Paribas. 2017. "The Bank for a Changing World" [advertisement]. https://cib.bnpparibas.com/our-regions/ americas_a-43-38.html

Carmody, Christine. 2012. "Considering Future Generations— Sustainability in Theory and Practice." *Economic Roundup*, November, pp. 65–91. https://treasury.gov.au/publication/ economic-roundup-issue-3-2012-2/

Center for Systemic Peace. 2015. *Global Trends in Armed Conflict*. Vienna, VA: Center for Systemic Peace. Retrieved February 9, 2018 (http://www.systemicpeace.org/CTfigures/war2015.jpg).

Crothers, Lane. 2012. *Globalization and American Popular Culture*. Lanham, MD: Roman & Littlefield.

Durkheim, Emile. 1893/1964. *The Division of Labor in Society*. New York: Free Press.

Durkheim, Emile. 1897/1966. *Suicide: A Study in Sociology*. New York: Free Press.

Freedom House. 2016. *Freedom in the World 2016*. Washington, DC: Freedom House. Retrieved February 9, 2018 (https://freedomhouse.org/report/freedom-world-2016/ maps-graphics).

Giddens, Anthony. 2003. *Runaway World: How Globalization Is Reshaping Our Lives*. New York: Routledge.

International Rescue Committee. 2014. *The Lost Boys of the Sudan*. New York: International Rescue Committee. Retrieved February 9, 2018 (http://www.rescue.org/blog/ lost-boys-sudan).

Landes, David S. 1999. *The Wealth and Poverty of Nations*. New York: Norton.

Lasswell, Harold D. 1960. *Politics: Who Gets What, When, How—with Postscript*. New York: Meridian Books.

Meyer, John W., John Boli, George M. Thomas, and Francisco O. Ramirez. 1997. "World Society and the Nation-State." *American Journal of Sociology* 103(1): 104–181.

Milgram, Stanley. 1967. "The Small World Problem." *Psychology Today,* May, pp. 60–67. Retrieved February 9, 2018 (http://snap.stanford.edu/class/cs224w-readings/mil- gram67smallworld.pdf).

Mills, C. Wright. 1959. *The Sociological Imagination*. New York: Oxford University Press.

Putnam, Robert D. 2000. *Bowling Alone: The Collapse and Revival of American Community*. New York: Simon & Schuster.

Reeves, Aaron, Martin McKee, David Gunnell, Shu-Sen Chang, Sanjay Basu, Benjamin Barr, and David Stuckler. 2015. "Economic Shocks, Resilience, and Male Suicides in the Great Recession: Cross-National Analysis of 20 EU Countries." *European Journal of Public Health,* 25(3): 404–409.

Reeves, Aaron, Martin McKee, and David Stuckler. 2014. "Economic Suicides in the Great Recession in Europe and North America." *British Journal of Psychiatry* 205(3): 246–247.

Rivoli, Pietra. 2009. *The Travels of a T-shirt in the Global Economy: An Economist Examines the Markets, Power, and Politics of World Trade*. Hoboken, NJ: John Wiley.

Scrivens, Katherine and Conal Smith. 2013. *Four Interpretations of Social Capital: An Agenda for Measurement* (OECD Statistics Working Paper No. 2013/06). Paris: OECD Publishing. doi:10.1787/5jzbcx010wmt-en

Sklair, Leslie. 1999. "Competing Conceptions of Globalization." *Journal of World Systems Research* 5(2): 143–163.

Tarun Bharat Sangh. N.d. *Adapting to Climate Change through Water Management in Eastern Rajasthan*. Rajasthan, India: Tarun Bharat Sangh. Retrieved February 9, 2018 (http:// tarunbharatsangh.in/portfolio_page/adapting-to-climate- change-through-water-management-in-eastern-rajasthan).

United Nations. 2015. *The Millennium Development Goals Report*. New York: United Nations. http://www.un.org/

millenniumgoals/2015_MDG_Report/pdf/MDG%20
2015%20rev%20(July%201).pdf

United Nations Development Programme. 2015. *UNDP
Human Development Report 2015.* New York: United Nations.
http://hdr.undp.org/sites/default/files/2015_human_devel-
opment_report.pdf

Wallerstein, Immanuel. 1974. *The Modern World System:
Capitalist Agriculture and the Origins of the European World-
Economy in the 16th Century.* New York: Academic Press.

Waste and Resources Action Programme. 2015. *Strategies to
Achieve Economic and Environmental Gains by Reducing
Food Waste.* Banbury, UK: Waste and Resources Action
Programme.

Watts, Duncan J. 1999. "Networks, Dynamics, and the Small-
World Phenomenon." *American Journal of Sociology* 105(2):
493–527.

Weber, Max. 1905/1976. The Protestant Ethic and the Spirit of
Capitalism. New York: Scribner.

Weber, Max. 1922/1978. *Economy and Society.* Berkeley:
University of California Press.

World Bank. N.d. *The World Bank Atlas Method—
Detailed Methodology.* Washington, DC: World Bank
Group. Retrieved February 9, 2018 (https://datahelpdesk
.worldbank.org/knowledgebase/articles/378832-what-is-
the-world-bank-atlas-method).

World Bank. 2017. *World Bank Country and Lending Groups.*
Washington, DC: World Bank Group. Retrieved February 9,
2018 (https://datahelpdesk.worldbank.org/knowledgebase/
articles/906519-world-bank-country-and-lending-groups).

World Economic Forum. 2014. *Global Risks 2014: Ninth
Edition.* Geneva: World Economic Forum.

Chapter 2

Acemoglu, Daron, Simon Johnson, and James A. Robinson.
2001. "The Colonial Origins of Comparative Development: An
Empirical Investigation." *American Economic Review* 91(5):
1369–1401.

Acemoglu, Daron, Simon Johnson, and James A. Robinson.
2002. "Reversal of Fortune: Geography and Institutions in the
Making of Modern World Income Distribution." *Quarterly
Journal of Economics* 117(4): 1231–1294.

Acemoglu, Daron and Alexander Wolitzky. 2011. "The
Economics of Labor Coercion." *Econometrica* 79(2): 555–600.

African Economist. 2015. "Africa's Top 100 Universities."
April 13, 2015. http://theafricaneconomist.com/africas-top-
100-universities-2015/ (Original link is broken; see https://
www.facebook.com/TheAfricanEconomist/)

Bairoch, Paul. 1993. *Economics and World History: Myths
and Paradoxes.* Chicago: University of Chicago Press.

Baldwin, Richard. 2006. *Trade and Industrialisation after
Globalisation's 2nd Unbundling: How Building and Joining
a Supply Chain Are Different and Why It Matters.* Cambridge,
MA: National Bureau of Economic Research.

Bridgman, Benjamin, Andrew Dugan, Mikhael Lal, Matthew
Osborne, and Shaunda Villones. 2012. "Accounting for
Household Production in the National Accounts, 1965–2010."
Survey of Current Business, pp. 23–36. Retrieved February 9,
2018 (https://www.bea.gov/scb/pdf/2012/05%20May/0512_
household.pdf).

Center for Systemic Peace. 2017. *Global Conflict Trends.*
Vienna, VA: Center for Systemic Peace. Retrieved April 26,
2018 (http://www.systemicpeace.org/conflicttrends.html).

Centers for Disease Control and Prevention. 2016. *Global
WASH Fast Facts.* Washington, DC: Department of Health and
Human Services, Centers for Disease Control and Prevention.
Retrieved February 9, 2018 (https://www.cdc.gov/healthywa-
ter/global/wash_statistics.html).

Centre for Applied Research. 2015. *Financial Flows and Tax
Havens.* Bergen: Norwegian School of Economics. Retrieved
February 9, 2018 (http://www.gfintegrity.org/wp-content/
uploads/2016/12/Financial_Flows-final.pdf).

Collier, Paul. 2007. *The Bottom Billion: Why the Poorest
Countries Are Failing and What Can Be Done about It.* Oxford,
UK: Oxford University Press.

Conference Board of Canada. 2011. *World Income Inequality:
Is the World Becoming More Unequal?* Ottawa, Ontario,
Canada: Conference Board of Canada. Retrieved February 9,
2018 (http://www.conferenceboard.ca/hcp/hot-topics/world
inequality.aspx).

DeSilver, Drew. 2014. *For Most Workers, Real Wages Have
Barely Budged for Decades.* Washington, DC: Pew Research
Center. Retrieved February 9, 2018 (http://www.pewresearch
.org/fact-tank/2014/10/09/for-most-workers-real-wages-
have-barely-budged-for-decades).

Dewan, Shaila. 2013. "Microcredit for Americans." *The New
York Times,* October 29, p. B1. Retrieved February 9, 2018
(http://www.nytimes.com/2013/10/29/business/micro-
credit-for-americans.html?_r=0).

Domhoff, William G. 2018. "Wealth, Income, and Power."
In *Who Rules America.* Santa Cruz: University of California,
Santa Cruz, Department of Sociology. Retrieved April 27, 2018
(https://whorulesamerica.ucsc.edu/power/wealth.html).

Donnelly, Grace. 2018. "Finland's Basic Income Experiment
Will End in 2019. *Fortune,* April 19. Retrieved April 26, 2018
(http://fortune.com/2018/04/19/finland-universal-basic-
income-experiment-ending).

Easterly, William and Ross Levine. 2016. "The European Origins of Economic Development." *Journal of Economic Growth* 21(3): 225–257.

Easterly, William and Tobias Pfutze. 2007. *Where Does the Money Go? Best and Worst Practices in Foreign Aid.* Washington, DC: Brookings Global Economy and Development.

Economist, The. 2013. "Poverty: Not Always with Us." *The Economist,* June 1. Retrieved February 9, 2018 (http://www.economist.com/news/briefing/21578643-world-has-astonishing-chance-take-billion-people-out-extreme-poverty-2030-not).

Edin, Kathryn J. and H. Luke Shaefer. 2015. *$2.00 a Day: Living on Almost Nothing in America.* New York: Houghton Mifflin Harcourt.

Elkins, Zachary, Tom Ginsburg, and Beth A. Simmons. 2013. "Getting to Rights: Treaty Ratification, Constitutional Convergence, and Human Rights Practice." *Harvard International Law Journal* 54(1)/University of Chicago, Public Law Working Paper No. 434. Retrieved February 9, 2018 (https://ssrn.com/abstract=2296607).

Farole, Thomas. 2013. *The Internal Geography of Trade: Lagging Regions and Global Markets.* Washington, DC: World Bank Group. Retrieved February 9, 2018 (http://documents.worldbank.org/curated/en/435791468147845613/The-internal-geography-of-trade-lagging-regions-and-global-markets)

Federal Financial Institutions Examination Council. 2016. *Economic Research and Data: Charge-Off and Delinquency Rates on Loans and Leases at Commercial Banks.* Washington, DC: Board of Governors of the Federal Reserve System. Retrieved February 9, 2018 (https://www.federalreserve.gov/releases/chargeoff/delallsa.htm).

Felipe, Jesus, Utsav Kumar, and Reynold Galope. 2017. "Middle-Income Transitions: Trap or Myth?" *Journal of the Asia Pacific Economy* 22(3): 429–453.

Felipe, Jesus, Aashish Mehta, and Changyong Rhee. 2018. "Manufacturing Matters . . . but It's the Jobs That Count." *Cambridge Journal of Economics,* February 19. Retrieved June 4, 2018 (https://doi.org/10.1093/cje/bex086).

Food and Agriculture Organization of the United Nations. 2015. *The State of Food and Agriculture: Social Protection and Agriculture—Breaking the Cycle of Rural Poverty.* Rome: Food and Agricultural Organization of the United Nations. Retrieved February 9, 2018 (http://www.fao.org/3/a-i4910e.pdf).

Förster, Michael, Ana Llena Nozal, and Céline Théveno. 2017. *The Socio-economic Divide in Europe.* Paris: OECD Publishing.

Ghosh, Jayati. 2016. "Inequality in India: Drivers and Consequences. In *World Social Science Report, 2016: Challenging Inequalities—Pathways to a Just World.* Paris: UNESCO/International Social Science Council. Retrieved February 9, 2018 (http://unesdoc.unesco.org/images/0024/002458/245825e.pdf).

Grindling, T. H. 2016. "Does Increasing the Minimum Wage Reduce Poverty in Developing Countries?" *IZA World of Labor: Evidence Based Policy Making.* Retrieved February 9, 2018 (http://wol.iza.org/articles/does-increasing-the-minimum-wage-reduce-poverty-in-developing-countries-1.pdf).

Gupta, Sanjeev, Hamid Davoodi, and Erwin Tiongson. 2001. "Corruption and the Provision of Health Care and Education Services." Pp. 111–141 in *The Political Economy of Corruption,* edited by Arvind K. Jain. London: Routledge.

Hanson, John R. 1988. "Third World Incomes before World War I: Some Comparisons." *Explorations in Economic History* 25: 323–336.

Hanson, John R. 1991. "Third World Incomes before World War I: Further Evidence." *Explorations in Economic History* 28: 367–379.

Hong, Gee Hee, Zsoka Koczan, Weicheng Lian, and Malhar Nabar. 2017. *The Disconnect between Unemployment and Wages.* Washington, DC: International Monetary Fund. Retrieved February 9, 2018 (https://blogs.imf.org/2017/09/27/the-disconnect-between-unemployment-and-wages).

Human Development Report Office Outreach. 2015. *What Is Human Development?* New York: Human Development Report Office, UN Human Development Programme. Retrieved February 9, 2018 (http://hdr.undp.org/en/content/what-human-development).

International Development Association and International Monetary Fund. 2016. "Heavily Indebted Poor Countries (HIPC) Initiative and Multilateral Debt Relief Initiative (MDRI)—Statistical Update." Washington, DC: World Bank Group. Retrieved February 9, 2018 (http://documents.worldbank.org/curated/en/123261467999692988/pdf/104810-BR-SecM2016-0137-IDA-SecM2016-0082-Box394885B-OUO-9.pdf).

International Labour Organization. 2016. *Global Wage Report 2016/17: Global Wage Growth Falls to Its Lowest Level in Four Years.* Geneva: International Labour Office. Retrieved February 9, 2018 (http://www.ilo.org/global/about-the-ilo/newsroom/news/WCMS_537790/lang--en/index.htm).

International Monetary Fund. 2017. *World Economic Outlook Update: A Shifting Global Economic Landscape.* Washington, DC: International Monetary Fund. Retrieved February 9, 2018 (http://www.imf.org/external/pubs/ft/weo/2017/update/01/pdf/0117.pdf).

Johnson, Matthew. 2015. "Is China Suffering from the Middle-Income Trap?" *Investopedia,* September 25. Retrieved February 9, 2018 (http://www.investopedia.com/articles/investing/092515/china-suffering-middleincome-trap.asp).

Keating, Giles, Michael O'Sullivan, Anthony Shorrocks, James B. Davies, and Rodrigo Lluberas. 2010. *Global Wealth Report 2010.* Zurich, Switzerland: Credit Suisse Research Institute. Retrieved February 9, 2018

(http://publications.credit-suisse.com/tasks/render/file/index
.cfm? fileid=88DC32A4-83E8-EB92-9D57B0F66437AC99).

Kippenberg, Juliane. 2015. *What . . . If Something Went Wrong: Child Labor in Small-Scale Gold Mines.* New York: Human Rights Watch. Retrieved February 9, 2018 (https://www
.hrw.org/sites/default/files/report_pdf/philippines0915_
brochure_web.pdf).

Kochhar, Rakesh. 2015. *Global Middle Class Is More Promise than Reality.* Washington, DC: Pew Research Center. Retrieved February 9, 2018 (http://www.pewglobal.org/2015/07/08/a-global-middle-class-is-more-promise-than-reality).

Landes, David S. 1999. *The Wealth and Poverty of Nations.* New York: Norton.

Lange, Matthew K. 2004. "British Colonial Legacies and Political Development." *World Development* 32(6): 905–922.

Li, Shi. 2016. "Recent Changes in Inequality in China." In *World Social Science Report, 2016: Challenging Inequalities— Pathways to a Just World.* Paris: UNESCO/International Social Science Council. Retrieved February 9, 2018 (http://
unesdoc.unesco.org/images/0024/002458/245825e.pdf).

Maddison, Angus. 1995. *Monitoring the World Economy, 1820–1992.* Paris: Development Centre of the Organisation for Economic Cooperation and Development.

Milanovic, Branko. 2011. *The Haves and the Have-Nots: A Brief and Idiosyncratic History of Global Inequality.* New York: Basic Books.

Miller, John W. 2011. "The $200,000-a-Year Mine Worker." *Wall Street Journal,* November 16. Retrieved April 28, 2018 (https://www.wsj.com/articles/SB10001424052970204621904577016172350869312).

Münch, Richard. 2016. *The Global Division of Labour: Development and Inequality in World Society* (International Political Economy Series). London: Palgrave Macmillan.

Mutume, Gumisai. 2007. "Africa Aims for a Scientific Revolution." *Africa Renewal Online.* Retrieved February 9, 2018 (http://www.un.org/africarenewal/magazine/october-2007/
africa-aims-scientific-revolution).

Nunn, Nathan. 2007. "Historical Legacies: A Model Linking Africa's Past to Its Current Underdevelopment." *Journal of Development Economics* 83: 157– 175.

Olken, Benjamin A. and Rohini Pande. 2012. *Corruption in Developing Countries.* Cambridge, MA: National Bureau of Economic Research. Retrieved February 9, 2018 (http://www
.nber.org/papers/w17398).

Organisation for Economic Cooperation and Development. 2011. *An Overview of Growing Income Inequalities in OECD Countries: Main Findings.* Paris: OECD Publishing. Retrieved April 26, 2018 (https://www.oecd.org/els/soc/49499779.pdf).

Organisation for Economic Cooperation and Development. 2014. *CleanGovBiz.* Paris: OECD Publishing. Retrieved February 9, 2018 (https://www.oecd.org/cleangovbiz/49693613.pdf).

Organisation for Economic Cooperation and Development. 2015. *Minimum Wages after the Crisis: Making Them Pay.* Paris: OECD Publishing. Retrieved February 9, 2018 (https://
www.oecd.org/social/Focus-on-Minimum-Wages-after-the-crisis-2015.pdf).

Organisation for Economic Cooperation and Development. 2017. *Understanding the Socio-economic Divide in Europe.* Paris: OECD Center for Opportunity and Equality. Retrieved April 26, 2018 (https://www.oecd.org/els/soc/cope-divide-europe-2017-background-report.pdf).

Oxfam International. 2014. *Working for the Few: Political Capture and Economic Inequality.* Boston: Oxfam International. Retrieved February 9, 2018 (https://www
.oxfam.org/sites/www.oxfam.org/files/bp-working-for-few-political-capture-economic-inequality-200114-summ-en.pdf).

Paap, Richard, Philip Hans Franses, and Dick van Dijk. 2005. "Does Africa Grow Slower than Asia, Latin America and the Middle East? Evidence from a New Data-Based Classification Method." *Journal of Development Economics* 77(2): 553–570.

Picketty, Thomas. 2014. *Capital in the Twenty-First Century.* Translated by Arthur Goldhammer. Cambridge, MA: Belknap Press of Harvard University Press.

Pritchett, Lant. 1997. "Divergence, Big Time." *Journal of Economic Perspectives* 11(3): 3–17.

Radelet, Steven. 2015. *The Great Surge: The Ascent of the Developing World.* New York: Simon & Schuster.

Rangan, V. Kasturi, Michael Chu, and Djordjija Petkoski. 2011. "The Globe: Segmenting the Base of the Pyramid." *Harvard Business Review* 2011, June. Retrieved February 9, 2018 (https://
hbr.org/2011/06/the-globe-segmenting-the-base-of-the-pyramid).

Roosevelt, Franklin D. 1932. *The Public Papers and Addresses of Franklin D. Roosevelt, Volume 1, 1928–32.* New York: Random House. Retrieved December 22, 2015 (http://newdeal.feri.org/
texts/456.htm)

Roser, Max. 2016. "Global Economic Inequality." *Our World in Data.* Retrieved February 9, 2018 (https://ourworldindata
.org/global-economic-inequality).

Roy, Rana. 2016. *The Cost of Air Pollution in Africa* (Working Paper No. 333). Paris: OECD Publishing. Retrieved February 9, 2018 (http://www.un.org/africarenewal/sites/www.un.org
.africarenewal/files/The_cost_%20of_air%20pollution_
in_%20Africa.pdf).

Ruben, Ruerd and Ricardo Fort. 2012. "The Impact of Fair Trade Certification for Coffee Farmers in Peru." *World Development* 40(3): 570–582.

Ruben, Ruerd, Ricardo Fort, and Guillermo Zúñiga-Arias. 2009. "Measuring the Impact of Fair Trade on Development." *Development in Practice* 19(6): 777–788.

Shambaugh, Jay, Ryan Nunn, Patrick Liu, and Greg Nantz. 2017. *Thirteen Facts about Wage Growth*. Washington, DC: Brookings Institution. Retrieved February 9, 2018 (https://www.brookings.edu/wp-content/uploads/2017/09/thp_20170926_thirteen_facts_wage_growth.pdf).

Shorrocks Anthony, James B. Davies, and Rodrigo Lluberas. 2015. *Global Wealth Databook 2015*. Zurich, Switzerland: Credit Suisse Research Institute. Retrieved February 9, 2018 (http://delangemars.nl/wp-content/uploads/2015/10/global-wealth-databook-20151.pdf).

Shorrocks Anthony, James B. Davies, Rodrigo Lluberas, and Antonios Koutsoukis. *Global Wealth Report 2016*. Zurich, Switzerland: Credit Suisse Research Institute. Retrieved February 9, 2018 (http://publications.credit-suisse.com/tasks/render/file/index.cfm?fileid=AD783798-ED07-E8C2-4405996B5B02A32E).

Sindzingre, Alice. 2005. "Reforms, Structure or Institutions? Assessing the Determinants of Growth in Low-Income Countries." *Third World Quarterly* 26(2): 281–305.

Stierli, Markus, Anthony Shorrocks, James B. Davies, Rodrigo Lluberas, and Antonios Koutsoukis. 2015. *Global Wealth Report 2015*. Zurich, Switzerland: Credit Suisse Research Institute. Retrieved February 9, 2018 (https://publications.credit-suisse.com/tasks/render/file/?fileID=F2425415-DCA7-80B8-EAD989AF9341D47E).

Stiglitz, Joseph. 2006. *Making Globalization Work*. New York: Norton.

Sutter, John D. 2012. "Slavery's Last Stronghold: The CNN Freedom Project—Ending Modern Day Slavery." *CNN News*. Retrieved February 9, 2018 (http://www.cnn.com/interactive/2012/03/world/mauritania.slaverys.last.stronghold).

Tafirenyika, Masimba. 2016. "Why Has Africa Failed to Industrialize?" *Africa Renewal Online,* August–November. New York: United Nations. Retrieved February 9, 2018 (http://www.un.org/africarenewal/magazine/august-2016/why-has-africa-failed-industrialize).

Transparency International. 2017. *Unmask the Corrupt*. Berlin: Transparency International. Retrieved February 9, 2018 (https://unmaskthecorrupt.org).

United Nations. 2015a. *Income Convergence or Persistent Inequalities among Countries? Development Issues No. 5*. New York: United Nations Development Strategy and Policy Analysis Unit in the Development Policy and Analysis Division of United Nations Department of Economic and Social Affairs. Retrieved February 9, 2018 (http://www.un.org/en/development/desa/policy/wess/wess_dev_issues/dsp_policy_05.pdf).

United Nations. 2015b. *Millennium Development Goals Report*. New York: United Nations. Retrieved February 9, 2018 (http://www.un.org/millenniumgoals/2015_MDG_Report/pdf/MDG%202015%20rev%20(July%201).pdf).

United Nations Development Programme. 2010. *Humanity Divided: Confronting Inequality in Developing Countries*. New York: United Nations. Retrieved February 9, 2018 (http://hdr.undp.org/sites/default/files/reports/270/hdr_2010_en_complete_reprint.pdf).

United Nations Development Programme. 2013. *Humanity Divided: Confronting Inequality in Developing Countries*. New York: United Nations. Retrieved February 9, 2018 (http://www.undp.org/content/dam/undp/library/Poverty%20Reduction/Inclusive%20development/Humanity%20Divided/HumanityDivided_Full-Report.pdf).

United Nations Development Programme. 2015. *Human Development Report 2015: Work for Human Development*. New York: United Nations. Retrieved February 9, 2018 (http://hdr.undp.org/sites/default/files/2015_human_development_report_0.pdf).

United Nations Educational, Scientific, and Cultural Organisation. 1998–2001a. *Eliminating Homelessness/Housing Humanity*. Geneva: UNESCO. Retrieved February 9, 2018 (http://www.unesco.org/education/tlsf/mods/theme_a/interact/www.worldgame.org/wwwproject/what03.shtml).

United Nations Educational, Scientific, and Cultural Organisation. 1998–2001b. *Securing Our Energy Future*. Geneva: UNESCO. Retrieved February 9, 2018 (http://www.unesco.org/education/tlsf/mods/theme_a/interact/www.worldgame.org/wwwproject/what07.shtml).

United Nations Office on Drugs and Crime. 2014. *Global Report on Trafficking in Persons 2014*. Vienna, Austria: United Nations Office on Drugs and Crime. Retrieved April 26, 2018 (https://www.unodc.org/documents/data-and-analysis/glotip/GLOTIP_2014_full_report.pdf).

United Nations Population Fund. 2006. *Gender Equality from Microfinance to Macro Change*. New York: United Nations Population Fund. Retrieved April 27, 2018 (http://www.unfpa.org/gender/micro.htm).

U.S. Agency for International Development. 2015. *Mobile Phones Tackling Poverty*. Washington, DC: USAID. Retrieved February 9, 2018 (https://www.usaid.gov/infographics/50th/mobile-phones-tacking-poverty).

Van Rooyen, Michael. 2013. "Effective Aid." *Harvard International Review* 35(2): 12–16.

Walk Free Foundation. 2016. *The Global Slavery Index*. Nedlands, Western Australia, Australia. Retrieved February 9, 2018 (https://www.globalslaveryindex.org/country/australia).

Wilkinson, Richard and Kate Pickett. (2009) *The Spirit Level: Why Greater Equality Makes Societies Stronger*. New York: Bloomsbury.

Wolff, Edward N. (2017). *A Century of Wealth in America*. Cambridge, MA: Harvard University Press.

World Bank. 1978. *World Development Report, 1978.* Washington, DC: World Bank Group. Retrieved February 9, 2018 (https://openknowledge.worldbank.org/bitstream/handle/10986/5961/WDR%201978%20-%20English.pdf?sequence=1).

World Bank. 2004. *The Costs of Corruption.* Washington, DC: World Bank Group. Retrieved February 9, 2018 (https://monthlyreview.org/2016/11/01/measuring-global-inequality).

World Bank. 2010. *The Cost to Developing Countries of Adapting to Climate Change: New Methods and Estimates.* Washington, DC: World Bank Group. Retrieved February 9, 2018 (http://siteresources.worldbank.org/EXTCC/Resources/EACC-june2010.pdf).

World Bank. 2012. *World Development Report: Gender Equity and Development.* Washington, DC: World Bank Group. Retrieved February 9, 2018 (http://siteresources.worldbank.org/INTWDR2012/Resources/7778105-1299699968583/7786210-1315936222006/Complete-Report.pdf).

World Bank. 2016a. *China: Overview.* Washington, DC: World Bank Group. Retrieved February 9, 2018 (http://www.worldbank.org/en/country/china/overview).

World Bank. 2016b. *World Development Report 2016: Digital Dividends.* Washington, DC: World Bank Group. doi:10.1596/978-1-4648-0671-1

World Economic Forum. 2009. *The Next Billions: Unleashing Business Potential in Untapped Markets.* Geneva: World Economic Forum. Retrieved February 9, 2018 (http://www3.weforum.org/docs/WEF_FB_UntappedMarkets_Report_2009.pdf).

World Economic Forum. 2016. *Latin America Is the World's Most Unequal Region: Here's How to Fix It.* Geneva: World Economic Forum.

World Health Organization. 2014. *Burden of Disease from the Joint Effects of Household and Ambient Air Pollution for 2012.* Geneva: World Health Organization. Retrieved February 9, 2018 (http://www.who.int/phe/health_topics/outdoorair/databases/FINAL_HAP_AAP_BoD_24March2014.pdf?ua=1).

World Health Organization. 2015. *Pneumonia.* Geneva: World Health Organization. Retrieved February 9, 2018 (http://www.who.int/mediacentre/factsheets/fs331/en).

World Health Organization. 2016. *Children: Reducing Mortality Fact Sheet.* Geneva: World Health Organization. Retrieved February 9, 2018 (http://www.who.int/mediacentre/factsheets/fs178/en).

Wortstall, Tim. 2017. "Chinese Wages Are Showing Paul Krugman Is Right Once Again." *Forbes,* March 1. Retrieved February 9, 2018 (https://www.forbes.com/sites/timworstall/2017/03/01/chinese-wages-are-showing-paul-krugman-is-right-once-again/#180f0d843fea).

Yates, Michael D. 2016. "Measuring Global Inequality." *Monthly Review: An Independent Socialist Magazine,* November. Accessed February 9, 2018 (https://monthlyreview.org/2016/11/01/measuring-global-inequality).

Zhuang, Juzhong, Ravi Kanbur, and Dalisay Maligalig. 2014. "Asia's Inequalities" In *Inequality in Asia and the Pacific: Trends, Drivers, and Policy Implications,* edited by Ravi Kanbur, Changyong Rhee, and Juzhong Zhuang. London: Routledge.

Chapter 3

Algarve Daily News. 2014. "Farm Workers See Wages Fall While Food Prices Drop." *Algarve Portugal: Algarve Daily News.* Retrieved February 9, 2018 (http://algarvedailynews.com/news/4252-farm-workers-see-wages-fall-while-food-prices-drop).

Allen, Patricia and Brooke Wilson. 2008. "Agrifood Inequalities: Globalization and Localization." *Development* 51(4): 534–540.

Arabi, U. and H. D. Ramya. 2013. "Hurdles in Implementing Food Security Bill." *Kurukshetra,* November, pp. 13–17. New Delhi: Publications Division Ministry of Information and Broadcasting, Government of India. Retrieved February 9, 2018 (http://iasscore.in/pdf/yojna/2.%20Hurdles%20in%20implementing%20food.pdf).

Breisinger, Clemens, Olivier Ecker, and Jean Francois Trinh Tan. 2015. "Conflict and Food Insecurity: How Do We Break the Links?" Chapter 7 in *Global Food Policy Report 2014–2015.* Washington, DC: International Food Policy Research Institute. Retrieved February 9, 2018 (https://www.ifpri.org/sites/default/files/gfpr/2015/feature_3086.html).

Brinkman, Henk-Jan and Cullen S. Hendrix. 2011. *Food Insecurity and Violent Conflict: Causes, Consequences, and Addressing the Challenges.* Rome: World Food Programme. Retrieved February 9, 2018 (https://ucanr.edu/blogs/food2025/blogfiles/14415.pdf).

Center for Sustainable Systems. 2017. *U.S. Food System Factsheet.* Ann Arbor: Center for Sustainable Systems, University of Michigan. Retrieved February 9, 2018 (http://css.umich.edu/sites/default/files/U.S._Food_System_Factsheet_CSS01-06_e2017.pdf).

Centers for Disease Control and Prevention. 2013. *Surveillance for Foodborne Disease Outbreaks, United States, 2013, Annual Report.* Washington, DC: Department of Health and Human Services, Centers for Disease Control and Prevention.

Department of Food and Public Distribution. 2014. *Village Grain Banks Scheme.* Mumbai: Ministry of Consumer Affairs, Food and Public Distribution, Government of India. Retrieved February 9, 2018 (http://dfpd.nic.in/writereaddata/images/pdf/Village-Grain-Banks-Scheme.pdf).

Department of Food and Public Distribution. 2015. *Public Distribution, NFSA & Computerisation: National Food Security Act, 2013.* Mumbai: Ministry of Consumer Affairs, Food and Public Distribution. Government of India. Retrieved February 9, 2018 (http://dfpd.nic.in/nfsa-act.htm).

De Schutter, Olivier. 2010. "Report Submitted by the Special Rapporteur on the Right to Food." Human Rights Council, Office of the High Commissioner on Human Rights. Retrieved February 9, 2018 (http://www2.ohchr.org/english/issues/food/docs/A-HRC-16-49.pdf).

De Schutter, Olivier. 2014. "Report of the Special Rapporteur on the Right to Food: Final Report—The Transformative Potential of the Right to Food." UN Human Rights Council, Office of the High Commissioner on Human Rights. Retrieved February 9, 2018 (http://www.srfood.org/images/stories/pdf/officialreports/20140310_finalreport_en.pdf).

Environmental Protection Agency. 2017. *Overview of Greenhouse Gases: Methane Emissions.* Washington, DC: Environmental Protection Agency. Retrieved February 9, 2018 (http://www3.epa.gov/climatechange/ghgemissions/gases/ch4.html).

European Commission. 2015. *Humanitarian Food Assistance Echo Fact Sheet.* Brussels: European Commission. Original no longer available. Most recent (retrieved February 9, 2018): http://ec.europa.eu/echo/files/aid/countries/factsheets/thematic/food_assistance_en.pdf;http://erccportal.jrc.ec.europa.eu/ECHO-Flash/Echo-Flash-Item/oid/7521/xmps/1974

Fan, Shenggen. 2015. "Food Policy in 2014–2015." Chapter 1 in *Strong Advances and Stubborn Setbacks in Global Food Policy Report 2014–2015.* Washington, DC: International Food Policy Research Institute. Retrieved February 9, 2018 (https://www.ifpri.org/sites/default/files/gfpr/2015/feature_3080.html).

Fick, Maggie. 2014. "How ISIS Uses Wheat Supplies to Tighten Its Control in Iraq." *Huffington Post,* September 30, updated November 30. Retrieved February 9, 2018 (http://www.huffingtonpost.com/2014/09/30/isis-wheat-iraq_n_5905560.html).

Food and Agricultural Organization of the United Nations. 2006. *Livestock's Long Shadow: Environmental Issues and Options.* Rome: Food and Agricultural Organization of the United Nations. Retrieved February 9, 2018 (ftp://ftp.fao.org/docrep/fao/010/a0701e/a0701e.pdf).

Food and Agricultural Organization of the United Nations. 2013. *FAO Statistical Yearbook: World Food and Agriculture.* Rome: Food and Agriculture Organization of the United Nations. Retrieved February 9, 2018 (http://www.fao.org/docrep/018/i3107e/i3107e.pdf).

Food and Agricultural Organization of the United Nations. 2015a. *Food Security Indicators.* Rome: Food and Agriculture Organization of the United Nations. Retrieved February 9, 2018 (http://www.fao.org/economic/ess/ess-fs/ess-fadata/en/#.VphPJk3bIfg).

Food and Agricultural Organization of the United Nations. 2015b. *The State of Food and Agriculture: Social Protection and Agriculture—Breaking the Cycle of Rural Poverty.* Rome: Food and Agriculture Organization of the United Nations. Retrieved February 9, 2018 (http://www.fao.org/3/a-i4910e.pdf).

Food and Agricultural Organization of the United Nations, International Fund for Agricultural Development, and World Food Programme. 2014. *The State of Food Insecurity in the World 2014: Strengthening the Enabling Environment for Food Security and Nutrition.* Rome: Food and Agriculture Organization of the United Nations. Retrieved February 9, 2018 (http://www.fao.org/3/a-i4030e.pdf).

Food and Agricultural Organization of the United Nations/World Health Organization. 2011. *Fruits and Vegetables Importance for Public Health.* Arusha, Tanzania: FAO/WHO Workshop on Promotion of the Production and Consumption of Fruits and Vegetables. Retrieved February 9, 2018 (http://www.fao.org/fileadmin/templates/agphome/documents/horticulture/WHO/arusha/F_V_public_health_XUEREB.pdf)

Grace, Delia and John McDermott. 2015. "Food Safety: Reducing and Managing Food Scares." Chapter 6 in *Global Food Policy Report 2014–2015.* Washington, DC: International Food Policy Research Institute. Retrieved February 9, 2018 (https://www.ifpri.org/sites/default/files/gfpr/2015/feature_3085.html).

Groom, Martha J., Elizabeth M. Gray, and Patricia A. Townsend. 2008. "Biofuels and Biodiversity: Principles for Creating Better Policies for Biofuel Production. *Conservation Biology* 22(3): 602–609.

Hendrix, Cullen and Henk-Jan Brinkman. 2013. "Food Insecurity and Conflict Dynamics: Causal Linkages and Complex Feedbacks." *Stability: International Journal of Security and Development* 2(2): art. 26. Retrieved February 9, 2018 (http://doi.org/10.5334/sta.bm).

Hesterman, Oran B. 2011. *Fair Food: Growing a Healthy, Sustainable Food System for All.* New York: Public Affairs.

Hoffman, Beth. 2013. *Behind the Brands: Food Justice and the "Big 10" Food and Beverage Companies.* Oxford, UK: Oxfam International.

Hudson, John C. 2011. "Agriculture." In *Encyclopedia of the Great Plains,* edited by David J. Wisehart. Lincoln: University of Nebraska–Lincoln. Retrieved February 9, 2018 (http://plainshumanities.unl.edu/encyclopedia/doc/egp.ag.001).

International Panel of Experts on Sustainable Food Systems. 2015. *The New Science of Sustainable Food Systems.* Rome: International Panel of Experts on Sustainable Food Systems. Retrieved February 9, 2018 (http://www.ipes-food.org/images/Reports/IPES_report01_1505_web_br_pages.pdf).

Kapur, Akash. 2014. "India's 'Plastic Man' Turns Litter into Paved Roads." *Bloomberg Business,* July 10. Retrieved February 9, 2018 (http://www.bloomberg.com/bw/articles/2014-07-10/indias-plastic-man-chemist-turns-litter-into-paved-roads).

Kaur, Manmeet. 2014. *India: WFP Reforms Ensure Food Reaches the Right Beneficiaries.* Rome: World Food Programme. Retrieved February 9, 2018 (https://www.wfp.org/stories/india-wfp-reforms-ensure-food-reaches-right-beneficiaries).

Kendall, Ann. 2005. "Applied Archaeology: Revitalizing Indigenous Agricultural Technology within an Andean Community." *Public Archaeology* 4: 205–221.

Montenegro, Maywa. 2015. "How Seed Laws Make Farmers' Seeds Illegal." *Alternet,* May 20. Retrieved February 9, 2018 (http://www.alternet.org/environment/how-seed-laws-make-farmers-seeds-illegal).

New York Times. 2008. "The World Food Crisis" [editorial]. *The New York Times,* April 10. Retrieved February 9, 2018 (http://www.nytimes.com/2008/04/10/opinion/10thu1.html).

Nicholson, Sarah. 2014. *Do European Agricultural Policies Encourage the Adoption of Unhealthy Diets?* Swindon, UK: Global Food Security. http://www.foodsecurity.ac.uk/blog/2014/06/do-european-agricultural-policies-encourage-the-adoption-of-unhealthy-diets/

Nunn, Nathan and Nancy Qian. 2014. "U.S. Food Aid and Civil Conflict." *American Economic Review* 104(6): 1630–1666.

Oxfam International. 2013. *Nothing Sweet about It: How Sugar Fuels Land Grabs.* Oxford, UK: Oxfam International. Retrieved February 9, 2018 (https://www.oxfam.org/sites/www.oxfam.org/files/nothingsweetaboutitmediabrief-embargoed2october2013.pdf).

Paul, James A. and Katarina Wahlberg. 2008. *A New Era of World Hunger? The Global Food Crisis Analyzed.* New York: Global Policy Forum. Retrieved February 9, 2018 (https://www.globalpolicy.org/world-hunger/48424-a-new-era-of-world-hunger.html).

Penn State Live. 2012. "Farm-Safety Expert: Beware of Toxic Gases from Manure Storages." *Penn State News,* October 4. University Park: Penn State University. Retrieved April 30, 2018 (http://news.psu.edu/story/146221/2012/10/04/farm-safety-expert-beware-toxic-gases-manure-storages).

Pimentel, David and Marcia Pimentel. 2003. "Sustainability of Meat-Based and Plant-Based Diets and the Environment." *American Journal of Clinical Nutrition* 78(3): 660–663.

Rediff News. 2013. "India's Food Crisis: Rotting Food-Grains, Hungry People." *Reddiff.com,* April 1. Retrieved February 9, 2018 (http://www.rediff.com/news/column/indias-food-crisis-rotting-food-grains-hungry-people/20130401.htm).

Rosenfeld, Allen. 2010. *The Fruit and Vegetable Consumption Challenge: How Federal Spending Falls Short of Addressing Public Health Needs.* Hockessin, DE: Produce for Better Health Foundation. Retrieved February 9, 2018 (http://www.pbhfoundation.org/pdfs/about/res/pbh_res/2010gapanalysis.pdf).

Ross, Stephanie Maxine. 2010. "Food for Thought, Part I: Foodborne Illness and Factory Farming." *Holistic Nursing Practice* 24(3): 169–173.

Saab, Anne. 2015. "Climate-Ready Seeds and Patent Rights: A Question of Climate (in) Justice?" *Global Jurist* 15(2): 219–235.

Shand, Hope. 1997. *Human Nature: Agricultural Biodiversity and Farm-Based Food Security.* Ottawa, Ontario, Canada: Rural Advancement Foundation International. Retrieved February 9, 2018 (http://www.etcgroup.org/sites/www.etcgroup.org/files/publication/538/01/other_human.pdf).

Shukla, Shyamala and Neeraj Gupta. 2014. *Grain Storage: Public–Private Partnerships.* Washington, DC: World Bank Group. Retrieved February 9, 2018 (http://www.ifc.org/wps/wcm/connect/e003f400485d33ba894efd299ede9589/PIQ_GrainStoragePPPs_ONLINE.pdf? MOD=AJPERES).

Sight and Life. 2012. *Micronutrients, Macro Impact: The Story of Vitamins and a Hungry World.* Basel, Switzerland: Sight and Life Press. Retrieved February 9, 2018 (https://sightandlife.org/blog/library_item/micronutrients-macro-impact-story-vitamins-hungry-world).

Tulchinsky, Theodore H. 2010. "Micronutrient Deficiency Conditions: Global Health Issues." *Public Health Reviews* 32: 243–255.

United Nations. 2015. *2015 Millennium Development Goal Report.* New York: United Nations. Retrieved February 9, 2018 (http://www.un.org/millenniumgoals/2015_MDG_Report/pdf/MDG%202015%20rev%20(July%201).pdf)

United Nations Conference on Trade and Development. 2010. *Agriculture at the Crossroads: Guaranteeing Food Security in a Changing Global Climate.* Geneva: UN Conference on Trade and Development. Retrieved February 9, 2018 (http://unctad.org/en/docs/presspb20108_en.pdf).

United Nations International Children's Emergency Fund, World Health Organization, and World Bank Group. 2015. *Levels and Trends in Child Malnutrition: Key Findings of the 2015 Edition.* Geneva: World Health Organization. Retrieved February 9, 2018 (http://www.who.int/nutgrowthdb/jme_brochure2015.pdf? ua=1).

Weinberger, Katrina and Thomas A. Lumpkin. 2005. *Horticulture for Poverty Alleviation: The Unfunded Revolution.* Taiwan: AVRDC—The World Vegetable Center. Retrieved February 9, 2018 (https://papers.ssrn.com/sol3/papers.cfm? abstract_id=781784).

Winders, William. 2009. *The Politics of Food Supply: U.S. Agricultural Policy in the World Economy.* New Haven, CT: Yale University Press.

World Bank. 2010. *Food Price Watch.* Washington, DC: World Bank Group.

World Bank. 2013. *Helping India Combat Persistently High Rates of Malnutrition.* Washington, DC: World Bank Group. Retrieved February 9, 2018 (http://www.worldbank.org/en/news/feature/2013/05/13/helping-india-combat-persistently-high-rates-of-malnutrition).

World Bank/International Center for Tropical Agriculture. 2015. *Climate-Smart Agriculture in Rwanda: CSA Country*

Profiles for Africa, Asia, and Latin America and the Caribbean Series. Washington, DC: World Bank Group. Retrieved February 9, 2018 (http://sdwebx.worldbank.org/climateportal/doc/agricultureProfiles/CSA%20RWANDA%20NOV%2018%202015.pdf).

World Food Programme. 2013. *State of School Feeding Worldwide.* Rome: World Food Programme. Retrieved February 9, 2018 (http://documents.wfp.org/stellent/groups/public/documents/communications/wfp257481.pdf).

World Food Programme. 2014. *Climate Impacts on Food Security and Nutrition: A Review of Existing Knowledge.* Rome: World Food Programme. Retrieved February 9, 2018 (http://documents.wfp.org/stellent/groups/public/documents/communications/wfp258981.pdf).

World Food Programme. 2015. *Global Food Security Update: Tracking Food Security Trends in Vulnerable Countries.* Rome: World Food Programme. Retrieved February 9, 2018 (http://vam.wfp.org/sites/global_update/December_2015/Index.htm).

World Food Programme. 2017. *Our Work: P4P Overview—Connecting Farmers to Markets.* Rome: World Food Programme. Retrieved February 9, 2018 (http://www.wfp.org/purchase-progress/overview).

World Health Organization. 2014. *Increasing Fruit and Vegetable Consumption to Reduce the Risk of Noncommunicable Diseases.* Geneva: World Health Organization. Retrieved February 9, 2018 (http://www.who.int/elena/titles/bbc/fruit_vegetables_ncds/en).

World Health Organization. 2015a. *Food Safety Fact Sheet No. 399.* Geneva: World Health Organization. Retrieved February 9, 2018 (http://www.who.int/mediacentre/factsheets/fs399/en).

World Health Organization. 2015b. *WHO Estimates of the Global Burden of Foodborne Diseases.* Geneva: World Health Organization. Retrieved February 9, 2018 (http://apps.who.int/iris/bitstream/10665/199350/1/9789241565165_eng.pdf? ua=1)

World Wide Fund for Nature. N.d. *Farming: Soil Erosion and Degradation.* Geneva: World Wide Fund for Nature. Retrieved February 9, 2018 (http://wwf.panda.org/what_we_do/footprint/agriculture/impacts/soil_erosion).

Yardley, Jim. 2007. "Beneath Booming Cities, China's Future Is Drying Up." *The New York Times,* November 14, p. A1. Retrieved February 9, 2018 (https://www.nytimes.com/2007/12/14/world/asia/14iht-28water-growth1.8754424.html).

Chapter 4

Alam, Maqsood and Margaret R. Hammerschlag. 2004. "SARS and Emerging Zoonoses." *Medscape* (CMP Healthcare Media). Retrieved February 10, 2018 (http://www.medscape.com/viewarticle/487377).

Alleyne, George, Agnes Binagwaho, Andy Haines, Selim Jahan, Rachel Nugent, Ariella Rojhani, and David Stuckler. 2013. "Embedding Non-communicable Diseases in the Post-2015 Development Agenda." *The Lancet* 381: 566–574.

Alwan, Ala, Tim Armstrong, Douglas Bettcher, Francesco Branca, Daniel Chisholm, Majid Ezzati, Richard Garfield, David MacLean, Colin Mathers, Shanthi Mendis, et al. 2011. *Global Status Report on Noncommunicable Diseases 2010.* Geneva: World Health Organization. http://www.who.int/nmh/publications/ncd_report_full_en.pdf

Andre, F. E., R. Booy, H. L. Bock, J. Clemens, S. K. Datta, T. J. John, B. W. Lee, S. Lolekha, H. Peltola, T. A. Ruff, et al. 2008. "Vaccination Greatly Reduces Disease, Disability, Death and Inequity Worldwide." *Bulletin of the World Health Organization* 86(2): 81–160.

Baker, Phillip and Sharon Friel. 2016. "Food Systems Transformations, Ultra-processed Food Markets and the Nutrition Transition in Asia." *Globalization and Health* 12: 80.

Başoğlu, Metin and Ebru Şalcioğlu. 2011. *A Mental Healthcare Model for Mass Trauma Survivors: Control-Focused Behavioral Treatment of Earthquake, War, and Torture Trauma.* Cambridge, UK: Cambridge University Press.

Case, Anne and Angus Deaton. 2017. *Mortality and Morbidity in the 21st Century* (prepared for the Brookings Panel on Economic Activity, March 23–24). Washington, DC: Brookings Institution.

Centers for Disease Control and Prevention. 2016a. *Pertussis in Other Countries.* Washington, DC: Department of Health and Human Services, Centers for Disease Control and Prevention. Retrieved February 10, 2018 (https://www.cdc.gov/pertussis/countries).

Centers for Disease Control and Prevention. 2016b. *Zoonotic Diseases.* Washington, DC: Department of Health and Human Services, Centers for Disease Control and Prevention. Retrieved February 10, 2018 (https://www.cdc.gov/onehealth/basics/zoonotic-diseases.html).

Centers for Disease Control and Prevention. 2017. *Measles History and Measles Cases and Outbreaks.* Washington, DC: Department of Health and Human Services, Centers for Disease Control and Prevention. Retrieved February 10, 2018 (https://www.cdc.gov/measles/about/history.html).

Chan, Savio and Michael Zakkour. 2014. *China's Super Consumers: What 1 Billion Customers Want and How to Sell It to Them.* Hoboken, NJ: John Wiley.

Charara, Raghid, Mohammad Forouzanfar, Mohsen Naghavi, Maziar Moradi-Lakeh, Ashkan Afshin, Theo Vos, Farah Daoud, Haidong Wang, Charbel El Bcheraoui, Ibrahim Khalil, et al. 2017. "The Burden of Mental Disorders in the Eastern Mediterranean Region, 1990–2013." *PLoS One* 12(1): e0169575.

Choi, Kyung-Hwa and Dong-Hyun Kim. 2015. "Trend of Suicide Rates According to Urbanity among Adolescents by Gender and

Suicide Method in Korea, 1997–2012." *International Journal of Environmental Research and Public Health* 12: 5129–5142.

Climate Central. 2016. *More Mosquito Days Increasing Zika Risk in U.S.* Princeton, NJ: Climate Central. Retrieved February 10, 2018 (http://www.climatecentral.org/news/more-mosquito-days-increasing-zika-risk-in-us-20553)

Coalition for Epidemic Preparedness Innovations. 2017. *CEPI: New Vaccines for a Safer World.* Retrieved February 10, 2018 (http://cepi.net/sites/default/files/CEPI_2pager_27_Apr_17.pdf).

De Vogli, Roberto, Anne Kouvonen, and David Gimeno. 2014. "The Influence of Market Deregulation on Fast Food Consumption and Body Mass Index: A Cross-National Time Series Analysis." *Bulletin of the World Health Organization* 92: 99A–107A. Retrieved February 10, 2018 (http://www.who.int/bulletin/volumes/92/2/13-120287/en).

Doucleff, Michaeleen and Jane Greenhalgh. 2017. "The Next Pandemic Could Be Dripping on Your Head." *Morning Edition* (National Public Radio), February 21. Retrieved February 10, 2018 (http://www.npr.org/sections/goatsandsoda).

Dugan, Andrew. 2013. "Fast Food Still Major Part of U.S. Diet." *Gallup News,* August 6. Retrieved February 10, 2018 (http://news.gallup.com/poll/163868/fast-food-major-part-diet.aspx).

Durkheim, Emile. 1897/1966. *Suicide: A Study in Sociology.* New York: Free Press.

Dye, Christopher, Ties Boerma, David Evans, Anthony Harris, Christian Lienhardt, Joanne McManus, et al. 2013. *The World Health Report 2013: Research for Universal Coverage.* Geneva: World Health Organization.

Economist, The. 2015. "Fast-Food Nations." *The Economist,* January 18. Retrieved February 10, 2018 (http://www.economist.com/fastfood).

Economist, The. 2017. "Winning the Endgame: A Global Attack on Long-Neglected Tropical Diseases Is Succeeding." *The Economist,* April 22. Retrieved February 10, 2018 (http://www.economist.com/news/international/21721133-donors-and-drug-firms-are-co-operating-defeat-ancient-plagues-global-attack).

Fellows, Peter and Martin Hilmi. 2011. *Selling Street and Snack Foods.* Rome: Food and Agriculture Organization of the United Nations. Retrieved February 10, 2018 (http://www.fao.org/docrep/015/i2474e/i2474e00.pdf).

Flahault, Antoine, Rafael Ruiz de Castaneda, and Isabelle Bolon. 2016. "Climate Change and Infectious Diseases." *Public Health Reviews* 37:21. Retrieved February 10, 2018 (https://link.springer.com/article/10.1186%2Fs40985-016-0035-2).

GBD 2015 Obesity Collaborators. 2017. "Health Effects of Overweight and Obesity in 195 Countries over 25 Years." *New England Journal of Medicine* 377(1): 13–27.

Gehlhar, Mark and Anita Regmi. 2005. "Factors Shaping Global Food Markets." Chapter 1 in *New Directions in Global Food Markets,* edited by Anita Regmi and Mark Gehlhar. Washington, DC: Economic Research Service/U.S. Department of Agriculture.

Habib, Samira Humaira and Soma Saha. 2010. "Burden of Non-communicable Disease: Global Overview." *Diabetes & Metabolic Syndrome: Clinical Research & Reviews* 4(1): 41–47.

The Hague Global Child Labour Conference. (2010). *Roadmap for Achieving the Elimination of the Worst Forms of Child Labour by 2016.* Geneva: The Hague Global Child Labour Conference. Retrieved February 10, 2018 (http://www.ilo.org/ILO-IPECinfo/product/viewProduct.do? productId=13453).

Harris, Ricci, Martin Tobias, Mona Jeffreys, Kiri Waldegrave, Saffron Karlsen, and James Nazroo. 2006. "Effects of Self-Reported Racial Discrimination and Deprivation on Māori Health and Inequalities in New Zealand: Cross-Sectional Study." *The Lancet* 367: 2005–2009.

Health Resources and Service Administration. 2017. "Shortage Areas." *Data Warehouse.* Washington, DC: Health Resources and Service Administration. Retrieved February 10, 2018 (https://datawarehouse.hrsa.gov/topics/shortageAreas.aspx).

Herkenrath, Mark, Claudia König, Hanno Scholtz, and Thomas Volken. 2005. "Convergence and Divergence in the Contemporary World System: An Introduction." *International Journal of Comparative Sociology* 46(5–6): 363–382.

Hodson, Hal. 2014. "Online Army Helps Map Guinea's Ebola Outbreak." *New Scientist,* April 9. Retrieved February 10, 2018 (https://www.newscientist.com/article/mg22229644.400-online-army-helps-map-guineas-ebola-outbreak).

Human Rights Watch. 2002. *Backgrounder: Child Labor in Agriculture.* New York: Human Rights Watch. Retrieved February 10, 2018 (https://www.hrw.org/legacy/backgrounder/crp/back0610.htm).

Human Rights Watch. 2014. *Tobacco's Hidden Children: Hazardous Child Labor in United States Tobacco Farming.* New York: Human Rights Watch. Retrieved February 10, 2018 (https://www.hrw.org/sites/default/files/reports/us0514_photoSumUploadwCvr.pdf).

Institute for Health Metrics and Evaluation. 2017. *Financing Global Health 2016: Development Assistance, Public and Private Health Spending for the Pursuit of Universal Health Coverage.* Seattle, WA: Institute for Health Metrics and Evaluation, University of Washington.

International Labour Organization–International Programme on the Elimination of Child Labor. 2013. *Making Progress against Child Labour—Global Estimates and Trends 2000–2012.* Geneva: International Labour Office. Retrieved February 10, 2018 (http://www.ilo.org/wcmsp5/groups/public/@ed_norm/@ipec/documents/publication/wcms_221513.pdf).

Jacobs, Andrew and Matt Richtel. 2017. "How Industry Got Brazil Hooked on Junk Food." *The New York Times,* September 16, p. A1,

Jorm, Anthony F., Sarah J. Bourchier, Stefan Cvetkovski, and Gavin Stewart. 2012. "Mental Health of Indigenous Australians: A Review of Findings from Community Surveys." *Medical Journal of Australia* 196(2): 118–121.

Keusch, Gerald T., Marguerite Pappaioanou, Mila C. González, Kimberly A. Scott, and Peggy Tsai, eds. 2009. *Sustaining Global Surveillance and Response to Emerging Zoonotic Diseases.* Washington, DC: National Academies Press. Retrieved February 10, 2018 (https://www.nap.edu/catalog/12625/sustaining-global-surveillance-and-response-to-emerging-zoonotic-diseases).

Kokkevi, Anna, Vassiliki Rotsika, Angeliki Arapaki, and Clive Richardson. 2011. "Changes in Associations between Psychosocial Factors and Suicide Attempts by Adolescents in Greece from 1984 to 2007." *European Journal of Public Health* 21(6): 694–698.

Lillie, Michelle. 2013. "Child Labor Blog Part III: Manufacturing in Asia." *Human Trafficking Search.* Brooklyn, NY: O. L. Pathy Family Foundation. Retrieved April 26, 2018 (http://humantrafficking-search.org/child-labor-blog-part-iii-manufacturing-in-asia).

MacGregor, Graham A. 2015. "Food and the Responsibility Deal: How the Salt Reduction Strategy Was Derailed." *British Medical Journal* 350: h1936.

Marsh, Sarah. 2017. "Suicide Is at Record Level among Students at UK Universities, Study Finds." *The Guardian,* September 2. Retrieved February 10, 2018 (https://www.theguardian.com/education/2017/sep/02/suicide-record-level-students-uk-universities-study).

McCoy, David, Sudeep Chand, and Devi Sridhar. 2009. "Global Health Funding: How Much, Where It Comes from, and Where It Goes." *Health Policy and Planning* 24(6): 407–417.

McLoughlin, A. B., M. S. Gould, and K. M. Malone. 2015. "Global Trends in Teenage Suicide: 2003–2014." *QJM: An International Journal of Medicine* 108(10): 765–780. Retrieved February 10, 2018 (https://academic.oup.com/qjmed/article/108/10/765/1620773/Global-trends-in-teenage-suicide-2003-2014).

McNeil, Donald G., Jr. 2017. "How a Tsunami in Japan Endangered Children in Cambodia." *The New York Times,* May 16, p. D6. Retrieved February 10, 2018 (https://www.nytimes.com/2017/05/15/health/tsunami-japan-cambodia-iodine-defiency.html).

Meek, Richard William, Hrushi Vyas, and Jane Violet Piddock. 2015. "Nonmedical Uses of Antibiotics: Time to Restrict Their Use?" *PLoS Biology* 13(10): e1002266.

Monteiro, Carlos A., Jean-Claude Moubarac, Geoffrey Cannon, and Barry Popkin. 2013. "Ultra-processed Products Are Becoming Dominant in the Global Food System." *Obesity Reviews* 14: 21–28.

Muller. Mike. 1974. *The Baby Killer.* London: War on Want. Retrieved February 10, 2018 (http://archive.babymilkaction.org/pdfs/babykiller.pdf).

Myers, Samuel L., Xiaoyan Gao, and Britt Cecconi Cruz. 2013. "Ethnic Minorities, Race, and Inequality in China: A New Perspective on Racial Dynamics." *Review of Black Political Economy* 40(3): 231–244.

National Public Radio. 2013. "Buried in Grain: NPR and CPI Examine the Danger and Weak Regulatory Response of Grain Bin Entrapments." *National Public Radio.* Retrieved February 10, 2018 (http://www.npr.org/series/174755100/buried-in-grain).

Nichonghaile, Clar. 2016. "Violet Shivutse: A Seat at the Table." In *Progress of the World's Women 2015–2016: Transforming Economies, Realizing Rights.* New York: United Nations. Retrieved February 10, 2018 (http://www.redvolver.it/storyborders/unwomen_ol/violet).

O'Neill, Jim (Project Chair). 2016. *Tackling Drug-Resistant Infections Globally: Final Report and Recommendations.* Review on microbial resistance commissioned by U.K. prime minister and supported by U.K. government and Wellcome Trust. Retrieved February 10, 2018 (https://amr-review.org/sites/default/files/160525_Final%20paper_with%20cover.pdf).

Organisation for Economic Cooperation and Development. N.d. "Aid (ODA) by Sector and Donor [DAC5]." *OECD.Stat.* Paris: OECD Publishing. Retrieved May 30, 2017.

Ouyang, Yusi and Per Pinstrup-Andersen. 2012. "Health Inequality between Ethnic Minority and Han Populations in China." *World Development* 40(7): 1452–1468.

Oxford Vaccination Group. 2017. *Measles.* Oxford, UK: Oxford University Vaccine Knowledge Project. Retrieved February 10, 2018 (http://vk.ovg.ox.ac.uk/measles).

Pack, Darrin. 2015. "Purdue Reports Grain Entrapments Up Nationwide in 2014." *Purdue University Agricultural News,* April 29. Retrieved February 10, 2018 (https://www.purdue.edu/newsroom/releases/2015/Q2/purdue-reports-grain-entrapments-up-nationwide-in-2014.html).

Popkin, Barry M., Linda S. Adair, and Shu Wen Ng. 2012. "NOW AND THEN: The Global Nutrition Transition: The Pandemic of Obesity in Developing Countries." *Nutrition Reviews* 70(1): 3–21.

Radhakrishnan, Rajiv and Chittaranjan Andrade. 2012. "Suicide: An Indian Perspective." *Indian Journal of Psychiatry* 54(4): 304–319.

Rataj, Elisabeth, Katharina Kunzweiler, and Susan Garthus-Niegel. 2016. "Extreme Weather Events in Developing Countries and Related Injuries and Mental Health Disorders—A Systematic Review." *BMC Public Health* 16:1020.

Rauscher, Kimberly J., Carol W. Runyan, Michael D. Schulman, and J. Michael Bowling. 2008. "U.S. Child Labor Violations in the Retail and Service Industries: Findings from a National Survey of Working Adolescents." *American Journal of Public Health* 98(9): 1693–1699.

Roth, Gregory, Catherine Johnson, Amanuel Abajobir, Foad Abd-Allah, Semaw Ferede Abera, Gebre Abyu, Muktar Ahmed, Baran Aksut, Tahiya Alam, Khurshid Alam, et al. 2017. "Global, Regional, and National Burden of Cardiovascular Diseases for 10 Causes, 1990 to 2015." *Journal of the American College of Cardiology* 70(1): 1–25.

SDG Collaborators. 2017. "Measuring Progress and Projecting Attainment on the Basis of Past Trends of the Health-Related Sustainable Development Goals in 188 Countries: An Analysis from the Global Burden of Disease Study 2016." *The Lancet* 390: 1423–1459.

Sejvar, James J. 2003. "West Nile Virus: An Historical Overview." *Ochsner Journal* 5(3): 6–10.

Simonsen, Lone, Peter Spreeuwenberg, Roger Lustig, Robert J. Taylor, Douglas M. Fleming, Madelon Kroneman, Maria D. Van Kerkhove, Anthony W. Mounts, W. John Paget, and the GLaMOR Collaborating Teams. 2013. "Global Mortality Estimates for the 2009 Influenza Pandemic from the GLaMOR Project: A Modeling Study." *PLoS Medicine* 10(11): e1001558.

Stephens, Carolyn, John Porter, Clive Nettleton, and Ruth Willis. 2006. "Disappearing, Displaced, and Undervalued: A Call to Action for Indigenous Health Worldwide." *The Lancet* 367: 2019–2028.

Tanielian, Terri and Lisa H. Jaycox, eds. 2008. *Invisible Wounds of War: Psychological and Cognitive Injuries, Their Consequences, and Services to Assist Recovery.* Santa Monica, CA: RAND.

Tebit, Dennis M. and Eric J. Arts. 2011. "Tracking a Century of Global Expansion and Evolution of HIV to Drive Understanding and to Combat Disease." *The Lancet Infectious Diseases* 11(1): 45–56.

Twenge, Jean M. 2017. "Have Smartphones Destroyed a Generation?" *The Atlantic,* September. Retrieved February 10, 2018 (https://www.theatlantic.com/magazine/archive/2017/09/has-the-smartphone-destroyed-a-generation/534198).

United Nations. 2014. *World Urbanization Prospects: The 2014 Revision.* New York: United Nations. Retrieved February 10, 2018 (https://esa.un.org/unpd/wup/publications/files/wup2014-highlights.pdf).

United Nations. 2015. *Millennium Development Goals Report 2015.* New York: United Nations. Retrieved February 10, 2018 (http://www.un.org/millenniumgoals/2015_MDG_Report/pdf/MDG%202015%20rev%20(July%201).pdf).

United Nations International. 2016. *State of the World's Children Report 2016.* New York: United Nations. Retrieved February 10, 2018 (https://www.unicef.org/publications/files/UNICEF_SOWC_2016.pdf).

U.S. Agency for International Development. 2017. *Neglected Tropical Diseases Program.* Washington, DC: United States Agency for International Development. Retrieved February 10, 2018 (https://www.neglecteddiseases.gov).

Uniting to Combat Neglected Tropical Diseases. 2015. *Reaching the Unreached: Fourth Progress Report of the London Declaration.* Haywards Heath, UK: United to Combat Neglected Tropical Diseases. Retrieved February 10, 2018 (http://uniting-tocombatntds.org/sites/all/themes/f1ux/images/fourth-report/en/pdfs/4th-Report-on-Progress_EN.pdf).

Upton, John. 2016. *Scientists Tease Out Climate Change's Role in Zika Spread.* Princeton, NJ: Climate Central. Retrieved February 10, 2018 (http://www.climatecentral.org/news/scientists-tease-out-climate-role-zika-spread-20582).

Ventola, C. Lee. 2015. "The Antibiotic Resistance Crisis, Part 1: Causes and Threats." *Pharmacy and Therapeutics* 40(4): 277–283.

Viergever, Rodrik F. and Thom C. C. Hendriks. 2016. "The 10 Largest Public and Philanthropic Funders of Health Research in the World: What They Fund and How They Distribute Their Funds." *Health Research Policy and Systems* 14: 12.

Werbart Törnblom, Annelie, Andrzej Werbart, and Per-Anders Rydelius. 2015. "Shame and Gender Differences in Paths to Youth Suicide: Parents' Perspective." *Qualitative Health Research* 25(8): 1099–1116.

World Health Organization. 2007. *Health of Indigenous Peoples Fact Sheet No. 326.* Geneva: World Health Organization. Retrieved February 10, 2018 (http://www.who.int/mediacentre/factsheets/fs326/en).

World Health Organization. 2010. *Health Systems Financing: The Path to Universal Coverage.* Geneva: World Health Organization. Retrieved February 10, 2018 (http://www.who.int/whr/2010/en).

World Health Organization. 2013. *Global Vaccine Action Plan 2011–2020.* Geneva: World Health Organization. Retrieved February 10, 2018 (http://www.who.int/immunization/global_vaccine_action_plan/GVAP_doc_2011_2020/en).

World Health Organization. 2014. *Global Status Report on Alcohol and Health.* Geneva: World Health Organization. Retrieved February 10, 2018 (http://www.who.int/substance_abuse/publications/global_alcohol_report/msbgsruprofiles.pdf).

World Health Organization. 2015a. *Measles Vaccination Has Saved an Estimated 17.1 Million Lives since 2000.* Geneva: World Health Organization. Retrieved February 10, 2018 (http://www.who.int/mediacentre/news/releases/2015/measles-vaccination/en).

World Health Organization. 2015b. *Prevention of Suicidal Behaviours: A Task for All.* Geneva: World Health Organization. Retrieved February 10, 2018 (http://www.who.int/mental_health/prevention/suicide/background/en).

World Health Organization. 2016a. *Monkeypox Factsheet.* Geneva: World Health Organization. Retrieved February 10, 2018 (http://www.who.int/mediacentre/factsheets/fs161/en).

World Health Organization. 2016b. *Uncovering Health Inequalities: A Path towards Leaving No One Behind.* Geneva: World Health Organization. Retrieved February 10, 2018 (http://www.who.int/features/2016/health-inequalities/en).

World Health Organization. 2017a. "Number of People Newly Infected with HIV/AIDS." *Global Health Observatory (GHO) Data.* Geneva: World Health Organization. Retrieved February 10, 2018 (http://www.who.int/gho/hiv/epidemic_status/inci dence/en).

World Health Organization. 2017b. *10 Facts about Obesity.* Geneva: World Health Organization. Retrieved February 10, 2018 (http://www.who.int/features/factfiles/obesity/en).

World Health Organization. 2017c. *Depression and Other Common Mental Disorders: Global Health Estimates.* Geneva: World Health Organization. Retrieved February 10, 2018 (http://apps.who.int/iris/bitstream/10665/254610/1/WHO-MSD-MER-2017.2-eng.pdf).

Chapter 5

Australian Bureau of Statistics. 2014. *Australian Social Trends, 2014: Exploring the Gap in Labour Market Outcomes for Aboriginal and Torres Strait Islander Peoples.* Canberra, Australia: Australian Bureau of Statistics. Retrieved February 10, 2018 (http://www.abs.gov.au/ausstats/abs@.nsf/Lookup/4102.0main+features72014).

Bawden, Anna. 2016. "'There Are Just Not Enough Teachers': Sciences Struggle to Recruit." *The Guardian,* September 15. Retrieved February 10, 2018 (https://www.theguardian .com/education/2015/sep/15/not-enough-teachers-science-shortage-teaching-jobs).

Das Shrestha, Deepesh. 2013. *Nepal: "I Would Have Gone Hungry without School Meals."* Rome: World Food Programme. Retrieved February 10, 2018 (https://www.wfp .org/stories/%E2%80%98i-would-have-gone-hungry-with-out-school-meals%E2%80%99).

Economist, The. 2017. "South Africa Has One of the World's Worst Education Systems." *The Economist,* January 7. Retrieved February 10, 2018 (http://www.economist .com/news/middle-east-and-africa/21713858-why-it-b ottom-class-south-africa-has-one-worlds-worst-education).

Epstein, Mark J. and Kristi Yuthas. 2012. "Redefining Education in the Developing World." *Stanford Social Innovation Review,* Winter. Retrieved February 10, 2018 (https://ssir.org/articles/entry/redefining_education_in_the_developing_world).

Ferreira, Francisco H. G. and Jérémie Gignoux. 2013. "The Measurement of Educational Inequality: Achievement and Opportunity." *World Bank Economic Review* 28(2): 210–246.

Freeman, Richard B., Stephen J. Machin, and Martina G. Viarengo. 2011. "Inequality of Educational Outcomes: International Evidence from Pisa." *Regional and Sectoral Economic Studies* 11(3): 5–20.

Global Citizen. 2014. "10 Barriers to Education around the World." *Global Citizen,* June 2 (updated January 24, 2018, with byline Phineas Rueckert). Retrieved February 10, 2018 (https://www.globalcitizen.org/en/content/10-barriers-to-education-around-the-world-2).

Global Partnership for Education. 2017. *Fund Education: Shape the Future—Case for Investment.* Washington, DC: Global Partnership for Education. Retrieved February 10, 2018 (http://www.globalpartnership.org/sites/default/files/2017-05-gpe-case-for-investment-updated.pdf).

Gramer, Robby. 2017. "Students in Kenya Block Streets with Desks to Protest Their School's Demolition." *Foreign Policy,* May 15. Retrieved February 10, 2018 (http://foreignpolicy .com/2017/05/15/students-in-kenya-block-streets-with-desks-to-protest-school-demolition-education-east-africa).

Hancock, LynNell. 2011. "Why Are Finland's Schools Successful?" *Smithsonian Magazine,* September. Retrieved February 10, 2018 (http://www.smithsonianmag.com/innovation/why-are-finlands-schools-successful-49859555).

Hill, Jason, Christina Stearns, and Chelsia Owens. 2015. Education and Certification Qualifications of Departmentalized Public High School-Level Teachers of Selected Subjects: Evidence from the 2011–12 Schools and Staffing Survey (NCES 2015-814). Washington, DC: Government Printing Office. Retrieved February 10, 2018 (https://nces.ed.gov/pubs2015/2015814.pdf).

Interagency Network for Education in Emergencies. 2012. *Minimum Standards for Education: Preparedness, Response, Recovery.* New York: Interagency Network for Education in Emergencies. Retrieved February 10, 2018 (https://www.unicef .org/eapro/Minimum_Standards_English_2010.pdf).

International Work Group for Indigenous Affairs. N.d. *Indigenous Peoples and Education.* Copenhagen, Denmark: International Work Group for Indigenous Affairs. http://www.iwgia .org/culture-and-identity/indigenous-peoples-and-education

Kamenetz, Anya, Steve Drummond, and Sami Yenigun. 2016. "The One-Room Schoolhouse That's a Model for the World." *Morning Edition* (National Public Radio), June 9. Retrieved February 10, 2018 (http://www.npr.org/sections/ed/2016/06/09/474976731/the-one-room-schoolhouse-thats-a-model-for-the-world).

Kremer, Michael and Alaka Holla. 2009. "Improving Education in the Developing World: What Have We Learned from Randomized Evaluations?" *Annual Review of Economics* 1: 513–542.

McFarland, J., B. Hussar, C. de Brey, T. Snyder, X. Wang, S. Wilkinson-Flicker, S. Gebrekristos, J. Zhang, A. Rathbun, A. Barmer, et al. 2017. *The Condition of Education 2017.* Washington, DC: U.S. Department of Education. Retrieved February 10, 2018 (https://nces.ed.gov/pubsearch/pubsinfo .asp? pubid=2017144).

Meyer, John W., Francisco O. Ramirez, and Yasemin Nuhoglu Soysal. 1992. "World Expansion of Mass Education, 1870–1980." *Sociology of Education* 65(2): 128–149.

Montt, Guillermo. 2011. "Cross-National Differences in Educational Achievement Inequality." *Sociology of Education* 84(1): 49–68.

Musu-Gillette, Lauren, Jennifer Robinson, Joel McFarland, Angelina KewalRamani, Anlan Zhang, and Sidney Wilkinson-Flicker. 2016. *Status and Trends in the Education of Racial and Ethnic Groups 2016*. Washington, DC: National Center for Educational Statistics. Retrieved February 10, 2018 (https://nces.ed.gov/pubs2016/2016007.pdf).

Organisation for Economic Cooperation and Development. 2010. *PISA 2009 Results: Overcoming Social Background—Equity in Learning Opportunities and Outcomes* (Vol. 2). Paris: OECD Publishing. Retrieved February 10, 2018 (http://dx.doi.org/10.1787/9789264091504-en).

Organisation for Economic Cooperation and Development. 2015. *PISA Data Explorer*. Paris: OECD Publishing. Retrieved February 10, 2018 (http://www.oecd.org/pisa/data).

Organisation for Economic Cooperation and Development. 2017. *Economic Policy Reforms 2017: Going for Growth*. Paris: OECD Publishing. Retrieved February 10, 2018 (http://www.keepeek.com/Digital-Asset-Management/oecd/economics/economic-policy-reforms-2017_growth-2017-en#page43).

Patten, Eileen. 2016. *Racial, Gender Wage Gaps Persist in U.S. Despite Some Progress*. Washington, DC: Pew Research Center. Retrieved February 10, 2018 (http://www.pewresearch.org/fact-tank/2016/07/01/racial-gender-wage-gaps-persist-in-u-s-despite-some-progress).

Pew Research Center. 2016. *On Views of Race and Inequality, Blacks and Whites Are Worlds Apart*. Washington, DC: Pew Research Center. Retrieved February 10, 2018 (http://www.pewsocialtrends.org/2016/06/27/on-views-of-race-and-inequality-blacks-and-whites-are-worlds-apart).

Revenga, Ana and Sudhir Shetty. 2012. "Empowering Women Is Smart Economics." *Finance & Development* 49(1). Retrieved February 10, 2018 (http://www.imf.org/external/pubs/ft/fandd/2012/03/revenga.htm#author).

Roser, Max and Mohamed Nagdy. 2016. "Primary Education." *Our World in Data*. Retrieved February 10, 2018 (https://ourworldindata.org/primary-education-and-schools).

Roudi-Fahimi, Farzaneh and Valentine M. Moghadam. 2003. *Empowering Women, Developing Society: Female Education in the Middle East and North Africa*. Washington, DC: Population Reference Bureau. Retrieved February 10, 2018 (http://www.prb.org/Publications/Reports/2003/EmpoweringWomenDevelopingSocietyFemaleEducationintheMiddleEastandNorthAfrica.aspx).

Shrestha, Deepesh. 2013. *Nepal: "I Would Have Gone Hungry without School Meals."* Rome: World Food Programme. Retrieved June 6, 2018 (https://www.wfp.org/stories/'i-would-have-gone-hungry-without-school-meals').

Tembon, Mercy. 2008. "Conclusions and Recommendations for the Way Forward." Pp. 279–305 in *Girls' Education in the 21st Century: Gender Equality, Empowerment, and Economic Growth*, edited by Mercy Tembon and Lucia Fort. Washington, DC: World Bank Group.

United Nations. 2015. *Millennium Development Goals Report 2015*. New York: United Nations. Retrieved February 10, 2018 (http://www.un.org/millenniumgoals/2015_MDG_Report/pdf/MDG%202015%20rev%20(July%201).pdf).

United Nations Educational, Scientific, and Cultural Organisation. 2015a. *Education 2030: Incheon Declaration and Framework for Action towards Inclusive and Equitable Quality Education and Lifelong Learning for All*. Paris: United Nations Educational, Scientific, and Cultural Organisation. Retrieved February 10, 2018, (http://www.unesco.org/fileadmin/MULTIMEDIA/HQ/ED/ED/pdf/FFA_Complet_Web-ENG.pdf).

United Nations Educational, Scientific, and Cultural Organisation. 2015b. *Education for All: Global Monitoring Report*. Paris: United Nations Educational, Scientific, and Cultural Organisation. Retrieved February 10, 2018 (http://unesdoc.unesco.org/images/0023/002322/232205e.pdf).

United Nations Educational, Scientific, and Cultural Organisation. 2016. *Education 2030 Incheon Declaration: Towards Inclusive and Equitable Quality Education and Lifelong Learning for All*. Paris: United Nations Educational, Scientific, and Cultural Organisation. Retrieved February 10, 2018 (http://unesdoc.unesco.org/images/0024/002456/245656E.pdf).

United Nations Educational, Scientific, and Cultural Organisation. 2017. *New Indicators and More Data for Countries in Every Region: Special Focus on New Indicators on Education Spending by Households and Governments*. Montreal, Canada: United Nations Educational, Scientific, and Cultural Organisation. Retrieved February 10, 2018 (http://uis.unesco.org/en/news/education-data-release-new-indicators-and-more-data-countries-every-region).

United Nations Educational, Scientific, and Cultural Organisation/United Nations International Children's Emergency Fund. 2015. *Fixing the Broken Promise of Education for All*. Montreal, Canada: United Nations Educational, Scientific, and Cultural Organisation. Retrieved February 10, 2018 (http://data.unicef.org/wp-content/uploads/2015/12/Global-OOSCreport-Full-web_217.pdf).

United Nations International Children's Emergency Fund. 2016. *Education Is Vital to Meeting the Sustainable Development Goals*. New York: United Nations International Children's Emergency Fund. Retrieved February 10, 2018 (https://data.unicef.org/topic/education/overview).

United Nations International Children's Emergency Fund Afghanistan. 2017. "Education Shaping Lives of Uprooted Children." *Medium*. Retrieved February 10, 2018 (https://

medium.com/@UNICEFAfghanistan/education-shaping-lives-of-children-on-the-move-fb5a94e4debd).

United Nations International Children's Emergency Fund Global Database. 2017. *Education: Current Status and Progress.* Montreal, Canada: United Nations Educational, Scientific, and Cultural Organisation. Retrieved February 10, 2018 (https://data.unicef.org/topic/education/secondary-education).

United Nations International Children's Emergency Fund/United Nations Educational, Scientific, and Cultural Organisation. 2007. *A Human Rights-Based Approach to Education for All.* New York/Paris: United Nations International Children's Emergency Fund/United Nations Educational, Scientific, and Cultural Organisation. Retrieved February 10, 2018 (https://www.unicef.org/publications/files/A_Human_Rights_Based_Approach_to_Education_for_All.pdf).

Wetzel, Deborah. 2013. *Brazil's Quiet Revolution.* Washington, DC: World Bank Group. Retrieved February 10, 2018 (http://www.worldbank.org/en/news/opinion/2013/11/04/bolsa-familia-Brazil-quiet-revolution).

Chapter 6

Appiah, Kwame Anthony. 2005. *The Ethics of Identity.* Princeton, NJ: Princeton University Press.

Association of Religion Data Archives. N.d. *National Profiles: China.* University Park, PA: The Pennsylvania State University. Retrieved February 10, 2018 (http://www.thearda.com/internationalData/countries/Country_52_3.asp).

Ayyar, Varsha and Lalit Khandare. 2012. "Mapping Color and Caste Discrimination in Indian Society." Pp. 71–95 in *The Melanin Millennium: Skin Color as 21st Century International Discourse,* edited by Ronald E. Hall. Dordrecht, The Netherlands: Springer.

Bielefeldt, Heiner. 2016. *Interim Report of the Special Rapporteur on Freedom of Religion or Belief.* New York: United Nations. Retrieved February 10, 2018 (http://www.ohchr.org/Documents/Issues/Religion/A-71-269_en.pdf).

Bird, Karen. 2014. "Ethnic Quotas and Ethnic Representation Worldwide." *International Political Science Review* 35(1): 12–26.

Blinken, Antony. 2016. *Release of the 2015 Annual Report on International Freedom (IRF).* Washington, DC: U.S. Department of State. Retrieved February 10, 2018 (https://uy.usembassy.gov/release-2015-annual-report-international-freedom-irf).

Branford, Sue. 2017. "Quilombolas' Community Land Rights under Attack by Brazilian Ruralists." *Mongabay: News and Inspiration from Nature's Frontline,* August 25. Retrieved February 10, 2018 (https://news.mongabay.com/2017/08/quilombolas-community-land-rights-under-attack-by-brazilian-ruralists).

Canaves, Sky. 2008. "In South Africa, Chinese Is the New Black." *The Wall Street Journal,* June 19. Retrieved February 10, 2018 (https://blogs.wsj.com/chinarealtime/2008/06/19/in-south-africa-chinese-is-the-new-black).

European Parliament. 2016. *The State of Freedom of Religion or Belief in the World: 2015 Annual Report.* Brussels: European Parliament. Retrieved February 10, 2018 (http://www.marketinginnovation.io/wp-content/uploads/2016/06/FoRB_Annual_Report_2015-Final.pdf).

Federal Bureau of Investigation. 2013. *Hate Crime Statistics 2012.* Washington, DC: Federal Bureau of Investigation. Retrieved February 10, 2018 (https://ucr.fbi.gov/hate-crime/2012/resource-pages/about-hate-crime).

Federal Bureau of Investigation. 2014. *Hate Crime Statistics 2013.* Washington, DC: Federal Bureau of Investigation. Retrieved February 10, 2018 (https://ucr.fbi.gov/hate-crime/2013/resource-pages/about-hate-crime).

Federal Bureau of Investigation. 2015. *Hate Crime Statistics 2014.* Washington, DC: Federal Bureau of Investigation. Retrieved February 10, 2018 (https://ucr.fbi.gov/hate-crime/2014/resource-pages/about-hate-crime).

Federal Bureau of Investigation. 2016. *Hate Crime Statistics 2015.* Washington, DC: Federal Bureau of Investigation. Retrieved February 10, 2018 (https://ucr.fbi.gov/hate-crime/2015/resource-pages/abouthatecrime_final).

Federal Bureau of Investigation. 2017. *Hate Crime Statistics 2016.* Washington, DC: Federal Bureau of Investigation. Retrieved February 10, 2018 (https://ucr.fbi.gov/crime-in-the-u.s/2016/crime-in-the-u.s.-2016/resource-pages/hate-crime-statistics).

Finke, Roger. 2013. "Origins and Consequences of Religious Restrictions: A Global Overview." *Sociology of Religion* 74: 1–17.

Finke, Roger and Robert R. Martin. 2014. "Ensuring Liberties: Understanding State Restrictions on Religious Freedoms." *Journal for the Scientific Study of Religion* 53(4): 687–705.

Finke, Roger, Dane R. Mataic, and Jonathan Fox. 2015. *Exploring the Trends and Consequences of Religious Registration: A Global Overview.* Washington, DC: Bureau of Democracy, Human Rights, and Labor and Office of International Religious Freedom. Retrieved February 10, 2018 (http://www.thearda.com/workingpapers/download/Trends%20&%20Consequences%20of_Religious%20Registration%20--%20ARDA%20copy.pdf).

Finke, Roger and Rodney Stark. 1988. "Religious Economies and Sacred Canopies: Religious Mobilization in American Cities, 1906." *American Sociological Review* 53(1): 41–49.

Fisher, Max. 2013. "A Fascinating Map of the World's Most and Least Racially Tolerant Countries." *The Washington Post.* May 15. Retrieved February 10, 2018 (https://www.washingtonpost.com/news/worldviews/wp/2013/

05/15/a-fascinating-map-of-the-worlds-most-and-least-racially-tolerant-countries/? utm_term=.f92241a4ef41).

Gaspar, Lúcia. 2011. *Quilombolas.* Pesquisa Escolar Online, Joaquim Nabuco Foundation. Retrieved February 10, 2018 (http://basilio.fundaj.gov.br/pesquisaescolar_en/index.php? option=com_content&id=1275: quilombolas).

Gordon-Reed, Annette. 2000. "Engaging Jefferson: Blacks and the Founding Fathers." *William and Mary Quarterly* 57(1): 171–182.

Green, P., Thomas McManus, and Alicia de la Cour Venning. 2015. *Countdown to Annihilation: Genocide in Myanmar.* London: International State Crime Initiative. Retrieved February 10, 2018 (http://statecrime.org/data/2015/10/ISCI-Rohingya-Report-PUBLISHED-VERSION.pdf).

Hersher, Rebecca. 2017. *Key Moments in the Dakota Access Pipeline Fight.* Washington, DC: National Public Radio. Retrieved June 6, 2018 (https://www.npr.org/sections/thetwo-way/2017/02/22/514988040/key-moments-in-the-dakota-access-pipeline-fight).

Human Rights Watch. 2013. *Discrimination, Inequality, and Poverty—A Human Rights Perspective.* New York: Human Rights Watch. Retrieved February 10, 2018 (https://www.hrw.org/news/2013/01/11/discrimination-inequality-and-poverty-human-rights-perspective).

Human Rights Watch. 2015. *One Passport, Two Systems: China's Restrictions on Foreign Travel by Tibetans and Others.* New York: Human Rights Watch. Retrieved February 10, 2018 (https://www.hrw.org/report/2015/07/13/one-passport-two-systems/chinas-restrictions-foreign-travel-tibetans-and-others).

Human Rights Watch. 2016. *China: Passports Arbitrarily Recalled in Xinjiang—Heightened Control over Travel for Residents of Uighur Muslim Region.* Retrieved February 10, 2018 (https://www.hrw.org/news/2016/11/21/china-passports-arbitrarily-recalled-xinjiang).

Human Rights Watch. 2017. *China Events of 2016.* New York: Human Rights Watch. Retrieved February 10, 2018 (https://www.hrw.org/world-report/2017/country-chapters/china-and-tibet#d91ede).

Hurst, Daniel. 2017. "Japan Racism Survey Reveals One in Three Foreigners Experience Discrimination." *The Guardian,* March 31. Retrieved February 10, 2018 (https://www.theguardian.com/world/2017/mar/31/japan-racism-survey-reveals-one-in-three-foreigners-experience-discrimination).

Indigenous Peoples Council on Biocolonialism. 2002. *The Kimberley Declaration.* Nixon, NV: Indigenous Peoples Council on Biocolonialism. Retrieved June 6, 2018 (http://www.ipcb.org/resolutions/htmls/kim_dec.html).

Inglehart, R., C. Haerpfer, A. Moreno, C. Welzel, K. Kizilova, J. Diez-Medrano, M. Lagos, P. Norris, E. Ponarin, B. Puranen, et al. (eds.). 2014. *World Values Survey: Round Six—Country-Pooled Datafile 2010–2014.* Madrid: JD Systems Institute. Retrieved February 10, 2018 (http://www.worldvaluessurvey.org/WVSDocumentationWV6.jsp).

International Work Group for Indigenous Affairs. 2016. *The Indigenous World 2016.* Copenhagen, Denmark: International Work Group for Indigenous Affairs. Retrieved February 10, 2018 (https://www.iwgia.org/images/publications/0740_THE_INDIGENOUS_ORLD_2016_final_eb.pdf).

Karmi, Ali. 2011. "The Curse of Being a Hazara." *Ali Karmi blog,* May 28. Retrieved February 10, 2018 (http://alikarimi.ca/tag/hazara-people).

Kristof, Nicholas. 2016. "A Wife's Wrenching Decision." *The New York Times,* January 14, p. A27. Retrieved February 10, 2018 (http://www.nytimes.com/2016/01/14/opinion/in-myanmar-a-wifes-wrenching-decision.html? ref=opinion).

Krogstad, Jens Manuel. 2015. *114th Congress Is Most Diverse Ever.* Washington, DC: Pew Research Center. Retrieved June 6, 2018 (http://www.pewresearch.org/fact-tank/2015/01/12/114th-congress-is-most-diverse-ever).

Lindblom, Alina, Elizabeth Marsh, Tasnim Motala, and Katherine Munyan. 2015. *Persecution of the Rohingya Muslims: Is Genocide Occurring in Myanmar's Rakhine State? A Legal Analysis* (prepared for Fortify Rights). New Haven, CT: Allard K. Lowenstein International Human Rights Clinic, Yale Law School. Retrieved February 10, 2018 (http://www.fortifyrights.org/downloads/Yale_Persecution_of_the_Rohingya_October_2015.pdf).

McCurry, Justin. 2016. "Japan to Conduct Racism Survey after Record Rise in Foreign Residents." *The Guardian,* October 31. Retrieved February 10, 2018 (https://www.theguardian.com/world/2016/oct/31/japan-to-conduct-first-racism-survey-after-record-rise-foreign-residents).

McDonald, Kevin. 2006. *Global Movements.* Malden, MA: Blackwell.

McDuie-Ra, Duncan. 2015. "'Is India Racist?': Murder, Migration and Mary Kom." *South Asia: Journal of South Asian Studies* 38(2): 1–16.

Ministry of Development of North Eastern Region. N.d. *Road Map (only NE).* New Delhi, India: Ministry of Development of North Eastern Region. Retrieved February 10, 2018 (http://www.mdoner.gov.in/node/1260).

Myers, Samuel L., Gao Xiaoyan, and Britt Ceconi Cruz. 2013. "Ethnic Minorities, Race, and Inequality in China: A New Perspective on Racial Dynamics." *Review of Black Political Economy* 40(3): 231–244.

National Association for the Advancement of Colored People. 2017. *Criminal Justice Fact Sheet.* Baltimore, MD: National Association for the Advancement of Colored People. Retrieved February 10, 2018 (http://www.naacp.org/criminal-justice-fact-sheet).

Organization of American States. 2011. *The Situation of People of African Descent in the Americas.* Washington, DC:

Organization of American States. Retrieved February 10, 2018 (https://www.oas.org/en/iachr/afro-descendants/docs/pdf/AFROS_2011_ENG.pdf).

Ouyang, Yusi and Per Pinstrup-Andersen. 2012. "Health Inequality between Ethnic Minority and Han Populations in China." *World Development* 40(7): 1452–1468.

Park, Sara. 2017. "Inventing Aliens: Immigration Control, 'Xenophobia' and Racism in Japan." *Race & Class* 58(3): 64–80.

Pew Research Center. 2015. *114th Congress Is More Diverse than Ever*. Washington, DC: Pew Research Center. Retrieved February 10, 2018 (http://www.pewresearch.org/fact-tank/2015/01/12/114th-congress-is-most-diverse-ever).

Pew Research Center. 2016a. *On Views of Race and Inequality, Blacks and Whites Are Worlds Apart*. Washington, DC: Pew Research Center. Retrieved February 10, 2018 (http://www.pewsocialtrends.org/2016/06/27/on-views-of-race-and-inequality-blacks-and-whites-are-worlds-apart).

Pew Research Center. 2016b. *Trends in Global Restrictions on Religion*. Washington, DC: Pew Research Center. Retrieved February 10, 2018 (http://assets.pewresearch.org/wp-content/uploads/sites/11/2016/06/Restrictions2016-Full-Report-FINAL.pdf)

Pfafman, Tessa M., Christopher J. Carpenter, and Yong Tang. 2015. "The Politics of Racism: Constructions of African Immigrants in China on ChinaSMACK." *Communication, Culture & Critique* 8:540–556.

Planas, Roque. 2014. "Brazil's 'Quilombo' Movement May Be the World's Largest Slavery Reparations Program." *Huffington Post,* July 10. Retrieved February 10, 2018 (http://www.huffingtonpost.com/2014/07/10/brazil-quilombos_n_5572236.html).

Reynolds, Andrew. 2006. *Electoral Systems and the Protection and Participation of Minorities*. London: Minority Rights Group International. Retrieved February 10, 2018 (http://minorityrights.org/publications/electoral-systems-and-the-protection-and-participation-of-minorities-october-2006).

Richardson, Sophie. 2016. *Intimidation as Governance in Tibet: China's Massive Military Drills Send Clear Message*. New York: Human Rights Watch. Retrieved February 10, 2018 (https://www.hrw.org/news/2016/11/25/intimidation-governance-tibet).

Roberts, Crystal. 2012. "Far from a Harmonious Society: Employment Discrimination in China." *Santa Clara Law Review* 52(4): 1531–1560.

Rushing, Elizabeth J. 2017. *How Many Internally Displaced Rohingya Are Trapped Inside Myanmar?* Geneva: Internal Displacement Monitoring Center, Norwegian Refugee Council.

Smedley, Audrey and Brian D. Smedley. 2011. *Race in North America: Origin and Evolution of a Worldview*. Boulder CO: Westview.

Snowden, Frank M., Jr. 1971. *Blacks in Antiquity: Ethiopians in the Greco-Roman Experience*. Cambridge, MA: Harvard University Press.

Sobolewska, Maria. 2013. "Party Strategies and the Descriptive Representation of Ethnic Minorities: The 2010 British General Election." *West European Politics* 36(3): 615–633.

Stokes, Bruce. 2016. *Hostile Neighbors: China vs. Japan*. Washington, DC: Pew Research Center. Retrieved February 10, 2018 (http://www.pewglobal.org/2016/09/13/hostile-neighbors-china-vs-japan).

Telles, Edward. 2007. "Discrimination against Indigenous Peoples: The Latin American Context." *UN Chronicle,* September. Retrieved February 10, 2018 (https://unchronicle.un.org/article/discrimination-against-indigenous-peoples-latin-american-context).

Tuttle, Gray. 2015. "China's Race Problem." *Foreign Affairs* May/June. Retrieved February 10, 2018 (https://www.foreignaffairs.com/articles/china/2015-04-20/china-s-race-problem).

United Nations. 2005. *Permanent Forum on Indigenous Issues: Report on the Fourth Session (16–27 May 2005)*. New York: United Nations Economic and Social Council. Retrieved February 10, 2018 (https://www.humanrights.gov.au/sites/default/files/content/social_justice/international_docs/pdf/unpfii_report_4th_session.pdf).

United Nations Development Programme. 2015. *Human Development Report 2015: Work for Human Development*. New York: United Nations Development Programme. Retrieved February 10, 2018 (http://hdr.undp.org/sites/default/files/2015_human_development_report.pdf).

United Nations High Commissioner for Refugees. 2014. *Global Action Plan to End 2014-24 Statelessness*. Geneva: United Nations High Commissioner for Refugees, Division of International Protection. Retrieved June 6, 2018 (http://www.unhcr.org/en-us/protection/statelessness/54621bf49/global-action-plan-end-statelessness-2014-2024.html).

U.S. Commission on International Religious Freedom. 2016. *USCIRF Annual Report 2016*. Washington, DC: U.S. Commission on International Religious Freedom. Retrieved February 10, 2018 (http://www.uscirf.gov/sites/default/files/USCIRF%202016%20Annual%20Report.pdf).

U.S. Department of Justice. 2016. *Religious Freedom in Focus, Volume 68: December 2016*. Washington, DC: U.S. Department of Justice. Retrieved February 10, 2018 (https://www.justice.gov/crt/religious-freedom-focus-volume-68-december2016#worship).

U.S. Department of State. 2016. *U.S. International Freedom Annual Report 2015*. Washington, DC: U.S. Department of State. Retrieved February 10, 2018 (https://www.state.gov/j/drl/rls/irf/2015religiousfreedom/index.htm#wrapper).

Wood, Peter. 1995. "'If Toads Could Speak': How the Myth of Race Took Hold and Flourished in the Minds of Europe's Renaissance Colonizers." Pp. 27–45 in *Racism and Anti-racism in World Perspective,* edited by Benjamin Bowser. Thousand Oaks, CA: Sage.

Yamamoto, Genzo. 2005. "Race and Racism: Asia." In *New Dictionary of the History of Ideas,* edited by Maryanne Cline Horowitz. Detroit, MI: Charles Scribner.

Zabriskie, Phil. 2008. "Hazaras: Afghanistan's Outsiders." *National Geographic,* February. Retrieved February 10, 2018 (http://ngm.nationalgeographic.com/2008/02/afghanistan-hazara/phil-zabriskie-text).

Zaretski, Robert. 2016. "How French Secularism Became Fundamentalist." *Foreign Policy.* April 7. Retrieved February 10, 2018 (http://foreignpolicy.com/2016/04/07/the-battle-for-the-french-secular-soul-laicite-charlie-hebdo).

Chapter 7

Allen, Erin. 2016. "Remember the Ladies." *Library of Congress Blog,* March 31. Washington, DC: U.S. Library of Congress. Retrieved February 10, 2018 (https://blogs.loc.gov/loc/2016/03/remember-the-ladies).

Altindag, Onur. 2016. "Son Preference, Fertility Decline, and the Nonmissing Girls of Turkey." *Demography* 53: 541–566.

Arab Foundation for Freedom and Equality. 2015. *Campaign Turns Population in Algeria against Homosexuals.* Beruit, Lebanon: Arab Foundation for Freedom and Equality. Retrieved February 10, 2018 (http://afemena.org/2015/08/13/campaigns-turns-population-in-algeria-against-homosexuals).

Borooah, Vani, Quy-Toan Do, Sriya Iyer, and Shareen Joshi. 2009. *Missing Women and India's Religious Demography.* Washington, DC: World Bank. Retrieved February 10, 2018 (https://papers.ssrn.com/sol3/papers.cfm? abstract_id=1498970).

Broadway, Barbara and R. Wilkins. 2017. *Probing the Effects of the Australian System of Minimum Wages on the Gender Wage Gap* (Melbourne Institute Working Paper No. 31/17). Retrieved May 9, 2018 (http://dx.doi.org/10.2139/ssrn.3082004).

Bureau of Labor Statistics. 2017. *Table 39: Median Weekly Earnings of Full Time Wage and Salary Workers.* Washington, DC: Bureau of Labor Statistics, U.S. Department of Labor. Retrieved May 9, 2018 (https://www.bls.gov/cps/cpsaat39.pdf).

Burri, Susanne and Sacha Prechal. 2008. *Gender Equality.* Brussels: European Commission Directorate-General for Employment, Social Affairs, and Equal Opportunities. Retrieved February 10, 2018 (http://ec.europa.eu/justice/gender-equality/files/your_rights/genderequalitylaw2008_en.pdf).

Buvinić, Mayra and Rebecca Furst-Nichols. 2016. "Promoting Women's Economic Empowerment." *The World Bank Research Observer* 31(1): 59–101.

Carroll, Aengus. 2016. *State Sponsored Homophobia 2016: A World Survey of Sexual Orientation Laws—Criminalisation, Protection and Recognition.* Geneva; International Lesbian, Gay,

Bisexual, Trans and Intersex Association. Retrieved February 10, 2018 (http://ilga.org/downloads/02_ILGA_State_Sponsored_Homophobia_2016_ENG_WEB_150516.pdf).

Central Adoption Resource Authority. 2016. *Adoption Statistics.* New Delhi, India: Ministry of Women & Child Development, Government of India. Retrieved February 10, 2018 (http://www.cara.nic.in/resource/adoption_Stattistics.html).

Children's Dignity Forum. 2009. *Peer Research Report on Child Marriage in Tarime District, Mara Region, Tanzania.* Dar es Salaam, Tanzania: Children's Dignity Forum and Foundation for Women's Health Research and Development. Retrieved February 10, 2018 (http://www.cdftz.org/files/Peer%20Research%20edited%20doc.pdf).

Davis, Alyssa and Elise Gould. 2015. *Closing the Pay Gap and Beyond: A Comprehensive Strategy for Improving Economic Security for Women and Families* (Briefing Paper No. 412). Washington, DC: Economic Policy Institute. Retrieved February 10, 2018 (http://www.epi.org/publication/closing-the-pay-gap-and-beyond).

Demirguc-Kunt, Asli, Leora Klapper, Dorothe Singer, and Peter Van Oudheusden. 2014. *The Global Findex Database 2014: Measuring Financial Inclusion around the World* (World Bank Policy Research Working Paper No. 7255). Washington, DC: World Bank. Retrieved February 10, 2018 (http://documents.worldbank.org/curated/en/187761468179367706/pdf/WPS7255.pdf#page=3).

Education GPS. 2015. *Jordan Student Performance (PISA 2015).* Paris: OECD Publishing. Retrieved February 10, 2018 (http://gpseducation.oecd.org/CountryProfile? primaryCountry=JOR&treshold=10&topic=PI).

Equality Now. 2015. *Beijing 20: Ending Sex Discrimination in the Law.* New York: Equality Now. Retrieved February 10, 2018 (https://www.equalitynow.org/sites/default/files/B+20_Report_EN.pdf).

Equality Now. 2016. The World's Shame: The Global Rape Epidemic—How Laws around the World Are Failing to Protect Women and Girls from Sexual Violence. New York: Equality Now. Retrieved February 10, 2018 (https://www.equalitynow.org/sites/default/files/EqualityNowRapeLawReport2017_Single%20Pages.pdf).

European Commission. N.d. *Legislation and Equality Plans.* Brussels: European Commission Directorate General for Justice and Consumers. Retrieved February 10, 2018 (http://ec.europa.eu/justice/gender-equality/gender-pay-gap/national-action/law/index_en.htm).

European Union Agency for Fundamental Rights. 2014. *European Union Lesbian, Gay, and Transgender Survey.* Luxembourg: Publications Office of the European Union.

Federal Bureau of Investigation. 2013. *Hate Crime Statistics 2012.* Washington, DC: Federal Bureau of Investigation.

Retrieved February 10, 2018 (https://ucr.fbi.gov/hate-crime/2012/resource-pages/about-hate-crime).

Federal Bureau of Investigation. 2014. *Hate Crime Statistics 2013*. Washington, DC: Federal Bureau of Investigation. Retrieved February 10, 2018 (https://ucr.fbi.gov/hate-crime/2013/resource-pages/about-hate-crime).

Federal Bureau of Investigation. 2015. *Hate Crime Statistics 2014*. Washington, DC: Federal Bureau of Investigation. Retrieved February 10, 2018 (https://ucr.fbi.gov/hate-crime/2014/resource-pages/about-hate-crime).

Federal Bureau of Investigation. 2016. *Hate Crime Statistics 2015*. Washington, DC: Federal Bureau of Investigation. Retrieved February 10, 2018 (https://ucr.fbi.gov/hate-crime/2015/resource-pages/abouthatecrime_final).

Federal Bureau of Investigation. 2017. *Hate Crime Statistics 2016*. Washington, DC: Federal Bureau of Investigation. Retrieved February 10, 2018 (https://ucr.fbi.gov/hate-crime/2016).

Feldblum, Chai R. and Victoria A. Lipnic. 2016. *Select Task Force on the Study of Harassment in the Workplace*. Washington, DC: Equal Employment Opportunity Commission. Retrieved February 10, 2018 (https://www.eeoc.gov/eeoc/task_force/harassment/report.cfm).

Fetterolf, Janell. 2017. *Many around the World Say Women's Equality Is Very Important*. Washington, DC: Pew Research Center. Retrieved February 10, 2018 (http://www.pewresearch.org/fact-tank/2017/01/19/many-around-the-world-say-womens-equality-is-very-important).

Filkins, Dexter. 2009. "Afghan Girls, Scarred by Acid, Defy Terror, Embracing School." *The New York Times,* January 13, p. A1. Retrieved February 10, 2018 (https://www.nytimes.com/2009/01/14/world/asia/14kandahar.html).

Gilles, Kate and Charlotte Feldman-Jacobs. 2013. *When Technology and Tradition Collide: From Gender Bias to Sex Selection*. Washington, DC: Population Reference Bureau. Retrieved February 10, 2018 (http://www.prb.org/Publications/Reports/2012/sex-selection.aspx).

Girls Not Brides. N.d. *What Is the Impact?* London: Girls Not Brides. Retrieved February 10, 2018 (http://www.girlsnotbrides.org/what-is-the-impact).

Hundal, Sunny. 2013. "India's 60 Million Women That Never Were." *Al Jazeera* (Opinion/India), August 8. Retrieved February 10, 2018 (http://www.aljazeera.com/indepth/opinion/2013/07/201372814110570679.html).

Inglehart, R., C. Haerpfer, A. Moreno, C. Welzel, K. Kizilova, J. Diez-Medrano, M. Lagos, P. Norris, E. Ponarin, B. Puranen, et al. (eds.). 2014. *World Values Survey: Round Six—Country-Pooled Datafile 2010–2014*. Madrid: JD Systems Institute. Retrieved February 10, 2018 (http://www.worldvaluessurvey.org/WVSDocumentationWV6.jsp).

International Labour Organization. 2014. *General Survey of the Reports on the Minimum Wage Fixing Convention, 1970 (No. 131), and the Minimum Wage Fixing Recommendation, 1970 (No. 135)*. Geneva: International Labour Organization. Retrieved February 10, 2018 (http://www.ilo.org/wcmsp5/groups/public/---ed_norm/---relconf/documents/meeting-document/wcms_235287.pdf).

Inter-Parliamentary Union. 2018. *Women in National Parliament*. Geneva: Inter-Parliamentary Union. Retrieved February 10, 2018 (http://www.ipu.org/wmn-e/world.htm).

James, Sandy E., Jody L. Herman, Susan Rankin, Mara Keisling, Lisa Mottet, and Ma'ayan Anafi. 2016. *The Report of the 2015 U.S. Transgender Survey*. Washington, DC: National Center for Transgender Equality. Retrieved February 10, 2018 (https://transequality.org/sites/default/files/docs/usts/USTS-Full-Report-Dec17.pdf).

Kanthak, Kristin and Jonathan Woon. 2015. "Women Don't Run? Election Aversion and Candidate Entry." *American Journal of Political Science* 59: 595–612.

Kantor, Jodi and Megan Twohey. 2017. "Harvey Weinstein Paid Off Sexual Harrassment Accusers for Decades." *The New York Times,* October 5, p. A1. Retrieved May 8, 2018 (https://www.nytimes.com/2017/10/05/us/harvey-weinstein-harassment-allegations.html).

Kimani, Mary. 2012. "Women Struggle to Secure Land Rights." *Africa Renewal* (Special Edition on Women 2012). Retrieved February 10, 2018 (http://www.un.org/africarenewal/magazine/special-edition-women-2012/women-struggle-secure-land-rights).

Klasen, Stephan and Francesca Lamanna. 2009. "The Impact of Gender Inequality in Education and Employment on Economic Growth: New Evidence for a Panel of Countries." *Feminist Economics* 15(3): 91–132.

Kristof, Nicholas. 2017. "As Donald Trump Denies Climate Change, These Kids Die of It." *The New York Times,* January 6, p. SR1. Retrieved February 10, 2018 (https://www.nytimes.com/2017/01/06/opinion/sunday/as-donald-trump-denies-climate-change-these-kids-die-of-it.html?_r=0 (see also video).

Larmer, Brook. 2013. "The Price of Marriage in China." *The New York Times,* March 10, p. BU1. Retrieved February 10, 2018 (http://www.nytimes.com/2013/03/10/business/in-a-changing-china-new-matchmaking-markets.html).

Le Strat, Yann, Caroline Dubertret, and Bernard Le Foll. 2011. "Child Marriage in the United States and Its Association with Mental Health in Women." *Pediatrics* 128(3): 524–530.

Meerkotter, Anneke and Graeme Reid. 2015. "Africa Rulings Move LGBT Rights Forward." *Jurist,* August 4. Retrieved February 10, 2018 (http://jurist.org/hotline/2015/08/meerkotter-reid-no-fault.php).

Milazzo, Annamaria. 2014. *Why Are Adult Women Missing?* Washington, DC: World Bank. Retrieved February 10, 2018 (http://documents.worldbank.org/curated/en/504091468049776276/pdf/WPS6802.pdf).

Nandera, Suzi. 2016. "Building Women's Economic Empowerment." *International Trade Forum,* March, pp. 20–21. Retrieved February 10, 2018 (http://www.intracen.org/news/Building-womens-economic-empowerment).

Nanes, Stefanie. 2015. "The Quota Encouraged Me to Run": Evaluating Jordan's Municipal Quota for Women." *Journal of Middle East Women's Studies* 11(3): 261–282.

National Crime Records Bureau. 2014. *Crime in India.* New Delhi: National Crime Records Bureau, Ministry of Home Affairs. Retrieved May 9, 2018 (http://www.ncrb.gov.in/StatPublications/CII/CII2014/Compendium%202014.pdf).

Newport, Frank. 2011. *Americans Prefer Boys to Girls, Just as They Did in 1941.* Princeton, NJ: Gallup. Retrieved May 8, 2018 (http://news.gallup.com/poll/148187/americans-prefer-boys-girls-1941.aspx).

Nwaubani, Adaobi Tricia. 2017. "LGBT Acceptance Slowly Grows in Nigeria, Despite Anti-gay Laws." *Thomson Reuters,* May 16. Retrieved May 10, 2018 (https://www.reuters.com/article/us-nigeria-lgbt-survey/lgbt-acceptance-slowly-grows-in-nigeria-despite-anti-gay-laws-idUSKCN18C2T8).

Organisation for Economic Cooperation and Development. 2015. *The ABC of Gender Equality in Education: Aptitude, Behaviour, Confidence.* Paris: OECD Publishing. Retrieved February 10, 2018 (http://dx.doi.org/10.1787/9789264229945-en).

Pande, Rohini and Anju Malhotra. 2006. *Son Preference and Daughter Neglect in India: What Happens to Living Girls?* Washington, DC: International Center for Research on Women. Retrieved February 10, 2018 (https://www.unfpa.org/sites/default/files/resource-pdf/UNFPA_Publication-39764.pdf).

Pew Research Center. 2015. *Women and Leadership.* Washington, DC: Pew Research Center. Retrieved February 10, 2018 (http://www.pewsocialtrends.org/2015/01/14/women-and-leadership).

Pörtner, Claus C. 2015. *Sex-Selective Abortions, Fertility, and Birth Spacing* (Policy Research Working Paper No. 7189). Washington, DC: World Bank Group. Retrieved February 10, 2018 (https://openknowledge.worldbank.org/handle/10986/21451).

Potok, Mark, 2011. "Anti-Gay Hate Crimes: Doing the Math." *Intelligence Report,* Winter. Montgomery, AL: Southern Poverty Law Center. Retrieved February 10, 2018 (https://www.splcenter.org/fighting-hate/intelligence-report/2011/anti-gay-hate-crimes-doing-math).

Powell, Catherine. 2017. "#MeToo Goes Global and Crosses Multiple Boundaries." *Blog Post,* December 14. New York: Council on Foreign Relations. Retrieved February 10, 2018 (https://www.cfr.org/blog/metoo-goes-global-and-crosses-multiple-boundaries).

Ramdani, Nabila. 2013. "'After the Wedding, Fear Set In': A Yemeni Child Bride's Story." *The Guardian,* October 1.

Retrieved February 10, 2018 (https://www.theguardian.com/lifeandstyle/2013/oct/01/story-yemen-child-bride).

Raney, Terri, Gustavo Anríquez, Andre Croppenstedt, Stefano Gerosa, Sarah Lowder, Ira Matuscke, and Jakob Skoet (State of Food and Agriculture [SOFA] Team) and Cheryl Doss. 2011. *The Role of Women in Agriculture.* Rome: Food and Agriculture Organization of the United Nations. Retrieved February 10, 2018 (http://www.fao.org/docrep/013/am307e/am307e00.pdf).

Rao, Nitya. 2011. *Women's Access to Land: An Asian Perspective.* Accra, Ghana: UN Women in cooperation with Food and Agricultural Organization of the United Nations, International Fund for Agricultural Development, and World Food Programme. Retrieved February 10, 2018 (http://www.un.org/womenwatch/daw/csw/csw56/egm/Rao-EP-3-EGM-RW-30Sep-2011.pdf).

Ripley, Amanda. 2017. "Boys Are Not Defective." *The Atlantic,* September 21. Retrieved February 10, 2018 (https://www.theatlantic.com/education/archive/2017/09/boys-are-not-defective/540204).

Schwindt-Bayer, Leslie A. 2010. *Political Power and Women's Representation in Latin America.* Oxford, UK: Oxford University Press.

Schwindt-Bayer, Leslie A. and William Mishler. 2005. "An Integrated Model of Women's Representation." *The Journal of Politics* 67(2): 407–428.

Stowe, Marilyn. 2016. *Child Marriage Scandal Rocks Tunisia.* London: Stowe Family Law. Retrieved February 10, 2018 (http://www.marilynstowe.co.uk/2016/12/15/child-marriage-scandal-rocks-tunisia).

Suarez, Paola A. 2017. "Child-Bride Marriage and Female Welfare." *European Journal of Law and Economics* 45(1): 1–28.

Tandon, Sneh Lata and Renu Sharma. 2006. "Female Foeticide and Infanticide in India: An Analysis of Crimes against Girl Children." *International Journal of Criminal Justice Sciences* 1(1).

Tripp, Aili Mari. 2016. "Women's Mobilisation for Legislative Political Representation in Africa." *Review of African Political Economy* 43(149): 382–399.

United Nations. 2013. *Measures Taken and Progress Achieved in the Promotion of Women and Political Participation: Report of the Secretary-General.* New York: United Nations. Retrieved February 10, 2018 (http://www.un.org/ga/search/view_doc.asp? symbol=A/68/184&Lang=E).

United Nations Development Programme. 2016. *Gender Inequality Index.* New York: United Nations Development Programme. Retrieved February 10, 2018 (http://hdr.undp.org/en/content/gender-inequality-index-gii).

United Nations Educational, Scientific, and Cultural Organization. 2015. *Education for All: 2015 Regional Review—Europe and North America.* Paris: United Nations Educational, Scientific, and Cultural Organization. Retrieved February 10,

2018 (https://www.unesco.de/fileadmin/medien/Dokumente/Bildung/2015_UNESCO_EFA_2015_Regional_Review_Europe_and_North_America.pdf).

United Nations High Commissioner for Human Rights. 2015. *Discrimination and Violence against Individuals Based on Their Sexual Orientation and Gender Identity.* New York: United Nations. Retrieved February 10, 2018 (http://www.ohchr.org/Documents/Issues/Discrimination/LGBT/A_HRC_29_23_One_pager_en.pdf).

United Nations Office of the High Commissioner on Human Rights. 2015. *Background Paper on Attacks against Girls Seeking to Access Education.* Geneva: UN Office of the High Commissioner on Human Rights. Retrieved February 10, 2018 (http://www.ohchr.org/Documents/HRBodies/CEDAW/Report_attacks_on_girls_Feb2015.pdf).

United Nations Population Fund. 2012. *Marrying Too Young: Ending Child Marriage.* New York: United Nations Population Fund. Retrieved February 10, 2018 (https://www.unfpa.org/sites/default/files/pub-pdf/MarryingTooYoung.pdf).

United Nations Population Fund. 2017. *New Study Finds Child Marriage Rising among Most Vulnerable Syrian Refugees.* United Nations Population Fund. Retrieved February 10, 2018 (http://www.unfpa.org/news/new-study-finds-child-marriage-rising-among-most-vulnerable-syrian-refugees#).

United Nations Women. 2015. *Progress of the World's Women 2015–2016: Transforming Economies, Realizing Rights.* New York: United Nations. Retrieved February 10, 2018 (http://progress.unwomen.org/en/2015/pdf/UNW_progressreport.pdf).

United Nations Women. 2016. *Facts and Figures: Ending Violence against Women.* New York: United Nations. Retrieved February 10, 2018 (http://www.unwomen.org/en/what-we-do/ending-violence-against-women/facts-and-figures#notes).

Vanneman, Reeve, Sonalde Desai, and Kriti Vikram. 2012. "Son Preference in India." Paper presented at the annual meeting of the Population Association of America, San Francisco. Retrieved February 10, 2018 (http://paa2012.princeton.edu/papers/122478).

Volden, Craig, Alan E. Wiseman, and Dana E. Wittmer. 2016. "Women's Issues and Their Fates in the U.S. Congress." *Political Science Research and Methods* 2016: 1–18.

Wallach, Jessica. 2016. *16 Days of Activism: The Link between Child Marriage and Violence.* Washington, DC: International Center for Research on Women. Retrieved February 10, 2018 (http://www.icrw.org/16-days-activism-link-child-marriage-violence).

Waters, Emily and Sue Yacka-Bible. 2017. *A Crisis of Hate: A Mid Year Report on Homicides against Lesbian, Gay, Bisexual and Transgender People.* New York: National Coalition of Anti-violence Programs. Retrieved February 10, 2018 (http://avp.org/wp-content/uploads/2017/08/NCAVP-A-Crisis-of-Hate-Final.pdf).

Women's Watch. N.d. *Directory of UN Resources on Gender and Women's Issues.* New York: UN Inter-Agency Network on Women and Gender Equality. Retrieved February 10, 2018 (http://www.un.org/womenwatch/directory/UN_entities_10.htm).

World Bank. 2012. *World Development Report: Gender Equality and Development.* Washington, DC: World Bank Group. Retrieved February 10, 2018 (https://siteresources.worldbank.org/INTWDR2012/Resources/7778105-1299699968583/7786210-1315936222006/Complete-Report.pdf).

World Bank. 2013. *Opening Doors: Gender Equality and Development in the Middle East and North Africa.* Washington, DC: World Bank Group. Retrieved February 10, 2018 (http://cmimarseille.org/fr/highlights/opening-doors-gender-equality-middle-east-and-north-africa).

World Economic Forum. 2017. *The Global Gender Gap Report 2017.* Geneva: World Economic Forum. Retrieved February 10, 2018 (http://www3.weforum.org/docs/WEF_GGGR_2017.pdf).

World Watch Monitor. 2016. "Child Marriage Becoming a 'Cloud of Crisis'—N. Nigerian Christian Leaders Warn President." *World Watch Monitor,* November 15. Retrieved February 10, 2018 (https://www.worldwatchmonitor.org/2016/11/4727148).

Zaidi, Batool and S. Philip Morgan. 2016. "In the Pursuit of Sons: Additional Births or Sex-Selective Abortion in Pakistan?" *Population and Development Review* 42(4): 693–710.

Zakaria, Rafia. 2017. "You Can't 'Empower' Us with Chickens." *The New York Times,* October 5, p. A23. Retrieved February 10, 2018 (https://www.nytimes.com/2017/10/05/opinion/the-myth-of-womens-empowerment.html) under the title "The Myth of Women's 'Empowerment.'"

Zillman, Claire. 2017. "Why Trump's Justice Department Just Increased the Stakes in the Fight for LGBT Workplace Rights." *Fortune,* July 27. Retrieved February 10, 2018 (http://fortune.com/2017/07/27/trump-department-justice-gay-workplace-discrimination).

Chapter 8

Aronowitz, Alexis A. 2013. *Human Trafficking, Human Misery: The Global Trade in Human Beings.* Lanham, MD: Scarecrow Press.

Artega, Maia. 2016. "Collaborative Technology Aids Super Bowl Trafficking Sting." *Thorn,* February 22. Accessed February 10, 2018 (https://www.wearethorn.org/blog/collaborative-tech-aids-super-bowl-trafficking-sting).

Associated Press. 2017. "2 Tons of Seized Ivory to Be Crushed in Central Park." *New York Post,* August 3. Retrieved February 10, 2018 (http://nypost.com/2017/08/03/2-tons-of-seized-ivory-to-be-crushed-in-central-park).

Bale, Rachael. 2016. "Demand for Fish Bladder May Wipe Out World's Rarest Ocean Mammal." *National Geographic Wildlife*

Watch, January 10. Retrieved February 10, 2018 (http://news .nationalgeographic.com/2016/01/160111-vaquita-totoaba-poaching-swim-bladders).

Bergman, Charles. 2009. "Wildlife Trafficking: A Reporter Follows the Lucrative, Illicit and Heartrending Trade in Stolen Wild Animals Deep into Ecuador's Rain Forest." *Smithsonian Magazine,* December. Retrieved February 10, 2018 (https:// www.smithsonianmag.com/travel/wildlife-trafficking-149079896)

Bjelopera, Jerome P. and Kristin M Finklea. 2012. *Organized Crime: An Evolving Challenge for U.S. Law Enforcement.* Washington, DC: Congressional Research Service. Retrieved February 10, 2018 (http://novacat.nova.edu:90/ record=b3012768~S13).

Centers for Disease Control and Prevention. 2013. *Sex Tourism.* Washington, DC: Department of Health and Human Services, Centers for Disease Control and Prevention. Retrieved February 10, 2018 (http://wwwnc.cdc.gov/travel/page/sex-tourism).

Colangelo, Lisa L. and Rich Schapiro. 2016. "Two Korean Children Kept as Slaves at Nightmare Queens Home Were Beaten, Forced to Do Hours of Unpaid Labor." *New York Daily News,* January 13. Retrieved February 10, 2018 (http://www .nydailynews.com/new-york/queens/korean-teens-slaves-beaten-queens-home-article-1.2494146).

Daniel-Wrabetz, Joana and Rita Penedo. 2015. "Trafficking in Human Beings in Time and Space: A Socioecological Perspective." Pp. 1–20 in *The Illegal Business of Human Trafficking,* edited by Maria Joao Guia. New York: Springer.

Dearden, Lizzie. 2015. "Isis 'Fatwa' on Female Sex Slaves Tells Militants How and When They Can Rape Captured Women and Girls." *The Independent,* December 29. Retrieved February 10, 2018 (http://www.independent.co.uk/news/world/middle-east/ isis-fatwa-on-female-sex-slaves-tells-militants-how-and-when-they-can-rape-captured-women-and-girls-a6789036.html).

De Compostela, Santiago. 2015. *Council of Europe Convention against Trafficking in Human Organs.* Brussels: Speeches and Op-Eds, Council of Europe. Retrieved February 10, 2018 (http://www.coe.int/en/web/secretary-general/-/council-of-europe-convention-against-trafficking-in-human-organs).

Desai, Radha. 2015. *Landmark Human Trafficking Case Ends with Bankruptcy for Signal International, Inc.* New York: Human Rights First. Retrieved February 10, 2018 (http://www. humanrightsfirst.org/blog/landmark-human-trafficking-case-ends-bankruptcy-signal-international-inc).

Dutch National Rapporteur on Trafficking in Human Beings and Sexual Violence against Children. (2013). *Trafficking in Human Beings* (ninth report of the Dutch National Rapporteur). The Hague, The Netherlands: Dutch National Rapporteur on Trafficking in Human Beings and Sexual Violence against Children. Retrieved February 10, 2018 (https://www .dutchrapporteur.nl/binaries/national-rapporteur-on-trafficking-in-human-beings-and-sexual-violence-against-children.ninth-report-of-the-dutch-national-rapporteur.2014_tcm24-35260.pdf).

Easton, Linda. 2015. "AP's Fish-Slaves Reporting Earns Gold Barlett & Steele Award." *Associated Press,* September 28. Retrieved February 10, 2018 (http://www.ap .org/Content/Press-Release/2015/APs-fish-slaves-reporting-earns-gold-Barlett-Steele-award).

End Slavery Now. 2015. *James Annan.* Cincinnati, OH: End Slavery Now. Retrieved February 10, 2018 (http://www .endslaverynow.org/blog/articles/james-annan).

Europol Public Information. 2011. *Trafficking in Human Beings in the European Union.* The Hague, The Netherlands: Networks in the South-East European Sphere. Retrieved February 10, 2018 (https://www.europol.europa.eu/node/468).

Gettleman, Jeffrey. 2016. "Kenya Burns Elephant Ivory Worth $105 Million to Defy Poachers." *The New York Times,* April 30. Retrieved May 10, 2018 (https://www.nytimes .com/2016/05/01/world/africa/kenya-burns-poached-elephant-ivory-uhuru-kenyatta.html).

Global Tiger Initiative Secretariat. 2013. *Global Tiger Recovery Program Implementation Plan: 2013–14.* Washington, DC: Global Tiger Initiative Secretariat, The World Bank. Retrieved February 10, 2018 (http://admin.indiaenvironmentportal.org .in/files/file/Global%20tiger%20recovery%20program%20 implementation%20plan%202013%E2%80%9314.pdf).

Goyenechea, Alejandra and Rosa A. Indenbaum. 2015. *Combating Wildlife Trafficking from Latin America to the United States.* Washington, DC: Defenders of Wildlife. Retrieved February 10, 2018 (https://defenders.org/sites/ default/files/publications/combating-wildlife-trafficking-from-latin-america-to-the-united-states-and-what-we-can-do-to-address-it.pdf).

Harris, Kamala. 2014. *Gangs without Borders.* Sacramento, CA: Office of the Attorney General, Transnational Organized Crime Special Project Team. Retrieved May 10, 2018 (https:// oag.ca.gov/sites/all/files/agweb/pdfs/toc/report_2014.pdf?).

Havocscope. 2016. *Value of the Illegal Wildlife Trade.* Havocscope: Global Black Market Information. Accessed February 10, 2018 (https://www.havocscope.com/value-of-the-illegal-wildlife-trade).

Hoff, Suzanne. 2011. "The Role of NGOs in Combating Human Trafficking and Supporting (Presumed) Trafficked Persons." Presented February 2011 to Council of Europe, Department of Information Society and Action against Crime, Directorate of Cooperation, Directorate General of Human Rights and Legal Affairs. Retrieved February 10, 2018 (http://docplayer .net/27507821-The-role-of-ngos-in-combating-human-trafficking-and-supporting-presumed-trafficked-persons.html).

ICE Newsroom. 2013. *123 Sexually Exploited Children Identified by HSI during "Operation Sunflower."* Washington, DC: Department of Homeland Security, U.S. Immigration and

Customs Enforcement. Retrieved February 10, 2018 (https://www.ice.gov/news/releases/123-sexually-exploited-children-identified-hsi-during-operation-sunflower).

International Labour Organization. 2015. *Fair Recruitment Initiative: Fostering Fair Recruitment Practices, Preventing Human Trafficking and Reducing the Costs of Labour Migration*. Geneva: International Labour Organization, Labour Migration Branch. Retrieved February 10, 2018 (http://www.ilo.org/wcmsp5/groups/public/---ed_norm/---declaration/documents/publication/wcms_320405.pdf).

International Labour Organization. 2016. *Forced Labour, Human Trafficking and Slavery*. Geneva: International Labour Organization. Retrieved February 10, 2018 (http://www.ilo.org/global/topics/forced-labour/lang--en/index.htm).

Interpol. 2014. *Against Organized Crime: Interpol Trafficking and Counterfeiting Casebook 2014*. Lyon, France: Interpol General Secretariat.

Interpol. 2016a. *Drugs, Criminals, Guns and Gold Intercepted in INTERPOL Border Operation in West Africa*. Lyon, France: Interpol Media Room. Retrieved February 10, 2018 (http://www.interpol.int/News-and-media/News/2016/N2016-022).

Interpol. 2016b. *Operations*. Lyon, France: Interpol. Retrieved February 10, 2018 (http://www.interpol.int/Crime-areas/Environmental-crime/Operations).

Interpol. 2016c. *Projects*. Lyon, France: Interpol. Retrieved February 10, 2018 (http://www.interpol.int/Crime-areas/Environmental-crime/Projects).

Kristof, Nicholas. 2015. "Meet a 21st-Century Slave." *The New York Times Sunday Review,* October 25, p. 9.

La Strada International. N.d. *Justice at Last: Access to Compensation for Trafficked Persons*. Amsterdam: La Strada International. Retrieved February 10, 2018 (http://lastradainternational.org/lsidocs/3234-Justice-at-last.pdf).

Lloyd, Paulette and Beth A. Simmons. 2014. "Framing for a New Transnational Legal Order: The Case of Human Trafficking." Chapter 12 in *Transnational Legal Orders,* edited by Terence Halliday and Gregory Shaffer. New York: Cambridge University Press. Retrieved February 10, 2018 (https://scholar.harvard.edu/files/bsimmons/files/chapter_12_lloyd_simmons_tlos.pdf).

Marshall, Monty G. and Benjamin R. Cole. 2014. *Global Report 2014: Conflict, Governance, and State Fragility*. Vienna, VA: Center for Systemic Peace.

Mathewson, Samantha. 2016. "Poaching and Trafficking: Strategic Steps to Save Animals." *Nature World News,* February 8. Retrieved February 10, 2018 (http://www.natureworldnews.com/articles/19764/20160208/trading-extinction-reducing-illegal-animal-poaching-trafficking.htm).

May, Channing. 2017. *Transnational Crime and the Developing World*. Washington, DC: Global Financial Integrity. Retrieved February 10, 2018 (https://illicittrade.com/reports/downloads/Transnational_Crime-final.pdf).

McDowell, Robin, Margie Mason, and Martha Mendoza. 2015. "AP Investigation: Slaves May Have Caught the Fish You Bought." *Associated Press,* March 25. Retrieved February 10, 2018 (http://www.ap.org/explore/seafood-from-slaves/ap-investigation-slaves-may-have-caught-the-fish-you-bought.html).

MTV EXIT Foundation. 2014. *End of Project Report*. Retrieved February 10, 2018 (http://press.mtvexit.org).

Mungai, Christine. 2015. "The Making of an African Narco-State: Drugs, Crime and Dirty Money Are New Big Threats." *Mail & Guardian Africa,* March 18. Retrieved February 10, 2018 (http://mgafrica.com/article/2015-03-18-the-making-of-a-narco-state).

National Labor Committee. 2003. *Sweatshop Owner Convicted of Human Trafficking*. Pittsburgh, PA: Institute for Global and Human Rights. Retrieved February 10, 2018 (http://www.globallabourrights.org/alerts/sweatshop-owner-convicted-of-human-trafficking).

National Labor Committee. 2008. *The Toyota You Don't Know*. Pittsburgh, PA: Institute for Global and Human Rights. Retrieved February 10, 2018 (http://www.globallabourrights.org/reports/the-toyota-you-dont-know).

Neme, Laura. 2015. "Scope and Scale of Illegal Wildlife Trade in Latin American Growing Rapidly." *Ecuador High Life,* November 5. Retrieved February 10, 2018 (http://ecuador-highlife.com/scope-and-scale-of-illegal-wildlife-trade-in-latin-american-growing-rapidly).

Neuman, William and Azam Ahmed. 2015. "Public Enemy? At Home in Mexico, 'El Chapo' Is Folk Hero No. 1." *The New York Times,* July 18, p. A1. Retrieved February 10, 2018 (https://www.nytimes.com/2015/07/18/world/americas/safe-haven-for-drug-kingpin-el-chapo-in-many-mexicans-hearts.html).

Newcomb, Randy. 2014. *Faith Leaders Pledge to End Modern-Day Slavery*. San Francisco: Humanity United. Retrieved February 10, 2018 (https://humanityunited.org/wp-content/uploads/2014/12/Declaration_004-1-1200x560.jpg).

Northam, Jackie. 2015. "The World's Most Trafficked Mammal Is One You May Never Have Heard of." *All Things Considered,* April 18. Washington, DC: National Public Radio. Retrieved February 10, 2018 (https://www.npr.org/sections/parallels/2015/08/18/432568915/the-worlds-most-trafficked-mammal-is-one-you-may-never-have-heard-of).

Office of the United Nations High Commissioner for Human Rights. 2000. Protocol to Prevent, Suppress, and Punish Trafficking in Persons, Especially Women and Children, supplementing the United Nations Convention against Transnational Organized Crime. Geneva: Office of the United Nations High Commissioner for Human Rights. Retrieved May 10, 2018 (http://www.ohchr.org/EN/ProfessionalInterest/Pages/ProtocolTraffickingInPersons.aspx).

Organization for Security and Cooperation in Europe. 2014. *How to Prevent Human Trafficking for Domestic Servitude in Diplomatic Households and Protect Private Domestic Workers.* Vienna, Austria: Organization for Security and Cooperation in Europe/Office of the Special Representative and Coordinator for Combating Trafficking in Human Beings. Retrieved February 10, 2018 (http://www.osce.org/handbook/domesticservitude? download=true).

Partnership for Freedom. 2016. *Meet the Rethink Supply Chains Finalists.* Retrieved February 10, 2018 (https://www.partnershipforfreedom.org/finalists-in-competition-to-combat-labor-trafficking-announced).

Polaris Project. 2015. *Sex Trafficking in the U.S.: A Closer Look at U.S. Citizen Victims.* Washington, DC: Polaris Project. Retrieved February 10, 2018 (https://polarisproject.org/sites/default/files/us-citizen-sex-trafficking.pdf).

Polaris Project. 2018. *Human Trafficking: Recognize the Signs.* Washington, DC: Polaris Project. Retrieved May 10, 2018 (https://polarisproject.org/human-trafficking/recognize-signs).

Scheper-Hughes, Nancy. 2015. "Human Trafficking in 'Fresh Organs' for Illicit Transplants." Pp. 76–90 in *Global Human Trafficking: Critical Issues and Contexts,* edited by Molly Dragiewicz. New York: Routledge.

Simmons, Beth A. and Daniel J. Hopkins. 2005. "The Constraining Power of International Treaties: Theories and Methods." *American Political Science Review* 99(4): 623–631.

Simpson, Cam. 2013. "An iPhone Tester Caught in Apple's Supply Chain." *Bloomberg Business,* November 7. Retrieved February 10, 2018 (http://www.bloomberg.com/bw/articles/2013-11-07/an-iphone-tester-caught-in-apples-supply-chain#p4).

Stoner, Sarah and Natalia Pervushina. 2013. *Reduced to Skin and Bones: An Updated Analysis of Tiger Seizures from 12 Tiger Range Countries (2000–2012).* Kuala Lumpur, Malaysia: TRAFFIC International.

Surtees, Rebecca. 2015. "The Trafficking of Seafarers and Fishers." Pp. 56–75 in *Global Human Trafficking: Critical Issues and Contexts,* edited by Molly Dragiewicz. New York: Routledge.

Udell, Richard A. 2015. "Operation Crash: Shutting Down the Illicit Trade in Rhino Horns and Elephant Ivory." *United States Attorneys' Bulletin,* September. Washington, DC: U.S. Department of Justice.

United Nations Office on Drugs and Crime. N.d. *Environmental Crime: Trafficking in Wildlife and Timber: Wildlife Trafficking Flows and Prices.* Retrieved February 10, 2018 (http://www.unodc.org/toc/en/crimes/environmental-crime.html).

United Nations Office on Drugs and Crime. 2000. *2000 UN Convention against Transnational Organized Crime.* Vienna, Austria: United Nations Office on Drugs and Crime. Retrieved February 10, 2018 (https://www.unodc.org/unodc/en/organized-crime/intro/UNTOC.html).

United Nations Office on Drugs and Crime. 2010. *The Globalization of Crime: A Transnational Organized Crime Threat Assessment.* Vienna, Austria: United Nations Office on Drugs and Crime. Retrieved February 10, 2018 (http://www.unodc.org/documents/data-and-analysis/tocta/TOCTA_Report_2010_low_res.pdf).

United Nations Office on Drugs and Crime. 2012. *New UNODC Campaign Highlights Transnational Organized Crime as a U.S. $870 Billion a Year Business.* Vienna, Austria: United Nations Office on Drugs and Crime. Retrieved February 10, 2018 (https://www.unodc.org/unodc/en/frontpage/2012/July/new-unodc-campaign-highlights-transnational-organized-crime-as-an-us-870-billion-a-year-business.html).

United Nations Office on Drugs and Crime. 2014. *Global Report on Trafficking in Persons.* Vienna, Austria: United Nations Office on Drugs and Crime. Retrieved February 10, 2018 (https://www.unodc.org/documents/data-and-analysis/glotip/GLOTIP_2014_full_report.pdf).

United Nations Office on Drugs and Crime. 2016. *World Wildlife Crime Report: Trafficking in Protected Species, 2016.* Vienna, Austria: United Nations Office on Drugs and Crime. Retrieved February 10, 2018 (https://www.unodc.org/documents/data-and-analysis/wildlife/World_Wildlife_Crime_Report_2016_final.pdf).

United Nations Treaty Collection. 2018. Depository 12.a.: Protocol to Prevent, Suppress and Punish Trafficking in Persons, Especially Women and Children, supplementing the United Nations Convention against Transnational Organized Crime. New York: Treaty Section, Office of Legal Affairs, United Nations. Retrieved May 10, 2018 (https://treaties.un.org/Pages/ViewDetails.aspx?src=IND&mtdsg_no=XVIII-12-a&chapter=18&lang=en).

Urbina, Ian. 2015. "Murder at Sea: Captured on Video, but Killers Go Free." *The New York Times,* July 20. Retrieved February 10, 2018 (http://www.nytimes.com/2015/07/20/world/middleeast/murder-at-sea-captured-on-video-but-killers-go-free.html? ref=topics&_r=0).

U.S. Agency for International Development. N.d. *Tag Archives for MTV EXIT.* Retrieved May 10, 2018 (https://blog.usaid.gov/tag/mtv-exit).

U.S. Agency for International Development. 2006. *Trafficking in Persons: USAID Response.* Washington, DC: U.S. Agency for International Development. Retrieved May 10, 2018 (http://www.northeastern.edu/humantrafficking/wp-content/uploads/Trafficking_in_Persons_USAIDS_Response.pdf).

U.S. Department of State. 2010. *Trafficking in Persons Report,* 10th edition. Washington, DC: Department of State, Office of the Undersecretary for Civilian Security, Democracy, and Human Rights. Retrieved February 10, 2018 (https://www.state.gov/documents/organization/142979.pdf).

U.S. Department of State. 2014. *Trafficking in Persons Report 2014.* Washington, DC: Department of State, Office of the Undersecretary for Civilian Security, Democracy, and Human

Rights. Retrieved February 10, 2018 (http://www.state.gov/j/tip/rls/tiprpt/2014).

U.S. Department of State. 2015. *Trafficking in Persons Report 2015.* Washington, DC: Department of State, Office of the Undersecretary for Civilian Security, Democracy, and Human Rights. Retrieved February 10, 2018 (http://www.state.gov/documents/organization/245365.pdf).

U.S. Immigration and Customs Enforcement. 2013. *Human Trafficking and Smuggling.* Washington, DC: Department of Homeland Security. Retrieved May 10, 2018 (https://www.ice.gov/factsheets/human-trafficking#wcm-survey-target-id).

van Dijk, Jan and Toine Spapens. 2014. "Transnational Organized Crime Networks across the World." Pp. 7–28 in *Transnational Organized Crime: An Overview from Six Continents,* edited by Jay S. Albanese and Philip L Reichel. Thousand Oaks, CA: Sage.

Welch, Megan. 2015. *Crush and Burn: Destroying Illegal Ivory—A Symbolic Gesture with Real Potential to Stop Wildlife Crime.* Washington, DC: World Wide Fund for Nature. Retrieved February 10, 2018 (http://www.worldwildlife.org/stories/crush-and-burn-destroying-illegal-ivory).

White, Gillian B. 2015. "All Your Clothes Are Made with Exploited Labor." *The Atlantic,* June 3. Retrieved May 10, 2018 (https://www.theatlantic.com/business/archive/2015/06/patagonia-labor-clothing-factory-exploitation/394658).

Wight. Andrew. 2013. "Animal Trafficking in Colombia: A $17M Industry." *Colombia Reports,* November 26. Retrieved February 10, 2018 (http://colombiareports.com/animal-trafficking).

Williams, Phil and Roy Godson. 2002. "Anticipating Organized and Transnational Crime." *Crime, Law and Social Change* 37(4): 311–355.

World Justice Project. 2016. *What Is the Rule of Law: The Four Universal Principles.* Washington, DC: World Justice Project. Retrieved February 10, 2018 (http://worldjusticeproject.org/what-rule-law).

World Wide Fund for Nature. 2016. *For the First Time in 100 Years, Tiger Numbers Are Growing.* Washington, DC: World Wide Fund for Nature. Retrieved February 10, 2018 (https://www.worldwildlife.org/stories/for-the-first-time-in-100-years-tiger-numbers-are-growing? link=btn&utm_campaign=species-tigers&utm_medium=email&utm_source=cons-update&utm_content=160411-ed).

Yachot, Noa. 2015. *VICTORY! U.S. Jury Awards $14 Million to Indian Guest Workers in Historic Labor Trafficking Case.* New York: American Civil Liberties Union. Retrieved February 10, 2018 (https://www.aclu.org/blog/speakeasy/victory-us-jury-awards-14-million-indian-guest-workers-historic-labor-trafficking).

Zhang, Sheldon X. (2012). *Trafficking of Migrant Laborers in San Diego County: Looking for a Hidden Population.* San Diego: Department of Sociology, San Diego State University.

Chapter 9

African Economic Development Institute. N.d. *West Africa and Drug Trafficking.* Los Angeles: African Economic Development Institute. Retrieved February 11, 2018 (http://www.africaecon.org/index.php/africa_business_reports/read/70).

Anders, Holger. 2015. "Expanding Arsenals: Insurgent Arms in Northern Mali." *Small Arms Survey 2015,* pp. 156–185. Retrieved February 11, 2018 (http://www.smallarmssurvey.org/fileadmin/docs/A-Yearbook/2015/eng/Small-Arms-Survey-2015-Chapter-06-EN.pdf).

Axe, David. 2015. "This Is How AK-47s Get to Paris." *The Daily Beast,* November 13. Retrieved February 11, 2018 (https://www.thedailybeast.com/this-is-how-ak-47s-get-to-paris).

Beaubien, Jason. 2011. "Mexican Cartels Spread Violence to Central America." *Morning Edition,* May 30. Washington, DC: National Public Radio. Retrieved February 11, 2018 (http://www.npr.org/2011/05/30/136690257/mexican-cartels-spread-violence-to-central-america).

Berman, Eric G. and Mihaela Racovita. 2015. *Under Attack and above Scrutiny? Arms and Ammunition Diversion from Peacekeepers in Sudan and South Sudan, 2002–14.* Geneva: Small Arms Survey. Retrieved February 11, 2018 (http://www.smallarmssurveysudan.org/fileadmin/docs/working-papers/HSBA-WP37-Peacekeeper-Diversions.pdf).

Broder, Jonathan. 2016. "Isis in Libya: How Muhammar Gaddafi's Anti-aircraft Missiles Are Falling into the Jihadists' Hands." *Independent,* March 11. London: Independent Digital News and Media. Retrieved February 11, 2018 (http://www.independent.co.uk/news/world/middle-east/isis-libya-muhammar-gaddafi-anti-aircraft-missiles-jihadists-a6926216.html).

Buxton, Julia. 2010. "The Historical Foundations of the Narcotic Drug Control Regime. Pp. 61–93 in *Innocent Bystanders: Developing Countries and the War on Drugs,* edited by Philip Keefer and Norman Loayza. Washington, DC: World Bank; New York: Palgrave Macmillan.

Call, Charles T. 2017. *Order from Chaos: What Guatemala's Political Crisis Means for Anti-corruption Efforts Everywhere.* Washington, DC: Brookings Institution. Retrieved February 11, 2018 (https://www.brookings.edu/blog/order-from-chaos/2017/09/07/what-guatemalas-political-crisis-means-for-anti-corruption-efforts-everywhere).

Carapic, Jovana. 2014. *Handgun Ownership and Armed Violence in the Western Balkans* (Issue Brief No. 4). Geneva: Small Arms Survey. Retrieved February 11, 2018 (http://www.smallarmssurvey.org/fileadmin/docs/G-Issue-briefs/SAS-AV-IB4-Western-Balkans.pdf).

Case, Anne and Agnus Deaton. 2017. *Mortality and Morbidity in the 21st Century* (Brookings Papers on Economic Activity). Washington, DC: Brookings Institution. Retrieved February 11, 2018 (https://www.brookings.edu/wp-content/uploads/2017/08/casetextsp17bpea.pdf).

Centers for Disease Control and Prevention. 2016. *Drug Overdose Death Data.* Washington, DC: Department of Health and Human Services, Centers for Disease Control and Prevention. Retrieved February 11, 2018 (https://www.cdc.gov/drugoverdose/data/statedeaths.html).

Chang, Ziv, Kenney Lu, Aaron Luo, Cedric Pernet, and Jay Yaneza. 2014. *Operation Iron Tiger: Exploring Chinese Cyber-Espionage Attacks on United States Defense Contractors.* Tokyo: Trend Labs. Retrieved February 11, 2018 (https://www.erai.com/CustomUploads/ca/wp/2015_12_wp_operation_iron_tiger.pdf).

Chivers, C. J. 2008. "Washington Blocks Exports of Munitions Firm Suspected of Fraud." *The New York Times.* April 4. Retrieved February 11, 2018 (http://www.nytimes.com/2008/04/04/washington/04ammo.html? ref=topics).

Chivers, C. J. 2016. "Facebook Groups Act as Weapons Bazaars for Militias." *The New York Times,* April 6. Retrieved May 10, 2018 (https://www.nytimes.com/2016/04/07/world/middleeast/facebook-weapons-syria-libya-iraq.html).

Chivers, C. J., Eric Schmitt, and Nicholas Wood. 2008. "Supplier under Scrutiny on Arms for Afghans." *The New York Times,* March 27. Retrieved February 11, 2018 (http://www.nytimes.com/2008/03/27/world/asia/27ammo.html).

Clough, Jonathan A. 2014. "World of Difference: The Budapest Convention on Cybercrime and the Challenges of Harmonisation." *Monash University Law Review* 40(3): 698–736; Monash University Faculty of Law Legal Studies Research Paper No. 2015/06.

Commercial Crime Services. 2015. *Social Media Spurs Online Sale of Fake Goods in UK.* London: International Chamber of Commerce. Retrieved February 11, 2018 (https://icc-ccs.org/news/1139-social-media-spurs-online-sale-of-fake-goods-in-uk).

Congressional Committee on Oversight and Government Reform. 2008. *The AEY Investigation.* Washington, DC: U.S. House of Representatives Committee on Oversight and Government Reform Majority Staff Analysis. Retrieved February 11, 2018 (https://democrats-oversight.house.gov/sites/democrats.oversight.house.gov/files/migrated/20080624102358.pdf).

Cook, Thomas R. 2011. "The Financial Arm of the FARC: A Threat Finance Perspective." *Journal of Strategic Security* 4(1): 19–36.

Denis, Elizabeth Gasiorowski. 2014. *Crackdown on Counterfeiting.* Geneva: International Organization for Standardizing. Retrieved February 11, 2018 (https://www.iso.org/news/2014/01/Ref1809.html).

Department of Justice. 2010. *73 Members and Associates of Organized Crime Enterprise, Others Indicted for Health Care Fraud Crimes Involving More than $163 Million.* Washington, DC: Department of Justice Office of Public Affairs. Retrieved February 11, 2018 (http://www.justice.gov/opa/pr/73-members-and-associates-organized-crime-enterprise-others-indicted-health-care-fraud-crimes).

Elfrink, Tim. 2016. "The Real Story behind the Movie War Dogs." *Miami New Times,* August 11. Retrieved February 11, 2018 (http://www.miaminewtimes.com/news/the-real-story-behind-the-movie-war-dogs-8674916).

Entous, Adam, Craig Timberg, and Elizabeth Dwoskin. 2017. "Russians Exploited Social Wedges." *The Washington Post,* September 26, p. A1.

European Union. 2017. *Report on EU Customs Enforcement of Intellectual Property Rights: Results at the EU Border 2016.* Luxembourg: Publications Office of the European Union. Retrieved February 11, 2018 (https://ec.europa.eu/taxation_customs/sites/taxation/files/report_on_eu_customs_enforcement_of_ipr_at_the_border_2017.pdf).

Europol and Office for Harmonization in the Internal Market. 2015. *2015 Situation Report on Counterfeiting in the European Union.* Retrieved February 11, 2018 (https://euipo.europa.eu/ohimportal/documents/11370/80606/2015+Situation+Report+on+Counterfeiting+in+the+EU).

Farge, Emma and Fernando Pereira. 2015. "Guinea Bissau Sidelines Top Brass in Bid to End Coups." *Reuters,* May 19. Retrieved February 11, 2018 (https://www.reuters.com/article/us-bissau-military-insight/guinea-bissau-sidelines-top-brass-in-bid-to-end-coups-idUSKBN0O41XS20150519).

Federal Bureau of Investigation. 2016. *Iranian DDoS Attacks: Conspiracy to Commit Computer Intrusion.* Washington, DC: Federal Bureau of Investigation. Retrieved May 10, 2018 (https://www.fbi.gov/wanted/cyber/iranian-ddos-attacks).

Geers, Kenneth, Darien Kindlund, Ned Moran, and Rob Rachwald. 2014. *WORLD WAR C: Understanding Nation-State Motives behind Today's Advanced Cyber Attacks.* Milpitas, CA: FireEye. Retrieved February 11, 2018 (https://www.fireeye.com/content/dam/fireeye-www/global/en/current-threats/pdfs/fireeye-wwc-report.pdf).

Gesellschaft für Internationale Zusammenarbeit. 2013. *Rethinking the Approach of Alternative Development: Principles and Standards of Rural Development in Drug Producing Areas.* Eschborn, Germany: Sectoral Programme of Rural Development, Federal Ministry for Economic Cooperation and Development, Department of Rural Development, Agriculture, and Food Security. Retrieved February 11, 2018 (https://www.giz.de/de/downloads/giz2013-en-alternative-development.pdf).

Global Intellectual Property Center. N.d. *Getting More than You Bargained For.* Washington, DC: U.S. Chamber of Commerce. Retrieved February 11, 2018 (http://dev.theglobalipcenter.com/wp-content/uploads/documents/15653_GIPCcounterfiet_Fin.pdf).

Global Intellectual Property Center. 2016. *Measuring the Magnitude of Global Counterfeiting.* Washington, DC: U.S. Chamber of Commerce. Retrieved February 11, 2018 (http://www.theglobalipcenter.com/wp-content/themes/gipc/map-index/assets/pdf/2016/GlobalCounterfeiting Report.pdf).

Goel, Vindu and Mike Isaac. 2016. "Facebook Moves to Ban Private Gun Sales on Its Site and Instagram." *The New York Times,* January 29. Retrieved May 10, 2018 (https://www.nytimes.com/2016/01/30/technology/facebook-gun-sales-ban.html).

Greenough, John. 2015. "The 'Connected Car' Is Creating a Massive New Business Opportunity for Auto, Tech, and Telecom Companies." *Business Insider,* February 19. Retrieved February 11, 2018 (http://www.businessinsider.com/connected-car-statistics-manufacturers-2015-2).

Group for Research and Information on Peace and Security. 2016. *Annual Report 2016.* Brussels: Group for Research and Information on Peace and Security. Retrieved February 11, 2018 (http://www.grip.org/sites/grip.org/files/PRESENTATION/RAPPORTS_ANNUELS/RAPPORTS_ACTIVITES/RGA_GRIP_EN_2016.pdf).

Harrell, Erika. 2015. *Victims of Identity Theft, 2014.* Washington, DC: U.S. Department of Justice. Retrieved February 11, 2018 (http://www.bjs.gov/content/pub/pdf/vit14.pdf).

Health Canada. 2017. *National Report: Apparent Opioid-Related Deaths (2016).* Ottawa, Ontario, Canada: Health Canada, Government of Canada. Retrieved February 11, 2018 (https://www.canada.ca/en/health-canada/services/substance-abuse/prescription-drug-abuse/opioids/national-report-apparent-opioid-related-deaths.html).

Hesseldahl, Arik. 2015. "Here's What Helped Sony's Hackers Break In: Zero-Day Vulnerability." *recode,* January 20. New York: Vox Media. Retrieved February 11, 2018 (https://www.recode.net/2015/1/20/11557888/heres-what-helped-sonys-hackers-break-in-zero-day-vulnerability).

Hollingsworth, Alex, Christopher J. Ruhm, and Kosali Simon. 2017. *Macroeconomic Conditions and Opioid Abuse* (NBER Working Paper No. 23192). Cambridge, MA: National Bureau of Economic Research. Retrieved February 11, 2018 (http://www.nber.org/papers/w23192).

Hollis, David. 2011. "Cyberwar Case Study: Georgia 2008." *Small Wars Journal,* January 6. Bethesda, MD: Small Wars Foundation. Retrieved February 11, 2018 (http://smallwarsjournal.com/jrnl/art/cyberwar-case-study-georgia-2008).

Information Security and Artificial Intelligence. 2013. "10 Crazy Cases of Identity Theft." Presented at 2010 International Conference on Information Security and Artificial Intelligence (ISAI 2010), Chengdu, China. Posted October 14, 2013. Retrieved February 11, 2018 (http://www.isai2010.org).

Intellectual Property Crime Group. 2015. *IP Crime Annual Report.* Newport, Wales, UK: Intellectual Property Crime Group Secretariat, Intellectual Property Office. Retrieved February 11, 2018 (https://www.gov.uk/government/uploads/system/uploads/attachment_data/file/461792/ip-crime-report-2014-15.pdf).

Internet Crime Complaint Center. 2018. *Internet Crime Report 2017.* Washington, DC: Internet Crime Complaint Center, Cyber Division, Federal Bureau of Investigation. Retrieved May 10, 2018 (https://pdf.ic3.gov/2017_IC3Report.pdf).

Interpol. 2014. *Countering Illicit Trade in Tobacco Products: A Guide for Policy-Makers.* Lyon, France: Interpol Office of Legal Affairs. Retrieved February 11, 2018 (https://www.interpol.int/Crime-areas/Trafficking-in-illicit-goods-and-counterfeiting/Legal-assistance/Legal-publications).

Interpol. 2017. *Hundreds of Tonnes of Illicit Medicines Seized in African Operation.* Lyon, France: Interpol. Retrieved February 11, 2018 (https://www.interpol.int/News-and-media/News/2017/N2017-107).

Jelsma, Martin. 2011. *The Development of International Drug Control: Lessons Learned and Strategic Challenges for the Future.* Geneva: Global Commission on Drug Policies. Retrieved May 10, 2018 (http://www.globalcommissionondrugs.org/wp-content/themes/gcdp_v1/pdf/Global_Com_Martin_Jelsma.pdf).

Jenzen-Jones, N. R. and Ian McCollum. 2017. *Web Trafficking: Analysing the Online Trade of Small Arms and Light Weapons in Libya.* Geneva: Small Arms Survey, Graduate Institute of International and Development Studies. Retrieved May 10, 2018 (http://www.smallarmssurvey.org/fileadmin/docs/F-Working-papers/SAS-SANA-WP26-Libya-web-trafficking.pdf).

Kaspersky. 2017. *Kaspersky Security Bulletin: Story of the Year 2017.* Woburn, MA: Kaspersky Labs US. Retrieved February 11, 2018 (https://cdn.securelist.com/files/2017/11/KSB_Story_of_the_Year_Ransomware_FINAL_eng.pdf).

Korolov, Maria. 2014. "10 Deadliest Differences of State Sponsored Attacks." *CSO Insider,* December 1. Framingham, MA: CXO Media. Retrieved February 11, 2018 (http://www.csoonline.com/article/2852855/advanced-persistent-threats/10-deadliest-differences-of-state-sponsored-attacks.html).

Lagon, Mark P. 2012. *A Global Trust for Rule of Law* (Policy Innovation Memorandum No. 26). New York: Council on Foreign Relations. Retrieved February 11, 2018 (https://www.cfr.org/sites/default/files/pdf/2012/09/Policy_Innovation_Memo26_Lagon.pdf).

Lawson, Guy. 2011. "The Stoner Arms Dealers: How Two American Kids Became Big-Time Weapons Dealers." *Rolling Stone,* March 16. Retrieved February 11, 2018 (http://www.rollingstone.com/politics/news/the-stoner-arms-dealers-20110316).

Lee, Brianna and Danielle Renwick. 2017. "Mexico's Drug War." *Foreign Affairs,* May 25. Retrieved February 11, 2018 (https://www.cfr.org/backgrounder/mexicos-drug-war).

May, Channing. 2017. *Transnational Crime and the Developing World.* Washington, DC: Global Financial Integrity. Retrieved February 11, 2018 (https://illicittrade.com/reports/downloads/Transnational_Crime-final.pdf).

McAfee. 2005. *Virtual Criminology Report: North American Study into Organized Crime and the Internet.* Santa Clara, CA: McAfee Labs Intel Security. Retrieved February 11, 2018 (http://www.cs.utsa.edu/~bylander/cs1023/mcafee_na_virtual_criminology_report.pdf).

McAfee. 2015a. *McAfee Labs 2016 Threats Predictions*. Santa Clara, CA: McAfee Labs Intel Security. Retrieved February 11, 2018 (http://www.mcafee.com/us/resources/reports/rp-threats-predictions-2016.pdf).

McAfee. 2015b. *McAfee Labs Threats Report: August 2015*. Santa Clara, CA: McAfee Labs Intel Security. Retrieved February 11, 2018 (https://www.mcafee.com/uk/security-awareness/articles/mcafee-labs-threats-report-aug-2015.aspx).

McAfee. 2016. *McAfee Labs Threats Report: June 2016*. Santa Clara, CA: McAfee Labs Intel Security. Retrieved February 11, 2018 (https://www.mcafee.com/us/resources/reports/rp-quarterly-threats-may-2016.pdf).

McDermott, Jeremy. 2013. "20 Years after Pablo: The Evolution of Colombia's Drug Trade." *InSight Crime,* December 3. Retrieved February 11, 2018 (http://www.insight-crime.org/news-analysis/20-years-after-pablo-the-evolution-of-colombias-drug-trade).

Microsoft Secure Blog Staff. 2016. "The Budapest Convention on Cybercrime—15th Anniversary." *Microsoft Secure,* November 17. Redmond, WA: Microsoft Secure Cloud. Retrieved February 11, 2018 (https://cloudblogs.microsoft.com/microsoftsecure/2016/11).

Morgan, Steve. 2017a. *Global Ransomware Damage Costs Predicted to Exceed $5 Billion in 2017*. Sausalito, CA: Cybersecurity Ventures. Retrieved February 11, 2018 (https://cybersecurityventures.com/ransomware-damage-report-2017-5-billion).

Morgan, Steve. 2017b. "Ransomware Damages Rise 15X in 2 Years to Hit $5 Billion in 2017." *Cybersecurity Business Report,* May 23. Framingham, MA: CSO and IDG Communications. Retrieved February 11, 2018 (https://www.csoonline.com/article/3197582/leadership-management/ransomware-damages-rise-15x-in-2-years-to-hit-5-billion-in-2017.html).

Paletta, Damian and Devlin Barrett. 2016. "DNC Hack Prompts Allegations of Russian Involvement." *The Wall Street Journal,* July 25. Retrieved February 11, 2018 (https://www.wsj.com/articles/dnc-hack-fits-pattern-of-past-russian-meddling-1469469535).

Pawlak, Patryk and Gergana Petkova. 2015. *State-Sponsored Hackers: Hybrid Armies?* Paris: European Union Institute for Security Studies. Retrieved February 11, 2018 (https://www.iss.europa.eu/sites/default/files/EUISSFiles/Alert_5_cyber___hacktors_.pdf).

Pennington Institute. 2017. *Australia's Continuing Overdose Tragedy*. Carlton, Victoria, Australia: Pennington Institute. Retrieved February 11, 2018 (http://www.penington.org.au/australias-continuing-overdose-tragedy).

Perlroth, Nicole. 2015. "In Search of Mistakes." *The New York Times,* June 11, p. F6. Retrieved February 11, 2018 (https://www.nytimes.com/2016/06/12/technology/the-chinese-hackers-in-the-back-office.html).

Perlroth, Nicole and Scott Shane. 2017. "How Israel Caught Russian Hackers Scouring the World for U.S. Secrets." *The New York Times,* October 11, p. A9. Retrieved February 11, 2018 (https://www.nytimes.com/2017/10/10/technology/kaspersky-lab-israel-russia-hacking.html).

Persi Paoli, Giacomo, Judith Aldridge, Nathan Ryan, and Richard Warnes. 2017. *Behind the Curtain: The Illicit Trade of Firearms, Explosives and Ammunition on the Dark Web*. Santa Monica, CA: RAND. Retrieved February 11, 2018 (https://www.rand.org/pubs/research_reports/RR2091.html).

Reuters. 2014. "Boko Haram Leader: We Will Sell the Girls on the Market." *The Guardian,* May 6. Retrieved February 11, 2018 (http://www.theguardian.com/world/video/2014/may/06/boko-haram-sell-girls-market-video).

Rogin, Josh. 2010. "The Top 10 Chinese Cyber Attacks (That We Know Of)." *Foreign Policy,* January 22. Retrieved February 11, 2018 (http://foreignpolicy.com/2010/01/22/the-top-10-chinese-cyber-attacks-that-we-know-of).

Saul, Heather. 2015. "Operation ISIS: Anonymous Takes Down Twitter and Facebook Accounts Associated with Extremist Group." *Independent,* February 10. Retrieved February 11, 2018 (http://www.independent.co.uk/life-style/gadgets-and-tech/operation-isis-anonymous-vows-to-take-down-accounts-and-associated-with-extremist-group-10035199.html).

Schemo, Diana Jean. 1998. "Colombian Peasants Seek Way Out of Drug Trade." *The New York Times,* February 28, p. A1. Retrieved February 11, 2018 (https://www.nytimes.com/1998/02/28/world/colombian-peasants-seek-way-out-of-drug-trade.html).

Schindler, Jacob. 2015. "As Counterfeit Hawkers Get Younger and Move to Social Media, Hong Kong Customs Fights Back with AI." *World Trademark Review,* July 29. Retrieved February 11, 2018 (http://www.worldtrademarkreview.com/Blog/detail.aspx?g=3481030a-6d99-423d-bf20-1deda4d898a1).

Schneier, Bruce. 2014. "Sony Made It Easy, but Any of Us Could Get Hacked." *The Wall Street Journal,* December 19. Retrieved February 11, 2018 (http://www.wsj.com/articles/sony-made-it-easy-but-any-of-us-could-get-hacked-1419002701).

Simmons, Beth A. and Daniel J. Hopkins. 2005. "The Constraining Power of International Treaties: Theories and Methods." *American Political Science Review* 99(4): 623–631.

Team Wall Street Survivor. 2015. "Alibaba Stock Price Falls after Counterfeit Goods Scandal." *Wall Street Survivor's Blog,* February 12. Retrieved February 11, 2018 (http://blog.wallstreetsurvivor.com/2015/02/12/alibaba-stock-price-falls-counterfeit-goods-scandal).

United Nations General Assembly. 2014. Outcome of the Fifth Biennial Meeting of States to Consider the Implementation of the Programme of Action to Prevent, Combat and Eradicate the Illicit Trade in Small Arms and Light Weapons in All Its Aspects. New York: United Nations General Assembly. Retrieved February 11, 2018 (https://papersmart.unmeetings .org/media2/3501333/aconf192bms2014wp1rev1.pdf).

United Nations Office on Drugs and Crime. 1959. *The Shanghai Opium Commission.* Vienna, Austria: United Nations Office on Drugs and Crime. Retrieved February 11, 2018 (https://www .unodc.org/unodc/en/data-and-analysis/bulletin/bulletin_ 1959-01-01_1_page006.html).

United Nations Office on Drugs and Crime. 2010. *The Globalization of Crime: A Transnational Organized Crime Threat Assessment.* Vienna, Austria: United Nations Office on Drugs and Crime. Retrieved February 11, 2018 (http://www .unodc.org/documents/data-and-analysis/tocta/TOCTA_ Report_2010_low_res.pdf).

United Nations Office on Drugs and Crime. 2011. *Crime and Its Deadly Link with Terrorism.* Vienna, Austria: United Nations Office on Drugs and Crime. Retrieved February 11, 2018 (https://www.unodc.org/unodc/en/frontpage/2011/March/ crime-and-its-deadly-connection-to-terrorism.html).

United Nations Office on Drugs and Crime. 2013a. *Comprehensive Study on Cybercrime: Draft.* Vienna, Austria: United Nations Office on Drugs and Crime. Retrieved February 11, 2018 (http://www.unodc.org/documents/organized-crime/ cybercrime/CYBERCRIME_STUDY_210213.pdf).

United Nations Office on Drugs and Crime. 2013b. Transnational Organized Crime in West Africa: A Threat Assessment. Vienna, Austria: United Nations Office on Drugs and Crime under responsibility of Regional Office for West and Central Africa. Retrieved February 11, 2018 (http://www.unodc.org/documents/ data-and-analysis/tocta/West_Africa_TOCTA_2013_EN.pdf).

United Nations Office on Drugs and Crime. 2015a. *World Drug Report 2015.* Vienna, Austria: United Nations Office on Drugs and Crime. Retrieved February 11, 2018 (http://www.unodc .org/documents/wdr2015/World_Drug_Report_2015.pdf).

United Nations Office on Drugs and Crime. 2015b. *Study on Firearms 2015: Study on the Transnational Nature of and Routes and Modus Operandi Used in Trafficking in Firearms.* Vienna, Austria: United Nations Office on Drugs and Crime. Retrieved February 11, 2018 (https://www.unodc.org/ documents/firearms-protocol/UNODC_Study_on_Firearms_ WEB.pdf).

United Nations Office on Drugs and Crime. 2017a. "Global Overview of Drug Demand and Supply: Booklet Two." In *World Drug Report 2017.* Vienna, Austria: Division for Policy Analysis and Public Affairs, United Nations Office on Drugs and Crime. Retrieved February 11, 2018 (http://www.unodc .org/wdr2017/field/Booklet_2_HEALTH.pdf).

United Nations Office on Drugs and Crime. 2017b. "Plant Based Drugs: Booklet Three." In *World Drug Report 2017.* Vienna, Austria: Division for Policy Analysis and Public Affairs, United Nations Office on Drugs and Crime. Retrieved February 11, 2018 (http://www.unodc.org/wdr2017/field/Booklet_3_ Plantbased_drugs.pdf).

United Nations Office on Drugs and Crime. 2017c. "The Drug Problem and Organized Crime, Illicit Financial Flows, Corruption and Terrorism: Booklet Five." *World Drug Report 2017.* Vienna, Austria: Division for Policy Analysis and Public Affairs, United Nations Office on Drugs and Crime. Retrieved February 11, 2018 (https://www.unodc.org/wdr2017/field/ Booklet_5_NEXUS.pdf).

United Nations Office on Drugs and Crime. 2017d. *Global Smart Update: Fentanyl and Its Analogues—50 Years On.* Vienna, Austria: Division for Policy Analysis and Public Affairs, United Nations Office on Drugs and Crime. Retrieved February 11, 2018 (http://www.unodc.org/documents/scientific/ Global_SMART_Update_17_web.pdf).

United Nations Office on Drugs and Crime. N.d. a. *Alternative Development—Drug Control through Rural Development.* Vienna, Austria: United Nations Office on Drugs and Crime. Retrieved February 11, 2018 (https://www.unodc.org/pdf/ publications/alt-development_rural-development.pdf).

United Nations Office on Drugs and Crime. N.d. b. *Drugs: Legal Framework: Background.* Vienna, Austria: United Nations Office on Drugs and Crime. Retrieved February 11, 2018 (http:// www.unodc.org/lpo-brazil/en/drogas/marco-legal.html).

United Nations Security Council. 2001. *Resolution 1373 (2001) Adopted by the Security Council at Its 4385th Meeting, on 28 September 2001.* New York: United Nations General Assembly. Retrieved February 11, 2018 (http://www.un.org/en/sc/ ctc/specialmeetings/2012/docs/United%20Nations%20 Security%20Council%20Resolution%201373%20(2001).pdf).

United Nations Security Council. 2014. *Resolution 2195 (2014) Adopted by the Security Council at Its 7351st Meeting, on 19 December 2014.* New York: United Nations General Assembly. Retrieved February 11, 2018 (https://www.un.org/en/sc/ctc/ docs/2015/N1470875_EN.pdf).

Unuchek, Roman and Victor Chebyshev. 2016. "Mobile Malware Evolution 2015." *Kaspersky Security Bulletin,* February 23. Moscow: AO Kaspersky Lab. Retrieved February 11, 2018 (https://securelist.com/analysis/kaspersky-security-bulletin/ 73839/mobile-malware-evolution-2015).

U.S. Customs and Border Protection. 2015. "More than 156,000 Hazardous Toys and 15,000 Counterfeit Knives Seized by CBP Baltimore." *Newsroom,* February 6. Washington, DC: U.S. Customs and Border Protection. Retrieved February 11, 2018 (https://www.cbp.gov/newsroom/local-media-release/ more-156000-hazardous-toys-and-15000-counterfeit-knives- seized-cbp).

U.S. Customs and Border Protection. 2017. *Intellectual Property Rights: Fiscal Year 2016 Seizure Statistics.* Washington, DC:

U.S. Customs and Border Protection Office of Trade, Department of Homeland Security. Retrieved February 11, 2018 (https://www.cbp.gov/sites/default/files/assets/documents/2018-Jan/FY2016%20IPR%20Seizure%20Statistics%20Book%20%28PDF%20Formatting%29_OT.pdf).

U.S. Department of State. 2017. *International Narcotics Control Strategy Report: Volume II—Money Laundering and Financial Crimes.* Washington, DC: Bureau for International Narcotics and Law Enforcement Affairs, United States Department of State. Retrieved February 11, 2018 (https://www.state.gov/documents/organization/268024.pdf).

Verizon. 2015. *2015 Databreach Investigations Report.* Basking Ridge, NJ: Verizon Enterprise Solutions. Retrieved February 11, 2018 (https://iapp.org/media/pdf/resource_center/Verizon_data-breach-investigation-report-2015.pdf).

Victor, Daniel. 2016. "Mac 'Ransomware' Attack Exposes Vulnerability of Apple Users." *The New York Times,* March 7, p. B2. Retrieved February 11, 2018 (http://www.nytimes.com/2016/03/08/business/mac-ransomware-attack-exposes-vulnerability-of-apple-users.html?_r=0).

Volz, Dustin. 2016. "U.S. Government Concludes Cyber Attack Caused Ukraine Power Outage." *Reuters U.S. Edition,* February 25. Retrieved February 11, 2018 (http://www.reuters.com/article/us-ukraine-cybersecurity-idUSKCN0VY30K).

Yagoub, Mimi. 2016a. "Are New Groups Already Moving In on FARC Drug Empire?" *InSight Crime,* August 19. Medellin, Colombia: InSight Crime. Retrieved February 11, 2018 (http://www.insightcrime.org/news-analysis/are-new-groups-moving-in-on-farc-drug-empire).

Yagoub, Mimi. 2016b. "Peru's New Homicide Index Shows Spiking Violence in Drug Port." *InSight Crime,* July 22. Medellin, Colombia: InSight Crime. Retrieved February 11, 2018 (http://www.insightcrime.org/news-briefs/peru-first-official-murder-stats-show-spiking-violence-in-drug-port).

Yagoub, Mimi. 2017. "Drug Seizures in Tumaco Make the 'Pacific Pearl' Colombia's Cocaine Capital." *InSight Crime,* May 29. Medellin, Colombia: InSight Crime. Retrieved February 11, 2018 (http://www.insightcrime.org/news-briefs/colombia-pacific-pearl-drug-seizures-tumaco-cocaine-capital).

Chapter 10

Abubakar, Aminu. 2015. "Grisly Discovery in Nigerian Town: Hundreds of Decomposed Corpses." *CNN World.* Retrieved May 10, 2018 (https://edition.cnn.com/2015/04/28/africa/nigeria-decomposed-bodies-boko-haram/index.html).

Almukhtar, Sarah, Tim Wallace, and Derek Watkins. 2016. "ISIS Has Lost Many of the Key Places It Once Controlled." *The New York Times,* July 3. Retrieved February 11, 2018 (https://www.nytimes.com/interactive/2016/06/18/world/middleeast/isis-control-places-cities.html?_r=0).

Benmelech, Efraim and Esteban F. Klor. 2016. *What Explains the Flow of Foreign Fighters to ISIS?* (NBER Working Paper No. 22190). Washington, DC: National Bureau of Economic Research. Retrieved February 11, 2018 (http://www.nber.org/papers/w22190).

Casey, Nicholas. 2016. "A Former Girl Soldier in Colombia Finds 'Life Is Hard' as a Civilian." *The New York Times,* April 27, p. A1. Retrieved February 11, 2018 (https://www.nytimes.com/2016/04/28/world/americas/colombia-farc-child-soldiers.html).

Center for Systemic Peace. 2014–2017. "Conflict Trends: Assessing the Qualities of Systemic Peace." Vienna, VA: Center for Systemic Peace. Retrieved February 11, 2018 (http://www.systemicpeace.org/CTfigures/CTfig09.htm, http://www.systemicpeace.org/CTfigures/CTfig17.htm, http://www.systemicpeace.org/conflicttrends.html, and http://www.systemicpeace.org/CTfigures/CTfig12.htm).

Center for Systemic Peace. 2017. *State Fragility and Warfare in the Global System 2016.* Vienna, VA: Center for Systemic Peace. Retrieved February 11, 2018 (http://www.systemicpeace.org/warlist/warlist.htm).

Center for Systemic Peace. N.d. *The Polity Project.* Vienna, VA: Center for Systemic Peace. Retrieved February 11, 2018 (http://www.systemicpeace.org/polityproject.html).

Chodorow, Adam. 2015. "Even ISIS Needs to Collect Taxes: Could That Threaten Its Rule?" *Slate,* December 7. Retrieved February 11, 2018 (http://www.slate.com/articles/business/moneybox/2015/12/isis_collects_taxes_and_its_effort_exposes_some_big_weaknesses.html).

Collier, Paul, Lani Elliott, Håvard Hegre, Anke Hoeffler, Marta Reynal-Querol, and Nicholas Sambanis. 2003. *Breaking the Conflict Trap: Civil War and Development Policy.* Washington, DC: World Bank Group; New York: Oxford University Press. Retrieved February 11, 2018 (http://documents.worldbank.org/curated/en/908361468779415791/310436360_2005000701000031/additional/multi0page.pdf).

Collier, Paul and Anke Hoeffler. 1998. "On Economic Causes of Civil War." *Oxford Economic Papers* 50(4): 563–573.

Cunningham, David E., Kristian Skrede Gleditsch, and Idean Salehyan. 2013. "Non-state Actors in Civil Wars: A New Dataset." *Conflict Management and Peace Science* 30(5): 516–531.

Escribà-Folch, Abel, Covadonga Meseguer, and Joseph Wright. 2015. "Remittances and Democratization." *International Studies Quarterly* 59(3): 571–586.

Fjelde, Hanne and Desiree Nilsson. 2012. "Rebels against Rebels: Explaining Violence between Rebel Groups." *Journal of Conflict Resolution* 56(4): 604–628.

Gates, Scott, Håvard Hegre, Håvard Mokleiv Nygard, and Håvard Strand. 2015. *The Consequences of Internal Armed*

Conflict for Development (Part 1). Sweden: Stockholm International Peace Research Institute. Retrieved February 11, 2018 (https://www.sipri.org/commentary/blog/2015/consequences-internal-armed-conflict-development-part-1).

Global Conflict Tracker. 2016. *Nagorno–Karabakh Conflict.* New York: Council on Foreign Relations. Retrieved February 11, 2018 (https://www.cfr.org/global/global-conflict-tracker/p32137#!/conflict/nagorno-karabakh-conflict).

Goldstone, Jack A., Robert H. Bates, David L. Epstein, Ted Robert Gurr, Michael B. Lustik, Monty G. Marshall, Jay Ulfelder, and Mark Woodward. 2010. "A Global Model for Forecasting Political Instability." *American Journal of Political Science* 54(1): 190–208.

Grim, Brian J. and Roger Finke. 2011. *The Price of Freedom Denied: Religious Persecution and Conflict in the 21st Century.* New York: Cambridge University Press.

Guha-Sapir, Debarati, Benjamin Schlüter, Jose Manuel Rodriguez-Llanes, Louis Lillywhite, and Madelyn Hsiao-Rei Hicks. 2018. "Patterns of Civilian and Child Deaths Due to War-Related Violence in Syria: A Comparative Analysis from the Violation Documentation Center Dataset, 2011–16." *Lancet Global Health* 6(1): e103–e110.

Human Rights Watch. 2016. *Nigeria: A Year On, No Word on 300 Abducted Children.* New York: Human Rights Watch. Retrieved May 11, 2018 (https://www.hrw.org/news/2016/03/29/nigeria-year-no-word-300-abducted-children).

International Dialogue. 2016. *A New Deal for Engagement in Fragile States.* Paris: International Network on Conflict and Fragility. Retrieved February 11, 2018 (https://www.pbsbdialogue.org/en).

Kaldor, Mary. 1999. *New and Old Wars: Organized Violence in a Global Era.* Cambridge, UK: Polity.

Kaldor, Mary. 2013. "In Defence of New Wars." *Stability: International Journal of Security and Development* 2(1): art. 4. Retrieved February 11, 2018 (http://doi.org/10.5334/sta.at).

Kibris, Arzu. 2015. "The Conflict Trap Revisited: Civil Conflict and Educational Achievement." *Journal of Conflict Resolution* 59(4): 645–670.

Lister, Charles. 2014. *Cutting off ISIS' Cash Flow.* Washington, DC: Brookings Institution. Retrieved February 11, 2018 (https://www.brookings.edu/blog/markaz/2014/10/24/cutting-off-isis-cash-flow).

Marshall, Monty G. and Benjamin R. Cole. 2009. *Global Report 2009: Conflict, Governance, and State Fragility.* Vienna, VA: Center for Systemic Peace; Fairfax, VA: Center for Global Policy, George Mason University. Retrieved February 11, 2018 (http://www.systemicpeace.org/vlibrary/GlobalReport2009.pdf).

Marshall, Monty G. and Benjamin R. Cole. 2014. *Global Report 2014: Conflict, Governance, and State Fragility.* Vienna, VA:

Center for Systemic Peace. Retrieved February 11, 2018 (http://www.systemicpeace.org/vlibrary/GlobalReport2014.pdf).

Marshall, Monty and Ted Robert Gurr. 2016. *Polity IV Project: Political Regime Characteristics and Transitions, 1800–2013.* Vienna, VA: Center for Systemic Peace. Retrieved February 11, 2018 (http://www.systemicpeace.org/polity/polity4x.htm).

Melander, Erik, Thérése Pettersson, and Lotta Themnér. 2016. "Organized Violence, 1989–2015." *Journal of Peace Research* 53(5): 727–742.

Mobjörk, Malin and Sebastian van Baalen. 2016. *Climate Change and Violent Conflict in East Africa—Implications for Policy.* Stockholm, Sweden: Stockholm University and Stockholm International Peace Research Institute. Retrieved February 11, 2018 (https://www.sipri.org/sites/default/files/Policy-brief%2C-Climate-change-and-violent-conflict%2C-April-2016.pdf).

Newman, Edward. 2004. "The 'New Wars' Debate: A Historical Perspective Is Needed." *Security Dialog* 35(2): 173–189.

Nilsson, Desirée. 2008. "Partial Peace: Rebel Groups Inside and Outside of Civil War Settlements." *Journal of Peace Research* 45(4): 479–495.

Nossiter, Adam. 2015. "Nigeria Says It Rescued Hundreds from Suspected Boko Haram Territory." *The New York Times,* April 28. Retrieved May 11, 2018 (https://www.nytimes.com/2015/04/29/world/africa/nigerian-army-claims-rescue-of-girls-and-women-from-boko-haram.html).

Organisation for Economic Co-operation and Development. 2001. *The DAC Guidelines: Helping to Prevent Violent Conflict.* Paris: OECD Publishing. Retrieved February 11, 2018 (http://www.oecd-ilibrary.org/development/helping-prevent-violent-conflict_9789264194786-en).

Organisation for Economic Co-operation and Development. 2016. *States of Fragility 2016: Understanding Violence.* Paris: OECD Publishing. Retrieved February 11, 2018 (http://www.oecd.org/dac/states-of-fragility-2016-9789264267213-en.htm).

Pettersson, Therese and Peter Wallensteen. 2015. "Armed Conflicts, 1946–2014." *Journal of Peace Research* 52(4): 536–550.

Pinker, Steven and Juan Manuel Santos. 2016. "Colombia's Milestone in World Peace." *The New York Times,* August 26, p. A17. Retrieved February 11, 2018 (https://www.nytimes.com/2016/08/26/opinion/colombias-milestone-in-world-peace.html).

Rice, Susan P. and Stewart Patrick. 2008. *Index of State Weakness in the Developing World.* Washington, DC: Brookings Institution.

Searcey, Dionne. 2018. "Kidnapped as Schoolgirls by Boko Haram; Here They Are Now." *The New York Times,* April 11. Retrieved June 10, 2018 (https://www.nytimes.com/inter

active/2018/04/11/world/africa/nigeria-boko-haram-girls.html).

Singer, J. David and Melvin Small. 1994. *Correlates of War Project: International and Civil War Data, 1816–1992* [computer file]. Ann Arbor, MI: Inter-University Consortium for Political and Social Research.

Slaughter, Anne-Marie. 2011. *The End of Twentieth-Century Warfare.* Washington, DC: Atlantic Council. Retrieved February 11, 2018 (http://www.atlanticcouncil.org/blogs/new-atlanticist/the-end-of-twentiethcentury-warfare).

Small, Melvin and J. David Singer. 1982. *Resort to Arms: International and Civil War, 1816–1980.* Beverly Hills, CA: Sage.

Smith, Dan. 1994. *War, Peace, and Third World Development* (Occasional Paper No. 16). Oslo, Norway: International Peace Institute. Retrieved February 11, 2018 (http://hdr.undp.org/en/content/war-peace-and-third-world-development).

Taranco, Oscar Fernandez. 2016. *A New Deal or a New Global Partnership for Conflict-Affected States?* Washington, DC: Brookings Institution. Retrieved February 11, 2018 (https://www.brookings.edu/blog/africa-in-focus/2016/03/30/a-new-deal-or-a-new-global-partnership-for-conflict-affected-states).

United Nations. 2013. *The Six Grave Violations against Children during Armed Conflict: The Legal Foundation.* New York: United Nations Office of the Special Representative of the Secretary-General for Children and Armed Conflict. Retrieved February 11, 2018 (https://childrenandarmedconflict.un.org/publications/WorkingPaper-1_SixGraveViolationsLegalFoundation.pdf).

United Nations International Children's Emergency Fund. 2016a. *Children in War and Conflict: Fast Facts.* New York: United Nations International Children's Emergency Fund. Retrieved February 11, 2018 (https://www.unicefusa.org/mission/emergencies/conflict).

United Nations International Children's Emergency Fund. 2016b. *145 Children Released [by] Armed Groups in South Sudan.* New York: United Nations International Children's Emergency Fund. Retrieved February 11, 2018 (https://www.unicef.org/media/media_92960.html).

United Nations International Children's Emergency Fund. 2016c. *Nigeria Regional Conflict: 10-Fold Increase in Number of Children Used in "Suicide" Attacks.* New York: United Nations International Children's Emergency Fund. Retrieved February 11, 2018 (http://www.unicef.org/infobycountry/media_90827.html).

White, Jeffrey B. 2008. *Some Thoughts on Irregular Warfare.* Washington, DC: Central Intelligence Agency Center for the Study of Intelligence. Retrieved February 11, 2018 (https://www.cia.gov/library/center-for-the-study-of-intelligence/csi-publications/csi-studies/studies/96unclass/iregular.htm).

Williams, Dodeye Uduak. 2014. "Relevance of Mary Kaldor's 'New Wars' Thesis in the 21st Century." *Journal of Law and Conflict Resolution* 6(5): 84–88.

Witte, Griff, Sudarsan Raghavan, and James McAuley. 2016. "Flow of Foreign Fighters Plummets as Islamic State Loses Its Edge." *The Washington Post,* September 9. Retrieved February 11, 2018 (https://www.washingtonpost.com/world/europe/flow-of-foreign-fighters-plummets-as-isis-loses-its-edge/2016/09/09/ed3e0dda-751b-11e6-9781-49e591781754_story.html? utm_term=.f177ac60bd4a).

Chapter 11

Achvarina, Vera and Simon F. Reich. 2006. "'No Place to Hide, Refugees, Displaced Persons, and the Recruitment of Child Soldiers." *International Security* 31(1): 127–164.

Al Jazeera. 2008. *Afghanistan's Refugee Challenge.* Doha, Qatar: Al Jazeera Media Network. Retrieved February 11, 2018 (http://www.aljazeera.com/focus/2008/08/2008812135027967466.html).

al-Miqdad, Faisal. N.d. "Iraqi refugees in Syria." *Forced Migration Review Special Issue.* Oxford, UK: Refugee Studies Centre, Department of International Development, University of Oxford. Retrieved May 11, 2018 (http://www.fmreview.org/sites/fmr/files/FMRdownloads/en/FMRpdfs/Iraq/08.pdf).

Americas Bureau, United Nations High Commissioner for Refugees. 2017. *The Comprehensive Regional Protection and Solutions Framework.* Geneva: United Nations High Commissioner for Refugees. Retrieved February 11, 2018 (http://www.unhcr.org/59d1f3594.pdf).

Amnesty International. 2016. *Pakistan: Deportation of Iconic "Afghan Girl" Is a Grave Injustice.* New York: Amnesty International. Retrieved February 11, 2018 (https://www.amnesty.org/en/latest/news/2016/11/deportation-of-iconic-afghan-girl-is-a-grave-injustice).

BBC News. 2016. *Migrant Crisis: Migration to Europe Explained in Seven Charts.* Retrieved February 11, 2018 (http://www.bbc.com/news/world-europe-34131911).

Blagrave, Patrick, Sweta Saxena, and Esteban Vesperoni. 2016. "Spillovers from China's Transition and from Migration." Pp. 171–202 in *Subdued Demand: Symptoms and Remedies.* Washington, DC: International Monetary Fund. Retrieved February 11, 2018 (http://www.imf.org/external/pubs/ft/weo/2016/02/pdf/c4.pdf).

Bruns, Bettina and Helga Zichner. 2016. "That's What Friends Are For—External Migration Management of the European Union in Its Eastern Neighborhood." Pp. 151–176 in *European Engagement under Review: Exporting Values, Rules, and Practices to the Post-Soviet Space,* edited by Vera Axyonova. Stuttgart, Germany: Fulda University of Applied Sciences.

Coles, Isabel and Shadia Nasralla. 2015. "The Migrant Truck Tragedy: 'I Feel Really Bad about What Happened.'" *Reuters*, November 12. Retrieved February 11, 2018 (http://www.reuters.com/investigates/special-report/europe-migrants-truck/#slideshow-truck).

Collett, Elizabeth. 2016. *The Paradox of the EU–Turkey Refugee Deal.* Washington, DC: Migration Policy Institute. Retrieved February 11, 2018 (http://www.migrationpolicy.org/news/paradox-eu-turkey-refugee-deal).

Connor, Phillip and Jens Manuel Krogstad. 2016. *Fewer Refugees Entering Europe than in 2015, but Asylum Backlog Still Growing.* Washington, DC: Pew Research Center. Retrieved February 11, 2018 (http://www.pewresearch.org/fact-tank/2016/09/06/fewer-refugees-entering-europe-than-in-2015-but-asylum-backlog-still-growing).

Cornish, Stephen. 2016. *We Must Uphold Promises to Global Refugee Community.* Toronto, Ontario, Canada: Médicines Sans Frontières. Retrieved February 11, 2018 (https://www.medecinssansfrontieres.ca/node/2922).

Das Shrestha, Deepesh. 2015. *Resettlement of Bhutanese Refugees Surpasses 100,000 Mark.* Geneva: United Nations High Commissioner for Refugees. Retrieved February 11, 2018 (http://www.unhcr.org/en-us/news/latest/2015/11/564dded46/resettlement-bhutanese-refugees-surpasses-100000-mark.html).

Development by Training Services. 2014. *Field Evaluation of Local Integration of Former Refugees in Zambia* (prepared for Office of Policy and Resource Planning, Bureau of Population, Refugees and Migration, U.S. Department of State). Retrieved February 11, 2018 (http://www.state.gov/documents/organization/235057.pdf).

Diop, Makhtar. 2016. *Africa: What Can We Learn from Africa's Approach to Forced Displacement?* Cologny, Switzerland: World Economic Forum. Retrieved February 11, 2018 (https://www.weforum.org/agenda/2016/06/what-can-we-learn-from-africas-approach-to-forced-displacement).

Ferris, Elizabeth. 2008. "Assessing the Impact of the Principles: An Unfinished Task." *Forced Migration Review.* Oxford, UK: Refugee Studies Centre, Oxford Department of International Development, University of Oxford. Retrieved February 11, 2018 (http://www.fmreview.org/GuidingPrinciples10/farris.html).

Getanda, Elijah Mironga, Chris Papadopoulos, and Hala Evans. 2015. "The Mental Health, Quality of Life and Life Satisfaction of Internally Displaced Persons Living in Nakuru County, Kenya." *BMC Public Health* 15: 755.

Hiskey, Jonathan T., Abby Córdova, Diana Orcés, and Mary Fran Malone. 2016. *Understanding the Central American Refugee Crisis.* Washington, DC: American Immigration Council. Retrieved February 11, 2018 (https://www.americanimmigrationcouncil.org/research/understanding-central-american-refugee-crisis).

Højen, Louise. 2015. *Colombia's "Invisible Crisis": Internally Displaced Persons.* Washington, DC: Council on Hemispheric Affairs. Retrieved February 11, 2018 (http://www.coha.org/colombias-invisible-crisis-internally-displaced-persons).

Human Rights Watch. 2016. *Kenya: Involuntary Refugee Returns to Somalia.* New York: Human Rights Watch. Retrieved February 11, 2018 (https://www.hrw.org/news/2016/09/14/kenya-involuntary-refugee-returns-somalia).

Hussien, Asad. 2016. "I Grew Up in the World's Biggest Refugee Camp—What Happens When It Closes?" *The Guardian,* September 23. Retrieved February 11, 2018 (https://www.theguardian.com/world/2016/sep/23/kenya-dadaab-refugee-camp-what-happens-when-it-closes-asad-hussein).

Igielnik, Ruth and Jens Manuel Krogstad. 2017. "Where Refugees to the U.S. Come From." *FACTANK,* February 3. Washington, DC: Pew Research Center. Retrieved February 11, 2018 (http://www.pewresearch.org/fact-tank/2016/06/17/where-refugees-to-the-u-s-come-from).

Internal Displacement Monitoring Center. 2016. *Global Report on Internal Displacement.* Oslo: Norwegian Refugee Council. Retrieved February 11, 2018 (http://internal-displacement.org/assets/publications/2016/2016-global-report-internal-displacement-IDMC.pdf).

Internal Displacement Monitoring Center. 2017. *Africa Report on Internal Displacement.* Oslo: Norwegian Refugee Council. Retrieved May 11, 2018 (https://reliefweb.int/sites/reliefweb.int/files/resources/20171206-Africa-report-2017-web.pdf).

Internal Displacement Monitoring Center. 2018. *Global Report on Internal Displacement.* Oslo: Norwegian Refugee Council. Retrieved May 11, 2018 (http://www.internal-displacement.org/sites/default/files/publications/documents/201805-final-GRID-2018_0.pdf).

International Labour Organization. 2013. *Assessment of Livelihood Opportunities for Returnees/Internally Displaced Persons and Host Communities in Afghanistan.* Kabul, Afghanistan: UNHCR Kabul. Retrieved February 11, 2018 (http://www.ilo.org/wcmsp5/groups/public/---asia/---ro-bangkok/---ilo-islamabad/documents/publication/wcms_213661.pdf).

Kallick, David Dyssegaard and Silva Mathema. 2016. *Refugee Integration in the United States.* Washington, DC: Center for American Progress. Retrieved February 11, 2018 (https://cdn.americanprogress.org/wp-content/uploads/2016/06/15112912/refugeeintegration.pdf).

Lima, Mauricio and Adam Nossiter. 2016. "'We Are Ready to Leave': France Clears Out Calais 'Jungle.'" *The New York Times,* October 24. Retrieved February 11, 2018 (http://www.nytimes.com/2016/10/25/world/europe/we-are-ready-to-leave-france-clears-out-the-jungle.html).

Millman, Joel. 2014. "The Battle for Gay Asylum: Why Sexual Minorities Have an Inside Track to a U.S. Green Card." *The

Wall Street Journal, June 13. Retrieved February 11, 2018 (http://www.wsj.com/articles/why-sexual-minorities-have-an-inside-track-to-a-u-s-green-card-1402676258).

Mørch, Maximillian. 2016. "Bhutan's Dark Secret: The Lhotshampa Expulsion." *The Diplomat,* September 21. Retrieved February 11, 2018 (https://thediplomat.com/2016/09/bhutans-dark-secret-the-lhotshampa-expulsion).

Nordland, Rod. 2016a. "An Afghan Boy Returns to a Land Nothing Like Home." *The New York Times,* November 12. Retrieved February 11, 2018 (https://www.nytimes.com/2016/11/13/world/asia/a-deported-afghan-boy-returns-to-a-land-nothing-like-home.html).

Nordland, Rod. 2016b. "'Sharbat Gula, Famed 'Afghan Girl,' Is Welcomed Back to Afghanistan." *The New York Times,* November 9. Retrieved February 11, 2018 (https://www.nytimes.com/2016/11/10/world/asia/afghan-girl-sharbat-gula-afghanistan-pakistan.html).

Norwegian Refugee Council. 2016. *Disaster and Climate Change.* Oslo: Norwegian Refugee Council. Retrieved February 11, 2018 (https://www.nrc.no/what-we-do/speaking-up-for-rights/climate-change).

Nossiter, Adam. 2016. "Paris Is the New Calais, with Scores of Migrants Arriving Daily." *The New York Times,* November 3. Retrieved May 11, 2018 (https://www.nytimes.com/2016/11/04/world/europe/paris-migrants-refugees.html).

Oeppen, Ceri. 2016. "'Leaving Afghanistan! Are You Sure?' European Efforts to Deter Potential Migrants through Information Campaigns." *Human Geography* 9(2): 57–68.

Office of Immigration Statistics. 2018. *Annual Flow Report: Refugees and Asylees 2016.* Washington, DC: Office of Immigration Statistics, Department of Homeland Security. Retrieved February 11, 2018 (https://www.dhs.gov/sites/default/files/publications/Refugees_Asylees_2016.pdf).

Organisation for Economic Cooperation and Development. 2016. *International Migration Outlook 2016.* Retrieved February 11, 2018 (http://www.oecd-ilibrary.org/social-issues-migration-health/international-migration-outlook-2016_migr_outlook-2016-en;jsessionid=1r8l1op5f4btw.x-oecd-live-03).

Pan, Laing. 2016. "Why China Isn't Hosting Syrian Refugees." *Foreign Policy,* February 26. Retrieved February 11, 2018 (http://foreignpolicy.com/2016/02/26/china-host-syrian-islam-refugee-crisis-migrant).

Pew Research Center. 2016. *The Shifting Origins of Refugees to the U.S. over Time.* Washington, DC: Pew Research Center. Retrieved February 11, 2018 (http://www.pewresearch.org/ft_16-09-14_refugeeskeyfacts_originsovertime).

Pillay, Navi. 2009. *Refugees and Migrants Are Widely Discriminated Against, Including in Rich Countries.* Geneva: United Nations High Commissioner for Refugees. Retrieved February 11, 2018 (http://www.unis.unvienna.org/unis/press-rels/2009/unisinf348.html).

Rasmussen, Sune Engel. 2016. "EU Signs Deal to Deport Unlimited Numbers of Afghan Asylum Seekers." *The Guardian,* October 3. Retrieved May 11, 2018 (https://www.theguardian.com/global-development/2016/oct/03/eu-european-union-signs-deal-deport-unlimited-numbers-afghan-asylum-seekers-afghanistan)

Reeves, Philip. 2016. "Feeling Unwanted in Germany, Some Afghan Migrants Head Home." *All Things Considered,* March 9. Washington, DC: National Public Radio. Retrieved February 11, 2018 (https://www.npr.org/sections/parallels/2016/03/09/469647719/feeling-unwanted-in-germany-some-afghan-migrants-head-home).

Sang-Hun, Choe. 2016. "Syrians Seeking Asylum in South Korea Find Only a Cold Shoulder." *The New York Times,* August 5, p. A4. Retrieved February 11, 2018 (https://www.nytimes.com/2016/08/06/world/asia/korea-refugees-syria.html).

Schmeidl, Susanne. 2009. "Repatriation to Afghanistan: Durable Solution or Responsibility Shifting?" *Forced Migration Review* 33: 20–22. Oxford, UK: Refugee Studies Center, University of Oxford. Retrieved February 11, 2018 (http://www.fmreview.org/sites/fmr/files/FMRdownloads/en/protracted/schmeidl.pdf).

Semple, Kirk. 2016. "Fleeing Gangs, Central American Families Surge toward U.S." *The New York Times,* November 12, p. A5. Retrieved February 11, 2018 (https://www.nytimes.com/2016/11/13/world/americas/fleeing-gangs-central-american-families-surge-toward-us.html).

Sharp, Jeremy. 2016. *Yemen's Civil War and Regional Intervention.* Washington, DC: Congressional Research Service. Retrieved February 11, 2018 (https://fas.org/sgp/crs/mideast/R43960.pdf).

Steer, Naomi. 2011. *A Sliver of Hope amid the Gloom.* UNHCR: Australia for United Nations High Commissioner for Refugees. Retrieved February 11, 2018 (http://blog.unrefugees.org.au/2011_07_01_archive.html).

United Nations. 2016. *International Migration Report Highlights.* New York: United Nations, Department of Economic and Social Affairs. Retrieved May 12, 2018 (http://www.un.org/en/development/desa/population/migration/publications/migrationreport/docs/MigrationReport2015_Highlights.pdf).

United Nations High Commissioner for Refugees. 2002. *Refugees and Others of Concern to UNHCR: 2000 Statistical Overview.* Geneva: United Nations High Commissioner for Refugees. Retrieved February 11, 2018 (http://www.Unhcr.Org/3d4e7bec5).

United Nations High Commissioner for Refugees. 2011. *Global Trends 2010.* Geneva: United Nations High Commissioner for Refugees. Retrieved February 11, 2018 (http://www.unhcr .org/4dfa11499.pdf).

United Nations High Commissioner for Refugees. 2015. *UNHCR Refugee Resettlement Trends 2015*. Geneva: United Nations High Commissioner for Refugees. Retrieved February 11, 2018 (http://www.unhcr.org/559ce97f9).

United Nations High Commissioner for Refugees. 2016a. *Global Trends: Forced Displacement in 2015*. Geneva: United Nations High Commissioner for Refugees. Retrieved February 11, 2018 (http://www.unhcr.org/en-us/statistics/unhcrstats/576408cd7/ unhcr-global-trends-2015.html; http://www.unhcr.org/globaltren ds/2015-GlobalTrends-annex-tables.zip).

United Nations High Commissioner for Refugees. 2016b. *Regional Response to the Northern Triangle of Central America Situation*. Geneva: United Nations High Commissioner for Refugees. Retrieved February 11, 2018 (http://www.refworld .org/docid/57fe2a944.html).

United Nations High Commissioner for Refugees. 2016c. *UNHCR Urges Governments: People Fleeing War to Be Considered as Refugees*. Geneva: United Nations High Commissioner for Refugees. Retrieved February 11, 2018 (http://www.unhcr .org/en-us/news/briefing/2016/12/584141ed4/unhcr-urges-governments-people-fleeing-war-considered-refugees.html

United Nations High Commissioner for Refugees. 2017. *Global Trends: Forced Displacement in 2016*. Geneva: United Nations High Commissioner for Refugees. Retrieved February 11, 2018 (http://www.unhcr.org/5943e8a34.pdf).

U.S. Customs and Border Protection. 2016. United States Border Patrol Southwest Family Unit Subject and Unaccompanied Alien Children Apprehensions Fiscal Year 2016: Statement by Secretary Johnson on Southwest Border Security. Washington, DC: Department of Homeland Security. Retrieved February 11, 2018 (https://www.cbp.gov/newsroom/ stats/southwest-border-unaccompanied-children/fy-2016).

U.S. Department of State. 2017. *Fact Sheet: Fiscal Year 2016 Refugee Admissions*. Washington, DC: U.S. Department of State Bureau of Population, Refugees, and Migration. Retrieved February 11, 2018 (https://www.state.gov/j/prm/releases/ factsheets/2017/266365.htm).

U.S. Immigration and Customs Enforcement. N.d. *FY 2015 ICE Immigration Removals*. Washington, DC: Office of Immigration and Customs Enforcement. Retrieved February 11, 2018 (https:// www.ice.gov/removal-statistics#wcm-survey-target-id).

Vongkiatkajorn, Kanyakrit. 2015. "The Year Southeast Asia Faced Its Own Refugee Crisis." *Vice News,* December 27. Retrieved February 11, 2018 (https://news.vice.com/article/ the-year-southeast-asia-faced-its-own-refugee-crisis).

Wararich, Omar. 2014. *Pakistan: Afghan Refugees Still Languish in Limbo*. New York: Amnesty International.

Retrieved February 11, 2018 (https://www.amnesty.org/en/ latest/news/2016/08/afghan-refugees-lives-in-limbo).

White, Josh. 2015. "How Calais' 'Jungle' Migrant Camp Has Now Become a Mini City—Complete with Restaurants, a Theatre, Book Shops and Free WiFi." *The Daily Mail.* December 6. Retrieved February 11, 2018 (http://www.dailymail.co.uk/ news/article-3348594/Restaurants-theatre-free-wifi-Calais-Jungle-migrant-camp-mini-city.html#ixzz4R0ZDxzFt).

Williamson, Hugh. 2017. *Japan Can Do More on Refugee Settlement*. New York: Human Rights Watch. Retrieved February 11, 2018 (https://www.hrw.org/news/2017/06/22/ japan-can-do-more-refugee-resettlement).

World Bank. 2018. *World Bank Development Indicators Interactive Database: Refugee Population by Country or Territory of Origin*. Washington, DC: World Bank Group. Retrieved May 11, 2018 (http://databank.worldbank.org/data/ reports.aspx?source=2&series=SM.POP.REFG.OR&country).

Chapter 12

Amnesty International. 2016a. *Refugees Welcome Index Shows Government Refugee Policies Out of Touch with Public Opinion*. London: Amnesty International UK Office. Retrieved February 12, 2018 (https://www.amnesty.org/en/latest/ news/2016/05/refugees-welcome-index-shows-government-refugee-policies-out-of-touch).

Amnesty International. 2016b. *Genuine Responsibility-Sharing: Amnesty International's Five Proposals*. London: Amnesty International. Retrieved February 12, 2018 (https:// www.amnesty.org/en/documents/ior40/4380/2016/en).

Balko, Radley. 2009. "The El Paso Miracle." *Reason,* July 6. Los Angeles: The Reason Foundation. Retrieved February 12, 2018 (http://reason.com/archives/2009/07/06/the-el-paso-miracle).

Benton, Meghan and Anne Nielsen. 2013. *Integrating Europe's Muslim Minorities: Public Anxieties, Policy Responses*. Washington, DC: Migration Policy Institute. Retrieved February 12, 2018 (http://www.migrationpolicy.org/article/ integrating-europes-muslim-minorities-public-anxieties-policy-responses).

Blagrave, Patrick, Sweta Saxena, and Esteban Vesperoni. 2016. "Spillovers from China's Transition and from Migration." Pp. 171–202 in *World Economic Outlook*: Subdued Demand—Symptoms and Remedies. Washington, DC: Spillover Task Force, International Monetary Fund. Retrieved February 12, 2018 (http://www.imf.org/external/pubs/ft/weo/2016/02/ pdf/c4.pdf).

Bradford, Anu. 2013. "Sharing the Risks and Rewards of Economic Migration." *University of Chicago Law Review* 80(29): 29–56.

Carling, Jørgen. 2008. "Interrogating Remittances: Core Question for Deeper Insight and Better Policies." Pp. 43–64 in *Migration and Development: Perspectives from the South,* edited by Stephen Castles and Raúl Delgado Wise. Geneva: International Organization for Migration.

Casey, Nicholas. 2016. "Climate Change Claims a Lake, and an Identity." *The New York Times,* July 7. Retrieved May 11, 2018 (https://www.nytimes.com/interactive/2016/07/07/world/americas/bolivia-climate-change-lake-poopo.html).

Center for American Entrepreneurship. 2017. *Immigrant Founders of the 2017 Fortune 500.* Washington, DC: Center for American Entrepreneurship. Retrieved February 12, 2018 (http://startupsusa.org/fortune500).

Collier, Paul. 2013. *Exodus: How Immigration Is Changing Our World.* Oxford, UK: Oxford University Press.

Cometto, Giorgio, Kate Tulenko, Adamson S. Muula, and Reudiger Krech. 2013. "Health Workforce Brain Drain: From Denouncing the Challenge to Solving the Problem." *PLoS Medicine* 10(9): e1001514.

Connor, Phillip. 2016. *International Migration: Key Findings from the U.S., Europe and the World.* Washington, DC: Pew Research Center. Retrieved February 12, 2018 (http://www.pewresearch.org/fact-tank/2016/12/15/international-migration-key-findings-from-the-u-s-europe-and-the-world).

Dustmann, Christian and Albrecht Glitz. 2011. "Migration and Education." Pp. 327–440 in *Handbook of the Economics of Education,* Volume 4, edited by Eric Alan Hanushek, Finis Welch, Stephen Machin, and Ludger Woessmann. Amsterdam: North-Holland.

Economist, The. 2012. "The Greatest Migration in History." *The Economist,* February 24. Retrieved February 12, 2018 (http://www.economist.com/blogs/freeexchange/2012/02/china).

Economist, The. 2017. "How Immigration Is Changing the Swedish Welfare State." *The Economist,* June 23. Retrieved February 12, 2018 (https://www.economist.com/the-economist-explains/2017/06/23/how-immigration-is-changing-the-swedish-welfare-state).

Economist Intelligence Unit. 2016. *Measuring Well-Governed Migration: The 2016 Migration Governance Index.* London: Economist Intelligence Unit. Retrieved February 12, 2018 (https://www.iom.int/sites/default/files/our_work/EIU-Migration-Governance-Index-20160429.pdf).

Ehrhart, Hélène, Maëlan Le Goff, Emmanuel Rocher, and Raju Jan Singh. 2014. *Does Migration Foster Exports? Evidence from Africa* (Policy Research Working Paper 6739). Washington, DC: World Bank African Division. Retrieved February 12, 2018 (https://openknowledge.worldbank.org/bitstream/handle/10986/16810/WPS6739.pdf? sequence=1).

Ewing, Walter A., Daniel E. Martínez, and Rubén G. Rumbaut. 2015. *The Criminalization of Immigration in the United States.* Washington, DC: American Immigration Council. Retrieved February 12, 2018 (https://www.americanimmigrationcouncil.org/sites/default/files/research/the_criminalization_of_immigration_in_the_united_states.pdf).

Federal Bureau of Investigation. 2017. *Crime in the United States 2016.* Washington, DC: Federal Bureau of Investigation. Retrieved February 12, 2018 (https://ucr.fbi.gov/crime-in-the-u.s/2016/crime-in-the-u.s.-2016).

Frey, William. 2017. *U.S. Immigration Levels Continue to Fuel Most Community Demographic Gains.* Washington, DC: Brookings Institution. Retrieved February 12, 2018 (https://www.brookings.edu/blog/the-avenue/2017/08/03/u-s-immigration-levels-continue-to-fuel-most-community-demographic-gains).

Inglehart, R., C. Haerpfer, A. Moreno, C. Welzel, K. Kizilova, J. Diez-Medrano, M. Lagos, P. Norris, E. Ponarin, B. Puranen, et al. (eds.). 2014. *World Values Survey: Round Six—Country-Pooled Datafile 2010–2014.* Madrid: JD Systems Institute. Retrieved February 10, 2018 (http://www.worldvaluessurvey.org/WVSDocumentationWV6.jsp).

Internal Displacement Monitoring Center. 2016. *Global Estimates 2015: People Displaced by Disasters.* Oslo: Norwegian Refugee Council. Retrieved February 12, 2018 (http://www.internal-displacement.org/assets/library/Media/201507-globalEstimates-2015/20150713-global-estimates-2015-en-v1.pdf).

International Organization for Migration. 2015. *World Migration Report 2015: Migrants and Cities—New Partnerships to Manage Mobility.* Geneva: International Organization for Migration. Retrieved February 12, 2018 (http://publications.iom.int/system/files/wmr2015_en.pdf).

Jaumotte, Florence, Ksenia Koloskova, and Sweta Saxena. 2016. *Impact of Migration on Income Levels in Advanced Economies.* Washington, DC: Spillover Task Force, International Monetary Fund. Retrieved February 12, 2018 (https://blogs.imf.org/2016/10/24/migrants-bring-economic-benefits-for-advanced-economies).

Johnson, Henry. 2015. "Hate Crimes against Muslims in the U.K. on the Rise." *Foreign Policy,* November 23. Retrieved February 12, 2018 (http://foreignpolicy.com/2015/11/23/hate-crimes-against-muslims-in-the-u-k-on-the-rise).

Liu, Joanne. 2017. *Europe Is Feeding a Criminal System of Abuse in Libya.* New York: Medecins Sans Frontieres/ Doctors without Borders. Retrieved February 12, 2018 (http://www.doctorswithoutborders.org/article/europe-feeding-criminal-system-abuse-libya).

Migration Policy Institute. 2016. *Top 10 Migration Issues of 2016* (Issue 10). Washington, DC: Migration Policy Institute. Retrieved February 12, 2018 (https://www.migrationpolicy.org/programs/migration-information-source/top-10-migration-issues-2016).

Mughan, Anthony and Pamela Paxton. 2006. "Anti-Immigrant Sentiment, Policy Preferences and Populist Party

Voting in Australia." *British Journal of Political Science* 36: 341–358.

Mutume, Gumisai. 2003. "Reversing Africa's Brain Drain." *Africa Recovery* 17(2): 1. New York: Africa Recovery, United Nations. (*Africa Recovery* is now *Africa Renewal.*)

Norwegian Refugee Council. 2015. "19.3 Million Displaced by Disasters but 'Mother Nature Not to Blame.'" Oslo: Norwegian Refugee Council. Retrieved May 11, 2018 (https://www.nrc.no/news/2015/july/19.3-million-displaced-by-disasters-but-mother-nature-not-to-blame).

Organisation for Economic Cooperation and Development. 2014. "Is Migration Good for the Economy?" *Migration Policy Debates,* May. Paris: OECD Publishing. Retrieved February 23, 2018 (https://www.oecd.org/migration/OECD%20Migration%20Policy%20Debates%20Numero%202.pdf).

Organisation for Economic Cooperation and Development. 2015. *International Migration Outlook 2015.* Paris: OECD Publishing. Retrieved February 12, 2018 (http://www.oecd-ilibrary.org/social-issues-migration-health/international-migration-outlook-2015/chile_migr_outlook-2015-12-en).

Organisation for Economic Cooperation and Development. 2016. *International Migration Outlook 2016.* Paris: OECD Publishing. Retrieved February 12, 2018 (http://www.oecd-ilibrary.org/social-issues-migration-health/international-migration-outlook_1999124x).

Organisation for Economic Cooperation and Development. 2018. *Foreign-Born Population (Indicator).* doi:10.1787/5a368e1b-en

Organisation for Economic Cooperation and Development–United Nations Department of Economic and Social Affairs. 2013. *World Migration in Figures.* Paris: Organisation for Economic Cooperation and Development, International Migration Division, and United Nations Department of Economic and Social Affairs, Population Division. Retrieved February 12, 2018 (http://www.oecd.org/els/mig/World-Migration-in-Figures.pdf).

Papademetriou, Demetrios G. and Meghan Benton. 2016. *From Fragmentation to Integration: Towards a 'Whole-of Society' Approach to Receiving and Settling Newcomers in Europe* (research paper for Vision Europe Summit 2016). Washington, DC: Migration Policy Institute. Retrieved February 12, 2018 (https://www.migrationpolicy.org/research/towards-whole-society-approach-receiving-and-settling-newcomers-europe).

Pew Research Center. 2015. *Post-1965 Immigration Wave Reshapes America's Racial and Ethnic Population Makeup.* Washington, DC: Pew Research Center. Retrieved February 12, 2018 (http://www.pewhispanic.org/2015/09/28/modern-immigration-wave-brings-59-million-to-u-s-driving-population-growth-and-change-through-2065).

United Nations. N.d. *Resources for Speakers on Global Issues: Refugees.* No longer accessible. Retrieved February 12, 2018: *Next Steps: New Dynamics of Displacement* (http://www.un.org/en/globalissues/briefingpapers/refugees/nextsteps.html); Faces behind the Figures (http://www.un.org/en/globalissues/briefingpapers/refugees/facesbehindthefigures.html); *Success Stories* (http://www.un.org/en/globalissues/briefingpapers/refugees/successstories.html).

United Nations. 2016a. *International Migration Report 2015.* New York: United Nations Department of Economic and Social Affairs. Retrieved February 12, 2018 (http://www.un.org/en/development/desa/population/migration/publications/migrationreport/docs/MigrationReport2015_Highlights.pdf).

United Nations. 2016b. "New York Declaration." *Refugees and Migrants.* Retrieved February 12, 2018 (http://refugeesmigrants.un.org/declaration).

United Nations Educational, Scientific, and Cultural Organization. 2017. *Learning to Live Together: Migrant/Migration.* Paris: United Nations Educational, Scientific, and Cultural Organization. Retrieved February 12, 2018 (http://www.unesco.org/new/en/social-and-human-sciences/themes/international-migration/glossary/migrant).

United Nations Office for Disaster Risk Reduction and Centre for Research on the Epidemiology of Disasters. 2016. *Poverty & Death: Disaster Mortality 1996–2015.* Geneva: United Nations Office for Disaster Risk Reduction. Retrieved May 11, 2018 (https://www.unisdr.org/files/50589_creddisastermortalityallfinalpdf.pdf).

United Nations Office of the High Commissioner on Human Rights. 2017. *Status of Ratification Interactive Dashboard.* Geneva: United Nations Office of the High Commissioner on Human Rights. Retrieved February 12, 2018 (http://indicators.ohchr.org).

United Nations Population Fund. 2006. *The State of the World Population 2006.* New York: United Nations Population Fund. Retrieved February 12, 2018 (http://www.unfpa.org/sites/default/files/pub-pdf/sowp06_en.pdf).

U.S. Agency for International Development. 2017. *Hurricane Matthew.* Washington, DC: U.S. Agency for International Development. Retrieved February 12, 2018 (https://www.usaid.gov/matthew).

Wise, Raúl Delgado and Humberto Márquez Covarrubias. 2007. "The Mexico–United States Migratory System: Dilemmas of Regional Integration, Development, and Emigration." Pp. 113–142 in *Migration and Development: Perspectives from the South,* edited by Stephen Castles and Raúl Delgado Wise. Geneva: International Organization for Migration. Retrieved May 11, 2018 (http://lawsdocbox.com/Immigration/73978811-Perspectives-from-the-south-editors-and-development-migration-raul-delgado-wise-stephen-castles-iom-international-organization-for-migration.html).

Woetzel, Jonathan, Lenny Mendonca, Janamitra Devan, Stefano Negri, Yangmel Hu, Luke Jordan, Xiujun Li, Alexander Maasry, Geoff Tsen, Flora Yu, et al. 2009.

Preparing for China's Urban Billion. McKinsey Global Institute, McKinsey & Company. Retrieved February 12, 2018 (https://www.mckinsey.com/global-themes/urbanization/preparing-for-chinas-urban-billion).

World Finance. 2015. "The Impact of Migration on Sender Countries." *World Finance,* April 22. London: World News Media. Retrieved February 12, 2018 (http://www.worldfinance.com/? s=The+impact+of+migration+on+sender+countries).

Chapter 13

Agency for Toxic Substances and Disease Registry. 2013. *Chromium Toxicity: Where Is Chromium Found?* Atlanta, GA: Agency for Toxic Substances and Disease Registry, Centers for Disease Control and Prevention. Retrieved February 12, 2018 (http://www.atsdr.cdc.gov/csem/csem.asp? csem=10&po=5).

Aide, T. Mitchell and H. Ricardo Grau. 2004. "Globalization, Migration, and Latin American Ecosystems." *Science* 305(5692): 1915–1916.

Ajero, May Antoniette, Dolors Armenteras, Jane Barr, Ricardo Barra, Ivar Baste, James Dobrowolski, Nicolai Dronin, Amir El-Sammak, Tom P. Evans, C. Max Finlayson, et al. 2012. *Geo 5: Global Environmental Outlook.* Nairobi, Kenya: United Nations Environment Programme.

Ajugwo, Anslem O. 2013. "Negative Effects of Gas Flaring: The Nigerian Experience." *Journal of Environment Pollution and Human Health* 1(1): 6–8.

Alcamo, Joseph. 2011. "Six Assertions about the Global Water Quality Challenge." Presented at Futures of European Waters Congress, March 24–25, 2011. Budapest, Hungary. (No longer available online.)

Allchin, Douglas. N.d. *The Poisoning of Minamata.* Retrieved February 12, 2018 (http://shipseducation.net/ethics/minamata.htm).

Arora, Rajat. 2015. "Government Makes Use of Plastic Waste in Road Construction Mandatory." *The Times of India,* November 26. Retrieved February 12, 2018 (http://articles.economic-times.indiatimes.com/2015-11-26/news/68582088_1_plastic-waste-road-construction-road-developers).

Associated Press. 2016. *Rio Water Pollution Stretches beyond Shoreline, AP Tests Show.* Retrieved February 12, 2018 (http://espn.go.com/olympics/story/_/id/14270878/rio-olympics-water-polluted-far-offshore-new-testing-shows).

Bernhardt, Angela. 2016. "Breaking the Cycle of Extreme Lead Poisoning in Pesarean, Indonesia." *Pure Earth Pollution Blog,* May 18. New York: Pure Earth Blacksmith Institute. Retrieved February 12, 2018 (http://www.pureearth.org/blog/lead-pollution-pesarean-indonesia).

Borchardt Mark A., Susan K. Spencer, Burney A. Kieke, Elisabetta Lambertini, and Frank J. Loge. 2012. "Viruses in Nondisinfected Drinking Water from Municipal Wells and Community Incidence of Acute Gastrointestinal Illness." *Environmental Health Perspectives* 120: 1272–1279.

Bouwman, Hindrik. 2012. *GEF Guidance on Emerging Chemicals Management Issues in Developing Countries and Countries with Economies in Transition* (Scientific and Technical Advisory Panel advisory document). Washington, DC: Global Environment Facility. Retrieved February 12, 2018 (https://www.thegef.org/sites/default/files/publications/GEF_Guidance_on_Emerging_Chemicals-Full-Report_0.pdf).

Breithaupt, Holger. 2006. "The Costs of REACH." *EMBO Reports* 7(10): 968–971.

Caiazzo, Fabio, Akshay Ashok, Ian A. Waitz, Steve H. L. Yim, and Steven R. H. Barrett. 2013. "Air Pollution and Early Deaths in the United States: I. Quantifying the Impact of Major Sectors in 2005." *Atmospheric Environment* 79: 198–208.

Carson, Rachel. 1962. *Silent Spring.* Boston: Houghton Mifflin (anniversary edition 2002).

Center for Sustainable Systems. 2016. *US Water Supply and Distribution: Factsheet.* Ann Arbor: University of Michigan. Retrieved February 12, 2018 (http://css.umich.edu/factsheets/us-water-supply-and-distribution-factsheet).

Centers for Disease Control and Prevention. 2015. *Global Water Sanitation and Hygiene (Global WASH).* Washington, DC: Department of Health and Human Services, Centers for Disease Control and Prevention. Retrieved February 12, 2018 (http://www.cdc.gov/healthywater/global/wash_statistics.html).

Chatain, Baptiste. 2013. "MEPs Ban Cadmium from Power Tool Batteries and Mercury from Button Cells." *European Parliament News.* Brussels: European Parliament Press Unit. Retrieved February 12, 2018 (http://www.europarl.europa.eu/news/en/news-room/20131004IPR21519/MEPs-ban-cadmium-from-power-tool-batteries-and-mercury-from-button-cells).

Chemical Hazards and Alternatives Toolbox. N.d. *Worldwide Regulation.* Retrieved February 12, 2018 (http://www.chem-hat.org/en/worldwide-regulation).

Classic Cars for Sale. 2014. *EU Proposes Chromium Plating Ban.* London: Bauer Consumer Media. Retrieved February 12, 2018 (http://www.classiccarsforsale.co.uk/news/classic-car-news/1404/eu-proposes-chrome-plating-ban).

Columbia Center for Children's Environmental Health. 2015. *Breathing Air Pollutants during Pregnancy Can Damage Child's Brain, Raise Risk of Cognitive and Behavioral Problems.* New York: Columbia University Mailman School of Public Health. Retrieved February 12, 2018 (http://ccceh.org/news/mar-25-2015-breathing-air-pollutants-during-pregnancy-can-damage-childs-brain-raise-risk-of-cognitive-and-behavioral-problems).

Columbia Center for Children's Environmental Health. 2016a. *Mothers and Newborns Study.* New York: Columbia University Mailman School of Public Health. Retrieved

February 12, 2018 (http://ccceh.org/our-research/featured-nyc-research-findings).

Columbia Center for Children's Environmental Health. 2016b. *Prenatal Exposure to Air Pollution Linked to Impulsivity, Emotional Problems in Children.* New York: Columbia University Mailman School of Public Health. Retrieved February 12, 2018 (http://ccceh.org/6820/homepage-feature/march-17-2016-prenatal-exposure-to-air-pollution-linked-to-impulsivity-emotional-problems-in-children).

Corcoran, Emily, Christian Nellemann, Elaine Baker, Robert Bos, David Osborn, and Heidi Savelli (eds.). 2010. *Sick Water? The Central Role of Wastewater Management in Sustainable Development.* Arendal, Norway: GRID–Arendal. Retrieved February 12, 2018 (http://www.grida.no/publications/218).

Dakkak, Amir. 2016. *Water Pollution Worries in Developing World.* Doha, Qatar: Echoing Sustainability in MENA. Retrieved February 12, 2018 (http://www.ecomena.org/water-pollution).

Dell, J., S. Tierney, G. Franco, R. G. Newell, R. Richards, J. Weyant, and T. J. Wilbanks. 2014. "Energy Supply and Use." Pp. 113–129 in *Climate Change Impacts in the United States: The Third National Climate Assessment,* edited by J. M. Melillo, Terese (T. C.) Richmond, and G. W. Yohe. Washington, DC: U.S. Global Change Research Program. Retrieved February 12, 2018 (http://s3.amazonaws.com/nca2014/high/NCA3_Climate_Change_Impacts_in_the_United%20States_HighRes.pdf).

Eilperin, Juliet and Daryll Fears. 2016. "Congress Is Overhauling an Outdated Law That Affects Nearly Every Product You Own." *The Washington Post,* May 19. Retrieved February 12, 2018 (https://www.washingtonpost.com/politics/congress-poised-to-pass-sweeping-reform-of-chemical-law/2016/05/18/0da5cd22-1d30-11e6-9c81-4be1c14fb8c8_story.html).

Environmental Protection Agency. 2016a. *National Rivers and Streams Assessment 2008–2009.* Washington, DC: Environmental Protection Agency. Retrieved February 12, 2018 (https://www.epa.gov/sites/production/files/2016-03/documents/nrsa_0809_march_2_final.pdf).

Environmental Protection Agency. 2016b. *TRI National Analysis 2014: Releases of Chemicals.* Washington, DC: Environmental Protection Agency. Retrieved February 12, 2018 (https://www.epa.gov/sites/production/files/2016-01/documents/tri_na_2014_complete_english.pdf).

Environmental Protection Agency. 2016c. *Volatile Organic Compounds' Impact on Indoor Air Quality.* Washington, DC: Environmental Protection Agency. Retrieved February 12, 2018 (https://www.epa.gov/indoor-air-quality-iaq/volatile-organic-compounds-impact-indoor-air-quality).

Environmental Protection Agency. 2017. *Determining the Prevalence of Contaminants in Treated and Untreated Drinking Water.* Washington, DC: Environmental Protection Agency. Retrieved February 12, 2018 (https://www.epa.gov/water-research/determining-prevalence-contaminants-treated-and-untreated-drinking-water).

Environmental Working Group. 2005. Body Burden: The Pollution in Newborns—Benchmark Investigation of Industrial Chemicals, Pollutants and Pesticides in Umbilical Cord Blood." Washington, DC: Environmental Working Group. Retrieved February 12, 2018 (https://www.ewg.org/research/body-burden-pollution-newborns#.WoIT1OdG2M8).

European Commission. N.d. *Circular Economy: Closing the Loop.* Brussels: European Parliamentary Research Service. Retrieved February 12, 2018 (http://www.europarl.europa.eu/RegData/etudes/BRIE/2016/573899/EPRS_BRI(2016)573899_EN.pdf).

European Environment Agency. N.d. *Water.* Copenhagen: European Environment Agency, European Union. Retrieved February 12, 2018 (https://www.eea.europa.eu/themes/water/#water).

European Environment Agency. 2016. *Persistent Organic Pollutant Emissions: Indicator Assessment.* Copenhagen: European Environment Agency, European Union. Retrieved February 12, 2018 (page archived December 20, 2016: http://www.eea.europa.eu/data-and-maps/indicators/eea32-persistent-organic-pollutant-pop-emissions-1/assessment-5).

Feigenbaum, James J. and Christopher Muller. 2016. "Lead Exposure and Violent Crime in the Early Twentieth Century." *Explorations in Economic History* 62: 51–86.

Food and Agriculture Organization. 2015. *The Global Forest Resources Assessment.* Rome: Food and Agriculture Organization of the United Nations. Retrieved February 12, 2018 (http://www.fao.org/3/a-i4808e.pdf).

Gail, William B. 2016. "A New Dark Age Looms." *The New York Times,* April 19, p. A25. Retrieved February 12, 2018 (https://www.nytimes.com/2016/04/19/opinion/a-new-dark-age-looms.html).

Gassert, Francis, Paul Reig, Tianyi Luo, and Andrew Maddocks. 2013. *Aqueduct Country and River Basin Rankings.* Washington, DC: World Resources Institute. Retrieved May 12, 2018 (http://www.wri.org/publication/aqueduct-country-river-basin-rankings).

Ghazoul, Jaboury, Zuzana Burivalova, John Garcia-Ulloa, and Lisa A. King. 2015. "Conceptualizing Forest Degradation." *Trends in Ecology & Evolution* 30(10): 622–632.

Global Environment Facility. 2013. *Mercury and the GEF.* Washington, DC: Global Environment Facility. Retrieved February 12, 2018 (https://www.thegef.org/sites/default/files/publications/GEF_Mercury-brochure-OCT7-2013_1_0.pdf).

Gourmelon, Gaelle. 2015. *Global Plastic Production Rises, Recycling Lags.* Washington, DC: Worldwatch Institute. Retrieved February 12, 2018 (http://www.worldwatch.org/global-plastic-production-rises-recycling-lags-0).

GRID–Arendal. 2009. *Vital Forest Graphics.* Arendal, Norway: GRID–Adrenal. Retrieved February 12, 2018 (https://www.grida.no/publications/152).

GRID–Arendal. 2010. "Ratio of Wastewater Treatment." From the collection *Sick Water—The Central Role of Wastewater Management in Sustainable Development*. Arendal, Norway: GRID–Arendal. Retrieved May 12, 2018 (http://www.grida.no/resources/7599).

GRID–Arendal. 2014. *State of the Rainforest 2014*. Arendal, Norway: GRID–Arendal and Rainforest Foundation. Retrieved February 12, 2018 (https://cld.bz/bookdata/iM6vBGo/basic-html/toc.html).

GRID–Arendal and United Nations Environment Programme. 2009. *Vital Forest Graphics*. Arendal, Norway: GRID–Arendal. Retrieved February 12, 2018 (https://www.grida.no/publications/152).

Gurdak, Jason. 2010a. "The High Plains Aquifer: Part One." *Prairie Fire*, May. Lincoln, NE. Prairie Fire Enterprises. Retrieved February 12, 2018 (http://www.prairiefirenewspaper.com/2010/05/the-high-plains-aquifer-part-one).

Gurdak Jason. 2010b. "The High Plains Aquifer: Part Two." *Prairie Fire*, June. Lincoln, NE. Prairie Fire Enterprises. Retrieved February 12, 2018 (http://www.prairiefirenewspaper.com/2010/06/the-high-plains-aquifer-part-two).

Heintz, James and Robert Pollin. 2011. *The Economic Benefits of a Green Chemical Industry in the United States*. Amherst: Political Economy Research Institute, University of Massachusetts. Retrieved February 12, 2018 (http://www.peri.umass.edu/fileadmin/pdf/other_publication_types/green_economics/Green_Chemistry_Report_FINAL.pdf).

Hinton, Jennifer J., Marcello M. Veiga, and Christian Beinhoff. 2003. "The Socio-economic Impacts of Artisanal and Small-Scale Mining in Developing Countries." In *Women and Artisanal Mining: Gender Roles and the Road Ahead,* edited by Gavin M. Hilson. Lisse, The Netherlands: Swets & Zeitlinger. Retrieved February 12, 2018 (http://siteresources.worldbank.org/INTOGMC/Resources/336099-1163605893612/hinton-rolereview.pdf).

Howard, Brian Clark. 2014. "Aral Sea's Eastern Basin Is Dry for First Time in 600 Years." *National Geographic,* October 2. Retrieved February 12, 2018 (http://news.nationalgeographic.com/news/2014/10/141001-aral-sea-shrinking-drought-water-environment).

International Energy Agency. 2012. "Water for Energy." Chapter 17 in *World Energy Outlook 2012*. Paris: Organisation for Economic Cooperation and Development/International Energy Agency. Retrieved February 12, 2018 (http://www.worldenergyoutlook.org/media/weowebsite/2012/WEO_2012_Water_Excerpt.pdf).

International Environmental Technology Centre. N.d. *Converting Waste Plastic into Fuel*. Osaka, Japan: United Nations Environment Programme, International Environmental Technology Centre. Retrieved February 12, 2018 (http://citeseerx.ist.psu.edu/showciting;jsessionid=C837CE546BF7229B8C[?]?[?]).

Kennedy, Merrit. 2016. "Lead Laced Water in Flint: A Step-by-Step Look at the Makings of a Crisis." *The Two-Way,* April 20. Washington, DC: National Public Radio. Retrieved February 12, 2018 (http://www.npr.org/sections/thetwo-way/2016/04/20/465545378/lead-laced-water-in-flint-a-step-by-step-look-at-the-makings-of-a-crisis).

Kissinger, Gabrielle, Martin Herold, and Veronique De Sy. 2012. *Drivers of Deforestation and Forest Degradation: A Synthesis Report for REDD+ Policymakers*. Vancouver, British Columbia, Canada: Lexeme Consulting. Retrieved February 12, 2018 (https://www.gov.uk/government/uploads/system/uploads/attachment_data/file/65505/6316-drivers-deforestation-report.pdf).

Kozacek, Codi. 2012. *Global Gold Rush: The Price of Mining Pursuits on the Water Supply*. Traverse City, MI: Circle of Blue. Retrieved February 12, 2018 (http://www.circleofblue.org/2012/world/global-gold-rush-the-price-of-mining-pursuits-on-water-supply).

Kristof, Nicholas. 2017. "Trumps Legacy: Damaged Brains." *The New York Times,* October 29. Retrieved February 12, 2018 (https://www.nytimes.com/interactive/2017/10/28/opinion/sunday/chlorpyrifos-dow-environmental-protection-agency.html).

Kulacki, Konrad J. and Bradley J. Cardinale. 2012. "Effects of Nano-Titanium Dioxide on Freshwater Algal Population Dynamics." *PLoS One* 7(10): e47130.

Lelieveld, J., J. S. Evans, M. Fnais, D. Giannadaki, and A. Pozzer. 2015. "The Contribution of Outdoor Air Pollution Sources to Premature Mortality on a Global Scale." *Nature* 525(7569): 367–371.

Lema, Meserecordias W., Jasper N. Ijumba, Karoli N. Njau, and Patrick A. Ndakidemi. 2014. "Environmental Contamination by Radionuclides and Heavy Metals through the Application of Phosphate Rocks during Farming and Mathematical Modeling of Their Impacts to the Ecosystem." *International Journal of Engineering Research and General Science* 2(4): 852–863.

Linos, Athena, Athanassios Petralias, Costas A. Christophi, Eleni Christoforidou, Paraskevi Kouroutou, Melina Stoltidis, Afroditi Veloudaki, Evangelia Tzala, Konstantinos C. Makris, and Margaret R. Karagas. 2011. "Oral Ingestion of Hexavalent Chromium through Drinking Water and Cancer Mortality in an Industrial Area of Greece—An Ecological Study." *Environmental Health* 10(50): 1–8.

Lohse, Sam. 2014. "Nano Contaminants: How Nanoparticles Get into the Environment." *Sustainable Nano,* May 13. Madison: University of Wisconsin, Center for Sustainable Nanotechnology. Retrieved February 12, 2018 (http://sustainable-nano.com/2014/05/13/nano-contaminants-how-nanoparticles-get-into-the-environment).

Lombroso, Linda. 2015. "Researcher Keeps Kids Safe from Chemicals." *Lohud* (part of USA Today Network),

March 8. Retrieved February 12, 2018 (http://www.lohud.com/story/news/health/2015/03/17/philip-landrigan-childrens-health/24914417).

Malaj, Egina, Peter C. von der Ohe, Matthias Grote, Ralph Kühne, Cédric P. Mondy, Philippe Usseglio-Polatera, Werner Brack, and Ralf B. Schäfer. 2014. "Organic Chemicals Jeopardize the Health of Freshwater Ecosystems on the Continental Scale." *Proceedings of the National Academy of Sciences of the United States of America* 111(26): 9549–9554.

Megevand, Carole. 2013. *Deforestation Trends in the Congo Basin: Reconciling Economic Growth and Forest Protection.* Washington, DC: World Bank Group. Retrieved February 12, 2018 (https://openknowledge.worldbank.org/handle/10986/12477).

Ministry of Environment and Urbanization, Republic of Turkey. 2015. *Implementation of Persistent Organic Pollutants Regulation in Turkey (POPs Project).* Ankara: Ministry of Environment and Urbanization, Republic of Turkey. Retrieved February 12, 2018 (http://www.csb.gov.tr/projeler/pops/index.php? Sayfa=sayfa&Tur=webmenu&Id=14987).

National Aeronautics and Space Administration. N.d. NASA Earth Observatory, EOS Project Science Office, NASA Goddard Space Flight Center. Retrieved February 12, 2018 (https://earthobservatory.nasa.gov).

National Aeronautics and Space Administration. 2015. *Study: Third of Big Groundwater Basins in Distress.* Retrieved February 12, 2018 (http://www.nasa.gov/jpl/grace/study-third-of-big-groundwater-basins-in-distress).

National Oceanic and Atmospheric Administration. 2008. *Nonpoint Source Pollution: Atmospheric Inputs.* Silver Spring, MD: National Oceanic and Atmospheric Administration. Retrieved February 12, 2018 (http://oceanservice.noaa.gov/education/kits/pollution/07input.html).

National Resources Defense Council. 2014. *Devil in the Deep Blue Sea.* Washington, DC: National Resources Defense Council. Retrieved February 12, 2018 (https://www.nrdc.org/onearth/devil-deep-blue-sea).

Payn, Tim, Jean-Michel Carnus, Peter Freer-Smith, Mark Kimberley, Walter Kollert, Shirong Liu, Christophe Orazio, Luiz Rodriguez, Luis Neves Silva, and Michael J. Wingfield. 2015. "Changes in Planted Forests and Future Global Implications." *Forest Ecology and Management* 352: 57–67.

Plant Chicago. N.d. *Closed Loop, Open Source.* Chicago: Plant Chicago. Retrieved February 12, 2018 (http://plantchicago.org).

Plumbing Manufacturers International. 2016. *Health and Safety: Lead.* Rolling Meadows, IL: Plumbing Manufacturers International. Retrieved February 12, 2018 (https://www.safeplumbing.org/health-safety/lead-in-plumbing).

Pure Earth. 2015. *Toxic Sites Identification Program.* New York: Pure Earth, Blacksmith Institute. Retrieved February 12, 2018 (http://www.pureearth.org/projects/toxic-sites-identification-program-tsip).

Pure Earth and Green Cross of Switzerland. 2016. *World's Worst Pollution Problems: The Toxins beneath Our Feet.* New York: Pure Earth; Zurich: Green Cross of Switzerland. Retrieved February 12, 2018 (http://www.worstpolluted.org/docs/WorldsWorst2016Spreads.pdf).

Raksit, Arpita. 2015. "Can the Circular Economy Work in the Developing World?" *Corporate Citizenship Briefing,* June 4. London: Corporate Citizenship. Retrieved February 12, 2018 (http://ccbriefing.corporate-citizenship.com/2015/06/04/can-the-circular-economy-work-in-the-developing-world).

Ramaswami, Abhishek. 2014. "Water Terrorism: How Militant Groups Are Taking Advantage of Climate Change Impacts." *Breaking Energy,* December 9. New York: Breaking Media. Retrieved February 12, 2018 (https://breakingenergy.com/2014/12/09/water-terrorism-how-militant-groups-are-taking-advantage-of-climate-change-impacts).

Ranson, Matthew, Brendan Cox, Cheryl Keenan, and Daniel Teitelbaum. 2015. "The Impact of Pollution Prevention on Toxic Environmental Releases from U.S. Manufacturing Facilities." *Environmental Science and Technology* 49(21): 12951–12957.

Richey, Alexandra S., Brian F. Thomas, Min-Hui Lo, John T. Reager, James S. Famiglietti, Katalyn Voss, Sean Swenson, and Matthew Rodell. 2015. "Quantifying Renewable Groundwater Stress with GRACE." *Water Resources Research* 51(7): 5217–5238.

Saini, Shivam. 2015. "A Dutch City Has Come Up with a Genius Plan That Could Eventually Eliminate Asphalt Roads." *Business Insider U.S. Edition,* July 21. Retrieved February 12, 2018 (http://www.businessinsider.com/a-dutch-city-is-planning-to-build-roads-from-recycled-plastic-2015-7).

Scientific and Technical Advisory Panel of the Global Environment Facility. 2012. *GEF Guidance on Emerging Chemicals Management Issues in Developing Countries and Countries with Economies in Transition.* Washington, DC: Global Environment Facility.

Senet, Stéphanie. 2016. "Circular Economy Way of Thinking Embraced across EU." *Journal de l'environnement,* June 3. Retrieved February 12, 2018 (http://www.euractiv.com/section/sustainable-dev/news/circular-economy-way-of-thinking-embraced-across-eu).

Shapiro, Ari. 2014. "In Arid Iraq, Control of Water Is Part of ISIS Arsenal." *All Things Considered,* October 12. Washington, DC: National Public Radio. Retrieved February 12, 2018 (http://www.npr.org/2014/10/12/355573903/in-arid-iraq-control-of-water-is-part-of-isis-arsenal).

Sloan, Sean and Jeffrey A. Sayer. 2015. "Forest Resources Assessment of 2015 Shows Positive Global Trends but Forest Loss and Degradation Persist in Poor Tropical Countries." *Forest Ecology and Management* 352(7): 134–145.

Thornton, Joe. 2002. *Environmental Impacts of Polyvinyl Chloride Building Materials.* Washington, DC: Healthy

Building Network. Retrieved February 12, 2018 (https://healthybuilding.net/uploads/files/environmental-impacts-of-polyvinyl-chloride-building-materials.pdf).

Tomlinson, George H., II. 1983. "Air Pollutants and Forest Decline." *Environmental Science and Technology* 17(6): 246A–256A.

United Nations. 2015. *The Millennium Development Goals Report.* New York: United Nations. Retrieved February 12, 2018 (http://www.un.org/millenniumgoals/2015_MDG_Report/pdf/MDG%202015%20rev%20(July%201).pdf).

United Nations Department of Economic and Social Affairs. 2014. *Transboundary Waters.* New York: United Nations Department of Economic and Social Affairs. Retrieved February 12, 2018 (http://www.un.org/waterforlifedecade/transboundary_waters.shtml).

United Nations Economic Commission for Europe. 2000. Protocol on Water and Health to the 1992 Convention on the Protection and Use of Transboundary Watercourses and International Lakes. New York: United Nations. Retrieved February 13, 2018 (https://www.ecolex.org/details/treaty/protocol-on-water-and-health-to-the-1992-convention-on-the-protection-and-use-of-transboundary-watercourses-and-international-lakes-tre-001306).

United Nations Economic Commission for Europe. 2014. *Model Provisions for Transboundary Groundwaters.* New York: United Nations. Retrieved February 13, 2018 (https://www.unece.org/fileadmin/DAM/env/water/publications/WAT_model_provisions/ece_mp.wat_40_eng.pdf).

United Nations Environment Programme. 2011. *The Basel Convention Overview.* Châtelaine, Switzerland: Secretariat of the Basel Convention. Retrieved February 12, 2018 (http://www.basel.int/TheConvention/Overview/tabid/1271/Default.aspx).

United Nations Environment Programme. 2013. *Mercury: Acting Now!* Geneva: United Nations Environment Programme, Chemicals Branch. Retrieved February 13, 2018 (http://wedocs.unep.org/bitstream/handle/20.500.11822/8356/-Mercury_%20acting%20now-2013Mercury%20Acting%20Now.pdf).

United Nations Environment Programme. 2016. *African Universities See Wealth in Waste.* Nairobi, Kenya: UN Environment Programme in Africa. Retrieved February 12, 2018 (http://web.unep.org/africa/news/african-universities-see-wealth-waste).

United Nations Environment Programme–DHI and United Nations Environment Programme. 2016. *Transboundary River Basins: Status and Trends.* Nairobi, Kenya: United Nations Environment Programme. Retrieved February 12, 2018 (http://twap-rivers.org/assets/GEF_TWAPRB_FullTechnicalReport.pdf).

United Nations General Assembly. 2010. Resolution adopted by the General Assembly on 28 July 2010 [without reference to a Main Committee (A/64/L.63/Rev. 1 and Add. 1)] 64/292: The human right to water and sanitation. New York: United Nations. Retrieved May 12, 2018 (https://www.un.org/es/comun/docs/?symbol=A/RES/64/292&lang=E).

Urbina, Ian. 2013. "Think Those Chemicals Have Been Tested?" *The New York Times Sunday Review,* April 13. Retrieved February 12, 2018 (http://www.nytimes.com/2013/04/14/sunday-review/think-those-chemicals-have-been-tested.html?_r=0).

van Lierop, Pieter, Erik Lindquist, Shiroma Sathyapal, and Gianluca Franceschini. 2015. "Global Forest Area Disturbance from Fire, Insect Pests, Diseases and Severe Weather Events." *Forest Ecology and Management* 352: 78–88.

Vanker, Aneesa, Whitney Barnett, Polite M. Nduru, Robert P. Gie, Peter D. Sly, and Heather J. Zar. 2015. "Home Environment and Indoor Air Pollution Exposure in an African Birth Cohort Study." *Building and Environment* 93: 72–83.

Vidal, John and Toby Helm. 2016. "Shock Figures to Reveal Deadly Toll of Global Air Pollution." *The Guardian,* January 16. Retrieved February 12, 2018 (https://www.theguardian.com/environment/2016/jan/16/world-heslth-organisation-figures-deadly-pollution-levels-world-biggest-cities).

Wilson, Michael P., Daniel A. Chia, and Bryan C. Ehlers. 2007. "Green Chemistry in California: A Framework for Leadership in Chemicals Policy and Innovation." *New Solutions: A Journal of Environmental and Occupational Health Policy* 16(4): 365–372.

World Bank. N.d. *Biodiversity and Forests at a Glance.* Washington, DC: World Bank Group. Retrieved February 12, 2018 (http://siteresources.worldbank.org/ESSDNETWORK/64158610-1111583197441/20488129/BiodiversityAndForestsAtAGlance.pdf).

World Bank. 2016. *Climate-Driven Water Scarcity Could Hit Economic Growth by Up to 6 Percent in Some Regions, Says World Bank.* Washington, DC: World Bank. Retrieved May 12, 2018 (http://www.worldbank.org/en/news/press-release/2016/05/03/climate-driven-water-scarcity-could-hit-economic-growth-by-up-to-6-percent-in-some-regions-says-world-bank).

World Economic Forum. 2014. *Towards the Circular Economy: Accelerating the Scale-Up across Global Supply Chains.* Geneva: World Economic Forum. Retrieved February 12, 2018 (http://www3.weforum.org/docs/WEF_ENV_TowardsCircularEconomy_Report_2014.pdf).

World Footwear. 2014. *European Union Imposes Restrictions to Chromium.* Portugal: APICCAPS (Portuguese Footwear, Components, and Leather Goods Manufacturers' Association). Retrieved February 12, 2018 (http://worldfootwear.com/news.asp?id=306&European_Union_imposes_restrictions_to_chromium).

World Health Organization. 2008. *Persistent Organic Pollutants: Children's Health and the Environment.* Geneva:

World Health Organization. Retrieved February 12, 2018 (http://www.who.int/ceh/capacity/POPs.pdf).

World Health Organization. 2012a. "Cholera 2011." *Weekly Epidemiological Record* 31–32(3): 289–304. Geneva: World Health Organization. Retrieved February 12, 2018 (http://www.who.int/wer/2012/wer8731_32.pdf).

World Health Organization. 2012b. *Global Costs and Benefits of Drinking-Water Supply and Sanitation Interventions to Reach the MDG Target and Universal Coverage.* Geneva: WHO Document Production Services. Retrieved February 13, 2018 (http://www.who.int/water_sanitation_health/publications/2012/globalcosts.pdf).

World Health Organization. 2015. *Antimicrobial Resistance: An Emerging Water, Sanitation and Hygiene Issue.* Geneva: World Health Organization. Retrieved February 12, 2018 (http://www.who.int/water_sanitation_health/publications/antimicrobial-resistance/en).

World Health Organization. 2016a. "Priority Risks and Future Trends." *Environment and Health in Developing Countries.* Geneva: Health and Environment Linkages Initiative, World Health Organization. Retrieved February 12, 2018 (http://www.who.int/heli/risks/ehindevcoun/en).

World Health Organization. 2016b. *Mercury and Health Factsheet.* Geneva: World Health Organization. Retrieved February 12, 2018 (http://www.who.int/mediacentre/factsheets/fs361/en).

World Wildlife Fund. N.d. *Rich Countries, Poor Water.* Zeist, The Netherlands: WWF Freshwater Programme. Retrieved February 12, 2018 (http://assets.wwf.org.uk/downloads/rich-countriespoorwater.pdf).

Yang, Xiaolin, Yuanquan Chen, Steven Pacenka, Wangsheng Gao, Min Zhang, Peng Sui, and Tammo S. Steenhuis. 2015. "Recharge and Groundwater Use in the North China Plain for Six Irrigated Crops for an Eleven Year Period." *PLoS One* 10(1): e115269.

Yardley, Jim. 2007. "Beneath China's Cities, China's Future Is Drying Up." *The New York Times,* September 28. Retrieved February 13, 2018 (http://www.nytimes.com/2007/09/28/world/asia/28water.html).

Chapter 14

Biello, David. 2014. "Can Carbon Capture Technology Be Part of the Climate Solution?" *Yale Environment 360,* September 8. New Haven, CT: Yale School of Forestry & Environmental Studies. Retrieved February 13, 2018 (http://e360.yale.edu/features/can_carbon_capture_technology_be_part_of_the_climate_solution).

Blanco, G., R. Gerlagh, S. Suh, J. Barrett, H. C. de Coninck, C. F. Diaz Morejon, R. Mathur, N. Nakicenovic, A. Ofosu Ahenkora, J. Pan, et al. 2014. "Drivers, Trends and Mitigation." Chapter 5 in *Climate Change 2014: Mitigation of Climate Change— Contribution of Working Group III to the Fifth Assessment Report of the Intergovernmental Panel on Climate Change,* edited by O. Edenhofer, R. Pichs-Madruga, Y. Sokona, E. Farahani, S. Kadner, K. Seyboth, A. Adler, I. Baum, S. Brunner, P. Eickemeier, et al. Cambridge, UK: Cambridge University Press. Retrieved February 13, 2018 (https://www.ipcc.ch/pdf/assessment-report/ar5/wg3/ipcc_wg3_ar5_chapter5.pdf).

Breisinger, Clemens, Olivier Ecker, and Jean Francois Trinh Tan. 2015. "Conflict and Food Insecurity: How Do We Break the Links?" Chapter 7 in *Global Food Policy Report 2014– 2015.* Washington, DC: International Food Policy Research Institute. Retrieved February 9, 2018 (https://www.ifpri.org/sites/default/files/gfpr/2015/feature_3086.html).

British Broadcasting Corporation. 2017. *Desertification: The People Whose Land Is Turning to Dust,* November 12. Retrieved February 13, 2018 (http://www.bbc.com/news/world-africa-34790661).

Bruckner, T., I. A. Bashmakov, Y. Mulugetta, H. Chum, A. de la Vega Navarro, J. Edmonds, A. Faaij, B. Fungtammasan, A. Garg, E. Hertwich, et al. 2014. "Energy Systems." Chapter 7 in *Climate Change 2014: Mitigation of Climate Change— Contribution of Working Group III to the Fifth Assessment Report of the Intergovernmental Panel on Climate Change,* edited by O. Edenhofer, R. Pichs-Madruga, Y. Sokona, E. Farahani, S. Kadner, K. Seyboth, A. Adler, I. Baum, S. Brunner, P. Eickemeier, et al. Cambridge, UK: Cambridge University Press. Retrieved February 13, 2018 (https://www.ipcc.ch/pdf/assessment-report/ar5/wg3/ipcc_wg3_ar5_chapter7.pdf).

Busby, Joshua W. 2007. *Climate Change and National Security: An Agenda for Action.* New York: Council on Foreign Relations. Retrieved February 13, 2018 (https://www.cfr.org/report/climate-change-and-national-security).

Center for Research on the Epidemology of Disasters. 2015. *The Human Cost of Weather Related Disasters 1995–2015.* New York: United Nations Office for Disaster Risk Reduction and Centre for Research on the Epidemiology of Disasters. Retrieved February 13, 2018 (https://www.unisdr.org/2015/docs/climatechange/COP21_WeatherDisastersReport_2015_FINAL.pdf).

Committee on the Status of Endangered Wildlife in Canada. 2011. *Wildlife Species Search: Walrus.* Quebec, Canada: Canadian Wildlife Service, Environment Canada.

Davenport, Coral and Campbell Robertson. 2016. "Resettling the First American 'Climate Refugees.'" *The New York Times,* May 2, p. A1. Retrieved February 13, 2018 (https://www.nytimes.com/2016/05/03/us/resettling-the-first-american-climate-refugees.html).

Dhillon, Amrit. 2017. "South Asia Floods: Mumbai Building Collapses as Monsoon Rains Wreak Havoc." *The Guardian,*

August 31. Retrieved February 13, 2018 (https://www.the-guardian.com/world/2017/aug/31/south-asia-floods-fears-death-toll-rise-india-pakistan-mumbai-building-collapses).

Di Liberto, Tom. 2017. "Former Hurricane Ophelia Batters Ireland." *ClimateWatch Magazine,* October 25. Silver Spring, MD: National Oceanic and Atmospheric Administration. Retrieved February 13, 2018 (https://www.climate.gov/news-features/event-tracker/former-hurricane-ophelia-batters-ireland).

Environmental Protection Agency. 2016. *Climate Change Indicators in the United States.* Washington, DC: Environmental Protection Agency. Retrieved February 13, 2018 (https://www3.epa.gov/climatechange/science/indicators/ghg).

Fitzgerald, Elliot. 2016. *10 Surprising Renewable Off-Grid Energy Sources.* Abingdon, UK: Smart Villages Research. Retrieved February 13, 2018 (http://e4sv.org/10-surprising-renewable-off-grid-energy-sourceseccentric-energy-off-grid-communities).

Fossheim, M., R. Primicerio, E. Johannesen, R. B. Ingvaldsen, M. M. Aschan, and A. V. Dolgov. 2015. *Climate Change Is Pushing Boreal Fish Northwards to the Arctic: The Case of the Barents Sea* (Arctic Report Card: Update for 2015). Silver Spring, MD: National Oceanic and Atmospheric Administration. Retrieved February 13, 2018 (https://www.arctic.noaa.gov/Report-Card/Report-Card-2015/ArtMID/5037/ArticleID/224/Climate-Change-is-Pushing-Boreal-Fish-Northwards-to-the-Arctic-The-Case-of-the-Barents-Sea).

Fountain, Henry. 2016. "Iceland Carbon Dioxide Storage Project Locks Away Gas, and Fast." *The New York Times,* June 9. Retrieved February 13, 2018 (https://www.nytimes.com/2016/06/10/science/carbon-capture-and-sequestration-iceland.html).

Glick, Daniel. N.d. "The Big Thaw." *National Geographic online,* republished from the pages of National Geographic Magazine. Washington DC: National Geographic Partners and National Geographic Society. Retrieved February 13, 2018 (http://environment.nationalgeographic.com/environment/global-warming/big-thaw/#page=2).

Global Terrorism Database. 2015. *Terrorist Attacks 2015.* College Park: National Consortium for the Study of Terrorism and Responses to Terrorism, University of Maryland. Retrieved February 13, 2018 (http://www.start.umd.edu/gtd/images/START_GlobalTerrorismDatabase_2015TerroristAttacks ConcentrationIntensityMap.jpg).

Holodny, Elena. 2016. "Extreme Weather Events Are on the Rise." *Business Insider,* March 23. Retrieved February 13, 2018 (http://www.businessinsider.com/extreme-weather-events-increasing-2016-3).

Hong, Eunkyoung, Robert Perkins, and Sarah Trainor. 2014. "Thaw Settlement Hazard of Permafrost Related to Climate Warming in Alaska." *Arctic* 67(1): 93–103. Retrieved February 13, 2018 (https://www.jstor.org/stable/24363724?).

Intergovernmental Panel on Climate Change. 2014: *Climate Change 2014: Synthesis Report* (Contribution of Working Groups I, II, and III to the *Fifth Assessment Report of the Intergovernmental Panel on Climate Change* [Core Writing Team, edited by R. K. Pachauri and L. A. Meyer]). Geneva: Intergovernmental Panel on Climate Change.

International Carbon Action Partnership. 2016. *Emissions Trading Worldwide: Status Report 2016.* Berlin: International Carbon Action Partnership. Retrieved February 13, 2018 (https://icapcarbonaction.com/en/status-report-2016).

Jacobson, Mark Z., Mark A. Delucchi, Zack A. F. Bauer, Savannah C. Goodman, William E. Chapman, Mary A. Cameron, et al. 2016. *100% Clean and Renewable Wind, Water, and Sunlight (WWS) All-Sector Energy Roadmaps for 139 Countries of the World.* Palo Alto, CA: Stanford University, Department of Civil and Environmental Engineering, Atmosphere/Energy Program. Retrieved February 13, 2018 (http://web.stanford.edu/group/efmh/jacobson/Articles/I/CountriesWWS.pdf).

Kazeem, Yomi. 2017. "Floods in Africa in August Killed 25 Times More People Than Hurricane Harvey Did." *Quartz Africa,* September 4. New York: Quartz Media. Retrieved February 13, 2018 (https://qz.com/1068790/floods-in-africa-in-august-killed-25-times-more-people-than-hurricane-harvey-did).

Kearney, Alanna. 2014. "The Battle May Be Over, but What about the War? Examining the ESA in the Crusade against Global Warming after In re Polar Bear Endangered Species Act Listing and Section 4(d) Rule Litigation." *The Villanova Environmental Law Journal* 25(2): 529. Retrieved May 13, 2018 (http://digitalcommons.law.villanova.edu/elj/vol25/iss2/5).

Kovacs, K. M., P. Lemons, J. G. MacCracken, and C. Lydersen. 2015. *Walruses in a Time of Climate Change.* Washington, DC: Arctic Program, National Oceanic and Atmospheric Administration. Retrieved May 12, 2018 (https://www.arctic.noaa.gov/Report-Card/Report-Card-2015/ArtMID/5037/ArticleID/226/Walruses-in-a-Time-of-Climate-Change).

Leahy, Stephen. 2018. "Polar Bears Really Are Starving Because of Global Warming, Study Shows." *National Geographic News,* February 1. Retrieved May 13, 2018 (https://news.national-geographic.com/2018/02/polar-bears-starve-melting-sea-ice-global-warming-study-beaufort-sea-environment).

Li, Can, N. Christina Hsu, Andrew M. Sayer, Nickolay A. Krotkov, Joshua S. Fu, Lok N. Lamsal, Jaehwa Lee, and Si-Chee Tsay. 2016. "Satellite Observation of Pollutant Emissions from Gas Flaring Activities Near the Arctic." *Atmospheric Environment* 133: 1–11.

Lindsey, Rebecca. 2017. "Climate Conditions behind Deadly October 2017 Wildfires in California." *ClimateWatch Magazine,* October 11. Silver Spring, MD: National Oceanic and Atmospheric Administration. Retrieved February 13, 2018 (https://www

.climate.gov/news-features/event-tracker/climate-conditions-behind-deadly-october-2017-wildfires-california).

Lone, Asma Khan. 2015. "How Can Climate Change Trigger Conflict in South Asia?" *Foreign Policy,* November 20. Retrieved February 13, 2018 (http://foreignpolicy.com/2015/11/20/how-can-climate-change-trigger-conflict-in-south-asia).

Lund University. 2015. "Melting Arctic Sea Ice Accelerates Methane Emissions." *ScienceDaily,* September 17. Retrieved February 13, 2018 (https://www.sciencedaily.com/releases/2015/09/150917091306.htm).

Madin, Kate. 2008. "Melting Ice Threatens Polar Bear Survival." *Oceanus Magazine,* April. Retrieved February 13, 2018 (http://www.whoi.edu/oceanus/feature/melting-ice-threatens-polar-bears-survival).

Makoye, Kizito. 2016. "Women Solar Entrepreneurs Drive East African Business Surge." *Reuters,* December 6. Retrieved February 13, 2018 (http://www.reuters.com/article/us-tanzania-solar-women-idUSKBN13V16N).

Met Office Hadley Centre and Climatic Research Unit. 2016. *2015: The Warmest Year on Record.* Exeter, UK: Met Office Hadley Centre. Retrieved February 13, 2018 (http://www.metoffice.gov.uk/news/releases/archive/2016/2015-global-temperature).

Meyer, John W., David John Frank, Ann Hironaka, Evan Schofer, and Nancy Brandon Tuma. 1997. "The Structuring of a World Environmental Regime, 1870–1990." *International Organization* 51(4): 623–651.

National Aeronautics and Space Administration. N.d. *How Much More Will the Earth Warm?* Greenbelt, MD: Earth Observatory, EOS Project Science Office, NASA Goddard Space Flight Center. Retrieved February 13, 2018 (http://earthobservatory.nasa.gov/Features/GlobalWarming/page5.php).

National Aeronautics and Space Administration. 2017a. *Carbon Dioxide.* Retrieved February 13, 2018 (https://climate.nasa.gov/vital-signs/carbon-dioxide).

National Aeronautics and Space Administration. 2017b. *Scientific Consensus: Earth's Climate Is Warming.* Retrieved February 13, 2018 (https://climate.nasa.gov/scientific-consensus).

National Aeronautics and Space Administration. 2017c. *Global Temperature.* Retrieved February 13, 2018 (https://climate.nasa.gov/vital-signs/global-temperature).

National Aeronautics and Space Administration. 2017d. *Ice Sheets.* Retrieved February 13, 2018 (https://climate.nasa.gov/vital-signs/land-ice).

National Aeronautics and Space Administration. 2017e. *Infographic: Sea Level Rise.* Retrieved February 13, 2018 (http://climate.nasa.gov/climate_resources/125).

National Aeronautics and Space Administration. 2017f. *Sea Level.* Retrieved February 13, 2018 (https://climate.nasa.gov/vital-signs/sea-level).

National Oceanic and Atmospheric Administration. 2016a. *Global Climate Report—April 2016.* Silver Spring, MD: National Oceanic and Atmospheric Administration. Retrieved February 13, 2018 (https://www.ncdc.noaa.gov/sotc/global/201604).

National Oceanic and Atmospheric Administration. 2016b. *Global Climate Report, Annual 2016.* Silver Spring, MD: National Oceanic and Atmospheric Administration. Retrieved February 13, 2018 (https://www.ncdc.noaa.gov/sotc/global/201613).

National Snow and Ice Data Center. 2013. *A Thawing, Rotting Arctic?* Boulder, CO: National Snow and Ice Data Center, University of Colorado, Boulder. Retrieved February 13, 2018 (https://nsidc.org/cryosphere/icelights/2013/05/thawing-rotting-arctic).

National Wildlife Federation. N.d. *Polar Bear.* Merrifield, VA: National Wildlife Federation. Retrieved February 13, 2018 (https://www.nwf.org/Educational-Resources/Wildlife-Guide/Mammals/Polar-Bear).

Pereira, Laura. 2017. "Climate Change Impacts on Agriculture across Africa." *Oxford Research Encyclopedia of Environmental Science,* November. Retrieved February 13, 2018 (http://environmentalscience.oxfordre.com/view/10.1093/acrefore/9780199389414.001.0001/acrefore-9780199389414-e-292).

Perovich, Donald K. and Christopher Polashenski. 2012. "Albedo Evolution of Seasonal Arctic Sea Ice." *Geophysical Research Letters* 39(8). doi:10.1029/2012GL051432

Pew Research Center. 2015. *Drought Tops Climate Change Concerns across All Regions.* Washington, DC: Pew Research Center, Global Attitudes and Trends. Retrieved February 13, 2018 (http://www.pewglobal.org/2015/11/05/global-concern-about-climate-change-broad-support-for-limiting-emissions/climate-change-report-26).

Popescu, Adam. 2016. "Love in the Time of Climate Change: Grizzlies and Polar Bears Are Now Mating." *The Washington Post,* May 23. Retrieved February 13, 2018 (https://www.washingtonpost.com/news/animalia/wp/2016/05/23/love-in-the-time-of-climate-change-grizzlies-and-polar-bears-are-now-mating).

Power, Jack. 2017. "Power Restored to All Homes following Storm Ophelia." *The Irish Times,* October 25. Retrieved February 13, 2018 (https://www.irishtimes.com/news/ireland/irish-news/power-restored-to-all-homes-following-storm-ophelia-1.3268267).

REN 21 Secretariat. 2016. *Renewables 2016: Global Status Report.* Paris: Renewable Energy Policy Network for the 21st Century. Retrieved February 13, 2018 (http://www.ren21.net/wp-content/uploads/2016/06/GSR_2016_Full_Report1.pdf).

REN 21 Secretariat. 2017. *Renewables 2017: Global Status Report.* Paris: Renewable Energy Policy Network for the 21st Century. Retrieved May 13, 2018 (http://www.ren21.net/

wp-content/uploads/2017/06/17-8399_GSR_2017_Full_Report_0621_Opt.pdf).

Roach, John. 2006. "Grizzly–Polar Bear Hybrid Found—But What Does It Mean?" *National Geographic News,* May 16. Retrieved February 13, 2018 (http://news.nationalgeographic.com/news/2006/05/polar-bears.html).

Royce, B. S. H. and S. H. Lam. 2013. *The Earth's Climate Sensitivity and Thermal Inertia.* Princeton, NJ: Department of Mechanical and Aerospace Engineering, Princeton University. Retrieved February 13, 2018 (https://www.princeton.edu/~lam/documents/RoyceLam2010.pdf).

Schuur, Edward A. G., Jason G. Vogel, Kathryn G. Crummer, Hanna Lee, James O. Sickman, and T. E. Osterkamp. 2009. "The Effect of Permafrost Thaw on Old Carbon Release and Net Carbon Exchange from Tundra." *Nature* 459(7246): 556–559.

Serdeczny, Olivia, Sophie Adams, Florent Baarsch, Dim Coumou, Alexander Robinson, William Hare, Michiel Schaeffer, Mahe Perrette, and Julia Reinhardt. 2016. "Climate Change Impacts in Sub-Saharan Africa: From Physical Changes to Their Social Repercussions." *Regional Environmental Change,* January. Retrieved February 13, 2018 (http://climate-analytics.org/files/ssa_final_published.pdf).

Shakhova, Natalia, Igor Semiletov, Orjan Gustafsson, Valentin Sergienko, Leopold Lobkovsky, Oleg Dudarev, Vladimir Tumskoy, Michael Grigoriev, Alexey Mazurov, Anatoly Salyuk, et al. 2017. "Current Rates and Mechanisms of Subsea Permafrost Degradation in the East Siberian Arctic Shelf." *Nature Communications* 8: 15872.

Smith, K. R., A. Woodward, D. Campbell-Lendrum, D. D. Chadee, Y. Honda, Q. Liu, J. M. Olwoch, B. Revich, and R. Sauerborn. 2014: "Human Health: Impacts, Adaptation, and Co-benefits. Pp. 709–754 in *Climate Change 2014: Impacts, Adaptation, and Vulnerability—Part A: Global and Sectoral Aspects: Contribution of Working Group II to the Fifth Assessment Report of the Intergovernmental Panel on Climate Change,* edited by C. B. Field, V. R. Barros, D. J. Dokken, K. J. Mach, M. D. Mastrandrea, T. E. Bilir, M. Chatterjee, K. L. Ebi, Y. O. Estrada, R. C. Genova, et al. Cambridge, UK: Cambridge University Press. Retrieved February 13, 2018 (https://www.ipcc.ch/pdf/assessment-report/ar5/wg2/WGIIAR5-Chap11_FINAL.pdf).

Union of Concerned Scientists. N.d. a. *Causes of Drought: What's the Climate Connection?* Cambridge, MA: Union of Concerned Scientists. Retrieved February 13, 2018 (http://www.ucsusa.org/global_warming/science_and_impacts/impacts/causes-of-drought-climate-change-connection.html#.WZNburpFyM8).

Union of Concerned Scientists. N.d. b. *Early Warning Signs of Global Warming: Arctic and Antarctic Warming.* Cambridge, MA: Union of Concerned Scientists. Retrieved February 13, 2018 (http://www.ucsusa.org/global_warming/science_and_impacts/impacts/early-warning-signs-of-global-1.html#.Vo DkQ_7bI5s).

United Nations. 2015. *Framework Convention on Climate Change: Conference of the Parties, Twenty-first session.* Paris: United Nations. Retrieved February 13, 2018 (https://unfccc.int/resource/docs/2015/cop21/eng/l09r01.pdf).

United Nations Convention to Combat Desertification. N.d. *Desertification: The Invisible Frontline.* Bonn, Germany: United Nations Convention to Combat Desertification. Retrieved February 13, 2018 (http://www.unccd.int/Lists/SiteDocumentLibrary/Publications/Desertification_The%20invisible_frontline.pdf).

United Nations Convention to Combat Desertification. 2014. *Desertification: The Invisible Frontline.* Bonn, Germany: United Nations Convention to Combat Desertification. Retrieved February 13, 2018 (http://www.unccd.int/Lists/SiteDocumentLibrary/Publications/Desertification_The%20invisible_frontline.pdf).

U.S. African Development Foundation. 2016. *Power Africa.* Retrieved February 13, 2018 (https://www.usaid.gov/powerafrica).

U.S. Department of State. 2008. *Map of Africa: Conflicts without Borders: Sub-national and Transnational Conflict-Affected Areas, January 2007–October 2008.* Washington, DC: U.S. Department of State. Retrieved February 13, 2018 (http://www.refworld.org/docid/49256ff12.html).

Weart, Spencer. 2016. *The Discovery of Global Warming.* College Park, MD: Center for the History of Physics, American Institute of Physics. Retrieved February 13, 2018 (January 2017 version now online: https://www.aip.org/history/climate/index.htm).

World Economic Forum. 2015. *Outlook on the Global Agenda 2015.* Geneva: World Economic Forum Global Agenda Councils.

World Health Organization–Western Pacific Region. 2012. *Strengthen Control of Vectorborne Diseases to Lessen the Impact of Climate Change in the Western Pacific Region with Focus on Cambodia, Mongolia and Papua New Guinea: Final Project Report.* Manila, Philippines: World Health Organization–Western Pacific Region. Retrieved February 13, 2018 (http://iris.wpro.who.int/handle/10665.1/6825).

World Meteorological Organization. 2013. *A Summary of Current Climate Change Findings and Figures.* Retrieved February 13, 2018 (https://library.wmo.int/pmb_ged/2013_info-note_climate-change.pdf).

World Wildlife Fund. 2012. *"Arctic Home" Generates over $2 Million in Donations for Polar Bear Conservation.* Washington, DC: World Wildlife Fund. Retrieved February 13, 2018 (http://www.worldwildlife.org/press-releases/arctic-home-generates-over-2-million-in-donations-for-polar-bear-conservation).

Ziska, Lewis H. and Paul J. Beggs. 2012. "Anthropogenic Climate Change and Allergen Exposure: The Role of Plant

Biology." *Journal of Allergy and Clinical Immunology* 129(1): 27–32.

Ziska, Lewis H., Paul R. Epstein, and William H. Schlesinger. 2009. "Rising CO2, Climate Change, and Public Health: Exploring the Links to Plant Biology." *Environmental Health Perspectives* 117(2): 155–158.

Chapter 15

100 Resilient Cities. 2017. "Defining Urban Resilience." *100 Resilient Cities.* New York: 100 Resilient Cities. Retrieved February 13, 2018 (http://www.100resilientcities.org/#/-_).

A. T. Kearney. 2017. *Global Cities 2017.* Chicago: A. T. Kearney. Retrieved February 13, 2018 (https://www.atkearney.com/documents/10192/12610750/Global+Cities+2017++Leaders+in+a+World+of+Disruptive+Innovation.pdf/c00b71dd-18ab-4d6b-8ae6-526e380d6cc4).

Adegboye, Kingsley. 2017. "We Are Not Part of Victoria Island, Lekki Flooding—Eko Atlantic." *Vanguard,* July 25. Lagos, Nigeria: Vanguard Media. Retrieved February 13, 2018 (https://www.vanguardngr.com/2017/07/not-part-victoria-island-lekki-flooding-eko-atlantic).

Airriess, Christopher. 2008. "The Geography of Secondary City Growth in a Globalized China: Comparing Douggan and Suzhou." *Journal of Urban History* 35(1): 134–149.

Allegheny County. 2017. *A Community Blueprint: Helping Immigrants Thrive in Allegheny County.* Pittsburgh, PA: Allegheny County, Department of Health and Human Services. Retrieved February 13, 2018 (http://www.alleghenycounty.us/Human-Services/Resources/Immigrants-Refugees/Immigrants-and-Internationals-Initiative/Immigrant-Community-Blueprint.aspx).

Allianz Risk Pulse. 2015. *The Megacity State: The World's Biggest Cities Shaping Our Future.* Munich: Allianz SE. Retrieved February 13, 2018 (https://www.allianz.com/v_1448643898000/media/press/document/Allianz_Risk_Pulse_Megacities_20151130-EN.pdf).

Amnesty International. 2016. *Brazil: Violence Has No Place in These Games.* London: Amnesty International. Retrieved February 13, 2018 (https://www.amnesty.org/en/documents/amr19/4088/2016/en).

Anderson, Cory. 2016. "10 Energy Efficient Building Materials." *Dengarden,* November 8. Berkeley, CA: HubPages. Retrieved February 13, 2018 (https://dengarden.com/home-improvement/10-Energy-Efficient-Building-Materials).

Angel, Shlomo and Somsook Boonyabancha. 1988. "Land Sharing as an Alternative to Eviction." *Third World Planning Review* 10(2): 107. Retrieved February 13, 2018 (https://www.researchgate.net/publication/279740303_Land_Sharing_as_an_Alternative_to_Eviction_The_Bangkok_Experience).

Armstrong, Amy. 2017. "How Are Cities Changing? Policy Trends for Developing Urban Resilience." *100 Resilient Cities,* November 13. New York: 100 Resilient Cities. Retrieved February 13, 2018 (http://www.100resilientcities.org/cities-changing-policy-trends-developing-urban-resilience).

Arsenault, Chris. 2016. "Fears for Poor as Brazil Cuts 'Minha Casa, Minha Vida' Housing Plan." *Reuters,* June 23. Retrieved February 13, 2018 (https://www.reuters.com/article/us-brazil-politics-landrights/fears-for-poor-as-brazil-cuts-minha-casa-minha-vida-housing-plan-idUSKCN0ZA03C).

Ayeyemi, Dayo. 2018. "$300m Credit: World Bank Scores Nigeria's Housing Finance Low." *New Telegraph,* February 13. Retrieved May 13, 2018 (https://newtelegraphonline.com/2018/02/300m-credit-world-bank-scores-nigerias-housing-finance-low).

Barbassa, Juliana. N.d. "What Went Wrong in Rio's Favelas?" *America's Quarterly* (special issue: "Fixing Brazil"). New York: Americas Society/Council of the Americas. Retrieved February 13, 2018 (http://www.americasquarterly.org/content/what-went-wrong-rios-favelas).

Beard, Mary. 2015. "Why Ancient Rome Matters." *The Guardian,* October 2. Retrieved February 13, 2018 (https://www.theguardian.com/books/2015/oct/02/mary-beard-why-ancient-rome-matters#img-1).

Berkowitz, Michael. 2013. "The Five Fastest Growing Cities." *100 Resilient Cities,* November 13. New York: 100 Resilient Cities. Retrieved February 13, 2018 (http://www.100resilientcities.org/blog/entry/the-five-fastest-growing-cities#/-_).

Bio Intelligence Service. 2015. *Assessing the Potential of the Cold Chain Sector to Reduce GHG Emissions through Food Loss and Waste Reduction.* Arlington, VA: Global Food Cold Chain Council. Retrieved February 13, 2018 (http://natural-leader.com/wp-content/uploads/2016/04/coldchainGH-Gemissionstudy.pdf).

Brown, Sarah. 2016. "How Is Rio Working to Improve Living Conditions in Favelas?" *Culture Trip,* October 13. London: Culture Trip. Retrieved February 13, 2018 (https://theculturetrip.com/south-america/brazil/articles/how-is-rio-working-to-improve-living-conditions-in-favelas).

Canada Green Building Council. 2016. *Zero Carbon Building Initiative.* Ottawa, Ontario: Canada Green Building Council. Retrieved February 13, 2018 (http://www.cagbc.org/CAGBC/Zero_Carbon/CAGBC/Zero_Carbon/The_CaGBC_Zero_Carbon_Building_Program.aspx? hkey=19498c4c-8025-465e-8ccc-4fa8428c785b).

Central Intelligence Agency. 2017. *The World Factbook.* Washington, DC: Central Intelligence Agency. Retrieved February 13, 2018 (https://www.cia.gov/library/publications/the-world-factbook).

Chade, Jamil. 2017. "Stadium Deals, Corruption and Bribery: The Questions at the Heart of Brazil's Olympic and World Cup 'Miracle.'" *The Guardian,* April 23. Retrieved February

13, 2018 (https://www.theguardian.com/sport/2017/apr/23/brazil-olympic-world-cup-corruption-bribery).

Chang, Nancy. 2008. "The Upside of Factory Girl Life in China." *Day to Day* (National Public Radio), October 14. Retrieved May 14, 2018 (https://www.npr.org/templates/story/story.php?storyId=95691866).

City of Pittsburgh. 2017. *ONEPGH: Pittsburgh's Resilience Strategy.* Pittsburgh, PA: City of Pittsburgh, Department of City Planning. Retrieved February 13, 2018 (http://lghttp.60358.nexesscdn.net/8046264/images/page/-/100rc/pdfs/Pittsburgh_-_Resilience_Strategy.pdf).

Cocco-Klein, Samantha. 2016. *Inequality.* New York: Global Urban Futures Project, Milano School of International Affairs, New School. Retrieved February 13, 2018 (https://www.globalurbanfutures.org/inequality).

Dignity Village. N.d. "Dignity Village." *Blog at Word Press.* Retrieved February 13, 2018 (https://dignityvillage.org).

Douglas, Bruce. 2015. "Brazil Officials Evict Families from Homes ahead of 2016 Olympic Games." *The Guardian,* October 28. Retrieved February 13, 2018 (https://www.theguardian.com/world/2015/oct/28/brazil-officials-evicting-families-2016-olympic-games).

Durkheim, Emile. 1893/1964. *The Division of Labor in Society.* New York: Free Press.

Ehlen, Mark A. 2014. "How Cities Can Learn from the Human Body's Systems." *100 Resilient Cities,* September 10. New York: 100 Resilient Cities. Retrieved February 13, 2018 (http://www.100resilientcities.org/how-cities-can-learn-from-the-human-bodys-systems).

Emsley, Clive, Tim Hitchcock, and Robert Shoemaker. 2015. "A Population History of London." *Old Bailey Proceedings Online.* Sheffield, UK: Old Bailey Proceedings Online. Retrieved February 13, 2018 (https://www.oldbaileyonline.org/static/Population-history-of-london.jsp).

Florida, Richard. 2002. *The Rise of the Creative Class.* New York: Basic Books.

Florida, Richard. 2014. "The Creative Class and Economic Development." *Economic Development Quarterly* 28(3): 196–205.

Gurgel, Thathiana. 2014. "The Growing Middle Class of Brazil's Slums." *This Big City,* May 6. Retrieved February 13, 2018 (http://thisbigcity.net/the-growing-middle-class-of-brazils-slums)

Healy, Meg and Sabrina Norris. 2016. "After Years of Waiting, Morar Carioca Finally Launched in Pica-Pau." *Rio on Watch,* May 12. Retrieved February 13, 2018 (http://www.rioonwatch.org/?p=28808).

Hine, Lewis Wickes. 1908. *National Child Labor Committee Collection.* Washington, DC: Library of Congress. Retrieved February 13, 2018 (http://www.loc.gov/pictures/collection/nclc/item/ncl2004001356/PP).

Hoelzel, Fabienne. 2016. "Which Way, Lagos?" Pp. 7–12 in *Urban Planning Processes in Lagos.* Abuja, Nigeria: Heinrich Böll Stiftung; Zurich: Fabulous Urban. Retrieved February 13, 2018 (https://ng.boell.org/sites/default/files/160206_urban_planning_processes_digital_new.pdf).

Holmes, Natalie and Alan Berube. 2016. *City and Metropolitan Inequality on the Rise, Driven by Declining Incomes.* Washington, DC: Brookings Institution. Retrieved February 13, 2018 (https://www.brookings.edu/research/city-and-metropolitan-inequality-on-the-rise-driven-by-declining-incomes).

Ibukun, Yinka, Sophie Mongalvy, and Antony Sguazzin. 2018. "Dream of a Lagos Champs–Élysées Banks on Nigerian Recovery." *Bloomberg,* May 30. Retrieved June 2, 2018 (https://www.bloomberg.com/news/articles/2018-05-29/eko-atlantic-city-eyes-2023-finish-as-nigeria-economy-rebounds).

International Organization for Migration. 2015. *World Migration Report 2015: Migrants and Cities—New Partnerships to Manage Mobility.* Geneva: International Organization for Migration. Retrieved February 13, 2018 (http://publications.iom.int/system/files/wmr2015_en.pdf).

Jacobs, Jane. 1961/1992. *The Life and Death of Great American Cities.* New York: Vintage Books.

Jenkins, Simon. 2014. "Vision of the Future or Criminal Eyesore: What Should Rio Do with Its Favelas?" *The Guardian.* April 30. Retrieved February 13, 2018 (https://www.theguardian.com/cities/2014/apr/30/rio-favelas-world-cup-olympics-vision-future-criminal-eyesore).

Khanna, Parag. 2010. "Beyond City Limits." *Foreign Policy,* August 6. Retrieved February 13, 2018 (http://foreignpolicy.com/2010/08/06/beyond-city-imits).

Kimari, Wangui. 2018. "Africa Needs to Drop the 'Youth Bulge' Discourse." *New Internationalist,* January 1. Retrieved March 17, 2018 (https://newint.org/features/2018/01/01/youth-bulge).

Kimmelman, Michael. 2017. "The Dutch Have Solutions to Rising Seas. The World Is Watching." *The New York Times,* June 15. Retrieved February 13, 2018 (https://www.nytimes.com/interactive/2017/06/15/world/europe/climate-change-rotterdam.html? rref=collection%2Fseriescollection%2Fchanging-climate-changing-cities).

King, Robin, Mariana Orloff, Terra Virsilas, and Tejas Pande. 2017. *Confronting the Urban Housing Crisis in the Global South: Adequate, Secure, and Affordable Housing* (working paper). Washington, DC: World Resources Institute. Retrieved February 13, 2018 (http://www.wri.org/wri-citiesforall/publication/towards-more-equal-city-confronting-urban-housing-crisis-global-south).

Landry, Charles. N.d. *Charles Landry.* (Creative City Index, Making Cities Great, and Charles Landry's Blog all link from this website). Retrieved February 13, 2018 (http://charleslandry.com).

Lawanson, Taibat. 2016. "Governing Lagos in the Urban Century: The Need for a Paradigm Shift." Pp. 219–222 in *Urban Planning Processes in Lagos.* Abuja, Nigeria: Heinrich Böll Stiftung; Zurich: Fabulous Urban. Retrieved February 13, 2018 (https://ng.boell.org/sites/default/files/160206_urban_planning_processes_digital_new.pdf).

Lumpp, Ray. 2013. "Seattle's Tent Cities Are a Local Reflection of Global Slum Housing Crisis." *The Seattle Globalist,* March 27. Retrieved February 13, 2018 (http://www.seattleglobalist.com/2013/03/27/seattles-tent-cities-local-reflection-of-global-slums/11743).

Mandyck, John. 2016. "Beyond the Jetsons' Dreams: The Future of Urbanization" (sponsored content by United Technologies). *The Atlantic.* Retrieved February 13, 2018 (http://www.theatlantic.com/sponsored/utc-growing-cities/beyond-the-jetsons-dreams-the-future-of-urbanization/807).

Marx, Benjamin, Thomas Stoker, and Tavneet Suri. 2013. "The Economics of Slums in the Developing World." *Journal of Economic Perspectives* 274: 187–210.

Marx, Karl. 1897/1992–1993. *Capital: A Critique of the Political Economy,* Volumes I–III. London: Penguin Classics.

McGranahan, Gordon and David Satterthwaite. 2014. *Urbanisation Concepts and Trends* (IIED working paper). London: International Institute for Environment and Development, Human Settlements Group. Retrieved February 13, 2018 (http://pubs.iied.org/pdfs/10709IIED.pdf).

McGuirk, Justin. 2016. "Failing the Informal City: How Rio de Janeiro's Mega Sporting Events Derailed the Legacy of Favela–Bairro." *Architectural Design* 86: 40–47.

Muggah, Robert. 2015. "A Manifesto for the Fragile City." *Journal of International Affairs* 68(2): 19–36.

Muggah, Robert. 2017. *These Are the Most Fragile Cities in the World—and This Is What We've Learned from Them.* Rio de Janeiro, Brazil: Igarapé Institute. Retrieved February 13, 2018 (https://igarape.org.br/en/estas-sao-as-cidades-mais-frageis-do-mundo-e-e-isso-o-que-aprendemos-com-elas).

Neuwirth, Robert. 2005a. *Shadow Cities: A Billion Squatters, a New Urban World.* New York: Routledge.

Neuwirth, Robert. 2005b. "The Hidden World of Shadow Cities." *TEDGlobal 2005,* taped in July. New York: TED Conferences. Retrieved February 13, 2018 (https://www.ted.com/talks/robert_neuwirth_on_our_shadow_cities/transcript? language=en#t-344000).

Onuoha, Mimi. 2017. "A 5-Mile Island Built to Save Lagos's Economy Has a Worrying Design Flaw." *Quartz Africa,* March 18. New York: Quartz Media. Retrieved February 13, 2018 (https://qz.com/923142/the-flaw-in-the-construction-of-eko-atlantic-island-in-lagos).

Organisation for Economic Cooperation and Development. 2015. *In It Together: Why Less Inequality Benefits All.* Paris: OECD Publishing. Retrieved February 13, 2018 (http://www.oecd.org/social/in-it-together-why-less-inequality-benefits-all-9789264235120-en.htm).

Osborn, Catherine. 2012a. "A History of Favela Upgrades Part I (1897–1988)." *Rio On Watch,* September 27. Retrieved February 13, 2018 (http://www.rioonwatch.org/?p=5295).

Osborn, Catherine. 2012b. "A History of Favela Upgrades Part II: Introducing Favela–Bairro (1988–2008)." *Rio On Watch,* November 26. Retrieved February 13, 2018 (http://www.rioonwatch.org/?p=5931).

Osborn, Catherine. 2013. "A History of Favela Upgrades Part III: Morar Carioca in Vision and Practice (2008–Present)." *Rio On Watch,* April 2. Retrieved February 13, 2018 (http://www.rioonwatch.org/?p=8136).

Participatory Slum Upgrading Programme. 2016. *Slum Almanac 2015/2016: Tracking Improvement in the Lives of Slum Dwellers.* Nairobi, Kenya: PSUP Team Nairobi, UN Habitat. Retrieved February 13, 2018 (https://unhabitat.org/slum-almanac-2015-2016).

Patel, Kamna. 2013. "A Successful Slum Upgrade in Durban: A Case of Formal Change and Informal Continuity." *Habitat International* 40: 211–217. Retrieved February 13, 2018 (http://www.sciencedirect.com/science/article/pii/S0197397513000490).

Perlman, Janice. 2010. *Favela: Four Decades of Living on the Edge in Rio de Janeiro.* New York: Oxford University Press.

Riffat, Saffa, Richard Powell, and Devrim Aydin. 2016. "Future Cities and Environmental Sustainability." *Future Cities and Environment* 2: 1. Retrieved February 13, 2018 (https://doi:10.1186/s40984-016-0014-2).

Rio Perfeitura. 2015. *Explaining Rio de Janeiro Habitational Policy.* Rio de Janeiro, Brazil: Rio Perfeitura. Retrieved February 13, 2018 (https://drive.google.com/file/d/0B1x0_cNhKxbDb094M1hraGVNekU/view).

Santos, Ana P. 2017. *UAE: Labor Day Tribute to a Migrant Mother.* Washington, DC: Pulitzer Center. Retrieved May 13, 2018 (https://pulitzercenter.org/reporting/uae-labor-day-tribute-migrant-mother).

Sassen, Saskia. 1991. *The Global City.* Princeton, NJ: Princeton University Press.

Sassen, Saskia. 2005. "The Global City: Introducing a Concept." *Brown Journal of World Affairs* 11(2): 27–43. Retrieved February 15, 2018 (http://www.saskiasassen.com/pdfs/publications/the-global-city-brown.pdf).

Sassen, Saskia. 2009. "The Other Workers in the Advanced Corporate Economy." *The Scholar and Feminist Online* 8(1). New York: Barnard Center for Research on Women. Retrieved February 13, 2018 (http://sfonline.barnard.edu/work/print_sassen.htm).

SHARE/WHEEL. 2017. *About Us.* Seattle, WA: Seattle Housing and Resource Effort and Women's Housing Equality and

Enhancement League. Retrieved February 13, 2018 (http://www.sharewheel.org/aboutus).

Shiva, Shruti. 2015. "Seven Lessons from a Successful Slum Upgrading Project." *Citiscope,* February 27. Retrieved February 13, 2018 (http://citiscope.org/story/2015/seven-lessons-successful-slum-upgrading-project).

Siemens. 2014. "City Climate Leadership Awards: Rio de Janeiro Climate Close-Up." *C40 Siemens.* Retrieved February 13, 2018 (https://www.siemens.com/press/pool/de/events/2014/infrastructure-cities/2014-06-CCLA/rio-climate-close-up.pdf).

Simmel, Georg. 1903/1971. "The Metropolis and Mental Life." Pp. 324–339 in *Georg Simmel: On Individuality and Social Forms,* edited by Daniel N. Levine. Chicago: University of Chicago Press.

Smith, Adam. 1776/1982. *The Wealth of Nations.* London. Penguin Classics.

Stokes, Elaisha. 2016. "The Drought That Preceded Syria's Civil War Was Likely the Worst in 900 Years." *Vice News,* March 3. Retrieved February 13, 2018 (https://news.vice.com/article/the-drought-that-preceded-syrias-civil-war-was-likely-the-worst-in-900-years).

Tönnies, Ferdinand. 1887/2004. *Community and Society.* New Brunswick, NJ: Transaction Publishers; East Lansing: Michigan State University Press.

Ummuna, Monika. 2016. "Forward." In *Urban Planning Processes in Lagos.* Abuja, Nigeria: Heinrich Böll Stiftung; Zurich: Fabulous Urban. Retrieved February 13, 2018 (https://ng.boell.org/sites/default/files/160206_urban_planning_processes_digital_new.pdf).

United Nations, Department of Economic and Social Affairs. 2013. *World Economic and Social Survey 2013: Sustainable Development Challenges.* New York: United Nations, Department of Economic and Social Affairs. Retrieved February 13, 2018 (https://sustainabledevelopment.un.org/content/documents/2843WESS2013.pdf).

United Nations, Department of Economic and Social Affairs. 2016. *The World's Cities in 2016—Data Booklet* (ST/ESA/SER.A/392). New York: United Nations, Department of Economic and Social Affairs, Population Division. Retrieved February 13, 2018 (http://www.un.org/en/development/desa/population/publications/pdf/urbanization/the_worlds_cities_in_2016_data_booklet.pdf).

UN Habitat. 2012. *State of Latin American and Caribbean Cities Report 2012: Towards a New Urban Transition.* Nairobi, Kenya: United Nations Human Settlements Programme. Retrieved February 13, 2018 (http://www.citiesalliance.org/sites/citiesalliance.org/files/SOLAC-ProjectOutput.pdf).

UN Habitat. 2016. "Urbanization as a Transformative Force." Chapter 2 in *World Cities Report 2016: Urbanization and Development.* Nairobi, Kenya. United Nations Human Settlements Programme. Retrieved February 13, 2018 (http://wcr.unhabitat.org/wp-content/uploads/2017/03/Chapter2-WCR-2016-1.pdf).

Uwaegbulam, Chinedu. 2015. "Low Supply, Demand in Eko Atlantic Scheme Drive Land Prices Higher." *Eko Atlantic,* June 21. Lagos, Nigeria: Eko Atlantic City. Retrieved February 13, 2018 (http://www.ekoatlantic.com/latestnews/lead-story-low-supply-demand-eko-atlantic-scheme-drive-land-prices-higher).

Waldron, Travis. 2016. "Nobody Asked Rio's Poor about the Olympics. So, They Yelled Louder." *HuffPost,* October 6. Retrieved February 13, 2018 (https://www.huffingtonpost.com/entry/rio-favelas-olympics-protest-legacy_us_57e572d2e4b0e28b2b53cfc8).

Watts, Jonathan. 2015. "The Rio Property Developer Hoping for a $1bn Olympic Legacy of His Own." *The Guardian,* August 4. Retrieved February 13, 2018 (https://www.theguardian.com/sport/2015/aug/04/rio-olympic-games-2016-property-developer-carlos-carvalho-barra).

Weber, Max. 1914/1978. "Bureaucracy." Pp. 956–1005 in *Economy and Society,* edited by G. Roth and C. Wittich. Berkeley: University of California Press.

White, Matthew. 2009. "The Rise of Cities in the 18th Century." *Georgian Britain,* October 14. London: The British Library. Retrieved February 13, 2018 (https://www.bl.uk/georgian-britain/articles/the-rise-of-cities-in-the-18th-century#sthash.l10Pa9pa.dpuf).

World Bank. 2001. "Favela–Bairro Project, Brazil." *Upgrading Urban Communities—A Resource Framework* (Version 04-16-01). Washington, DC: World Bank Group. Retrieved February 15, 2018 (http://web.mit.edu/urbanupgrading/upgrading/case-examples/ce-BL-fav.html).

World Health Organization and UN Habitat. 2010. *Hidden Cities: Unmasking and Overcoming Health Inequities in Urban Settings.* Kobe, Japan: WHO Kobe Center Publications. Retrieved February 13, 2018 (http://www.who.int/kobe_centre/publications/hidden_cities2010/en).

Yardley, Jim. 2011. "In One Slum, Misery, Work, Politics and Hope." *The New York Times,* December 28. Retrieved February 13, 2018 (http://www.nytimes.com/2011/12/29/world/asia/in-indian-slum-misery-work-politics-and-hope.html).

Zielinski, Susan. 2012. "The New Mobility." *McKinsey Insights,* October. New York: McKinsey. Retrieved February 13, 2018 (https://www.mckinsey.com/industries/public-sector/our-insights/the-new-mobility).

Chapter 16

Abramowitz, Michael J. 2017. "Hobbling a Champion of Global Press Freedom." In *Freedom of the Press 2017.* Washington, DC: Freedom House. Retrieved February 15, 2018 (https://freedomhouse.org/report/freedom-press/freedom-press-2017).

Ames, Barry. 2002. *The Deadlock of Democracy in Brazil.* Ann Arbor: University of Michigan Press.

Asian Infrastructure Investment Bank. 2014–2017. *Policies and Strategies.* Beijing: Asian Infrastructure Investment Bank. Retrieved February 15, 2018 (https://www.aiib.org/en/policies-strategies).

Babones, Salvadore. 2018. "China's Constitutional Amendments Are All about the Party, Not the President." *Forbes,* March 11. Retrieved May 13, 2018 (https://www.forbes.com/sites/salvatorebabones/2018/03/11/chinas-constitutional-amendments-are-all-about-the-party-not-the-president/#7b6da5771615).

Bamyeh, Mohammed A. 2011. "Anarchist Method, Liberal Intention, Authoritarian Lesson: The Arab Spring between Three Enlightenments." *Lib.com,* July 31. Retrieved February 15, 2018 (https://libcom.org/library/anarchist-liberal-authoritarian-enlightenments-notes-arab-spring).

Beck, Julie. 2017. "The Tricky Psychology of Holding Government Accountable." *The Atlantic,* January 12. Retrieved February 15, 2018 (https://www.theatlantic.com/science/archive/2017/01/government-accountability-psychology/512888).

Beck, Ulrich. 1992. *Risk Society.* London: Sage.

Beck, Ulrich. 2009. "World Risk Society and Manufactured Uncertainties." *IRIS: European Journal of Philosophy and Public Debate,* October, pp. 291–299. Retrieved February 15, 2018 (http://www.fupress.net/index.php/iris/article/view/3304/2906).

Bradford, Colin I. and Johannes F. Linn. 2007. *Reform of Global Governance: Priorities for Action* (Brookings Policy Brief Series No. 163). Washington, DC: Brookings Institution. Retrieved February 15, 2018 (https://www.brookings.edu/wp-content/uploads/2016/06/pb163.pdf).

Bretton Woods Project. 2016. *IMF & World Bank Decision-Making and Governance.* London: Bretton Woods Project. Retrieved February 15, 2018 (http://www.brettonwoodsproject.org/2016/03/imf-world-bank-decision-making-and-governance-existing-structures-and-reform-processes).

Buckley, Chris. 2017. "A Spring Thaw? Trump Now Has 'Very Good' Words for China's Leader." *The New York Times,* April 30. Retrieved May 13, 2018 (https://www.nytimes.com/2017/04/29/world/asia/trump-xi-jinping-china.html).

Cassese, Sabino. 2005. "The Globalization of Law." *New York University Journal of International Law and Politics* 37(4): 973–994.

Cave, Tamasin and Andy Rowell. 2015. *A Quiet Word: Lobbying, Crony Capitalism and Broken Politics in Britain.* London: Vintage.

Center for Deliberative Democracy. N.d. *What Is Deliberative Polling?* Stanford, CA: Stanford University Center for Deliberative Democracy. Retrieved February 15, 2018 (http://cdd.stanford.edu/what-is-deliberative-polling).

China Global Television Network. 2018. *History of Amendments to China's Constitution.* Beijing: China Global Television Network. Retrieved May 13, 2018 (https://news.cgtn.com/news/784d6a4d79677a6333566d54/share_p.html).

CSO Partnership for Development Effectiveness. 2010. *Istanbul Development Effectiveness Principles.* Istanbul: Open Forum for CSO Development Effectiveness. Retrieved February 15, 2018 (http://csopartnership.org/wp-content/uploads/2016/01/hlf4_72.pdf).

Davies, Thomas Richard. 2008. *The Rise and Fall of Transnational Civil Society: The Evolution of International Non-Governmental Organizations since 1839* (Report No. CUTP/003). London: Department of International Politics, City University London. Retrieved February 15, 2018 (http://openaccess.city.ac.uk/1287).

Doherty, Carroll, Jocelyn Kiley, and Bridget Johnson. 2017. *In First Months, Views of Trump Are Already Strongly Felt, Deeply Polarized.* Washington, DC: Pew Research Center. Retrieved February 15, 2018 (http://assets.pewresearch.org/wp-content/uploads/sites/5/2017/02/17094915/02-16-17-Political-release.pdf).

Donno, Daniela. 2013. *Defending Democratic Norms: International Actors and the Politics of Electoral Misconduct.* Oxford, UK: Oxford University Press.

Drake, Bruce and Jacob Poushter. 2016. *In Views of Diversity, Many Europeans Are Less Positive than Americans.* Washington, DC: Pew Research Center. Retrieved February 15, 2018 (http://www.pewresearch.org/fact-tank/2016/07/12/in-views-of-diversity-many-europeans-are-less-positive-than-americans).

Drutman, Lee. 2015. "How Corporate Lobbyists Conquered American Democracy." *The Atlantic,* April 20. Retrieved February 15, 2018 (https://www.theatlantic.com/business/archive/2015/04/how-corporate-lobbyists-conquered-american-democracy/390822).

Eisenhower, Dwight D. 1961. *Military–Industrial Complex Speech, Dwight D. Eisenhower, 1961.* New Haven, CT: The Avalon Project, Lillian Goldman Law Library, Yale Law School. Retrieved February 15, 2018 (http://avalon.law.yale.edu/20th_century/eisenhower001.asp).

Fishkin, James S., Baogang He, Robert C. Luskin, and Alice Siu. 2010. "Deliberative Democracy in an Unlikely Place: Deliberative Polling in China." *British Journal of Political Science* 40(2): 435–448.

Freedom House. 2017. *Nations in Transit 2017.* New York: Freedom House. Retrieved February 15, 2018 (https://freedomhouse.org/report/nations-transit/nations-transit-2017).

Fukuyama, Francis. (2013). "What Is Governance?" *Governance: An International Journal of Policy, Administration, and Institutions* 26(3): 347–368.

Grant, Ruth W. and Robert O. Keohane. 2005. "Accountability and Abuse of Power in World Politics." *American Political Science Review* 99(1): 29–43.

Haggard, Stephan and Lydia Tiede. 2010. "The Rule of Law and Economic Growth: Where Are We?" Presented at the University of Texas School of Law Conference on Measuring the Rule of Law, March 25–26. Retrieved February 15, 2018 (https://law.utexas.edu/conferences/measuring/The%20 Papers/ruleoflawconference.Haggard&Tiede.Rule%20of%20 Law.March13.2010.pdf).

Heinrich, Finn. 2017. *Corruption and Inequality: How Populists Mislead People.* Berlin: Transparency International. Retrieved February 15, 2018 (http://www.transparency.org/news/feature/ corruption_and_inequality_how_populists_mislead_people).

Holmes, Leslie. 2009. "Good Guys, Bad Guys: Transnational Corporations, Rational Choice Theory, and Power Crime." *Crime, Law and Social Change* 51: 383–397.

IBON International. 2014. *Civil Society Accountability: To Whom and for Whom?* (prepared for 2014 Development Cooperation Forum, DCF Germany High-Level Symposium: "Accountable and Effective Development Cooperation in a Post-2015 Era." New York: United Nations Economic and Social Council. Retrieved February 15, 2018 (http://www .un.org/en/ecosoc/newfunct/pdf13/dcf_germany_policy_ brief_2_cso_accountability.pdf).

Inglehart, R., C. Haerpfer, A. Moreno, C. Welzel, K. Kizilova, J. Diez-Medrano, M. Lagos, P. Norris, E. Ponarin, B. Puranen, et al. (eds.). 2014. *World Values Survey: Round Six—Country-Pooled Datafile 2010–2014.* Madrid: JD Systems Institute. Retrieved February 10, 2018 (http://www.worldvaluessurvey .org/WVSDocumentationWV6.jsp).

Jackman, Simon and Lynn Vavreck. 2011. "Cosmopolitanism." Pp. 70–96 in *Facing the Challenge of Democracy: Explorations in the Analysis of Public Opinion and Political Participation,* edited by Paul M. Sniderman and Benjamin Highton. Princeton, NJ: Princeton University Press.

Jackson, Isabella. 2018. "Why China Won't Let People Compare Xi Jinping with an Imperial Predecessor." *The Conversation,* March 5. Boston: The Conversation. Retrieved May 13, 2018 (https://theconversation.com/why-china-wont-let-people-compare-xi-jinping-with-an-imperial-predecessor-92617).

Kaldor, Mary. 2003. *Global Civil Society: An Answer to War.* Cambridge, UK: Polity.

Keane, John. 2003. *Global Civil Society?* Cambridge, UK: Cambridge University Press.

Kelly, Kate. 2017. "Edge or Liability? White House ties may cut two ways for Goldman." *The New York Times,* March 16, p. B1. Retrieved February 15, 2018 (https://www.nytimes .com/2017/03/16/business/dealbook/goldman-sachs-white-house-relationship.html).

Keohane, Robert O. 2002. "Governing Globalization in a Partially Globalized World." Pp. 325–348 in *Governing Globalization: Power, Authority and Global Governance,* edited by David Held and Anthony McGrew. Cambridge, UK: Polity.

Kessler, Glenn. 2012. "When Did McConnell Say He Wanted to Make Obama a 'One-Term President'?" *The Washington Post,* September 25. Retrieved February 15, 2018 (https:// www.washingtonpost.com/blogs/fact-checker/post/ when-did-mcconnell-say-he-wanted-to-make-obama-a-one-term-president/2012/09/24/79fd5cd8-0696-11e2-afff-d6c7f20a83bf_blog.html? utm_term=.6482637e5bc5).

Klaas, Brian. 2016. *The Despot's Accomplice: How the West Is Aiding and Abetting the Decline of Democracy.* New York: Oxford University Press.

Koenig-Archibugi, Mathias. 2002. "Mapping Global Governance." Pp. 46–69 in *Governing Globalization: Power, Authority and Global Governance,* edited by David Held and Anthony McGrew. Cambridge, UK: Polity.

Kuper, Andrew. 2007. "Reconstructing Global Governance: Eight Innovations." Pp. 225–239 in *Globalization Theory: Approaches and Controversies,* edited by David Held and Anthony McGrew. Cambridge, UK: Polity.

Kwong, Jessica. 2017. "Russia and China Military Drills Target Both North Korea and U.S." *Newsweek.* Retrieved February 15, 2018 (http://www.newsweek.com/russia-and-china-drills-target-both-north-korea-and-us-746281).

Lazare, Sarah. 2015. "From DOE to CEO: Revolving Door Spins in Washington as Top Official Hired by Nuclear Company." *Common Dreams,* March 16. Portland, ME: Common Dreams. Retrieved February 15, 2018 (https://www.commondreams .org/news/2015/03/16/doe-ceo-revolving-door-spins-washington-top-official-hired-nuclear-company).

League of Nations. 1924. *The Covenant of the League of Nations (including amendments adopted to December, 1924.* New Haven, CT: The Avalon Project, Lillian Goldman Law Library, Yale Law School. Retrieved February 15, 2018 (http:// avalon.law.yale.edu/20th_century/leagcov.asp).

Lerner, Jennifer S. and Philip E. Tetlock. 2003. "Bridging Individual, Interpersonal, and Institutional Approaches to Judgment and Choice: The Impact of Accountability on Cognitive Bias." Pp. 431–457 in *Emerging Perspectives in Judgment and Decision Making,* edited by S. Schneider and J. Shanteau. Cambridge, UK: Cambridge University Press.

Lipton, Eric. 2017. "Icahn Raises Ethics Flags with Dual Roles as Investor and Trump Adviser." *The New York Times,* March 26. Retrieved February 15, 2018 (https://www.nytimes .com/2017/03/26/us/politics/carl-icahn-trump-adviser-red-flags-ethics.html).

Maiello, Michael. 2009. "Corruption, American Style." *Forbes,* January 22. Retrieved February 15, 2018 (https://www.forbes .com/2009/01/22/corruption-lobbying-bribes-biz-corruption09-cx_mm_0122maiello.html#4334cf40224e)

Marshall, Monty G. and Benjamin R. Cole. 2014. *Global Report 2014: Conflict, Governance and State Fragility.* Vienna, VA: Center for Systemic Peace.

Meier, Barry. 2018. "Origins of an Epidemic: Purdue Pharma Knew Its Opioids Were Widely Abused." *The New York Times,* May 29. Retrieved June 5, 2018 (https://www.nytimes.com/2018/05/29/health/purdue-opioids-oxycontin.html).

Meyer, John, David John Frank, Ann Hironka, Evan Schofer, and Nancy Brandon Tuma. 1997. "The Structuring of a World Environmental Regime, 1870–1990." *International Organization* 51(4): 623–651.

Ministry of Foreign Affairs. 2015. Xi Jinping Attends the Opening Ceremony of the Johannesburg Summit of the Forum on China–Africa Cooperation and Delivers a Speech, Proposing to Upgrade China–Africa Relations to Comprehensive Strategic and Cooperative Partnership, Comprehensively Expounding China's African Policy and Announcing Major Measures to Deepen China–Africa Cooperation. Beijing: Ministry of Foreign Affairs of the People's Republic of China. Retrieved February 15, 2018 (http://www.fmprc.gov.cn/mfa_eng/topics_665678/xjpffgcxqh-bhbldhdjbbwnfjxgsfwbfnfyhnsbzczfhzltfh/t1322278.shtml).

Mullany, Gerry and Sang-Hun Choe. 2017. "Huge North Korean Artillery Drills Come as China Tries to Ease Tensions." *The New York Times,* April 26, p. A6.

Olken, Benjamin A. and Rohini Pande. 2012. *Corruption in Developing Countries.* Cambridge, MA: Abdul Latif Jameel Poverty Action Lab, Governance Initiative. Retrieved February 15, 2018 (http://economics.mit.edu/files/7589).

O'Neil, Colin. 2017. *Sonny Perdue's Revolving Door Policy Already in Action.* Washington. DC: Environmental Working Group. Retrieved February 15, 2018 (http://www.ewg.org/planet-trump/2017/03/sonny-perdues-revolving-door-policy-already-action).

Organisation for Economic Cooperation and Development. 2013. *How's Life 2013: Measuring Well-Being.* Paris: OECD Publishing. Retrieved February 15, 2018 (http://www.oecd.org/std/3013071e.pdf).

Organisation for Economic Cooperation and Development. 2014. *OECD Foreign Bribery Report: An Analysis of the Crime of Bribery of Foreign Public Officials.* Paris: OECD Publishing. Retrieved February 15, 2018. Retrieved February 15, 2018 (http://www.oecd.org/corruption/oecd-foreign-bribery-report-9789264226616-en.htm).

Organisation for Economic Cooperation and Development. 2017a. *2016 Data on Enforcement of the Anti-Bribery Convention.* Paris: OECD Publishing. Retrieved February 15, 2018 (http://www.oecd.org/daf/anti-bribery/Anti-Bribery-Convention-Enforcement-Data-2016.pdf).

Organisation for Economic Cooperation and Development. 2017b. *Fighting the Crime of Foreign Bribery.* Paris: OECD Publishing. Retrieved February 15, 2018 (http://www.oecd.org/corruption/Fighting-the-crime-of-foreign-bribery.pdf).

Pew Research Center. 2015. *Beyond Distrust: How Americans View Their Government.* Washington, DC: Pew Research Center. Retrieved February 15, 2018 (http://www.people-press.org/files/2015/11/11-23-2015-Governance-release.pdf).

Putnam, Robert D. 1993. *Making Democracy Work: Civic Traditions in Modern Italy.* Princeton, NJ: Princeton University Press.

Putnam, Robert D. 2000. *Bowling Alone: The Collapse and Revival of American Community.* New York: Simon & Schuster.

Reporters Sans Frontières (Reporters without Borders). 2017. *Journalism Weakened by Democracy's Erosion.* Paris: Reporters Sans Frontières. Retrieved February 15, 2018 (https://rsf.org/en/journalism-weakened-democracys-erosion).

Rutzen, Douglas. 2015. "A Global Assault on Nonprofits." *Global Investigative Journalism Network,* November 30. Los Angeles: Institute for Nonprofit News. Retrieved February 15, 2018 (https://gijn.org/2015/11/30/the-global-assault-on-nonprofits).

Saloojee, Yussuf and Elif Dagli. 2000. "Tobacco Industry Tactics for Resisting Public Policy on Health." *Bulletin of the World Health Organization* 78(7): 902–910. Retrieved February 15, 2018 (http://www.who.int/bulletin/archives/78(7)902.pdf).

Scrivens, Katherine and Conal Smith. 2013. *Four Interpretations of Social Capital: An Agenda for Measurement* (Working Paper No. 55). Paris: OECD Statistics Directorate. Retrieved February 15, 2018 (http://www.oecd.org/officialdocuments/publicdisplaydocumentpdf/? cote=STD/DOC(2013)6&docLanguage=En).

Simmons, Beth A. 2000. "International Law and State Behavior: Commitment and Compliance in International Monetary Affairs." *American Political Science Review* 94(4): 819–835.

Talbott, Strobe. 2017. Comments at "Major Powers and Global Governance: Megatrends and Grand Challenges" Conference, October 30. Beijing: Brookings–Tsinghua Center for Public Policy, Brookings Institution. Retrieved February 15, 2018 (https://www.brookings.edu/wp-content/uploads/2017/10/20171030_english-transcript.pdf).

Tarabay, Jamie. 2017. "Russia's Power Play in North Korea Aimed at Both China and US." *CNN World,* December 7. Retrieved February 15, 2018 (http://www.cnn.com/2017/09/01/asia/russia-north-korea-analysis/index.html).

Tetlock, Philip, E. 2005. *Expert Political Judgment: How Good Is It? How Can We Know?* Princeton, NJ: Princeton University Press.

Thomas, Daniel C. 2001. *The Helsinki Effect: International Norms, Human Rights, and the Demise of Communism.* Princeton, NJ: Princeton University Press.

Tomlinson, Brian. 2012. *CSOs on the Road from Accra to Busan: CSO Initiatives to Strengthen Development Effectiveness.* Quezon City, Philippines: IBON Books. Retrieved February 15, 2018 (http://concordeurope.org/wp-content/uploads/2012/09/csos_on_the_road_from_accra_to_busan_final.pdf?1855fc).

Transparency International. 2010. *Regulating the Revolving Door* (Working Paper No. 06/2010). Berlin: Transparency International. Retrieved February 15, 2018 (https://www.transparency.org/whatwedo/publication/working_paper_06_2010_regulating_the_revolving_door).

Transparency International. 2013. *Global Corruption Barometer 2013: Report.* Berlin: Transparency International. Retrieved February 15, 2018 (http://www.transparency.org/gcb2013/report).

United Nations. 1945. *Preamble to the Charter of the United Nations and Statute of the International Court of Justice.* New York: United Nations. Retrieved February 15, 2018 (http://www.un.org/en/sections/un-charter/preamble/index.html).

United Nations Foundation. 2013. *What We Do.* New York: United Nations. Retrieved February 15, 2018 (http://www.unfoundation.org/what-we-do/working-with-the-un).

U.S. Constitutional Convention. 1787. *We, the People of the United States, In Order to Form a More Perfect Union. . . .* Providence, RI: John Carter (printer). Broadside Collection (Library of Congress). Retrieved May 15, 2018 (https://www.loc.gov/item/90898138).

van der Meer, Tom W. G. 2017. "Political Trust and the 'Crisis of Democracy.'" *Oxford Research Encyclopedia of Politics,* January. New York: Oxford University Press. Retrieved February 15, 2018 (http://politics.oxfordre.com/view/10.1093/acrefore/9780190228637.001.0001/acrefore-9780190228637-e-77).

Wike, Richard, Bruce Stokes, and Rhonda Stewart. 2016. *Europeans Fear Wave of Refugees Will Mean More Terrorism, Fewer Jobs.* Washington, DC: Pew Research Center. Retrieved February 15, 2018 (http://www.pewglobal.org/files/2016/07/Pew-Research-Center-EU-Refugees-and-National-Identity-Report-FINAL-July-11-2016.pdf).

World Bank. 2006. *Crime, Violence and Economic Development in Brazil: Elements for Effective Public Policy* (Working Paper No. 36525). Washington, DC: World Bank.

World Values Survey. N.d. *World Values Survey Wave 6: 2010–2014.* Vienna, Austria: Institute for Comparative Survey Research. Retrieved February 15, 2018 (http://www.worldvaluessurvey.org/WVSOnline.jsp).

Index